W9-BRD-724

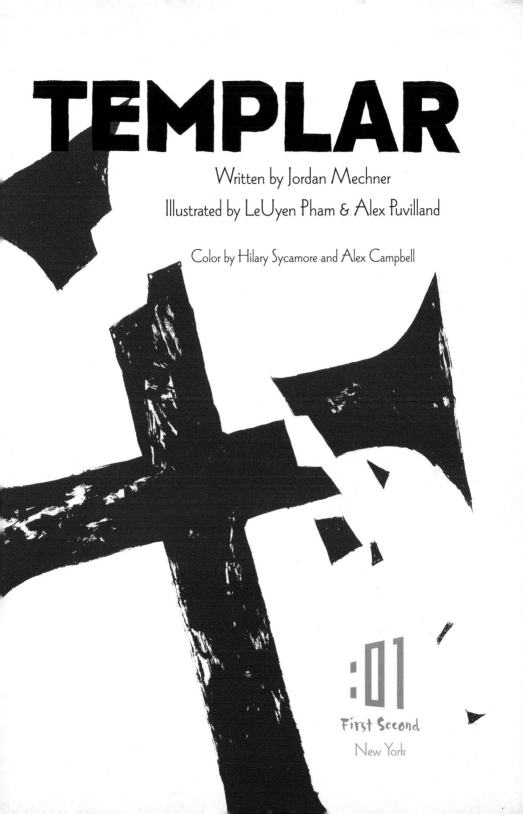

TEMPLAR

Written by Jordan Mechner

Illustrated by LeUyen Pham & Alex Puvilland

Color by Hilary Sycamore and Alex Campbell

:01

First Second

New York

*To Jane and Ethan, who waited patiently for
this book and are now old enough to read it*
—J.M.

To Adrien, of course
—A.P. & L.P.

First Second
New York

Text copyright © 2013 by Jordan Mechner
Illustrations copyright © 2013 by Alex Puvilland and LeUyen Pham
Coloring by Hilary Sycamore (lead) and Alex Campbell of Sky Blue Ink

Published by First Second
First Second is an imprint of Roaring Brook Press, a division of Holtzbrinck Publishing
Holdings Limited Partnership
175 Fifth Avenue, New York, New York 10010
All rights reserved

Cataloging-in-Publication Data is on file at the Library of Congress

ISBN: 978-1-59643-393-9

First Second books are available for special promotions and premiums.
For details, contact: Director of Special Markets, Holtzbrinck Publishers.

First edition 2013

Book design by Danica Novgorodoff
Printed in China

10 9 8 7 6 5 4 3 2

TEMPLAR

PREFACE iv

Book One • Solomon's Thieves

CHAPTER 1. The Fall 3
CHAPTER 2. "I Have Told the Whole Truth . . ." 49
CHAPTER 3. The Secret 87

Book Two • The Bishops

CHAPTER 4. The Fortress 137
CHAPTER 5. The Innocents. 185
CHAPTER 6. Saint-Antoine 231

Book Three • The Grail

CHAPTER 7. The Plan. 287
CHAPTER 8. Solomon's Treasure. 355
CHAPTER 9. The River. 399

AFTERWORD 470

Preface

A lunatic is easily recognized...
You can tell him by the liberties he takes
with common sense, by his flashes of
inspiration, and by the fact that sooner or
later he brings up the Templars.

– UMBERTO ECO,
FOUCAULT'S PENDULUM

I'VE BEEN FASCINATED BY THE KNIGHTS TEMPLAR ever since I came across them in the course of research to write *The Last Express*—and again, years later, while writing *Prince of Persia: The Sands of Time.* This should be no surprise; as Umberto Eco has noted, everything has something to do with the Templars.

One of the perks of making up stories for a living, be they screenplays, video games, or novels, is that it offers an excuse to read lots of books in the name of research. For a writer, one of the greatest joys is that moment when, seeking background material for one story, you stumble onto a better one.

My original, or rather deeply unoriginal, thought was that the Templars would make a nifty background for a conspiracy thriller. I spent a few years developing various ideas along those lines before losing heart. I'd read so many stories in which a clandestine society tracing its lineage back to the Templars guarded the Ark of the Covenant, Christ's bloodline, the Holy Grail, or some other long-buried secret that would shake civilization to its foundations if, etc., that I couldn't persuade myself the world needed another one. (I was wrong, of course. It was 2002, and the world still needed *The Da Vinci Code*, *National Treasure*, and *Assassin's Creed.*)

Out of all that historical and pseudo-historical research, what gripped my imagination more than any speculative latter-day conspiracy theory was the *actual* story of the spectacular rise and shocking downfall of the Knights of the Temple—a scandal that shook the fourteenth century and reverberates to this day. Bizarrely, although it's well documented for something that happened 700 years ago, it was a piece of history I'd never seen dramatized—not in a movie, not in a novel, not in a video game.

The back story in a nutshell: Formed during the Crusades, the Templars gained fame as the noblest and bravest knights in Christendom. Like Western gunslingers or Japanese samurai, their legend grew, attracting new recruits, donations, and privileges. Boys dreamed of becoming Templars when they grew up. They were the Jedi of their time. By their peak in the thirteenth century, the Knights Templar had grown into a religious, military, and banking organization whose assets, power, and reach rivaled any of the kings of Europe. They flourished, inviolate (and tax-free), under the protection of an all-powerful Catholic Church and Pope.

Then, one October dawn in 1307, the King of France ordered the simultaneous mass arrest of all Templars in his kingdom—15,000 of them, from the lowliest serving brother to the Grand Master himself. The Templars were hauled before the Inquisition and accused of witchcraft, heresy, sodomy—the most evil crimes in their world. It's as if the FBI were to raid the U.S. Marines, confiscate their weapons and assets, and arrest every soldier on charges of treason and terrorism.

The Templar trial was a sensation. The king's chief minister, Guillaume de Nogaret, had shrewdly judged the tenor of the times. He staged the first modern political show trial, using tactics that would work equally well for Stalin and McCarthy more than six centuries later: Prisoners who denied the charges were tortured until they confessed, which proved that those who hadn't confessed were lying. Faced with a public-relations disaster, the Pope backed down, sacrificing his once-mighty Templars to ensure his own political survival. The Order of the Temple was shattered, never to rise again.

The more I read about the trial, the more I sympathized with these Templars. Not so much the historical figures like the martyred Grand Master Jacques de Molay, but the rank and file—regular knights (and their support staff) who'd donated their worldly goods and taken the vows. They'd spent years in a Middle Eastern war zone, risking their lives in what the Pope and Church had told them was a just and holy cause, and came home to find themselves scapegoats—pawns in a political chess game their simple ideals of chivalry and brotherhood hadn't equipped them for.

I wanted to do a story about *those* guys—ordinary enlisted men who slipped through the cracks of history.

Reading between the lines of the Templar trial records, I got the feeling that it had been the troublemakers, the ones with a slightly scoundrelly streak, who had a better chance of slipping through the net, while the morally blameless knights who followed the rules went dutifully like lambs to the slaughter. This resonated all too well with my own family's experience of twentieth-century European history.

Medieval society was particularly inhospitable to those on its fringes. Without a family, a trade, a legitimate means of support, escaped Templars would have been by definition outlaws. Here were guys with special military skills who had been out of civilian life for years, whose whole world was the monastery, the barracks, and the battlefield—thrown out into the cold, hunted by the king's men. What would they do, how would they survive, in a city like Paris?

This speculation provided the spark for *Templar*. I wanted to weave an adventure yarn in the spirit of Alexandre Dumas, about a bunch of unlikely heroes whose main interests are fighting, gambling, drinking, and women (even though the last three are prohibited) and, caught in the backwash of history, have no one left to turn to but each other.

Here it is.

My thanks to all who've helped me with the research and the weaving over the past six years; to Mark Siegel and the team at First Second for their unwavering support and willingness to publish such a thick book; and most especially to the amazing husband-and-wife artistic team of LeUyen Pham and Alex Puvilland, who've brought the world and characters of *Templar* to vibrant life. Their unflagging creative energy and commitment went beyond illustration. They never stopped seeking ways to make our story better, sharper, even when it meant rewriting and redrawing pages that were already done. They've been the best collaborators a writer could wish for.

I hope you enjoy this book as much as we've enjoyed making it. And remember—it's all *absolutely true.* Well, some of it.

Jordan Mechner
New York
April 2012

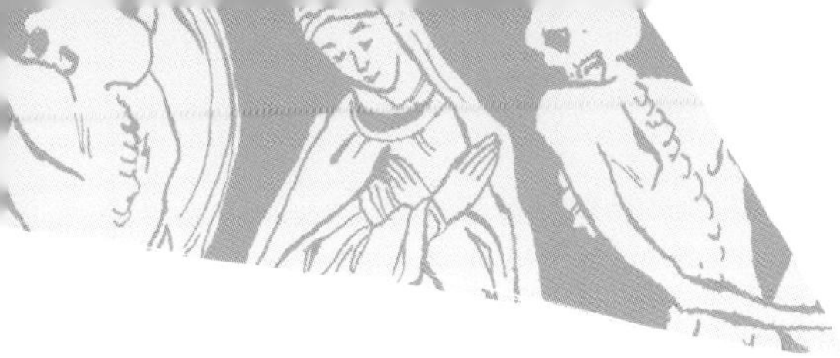

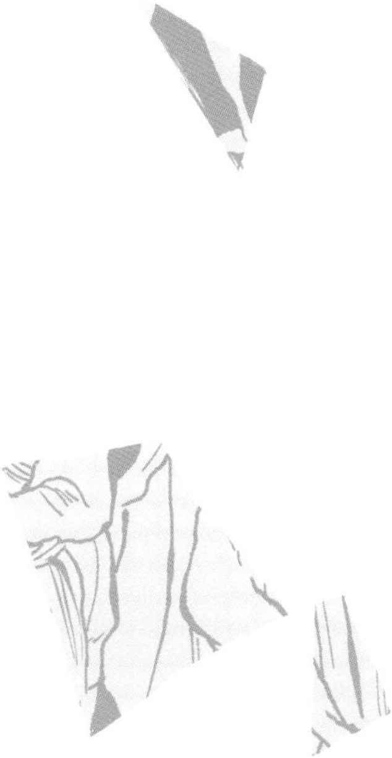

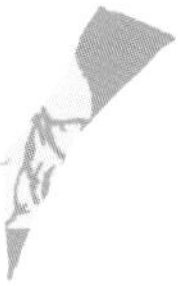

Book One • Solomon's Thieves

From humble beginnings the Knights Templar rose to become the most powerful military monastic order of the medieval world.

Pledged to protect pilgrims during the Crusades, the Templars became heroes to Christians everywhere. Their fighting prowess was legendary. The sight of their white cloaks and red crosses inspired the faithful and struck terror into their enemies. Young men rushed to join the Order, taking vows of poverty, chastity, and obedience to fight for God.

By the thirteenth century the Order commanded thousands of men, ships, and castles in every country in Europe. Considered untouchable, the Templars owed allegiance to no king—only to the Pope himself.

But the Crusades were an expensive, blood-soaked failure. In 1291, after two centuries of warfare, the Muslims drove the Christian armies from the Holy Land once and for all.

For the Templars, it was the beginning of the end . . .

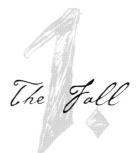

1. The Fall

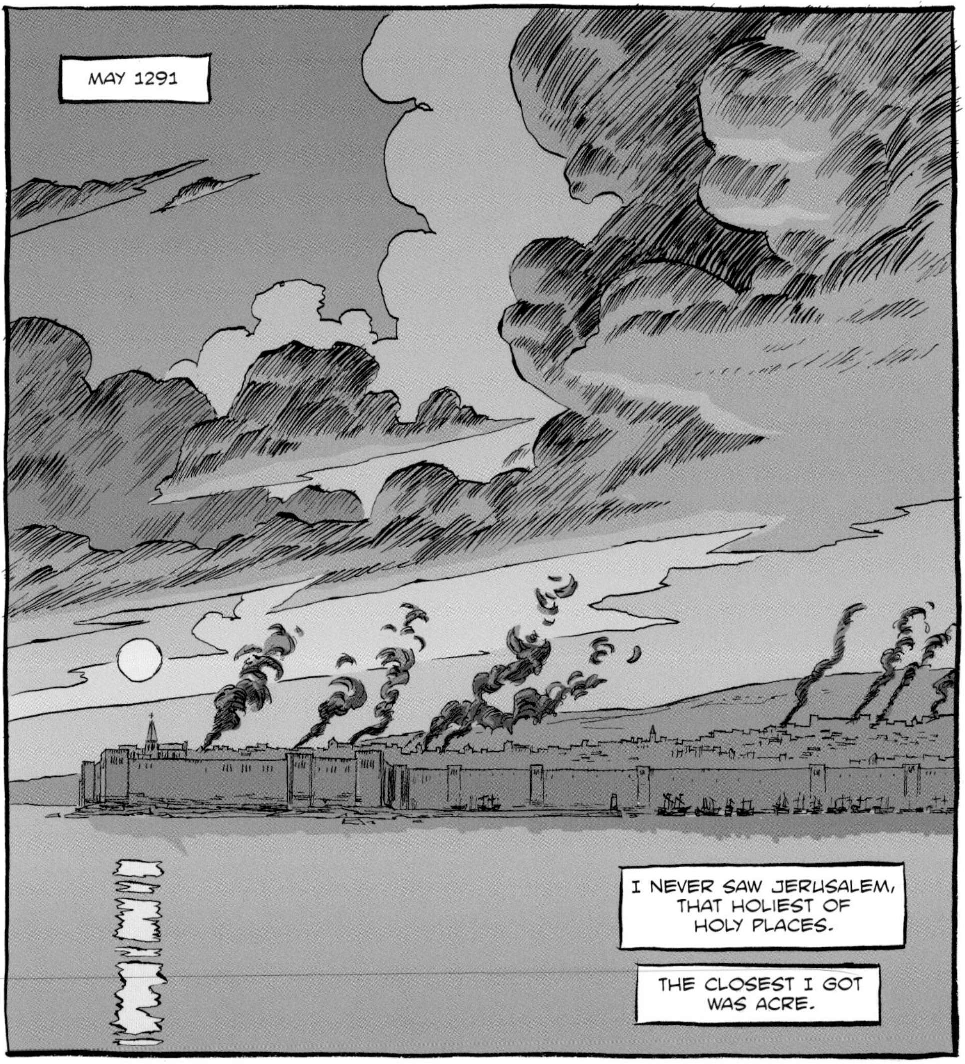
MAY 1291
I NEVER SAW JERUSALEM, THAT HOLIEST OF HOLY PLACES.
THE CLOSEST I GOT WAS ACRE.

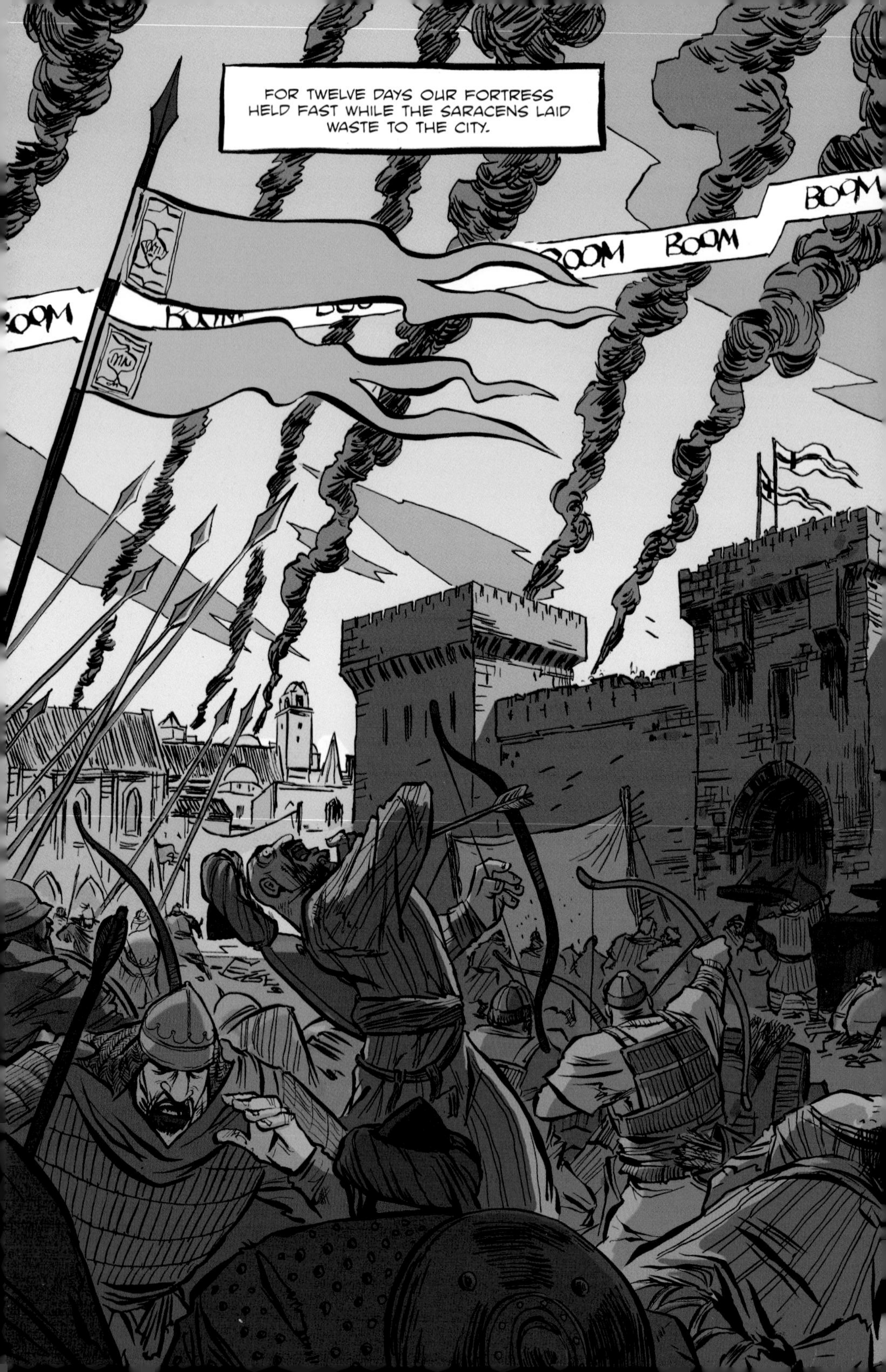
FOR TWELVE DAYS OUR FORTRESS HELD FAST WHILE THE SARACENS LAID WASTE TO THE CITY.
BOOM
BOOM
BOOM

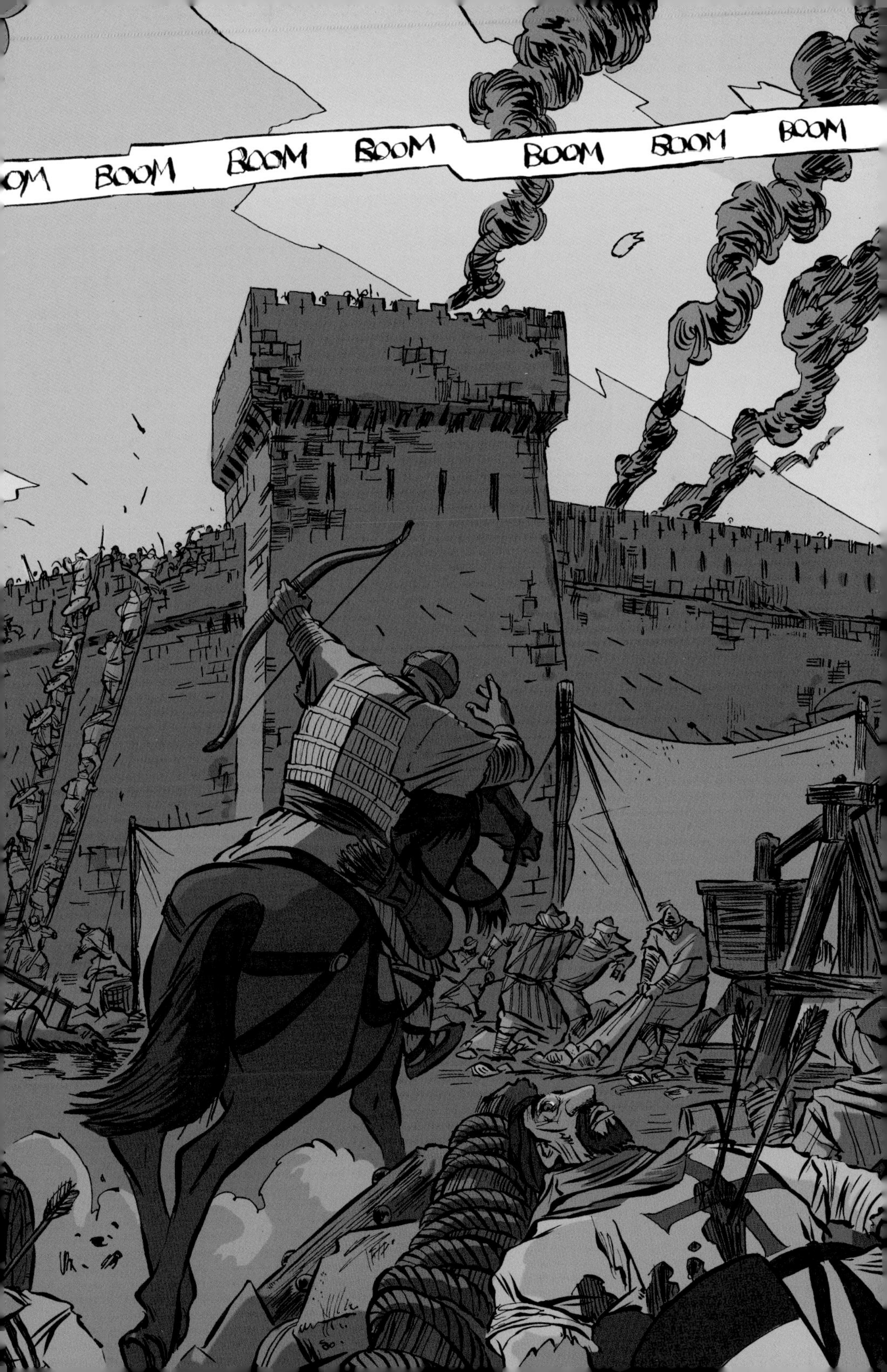
OOM BOOM BOOM BOOM BOOM BOOM BOOM

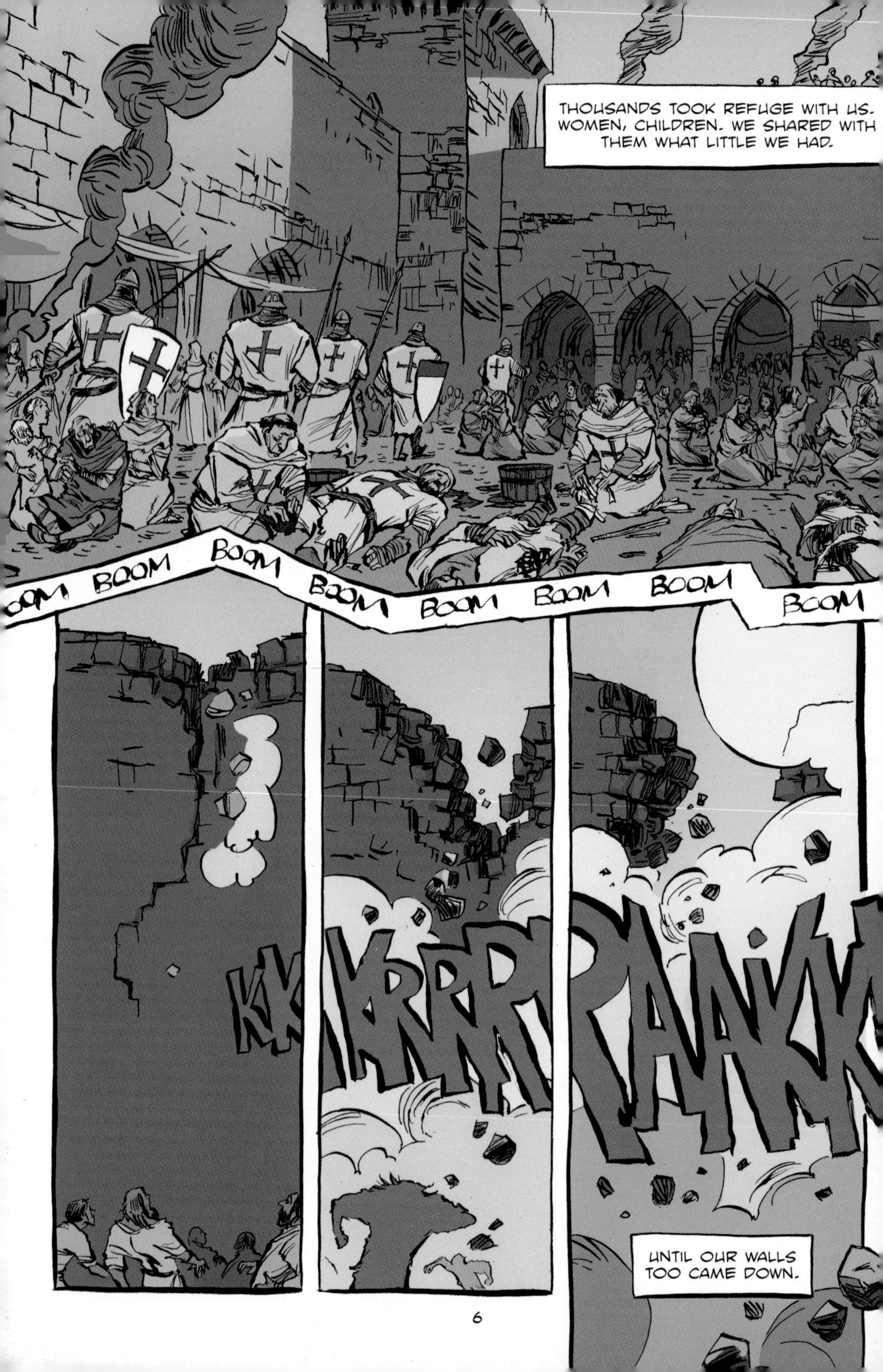
THOUSANDS TOOK REFUGE WITH US. WOMEN, CHILDREN. WE SHARED WITH THEM WHAT LITTLE WE HAD.
BOOM BOOM BOOM BOOM BOOM BOOM BOOM BOOM
KKRRRRAAKK
UNTIL OUR WALLS TOO CAME DOWN.

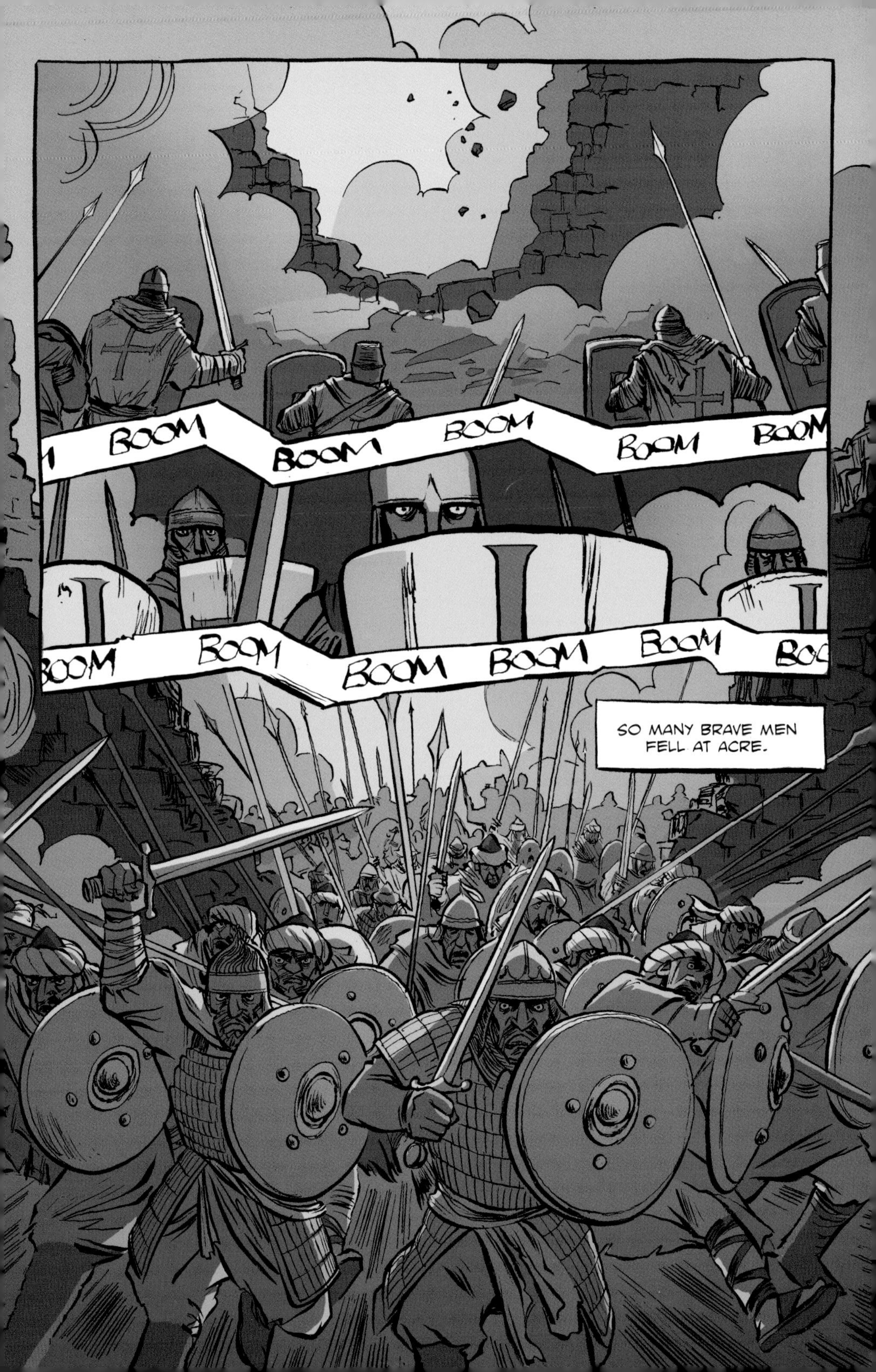

BOOM BOOM BOOM BOOM BOOM BOOM
BOOM BOOM BOOM BOOM BOOM
SO MANY BRAVE MEN FELL AT ACRE.

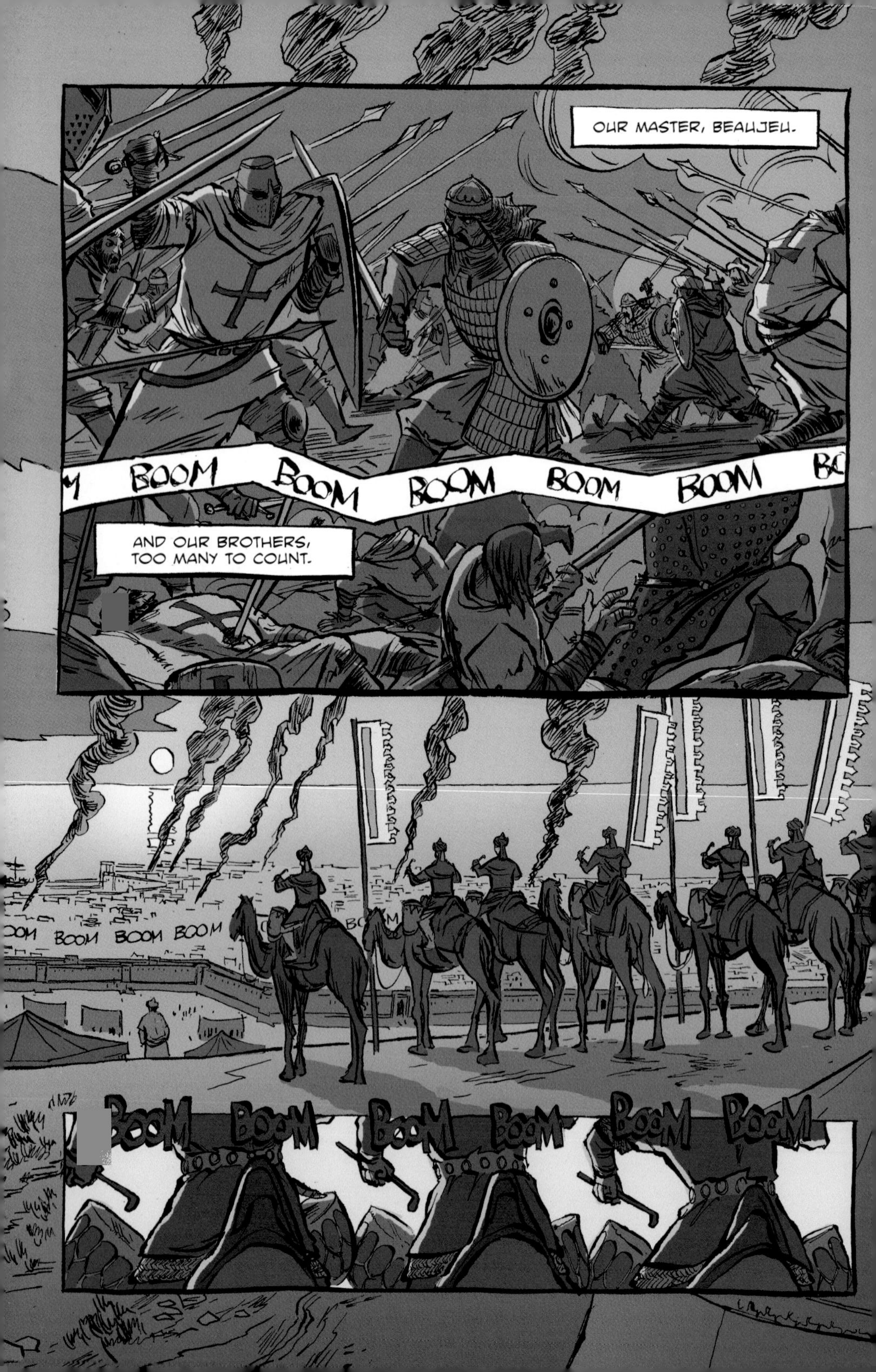
OUR MASTER, BEAUJEU.
BOOM BOOM BOOM BOOM BOOM
AND OUR BROTHERS, TOO MANY TO COUNT.
BOOM BOOM BOOM
BOOM BOOM BOOM BOOM BOOM BOOM

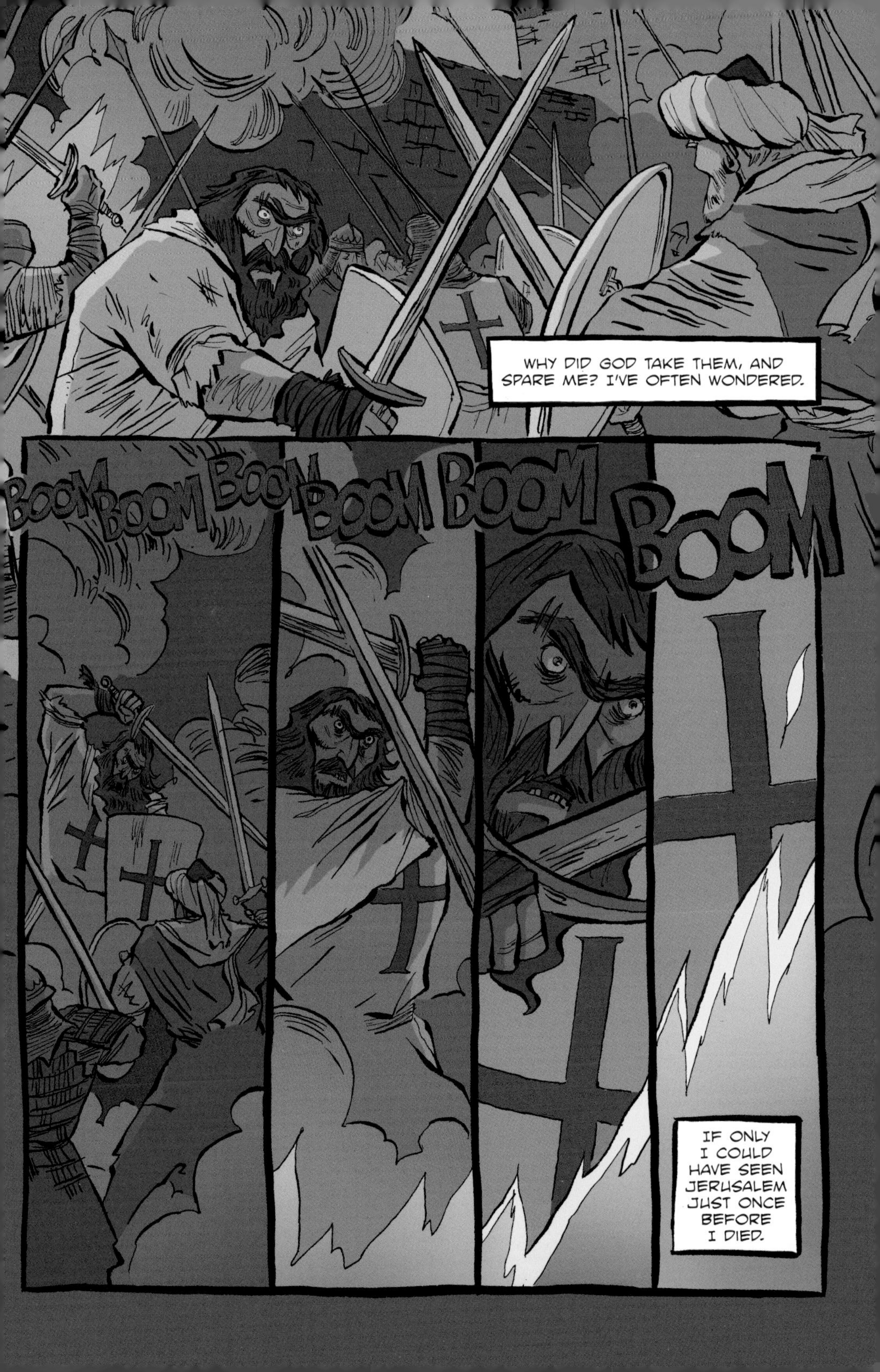
WHY DID GOD TAKE THEM, AND SPARE ME? I'VE OFTEN WONDERED.
BOOM BOOM BOOM BOOM BOOM BOOM
IF ONLY I COULD HAVE SEEN JERUSALEM JUST ONCE BEFORE I DIED.

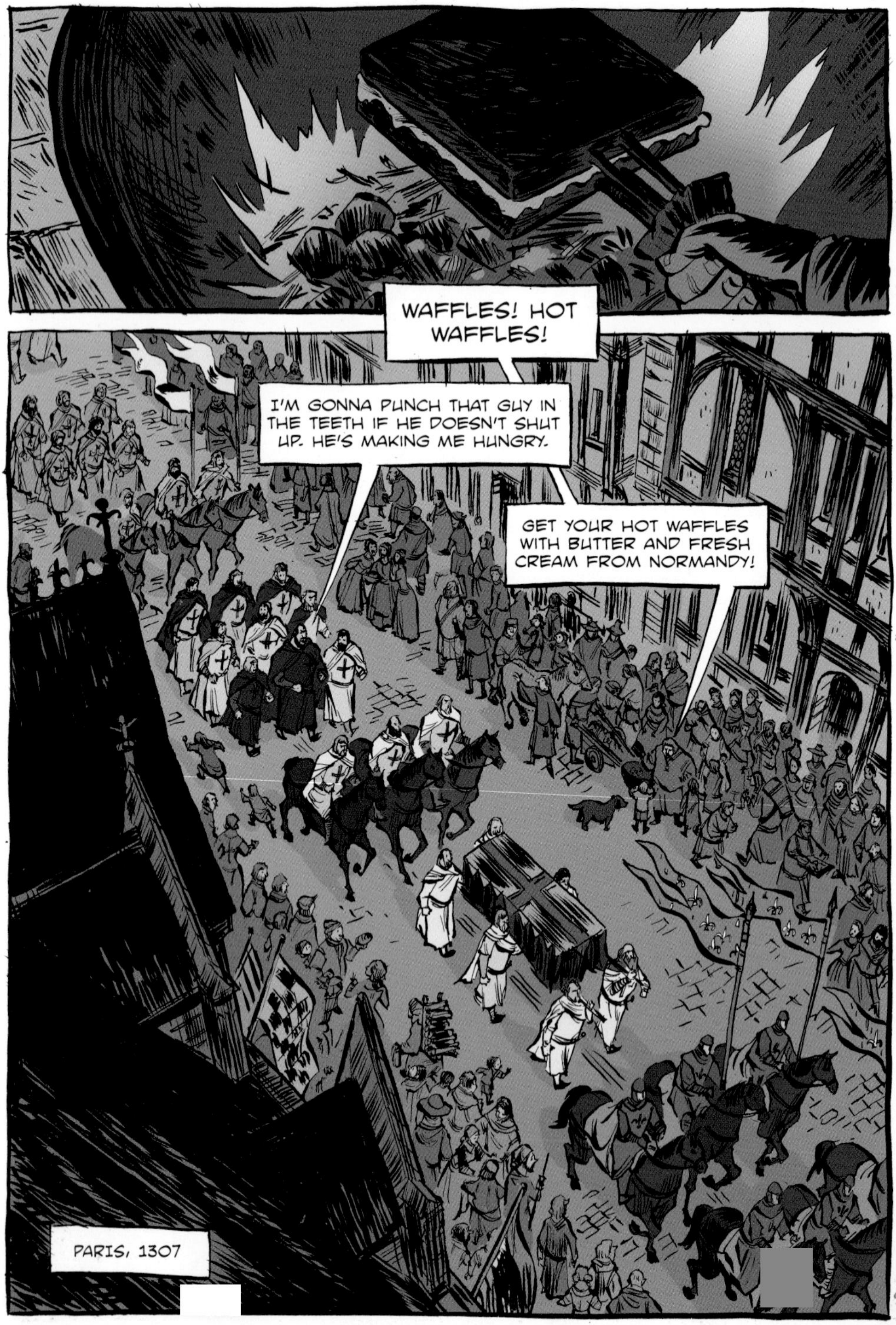
WAFFLES! HOT WAFFLES!
I'M GONNA PUNCH THAT GUY IN THE TEETH IF HE DOESN'T SHUT UP. HE'S MAKING ME HUNGRY.
GET YOUR HOT WAFFLES WITH BUTTER AND FRESH CREAM FROM NORMANDY!
PARIS, 1307

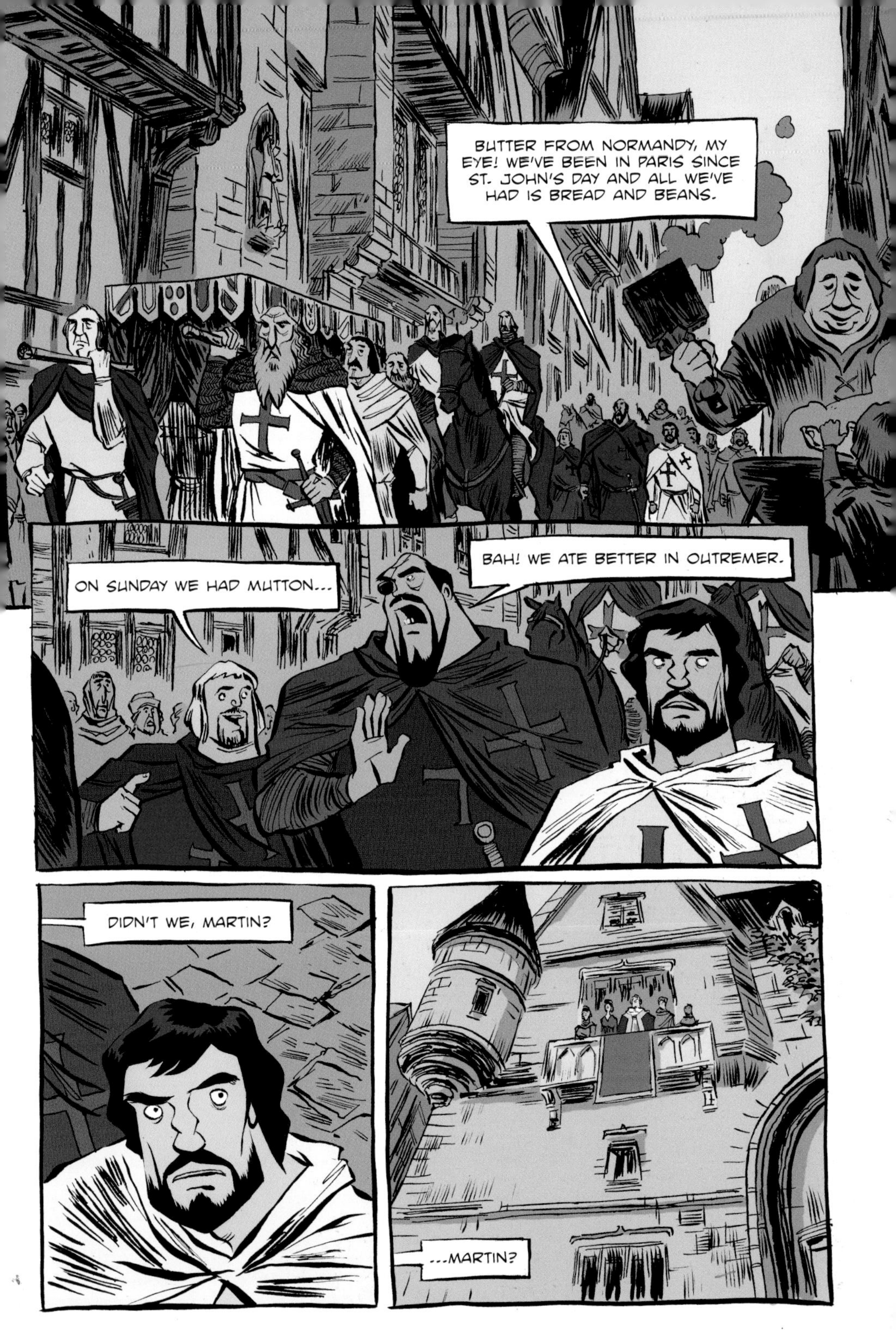
BUTTER FROM NORMANDY, MY EYE! WE'VE BEEN IN PARIS SINCE ST. JOHN'S DAY AND ALL WE'VE HAD IS BREAD AND BEANS.
ON SUNDAY WE HAD MUTTON...
BAH! WE ATE BETTER IN OUTREMER.
DIDN'T WE, MARTIN?
...MARTIN?

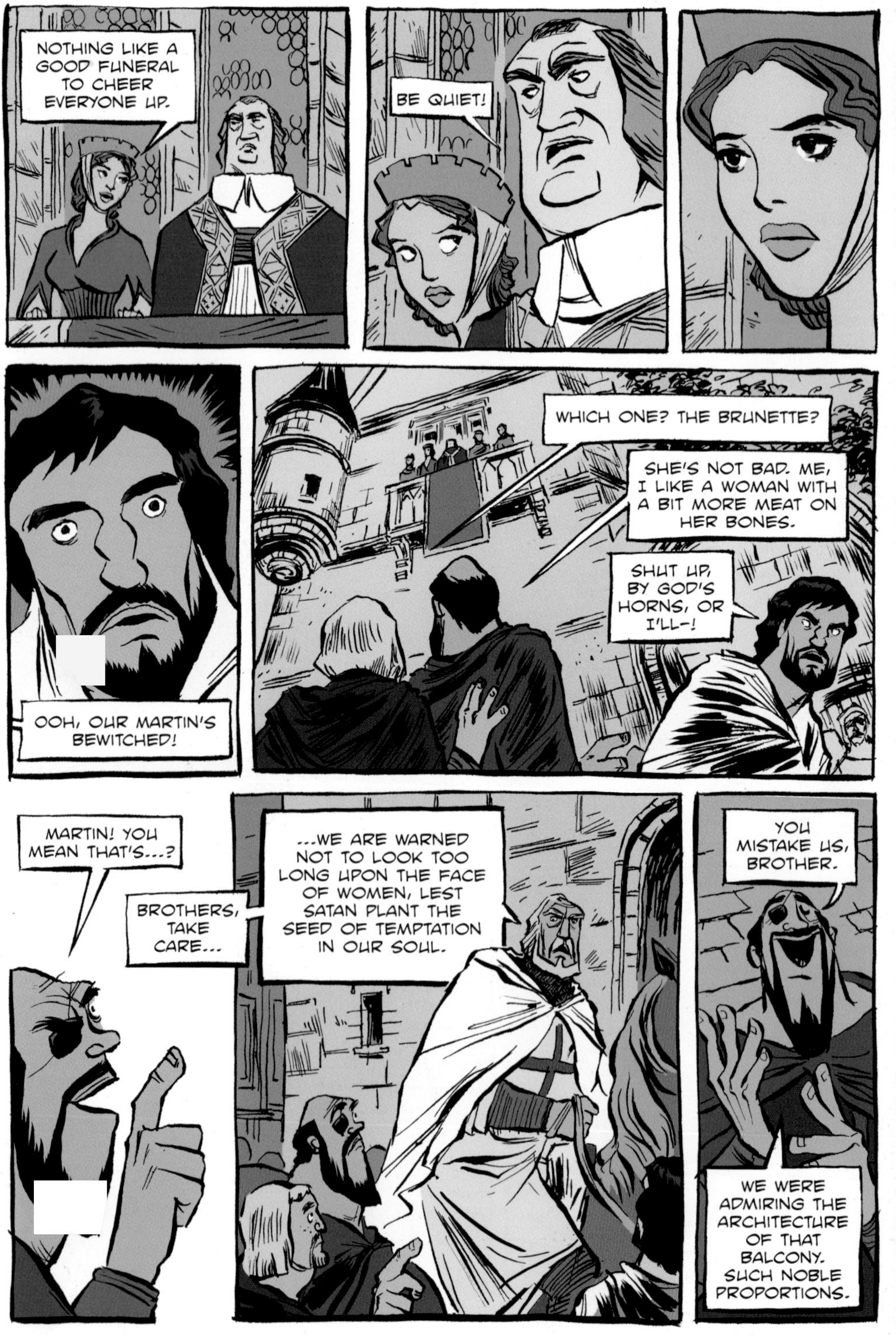
NOTHING LIKE A GOOD FUNERAL TO CHEER EVERYONE UP.
BE QUIET!
WHICH ONE? THE BRUNETTE?
SHE'S NOT BAD. ME, I LIKE A WOMAN WITH A BIT MORE MEAT ON HER BONES.
SHUT UP, BY GOD'S HORNS, OR I'LL-!
OOH, OUR MARTIN'S BEWITCHED!
MARTIN! YOU MEAN THAT'S...?
BROTHERS, TAKE CARE...
...WE ARE WARNED NOT TO LOOK TOO LONG UPON THE FACE OF WOMEN, LEST SATAN PLANT THE SEED OF TEMPTATION IN OUR SOUL.
YOU MISTAKE US, BROTHER.
WE WERE ADMIRING THE ARCHITECTURE OF THAT BALCONY. SUCH NOBLE PROPORTIONS.

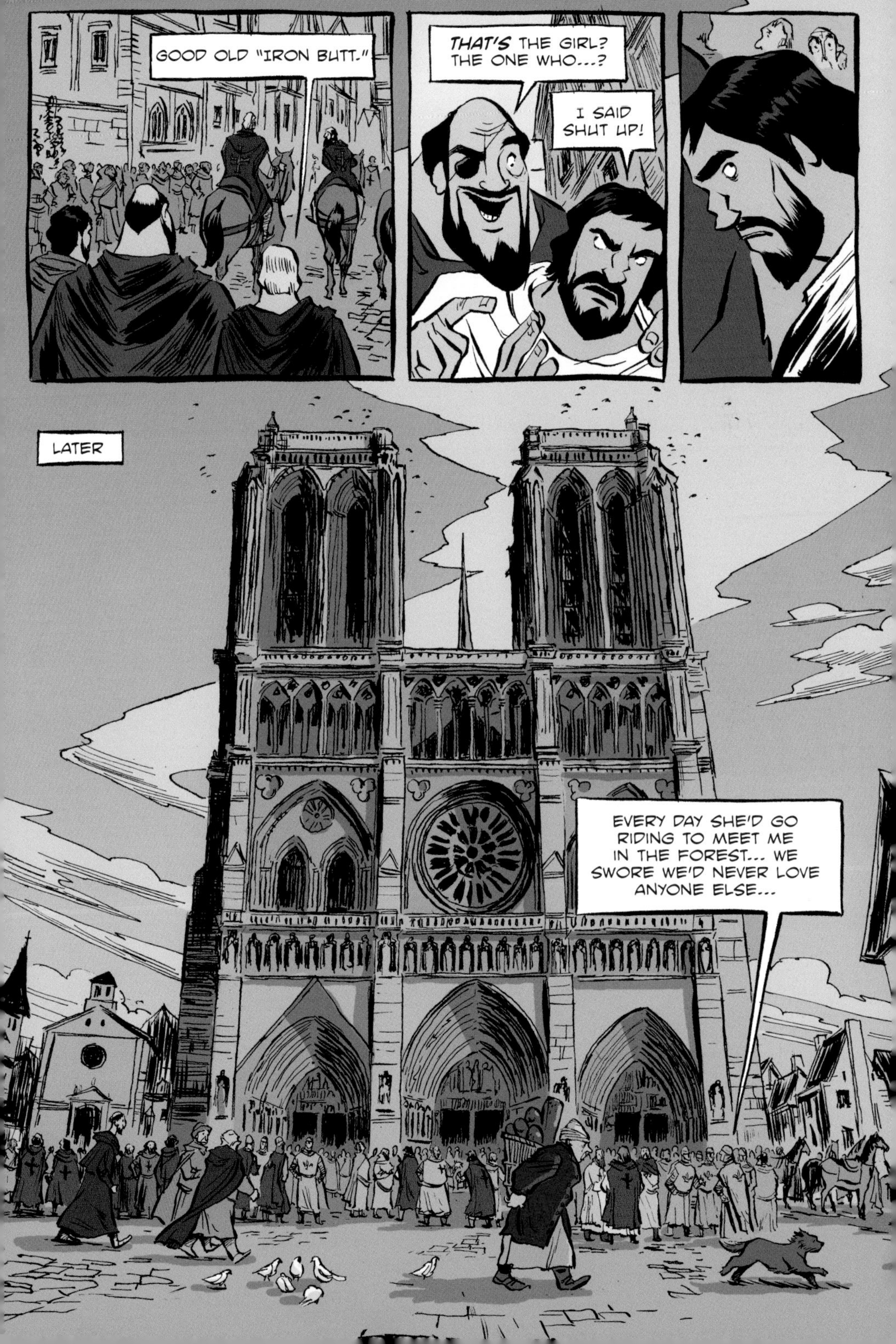
GOOD OLD "IRON BUTT."
THAT'S THE GIRL? THE ONE WHO...?
I SAID SHUT UP!
LATER
EVERY DAY SHE'D GO RIDING TO MEET ME IN THE FOREST... WE SWORE WE'D NEVER LOVE ANYONE ELSE...

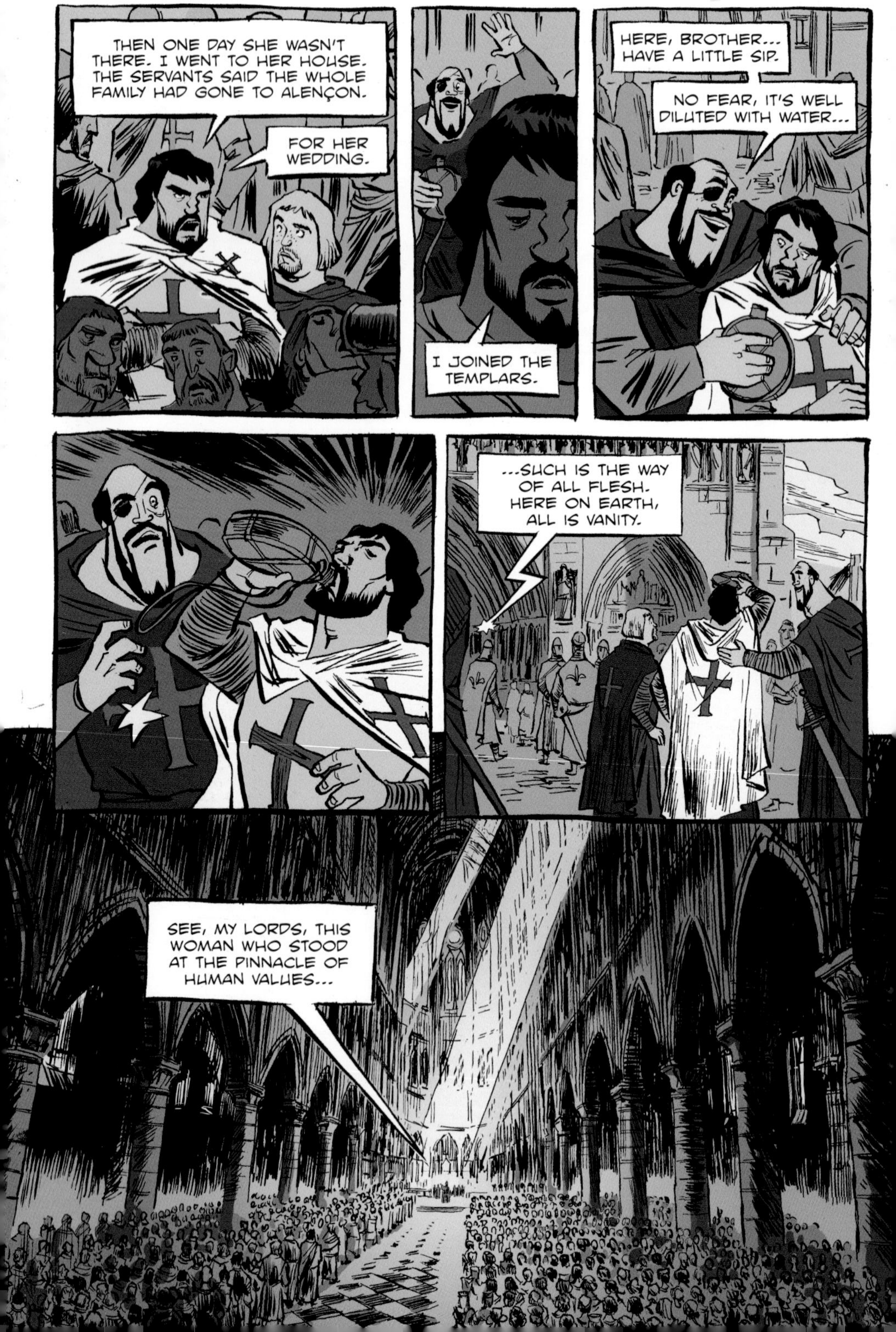
THEN ONE DAY SHE WASN'T THERE. I WENT TO HER HOUSE. THE SERVANTS SAID THE WHOLE FAMILY HAD GONE TO ALENÇON.
FOR HER WEDDING.
I JOINED THE TEMPLARS.
HERE, BROTHER... HAVE A LITTLE SIP.
NO FEAR, IT'S WELL DILUTED WITH WATER...
...SUCH IS THE WAY OF ALL FLESH. HERE ON EARTH, ALL IS VANITY.
SEE, MY LORDS, THIS WOMAN WHO STOOD AT THE PINNACLE OF HUMAN VALUES...

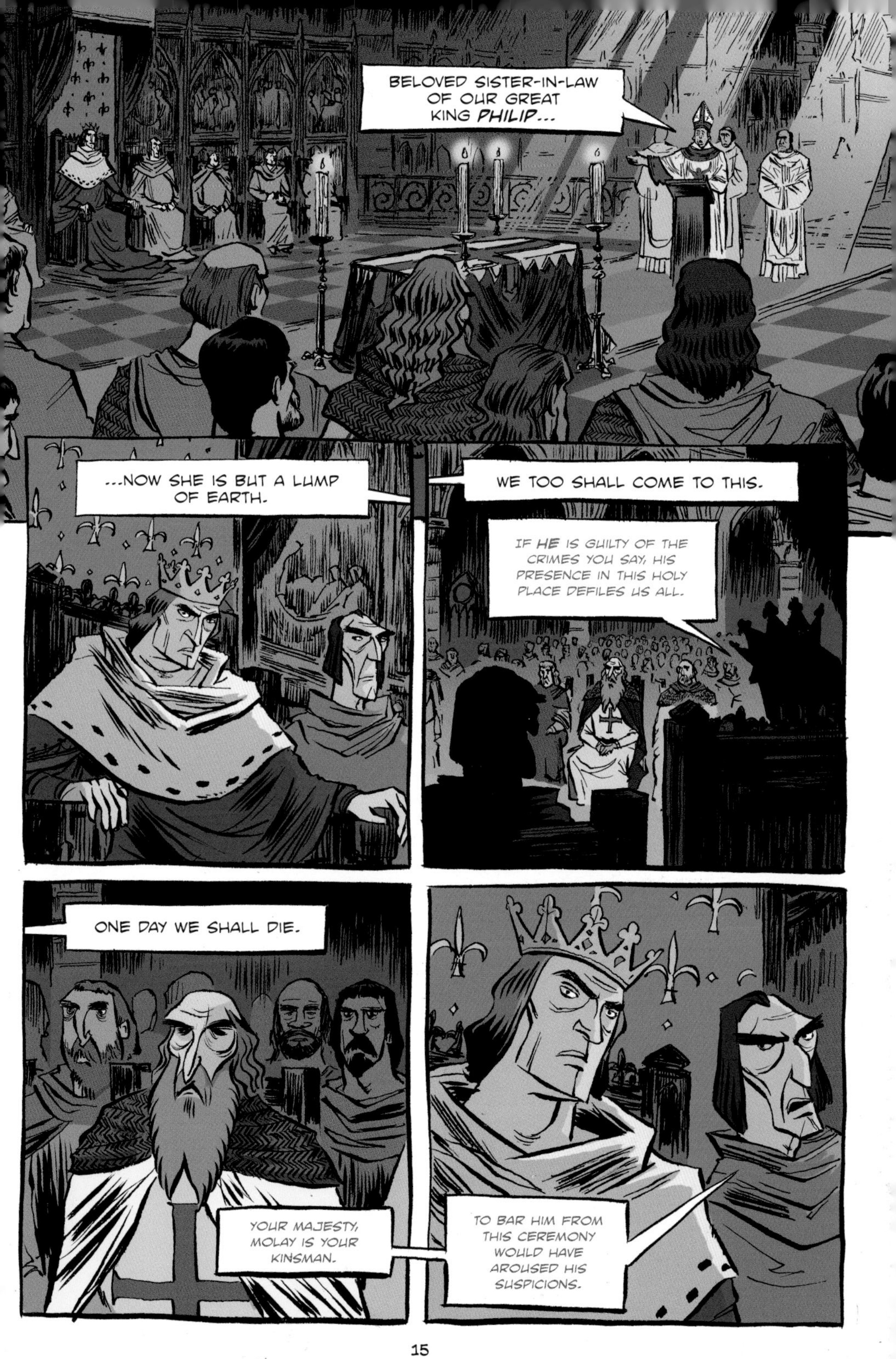
BELOVED SISTER-IN-LAW OF OUR GREAT KING PHILIP...
...NOW SHE IS BUT A LUMP OF EARTH.
WE TOO SHALL COME TO THIS.
IF HE IS GUILTY OF THE CRIMES YOU SAY, HIS PRESENCE IN THIS HOLY PLACE DEFILES US ALL.
ONE DAY WE SHALL DIE.
YOUR MAJESTY, MOLAY IS YOUR KINSMAN.
TO BAR HIM FROM THIS CEREMONY WOULD HAVE AROUSED HIS SUSPICIONS.

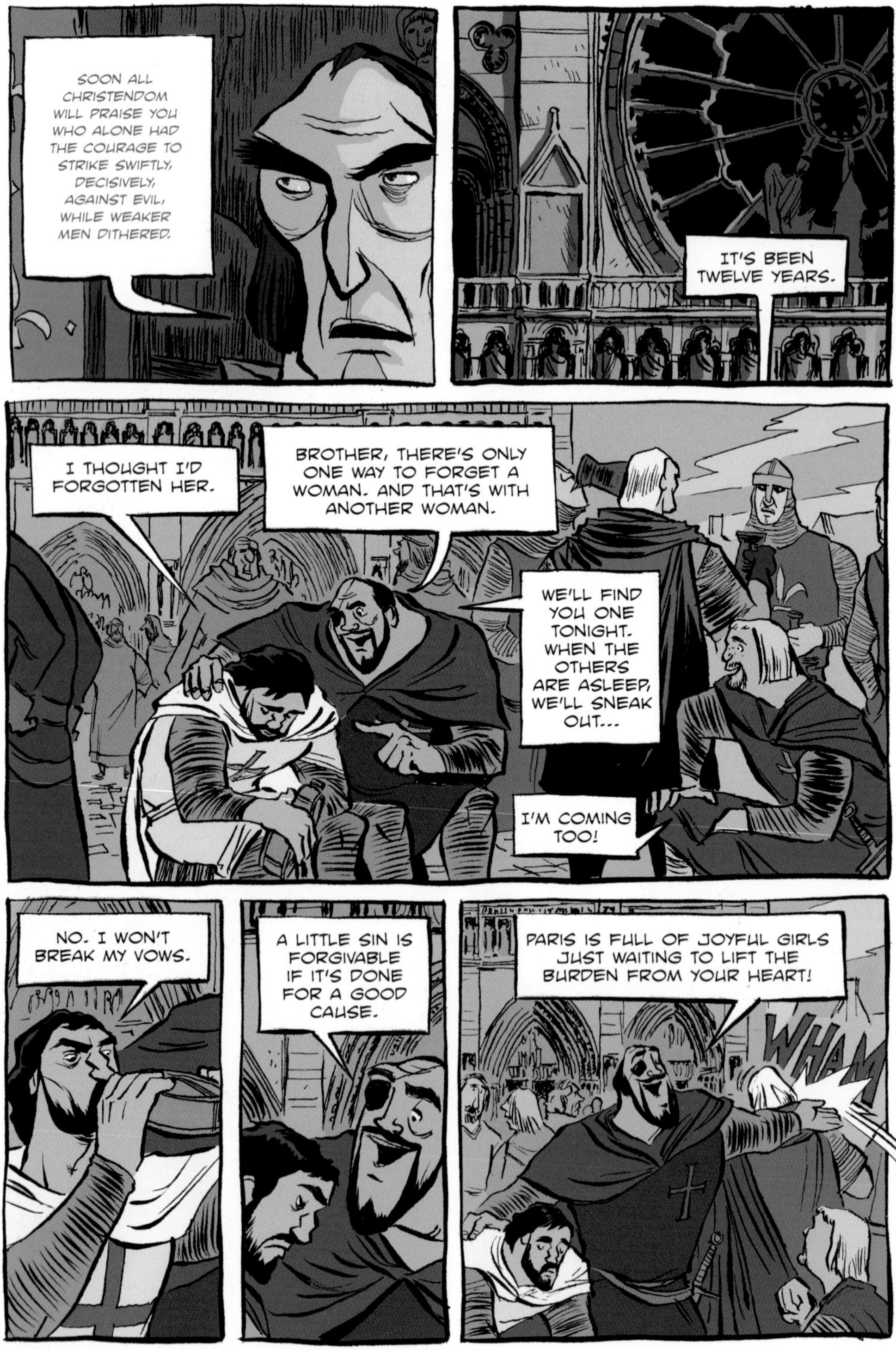
SOON ALL CHRISTENDOM WILL PRAISE YOU WHO ALONE HAD THE COURAGE TO STRIKE SWIFTLY, DECISIVELY, AGAINST EVIL, WHILE WEAKER MEN DITHERED.
IT'S BEEN TWELVE YEARS.
I THOUGHT I'D FORGOTTEN HER.
BROTHER, THERE'S ONLY ONE WAY TO FORGET A WOMAN. AND THAT'S WITH ANOTHER WOMAN.
WE'LL FIND YOU ONE TONIGHT. WHEN THE OTHERS ARE ASLEEP, WE'LL SNEAK OUT...
I'M COMING TOO!
NO. I WON'T BREAK MY VOWS.
A LITTLE SIN IS FORGIVABLE IF IT'S DONE FOR A GOOD CAUSE.
PARIS IS FULL OF JOYFUL GIRLS JUST WAITING TO LIFT THE BURDEN FROM YOUR HEART!
WHAM

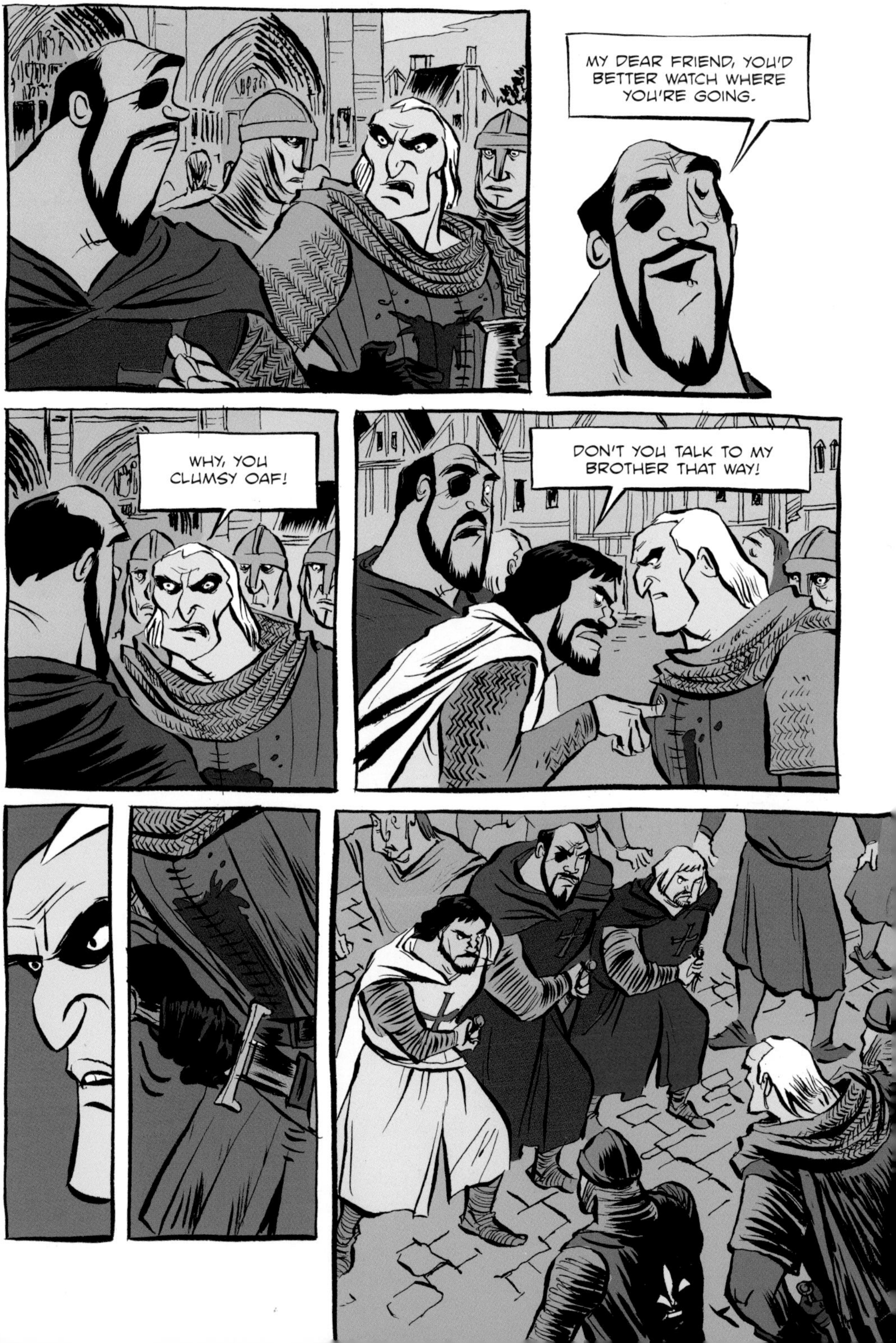
MY DEAR FRIEND, YOU'D BETTER WATCH WHERE YOU'RE GOING.
WHY, YOU CLUMSY OAF!
DON'T YOU TALK TO MY BROTHER THAT WAY!

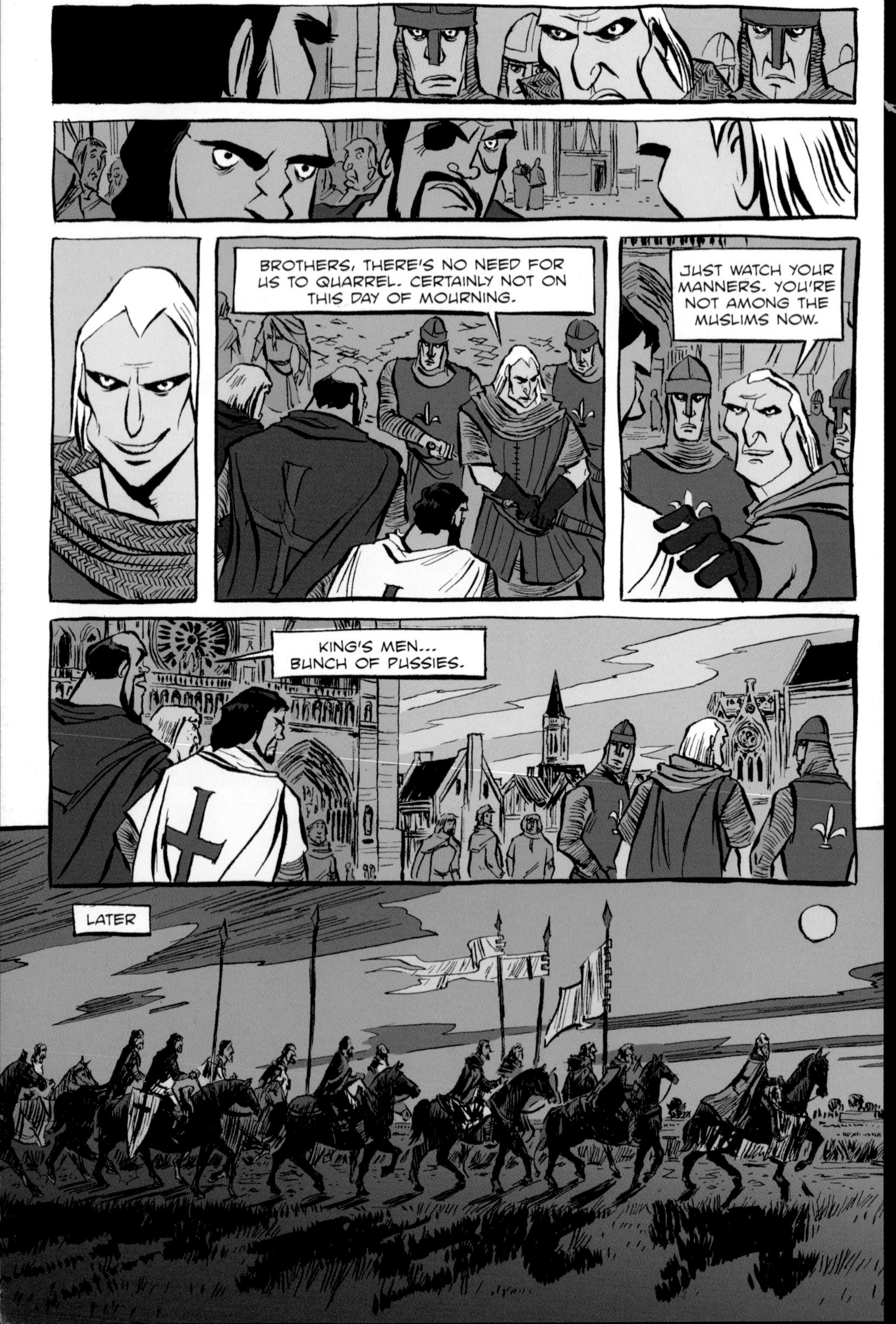
BROTHERS, THERE'S NO NEED FOR US TO QUARREL. CERTAINLY NOT ON THIS DAY OF MOURNING.
JUST WATCH YOUR MANNERS. YOU'RE NOT AMONG THE MUSLIMS NOW.
KING'S MEN... BUNCH OF PUSSIES.
LATER

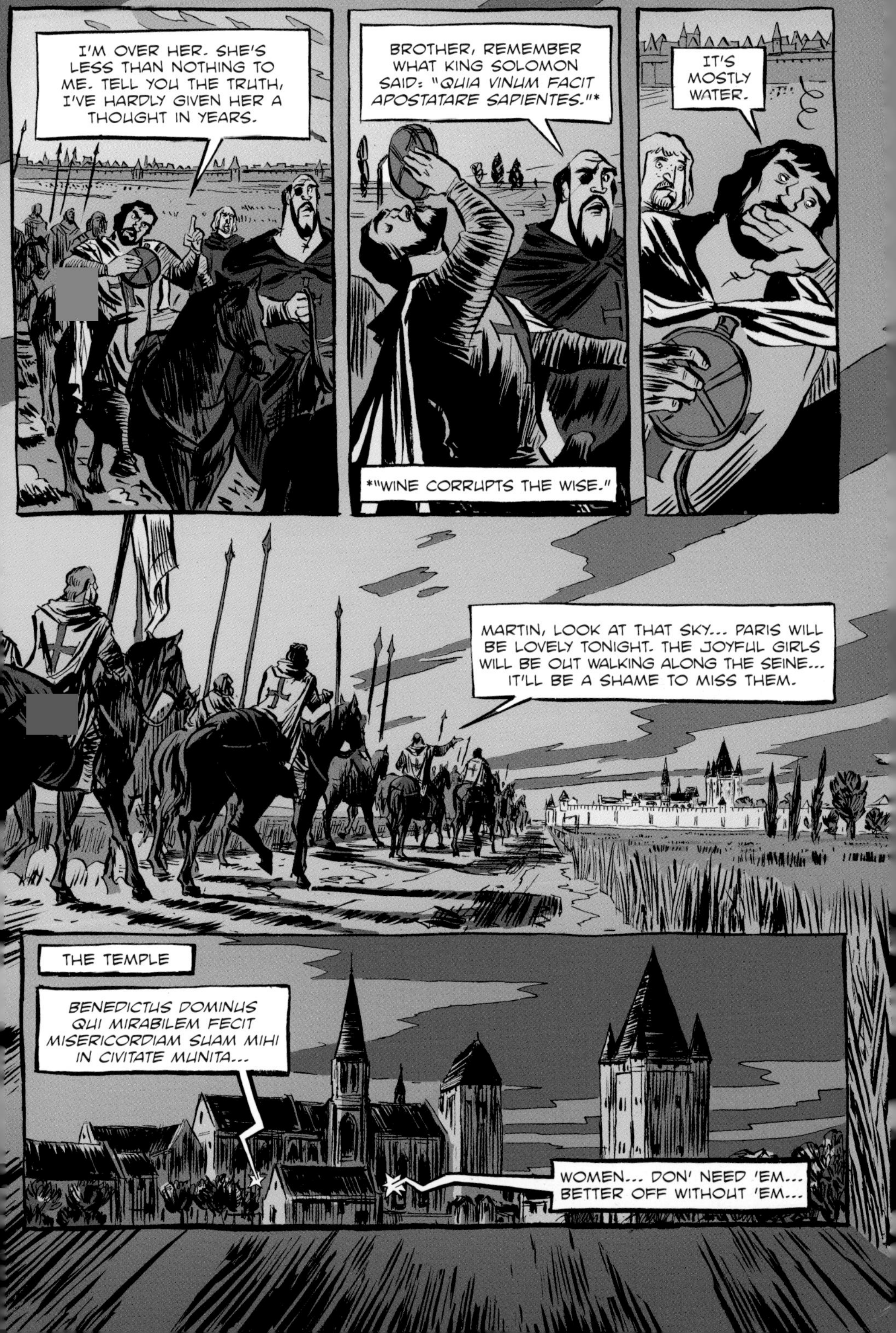
I'M OVER HER. SHE'S LESS THAN NOTHING TO ME. TELL YOU THE TRUTH, I'VE HARDLY GIVEN HER A THOUGHT IN YEARS.
BROTHER, REMEMBER WHAT KING SOLOMON SAID: "*QUIA VINUM FACIT APOSTATARE SAPIENTES.*"*
*"WINE CORRUPTS THE WISE."
IT'S MOSTLY WATER.
MARTIN, LOOK AT THAT SKY... PARIS WILL BE LOVELY TONIGHT. THE JOYFUL GIRLS WILL BE OUT WALKING ALONG THE SEINE... IT'LL BE A SHAME TO MISS THEM.
THE TEMPLE
BENEDICTUS DOMINUS QUI MIRABILEM FECIT MISERICORDIAM SUAM MIHI IN CIVITATE MUNITA...
WOMEN... DON' NEED 'EM... BETTER OFF WITHOUT 'EM...

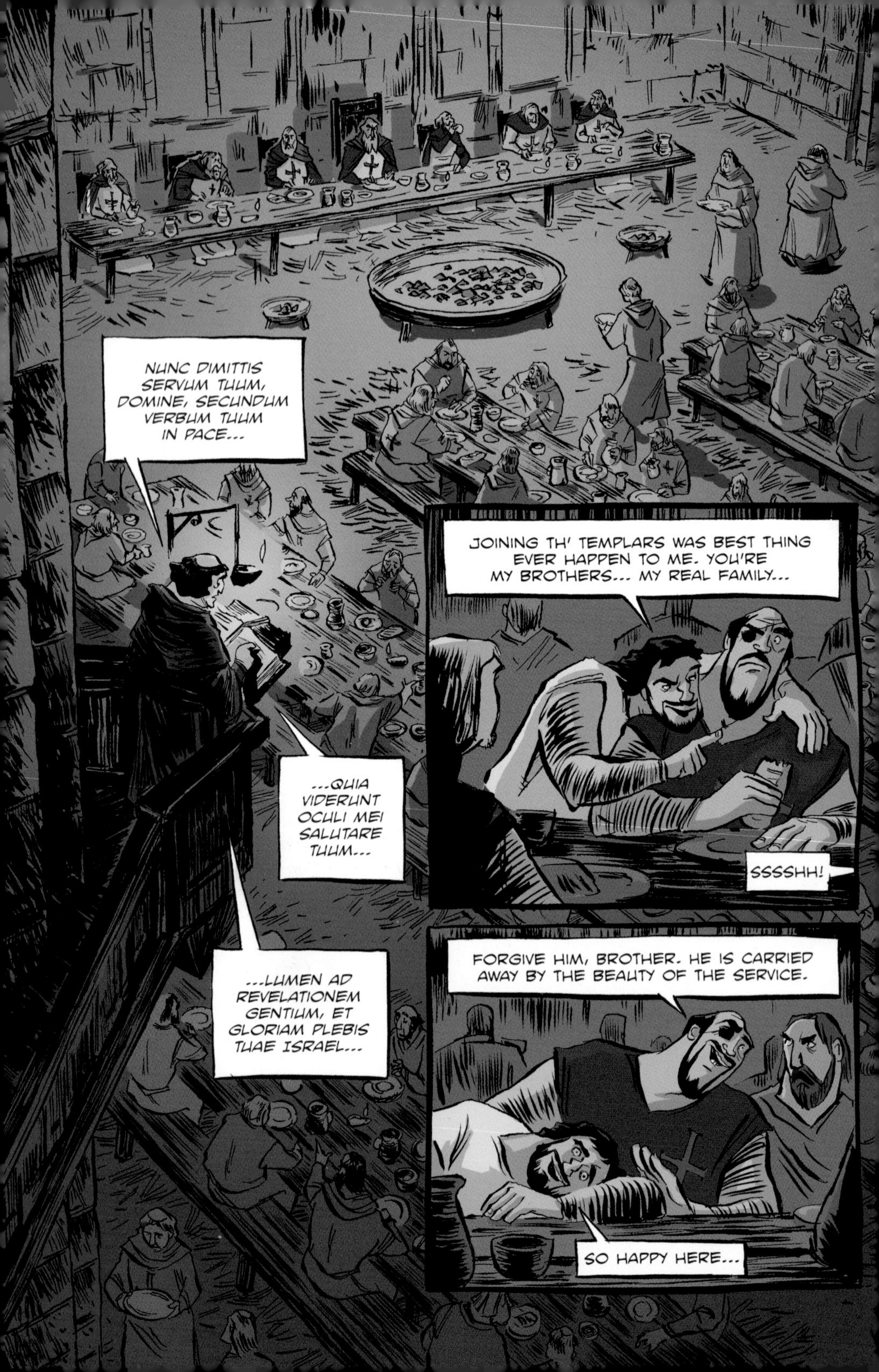
NUNC DIMITTIS SERVUM TUUM, DOMINE, SECUNDUM VERBUM TUUM IN PACE...
...QUIA VIDERUNT OCULI MEI SALUTARE TUUM...
...LUMEN AD REVELATIONEM GENTIUM, ET GLORIAM PLEBIS TUAE ISRAEL...
JOINING TH' TEMPLARS WAS BEST THING EVER HAPPEN TO ME. YOU'RE MY BROTHERS... MY REAL FAMILY...
SSSSHH!
FORGIVE HIM, BROTHER. HE IS CARRIED AWAY BY THE BEAUTY OF THE SERVICE.
SO HAPPY HERE...

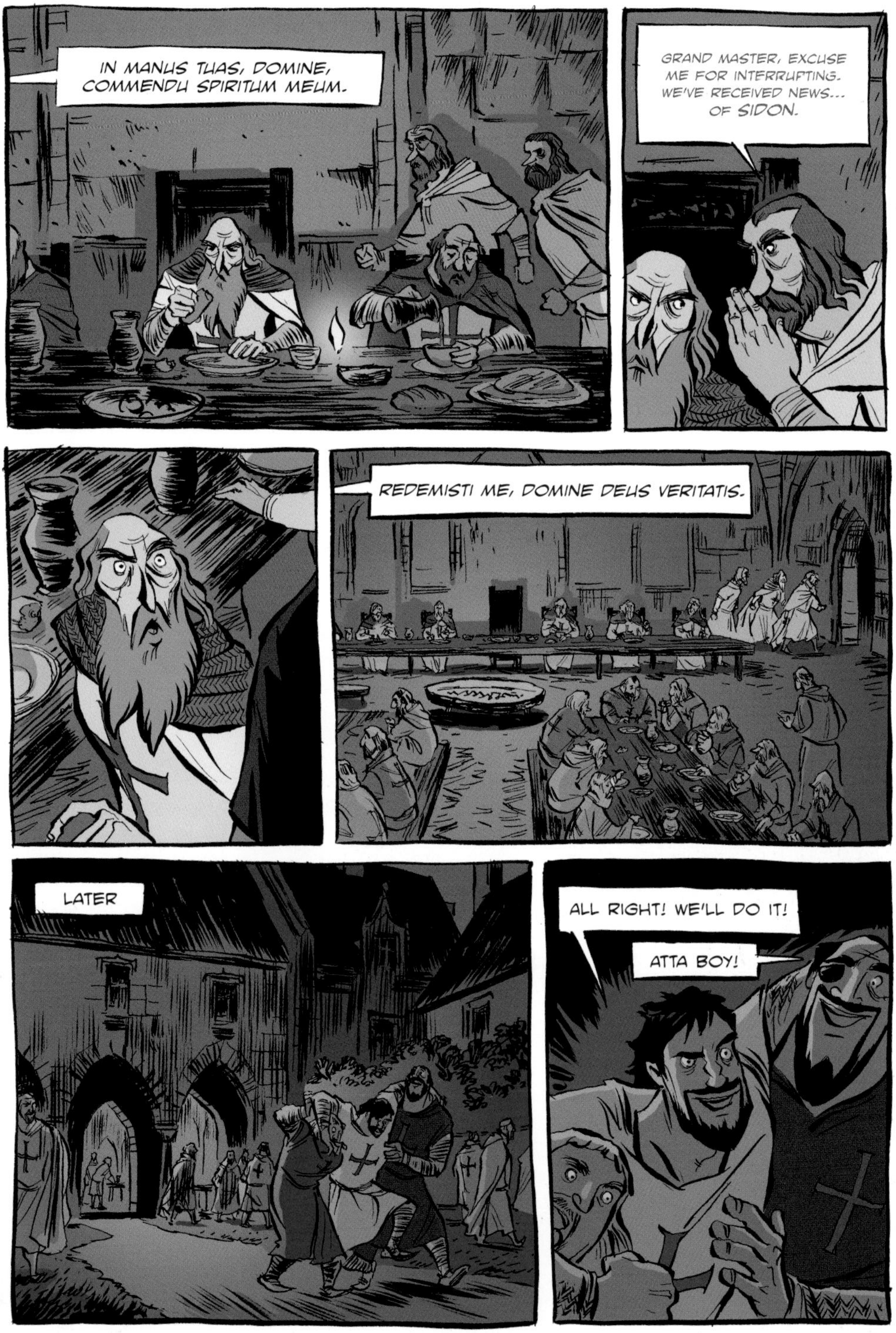
IN MANUS TUAS, DOMINE, COMMENDU SPIRITUM MEUM.
GRAND MASTER, EXCUSE ME FOR INTERRUPTING. WE'VE RECEIVED NEWS... OF SIDON.
REDEMISTI ME, DOMINE DEUS VERITATIS.
LATER
ALL RIGHT! WE'LL DO IT!
ATTA BOY!

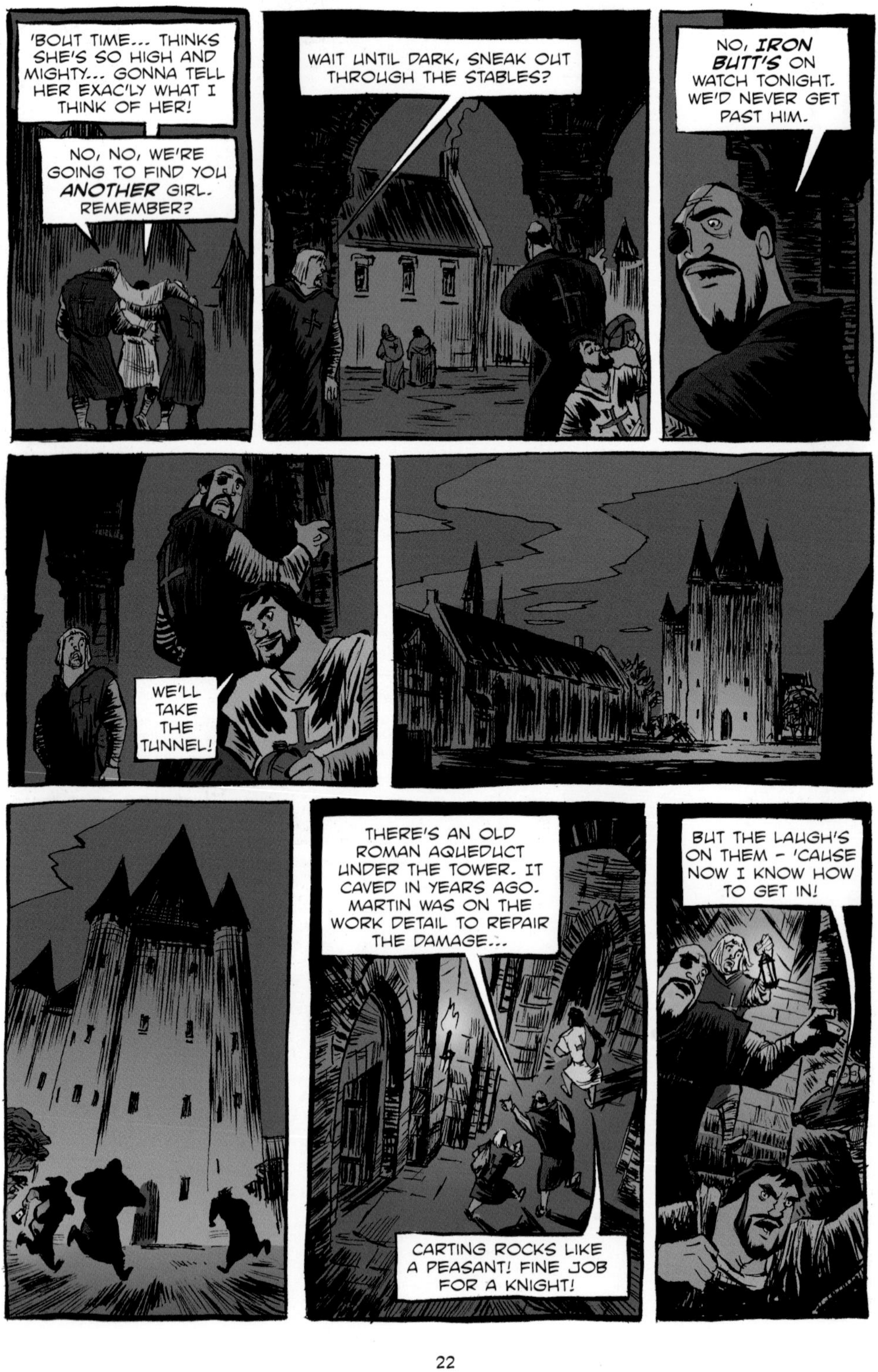
'BOUT TIME... THINKS SHE'S SO HIGH AND MIGHTY... GONNA TELL HER EXAC'LY WHAT I THINK OF HER!
NO, NO, WE'RE GOING TO FIND YOU ANOTHER GIRL. REMEMBER?
WAIT UNTIL DARK, SNEAK OUT THROUGH THE STABLES?
NO, IRON BUTT'S ON WATCH TONIGHT. WE'D NEVER GET PAST HIM.
WE'LL TAKE THE TUNNEL!
THERE'S AN OLD ROMAN AQUEDUCT UNDER THE TOWER. IT CAVED IN YEARS AGO. MARTIN WAS ON THE WORK DETAIL TO REPAIR THE DAMAGE...
CARTING ROCKS LIKE A PEASANT! FINE JOB FOR A KNIGHT!
BUT THE LAUGH'S ON THEM - 'CAUSE NOW I KNOW HOW TO GET IN!

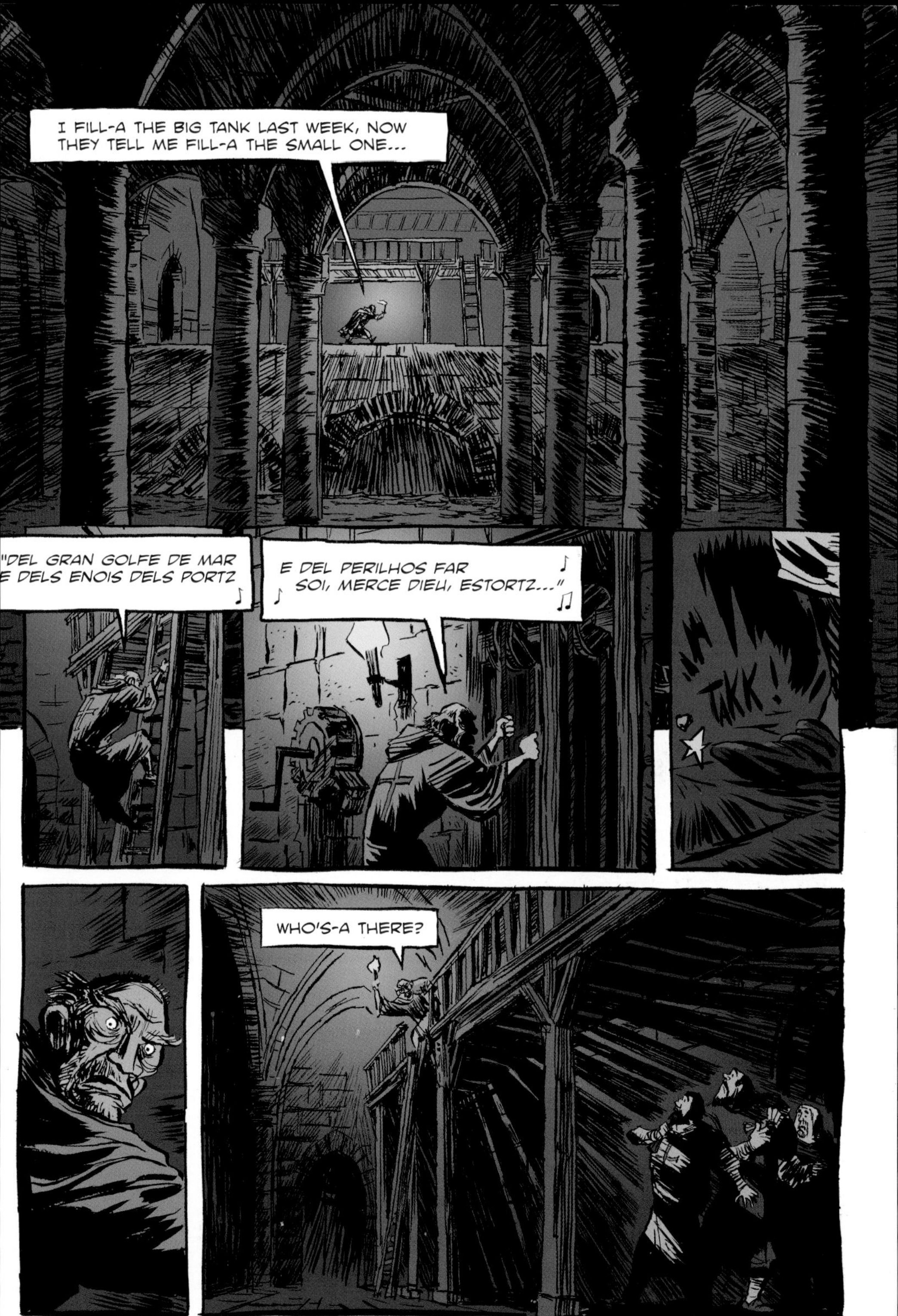
I FILL-A THE BIG TANK LAST WEEK, NOW THEY TELL ME FILL-A THE SMALL ONE...
"DEL GRAN GOLFE DE MAR E DELS ENOIS DELS PORTZ
E DEL PERILHOS FAR SOI, MERCE DIEU, ESTORTZ..."
TAKK!
WHO'S-A THERE?

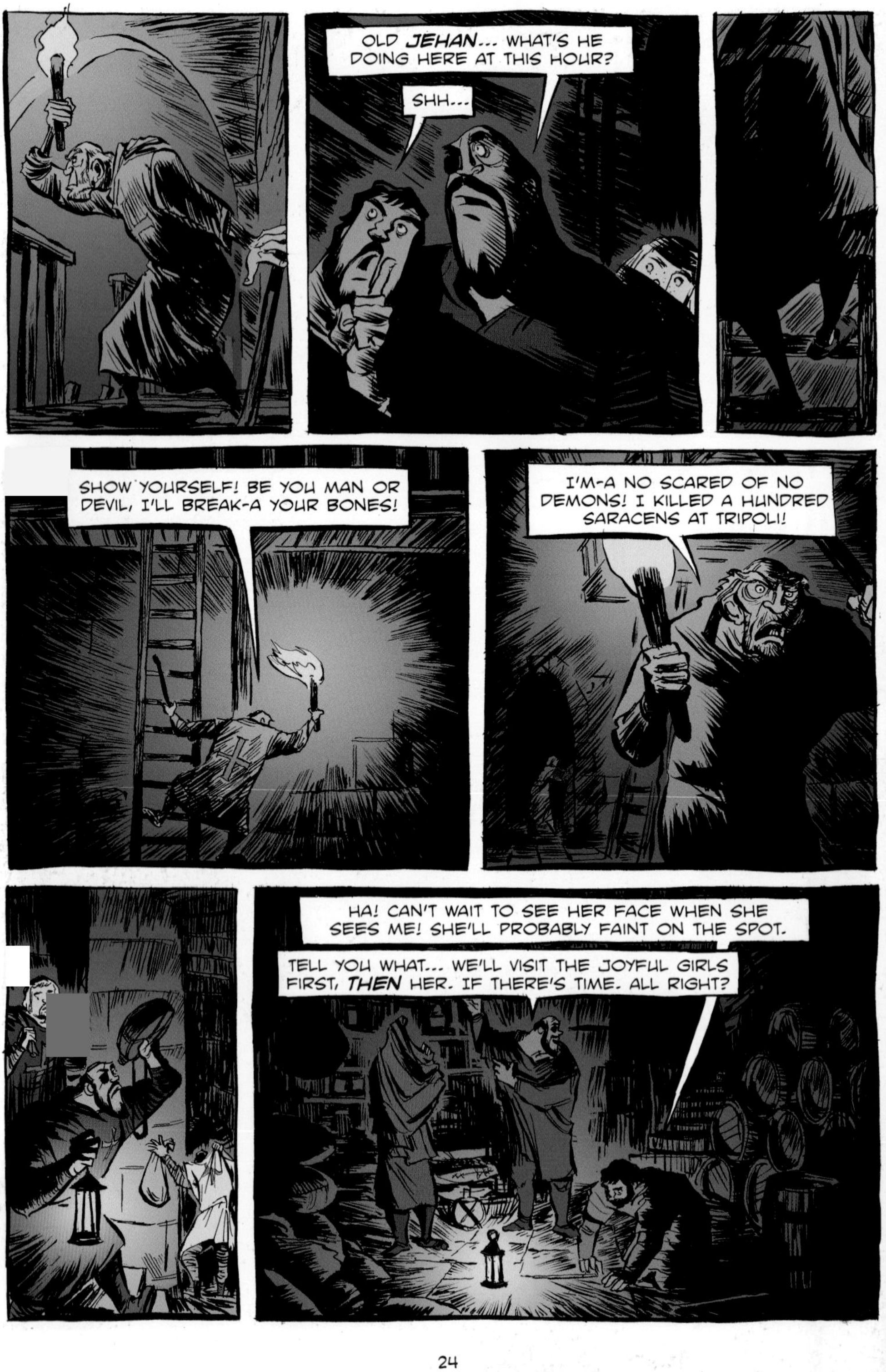
OLD JEHAN... WHAT'S HE DOING HERE AT THIS HOUR?
SHH...
SHOW YOURSELF! BE YOU MAN OR DEVIL, I'LL BREAK-A YOUR BONES!
I'M-A NO SCARED OF NO DEMONS! I KILLED A HUNDRED SARACENS AT TRIPOLI!
HA! CAN'T WAIT TO SEE HER FACE WHEN SHE SEES ME! SHE'LL PROBABLY FAINT ON THE SPOT.
TELL YOU WHAT... WE'LL VISIT THE JOYFUL GIRLS FIRST, THEN HER. IF THERE'S TIME. ALL RIGHT?

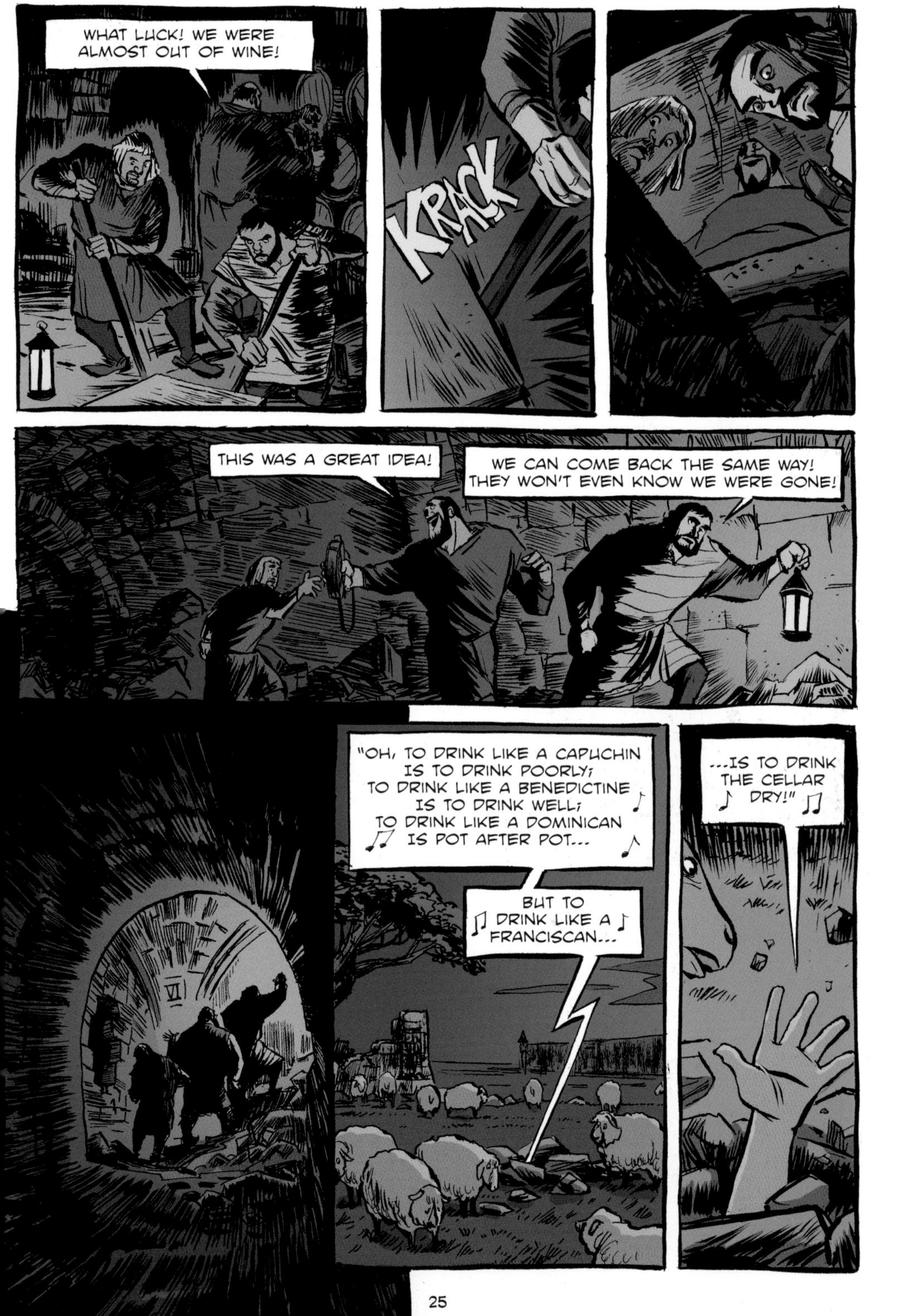

WHAT LUCK! WE WERE ALMOST OUT OF WINE!
KRACK
THIS WAS A GREAT IDEA!
WE CAN COME BACK THE SAME WAY! THEY WON'T EVEN KNOW WE WERE GONE!
VI
"OH, TO DRINK LIKE A CAPUCHIN IS TO DRINK POORLY; TO DRINK LIKE A BENEDICTINE IS TO DRINK WELL; TO DRINK LIKE A DOMINICAN IS POT AFTER POT...
BUT TO DRINK LIKE A FRANCISCAN...
...IS TO DRINK THE CELLAR DRY!"

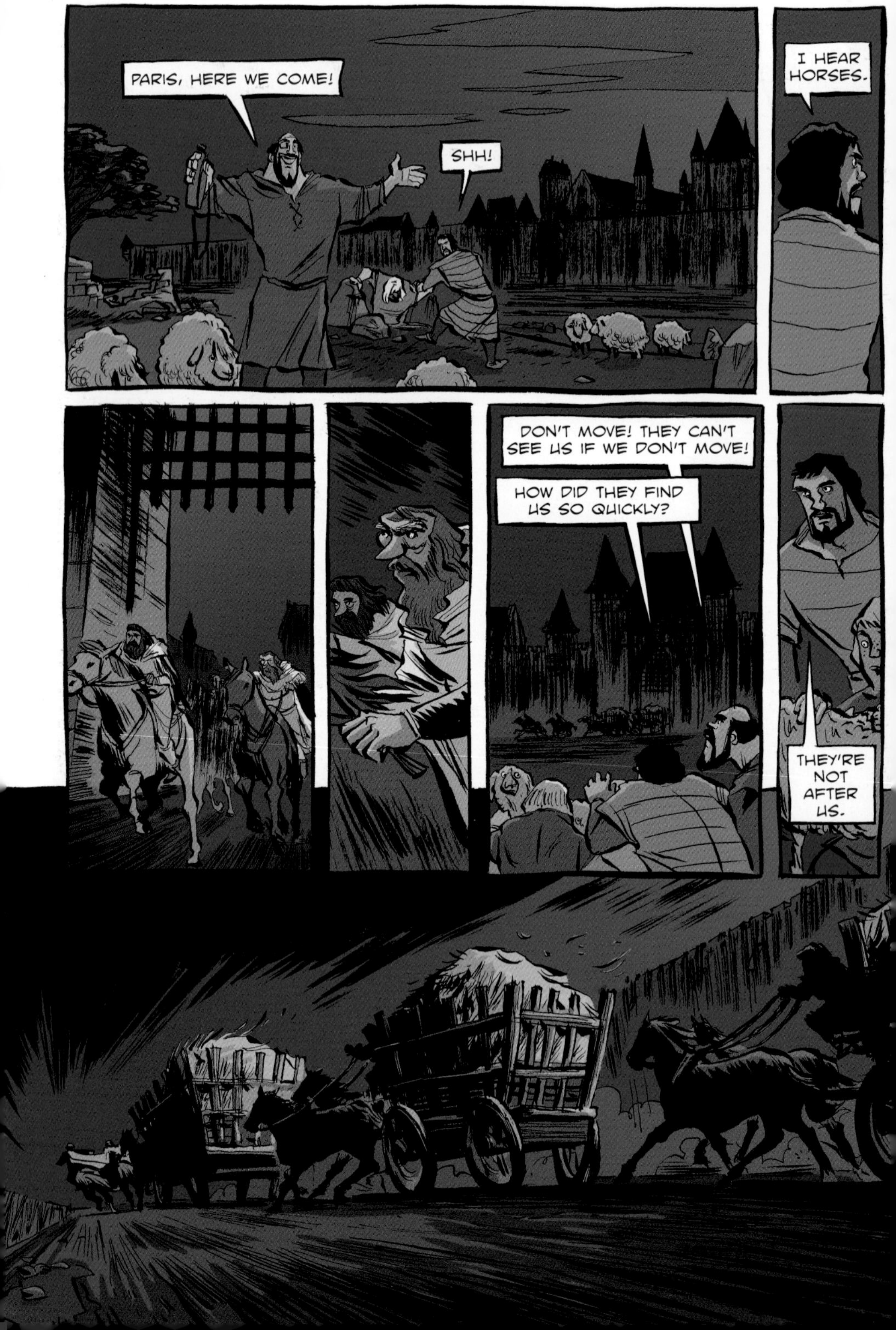

PARIS, HERE WE COME!
SHH!
I HEAR HORSES.
DON'T MOVE! THEY CAN'T SEE US IF WE DON'T MOVE!
HOW DID THEY FIND US SO QUICKLY?
THEY'RE NOT AFTER US.

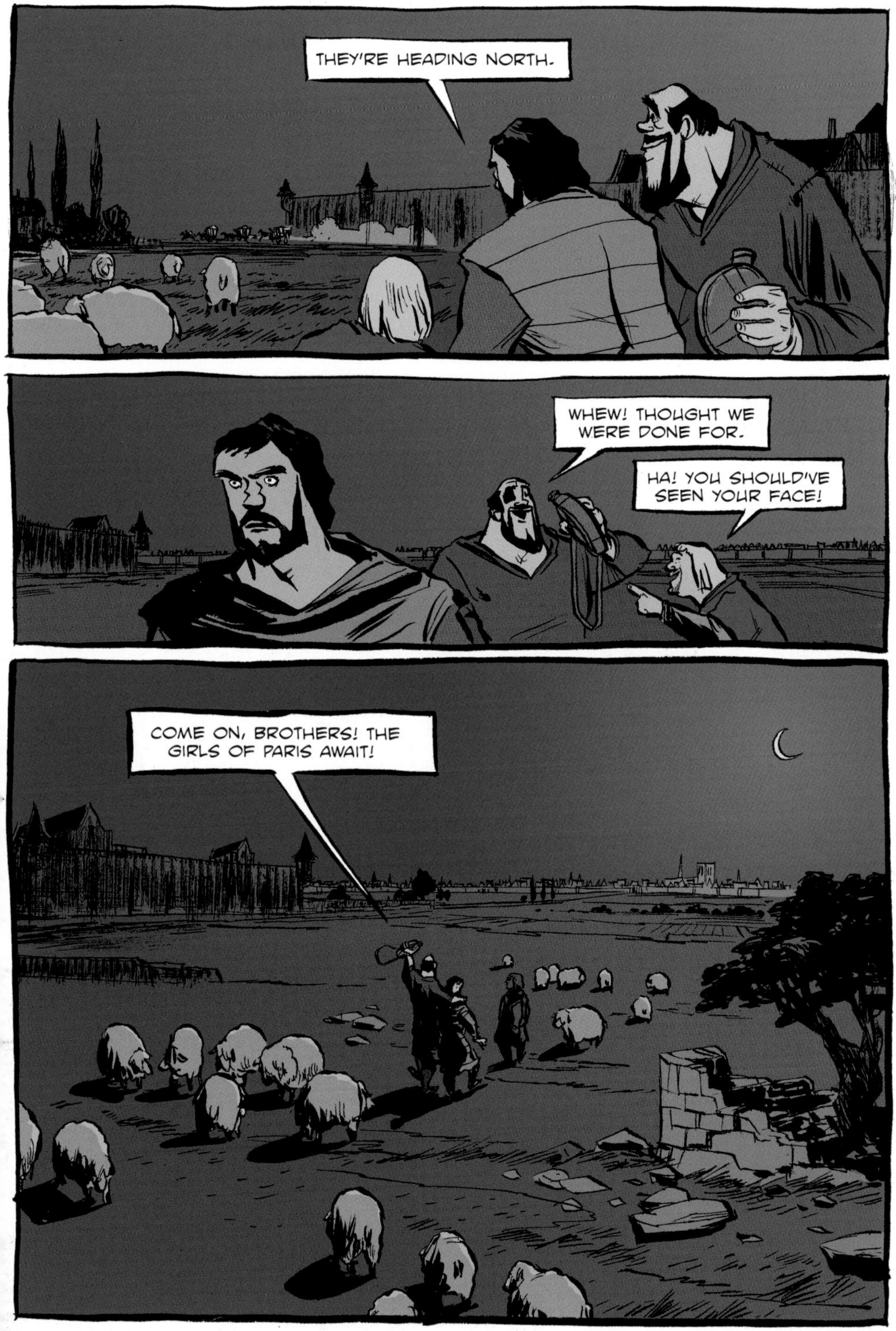
THEY'RE HEADING NORTH.
WHEW! THOUGHT WE WERE DONE FOR.
HA! YOU SHOULD'VE SEEN YOUR FACE!
COME ON, BROTHERS! THE GIRLS OF PARIS AWAIT!

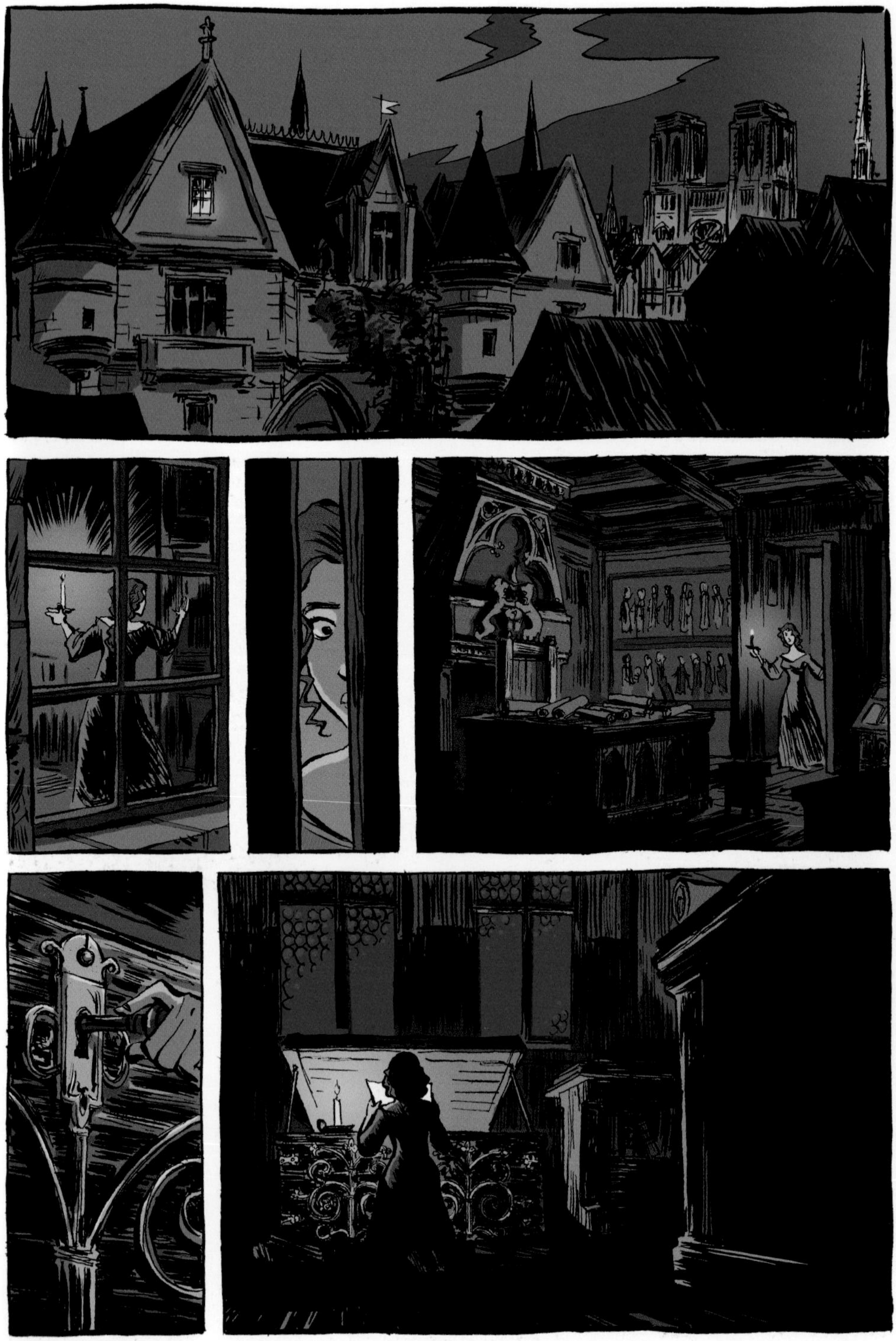

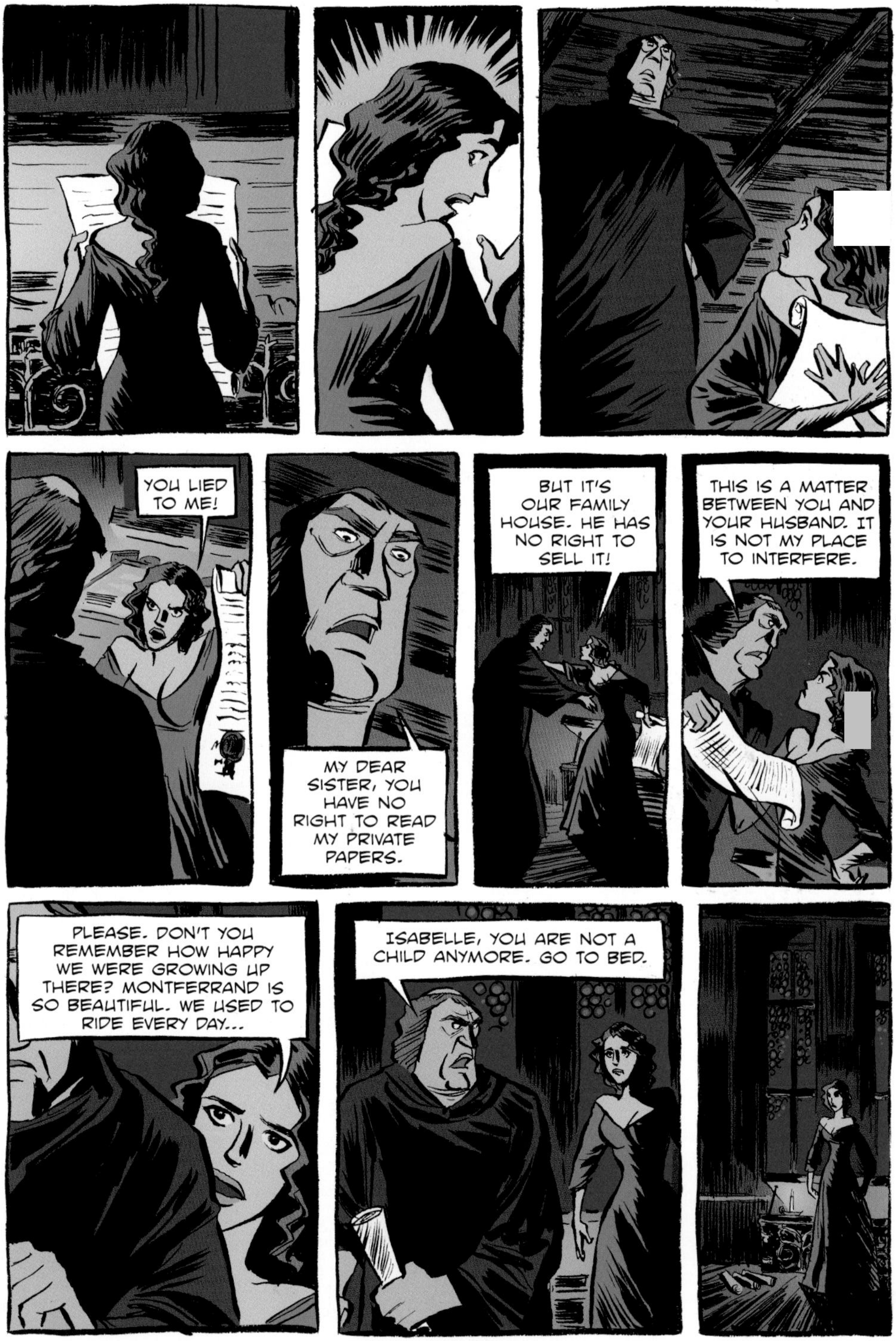
YOU LIED TO ME!
MY DEAR SISTER, YOU HAVE NO RIGHT TO READ MY PRIVATE PAPERS.
BUT IT'S OUR FAMILY HOUSE. HE HAS NO RIGHT TO SELL IT!
THIS IS A MATTER BETWEEN YOU AND YOUR HUSBAND. IT IS NOT MY PLACE TO INTERFERE.
PLEASE. DON'T YOU REMEMBER HOW HAPPY WE WERE GROWING UP THERE? MONTFERRAND IS SO BEAUTIFUL. WE USED TO RIDE EVERY DAY...
ISABELLE, YOU ARE NOT A CHILD ANYMORE. GO TO BED.

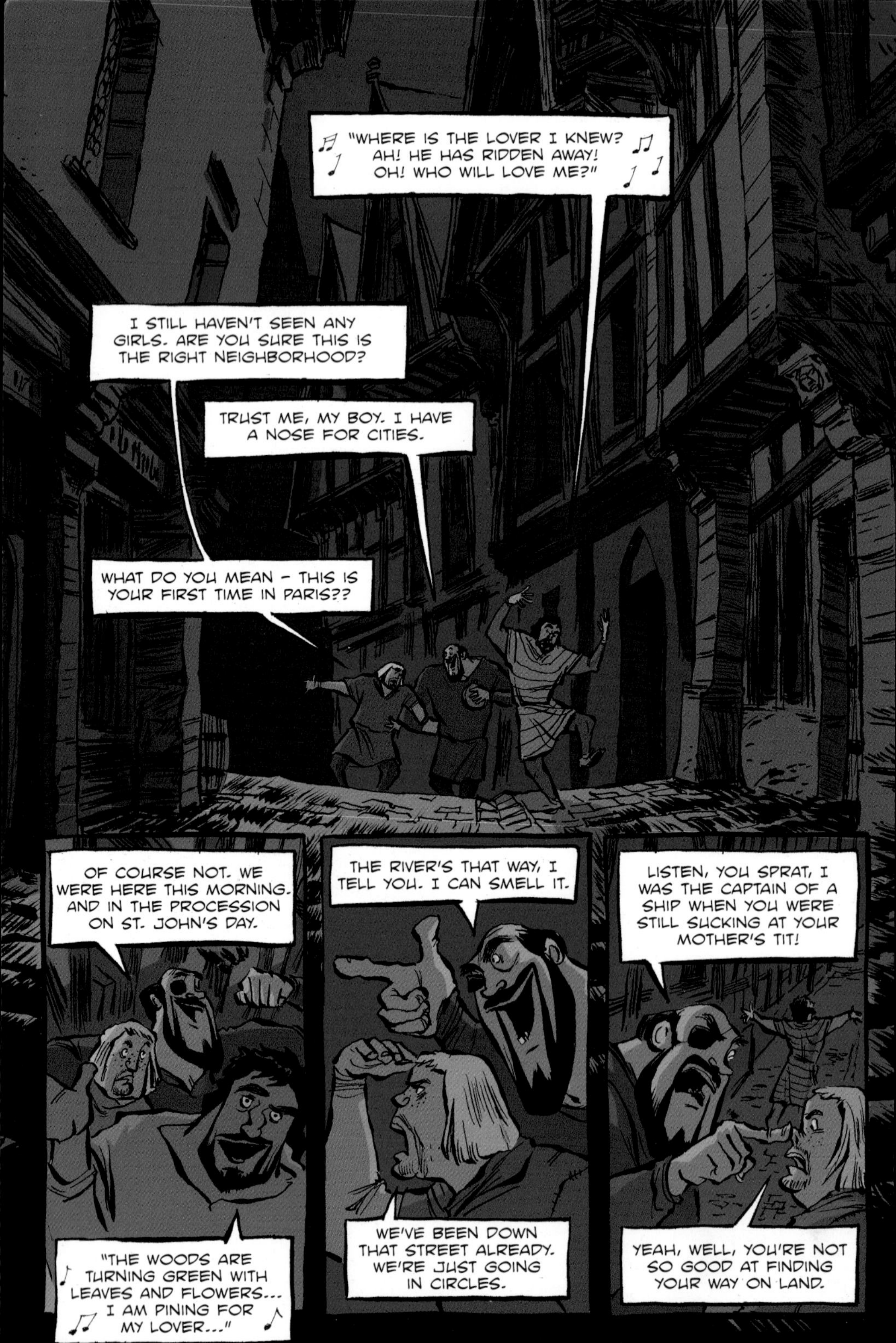
"WHERE IS THE LOVER I KNEW? AH! HE HAS RIDDEN AWAY! OH! WHO WILL LOVE ME?"
I STILL HAVEN'T SEEN ANY GIRLS. ARE YOU SURE THIS IS THE RIGHT NEIGHBORHOOD?
TRUST ME, MY BOY. I HAVE A NOSE FOR CITIES.
WHAT DO YOU MEAN – THIS IS YOUR FIRST TIME IN PARIS??
OF COURSE NOT. WE WERE HERE THIS MORNING. AND IN THE PROCESSION ON ST. JOHN'S DAY.
"THE WOODS ARE TURNING GREEN WITH LEAVES AND FLOWERS... I AM PINING FOR MY LOVER..."
THE RIVER'S THAT WAY, I TELL YOU. I CAN SMELL IT.
WE'VE BEEN DOWN THAT STREET ALREADY. WE'RE JUST GOING IN CIRCLES.
LISTEN, YOU SPRAT, I WAS THE CAPTAIN OF A SHIP WHEN YOU WERE STILL SUCKING AT YOUR MOTHER'S TIT!
YEAH, WELL, YOU'RE NOT SO GOOD AT FINDING YOUR WAY ON LAND.

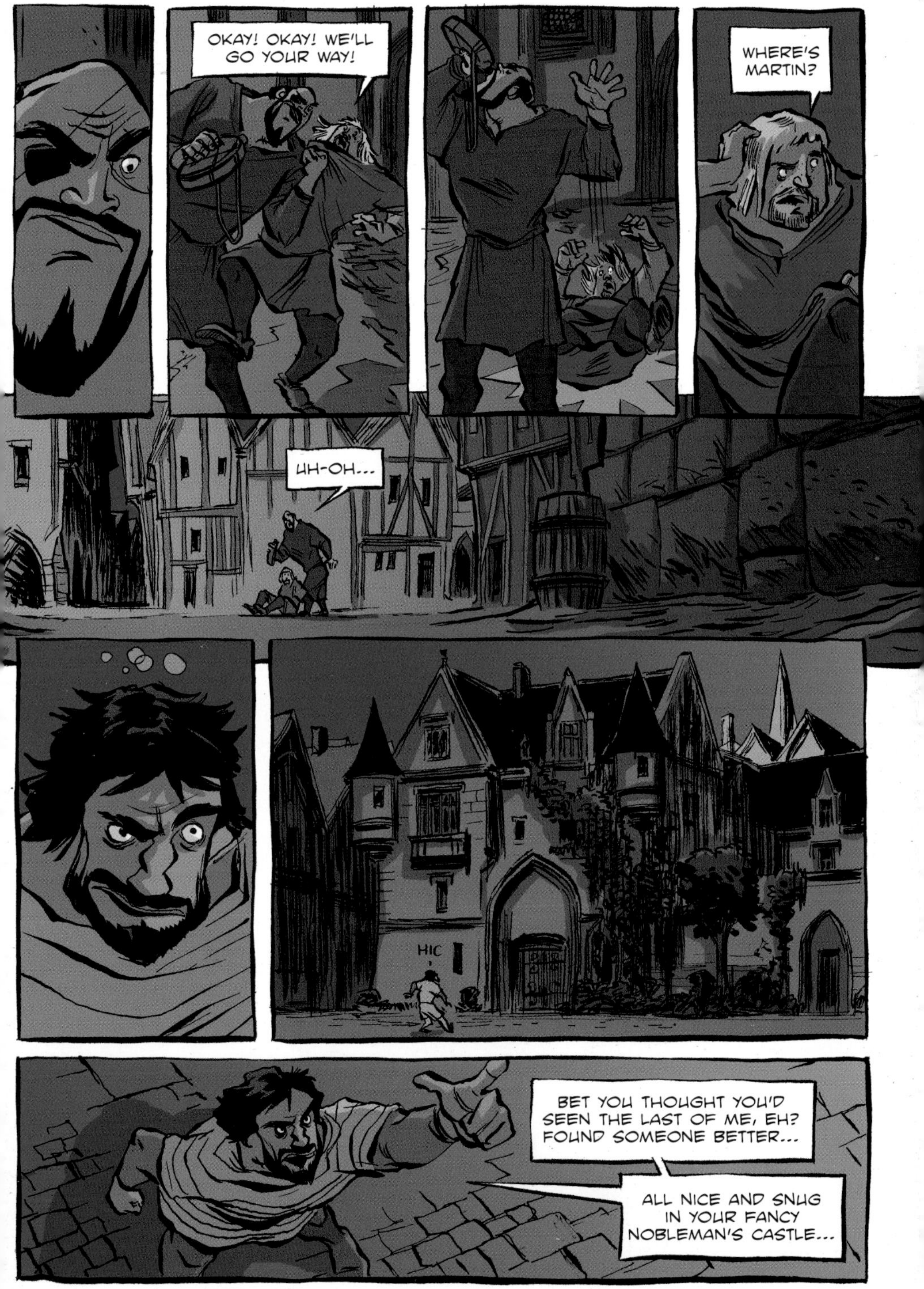
OKAY! OKAY! WE'LL GO YOUR WAY!
WHERE'S MARTIN?
UH-OH...
HIC
BET YOU THOUGHT YOU'D SEEN THE LAST OF ME, EH? FOUND SOMEONE BETTER...
ALL NICE AND SNUG IN YOUR FANCY NOBLEMAN'S CASTLE...

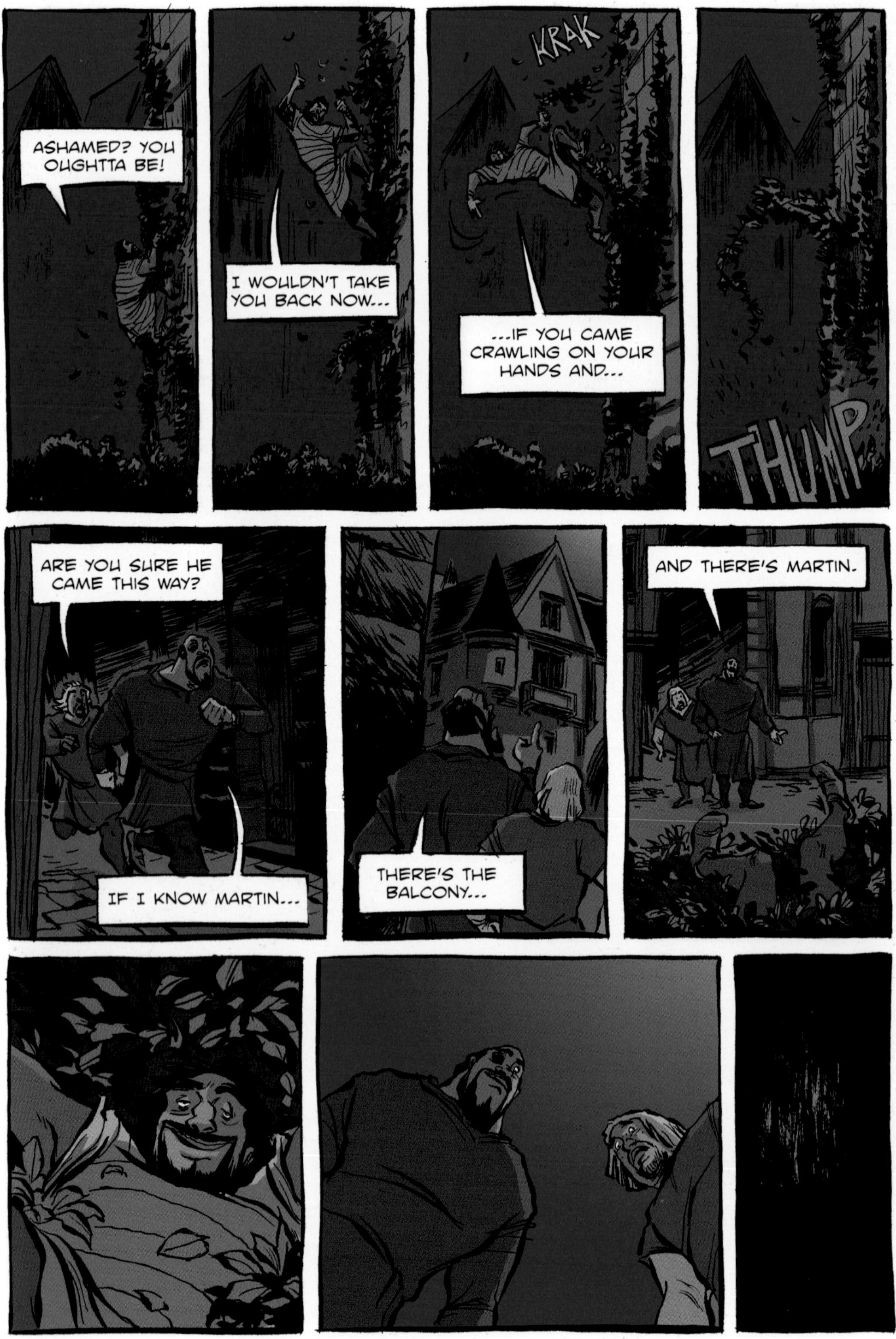
ASHAMED? YOU OUGHTTA BE!
I WOULDN'T TAKE YOU BACK NOW...
KRAK
...IF YOU CAME CRAWLING ON YOUR HANDS AND...
THUMP
ARE YOU SURE HE CAME THIS WAY?
IF I KNOW MARTIN...
THERE'S THE BALCONY...
AND THERE'S MARTIN.

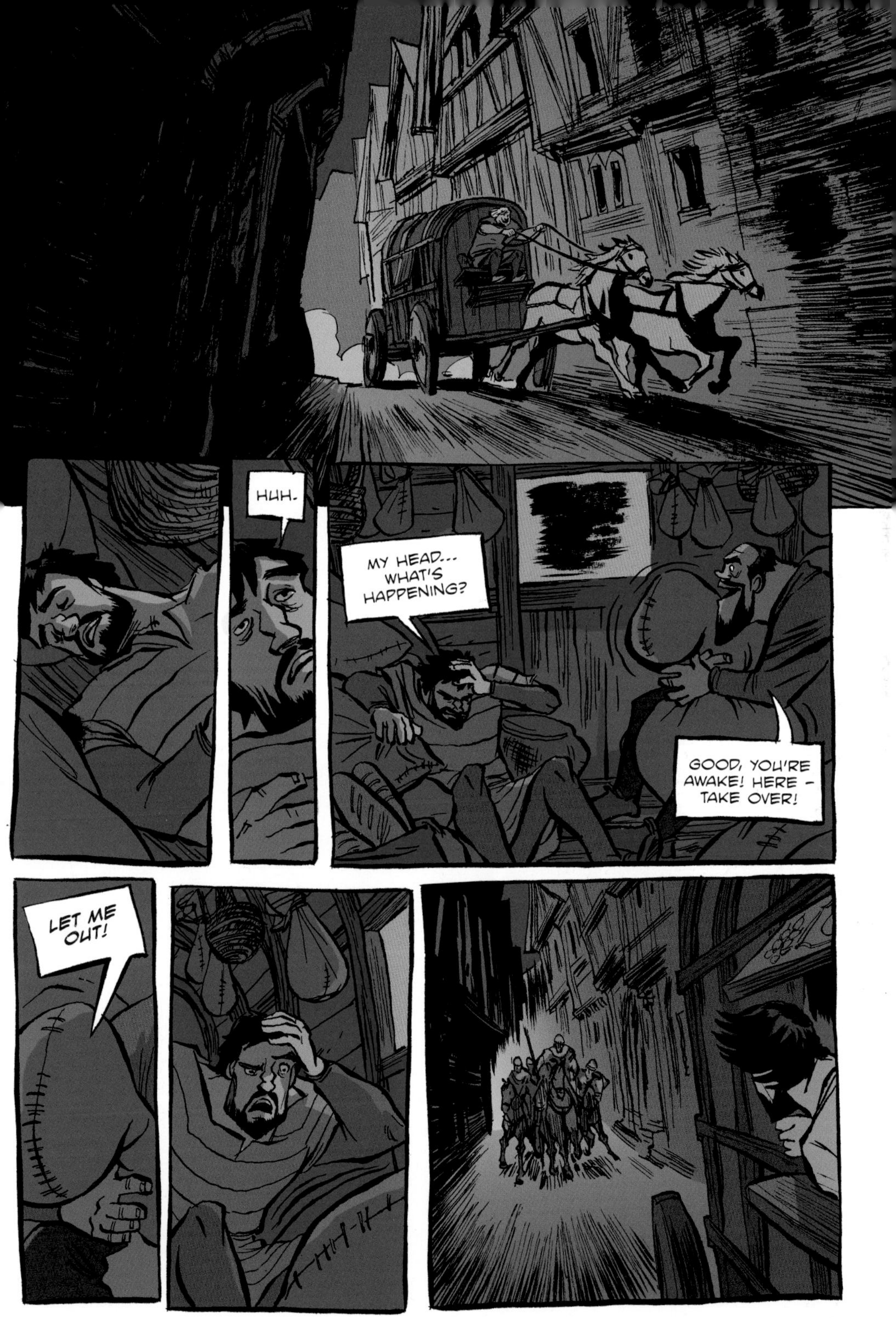
HUH.
MY HEAD... WHAT'S HAPPENING?
GOOD, YOU'RE AWAKE! HERE - TAKE OVER!
LET ME OUT!

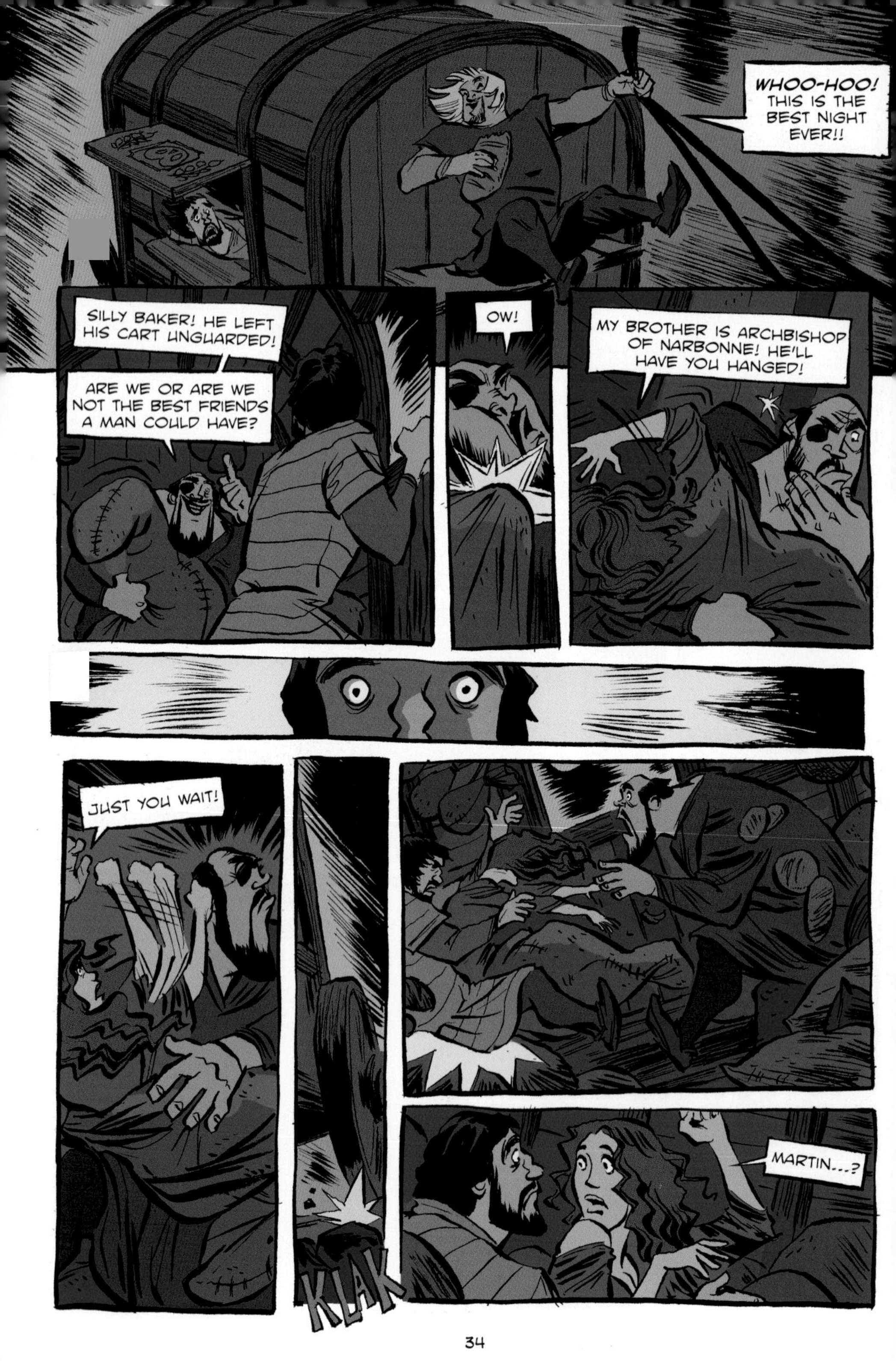
WHOO-HOO! THIS IS THE BEST NIGHT EVER!!
SILLY BAKER! HE LEFT HIS CART UNGUARDED!
ARE WE OR ARE WE NOT THE BEST FRIENDS A MAN COULD HAVE?
OW!
MY BROTHER IS ARCHBISHOP OF NARBONNE! HE'LL HAVE YOU HANGED!
JUST YOU WAIT!
KLAK
MARTIN...?

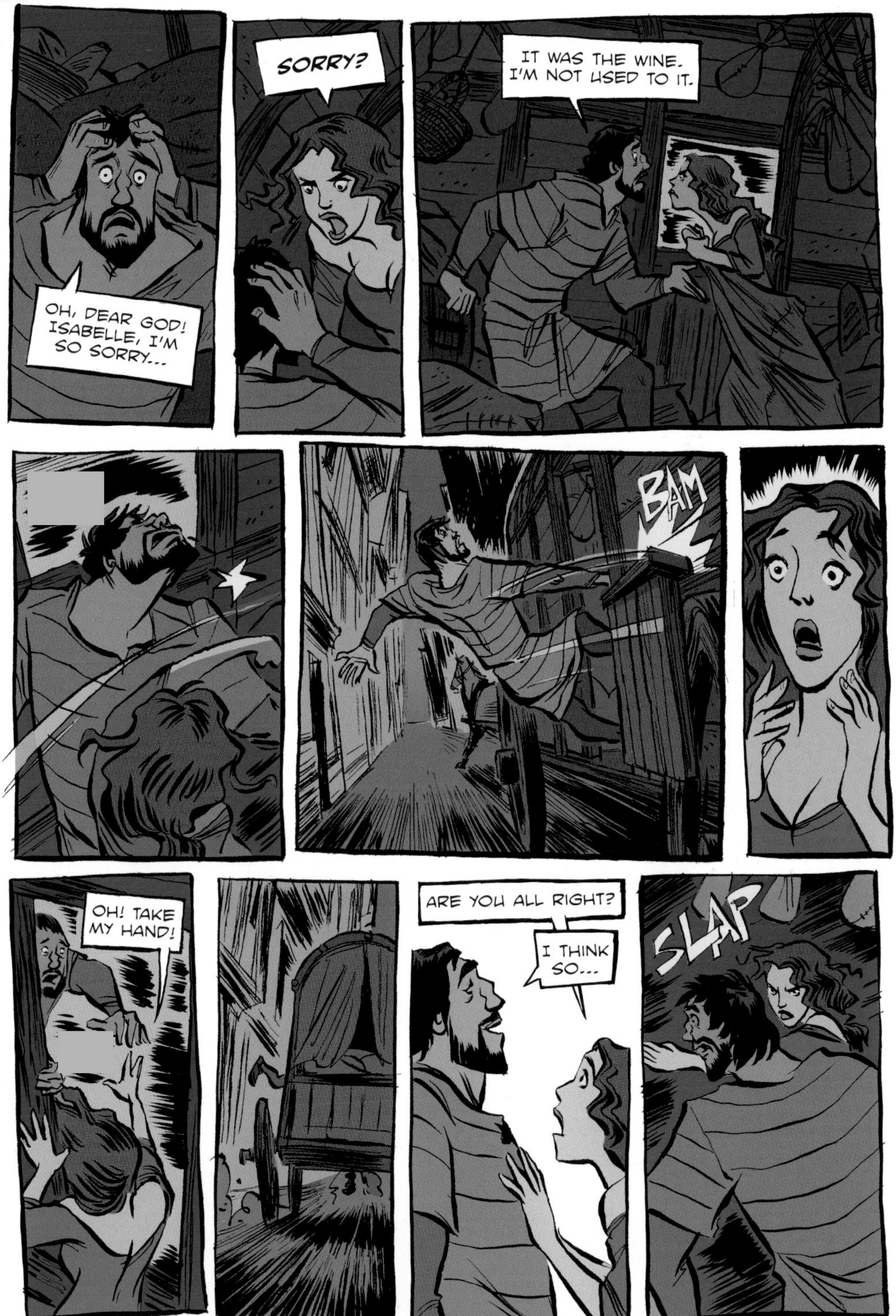
OH, DEAR GOD! ISABELLE, I'M SO SORRY...
SORRY?
IT WAS THE WINE. I'M NOT USED TO IT.
BAM
OH! TAKE MY HAND!
ARE YOU ALL RIGHT?
I THINK SO...
SLAP

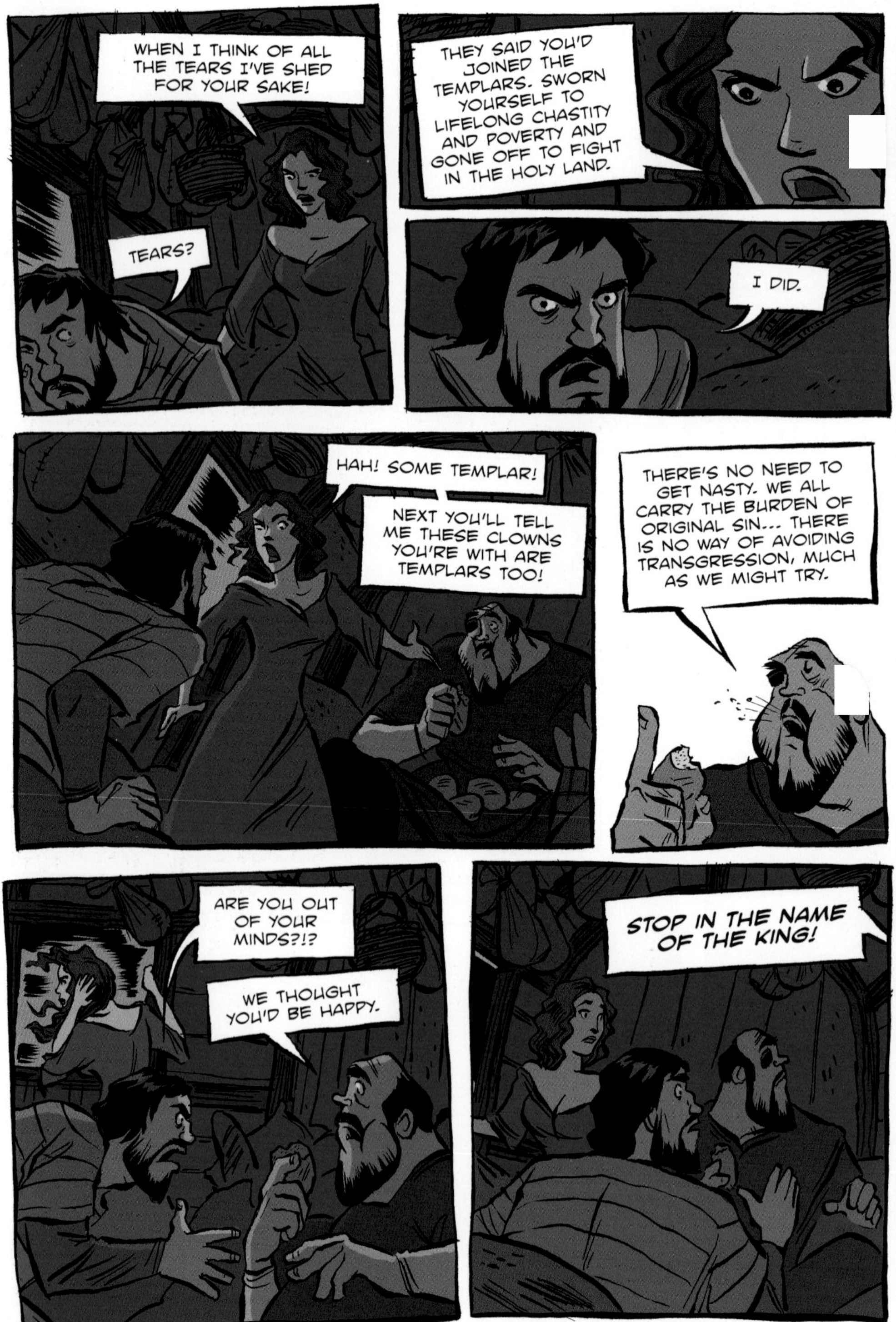
WHEN I THINK OF ALL THE TEARS I'VE SHED FOR YOUR SAKE!
TEARS?
THEY SAID YOU'D JOINED THE TEMPLARS. SWORN YOURSELF TO LIFELONG CHASTITY AND POVERTY AND GONE OFF TO FIGHT IN THE HOLY LAND.
I DID.
HAH! SOME TEMPLAR!
NEXT YOU'LL TELL ME THESE CLOWNS YOU'RE WITH ARE TEMPLARS TOO!
THERE'S NO NEED TO GET NASTY. WE ALL CARRY THE BURDEN OF ORIGINAL SIN... THERE IS NO WAY OF AVOIDING TRANSGRESSION, MUCH AS WE MIGHT TRY.
ARE YOU OUT OF YOUR MINDS?!?
WE THOUGHT YOU'D BE HAPPY.
STOP IN THE NAME OF THE KING!

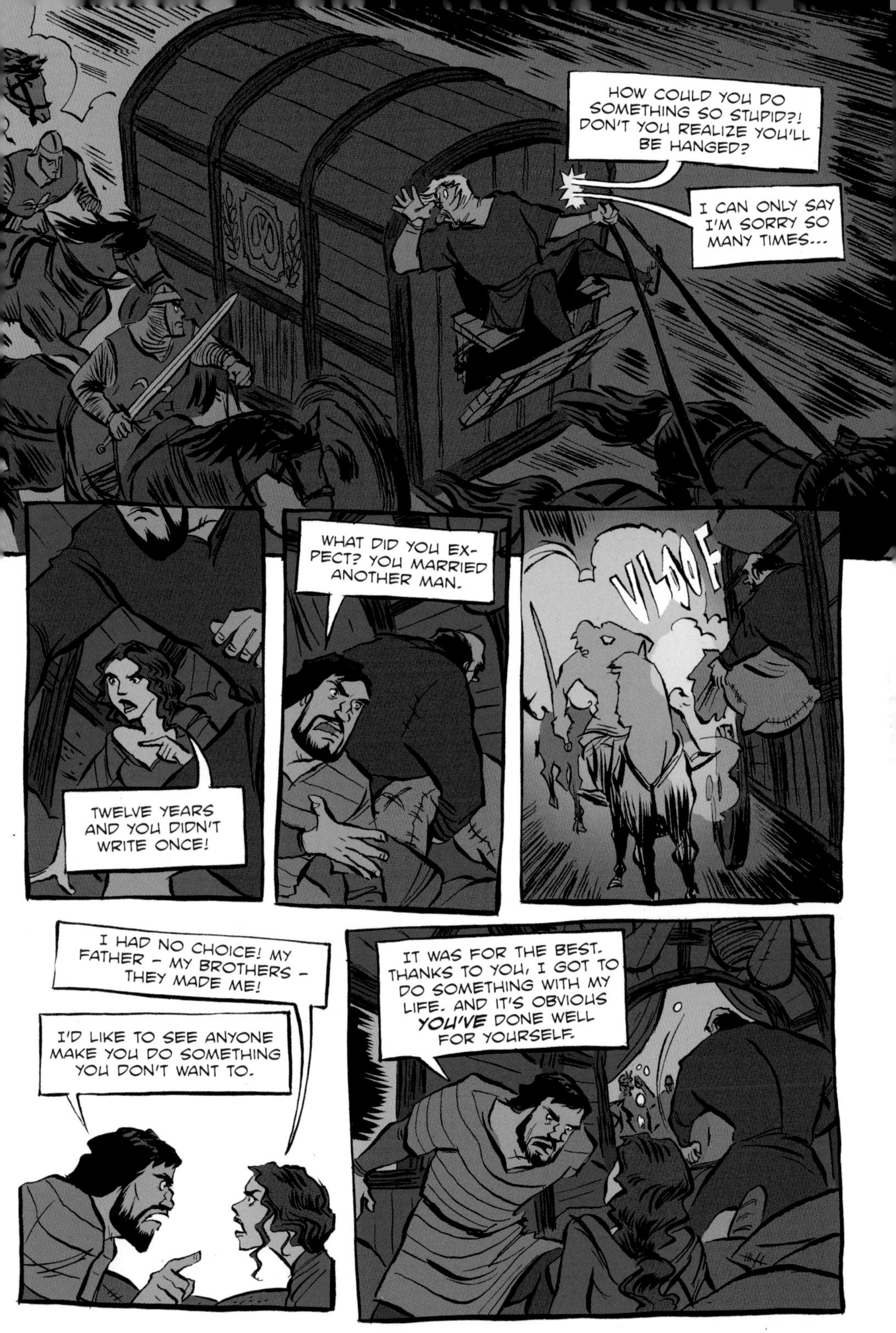
HOW COULD YOU DO SOMETHING SO STUPID?! DON'T YOU REALIZE YOU'LL BE HANGED?
I CAN ONLY SAY I'M SORRY SO MANY TIMES...
TWELVE YEARS AND YOU DIDN'T WRITE ONCE!
WHAT DID YOU EX-PECT? YOU MARRIED ANOTHER MAN.
VLSOOF
I HAD NO CHOICE! MY FATHER – MY BROTHERS – THEY MADE ME!
I'D LIKE TO SEE ANYONE MAKE YOU DO SOMETHING YOU DON'T WANT TO.
IT WAS FOR THE BEST. THANKS TO YOU, I GOT TO DO SOMETHING WITH MY LIFE. AND IT'S OBVIOUS *YOU'VE* DONE WELL FOR YOURSELF.

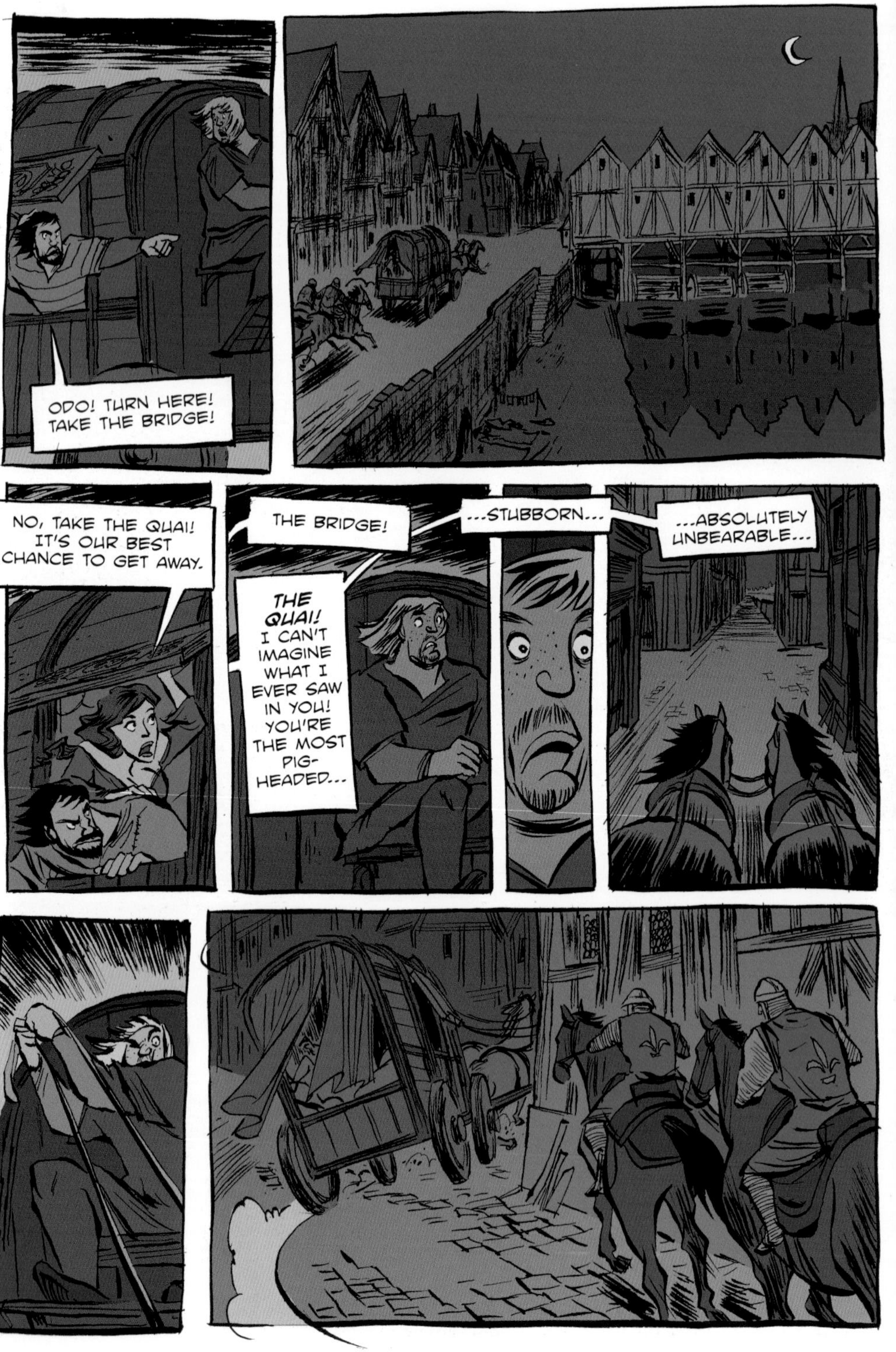
ODO! TURN HERE! TAKE THE BRIDGE!
NO, TAKE THE QUAI! IT'S OUR BEST CHANCE TO GET AWAY.
THE BRIDGE!
THE QUAI! I CAN'T IMAGINE WHAT I EVER SAW IN YOU! YOU'RE THE MOST PIG-HEADED...
...STUBBORN...
...ABSOLUTELY UNBEARABLE...

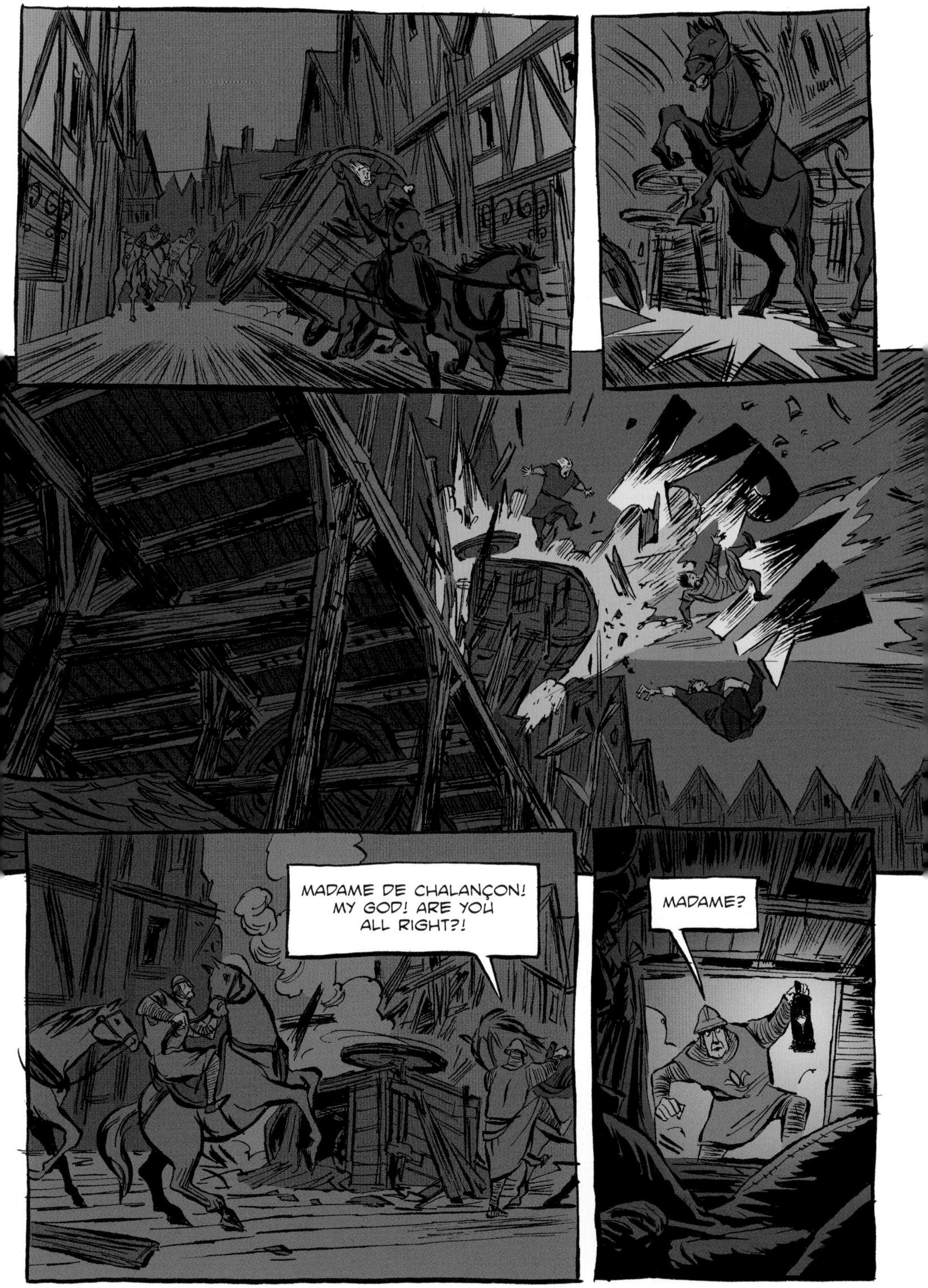
MADAME DE CHALANÇON! MY GOD! ARE YOU ALL RIGHT?!
MADAME?

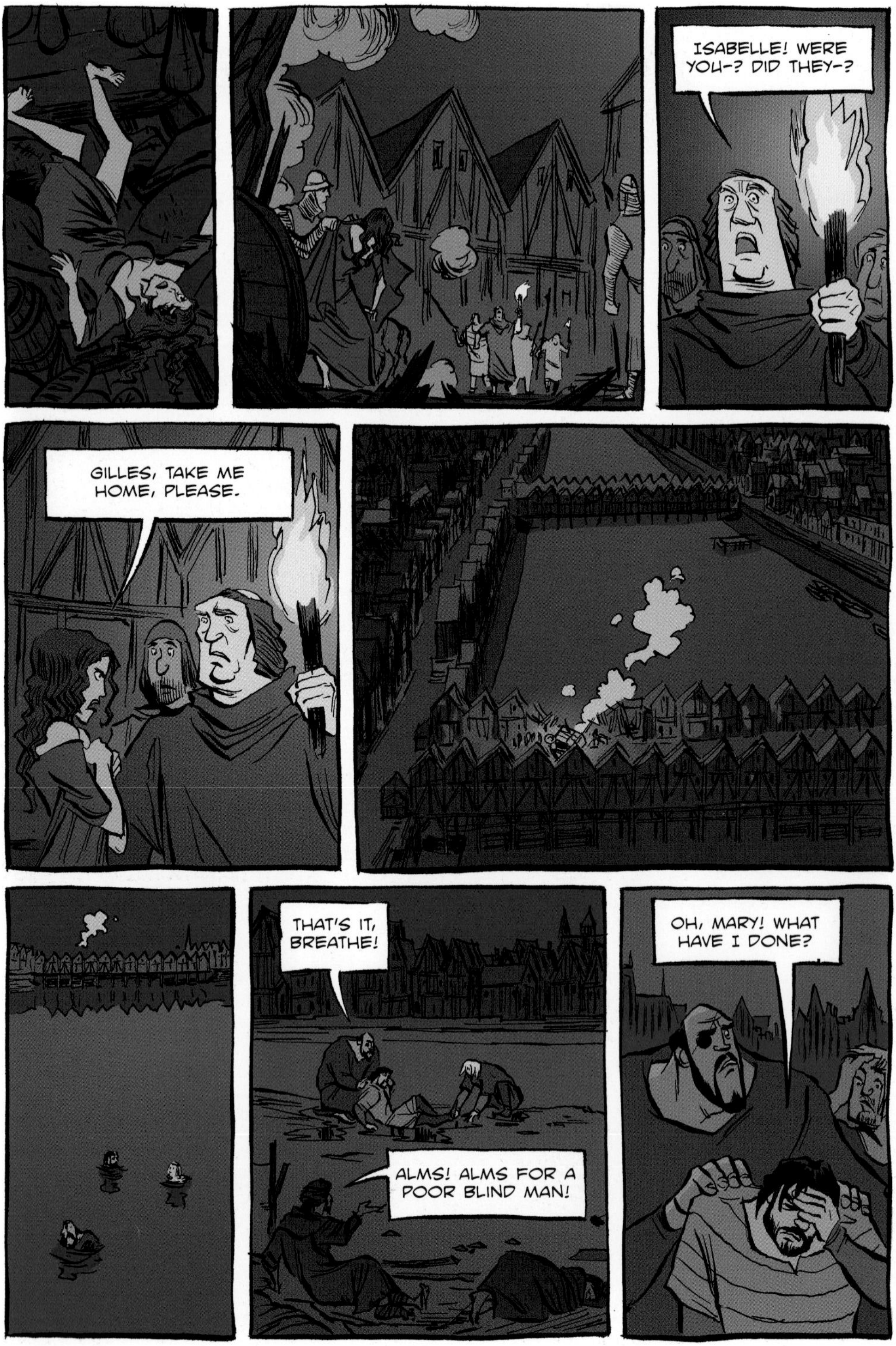
ISABELLE! WERE YOU-? DID THEY-?
GILLES, TAKE ME HOME, PLEASE.
THAT'S IT, BREATHE!
ALMS! ALMS FOR A POOR BLIND MAN!
OH, MARY! WHAT HAVE I DONE?

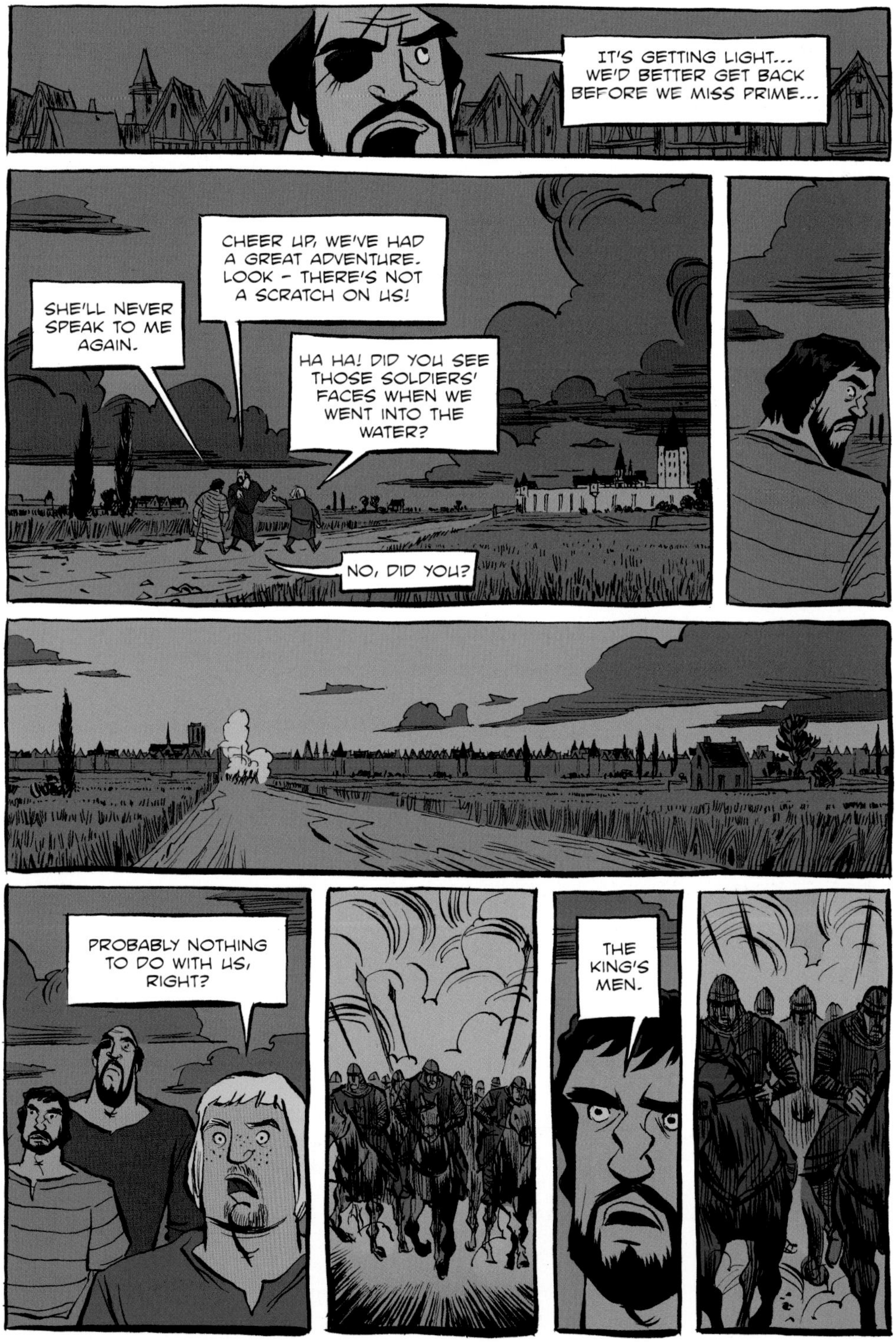
IT'S GETTING LIGHT... WE'D BETTER GET BACK BEFORE WE MISS PRIME...
SHE'LL NEVER SPEAK TO ME AGAIN.
CHEER UP, WE'VE HAD A GREAT ADVENTURE. LOOK - THERE'S NOT A SCRATCH ON US!
HA HA! DID YOU SEE THOSE SOLDIERS' FACES WHEN WE WENT INTO THE WATER?
NO, DID YOU?
PROBABLY NOTHING TO DO WITH US, RIGHT?
THE KING'S MEN.

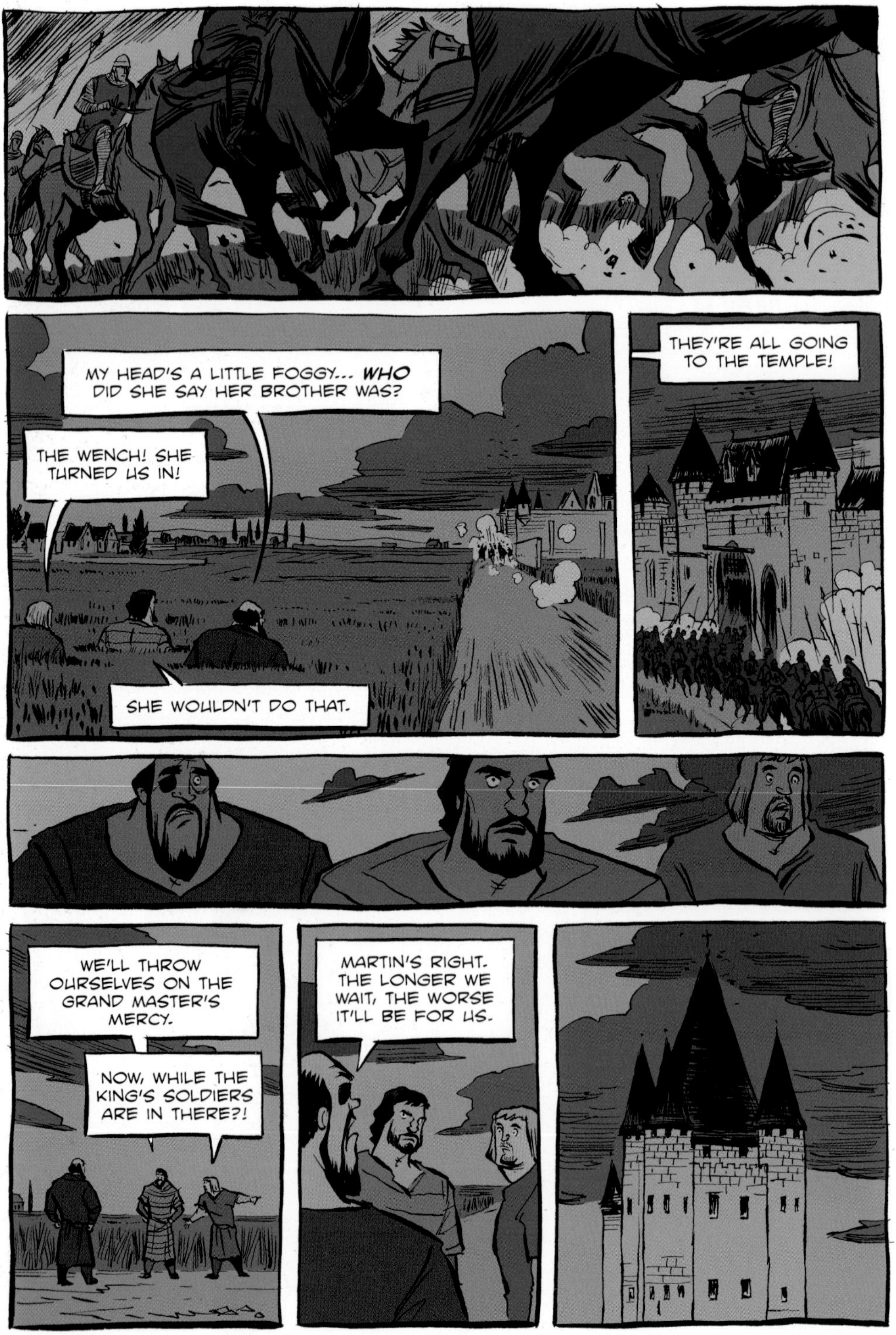
MY HEAD'S A LITTLE FOGGY... WHO DID SHE SAY HER BROTHER WAS?
THE WENCH! SHE TURNED US IN!
SHE WOULDN'T DO THAT.
THEY'RE ALL GOING TO THE TEMPLE!
WE'LL THROW OURSELVES ON THE GRAND MASTER'S MERCY.
NOW, WHILE THE KING'S SOLDIERS ARE IN THERE?!
MARTIN'S RIGHT. THE LONGER WE WAIT, THE WORSE IT'LL BE FOR US.

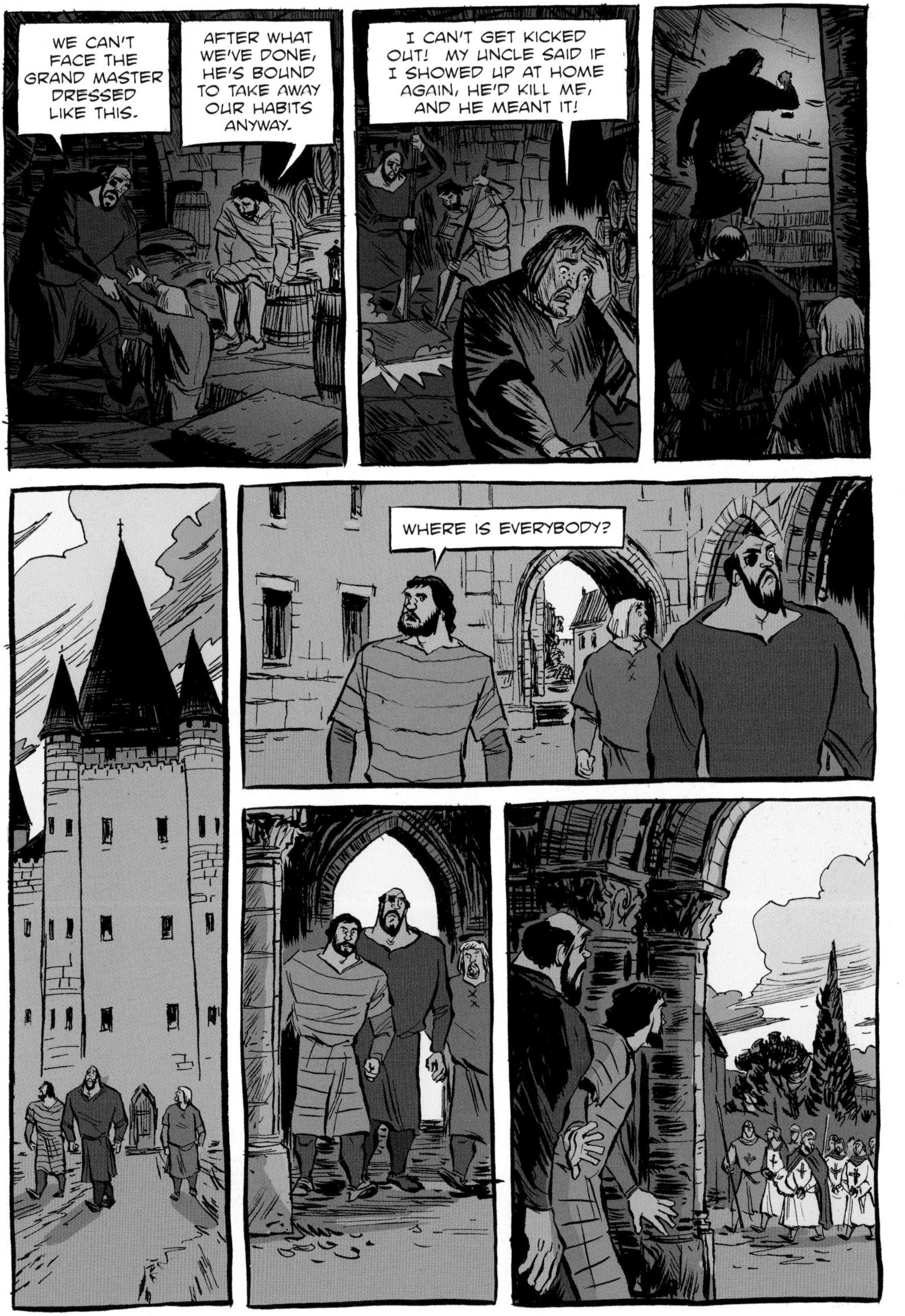
WE CAN'T FACE THE GRAND MASTER DRESSED LIKE THIS.
AFTER WHAT WE'VE DONE, HE'S BOUND TO TAKE AWAY OUR HABITS ANYWAY.
I CAN'T GET KICKED OUT! MY UNCLE SAID IF I SHOWED UP AT HOME AGAIN, HE'D KILL ME, AND HE MEANT IT!
WHERE IS EVERYBODY?

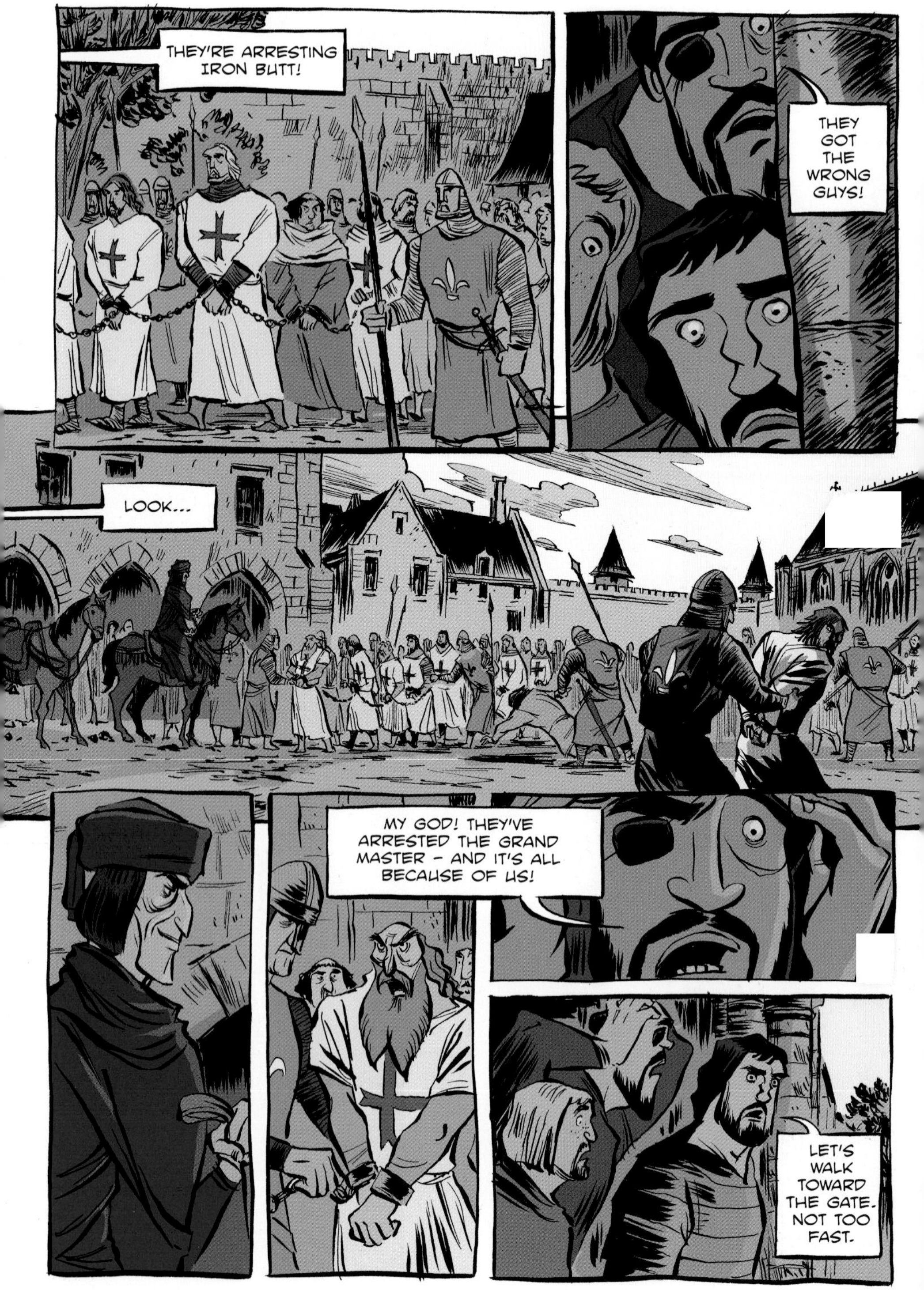
THEY'RE ARRESTING IRON BUTT!
THEY GOT THE WRONG GUYS!
LOOK...
MY GOD! THEY'VE ARRESTED THE GRAND MASTER - AND IT'S ALL BECAUSE OF US!
LET'S WALK TOWARD THE GATE. NOT TOO FAST.

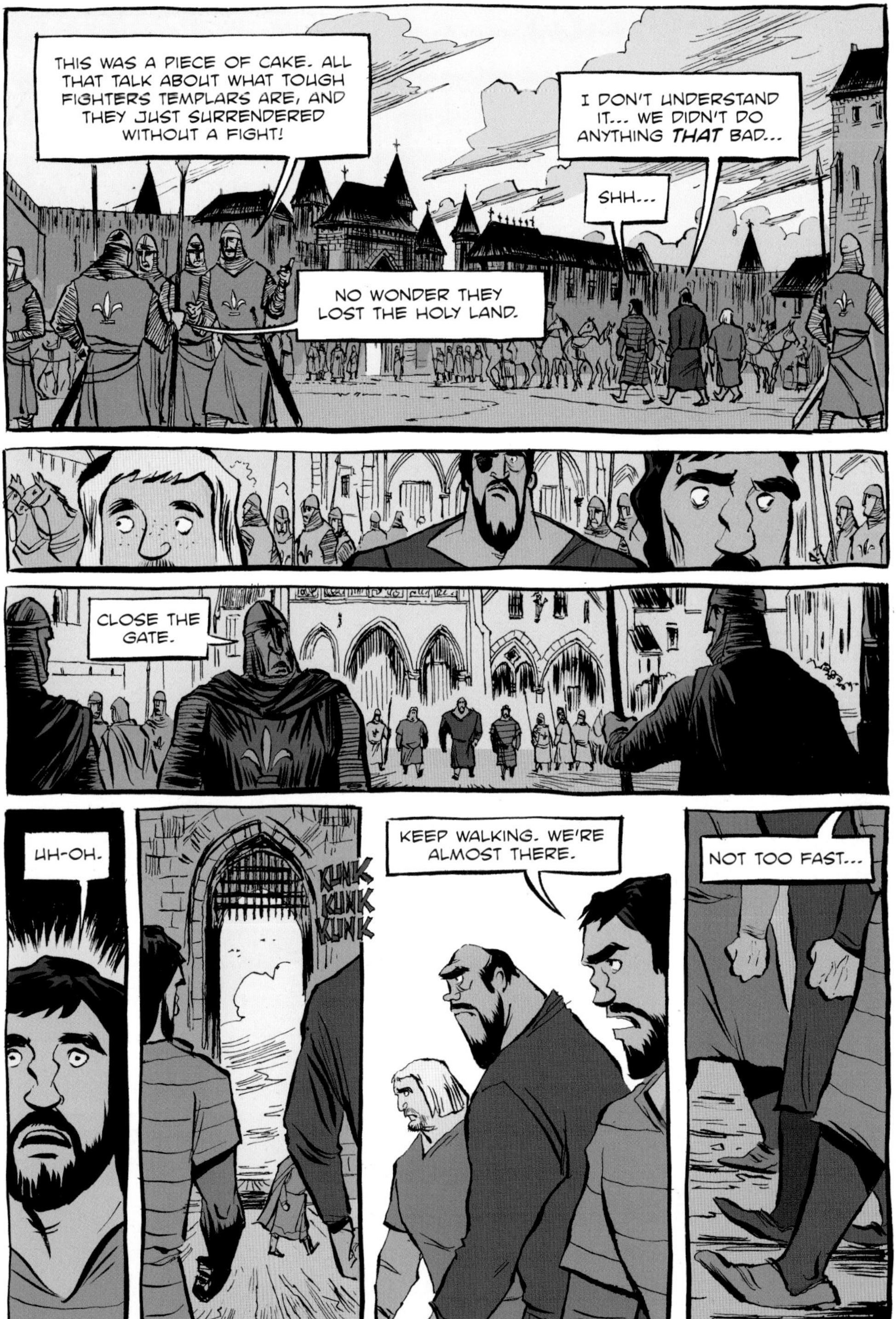
THIS WAS A PIECE OF CAKE. ALL THAT TALK ABOUT WHAT TOUGH FIGHTERS TEMPLARS ARE, AND THEY JUST SURRENDERED WITHOUT A FIGHT!
NO WONDER THEY LOST THE HOLY LAND.
I DON'T UNDERSTAND IT... WE DIDN'T DO ANYTHING THAT BAD...
SHH...
CLOSE THE GATE.
UH-OH.
KUNK KUNK KUNK
KEEP WALKING. WE'RE ALMOST THERE.
NOT TOO FAST...

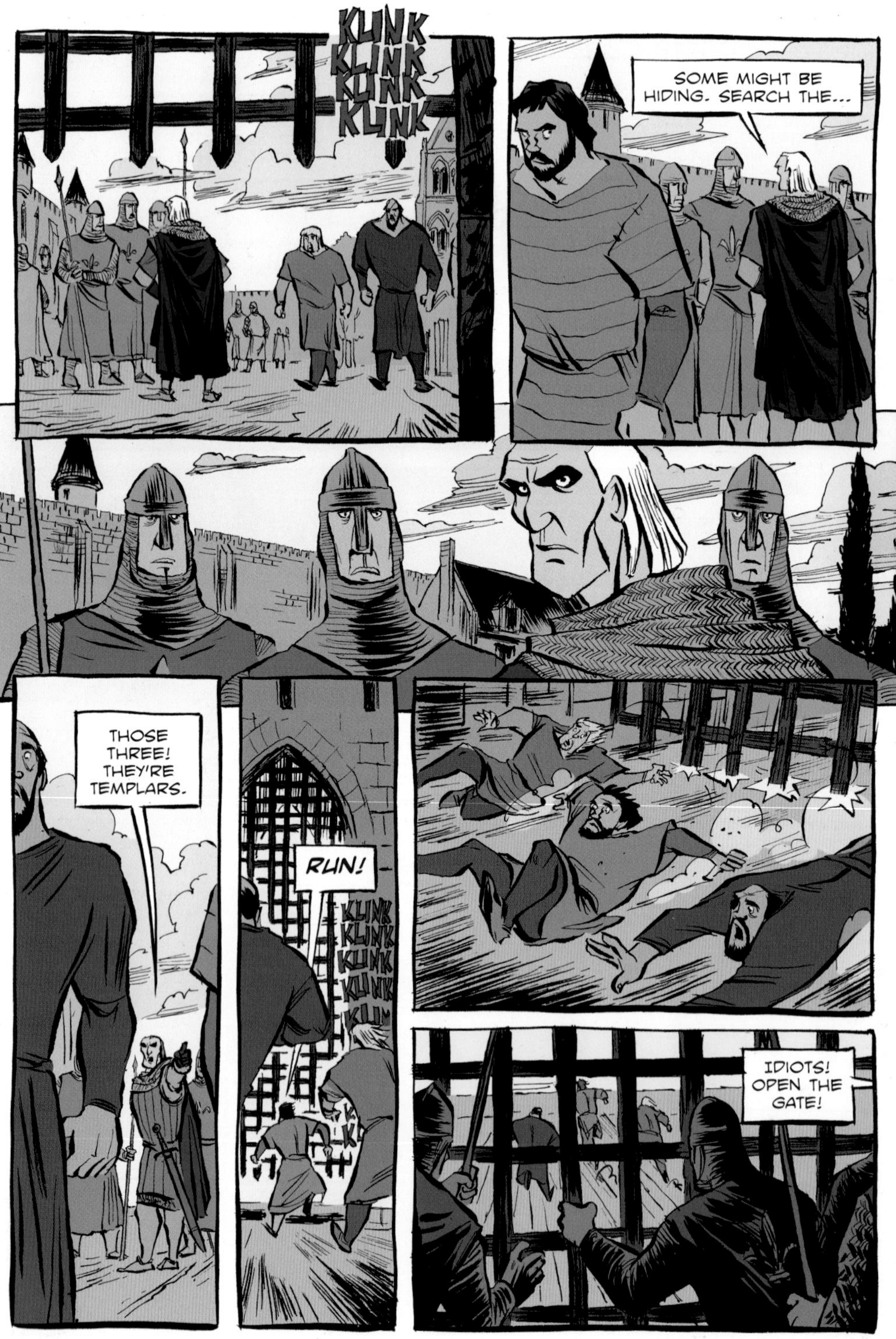
KLUNK
KLINK
KLUNK
KLUNK
SOME MIGHT BE HIDING. SEARCH THE...
THOSE THREE! THEY'RE TEMPLARS.
RUN!
KLUNK
KLINK
KLUNK
KLUNK
IDIOTS! OPEN THE GATE!

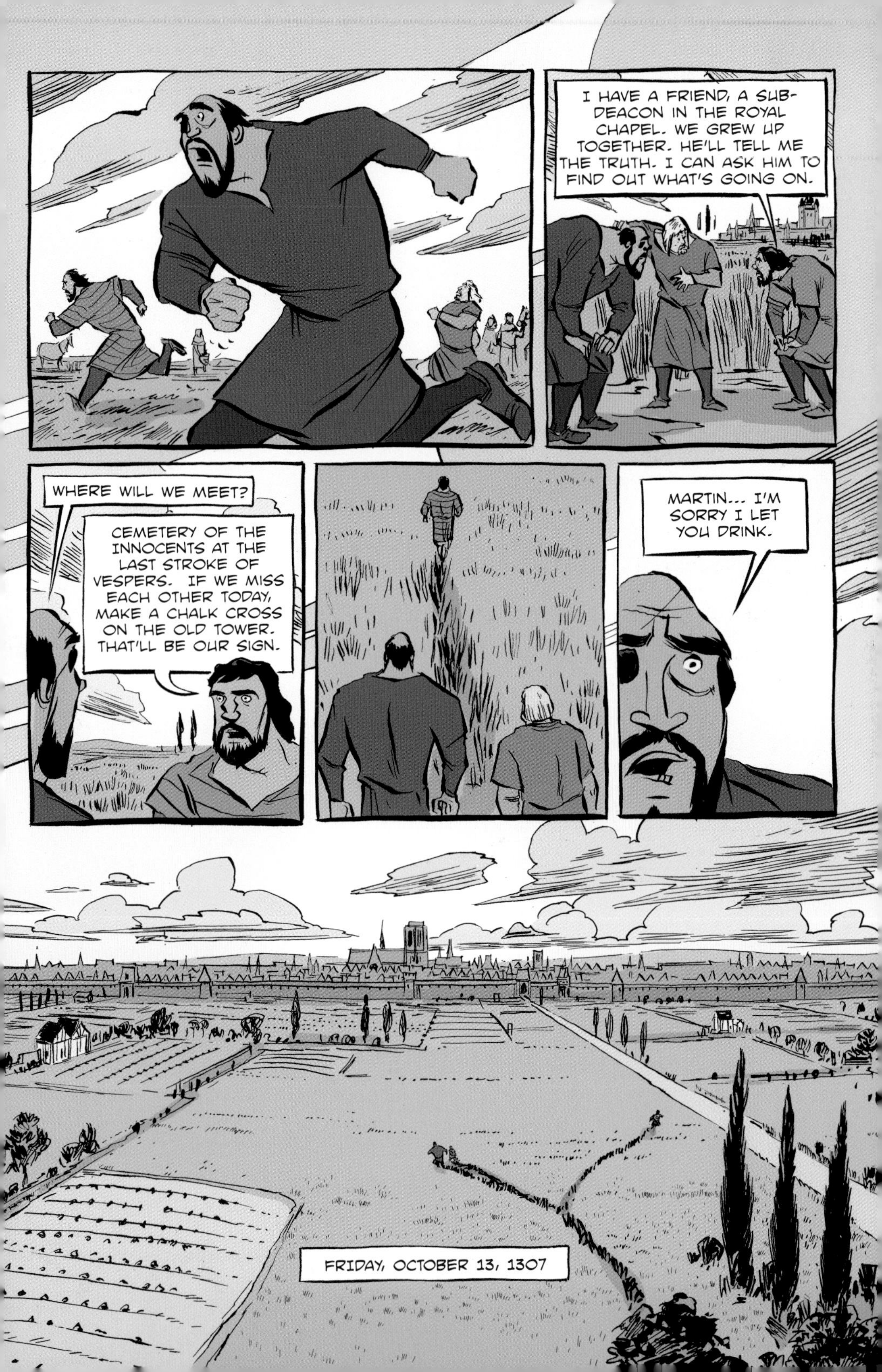
I HAVE A FRIEND, A SUB-DEACON IN THE ROYAL CHAPEL. WE GREW UP TOGETHER. HE'LL TELL ME THE TRUTH. I CAN ASK HIM TO FIND OUT WHAT'S GOING ON.
WHERE WILL WE MEET?
CEMETERY OF THE INNOCENTS AT THE LAST STROKE OF VESPERS. IF WE MISS EACH OTHER TODAY, MAKE A CHALK CROSS ON THE OLD TOWER. THAT'LL BE OUR SIGN.
MARTIN... I'M SORRY I LET YOU DRINK.
FRIDAY, OCTOBER 13, 1307

2.
"I Have Told the Whole Truth..."

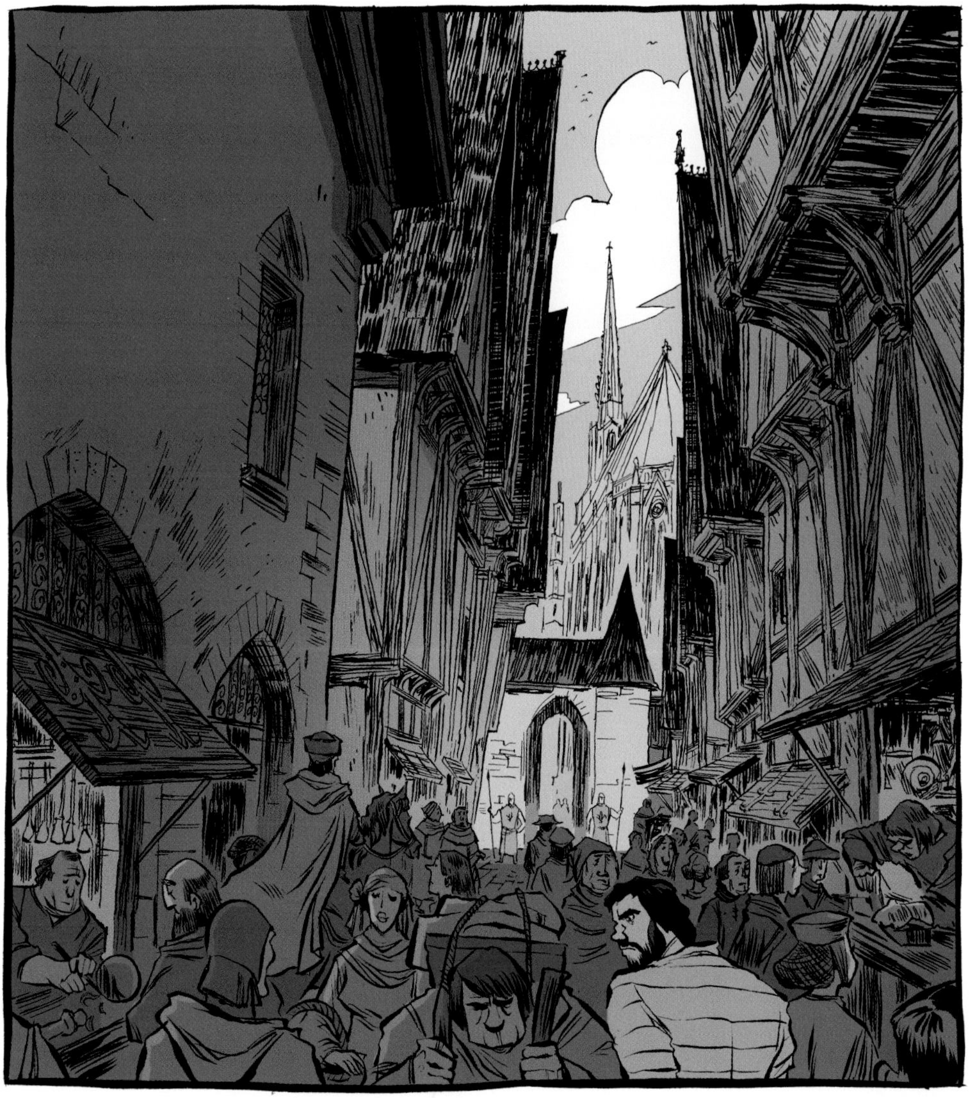

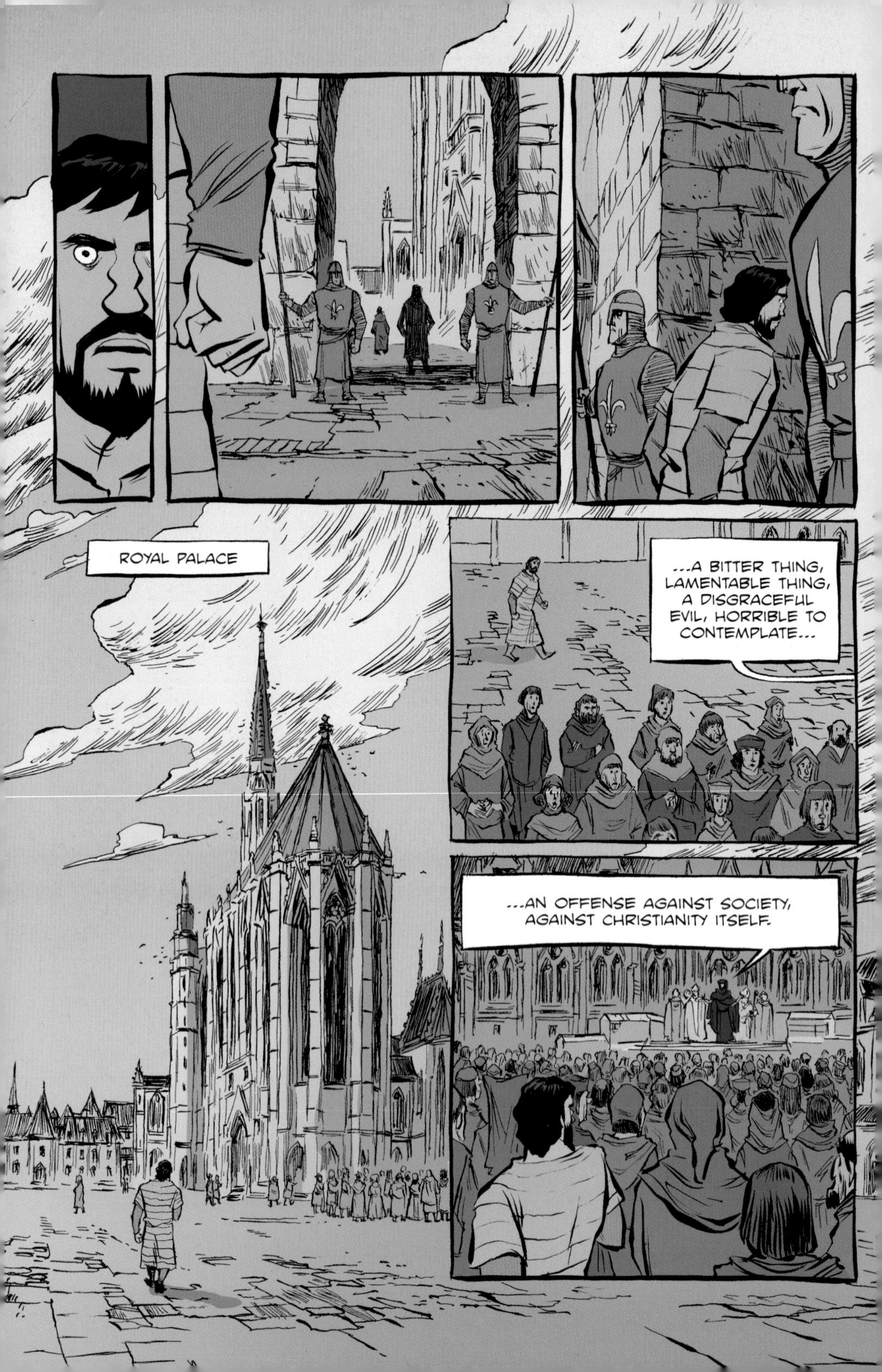
ROYAL PALACE
...A BITTER THING, LAMENTABLE THING, A DISGRACEFUL EVIL, HORRIBLE TO CONTEMPLATE...
...AN OFFENSE AGAINST SOCIETY, AGAINST CHRISTIANITY ITSELF.

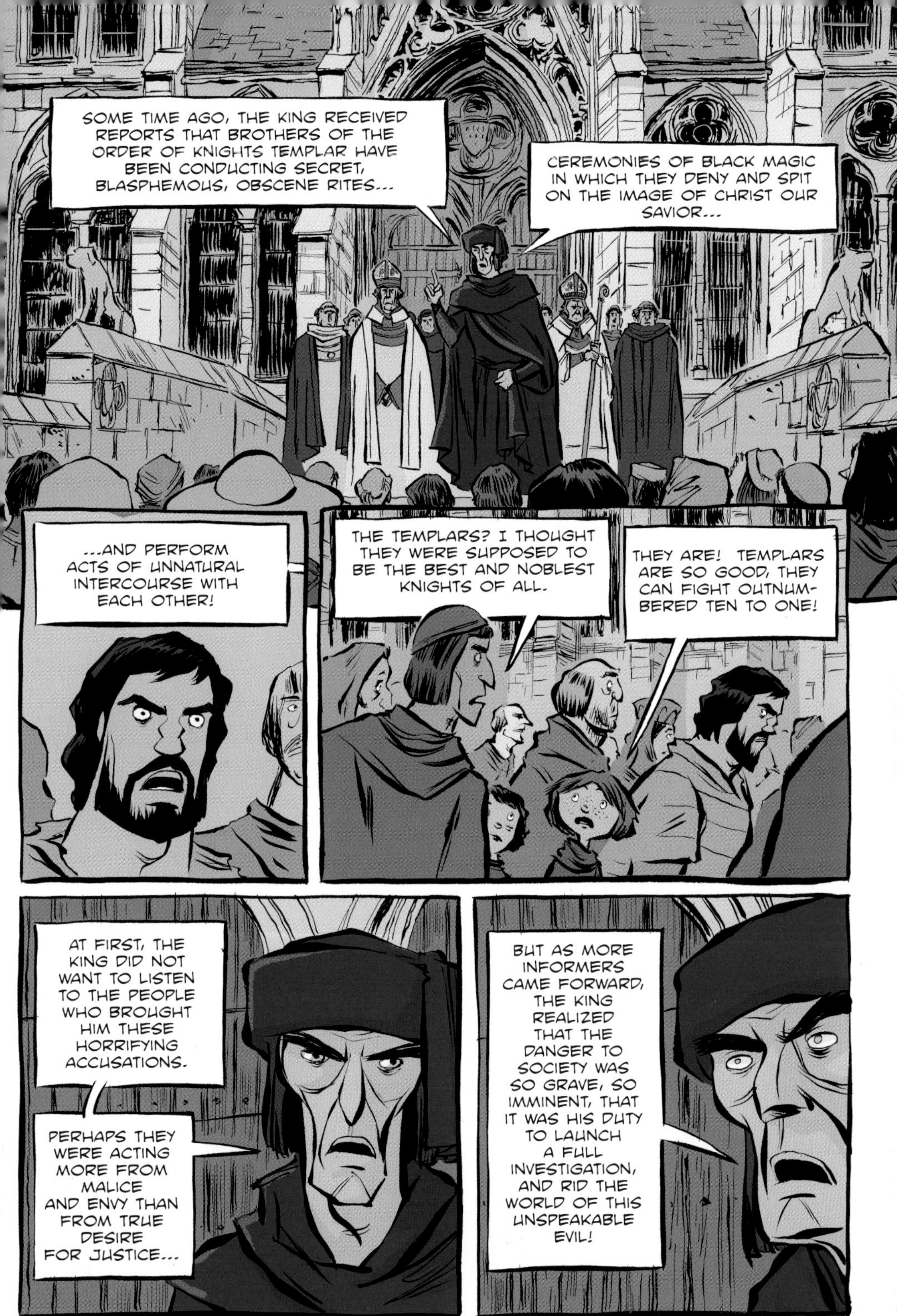
SOME TIME AGO, THE KING RECEIVED REPORTS THAT BROTHERS OF THE ORDER OF KNIGHTS TEMPLAR HAVE BEEN CONDUCTING SECRET, BLASPHEMOUS, OBSCENE RITES...
CEREMONIES OF BLACK MAGIC IN WHICH THEY DENY AND SPIT ON THE IMAGE OF CHRIST OUR SAVIOR...
...AND PERFORM ACTS OF UNNATURAL INTERCOURSE WITH EACH OTHER!
THE TEMPLARS? I THOUGHT THEY WERE SUPPOSED TO BE THE BEST AND NOBLEST KNIGHTS OF ALL.
THEY ARE! TEMPLARS ARE SO GOOD, THEY CAN FIGHT OUTNUMBERED TEN TO ONE!
AT FIRST, THE KING DID NOT WANT TO LISTEN TO THE PEOPLE WHO BROUGHT HIM THESE HORRIFYING ACCUSATIONS.
PERHAPS THEY WERE ACTING MORE FROM MALICE AND ENVY THAN FROM TRUE DESIRE FOR JUSTICE...
BUT AS MORE INFORMERS CAME FORWARD, THE KING REALIZED THAT THE DANGER TO SOCIETY WAS SO GRAVE, SO IMMINENT, THAT IT WAS HIS DUTY TO LAUNCH A FULL INVESTIGATION, AND RID THE WORLD OF THIS UNSPEAKABLE EVIL!

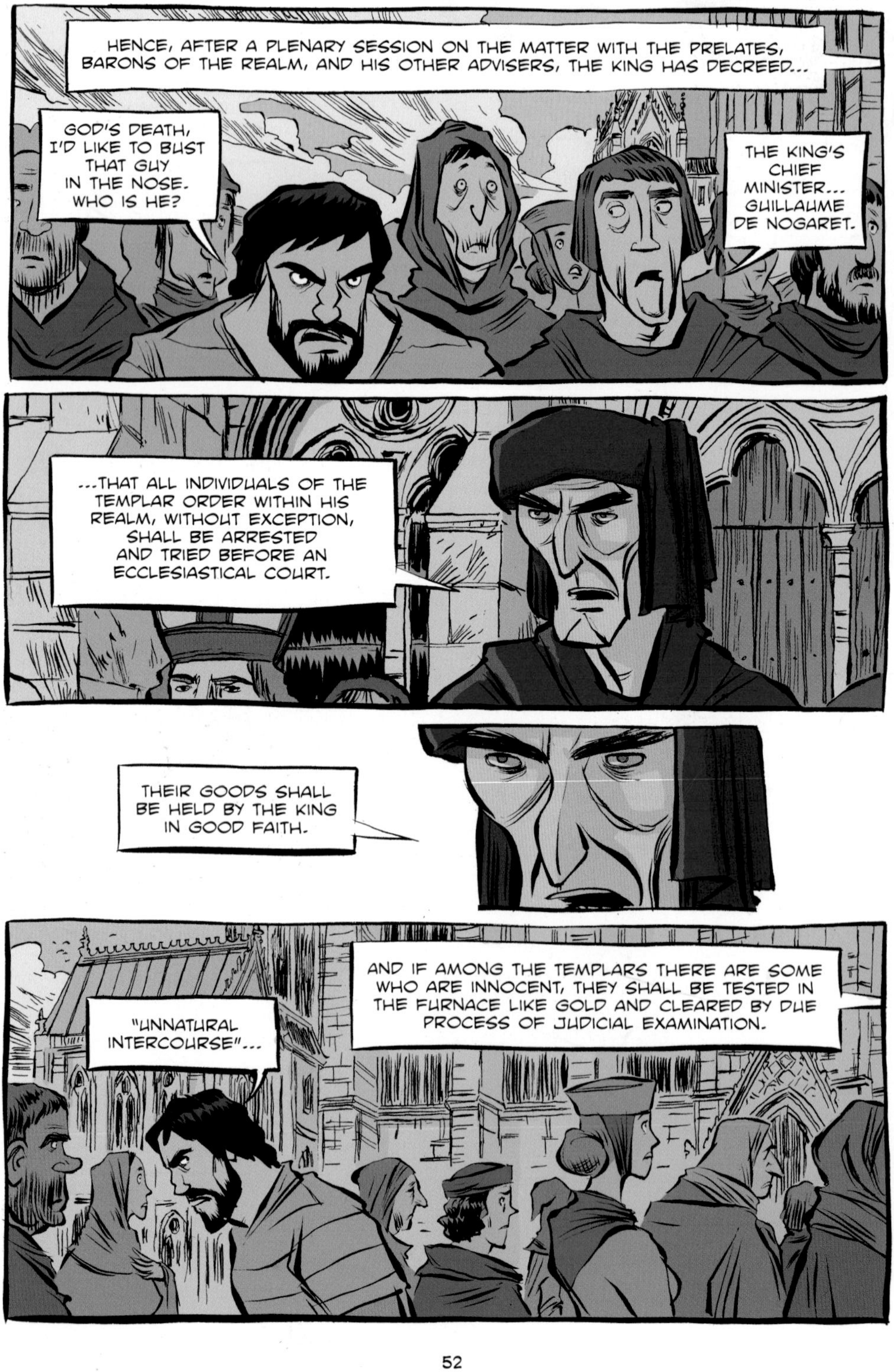
HENCE, AFTER A PLENARY SESSION ON THE MATTER WITH THE PRELATES, BARONS OF THE REALM, AND HIS OTHER ADVISERS, THE KING HAS DECREED...
GOD'S DEATH, I'D LIKE TO BUST THAT GUY IN THE NOSE. WHO IS HE?
THE KING'S CHIEF MINISTER... GUILLAUME DE NOGARET.
...THAT ALL INDIVIDUALS OF THE TEMPLAR ORDER WITHIN HIS REALM, WITHOUT EXCEPTION, SHALL BE ARRESTED AND TRIED BEFORE AN ECCLESIASTICAL COURT.
THEIR GOODS SHALL BE HELD BY THE KING IN GOOD FAITH.
AND IF AMONG THE TEMPLARS THERE ARE SOME WHO ARE INNOCENT, THEY SHALL BE TESTED IN THE FURNACE LIKE GOLD AND CLEARED BY DUE PROCESS OF JUDICIAL EXAMINATION.
"UNNATURAL INTERCOURSE"...

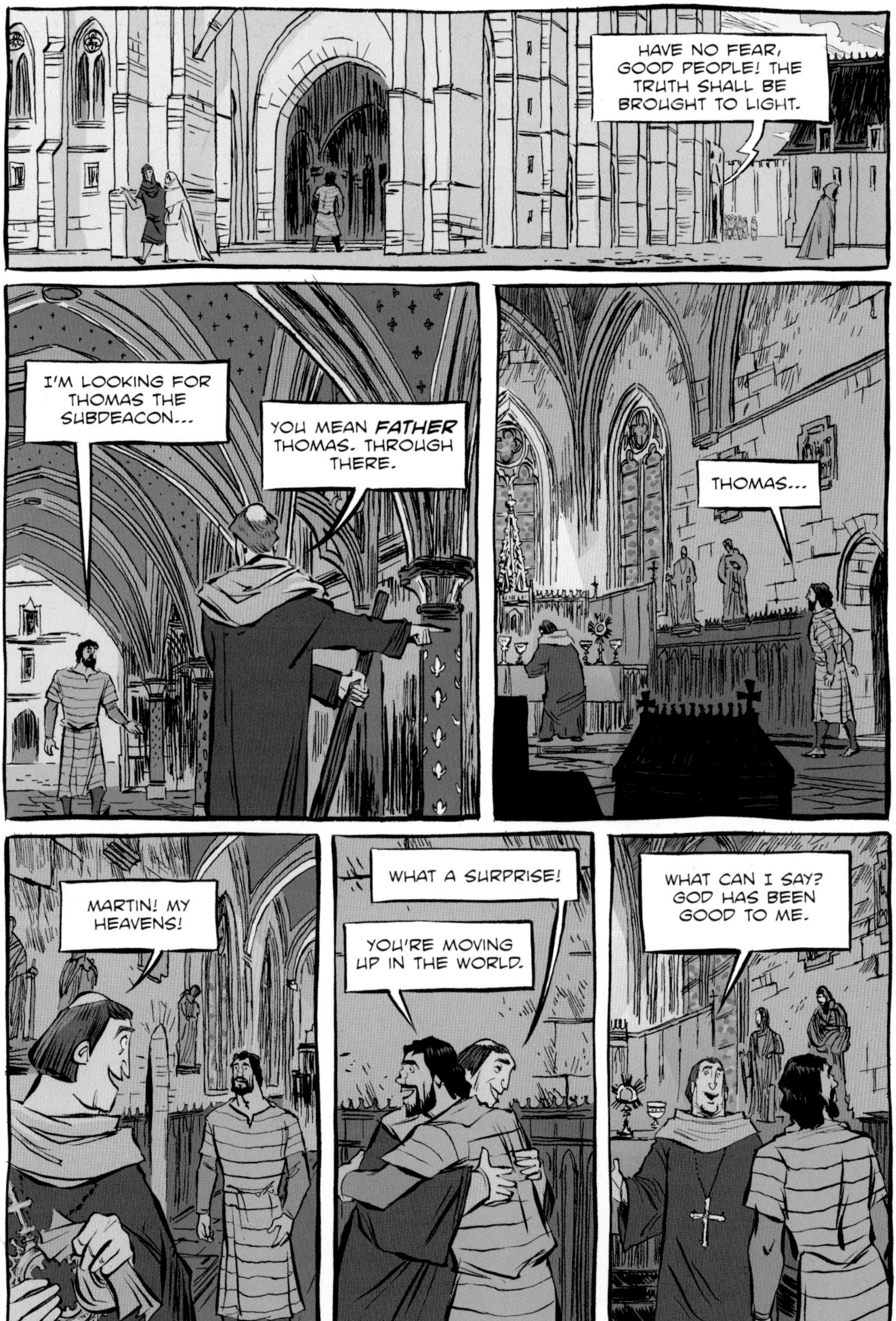
HAVE NO FEAR, GOOD PEOPLE! THE TRUTH SHALL BE BROUGHT TO LIGHT.
I'M LOOKING FOR THOMAS THE SUBDEACON...
YOU MEAN **FATHER** THOMAS. THROUGH THERE.
THOMAS...
MARTIN! MY HEAVENS!
WHAT A SURPRISE!
YOU'RE MOVING UP IN THE WORLD.
WHAT CAN I SAY? GOD HAS BEEN GOOD TO ME.

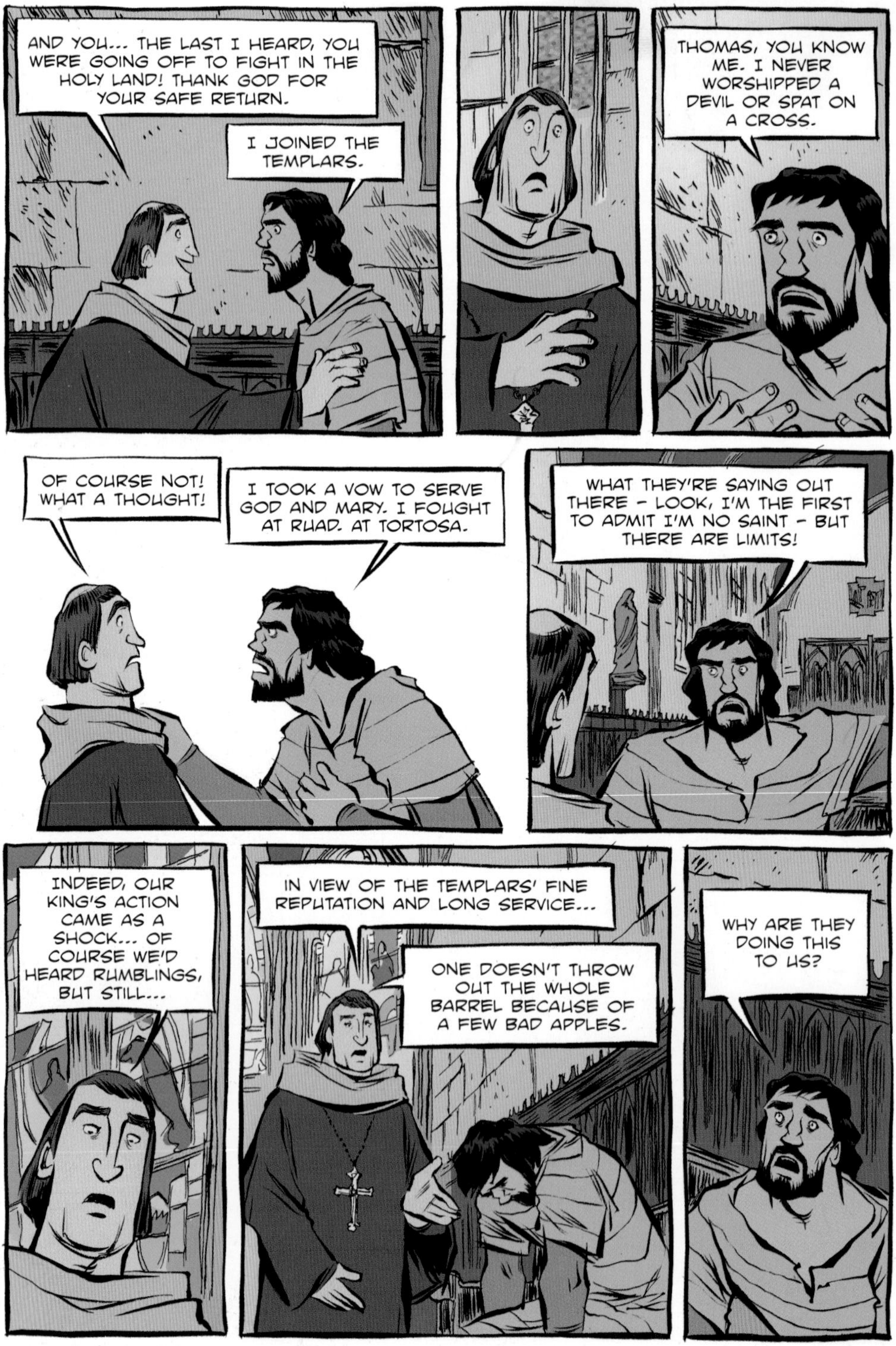
AND YOU... THE LAST I HEARD, YOU WERE GOING OFF TO FIGHT IN THE HOLY LAND! THANK GOD FOR YOUR SAFE RETURN.
I JOINED THE TEMPLARS.
THOMAS, YOU KNOW ME. I NEVER WORSHIPPED A DEVIL OR SPAT ON A CROSS.
OF COURSE NOT! WHAT A THOUGHT!
I TOOK A VOW TO SERVE GOD AND MARY. I FOUGHT AT RUAD. AT TORTOSA.
WHAT THEY'RE SAYING OUT THERE - LOOK, I'M THE FIRST TO ADMIT I'M NO SAINT - BUT THERE ARE LIMITS!
INDEED, OUR KING'S ACTION CAME AS A SHOCK... OF COURSE WE'D HEARD RUMBLINGS, BUT STILL...
IN VIEW OF THE TEMPLARS' FINE REPUTATION AND LONG SERVICE...
ONE DOESN'T THROW OUT THE WHOLE BARREL BECAUSE OF A FEW BAD APPLES.
WHY ARE THEY DOING THIS TO US?

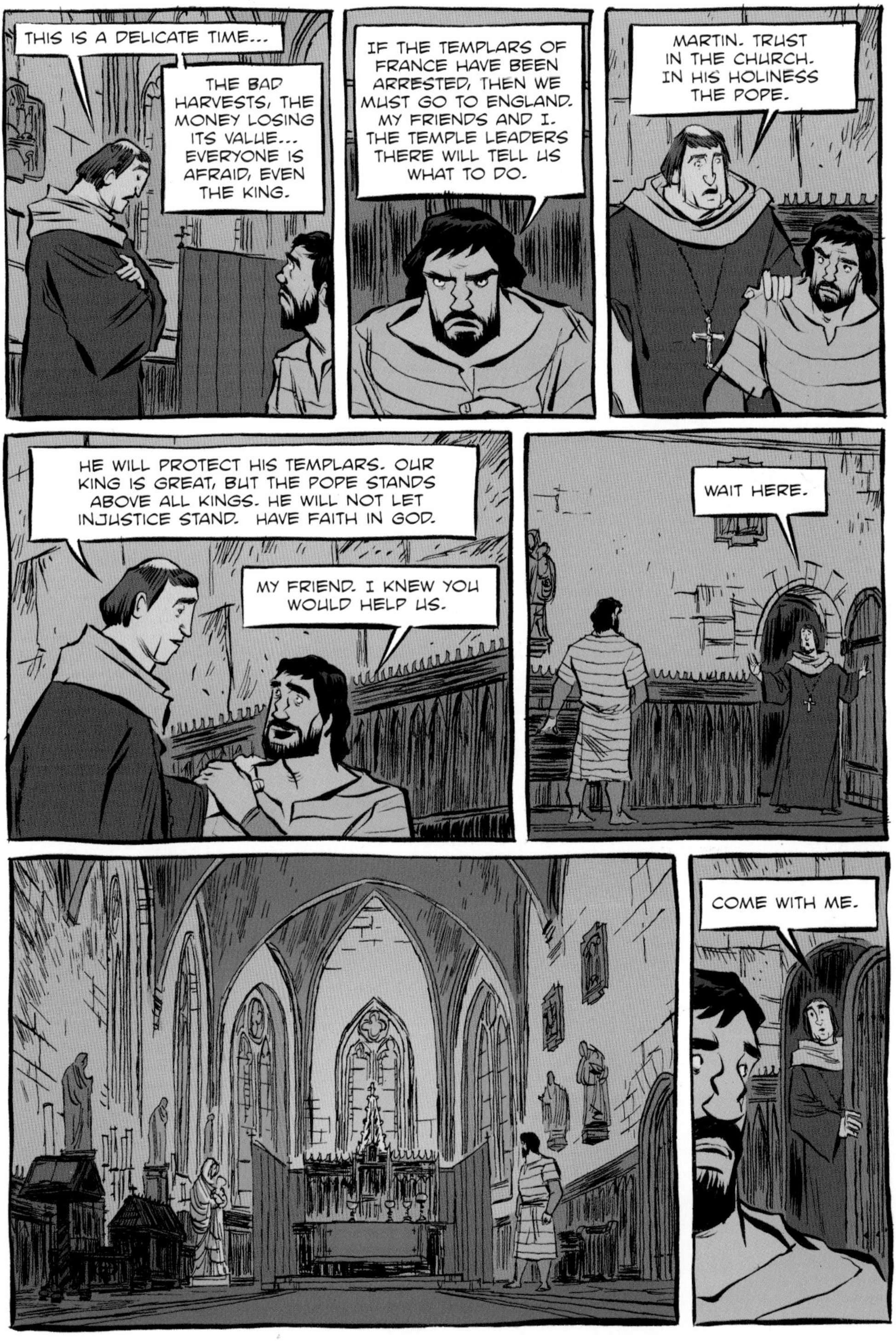
THIS IS A DELICATE TIME...
THE BAD HARVESTS, THE MONEY LOSING ITS VALUE... EVERYONE IS AFRAID, EVEN THE KING.
IF THE TEMPLARS OF FRANCE HAVE BEEN ARRESTED, THEN WE MUST GO TO ENGLAND. MY FRIENDS AND I. THE TEMPLE LEADERS THERE WILL TELL US WHAT TO DO.
MARTIN. TRUST IN THE CHURCH. IN HIS HOLINESS THE POPE.
HE WILL PROTECT HIS TEMPLARS. OUR KING IS GREAT, BUT THE POPE STANDS ABOVE ALL KINGS. HE WILL NOT LET INJUSTICE STAND. HAVE FAITH IN GOD.
MY FRIEND. I KNEW YOU WOULD HELP US.
WAIT HERE.
COME WITH ME.

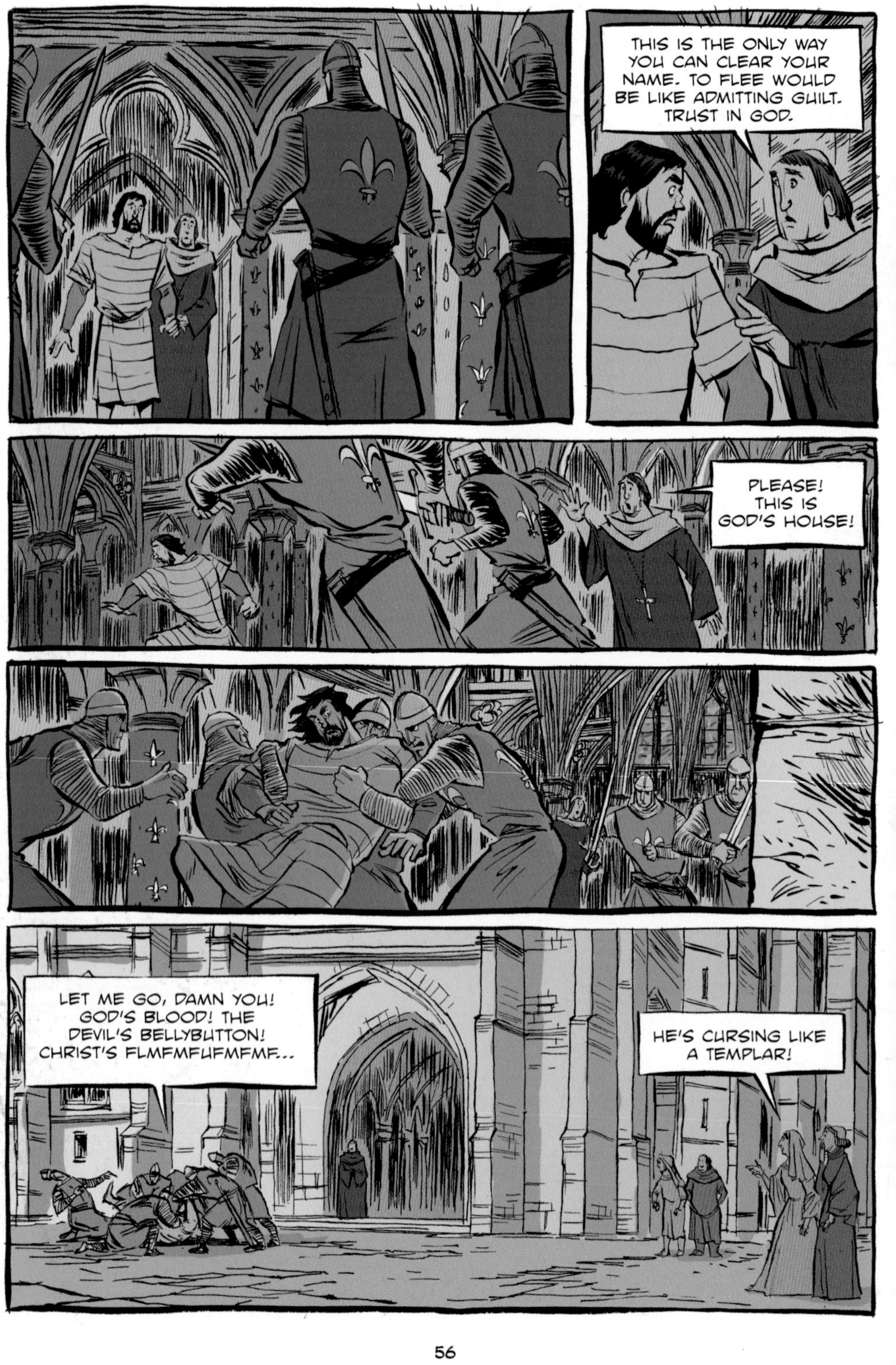
THIS IS THE ONLY WAY YOU CAN CLEAR YOUR NAME. TO FLEE WOULD BE LIKE ADMITTING GUILT. TRUST IN GOD.
PLEASE! THIS IS GOD'S HOUSE!
LET ME GO, DAMN YOU! GOD'S BLOOD! THE DEVIL'S BELLYBUTTON! CHRIST'S FLMFMFUFMFMF...
HE'S CURSING LIKE A TEMPLAR!

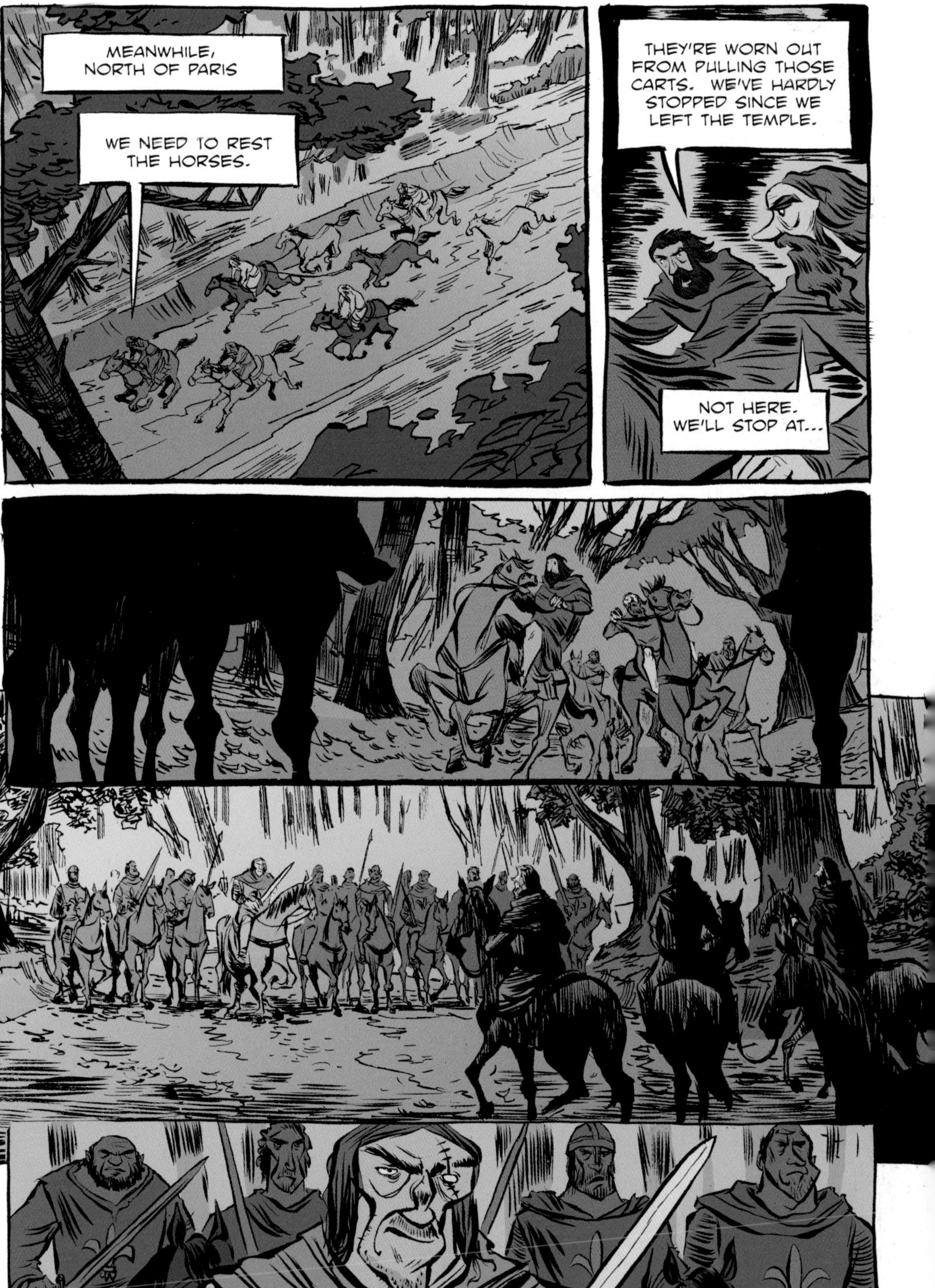
MEANWHILE, NORTH OF PARIS
WE NEED TO REST THE HORSES.
THEY'RE WORN OUT FROM PULLING THOSE CARTS. WE'VE HARDLY STOPPED SINCE WE LEFT THE TEMPLE.
NOT HERE. WE'LL STOP AT...

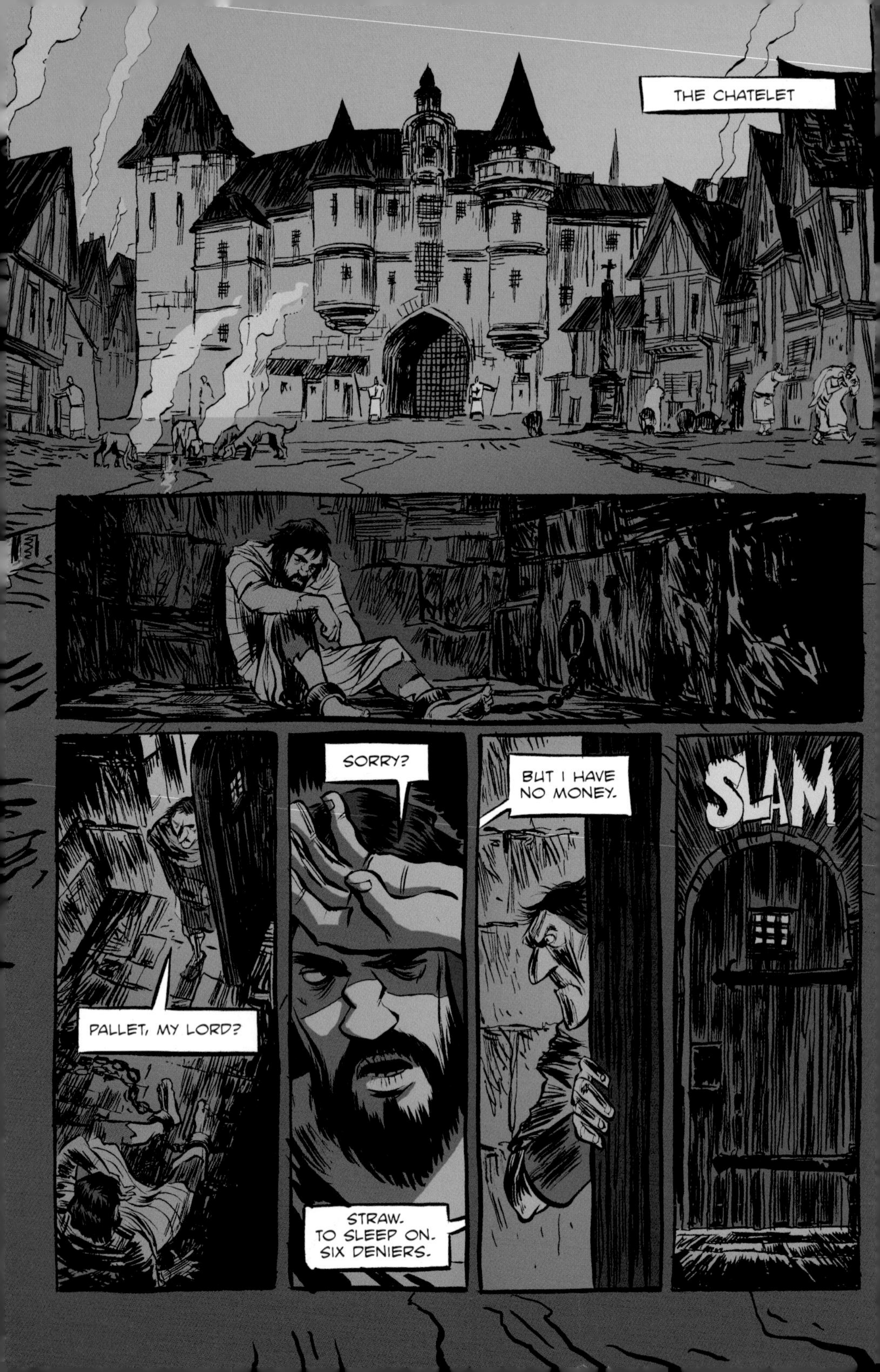
THE CHATELET
PALLET, MY LORD?
SORRY?
STRAW. TO SLEEP ON. SIX DENIERS.
BUT I HAVE NO MONEY.
SLAM

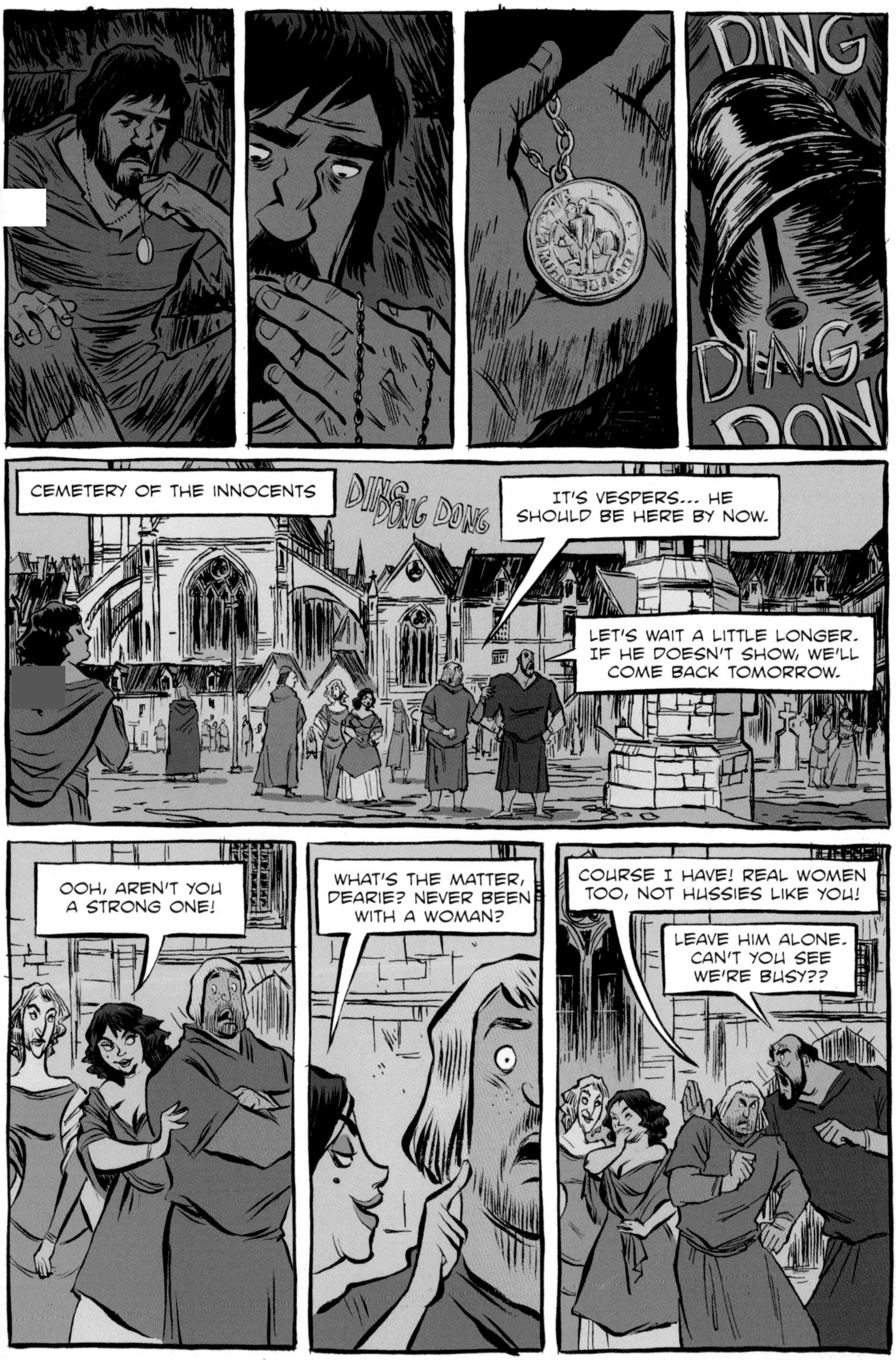
DING
DING
DONG
CEMETERY OF THE INNOCENTS
DING DONG DONG
IT'S VESPERS... HE SHOULD BE HERE BY NOW.
LET'S WAIT A LITTLE LONGER. IF HE DOESN'T SHOW, WE'LL COME BACK TOMORROW.
OOH, AREN'T YOU A STRONG ONE!
WHAT'S THE MATTER, DEARIE? NEVER BEEN WITH A WOMAN?
COURSE I HAVE! REAL WOMEN TOO, NOT HUSSIES LIKE YOU!
LEAVE HIM ALONE. CAN'T YOU SEE WE'RE BUSY??

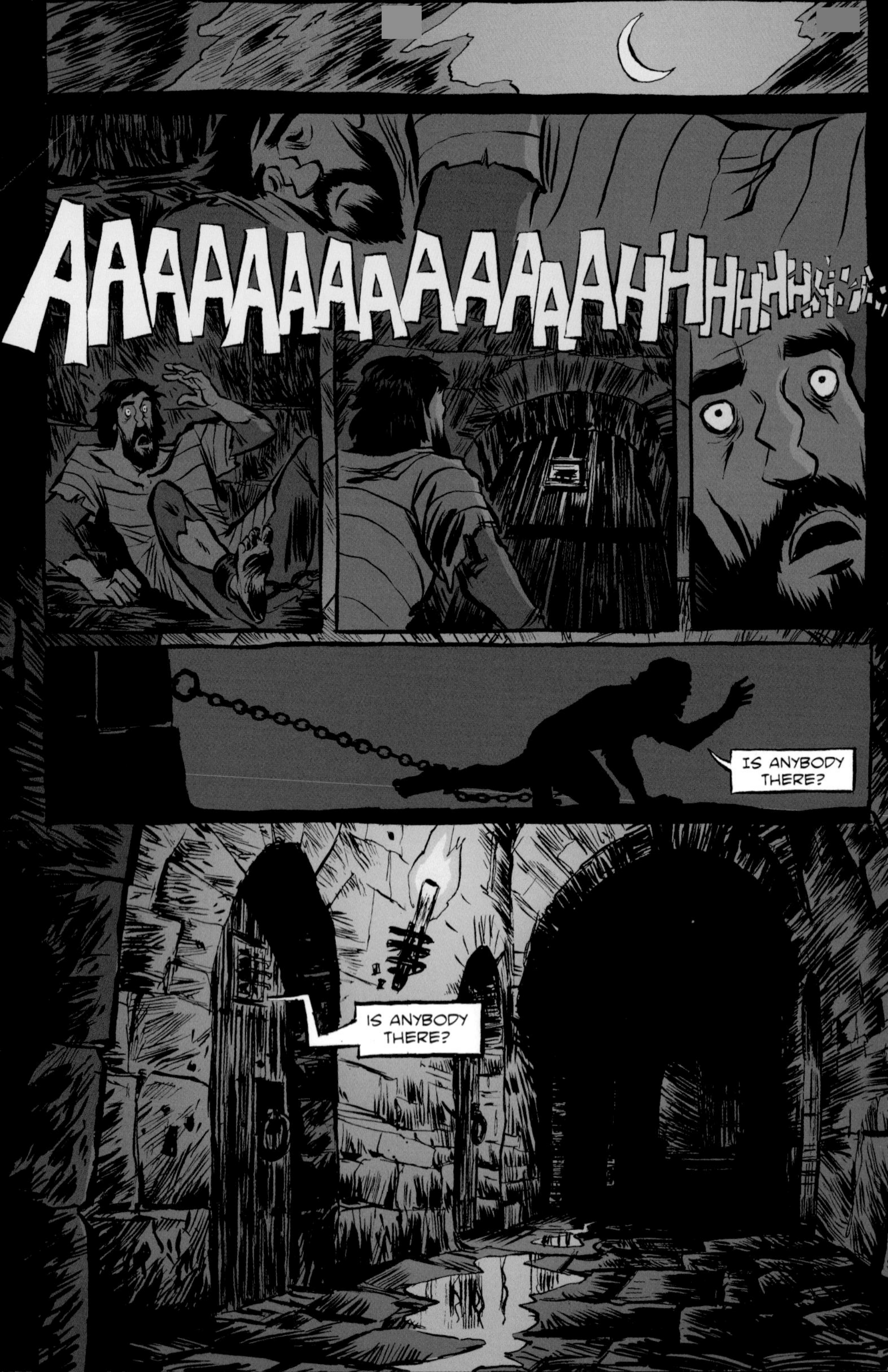
AAAAAAAAAAAAAHHHH
IS ANYBODY THERE?
IS ANYBODY THERE?

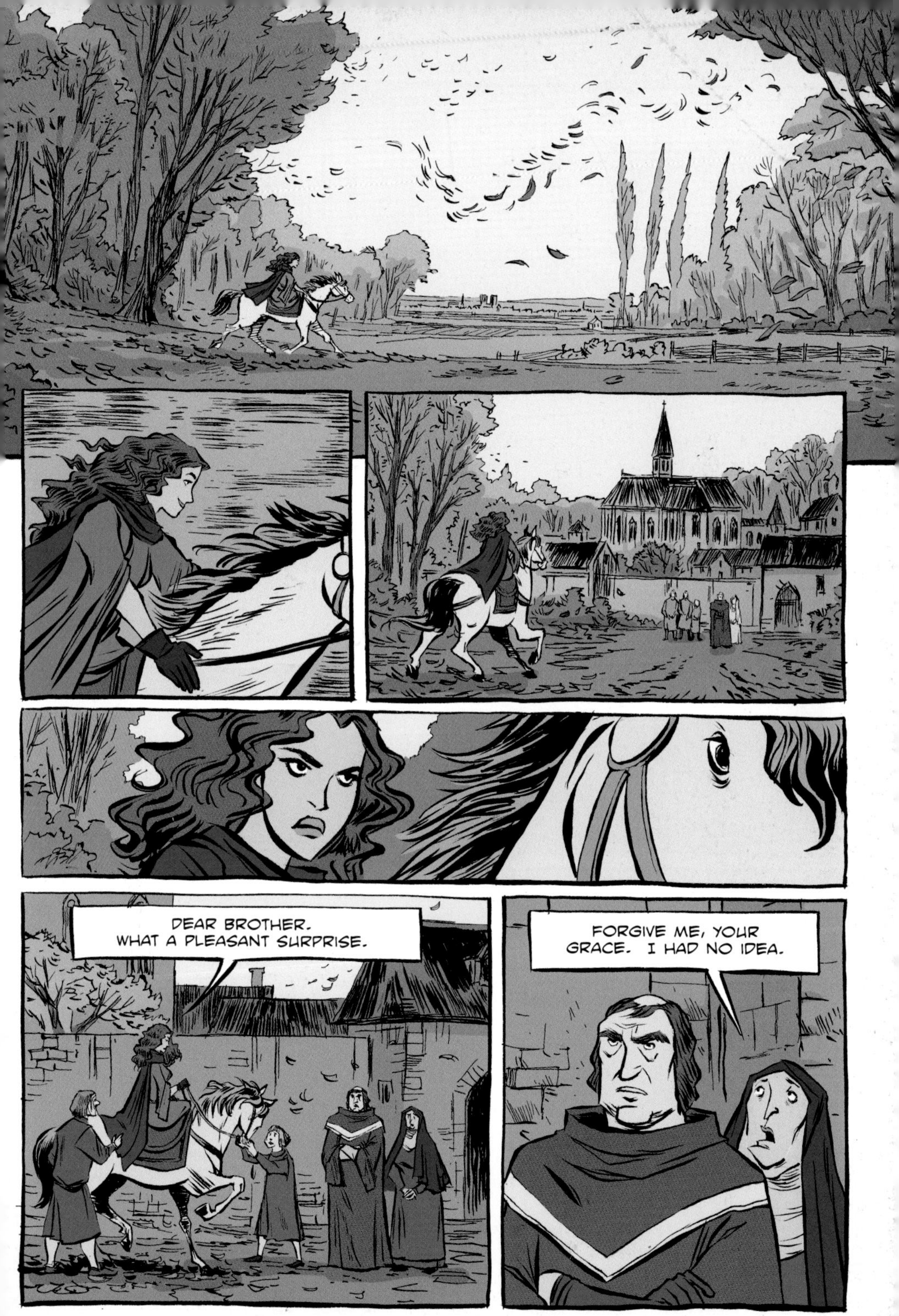
DEAR BROTHER.
WHAT A PLEASANT SURPRISE.
FORGIVE ME, YOUR GRACE. I HAD NO IDEA.

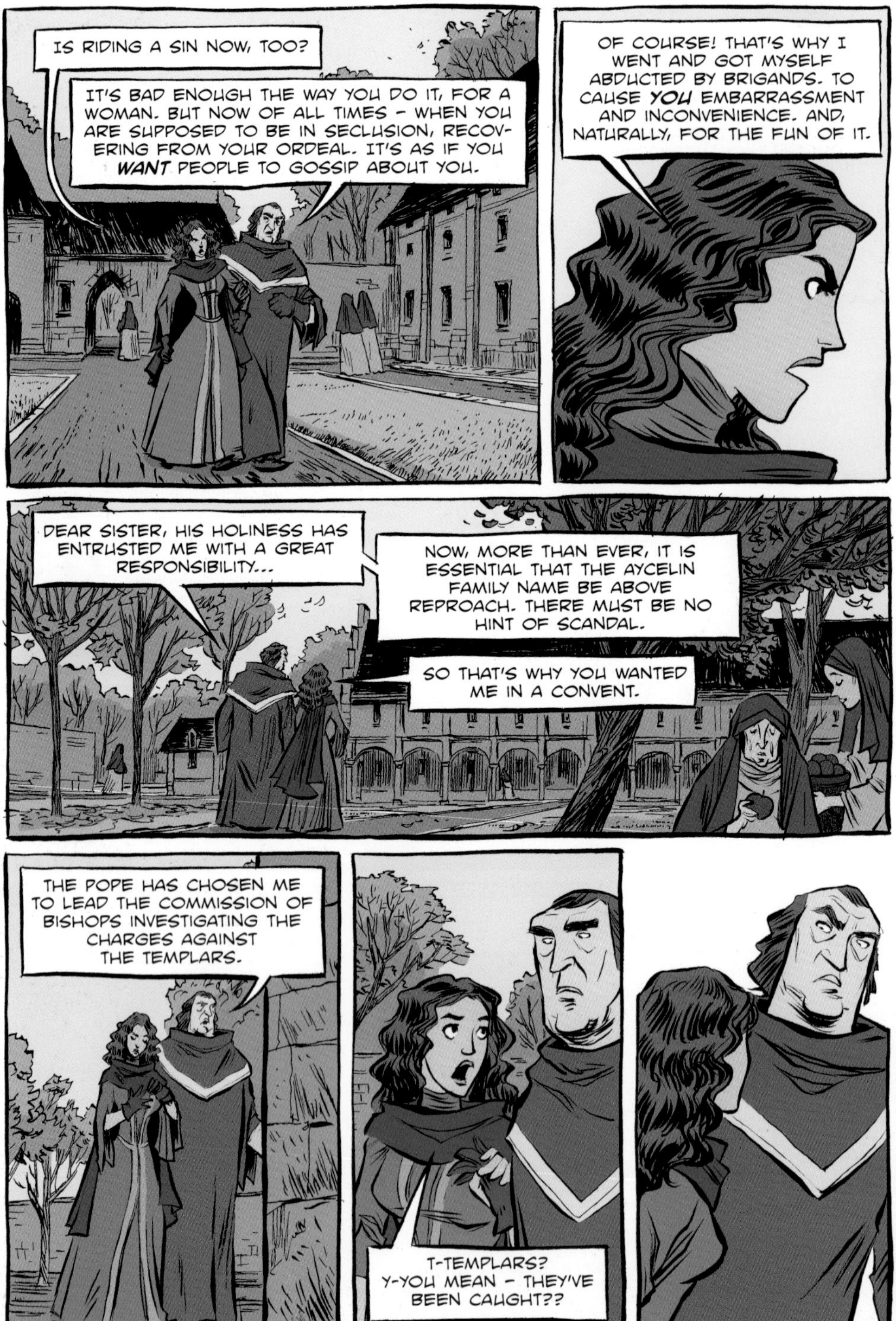
IS RIDING A SIN NOW, TOO?
IT'S BAD ENOUGH THE WAY YOU DO IT, FOR A WOMAN. BUT NOW OF ALL TIMES - WHEN YOU ARE SUPPOSED TO BE IN SECLUSION, RECOVERING FROM YOUR ORDEAL. IT'S AS IF YOU WANT PEOPLE TO GOSSIP ABOUT YOU.
OF COURSE! THAT'S WHY I WENT AND GOT MYSELF ABDUCTED BY BRIGANDS. TO CAUSE YOU EMBARRASSMENT AND INCONVENIENCE. AND, NATURALLY, FOR THE FUN OF IT.
DEAR SISTER, HIS HOLINESS HAS ENTRUSTED ME WITH A GREAT RESPONSIBILITY...
NOW, MORE THAN EVER, IT IS ESSENTIAL THAT THE AYCELIN FAMILY NAME BE ABOVE REPROACH. THERE MUST BE NO HINT OF SCANDAL.
SO THAT'S WHY YOU WANTED ME IN A CONVENT.
THE POPE HAS CHOSEN ME TO LEAD THE COMMISSION OF BISHOPS INVESTIGATING THE CHARGES AGAINST THE TEMPLARS.
T-TEMPLARS? Y-YOU MEAN - THEY'VE BEEN CAUGHT??

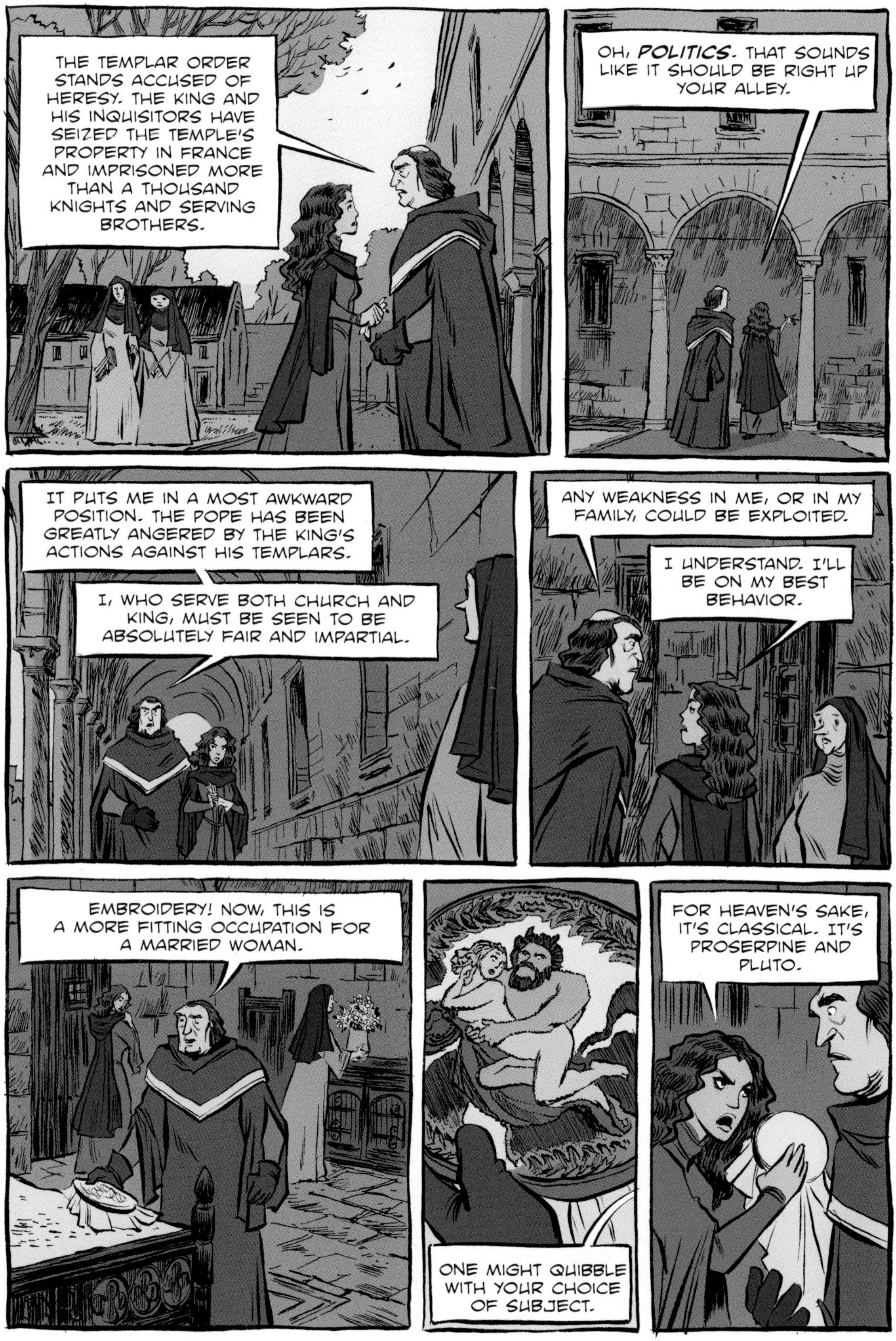
THE TEMPLAR ORDER STANDS ACCUSED OF HERESY. THE KING AND HIS INQUISITORS HAVE SEIZED THE TEMPLE'S PROPERTY IN FRANCE AND IMPRISONED MORE THAN A THOUSAND KNIGHTS AND SERVING BROTHERS.
OH, *POLITICS*. THAT SOUNDS LIKE IT SHOULD BE RIGHT UP YOUR ALLEY.
IT PUTS ME IN A MOST AWKWARD POSITION. THE POPE HAS BEEN GREATLY ANGERED BY THE KING'S ACTIONS AGAINST HIS TEMPLARS.
I, WHO SERVE BOTH CHURCH AND KING, MUST BE SEEN TO BE ABSOLUTELY FAIR AND IMPARTIAL.
ANY WEAKNESS IN ME, OR IN MY FAMILY, COULD BE EXPLOITED.
I UNDERSTAND. I'LL BE ON MY BEST BEHAVIOR.
EMBROIDERY! NOW, THIS IS A MORE FITTING OCCUPATION FOR A MARRIED WOMAN.
ONE MIGHT QUIBBLE WITH YOUR CHOICE OF SUBJECT.
FOR HEAVEN'S SAKE, IT'S CLASSICAL. IT'S PROSERPINE AND PLUTO.

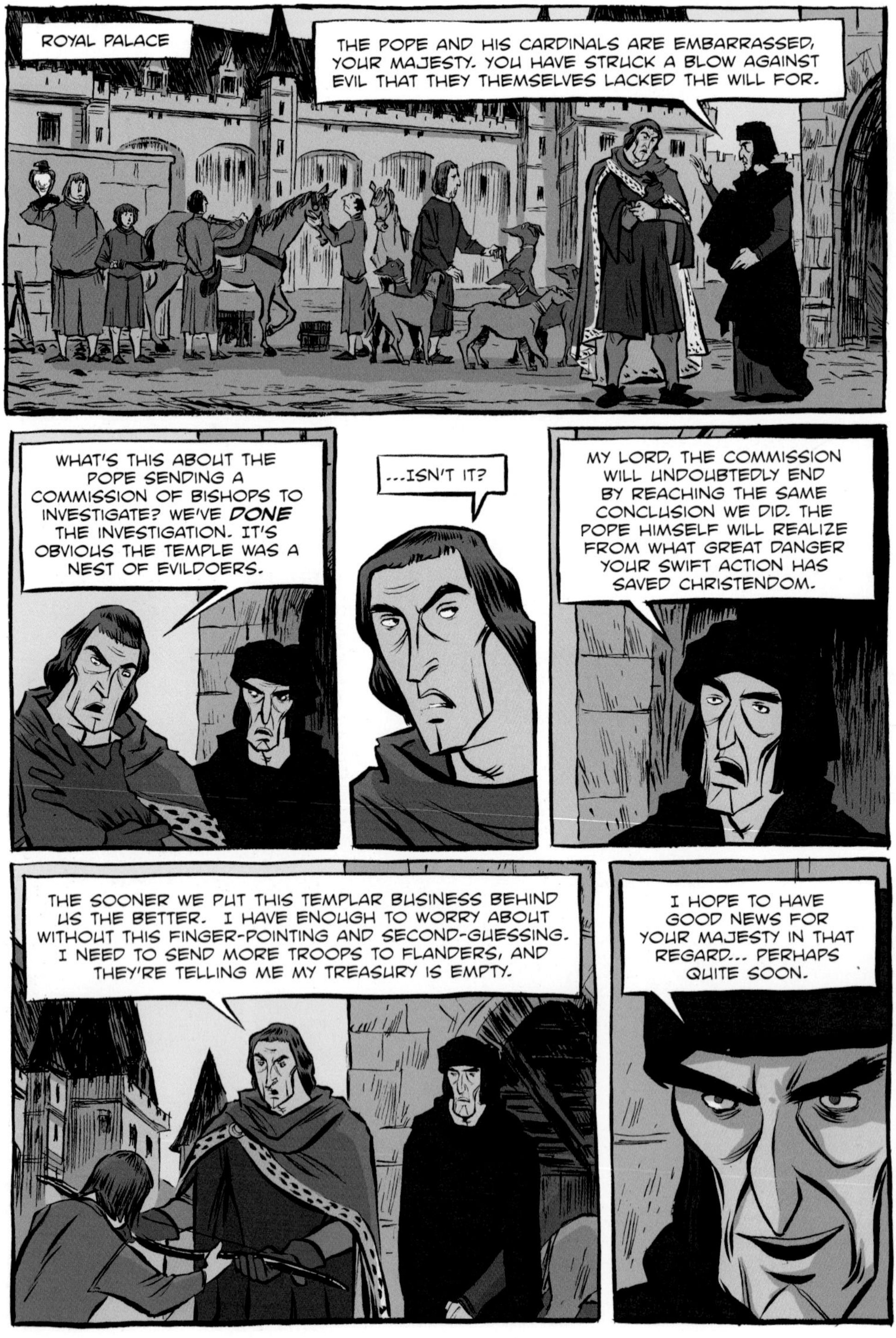
ROYAL PALACE
THE POPE AND HIS CARDINALS ARE EMBARRASSED, YOUR MAJESTY. YOU HAVE STRUCK A BLOW AGAINST EVIL THAT THEY THEMSELVES LACKED THE WILL FOR.
WHAT'S THIS ABOUT THE POPE SENDING A COMMISSION OF BISHOPS TO INVESTIGATE? WE'VE DONE THE INVESTIGATION. IT'S OBVIOUS THE TEMPLE WAS A NEST OF EVILDOERS.
...ISN'T IT?
MY LORD, THE COMMISSION WILL UNDOUBTEDLY END BY REACHING THE SAME CONCLUSION WE DID. THE POPE HIMSELF WILL REALIZE FROM WHAT GREAT DANGER YOUR SWIFT ACTION HAS SAVED CHRISTENDOM.
THE SOONER WE PUT THIS TEMPLAR BUSINESS BEHIND US THE BETTER. I HAVE ENOUGH TO WORRY ABOUT WITHOUT THIS FINGER-POINTING AND SECOND-GUESSING. I NEED TO SEND MORE TROOPS TO FLANDERS, AND THEY'RE TELLING ME MY TREASURY IS EMPTY.
I HOPE TO HAVE GOOD NEWS FOR YOUR MAJESTY IN THAT REGARD... PERHAPS QUITE SOON.

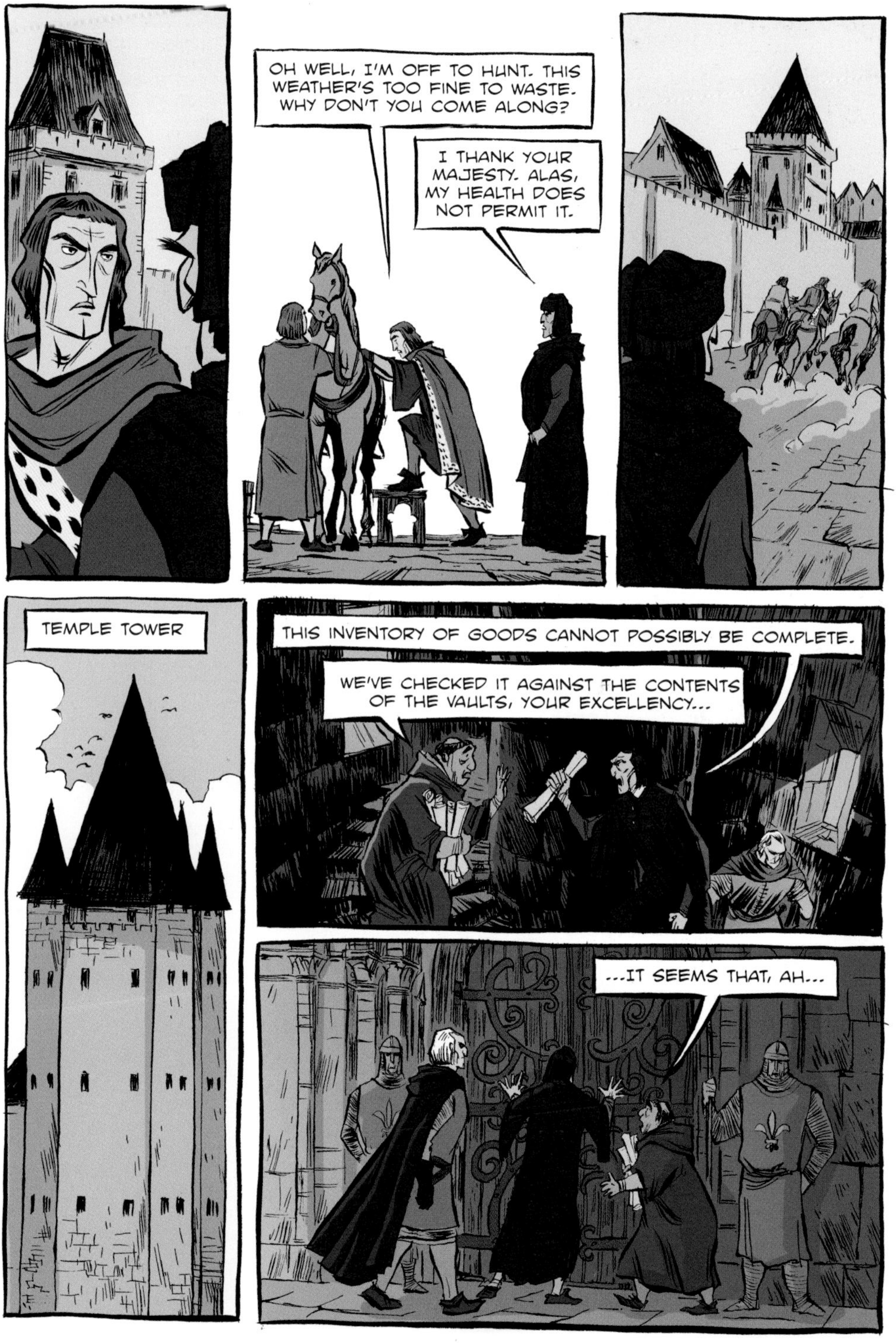
OH WELL, I'M OFF TO HUNT. THIS WEATHER'S TOO FINE TO WASTE. WHY DON'T YOU COME ALONG?
I THANK YOUR MAJESTY. ALAS, MY HEALTH DOES NOT PERMIT IT.
TEMPLE TOWER
THIS INVENTORY OF GOODS CANNOT POSSIBLY BE COMPLETE.
WE'VE CHECKED IT AGAINST THE CONTENTS OF THE VAULTS, YOUR EXCELLENCY...
...IT SEEMS THAT, AH...

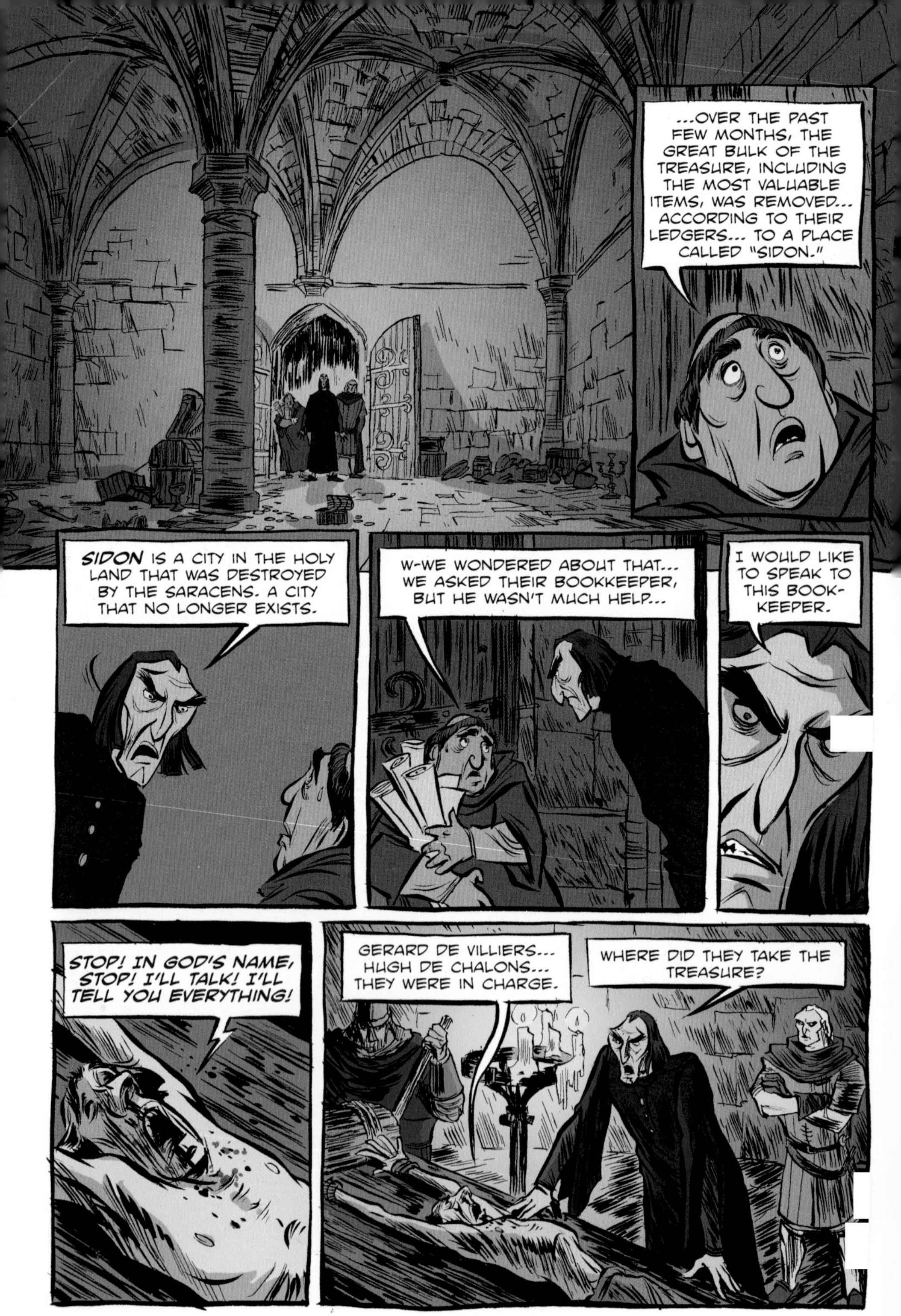
...OVER THE PAST FEW MONTHS, THE GREAT BULK OF THE TREASURE, INCLUDING THE MOST VALUABLE ITEMS, WAS REMOVED... ACCORDING TO THEIR LEDGERS... TO A PLACE CALLED "SIDON."
SIDON IS A CITY IN THE HOLY LAND THAT WAS DESTROYED BY THE SARACENS. A CITY THAT NO LONGER EXISTS.
W-WE WONDERED ABOUT THAT... WE ASKED THEIR BOOKKEEPER, BUT HE WASN'T MUCH HELP...
I WOULD LIKE TO SPEAK TO THIS BOOK-KEEPER.
STOP! IN GOD'S NAME, STOP! I'LL TALK! I'LL TELL YOU EVERYTHING!
GERARD DE VILLIERS... HUGH DE CHALONS... THEY WERE IN CHARGE.
WHERE DID THEY TAKE THE TREASURE?

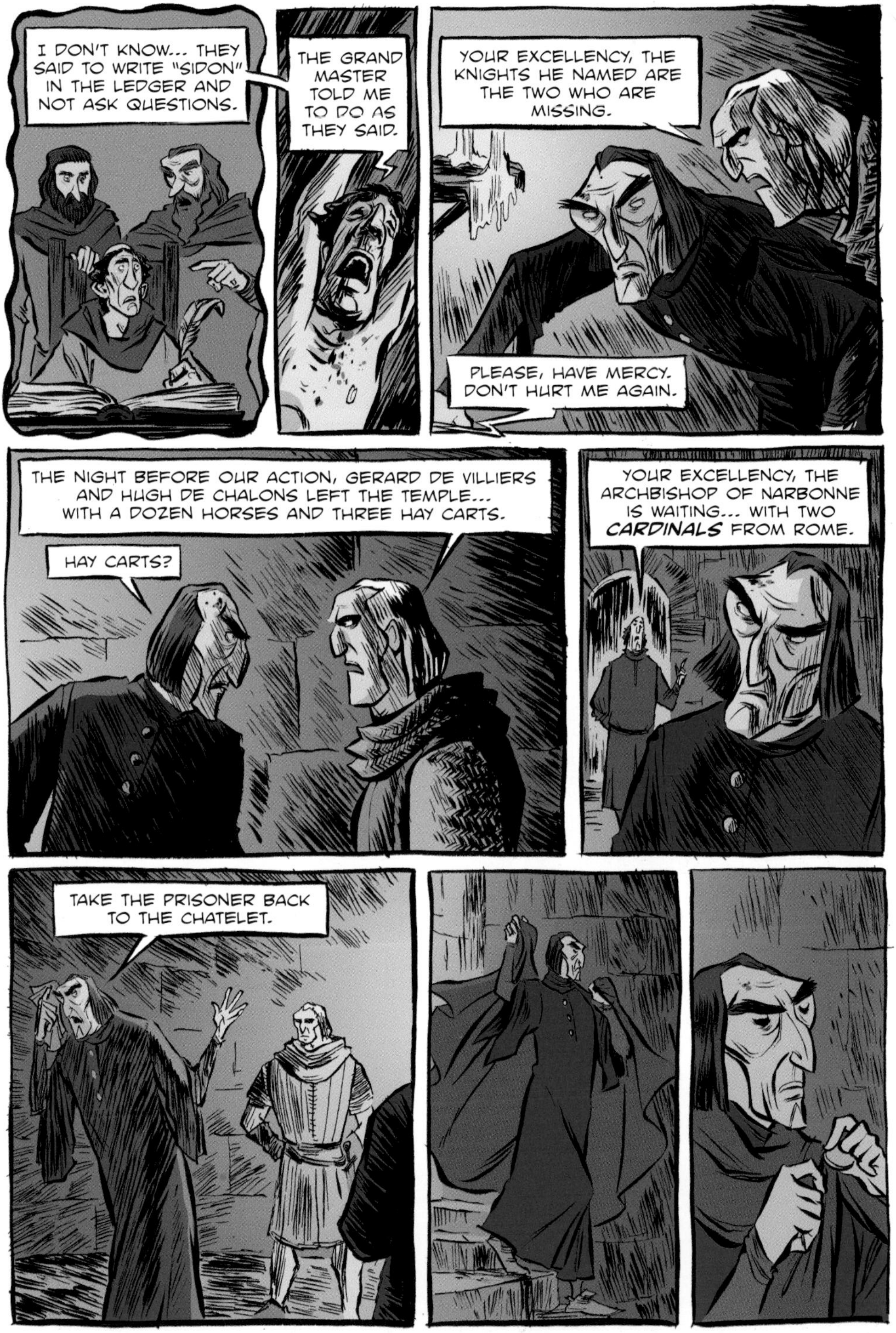
I DON'T KNOW... THEY SAID TO WRITE "SIDON" IN THE LEDGER AND NOT ASK QUESTIONS.
THE GRAND MASTER TOLD ME TO DO AS THEY SAID.
YOUR EXCELLENCY, THE KNIGHTS HE NAMED ARE THE TWO WHO ARE MISSING.
PLEASE, HAVE MERCY. DON'T HURT ME AGAIN.
THE NIGHT BEFORE OUR ACTION, GERARD DE VILLIERS AND HUGH DE CHALONS LEFT THE TEMPLE... WITH A DOZEN HORSES AND THREE HAY CARTS.
HAY CARTS?
YOUR EXCELLENCY, THE ARCHBISHOP OF NARBONNE IS WAITING... WITH TWO CARDINALS FROM ROME.
TAKE THE PRISONER BACK TO THE CHATELET.

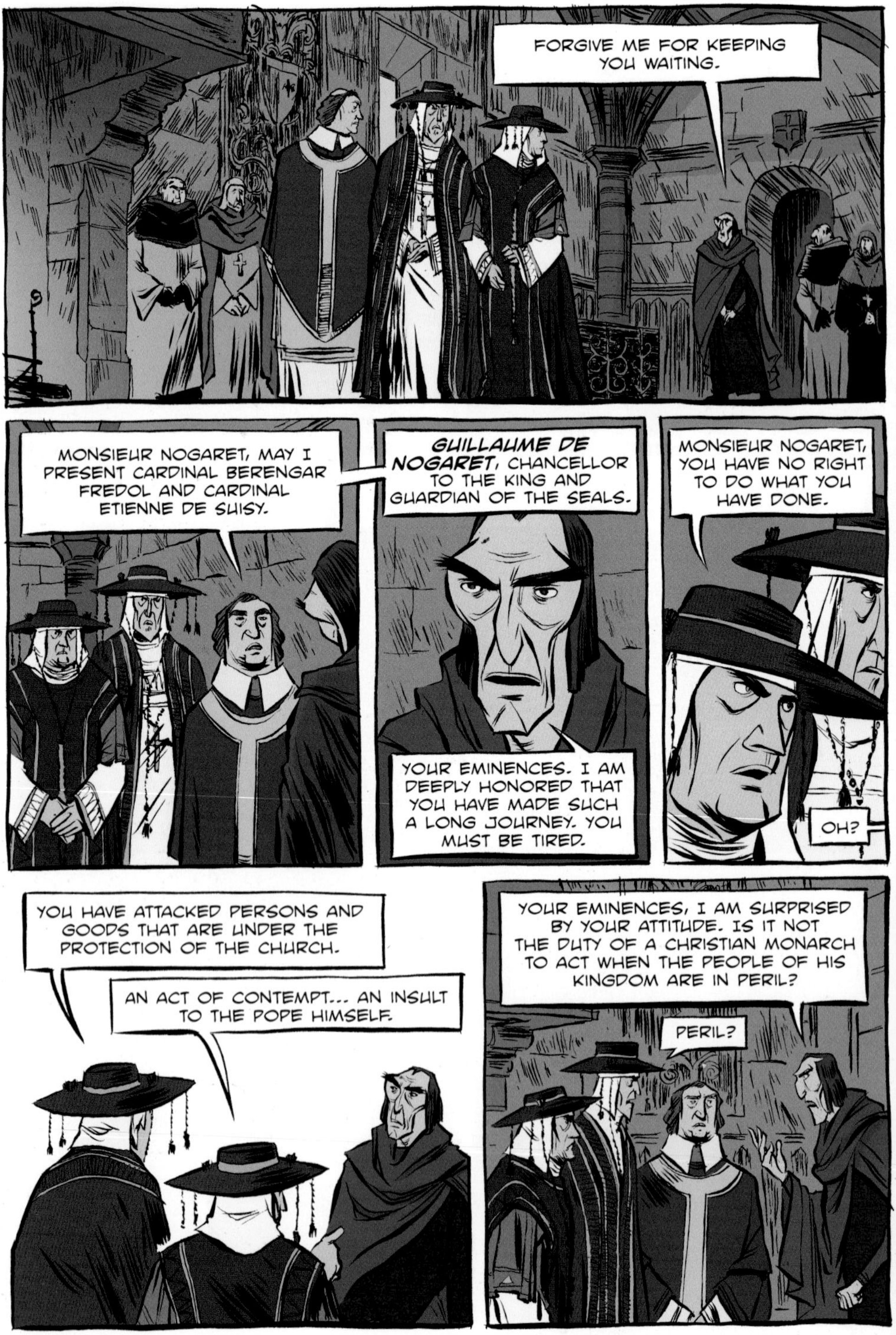
FORGIVE ME FOR KEEPING YOU WAITING.
MONSIEUR NOGARET, MAY I PRESENT CARDINAL BERENGAR FREDOL AND CARDINAL ETIENNE DE SUISY.
GUILLAUME DE NOGARET, CHANCELLOR TO THE KING AND GUARDIAN OF THE SEALS.
YOUR EMINENCES. I AM DEEPLY HONORED THAT YOU HAVE MADE SUCH A LONG JOURNEY. YOU MUST BE TIRED.
MONSIEUR NOGARET, YOU HAVE NO RIGHT TO DO WHAT YOU HAVE DONE.
OH?
YOU HAVE ATTACKED PERSONS AND GOODS THAT ARE UNDER THE PROTECTION OF THE CHURCH.
AN ACT OF CONTEMPT... AN INSULT TO THE POPE HIMSELF.
YOUR EMINENCES, I AM SURPRISED BY YOUR ATTITUDE. IS IT NOT THE DUTY OF A CHRISTIAN MONARCH TO ACT WHEN THE PEOPLE OF HIS KINGDOM ARE IN PERIL?
PERIL?

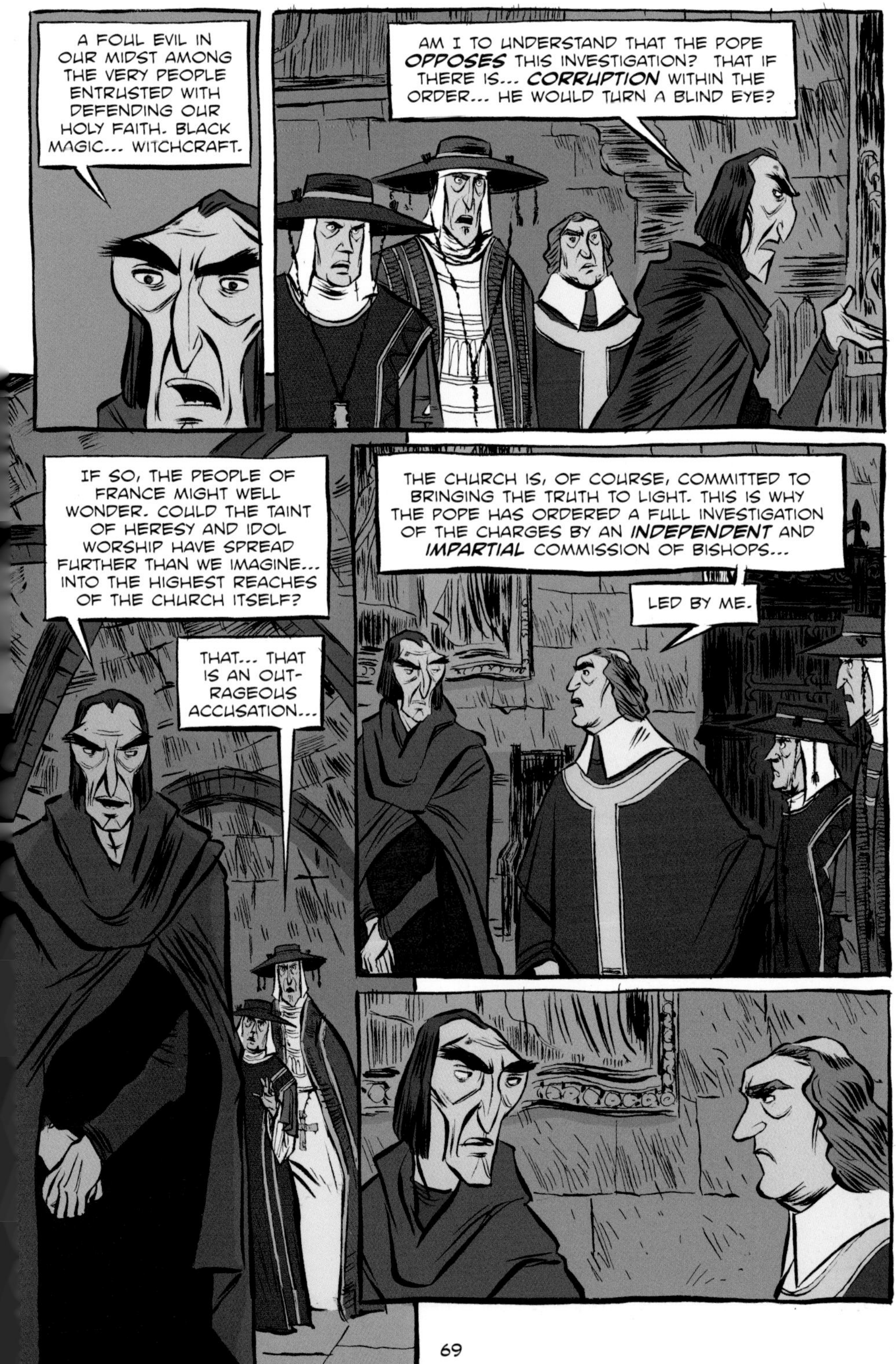
A FOUL EVIL IN OUR MIDST AMONG THE VERY PEOPLE ENTRUSTED WITH DEFENDING OUR HOLY FAITH. BLACK MAGIC... WITCHCRAFT.
AM I TO UNDERSTAND THAT THE POPE OPPOSES THIS INVESTIGATION? THAT IF THERE IS... CORRUPTION WITHIN THE ORDER... HE WOULD TURN A BLIND EYE?
IF SO, THE PEOPLE OF FRANCE MIGHT WELL WONDER. COULD THE TAINT OF HERESY AND IDOL WORSHIP HAVE SPREAD FURTHER THAN WE IMAGINE... INTO THE HIGHEST REACHES OF THE CHURCH ITSELF?
THAT... THAT IS AN OUTRAGEOUS ACCUSATION...
THE CHURCH IS, OF COURSE, COMMITTED TO BRINGING THE TRUTH TO LIGHT. THIS IS WHY THE POPE HAS ORDERED A FULL INVESTIGATION OF THE CHARGES BY AN INDEPENDENT AND IMPARTIAL COMMISSION OF BISHOPS...
LED BY ME.

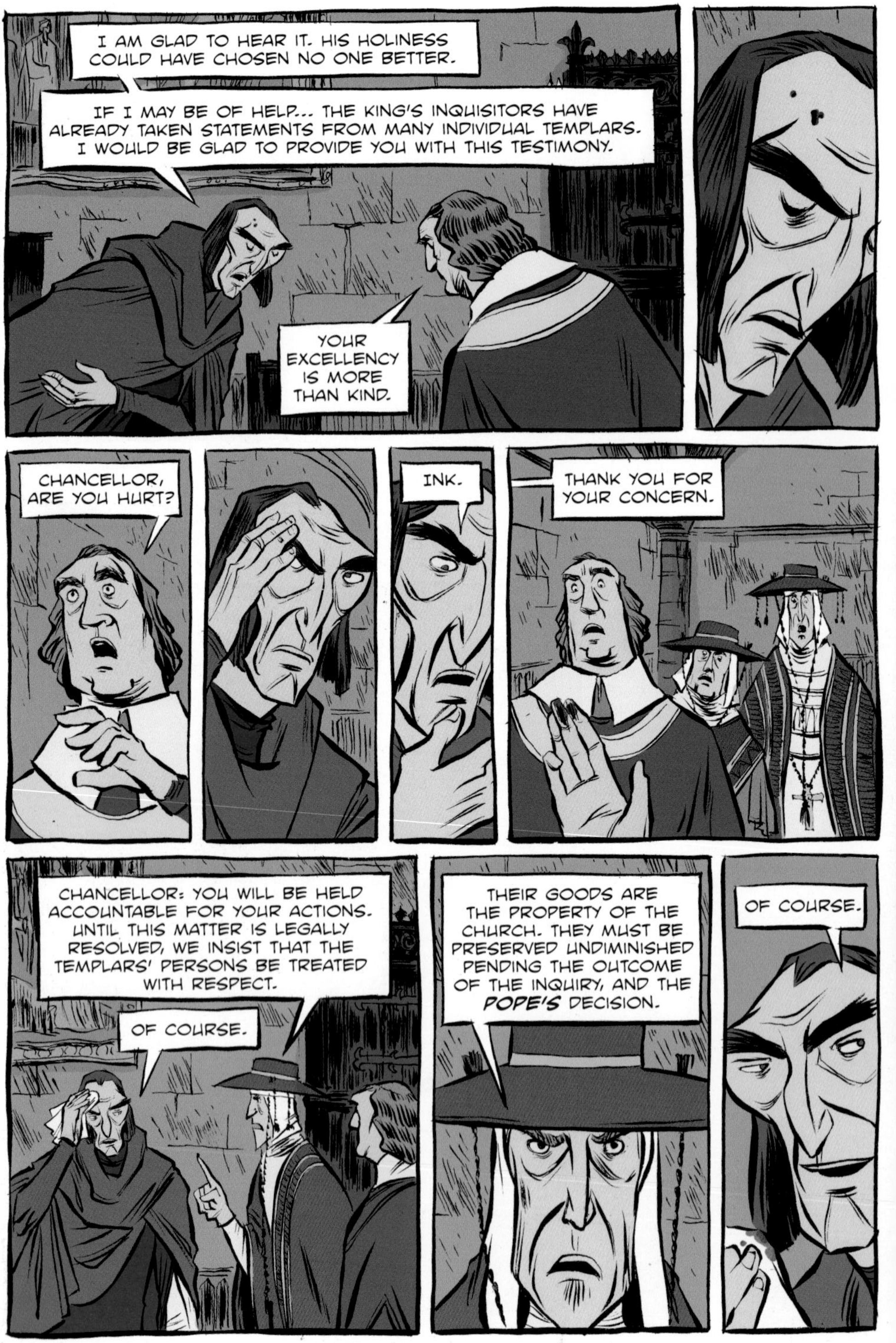
I AM GLAD TO HEAR IT. HIS HOLINESS COULD HAVE CHOSEN NO ONE BETTER.
IF I MAY BE OF HELP... THE KING'S INQUISITORS HAVE ALREADY TAKEN STATEMENTS FROM MANY INDIVIDUAL TEMPLARS. I WOULD BE GLAD TO PROVIDE YOU WITH THIS TESTIMONY.
YOUR EXCELLENCY IS MORE THAN KIND.
CHANCELLOR, ARE YOU HURT?
INK.
THANK YOU FOR YOUR CONCERN.
CHANCELLOR: YOU WILL BE HELD ACCOUNTABLE FOR YOUR ACTIONS. UNTIL THIS MATTER IS LEGALLY RESOLVED, WE INSIST THAT THE TEMPLARS' PERSONS BE TREATED WITH RESPECT.
OF COURSE.
THEIR GOODS ARE THE PROPERTY OF THE CHURCH. THEY MUST BE PRESERVED UNDIMINISHED PENDING THE OUTCOME OF THE INQUIRY, AND THE ***POPE'S*** DECISION.
OF COURSE.

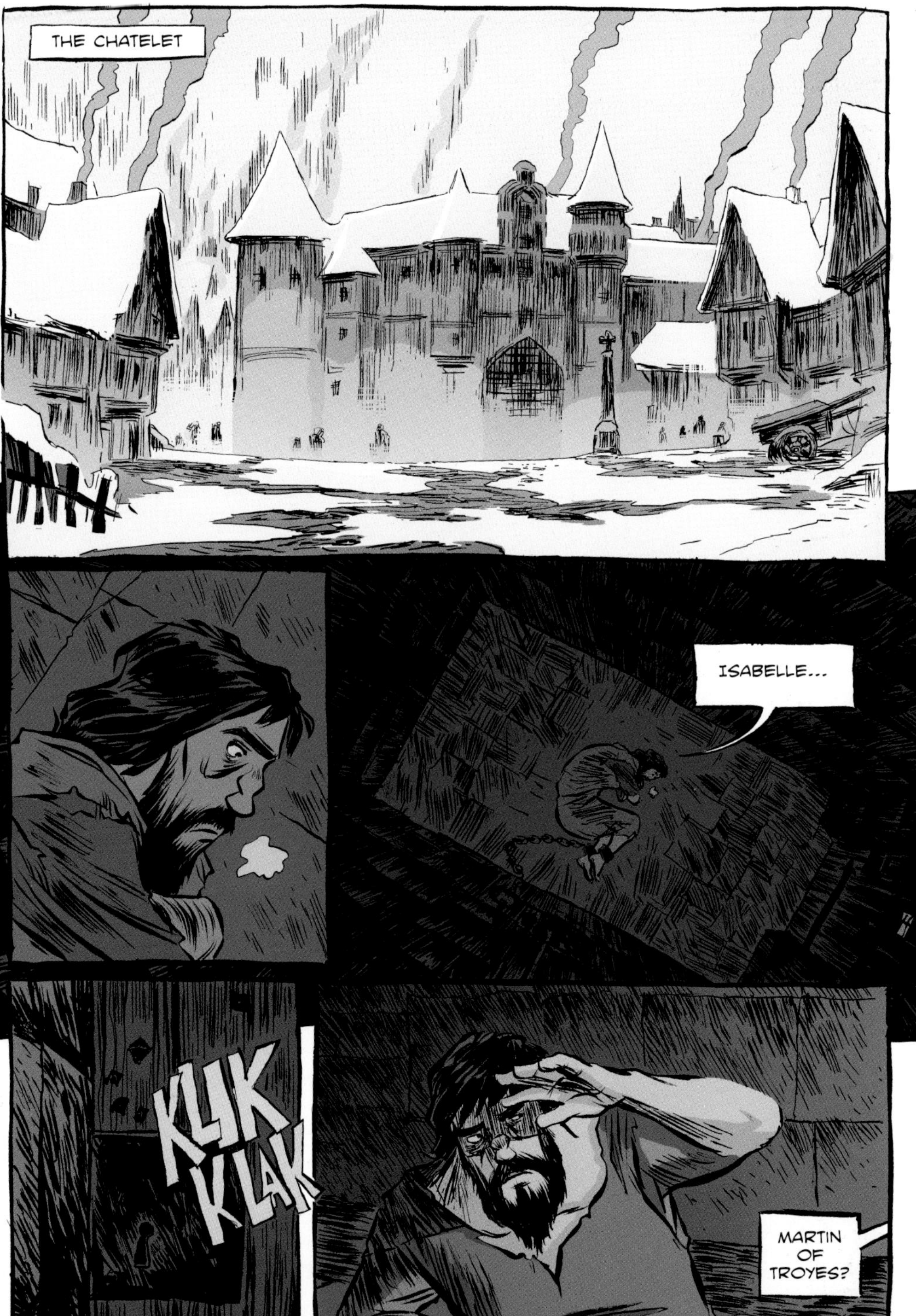
THE CHATELET
ISABELLE...
KLIK
KLAK
MARTIN OF TROYES?

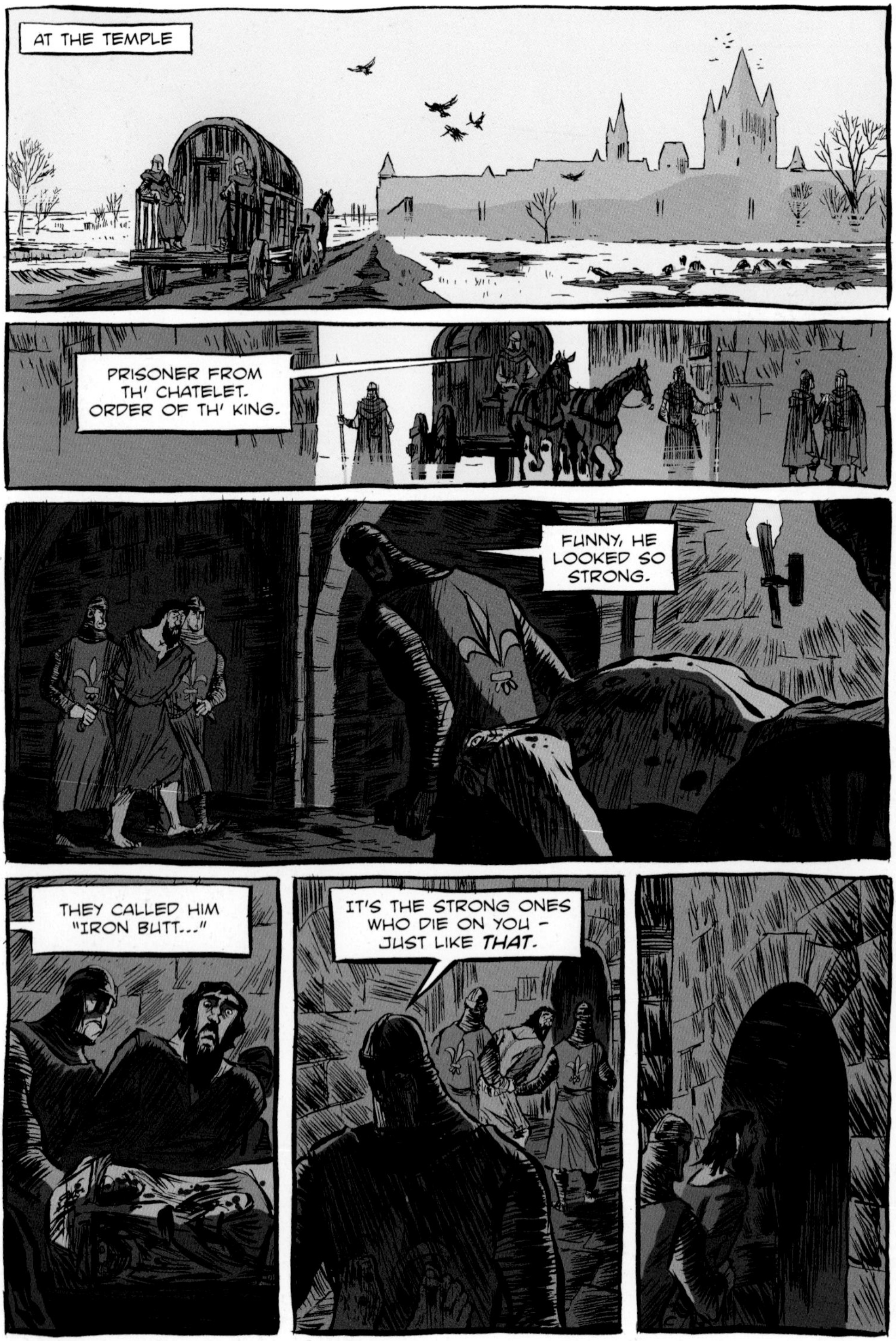
AT THE TEMPLE
PRISONER FROM TH' CHATELET. ORDER OF TH' KING.
FUNNY, HE LOOKED SO STRONG.
THEY CALLED HIM "IRON BUTT..."
IT'S THE STRONG ONES WHO DIE ON YOU - JUST LIKE *THAT*.

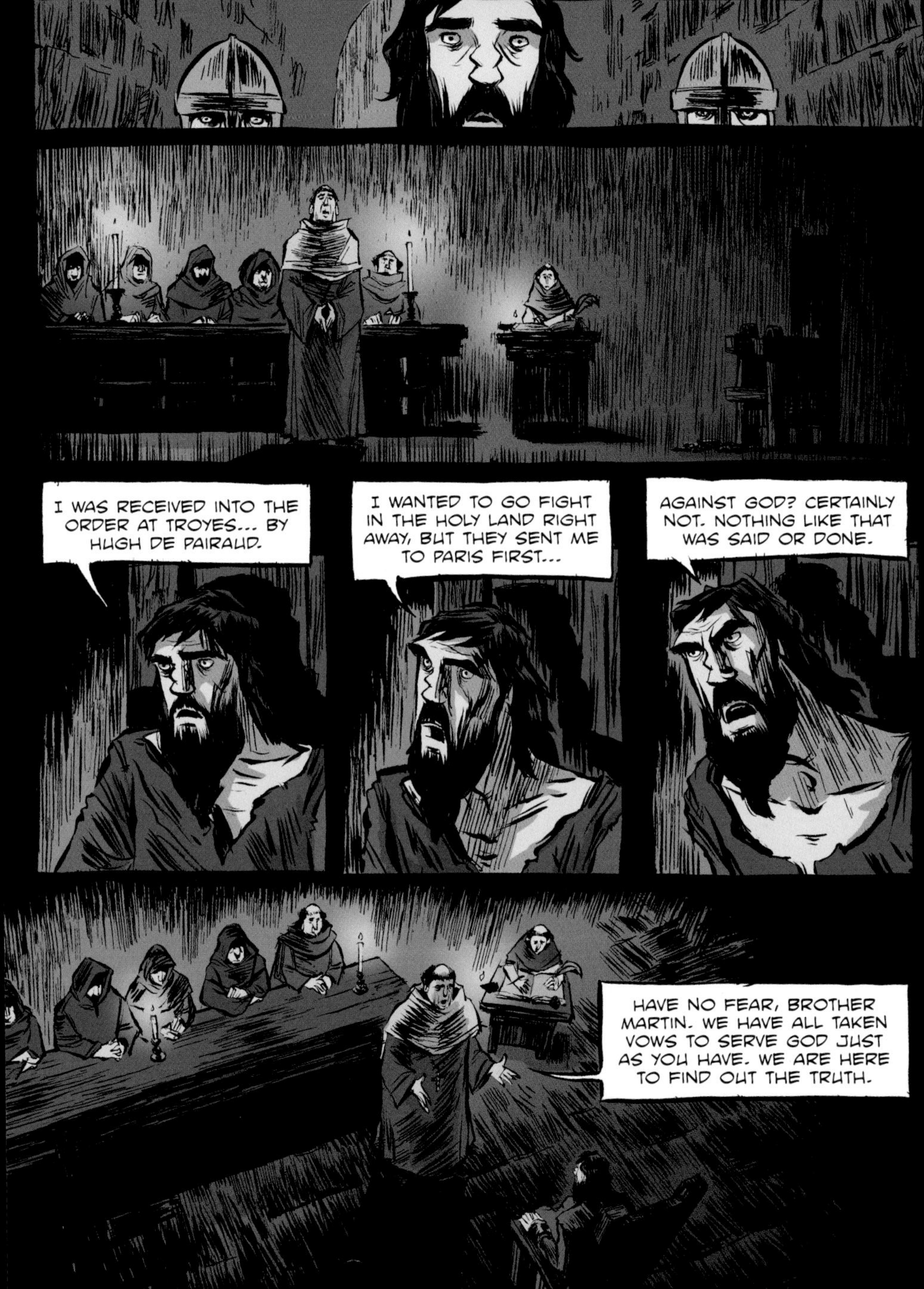
I WAS RECEIVED INTO THE ORDER AT TROYES... BY HUGH DE PAIRAUD.
I WANTED TO GO FIGHT IN THE HOLY LAND RIGHT AWAY, BUT THEY SENT ME TO PARIS FIRST...
AGAINST GOD? CERTAINLY NOT. NOTHING LIKE THAT WAS SAID OR DONE.
HAVE NO FEAR, BROTHER MARTIN. WE HAVE ALL TAKEN VOWS TO SERVE GOD JUST AS YOU HAVE. WE ARE HERE TO FIND OUT THE TRUTH.

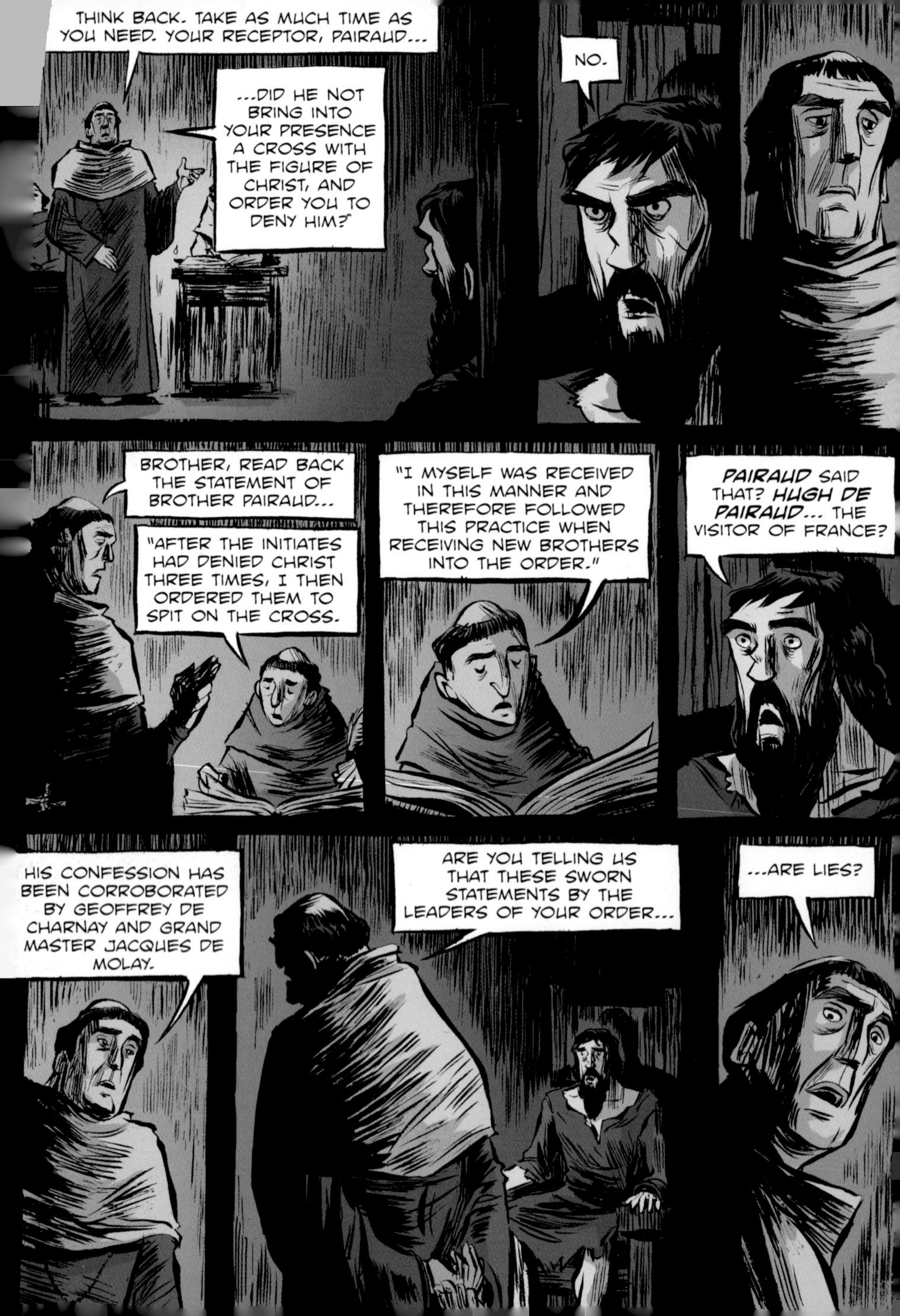
THINK BACK. TAKE AS MUCH TIME AS YOU NEED. YOUR RECEPTOR, PAIRAUD...
...DID HE NOT BRING INTO YOUR PRESENCE A CROSS WITH THE FIGURE OF CHRIST, AND ORDER YOU TO DENY HIM?"
NO.
BROTHER, READ BACK THE STATEMENT OF BROTHER PAIRAUD...
"AFTER THE INITIATES HAD DENIED CHRIST THREE TIMES, I THEN ORDERED THEM TO SPIT ON THE CROSS.
"I MYSELF WAS RECEIVED IN THIS MANNER AND THEREFORE FOLLOWED THIS PRACTICE WHEN RECEIVING NEW BROTHERS INTO THE ORDER."
PAIRAUD SAID THAT? ***HUGH DE PAIRAUD***... THE VISITOR OF FRANCE?
HIS CONFESSION HAS BEEN CORROBORATED BY GEOFFREY DE CHARNAY AND GRAND MASTER JACQUES DE MOLAY.
ARE YOU TELLING US THAT THESE SWORN STATEMENTS BY THE LEADERS OF YOUR ORDER...
...ARE LIES?

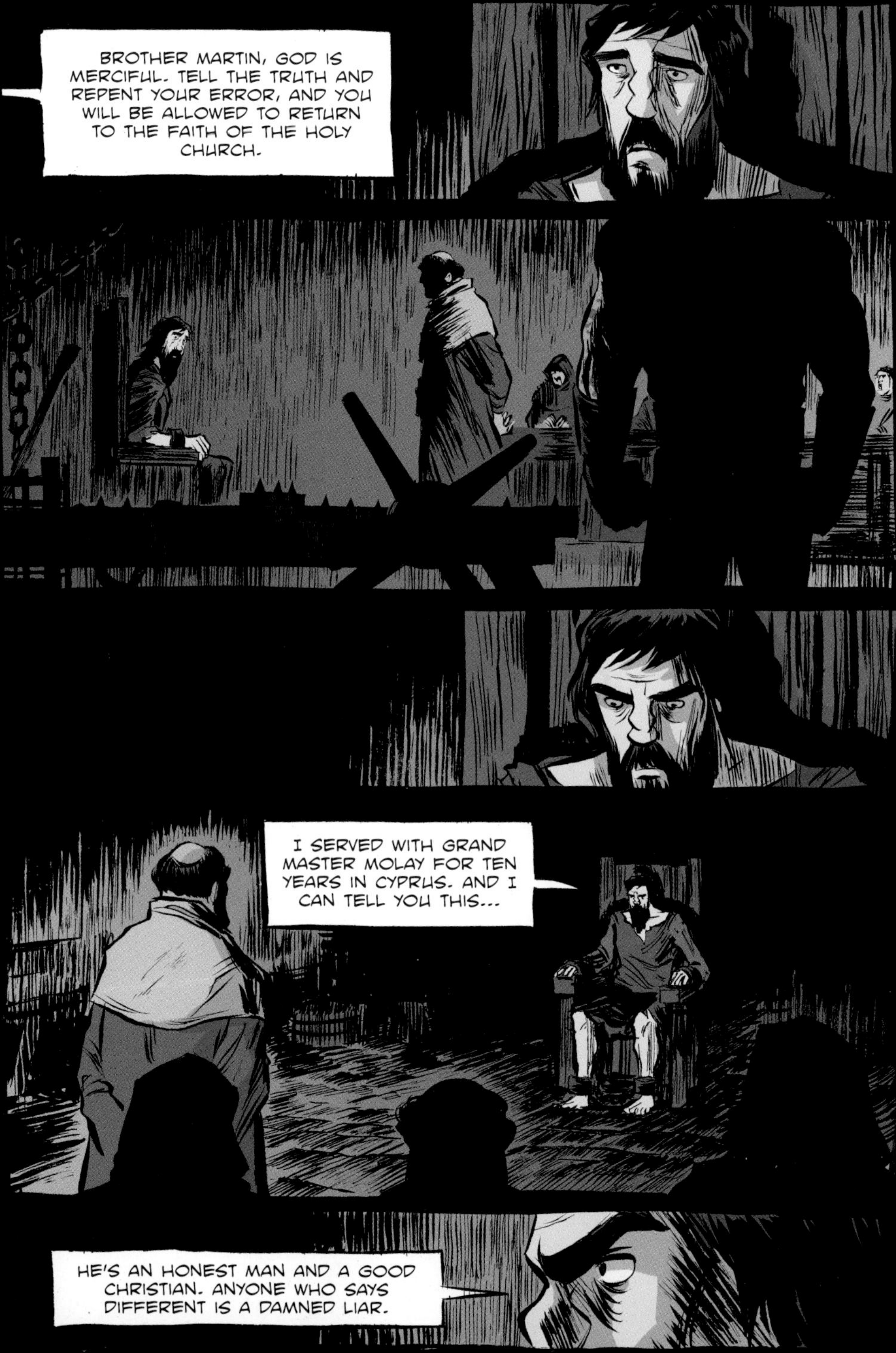
BROTHER MARTIN, GOD IS MERCIFUL. TELL THE TRUTH AND REPENT YOUR ERROR, AND YOU WILL BE ALLOWED TO RETURN TO THE FAITH OF THE HOLY CHURCH.
I SERVED WITH GRAND MASTER MOLAY FOR TEN YEARS IN CYPRUS. AND I CAN TELL YOU THIS...
HE'S AN HONEST MAN AND A GOOD CHRISTIAN. ANYONE WHO SAYS DIFFERENT IS A DAMNED LIAR.

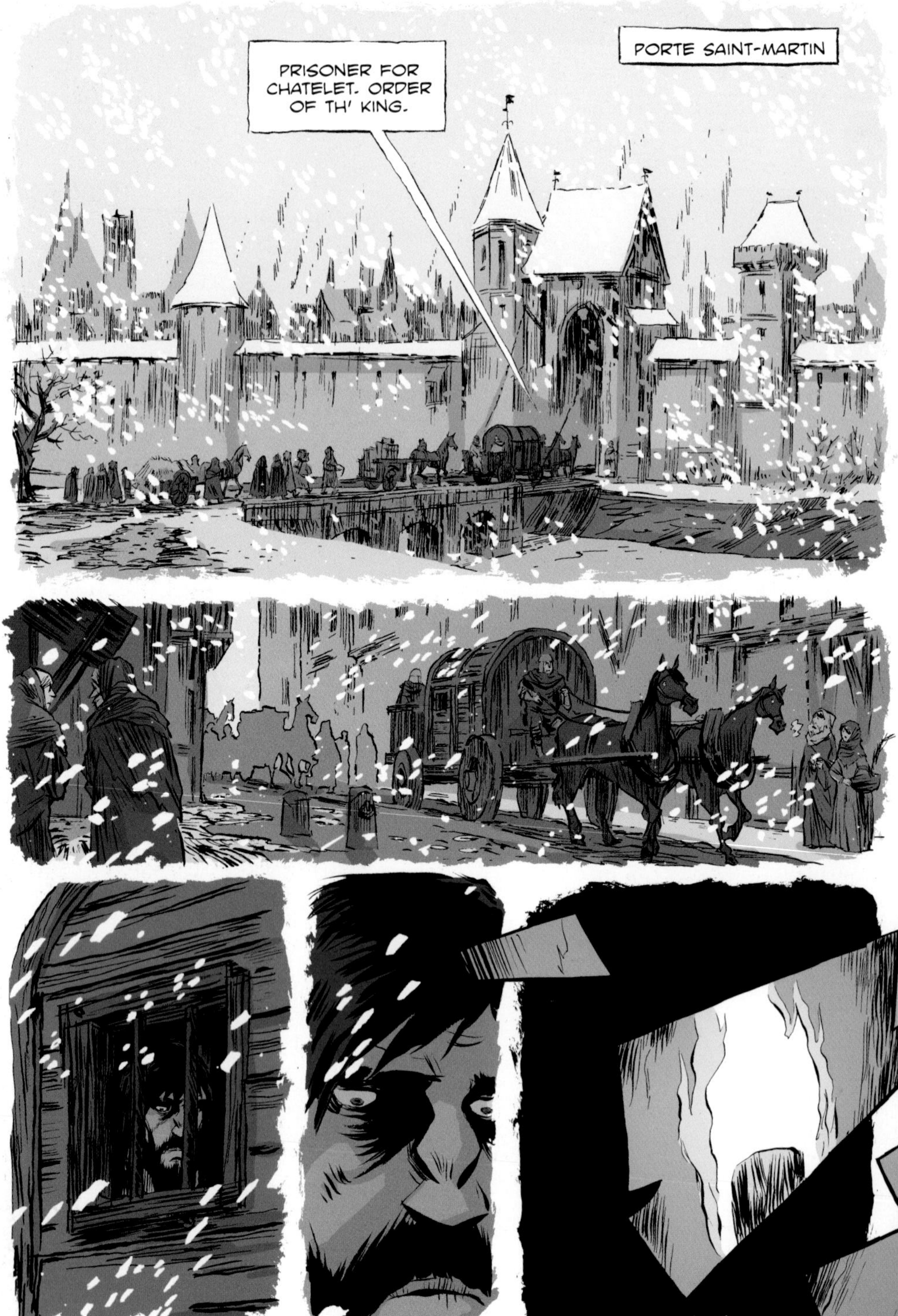
PORTE SAINT-MARTIN
PRISONER FOR CHATELET. ORDER OF TH' KING.

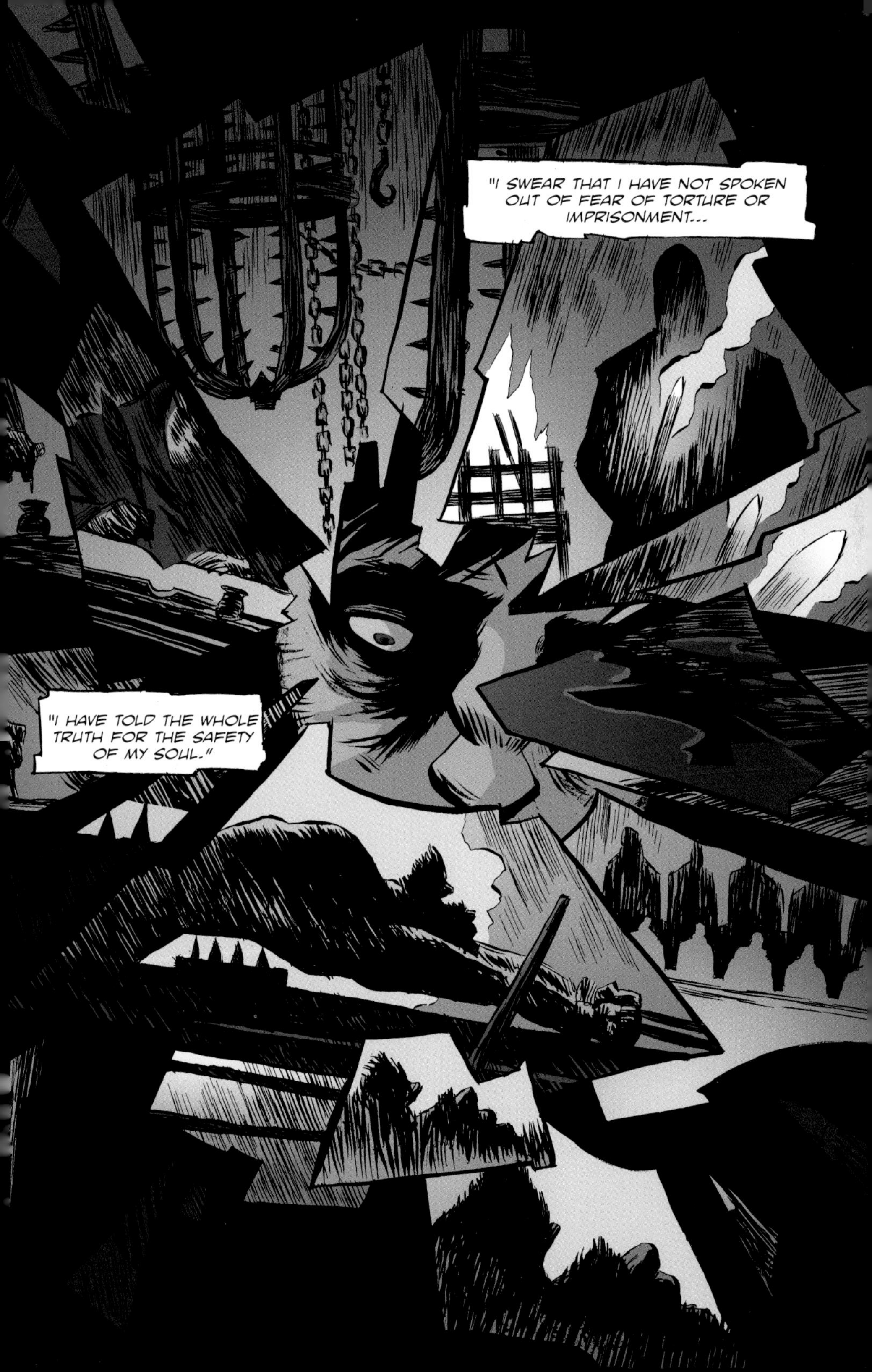
"I SWEAR THAT I HAVE NOT SPOKEN OUT OF FEAR OF TORTURE OR IMPRISONMENT...
"I HAVE TOLD THE WHOLE TRUTH FOR THE SAFETY OF MY SOUL."

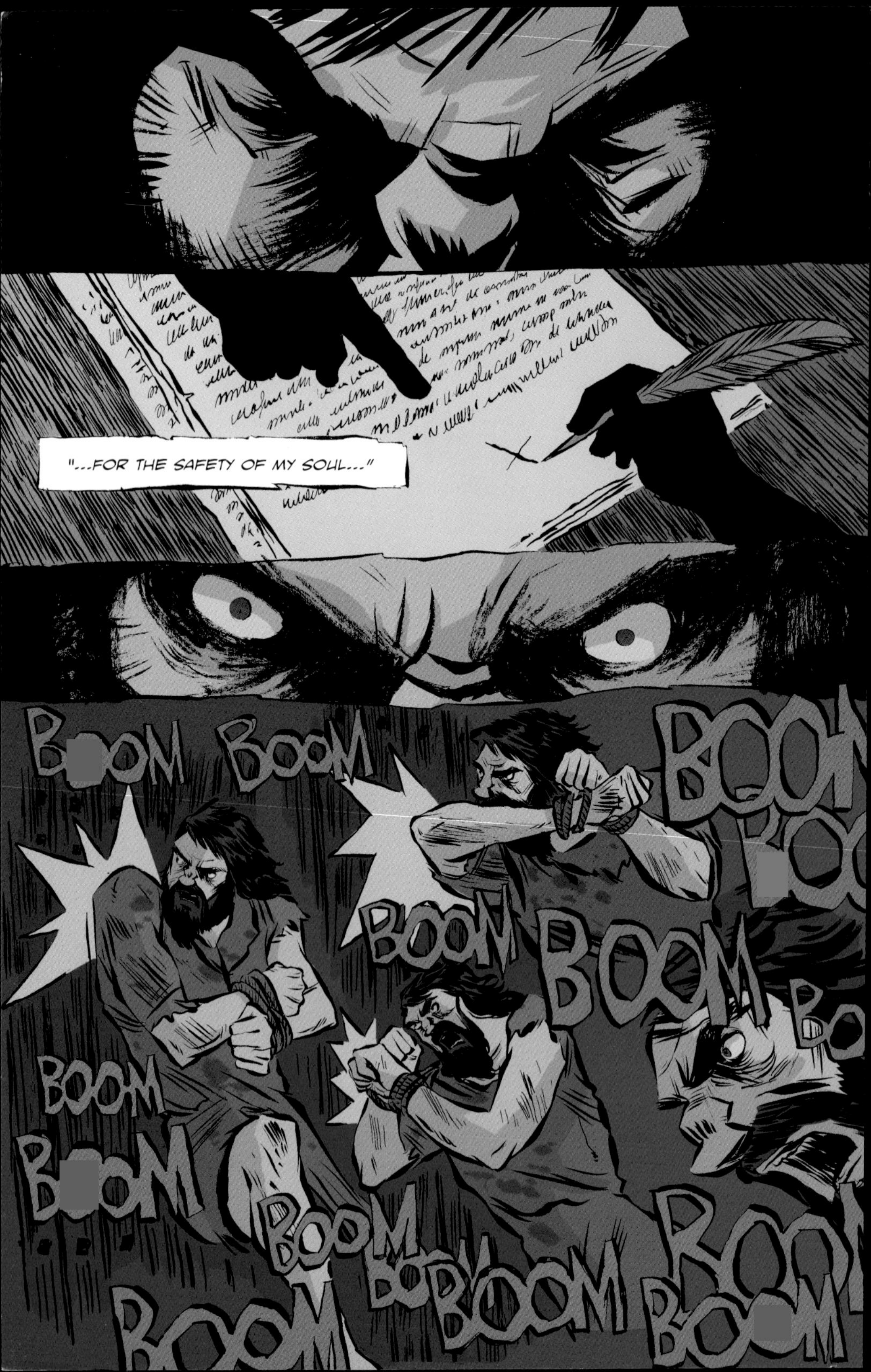
"...FOR THE SAFETY OF MY SOUL..."
BOOM
BOOM
BOOM
BOOM
BOOM
BOOM
BOOM

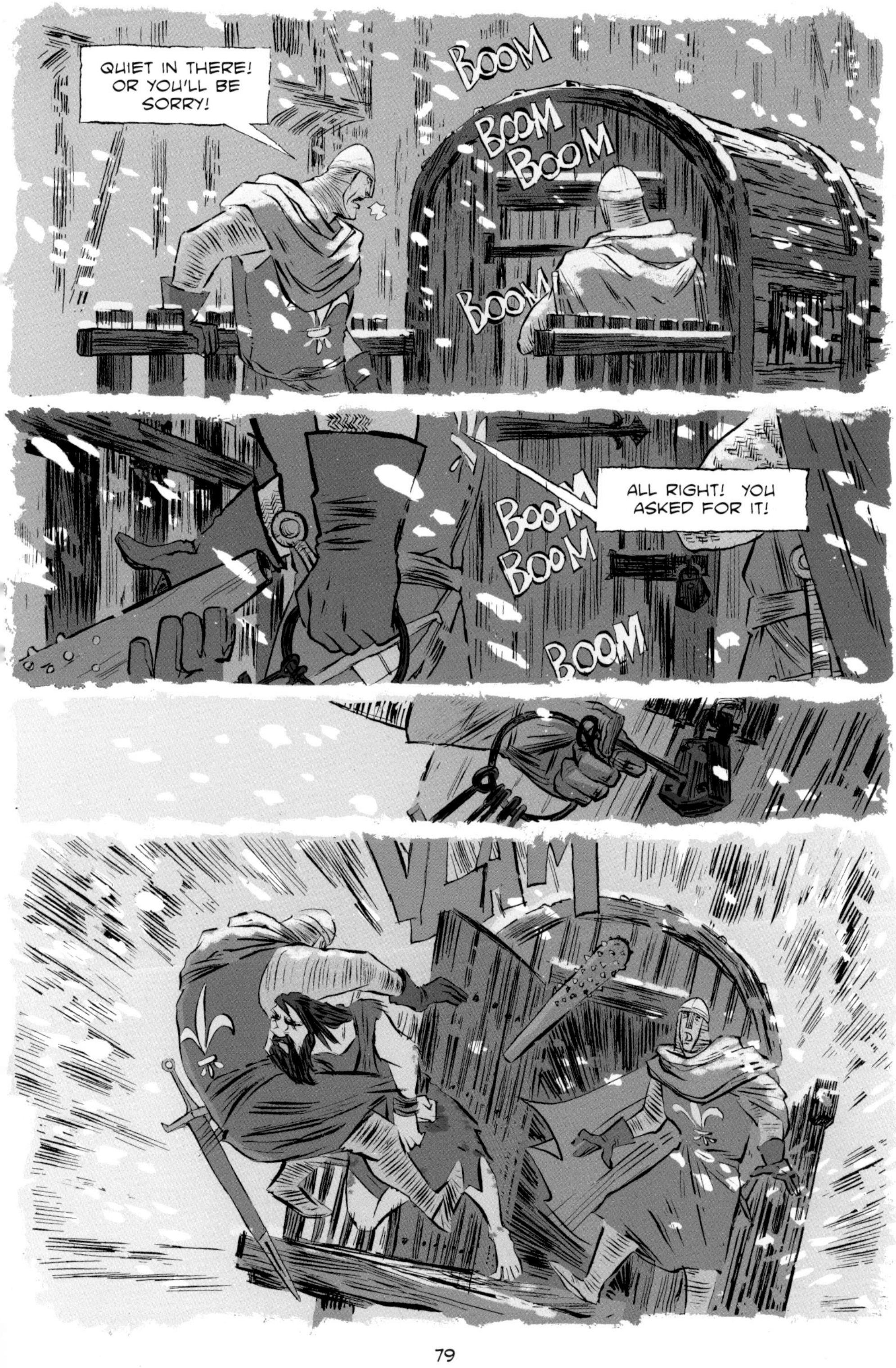
QUIET IN THERE! OR YOU'LL BE SORRY!
BOOM
BOOM
BOOM
BOOM
BOOM
ALL RIGHT! YOU ASKED FOR IT!
BOOM
BOOM
BOOM

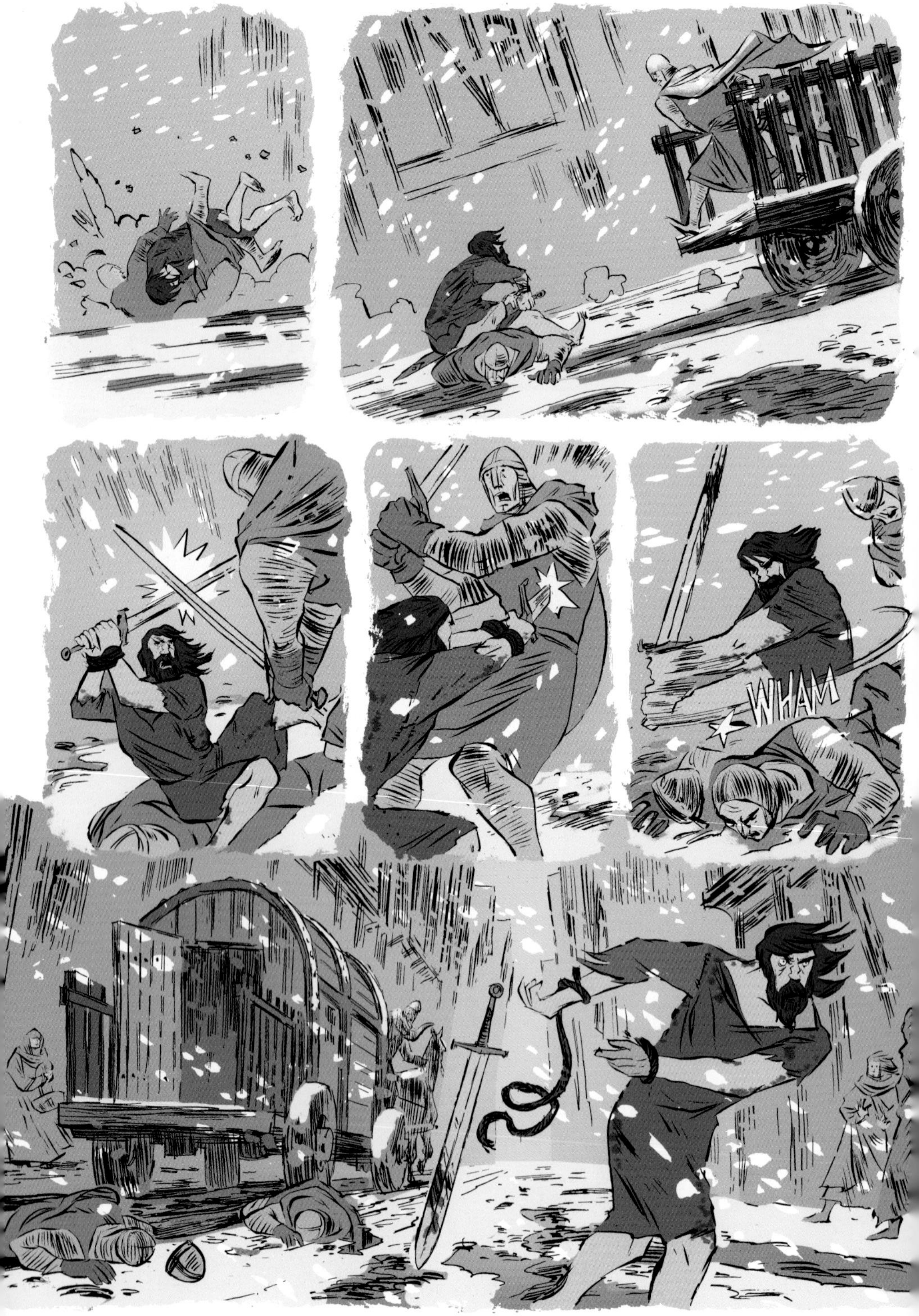
WHAM

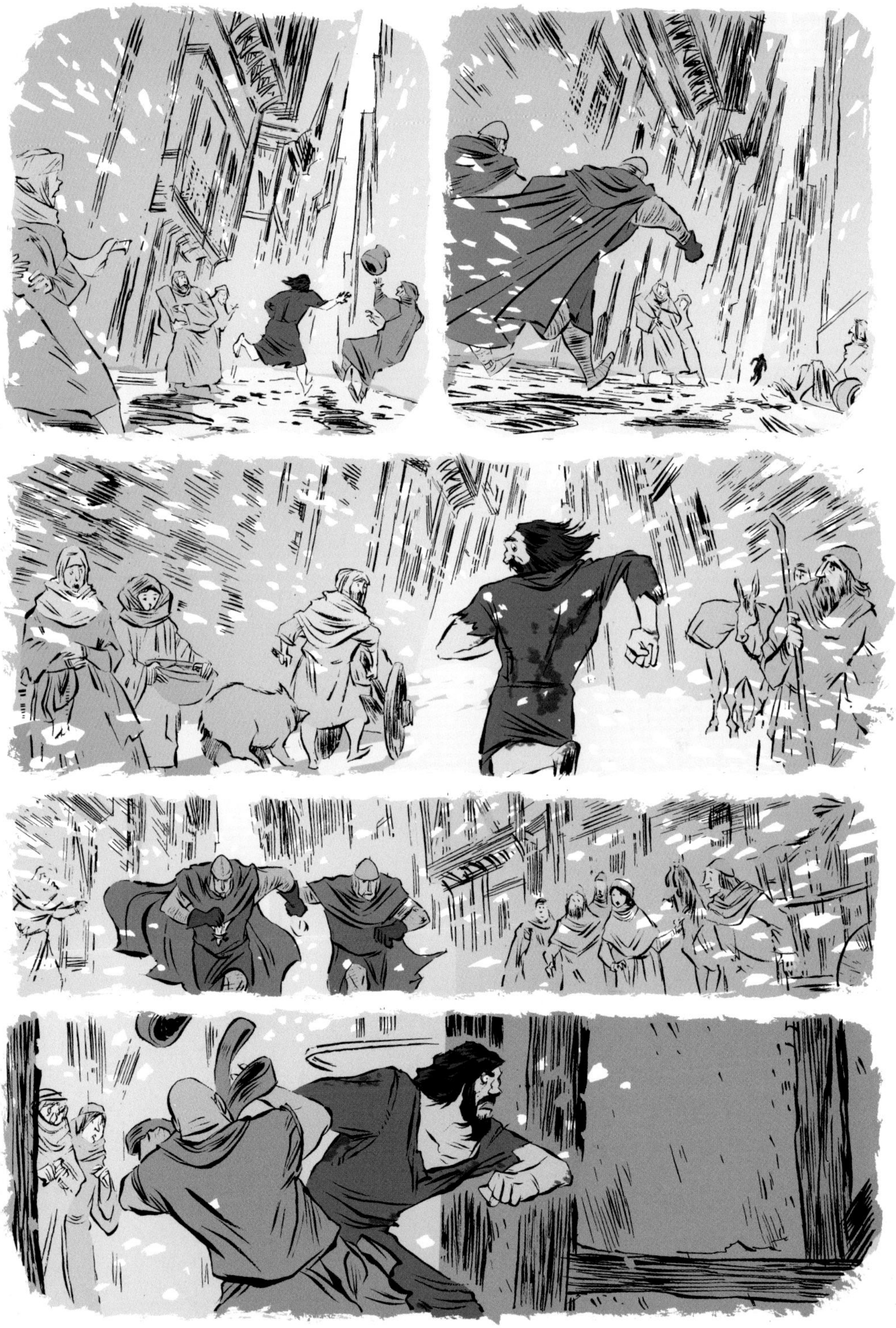

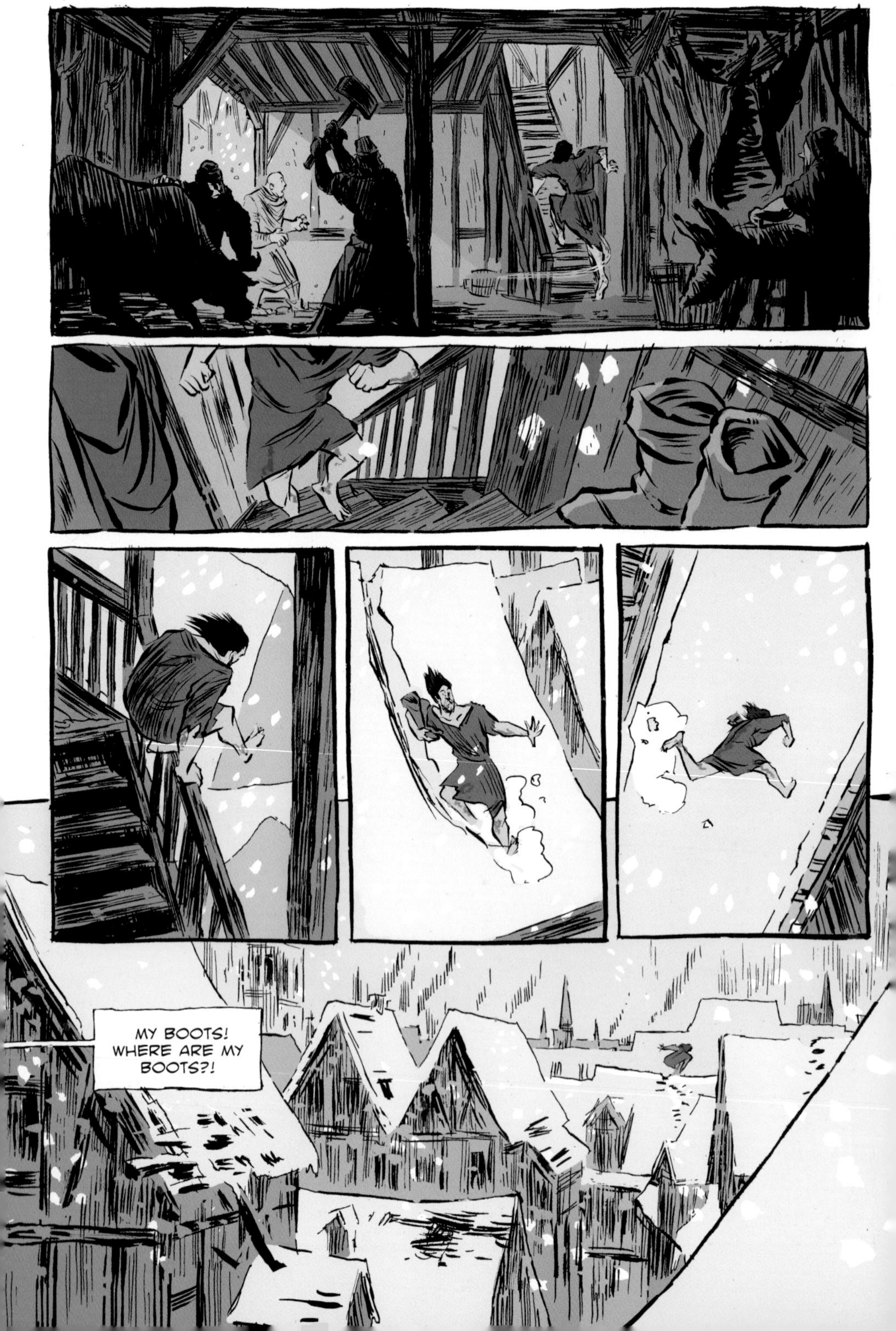
MY BOOTS! WHERE ARE MY BOOTS?!

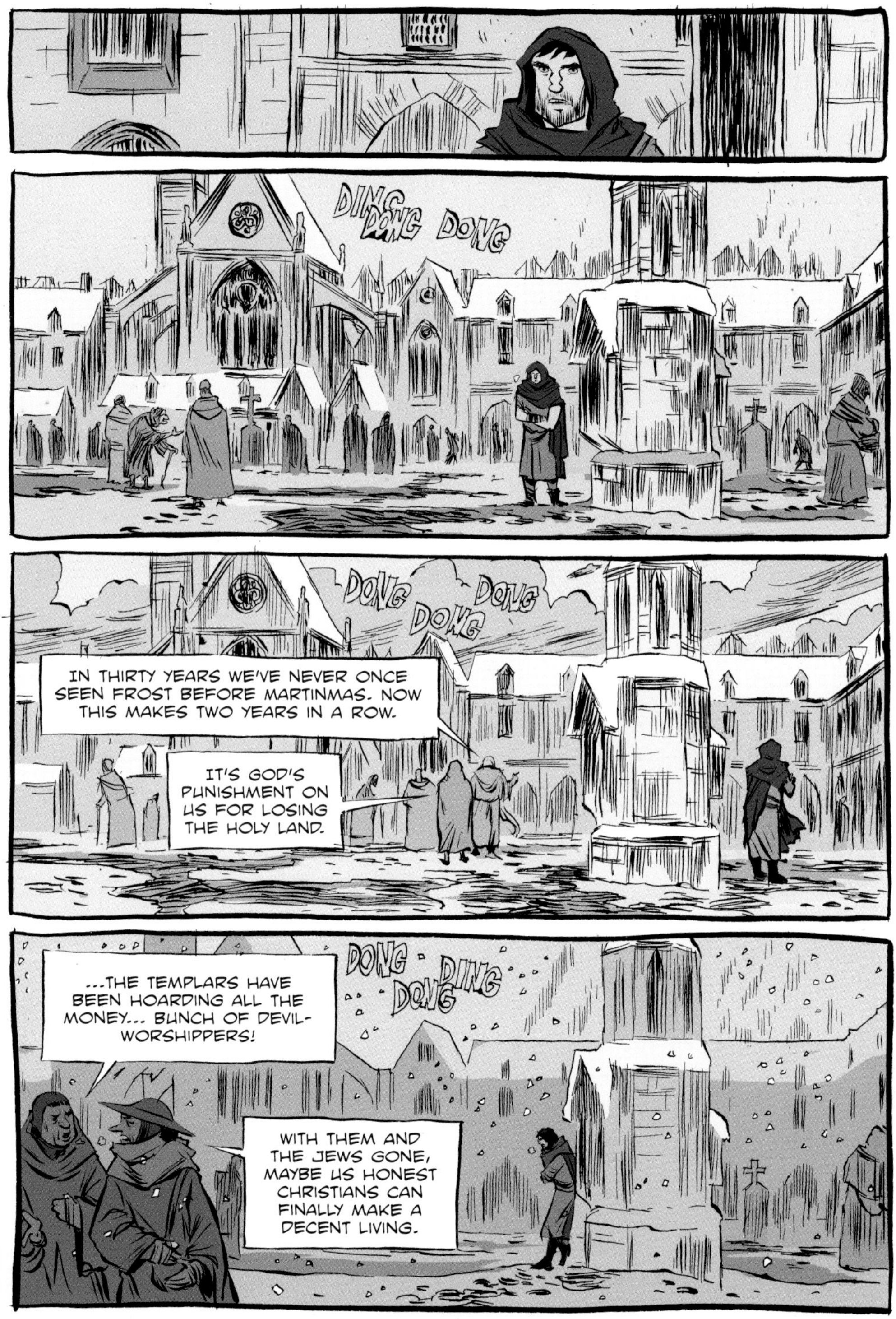
DING DONG DONG
DONG DONG DONG
IN THIRTY YEARS WE'VE NEVER ONCE SEEN FROST BEFORE MARTINMAS. NOW THIS MAKES TWO YEARS IN A ROW.
IT'S GOD'S PUNISHMENT ON US FOR LOSING THE HOLY LAND.
DONG DONG DING
...THE TEMPLARS HAVE BEEN HOARDING ALL THE MONEY... BUNCH OF DEVIL-WORSHIPPERS!
WITH THEM AND THE JEWS GONE, MAYBE US HONEST CHRISTIANS CAN FINALLY MAKE A DECENT LIVING.

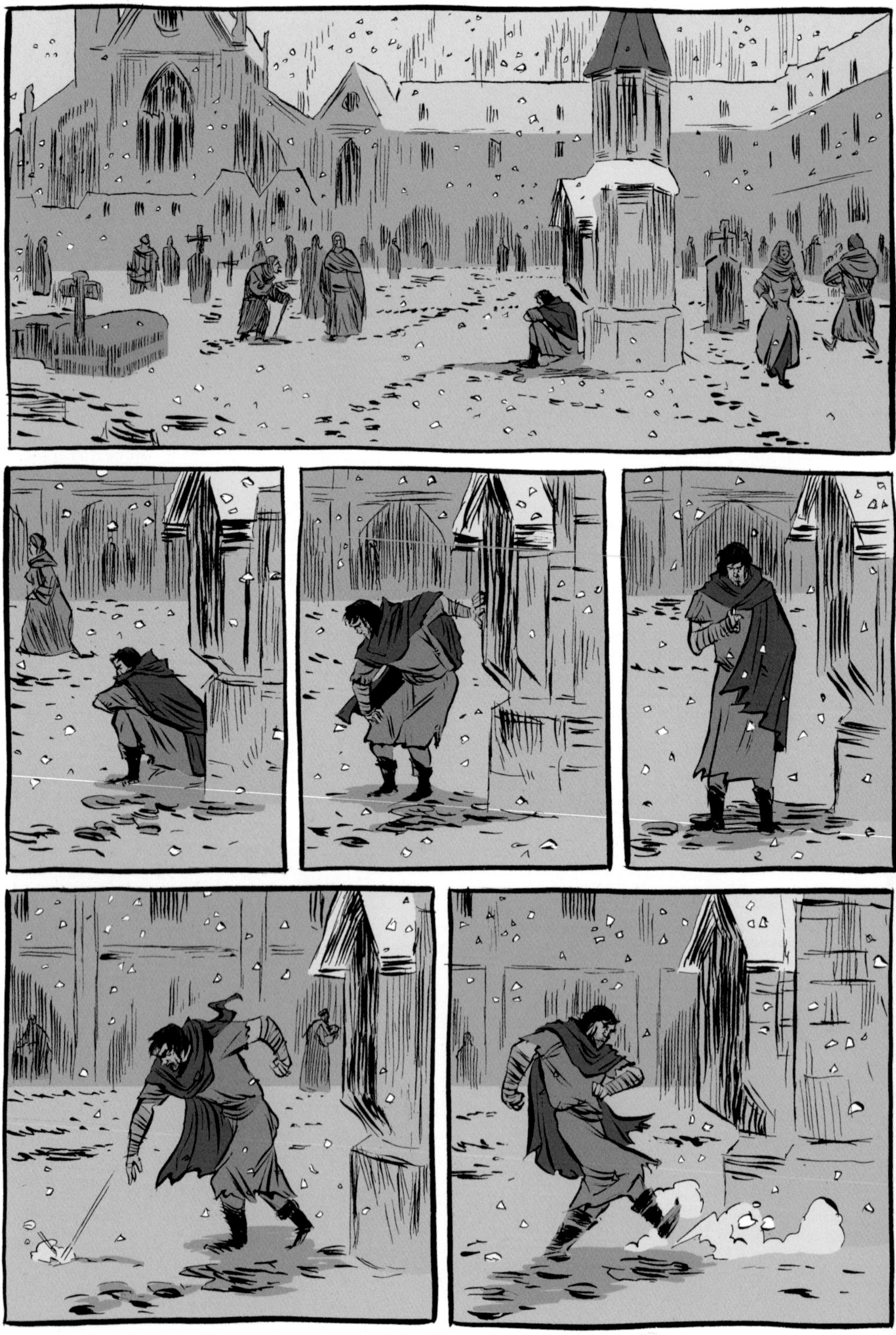

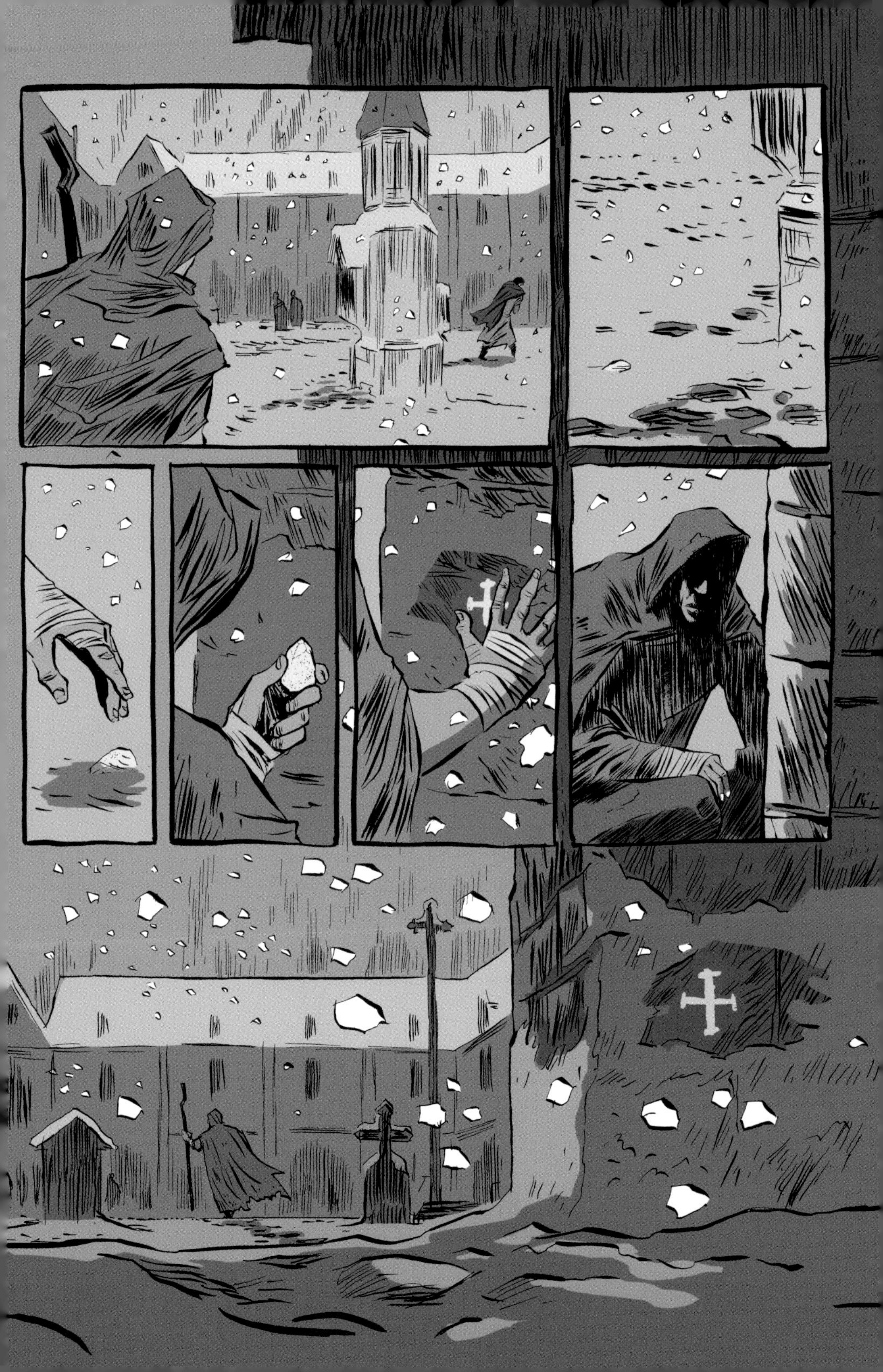

3. The Secret

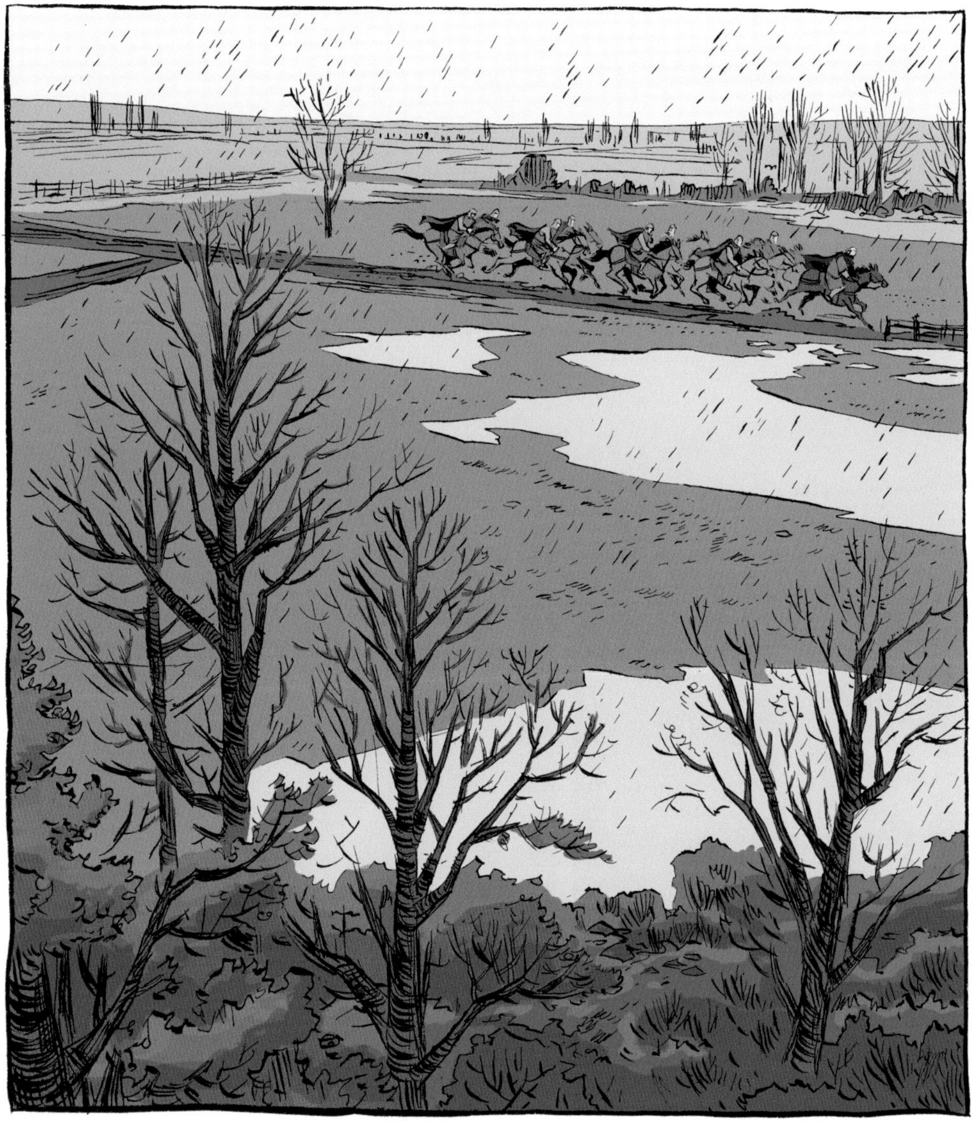

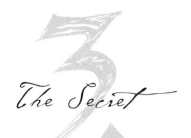

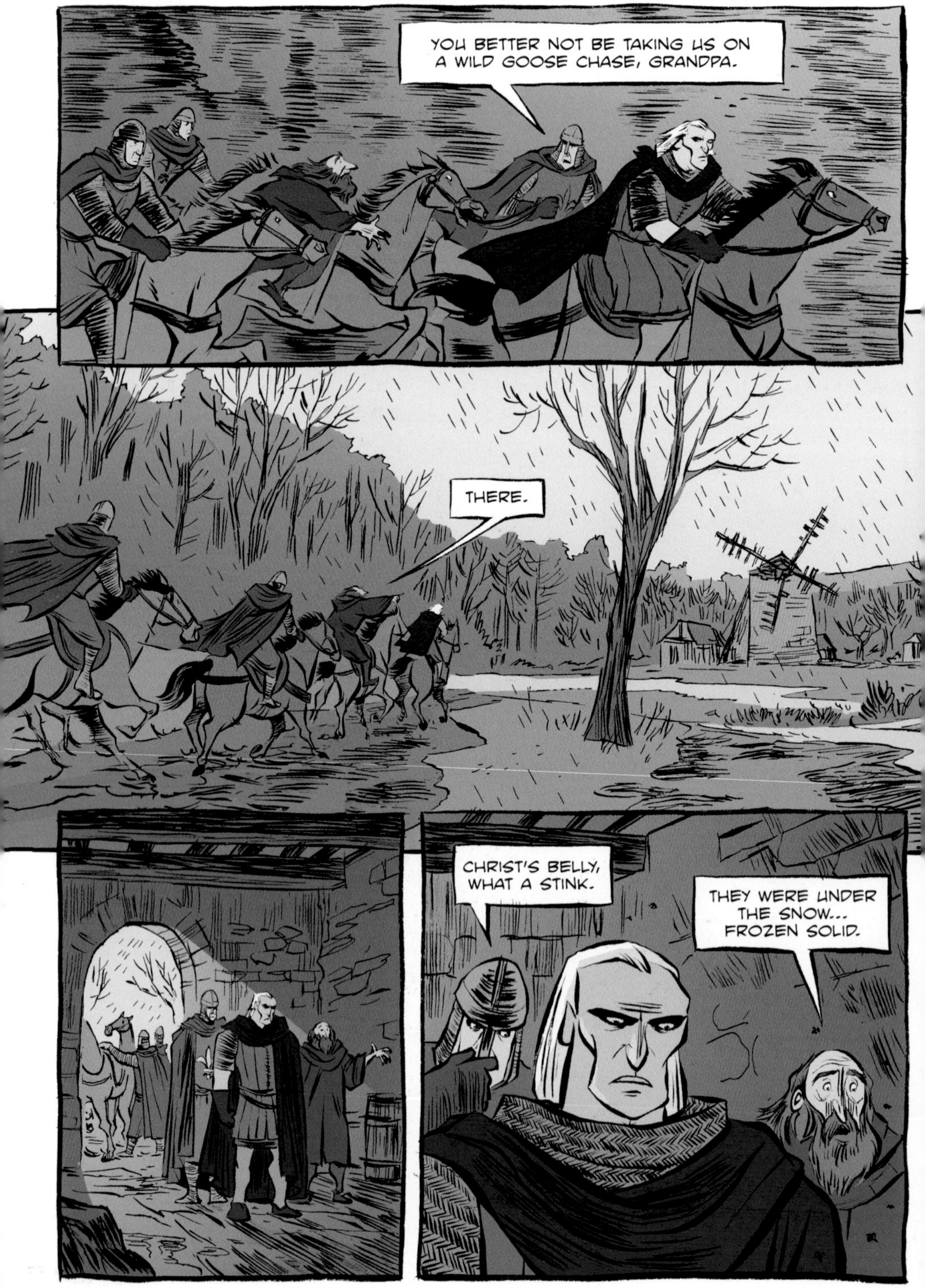
YOU BETTER NOT BE TAKING US ON A WILD GOOSE CHASE, GRANDPA.
THERE.
CHRIST'S BELLY, WHAT A STINK.
THEY WERE UNDER THE SNOW... FROZEN SOLID.

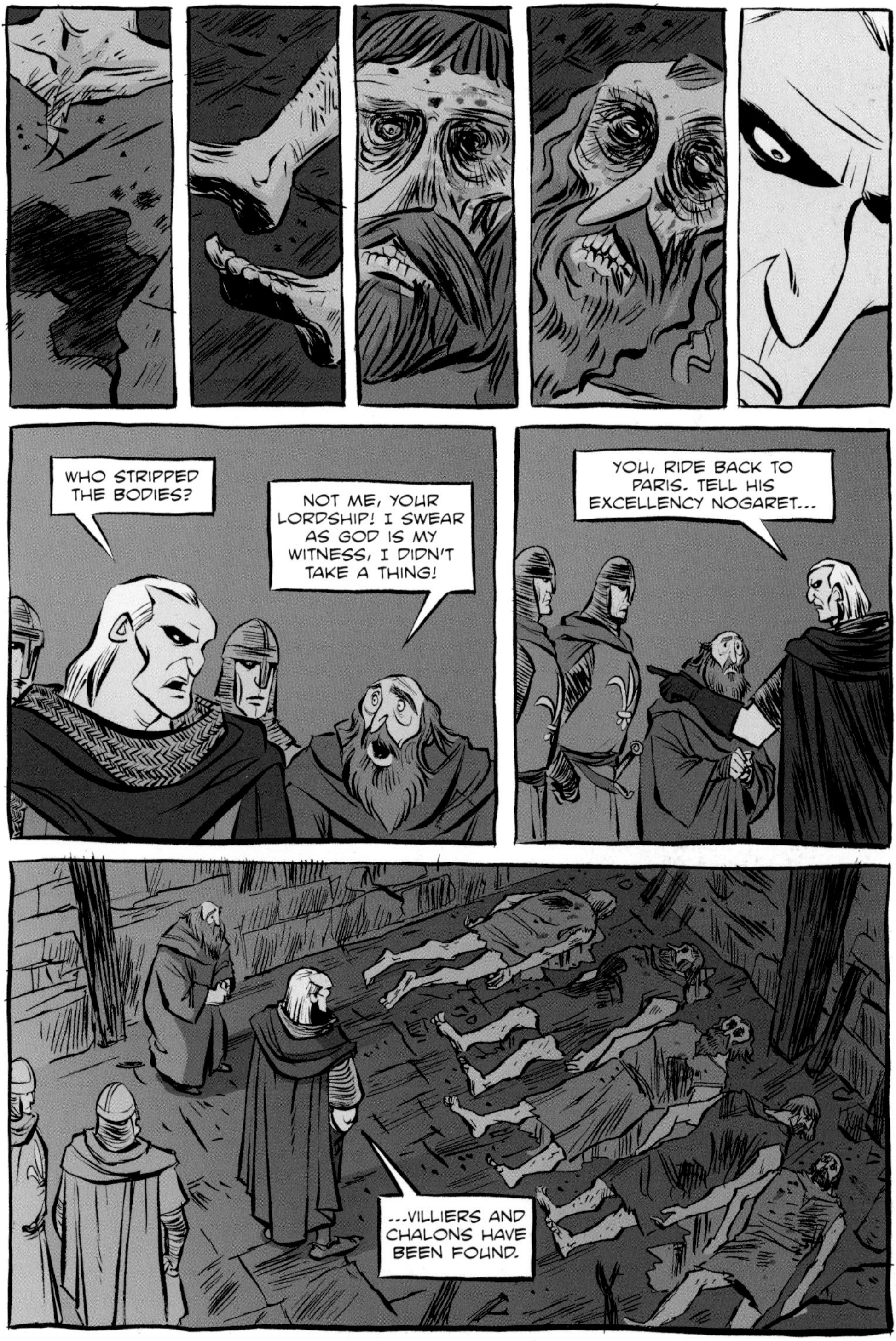
WHO STRIPPED THE BODIES?
NOT ME, YOUR LORDSHIP! I SWEAR AS GOD IS MY WITNESS, I DIDN'T TAKE A THING!
YOU, RIDE BACK TO PARIS. TELL HIS EXCELLENCY NOGARET...
...VILLIERS AND CHALONS HAVE BEEN FOUND.

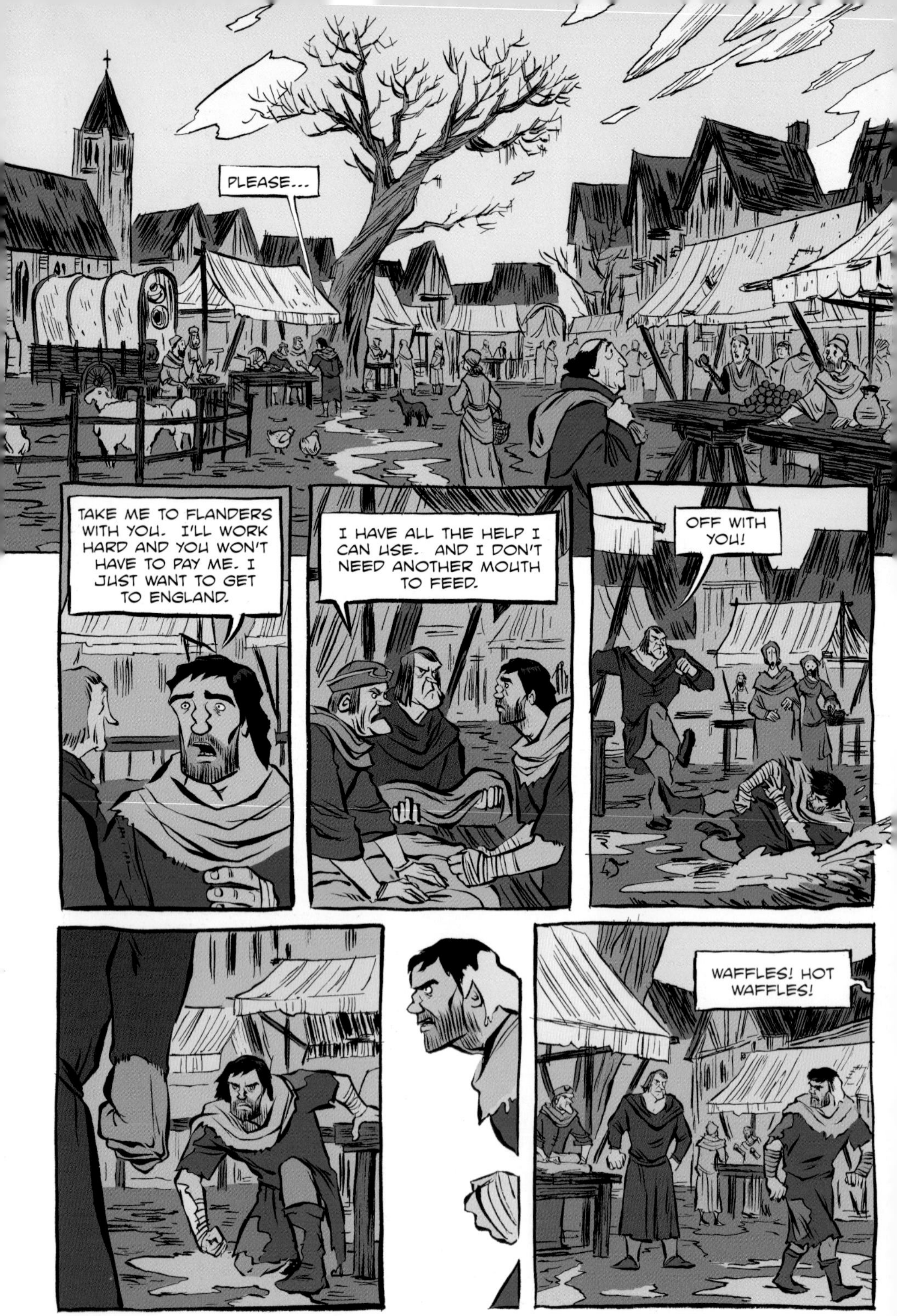
PLEASE...
TAKE ME TO FLANDERS WITH YOU. I'LL WORK HARD AND YOU WON'T HAVE TO PAY ME. I JUST WANT TO GET TO ENGLAND.
I HAVE ALL THE HELP I CAN USE. AND I DON'T NEED ANOTHER MOUTH TO FEED.
OFF WITH YOU!
WAFFLES! HOT WAFFLES!

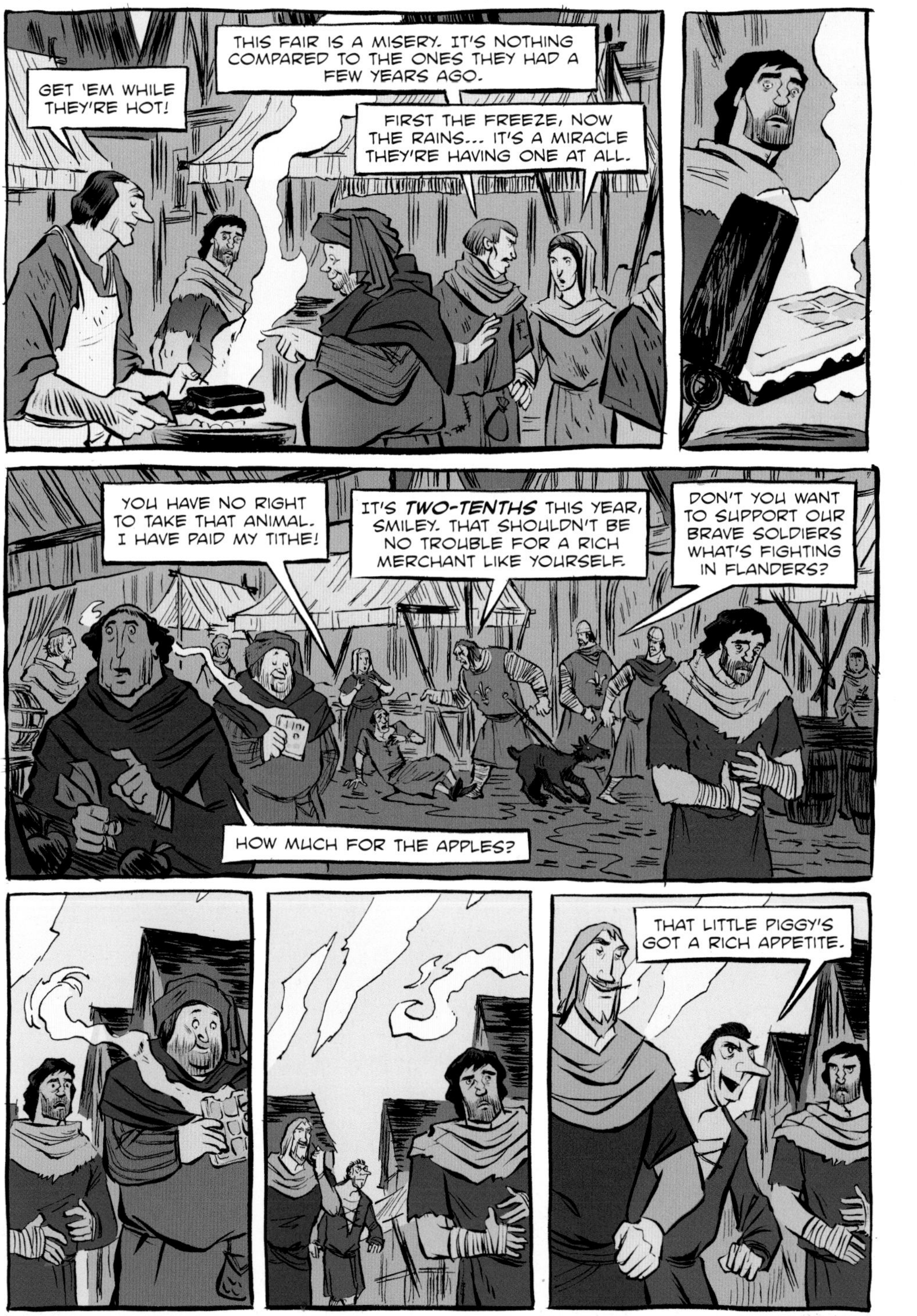
GET 'EM WHILE THEY'RE HOT!
THIS FAIR IS A MISERY. IT'S NOTHING COMPARED TO THE ONES THEY HAD A FEW YEARS AGO.
FIRST THE FREEZE, NOW THE RAINS... IT'S A MIRACLE THEY'RE HAVING ONE AT ALL.
YOU HAVE NO RIGHT TO TAKE THAT ANIMAL. I HAVE PAID MY TITHE!
IT'S *TWO-TENTHS* THIS YEAR, SMILEY. THAT SHOULDN'T BE NO TROUBLE FOR A RICH MERCHANT LIKE YOURSELF.
DON'T YOU WANT TO SUPPORT OUR BRAVE SOLDIERS WHAT'S FIGHTING IN FLANDERS?
HOW MUCH FOR THE APPLES?
THAT LITTLE PIGGY'S GOT A RICH APPETITE.

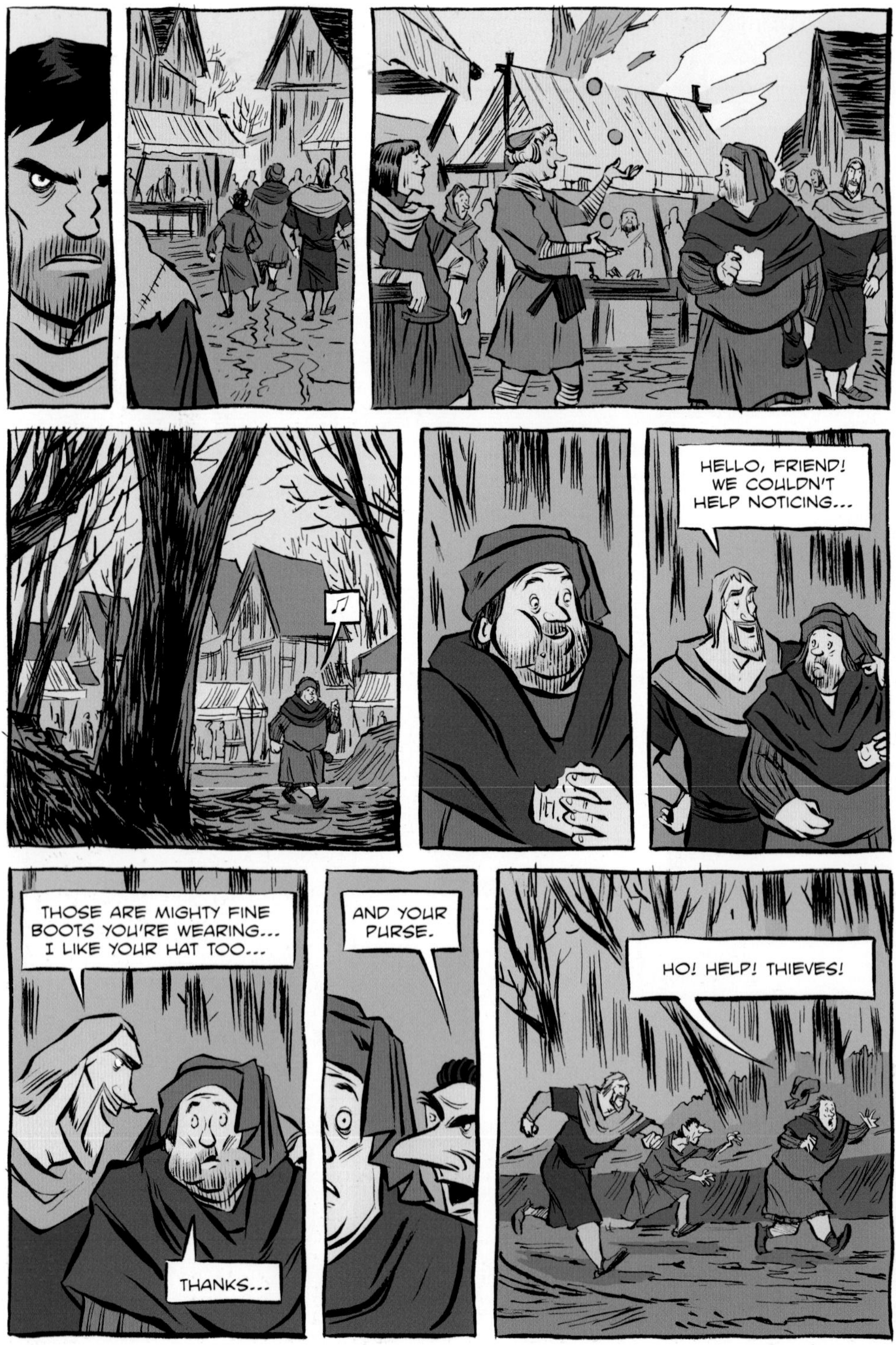
HELLO, FRIEND! WE COULDN'T HELP NOTICING...
THOSE ARE MIGHTY FINE BOOTS YOU'RE WEARING... I LIKE YOUR HAT TOO...
THANKS...
AND YOUR PURSE.
HO! HELP! THIEVES!

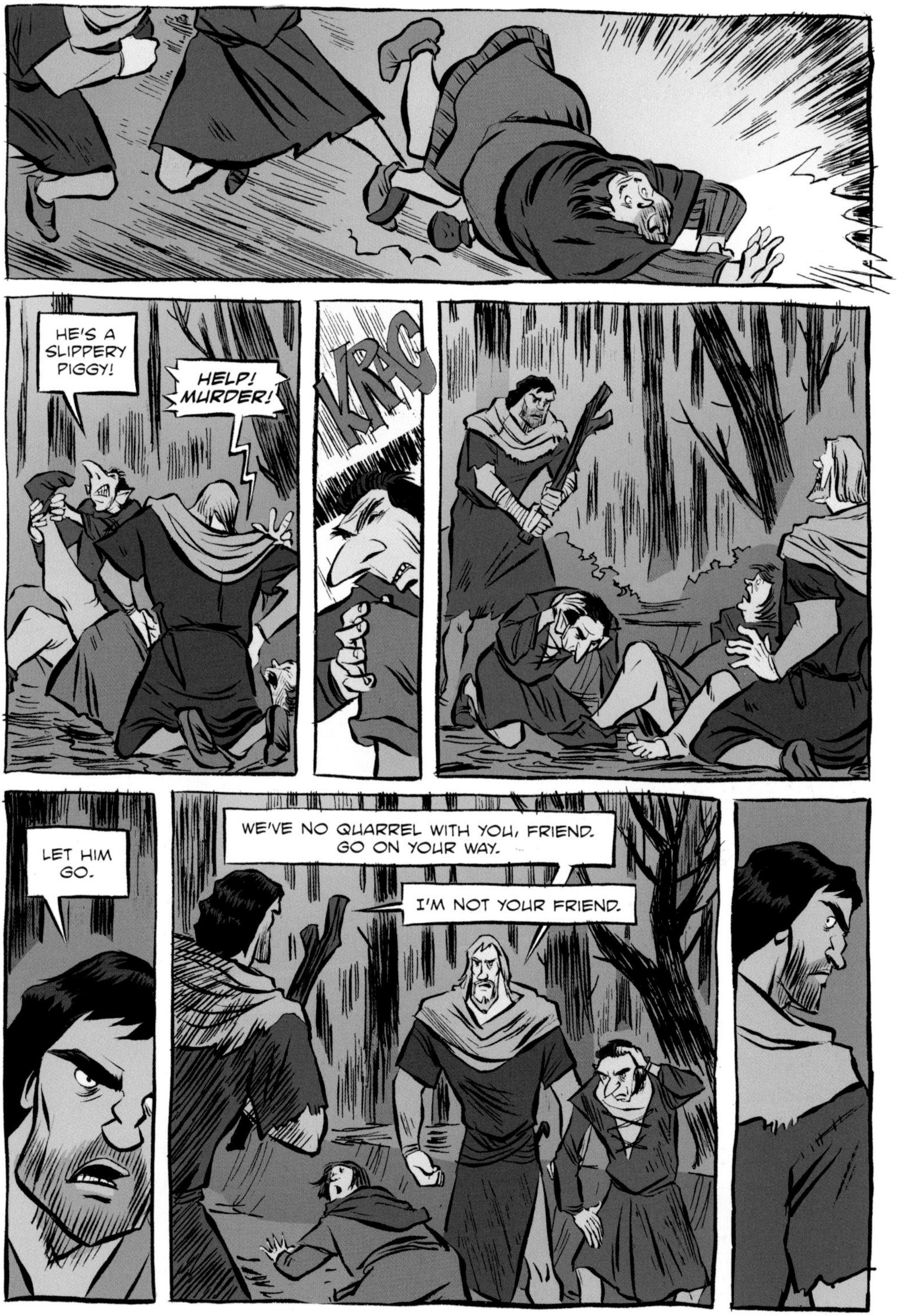
HE'S A SLIPPERY PIGGY!
HELP! MURDER!
KRAC
LET HIM GO.
WE'VE NO QUARREL WITH YOU, FRIEND. GO ON YOUR WAY.
I'M NOT YOUR FRIEND.

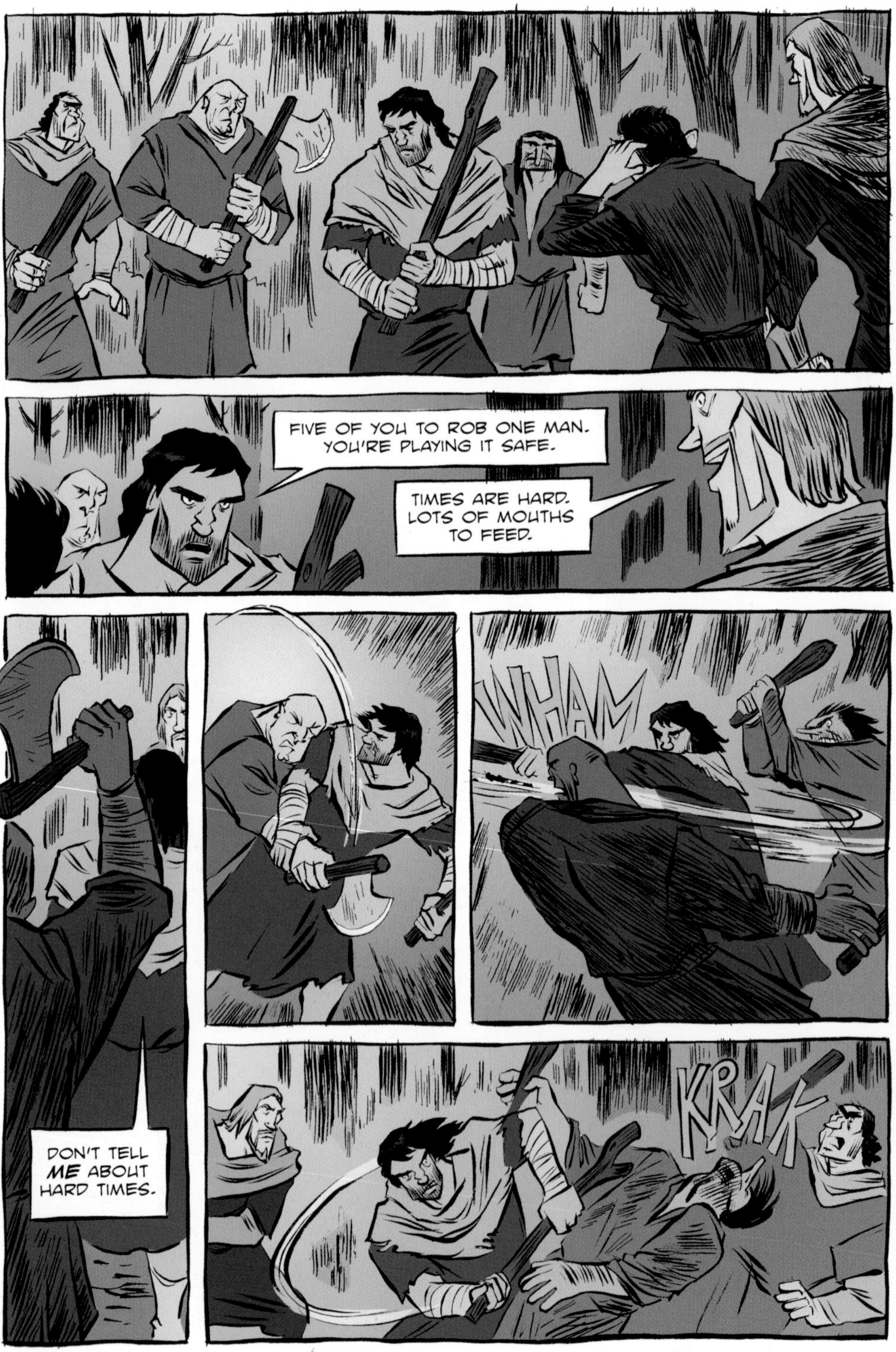
FIVE OF YOU TO ROB ONE MAN. YOU'RE PLAYING IT SAFE.
TIMES ARE HARD. LOTS OF MOUTHS TO FEED.
WHAM
DON'T TELL ***ME*** ABOUT HARD TIMES.
KRAK

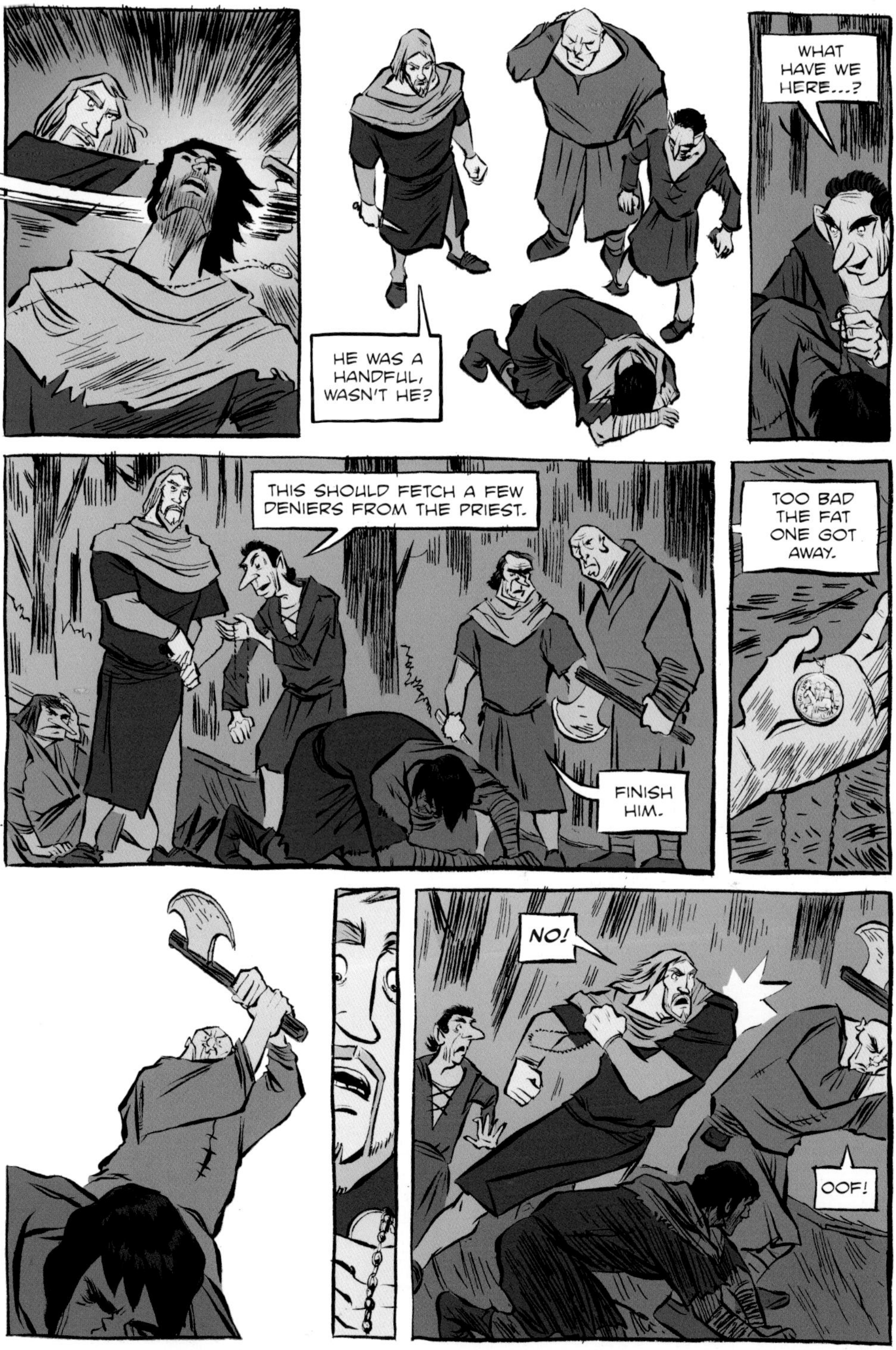
HE WAS A HANDFUL, WASN'T HE?
WHAT HAVE WE HERE...?
THIS SHOULD FETCH A FEW DENIERS FROM THE PRIEST.
FINISH HIM.
TOO BAD THE FAT ONE GOT AWAY.
NO!
OOF!

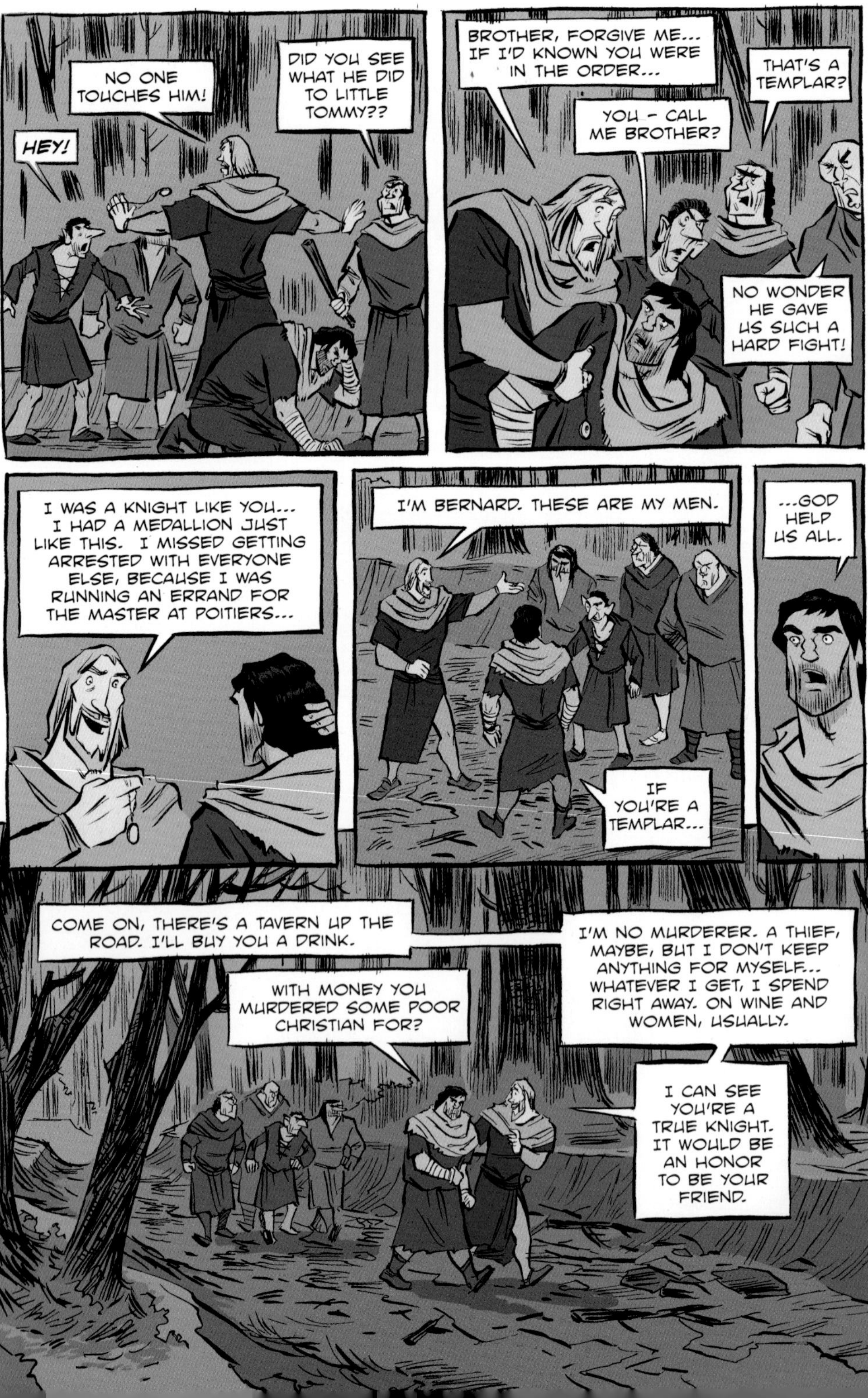
HEY!
NO ONE TOUCHES HIM!
DID YOU SEE WHAT HE DID TO LITTLE TOMMY??
BROTHER, FORGIVE ME... IF I'D KNOWN YOU WERE IN THE ORDER...
YOU - CALL ME BROTHER?
THAT'S A TEMPLAR?
NO WONDER HE GAVE US SUCH A HARD FIGHT!
I WAS A KNIGHT LIKE YOU... I HAD A MEDALLION JUST LIKE THIS. I MISSED GETTING ARRESTED WITH EVERYONE ELSE, BECAUSE I WAS RUNNING AN ERRAND FOR THE MASTER AT POITIERS...
I'M BERNARD. THESE ARE MY MEN.
IF YOU'RE A TEMPLAR...
...GOD HELP US ALL.
COME ON, THERE'S A TAVERN UP THE ROAD. I'LL BUY YOU A DRINK.
WITH MONEY YOU MURDERED SOME POOR CHRISTIAN FOR?
I'M NO MURDERER. A THIEF, MAYBE, BUT I DON'T KEEP ANYTHING FOR MYSELF... WHATEVER I GET, I SPEND RIGHT AWAY. ON WINE AND WOMEN, USUALLY.
I CAN SEE YOU'RE A TRUE KNIGHT. IT WOULD BE AN HONOR TO BE YOUR FRIEND.

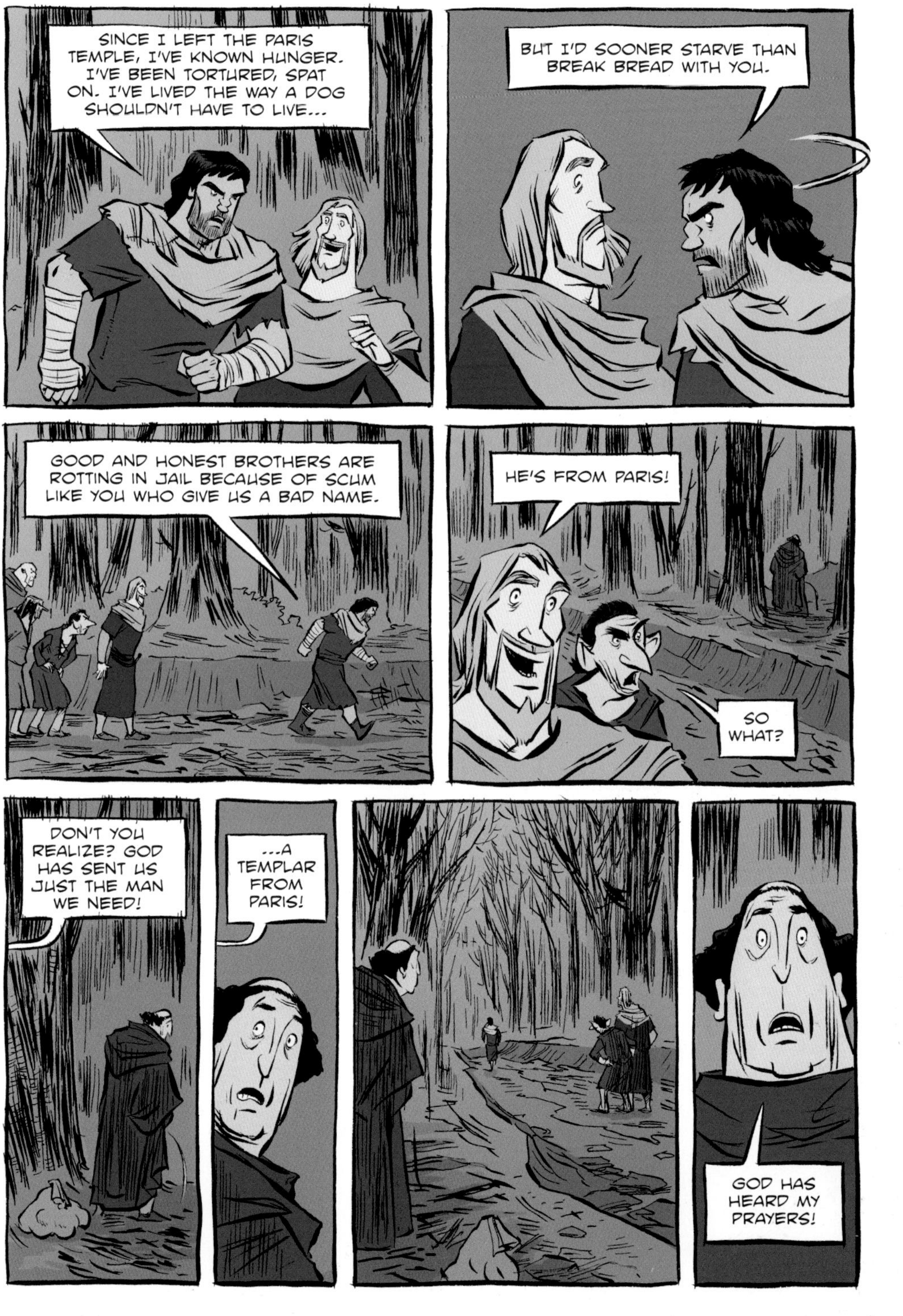
SINCE I LEFT THE PARIS TEMPLE, I'VE KNOWN HUNGER. I'VE BEEN TORTURED, SPAT ON. I'VE LIVED THE WAY A DOG SHOULDN'T HAVE TO LIVE...
BUT I'D SOONER STARVE THAN BREAK BREAD WITH YOU.
GOOD AND HONEST BROTHERS ARE ROTTING IN JAIL BECAUSE OF SCUM LIKE YOU WHO GIVE US A BAD NAME.
HE'S FROM PARIS!
SO WHAT?
DON'T YOU REALIZE? GOD HAS SENT US JUST THE MAN WE NEED!
...A TEMPLAR FROM PARIS!
GOD HAS HEARD MY PRAYERS!

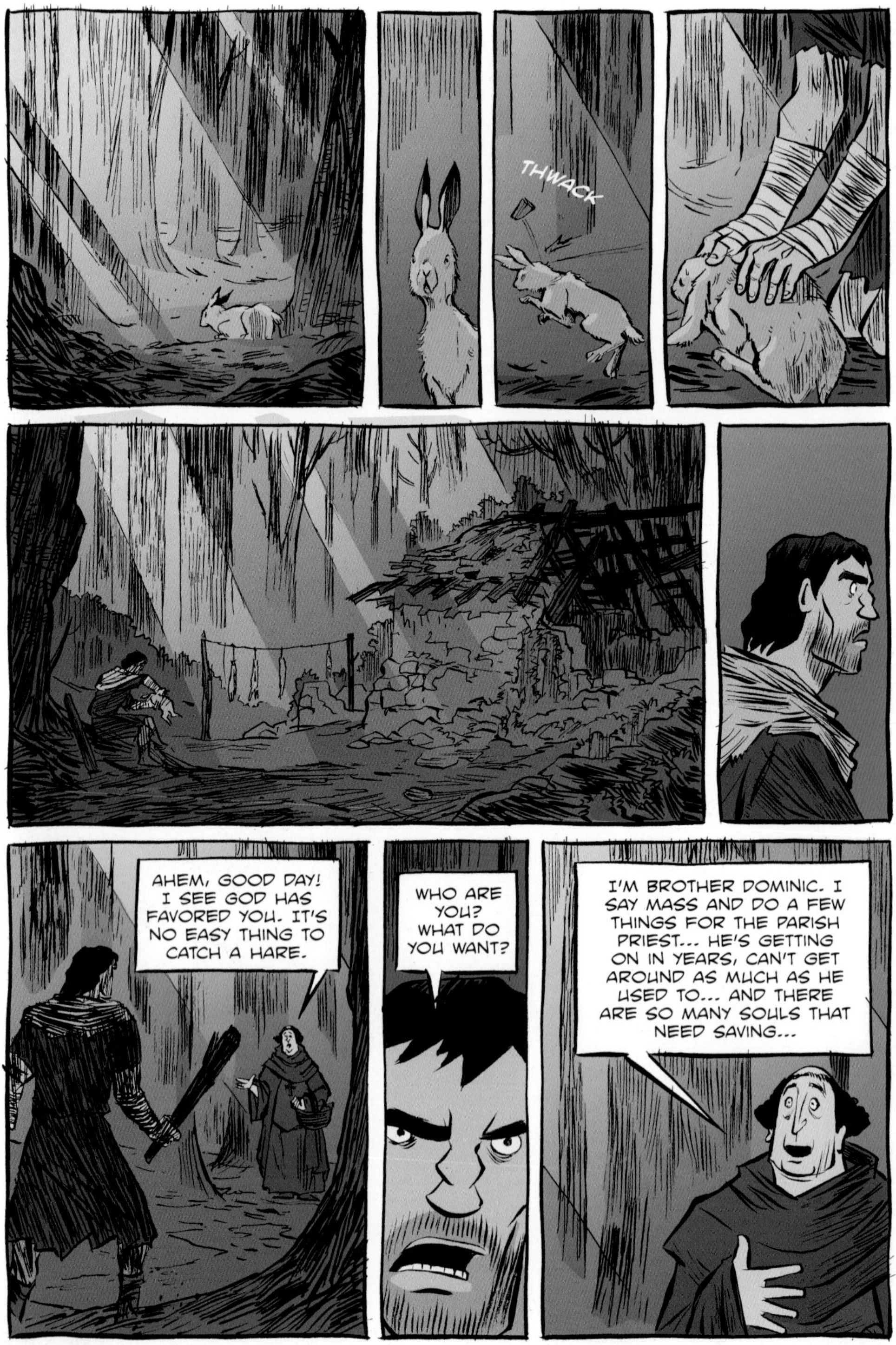
THWACK
AHEM, GOOD DAY! I SEE GOD HAS FAVORED YOU. IT'S NO EASY THING TO CATCH A HARE.
WHO ARE YOU? WHAT DO YOU WANT?
I'M BROTHER DOMINIC. I SAY MASS AND DO A FEW THINGS FOR THE PARISH PRIEST... HE'S GETTING ON IN YEARS, CAN'T GET AROUND AS MUCH AS HE USED TO... AND THERE ARE SO MANY SOULS THAT NEED SAVING...

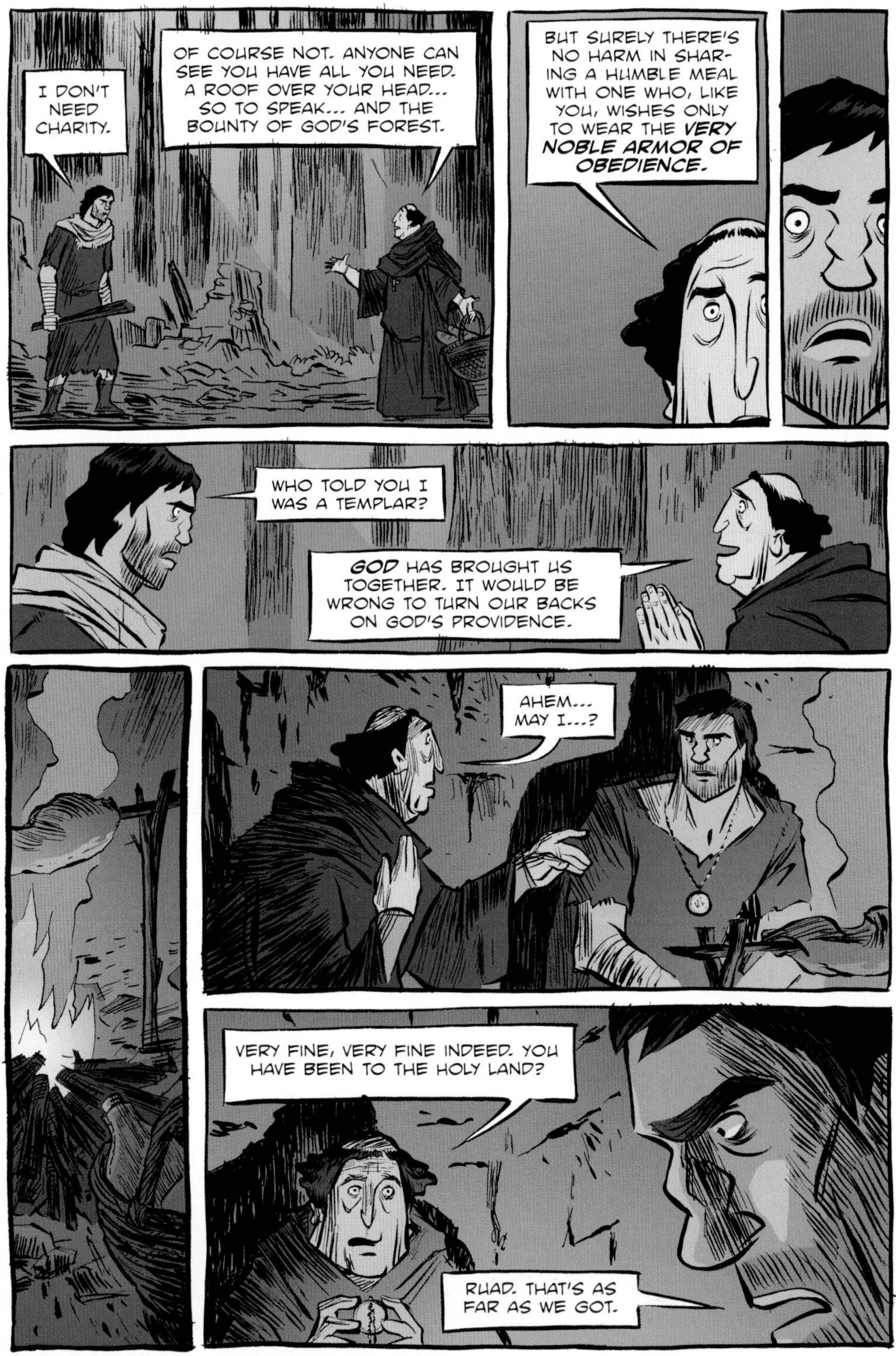
I DON'T NEED CHARITY.
OF COURSE NOT. ANYONE CAN SEE YOU HAVE ALL YOU NEED. A ROOF OVER YOUR HEAD... SO TO SPEAK... AND THE BOUNTY OF GOD'S FOREST.
BUT SURELY THERE'S NO HARM IN SHARING A HUMBLE MEAL WITH ONE WHO, LIKE YOU, WISHES ONLY TO WEAR THE VERY NOBLE ARMOR OF OBEDIENCE.
WHO TOLD YOU I WAS A TEMPLAR?
GOD HAS BROUGHT US TOGETHER. IT WOULD BE WRONG TO TURN OUR BACKS ON GOD'S PROVIDENCE.
AHEM... MAY I...?
VERY FINE, VERY FINE INDEED. YOU HAVE BEEN TO THE HOLY LAND?
RUAD. THAT'S AS FAR AS WE GOT.

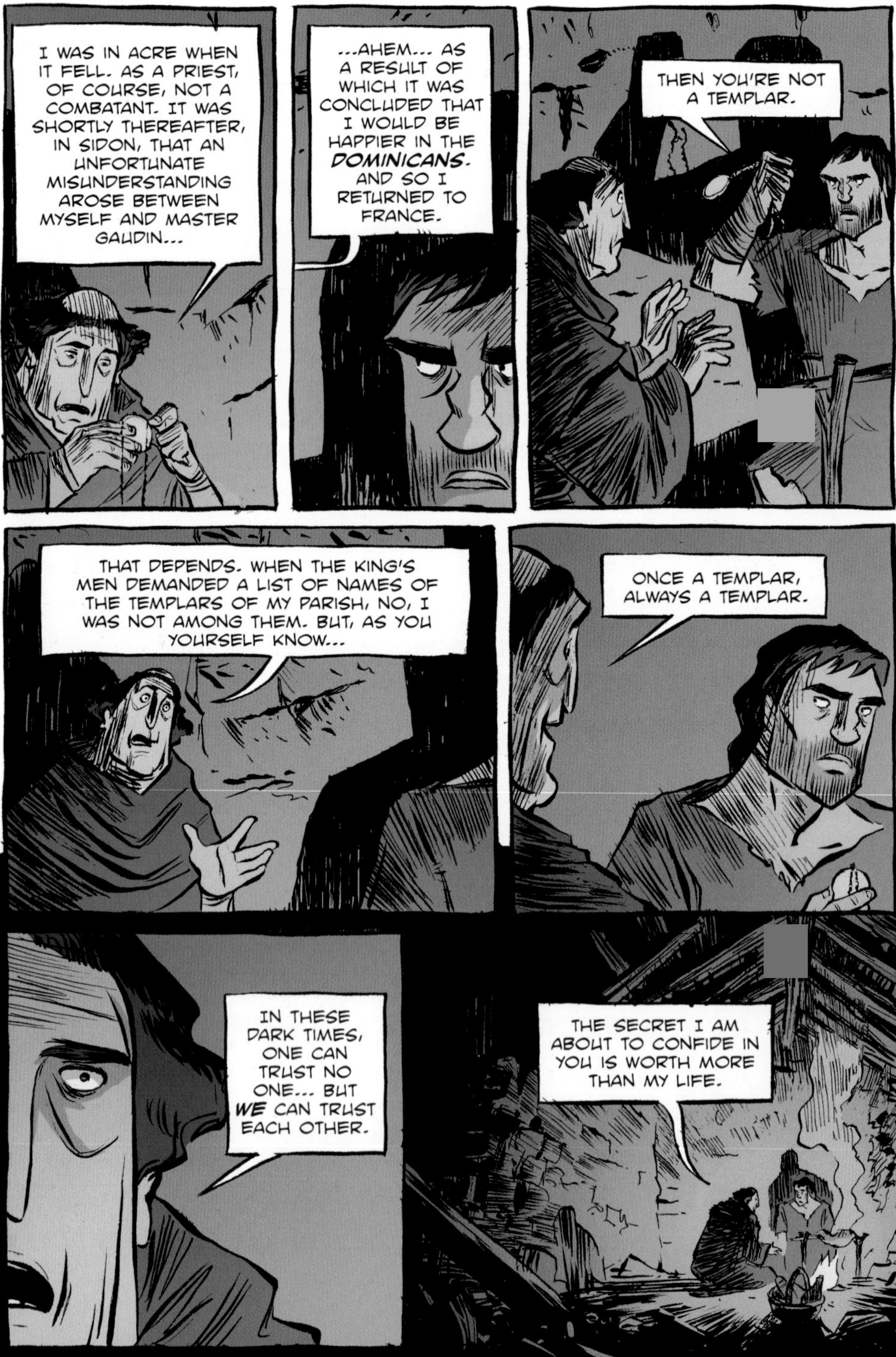

I WAS IN ACRE WHEN IT FELL. AS A PRIEST, OF COURSE, NOT A COMBATANT. IT WAS SHORTLY THEREAFTER, IN SIDON, THAT AN UNFORTUNATE MISUNDERSTANDING AROSE BETWEEN MYSELF AND MASTER GAUDIN...
...AHEM... AS A RESULT OF WHICH IT WAS CONCLUDED THAT I WOULD BE HAPPIER IN THE DOMINICANS. AND SO I RETURNED TO FRANCE.
THEN YOU'RE NOT A TEMPLAR.
THAT DEPENDS. WHEN THE KING'S MEN DEMANDED A LIST OF NAMES OF THE TEMPLARS OF MY PARISH, NO, I WAS NOT AMONG THEM. BUT, AS YOU YOURSELF KNOW...
ONCE A TEMPLAR, ALWAYS A TEMPLAR.
IN THESE DARK TIMES, ONE CAN TRUST NO ONE... BUT WE CAN TRUST EACH OTHER.
THE SECRET I AM ABOUT TO CONFIDE IN YOU IS WORTH MORE THAN MY LIFE.

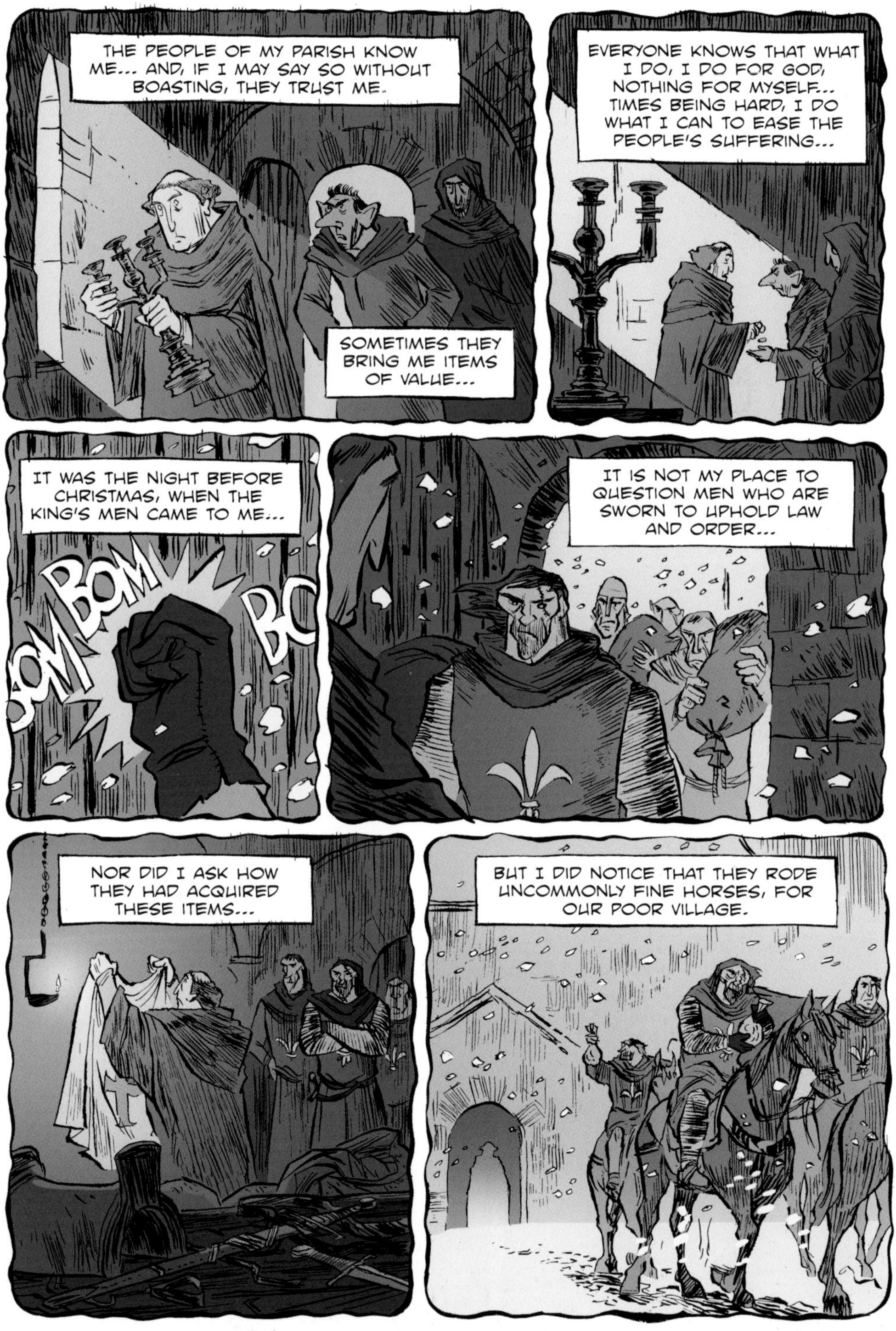
THE PEOPLE OF MY PARISH KNOW ME... AND, IF I MAY SAY SO WITHOUT BOASTING, THEY TRUST ME.
SOMETIMES THEY BRING ME ITEMS OF VALUE...
EVERYONE KNOWS THAT WHAT I DO, I DO FOR GOD, NOTHING FOR MYSELF... TIMES BEING HARD, I DO WHAT I CAN TO EASE THE PEOPLE'S SUFFERING...
IT WAS THE NIGHT BEFORE CHRISTMAS, WHEN THE KING'S MEN CAME TO ME...
BOM BOM BOM BO
IT IS NOT MY PLACE TO QUESTION MEN WHO ARE SWORN TO UPHOLD LAW AND ORDER...
NOR DID I ASK HOW THEY HAD ACQUIRED THESE ITEMS...
BUT I DID NOTICE THAT THEY RODE UNCOMMONLY FINE HORSES, FOR OUR POOR VILLAGE.

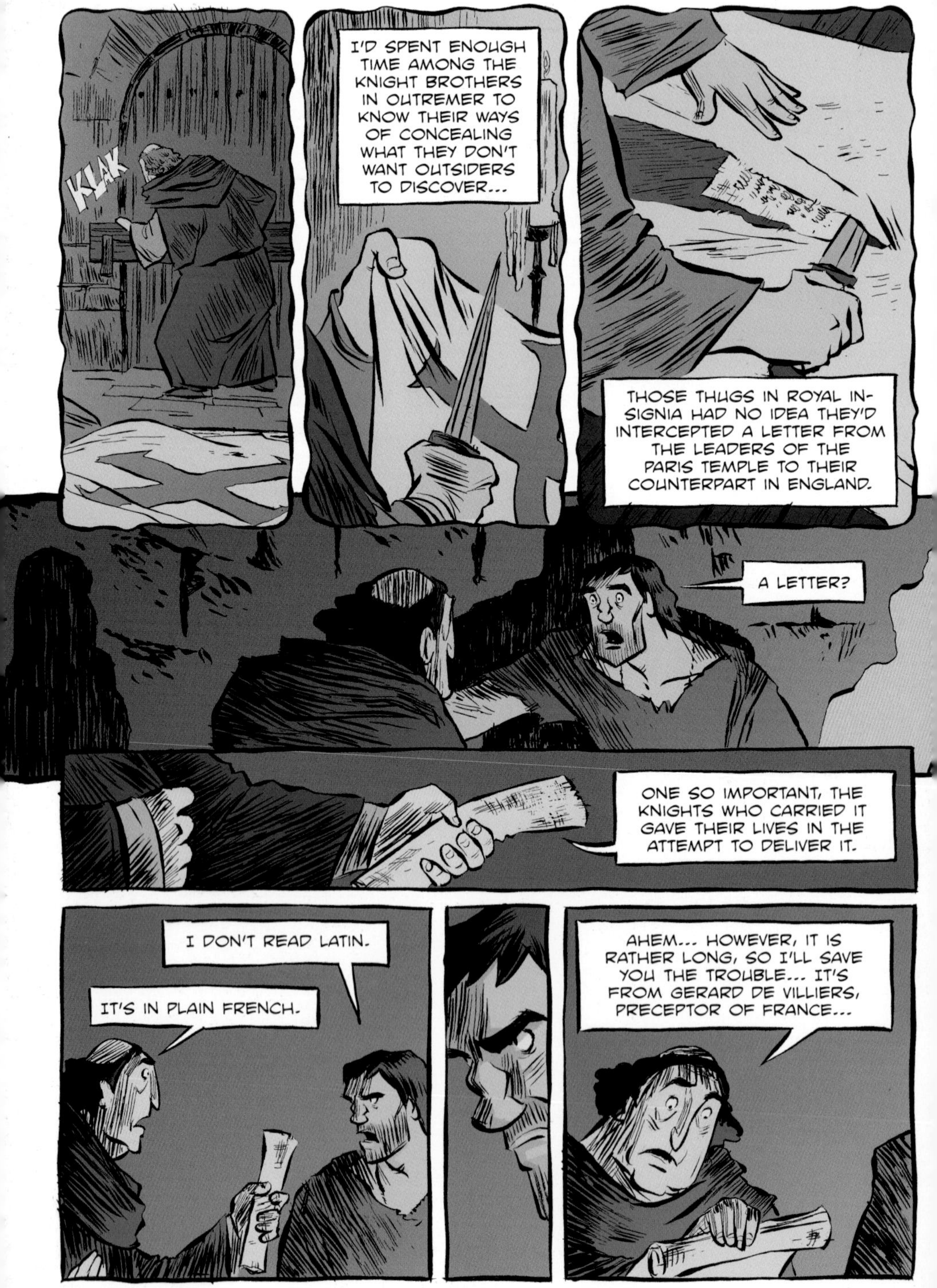
KLAK
I'D SPENT ENOUGH TIME AMONG THE KNIGHT BROTHERS IN OUTREMER TO KNOW THEIR WAYS OF CONCEALING WHAT THEY DON'T WANT OUTSIDERS TO DISCOVER...
THOSE THUGS IN ROYAL INSIGNIA HAD NO IDEA THEY'D INTERCEPTED A LETTER FROM THE LEADERS OF THE PARIS TEMPLE TO THEIR COUNTERPART IN ENGLAND.
A LETTER?
ONE SO IMPORTANT, THE KNIGHTS WHO CARRIED IT GAVE THEIR LIVES IN THE ATTEMPT TO DELIVER IT.
I DON'T READ LATIN.
IT'S IN PLAIN FRENCH.
AHEM... HOWEVER, IT IS RATHER LONG, SO I'LL SAVE YOU THE TROUBLE... IT'S FROM GERARD DE VILLIERS, PRECEPTOR OF FRANCE...

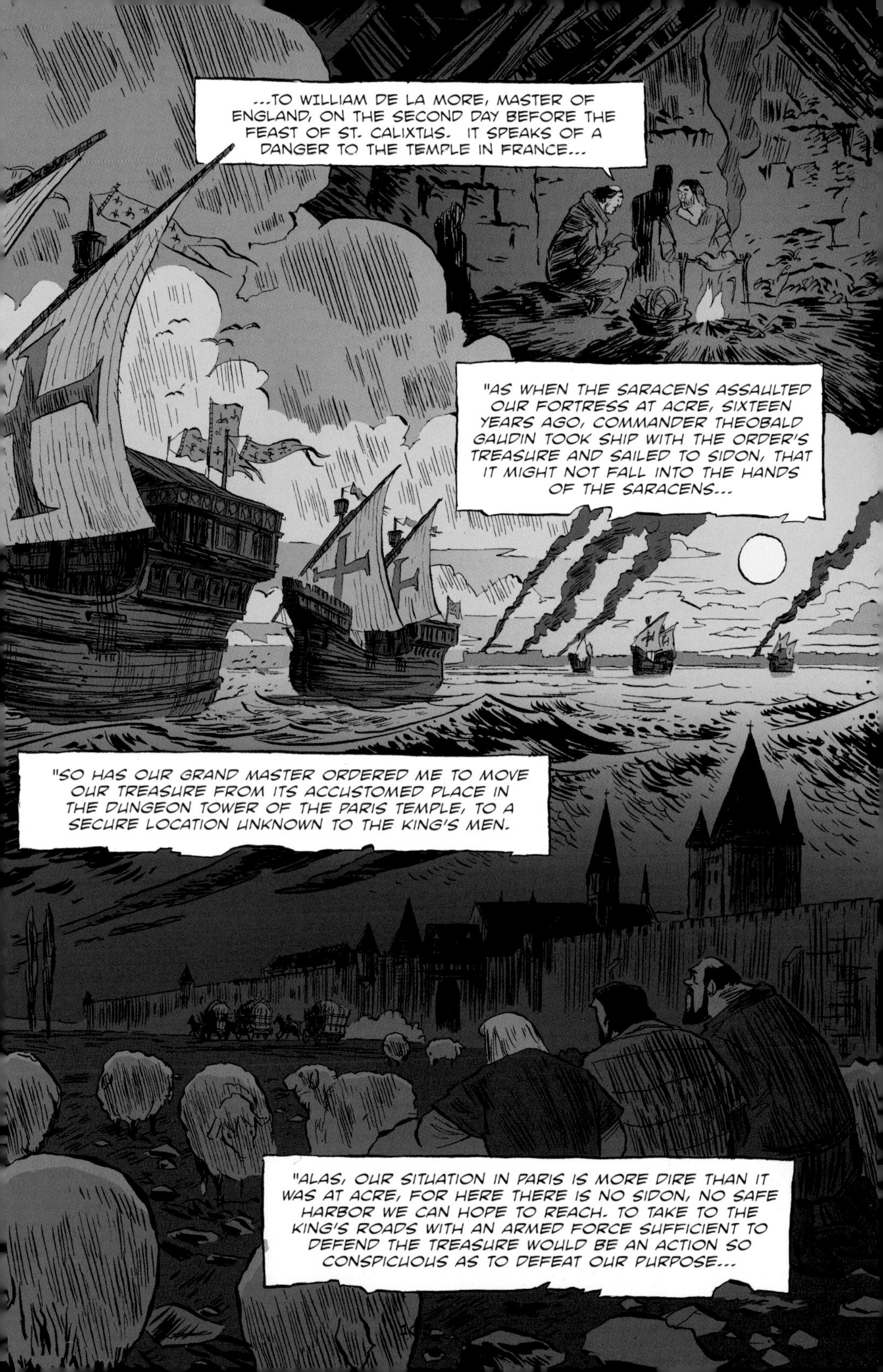
...TO WILLIAM DE LA MORE, MASTER OF ENGLAND, ON THE SECOND DAY BEFORE THE FEAST OF ST. CALIXTUS. IT SPEAKS OF A DANGER TO THE TEMPLE IN FRANCE...
"AS WHEN THE SARACENS ASSAULTED OUR FORTRESS AT ACRE, SIXTEEN YEARS AGO, COMMANDER THEOBALD GAUDIN TOOK SHIP WITH THE ORDER'S TREASURE AND SAILED TO SIDON, THAT IT MIGHT NOT FALL INTO THE HANDS OF THE SARACENS...
"SO HAS OUR GRAND MASTER ORDERED ME TO MOVE OUR TREASURE FROM ITS ACCUSTOMED PLACE IN THE DUNGEON TOWER OF THE PARIS TEMPLE, TO A SECURE LOCATION UNKNOWN TO THE KING'S MEN.
"ALAS, OUR SITUATION IN PARIS IS MORE DIRE THAN IT WAS AT ACRE, FOR HERE THERE IS NO SIDON, NO SAFE HARBOR WE CAN HOPE TO REACH. TO TAKE TO THE KING'S ROADS WITH AN ARMED FORCE SUFFICIENT TO DEFEND THE TREASURE WOULD BE AN ACTION SO CONSPICUOUS AS TO DEFEAT OUR PURPOSE...

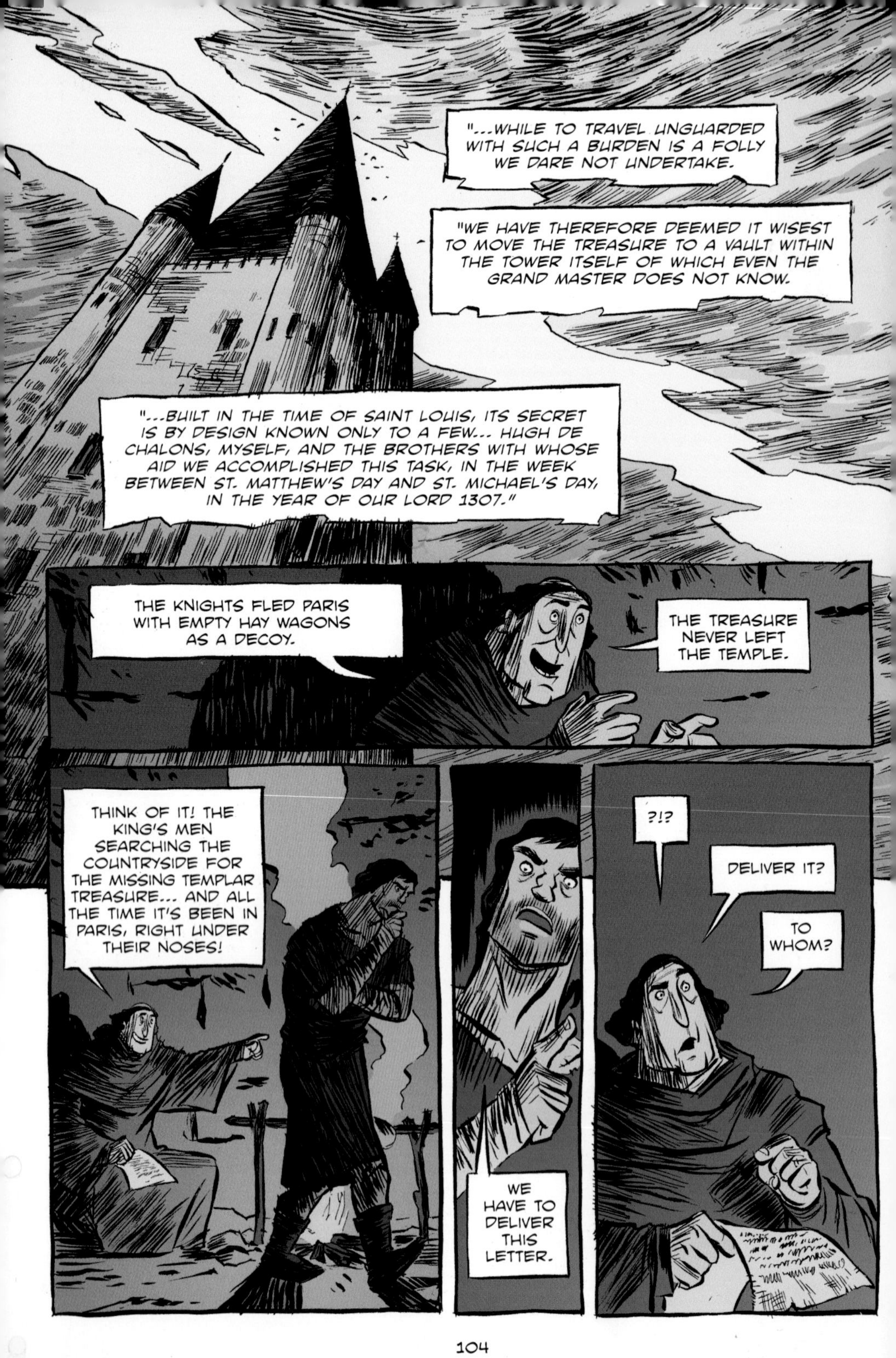
"...WHILE TO TRAVEL UNGUARDED WITH SUCH A BURDEN IS A FOLLY WE DARE NOT UNDERTAKE.
"WE HAVE THEREFORE DEEMED IT WISEST TO MOVE THE TREASURE TO A VAULT WITHIN THE TOWER ITSELF OF WHICH EVEN THE GRAND MASTER DOES NOT KNOW.
"...BUILT IN THE TIME OF SAINT LOUIS, ITS SECRET IS BY DESIGN KNOWN ONLY TO A FEW... HUGH DE CHALONS, MYSELF, AND THE BROTHERS WITH WHOSE AID WE ACCOMPLISHED THIS TASK, IN THE WEEK BETWEEN ST. MATTHEW'S DAY AND ST. MICHAEL'S DAY, IN THE YEAR OF OUR LORD 1307."
THE KNIGHTS FLED PARIS WITH EMPTY HAY WAGONS AS A DECOY.
THE TREASURE NEVER LEFT THE TEMPLE.
THINK OF IT! THE KING'S MEN SEARCHING THE COUNTRYSIDE FOR THE MISSING TEMPLAR TREASURE... AND ALL THE TIME IT'S BEEN IN PARIS, RIGHT UNDER THEIR NOSES!
WE HAVE TO DELIVER THIS LETTER.
?!?
DELIVER IT?
TO WHOM?

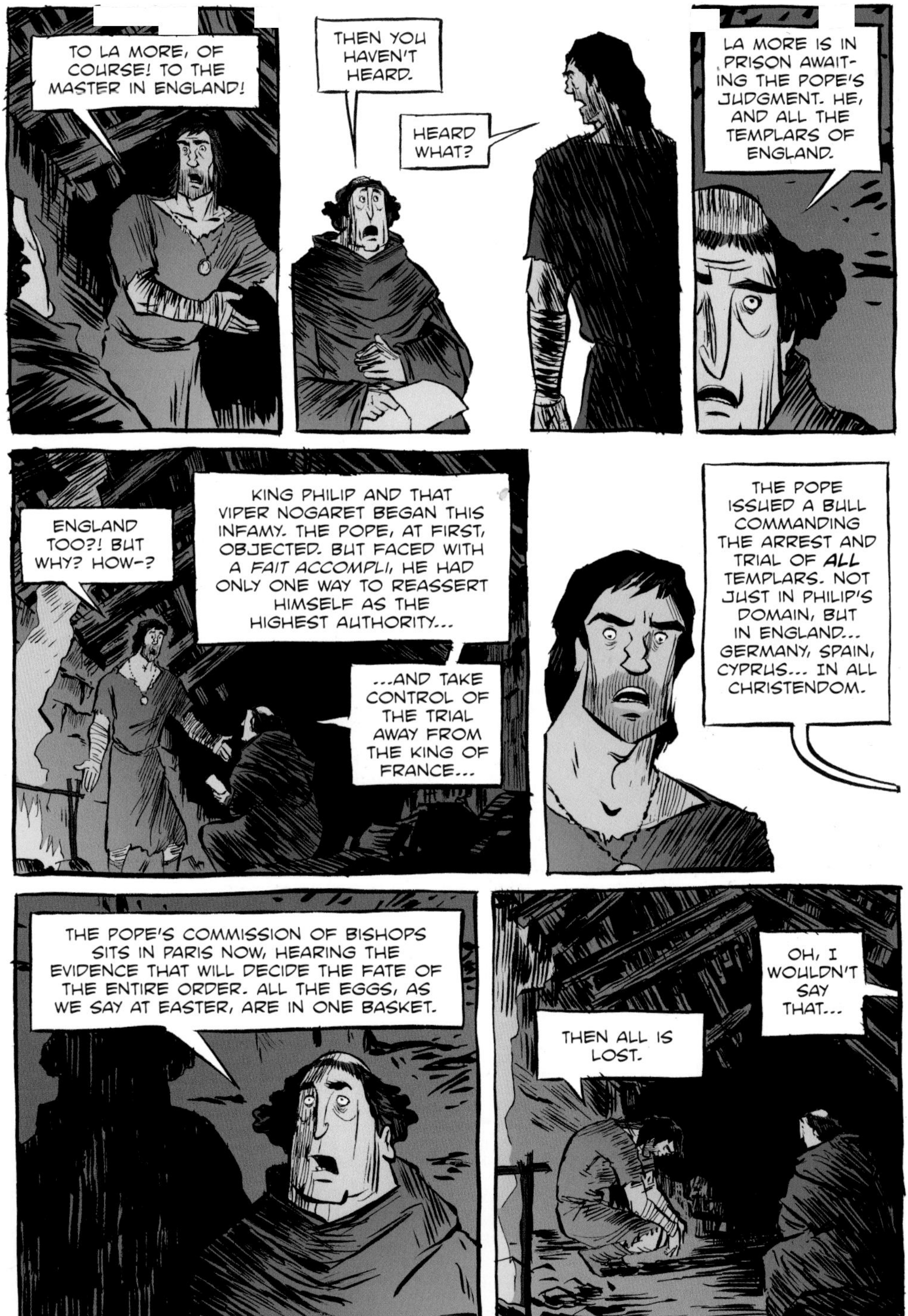
TO LA MORE, OF COURSE! TO THE MASTER IN ENGLAND!
THEN YOU HAVEN'T HEARD.
HEARD WHAT?
LA MORE IS IN PRISON AWAITING THE POPE'S JUDGMENT. HE, AND ALL THE TEMPLARS OF ENGLAND.
ENGLAND TOO?! BUT WHY? HOW-?
KING PHILIP AND THAT VIPER NOGARET BEGAN THIS INFAMY. THE POPE, AT FIRST, OBJECTED. BUT FACED WITH A *FAIT ACCOMPLI*, HE HAD ONLY ONE WAY TO REASSERT HIMSELF AS THE HIGHEST AUTHORITY...
...AND TAKE CONTROL OF THE TRIAL AWAY FROM THE KING OF FRANCE...
THE POPE ISSUED A BULL COMMANDING THE ARREST AND TRIAL OF ***ALL*** TEMPLARS. NOT JUST IN PHILIP'S DOMAIN, BUT IN ENGLAND... GERMANY, SPAIN, CYPRUS... IN ALL CHRISTENDOM.
THE POPE'S COMMISSION OF BISHOPS SITS IN PARIS NOW, HEARING THE EVIDENCE THAT WILL DECIDE THE FATE OF THE ENTIRE ORDER. ALL THE EGGS, AS WE SAY AT EASTER, ARE IN ONE BASKET.
THEN ALL IS LOST.
OH, I WOULDN'T SAY THAT...

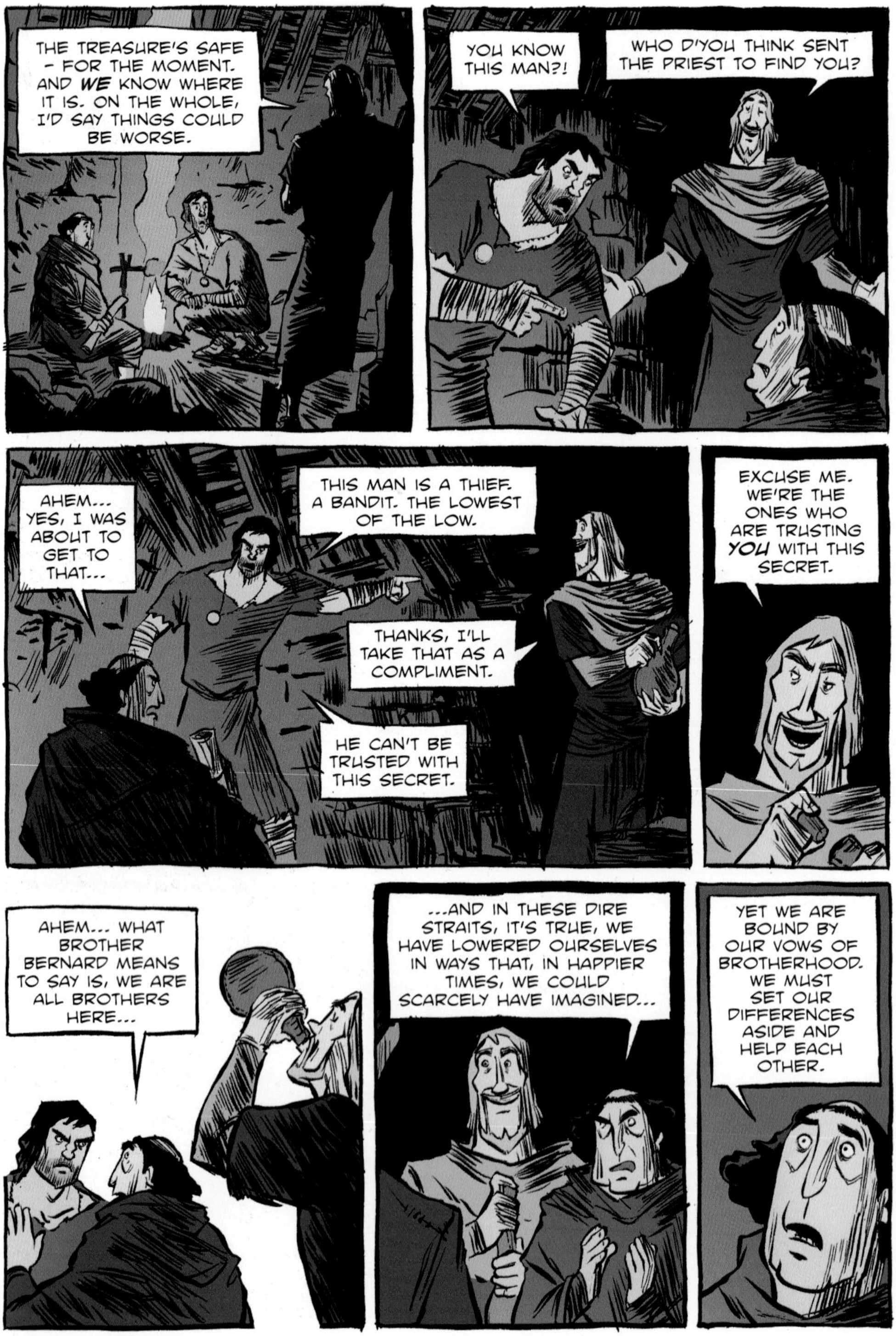

THE TREASURE'S SAFE - FOR THE MOMENT. AND **WE** KNOW WHERE IT IS. ON THE WHOLE, I'D SAY THINGS COULD BE WORSE.
YOU KNOW THIS MAN?!
WHO D'YOU THINK SENT THE PRIEST TO FIND YOU?
AHEM... YES, I WAS ABOUT TO GET TO THAT...
THIS MAN IS A THIEF. A BANDIT. THE LOWEST OF THE LOW.
THANKS, I'LL TAKE THAT AS A COMPLIMENT.
HE CAN'T BE TRUSTED WITH THIS SECRET.
EXCUSE ME. WE'RE THE ONES WHO ARE TRUSTING **YOU** WITH THIS SECRET.
AHEM... WHAT BROTHER BERNARD MEANS TO SAY IS, WE ARE ALL BROTHERS HERE...
...AND IN THESE DIRE STRAITS, IT'S TRUE, WE HAVE LOWERED OURSELVES IN WAYS THAT, IN HAPPIER TIMES, WE COULD SCARCELY HAVE IMAGINED...
YET WE ARE BOUND BY OUR VOWS OF BROTHERHOOD. WE MUST SET OUR DIFFERENCES ASIDE AND HELP EACH OTHER.

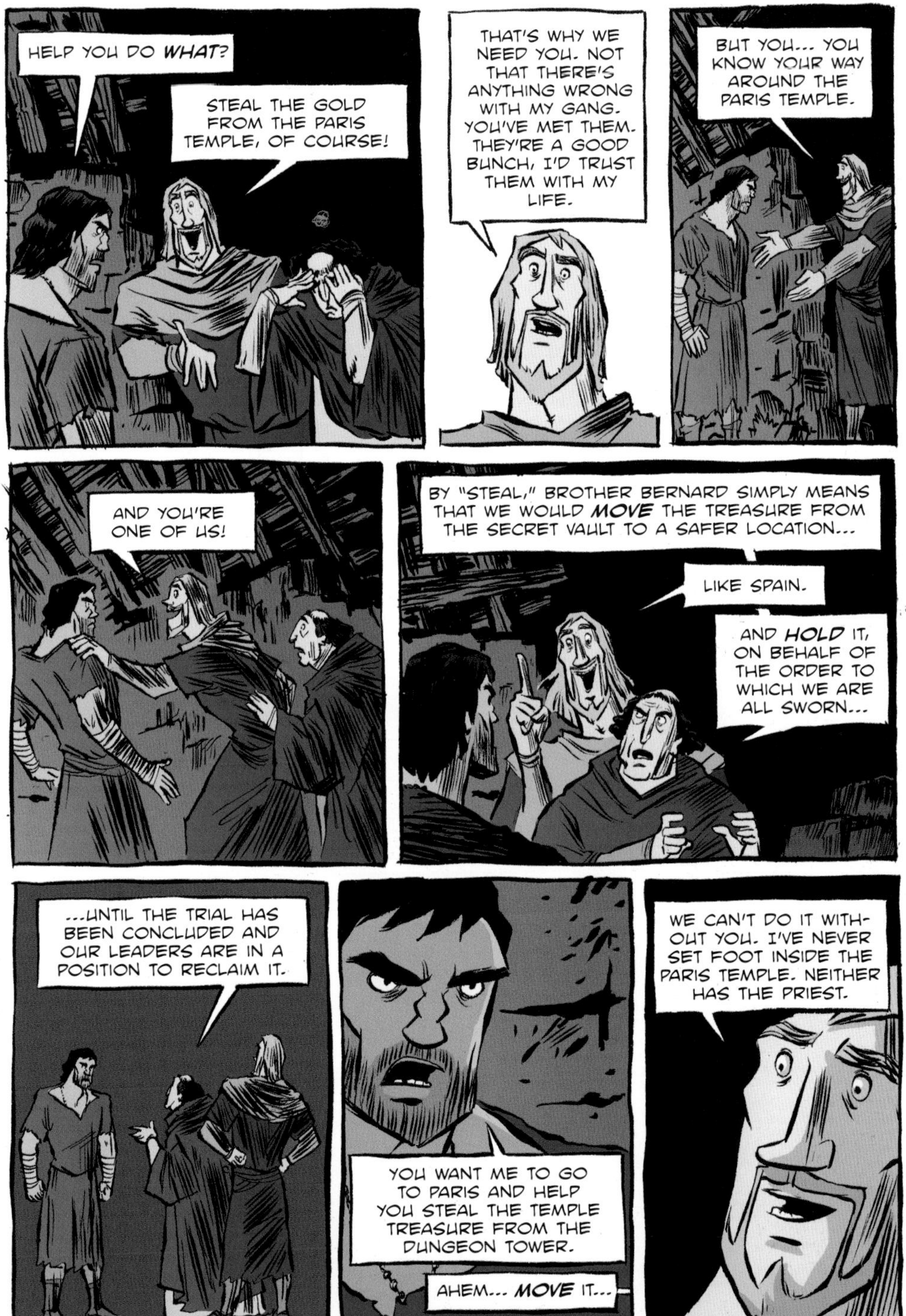
HELP YOU DO WHAT?
STEAL THE GOLD FROM THE PARIS TEMPLE, OF COURSE!
THAT'S WHY WE NEED YOU. NOT THAT THERE'S ANYTHING WRONG WITH MY GANG. YOU'VE MET THEM. THEY'RE A GOOD BUNCH, I'D TRUST THEM WITH MY LIFE.
BUT YOU... YOU KNOW YOUR WAY AROUND THE PARIS TEMPLE.
AND YOU'RE ONE OF US!
BY "STEAL," BROTHER BERNARD SIMPLY MEANS THAT WE WOULD MOVE THE TREASURE FROM THE SECRET VAULT TO A SAFER LOCATION...
LIKE SPAIN.
AND HOLD IT, ON BEHALF OF THE ORDER TO WHICH WE ARE ALL SWORN...
...UNTIL THE TRIAL HAS BEEN CONCLUDED AND OUR LEADERS ARE IN A POSITION TO RECLAIM IT.
YOU WANT ME TO GO TO PARIS AND HELP YOU STEAL THE TEMPLE TREASURE FROM THE DUNGEON TOWER.
AHEM... MOVE IT...
WE CAN'T DO IT WITHOUT YOU. I'VE NEVER SET FOOT INSIDE THE PARIS TEMPLE. NEITHER HAS THE PRIEST.

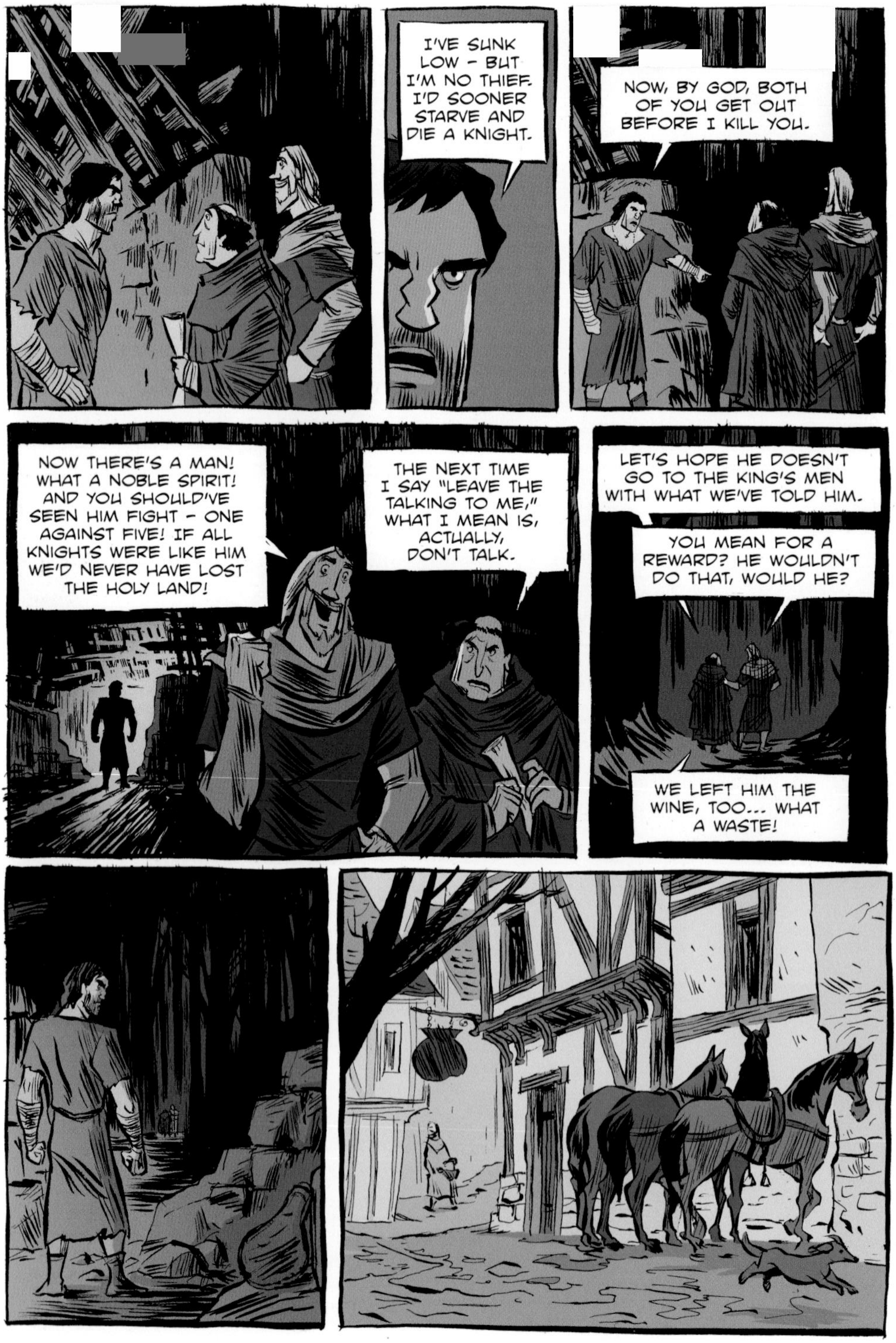
I'VE SUNK LOW - BUT I'M NO THIEF. I'D SOONER STARVE AND DIE A KNIGHT.
NOW, BY GOD, BOTH OF YOU GET OUT BEFORE I KILL YOU.
NOW THERE'S A MAN! WHAT A NOBLE SPIRIT! AND YOU SHOULD'VE SEEN HIM FIGHT - ONE AGAINST FIVE! IF ALL KNIGHTS WERE LIKE HIM WE'D NEVER HAVE LOST THE HOLY LAND!
THE NEXT TIME I SAY "LEAVE THE TALKING TO ME," WHAT I MEAN IS, ACTUALLY, DON'T TALK.
LET'S HOPE HE DOESN'T GO TO THE KING'S MEN WITH WHAT WE'VE TOLD HIM.
YOU MEAN FOR A REWARD? HE WOULDN'T DO THAT, WOULD HE?
WE LEFT HIM THE WINE, TOO... WHAT A WASTE!

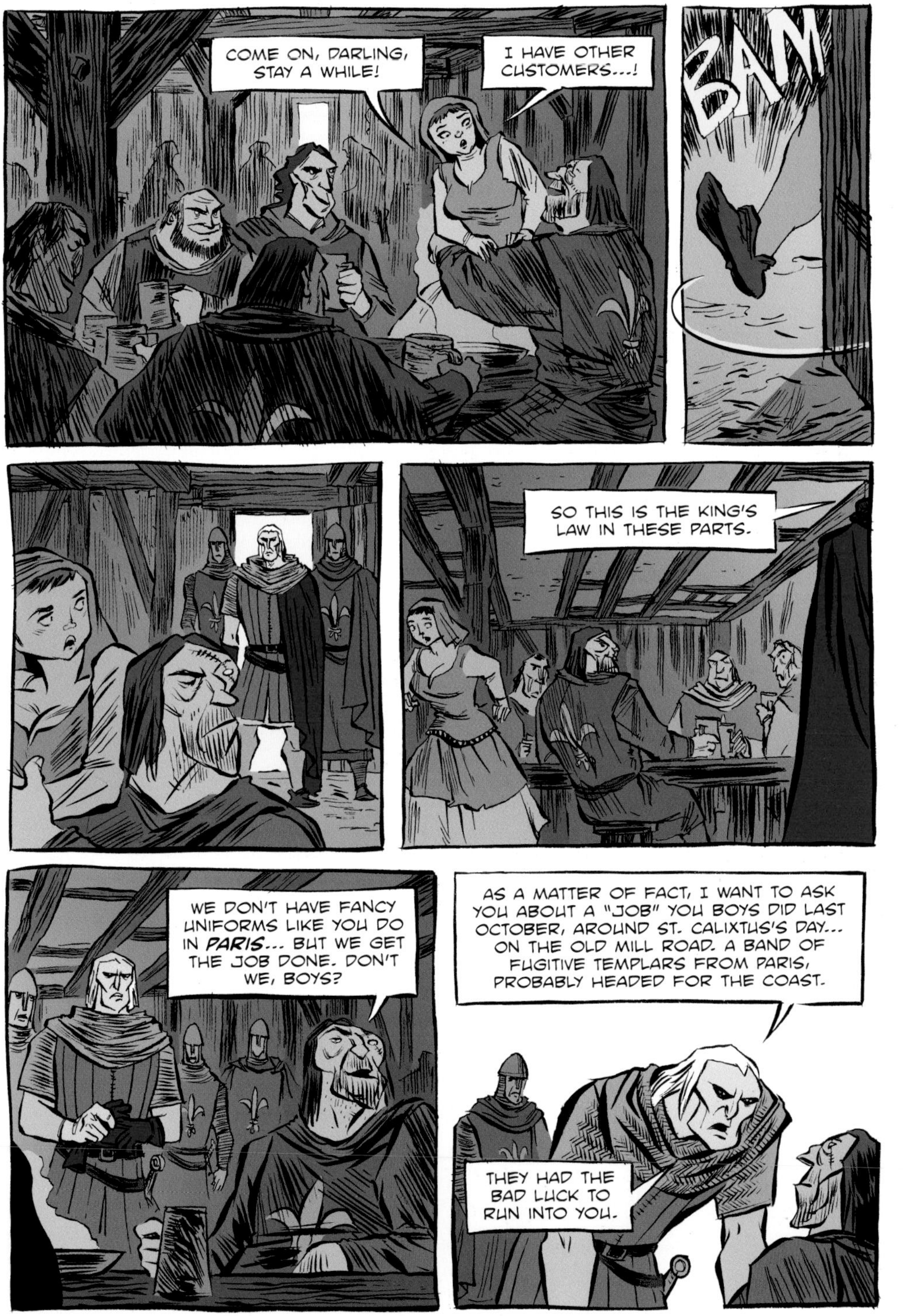
COME ON, DARLING, STAY A WHILE!
I HAVE OTHER CUSTOMERS...!
BAM
SO THIS IS THE KING'S LAW IN THESE PARTS.
WE DON'T HAVE FANCY UNIFORMS LIKE YOU DO IN *PARIS*... BUT WE GET THE JOB DONE. DON'T WE, BOYS?
AS A MATTER OF FACT, I WANT TO ASK YOU ABOUT A "JOB" YOU BOYS DID LAST OCTOBER, AROUND ST. CALIXTUS'S DAY... ON THE OLD MILL ROAD. A BAND OF FUGITIVE TEMPLARS FROM PARIS, PROBABLY HEADED FOR THE COAST.
THEY HAD THE BAD LUCK TO RUN INTO YOU.

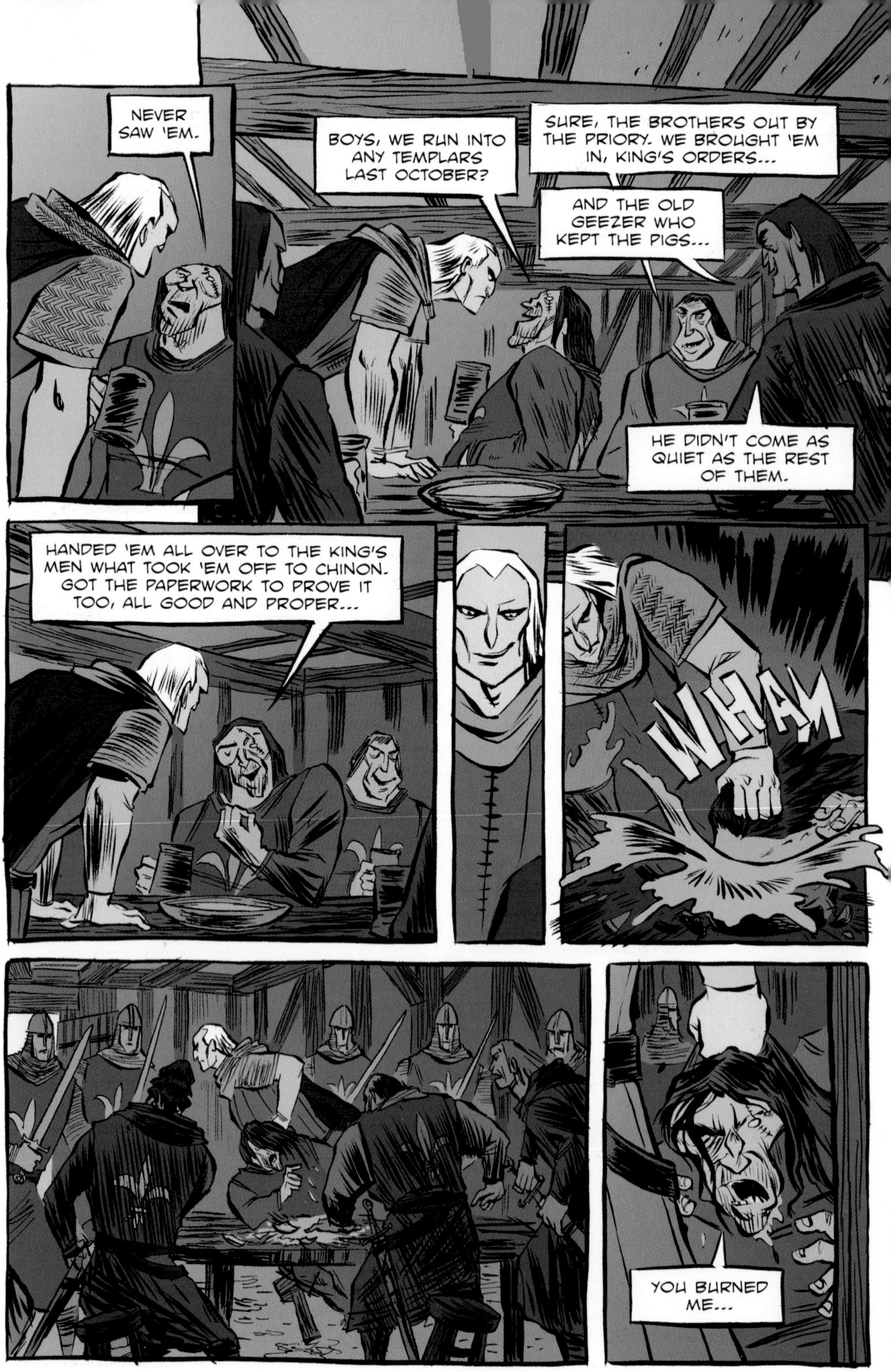
NEVER SAW 'EM.
BOYS, WE RUN INTO ANY TEMPLARS LAST OCTOBER?
SURE, THE BROTHERS OUT BY THE PRIORY. WE BROUGHT 'EM IN, KING'S ORDERS...
AND THE OLD GEEZER WHO KEPT THE PIGS...
HE DIDN'T COME AS QUIET AS THE REST OF THEM.
HANDED 'EM ALL OVER TO THE KING'S MEN WHAT TOOK 'EM OFF TO CHINON. GOT THE PAPERWORK TO PROVE IT TOO, ALL GOOD AND PROPER...
WHAM
YOU BURNED ME...

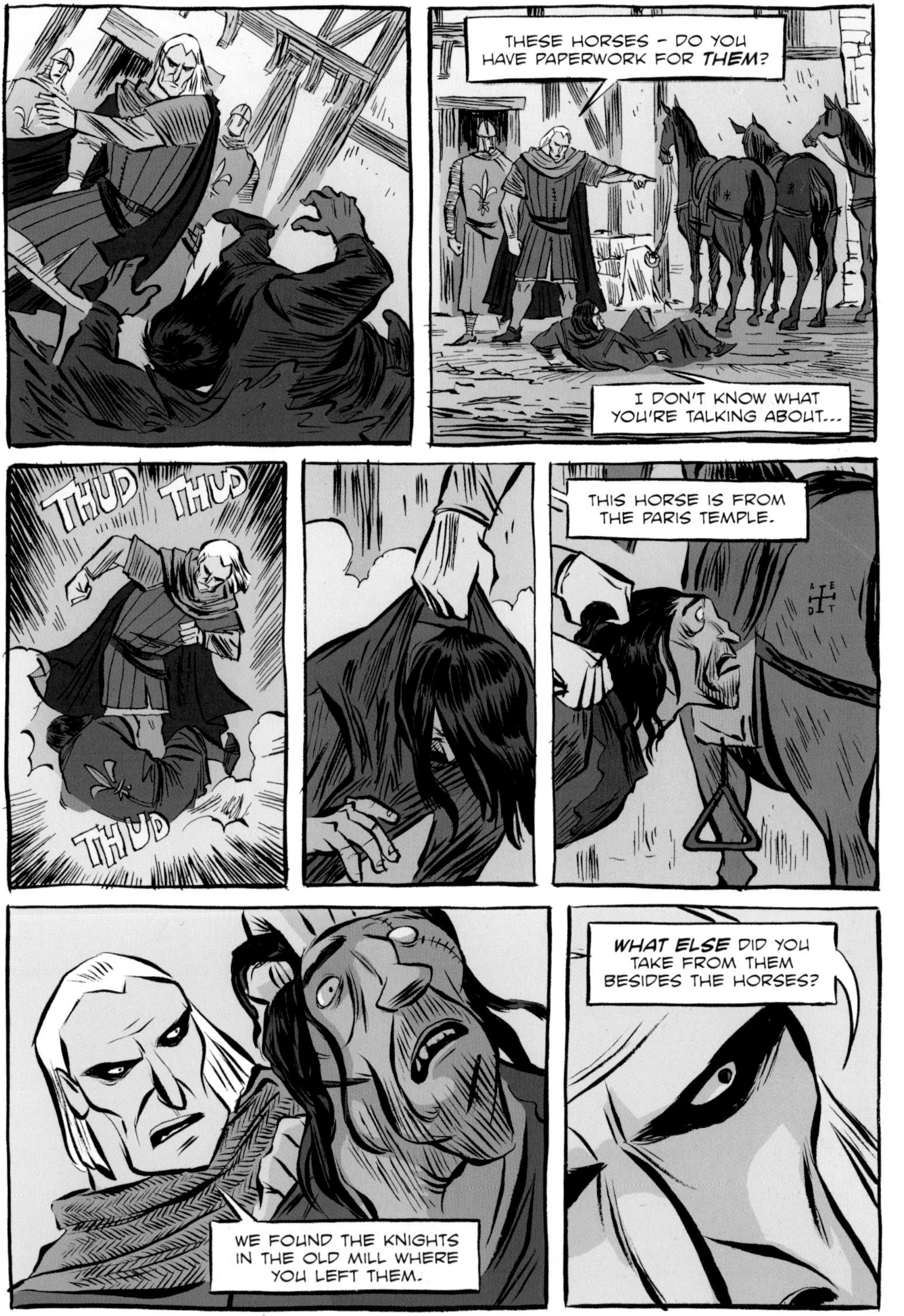
THESE HORSES - DO YOU HAVE PAPERWORK FOR THEM?
I DON'T KNOW WHAT YOU'RE TALKING ABOUT...
THUD
THUD
THUD
THIS HORSE IS FROM THE PARIS TEMPLE.
WE FOUND THE KNIGHTS IN THE OLD MILL WHERE YOU LEFT THEM.
WHAT ELSE DID YOU TAKE FROM THEM BESIDES THE HORSES?

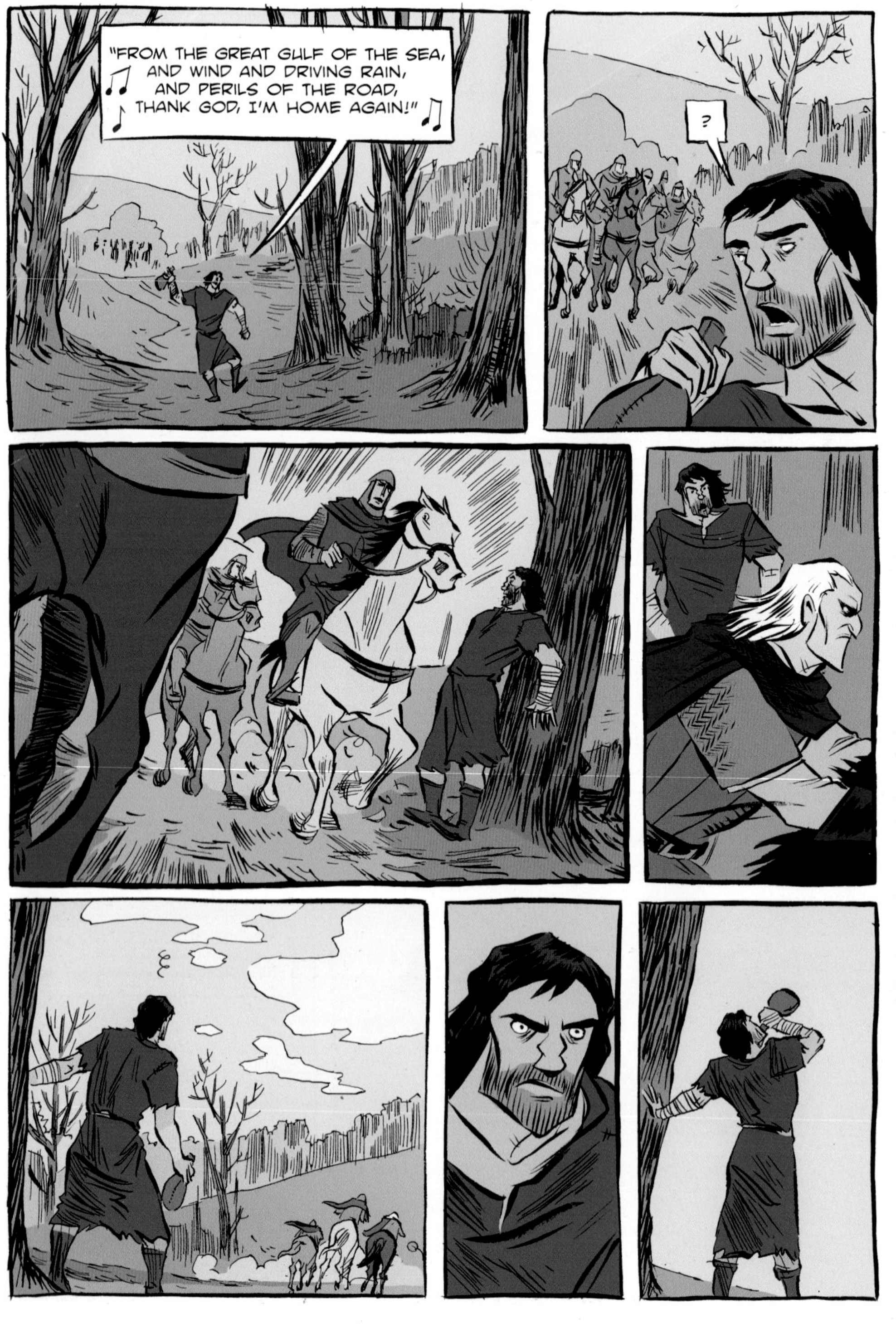
"FROM THE GREAT GULF OF THE SEA, AND WIND AND DRIVING RAIN, AND PERILS OF THE ROAD, THANK GOD, I'M HOME AGAIN!"
?

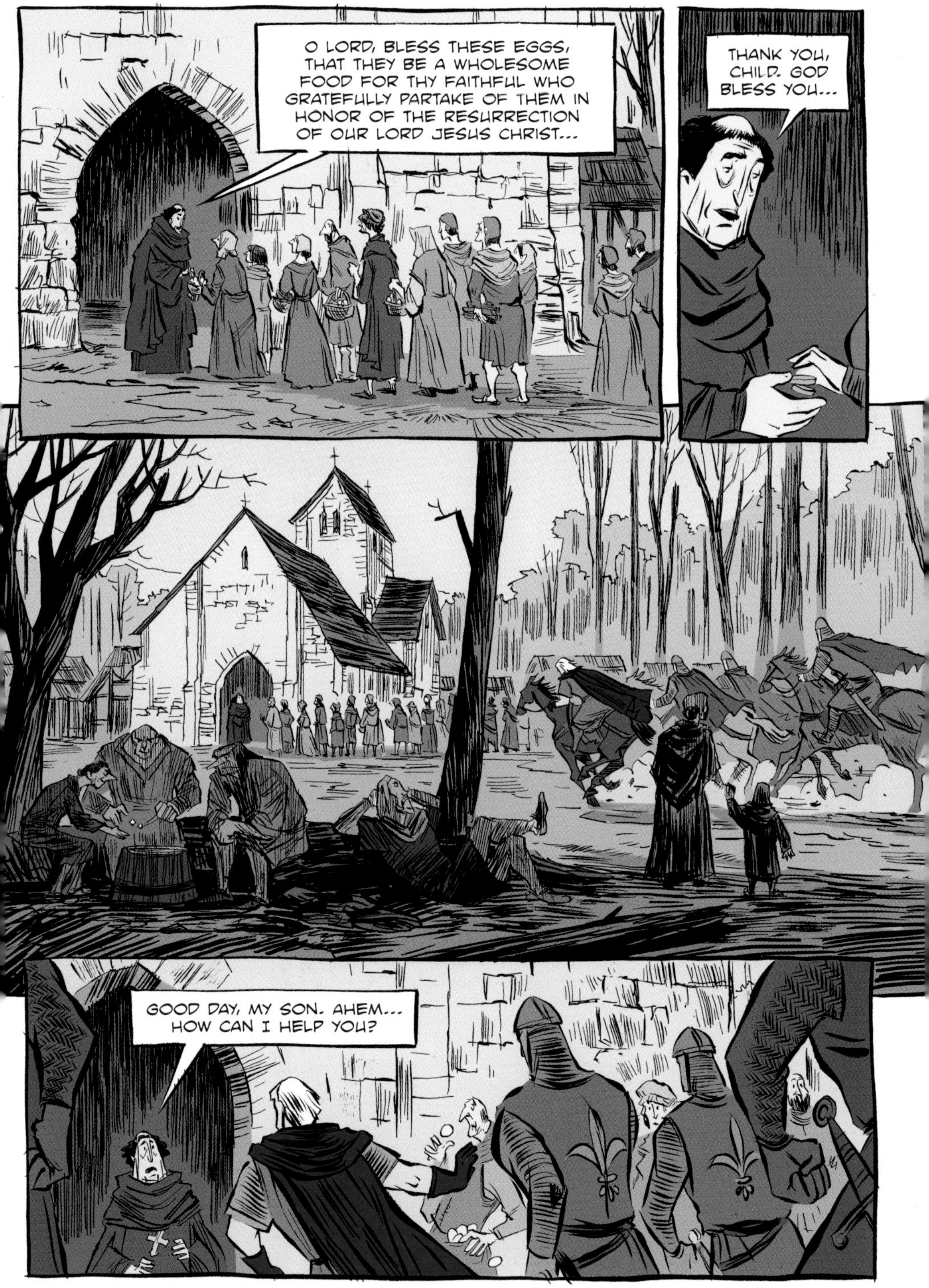
O LORD, BLESS THESE EGGS, THAT THEY BE A WHOLESOME FOOD FOR THY FAITHFUL WHO GRATEFULLY PARTAKE OF THEM IN HONOR OF THE RESURRECTION OF OUR LORD JESUS CHRIST...
THANK YOU, CHILD. GOD BLESS YOU...
GOOD DAY, MY SON. AHEM... HOW CAN I HELP YOU?

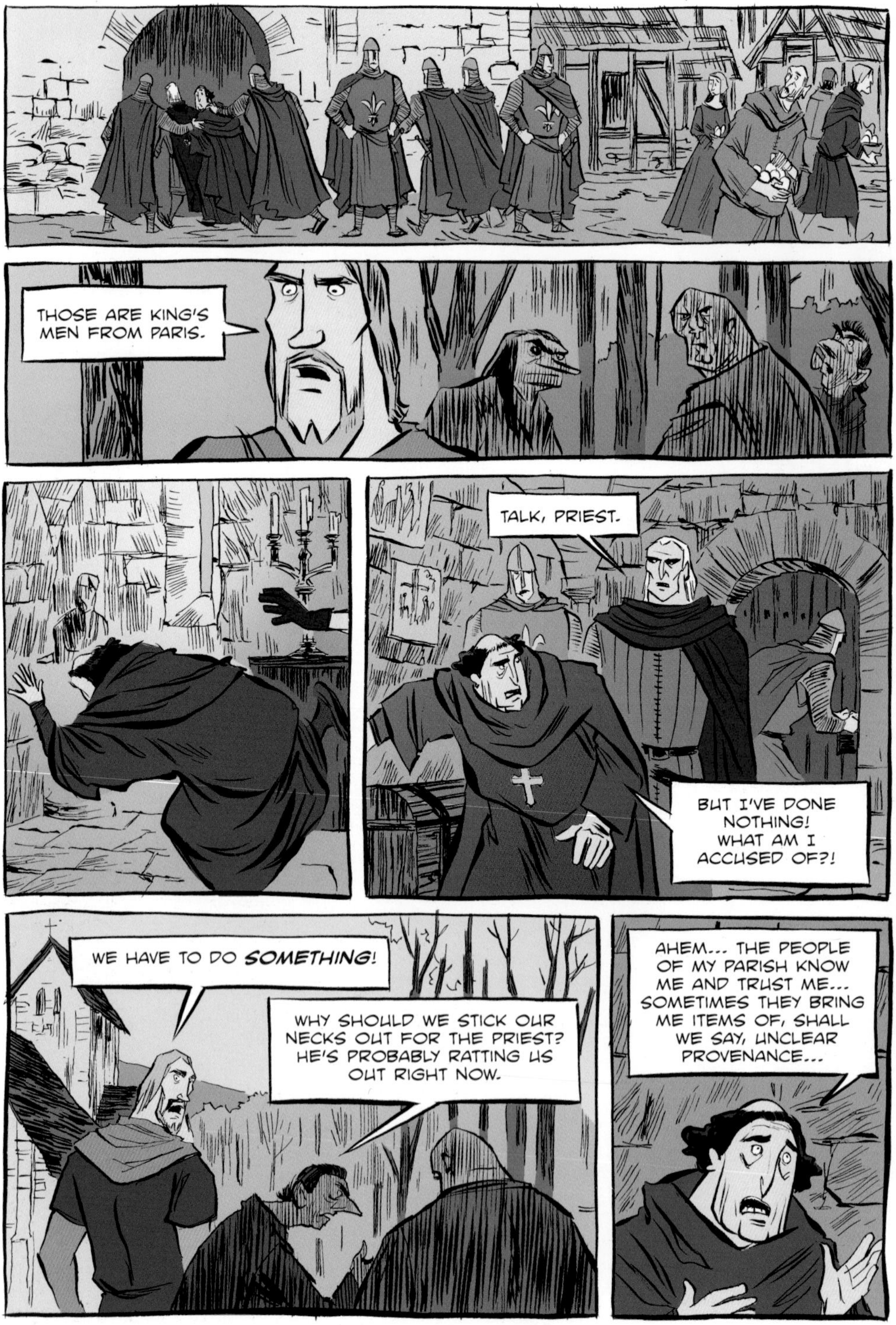
THOSE ARE KING'S MEN FROM PARIS.
TALK, PRIEST.
BUT I'VE DONE NOTHING! WHAT AM I ACCUSED OF?!
WE HAVE TO DO SOMETHING!
WHY SHOULD WE STICK OUR NECKS OUT FOR THE PRIEST? HE'S PROBABLY RATTING US OUT RIGHT NOW.
AHEM... THE PEOPLE OF MY PARISH KNOW ME AND TRUST ME... SOMETIMES THEY BRING ME ITEMS OF, SHALL WE SAY, UNCLEAR PROVENANCE...

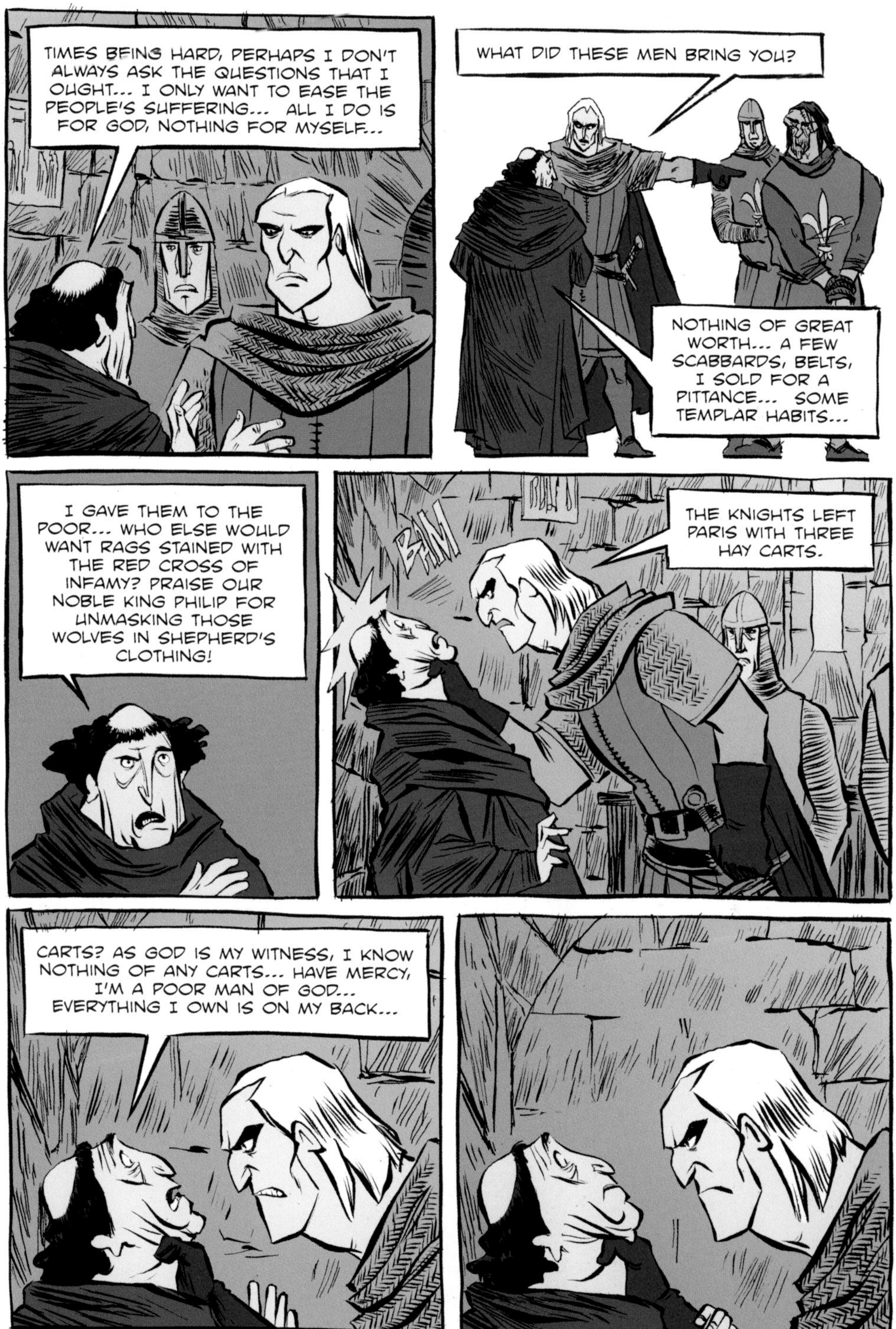
TIMES BEING HARD, PERHAPS I DON'T ALWAYS ASK THE QUESTIONS THAT I OUGHT... I ONLY WANT TO EASE THE PEOPLE'S SUFFERING... ALL I DO IS FOR GOD, NOTHING FOR MYSELF...
WHAT DID THESE MEN BRING YOU?
NOTHING OF GREAT WORTH... A FEW SCABBARDS, BELTS, I SOLD FOR A PITTANCE... SOME TEMPLAR HABITS...
I GAVE THEM TO THE POOR... WHO ELSE WOULD WANT RAGS STAINED WITH THE RED CROSS OF INFAMY? PRAISE OUR NOBLE KING PHILIP FOR UNMASKING THOSE WOLVES IN SHEPHERD'S CLOTHING!
BAM
THE KNIGHTS LEFT PARIS WITH THREE HAY CARTS.
CARTS? AS GOD IS MY WITNESS, I KNOW NOTHING OF ANY CARTS... HAVE MERCY, I'M A POOR MAN OF GOD... EVERYTHING I OWN IS ON MY BACK...

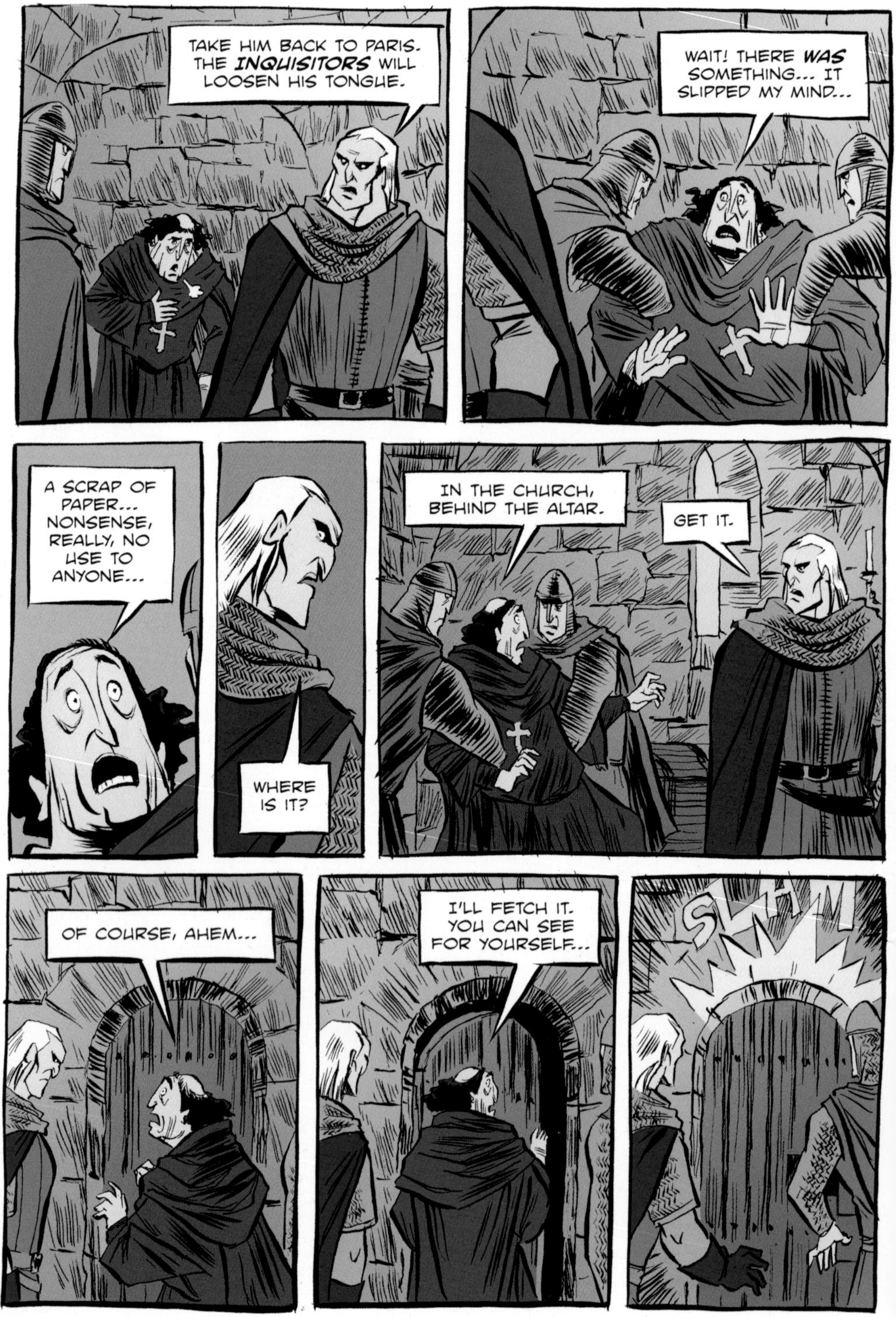
TAKE HIM BACK TO PARIS. THE INQUISITORS WILL LOOSEN HIS TONGUE.
WAIT! THERE WAS SOMETHING... IT SLIPPED MY MIND...
A SCRAP OF PAPER... NONSENSE, REALLY, NO USE TO ANYONE...
WHERE IS IT?
IN THE CHURCH, BEHIND THE ALTAR.
GET IT.
OF COURSE, AHEM...
I'LL FETCH IT. YOU CAN SEE FOR YOURSELF...

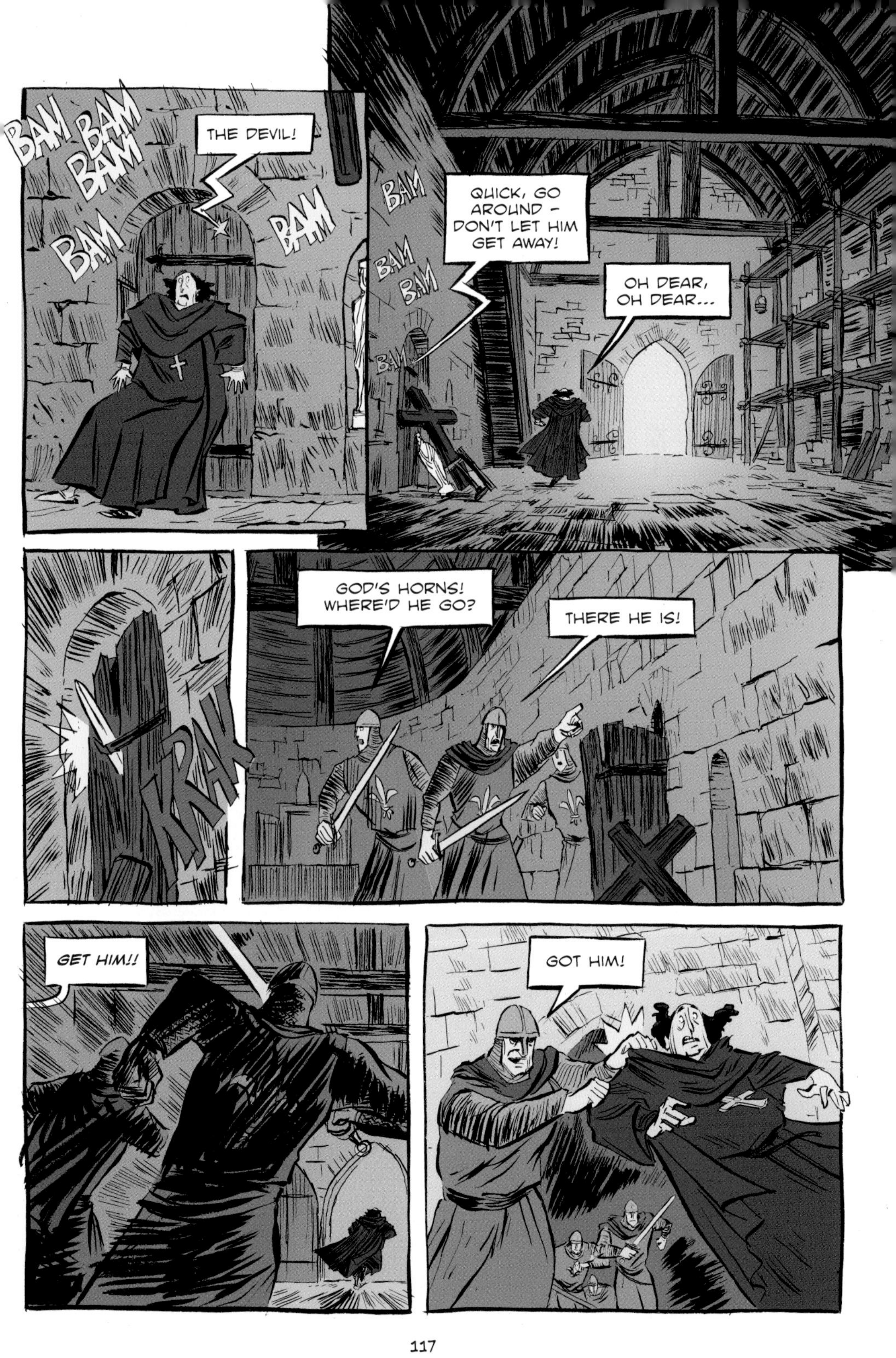
BAM BAM BAM
BAM
THE DEVIL!
BAM
BAM
BAM BAM
BAM
QUICK, GO AROUND – DON'T LET HIM GET AWAY!
OH DEAR, OH DEAR...
KRAK
GOD'S HORNS! WHERE'D HE GO?
THERE HE IS!
GET HIM!!
GOT HIM!

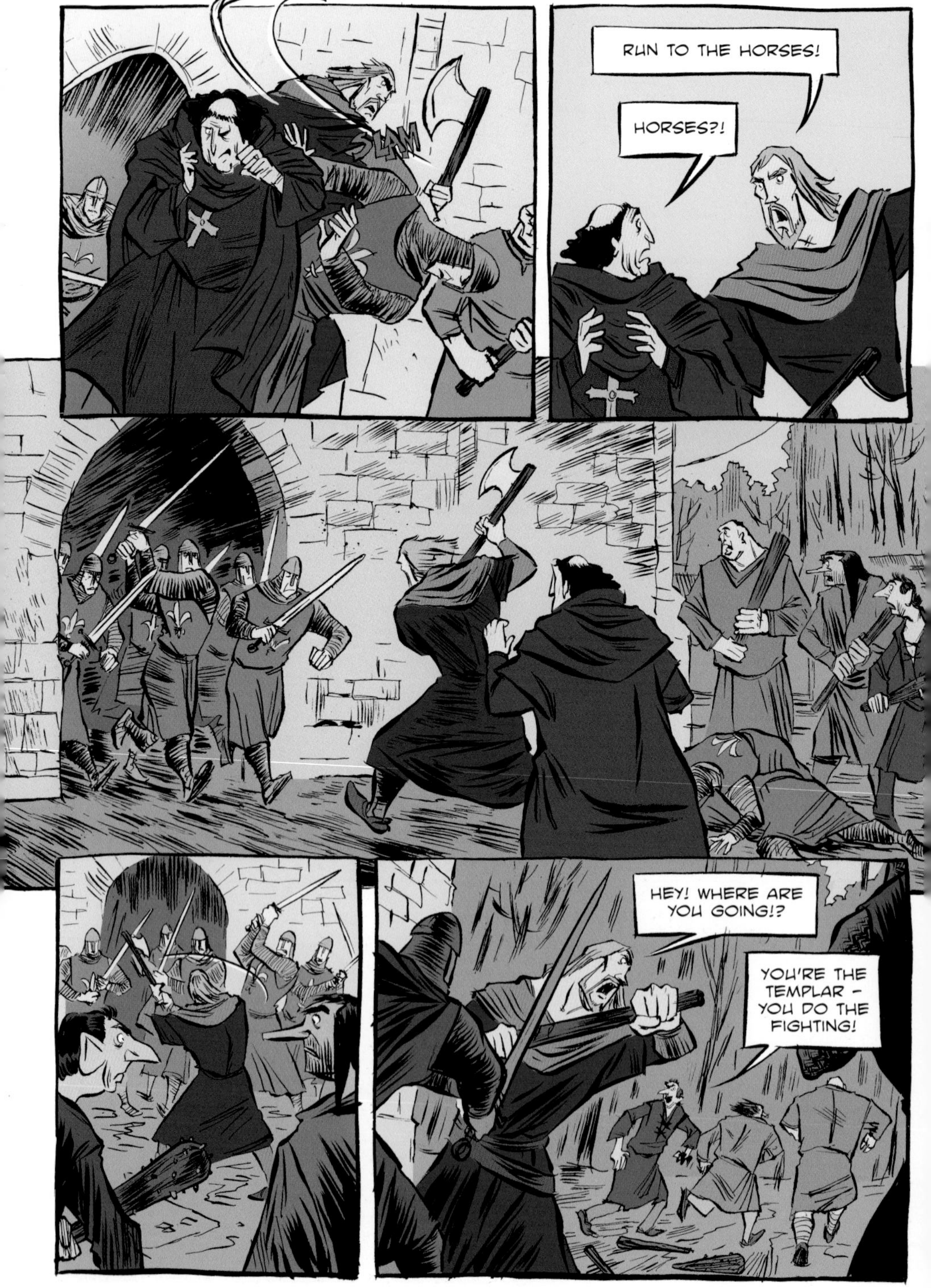
SLAM
RUN TO THE HORSES!
HORSES?!
HEY! WHERE ARE YOU GOING!?
YOU'RE THE TEMPLAR - YOU DO THE FIGHTING!

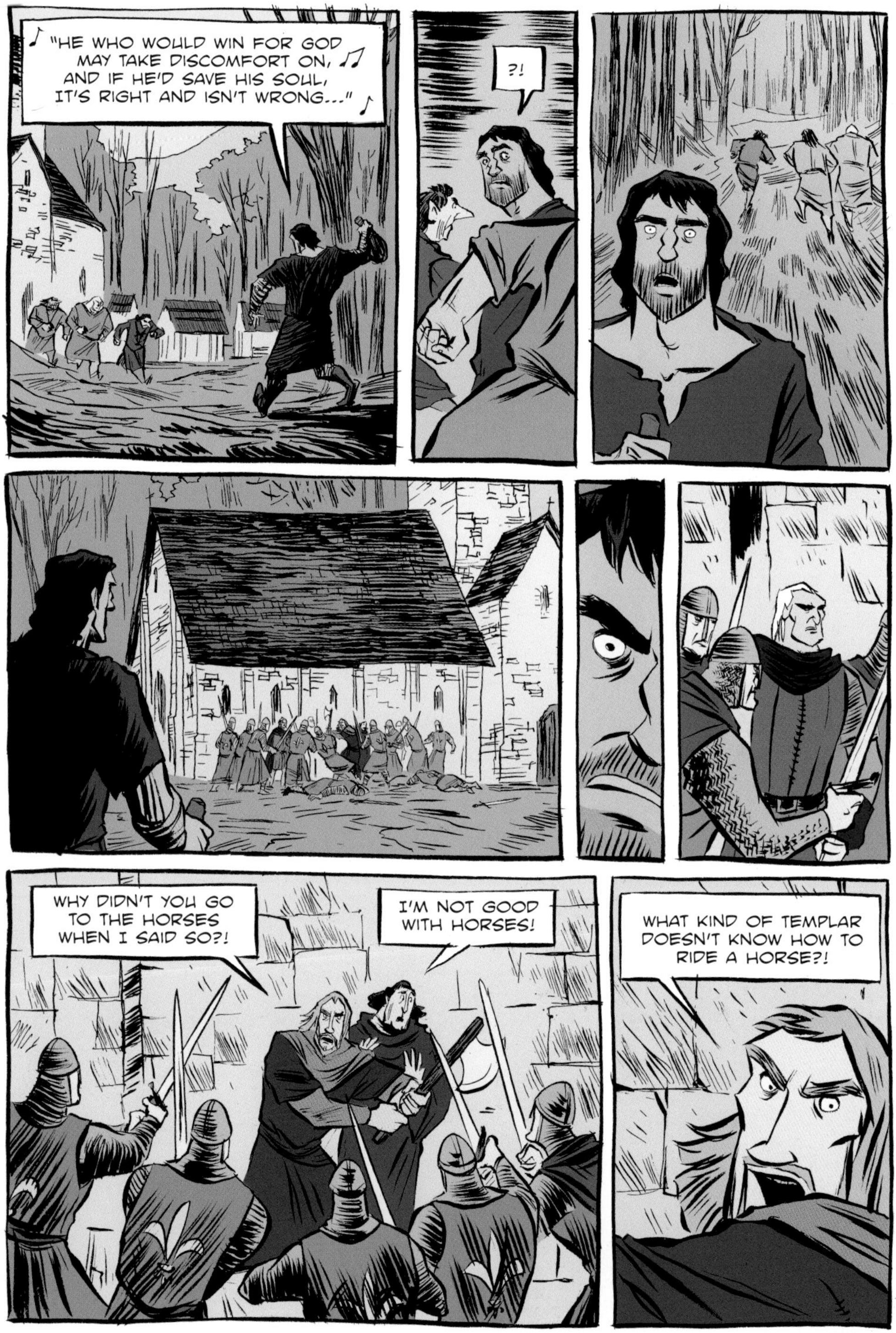
"HE WHO WOULD WIN FOR GOD MAY TAKE DISCOMFORT ON, AND IF HE'D SAVE HIS SOUL, IT'S RIGHT AND ISN'T WRONG..."
?!
WHY DIDN'T YOU GO TO THE HORSES WHEN I SAID SO?!
I'M NOT GOOD WITH HORSES!
WHAT KIND OF TEMPLAR DOESN'T KNOW HOW TO RIDE A HORSE?!

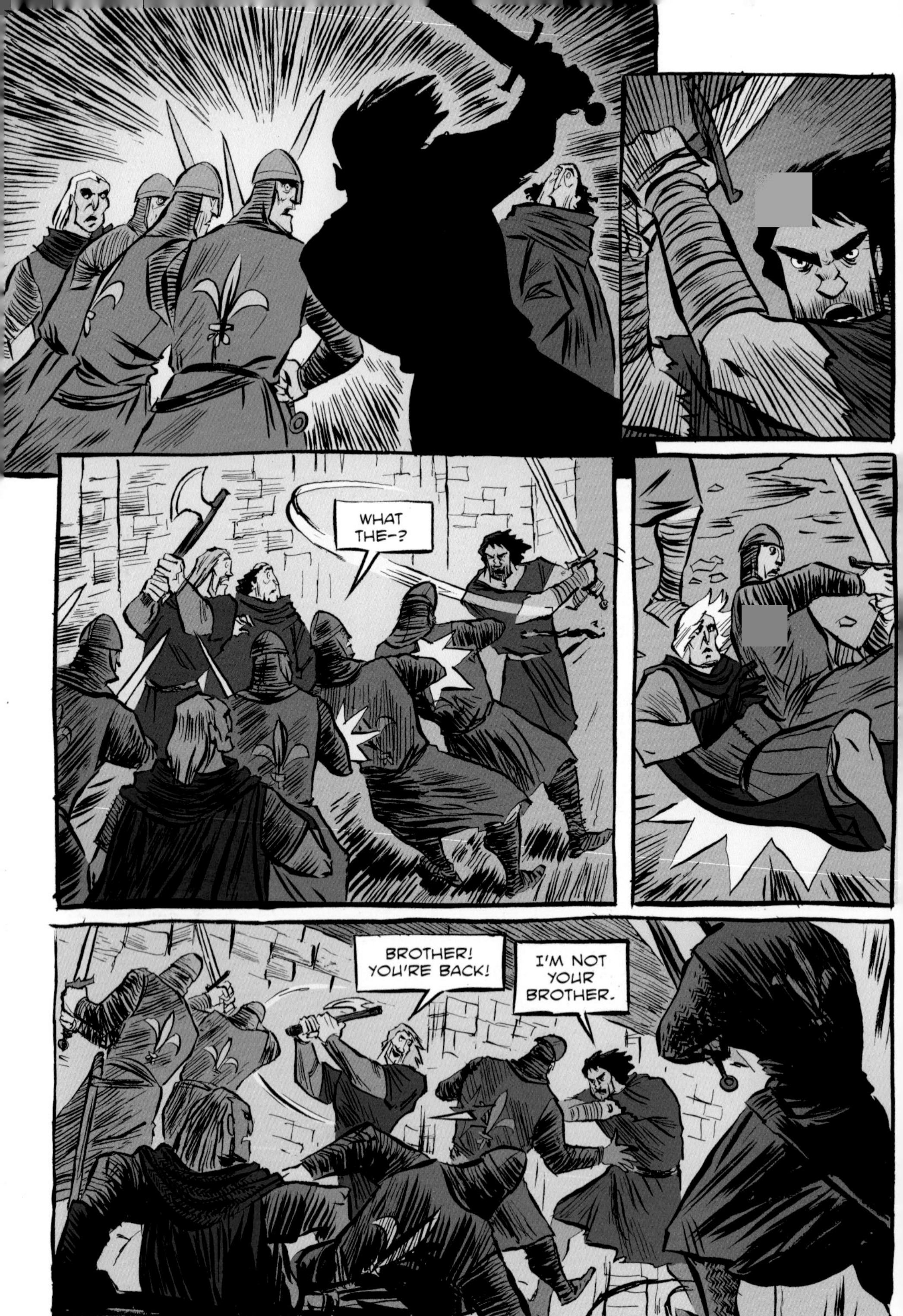
WHAT THE-?
BROTHER! YOU'RE BACK!
I'M NOT YOUR BROTHER.

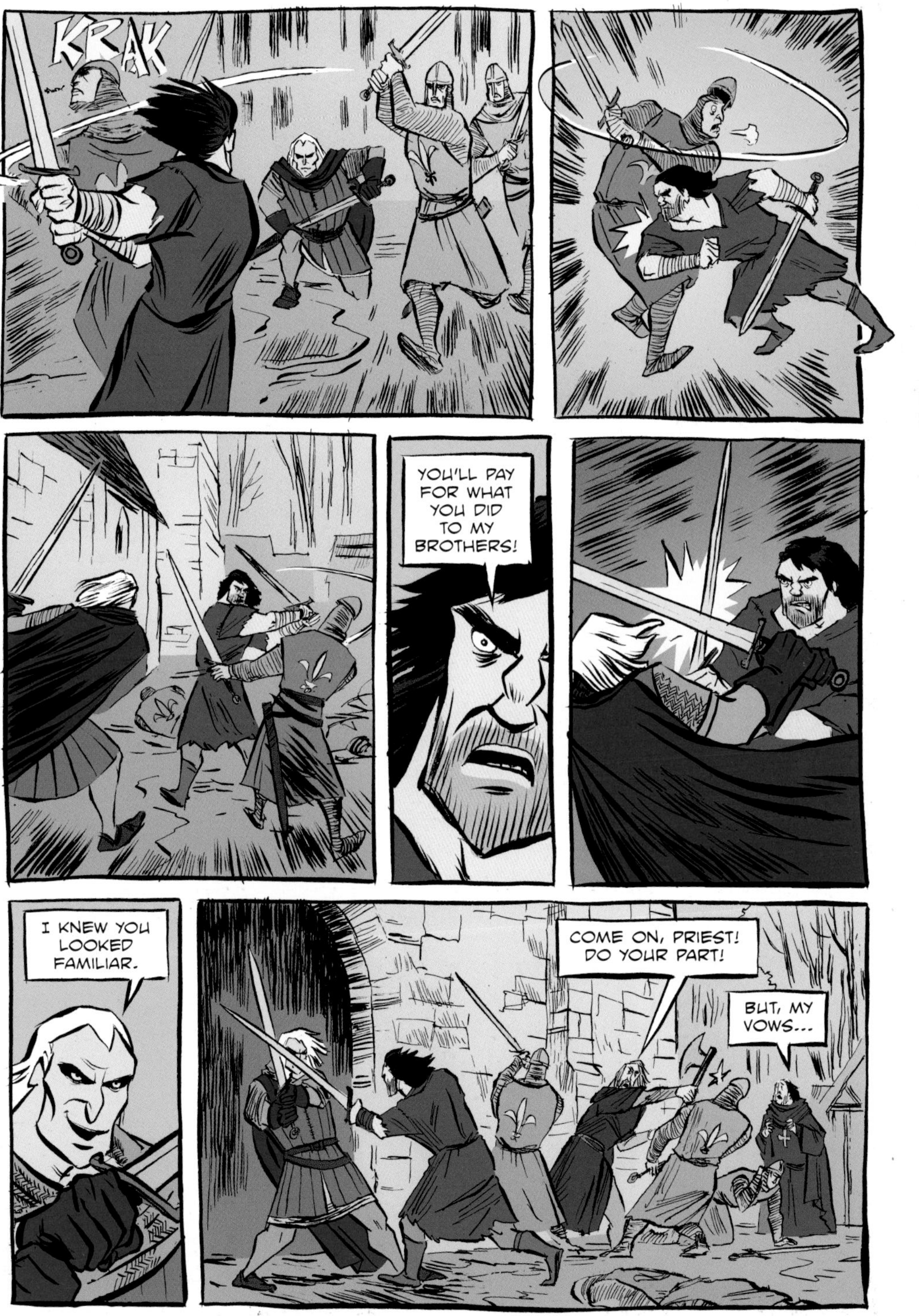
KRAK
YOU'LL PAY FOR WHAT YOU DID TO MY BROTHERS!
I KNEW YOU LOOKED FAMILIAR.
COME ON, PRIEST! DO YOUR PART!
BUT, MY VOWS...

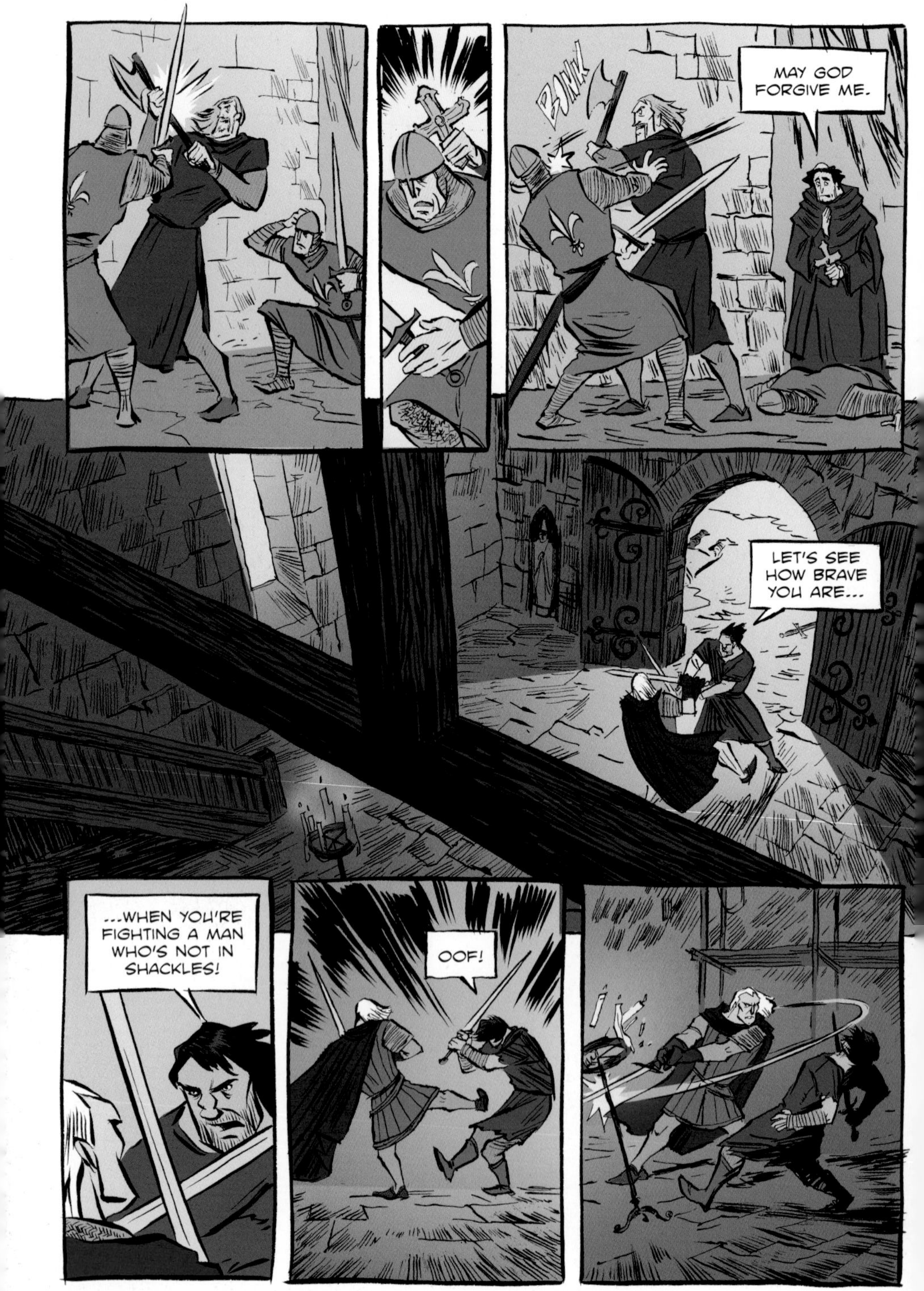
BONK
MAY GOD FORGIVE ME.
LET'S SEE HOW BRAVE YOU ARE...
...WHEN YOU'RE FIGHTING A MAN WHO'S NOT IN SHACKLES!
OOF!

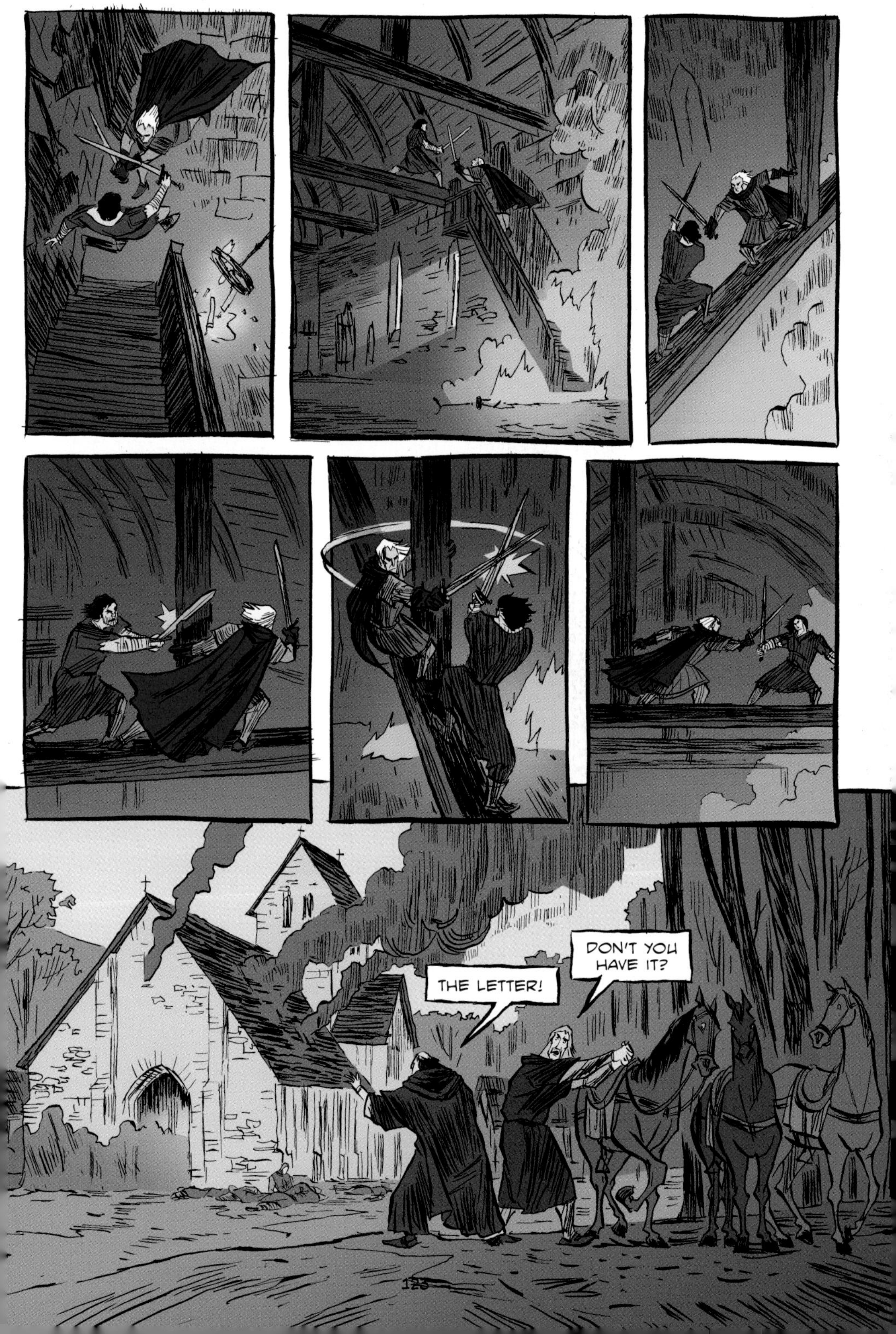
THE LETTER!
DON'T YOU HAVE IT?

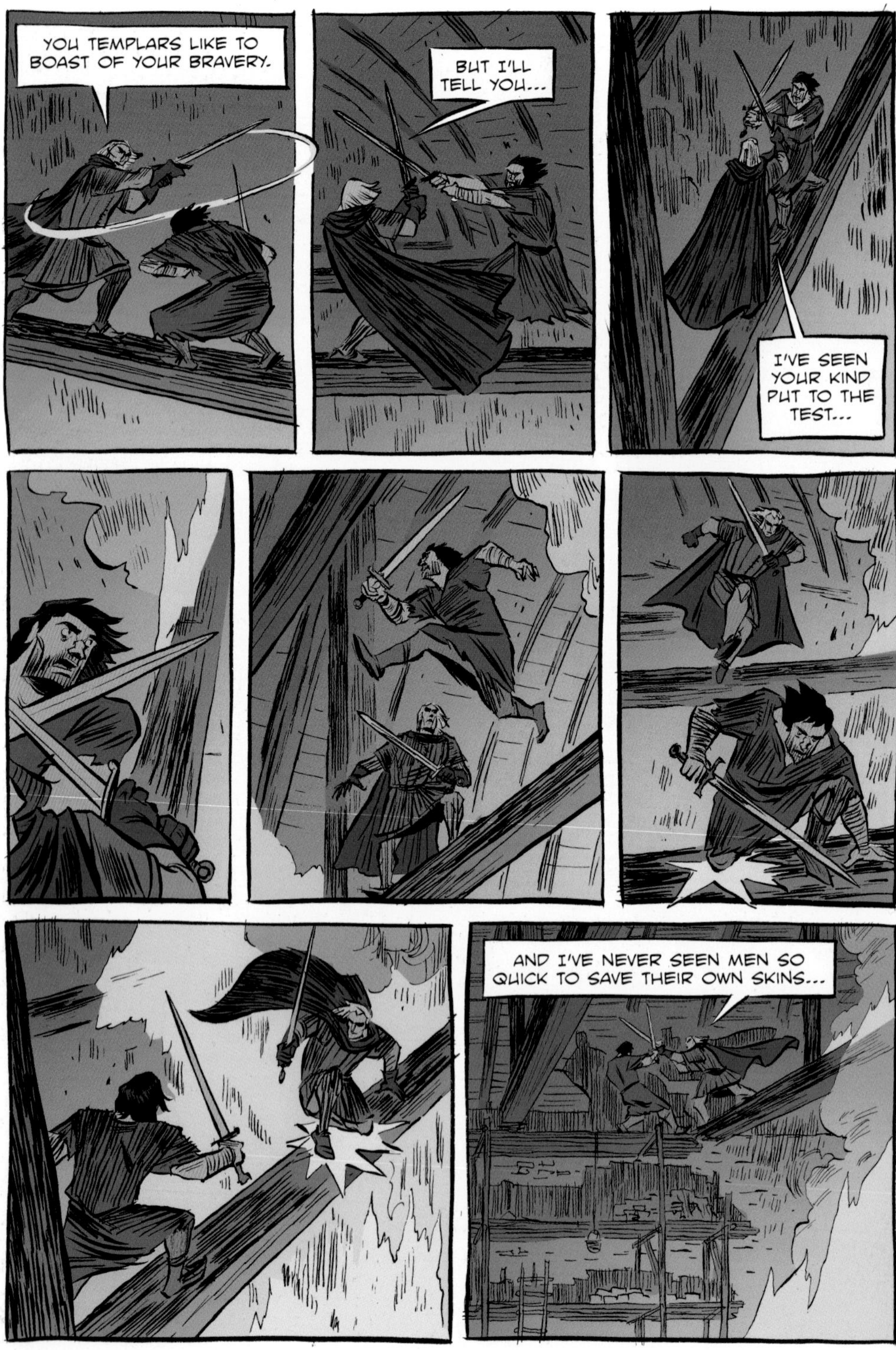
YOU TEMPLARS LIKE TO BOAST OF YOUR BRAVERY.
BUT I'LL TELL YOU...
I'VE SEEN YOUR KIND PUT TO THE TEST...
AND I'VE NEVER SEEN MEN SO QUICK TO SAVE THEIR OWN SKINS...

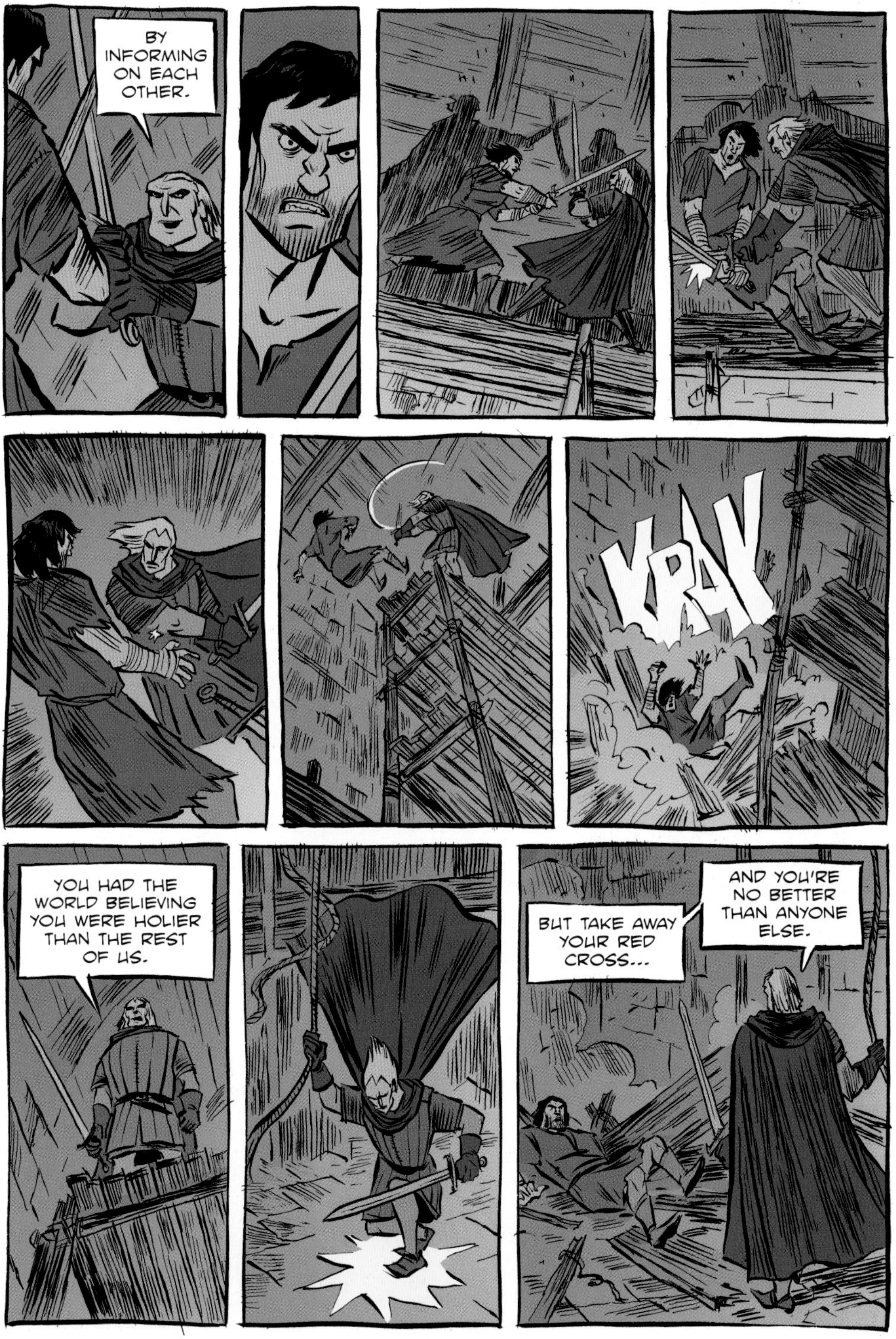
BY INFORMING ON EACH OTHER.
KRAK
YOU HAD THE WORLD BELIEVING YOU WERE HOLIER THAN THE REST OF US.
BUT TAKE AWAY YOUR RED CROSS...
AND YOU'RE NO BETTER THAN ANYONE ELSE.

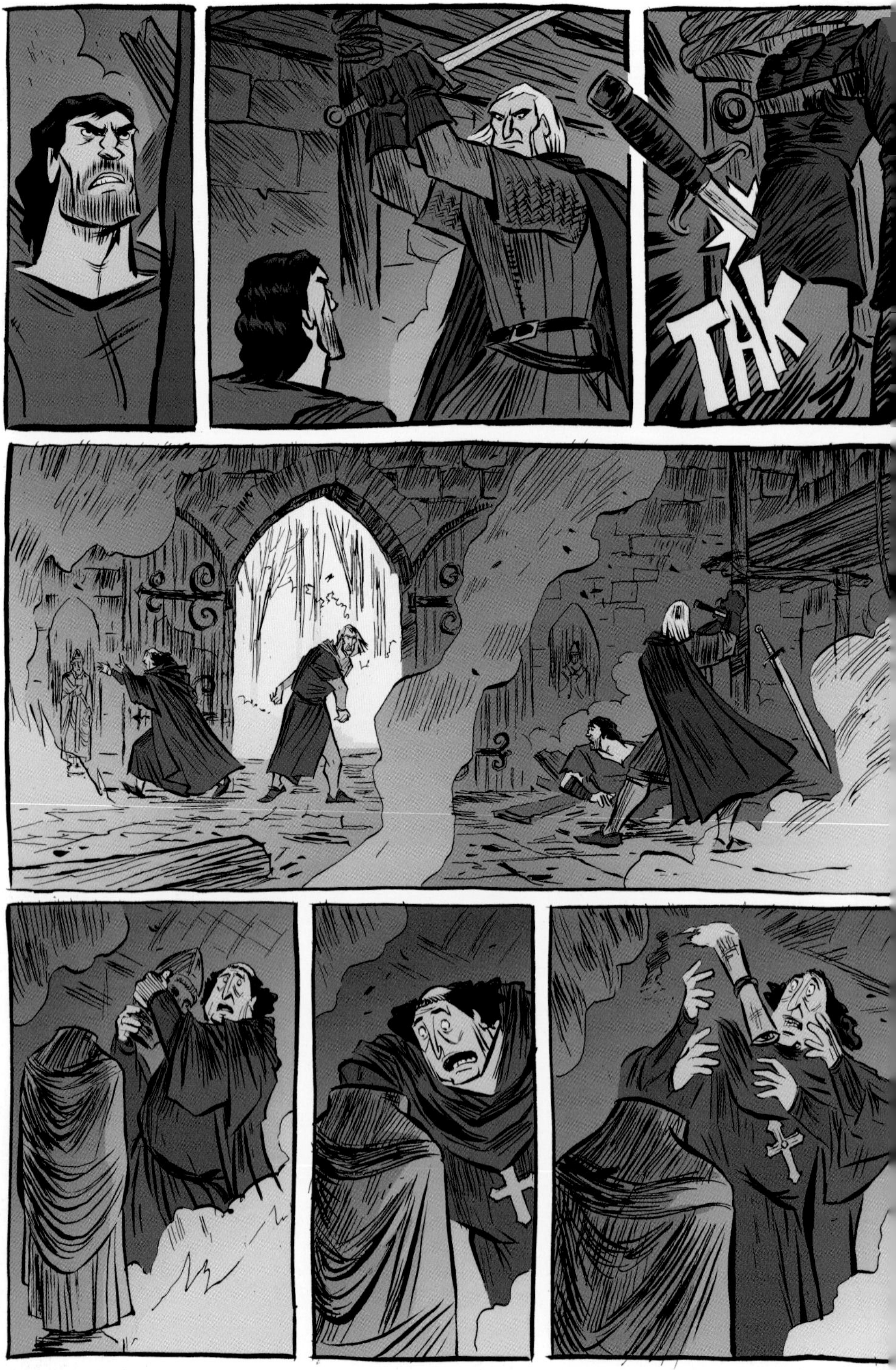
TAK

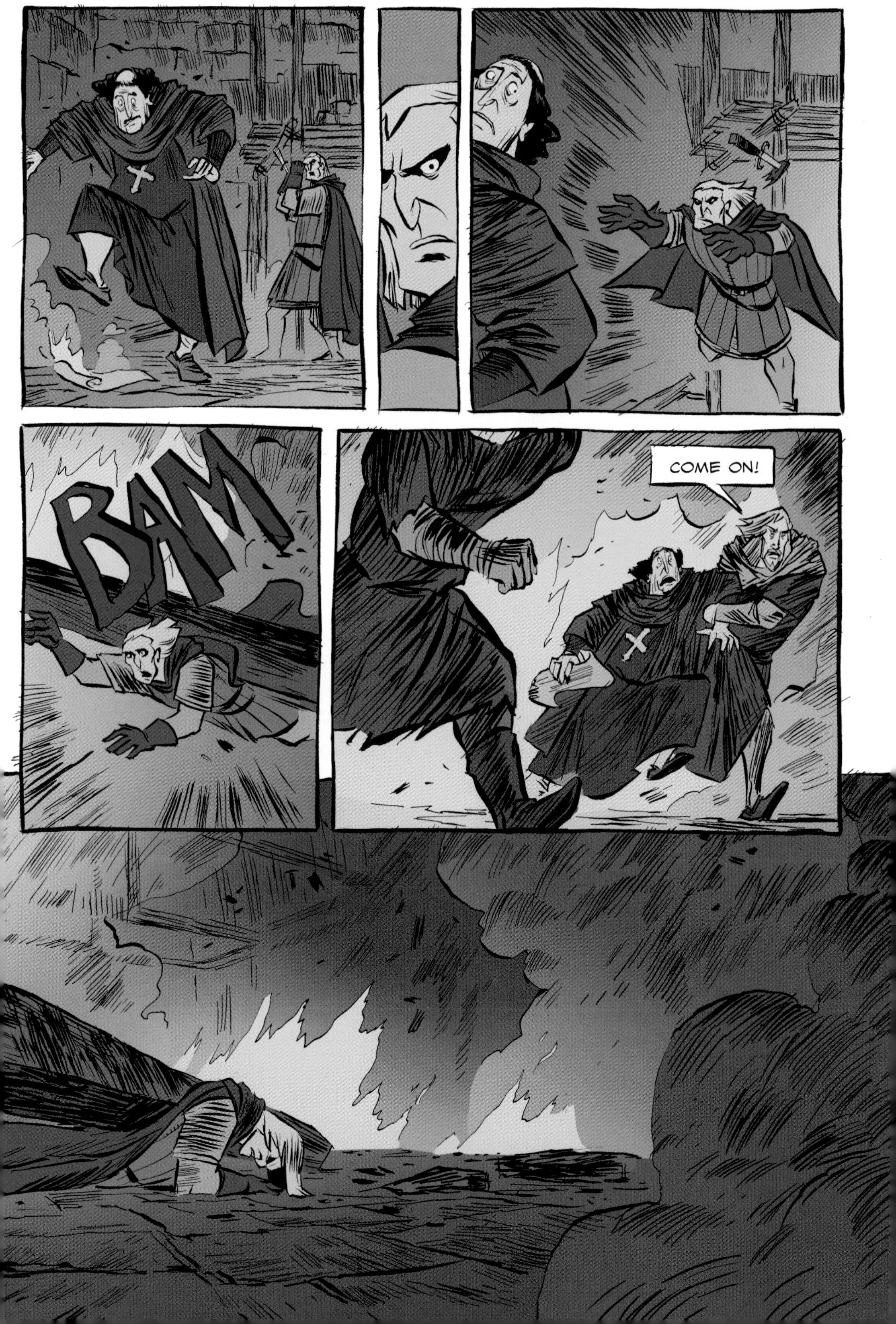
BAM
COME ON!

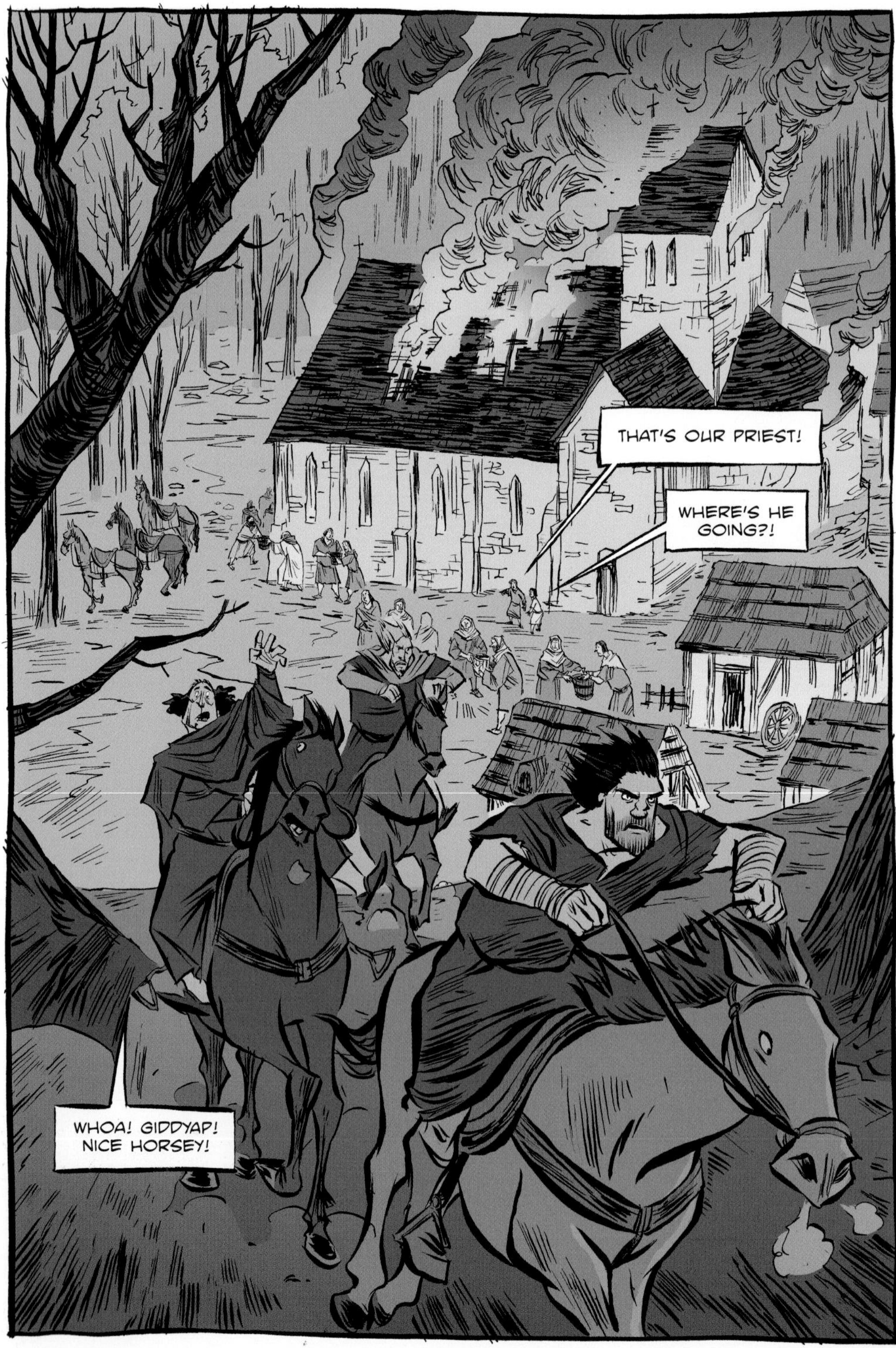
THAT'S OUR PRIEST!
WHERE'S HE GOING?!
WHOA! GIDDYAP! NICE HORSEY!

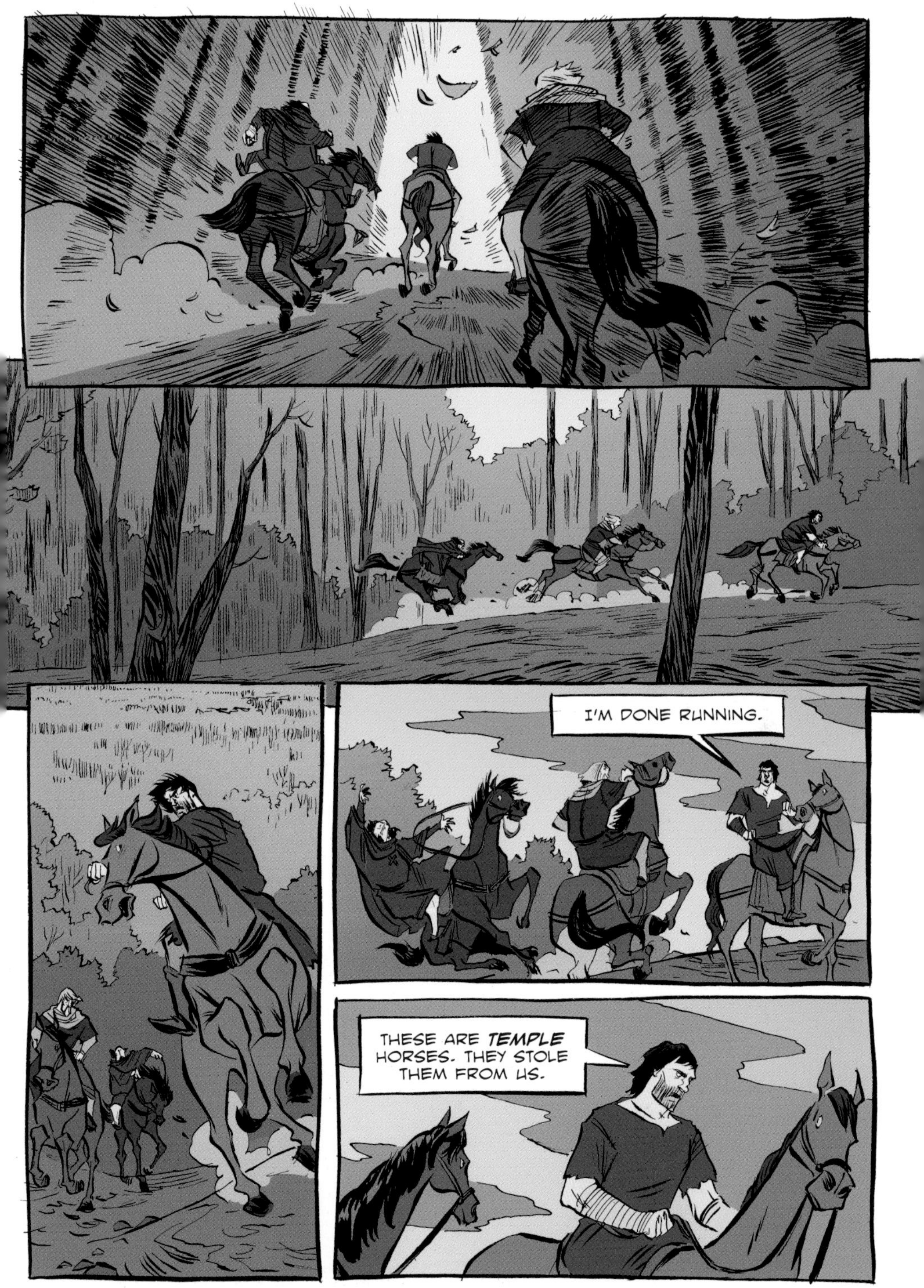
I'M DONE RUNNING.
THESE ARE *TEMPLE* HORSES. THEY STOLE THEM FROM US.

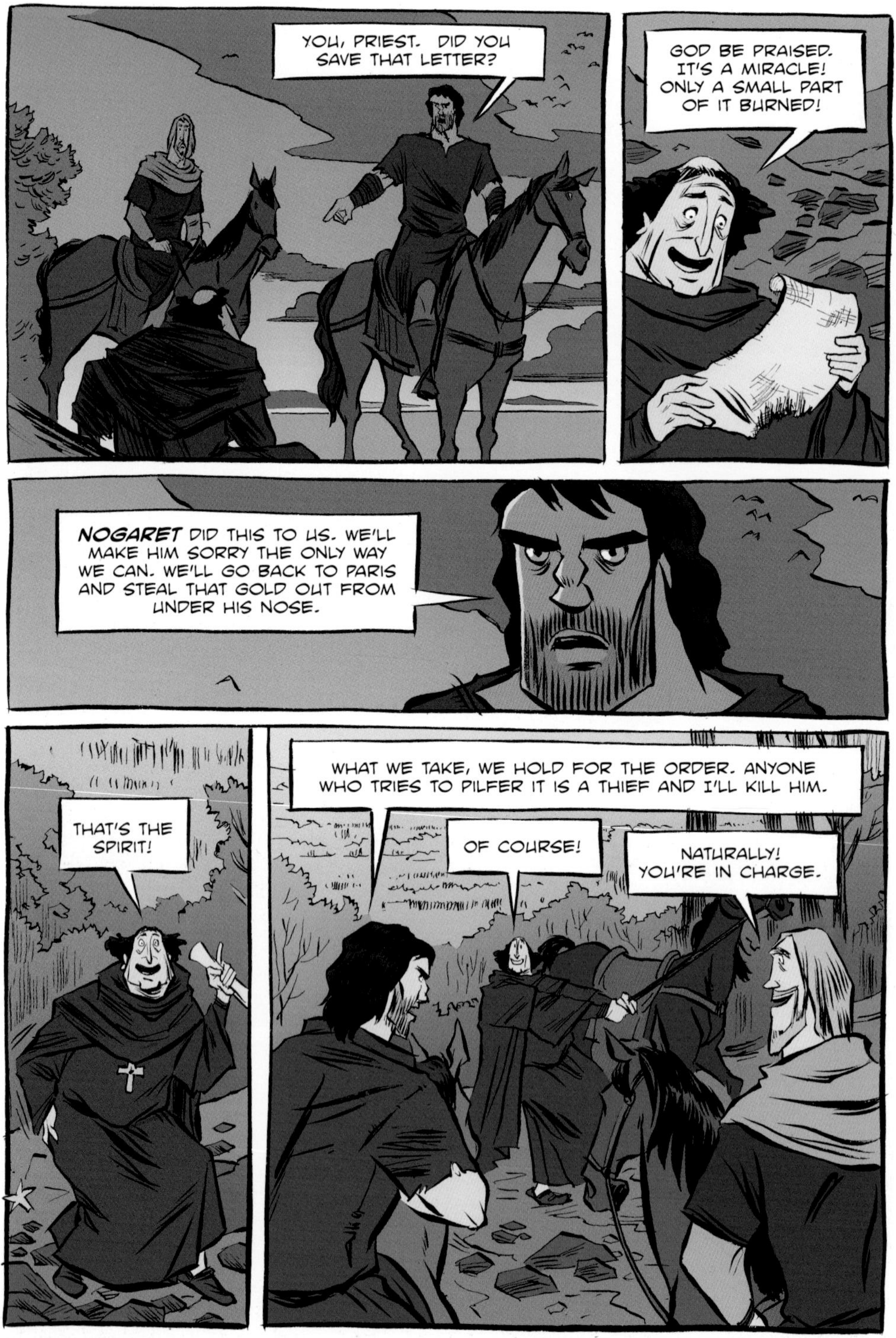
YOU, PRIEST. DID YOU SAVE THAT LETTER?
GOD BE PRAISED. IT'S A MIRACLE! ONLY A SMALL PART OF IT BURNED!
NOGARET DID THIS TO US. WE'LL MAKE HIM SORRY THE ONLY WAY WE CAN. WE'LL GO BACK TO PARIS AND STEAL THAT GOLD OUT FROM UNDER HIS NOSE.
THAT'S THE SPIRIT!
WHAT WE TAKE, WE HOLD FOR THE ORDER. ANYONE WHO TRIES TO PILFER IT IS A THIEF AND I'LL KILL HIM.
OF COURSE!
NATURALLY! YOU'RE IN CHARGE.

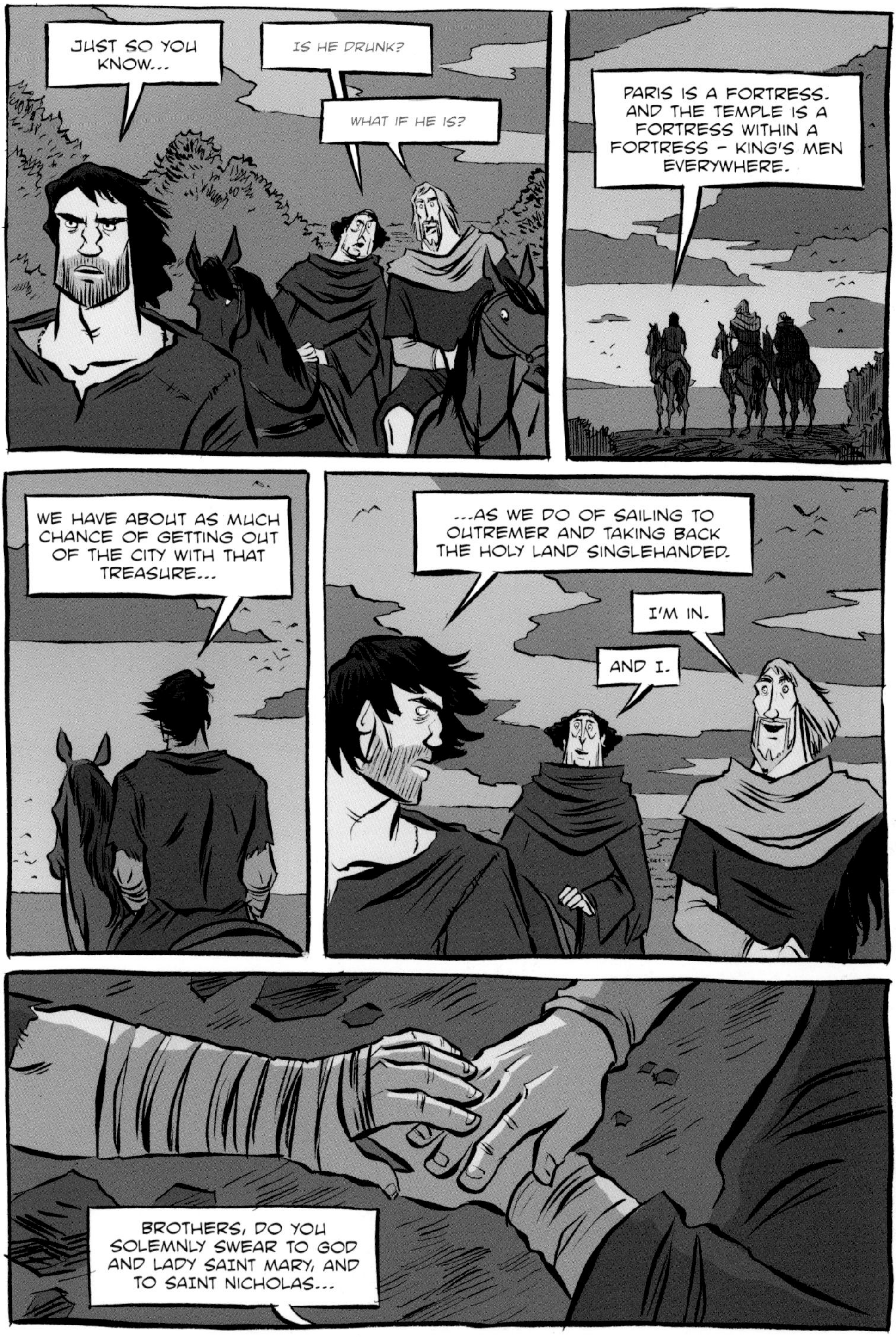

JUST SO YOU KNOW...
IS HE DRUNK?
WHAT IF HE IS?
PARIS IS A FORTRESS. AND THE TEMPLE IS A FORTRESS WITHIN A FORTRESS - KING'S MEN EVERYWHERE.
WE HAVE ABOUT AS MUCH CHANCE OF GETTING OUT OF THE CITY WITH THAT TREASURE...
...AS WE DO OF SAILING TO OUTREMER AND TAKING BACK THE HOLY LAND SINGLEHANDED.
I'M IN.
AND I.
BROTHERS, DO YOU SOLEMNLY SWEAR TO GOD AND LADY SAINT MARY, AND TO SAINT NICHOLAS...

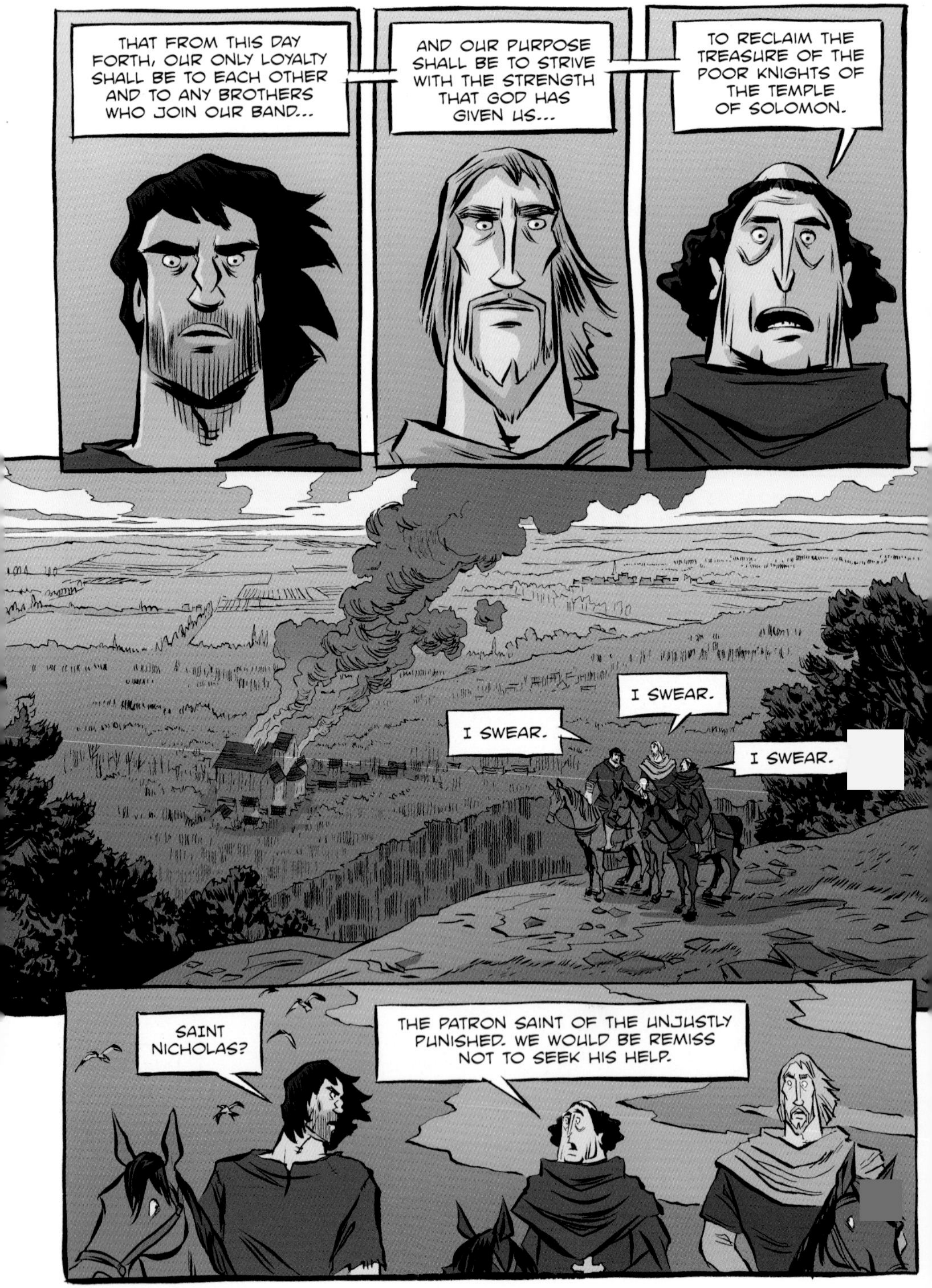
THAT FROM THIS DAY FORTH, OUR ONLY LOYALTY SHALL BE TO EACH OTHER AND TO ANY BROTHERS WHO JOIN OUR BAND...
AND OUR PURPOSE SHALL BE TO STRIVE WITH THE STRENGTH THAT GOD HAS GIVEN US...
TO RECLAIM THE TREASURE OF THE POOR KNIGHTS OF THE TEMPLE OF SOLOMON.
I SWEAR.
I SWEAR.
I SWEAR.
SAINT NICHOLAS?
THE PATRON SAINT OF THE UNJUSTLY PUNISHED. WE WOULD BE REMISS NOT TO SEEK HIS HELP.

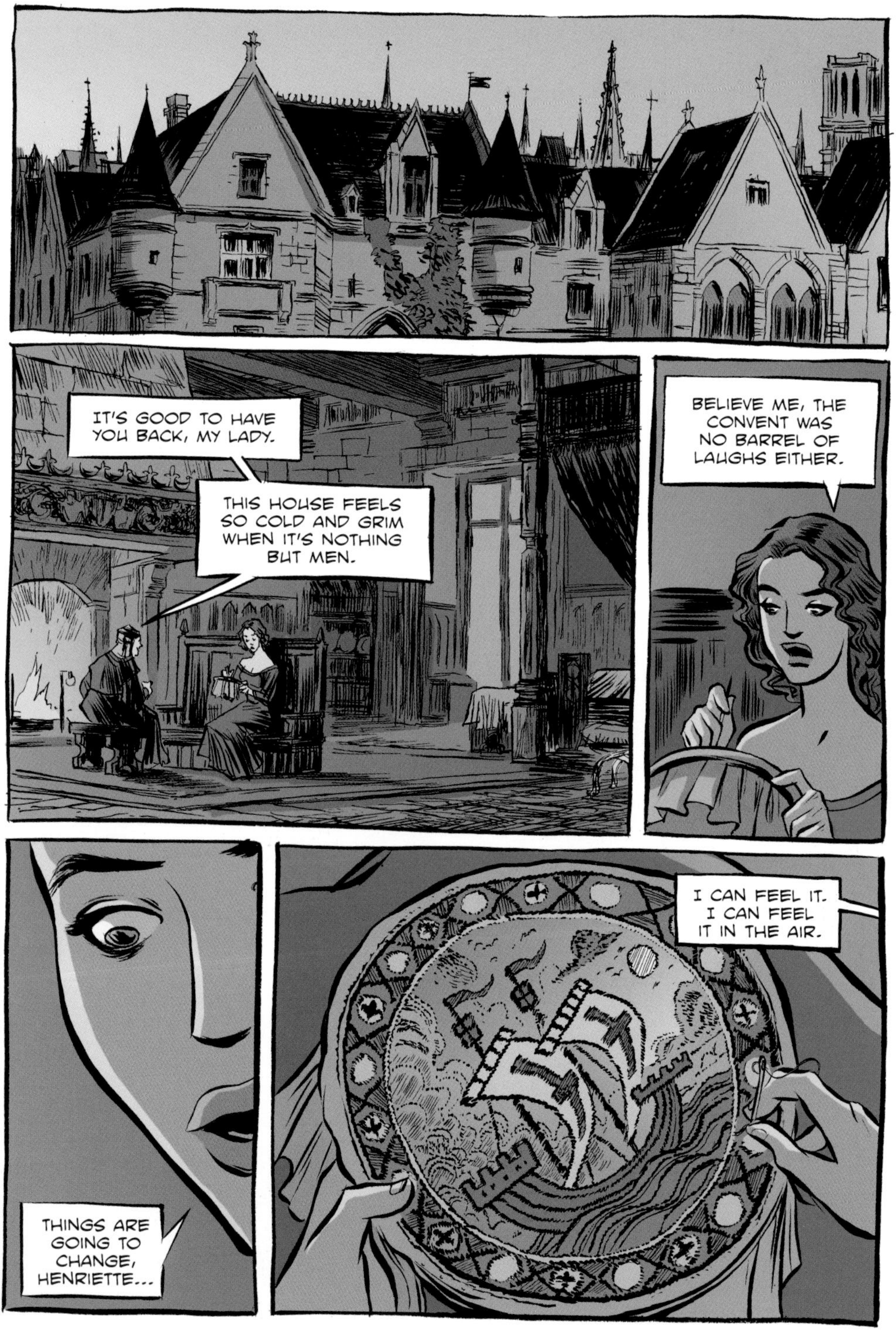
IT'S GOOD TO HAVE YOU BACK, MY LADY.
THIS HOUSE FEELS SO COLD AND GRIM WHEN IT'S NOTHING BUT MEN.
BELIEVE ME, THE CONVENT WAS NO BARREL OF LAUGHS EITHER.
THINGS ARE GOING TO CHANGE, HENRIETTE...
I CAN FEEL IT. I CAN FEEL IT IN THE AIR.

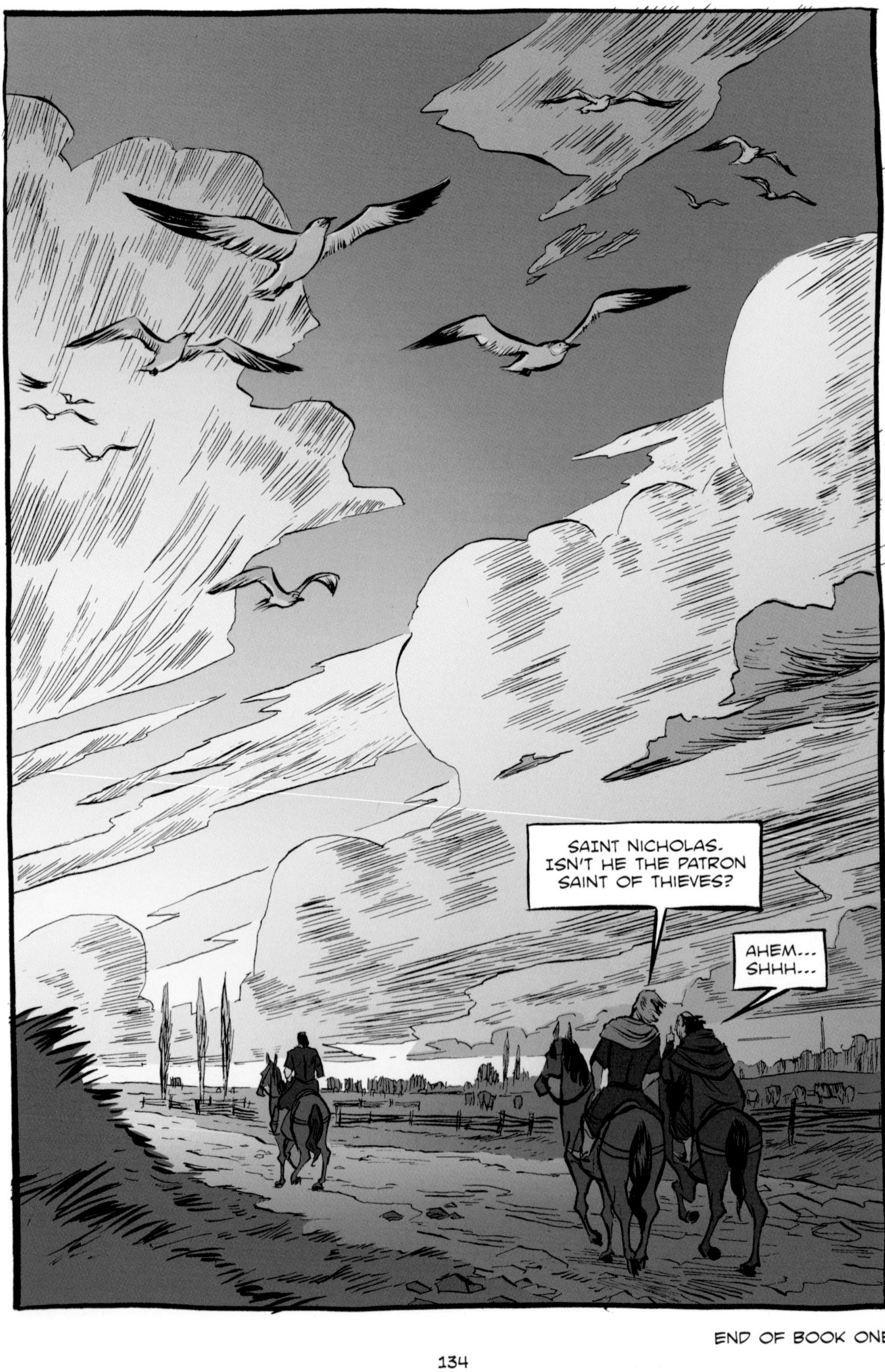
SAINT NICHOLAS. ISN'T HE THE PATRON SAINT OF THIEVES?
AHEM... SHHH...

END OF BOOK ONE

Book Two • The Bishops

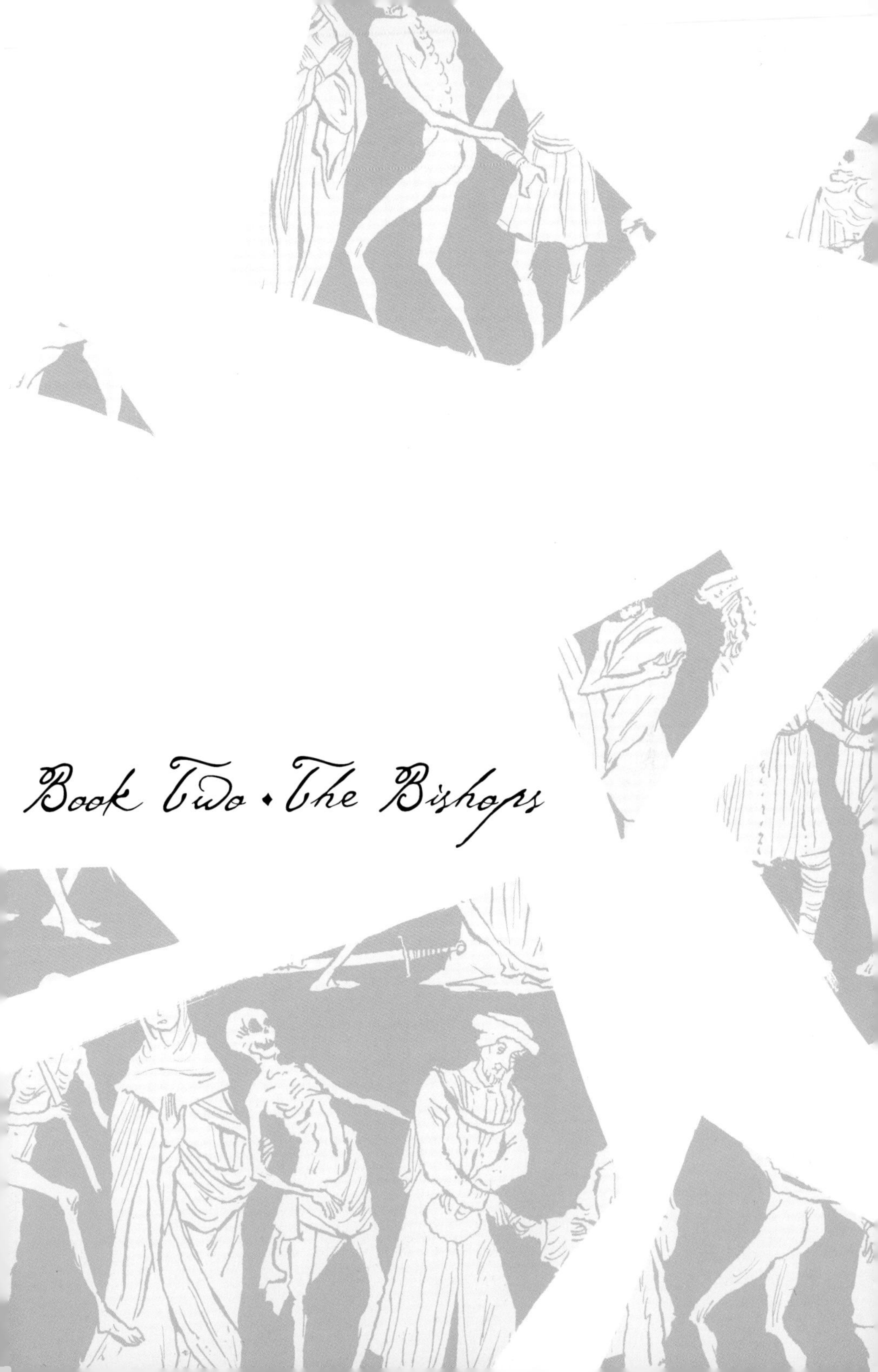

4. The Fortress

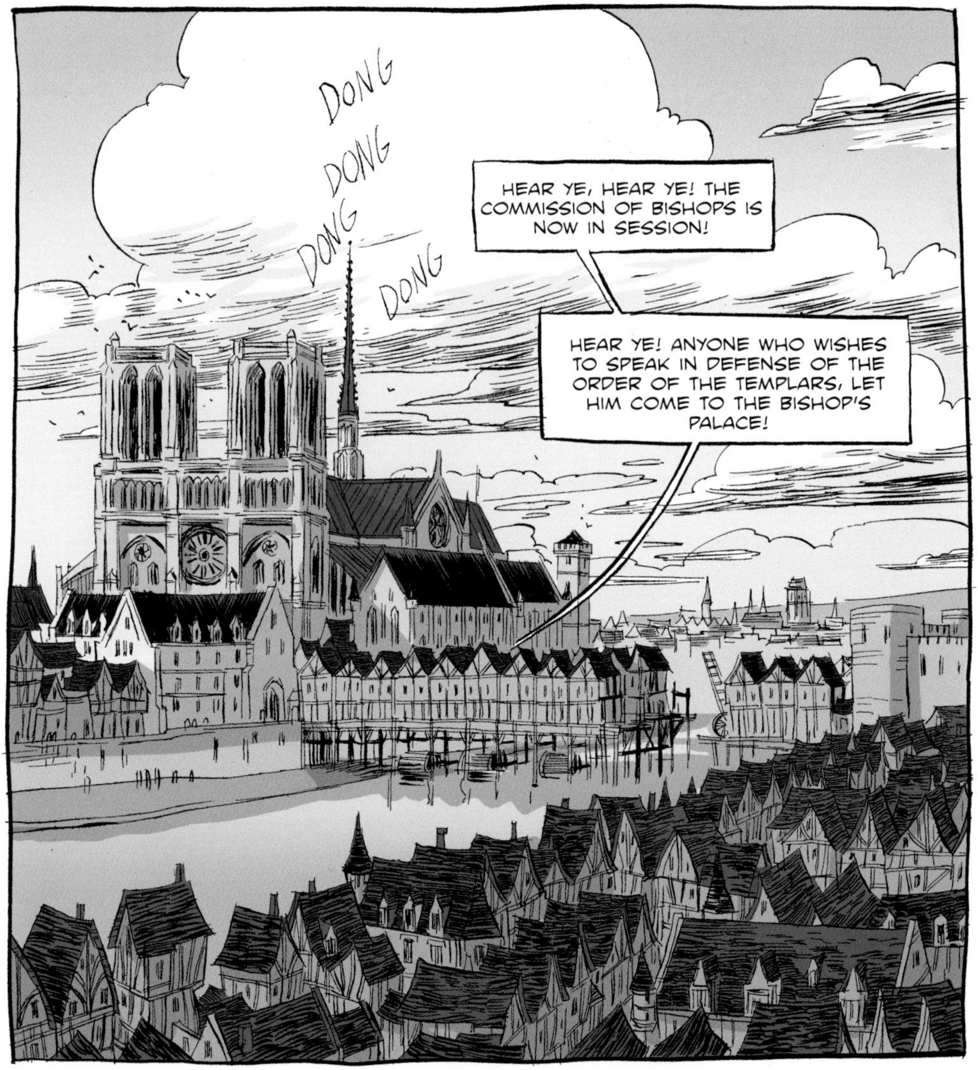
DONG
DONG
DONG
DONG
HEAR YE, HEAR YE! THE COMMISSION OF BISHOPS IS NOW IN SESSION!
HEAR YE! ANYONE WHO WISHES TO SPEAK IN DEFENSE OF THE ORDER OF THE TEMPLARS, LET HIM COME TO THE BISHOP'S PALACE!

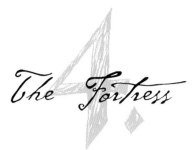

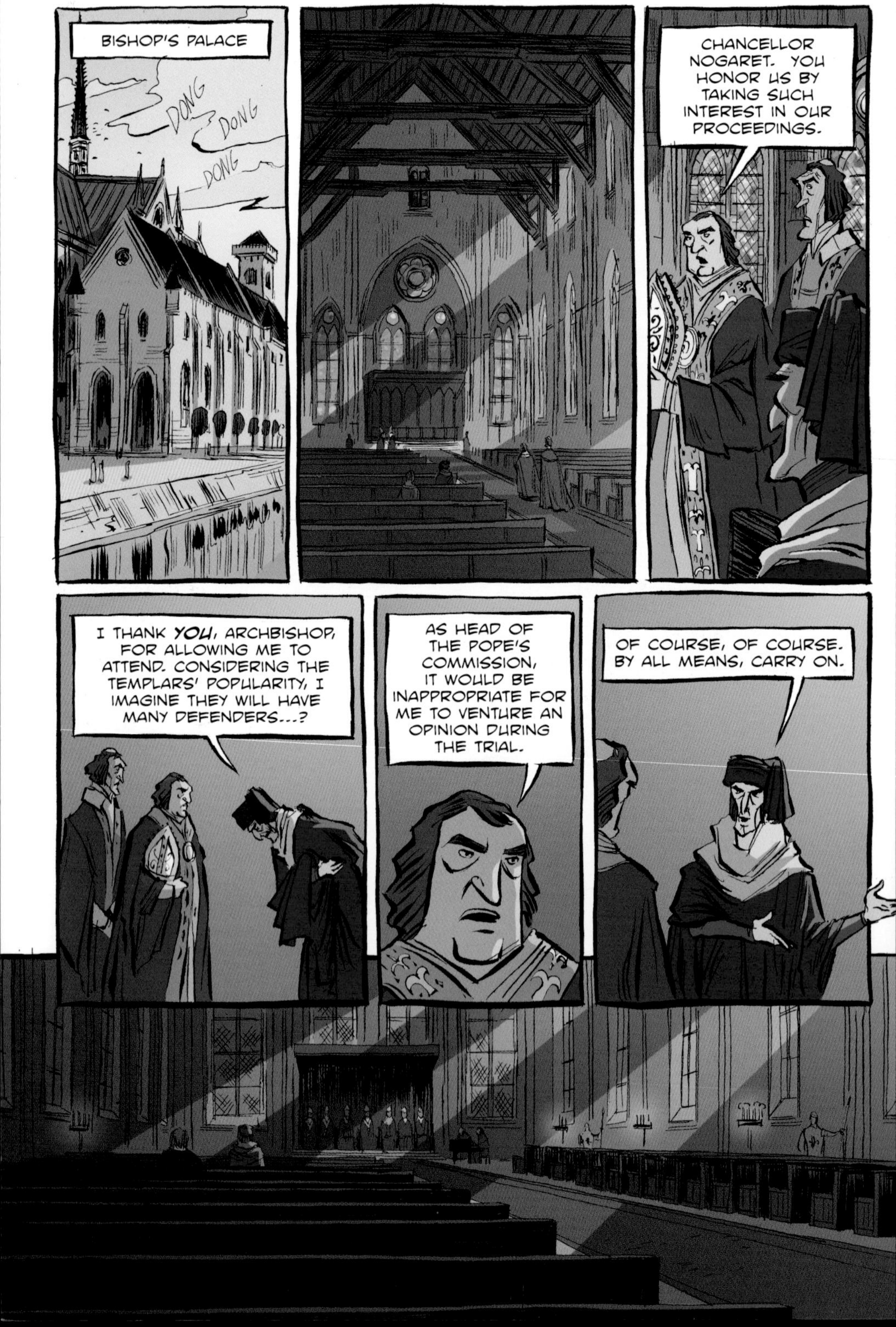
BISHOP'S PALACE
DONG DONG DONG
CHANCELLOR NOGARET. YOU HONOR US BY TAKING SUCH INTEREST IN OUR PROCEEDINGS.
I THANK YOU, ARCHBISHOP, FOR ALLOWING ME TO ATTEND. CONSIDERING THE TEMPLARS' POPULARITY, I IMAGINE THEY WILL HAVE MANY DEFENDERS...?
AS HEAD OF THE POPE'S COMMISSION, IT WOULD BE INAPPROPRIATE FOR ME TO VENTURE AN OPINION DURING THE TRIAL.
OF COURSE, OF COURSE. BY ALL MEANS, CARRY ON.

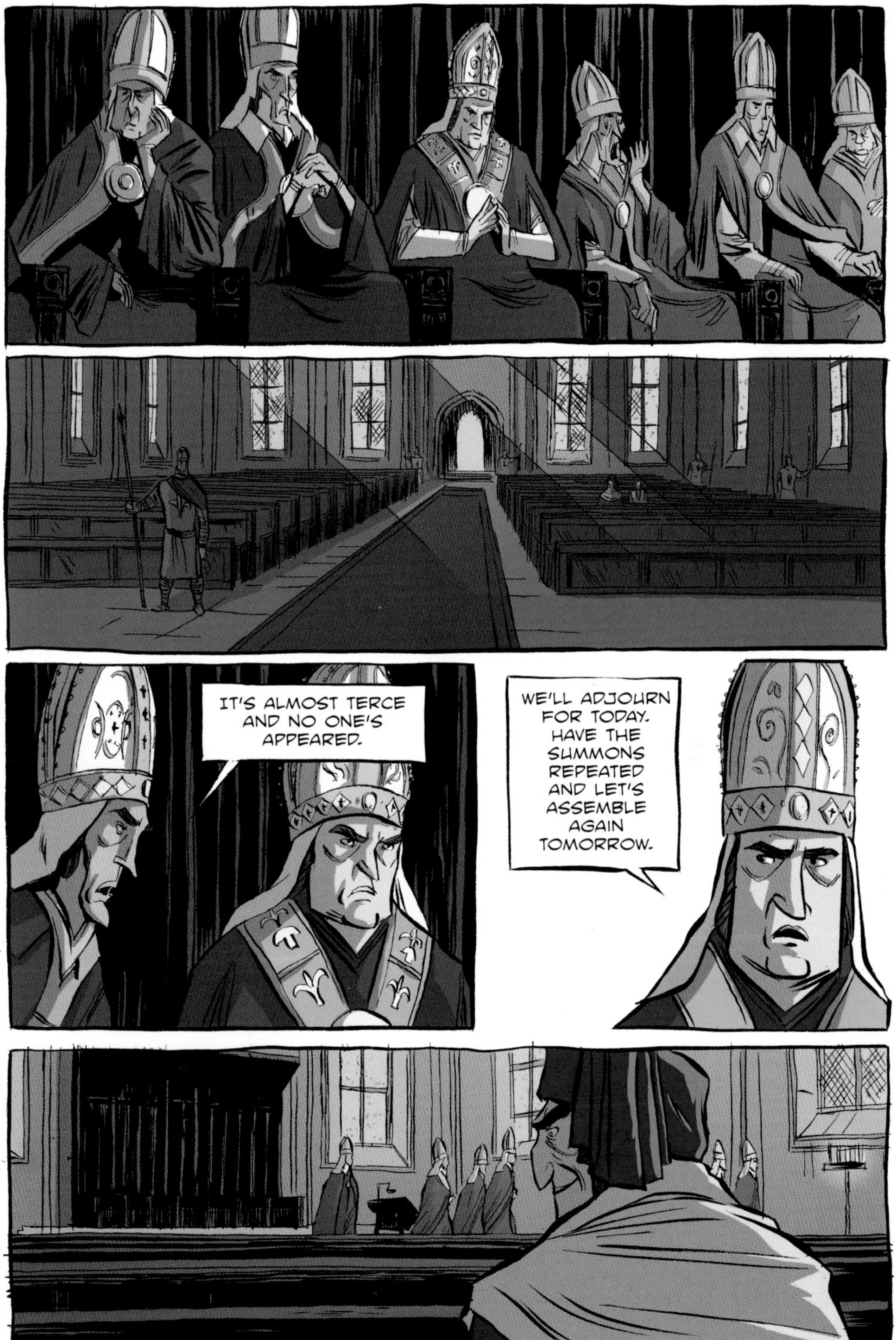
IT'S ALMOST TERCE AND NO ONE'S APPEARED.
WE'LL ADJOURN FOR TODAY. HAVE THE SUMMONS REPEATED AND LET'S ASSEMBLE AGAIN TOMORROW.

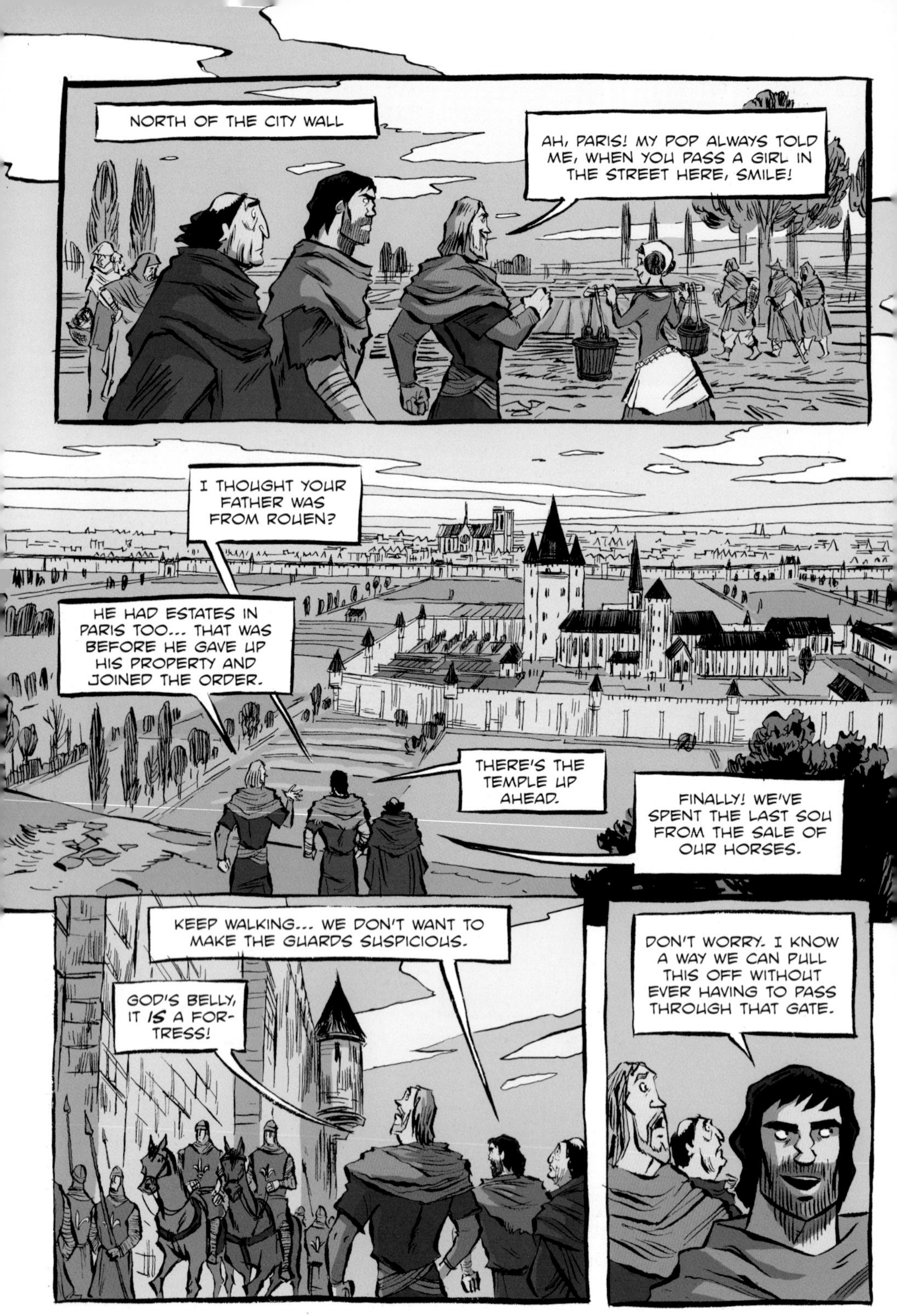
NORTH OF THE CITY WALL
AH, PARIS! MY POP ALWAYS TOLD ME, WHEN YOU PASS A GIRL IN THE STREET HERE, SMILE!
I THOUGHT YOUR FATHER WAS FROM ROUEN?
HE HAD ESTATES IN PARIS TOO... THAT WAS BEFORE HE GAVE UP HIS PROPERTY AND JOINED THE ORDER.
THERE'S THE TEMPLE UP AHEAD.
FINALLY! WE'VE SPENT THE LAST SOU FROM THE SALE OF OUR HORSES.
KEEP WALKING... WE DON'T WANT TO MAKE THE GUARDS SUSPICIOUS.
GOD'S BELLY, IT *IS* A FORTRESS!
DON'T WORRY. I KNOW A WAY WE CAN PULL THIS OFF WITHOUT EVER HAVING TO PASS THROUGH THAT GATE.

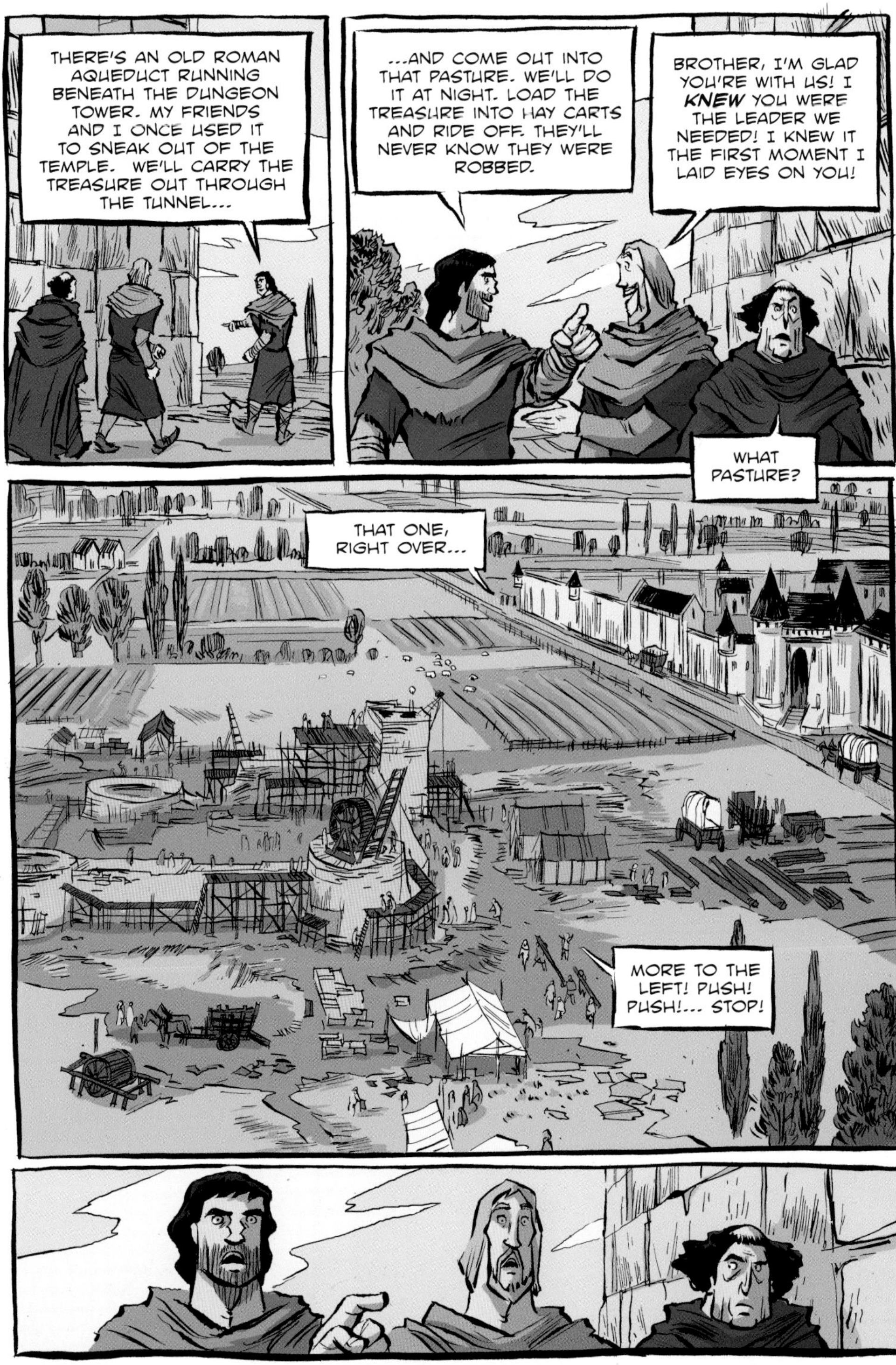
THERE'S AN OLD ROMAN AQUEDUCT RUNNING BENEATH THE DUNGEON TOWER. MY FRIENDS AND I ONCE USED IT TO SNEAK OUT OF THE TEMPLE. WE'LL CARRY THE TREASURE OUT THROUGH THE TUNNEL...
...AND COME OUT INTO THAT PASTURE. WE'LL DO IT AT NIGHT. LOAD THE TREASURE INTO HAY CARTS AND RIDE OFF. THEY'LL NEVER KNOW THEY WERE ROBBED.
BROTHER, I'M GLAD YOU'RE WITH US! I **KNEW** YOU WERE THE LEADER WE NEEDED! I KNEW IT THE FIRST MOMENT I LAID EYES ON YOU!
WHAT PASTURE?
THAT ONE, RIGHT OVER...
MORE TO THE LEFT! PUSH! PUSH!... STOP!

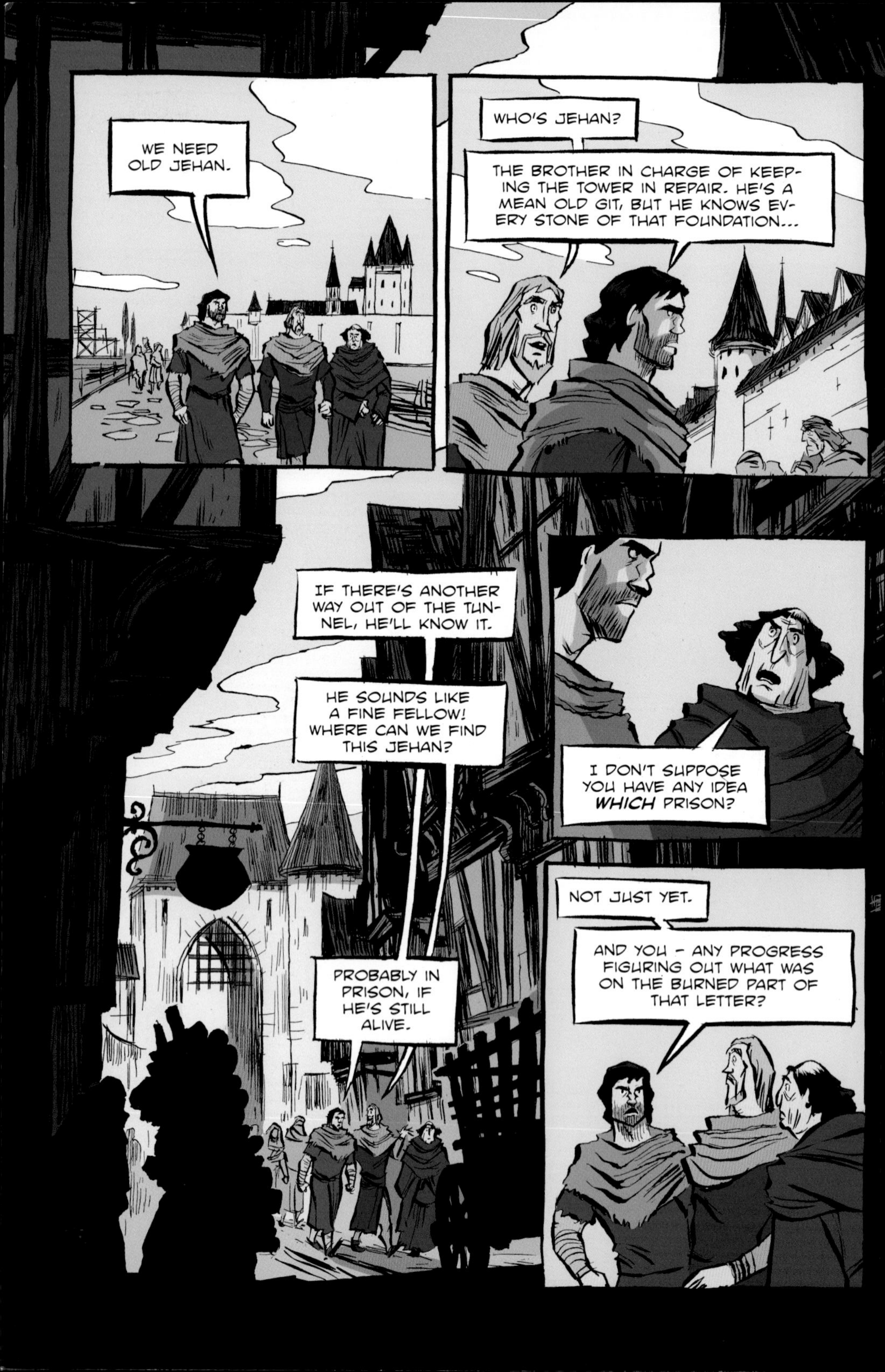
WE NEED OLD JEHAN.
WHO'S JEHAN?
THE BROTHER IN CHARGE OF KEEPING THE TOWER IN REPAIR. HE'S A MEAN OLD GIT, BUT HE KNOWS EVERY STONE OF THAT FOUNDATION...
IF THERE'S ANOTHER WAY OUT OF THE TUNNEL, HE'LL KNOW IT.
HE SOUNDS LIKE A FINE FELLOW! WHERE CAN WE FIND THIS JEHAN?
PROBABLY IN PRISON, IF HE'S STILL ALIVE.
I DON'T SUPPOSE YOU HAVE ANY IDEA *WHICH* PRISON?
NOT JUST YET.
AND YOU - ANY PROGRESS FIGURING OUT WHAT WAS ON THE BURNED PART OF THAT LETTER?

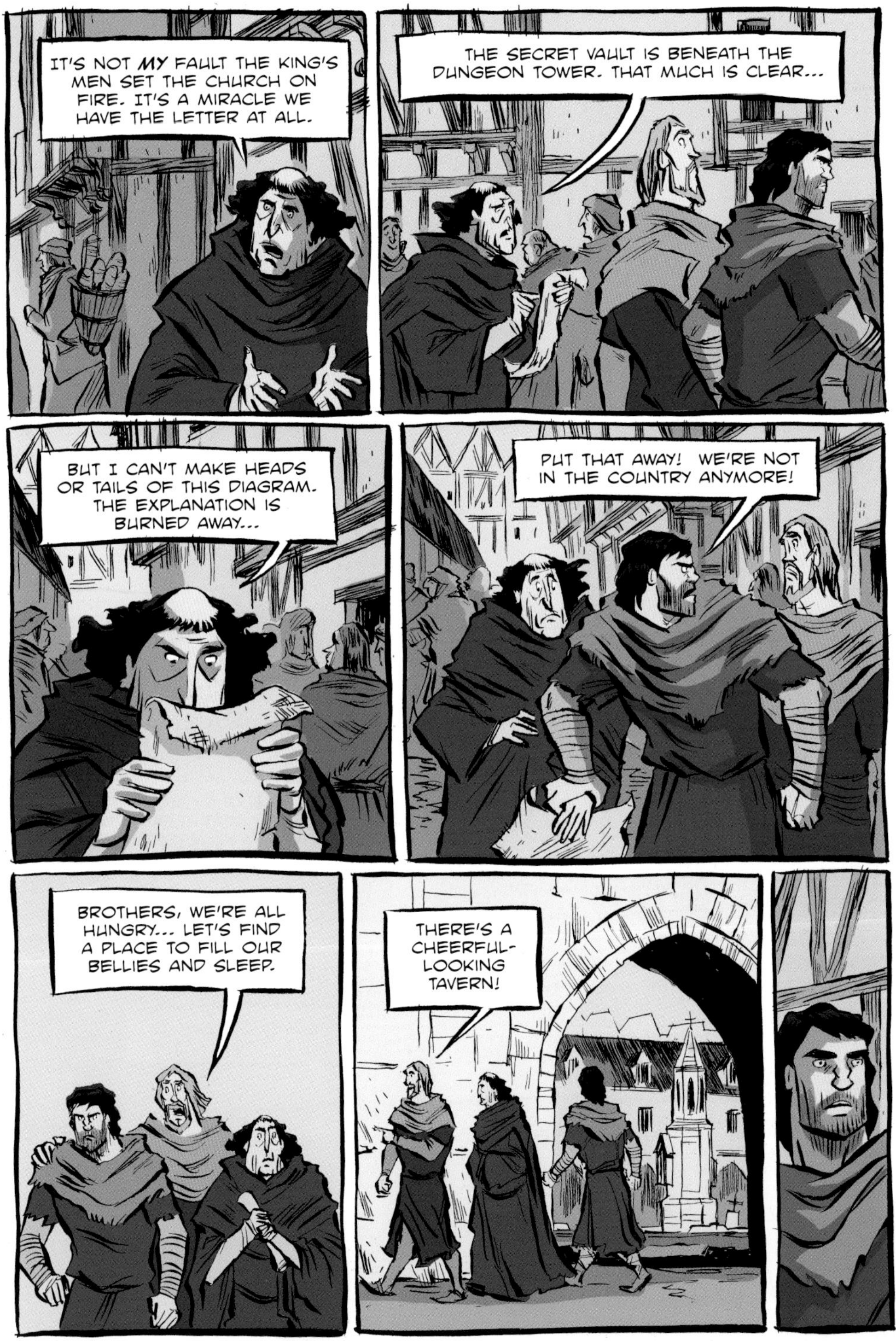

IT'S NOT *MY* FAULT THE KING'S MEN SET THE CHURCH ON FIRE. IT'S A MIRACLE WE HAVE THE LETTER AT ALL.
THE SECRET VAULT IS BENEATH THE DUNGEON TOWER. THAT MUCH IS CLEAR...
BUT I CAN'T MAKE HEADS OR TAILS OF THIS DIAGRAM. THE EXPLANATION IS BURNED AWAY...
PUT THAT AWAY! WE'RE NOT IN THE COUNTRY ANYMORE!
BROTHERS, WE'RE ALL HUNGRY... LET'S FIND A PLACE TO FILL OUR BELLIES AND SLEEP.
THERE'S A CHEERFUL-LOOKING TAVERN!

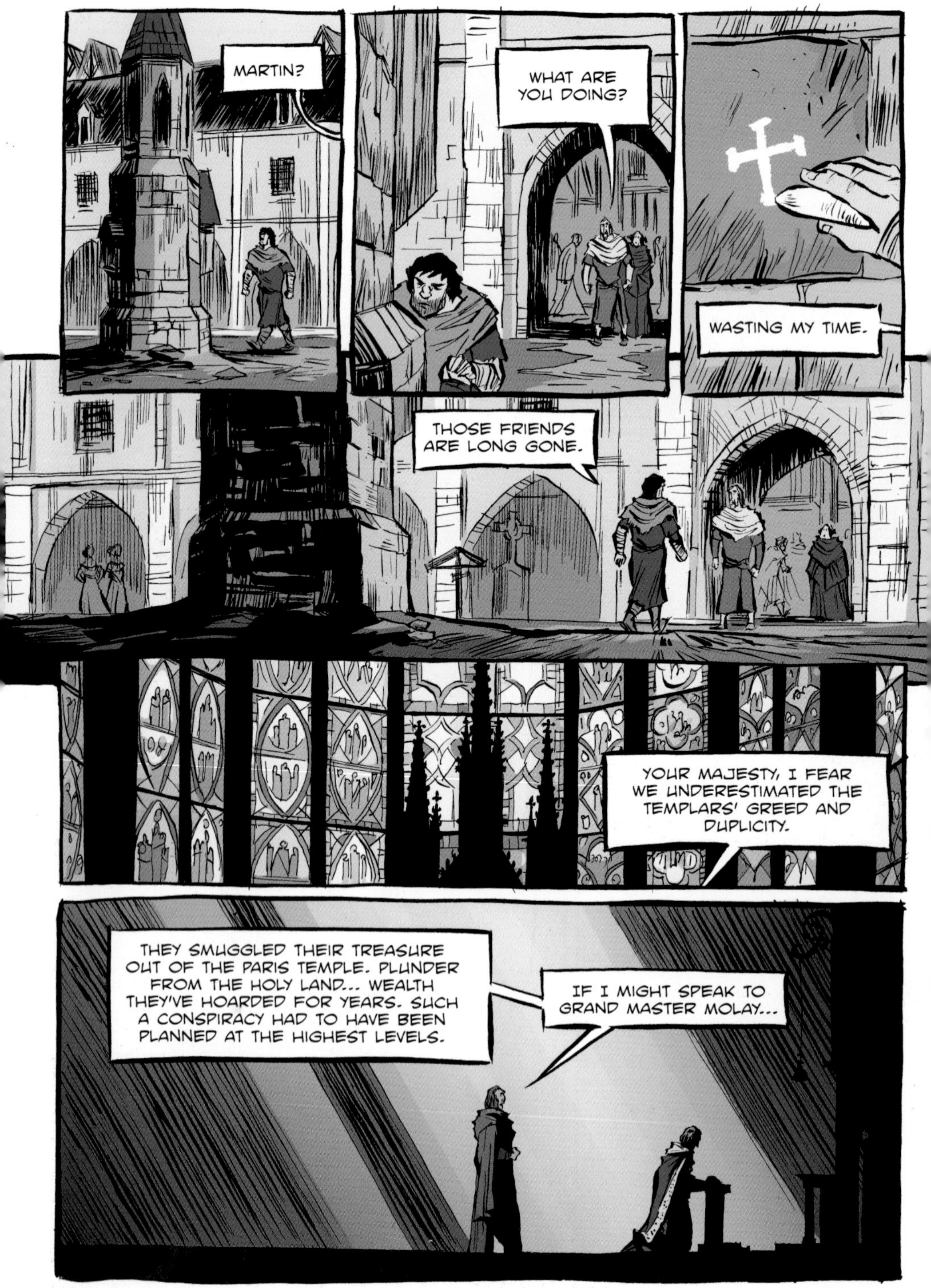
MARTIN?
WHAT ARE YOU DOING?
WASTING MY TIME.
THOSE FRIENDS ARE LONG GONE.
YOUR MAJESTY, I FEAR WE UNDERESTIMATED THE TEMPLARS' GREED AND DUPLICITY.
THEY SMUGGLED THEIR TREASURE OUT OF THE PARIS TEMPLE. PLUNDER FROM THE HOLY LAND... WEALTH THEY'VE HOARDED FOR YEARS. SUCH A CONSPIRACY HAD TO HAVE BEEN PLANNED AT THE HIGHEST LEVELS.
IF I MIGHT SPEAK TO GRAND MASTER MOLAY...

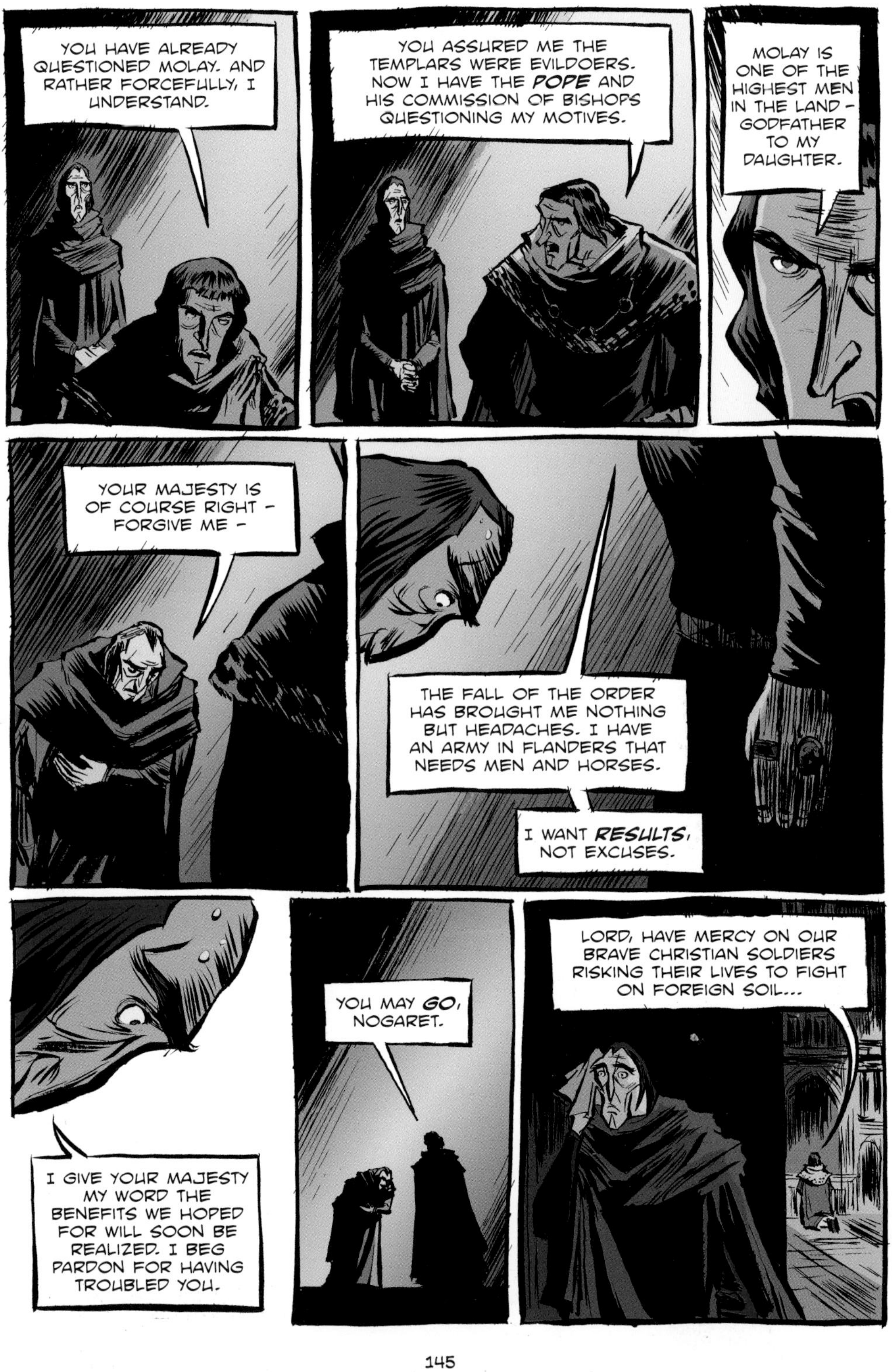
YOU HAVE ALREADY QUESTIONED MOLAY. AND RATHER FORCEFULLY, I UNDERSTAND.
YOU ASSURED ME THE TEMPLARS WERE EVILDOERS. NOW I HAVE THE **POPE** AND HIS COMMISSION OF BISHOPS QUESTIONING MY MOTIVES.
MOLAY IS ONE OF THE HIGHEST MEN IN THE LAND - GODFATHER TO MY DAUGHTER.
YOUR MAJESTY IS OF COURSE RIGHT - FORGIVE ME -
THE FALL OF THE ORDER HAS BROUGHT ME NOTHING BUT HEADACHES. I HAVE AN ARMY IN FLANDERS THAT NEEDS MEN AND HORSES.
I WANT **RESULTS**, NOT EXCUSES.
I GIVE YOUR MAJESTY MY WORD THE BENEFITS WE HOPED FOR WILL SOON BE REALIZED. I BEG PARDON FOR HAVING TROUBLED YOU.
YOU MAY **GO**, NOGARET.
LORD, HAVE MERCY ON OUR BRAVE CHRISTIAN SOLDIERS RISKING THEIR LIVES TO FIGHT ON FOREIGN SOIL...

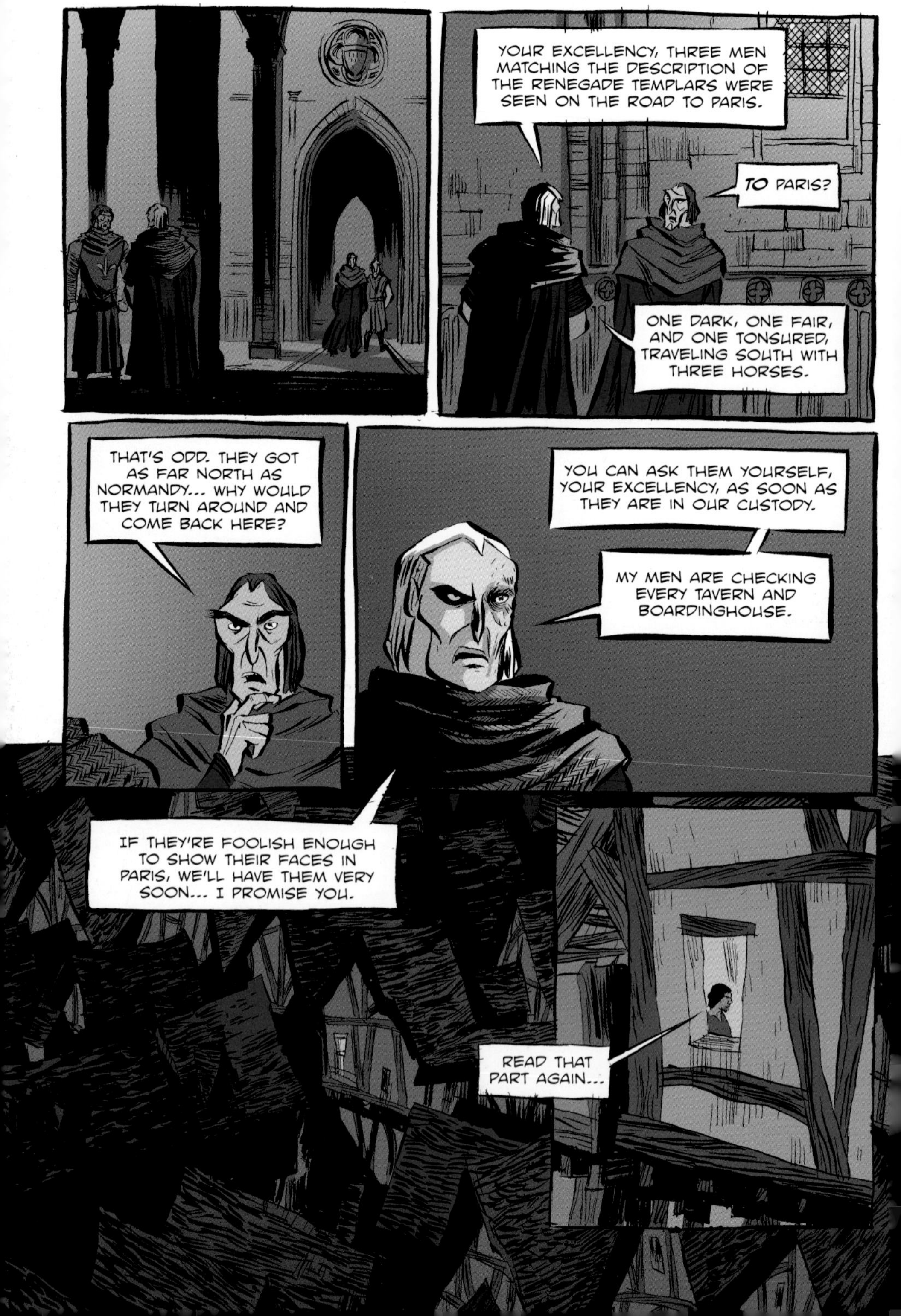
YOUR EXCELLENCY, THREE MEN MATCHING THE DESCRIPTION OF THE RENEGADE TEMPLARS WERE SEEN ON THE ROAD TO PARIS.
TO PARIS?
ONE DARK, ONE FAIR, AND ONE TONSURED, TRAVELING SOUTH WITH THREE HORSES.
THAT'S ODD. THEY GOT AS FAR NORTH AS NORMANDY... WHY WOULD THEY TURN AROUND AND COME BACK HERE?
YOU CAN ASK THEM YOURSELF, YOUR EXCELLENCY, AS SOON AS THEY ARE IN OUR CUSTODY.
MY MEN ARE CHECKING EVERY TAVERN AND BOARDINGHOUSE.
IF THEY'RE FOOLISH ENOUGH TO SHOW THEIR FACES IN PARIS, WE'LL HAVE THEM VERY SOON... I PROMISE YOU.
READ THAT PART AGAIN...

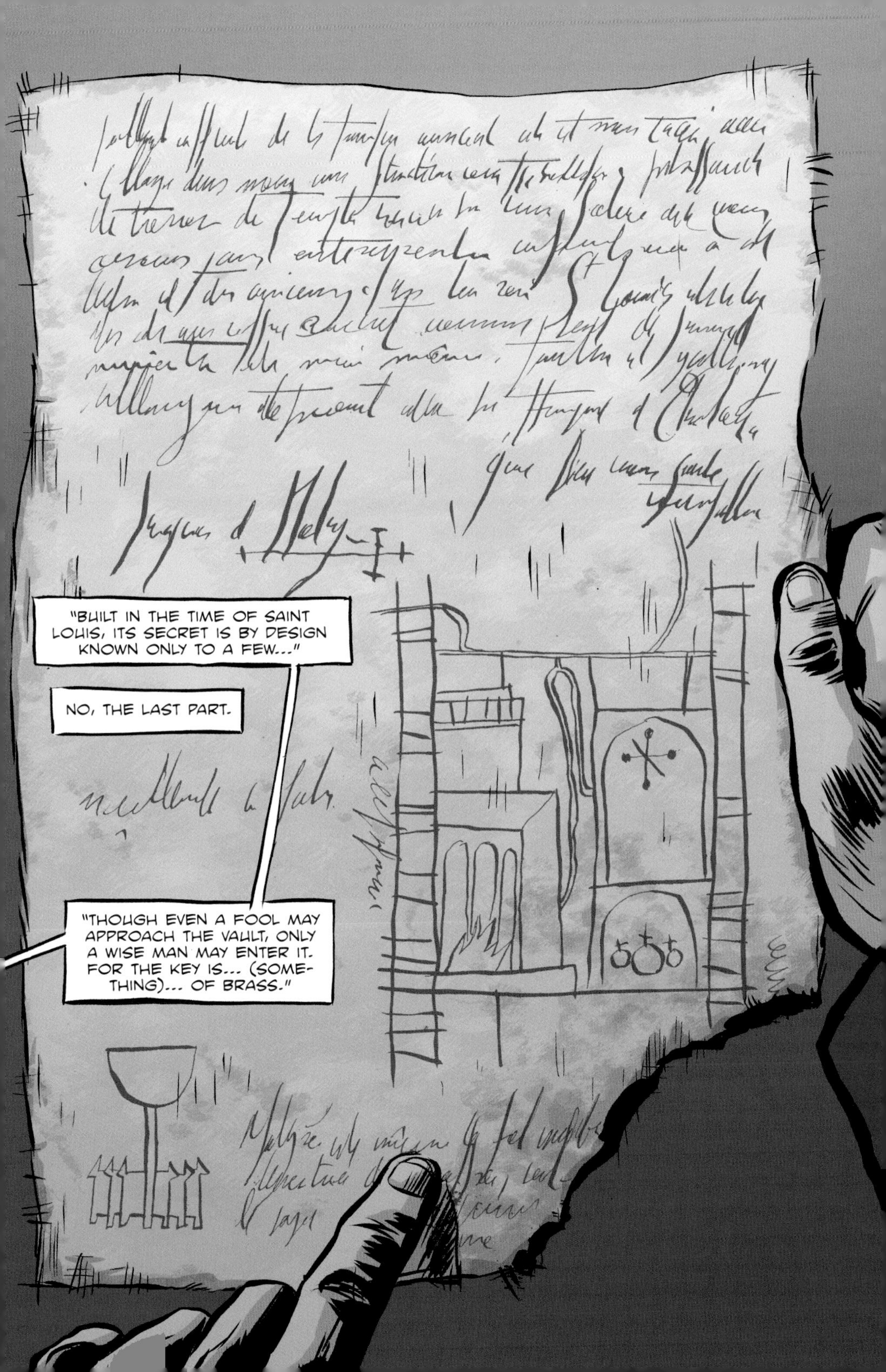
"BUILT IN THE TIME OF SAINT LOUIS, ITS SECRET IS BY DESIGN KNOWN ONLY TO A FEW..."
NO, THE LAST PART.
"THOUGH EVEN A FOOL MAY APPROACH THE VAULT, ONLY A WISE MAN MAY ENTER IT. FOR THE KEY IS... (SOMETHING)... OF BRASS."

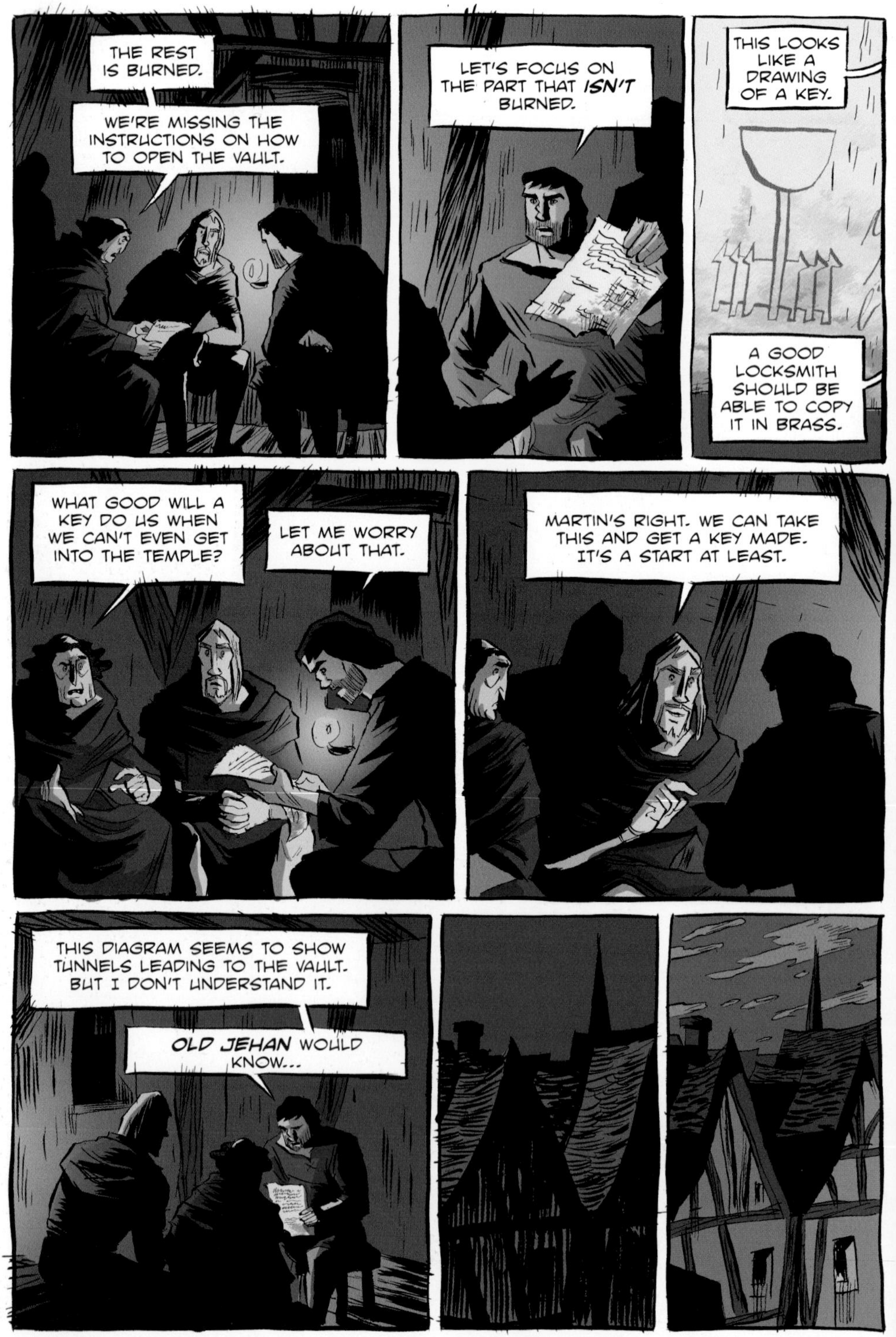
THE REST IS BURNED.
WE'RE MISSING THE INSTRUCTIONS ON HOW TO OPEN THE VAULT.
LET'S FOCUS ON THE PART THAT *ISN'T* BURNED.
THIS LOOKS LIKE A DRAWING OF A KEY.
A GOOD LOCKSMITH SHOULD BE ABLE TO COPY IT IN BRASS.
WHAT GOOD WILL A KEY DO US WHEN WE CAN'T EVEN GET INTO THE TEMPLE?
LET ME WORRY ABOUT THAT.
MARTIN'S RIGHT. WE CAN TAKE THIS AND GET A KEY MADE. IT'S A START AT LEAST.
THIS DIAGRAM SEEMS TO SHOW TUNNELS LEADING TO THE VAULT. BUT I DON'T UNDERSTAND IT.
OLD JEHAN WOULD KNOW...

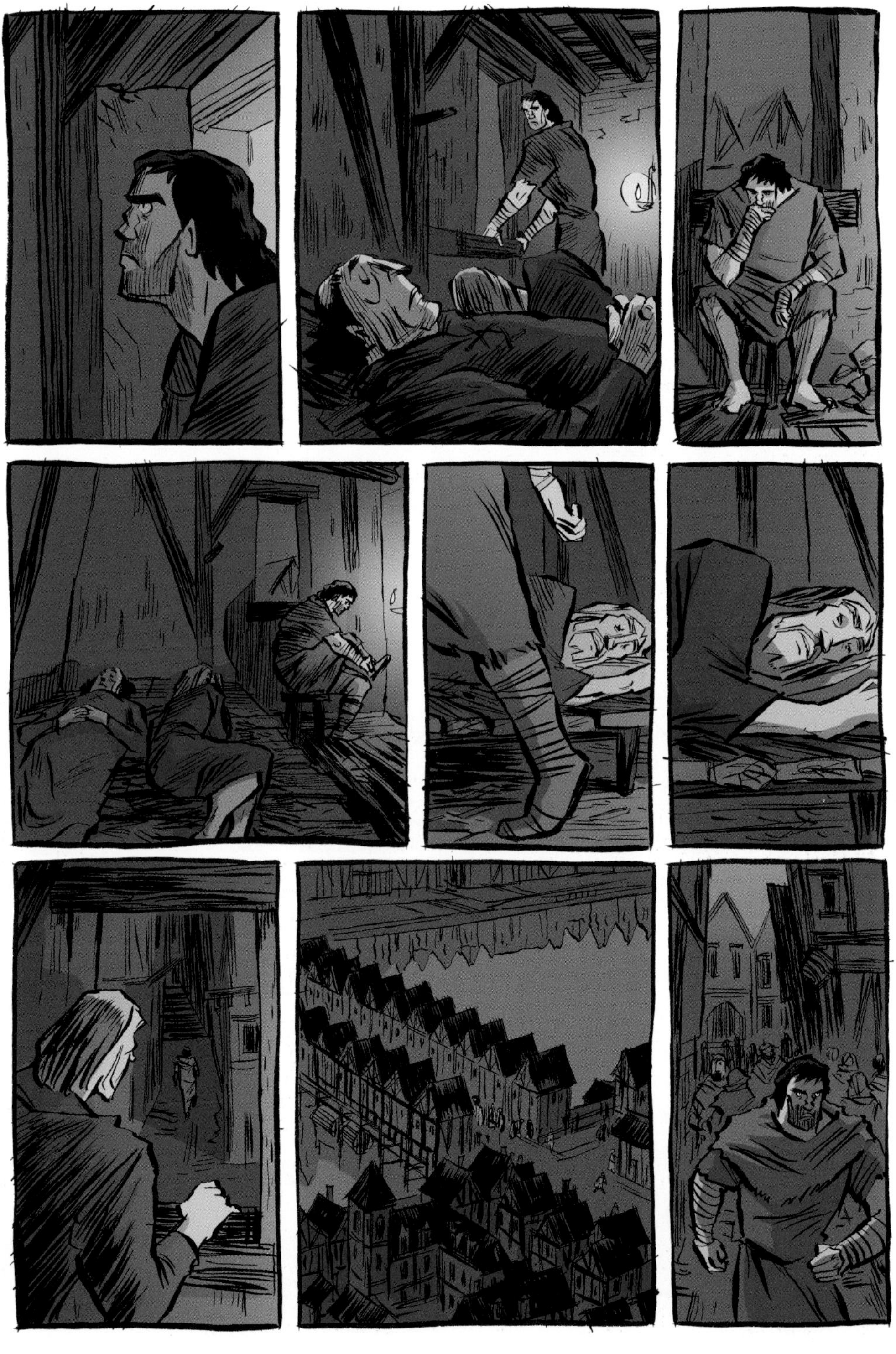

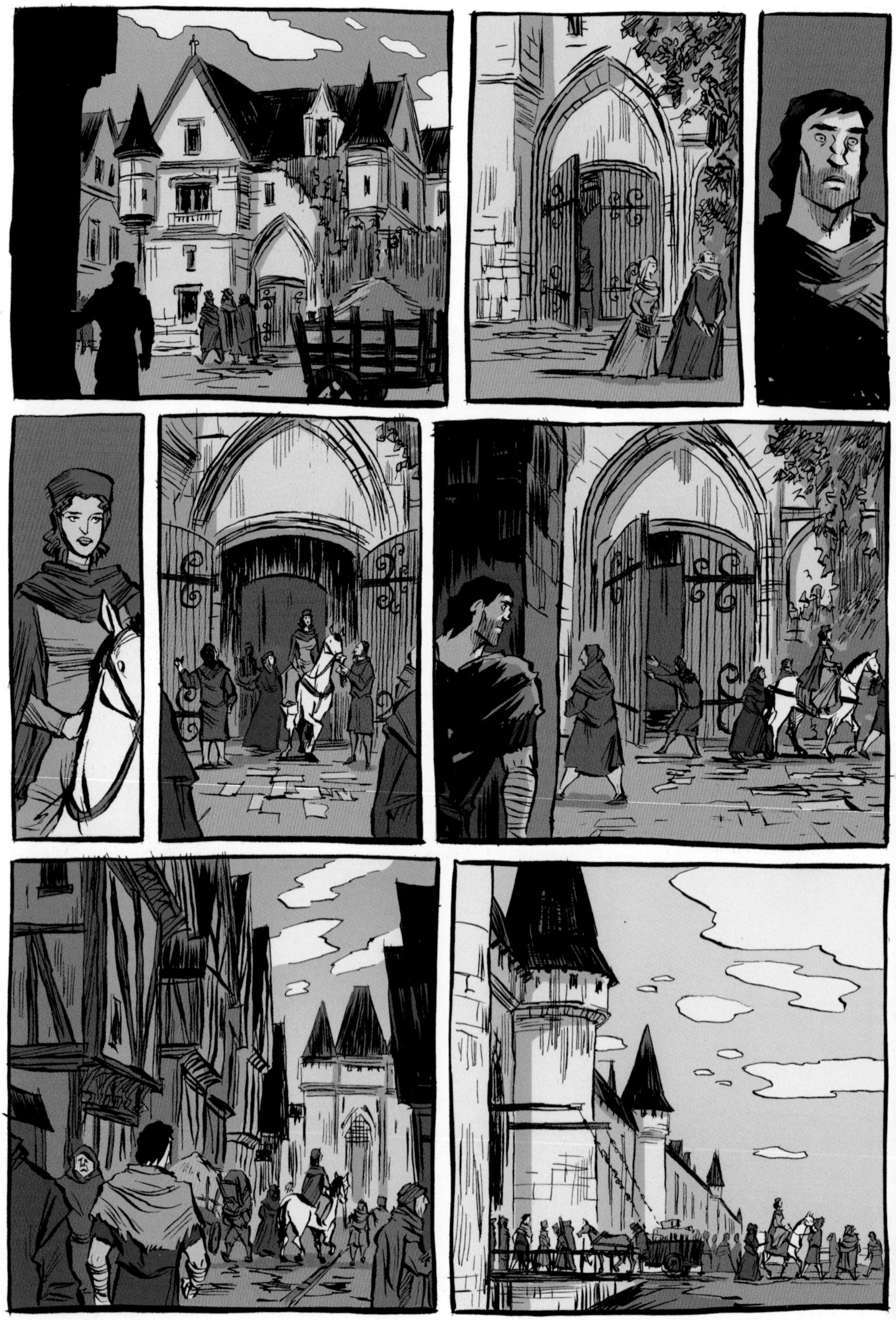

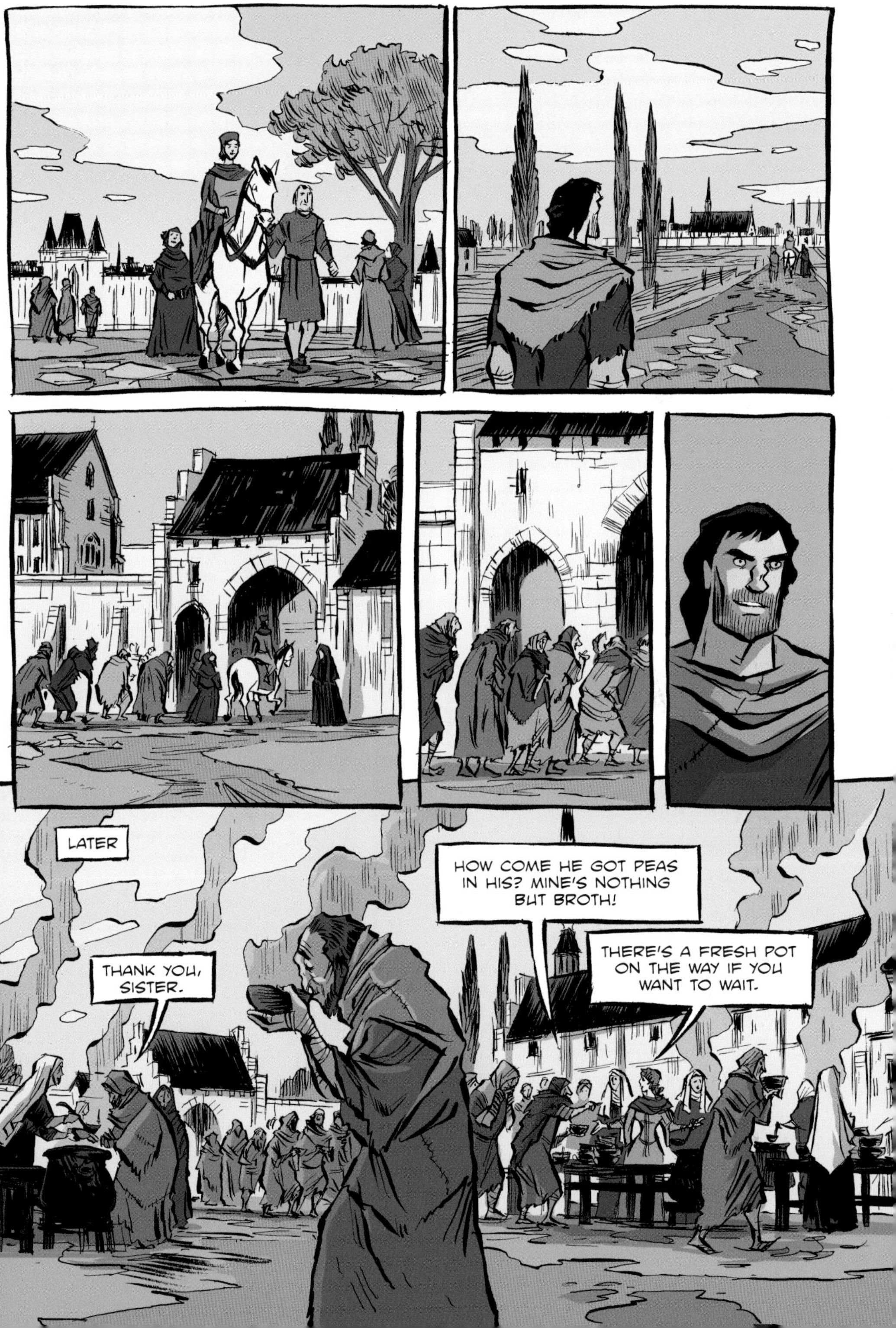
LATER
THANK YOU, SISTER.
HOW COME HE GOT PEAS IN HIS? MINE'S NOTHING BUT BROTH!
THERE'S A FRESH POT ON THE WAY IF YOU WANT TO WAIT.

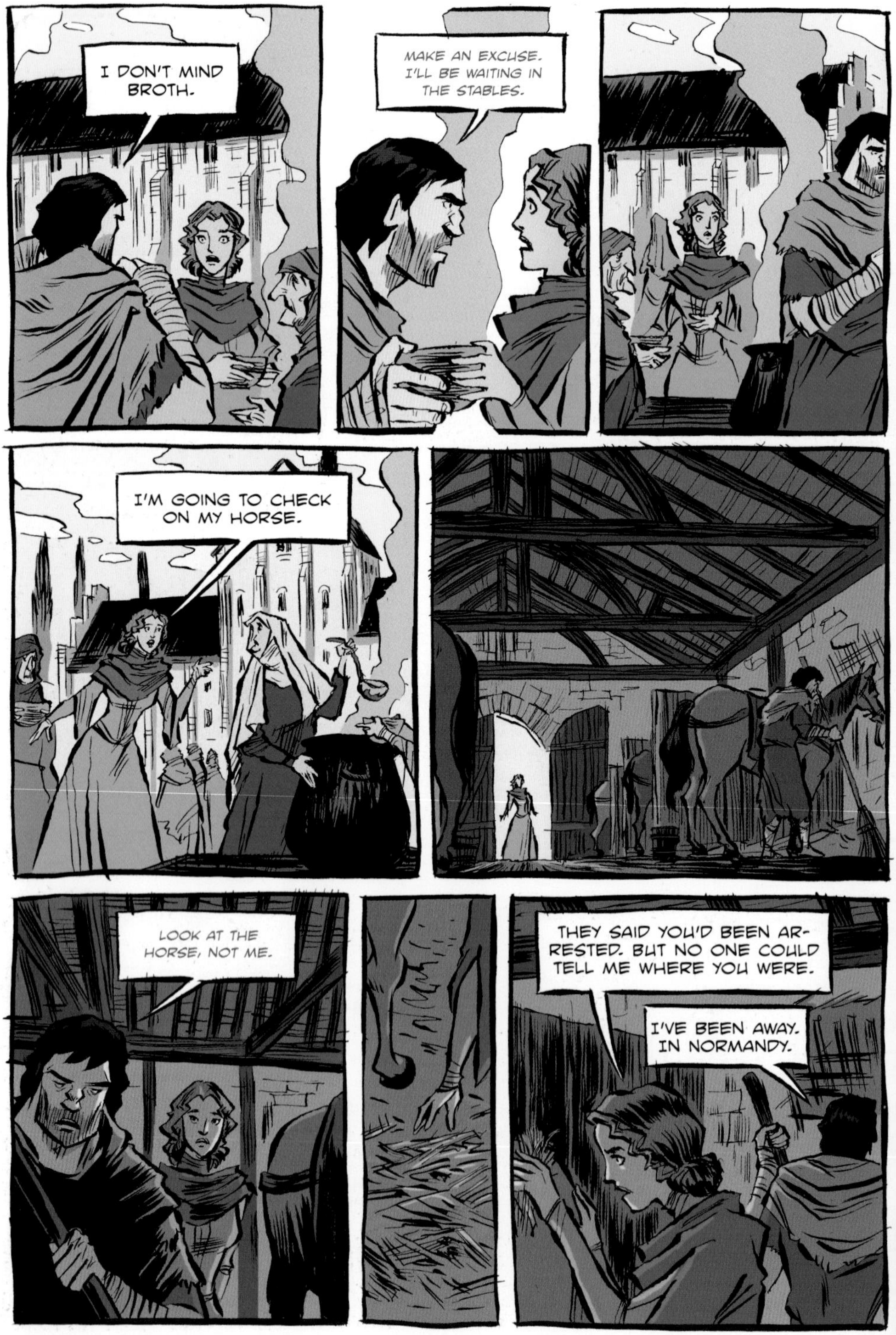
I DON'T MIND BROTH.
MAKE AN EXCUSE. I'LL BE WAITING IN THE STABLES.
I'M GOING TO CHECK ON MY HORSE.
LOOK AT THE HORSE, NOT ME.
THEY SAID YOU'D BEEN ARRESTED. BUT NO ONE COULD TELL ME WHERE YOU WERE.
I'VE BEEN AWAY. IN NORMANDY.

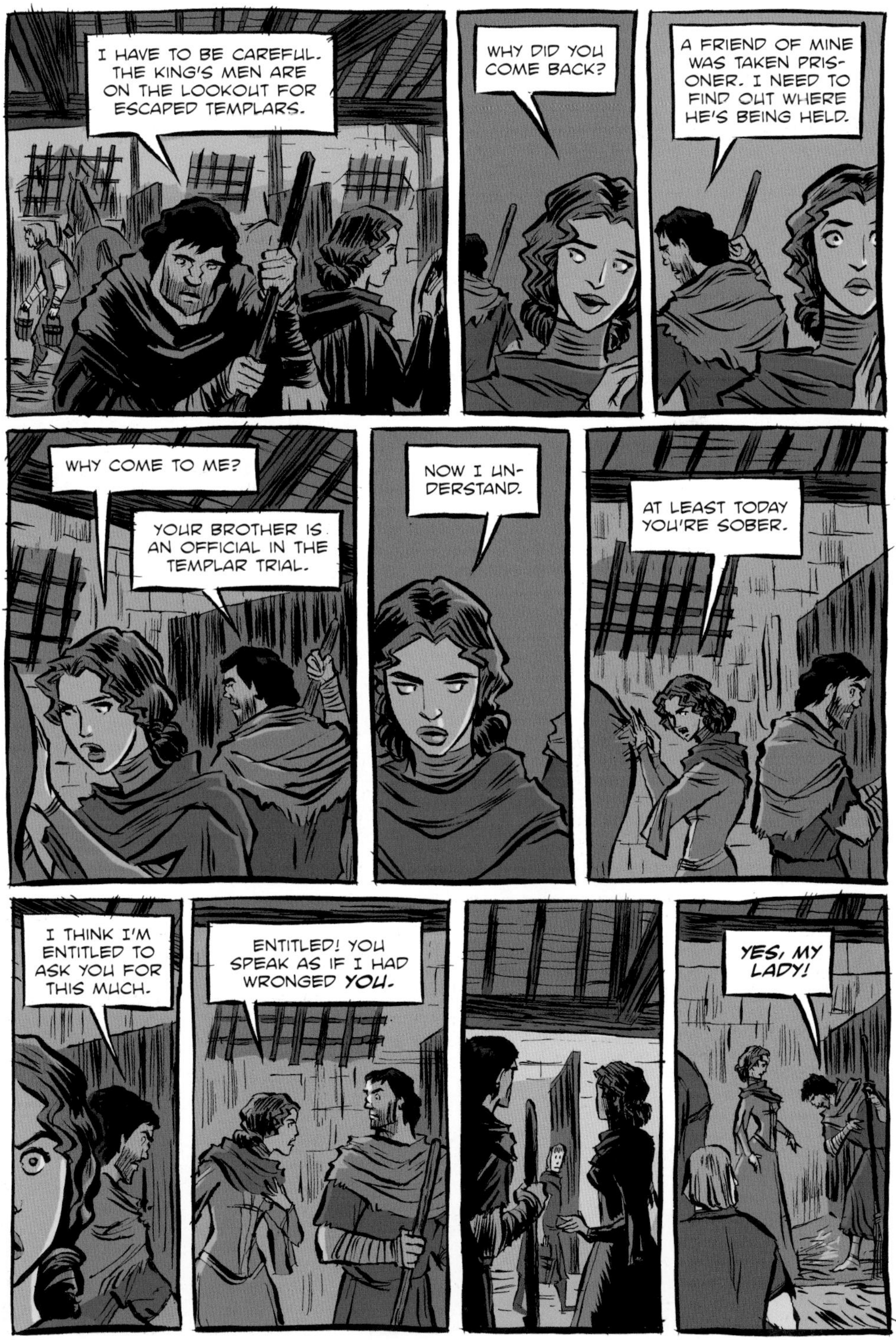
I HAVE TO BE CAREFUL. THE KING'S MEN ARE ON THE LOOKOUT FOR ESCAPED TEMPLARS.
WHY DID YOU COME BACK?
A FRIEND OF MINE WAS TAKEN PRISONER. I NEED TO FIND OUT WHERE HE'S BEING HELD.
WHY COME TO ME?
YOUR BROTHER IS AN OFFICIAL IN THE TEMPLAR TRIAL.
NOW I UNDERSTAND.
AT LEAST TODAY YOU'RE SOBER.
I THINK I'M ENTITLED TO ASK YOU FOR THIS MUCH.
ENTITLED! YOU SPEAK AS IF I HAD WRONGED *YOU*.
YES, MY LADY!

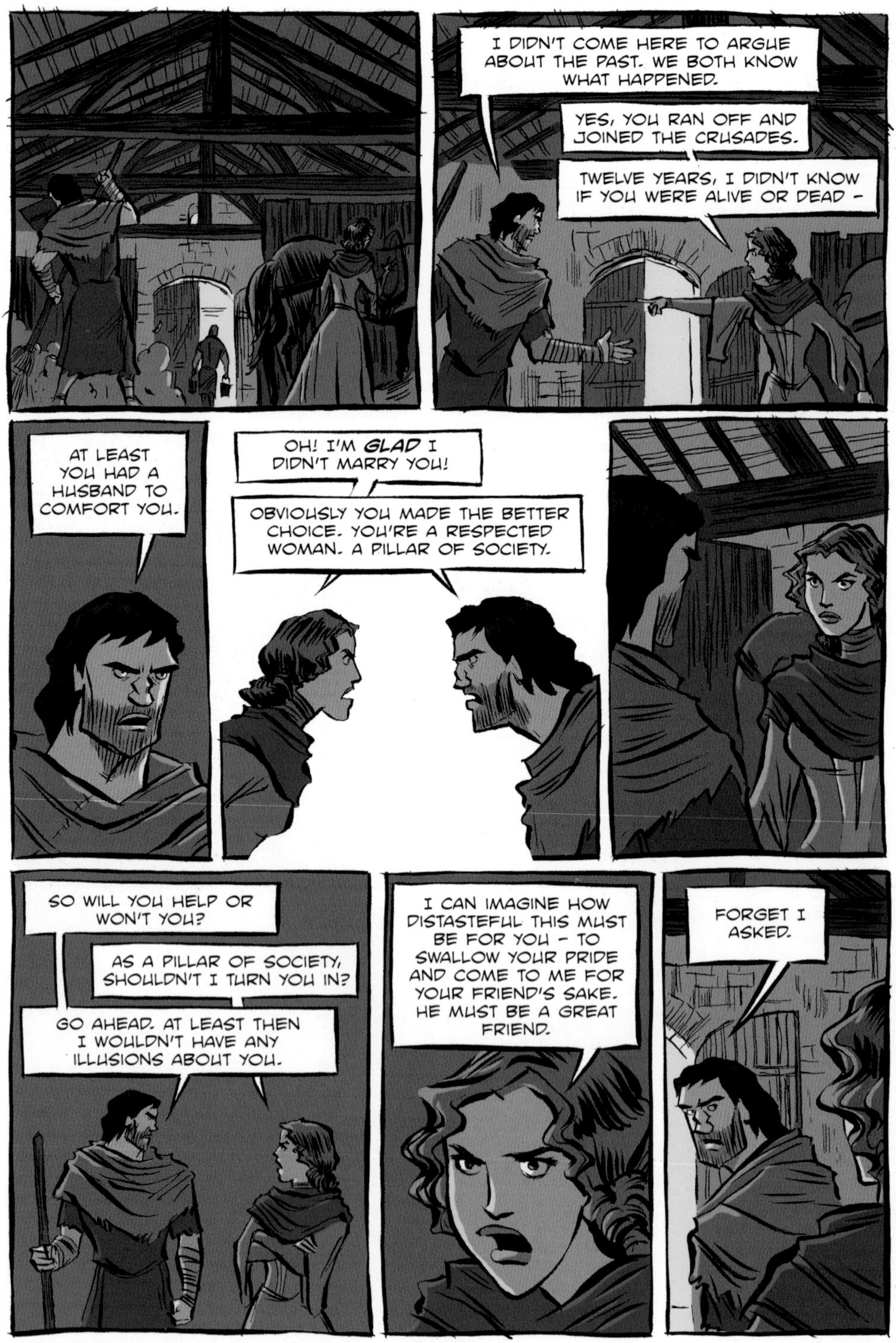
I DIDN'T COME HERE TO ARGUE ABOUT THE PAST. WE BOTH KNOW WHAT HAPPENED.
YES, YOU RAN OFF AND JOINED THE CRUSADES.
TWELVE YEARS, I DIDN'T KNOW IF YOU WERE ALIVE OR DEAD -
AT LEAST YOU HAD A HUSBAND TO COMFORT YOU.
OH! I'M *GLAD* I DIDN'T MARRY YOU!
OBVIOUSLY YOU MADE THE BETTER CHOICE. YOU'RE A RESPECTED WOMAN. A PILLAR OF SOCIETY.
SO WILL YOU HELP OR WON'T YOU?
AS A PILLAR OF SOCIETY, SHOULDN'T I TURN YOU IN?
GO AHEAD. AT LEAST THEN I WOULDN'T HAVE ANY ILLUSIONS ABOUT YOU.
I CAN IMAGINE HOW DISTASTEFUL THIS MUST BE FOR YOU - TO SWALLOW YOUR PRIDE AND COME TO ME FOR YOUR FRIEND'S SAKE. HE MUST BE A GREAT FRIEND.
FORGET I ASKED.

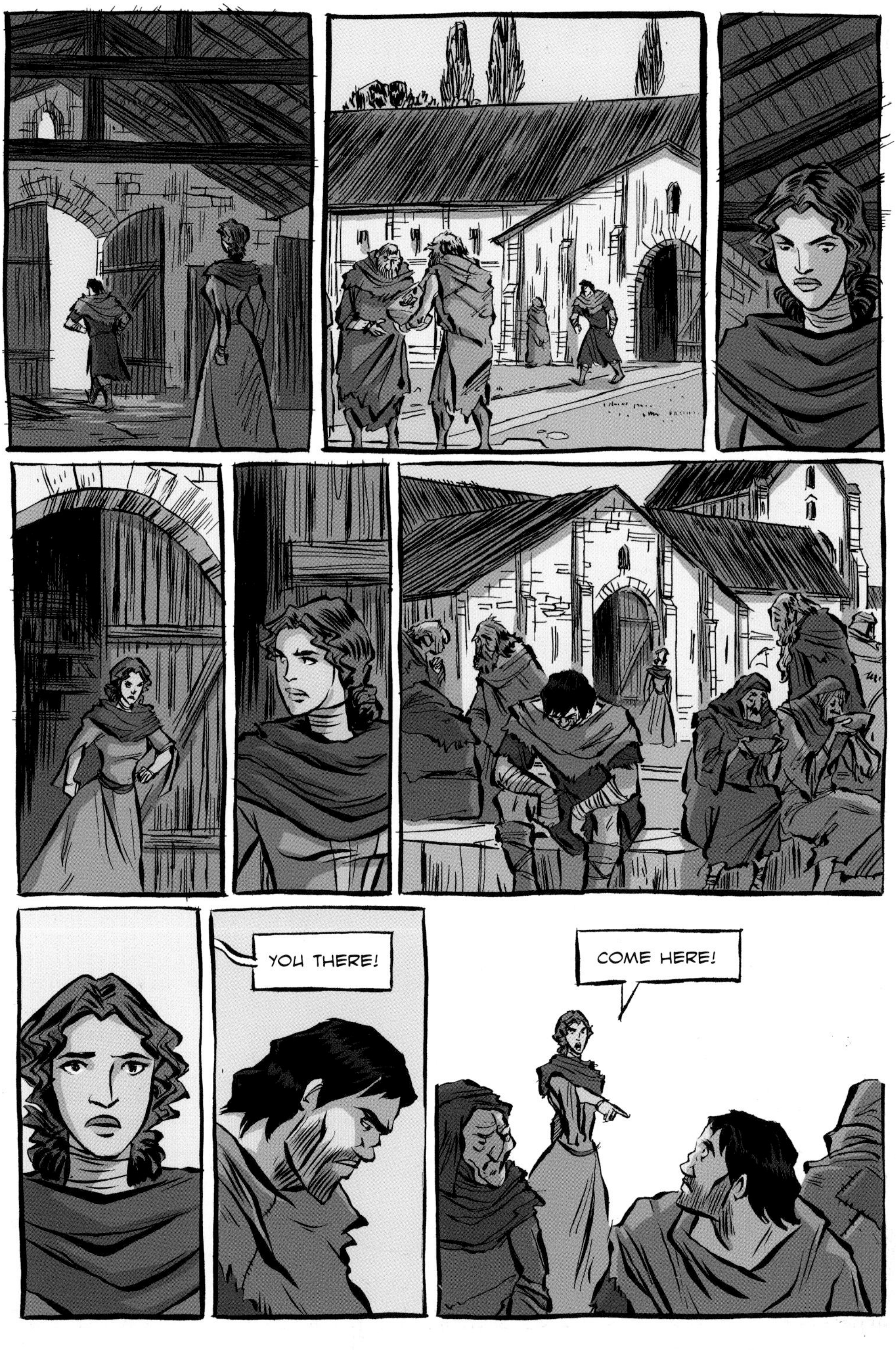
YOU THERE!
COME HERE!

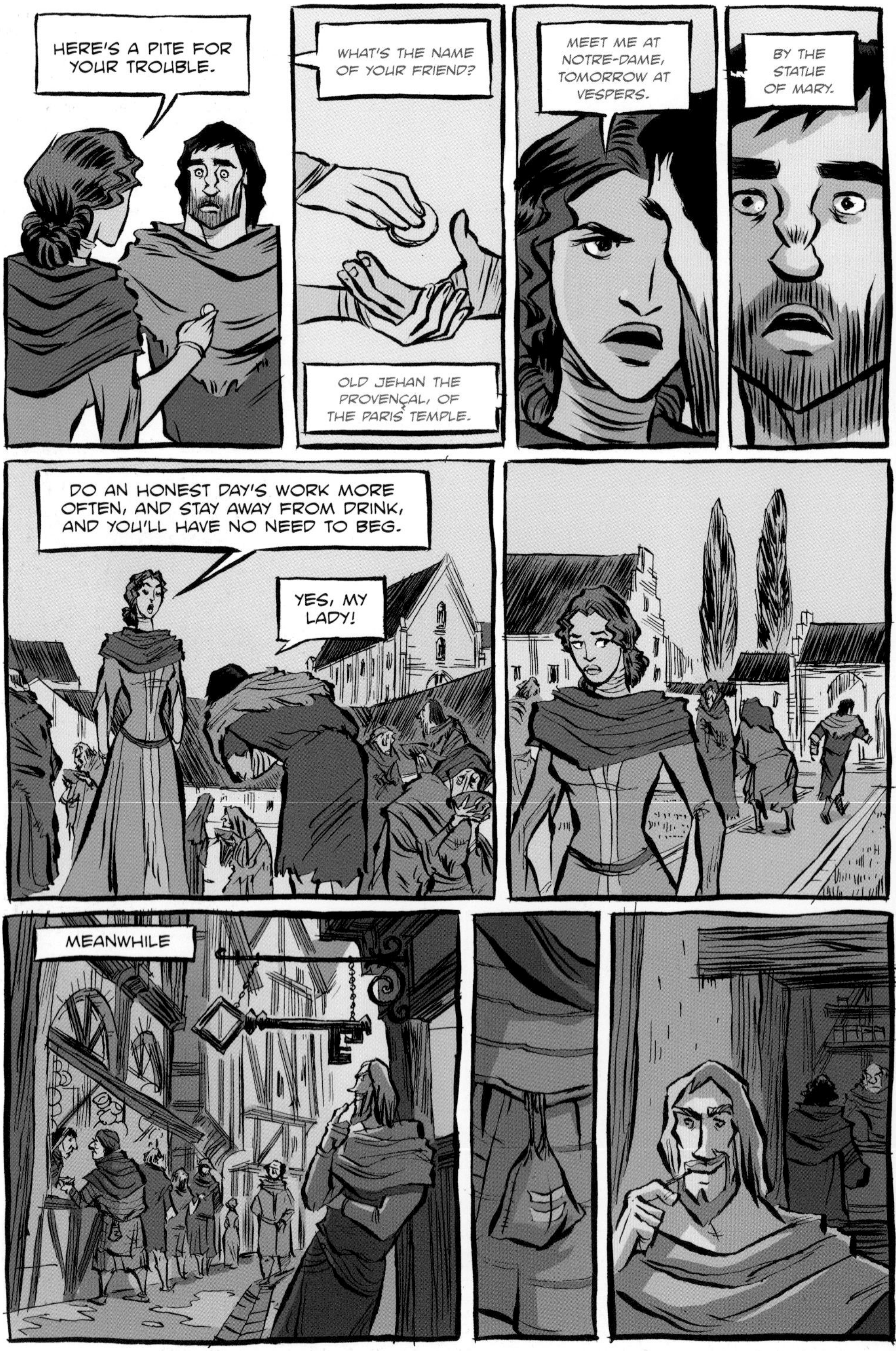
HERE'S A PITE FOR YOUR TROUBLE.
WHAT'S THE NAME OF YOUR FRIEND?
OLD JEHAN THE PROVENÇAL, OF THE PARIS TEMPLE.
MEET ME AT NOTRE-DAME, TOMORROW AT VESPERS.
BY THE STATUE OF MARY.
DO AN HONEST DAY'S WORK MORE OFTEN, AND STAY AWAY FROM DRINK, AND YOU'LL HAVE NO NEED TO BEG.
YES, MY LADY!
MEANWHILE

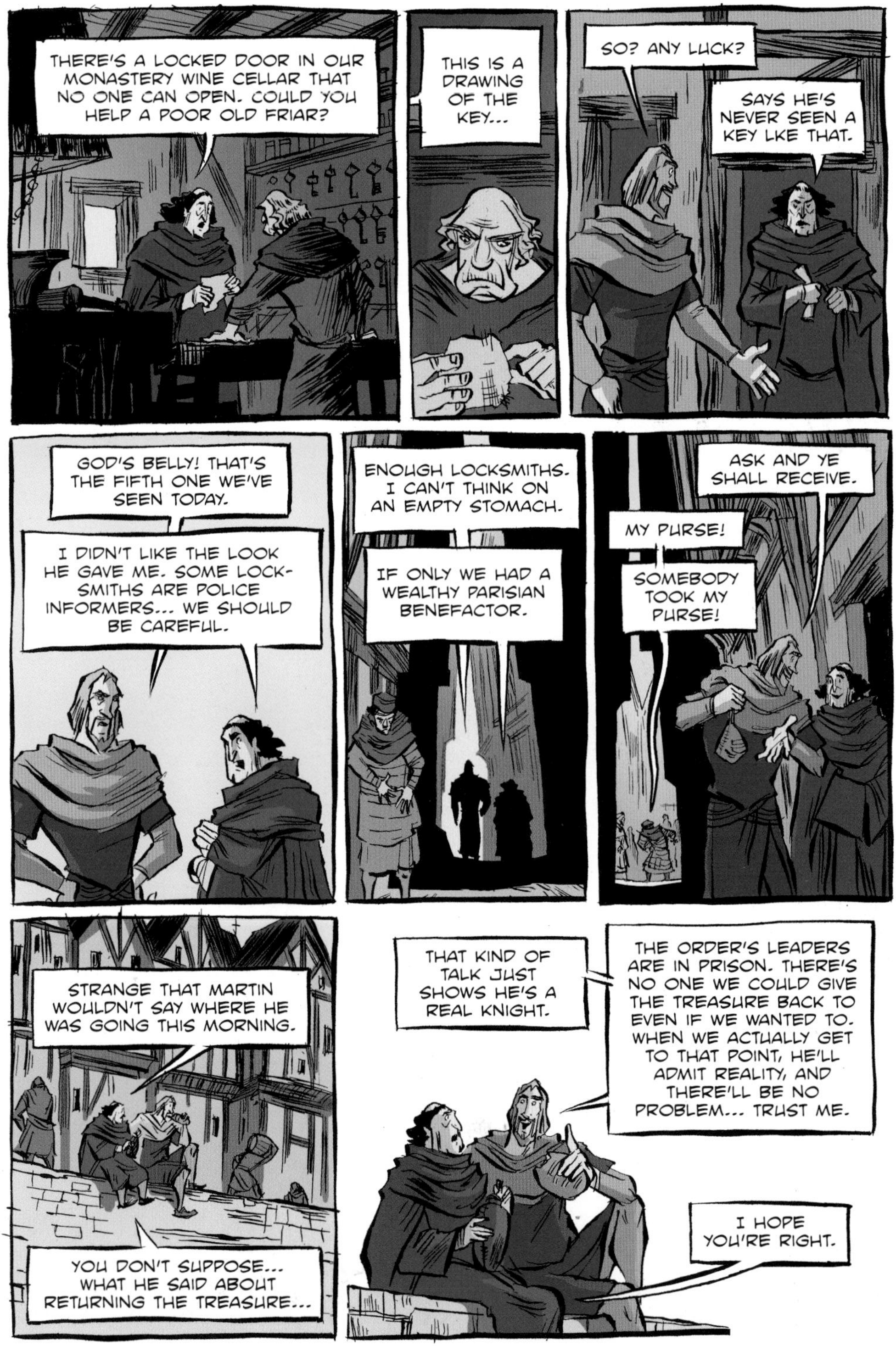
THERE'S A LOCKED DOOR IN OUR MONASTERY WINE CELLAR THAT NO ONE CAN OPEN. COULD YOU HELP A POOR OLD FRIAR?
THIS IS A DRAWING OF THE KEY...
SO? ANY LUCK?
SAYS HE'S NEVER SEEN A KEY LKE THAT.
GOD'S BELLY! THAT'S THE FIFTH ONE WE'VE SEEN TODAY.
I DIDN'T LIKE THE LOOK HE GAVE ME. SOME LOCK-SMITHS ARE POLICE INFORMERS... WE SHOULD BE CAREFUL.
ENOUGH LOCKSMITHS. I CAN'T THINK ON AN EMPTY STOMACH.
IF ONLY WE HAD A WEALTHY PARISIAN BENEFACTOR.
ASK AND YE SHALL RECEIVE.
MY PURSE!
SOMEBODY TOOK MY PURSE!
STRANGE THAT MARTIN WOULDN'T SAY WHERE HE WAS GOING THIS MORNING.
YOU DON'T SUPPOSE... WHAT HE SAID ABOUT RETURNING THE TREASURE...
THAT KIND OF TALK JUST SHOWS HE'S A REAL KNIGHT.
THE ORDER'S LEADERS ARE IN PRISON. THERE'S NO ONE WE COULD GIVE THE TREASURE BACK TO EVEN IF WE WANTED TO. WHEN WE ACTUALLY GET TO THAT POINT, HE'LL ADMIT REALITY, AND THERE'LL BE NO PROBLEM... TRUST ME.
I HOPE YOU'RE RIGHT.

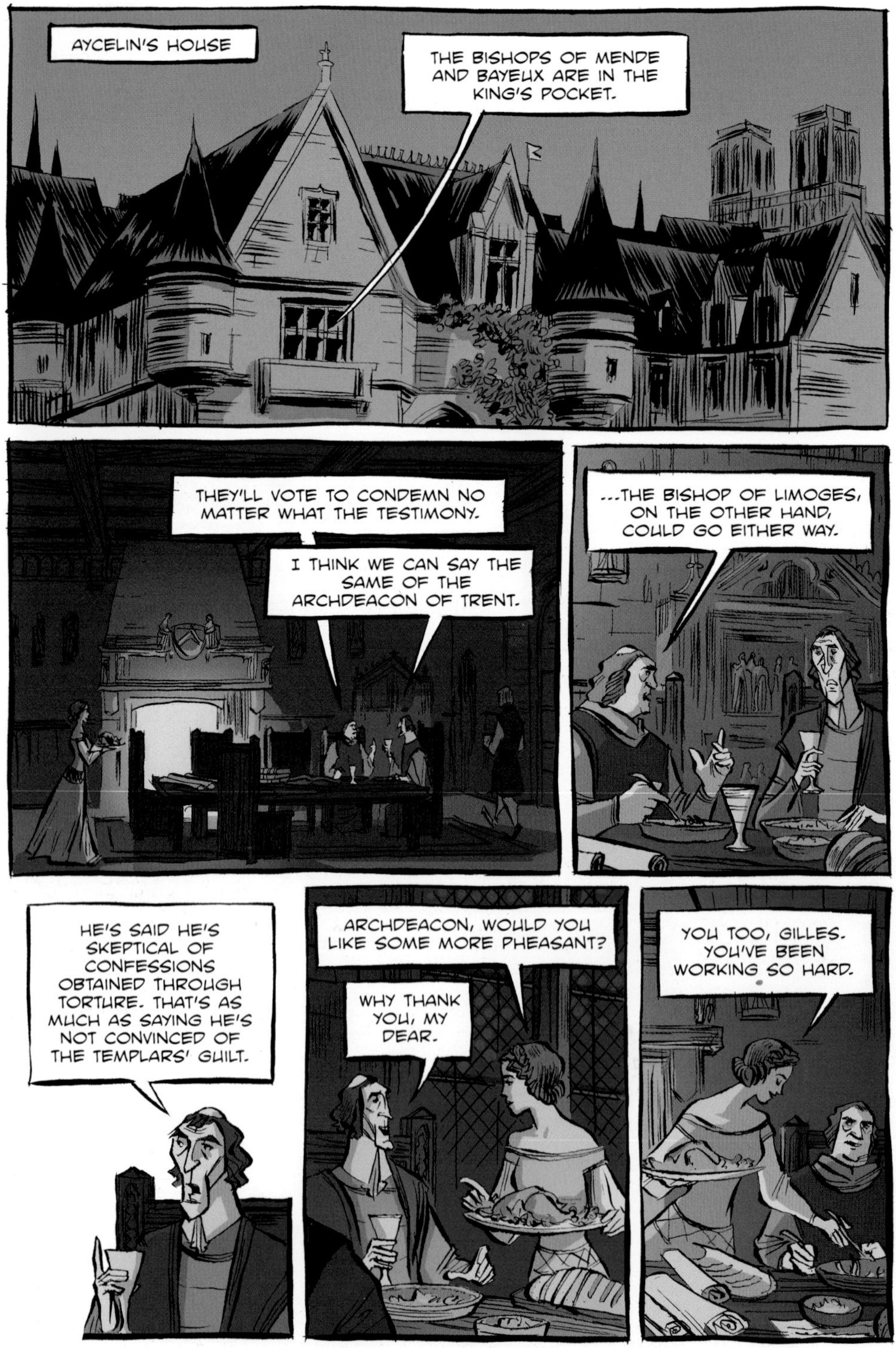
AYCELIN'S HOUSE
THE BISHOPS OF MENDE AND BAYEUX ARE IN THE KING'S POCKET.
THEY'LL VOTE TO CONDEMN NO MATTER WHAT THE TESTIMONY.
I THINK WE CAN SAY THE SAME OF THE ARCHDEACON OF TRENT.
...THE BISHOP OF LIMOGES, ON THE OTHER HAND, COULD GO EITHER WAY.
HE'S SAID HE'S SKEPTICAL OF CONFESSIONS OBTAINED THROUGH TORTURE. THAT'S AS MUCH AS SAYING HE'S NOT CONVINCED OF THE TEMPLARS' GUILT.
ARCHDEACON, WOULD YOU LIKE SOME MORE PHEASANT?
WHY THANK YOU, MY DEAR.
YOU TOO, GILLES. YOU'VE BEEN WORKING SO HARD.

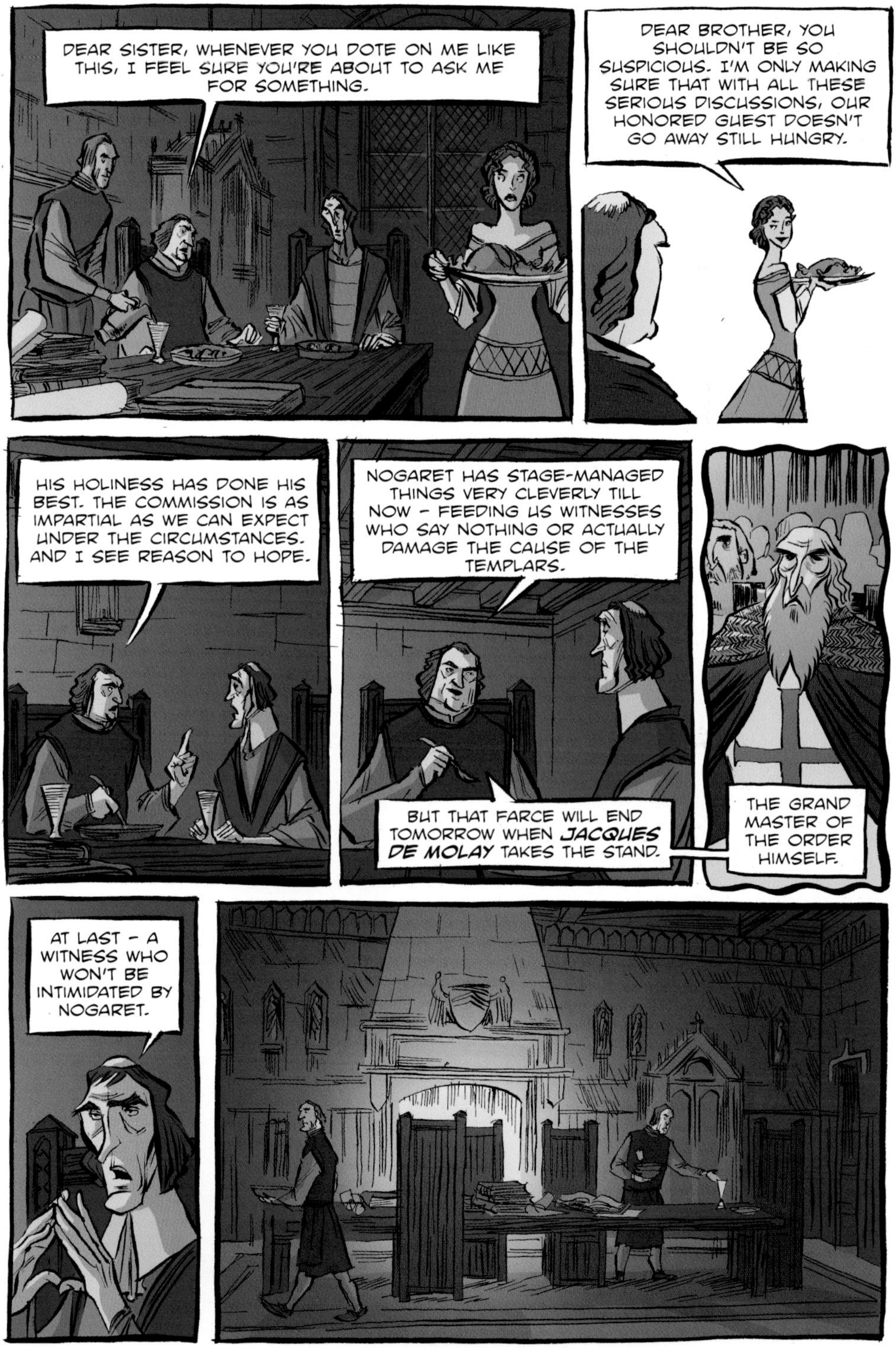
DEAR SISTER, WHENEVER YOU DOTE ON ME LIKE THIS, I FEEL SURE YOU'RE ABOUT TO ASK ME FOR SOMETHING.
DEAR BROTHER, YOU SHOULDN'T BE SO SUSPICIOUS. I'M ONLY MAKING SURE THAT WITH ALL THESE SERIOUS DISCUSSIONS, OUR HONORED GUEST DOESN'T GO AWAY STILL HUNGRY.
HIS HOLINESS HAS DONE HIS BEST. THE COMMISSION IS AS IMPARTIAL AS WE CAN EXPECT UNDER THE CIRCUMSTANCES. AND I SEE REASON TO HOPE.
NOGARET HAS STAGE-MANAGED THINGS VERY CLEVERLY TILL NOW – FEEDING US WITNESSES WHO SAY NOTHING OR ACTUALLY DAMAGE THE CAUSE OF THE TEMPLARS.
BUT THAT FARCE WILL END TOMORROW WHEN JACQUES DE MOLAY TAKES THE STAND.
THE GRAND MASTER OF THE ORDER HIMSELF.
AT LAST – A WITNESS WHO WON'T BE INTIMIDATED BY NOGARET.

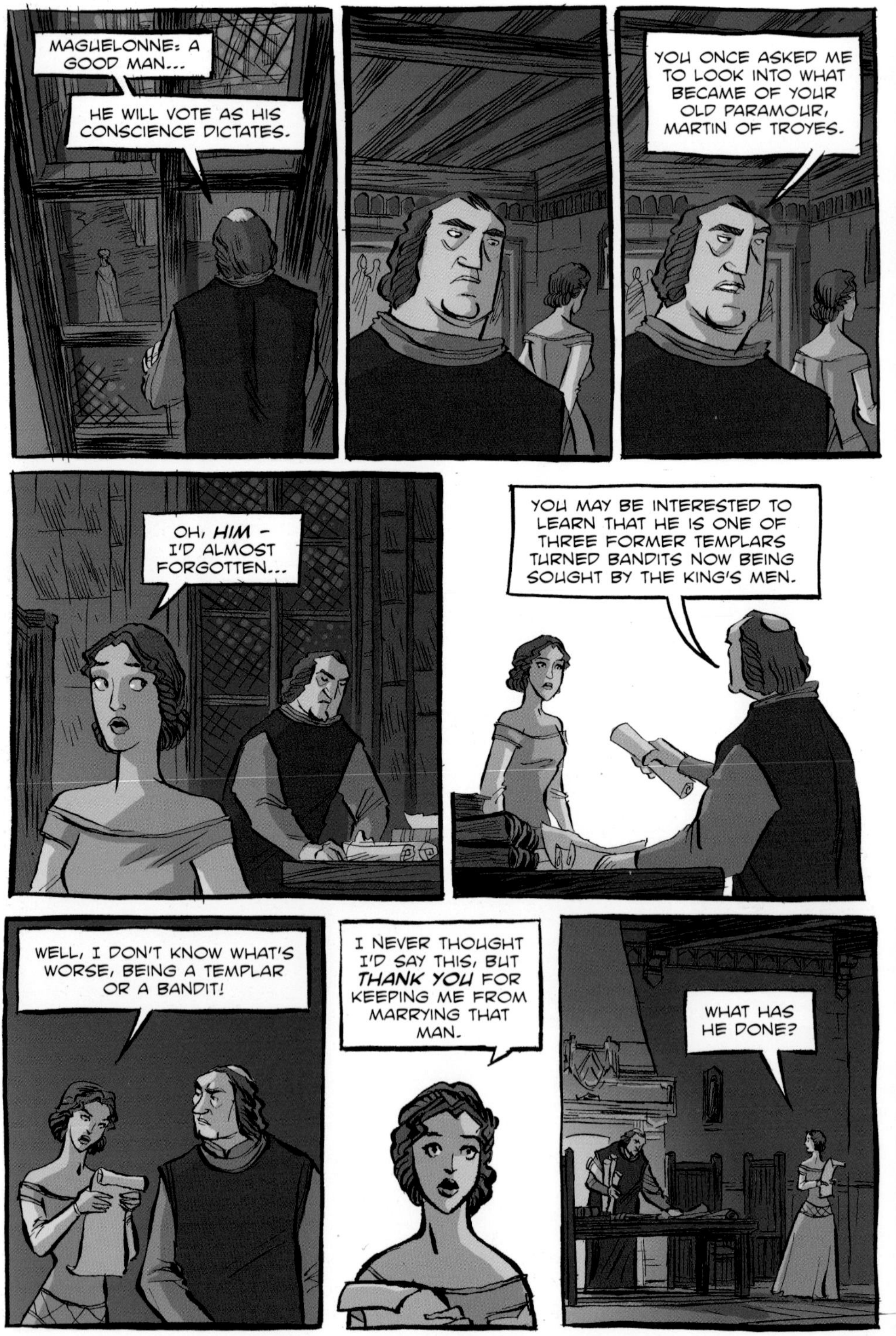
MAGUELONNE: A GOOD MAN...
HE WILL VOTE AS HIS CONSCIENCE DICTATES.
YOU ONCE ASKED ME TO LOOK INTO WHAT BECAME OF YOUR OLD PARAMOUR, MARTIN OF TROYES.
OH, *HIM* - I'D ALMOST FORGOTTEN...
YOU MAY BE INTERESTED TO LEARN THAT HE IS ONE OF THREE FORMER TEMPLARS TURNED BANDITS NOW BEING SOUGHT BY THE KING'S MEN.
WELL, I DON'T KNOW WHAT'S WORSE, BEING A TEMPLAR OR A BANDIT!
I NEVER THOUGHT I'D SAY THIS, BUT *THANK YOU* FOR KEEPING ME FROM MARRYING THAT MAN.
WHAT HAS HE DONE?

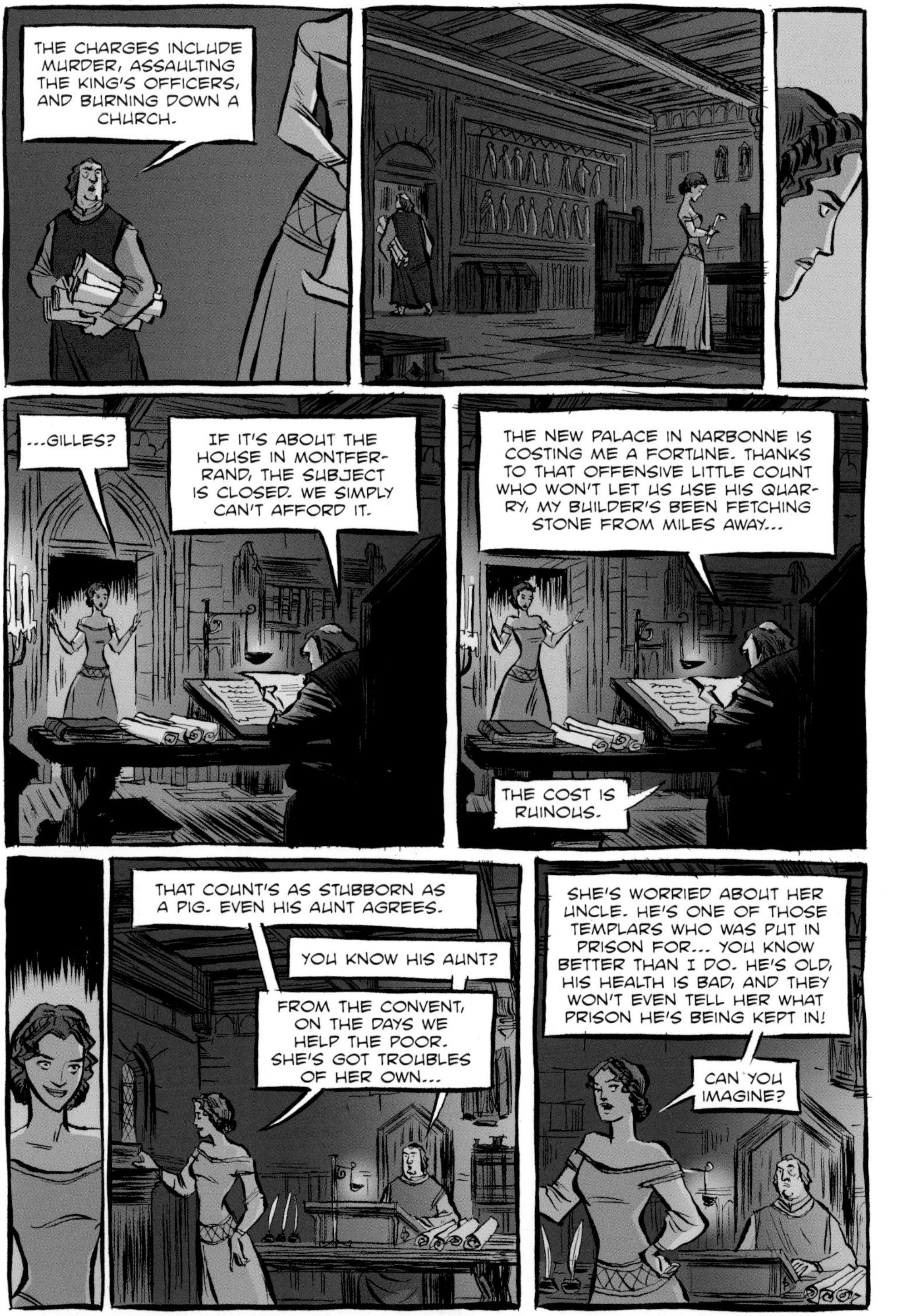
THE CHARGES INCLUDE MURDER, ASSAULTING THE KING'S OFFICERS, AND BURNING DOWN A CHURCH.
...GILLES?
IF IT'S ABOUT THE HOUSE IN MONTFERRAND, THE SUBJECT IS CLOSED. WE SIMPLY CAN'T AFFORD IT.
THE NEW PALACE IN NARBONNE IS COSTING ME A FORTUNE. THANKS TO THAT OFFENSIVE LITTLE COUNT WHO WON'T LET US USE HIS QUARRY, MY BUILDER'S BEEN FETCHING STONE FROM MILES AWAY...
THE COST IS RUINOUS.
THAT COUNT'S AS STUBBORN AS A PIG. EVEN HIS AUNT AGREES.
YOU KNOW HIS AUNT?
FROM THE CONVENT, ON THE DAYS WE HELP THE POOR. SHE'S GOT TROUBLES OF HER OWN...
SHE'S WORRIED ABOUT HER UNCLE. HE'S ONE OF THOSE TEMPLARS WHO WAS PUT IN PRISON FOR... YOU KNOW BETTER THAN I DO. HE'S OLD, HIS HEALTH IS BAD, AND THEY WON'T EVEN TELL HER WHAT PRISON HE'S BEING KEPT IN!
CAN YOU IMAGINE?

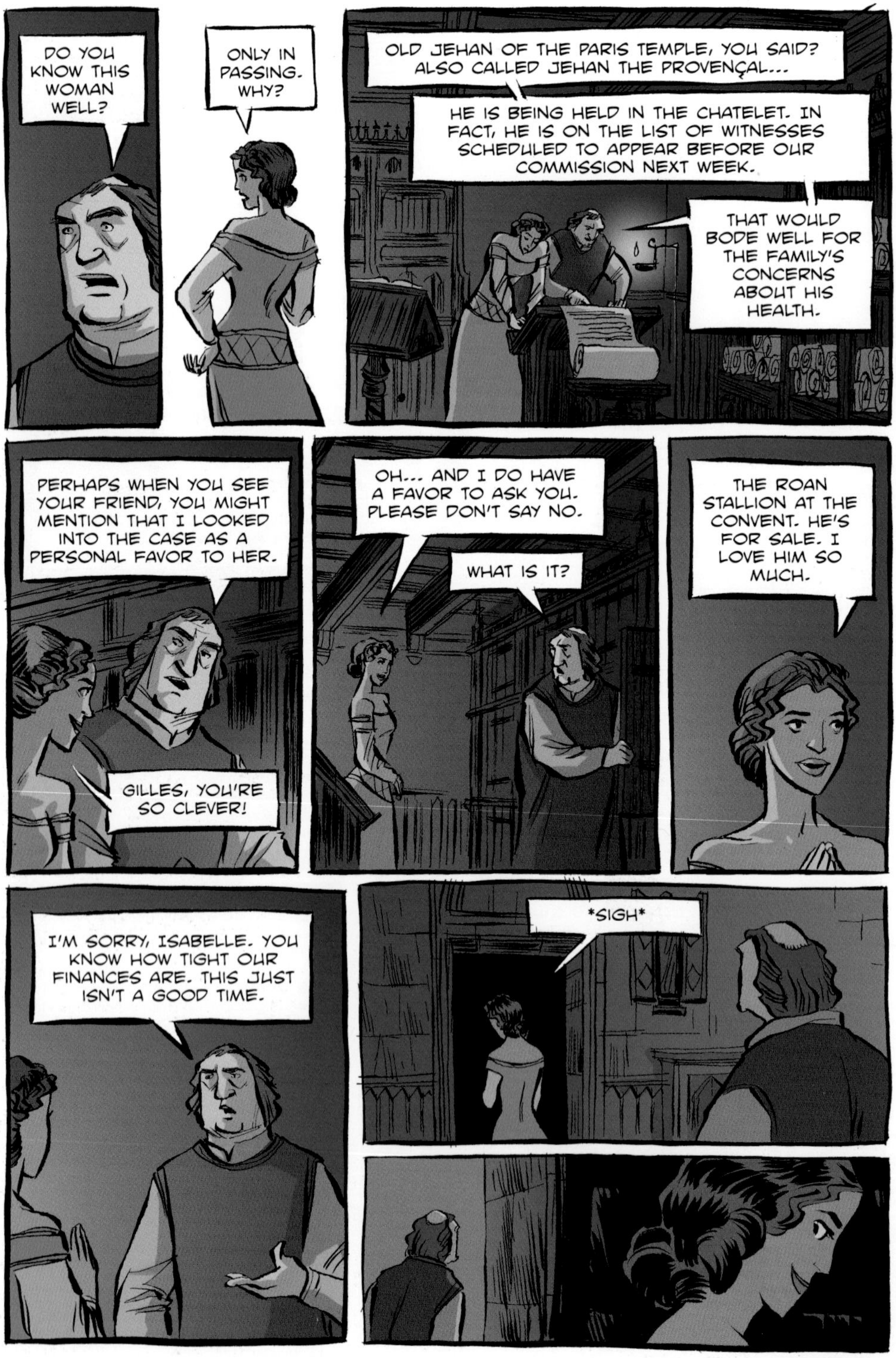
DO YOU KNOW THIS WOMAN WELL?
ONLY IN PASSING. WHY?
OLD JEHAN OF THE PARIS TEMPLE, YOU SAID? ALSO CALLED JEHAN THE PROVENÇAL...
HE IS BEING HELD IN THE CHATELET. IN FACT, HE IS ON THE LIST OF WITNESSES SCHEDULED TO APPEAR BEFORE OUR COMMISSION NEXT WEEK.
THAT WOULD BODE WELL FOR THE FAMILY'S CONCERNS ABOUT HIS HEALTH.
PERHAPS WHEN YOU SEE YOUR FRIEND, YOU MIGHT MENTION THAT I LOOKED INTO THE CASE AS A PERSONAL FAVOR TO HER.
GILLES, YOU'RE SO CLEVER!
OH... AND I DO HAVE A FAVOR TO ASK YOU. PLEASE DON'T SAY NO.
WHAT IS IT?
THE ROAN STALLION AT THE CONVENT. HE'S FOR SALE. I LOVE HIM SO MUCH.
I'M SORRY, ISABELLE. YOU KNOW HOW TIGHT OUR FINANCES ARE. THIS JUST ISN'T A GOOD TIME.
SIGH

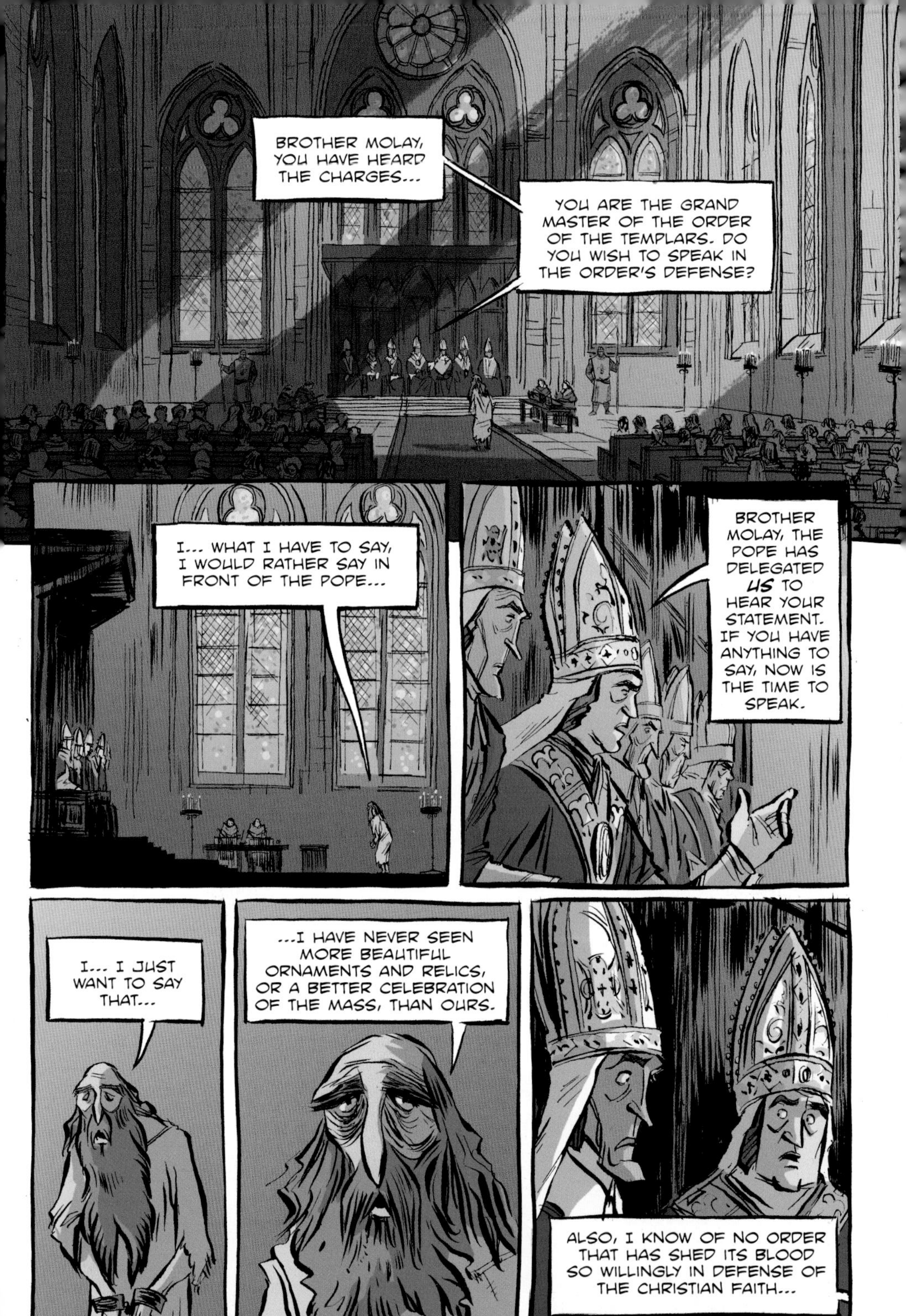
BROTHER MOLAY, YOU HAVE HEARD THE CHARGES...
YOU ARE THE GRAND MASTER OF THE ORDER OF THE TEMPLARS. DO YOU WISH TO SPEAK IN THE ORDER'S DEFENSE?
I... WHAT I HAVE TO SAY, I WOULD RATHER SAY IN FRONT OF THE POPE...
BROTHER MOLAY, THE POPE HAS DELEGATED *US* TO HEAR YOUR STATEMENT. IF YOU HAVE ANYTHING TO SAY, NOW IS THE TIME TO SPEAK.
I... I JUST WANT TO SAY THAT...
...I HAVE NEVER SEEN MORE BEAUTIFUL ORNAMENTS AND RELICS, OR A BETTER CELEBRATION OF THE MASS, THAN OURS.
ALSO, I KNOW OF NO ORDER THAT HAS SHED ITS BLOOD SO WILLINGLY IN DEFENSE OF THE CHRISTIAN FAITH...

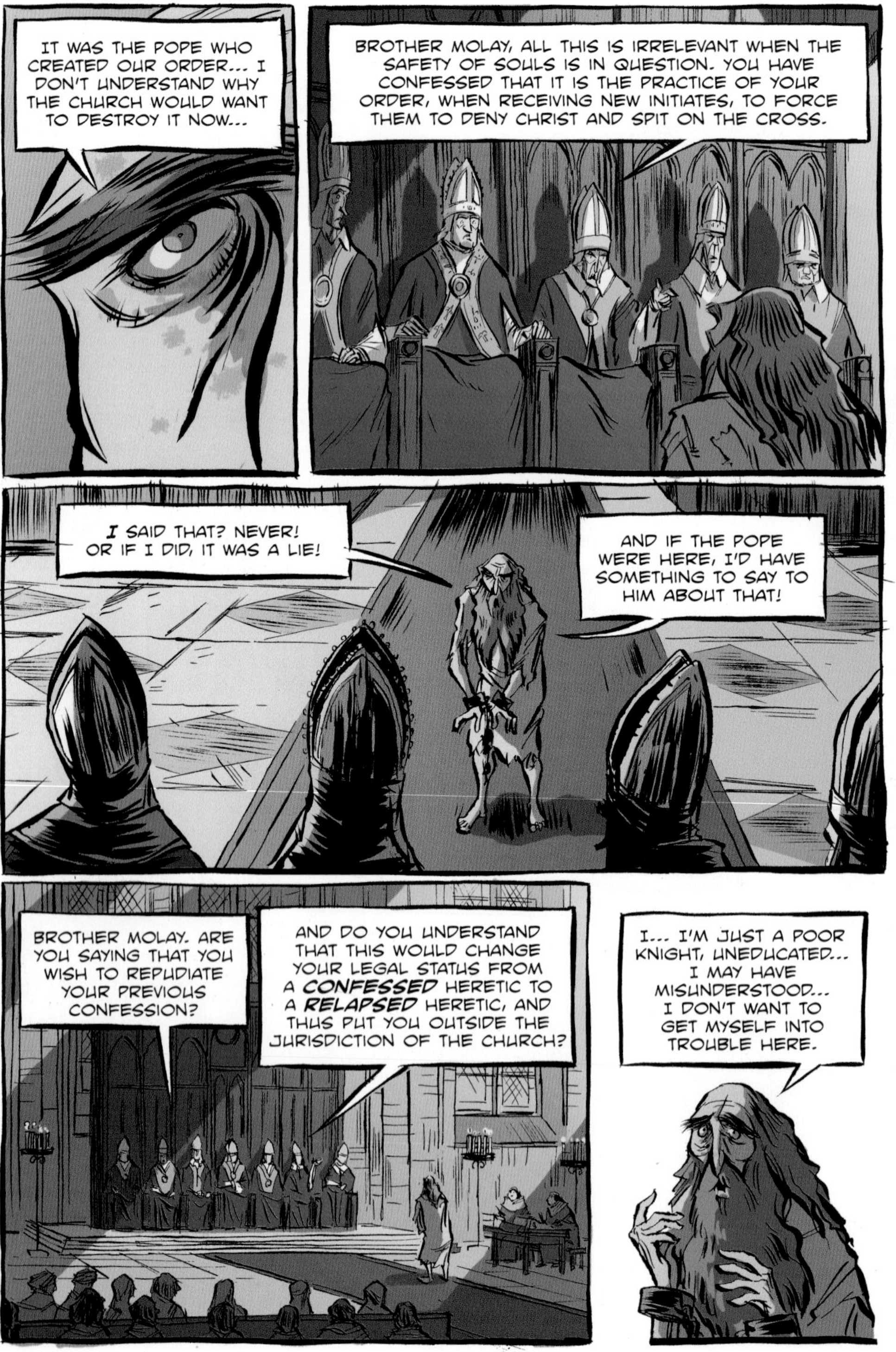
IT WAS THE POPE WHO CREATED OUR ORDER... I DON'T UNDERSTAND WHY THE CHURCH WOULD WANT TO DESTROY IT NOW...
BROTHER MOLAY, ALL THIS IS IRRELEVANT WHEN THE SAFETY OF SOULS IS IN QUESTION. YOU HAVE CONFESSED THAT IT IS THE PRACTICE OF YOUR ORDER, WHEN RECEIVING NEW INITIATES, TO FORCE THEM TO DENY CHRIST AND SPIT ON THE CROSS.
I SAID THAT? NEVER! OR IF I DID, IT WAS A LIE!
AND IF THE POPE WERE HERE, I'D HAVE SOMETHING TO SAY TO HIM ABOUT THAT!
BROTHER MOLAY. ARE YOU SAYING THAT YOU WISH TO REPUDIATE YOUR PREVIOUS CONFESSION?
AND DO YOU UNDERSTAND THAT THIS WOULD CHANGE YOUR LEGAL STATUS FROM A ***CONFESSED*** HERETIC TO A ***RELAPSED*** HERETIC, AND THUS PUT YOU OUTSIDE THE JURISDICTION OF THE CHURCH?
I... I'M JUST A POOR KNIGHT, UNEDUCATED... I MAY HAVE MISUNDERSTOOD... I DON'T WANT TO GET MYSELF INTO TROUBLE HERE.

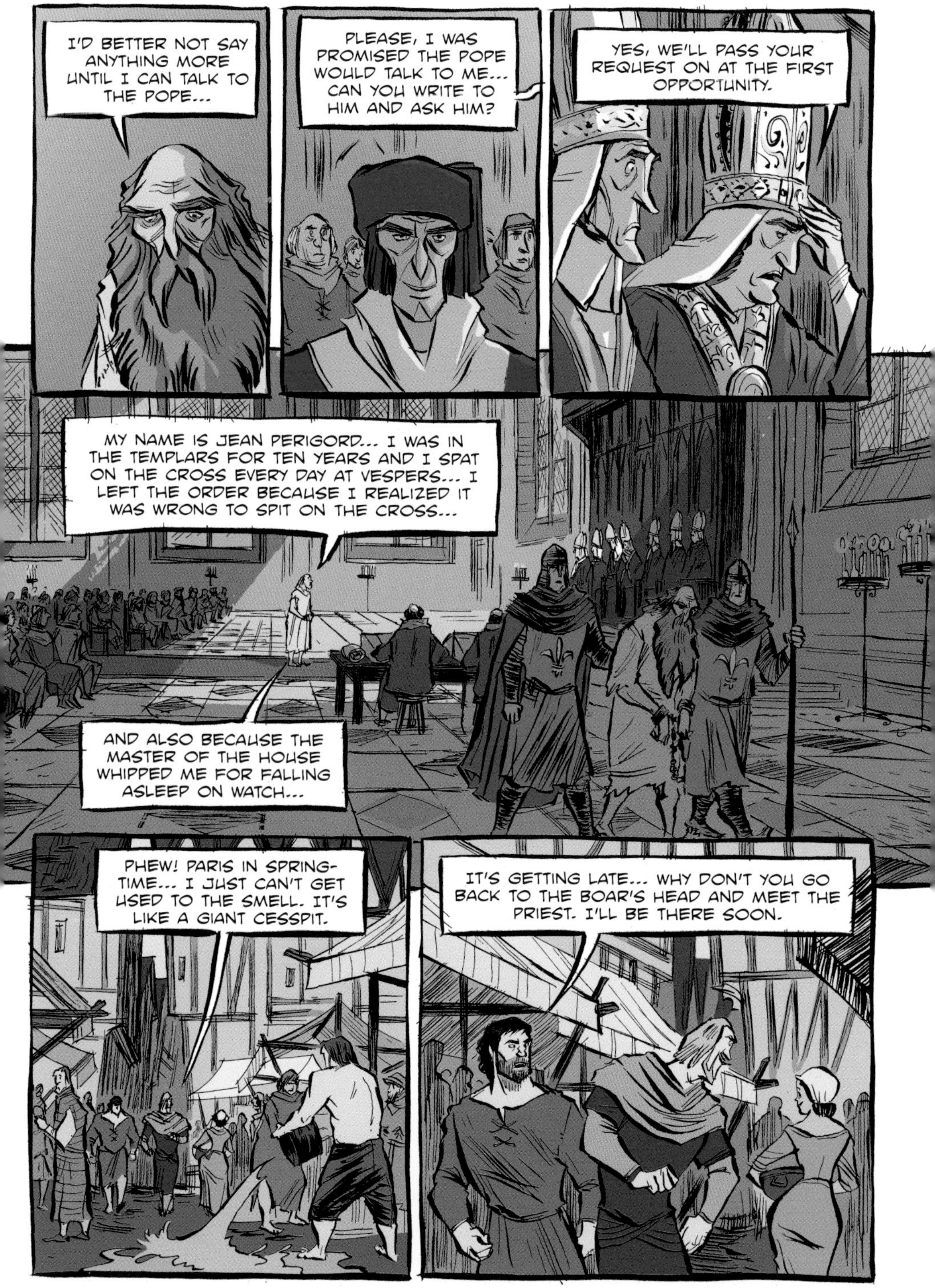
I'D BETTER NOT SAY ANYTHING MORE UNTIL I CAN TALK TO THE POPE...
PLEASE, I WAS PROMISED THE POPE WOULD TALK TO ME... CAN YOU WRITE TO HIM AND ASK HIM?
YES, WE'LL PASS YOUR REQUEST ON AT THE FIRST OPPORTUNITY.
MY NAME IS JEAN PERIGORD... I WAS IN THE TEMPLARS FOR TEN YEARS AND I SPAT ON THE CROSS EVERY DAY AT VESPERS... I LEFT THE ORDER BECAUSE I REALIZED IT WAS WRONG TO SPIT ON THE CROSS...
AND ALSO BECAUSE THE MASTER OF THE HOUSE WHIPPED ME FOR FALLING ASLEEP ON WATCH...
PHEW! PARIS IN SPRING-TIME... I JUST CAN'T GET USED TO THE SMELL. IT'S LIKE A GIANT CESSPIT.
IT'S GETTING LATE... WHY DON'T YOU GO BACK TO THE BOAR'S HEAD AND MEET THE PRIEST. I'LL BE THERE SOON.

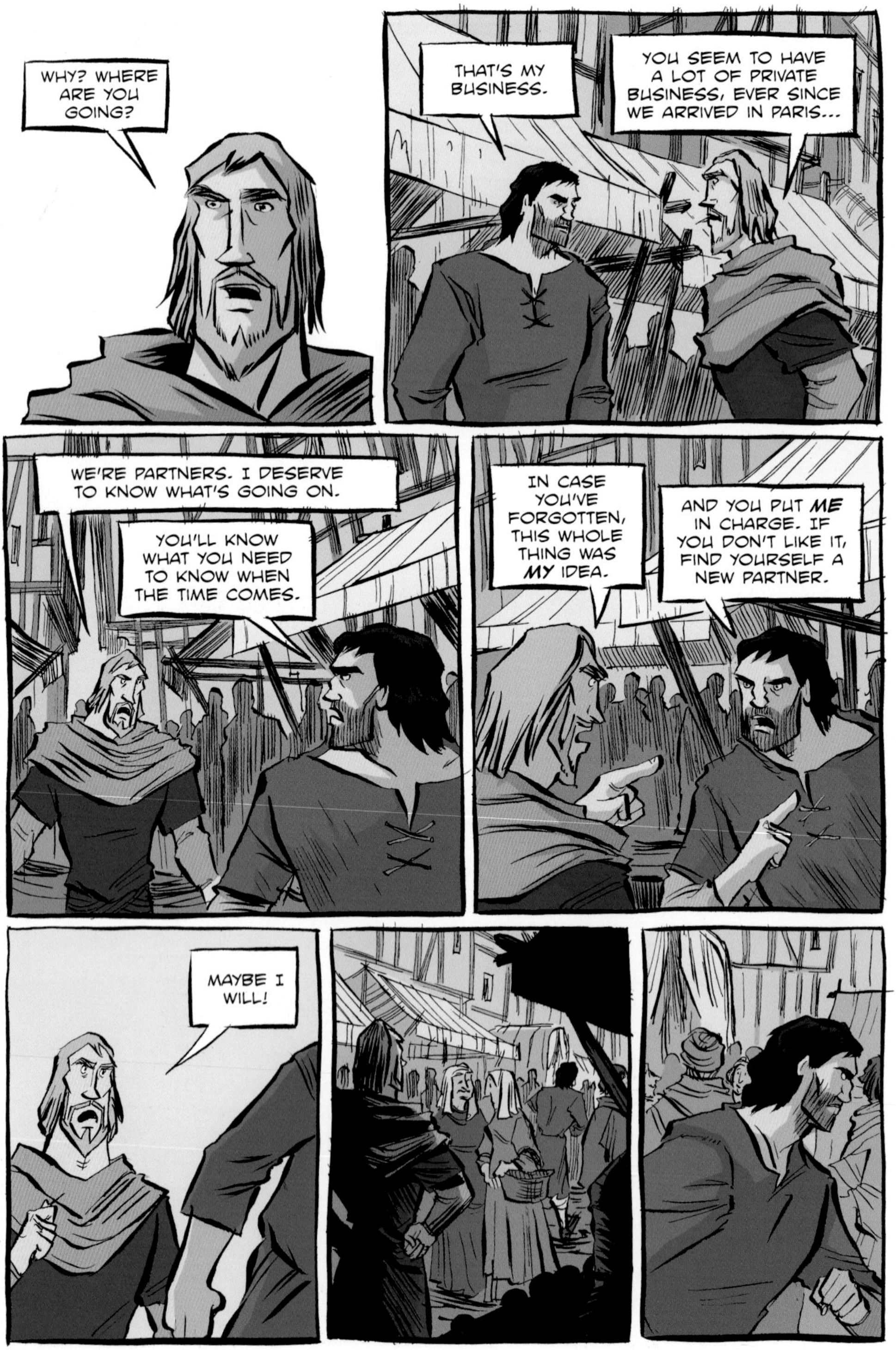
WHY? WHERE ARE YOU GOING?
THAT'S MY BUSINESS.
YOU SEEM TO HAVE A LOT OF PRIVATE BUSINESS, EVER SINCE WE ARRIVED IN PARIS...
WE'RE PARTNERS. I DESERVE TO KNOW WHAT'S GOING ON.
YOU'LL KNOW WHAT YOU NEED TO KNOW WHEN THE TIME COMES.
IN CASE YOU'VE FORGOTTEN, THIS WHOLE THING WAS *MY* IDEA.
AND YOU PUT *ME* IN CHARGE. IF YOU DON'T LIKE IT, FIND YOURSELF A NEW PARTNER.
MAYBE I WILL!

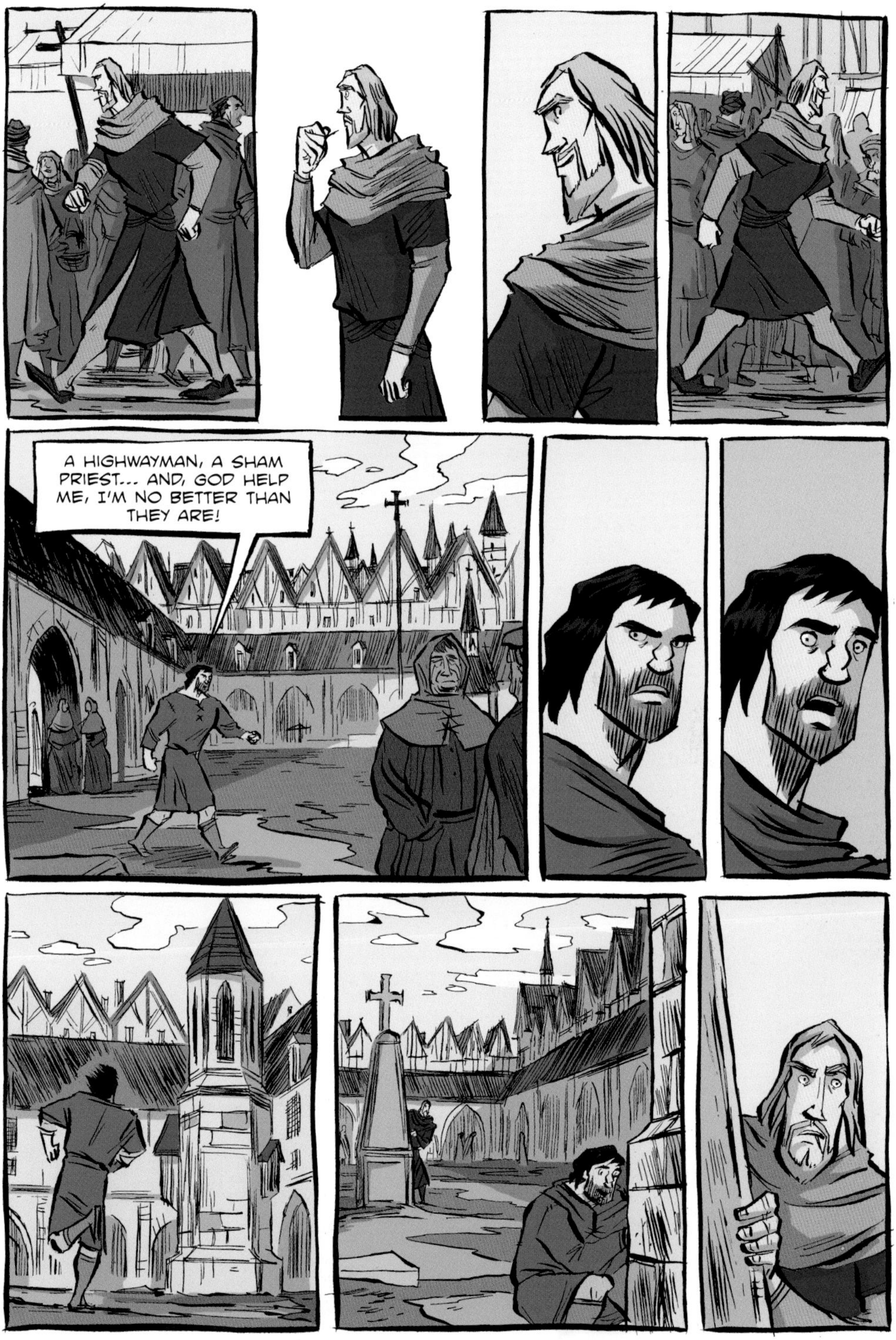
A HIGHWAYMAN, A SHAM PRIEST... AND, GOD HELP ME, I'M NO BETTER THAN THEY ARE!

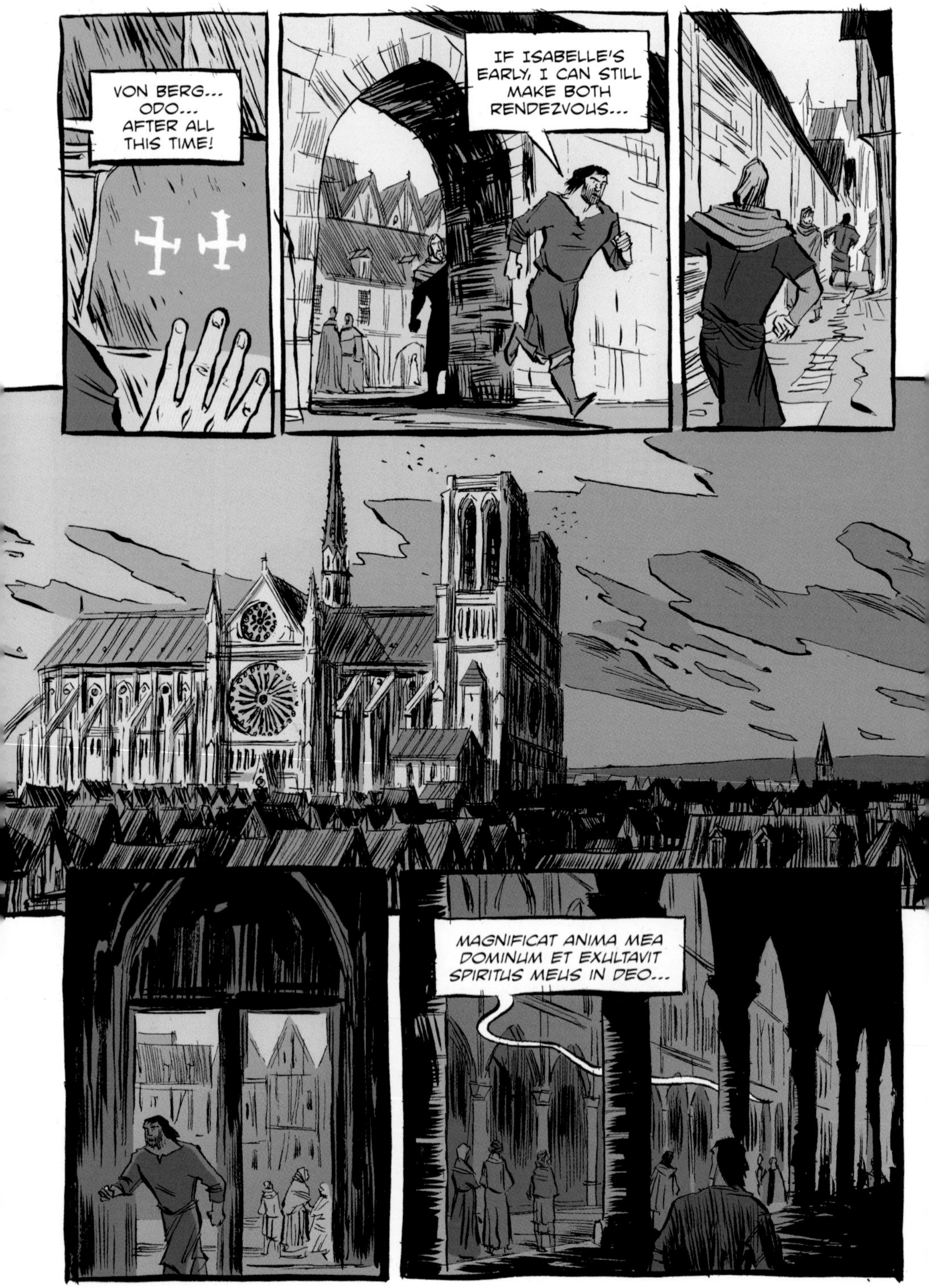
VON BERG... ODO... AFTER ALL THIS TIME!
IF ISABELLE'S EARLY, I CAN STILL MAKE BOTH RENDEZVOUS...
MAGNIFICAT ANIMA MEA DOMINUM ET EXULTAVIT SPIRITUS MEUS IN DEO...

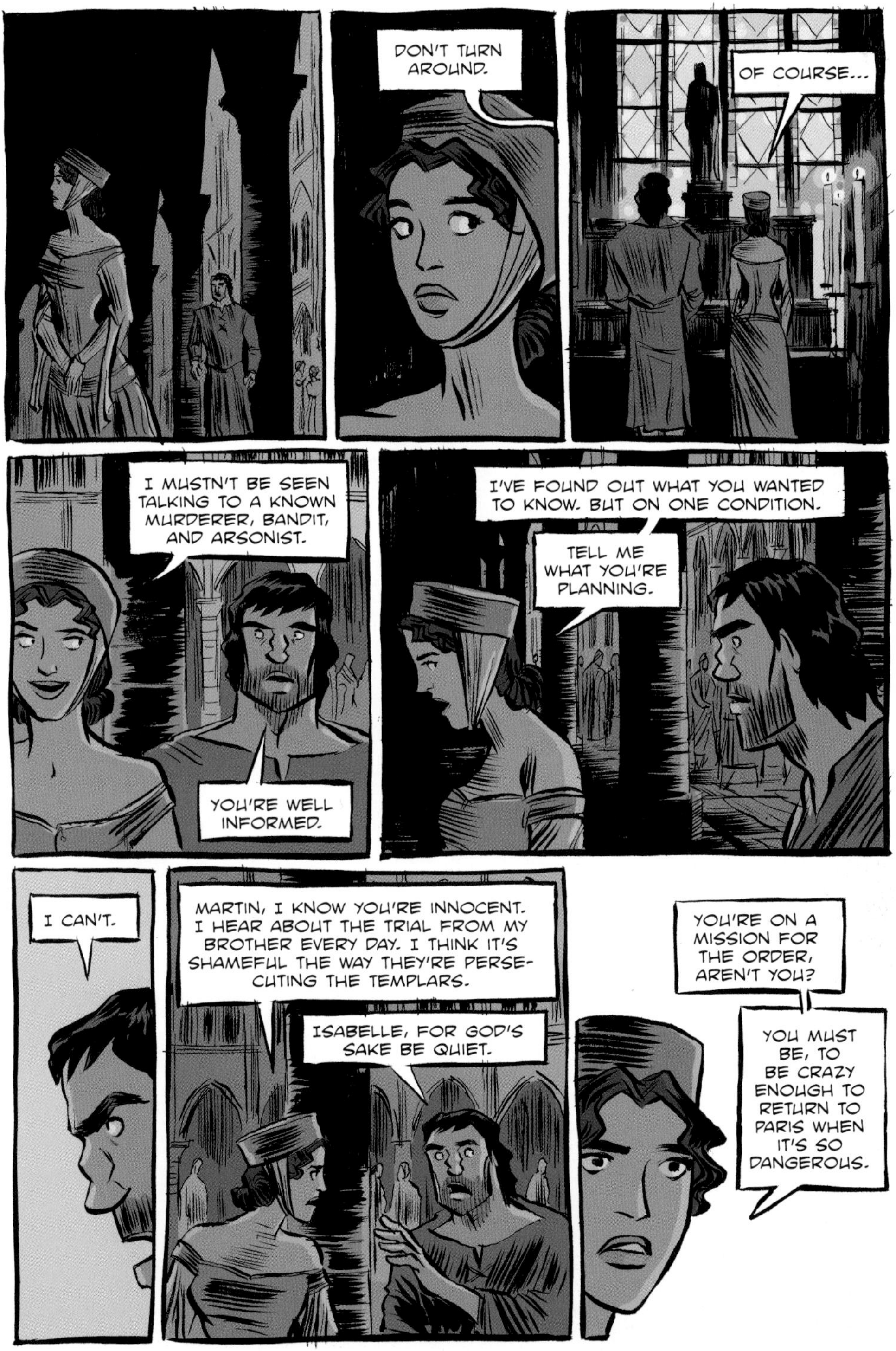
DON'T TURN AROUND.
OF COURSE...
I MUSTN'T BE SEEN TALKING TO A KNOWN MURDERER, BANDIT, AND ARSONIST.
YOU'RE WELL INFORMED.
I'VE FOUND OUT WHAT YOU WANTED TO KNOW. BUT ON ONE CONDITION.
TELL ME WHAT YOU'RE PLANNING.
I CAN'T.
MARTIN, I KNOW YOU'RE INNOCENT. I HEAR ABOUT THE TRIAL FROM MY BROTHER EVERY DAY. I THINK IT'S SHAMEFUL THE WAY THEY'RE PERSE-CUTING THE TEMPLARS.
ISABELLE, FOR GOD'S SAKE BE QUIET.
YOU'RE ON A MISSION FOR THE ORDER, AREN'T YOU?
YOU MUST BE, TO BE CRAZY ENOUGH TO RETURN TO PARIS WHEN IT'S SO DANGEROUS.

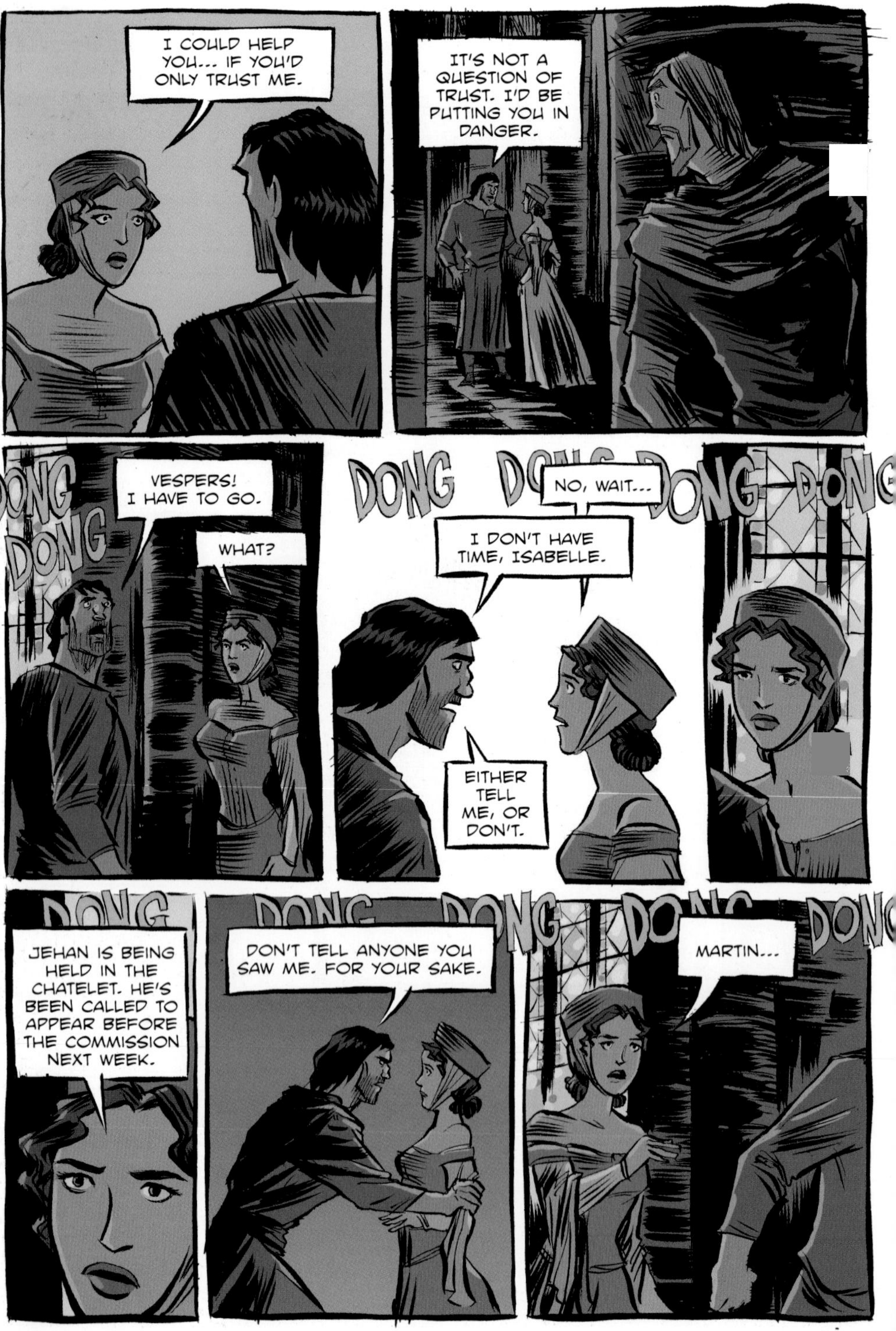
I COULD HELP YOU... IF YOU'D ONLY TRUST ME.
IT'S NOT A QUESTION OF TRUST. I'D BE PUTTING YOU IN DANGER.
DONG DONG
VESPERS! I HAVE TO GO.
WHAT?
DONG
NO, WAIT...
I DON'T HAVE TIME, ISABELLE.
EITHER TELL ME, OR DON'T.
DONG DONG
JEHAN IS BEING HELD IN THE CHATELET. HE'S BEEN CALLED TO APPEAR BEFORE THE COMMISSION NEXT WEEK.
DON'T TELL ANYONE YOU SAW ME. FOR YOUR SAKE.
DONG
MARTIN...

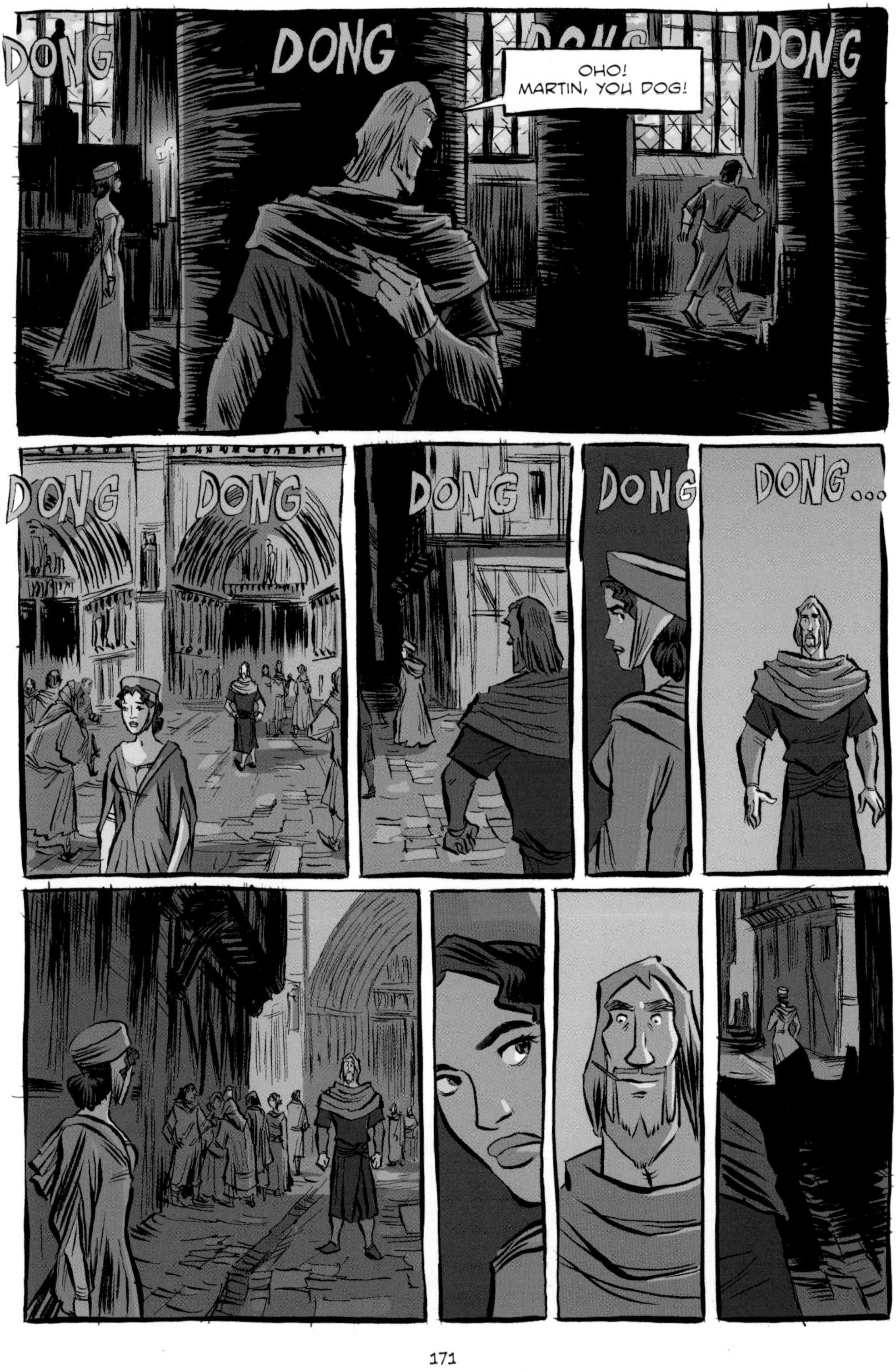
DONG
DONG
OHO!
MARTIN, YOU DOG!
DONG
DONG
DONG
DONG
DONG
DONG...

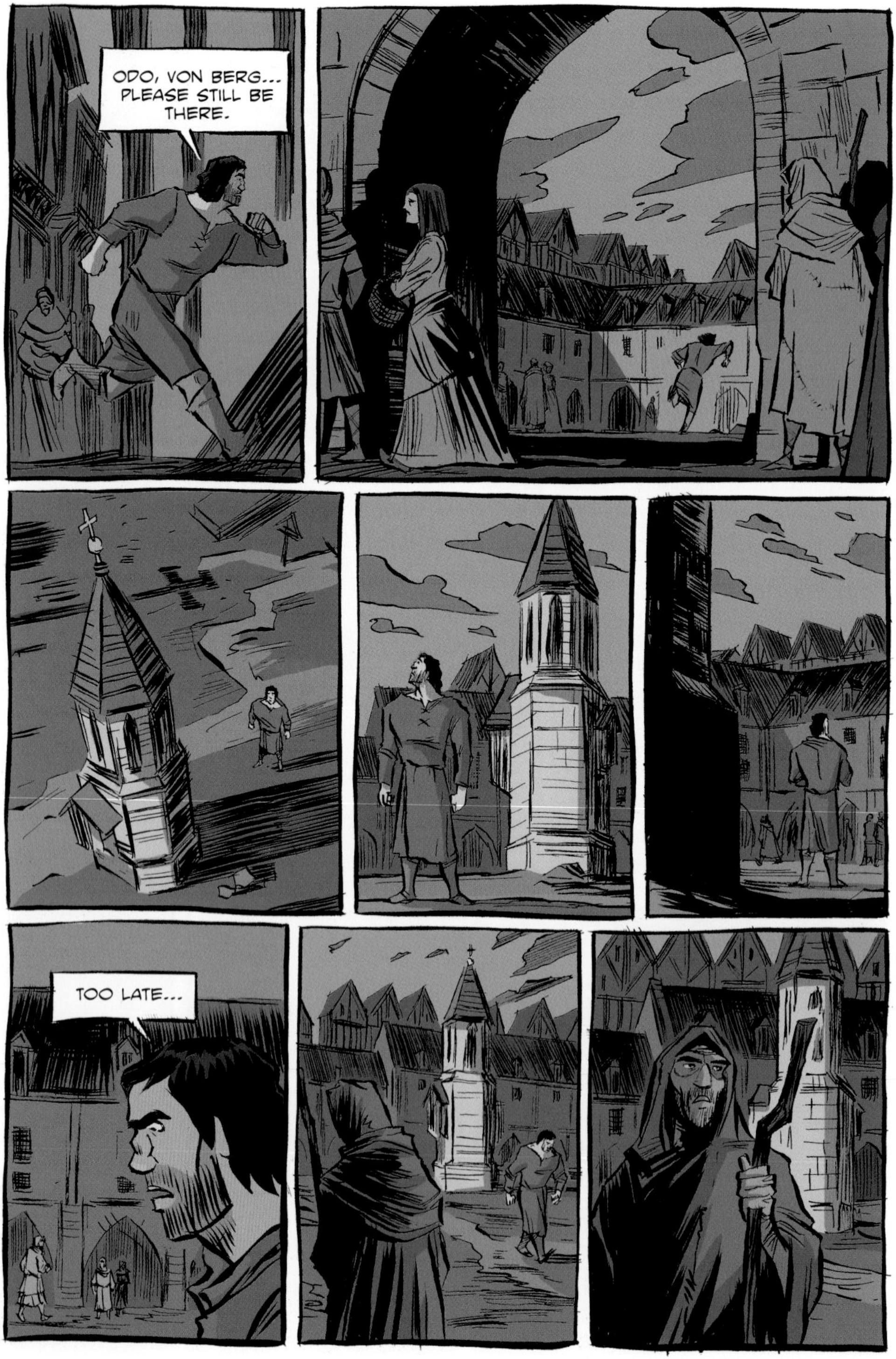
ODO, VON BERG... PLEASE STILL BE THERE.
TOO LATE...

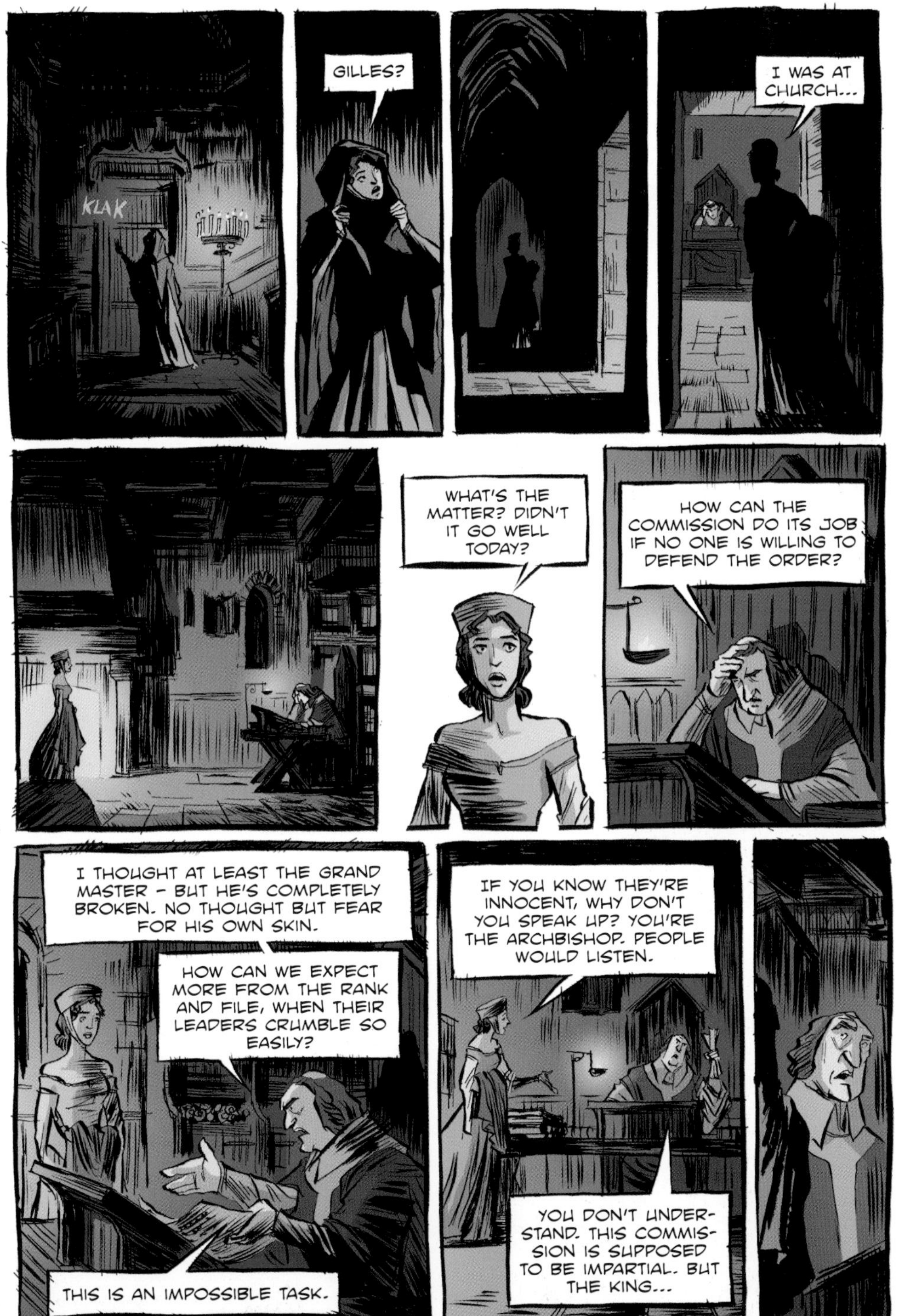
KLAK
GILLES?
I WAS AT CHURCH...
WHAT'S THE MATTER? DIDN'T IT GO WELL TODAY?
HOW CAN THE COMMISSION DO ITS JOB IF NO ONE IS WILLING TO DEFEND THE ORDER?
I THOUGHT AT LEAST THE GRAND MASTER - BUT HE'S COMPLETELY BROKEN. NO THOUGHT BUT FEAR FOR HIS OWN SKIN.
HOW CAN WE EXPECT MORE FROM THE RANK AND FILE, WHEN THEIR LEADERS CRUMBLE SO EASILY?
THIS IS AN IMPOSSIBLE TASK.
IF YOU KNOW THEY'RE INNOCENT, WHY DON'T YOU SPEAK UP? YOU'RE THE ARCHBISHOP. PEOPLE WOULD LISTEN.
YOU DON'T UNDERSTAND. THIS COMMISSION IS SUPPOSED TO BE IMPARTIAL. BUT THE KING...

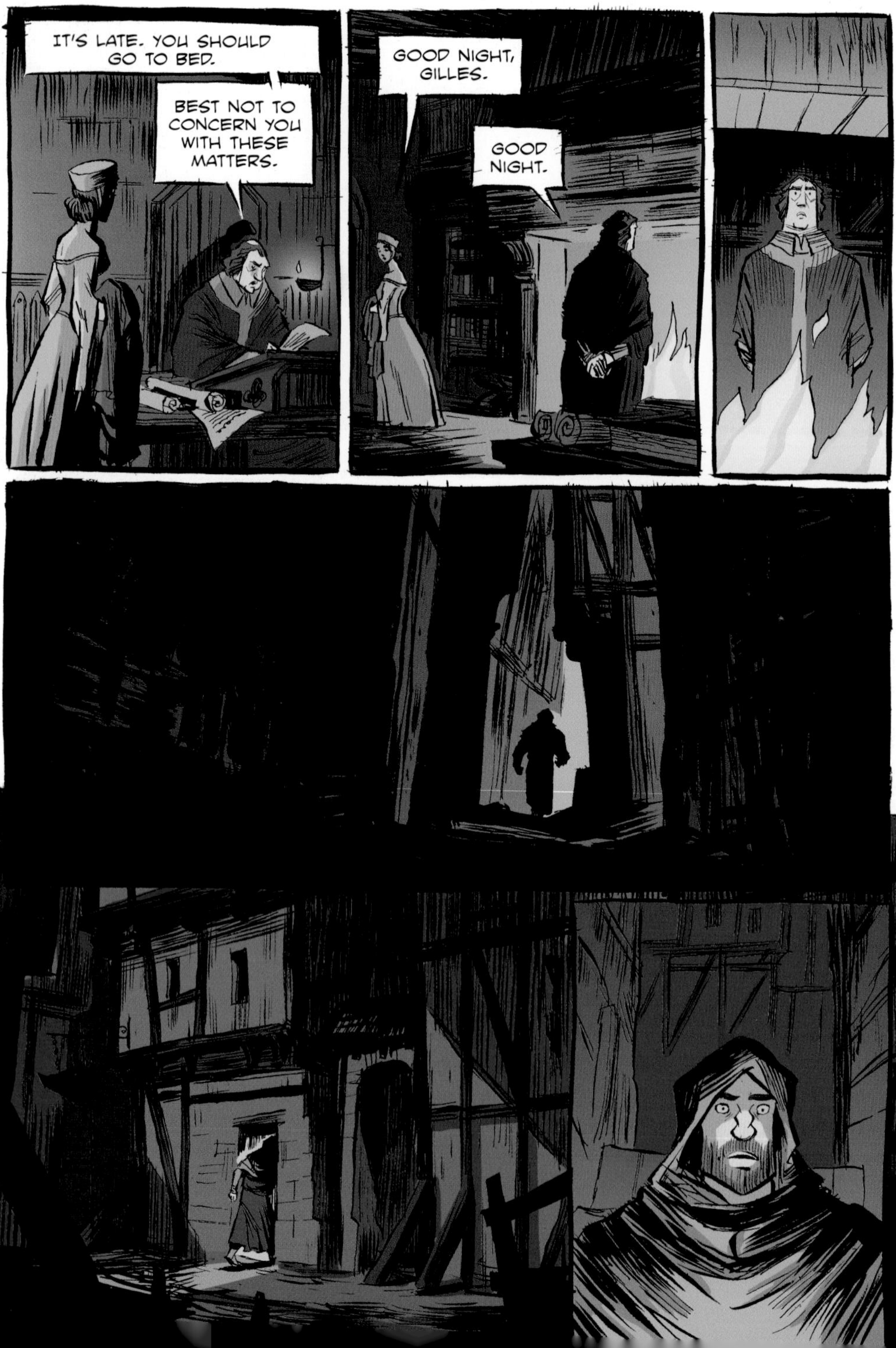
IT'S LATE. YOU SHOULD GO TO BED.
BEST NOT TO CONCERN YOU WITH THESE MATTERS.
GOOD NIGHT, GILLES.
GOOD NIGHT.

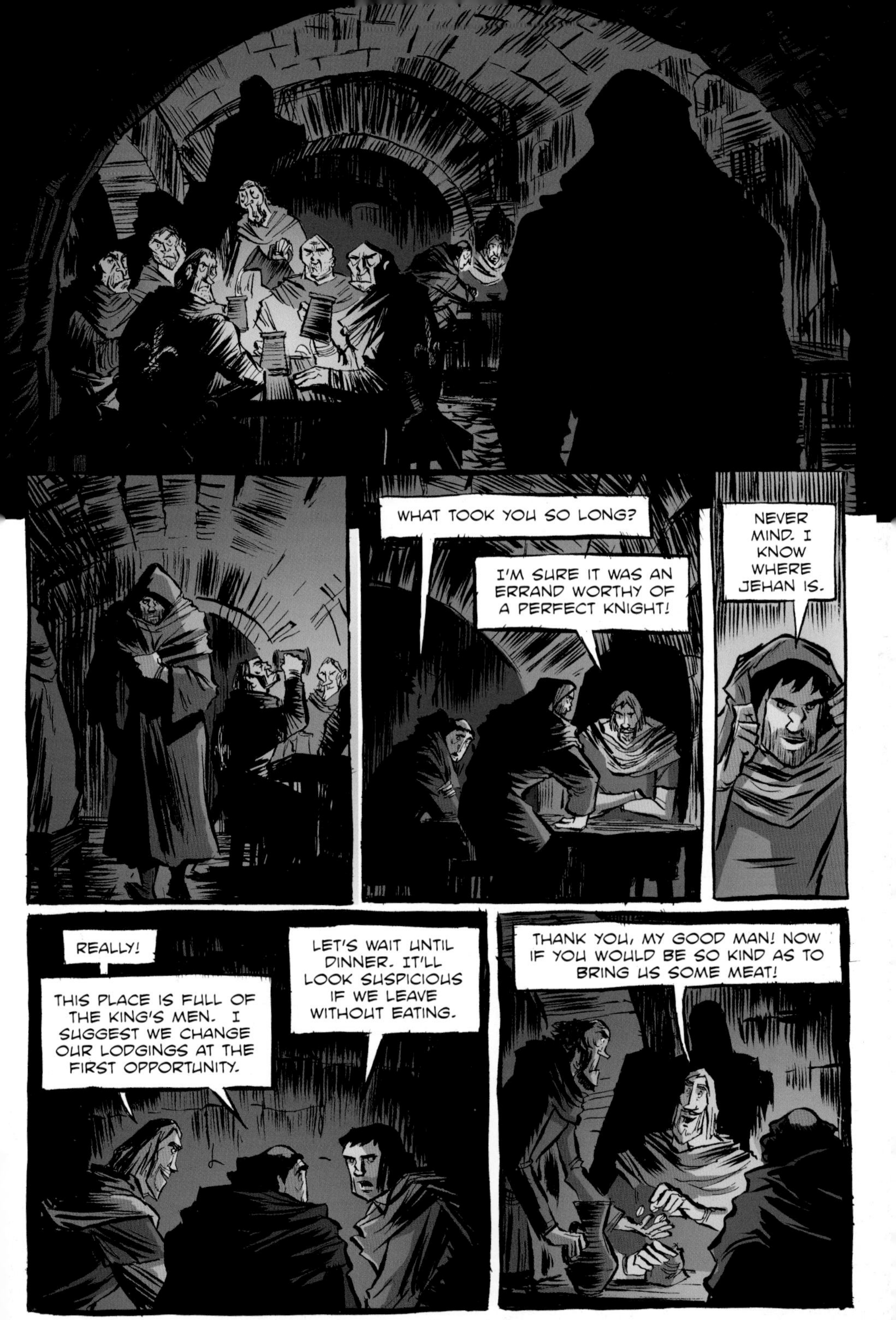
WHAT TOOK YOU SO LONG?
I'M SURE IT WAS AN ERRAND WORTHY OF A PERFECT KNIGHT!
NEVER MIND. I KNOW WHERE JEHAN IS.
REALLY!
THIS PLACE IS FULL OF THE KING'S MEN. I SUGGEST WE CHANGE OUR LODGINGS AT THE FIRST OPPORTUNITY.
LET'S WAIT UNTIL DINNER. IT'LL LOOK SUSPICIOUS IF WE LEAVE WITHOUT EATING.
THANK YOU, MY GOOD MAN! NOW IF YOU WOULD BE SO KIND AS TO BRING US SOME MEAT!

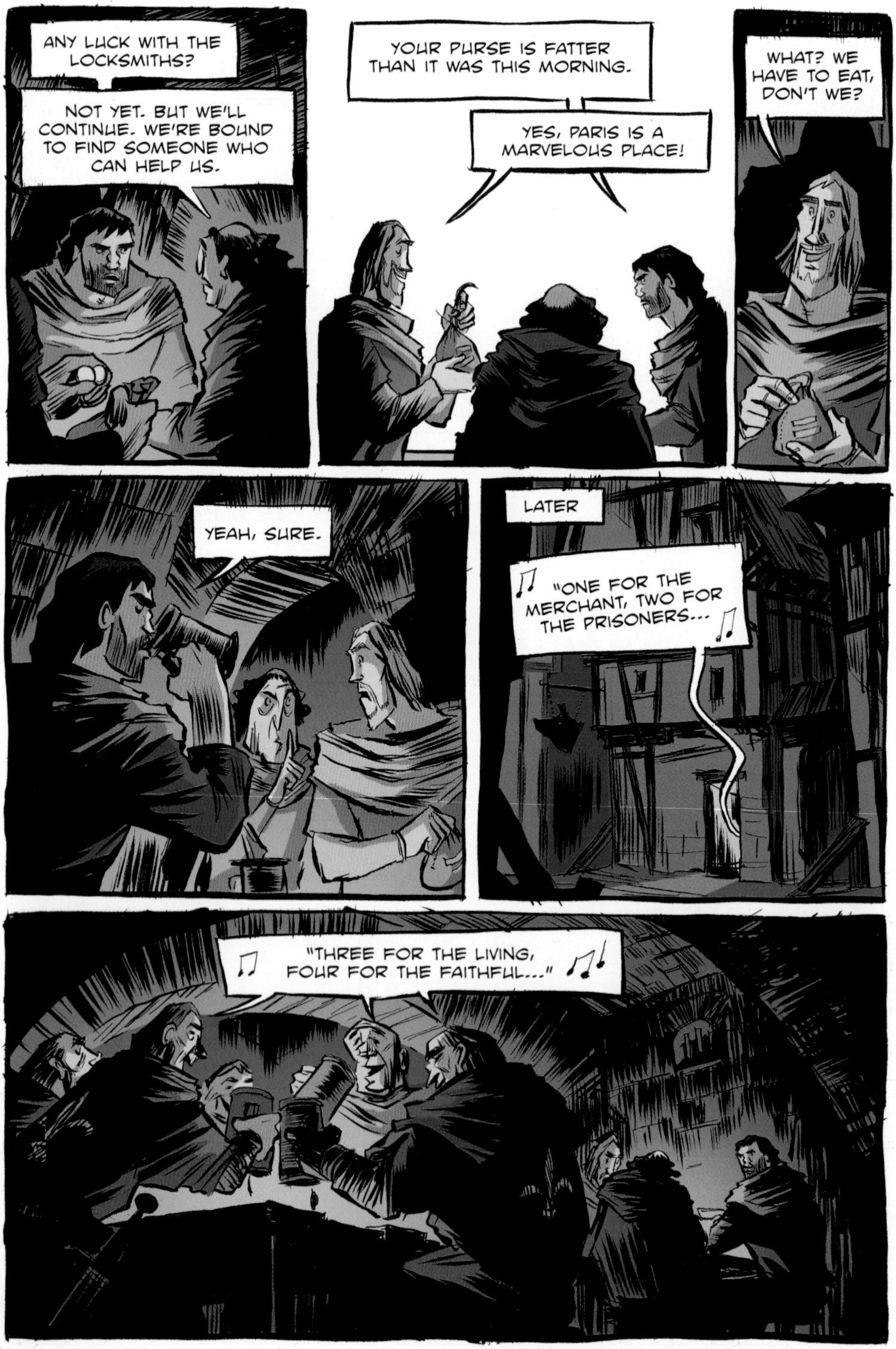
ANY LUCK WITH THE LOCKSMITHS?
NOT YET. BUT WE'LL CONTINUE. WE'RE BOUND TO FIND SOMEONE WHO CAN HELP US.
YOUR PURSE IS FATTER THAN IT WAS THIS MORNING.
YES, PARIS IS A MARVELOUS PLACE!
WHAT? WE HAVE TO EAT, DON'T WE?
YEAH, SURE.
LATER
"ONE FOR THE MERCHANT, TWO FOR THE PRISONERS...
"THREE FOR THE LIVING, FOUR FOR THE FAITHFUL..."

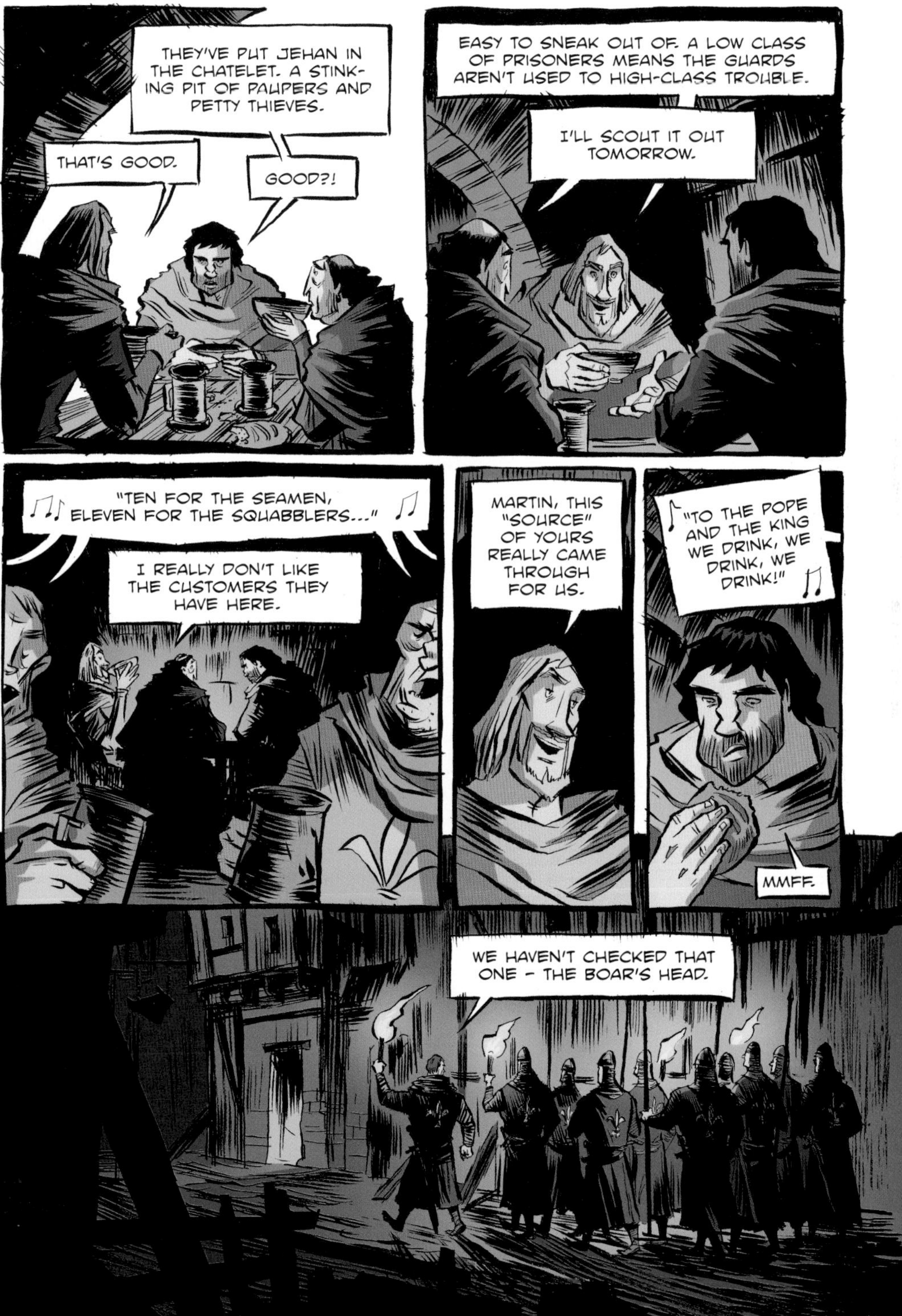
THEY'VE PUT JEHAN IN THE CHATELET. A STINKING PIT OF PAUPERS AND PETTY THIEVES.
THAT'S GOOD.
GOOD?!
EASY TO SNEAK OUT OF. A LOW CLASS OF PRISONERS MEANS THE GUARDS AREN'T USED TO HIGH-CLASS TROUBLE.
I'LL SCOUT IT OUT TOMORROW.
"TEN FOR THE SEAMEN, ELEVEN FOR THE SQUABBLERS..."
I REALLY DON'T LIKE THE CUSTOMERS THEY HAVE HERE.
MARTIN, THIS "SOURCE" OF YOURS REALLY CAME THROUGH FOR US.
"TO THE POPE AND THE KING WE DRINK, WE DRINK, WE DRINK!"
MMFF.
WE HAVEN'T CHECKED THAT ONE – THE BOAR'S HEAD.

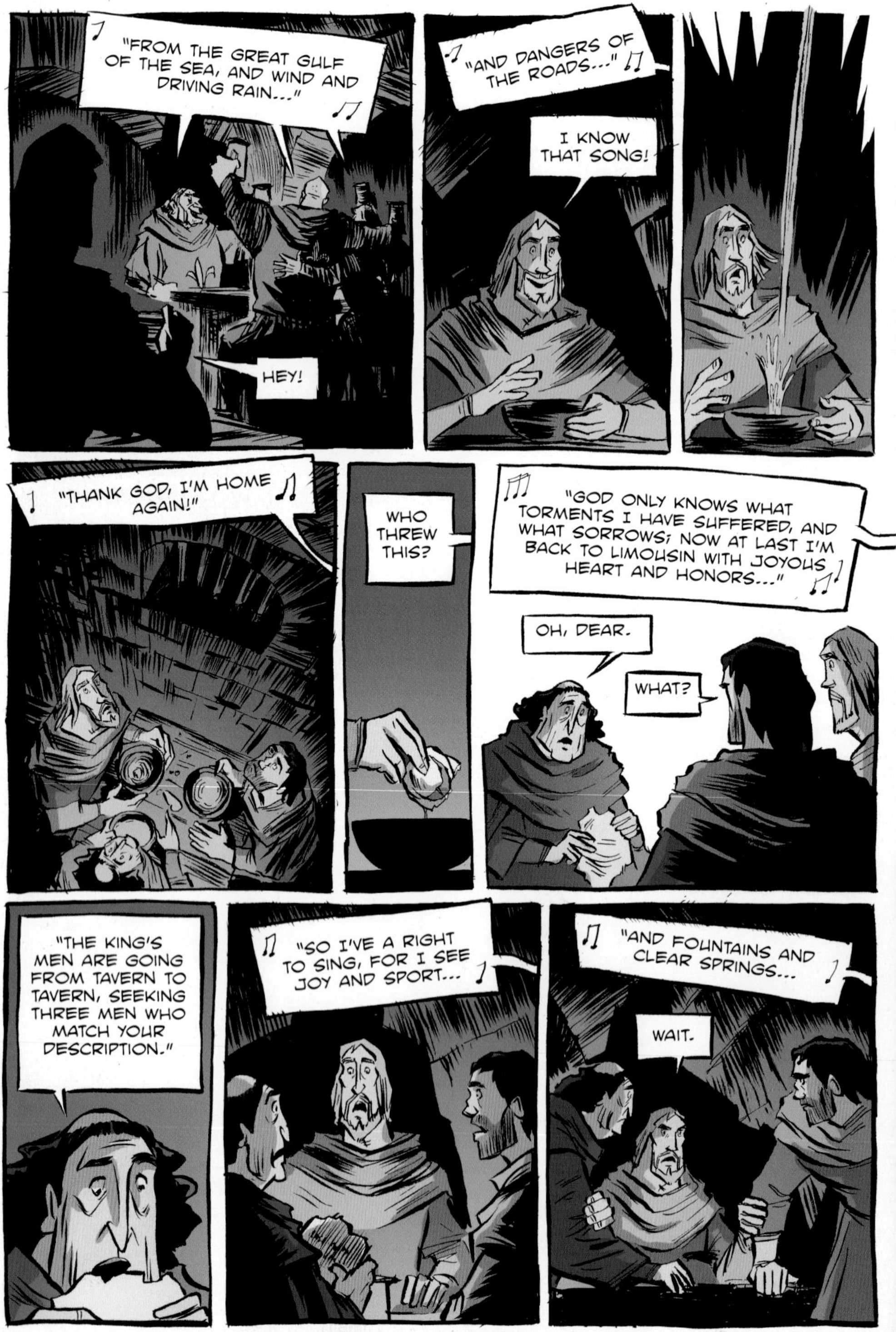
"FROM THE GREAT GULF OF THE SEA, AND WIND AND DRIVING RAIN..."
HEY!
"AND DANGERS OF THE ROADS..."
I KNOW THAT SONG!
"THANK GOD, I'M HOME AGAIN!"
WHO THREW THIS?
"GOD ONLY KNOWS WHAT TORMENTS I HAVE SUFFERED, AND WHAT SORROWS; NOW AT LAST I'M BACK TO LIMOUSIN WITH JOYOUS HEART AND HONORS..."
OH, DEAR.
WHAT?
"THE KING'S MEN ARE GOING FROM TAVERN TO TAVERN, SEEKING THREE MEN WHO MATCH YOUR DESCRIPTION."
"SO I'VE A RIGHT TO SING, FOR I SEE JOY AND SPORT...
"AND FOUNTAINS AND CLEAR SPRINGS...
WAIT.

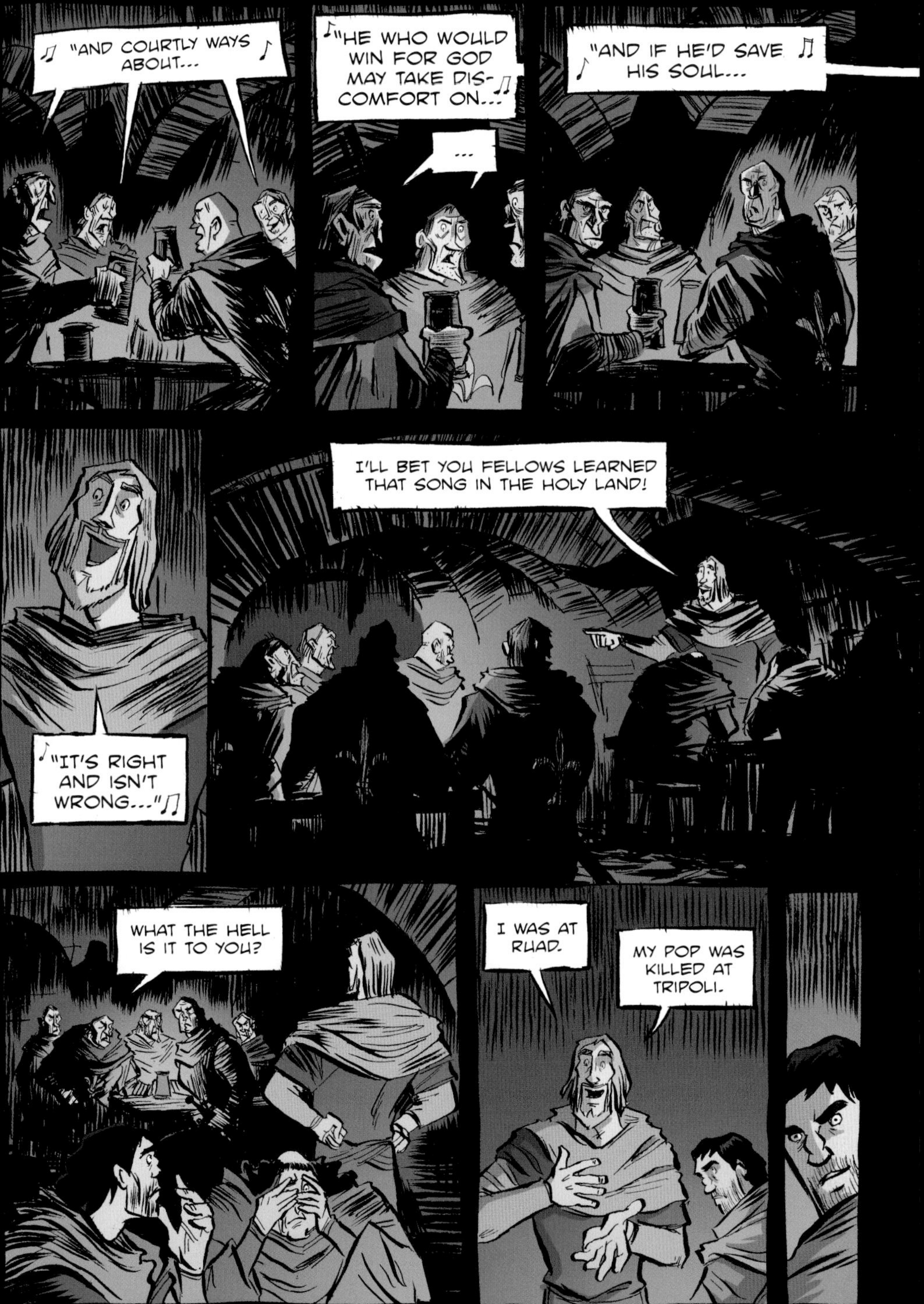
♫ "AND COURTLY WAYS ABOUT... ♪
♪"HE WHO WOULD WIN FOR GOD MAY TAKE DIS-COMFORT ON...♫
...
♪ "AND IF HE'D SAVE HIS SOUL... ♫
I'LL BET YOU FELLOWS LEARNED THAT SONG IN THE HOLY LAND!
♪"IT'S RIGHT AND ISN'T WRONG..."♫
WHAT THE HELL IS IT TO YOU?
I WAS AT RUAD.
MY POP WAS KILLED AT TRIPOLI.

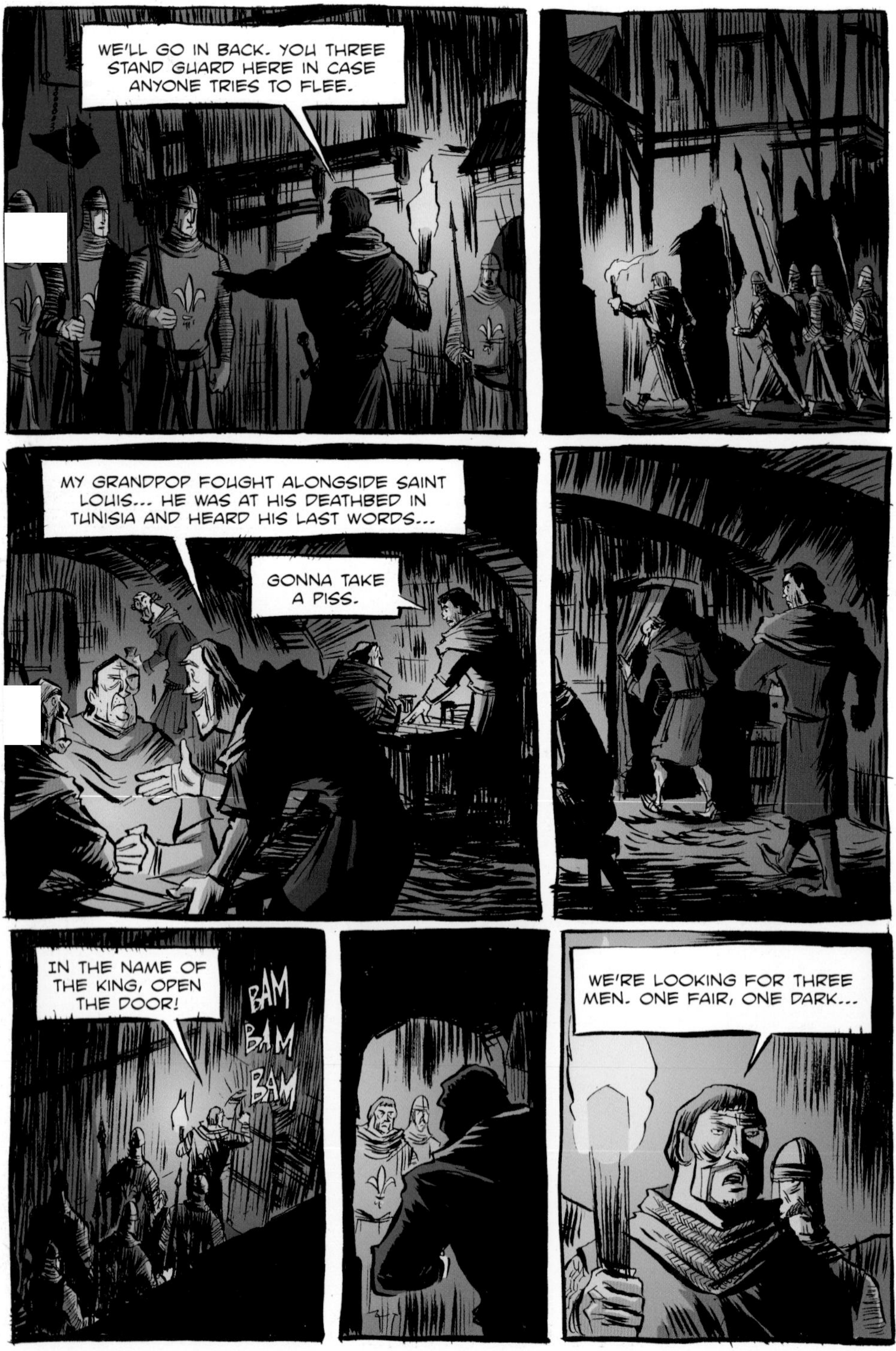

WE'LL GO IN BACK. YOU THREE STAND GUARD HERE IN CASE ANYONE TRIES TO FLEE.
MY GRANDPOP FOUGHT ALONGSIDE SAINT LOUIS... HE WAS AT HIS DEATHBED IN TUNISIA AND HEARD HIS LAST WORDS...
GONNA TAKE A PISS.
IN THE NAME OF THE KING, OPEN THE DOOR!
BAM
BAM
BAM
WE'RE LOOKING FOR THREE MEN. ONE FAIR, ONE DARK...

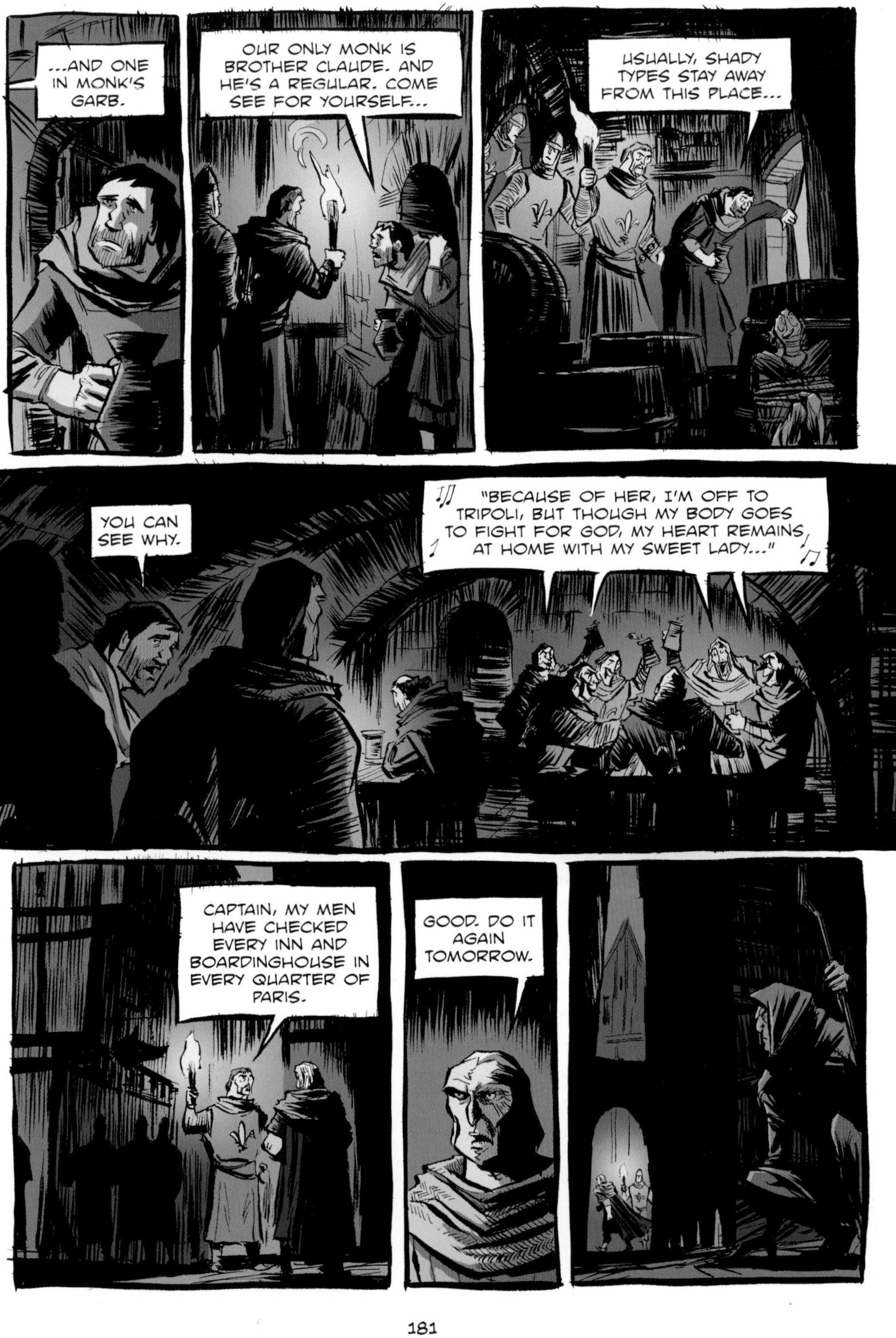
...AND ONE IN MONK'S GARB.
OUR ONLY MONK IS BROTHER CLAUDE. AND HE'S A REGULAR. COME SEE FOR YOURSELF...
USUALLY, SHADY TYPES STAY AWAY FROM THIS PLACE...
YOU CAN SEE WHY.
"BECAUSE OF HER, I'M OFF TO TRIPOLI, BUT THOUGH MY BODY GOES TO FIGHT FOR GOD, MY HEART REMAINS AT HOME WITH MY SWEET LADY..."
CAPTAIN, MY MEN HAVE CHECKED EVERY INN AND BOARDINGHOUSE IN EVERY QUARTER OF PARIS.
GOOD. DO IT AGAIN TOMORROW.

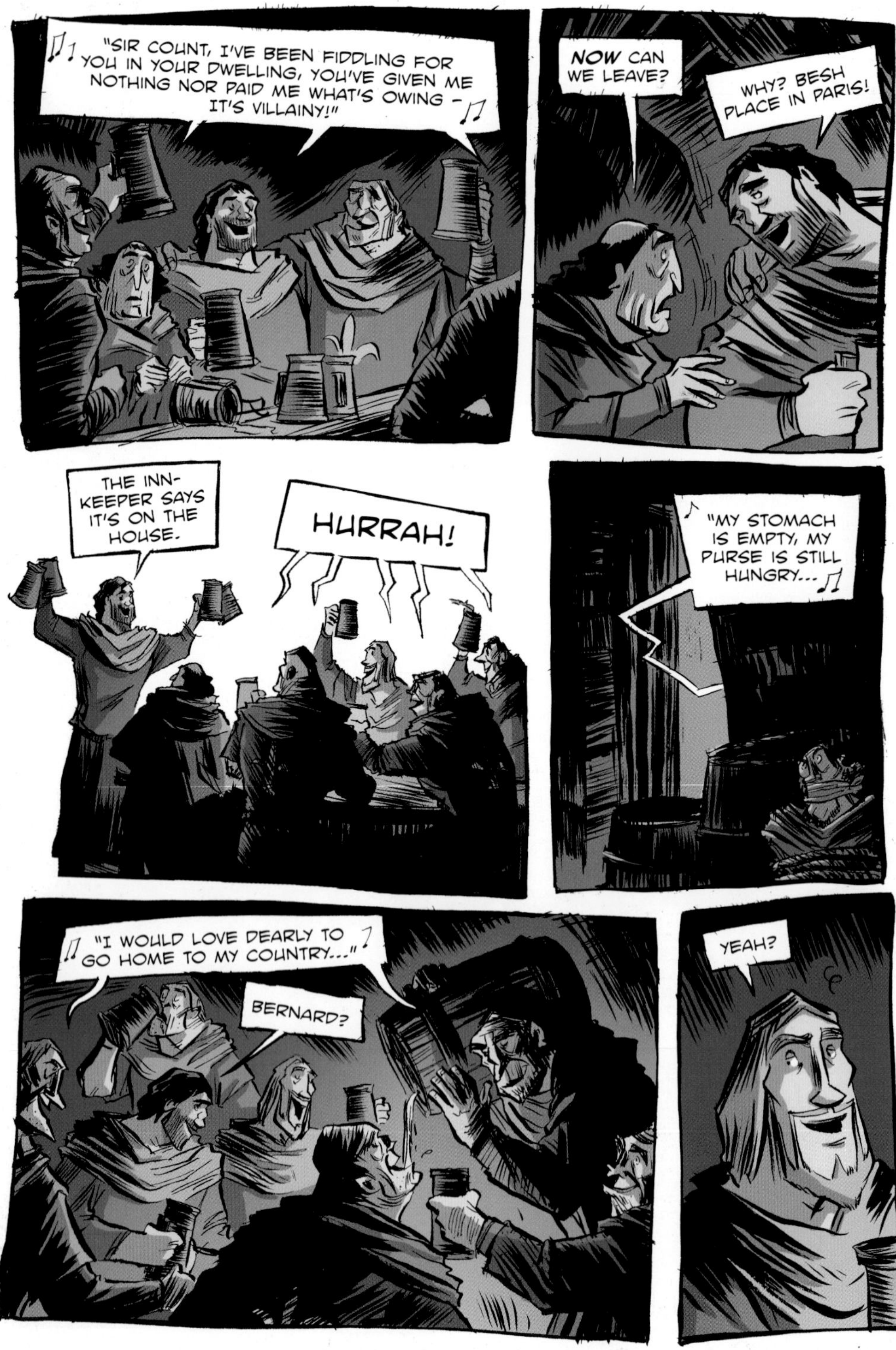
"SIR COUNT, I'VE BEEN FIDDLING FOR YOU IN YOUR DWELLING, YOU'VE GIVEN ME NOTHING NOR PAID ME WHAT'S OWING – IT'S VILLAINY!"
NOW CAN WE LEAVE?
WHY? BESH PLACE IN PARIS!
THE INN-KEEPER SAYS IT'S ON THE HOUSE.
HURRAH!
"MY STOMACH IS EMPTY, MY PURSE IS STILL HUNGRY...
"I WOULD LOVE DEARLY TO GO HOME TO MY COUNTRY..."
BERNARD?
YEAH?

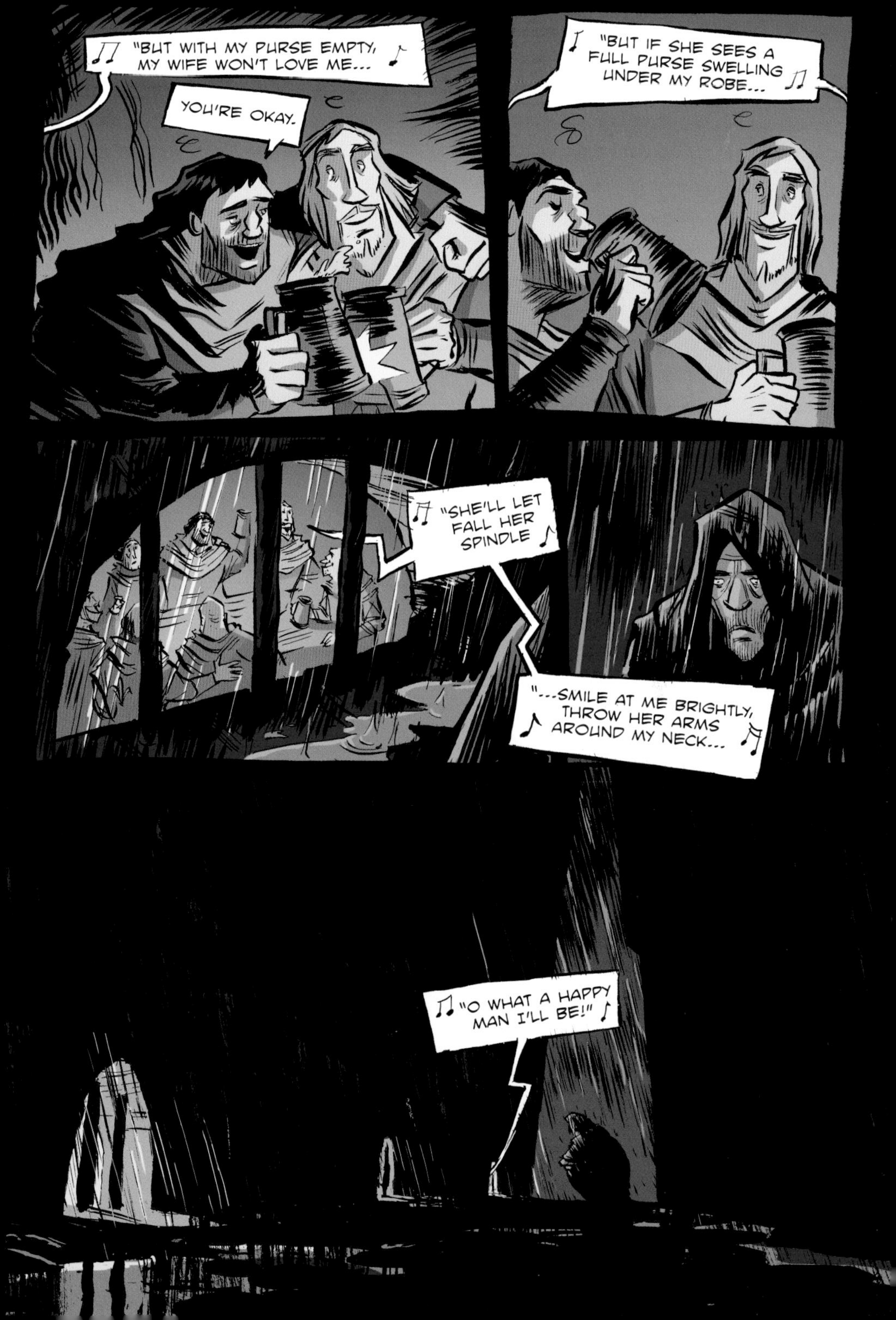
"BUT WITH MY PURSE EMPTY, MY WIFE WON'T LOVE ME...
YOU'RE OKAY.
"BUT IF SHE SEES A FULL PURSE SWELLING UNDER MY ROBE...
"SHE'LL LET FALL HER SPINDLE
"...SMILE AT ME BRIGHTLY, THROW HER ARMS AROUND MY NECK...
"O WHAT A HAPPY MAN I'LL BE!"

5. The Innocents

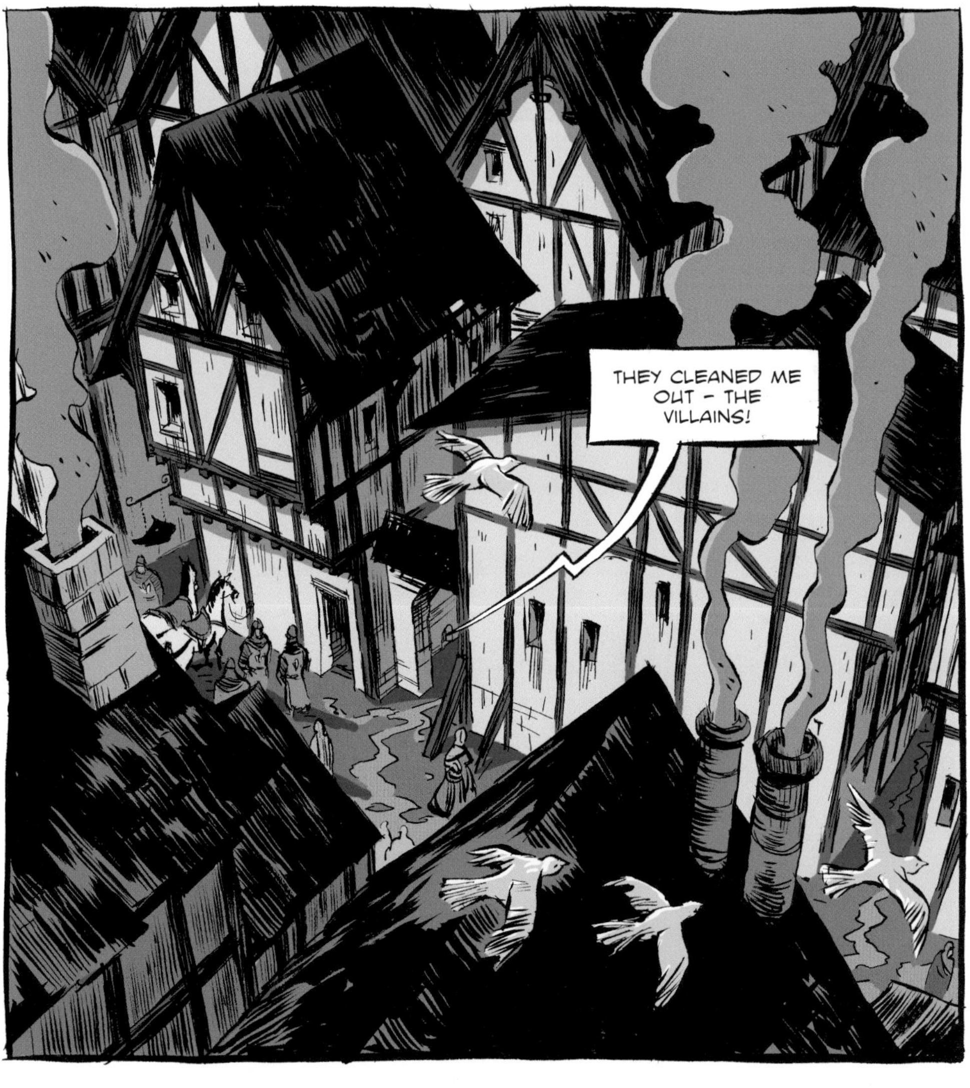
THEY CLEANED ME OUT – THE VILLAINS!

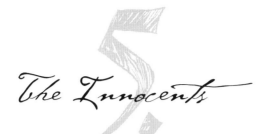

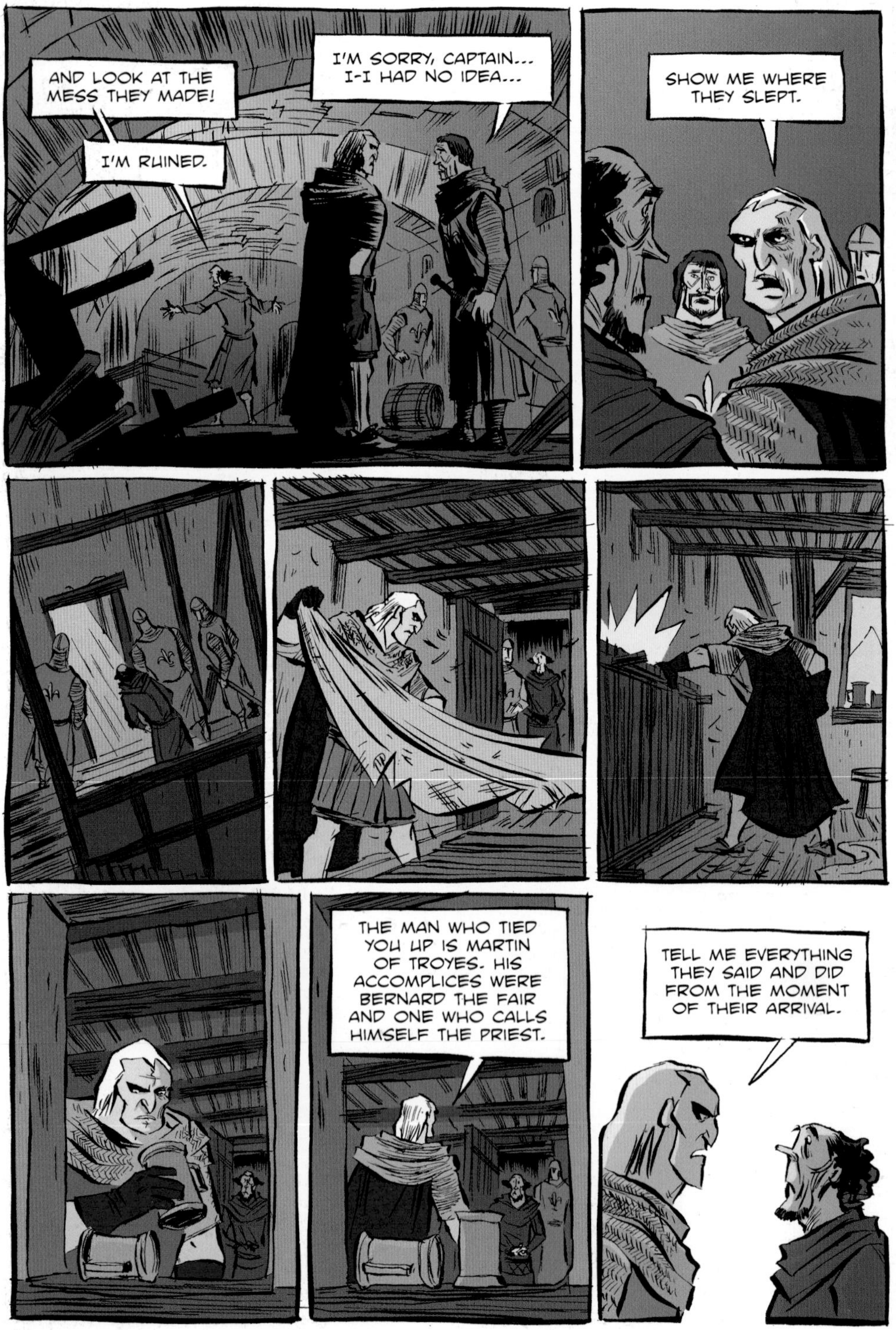
AND LOOK AT THE MESS THEY MADE!
I'M RUINED.
I'M SORRY, CAPTAIN... I-I HAD NO IDEA...
SHOW ME WHERE THEY SLEPT.
THE MAN WHO TIED YOU UP IS MARTIN OF TROYES. HIS ACCOMPLICES WERE BERNARD THE FAIR AND ONE WHO CALLS HIMSELF THE PRIEST.
TELL ME EVERYTHING THEY SAID AND DID FROM THE MOMENT OF THEIR ARRIVAL.

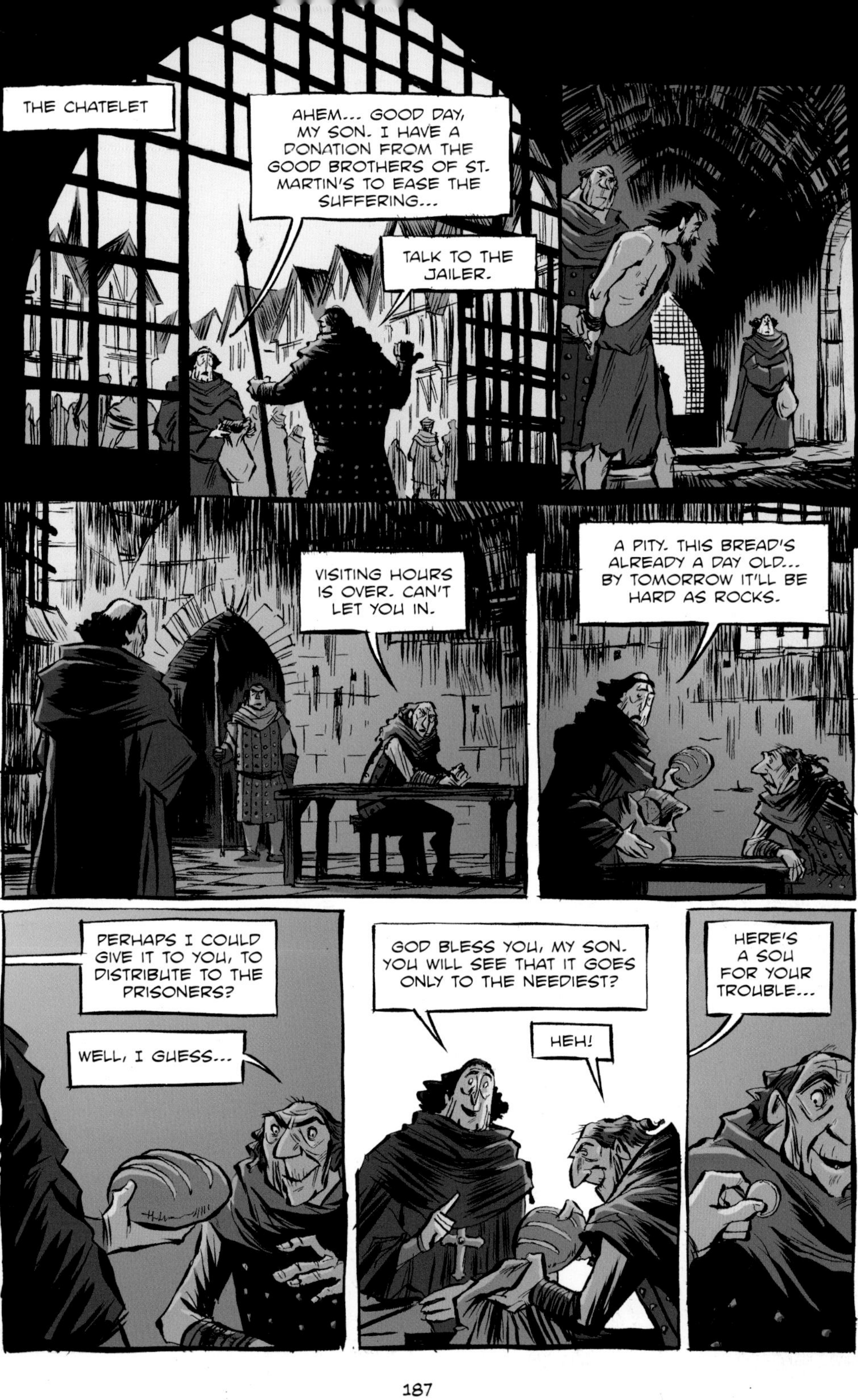
THE CHATELET
AHEM... GOOD DAY, MY SON. I HAVE A DONATION FROM THE GOOD BROTHERS OF ST. MARTIN'S TO EASE THE SUFFERING...
TALK TO THE JAILER.
VISITING HOURS IS OVER. CAN'T LET YOU IN.
A PITY. THIS BREAD'S ALREADY A DAY OLD... BY TOMORROW IT'LL BE HARD AS ROCKS.
PERHAPS I COULD GIVE IT TO YOU, TO DISTRIBUTE TO THE PRISONERS?
WELL, I GUESS...
GOD BLESS YOU, MY SON. YOU WILL SEE THAT IT GOES ONLY TO THE NEEDIEST?
HEH!
HERE'S A SOU FOR YOUR TROUBLE...

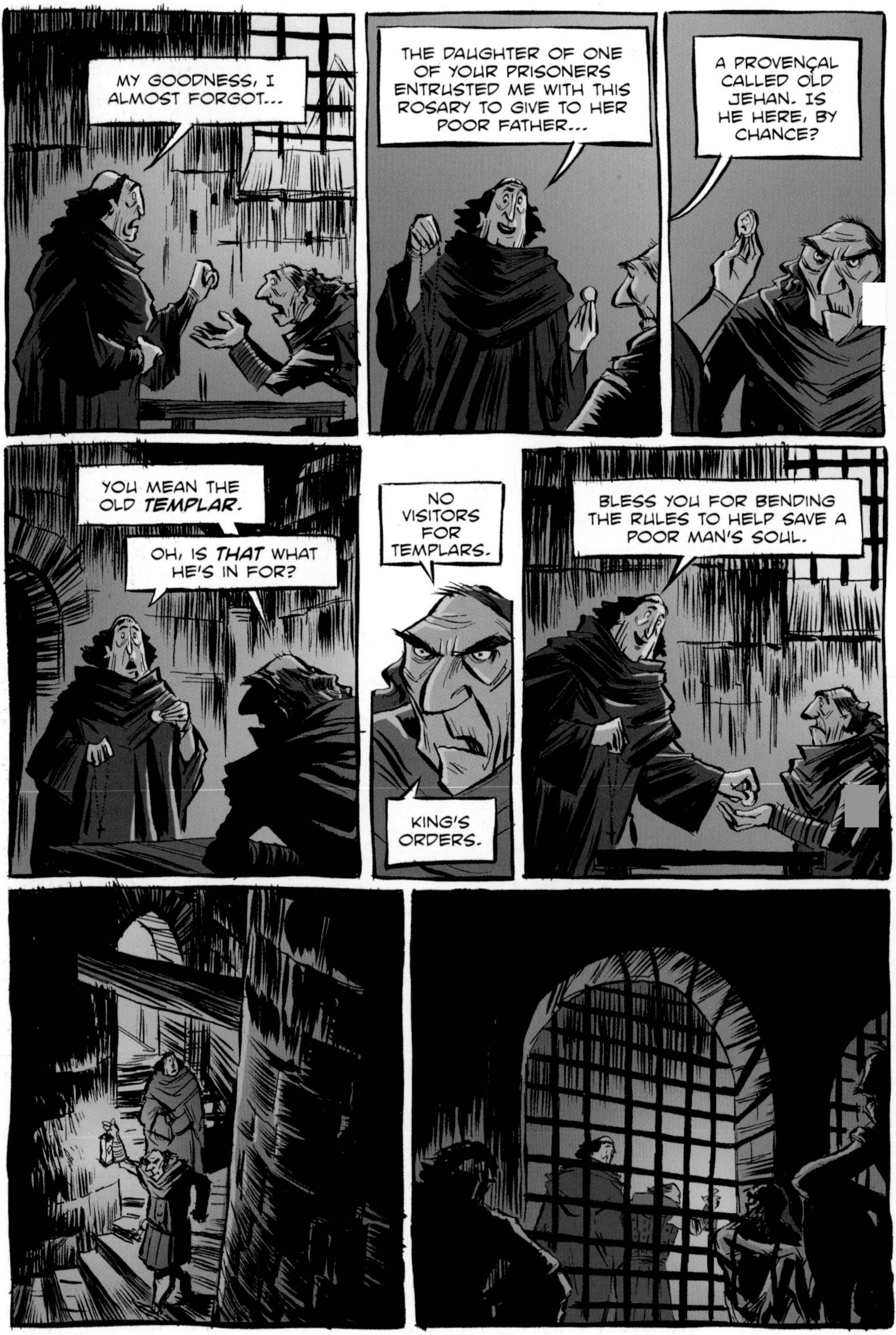
MY GOODNESS, I ALMOST FORGOT...
THE DAUGHTER OF ONE OF YOUR PRISONERS ENTRUSTED ME WITH THIS ROSARY TO GIVE TO HER POOR FATHER...
A PROVENÇAL CALLED OLD JEHAN. IS HE HERE, BY CHANCE?
YOU MEAN THE OLD *TEMPLAR*.
OH, IS *THAT* WHAT HE'S IN FOR?
NO VISITORS FOR TEMPLARS.
KING'S ORDERS.
BLESS YOU FOR BENDING THE RULES TO HELP SAVE A POOR MAN'S SOUL.

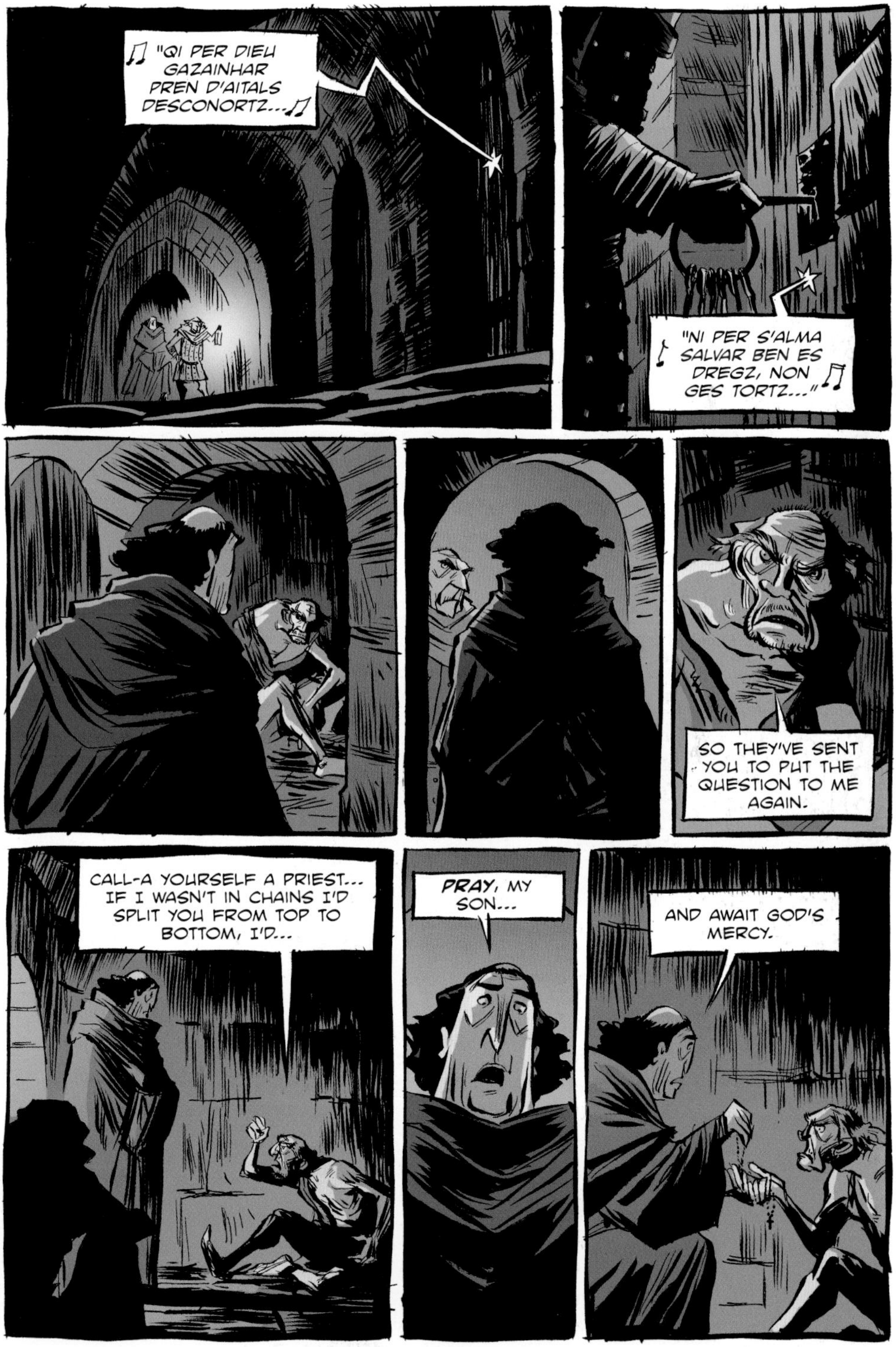
"QI PER DIEU GAZAINHAR PREN D'AITALS DESCONORTZ...
"NI PER S'ALMA SALVAR BEN ES DREGZ, NON GES TORTZ..."
SO THEY'VE SENT YOU TO PUT THE QUESTION TO ME AGAIN.
CALL-A YOURSELF A PRIEST... IF I WASN'T IN CHAINS I'D SPLIT YOU FROM TOP TO BOTTOM, I'D...
PRAY, MY SON...
AND AWAIT GOD'S MERCY.

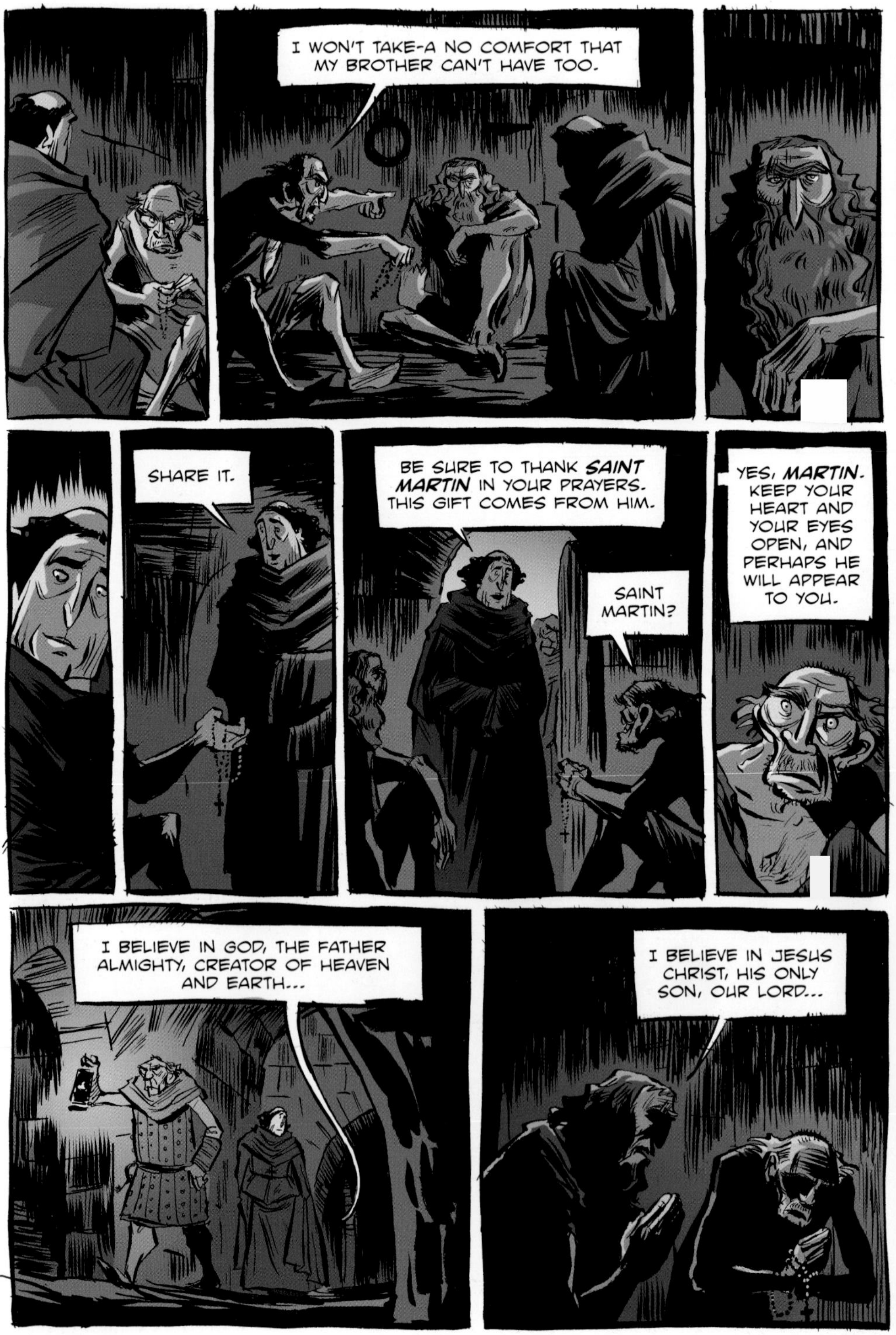
I WON'T TAKE-A NO COMFORT THAT MY BROTHER CAN'T HAVE TOO.
SHARE IT.
BE SURE TO THANK SAINT MARTIN IN YOUR PRAYERS. THIS GIFT COMES FROM HIM.
SAINT MARTIN?
YES, MARTIN. KEEP YOUR HEART AND YOUR EYES OPEN, AND PERHAPS HE WILL APPEAR TO YOU.
I BELIEVE IN GOD, THE FATHER ALMIGHTY, CREATOR OF HEAVEN AND EARTH...
I BELIEVE IN JESUS CHRIST, HIS ONLY SON, OUR LORD...

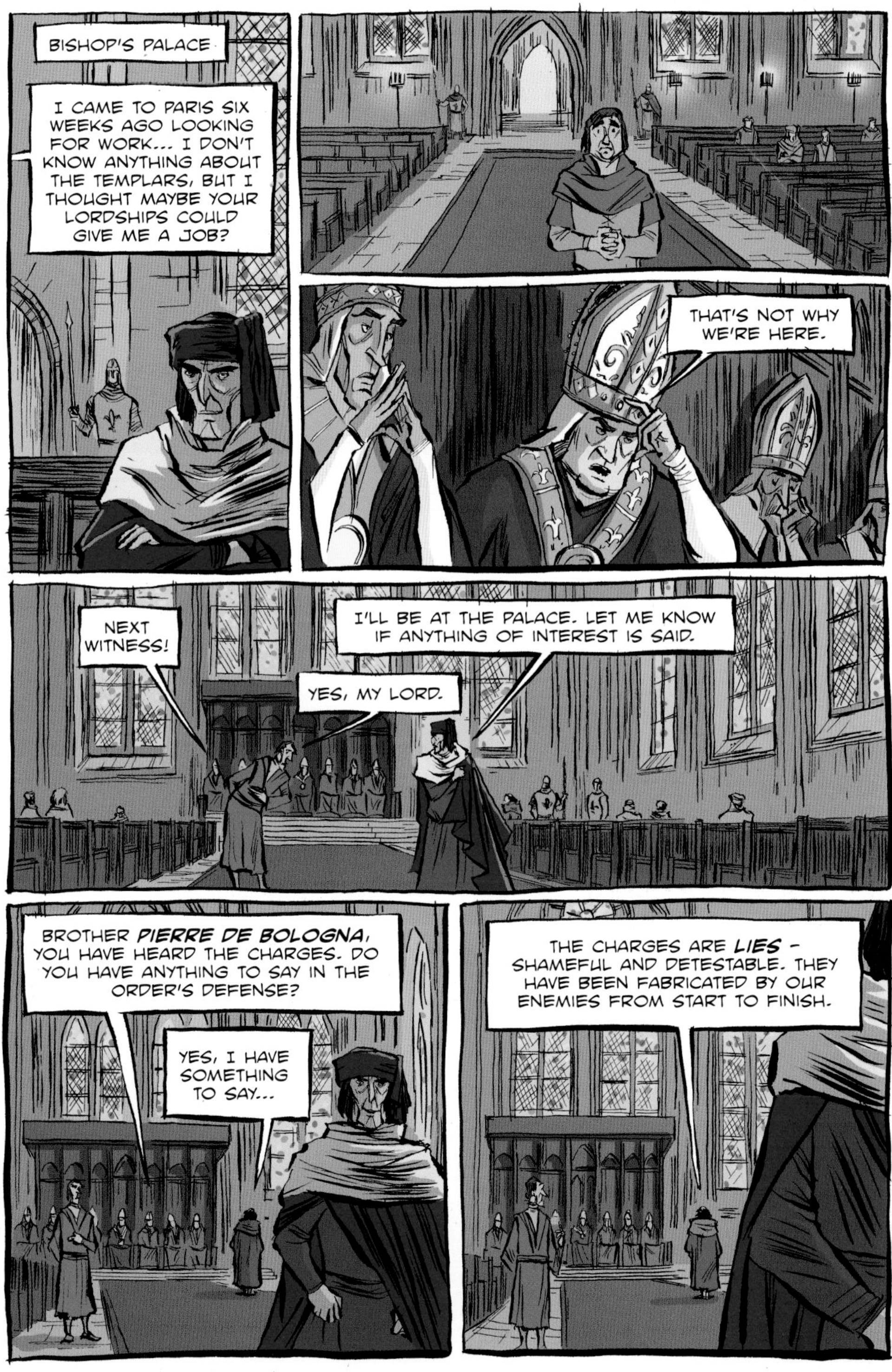
BISHOP'S PALACE
I CAME TO PARIS SIX WEEKS AGO LOOKING FOR WORK... I DON'T KNOW ANYTHING ABOUT THE TEMPLARS, BUT I THOUGHT MAYBE YOUR LORDSHIPS COULD GIVE ME A JOB?
THAT'S NOT WHY WE'RE HERE.
NEXT WITNESS!
I'LL BE AT THE PALACE. LET ME KNOW IF ANYTHING OF INTEREST IS SAID.
YES, MY LORD.
BROTHER *PIERRE DE BOLOGNA*, YOU HAVE HEARD THE CHARGES. DO YOU HAVE ANYTHING TO SAY IN THE ORDER'S DEFENSE?
YES, I HAVE SOMETHING TO SAY...
THE CHARGES ARE *LIES* - SHAMEFUL AND DETESTABLE. THEY HAVE BEEN FABRICATED BY OUR ENEMIES FROM START TO FINISH.

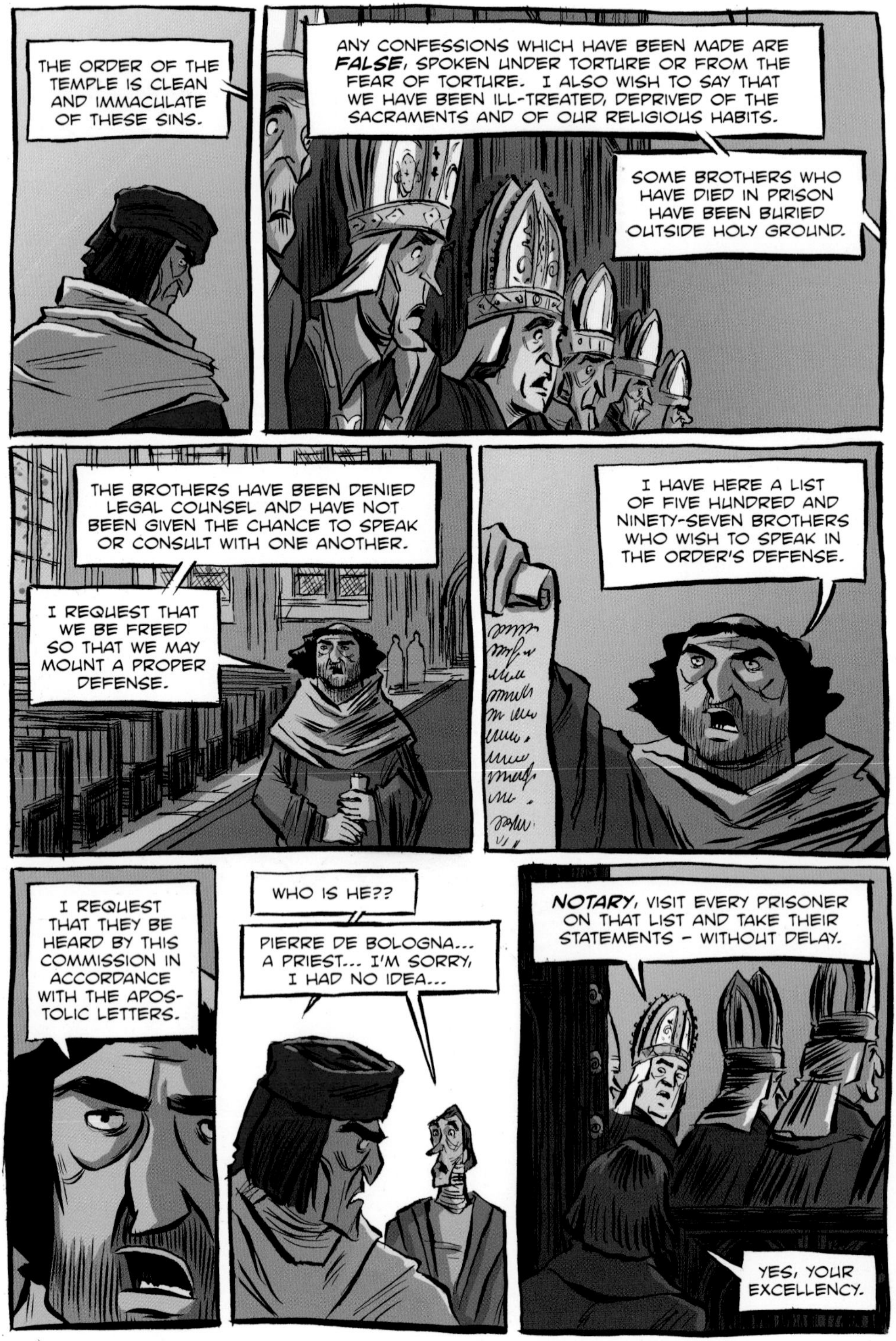
THE ORDER OF THE TEMPLE IS CLEAN AND IMMACULATE OF THESE SINS.
ANY CONFESSIONS WHICH HAVE BEEN MADE ARE FALSE, SPOKEN UNDER TORTURE OR FROM THE FEAR OF TORTURE. I ALSO WISH TO SAY THAT WE HAVE BEEN ILL-TREATED, DEPRIVED OF THE SACRAMENTS AND OF OUR RELIGIOUS HABITS.
SOME BROTHERS WHO HAVE DIED IN PRISON HAVE BEEN BURIED OUTSIDE HOLY GROUND.
THE BROTHERS HAVE BEEN DENIED LEGAL COUNSEL AND HAVE NOT BEEN GIVEN THE CHANCE TO SPEAK OR CONSULT WITH ONE ANOTHER.
I REQUEST THAT WE BE FREED SO THAT WE MAY MOUNT A PROPER DEFENSE.
I HAVE HERE A LIST OF FIVE HUNDRED AND NINETY-SEVEN BROTHERS WHO WISH TO SPEAK IN THE ORDER'S DEFENSE.
I REQUEST THAT THEY BE HEARD BY THIS COMMISSION IN ACCORDANCE WITH THE APOSTOLIC LETTERS.
WHO IS HE??
PIERRE DE BOLOGNA... A PRIEST... I'M SORRY, I HAD NO IDEA...
NOTARY, VISIT EVERY PRISONER ON THAT LIST AND TAKE THEIR STATEMENTS - WITHOUT DELAY.
YES, YOUR EXCELLENCY.

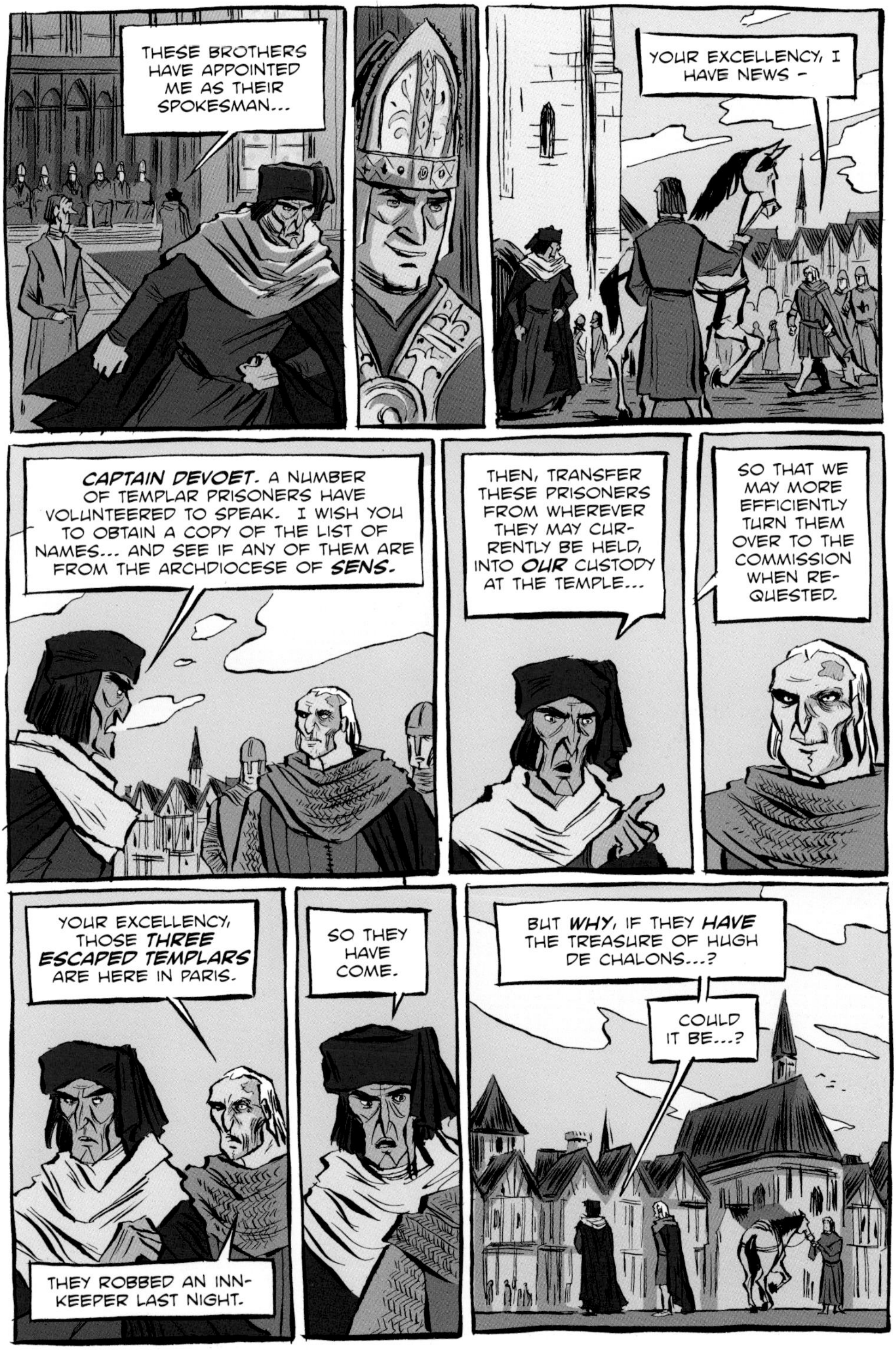
THESE BROTHERS HAVE APPOINTED ME AS THEIR SPOKESMAN...
YOUR EXCELLENCY, I HAVE NEWS -
CAPTAIN DEVOET. A NUMBER OF TEMPLAR PRISONERS HAVE VOLUNTEERED TO SPEAK. I WISH YOU TO OBTAIN A COPY OF THE LIST OF NAMES... AND SEE IF ANY OF THEM ARE FROM THE ARCHDIOCESE OF SENS.
THEN, TRANSFER THESE PRISONERS FROM WHEREVER THEY MAY CURRENTLY BE HELD, INTO OUR CUSTODY AT THE TEMPLE...
SO THAT WE MAY MORE EFFICIENTLY TURN THEM OVER TO THE COMMISSION WHEN REQUESTED.
YOUR EXCELLENCY, THOSE THREE ESCAPED TEMPLARS ARE HERE IN PARIS.
THEY ROBBED AN INNKEEPER LAST NIGHT.
SO THEY HAVE COME.
BUT WHY, IF THEY HAVE THE TREASURE OF HUGH DE CHALONS...?
COULD IT BE...?

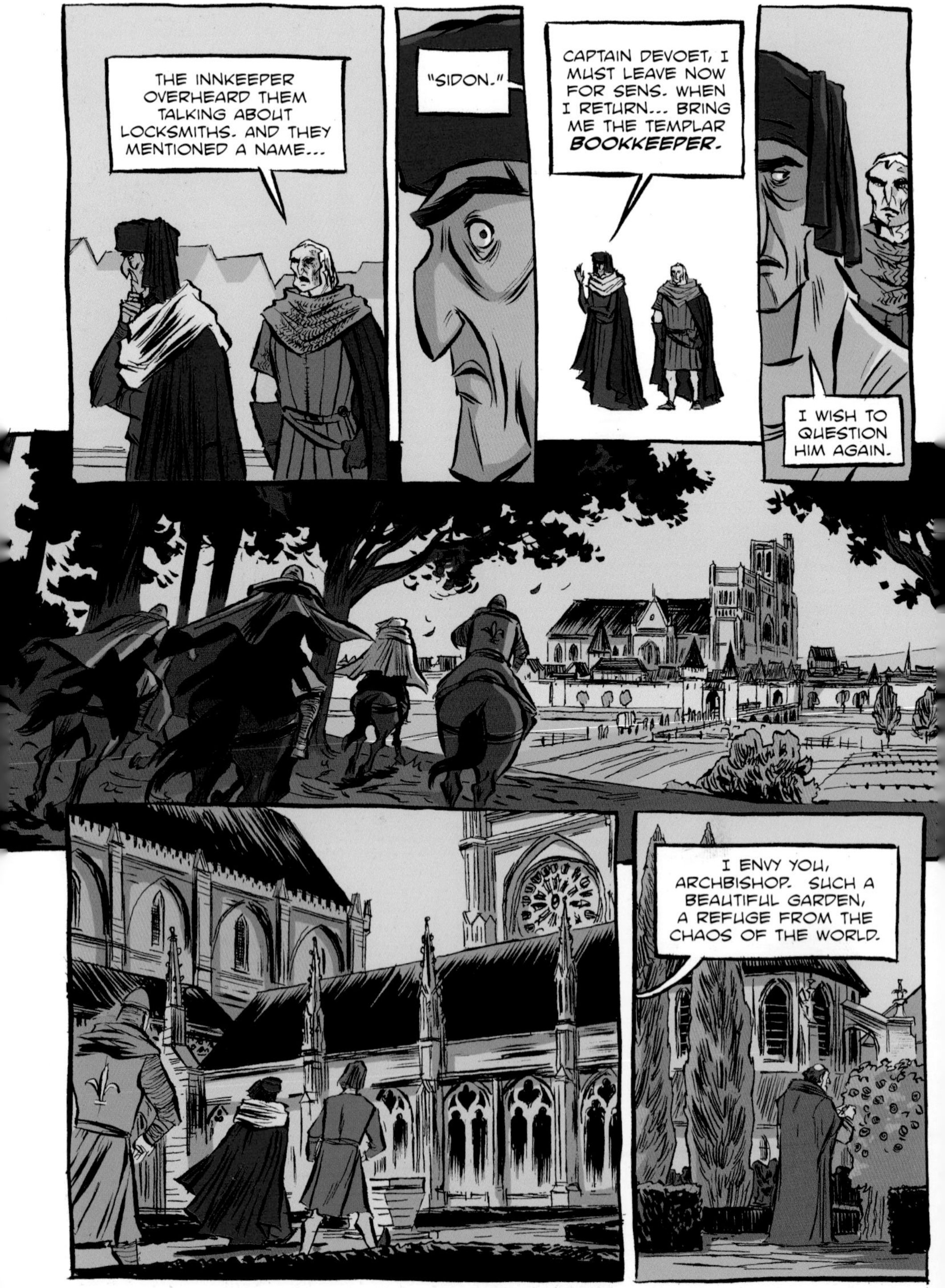
THE INNKEEPER OVERHEARD THEM TALKING ABOUT LOCKSMITHS. AND THEY MENTIONED A NAME...
"SIDON."
CAPTAIN DEVOET, I MUST LEAVE NOW FOR SENS. WHEN I RETURN... BRING ME THE TEMPLAR BOOKKEEPER.
I WISH TO QUESTION HIM AGAIN.
I ENVY YOU, ARCHBISHOP. SUCH A BEAUTIFUL GARDEN, A REFUGE FROM THE CHAOS OF THE WORLD.

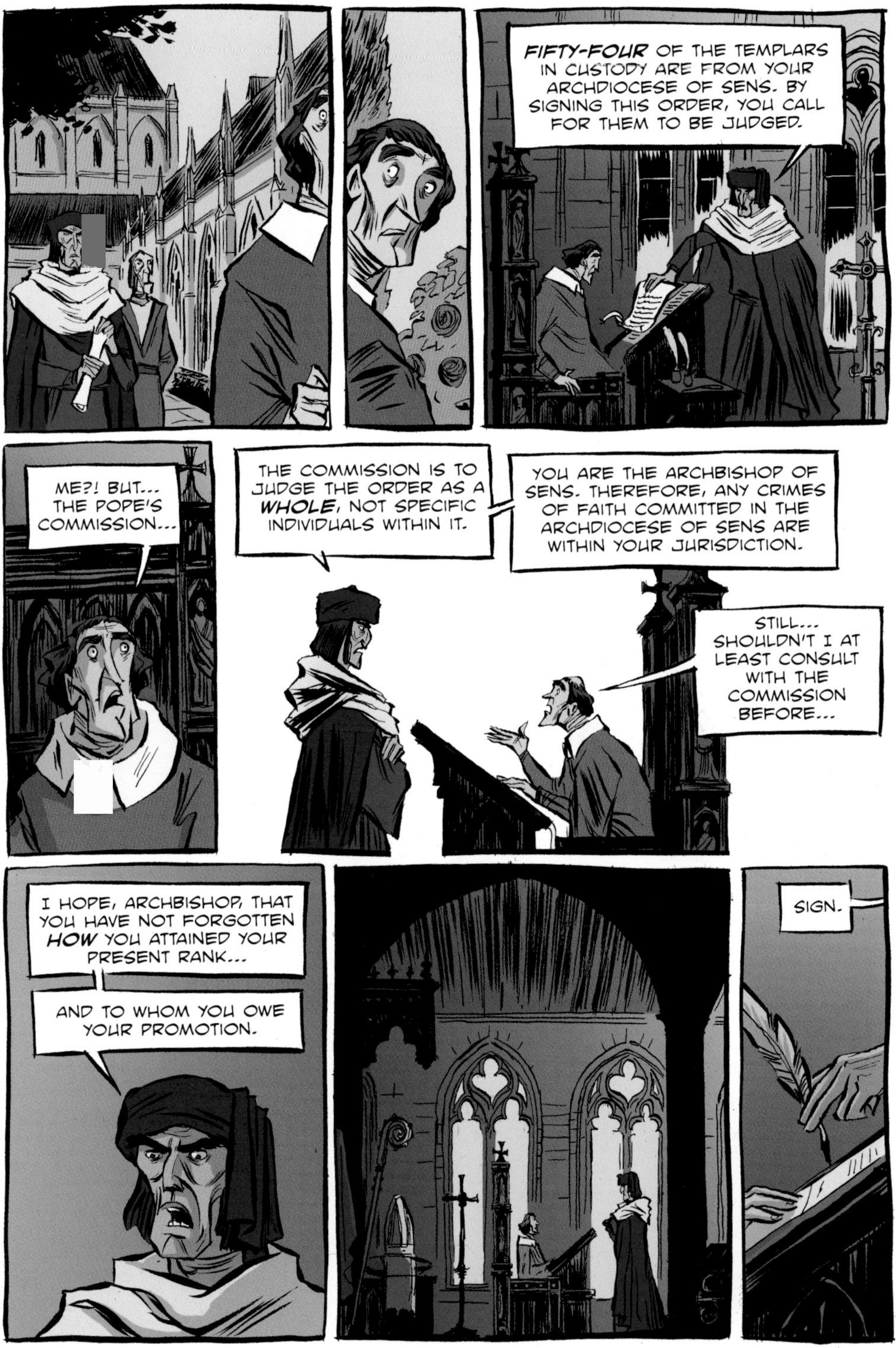
FIFTY-FOUR OF THE TEMPLARS IN CUSTODY ARE FROM YOUR ARCHDIOCESE OF SENS. BY SIGNING THIS ORDER, YOU CALL FOR THEM TO BE JUDGED.
ME?! BUT... THE POPE'S COMMISSION...
THE COMMISSION IS TO JUDGE THE ORDER AS A WHOLE, NOT SPECIFIC INDIVIDUALS WITHIN IT.
YOU ARE THE ARCHBISHOP OF SENS. THEREFORE, ANY CRIMES OF FAITH COMMITTED IN THE ARCHDIOCESE OF SENS ARE WITHIN YOUR JURISDICTION.
STILL... SHOULDN'T I AT LEAST CONSULT WITH THE COMMISSION BEFORE...
I HOPE, ARCHBISHOP, THAT YOU HAVE NOT FORGOTTEN HOW YOU ATTAINED YOUR PRESENT RANK...
AND TO WHOM YOU OWE YOUR PROMOTION.
SIGN.

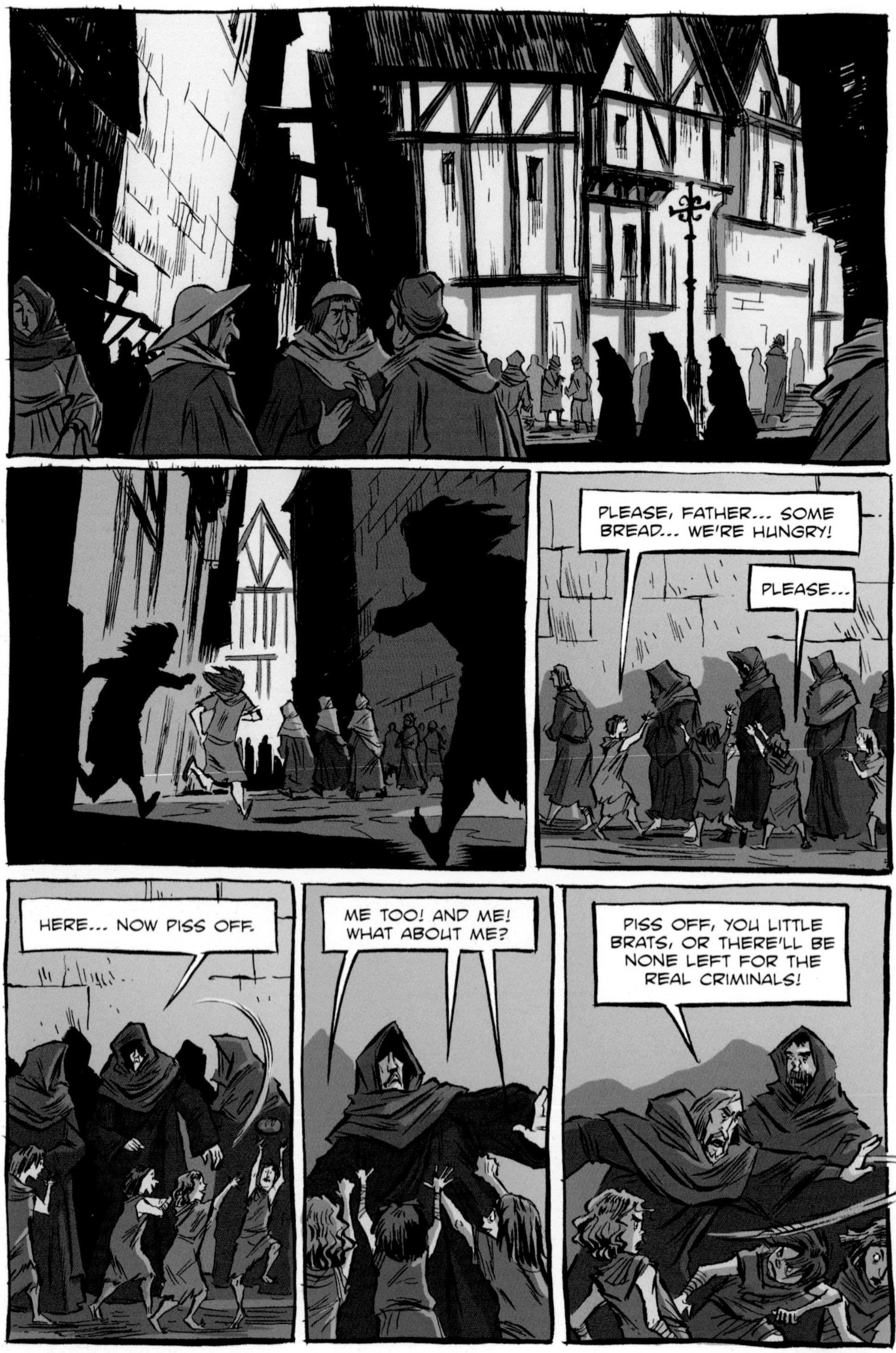
PLEASE, FATHER... SOME BREAD... WE'RE HUNGRY!
PLEASE...
HERE... NOW PISS OFF.
ME TOO! AND ME! WHAT ABOUT ME?
PISS OFF, YOU LITTLE BRATS, OR THERE'LL BE NONE LEFT FOR THE REAL CRIMINALS!

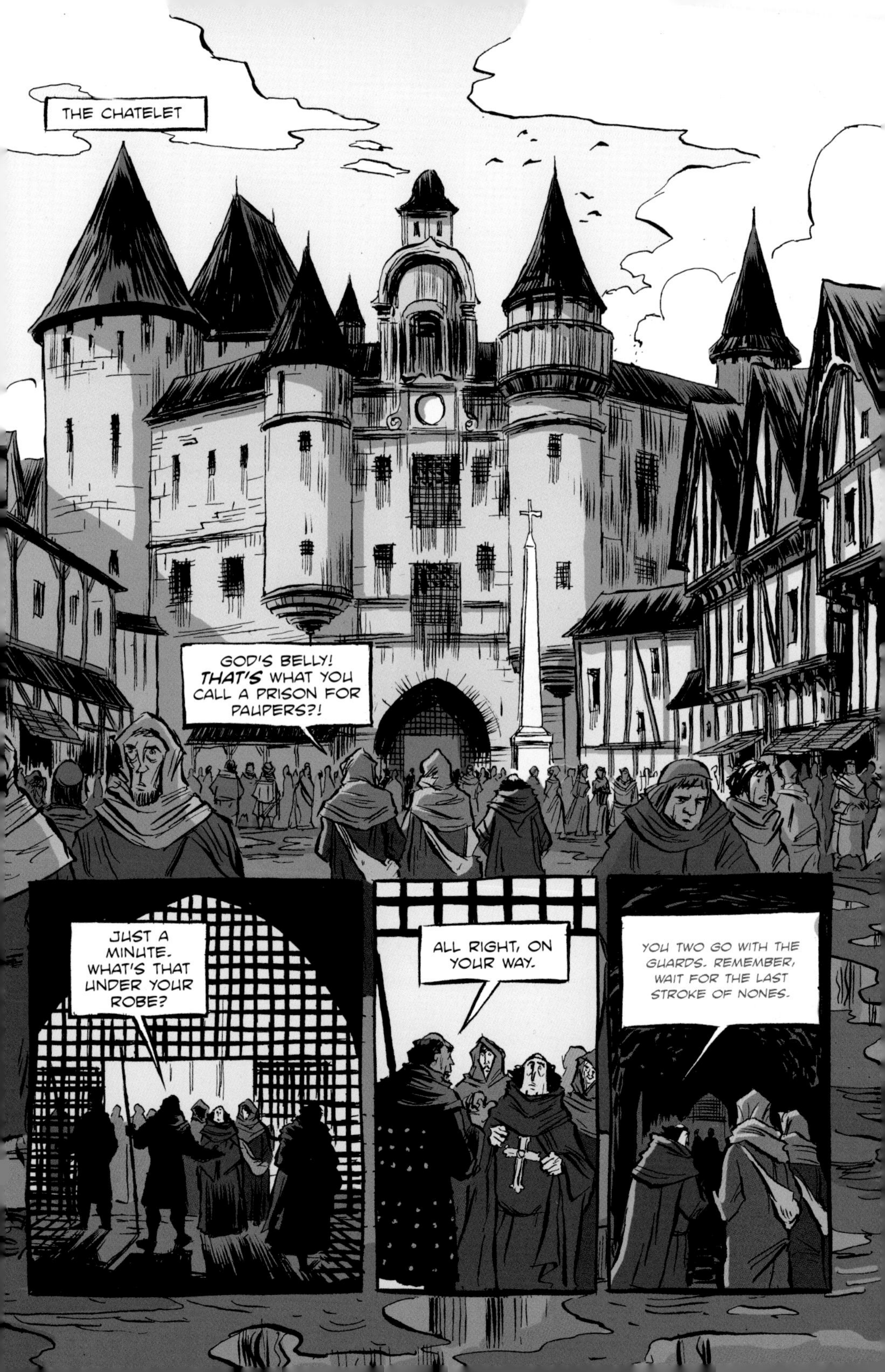

THE CHATELET
GOD'S BELLY! THAT'S WHAT YOU CALL A PRISON FOR PAUPERS?!
JUST A MINUTE. WHAT'S THAT UNDER YOUR ROBE?
ALL RIGHT, ON YOUR WAY.
YOU TWO GO WITH THE GUARDS. REMEMBER, WAIT FOR THE LAST STROKE OF NONES.

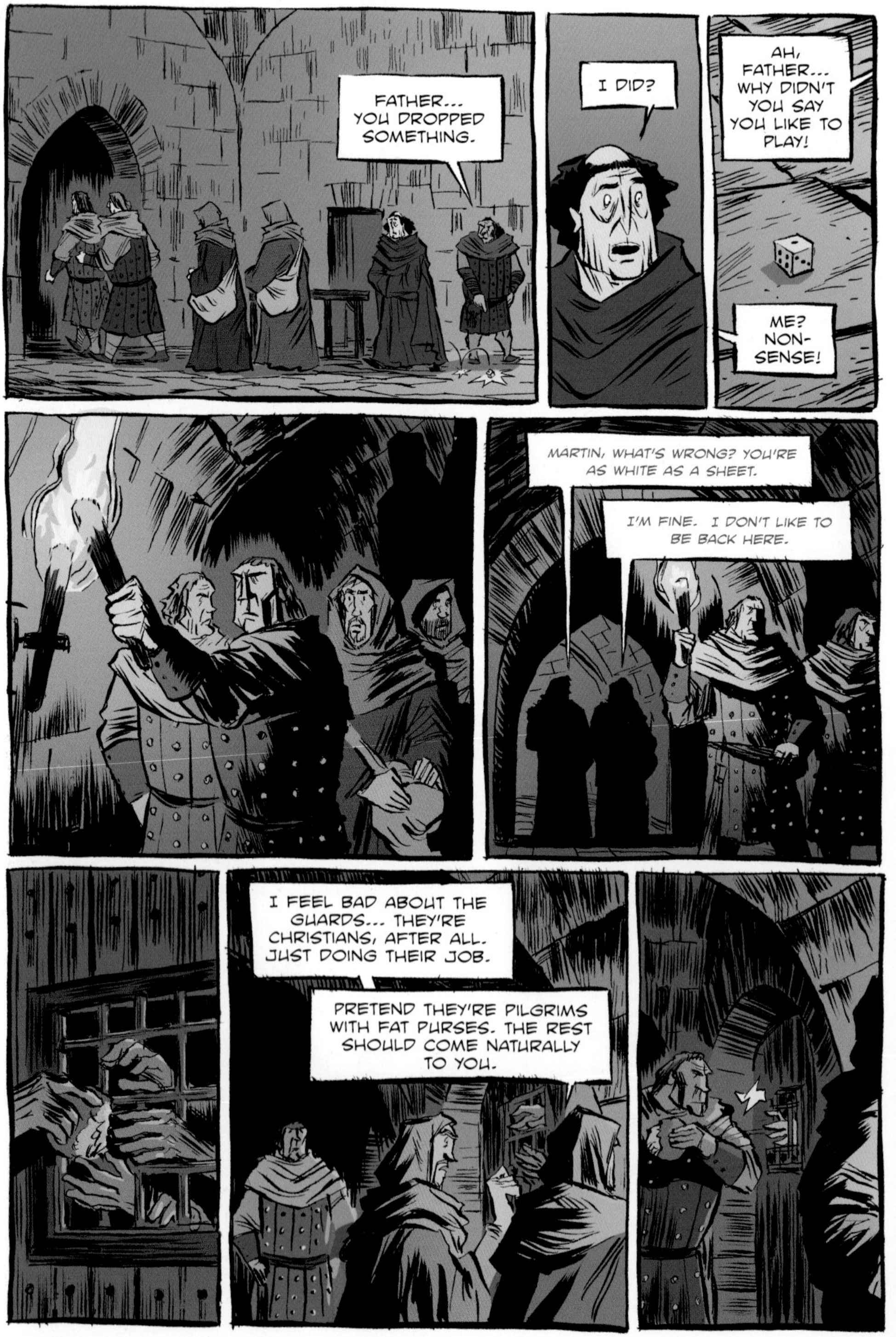
FATHER... YOU DROPPED SOMETHING.
I DID?
AH, FATHER... WHY DIDN'T YOU SAY YOU LIKE TO PLAY!
ME? NON-SENSE!
MARTIN, WHAT'S WRONG? YOU'RE AS WHITE AS A SHEET.
I'M FINE. I DON'T LIKE TO BE BACK HERE.
I FEEL BAD ABOUT THE GUARDS... THEY'RE CHRISTIANS, AFTER ALL. JUST DOING THEIR JOB.
PRETEND THEY'RE PILGRIMS WITH FAT PURSES. THE REST SHOULD COME NATURALLY TO YOU.

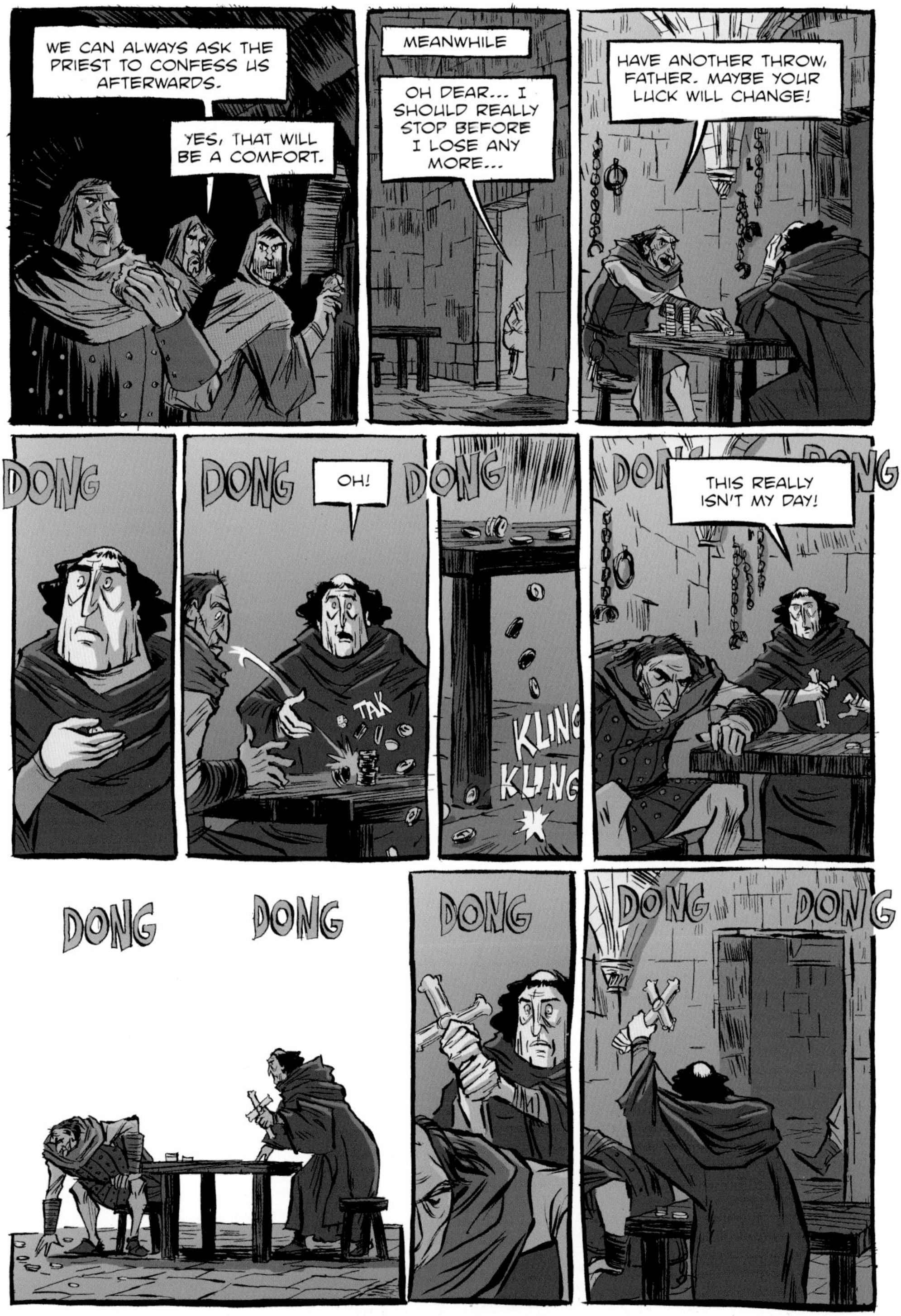
WE CAN ALWAYS ASK THE PRIEST TO CONFESS US AFTERWARDS.
YES, THAT WILL BE A COMFORT.
MEANWHILE
OH DEAR... I SHOULD REALLY STOP BEFORE I LOSE ANY MORE...
HAVE ANOTHER THROW, FATHER. MAYBE YOUR LUCK WILL CHANGE!
DONG
DONG
OH!
TAK
DONG
KLING
KLING
THIS REALLY ISN'T MY DAY!
DONG
DONG
DONG
DONG
DONG

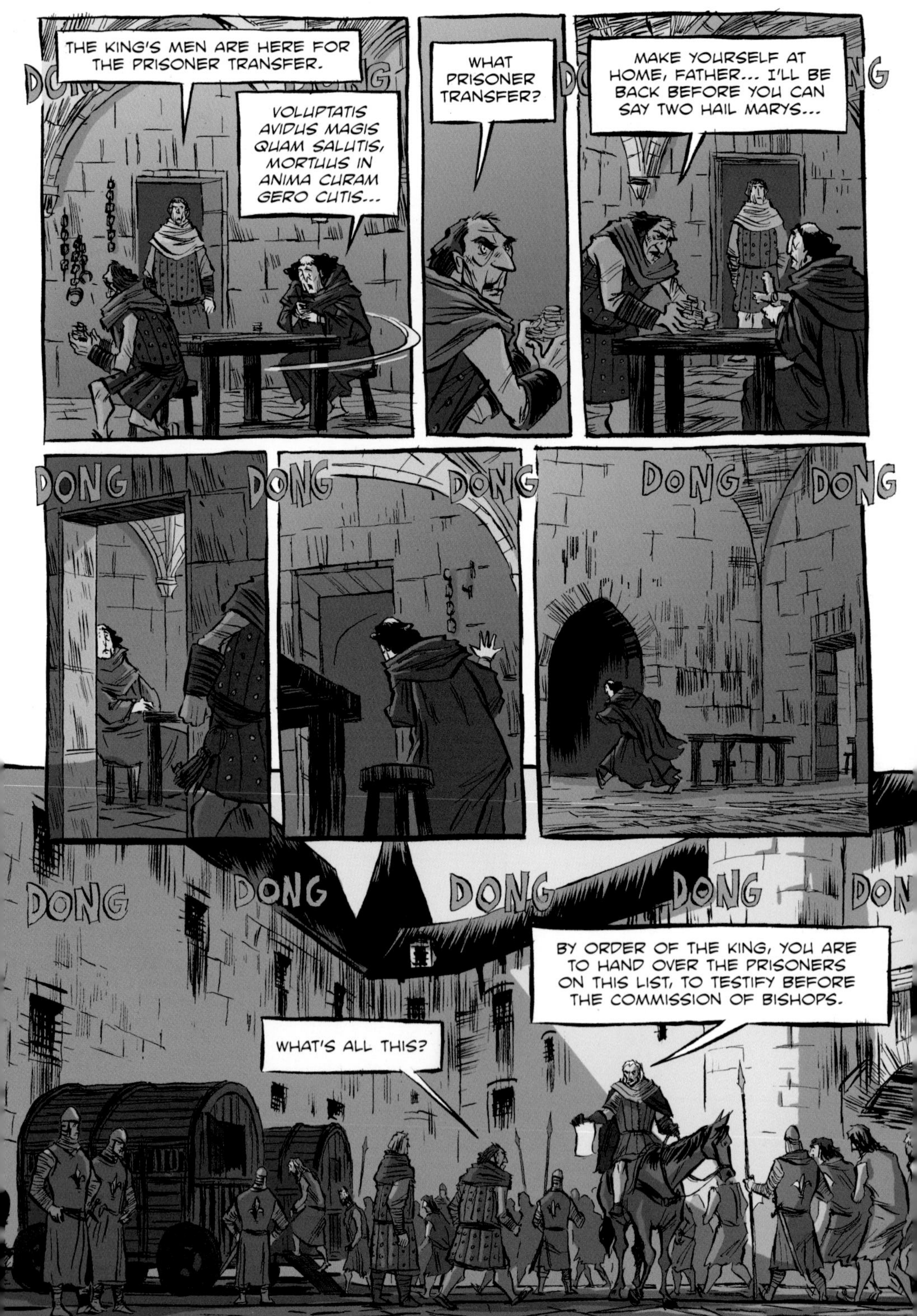
DONG DONG
THE KING'S MEN ARE HERE FOR THE PRISONER TRANSFER.
VOLUPTATIS AVIDUS MAGIS QUAM SALUTIS, MORTUUS IN ANIMA CURAM GERO CUTIS...
WHAT PRISONER TRANSFER?
MAKE YOURSELF AT HOME, FATHER... I'LL BE BACK BEFORE YOU CAN SAY TWO HAIL MARYS...
DONG
DONG
DONG
DONG
DONG
DONG
DONG
DONG
DONG
BY ORDER OF THE KING, YOU ARE TO HAND OVER THE PRISONERS ON THIS LIST, TO TESTIFY BEFORE THE COMMISSION OF BISHOPS.
WHAT'S ALL THIS?

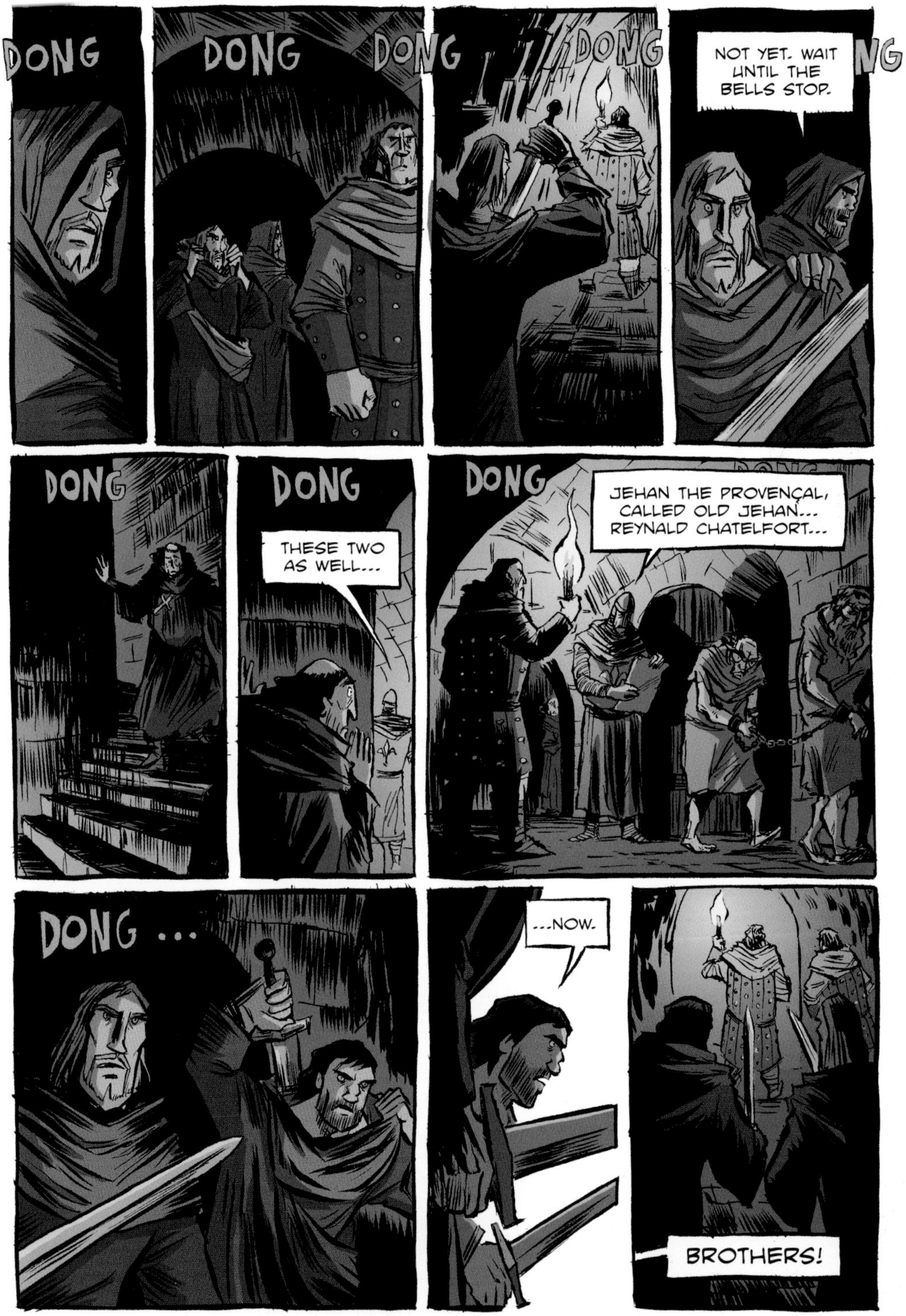
DONG
DONG
DONG
DONG
NOT YET. WAIT UNTIL THE BELLS STOP.
NG
DONG
DONG
THESE TWO AS WELL...
DONG
JEHAN THE PROVENÇAL, CALLED OLD JEHAN... REYNALD CHATELFORT...
DONG ...
...NOW.
BROTHERS!

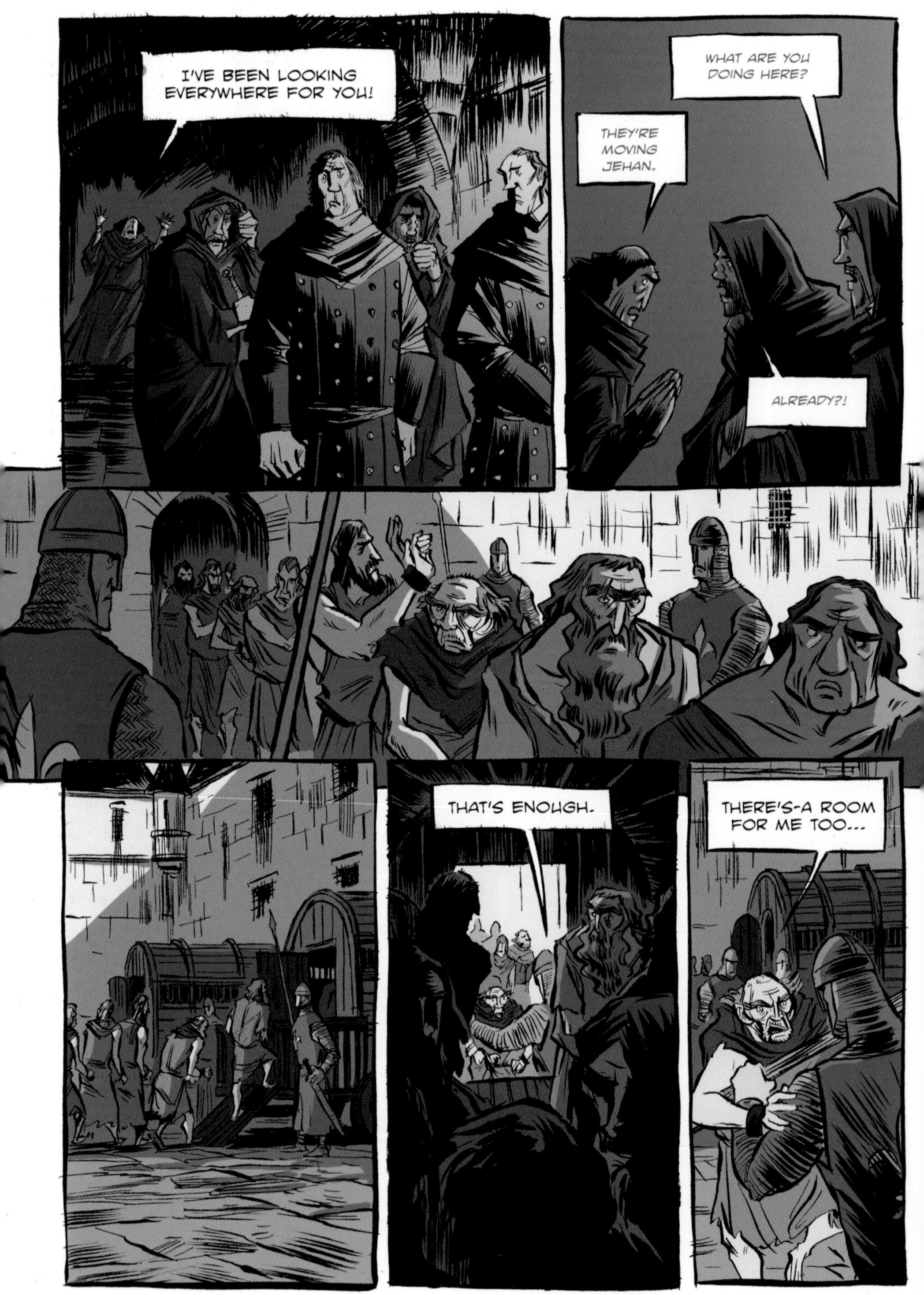
I'VE BEEN LOOKING EVERYWHERE FOR YOU!
WHAT ARE YOU DOING HERE?
THEY'RE MOVING JEHAN.
ALREADY?!
THAT'S ENOUGH.
THERE'S-A ROOM FOR ME TOO...

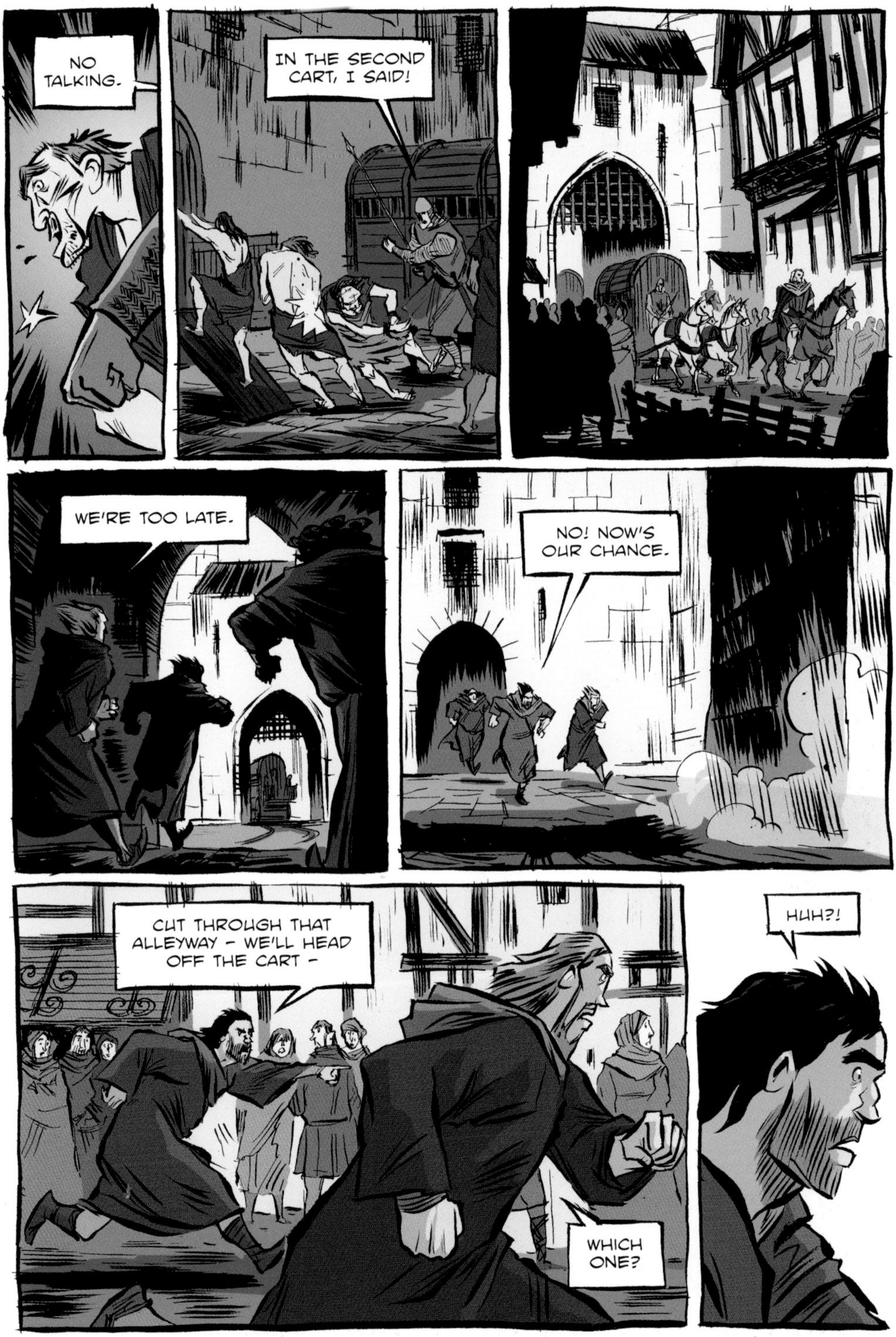
NO TALKING.
IN THE SECOND CART, I SAID!
WE'RE TOO LATE.
NO! NOW'S OUR CHANCE.
CUT THROUGH THAT ALLEYWAY - WE'LL HEAD OFF THE CART -
WHICH ONE?
HUH?!

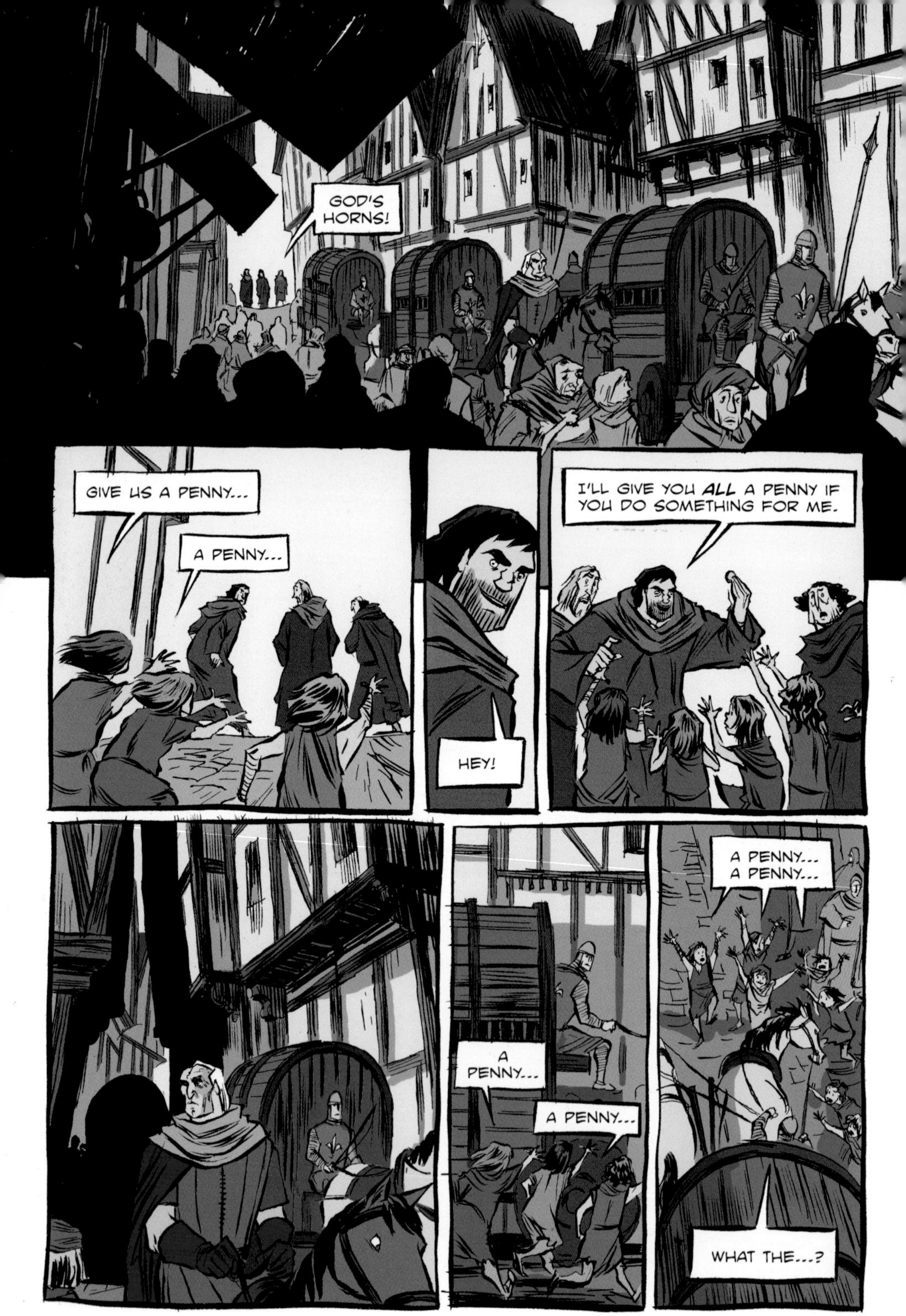
GOD'S HORNS!
GIVE US A PENNY...
A PENNY...
HEY!
I'LL GIVE YOU ALL A PENNY IF YOU DO SOMETHING FOR ME.
A PENNY...
A PENNY...
A PENNY... A PENNY...
WHAT THE...?

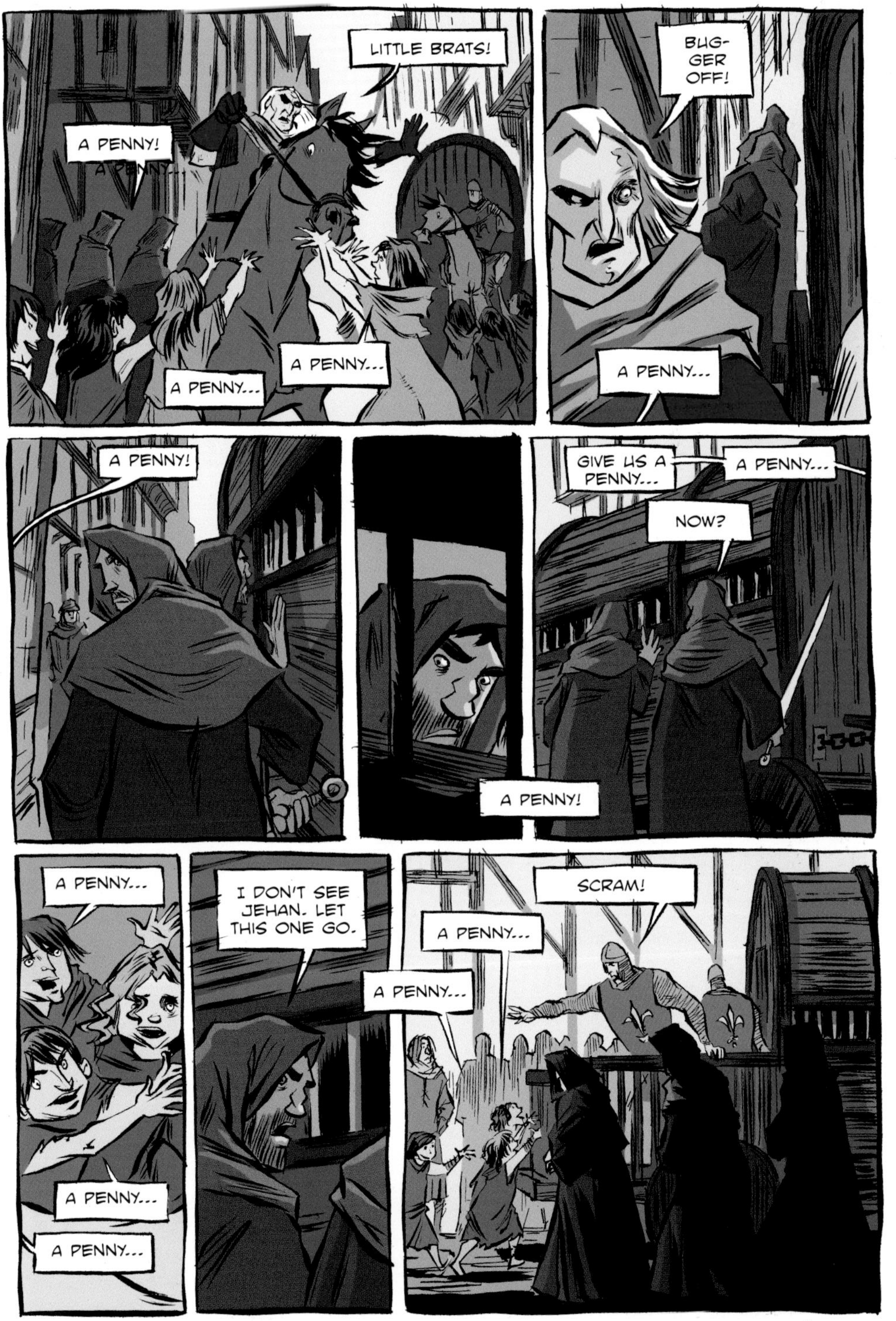

LITTLE BRATS!
A PENNY! A PENNY...
A PENNY...
A PENNY...
BUG-GER OFF!
A PENNY...
A PENNY!
A PENNY!
GIVE US A PENNY...
A PENNY...
NOW?
A PENNY...
A PENNY...
A PENNY...
I DON'T SEE JEHAN. LET THIS ONE GO.
SCRAM!
A PENNY...
A PENNY...

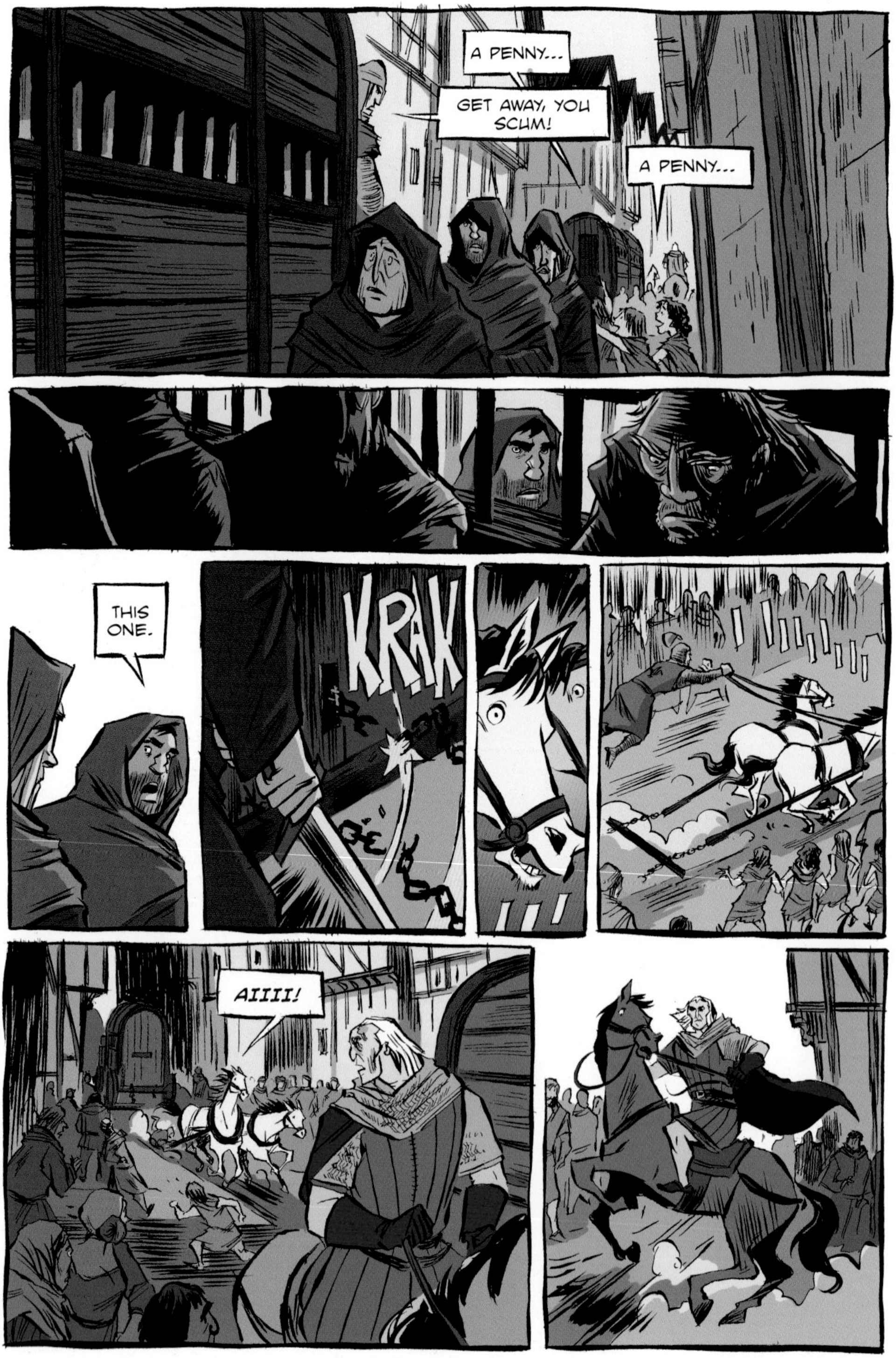
A PENNY...
GET AWAY, YOU SCUM!
A PENNY...
THIS ONE.
KRAK
AIIII!

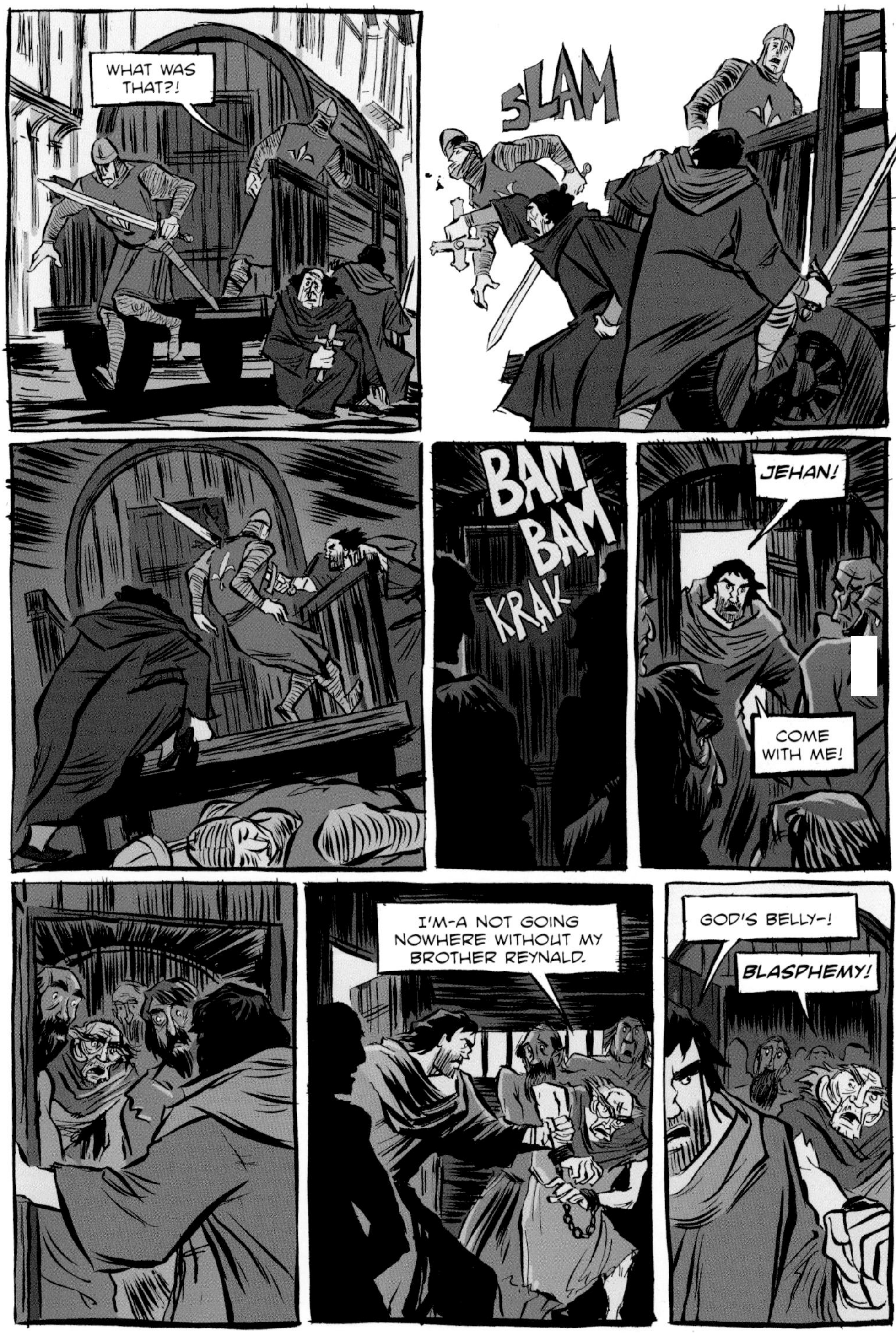
WHAT WAS THAT?!
SLAM
BAM
BAM
KRAK
JEHAN!
COME WITH ME!
I'M-A NOT GOING NOWHERE WITHOUT MY BROTHER REYNALD.
GOD'S BELLY-!
BLASPHEMY!

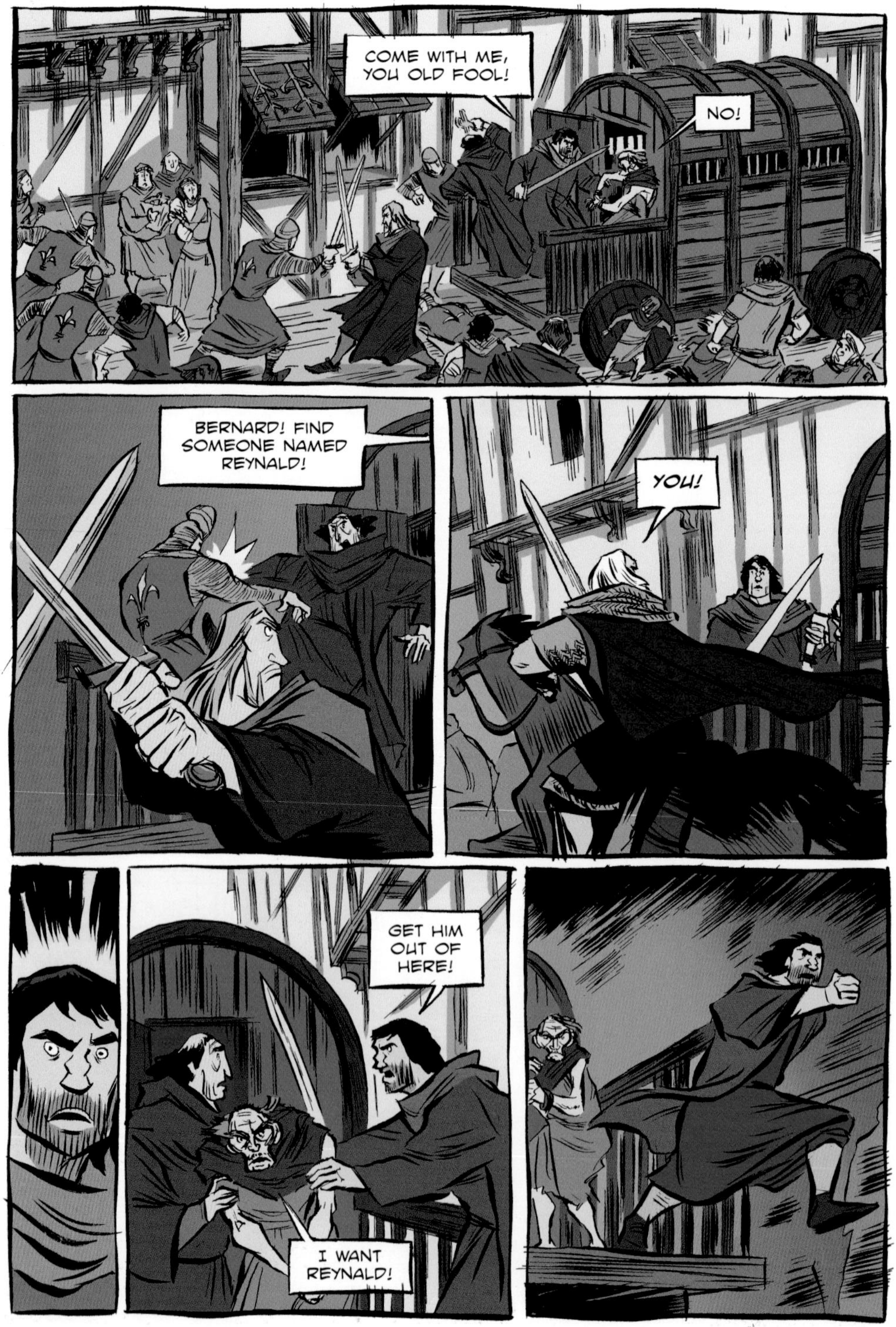
COME WITH ME, YOU OLD FOOL!
NO!
BERNARD! FIND SOMEONE NAMED REYNALD!
YOU!
GET HIM OUT OF HERE!
I WANT REYNALD!

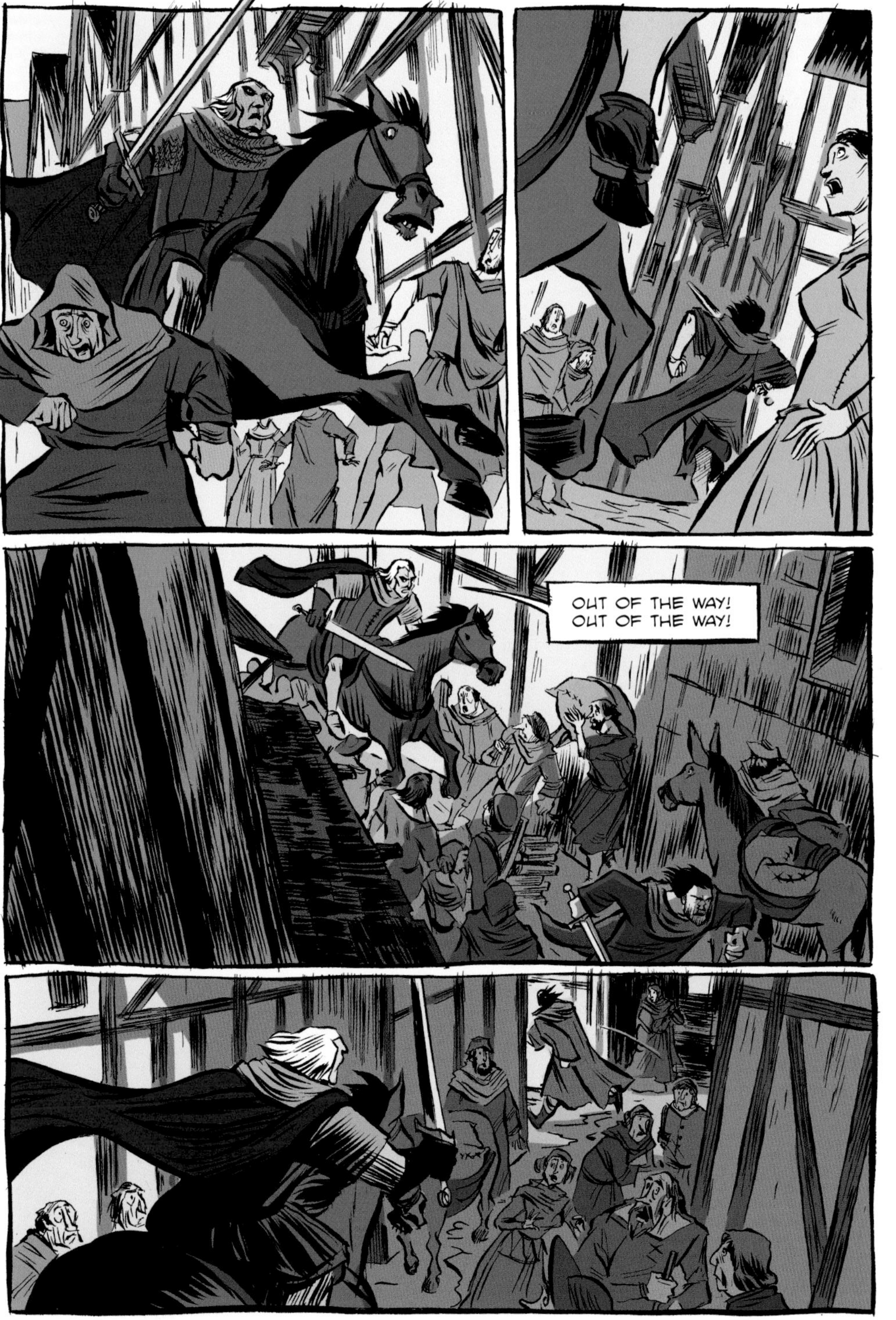
OUT OF THE WAY!
OUT OF THE WAY!

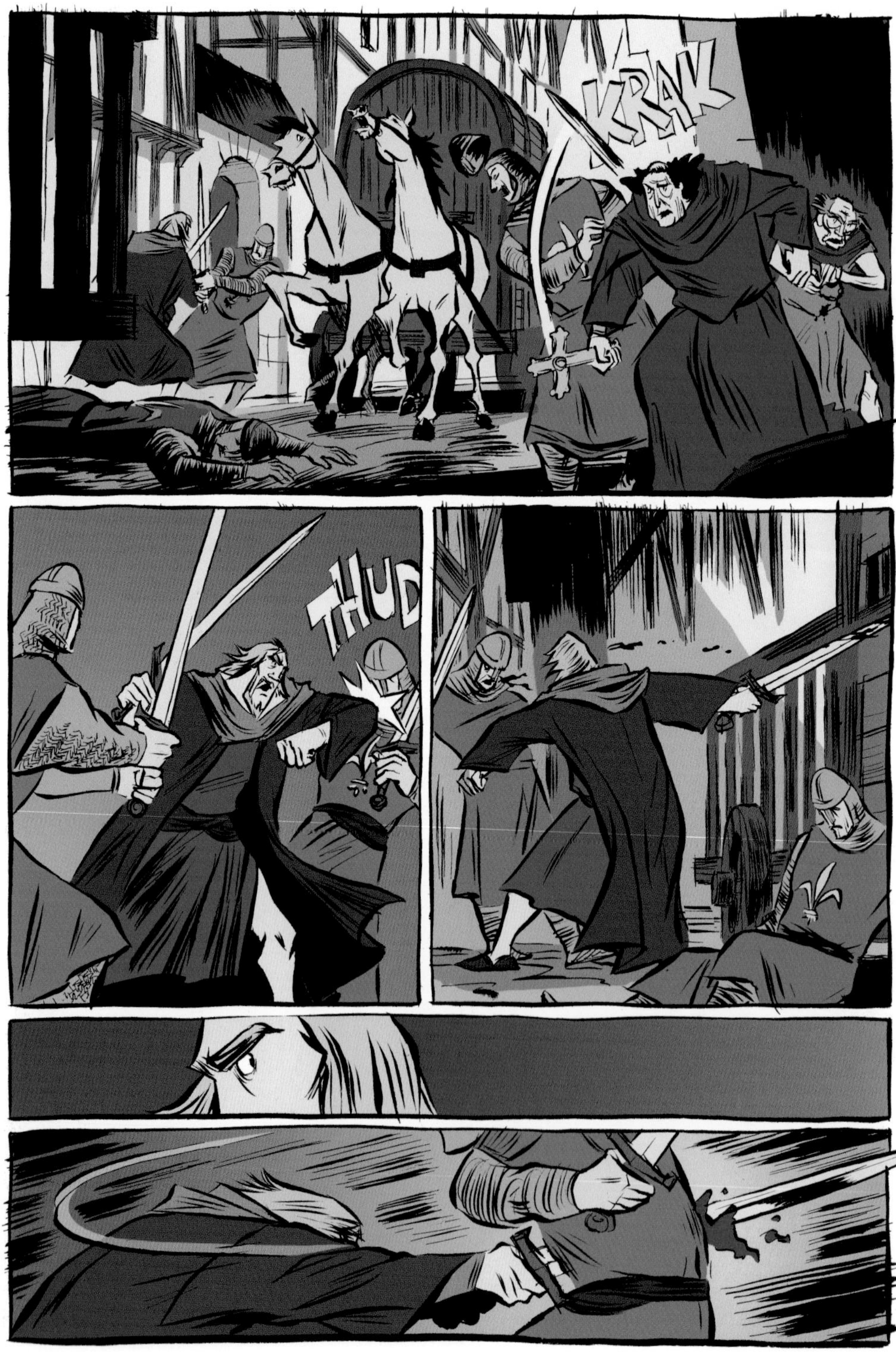
KRAK
THUD

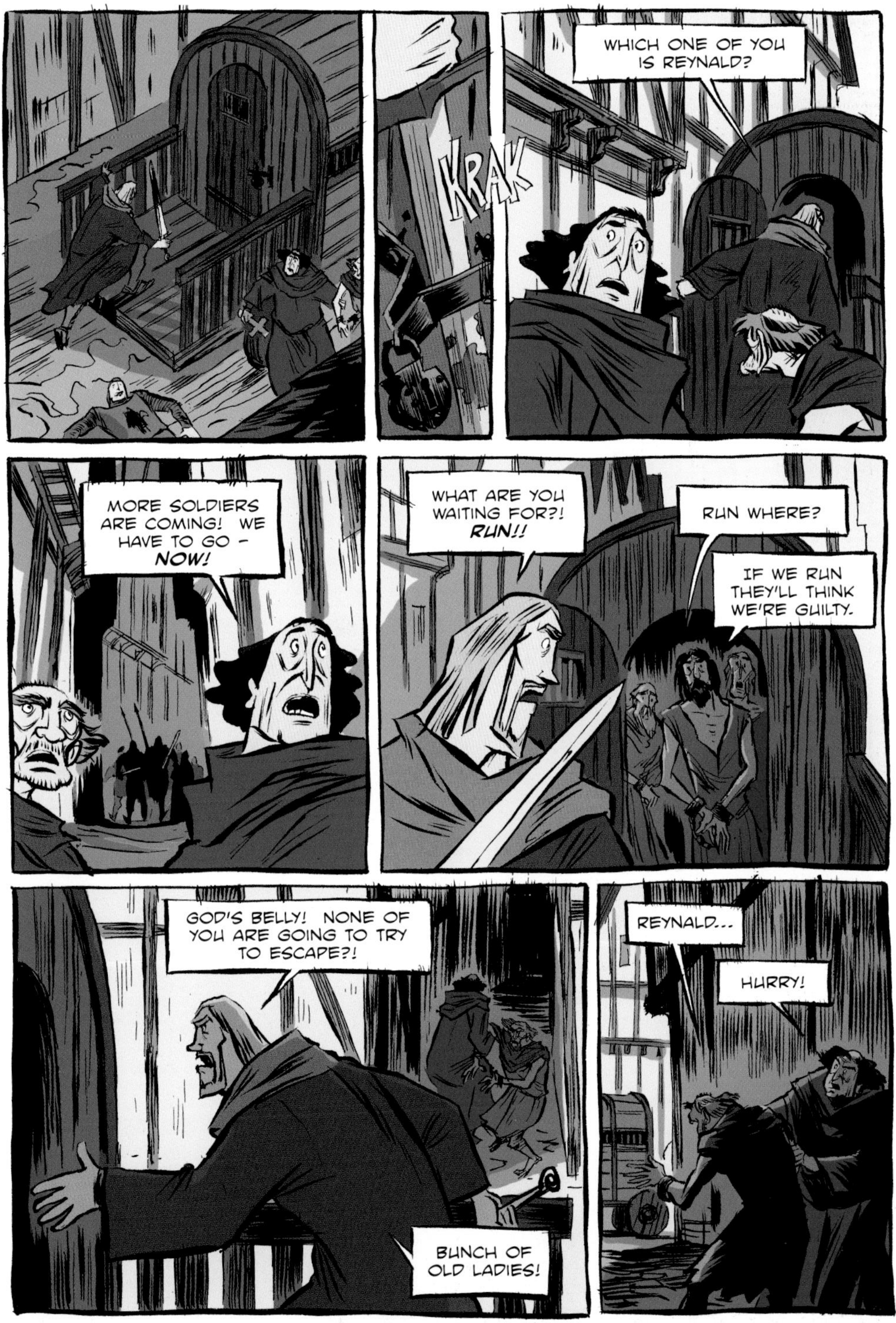
KRAK
WHICH ONE OF YOU IS REYNALD?
MORE SOLDIERS ARE COMING! WE HAVE TO GO - NOW!
WHAT ARE YOU WAITING FOR?! RUN!!
RUN WHERE?
IF WE RUN THEY'LL THINK WE'RE GUILTY.
GOD'S BELLY! NONE OF YOU ARE GOING TO TRY TO ESCAPE?!
BUNCH OF OLD LADIES!
REYNALD...
HURRY!

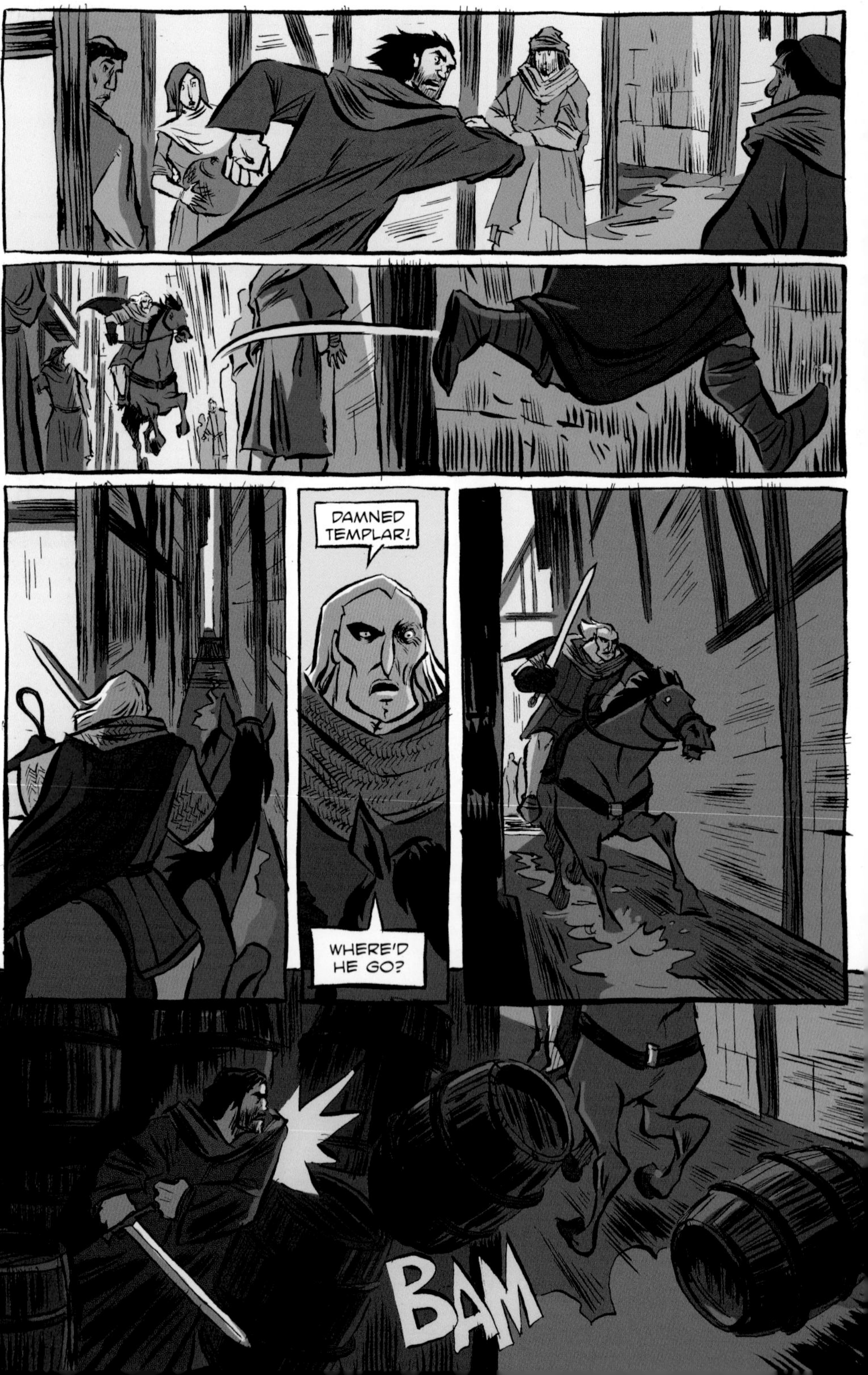
DAMNED TEMPLAR!
WHERE'D HE GO?
BAM

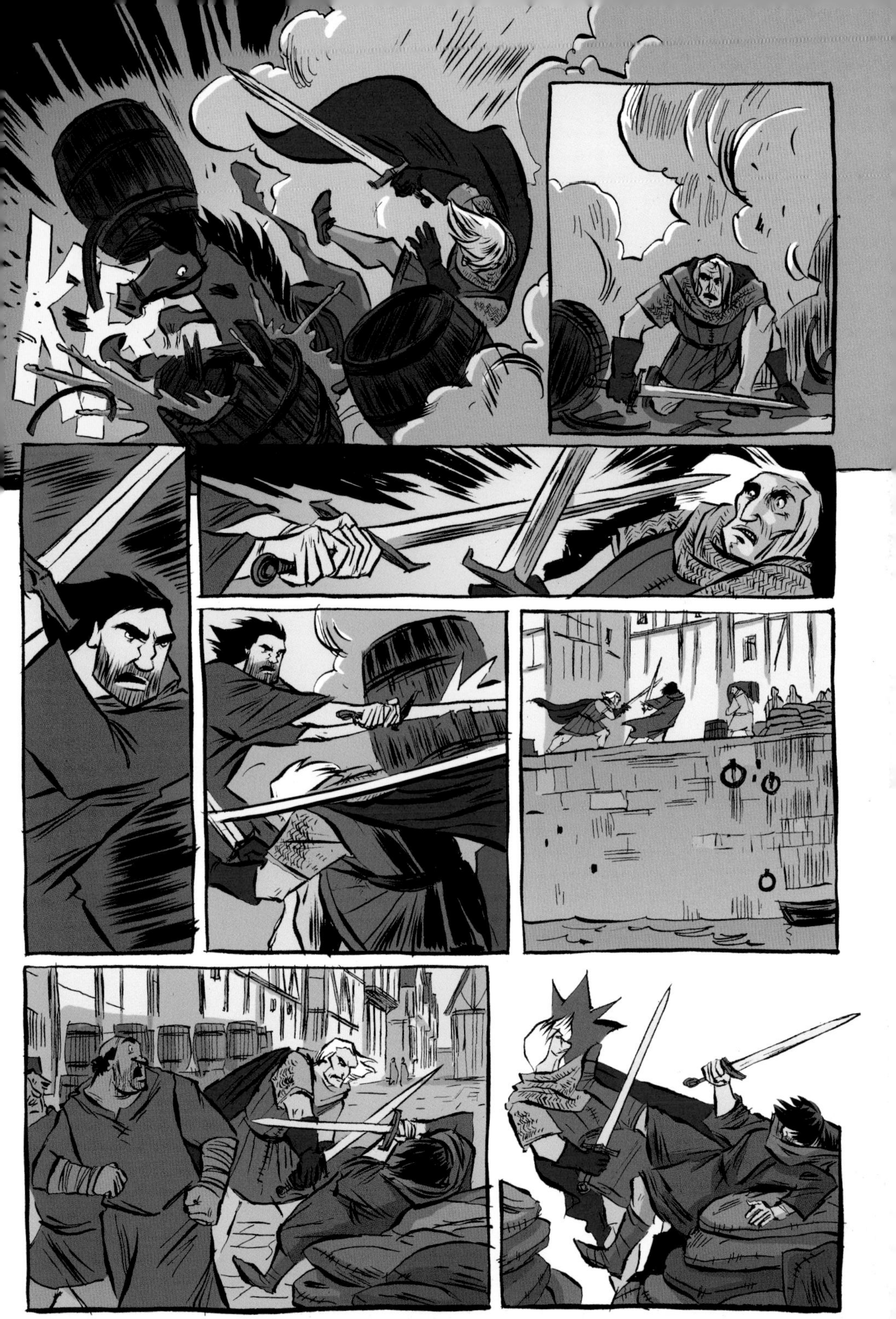

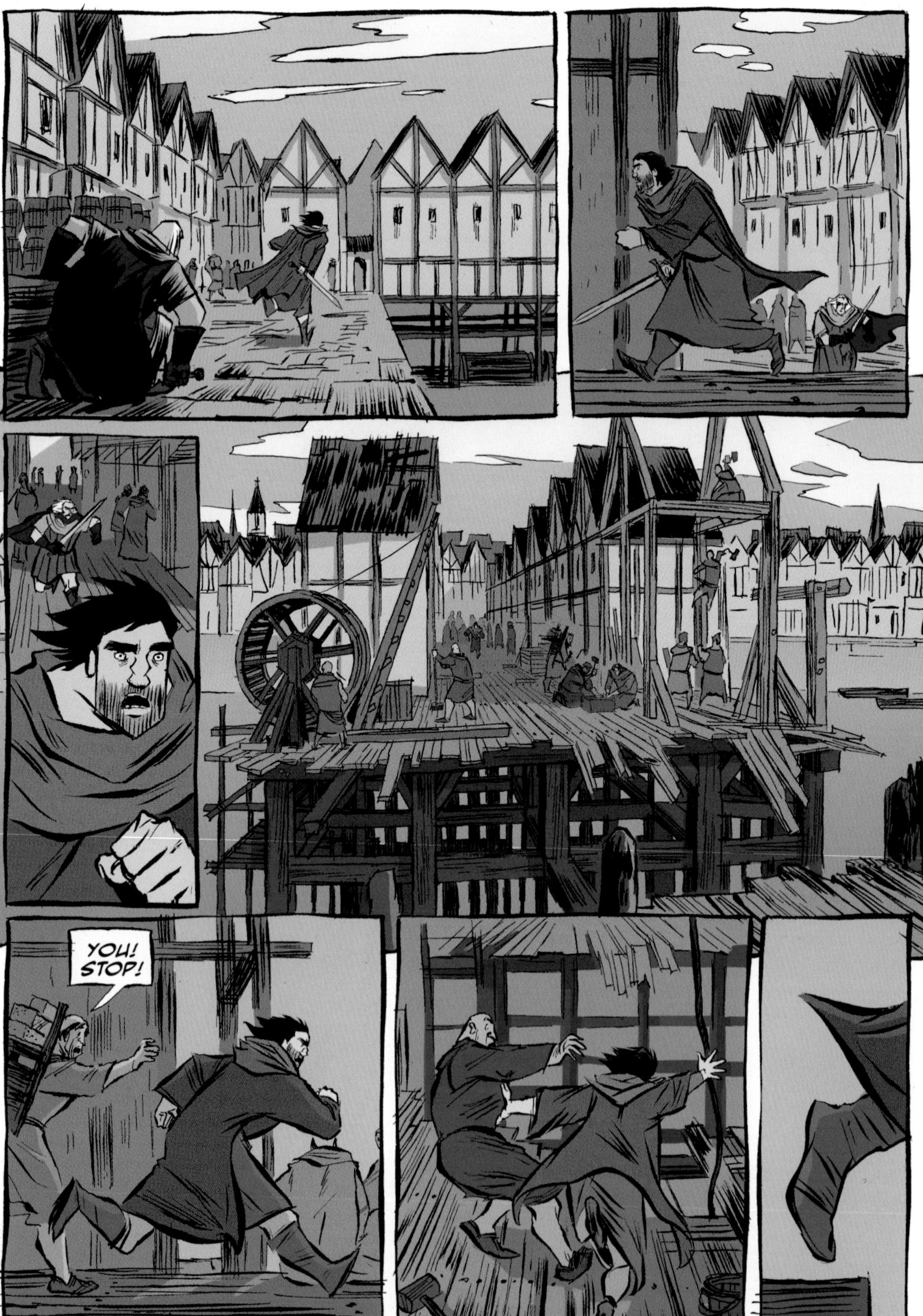
YOU! STOP!

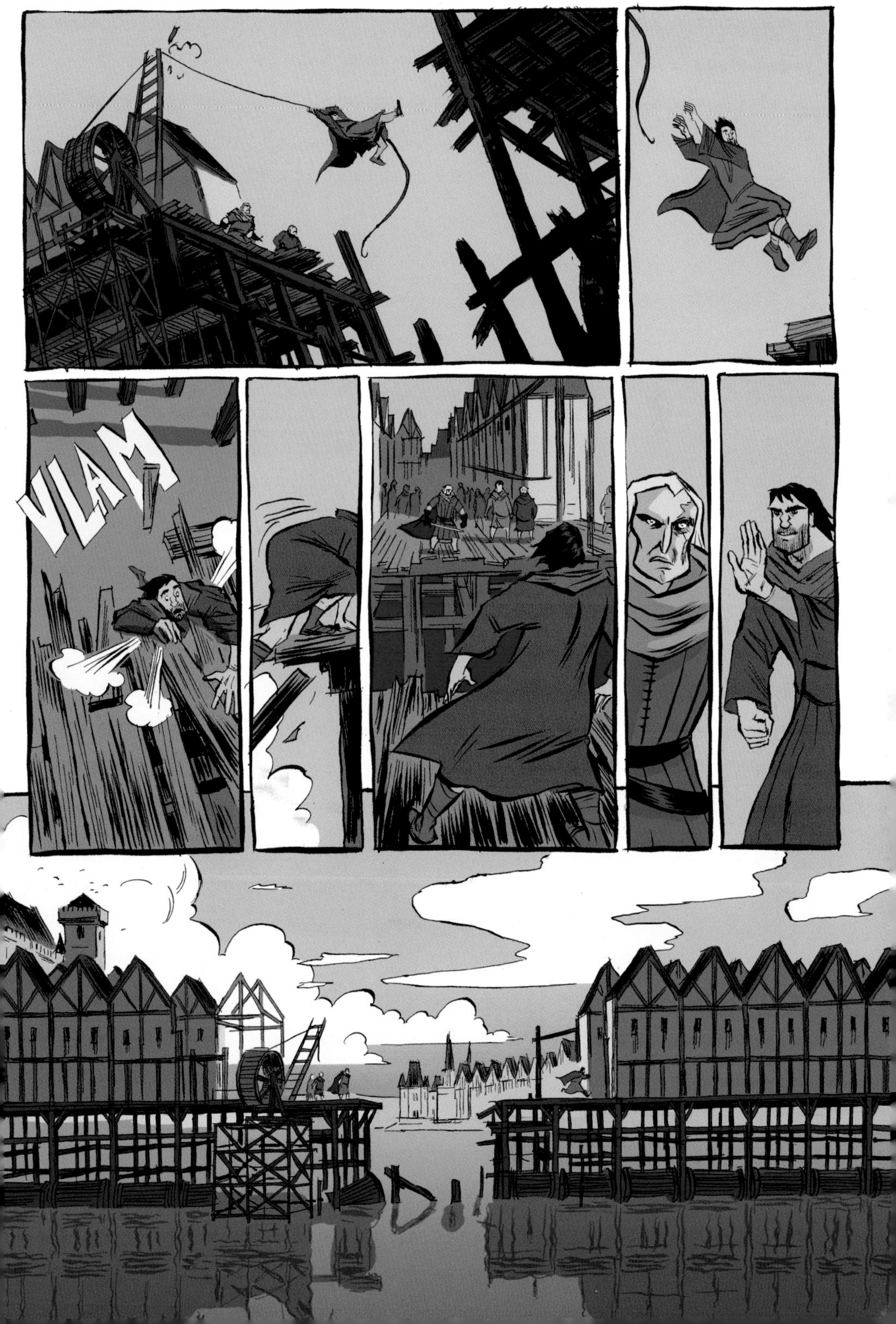
VLAM

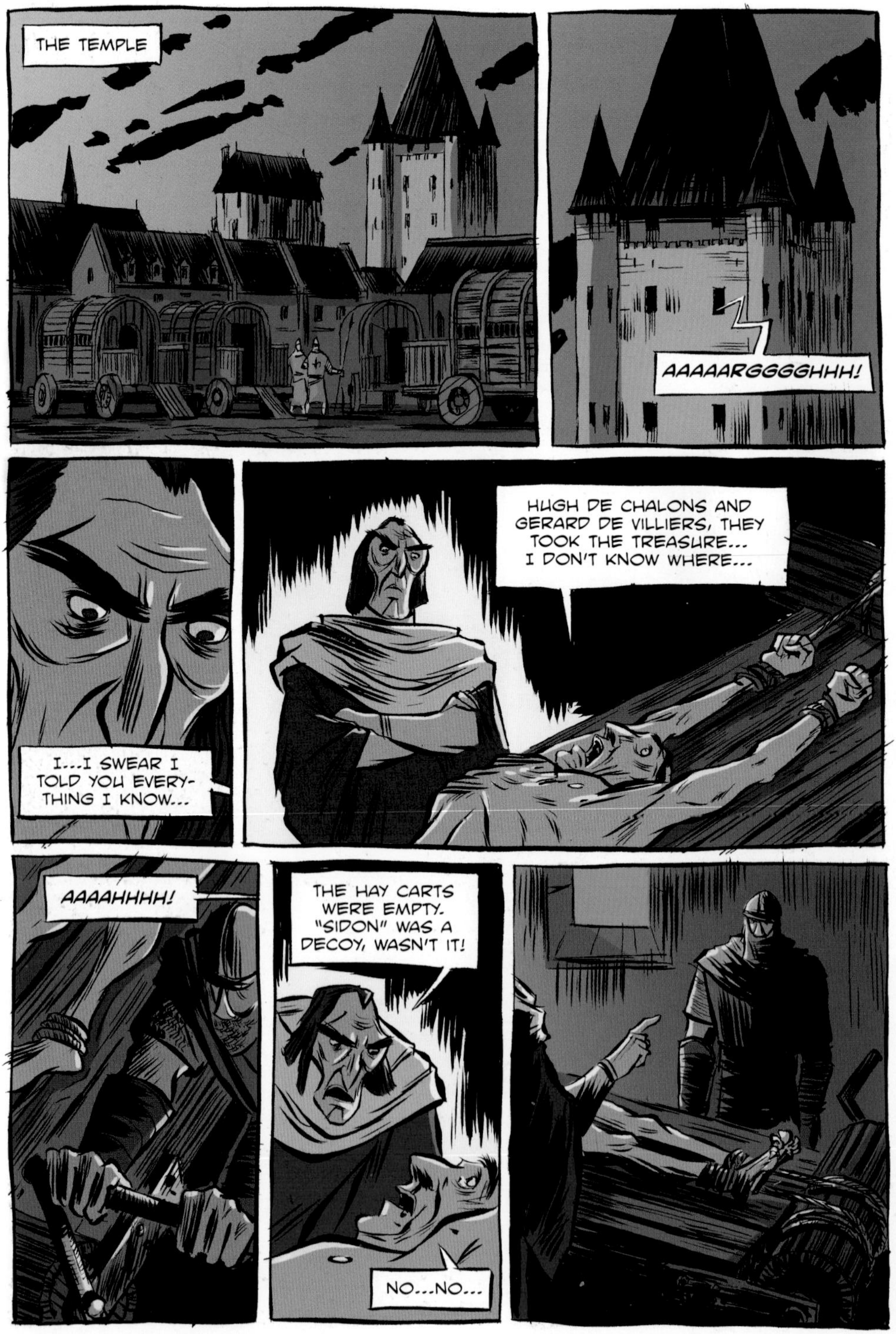
THE TEMPLE
AAAAARGGGGHHH!
I...I SWEAR I TOLD YOU EVERY-THING I KNOW...
HUGH DE CHALONS AND GERARD DE VILLIERS, THEY TOOK THE TREASURE... I DON'T KNOW WHERE...
AAAAHHHH!
THE HAY CARTS WERE EMPTY. "SIDON" WAS A DECOY, WASN'T IT!
NO...NO...

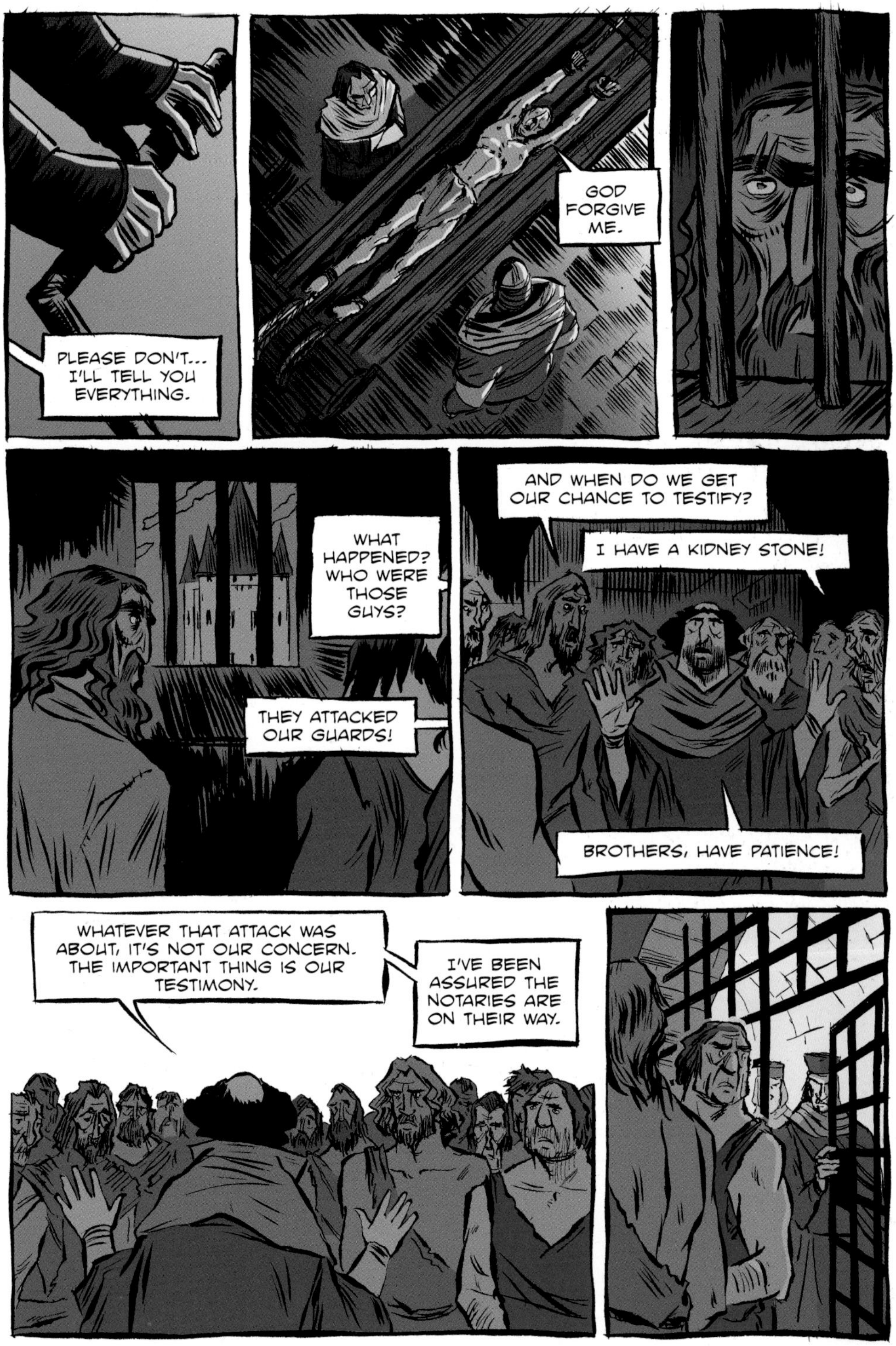
PLEASE DON'T... I'LL TELL YOU EVERYTHING.
GOD FORGIVE ME.
WHAT HAPPENED? WHO WERE THOSE GUYS?
THEY ATTACKED OUR GUARDS!
AND WHEN DO WE GET OUR CHANCE TO TESTIFY?
I HAVE A KIDNEY STONE!
BROTHERS, HAVE PATIENCE!
WHATEVER THAT ATTACK WAS ABOUT, IT'S NOT OUR CONCERN. THE IMPORTANT THING IS OUR TESTIMONY.
I'VE BEEN ASSURED THE NOTARIES ARE ON THEIR WAY.

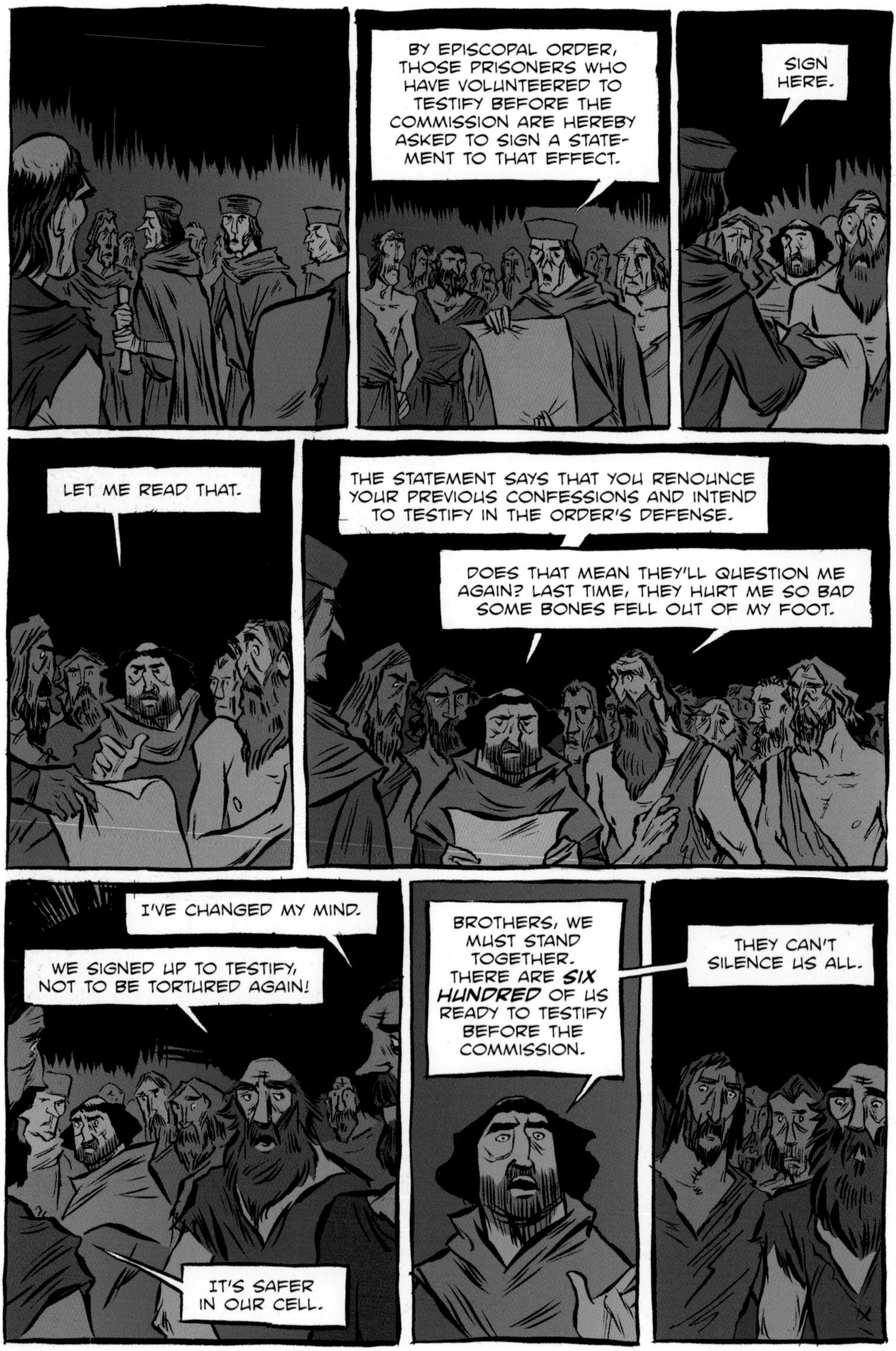
BY EPISCOPAL ORDER, THOSE PRISONERS WHO HAVE VOLUNTEERED TO TESTIFY BEFORE THE COMMISSION ARE HEREBY ASKED TO SIGN A STATEMENT TO THAT EFFECT.
SIGN HERE.
LET ME READ THAT.
THE STATEMENT SAYS THAT YOU RENOUNCE YOUR PREVIOUS CONFESSIONS AND INTEND TO TESTIFY IN THE ORDER'S DEFENSE.
DOES THAT MEAN THEY'LL QUESTION ME AGAIN? LAST TIME, THEY HURT ME SO BAD SOME BONES FELL OUT OF MY FOOT.
I'VE CHANGED MY MIND.
WE SIGNED UP TO TESTIFY, NOT TO BE TORTURED AGAIN!
IT'S SAFER IN OUR CELL.
BROTHERS, WE MUST STAND TOGETHER. THERE ARE *SIX HUNDRED* OF US READY TO TESTIFY BEFORE THE COMMISSION.
THEY CAN'T SILENCE US ALL.

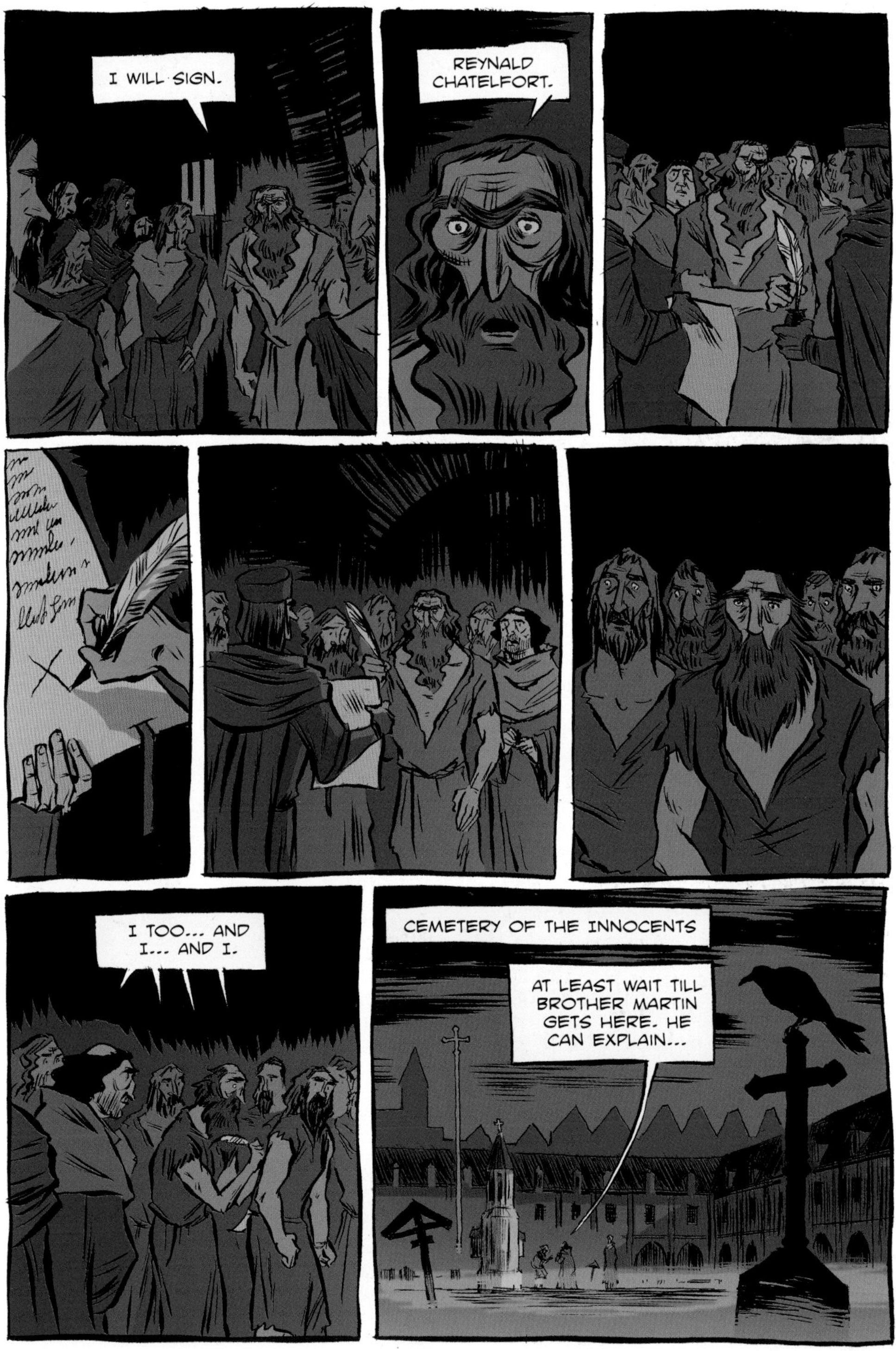

I WILL SIGN.
REYNALD CHATELFORT.
I TOO... AND I... AND I.
CEMETERY OF THE INNOCENTS
AT LEAST WAIT TILL BROTHER MARTIN GETS HERE. HE CAN EXPLAIN...

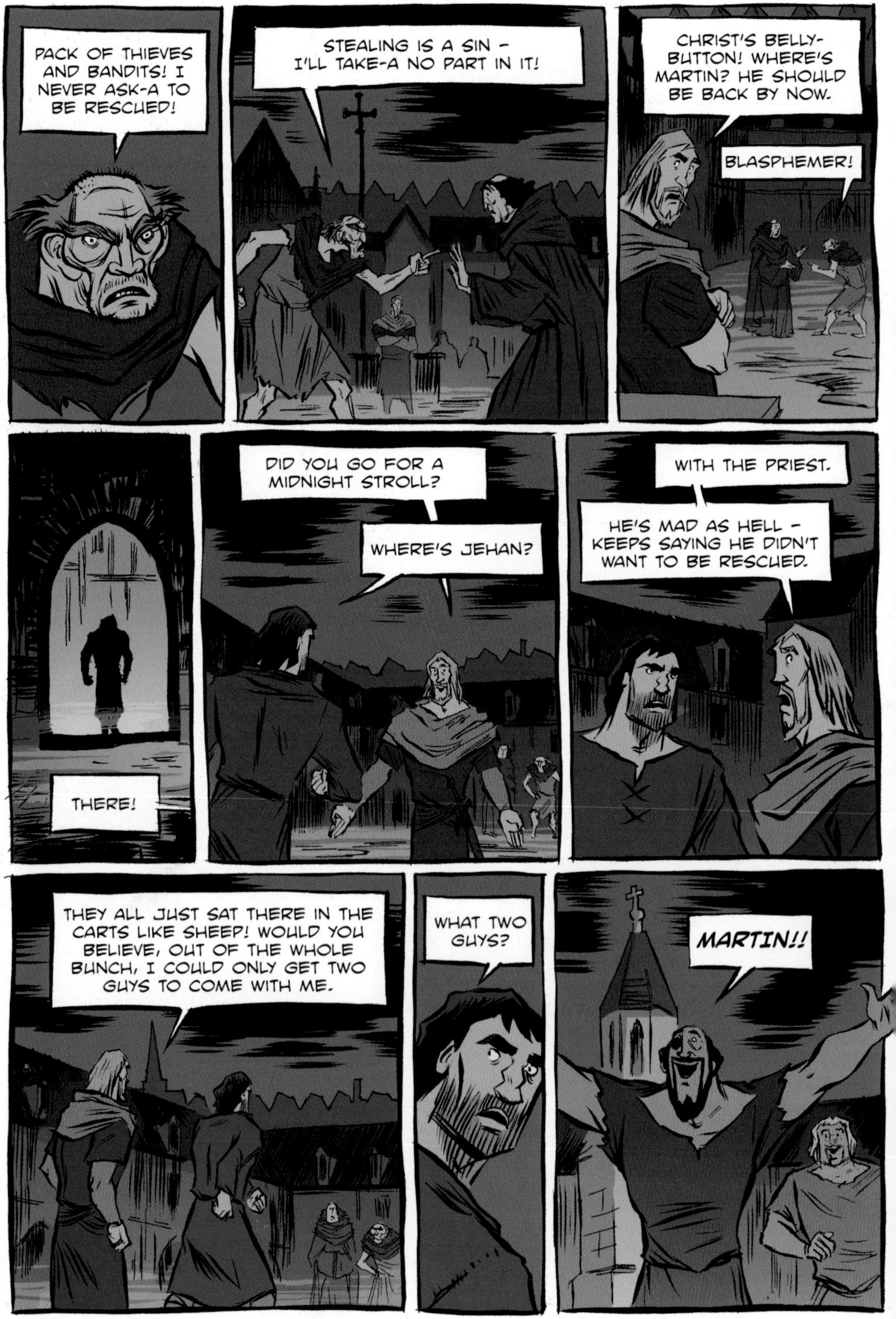
PACK OF THIEVES AND BANDITS! I NEVER ASK-A TO BE RESCUED!
STEALING IS A SIN - I'LL TAKE-A NO PART IN IT!
CHRIST'S BELLY-BUTTON! WHERE'S MARTIN? HE SHOULD BE BACK BY NOW.
BLASPHEMER!
THERE!
DID YOU GO FOR A MIDNIGHT STROLL?
WHERE'S JEHAN?
WITH THE PRIEST.
HE'S MAD AS HELL - KEEPS SAYING HE DIDN'T WANT TO BE RESCUED.
THEY ALL JUST SAT THERE IN THE CARTS LIKE SHEEP! WOULD YOU BELIEVE, OUT OF THE WHOLE BUNCH, I COULD ONLY GET TWO GUYS TO COME WITH ME.
WHAT TWO GUYS?
MARTIN!!

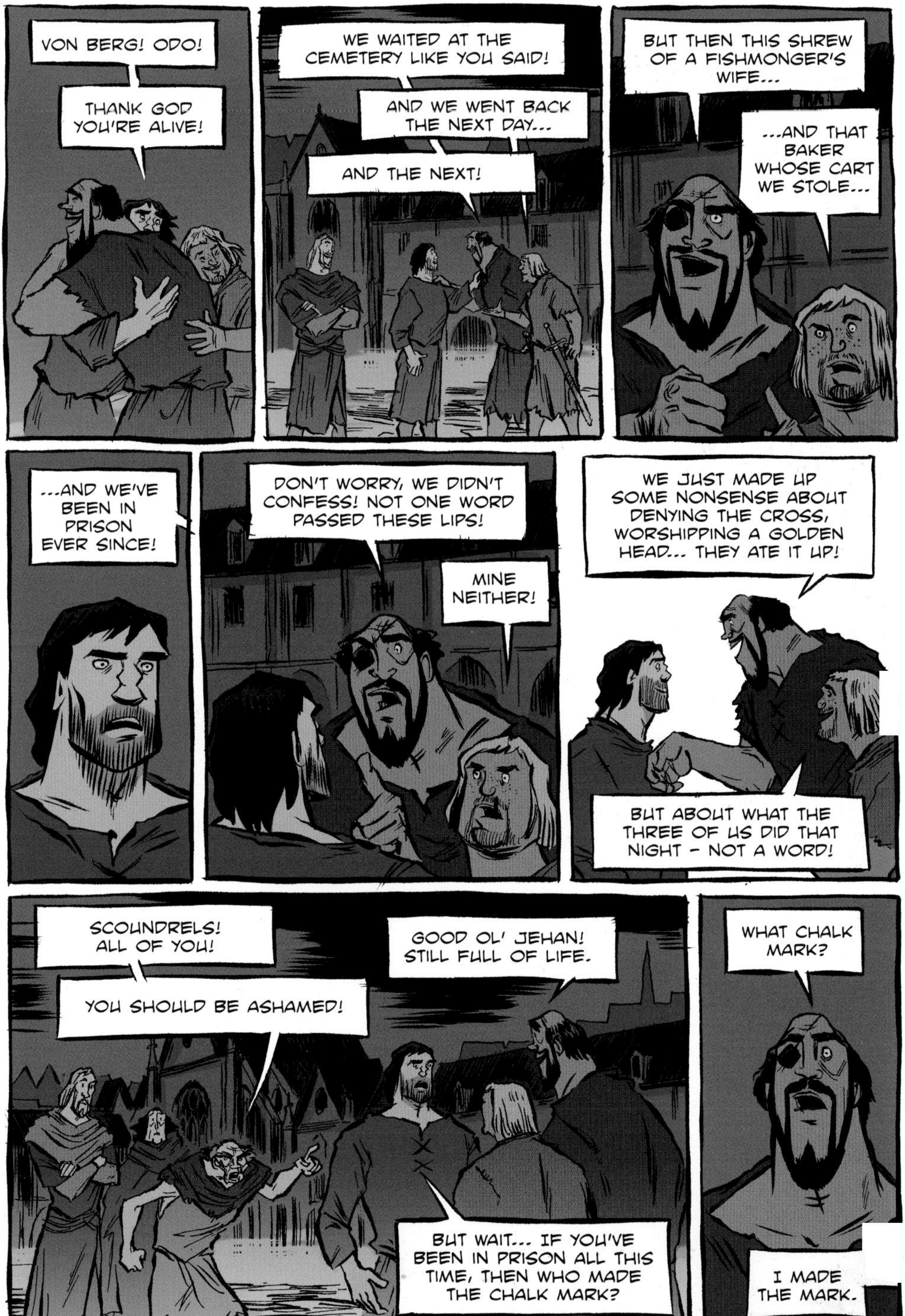
VON BERG! ODO!
THANK GOD YOU'RE ALIVE!
WE WAITED AT THE CEMETERY LIKE YOU SAID!
AND WE WENT BACK THE NEXT DAY...
AND THE NEXT!
BUT THEN THIS SHREW OF A FISHMONGER'S WIFE...
...AND THAT BAKER WHOSE CART WE STOLE...
...AND WE'VE BEEN IN PRISON EVER SINCE!
DON'T WORRY, WE DIDN'T CONFESS! NOT ONE WORD PASSED THESE LIPS!
MINE NEITHER!
WE JUST MADE UP SOME NONSENSE ABOUT DENYING THE CROSS, WORSHIPPING A GOLDEN HEAD... THEY ATE IT UP!
BUT ABOUT WHAT THE THREE OF US DID THAT NIGHT - NOT A WORD!
SCOUNDRELS! ALL OF YOU!
YOU SHOULD BE ASHAMED!
GOOD OL' JEHAN! STILL FULL OF LIFE.
BUT WAIT... IF YOU'VE BEEN IN PRISON ALL THIS TIME, THEN WHO MADE THE CHALK MARK?
WHAT CHALK MARK?
I MADE THE MARK.

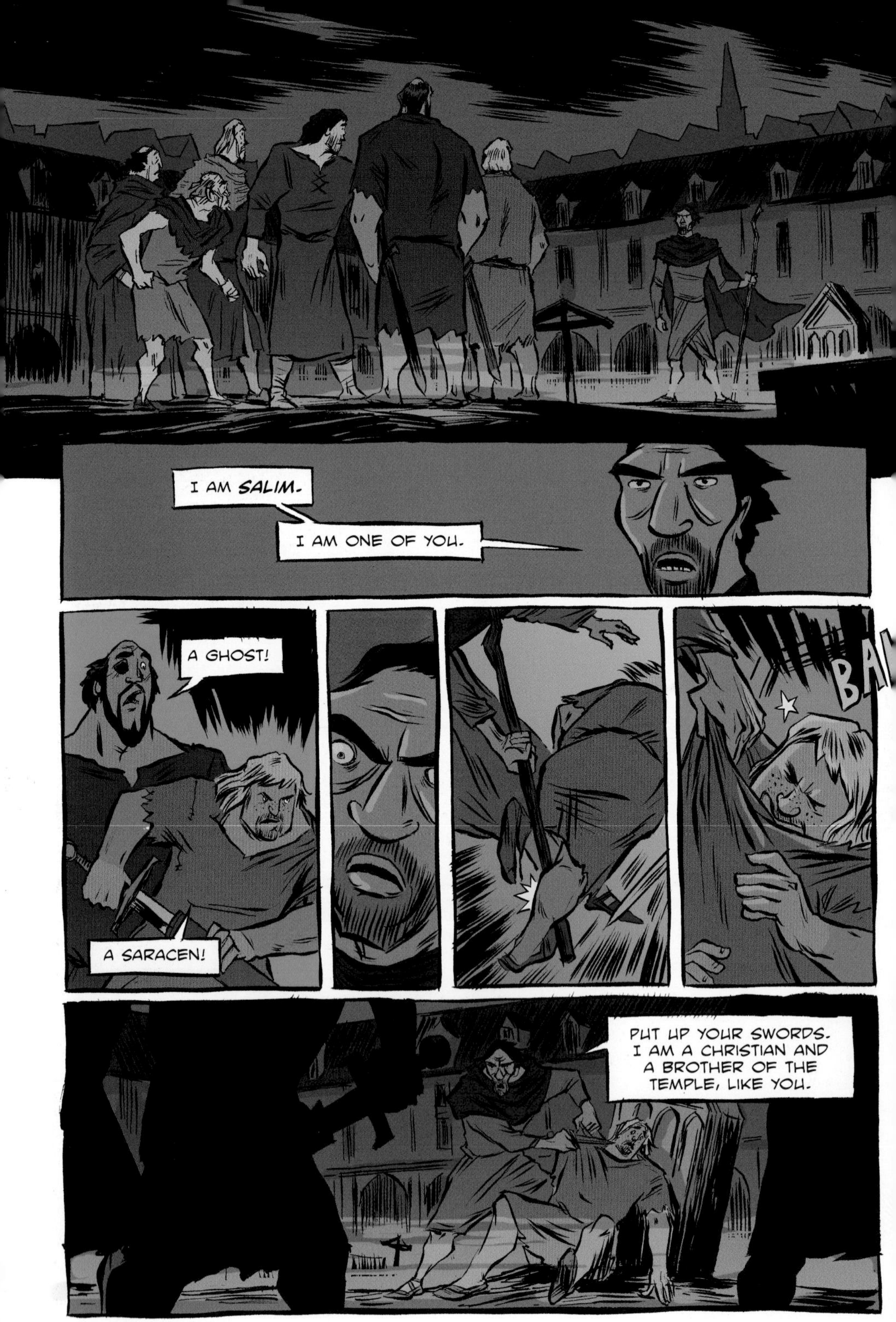

I AM SALIM.
I AM ONE OF YOU.
A GHOST!
A SARACEN!
PUT UP YOUR SWORDS. I AM A CHRISTIAN AND A BROTHER OF THE TEMPLE, LIKE YOU.

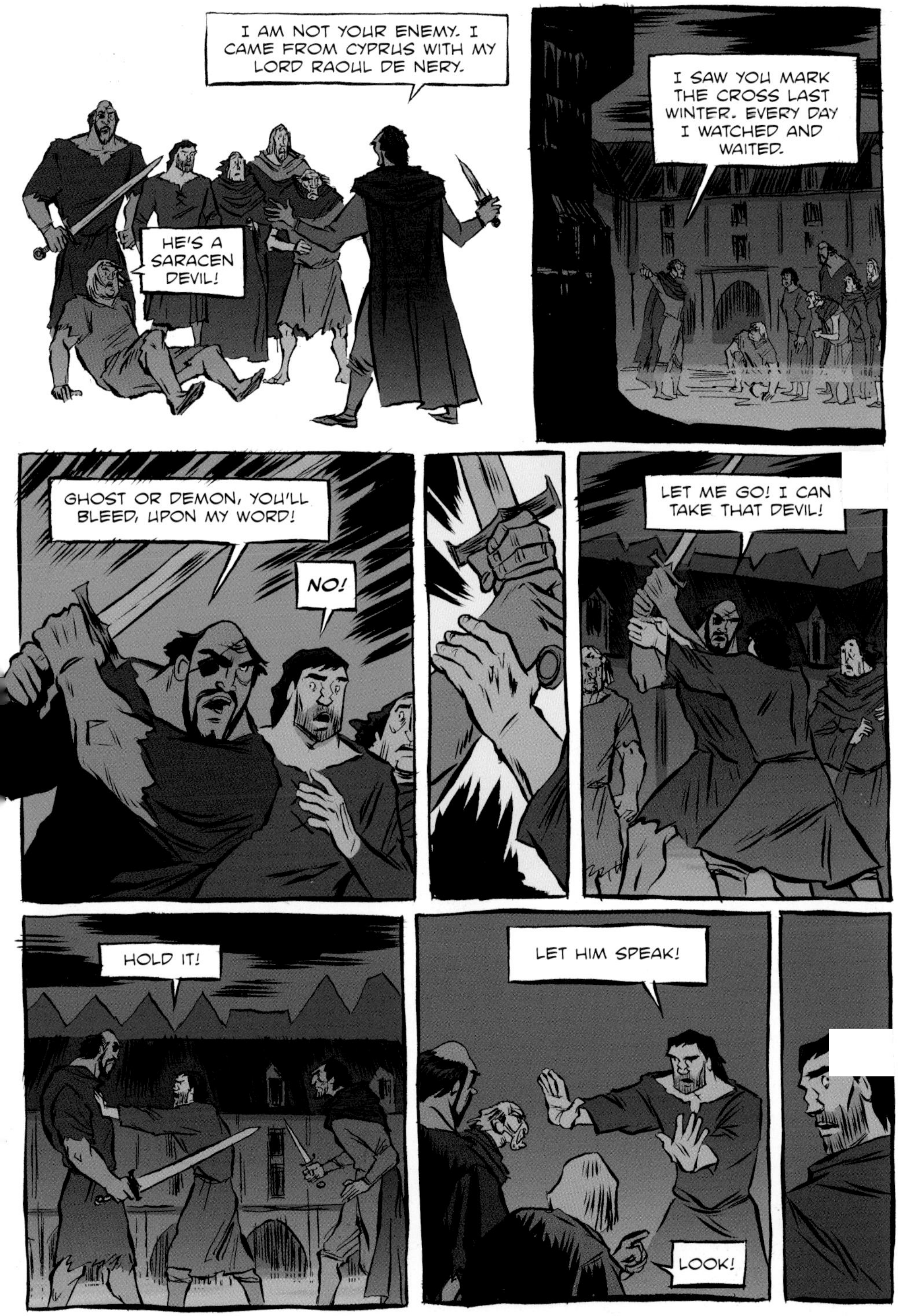

I AM NOT YOUR ENEMY. I CAME FROM CYPRUS WITH MY LORD RAOUL DE NERY.
HE'S A SARACEN DEVIL!
I SAW YOU MARK THE CROSS LAST WINTER. EVERY DAY I WATCHED AND WAITED.
GHOST OR DEMON, YOU'LL BLEED, UPON MY WORD!
NO!
LET ME GO! I CAN TAKE THAT DEVIL!
HOLD IT!
LET HIM SPEAK!
LOOK!

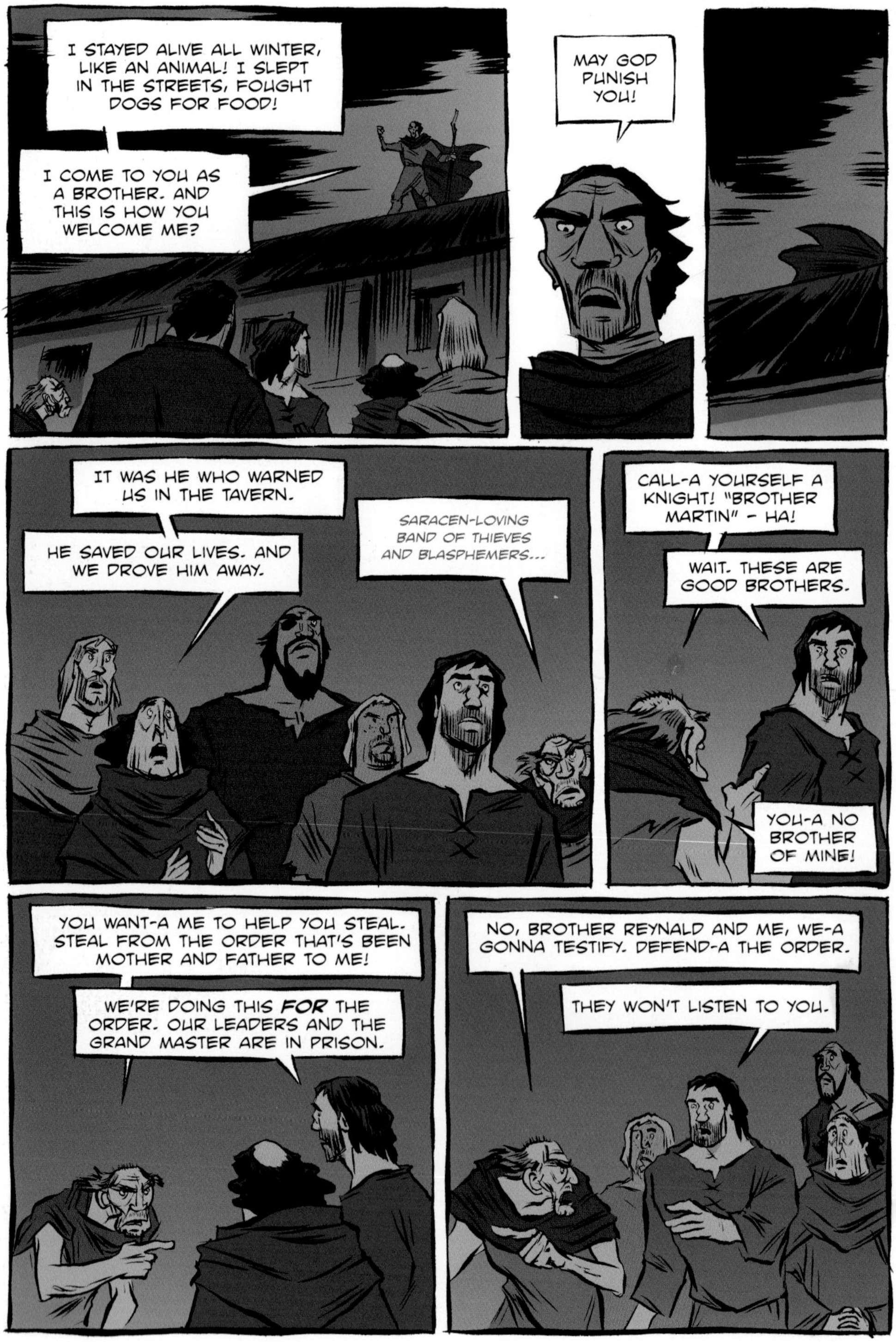

I STAYED ALIVE ALL WINTER, LIKE AN ANIMAL! I SLEPT IN THE STREETS, FOUGHT DOGS FOR FOOD!
I COME TO YOU AS A BROTHER. AND THIS IS HOW YOU WELCOME ME?
MAY GOD PUNISH YOU!
IT WAS HE WHO WARNED US IN THE TAVERN.
HE SAVED OUR LIVES. AND WE DROVE HIM AWAY.
SARACEN-LOVING BAND OF THIEVES AND BLASPHEMERS...
CALL-A YOURSELF A KNIGHT! "BROTHER MARTIN" - HA!
WAIT. THESE ARE GOOD BROTHERS.
YOU-A NO BROTHER OF MINE!
YOU WANT-A ME TO HELP YOU STEAL. STEAL FROM THE ORDER THAT'S BEEN MOTHER AND FATHER TO ME!
WE'RE DOING THIS **FOR** THE ORDER. OUR LEADERS AND THE GRAND MASTER ARE IN PRISON.
NO, BROTHER REYNALD AND ME, WE-A GONNA TESTIFY. DEFEND-A THE ORDER.
THEY WON'T LISTEN TO YOU.

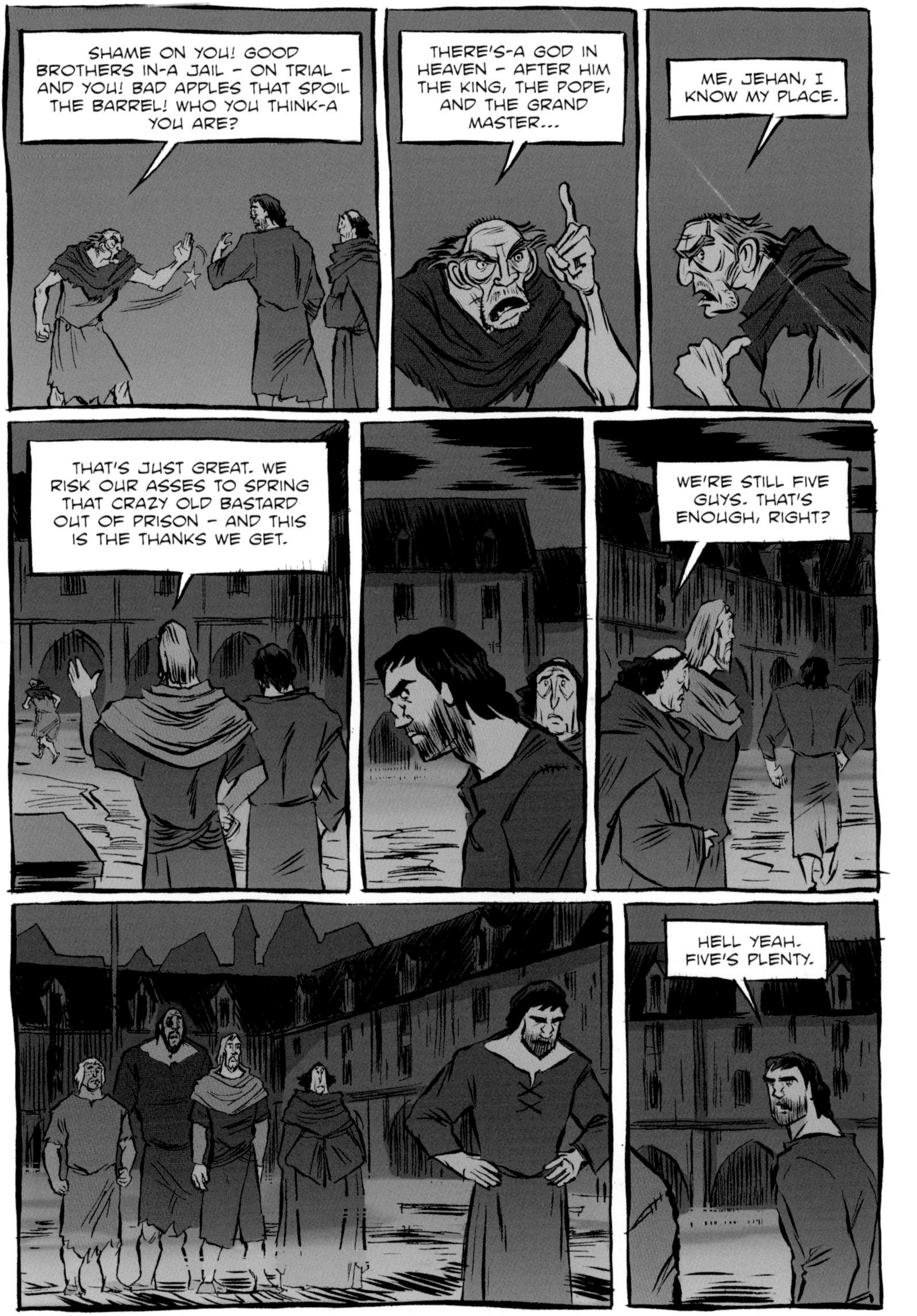
SHAME ON YOU! GOOD BROTHERS IN-A JAIL - ON TRIAL - AND YOU! BAD APPLES THAT SPOIL THE BARREL! WHO YOU THINK-A YOU ARE?
THERE'S-A GOD IN HEAVEN - AFTER HIM THE KING, THE POPE, AND THE GRAND MASTER...
ME, JEHAN, I KNOW MY PLACE.
THAT'S JUST GREAT. WE RISK OUR ASSES TO SPRING THAT CRAZY OLD BASTARD OUT OF PRISON - AND THIS IS THE THANKS WE GET.
WE'RE STILL FIVE GUYS. THAT'S ENOUGH, RIGHT?
HELL YEAH. FIVE'S PLENTY.

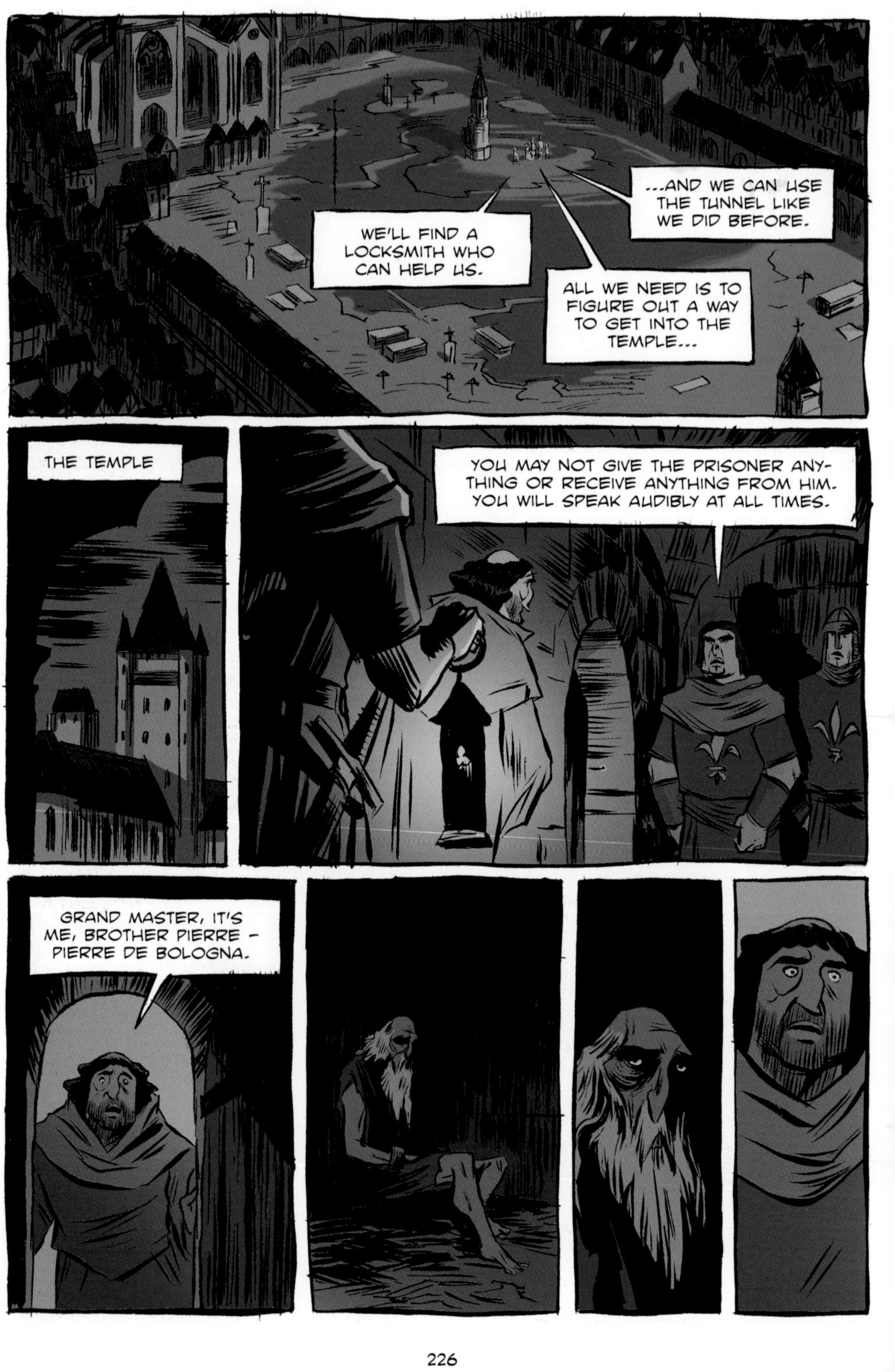
WE'LL FIND A LOCKSMITH WHO CAN HELP US.
ALL WE NEED IS TO FIGURE OUT A WAY TO GET INTO THE TEMPLE...
...AND WE CAN USE THE TUNNEL LIKE WE DID BEFORE.
THE TEMPLE
YOU MAY NOT GIVE THE PRISONER ANYTHING OR RECEIVE ANYTHING FROM HIM. YOU WILL SPEAK AUDIBLY AT ALL TIMES.
GRAND MASTER, IT'S ME, BROTHER PIERRE - PIERRE DE BOLOGNA.

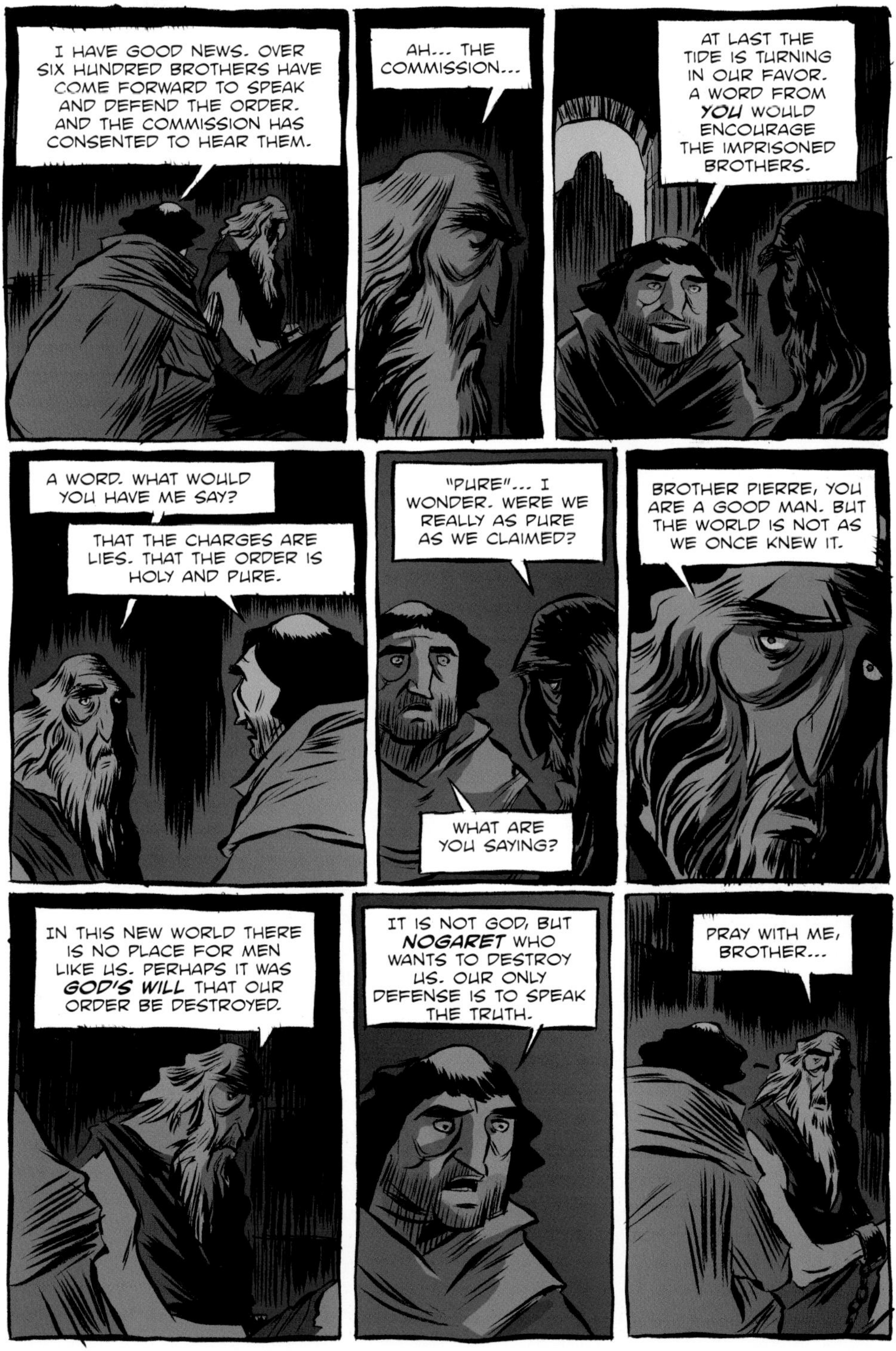
I HAVE GOOD NEWS. OVER SIX HUNDRED BROTHERS HAVE COME FORWARD TO SPEAK AND DEFEND THE ORDER. AND THE COMMISSION HAS CONSENTED TO HEAR THEM.
AH... THE COMMISSION...
AT LAST THE TIDE IS TURNING IN OUR FAVOR. A WORD FROM ***YOU*** WOULD ENCOURAGE THE IMPRISONED BROTHERS.
A WORD. WHAT WOULD YOU HAVE ME SAY?
THAT THE CHARGES ARE LIES. THAT THE ORDER IS HOLY AND PURE.
"PURE"... I WONDER. WERE WE REALLY AS PURE AS WE CLAIMED?
WHAT ARE YOU SAYING?
BROTHER PIERRE, YOU ARE A GOOD MAN. BUT THE WORLD IS NOT AS WE ONCE KNEW IT.
IN THIS NEW WORLD THERE IS NO PLACE FOR MEN LIKE US. PERHAPS IT WAS ***GOD'S WILL*** THAT OUR ORDER BE DESTROYED.
IT IS NOT GOD, BUT ***NOGARET*** WHO WANTS TO DESTROY US. OUR ONLY DEFENSE IS TO SPEAK THE TRUTH.
PRAY WITH ME, BROTHER...

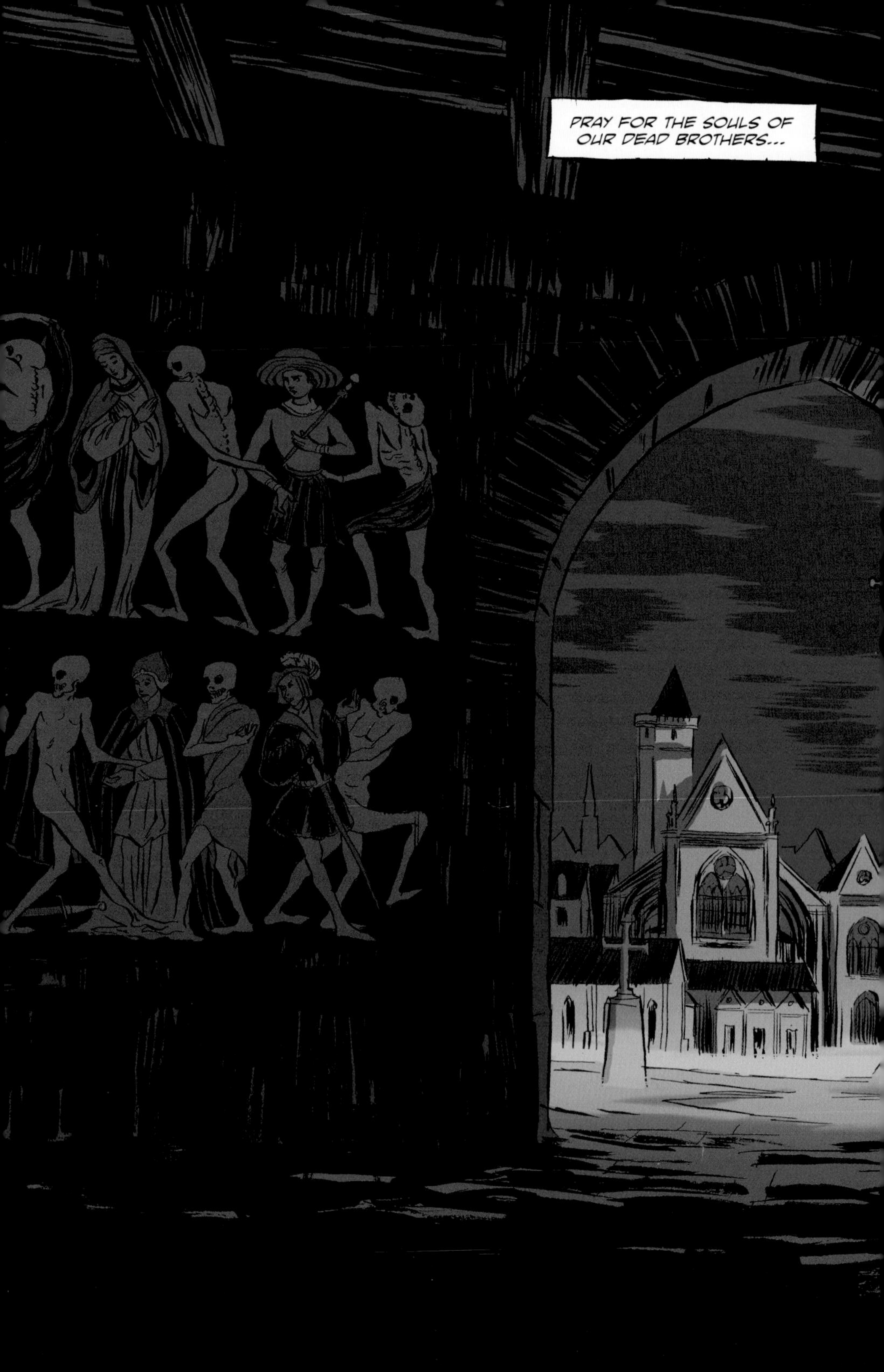
PRAY FOR THE SOULS OF OUR DEAD BROTHERS...

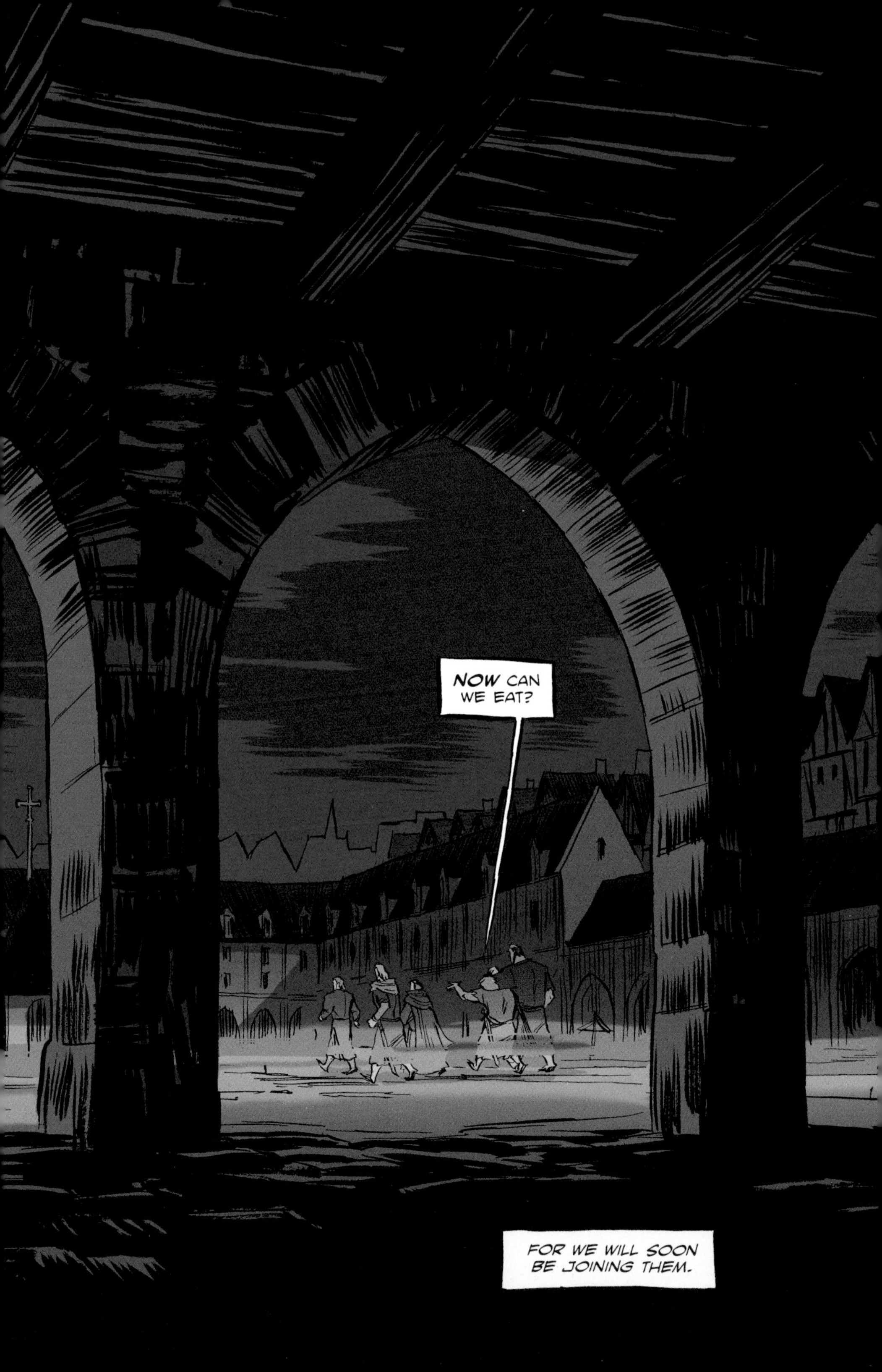
NOW CAN WE EAT?
FOR WE WILL SOON BE JOINING THEM.

6. Saint-Antoine

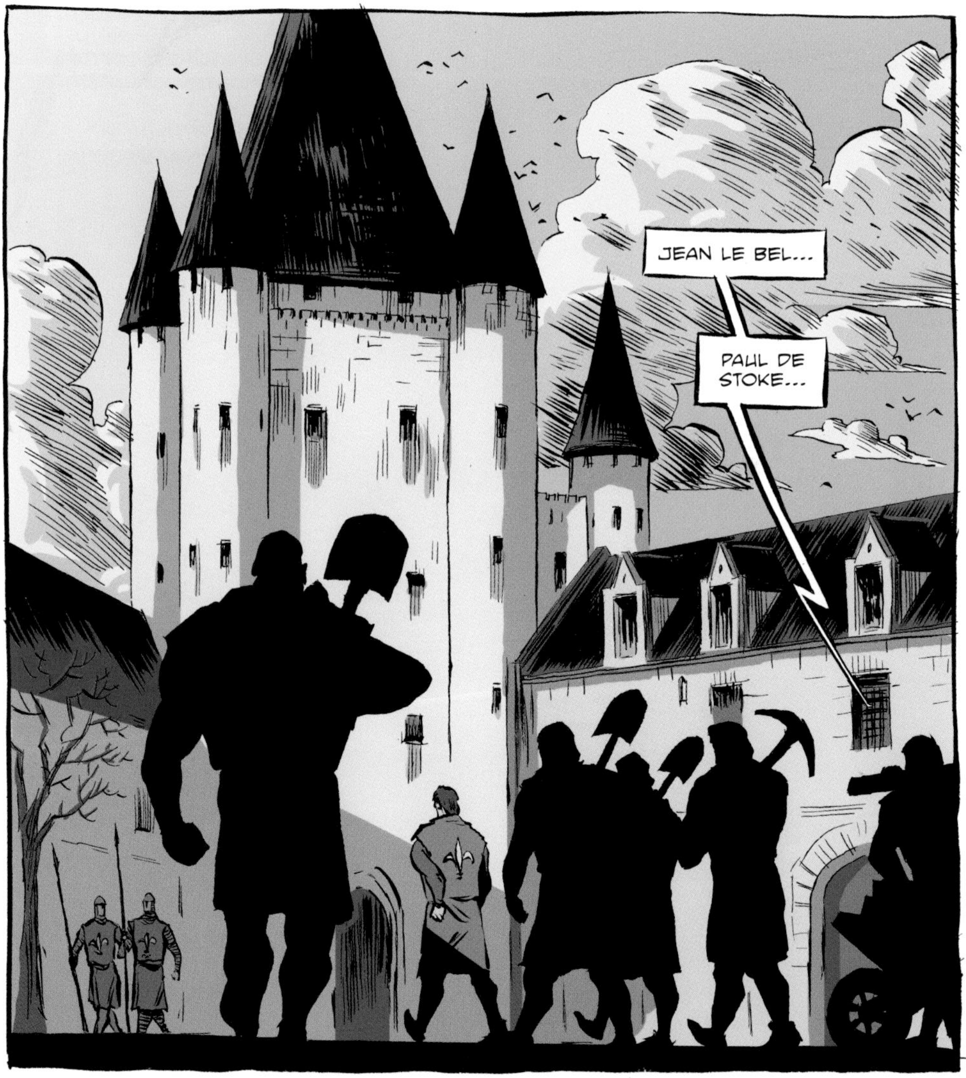
JEAN LE BEL...
PAUL DE STOKE...

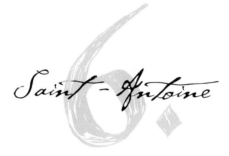

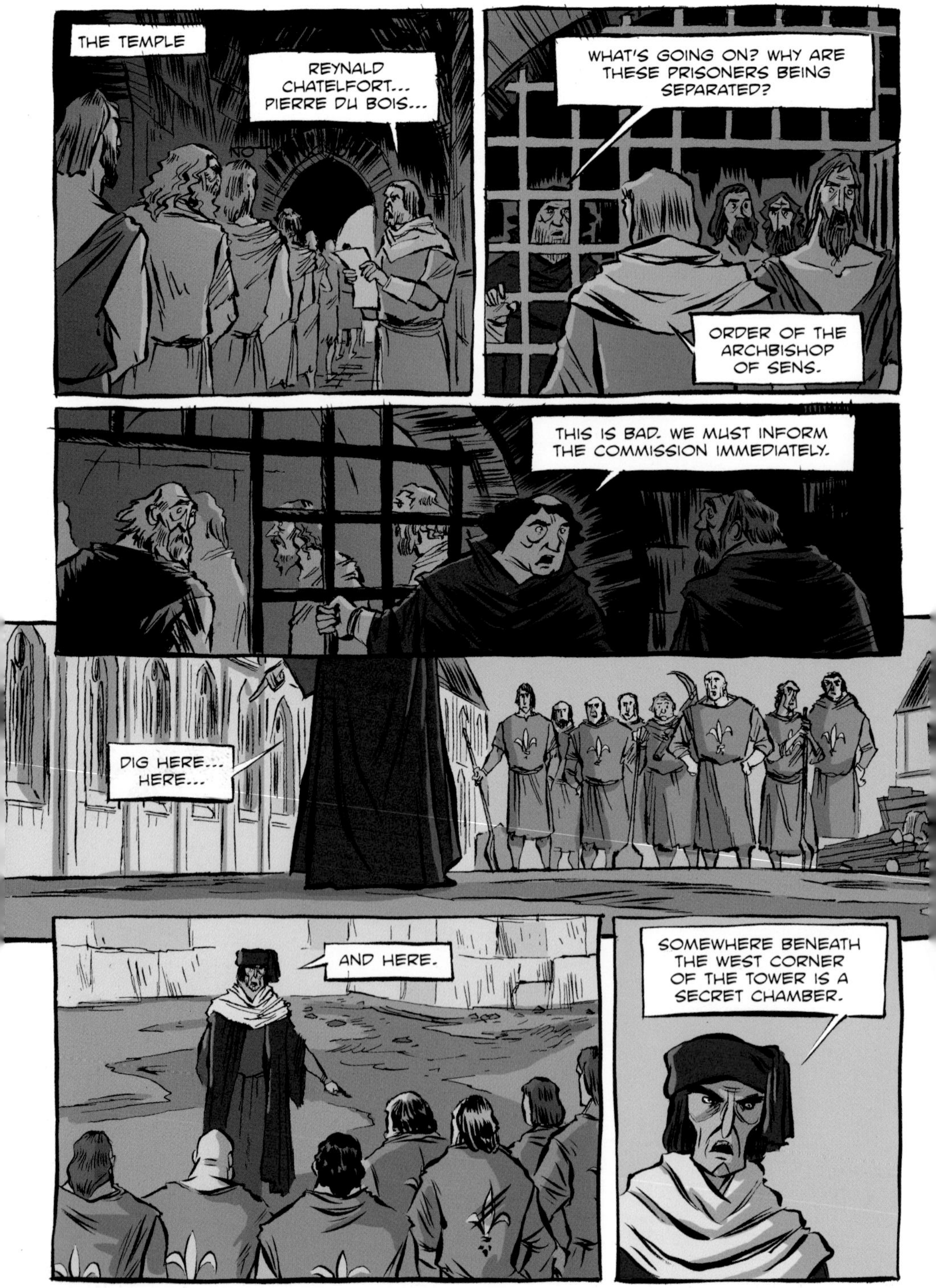
THE TEMPLE
REYNALD CHATELFORT... PIERRE DU BOIS...
WHAT'S GOING ON? WHY ARE THESE PRISONERS BEING SEPARATED?
ORDER OF THE ARCHBISHOP OF SENS.
THIS IS BAD. WE MUST INFORM THE COMMISSION IMMEDIATELY.
DIG HERE... HERE...
AND HERE.
SOMEWHERE BENEATH THE WEST CORNER OF THE TOWER IS A SECRET CHAMBER.

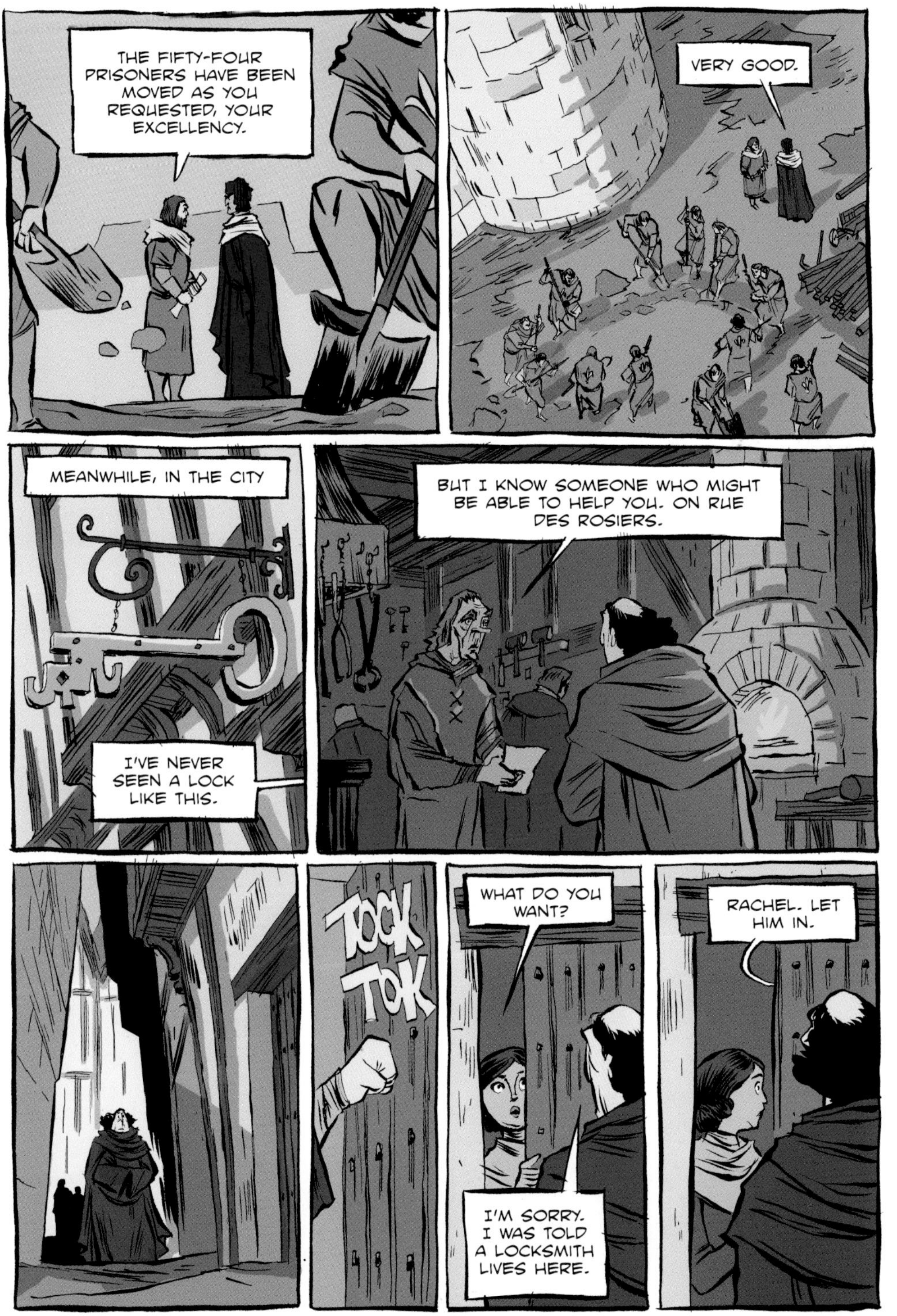
THE FIFTY-FOUR PRISONERS HAVE BEEN MOVED AS YOU REQUESTED, YOUR EXCELLENCY.
VERY GOOD.
MEANWHILE, IN THE CITY
I'VE NEVER SEEN A LOCK LIKE THIS.
BUT I KNOW SOMEONE WHO MIGHT BE ABLE TO HELP YOU. ON RUE DES ROSIERS.
TOCK
TOK
WHAT DO YOU WANT?
I'M SORRY. I WAS TOLD A LOCKSMITH LIVES HERE.
RACHEL. LET HIM IN.

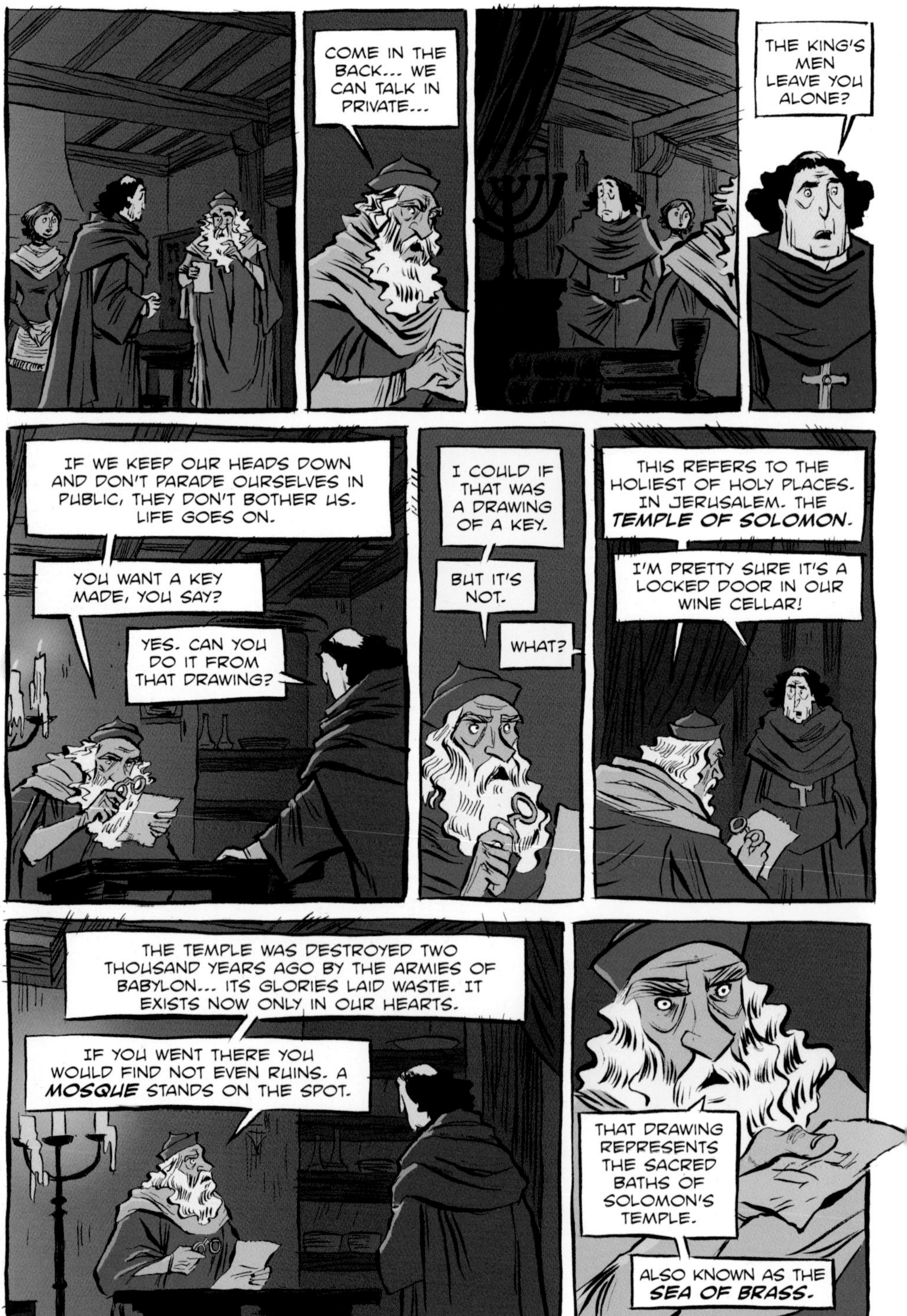
COME IN THE BACK... WE CAN TALK IN PRIVATE...
THE KING'S MEN LEAVE YOU ALONE?
IF WE KEEP OUR HEADS DOWN AND DON'T PARADE OURSELVES IN PUBLIC, THEY DON'T BOTHER US. LIFE GOES ON.
YOU WANT A KEY MADE, YOU SAY?
YES. CAN YOU DO IT FROM THAT DRAWING?
I COULD IF THAT WAS A DRAWING OF A KEY.
BUT IT'S NOT.
WHAT?
THIS REFERS TO THE HOLIEST OF HOLY PLACES. IN JERUSALEM. THE ***TEMPLE OF SOLOMON***.
I'M PRETTY SURE IT'S A LOCKED DOOR IN OUR WINE CELLAR!
THE TEMPLE WAS DESTROYED TWO THOUSAND YEARS AGO BY THE ARMIES OF BABYLON... ITS GLORIES LAID WASTE. IT EXISTS NOW ONLY IN OUR HEARTS.
IF YOU WENT THERE YOU WOULD FIND NOT EVEN RUINS. A ***MOSQUE*** STANDS ON THE SPOT.
THAT DRAWING REPRESENTS THE SACRED BATHS OF SOLOMON'S TEMPLE.
ALSO KNOWN AS THE ***SEA OF BRASS***.

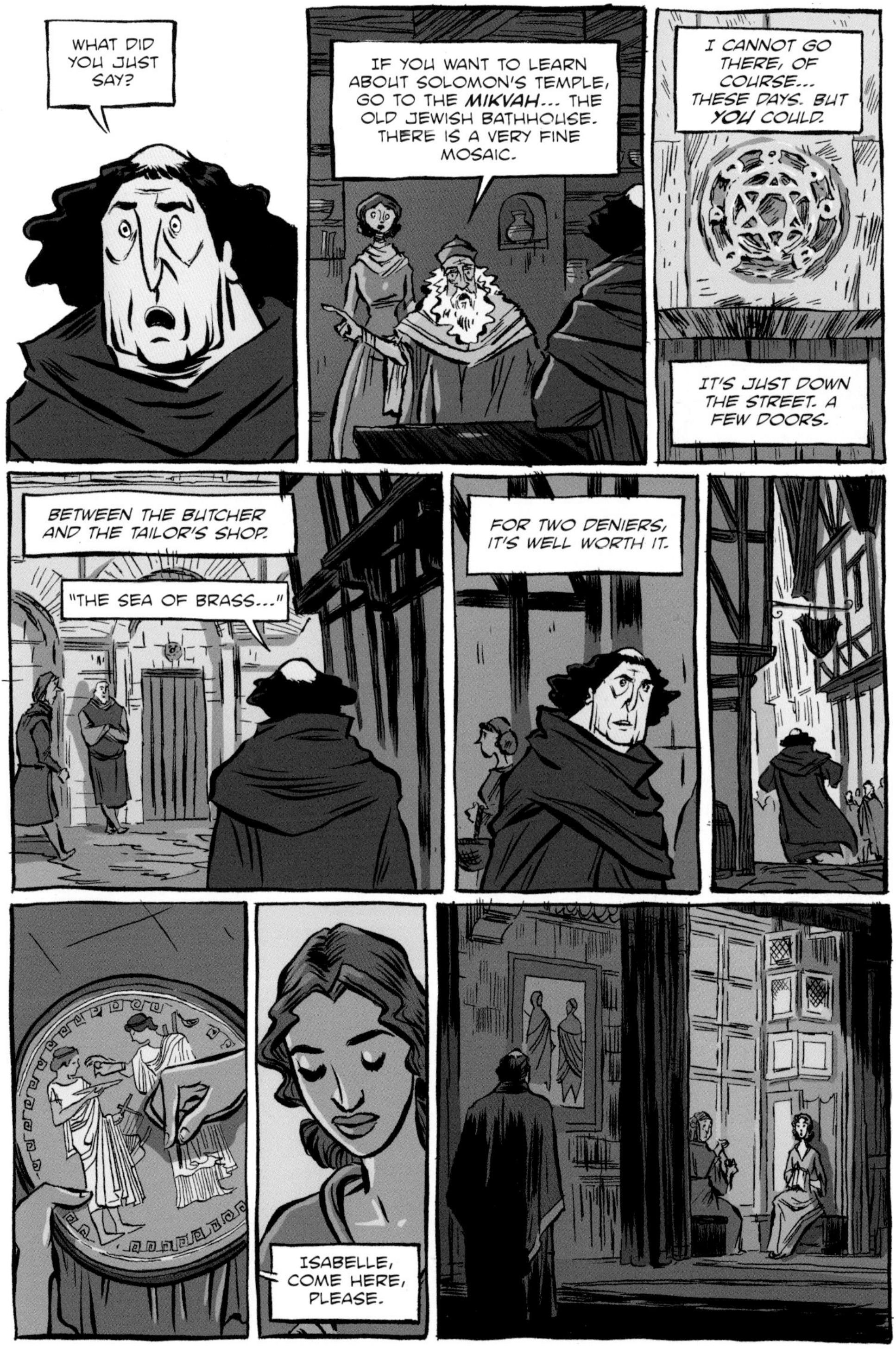
WHAT DID YOU JUST SAY?
IF YOU WANT TO LEARN ABOUT SOLOMON'S TEMPLE, GO TO THE MIKVAH... THE OLD JEWISH BATHHOUSE. THERE IS A VERY FINE MOSAIC.
I CANNOT GO THERE, OF COURSE... THESE DAYS. BUT YOU COULD.
IT'S JUST DOWN THE STREET. A FEW DOORS.
BETWEEN THE BUTCHER AND THE TAILOR'S SHOP.
"THE SEA OF BRASS..."
FOR TWO DENIERS, IT'S WELL WORTH IT.
ISABELLE, COME HERE, PLEASE.

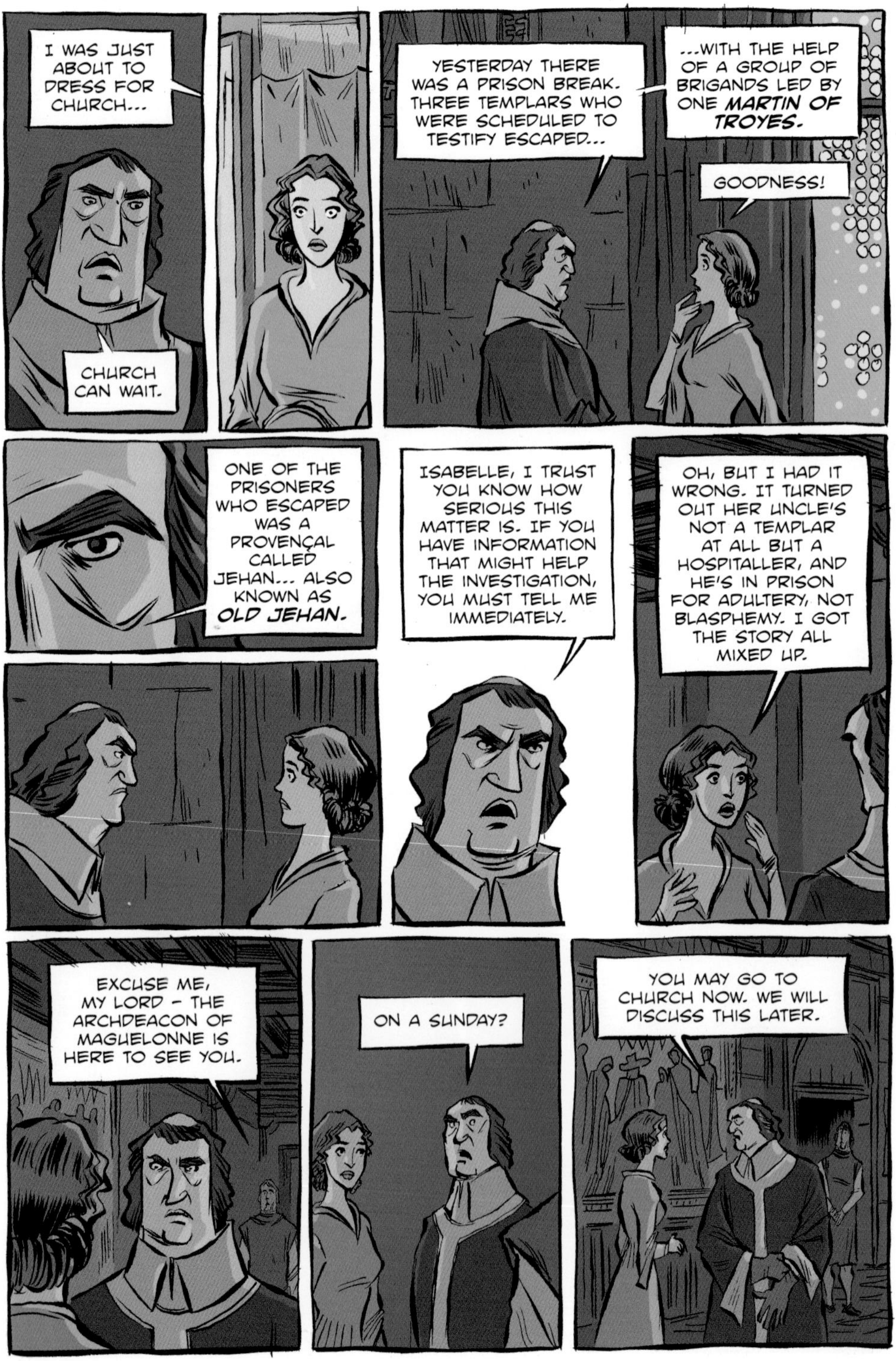
I WAS JUST ABOUT TO DRESS FOR CHURCH...
CHURCH CAN WAIT.
YESTERDAY THERE WAS A PRISON BREAK. THREE TEMPLARS WHO WERE SCHEDULED TO TESTIFY ESCAPED...
...WITH THE HELP OF A GROUP OF BRIGANDS LED BY ONE ***MARTIN OF TROYES.***
GOODNESS!
ONE OF THE PRISONERS WHO ESCAPED WAS A PROVENÇAL CALLED JEHAN... ALSO KNOWN AS ***OLD JEHAN.***
ISABELLE, I TRUST YOU KNOW HOW SERIOUS THIS MATTER IS. IF YOU HAVE INFORMATION THAT MIGHT HELP THE INVESTIGATION, YOU MUST TELL ME IMMEDIATELY.
OH, BUT I HAD IT WRONG. IT TURNED OUT HER UNCLE'S NOT A TEMPLAR AT ALL BUT A HOSPITALLER, AND HE'S IN PRISON FOR ADULTERY, NOT BLASPHEMY. I GOT THE STORY ALL MIXED UP.
EXCUSE ME, MY LORD – THE ARCHDEACON OF MAGUELONNE IS HERE TO SEE YOU.
ON A SUNDAY?
YOU MAY GO TO CHURCH NOW. WE WILL DISCUSS THIS LATER.

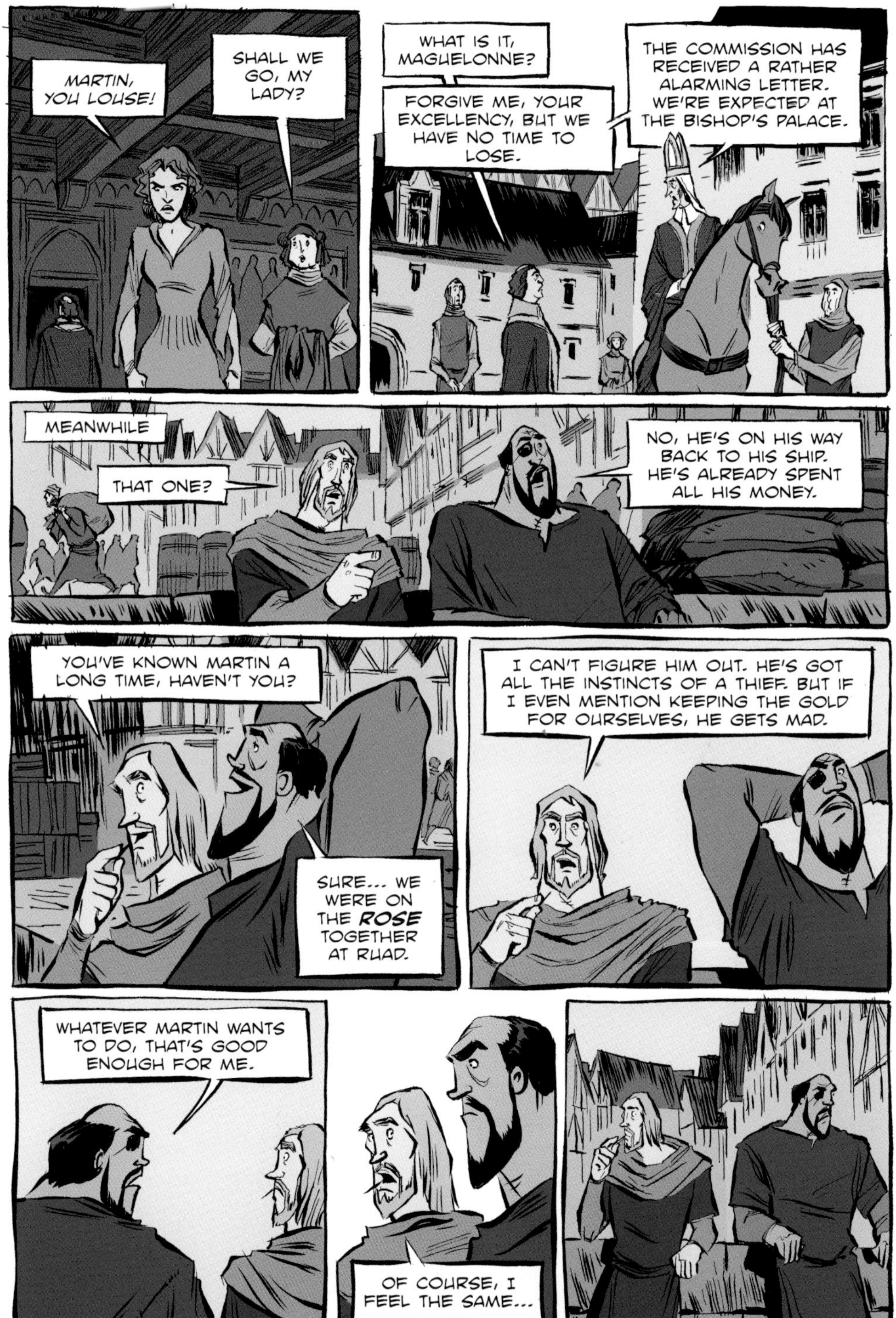

MARTIN, YOU LOUSE!
SHALL WE GO, MY LADY?
WHAT IS IT, MAGUELONNE?
FORGIVE ME, YOUR EXCELLENCY, BUT WE HAVE NO TIME TO LOSE.
THE COMMISSION HAS RECEIVED A RATHER ALARMING LETTER. WE'RE EXPECTED AT THE BISHOP'S PALACE.
MEANWHILE
THAT ONE?
NO, HE'S ON HIS WAY BACK TO HIS SHIP. HE'S ALREADY SPENT ALL HIS MONEY.
YOU'VE KNOWN MARTIN A LONG TIME, HAVEN'T YOU?
SURE... WE WERE ON THE ROSE TOGETHER AT RUAD.
I CAN'T FIGURE HIM OUT. HE'S GOT ALL THE INSTINCTS OF A THIEF. BUT IF I EVEN MENTION KEEPING THE GOLD FOR OURSELVES, HE GETS MAD.
WHATEVER MARTIN WANTS TO DO, THAT'S GOOD ENOUGH FOR ME.
OF COURSE, I FEEL THE SAME...

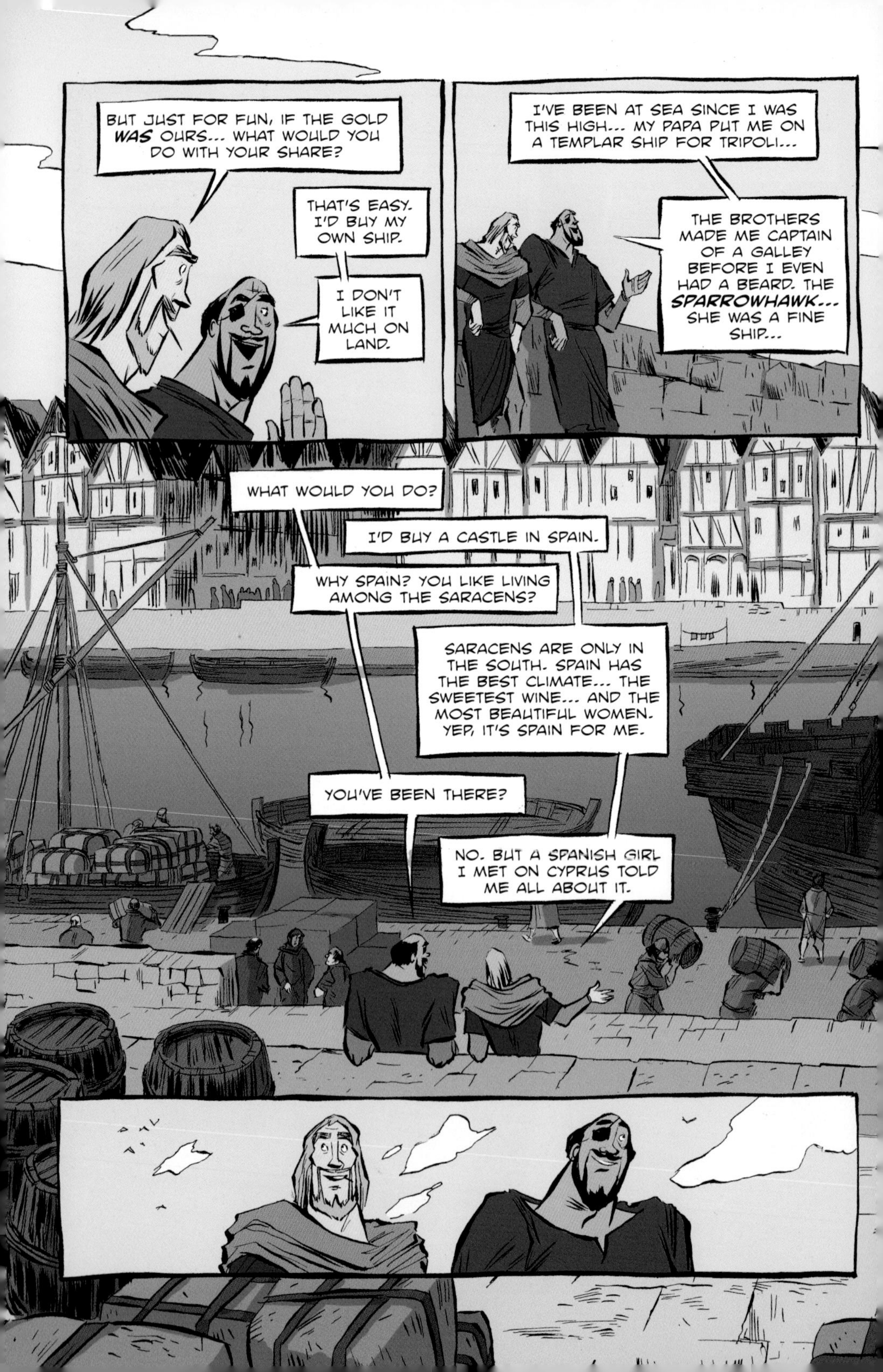
BUT JUST FOR FUN, IF THE GOLD **WAS** OURS... WHAT WOULD YOU DO WITH YOUR SHARE?
THAT'S EASY. I'D BUY MY OWN SHIP.
I DON'T LIKE IT MUCH ON LAND.
I'VE BEEN AT SEA SINCE I WAS THIS HIGH... MY PAPA PUT ME ON A TEMPLAR SHIP FOR TRIPOLI...
THE BROTHERS MADE ME CAPTAIN OF A GALLEY BEFORE I EVEN HAD A BEARD. THE ***SPARROWHAWK...*** SHE WAS A FINE SHIP...
WHAT WOULD YOU DO?
I'D BUY A CASTLE IN SPAIN.
WHY SPAIN? YOU LIKE LIVING AMONG THE SARACENS?
SARACENS ARE ONLY IN THE SOUTH. SPAIN HAS THE BEST CLIMATE... THE SWEETEST WINE... AND THE MOST BEAUTIFUL WOMEN. YEP, IT'S SPAIN FOR ME.
YOU'VE BEEN THERE?
NO. BUT A SPANISH GIRL I MET ON CYPRUS TOLD ME ALL ABOUT IT.

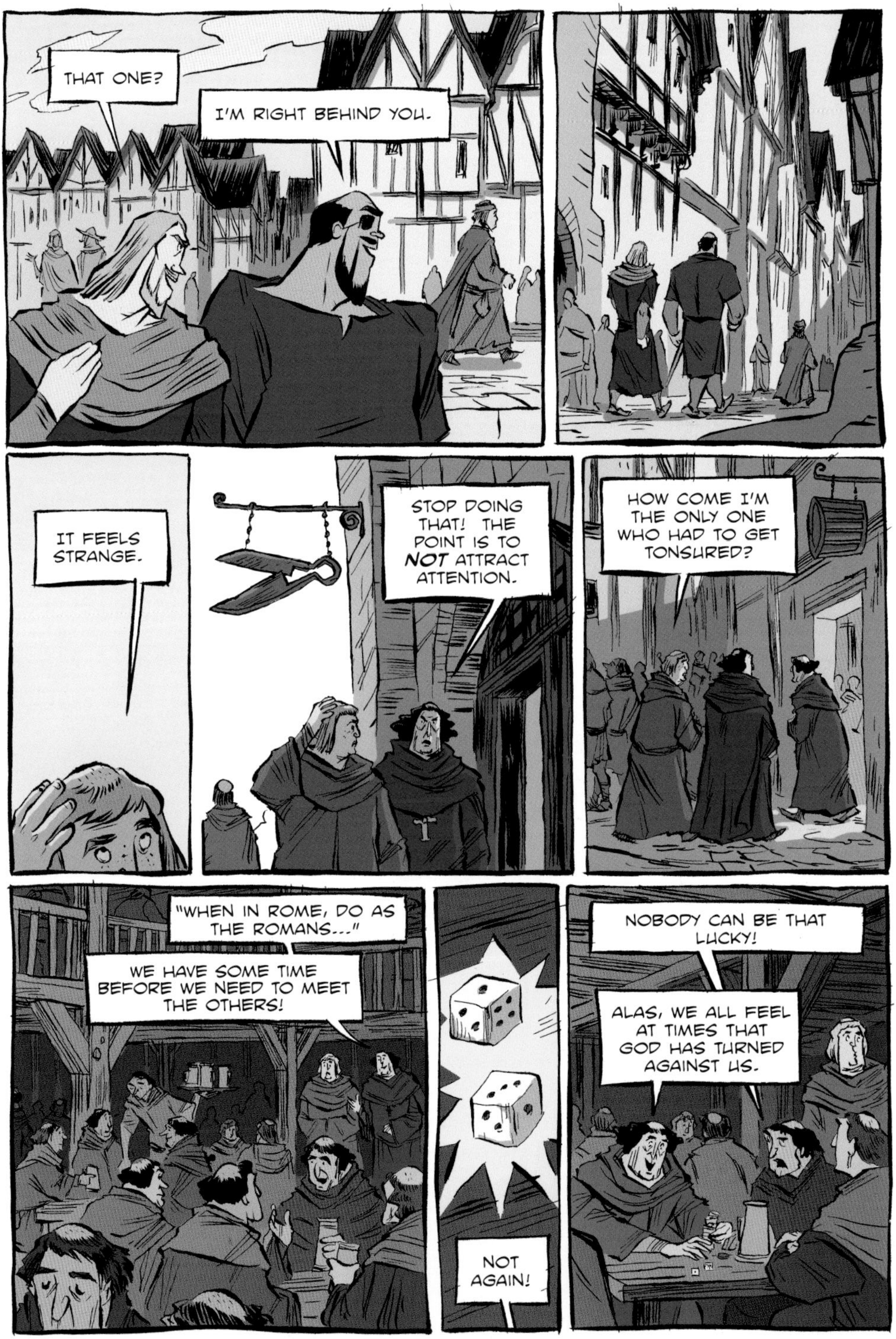
THAT ONE?
I'M RIGHT BEHIND YOU.
IT FEELS STRANGE.
STOP DOING THAT! THE POINT IS TO NOT ATTRACT ATTENTION.
HOW COME I'M THE ONLY ONE WHO HAD TO GET TONSURED?
"WHEN IN ROME, DO AS THE ROMANS..."
WE HAVE SOME TIME BEFORE WE NEED TO MEET THE OTHERS!
NOT AGAIN!
NOBODY CAN BE THAT LUCKY!
ALAS, WE ALL FEEL AT TIMES THAT GOD HAS TURNED AGAINST US.

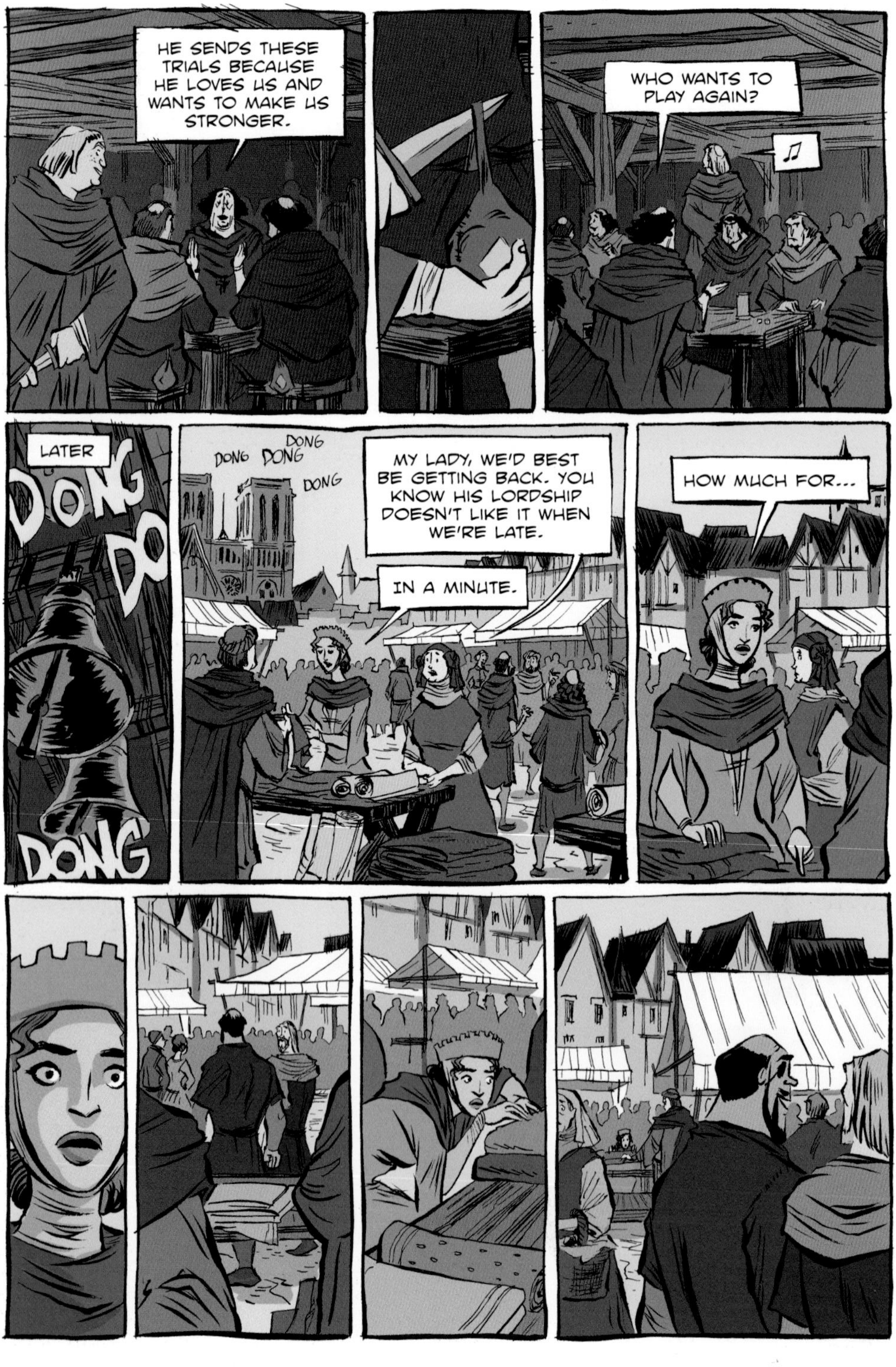
HE SENDS THESE TRIALS BECAUSE HE LOVES US AND WANTS TO MAKE US STRONGER.
WHO WANTS TO PLAY AGAIN?
♫
LATER
DONG DO
DONG
DONG DONG DONG
DONG
MY LADY, WE'D BEST BE GETTING BACK. YOU KNOW HIS LORDSHIP DOESN'T LIKE IT WHEN WE'RE LATE.
IN A MINUTE.
HOW MUCH FOR...

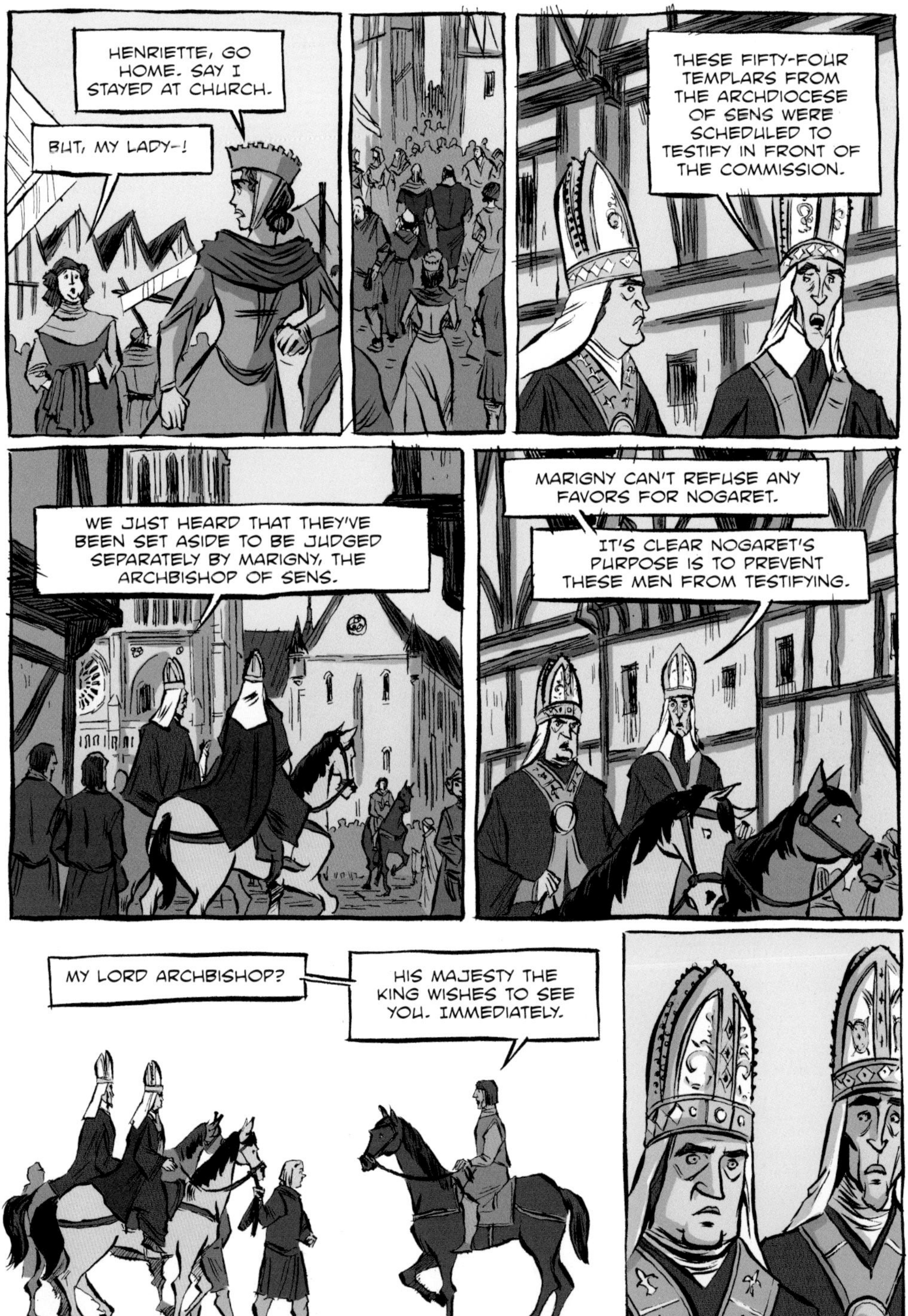
HENRIETTE, GO HOME. SAY I STAYED AT CHURCH.
BUT, MY LADY-!
THESE FIFTY-FOUR TEMPLARS FROM THE ARCHDIOCESE OF SENS WERE SCHEDULED TO TESTIFY IN FRONT OF THE COMMISSION.
WE JUST HEARD THAT THEY'VE BEEN SET ASIDE TO BE JUDGED SEPARATELY BY MARIGNY, THE ARCHBISHOP OF SENS.
MARIGNY CAN'T REFUSE ANY FAVORS FOR NOGARET.
IT'S CLEAR NOGARET'S PURPOSE IS TO PREVENT THESE MEN FROM TESTIFYING.
MY LORD ARCHBISHOP?
HIS MAJESTY THE KING WISHES TO SEE YOU. IMMEDIATELY.

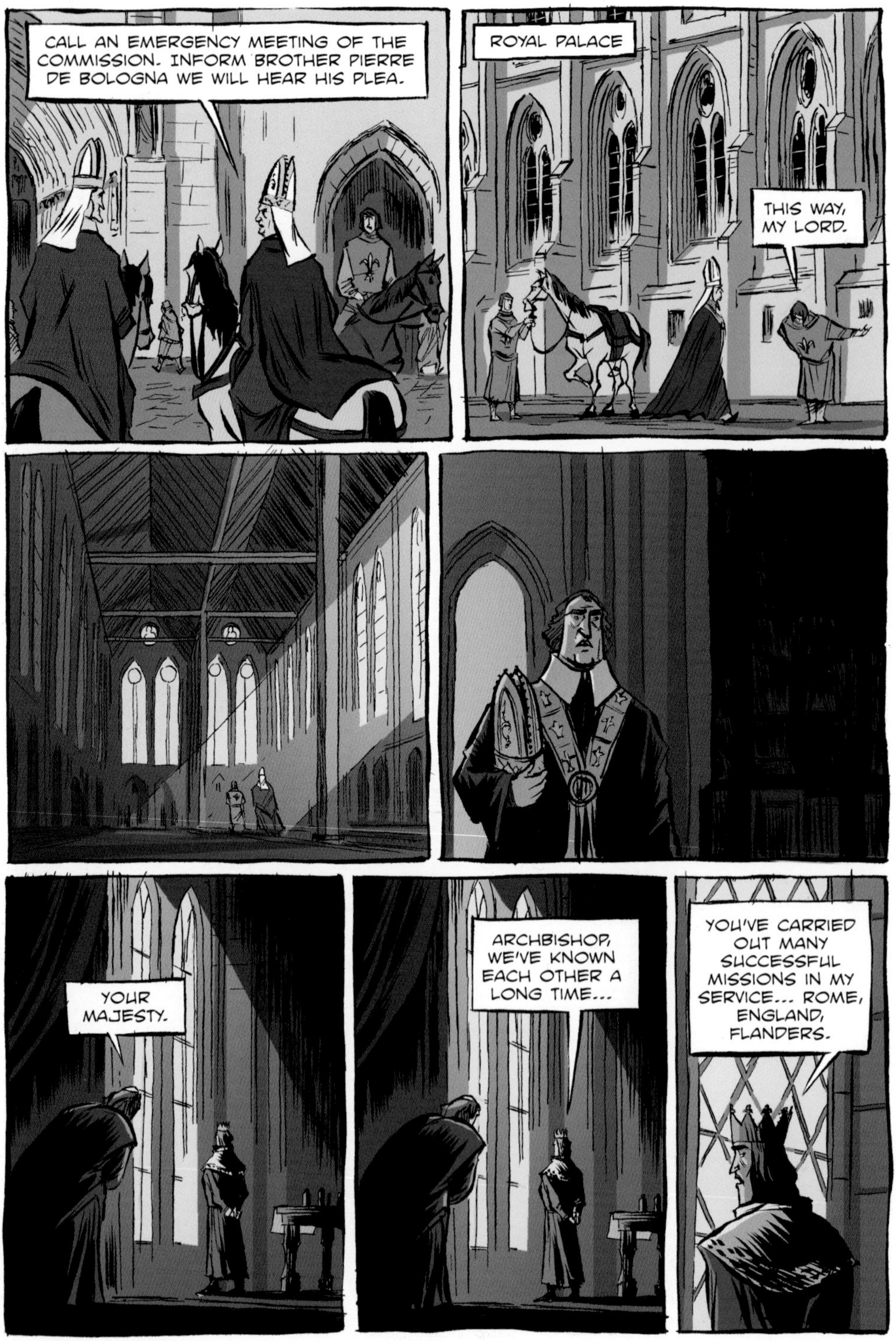
CALL AN EMERGENCY MEETING OF THE COMMISSION. INFORM BROTHER PIERRE DE BOLOGNA WE WILL HEAR HIS PLEA.
ROYAL PALACE
THIS WAY, MY LORD.
YOUR MAJESTY.
ARCHBISHOP, WE'VE KNOWN EACH OTHER A LONG TIME...
YOU'VE CARRIED OUT MANY SUCCESSFUL MISSIONS IN MY SERVICE... ROME, ENGLAND, FLANDERS.

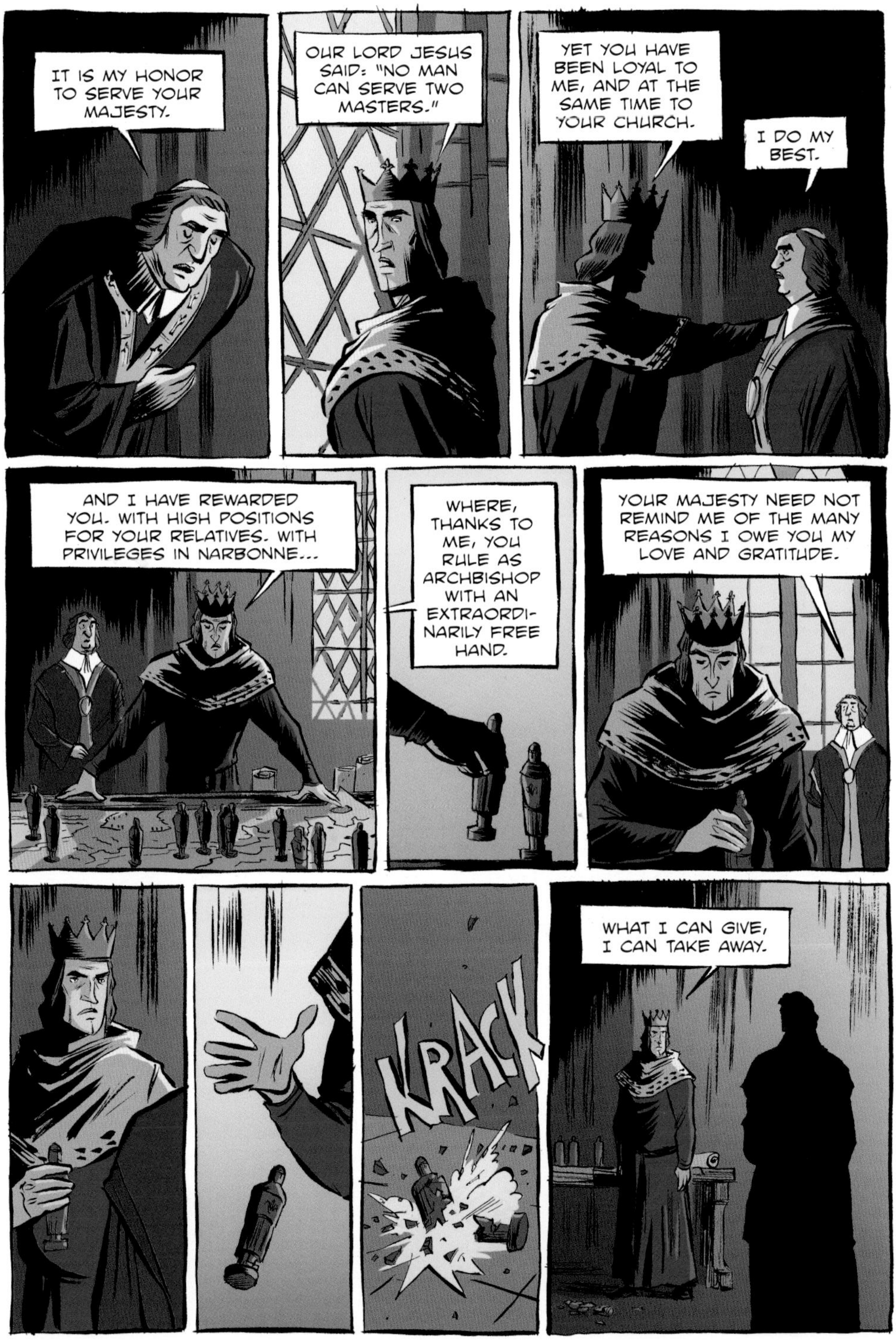
IT IS MY HONOR TO SERVE YOUR MAJESTY.
OUR LORD JESUS SAID: "NO MAN CAN SERVE TWO MASTERS."
YET YOU HAVE BEEN LOYAL TO ME, AND AT THE SAME TIME TO YOUR CHURCH.
I DO MY BEST.
AND I HAVE REWARDED YOU. WITH HIGH POSITIONS FOR YOUR RELATIVES. WITH PRIVILEGES IN NARBONNE...
WHERE, THANKS TO ME, YOU RULE AS ARCHBISHOP WITH AN EXTRAORDINARILY FREE HAND.
YOUR MAJESTY NEED NOT REMIND ME OF THE MANY REASONS I OWE YOU MY LOVE AND GRATITUDE.
KRACK
WHAT I CAN GIVE, I CAN TAKE AWAY.

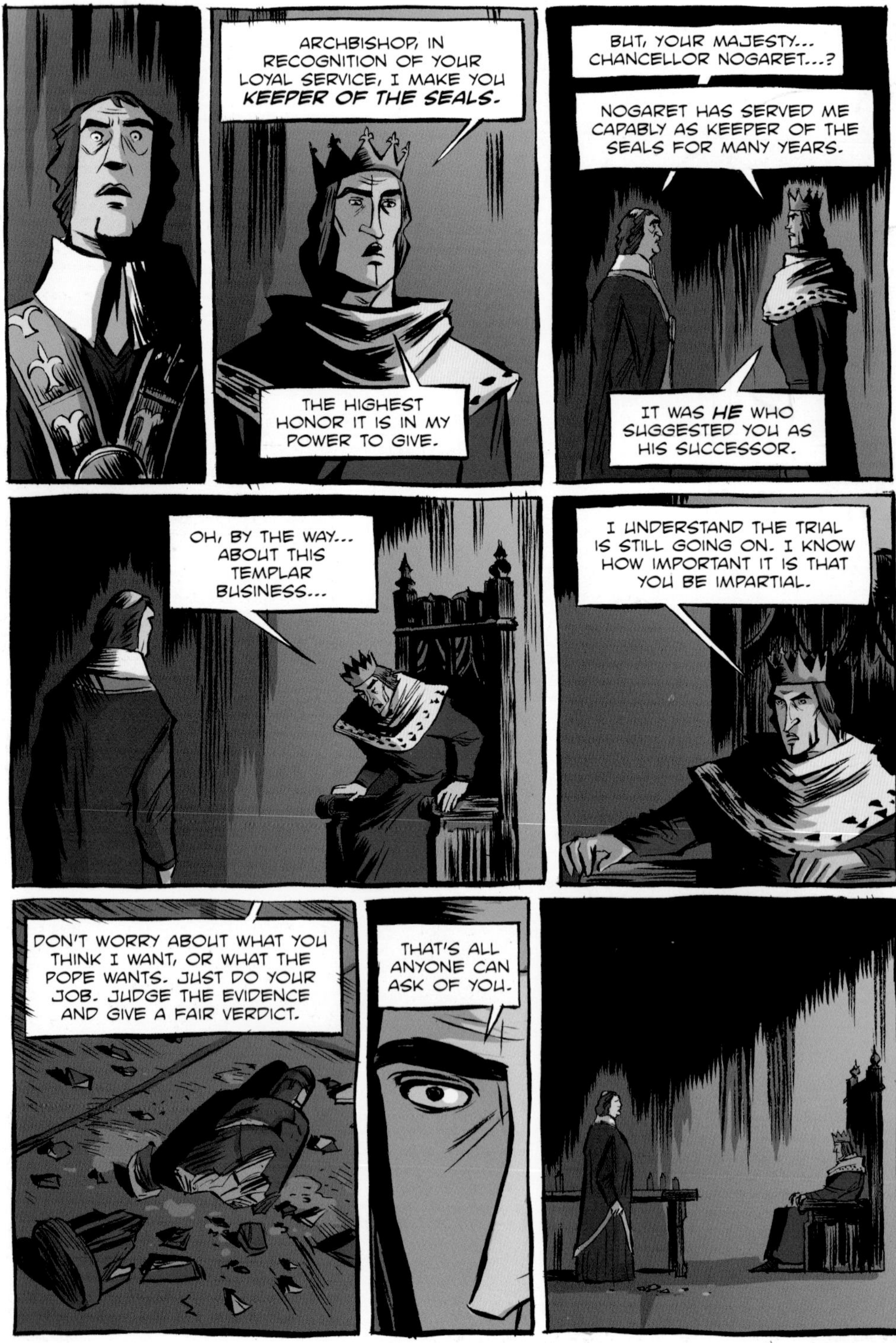
ARCHBISHOP, IN RECOGNITION OF YOUR LOYAL SERVICE, I MAKE YOU **KEEPER OF THE SEALS.**
THE HIGHEST HONOR IT IS IN MY POWER TO GIVE.
BUT, YOUR MAJESTY... CHANCELLOR NOGARET...?
NOGARET HAS SERVED ME CAPABLY AS KEEPER OF THE SEALS FOR MANY YEARS.
IT WAS **HE** WHO SUGGESTED YOU AS HIS SUCCESSOR.
OH, BY THE WAY... ABOUT THIS TEMPLAR BUSINESS...
I UNDERSTAND THE TRIAL IS STILL GOING ON. I KNOW HOW IMPORTANT IT IS THAT YOU BE IMPARTIAL.
DON'T WORRY ABOUT WHAT YOU THINK I WANT, OR WHAT THE POPE WANTS. JUST DO YOUR JOB. JUDGE THE EVIDENCE AND GIVE A FAIR VERDICT.
THAT'S ALL ANYONE CAN ASK OF YOU.

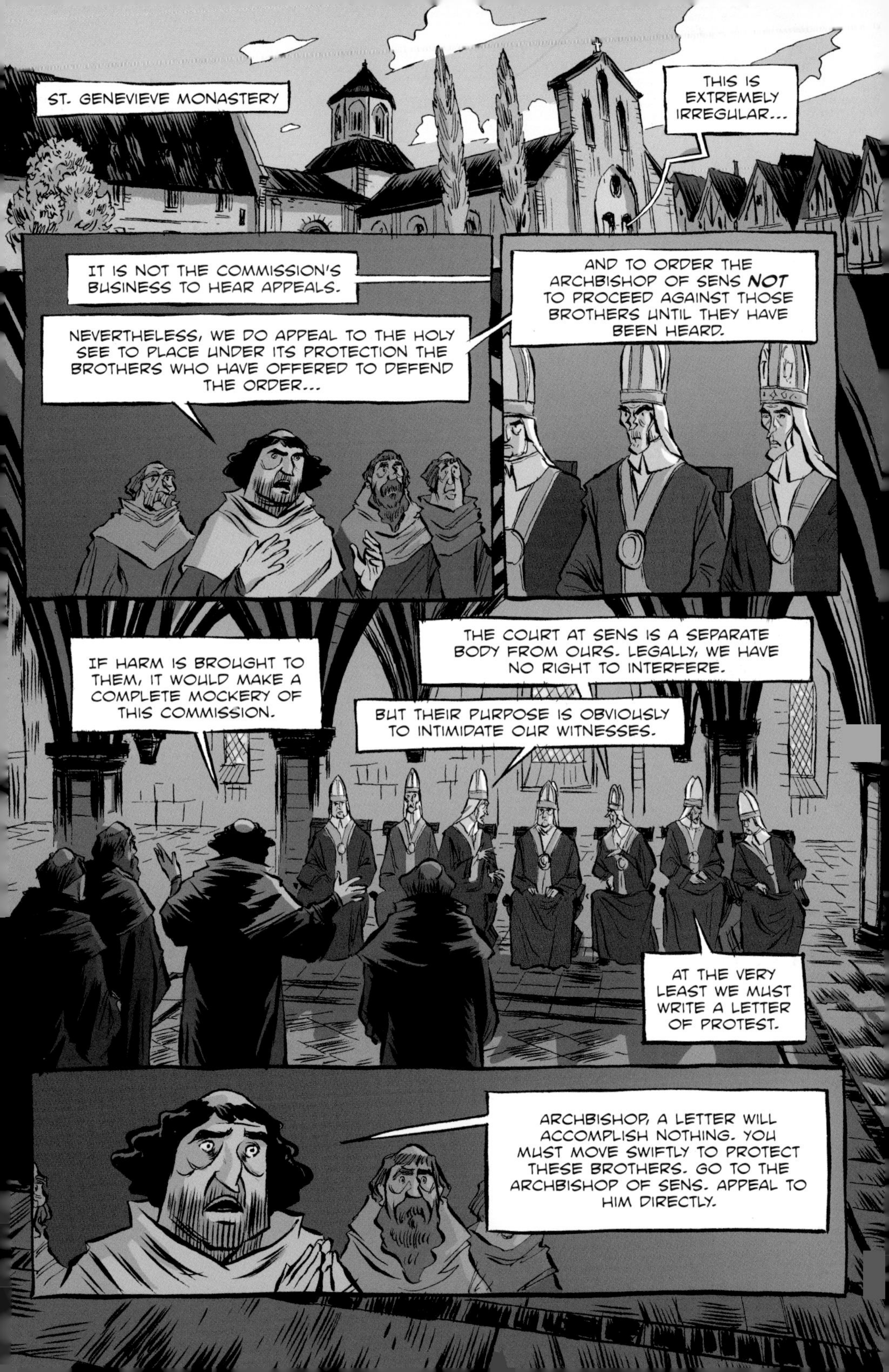

ST. GENEVIEVE MONASTERY
THIS IS EXTREMELY IRREGULAR...
IT IS NOT THE COMMISSION'S BUSINESS TO HEAR APPEALS.
NEVERTHELESS, WE DO APPEAL TO THE HOLY SEE TO PLACE UNDER ITS PROTECTION THE BROTHERS WHO HAVE OFFERED TO DEFEND THE ORDER...
AND TO ORDER THE ARCHBISHOP OF SENS *NOT* TO PROCEED AGAINST THOSE BROTHERS UNTIL THEY HAVE BEEN HEARD.
IF HARM IS BROUGHT TO THEM, IT WOULD MAKE A COMPLETE MOCKERY OF THIS COMMISSION.
THE COURT AT SENS IS A SEPARATE BODY FROM OURS. LEGALLY, WE HAVE NO RIGHT TO INTERFERE.
BUT THEIR PURPOSE IS OBVIOUSLY TO INTIMIDATE OUR WITNESSES.
AT THE VERY LEAST WE MUST WRITE A LETTER OF PROTEST.
ARCHBISHOP, A LETTER WILL ACCOMPLISH NOTHING. YOU MUST MOVE SWIFTLY TO PROTECT THESE BROTHERS. GO TO THE ARCHBISHOP OF SENS. APPEAL TO HIM DIRECTLY.

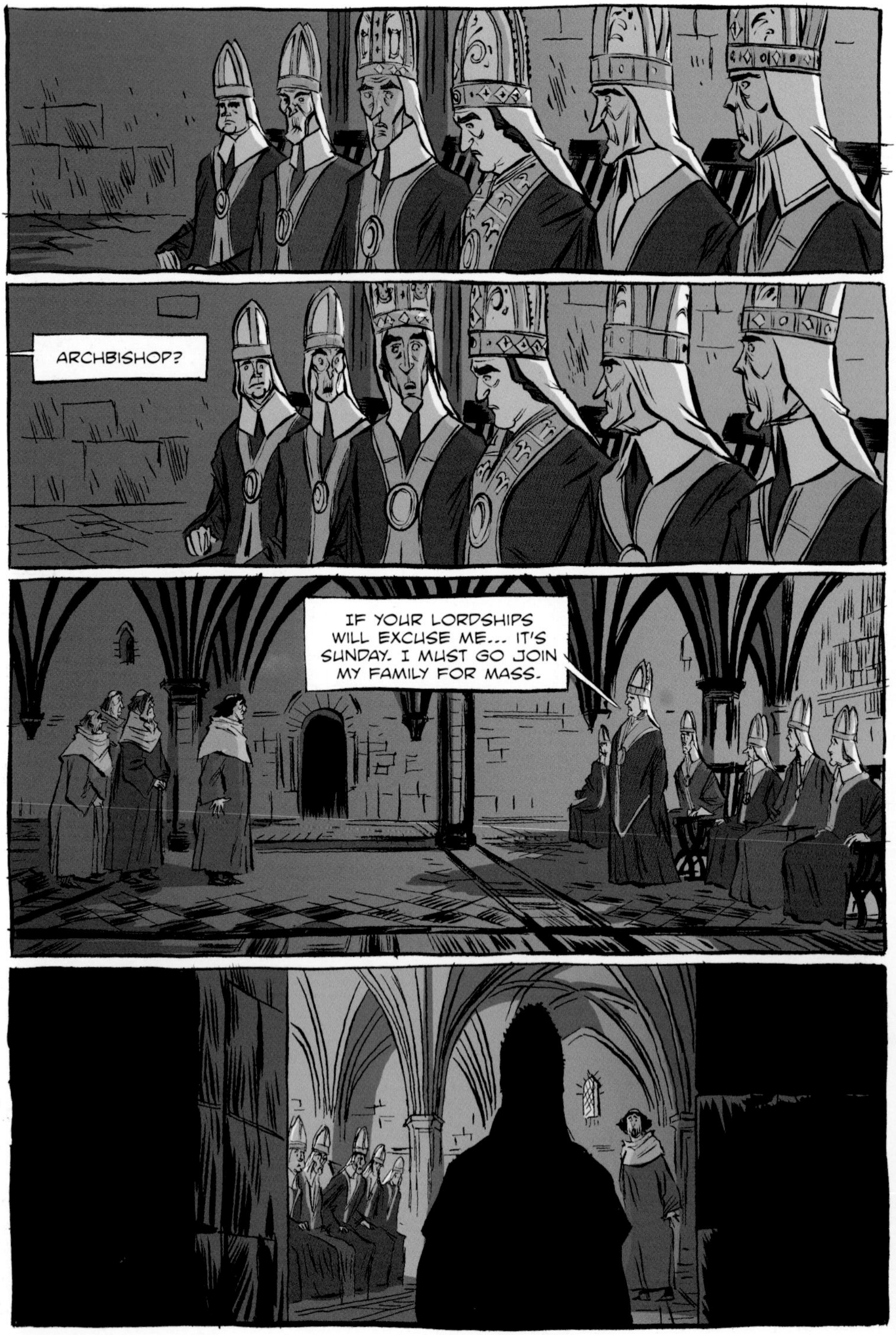
ARCHBISHOP?
IF YOUR LORDSHIPS WILL EXCUSE ME... IT'S SUNDAY. I MUST GO JOIN MY FAMILY FOR MASS.

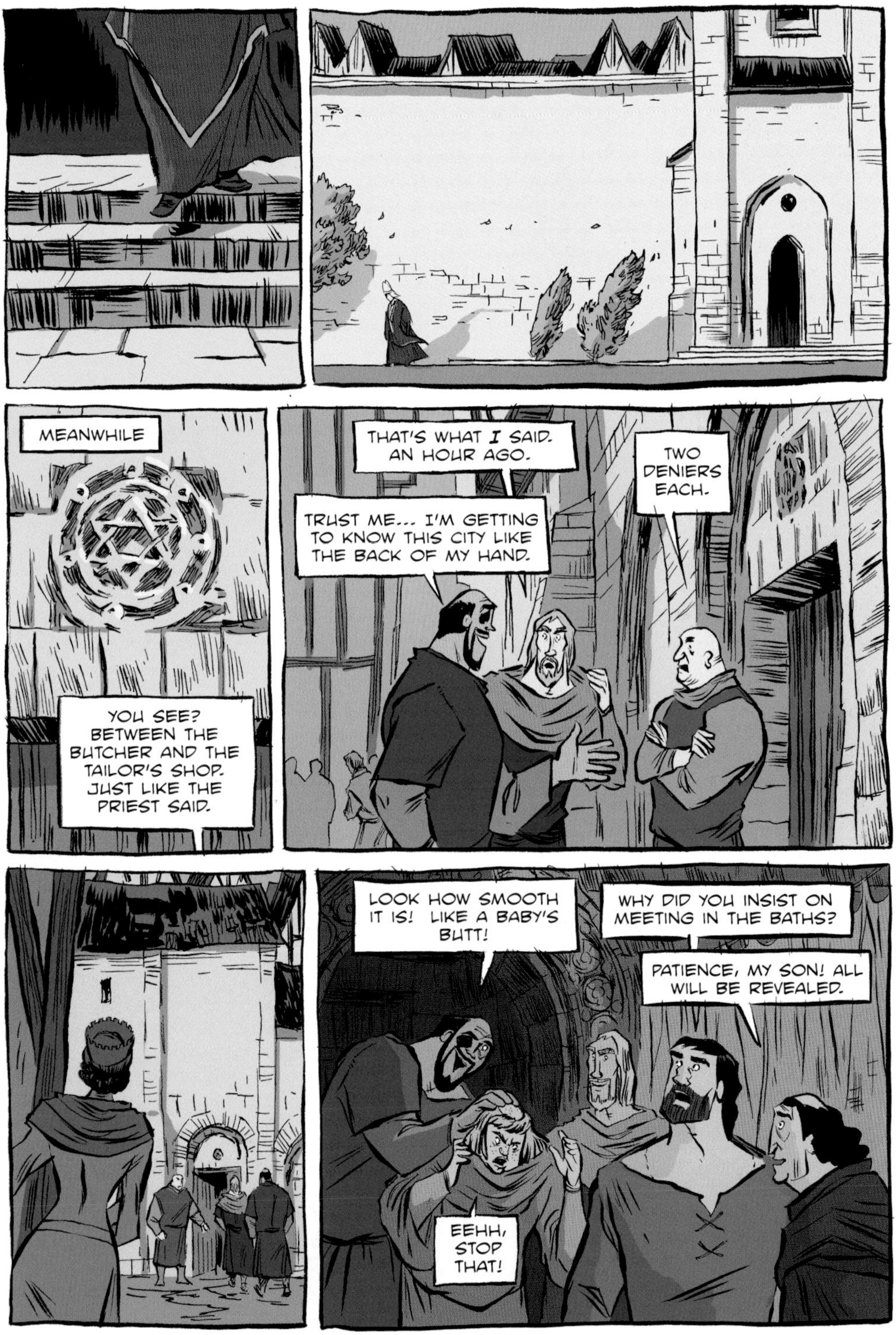
MEANWHILE
YOU SEE? BETWEEN THE BUTCHER AND THE TAILOR'S SHOP. JUST LIKE THE PRIEST SAID.
THAT'S WHAT I SAID. AN HOUR AGO.
TRUST ME... I'M GETTING TO KNOW THIS CITY LIKE THE BACK OF MY HAND.
TWO DENIERS EACH.
LOOK HOW SMOOTH IT IS! LIKE A BABY'S BUTT!
EEHH, STOP THAT!
WHY DID YOU INSIST ON MEETING IN THE BATHS?
PATIENCE, MY SON! ALL WILL BE REVEALED.

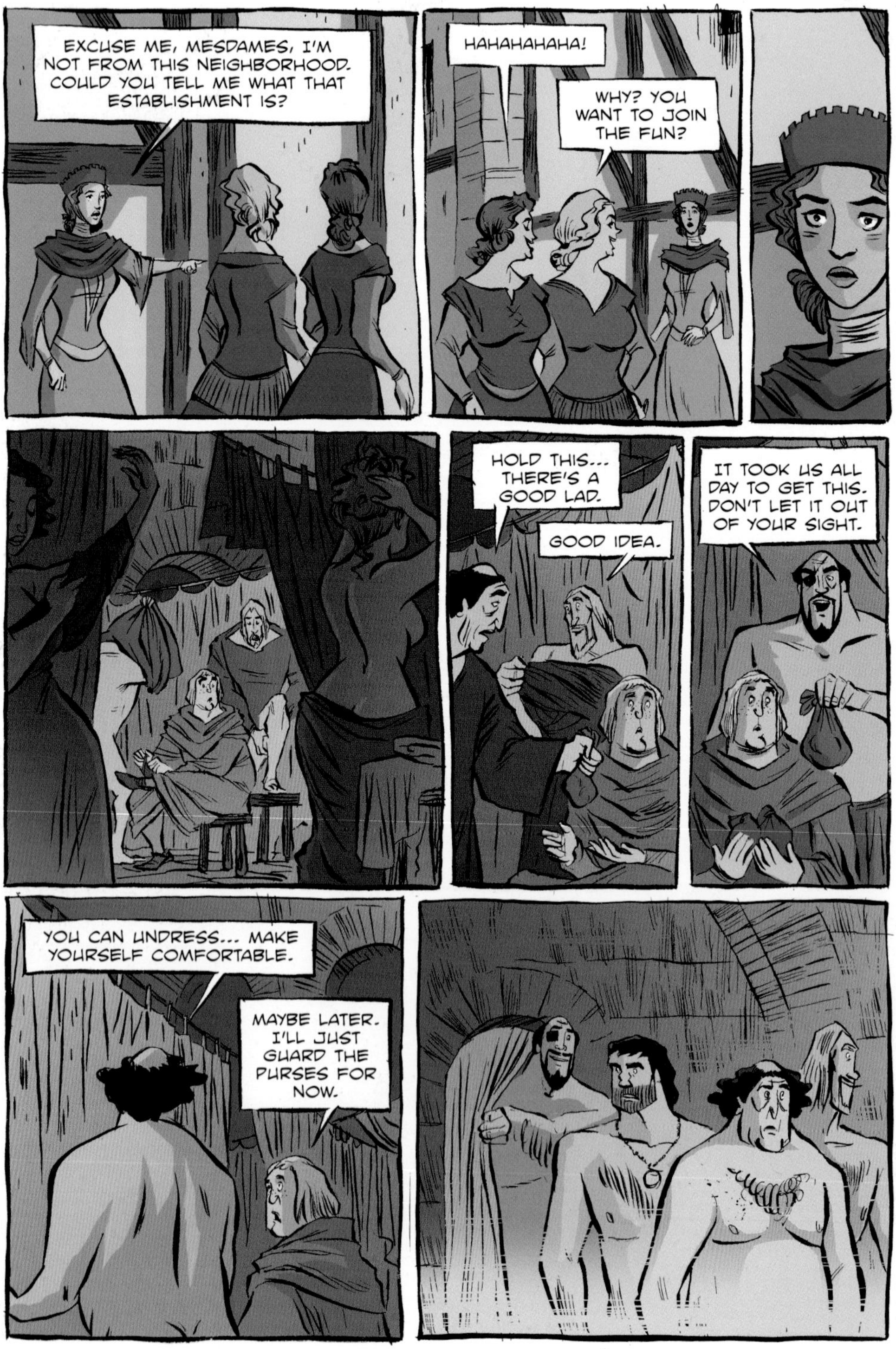
EXCUSE ME, MESDAMES, I'M NOT FROM THIS NEIGHBORHOOD. COULD YOU TELL ME WHAT THAT ESTABLISHMENT IS?
HAHAHAHAHA!
WHY? YOU WANT TO JOIN THE FUN?
HOLD THIS... THERE'S A GOOD LAD.
GOOD IDEA.
IT TOOK US ALL DAY TO GET THIS. DON'T LET IT OUT OF YOUR SIGHT.
YOU CAN UNDRESS... MAKE YOURSELF COMFORTABLE.
MAYBE LATER. I'LL JUST GUARD THE PURSES FOR NOW.

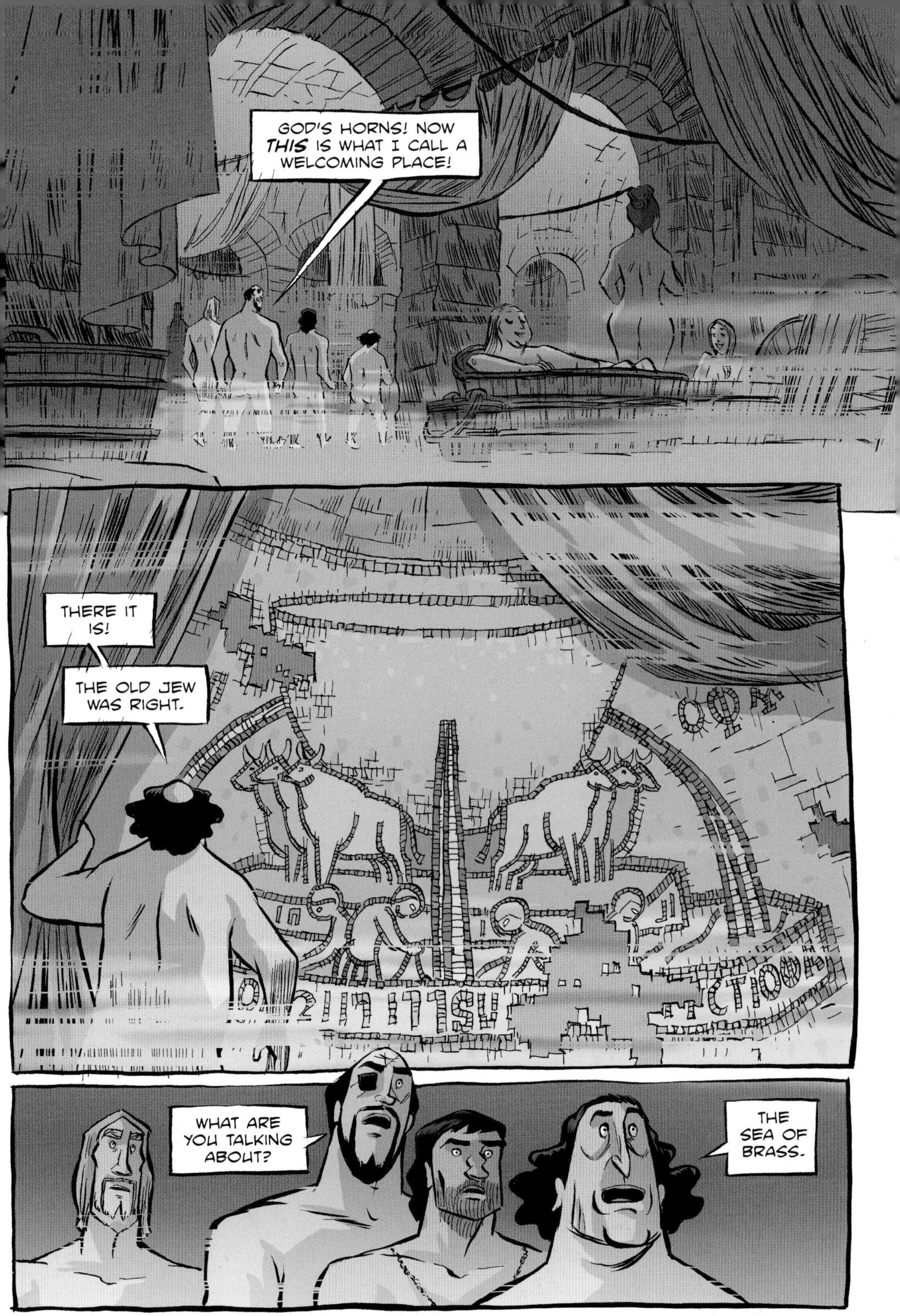
GOD'S HORNS! NOW *THIS* IS WHAT I CALL A WELCOMING PLACE!
THERE IT IS!
THE OLD JEW WAS RIGHT.
WHAT ARE YOU TALKING ABOUT?
THE SEA OF BRASS.

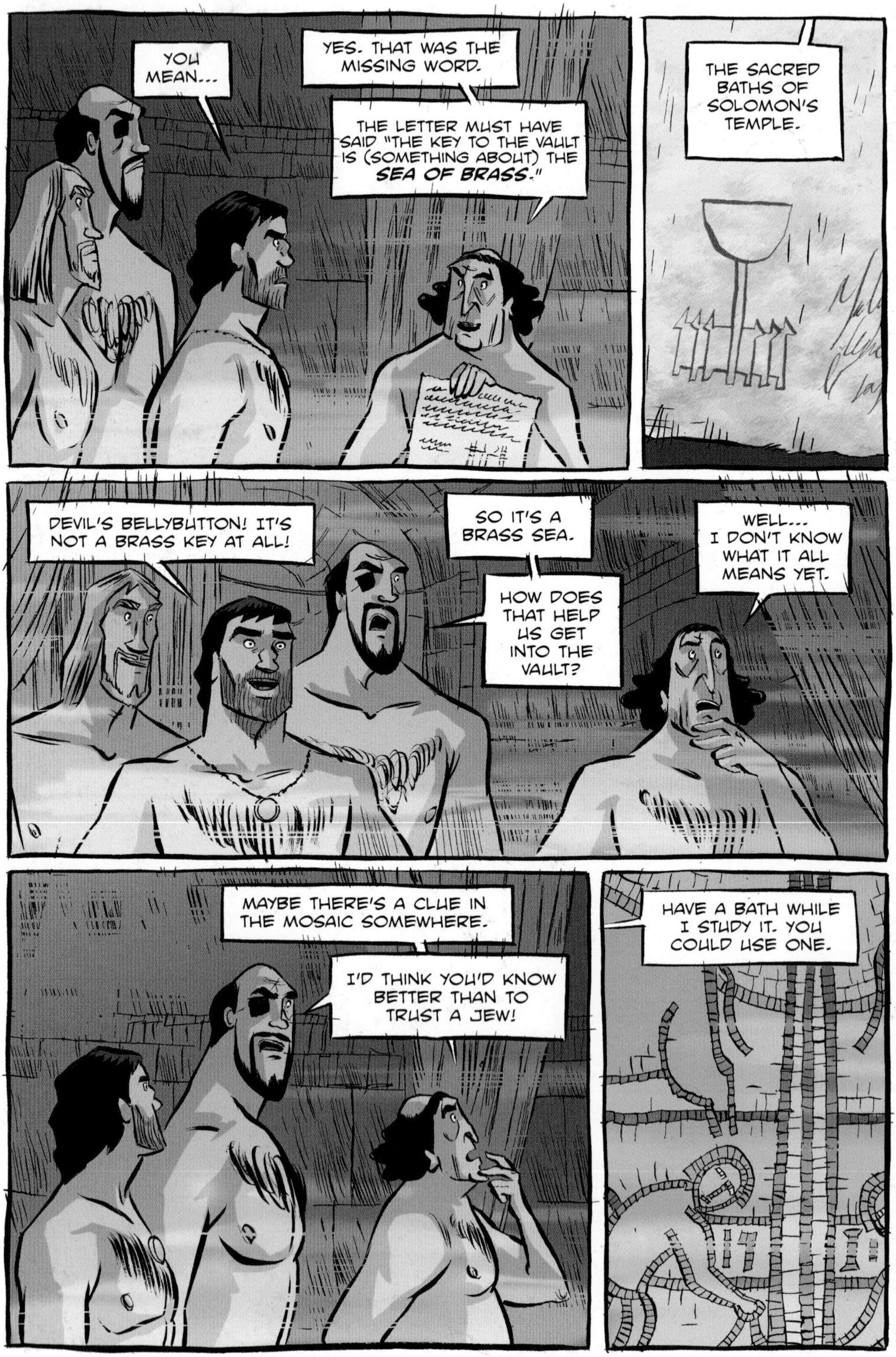
YOU MEAN...
YES. THAT WAS THE MISSING WORD.
THE LETTER MUST HAVE SAID "THE KEY TO THE VAULT IS (SOMETHING ABOUT) THE SEA OF BRASS."
THE SACRED BATHS OF SOLOMON'S TEMPLE.
DEVIL'S BELLYBUTTON! IT'S NOT A BRASS KEY AT ALL!
SO IT'S A BRASS SEA.
HOW DOES THAT HELP US GET INTO THE VAULT?
WELL... I DON'T KNOW WHAT IT ALL MEANS YET.
MAYBE THERE'S A CLUE IN THE MOSAIC SOMEWHERE.
I'D THINK YOU'D KNOW BETTER THAN TO TRUST A JEW!
HAVE A BATH WHILE I STUDY IT. YOU COULD USE ONE.

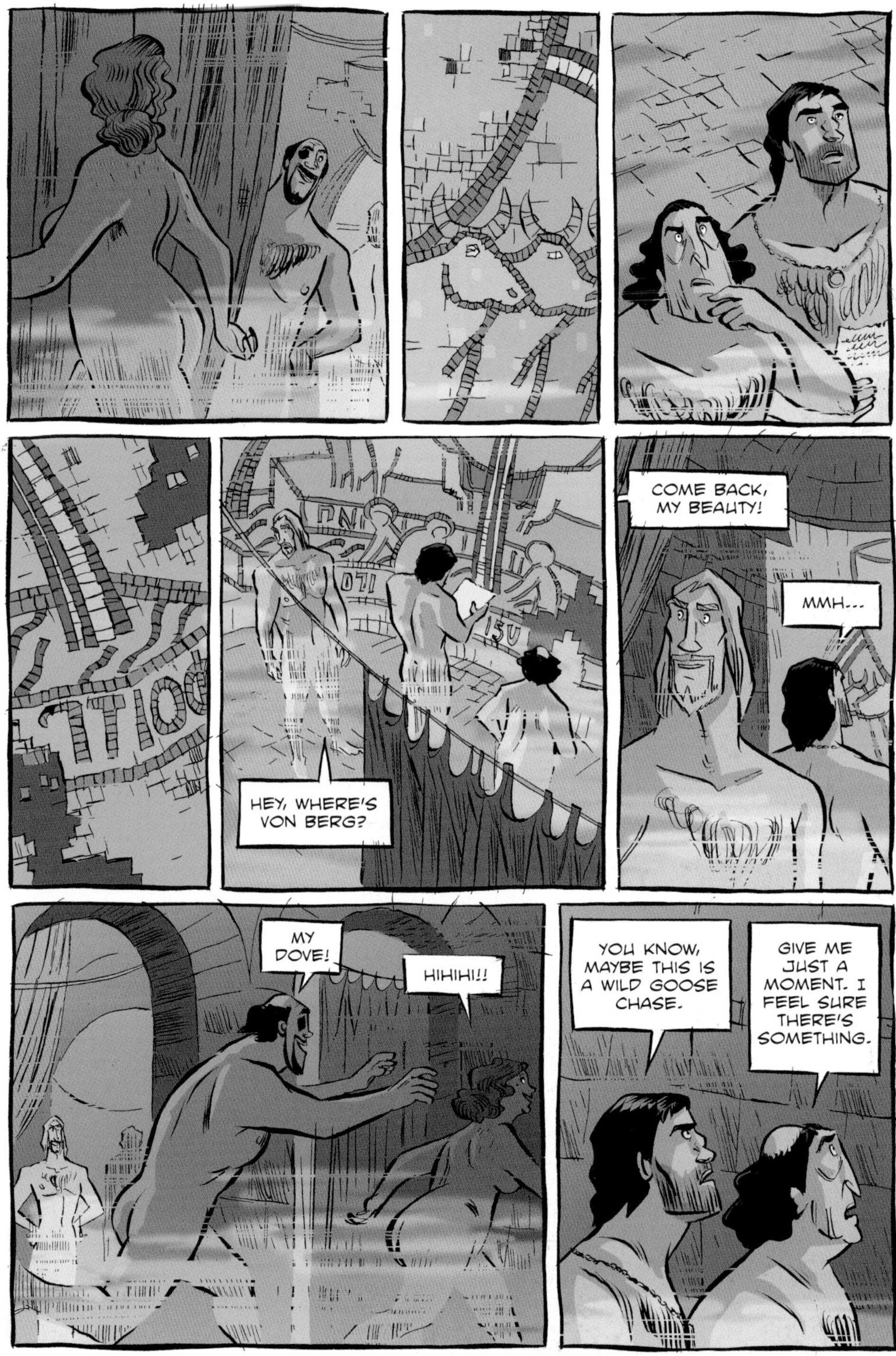
HEY, WHERE'S VON BERG?
COME BACK, MY BEAUTY!
MMH...
MY DOVE!
HIHIHI!!
YOU KNOW, MAYBE THIS IS A WILD GOOSE CHASE.
GIVE ME JUST A MOMENT. I FEEL SURE THERE'S SOMETHING.

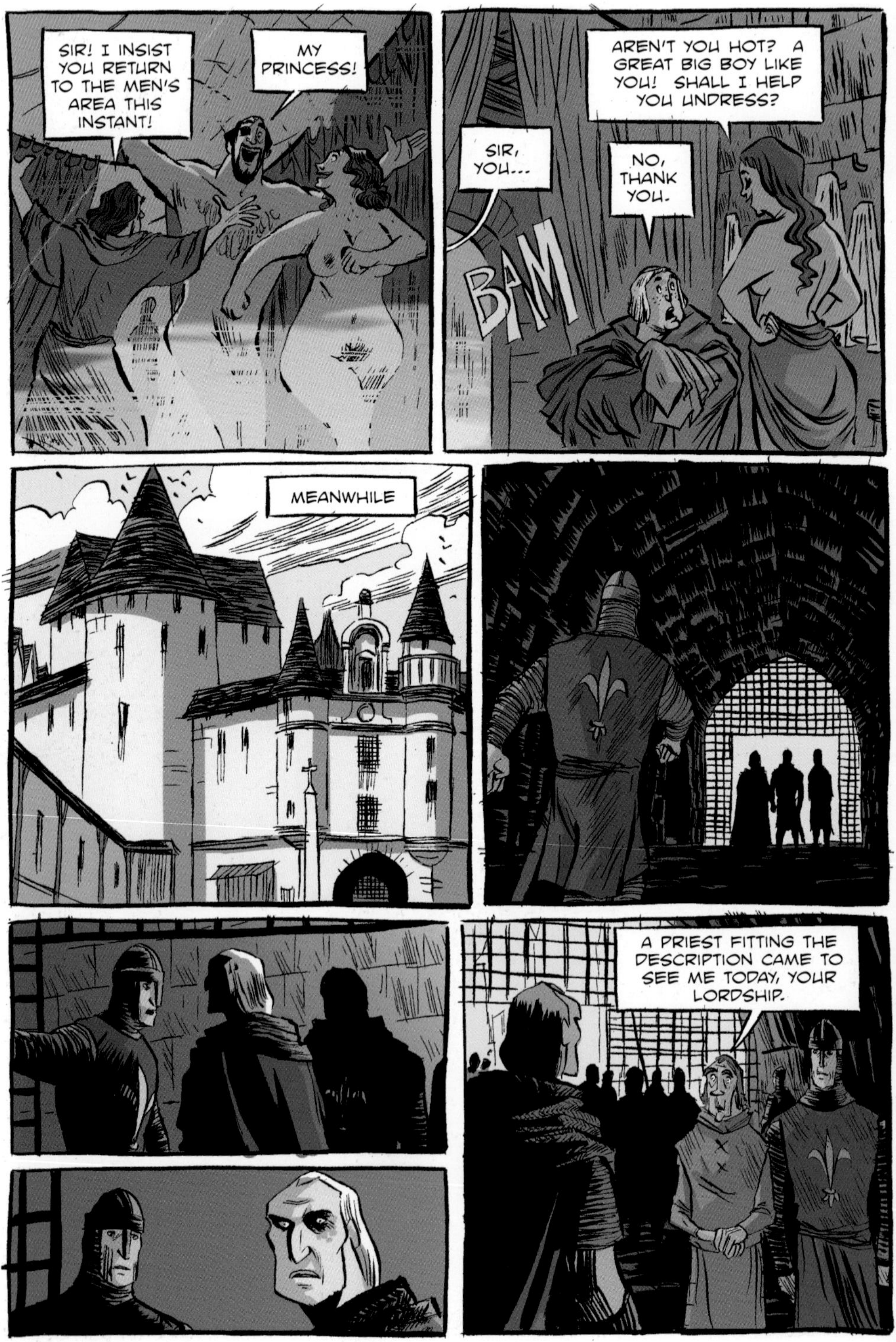
SIR! I INSIST YOU RETURN TO THE MEN'S AREA THIS INSTANT!
MY PRINCESS!
SIR, YOU...
BAM
AREN'T YOU HOT? A GREAT BIG BOY LIKE YOU! SHALL I HELP YOU UNDRESS?
NO, THANK YOU.
MEANWHILE
A PRIEST FITTING THE DESCRIPTION CAME TO SEE ME TODAY, YOUR LORDSHIP.

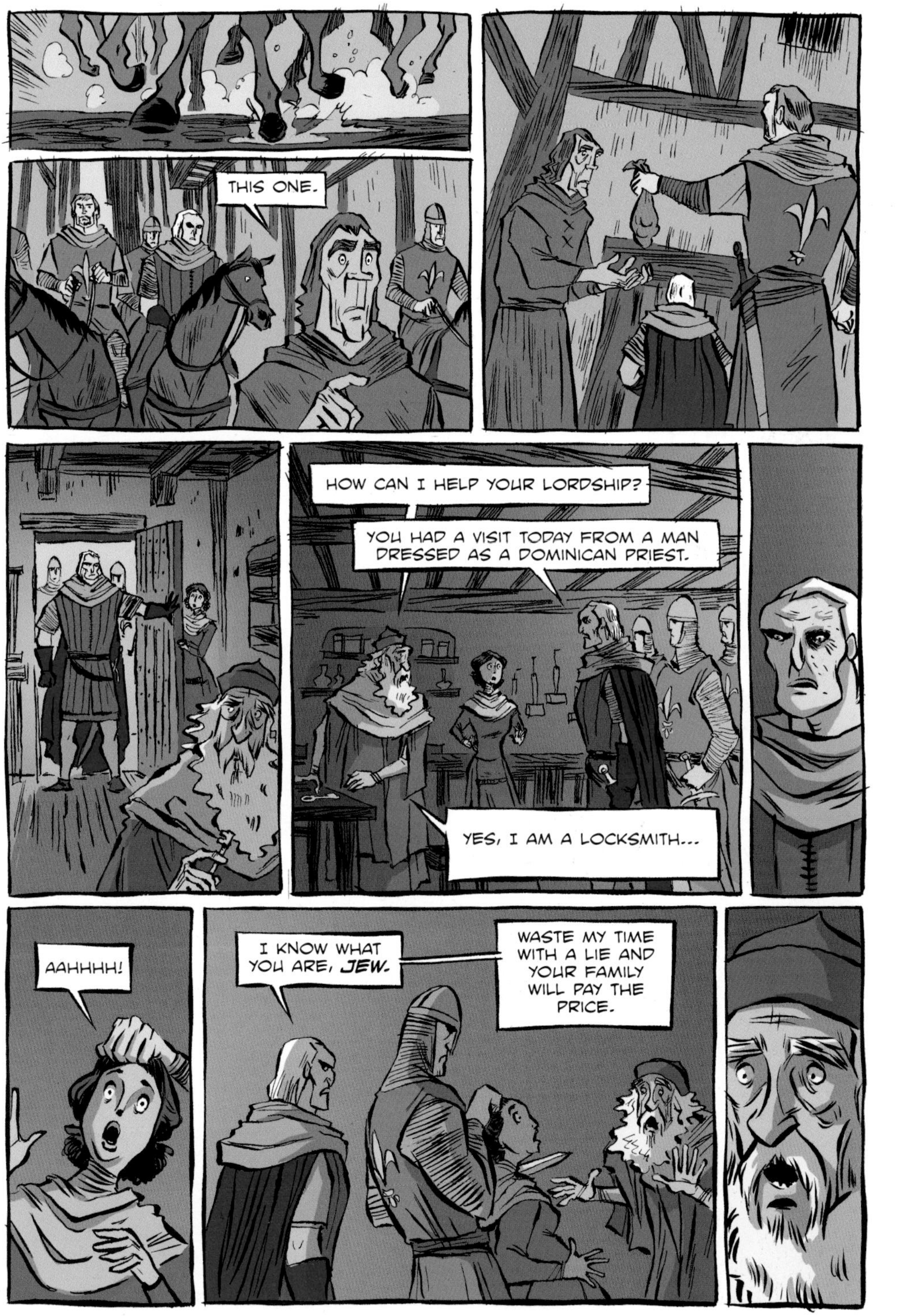
THIS ONE.
HOW CAN I HELP YOUR LORDSHIP?
YOU HAD A VISIT TODAY FROM A MAN DRESSED AS A DOMINICAN PRIEST.
YES, I AM A LOCKSMITH...
AAHHHH!
I KNOW WHAT YOU ARE, JEW.
WASTE MY TIME WITH A LIE AND YOUR FAMILY WILL PAY THE PRICE.

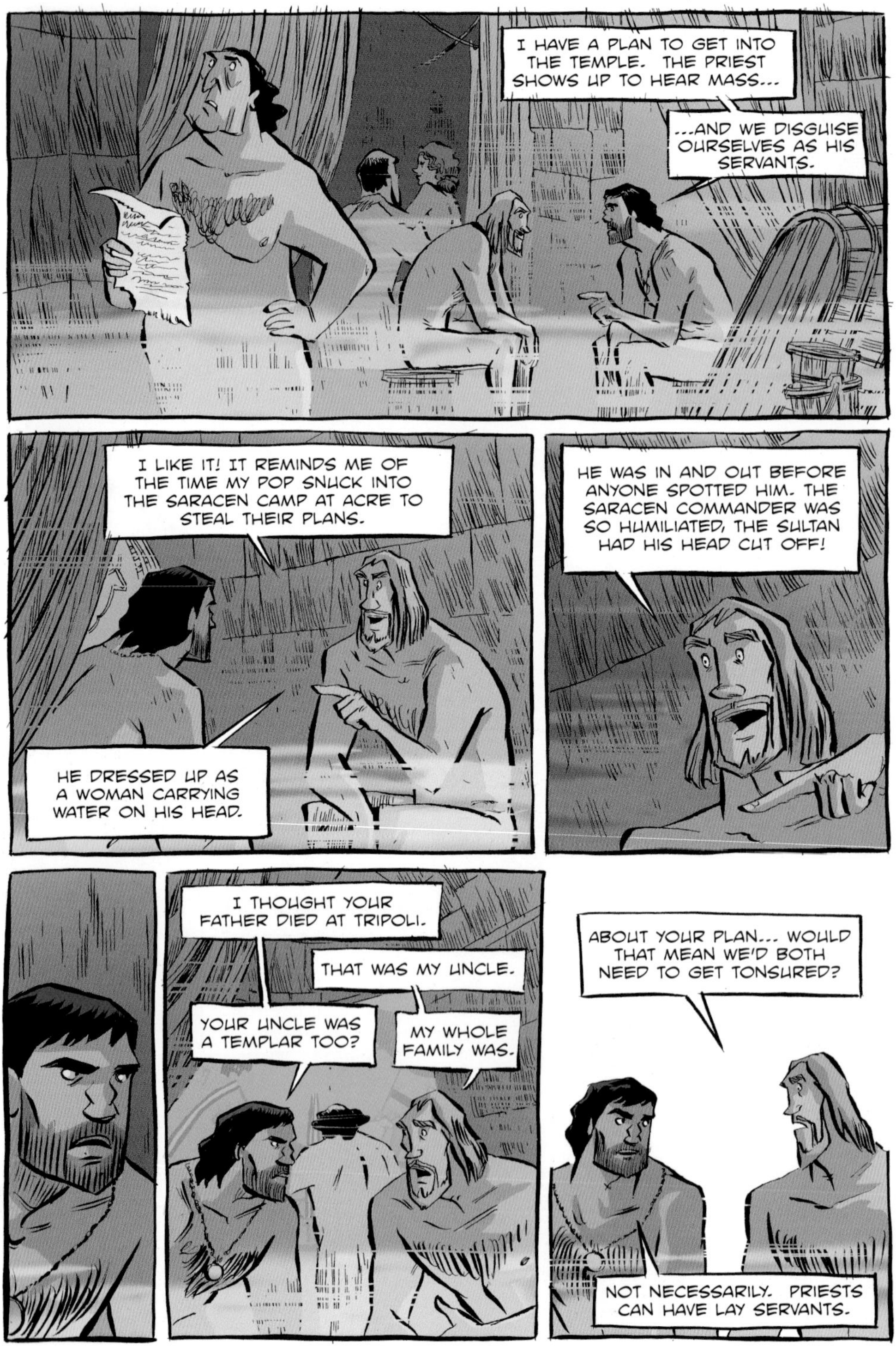
I HAVE A PLAN TO GET INTO THE TEMPLE. THE PRIEST SHOWS UP TO HEAR MASS...
...AND WE DISGUISE OURSELVES AS HIS SERVANTS.
I LIKE IT! IT REMINDS ME OF THE TIME MY POP SNUCK INTO THE SARACEN CAMP AT ACRE TO STEAL THEIR PLANS.
HE DRESSED UP AS A WOMAN CARRYING WATER ON HIS HEAD.
HE WAS IN AND OUT BEFORE ANYONE SPOTTED HIM. THE SARACEN COMMANDER WAS SO HUMILIATED, THE SULTAN HAD HIS HEAD CUT OFF!
I THOUGHT YOUR FATHER DIED AT TRIPOLI.
THAT WAS MY UNCLE.
YOUR UNCLE WAS A TEMPLAR TOO?
MY WHOLE FAMILY WAS.
ABOUT YOUR PLAN... WOULD THAT MEAN WE'D BOTH NEED TO GET TONSURED?
NOT NECESSARILY. PRIESTS CAN HAVE LAY SERVANTS.

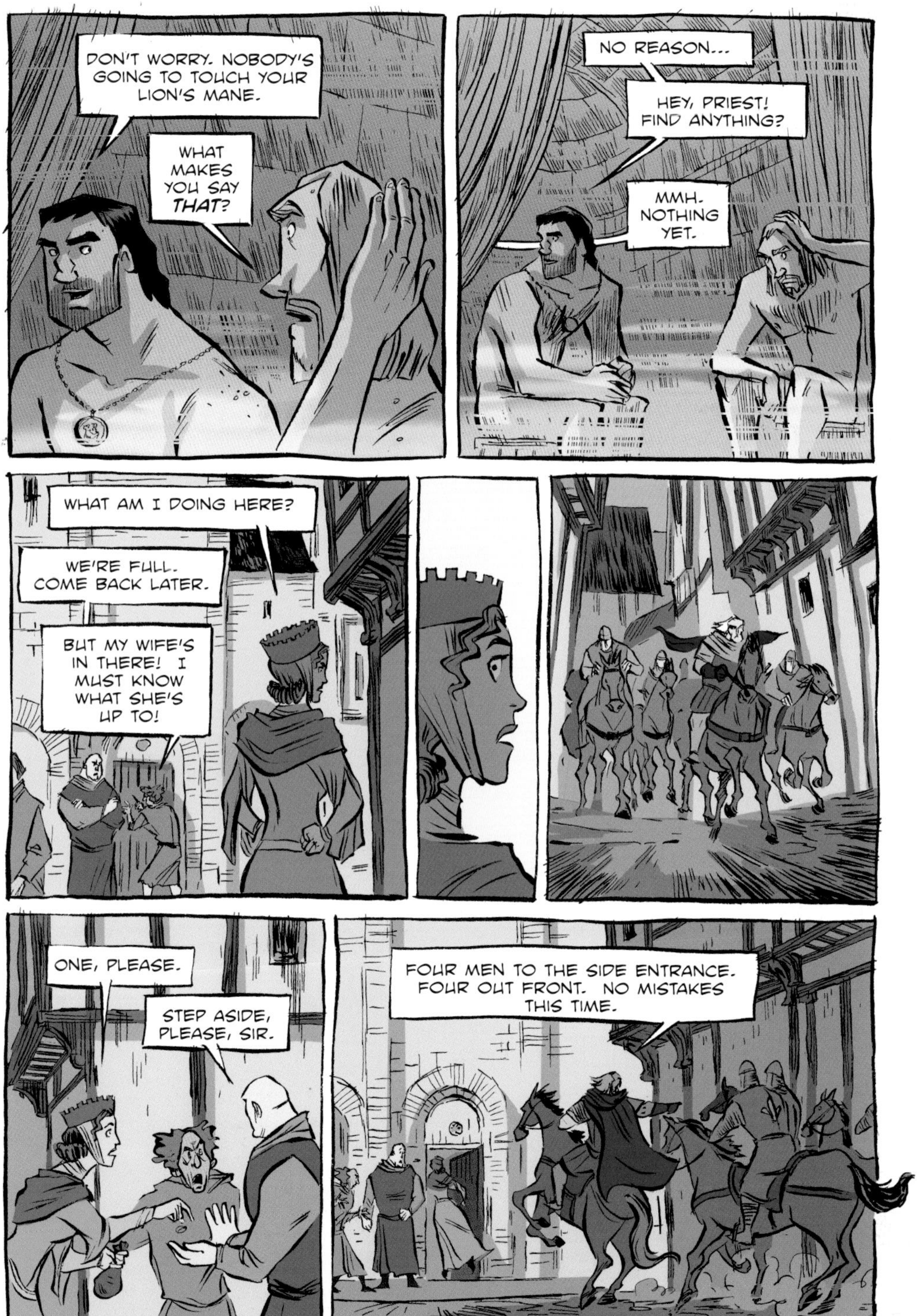
DON'T WORRY. NOBODY'S GOING TO TOUCH YOUR LION'S MANE.
WHAT MAKES YOU SAY *THAT*?
NO REASON...
HEY, PRIEST! FIND ANYTHING?
MMH. NOTHING YET.
WHAT AM I DOING HERE?
WE'RE FULL. COME BACK LATER.
BUT MY WIFE'S IN THERE! I MUST KNOW WHAT SHE'S UP TO!
ONE, PLEASE.
STEP ASIDE, PLEASE, SIR.
FOUR MEN TO THE SIDE ENTRANCE. FOUR OUT FRONT. NO MISTAKES THIS TIME.

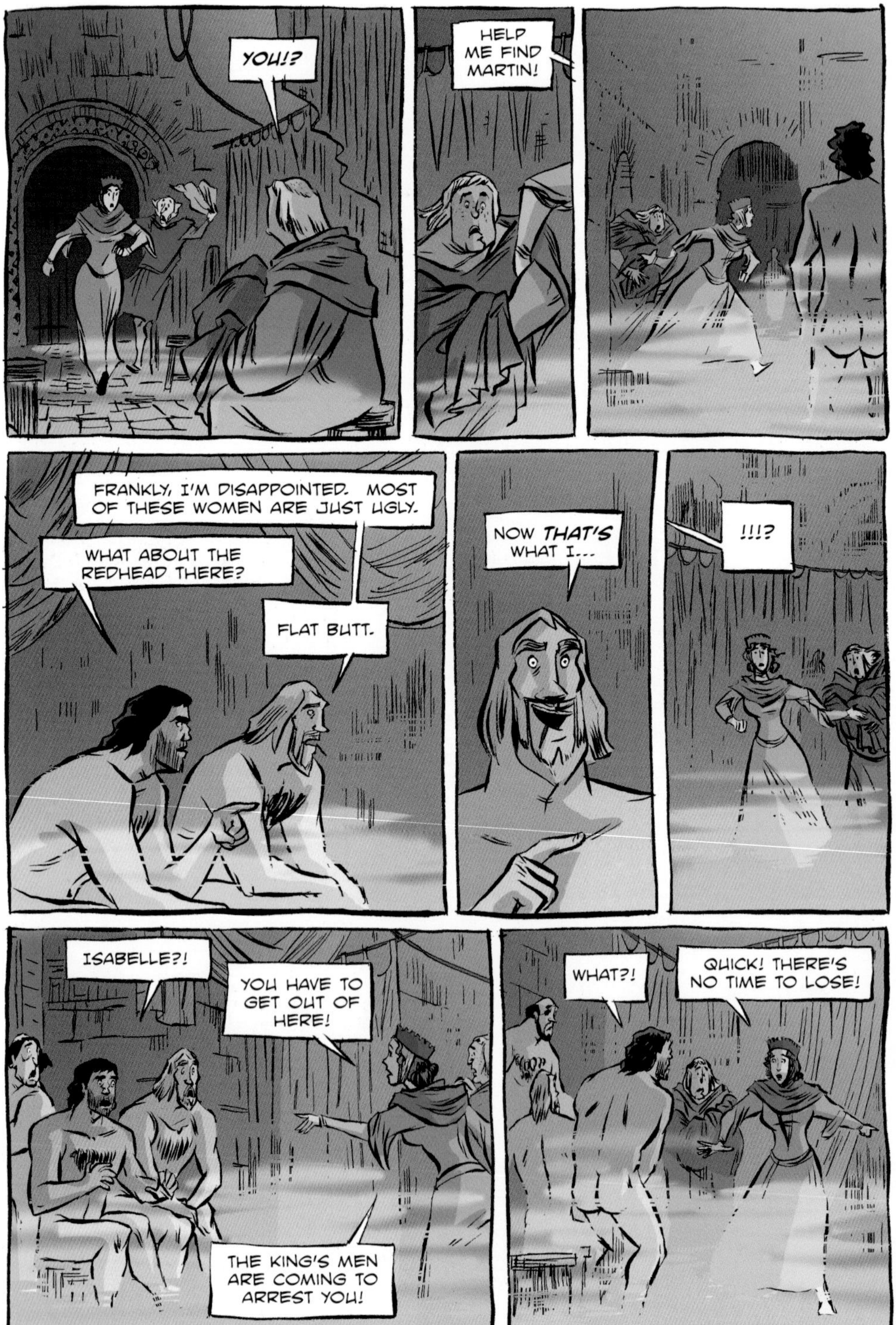
YOU!?
HELP ME FIND MARTIN!
FRANKLY, I'M DISAPPOINTED. MOST OF THESE WOMEN ARE JUST UGLY.
WHAT ABOUT THE REDHEAD THERE?
FLAT BUTT.
NOW THAT'S WHAT I...
!!!?
ISABELLE?!
YOU HAVE TO GET OUT OF HERE!
THE KING'S MEN ARE COMING TO ARREST YOU!
WHAT?!
QUICK! THERE'S NO TIME TO LOSE!

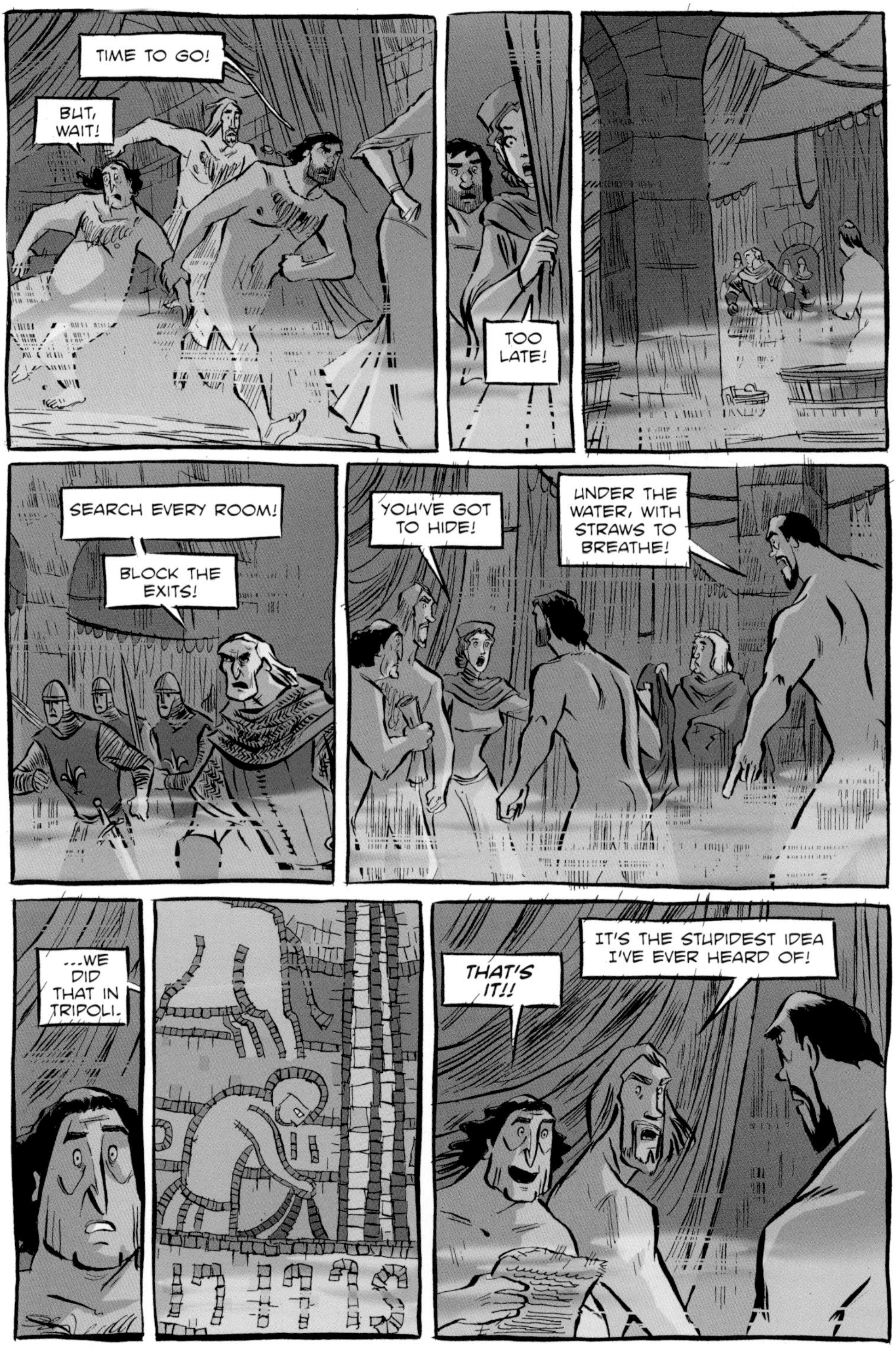
TIME TO GO!
BUT, WAIT!
TOO LATE!
SEARCH EVERY ROOM!
BLOCK THE EXITS!
YOU'VE GOT TO HIDE!
UNDER THE WATER, WITH STRAWS TO BREATHE!
...WE DID THAT IN TRIPOLI.
THAT'S IT!!
IT'S THE STUPIDEST IDEA I'VE EVER HEARD OF!

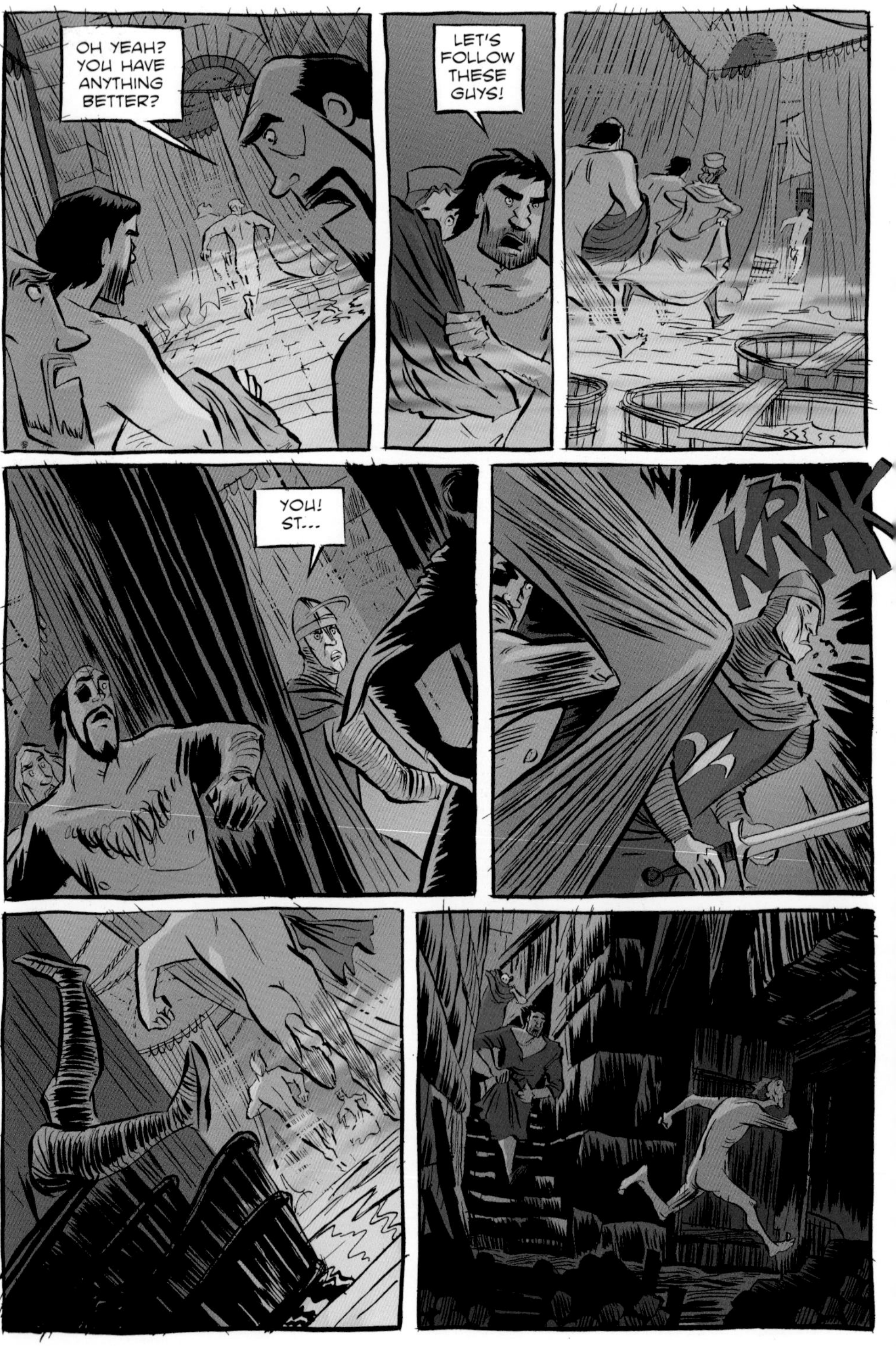
OH YEAH? YOU HAVE ANYTHING BETTER?
LET'S FOLLOW THESE GUYS!
YOU! ST...
KRAK

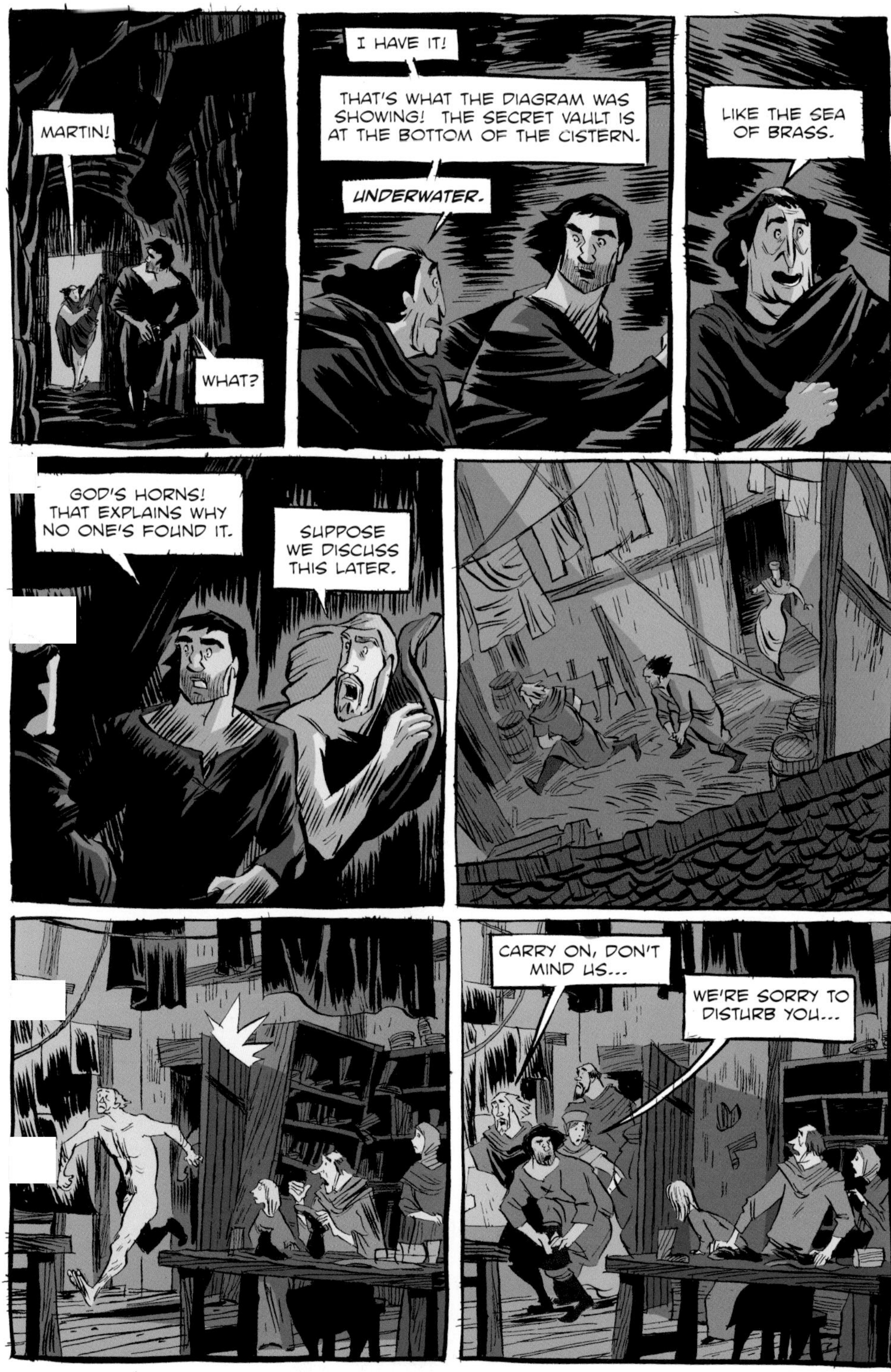
MARTIN!
WHAT?
I HAVE IT!
THAT'S WHAT THE DIAGRAM WAS SHOWING! THE SECRET VAULT IS AT THE BOTTOM OF THE CISTERN.
UNDERWATER.
LIKE THE SEA OF BRASS.
GOD'S HORNS! THAT EXPLAINS WHY NO ONE'S FOUND IT.
SUPPOSE WE DISCUSS THIS LATER.
CARRY ON, DON'T MIND US...
WE'RE SORRY TO DISTURB YOU...

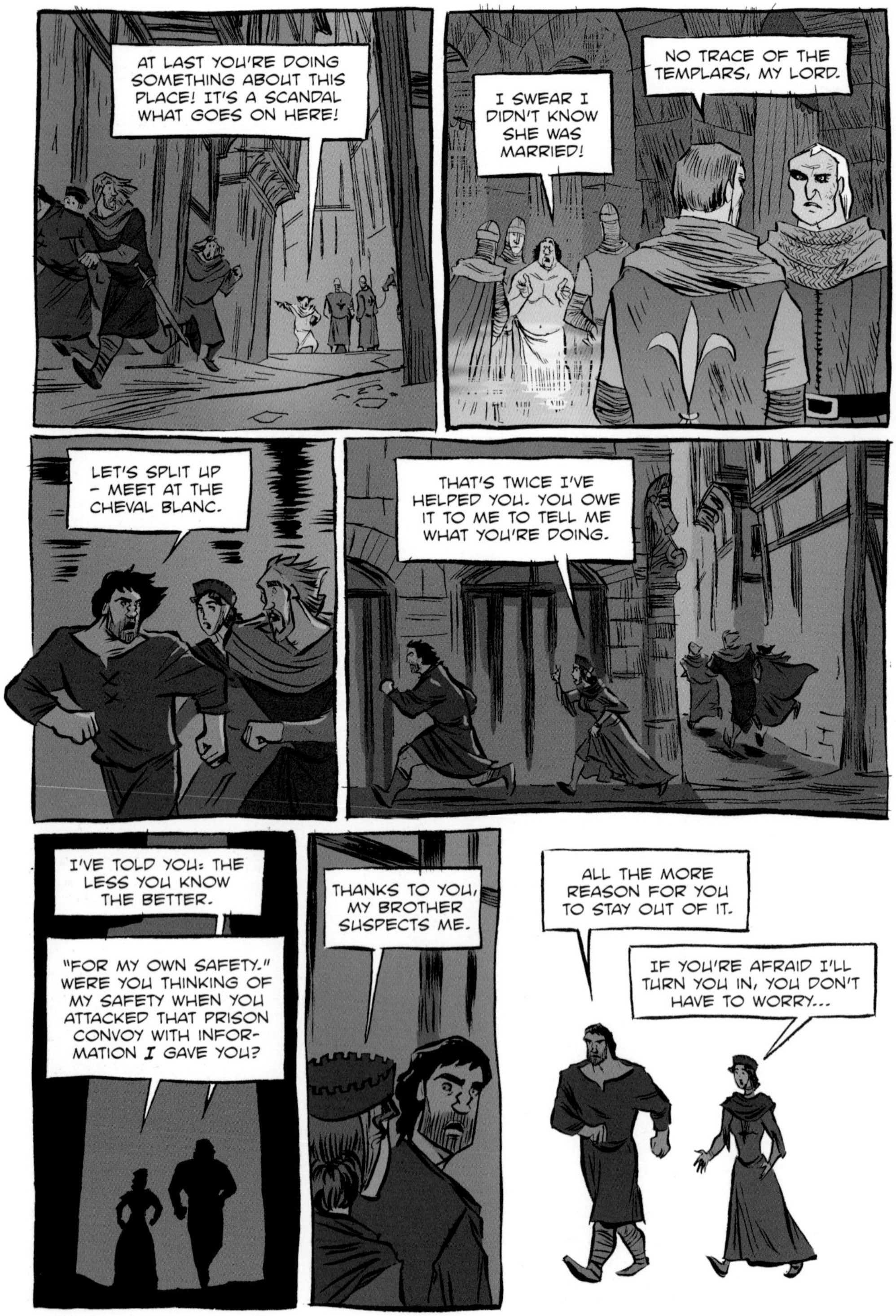
AT LAST YOU'RE DOING SOMETHING ABOUT THIS PLACE! IT'S A SCANDAL WHAT GOES ON HERE!
I SWEAR I DIDN'T KNOW SHE WAS MARRIED!
NO TRACE OF THE TEMPLARS, MY LORD.
LET'S SPLIT UP - MEET AT THE CHEVAL BLANC.
THAT'S TWICE I'VE HELPED YOU. YOU OWE IT TO ME TO TELL ME WHAT YOU'RE DOING.
I'VE TOLD YOU: THE LESS YOU KNOW THE BETTER.
"FOR MY OWN SAFETY." WERE YOU THINKING OF MY SAFETY WHEN YOU ATTACKED THAT PRISON CONVOY WITH INFORMATION *I* GAVE YOU?
THANKS TO YOU, MY BROTHER SUSPECTS ME.
ALL THE MORE REASON FOR YOU TO STAY OUT OF IT.
IF YOU'RE AFRAID I'LL TURN YOU IN, YOU DON'T HAVE TO WORRY...

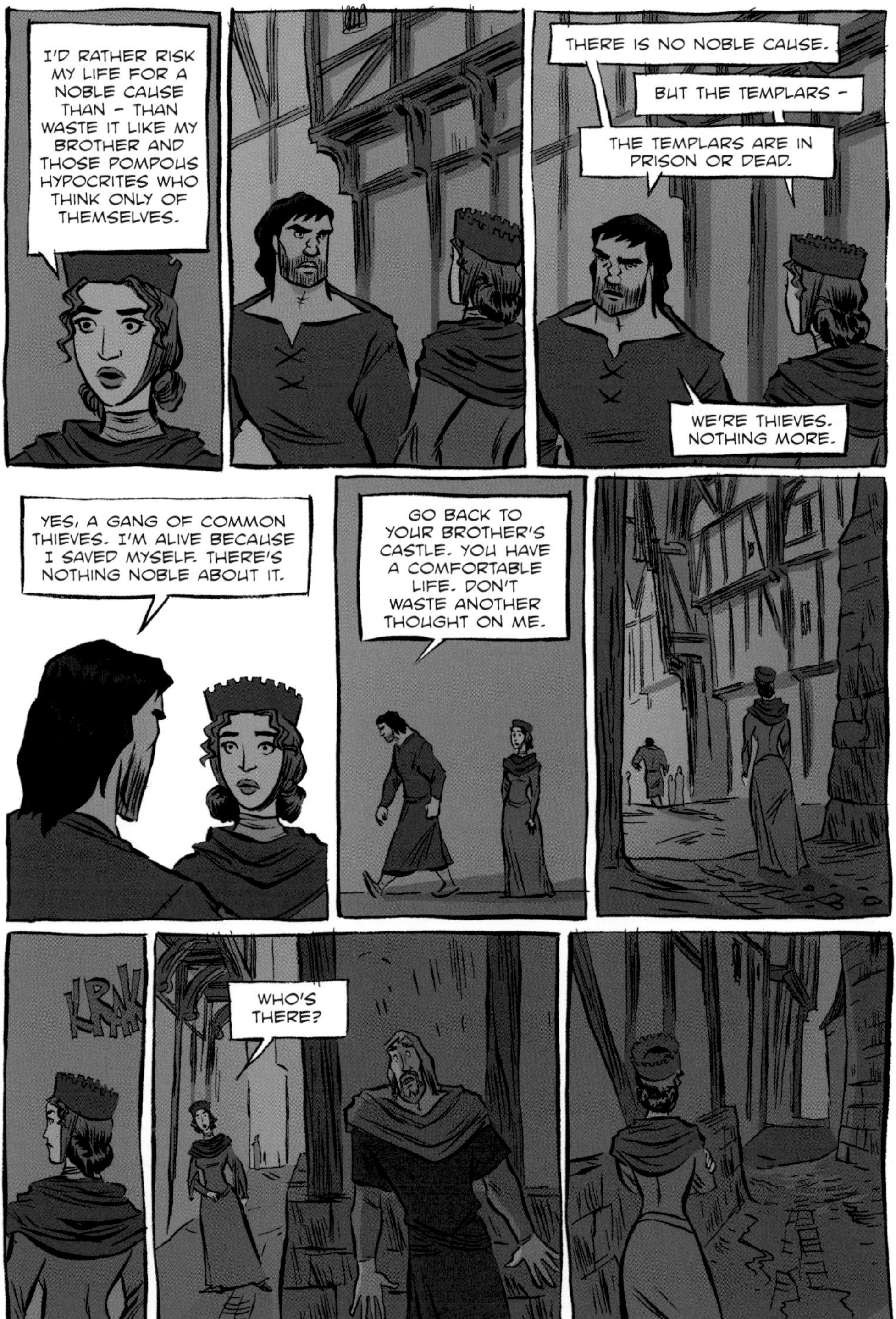
I'D RATHER RISK MY LIFE FOR A NOBLE CAUSE THAN – THAN WASTE IT LIKE MY BROTHER AND THOSE POMPOUS HYPOCRITES WHO THINK ONLY OF THEMSELVES.
THERE IS NO NOBLE CAUSE.
BUT THE TEMPLARS –
THE TEMPLARS ARE IN PRISON OR DEAD.
WE'RE THIEVES. NOTHING MORE.
YES, A GANG OF COMMON THIEVES. I'M ALIVE BECAUSE I SAVED MYSELF. THERE'S NOTHING NOBLE ABOUT IT.
GO BACK TO YOUR BROTHER'S CASTLE. YOU HAVE A COMFORTABLE LIFE. DON'T WASTE ANOTHER THOUGHT ON ME.
KLRAK
WHO'S THERE?

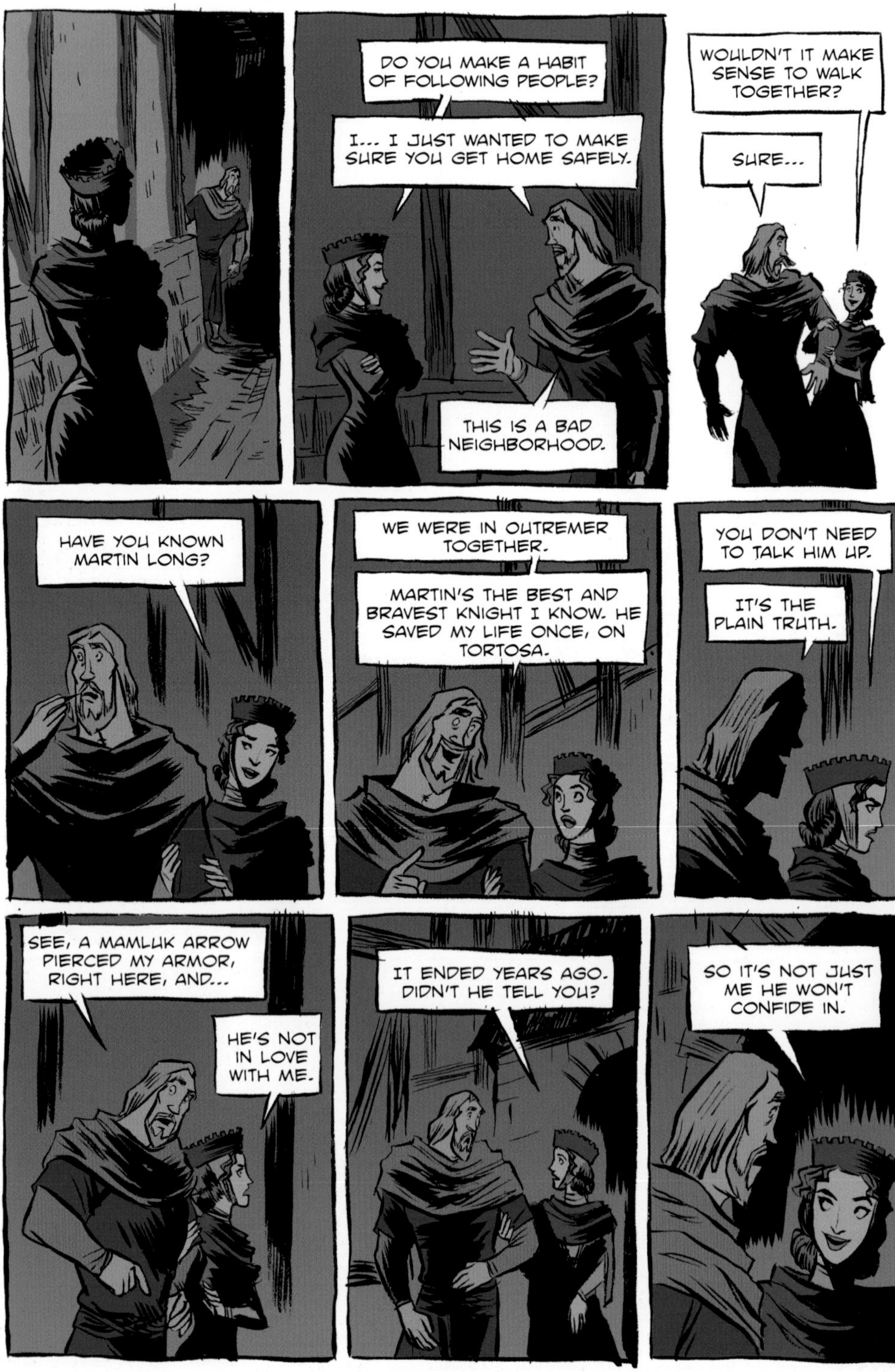
DO YOU MAKE A HABIT OF FOLLOWING PEOPLE?
I... I JUST WANTED TO MAKE SURE YOU GET HOME SAFELY.
THIS IS A BAD NEIGHBORHOOD.
WOULDN'T IT MAKE SENSE TO WALK TOGETHER?
SURE...
HAVE YOU KNOWN MARTIN LONG?
WE WERE IN OUTREMER TOGETHER.
MARTIN'S THE BEST AND BRAVEST KNIGHT I KNOW. HE SAVED MY LIFE ONCE, ON TORTOSA.
YOU DON'T NEED TO TALK HIM UP.
IT'S THE PLAIN TRUTH.
SEE, A MAMLUK ARROW PIERCED MY ARMOR, RIGHT HERE, AND...
HE'S NOT IN LOVE WITH ME.
IT ENDED YEARS AGO. DIDN'T HE TELL YOU?
SO IT'S NOT JUST ME HE WON'T CONFIDE IN.

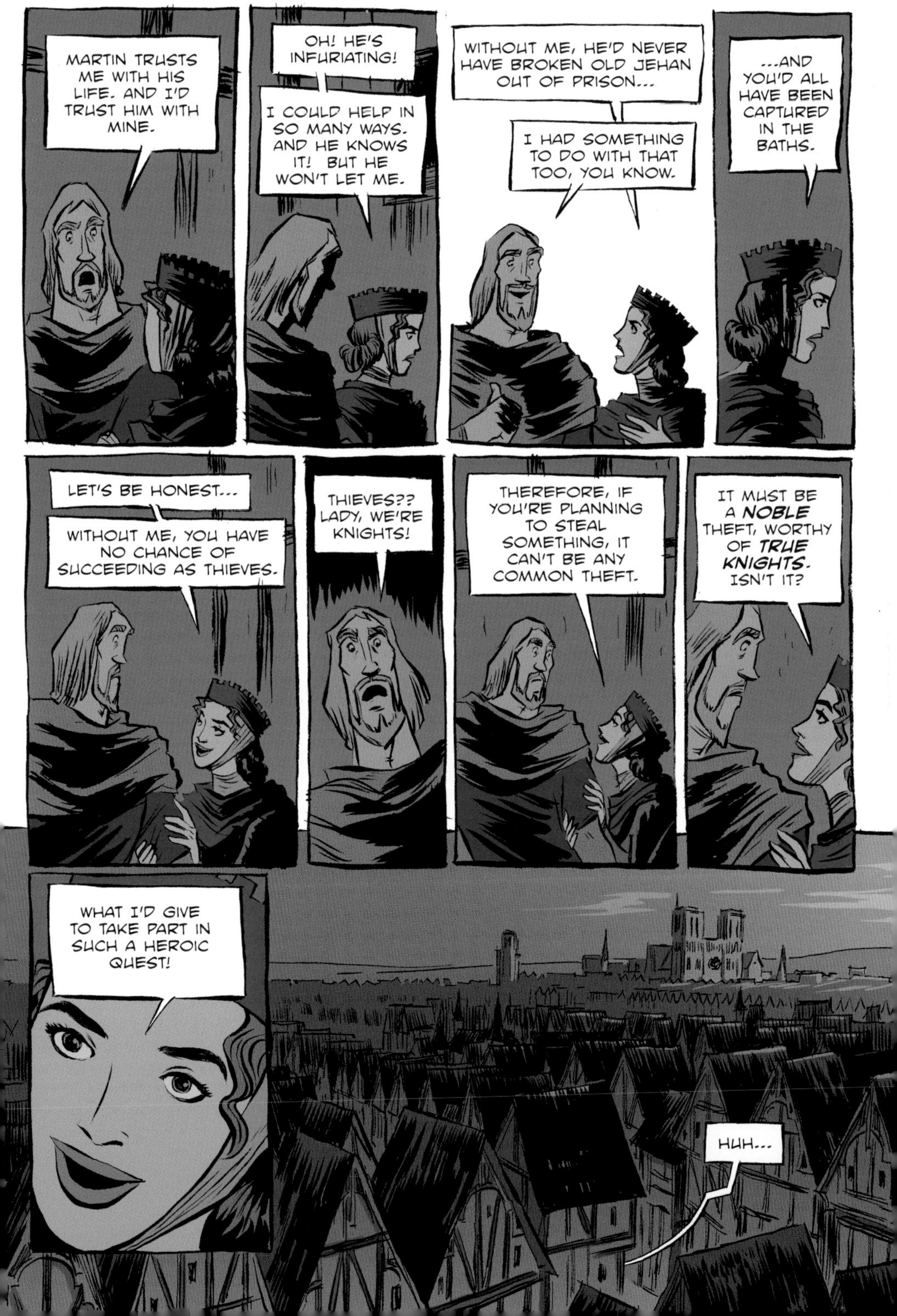
MARTIN TRUSTS ME WITH HIS LIFE. AND I'D TRUST HIM WITH MINE.
OH! HE'S INFURIATING!
I COULD HELP IN SO MANY WAYS. AND HE KNOWS IT! BUT HE WON'T LET ME.
WITHOUT ME, HE'D NEVER HAVE BROKEN OLD JEHAN OUT OF PRISON...
I HAD SOMETHING TO DO WITH THAT TOO, YOU KNOW.
...AND YOU'D ALL HAVE BEEN CAPTURED IN THE BATHS.
LET'S BE HONEST...
WITHOUT ME, YOU HAVE NO CHANCE OF SUCCEEDING AS THIEVES.
THIEVES?? LADY, WE'RE KNIGHTS!
THEREFORE, IF YOU'RE PLANNING TO STEAL SOMETHING, IT CAN'T BE ANY COMMON THEFT.
IT MUST BE A ***NOBLE*** THEFT, WORTHY OF ***TRUE KNIGHTS***. ISN'T IT?
WHAT I'D GIVE TO TAKE PART IN SUCH A HEROIC QUEST!
HUH...

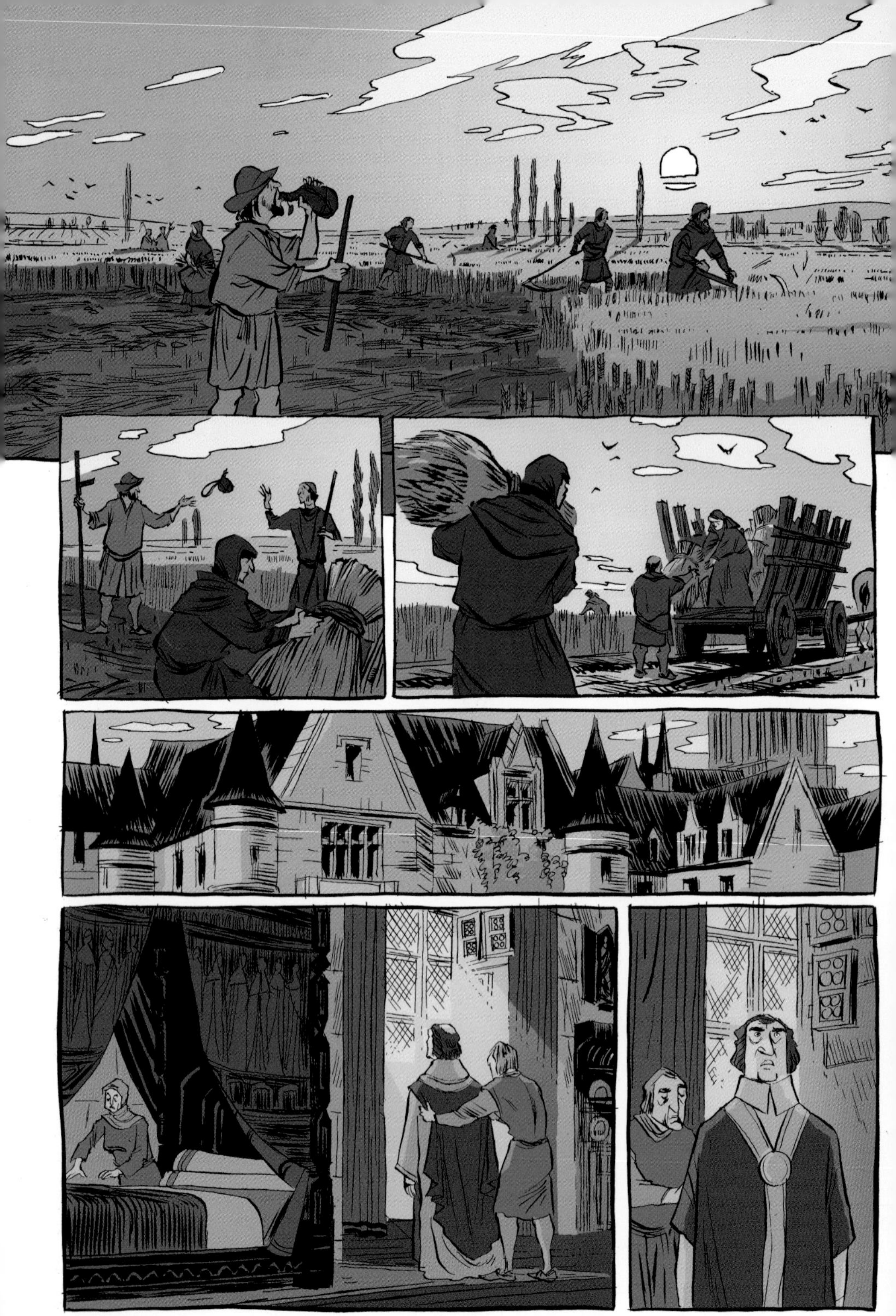

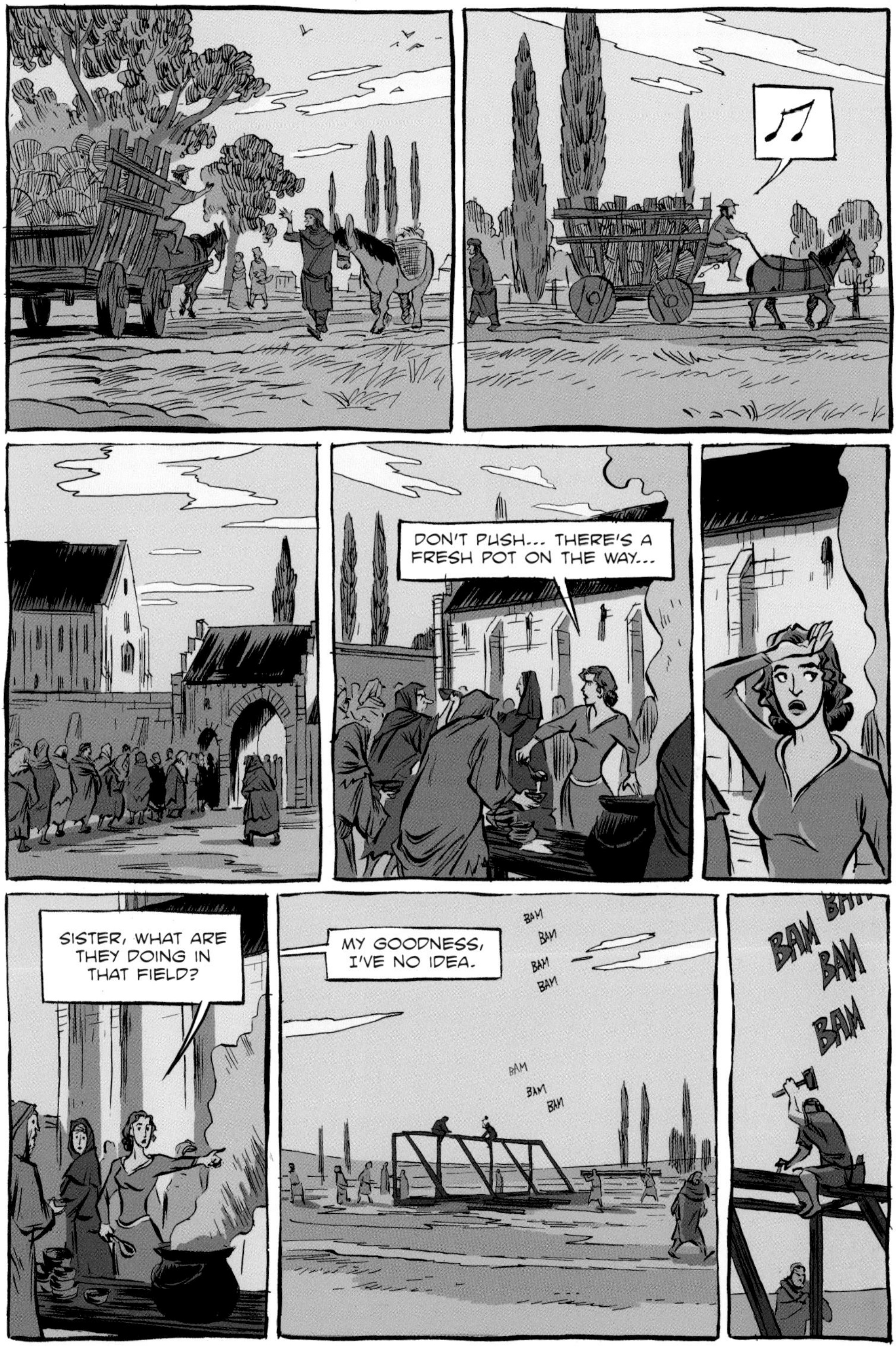
♫
DON'T PUSH... THERE'S A FRESH POT ON THE WAY...
SISTER, WHAT ARE THEY DOING IN THAT FIELD?
MY GOODNESS, I'VE NO IDEA.
BAM BAM BAM BAM
BAM BAM BAM
BAM BAM BAM BAM

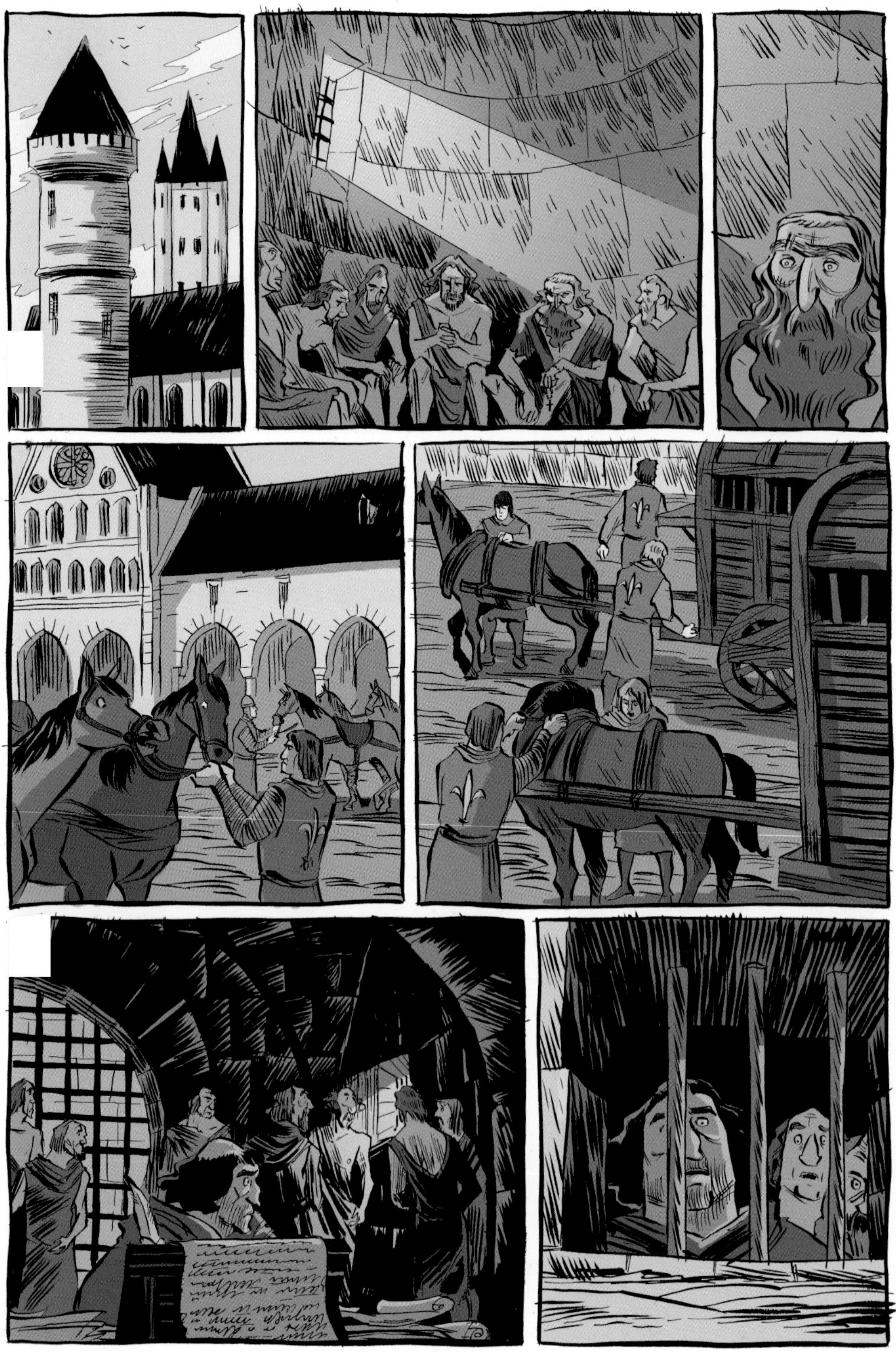

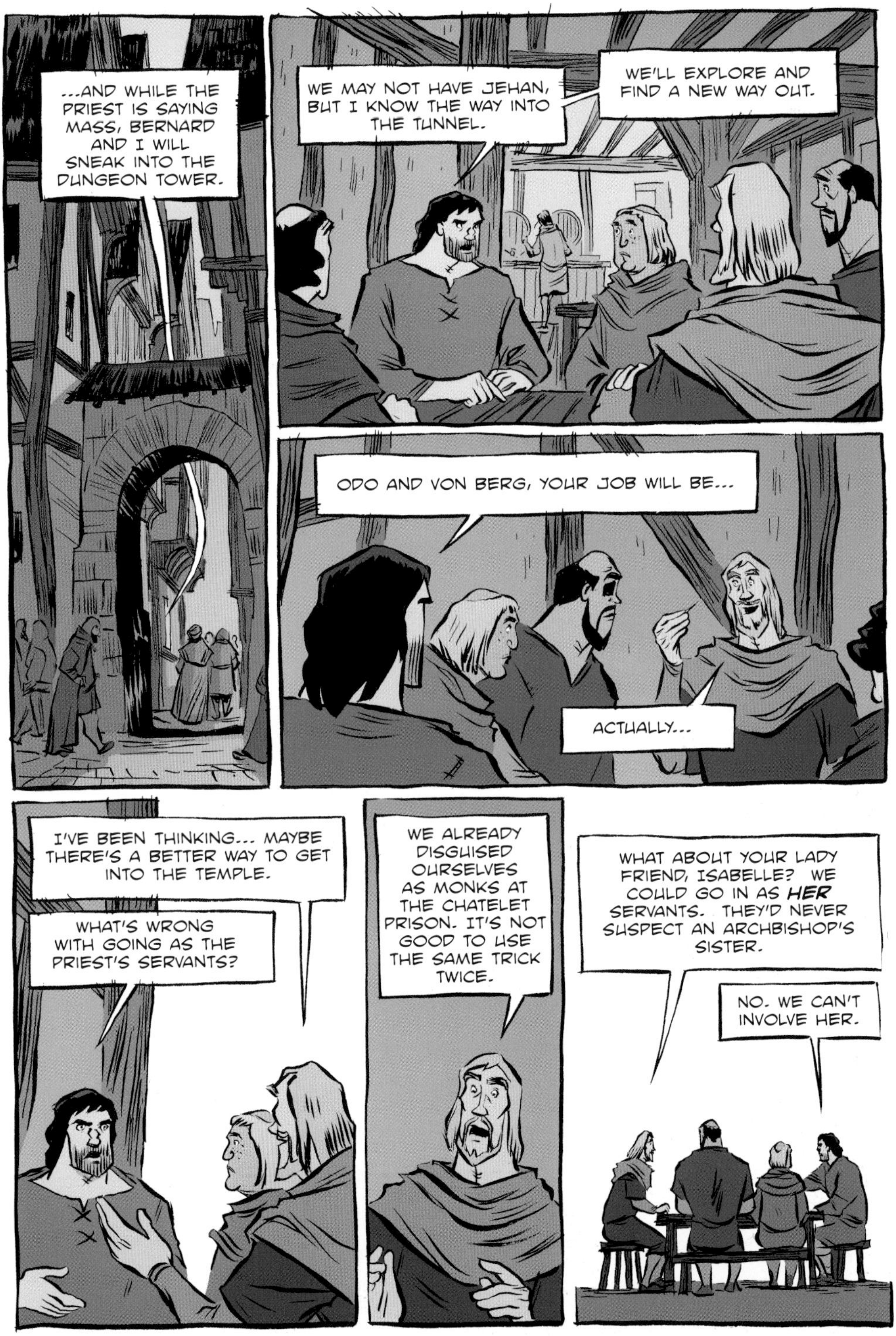
...AND WHILE THE PRIEST IS SAYING MASS, BERNARD AND I WILL SNEAK INTO THE DUNGEON TOWER.
WE MAY NOT HAVE JEHAN, BUT I KNOW THE WAY INTO THE TUNNEL.
WE'LL EXPLORE AND FIND A NEW WAY OUT.
ODO AND VON BERG, YOUR JOB WILL BE...
ACTUALLY...
I'VE BEEN THINKING... MAYBE THERE'S A BETTER WAY TO GET INTO THE TEMPLE.
WHAT'S WRONG WITH GOING AS THE PRIEST'S SERVANTS?
WE ALREADY DISGUISED OURSELVES AS MONKS AT THE CHATELET PRISON. IT'S NOT GOOD TO USE THE SAME TRICK TWICE.
WHAT ABOUT YOUR LADY FRIEND, ISABELLE? WE COULD GO IN AS ***HER*** SERVANTS. THEY'D NEVER SUSPECT AN ARCHBISHOP'S SISTER.
NO. WE CAN'T INVOLVE HER.

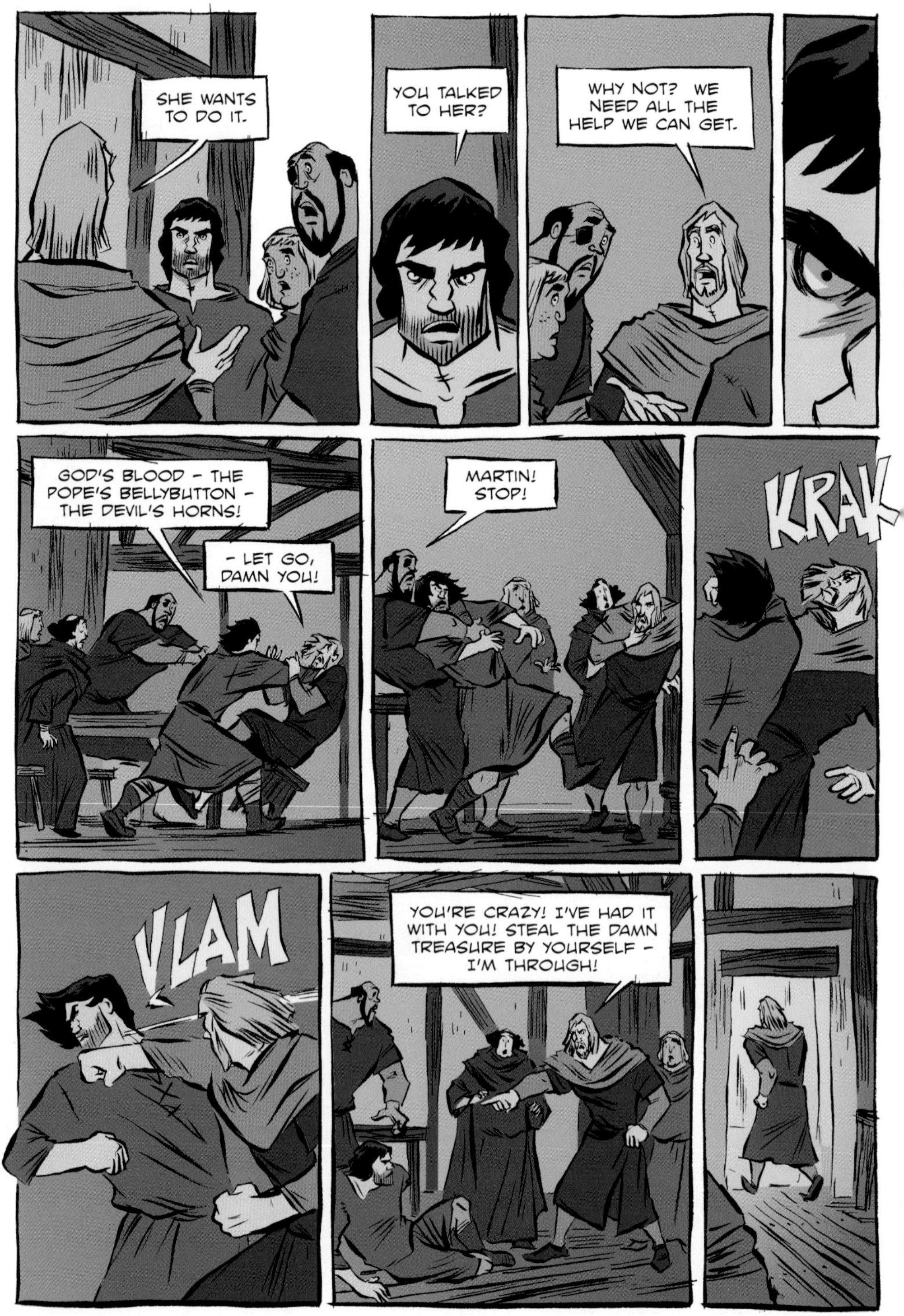
SHE WANTS TO DO IT.
YOU TALKED TO HER?
WHY NOT? WE NEED ALL THE HELP WE CAN GET.
GOD'S BLOOD - THE POPE'S BELLYBUTTON - THE DEVIL'S HORNS!
- LET GO, DAMN YOU!
MARTIN! STOP!
KRAK
VLAM
YOU'RE CRAZY! I'VE HAD IT WITH YOU! STEAL THE DAMN TREASURE BY YOURSELF - I'M THROUGH!

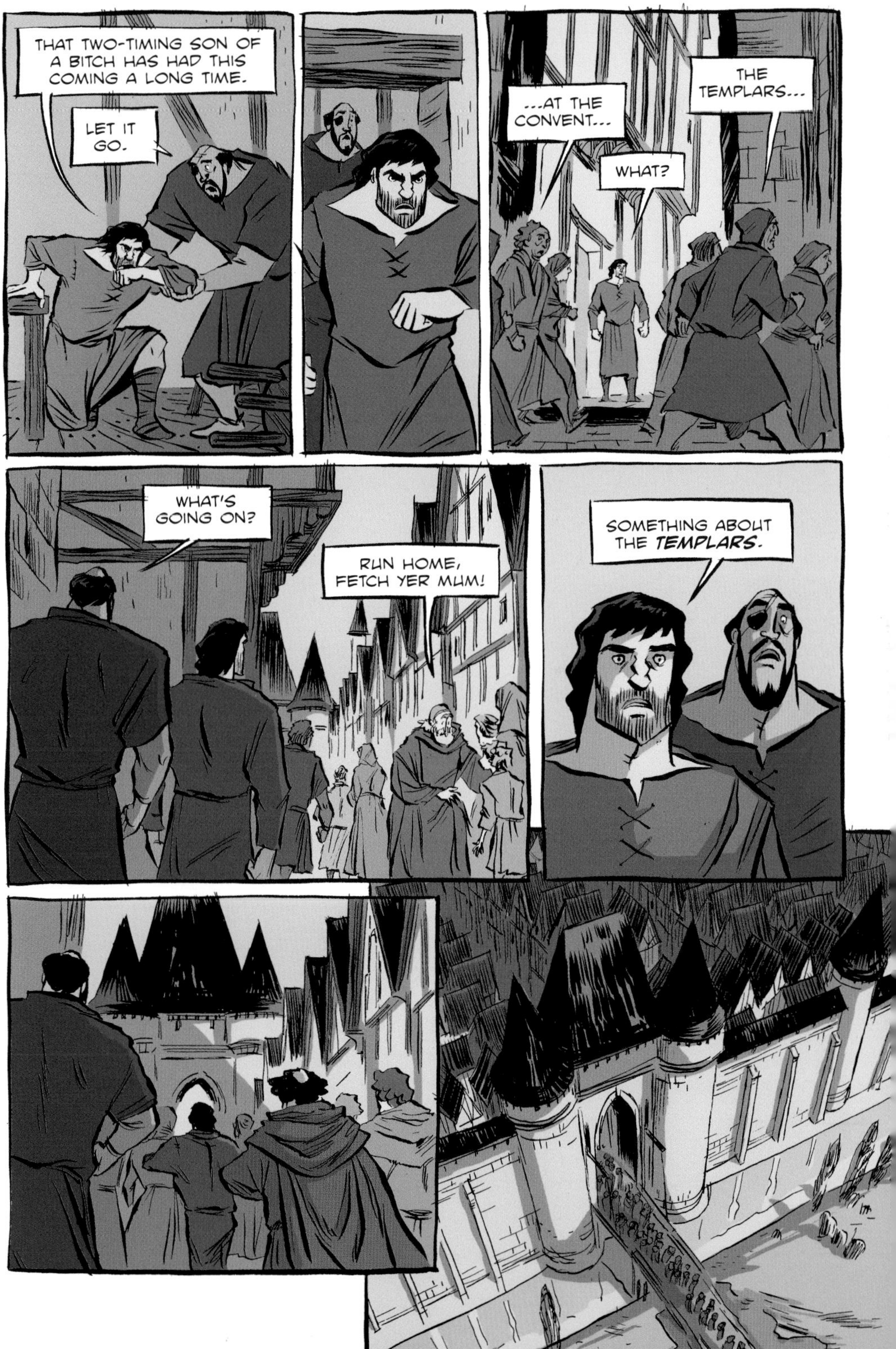
THAT TWO-TIMING SON OF A BITCH HAS HAD THIS COMING A LONG TIME.
LET IT GO.
...AT THE CONVENT...
WHAT?
THE TEMPLARS...
WHAT'S GOING ON?
RUN HOME, FETCH YER MUM!
SOMETHING ABOUT THE TEMPLARS.

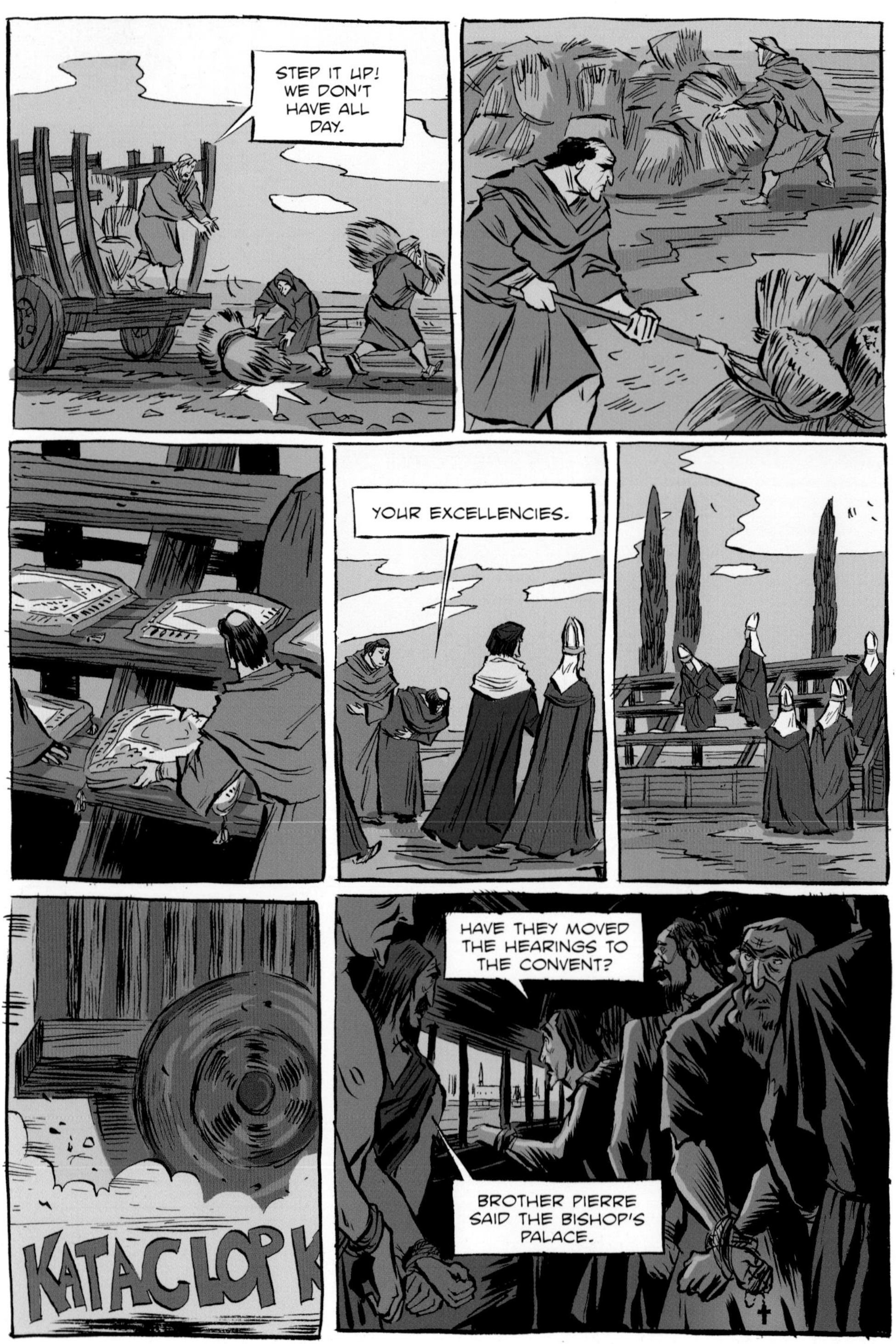
STEP IT UP! WE DON'T HAVE ALL DAY.
YOUR EXCELLENCIES.
KATACLOP K
HAVE THEY MOVED THE HEARINGS TO THE CONVENT?
BROTHER PIERRE SAID THE BISHOP'S PALACE.

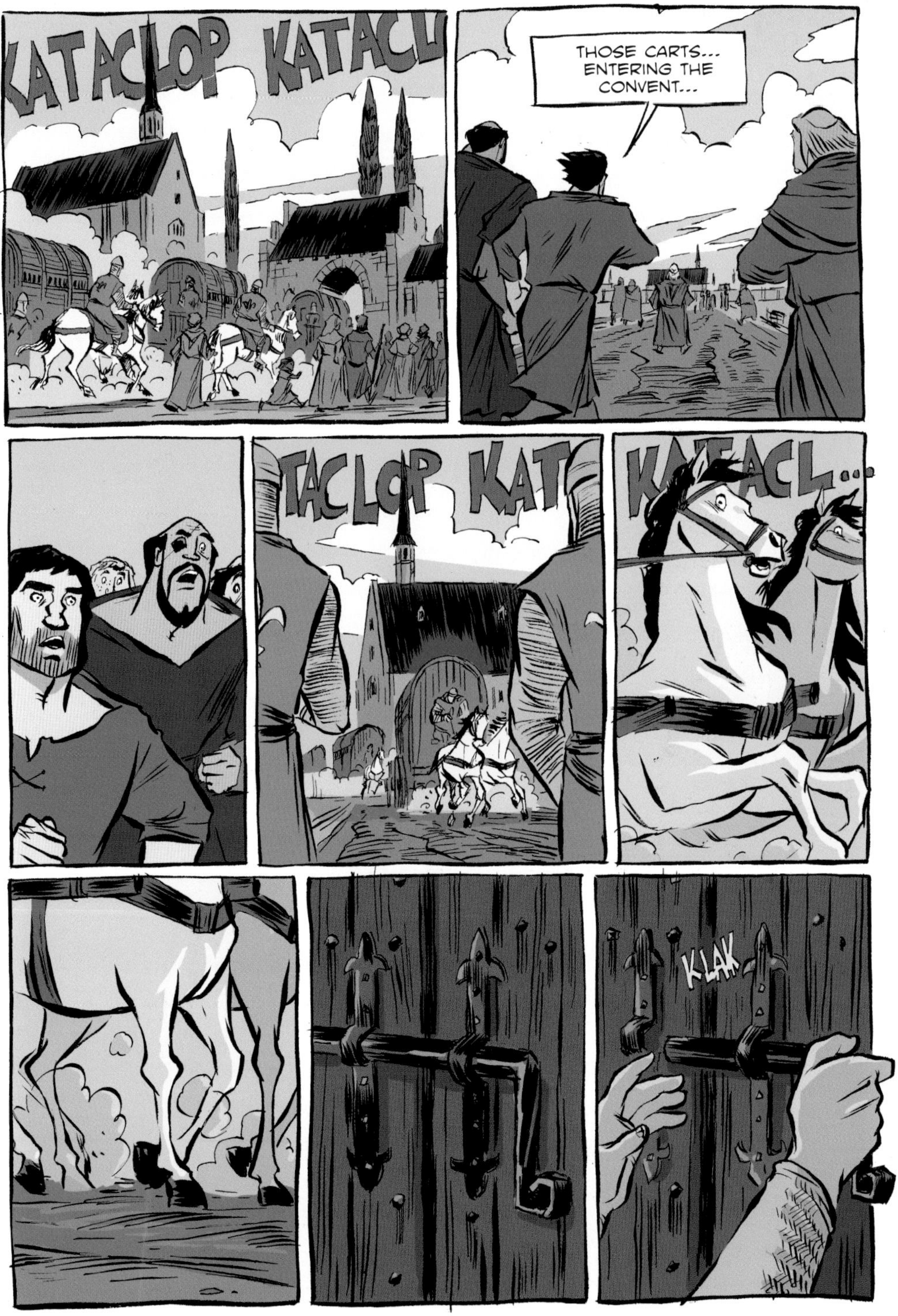

KATACLOP KATACL
THOSE CARTS... ENTERING THE CONVENT...
TACLOP KAT
KATACL...
KLAK

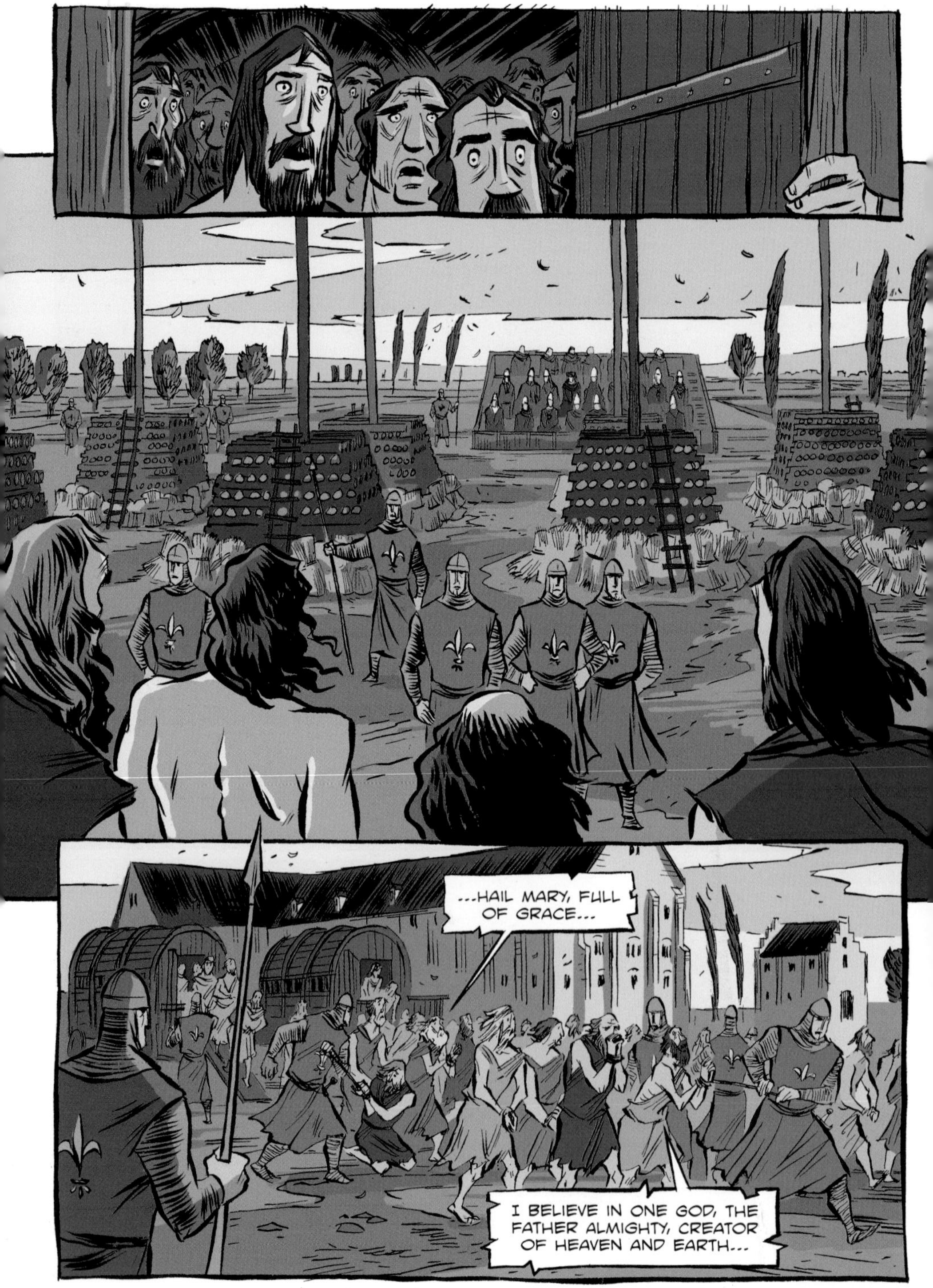
...HAIL MARY, FULL OF GRACE...
I BELIEVE IN ONE GOD, THE FATHER ALMIGHTY, CREATOR OF HEAVEN AND EARTH...

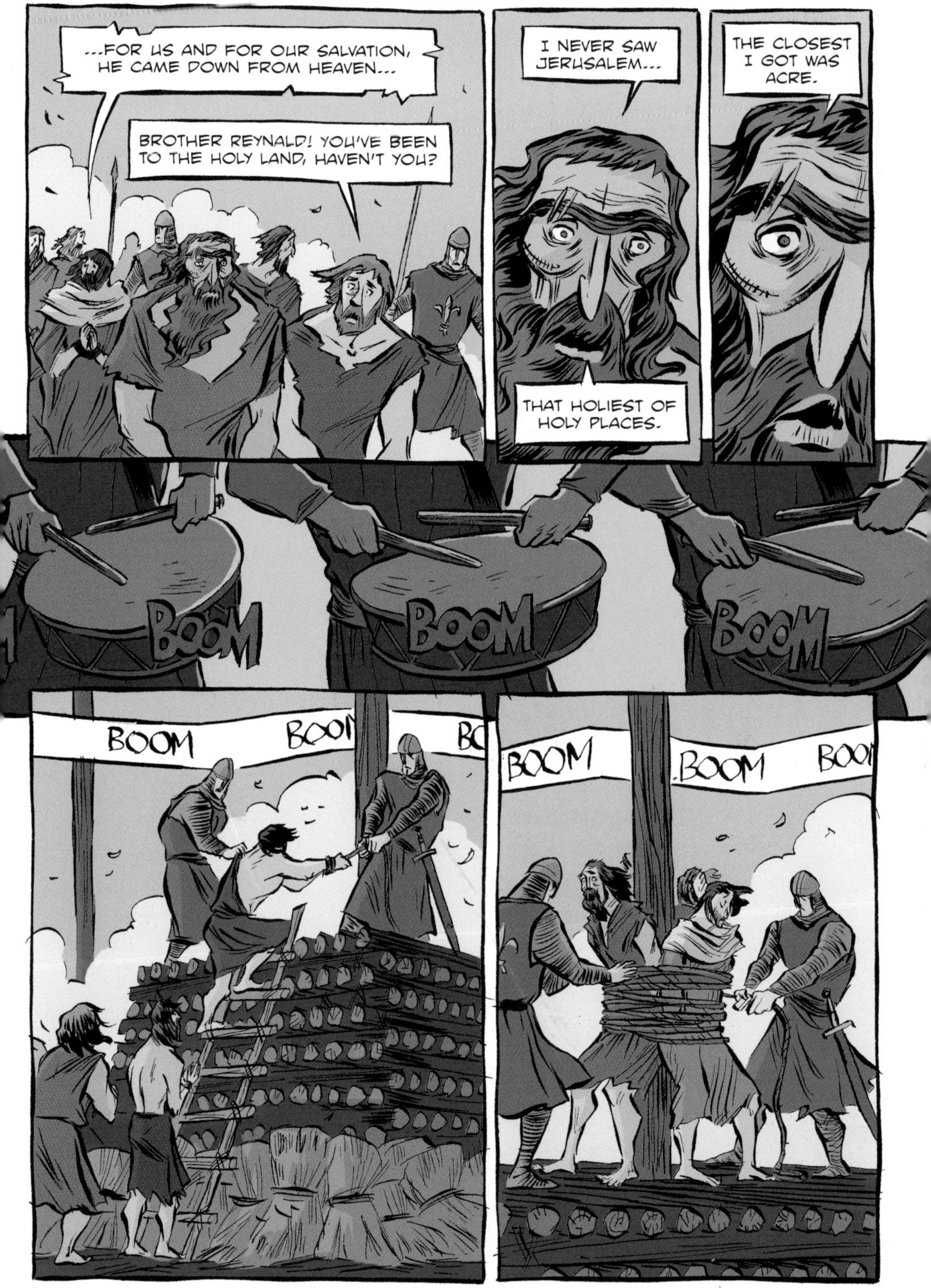
...FOR US AND FOR OUR SALVATION, HE CAME DOWN FROM HEAVEN...
BROTHER REYNALD! YOU'VE BEEN TO THE HOLY LAND, HAVEN'T YOU?
I NEVER SAW JERUSALEM...
THAT HOLIEST OF HOLY PLACES.
THE CLOSEST I GOT WAS ACRE.
BOOM
BOOM
BOOM
BOOM
BOOM
BOOM
BOOM

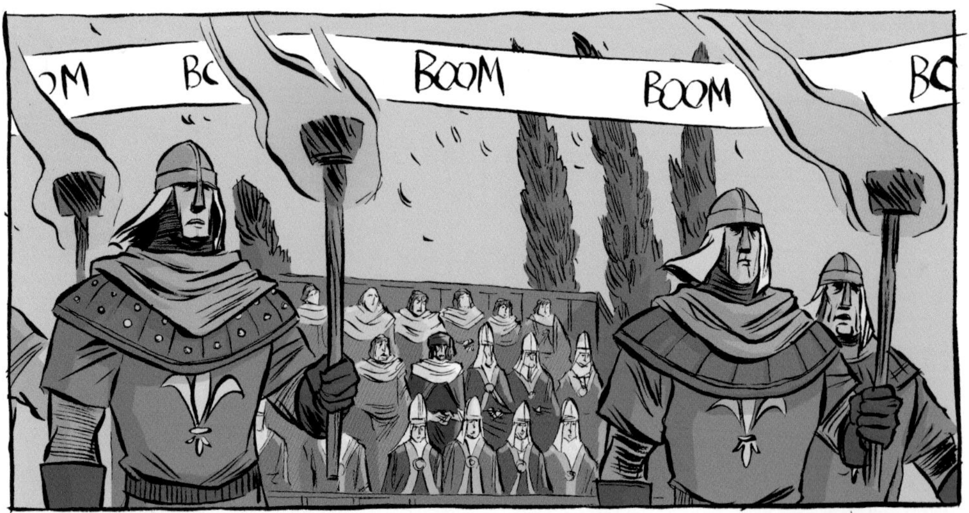
OM
BO
BOOM
BOOM
BO

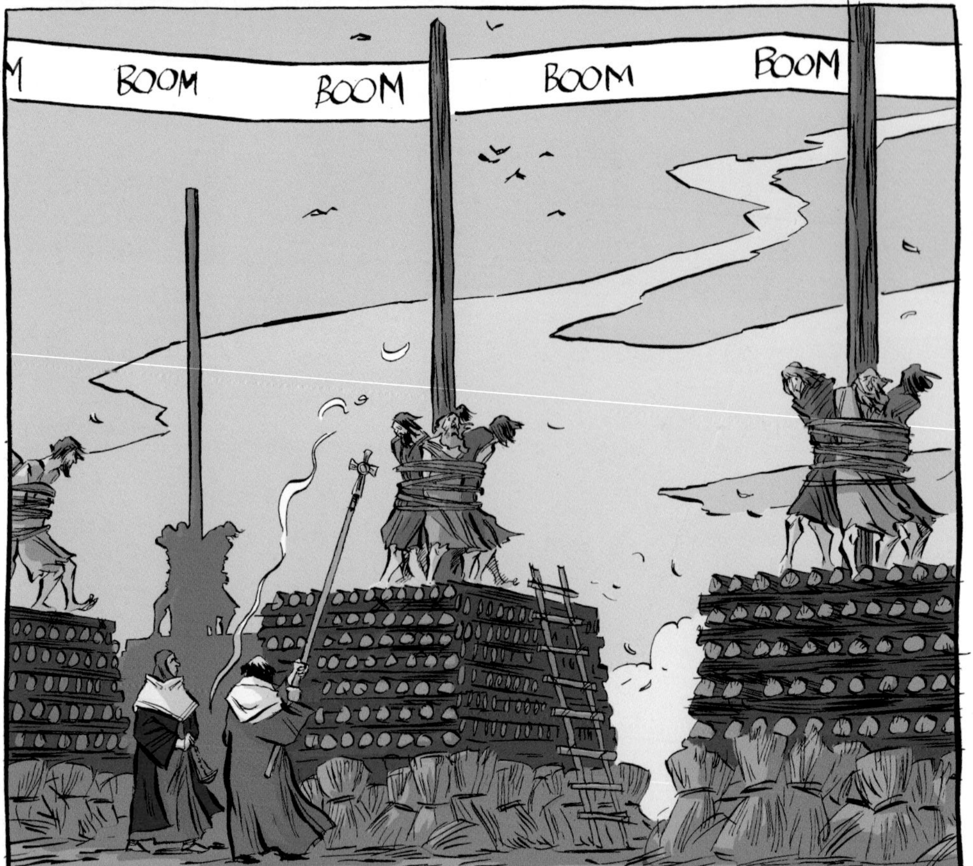
M
BOOM
BOOM
BOOM
BOOM

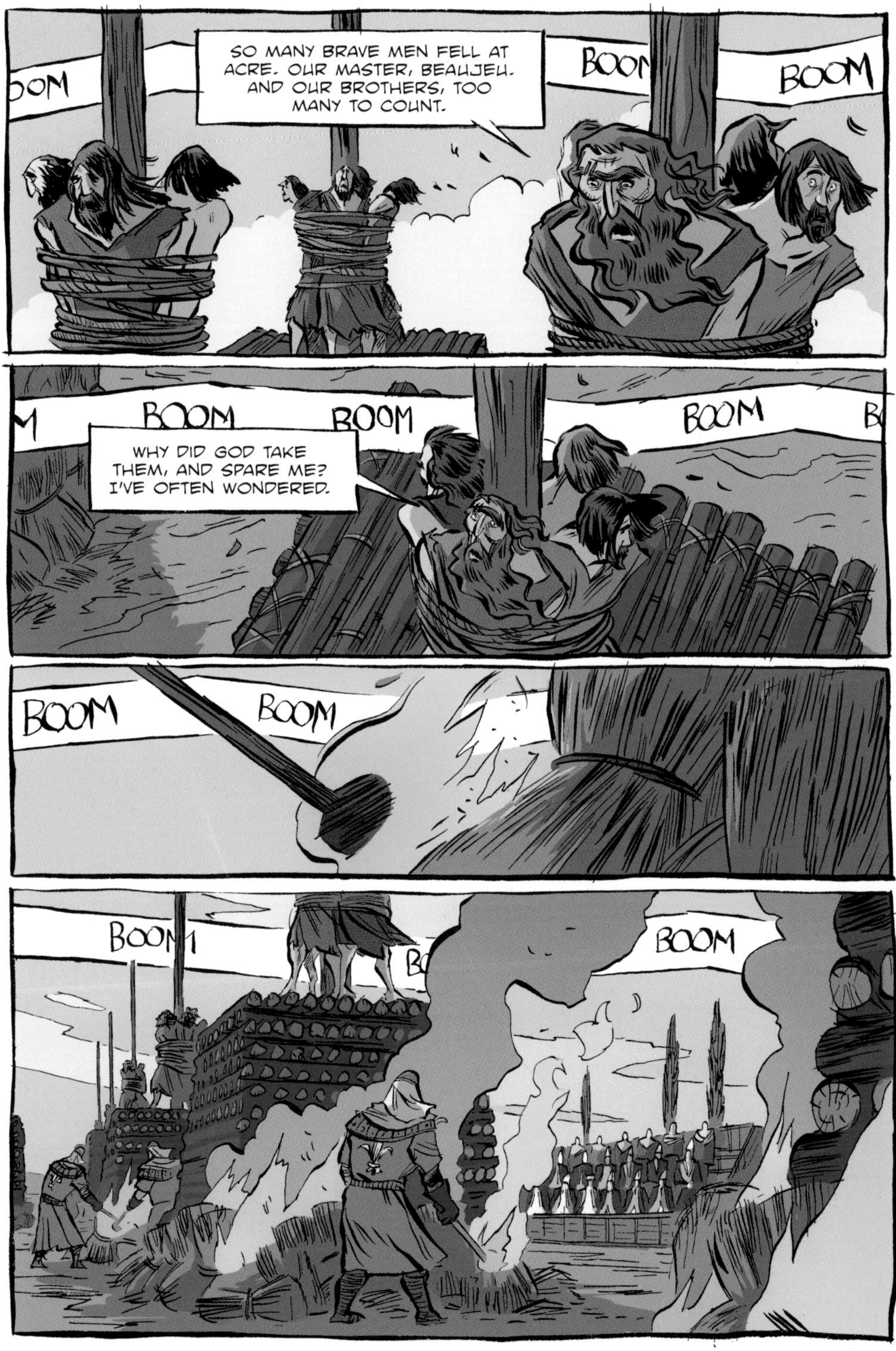

OOM
SO MANY BRAVE MEN FELL AT ACRE. OUR MASTER, BEAUJEU. AND OUR BROTHERS, TOO MANY TO COUNT.
BOOM
BOOM
M
BOOM
BOOM
WHY DID GOD TAKE THEM, AND SPARE ME? I'VE OFTEN WONDERED.
BOOM
BOOM
BOOM
BOOM
BOOM

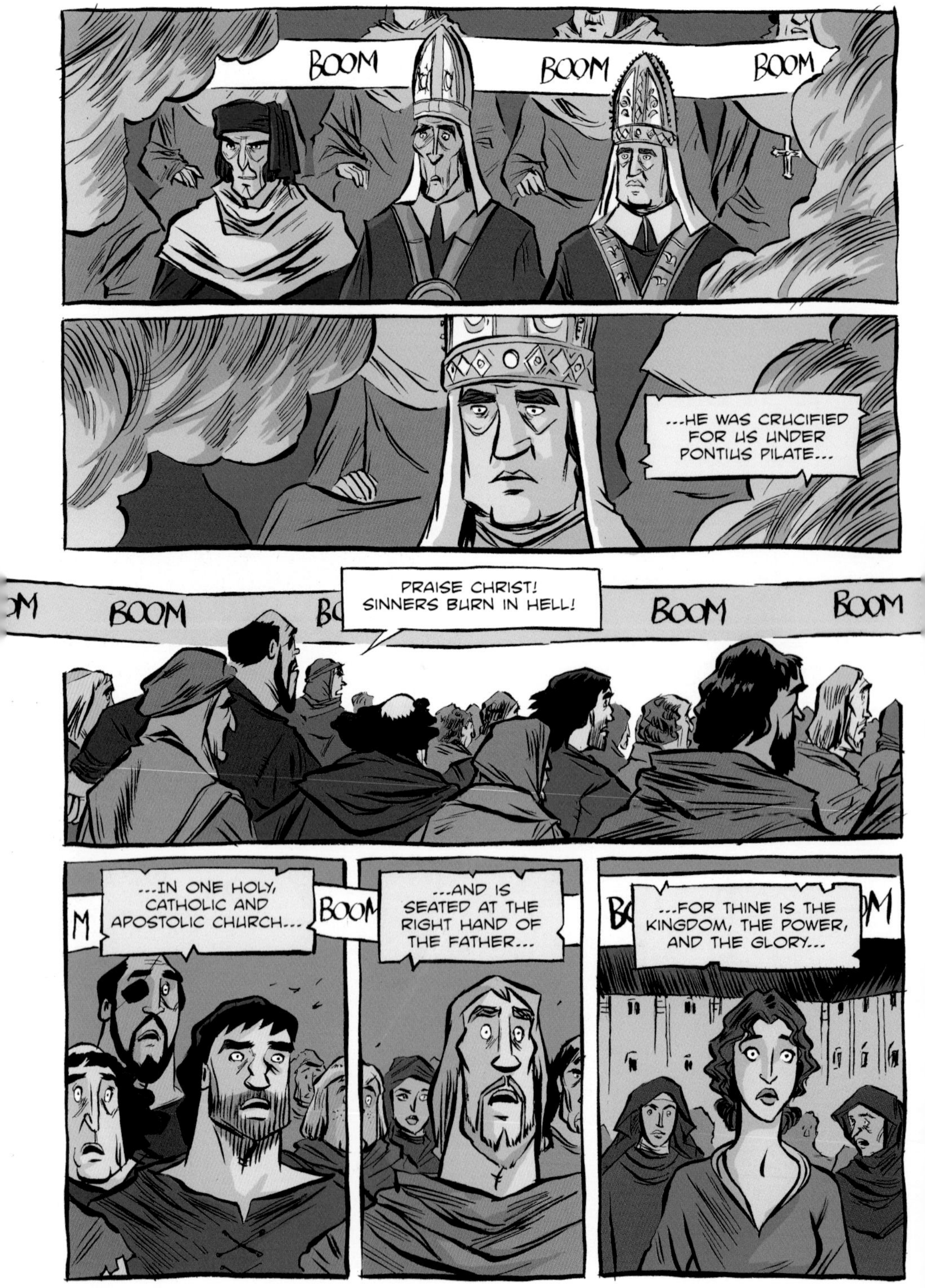
BOOM
BOOM
BOOM
...HE WAS CRUCIFIED FOR US UNDER PONTIUS PILATE...
BOOM
PRAISE CHRIST! SINNERS BURN IN HELL!
BOOM
BOOM
...IN ONE HOLY, CATHOLIC AND APOSTOLIC CHURCH...
...AND IS SEATED AT THE RIGHT HAND OF THE FATHER...
...FOR THINE IS THE KINGDOM, THE POWER, AND THE GLORY...

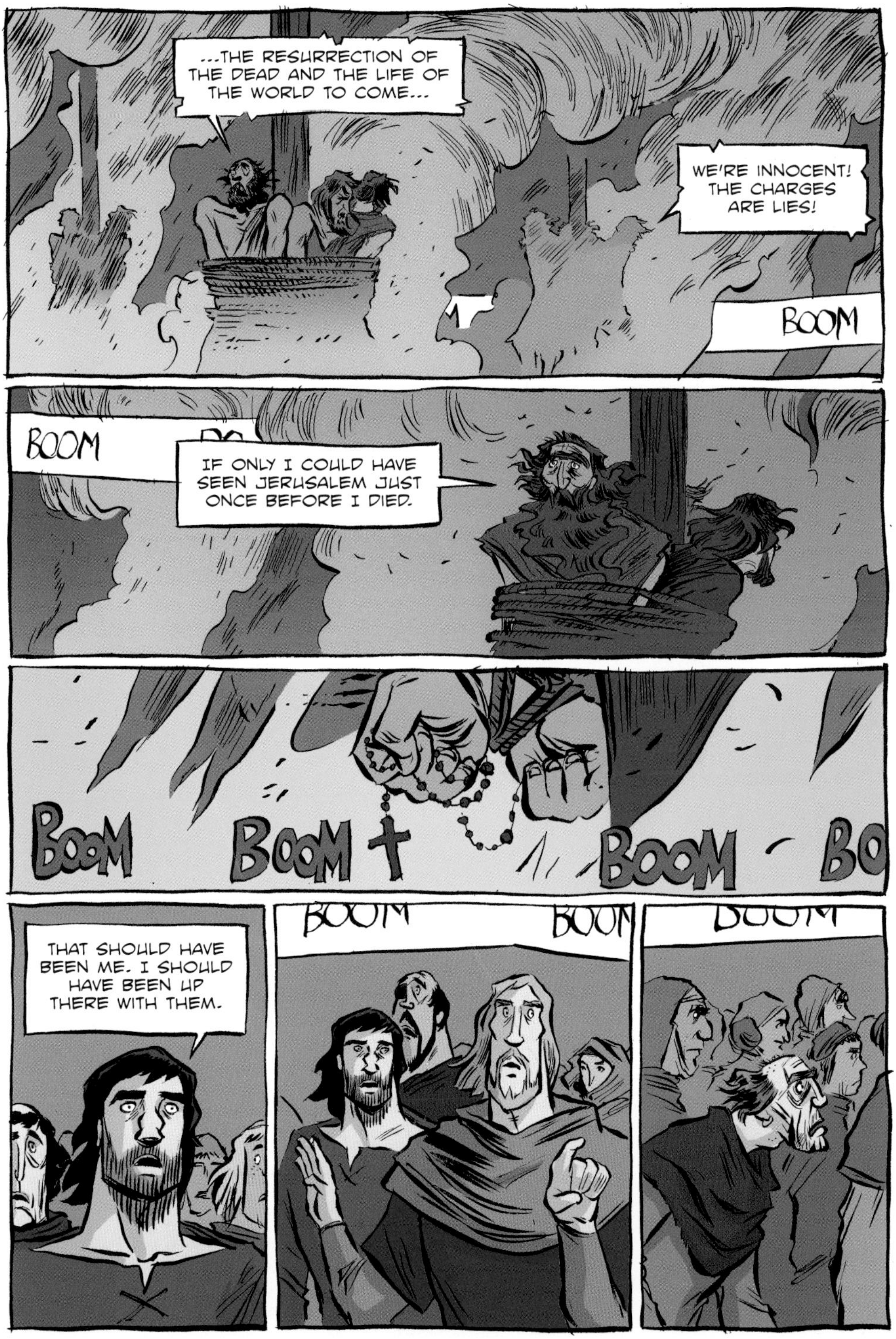
...THE RESURRECTION OF THE DEAD AND THE LIFE OF THE WORLD TO COME...
WE'RE INNOCENT! THE CHARGES ARE LIES!
BOOM
BOOM
IF ONLY I COULD HAVE SEEN JERUSALEM JUST ONCE BEFORE I DIED.
BOOM
BOOM
BOOM
THAT SHOULD HAVE BEEN ME. I SHOULD HAVE BEEN UP THERE WITH THEM.

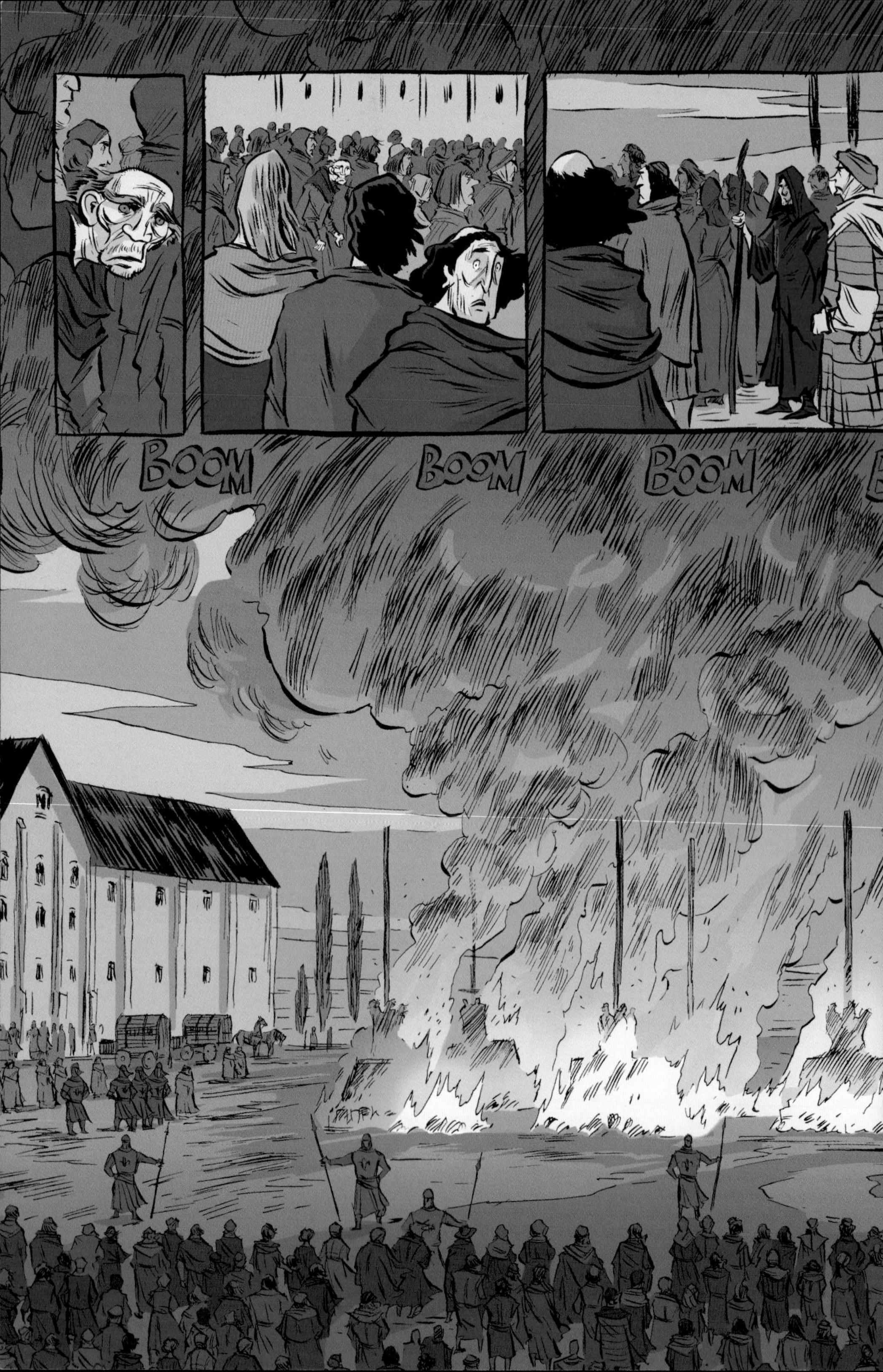
BOOM
BOOM
BOOM

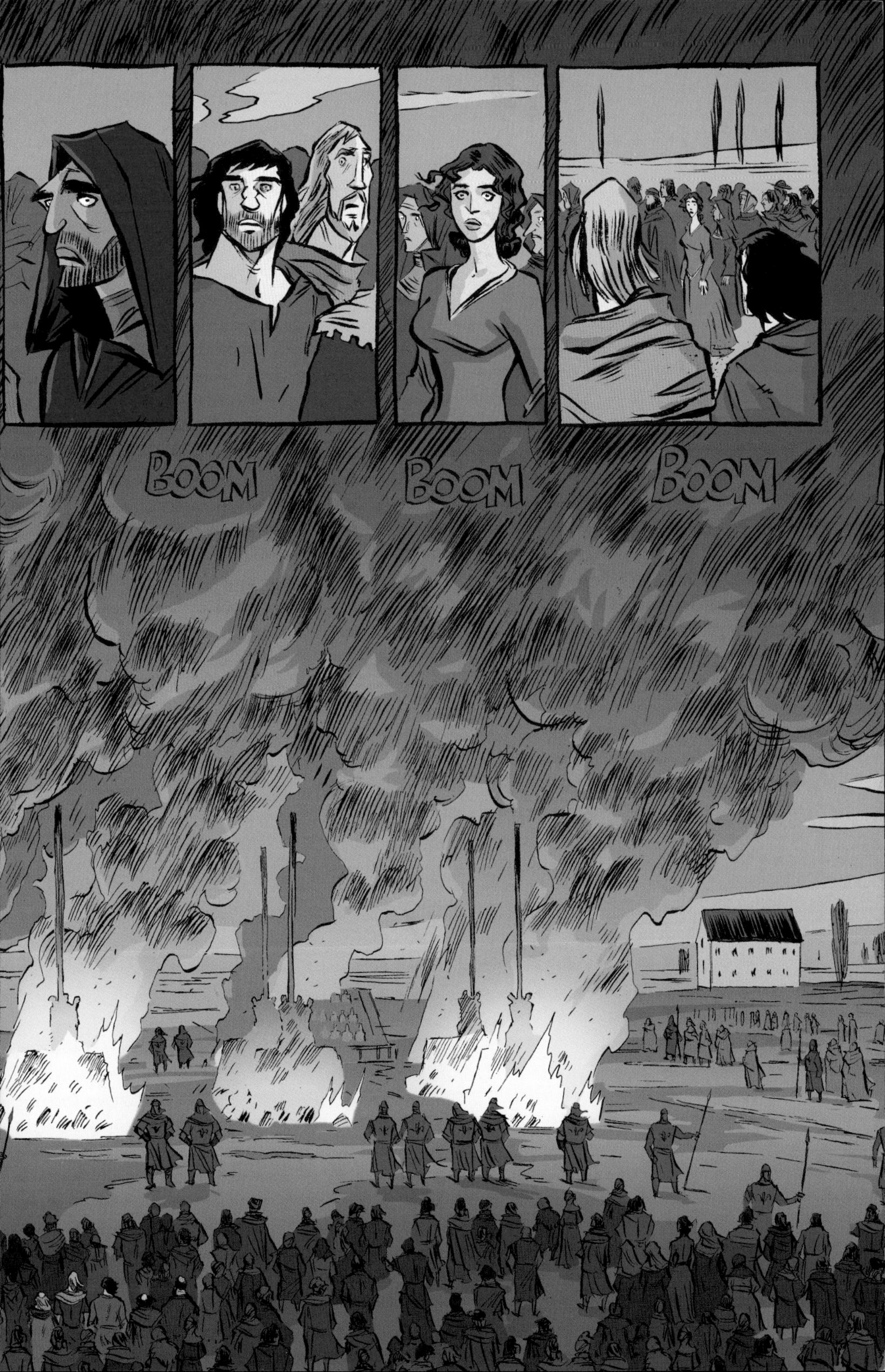
BOOM
BOOM
BOOM

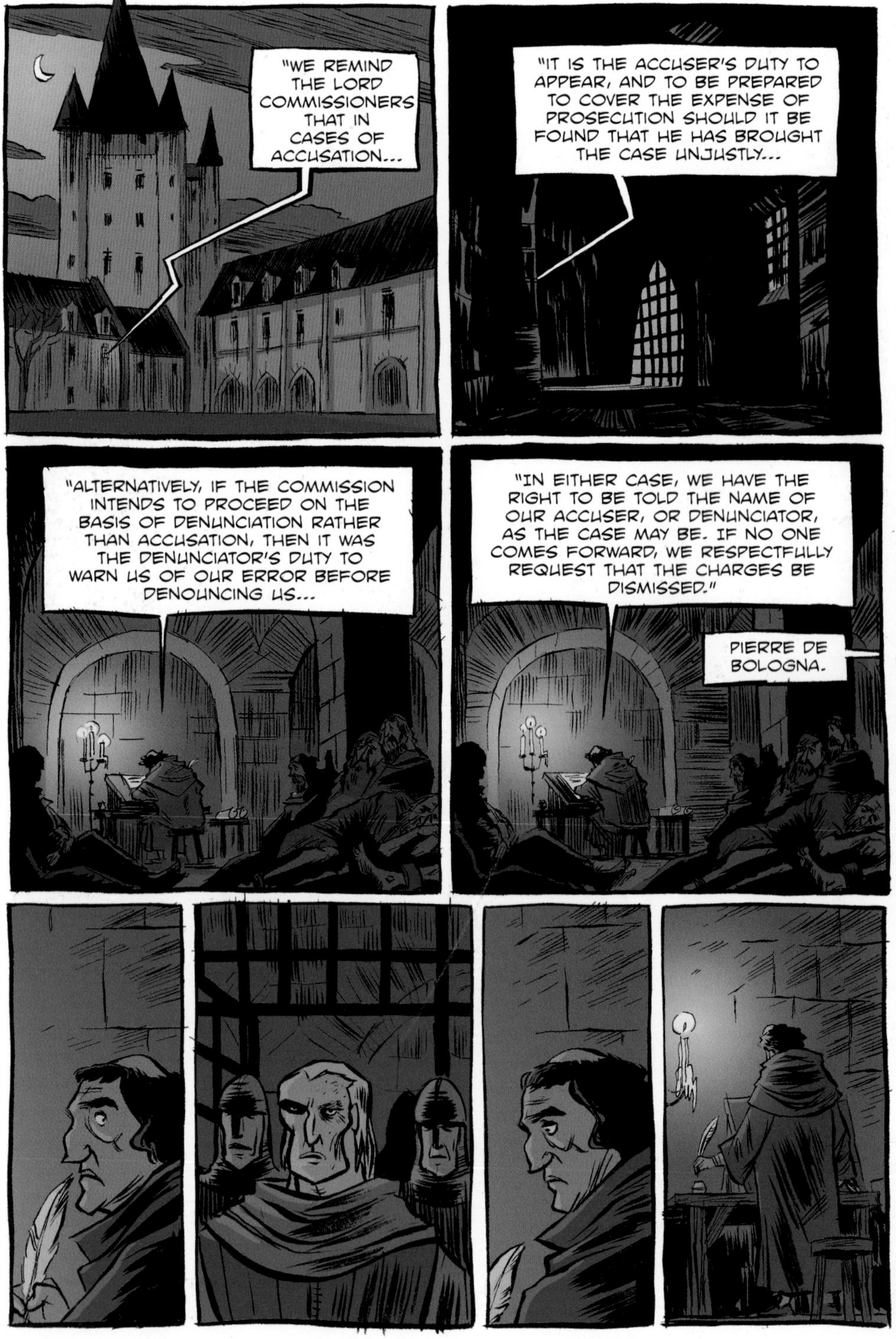
"WE REMIND THE LORD COMMISSIONERS THAT IN CASES OF ACCUSATION...
"IT IS THE ACCUSER'S DUTY TO APPEAR, AND TO BE PREPARED TO COVER THE EXPENSE OF PROSECUTION SHOULD IT BE FOUND THAT HE HAS BROUGHT THE CASE UNJUSTLY...
"ALTERNATIVELY, IF THE COMMISSION INTENDS TO PROCEED ON THE BASIS OF DENUNCIATION RATHER THAN ACCUSATION, THEN IT WAS THE DENUNCIATOR'S DUTY TO WARN US OF OUR ERROR BEFORE DENOUNCING US...
"IN EITHER CASE, WE HAVE THE RIGHT TO BE TOLD THE NAME OF OUR ACCUSER, OR DENUNCIATOR, AS THE CASE MAY BE. IF NO ONE COMES FORWARD, WE RESPECTFULLY REQUEST THAT THE CHARGES BE DISMISSED."
PIERRE DE BOLOGNA.

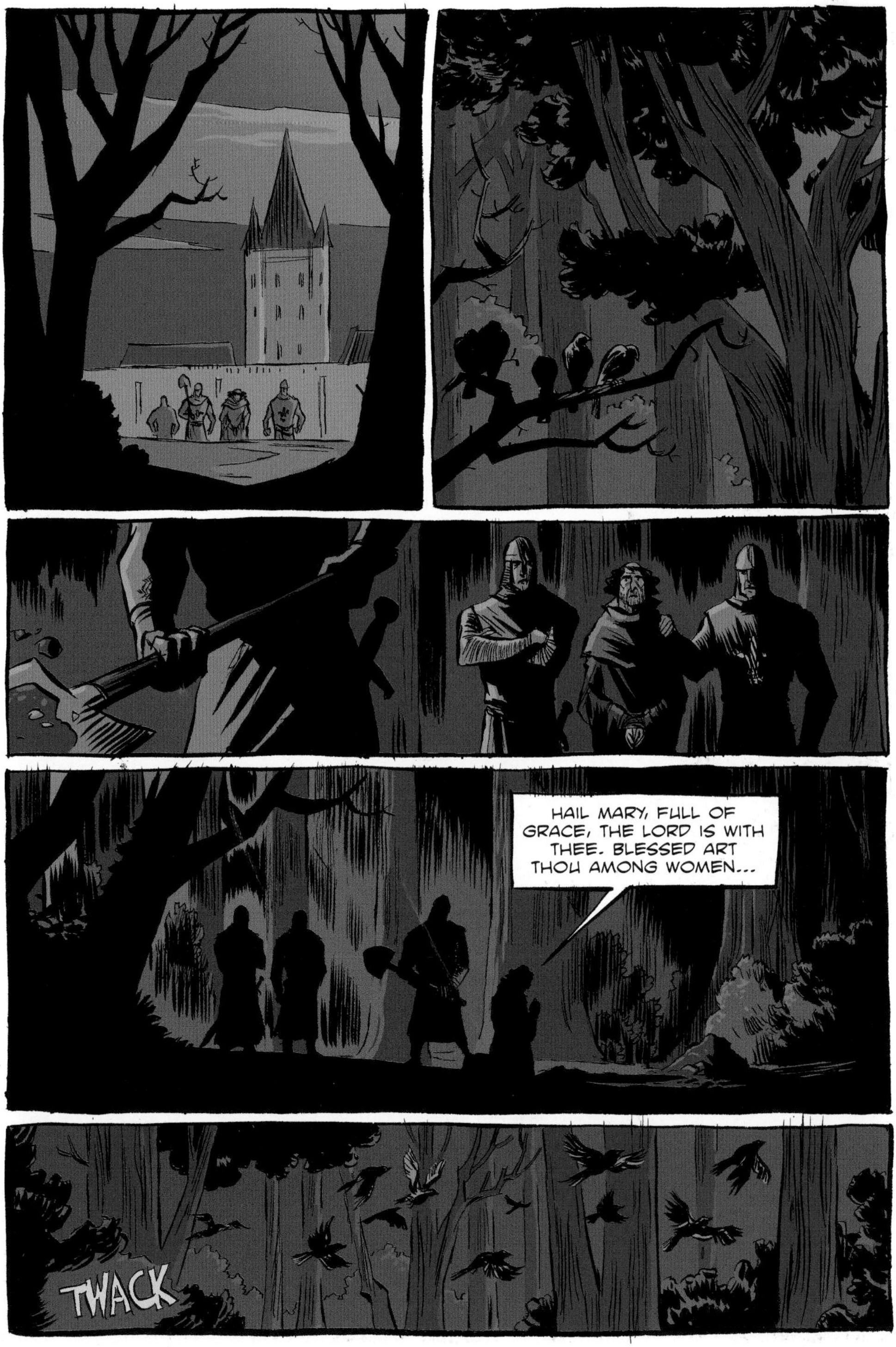
HAIL MARY, FULL OF GRACE, THE LORD IS WITH THEE. BLESSED ART THOU AMONG WOMEN...
TWACK

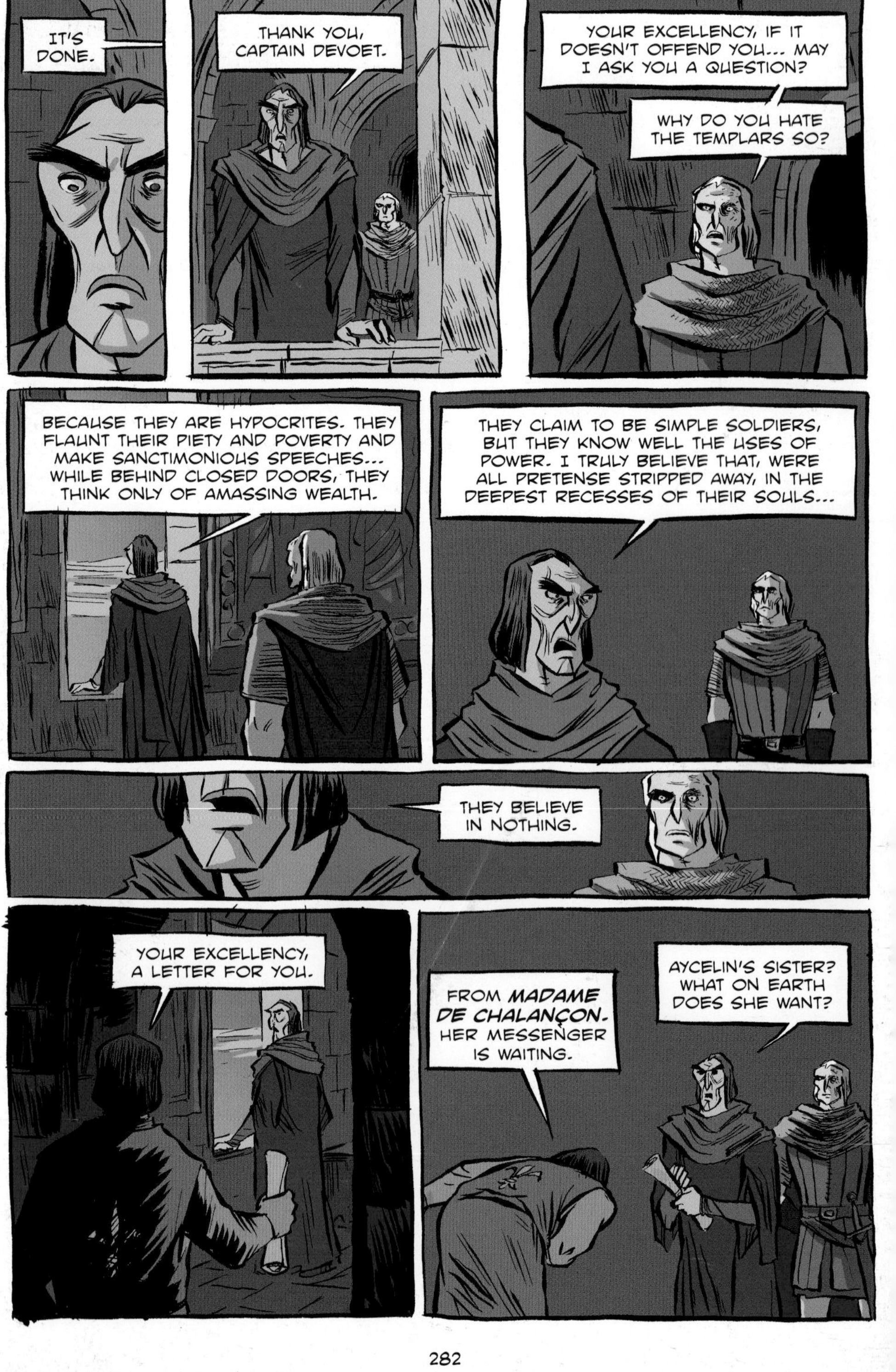
IT'S DONE.
THANK YOU, CAPTAIN DEVOET.
YOUR EXCELLENCY, IF IT DOESN'T OFFEND YOU... MAY I ASK YOU A QUESTION?
WHY DO YOU HATE THE TEMPLARS SO?
BECAUSE THEY ARE HYPOCRITES. THEY FLAUNT THEIR PIETY AND POVERTY AND MAKE SANCTIMONIOUS SPEECHES... WHILE BEHIND CLOSED DOORS, THEY THINK ONLY OF AMASSING WEALTH.
THEY CLAIM TO BE SIMPLE SOLDIERS, BUT THEY KNOW WELL THE USES OF POWER. I TRULY BELIEVE THAT, WERE ALL PRETENSE STRIPPED AWAY, IN THE DEEPEST RECESSES OF THEIR SOULS...
THEY BELIEVE IN NOTHING.
YOUR EXCELLENCY, A LETTER FOR YOU.
FROM *MADAME DE CHALANÇON*. HER MESSENGER IS WAITING.
AYCELIN'S SISTER? WHAT ON EARTH DOES SHE WANT?

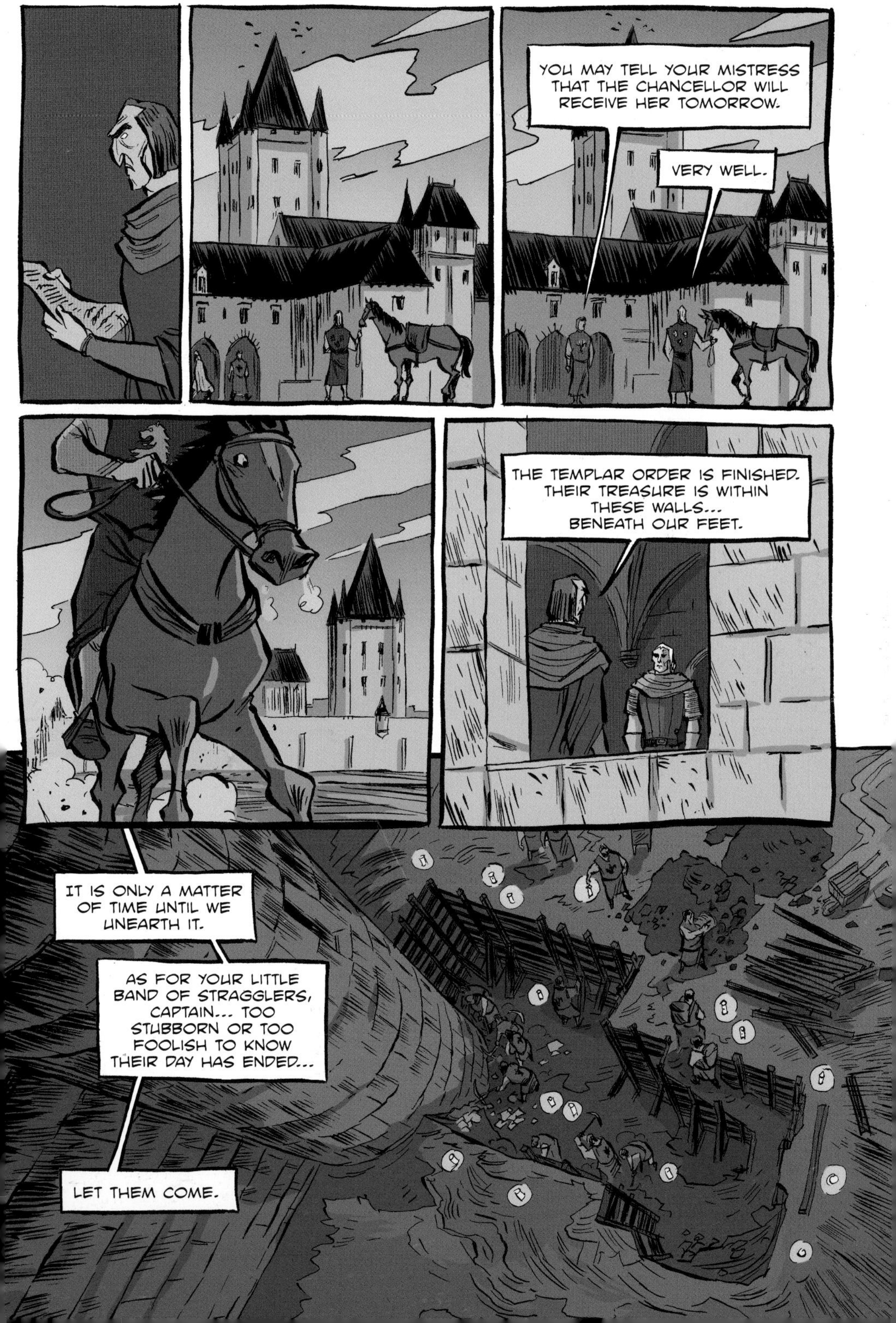
YOU MAY TELL YOUR MISTRESS THAT THE CHANCELLOR WILL RECEIVE HER TOMORROW.
VERY WELL.
THE TEMPLAR ORDER IS FINISHED. THEIR TREASURE IS WITHIN THESE WALLS... BENEATH OUR FEET.
IT IS ONLY A MATTER OF TIME UNTIL WE UNEARTH IT.
AS FOR YOUR LITTLE BAND OF STRAGGLERS, CAPTAIN... TOO STUBBORN OR TOO FOOLISH TO KNOW THEIR DAY HAS ENDED...
LET THEM COME.

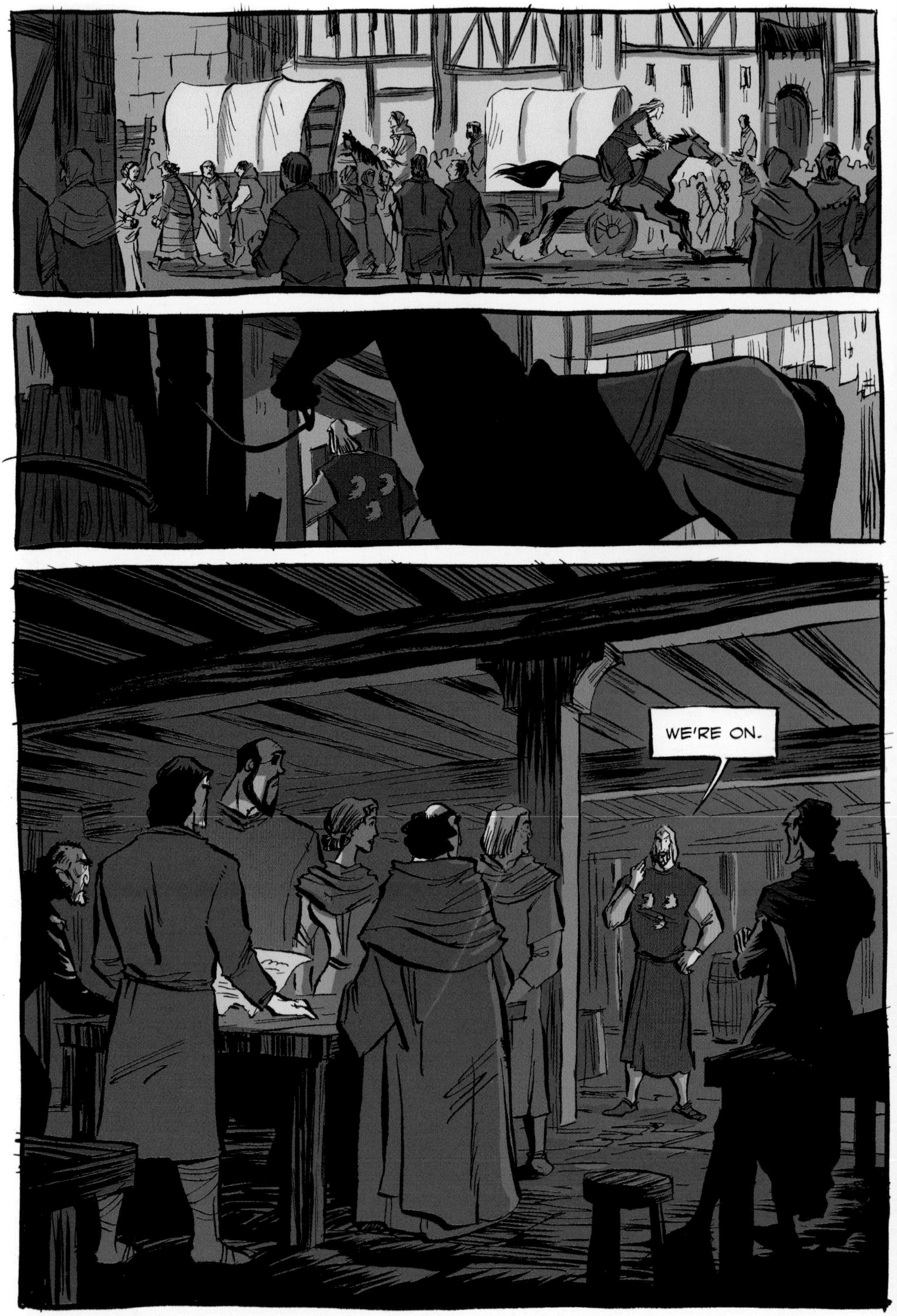
WE'RE ON.

END OF BOOK TWO

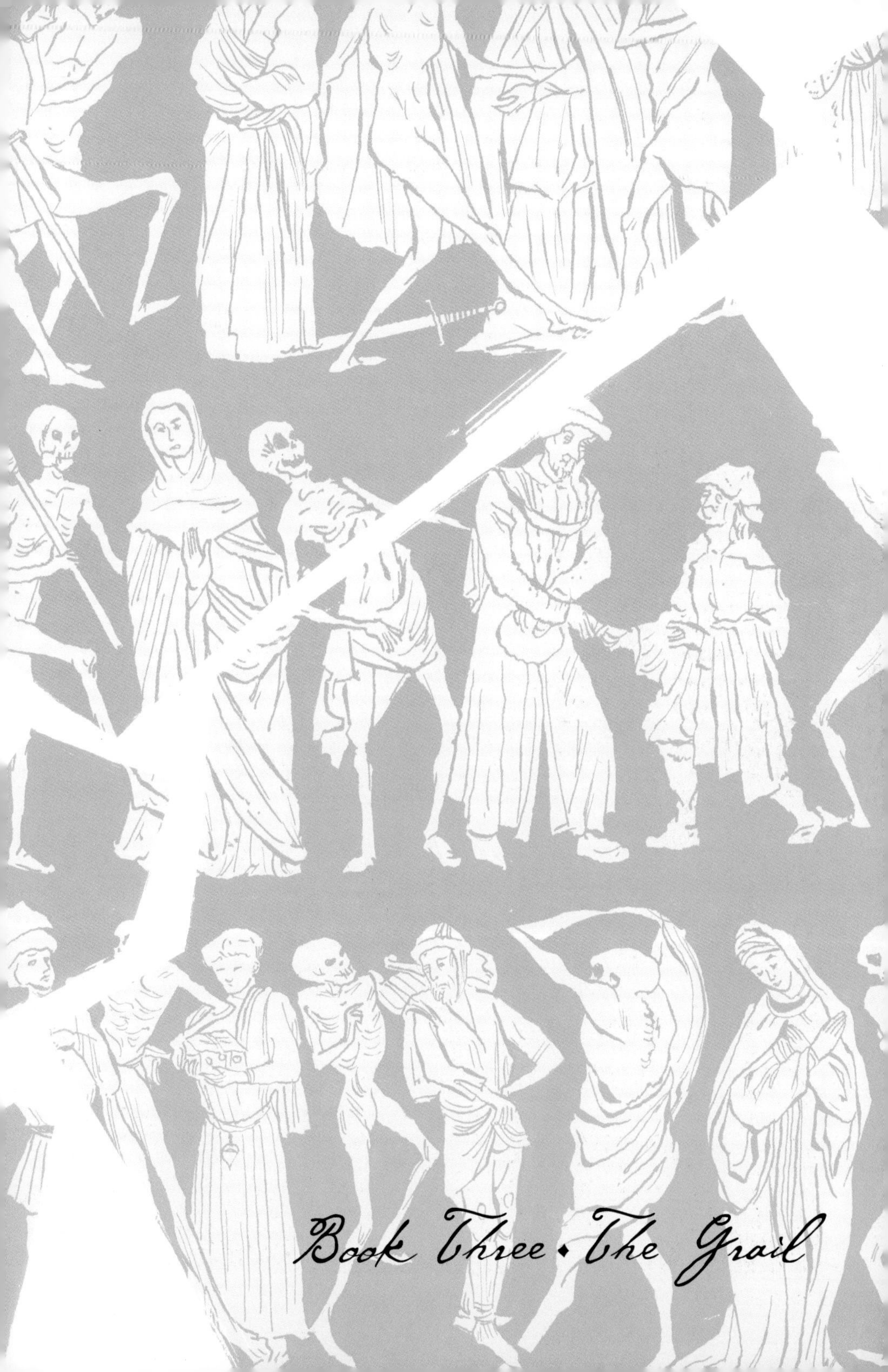

Book Three • The Grail

7. The Plan

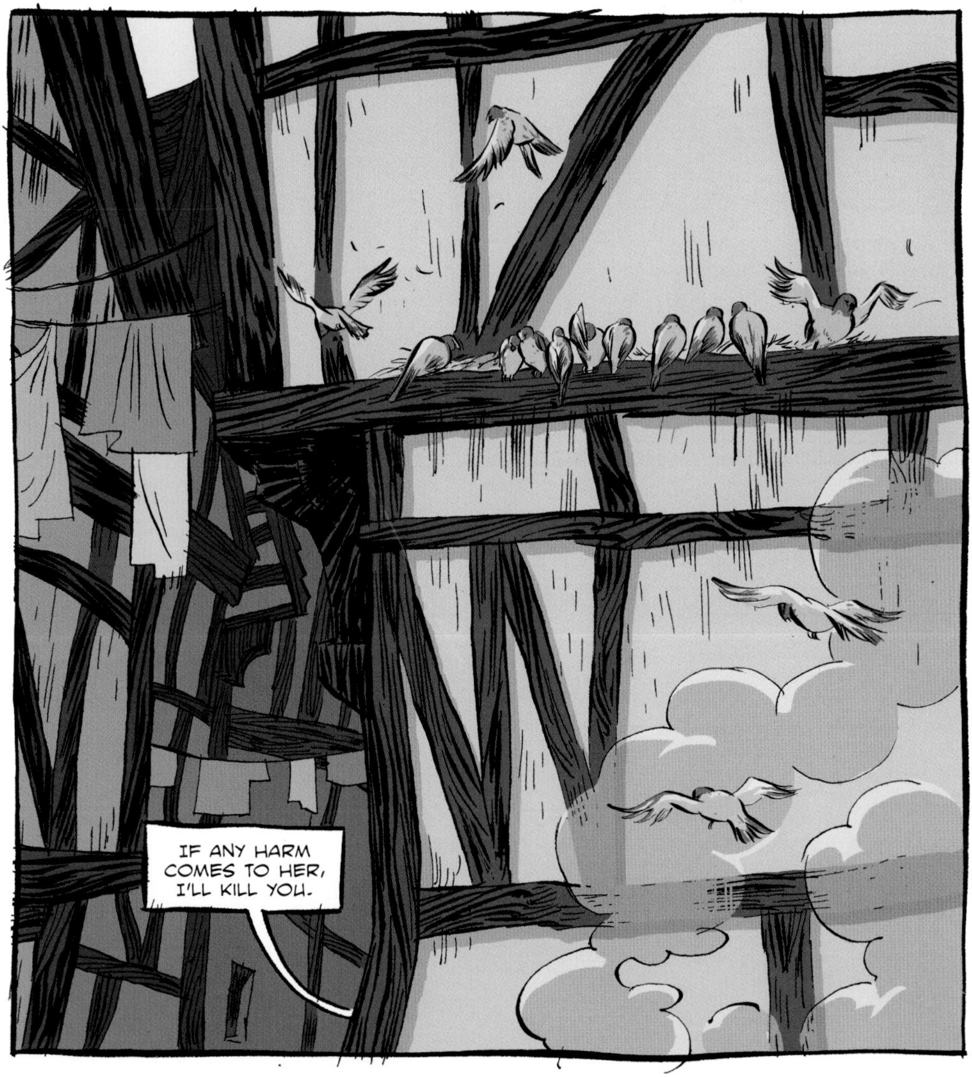
IF ANY HARM COMES TO HER, I'LL KILL YOU.

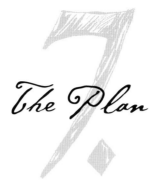

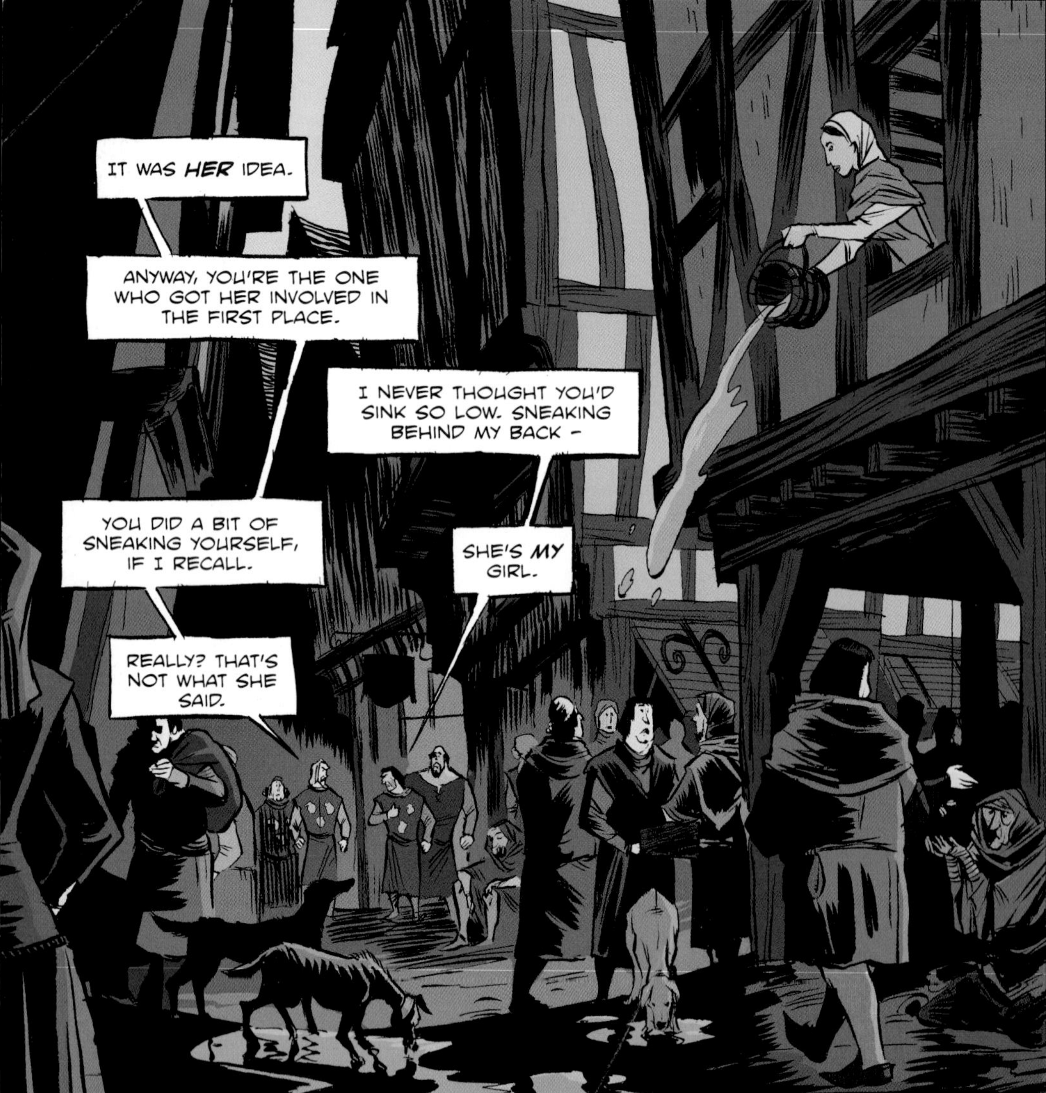
IT WAS HER IDEA.
ANYWAY, YOU'RE THE ONE WHO GOT HER INVOLVED IN THE FIRST PLACE.
I NEVER THOUGHT YOU'D SINK SO LOW. SNEAKING BEHIND MY BACK -
YOU DID A BIT OF SNEAKING YOURSELF, IF I RECALL.
SHE'S MY GIRL.
REALLY? THAT'S NOT WHAT SHE SAID.

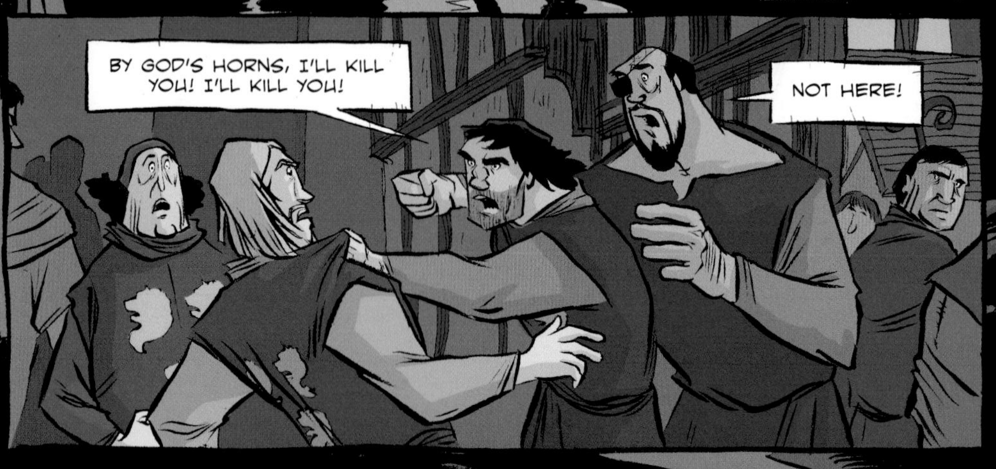
BY GOD'S HORNS, I'LL KILL YOU! I'LL KILL YOU!
NOT HERE!

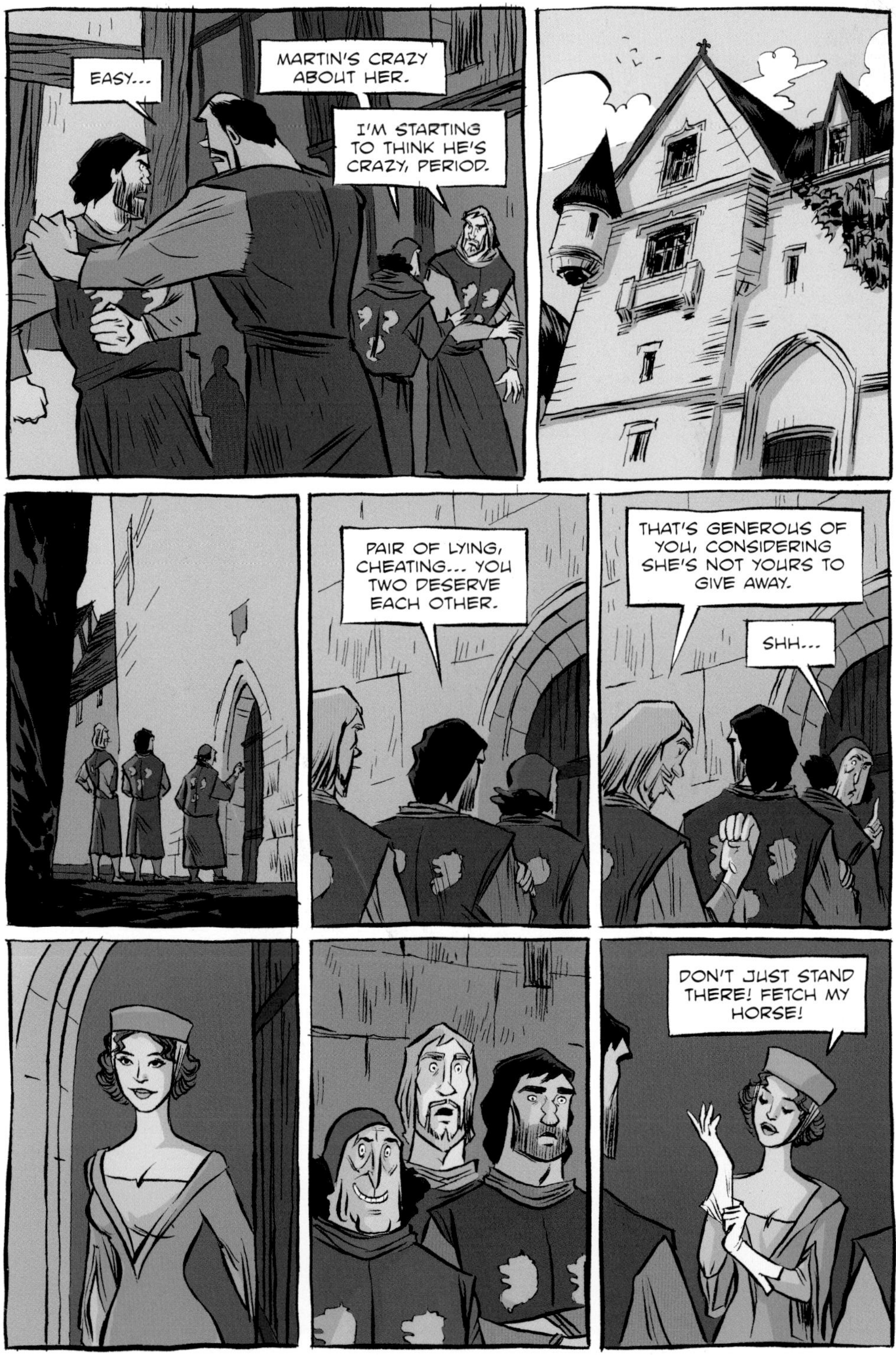
EASY...
MARTIN'S CRAZY ABOUT HER.
I'M STARTING TO THINK HE'S CRAZY, PERIOD.
PAIR OF LYING, CHEATING... YOU TWO DESERVE EACH OTHER.
THAT'S GENEROUS OF YOU, CONSIDERING SHE'S NOT YOURS TO GIVE AWAY.
SHH...
DON'T JUST STAND THERE! FETCH MY HORSE!

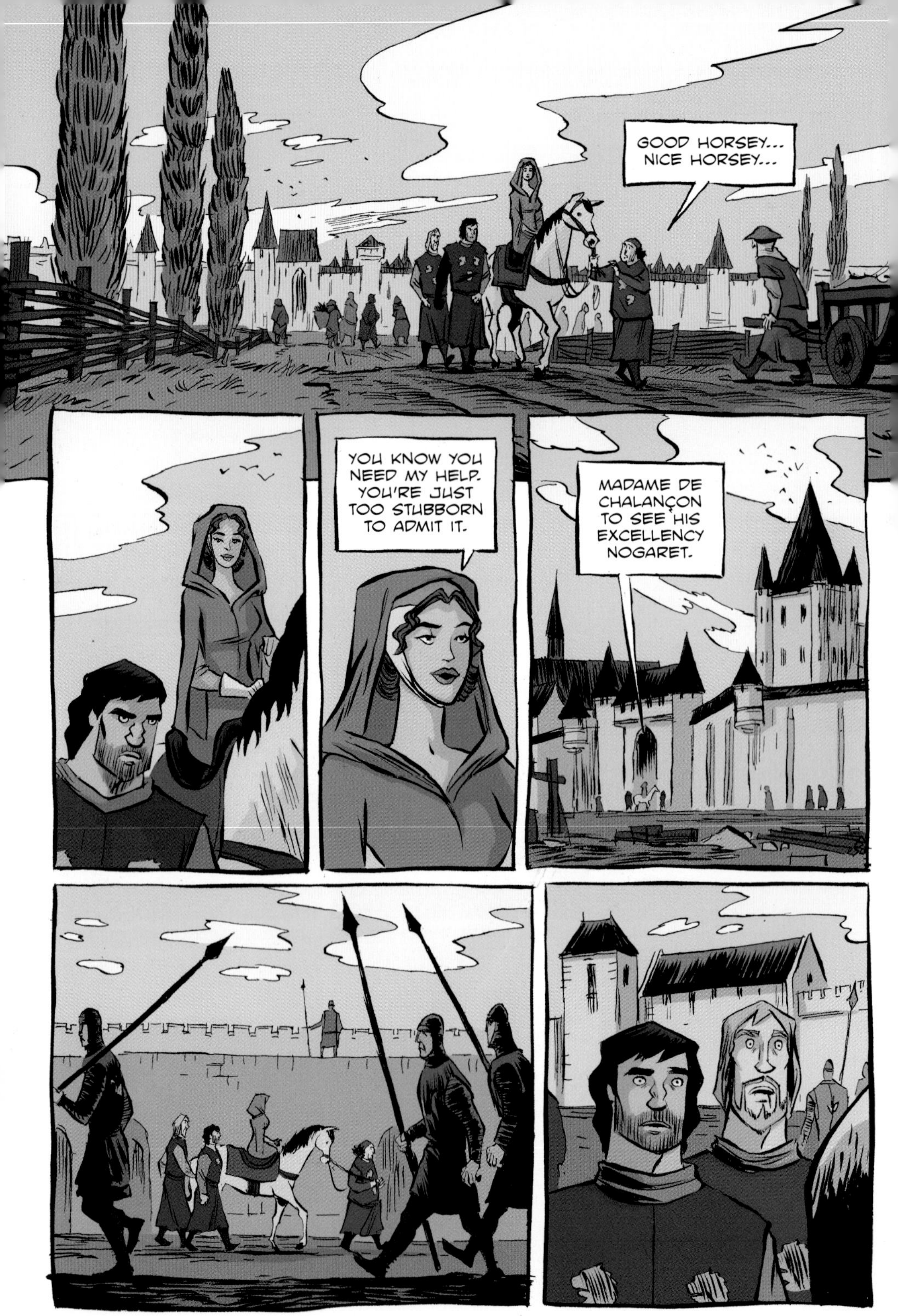
GOOD HORSEY... NICE HORSEY...
YOU KNOW YOU NEED MY HELP. YOU'RE JUST TOO STUBBORN TO ADMIT IT.
MADAME DE CHALANÇON TO SEE HIS EXCELLENCY NOGARET.

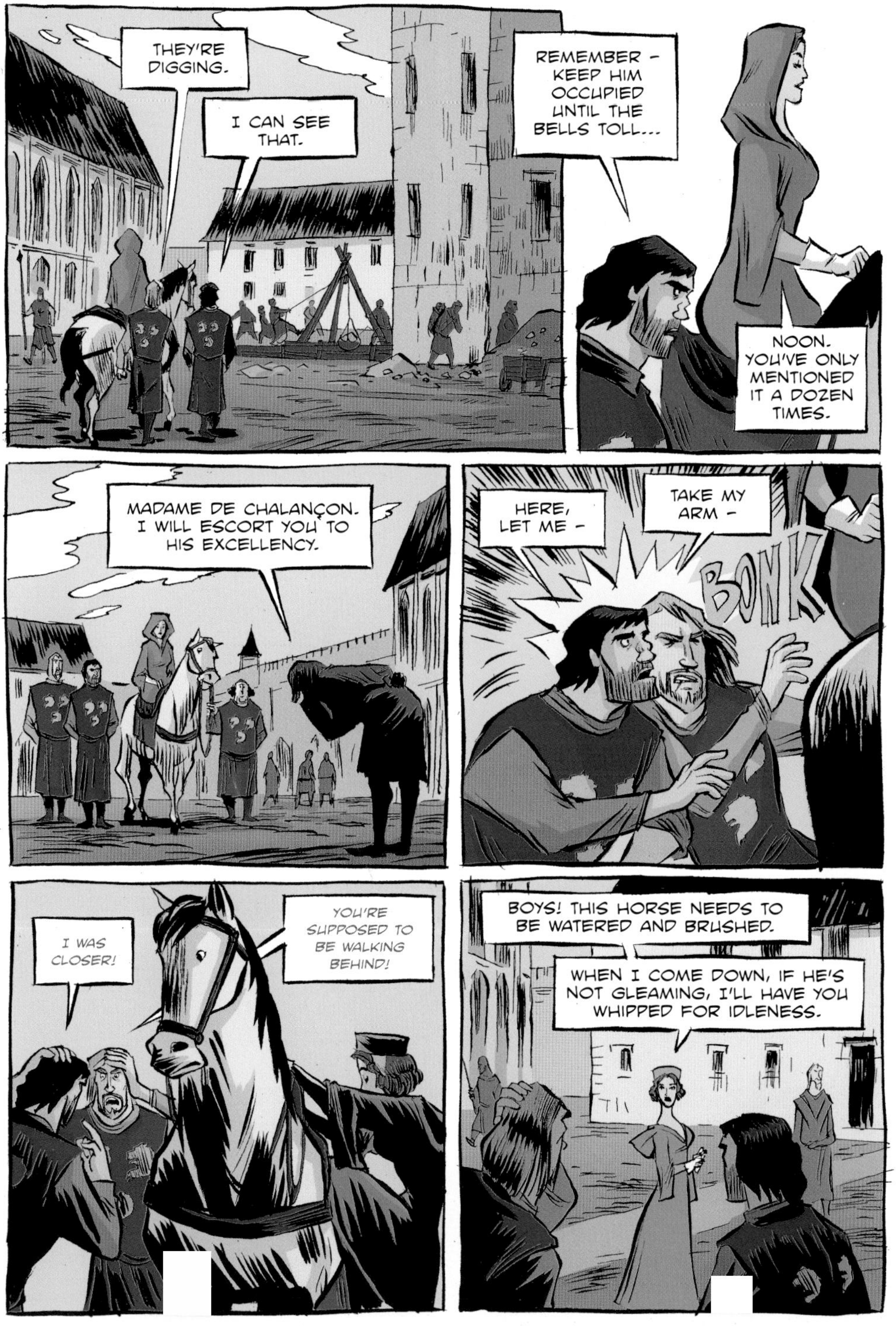
THEY'RE DIGGING.
I CAN SEE THAT.
REMEMBER - KEEP HIM OCCUPIED UNTIL THE BELLS TOLL...
NOON. YOU'VE ONLY MENTIONED IT A DOZEN TIMES.
MADAME DE CHALANÇON. I WILL ESCORT YOU TO HIS EXCELLENCY.
HERE, LET ME -
TAKE MY ARM -
BONK
I WAS CLOSER!
YOU'RE SUPPOSED TO BE WALKING BEHIND!
BOYS! THIS HORSE NEEDS TO BE WATERED AND BRUSHED.
WHEN I COME DOWN, IF HE'S NOT GLEAMING, I'LL HAVE YOU WHIPPED FOR IDLENESS.

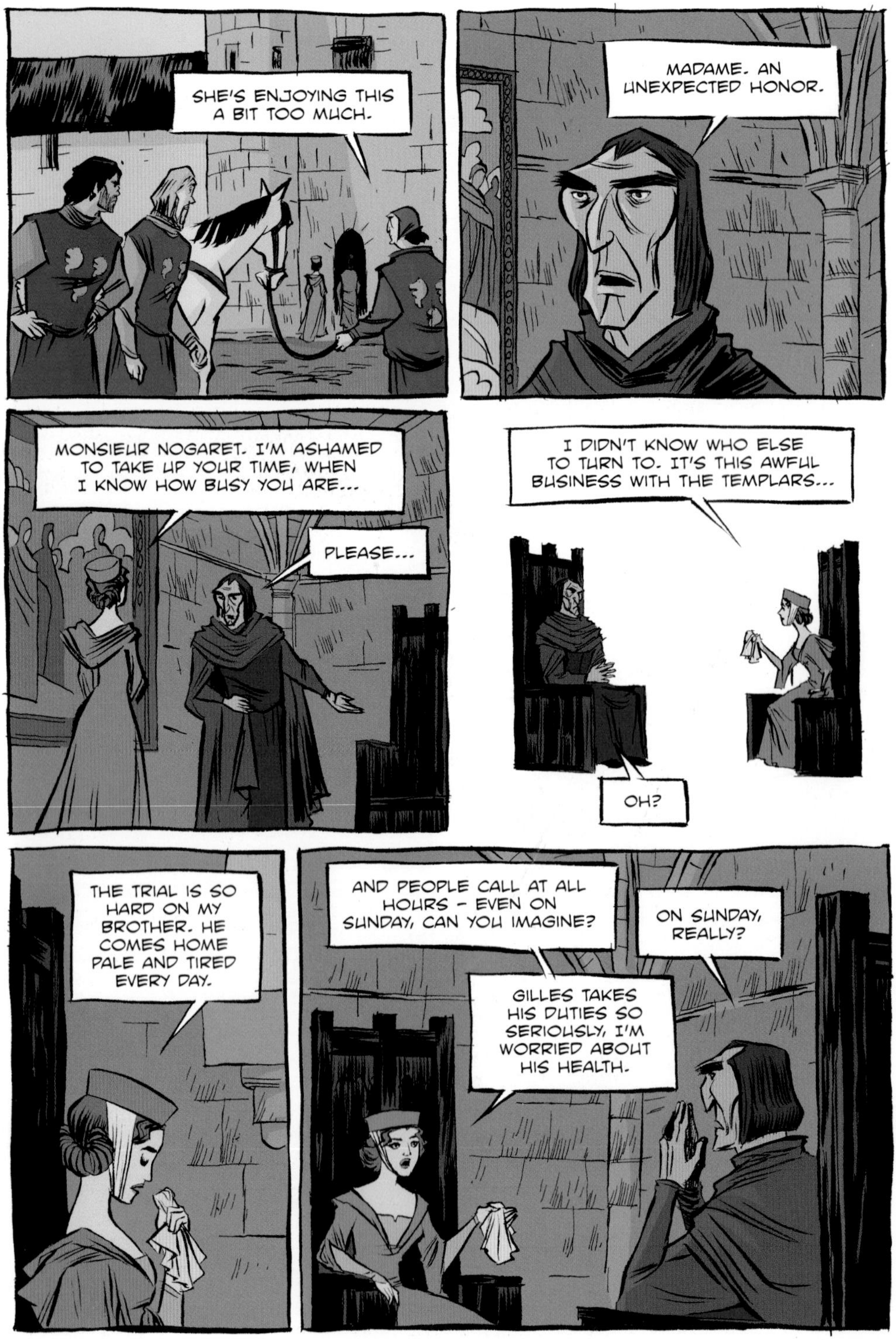
SHE'S ENJOYING THIS A BIT TOO MUCH.
MADAME. AN UNEXPECTED HONOR.
MONSIEUR NOGARET. I'M ASHAMED TO TAKE UP YOUR TIME, WHEN I KNOW HOW BUSY YOU ARE...
PLEASE...
I DIDN'T KNOW WHO ELSE TO TURN TO. IT'S THIS AWFUL BUSINESS WITH THE TEMPLARS...
OH?
THE TRIAL IS SO HARD ON MY BROTHER. HE COMES HOME PALE AND TIRED EVERY DAY.
AND PEOPLE CALL AT ALL HOURS - EVEN ON SUNDAY, CAN YOU IMAGINE?
ON SUNDAY, REALLY?
GILLES TAKES HIS DUTIES SO SERIOUSLY, I'M WORRIED ABOUT HIS HEALTH.

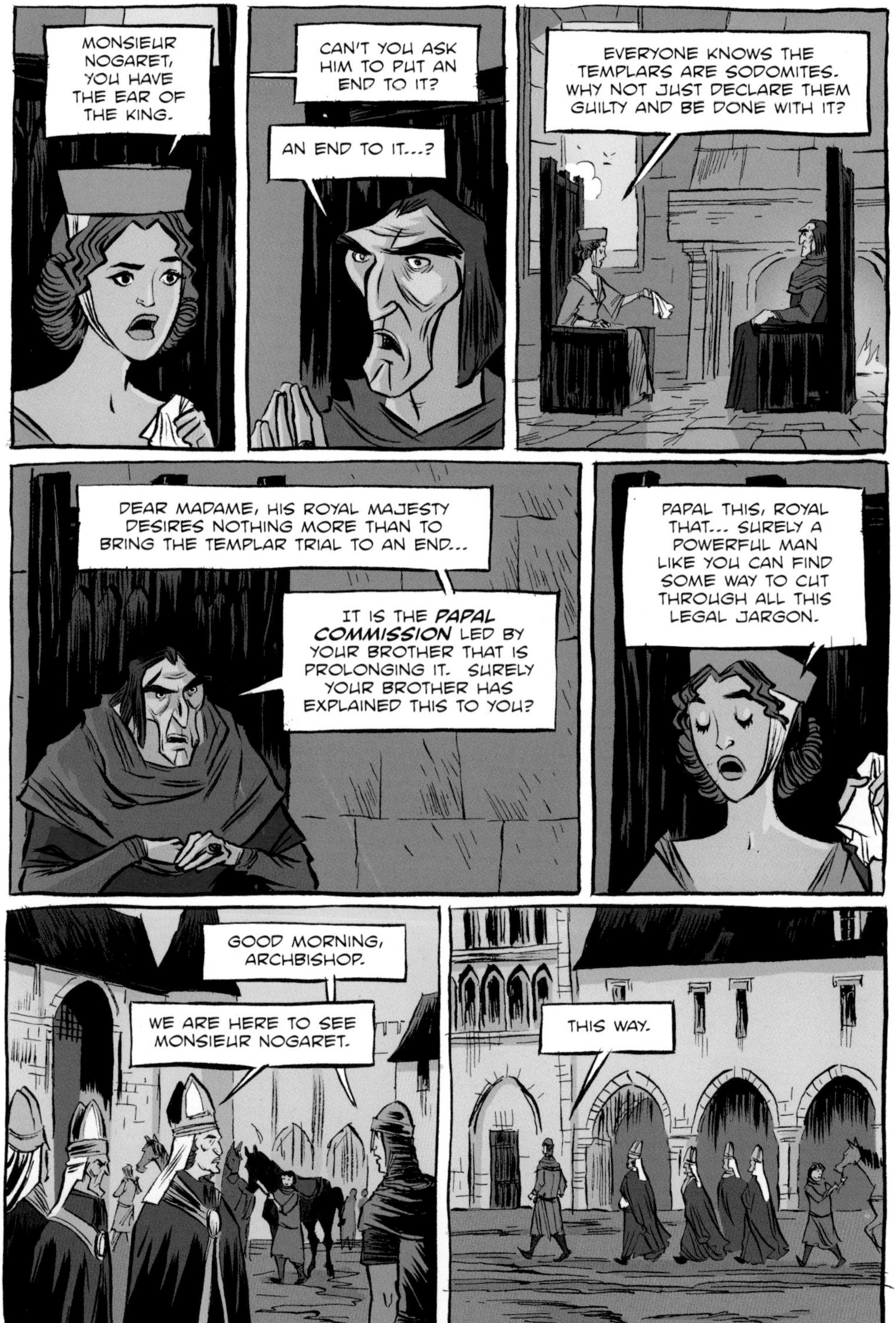
MONSIEUR NOGARET, YOU HAVE THE EAR OF THE KING.
CAN'T YOU ASK HIM TO PUT AN END TO IT?
AN END TO IT...?
EVERYONE KNOWS THE TEMPLARS ARE SODOMITES. WHY NOT JUST DECLARE THEM GUILTY AND BE DONE WITH IT?
DEAR MADAME, HIS ROYAL MAJESTY DESIRES NOTHING MORE THAN TO BRING THE TEMPLAR TRIAL TO AN END...
IT IS THE *PAPAL COMMISSION* LED BY YOUR BROTHER THAT IS PROLONGING IT. SURELY YOUR BROTHER HAS EXPLAINED THIS TO YOU?
PAPAL THIS, ROYAL THAT... SURELY A POWERFUL MAN LIKE YOU CAN FIND SOME WAY TO CUT THROUGH ALL THIS LEGAL JARGON.
GOOD MORNING, ARCHBISHOP.
WE ARE HERE TO SEE MONSIEUR NOGARET.
THIS WAY.

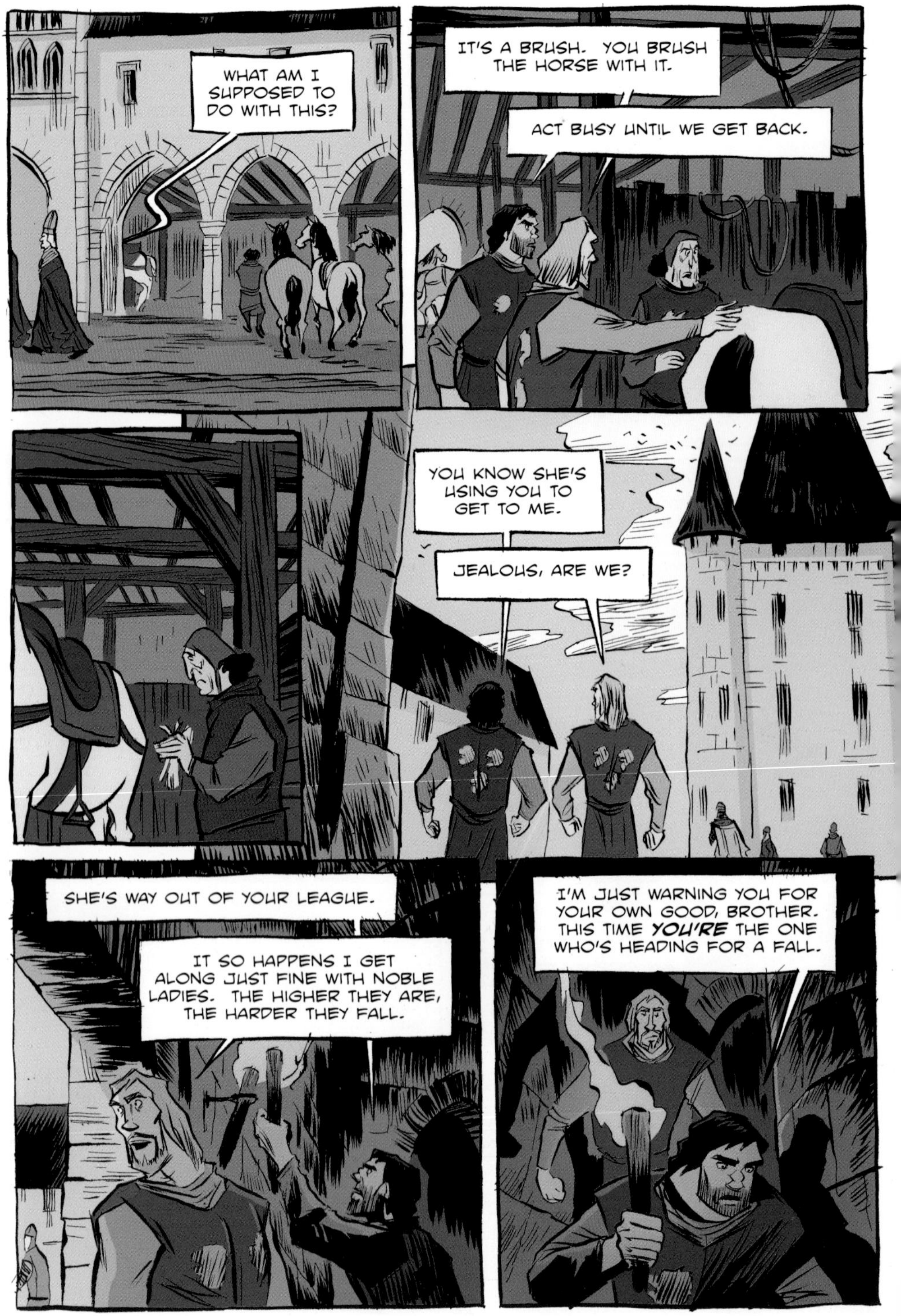
WHAT AM I SUPPOSED TO DO WITH THIS?
IT'S A BRUSH. YOU BRUSH THE HORSE WITH IT.
ACT BUSY UNTIL WE GET BACK.
YOU KNOW SHE'S USING YOU TO GET TO ME.
JEALOUS, ARE WE?
SHE'S WAY OUT OF YOUR LEAGUE.
IT SO HAPPENS I GET ALONG JUST FINE WITH NOBLE LADIES. THE HIGHER THEY ARE, THE HARDER THEY FALL.
I'M JUST WARNING YOU FOR YOUR OWN GOOD, BROTHER. THIS TIME *YOU'RE* THE ONE WHO'S HEADING FOR A FALL.

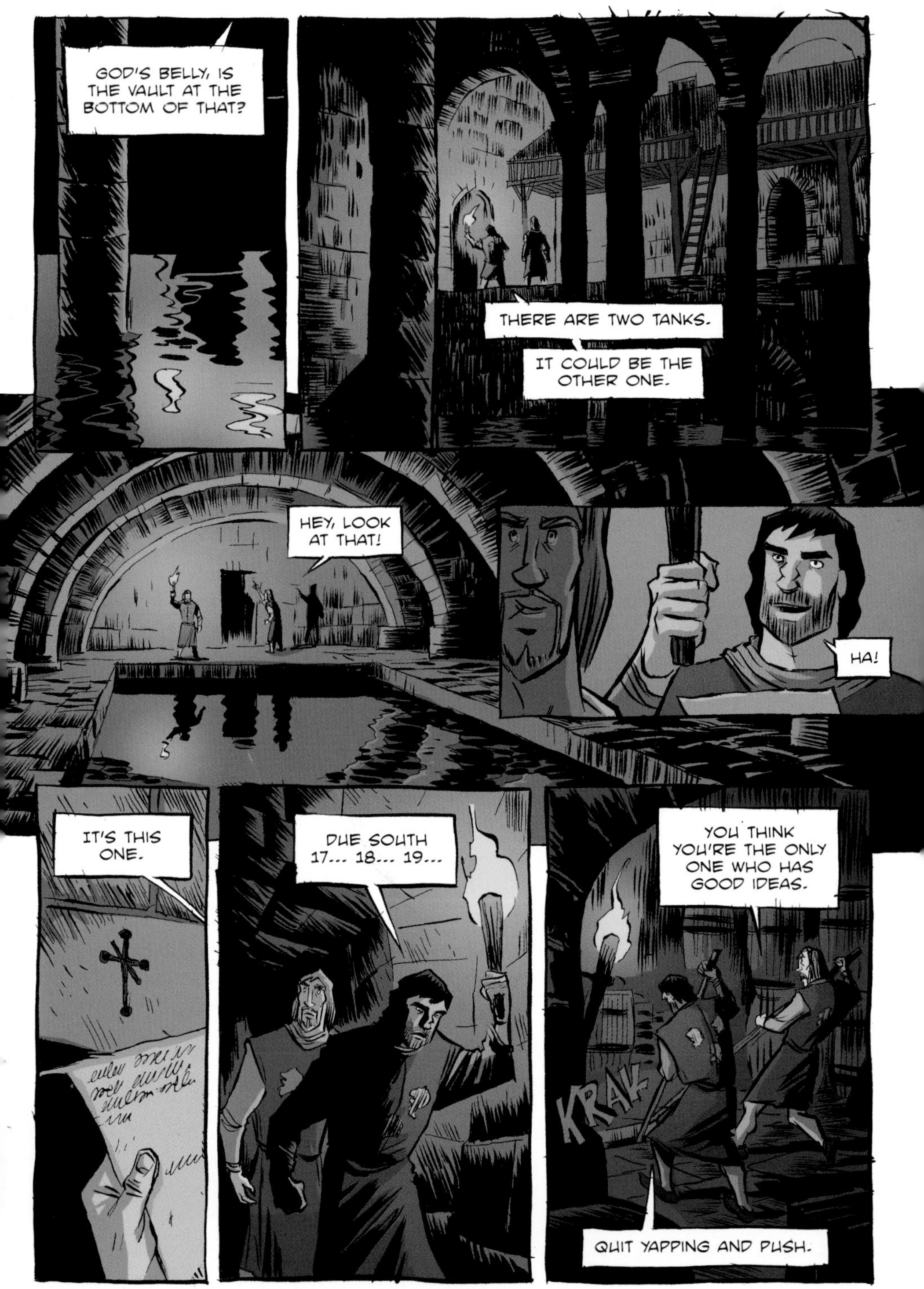
GOD'S BELLY, IS THE VAULT AT THE BOTTOM OF THAT?
THERE ARE TWO TANKS.
IT COULD BE THE OTHER ONE.
HEY, LOOK AT THAT!
HA!
IT'S THIS ONE.
DUE SOUTH 17... 18... 19...
YOU THINK YOU'RE THE ONLY ONE WHO HAS GOOD IDEAS.
KRAK
QUIT YAPPING AND PUSH.

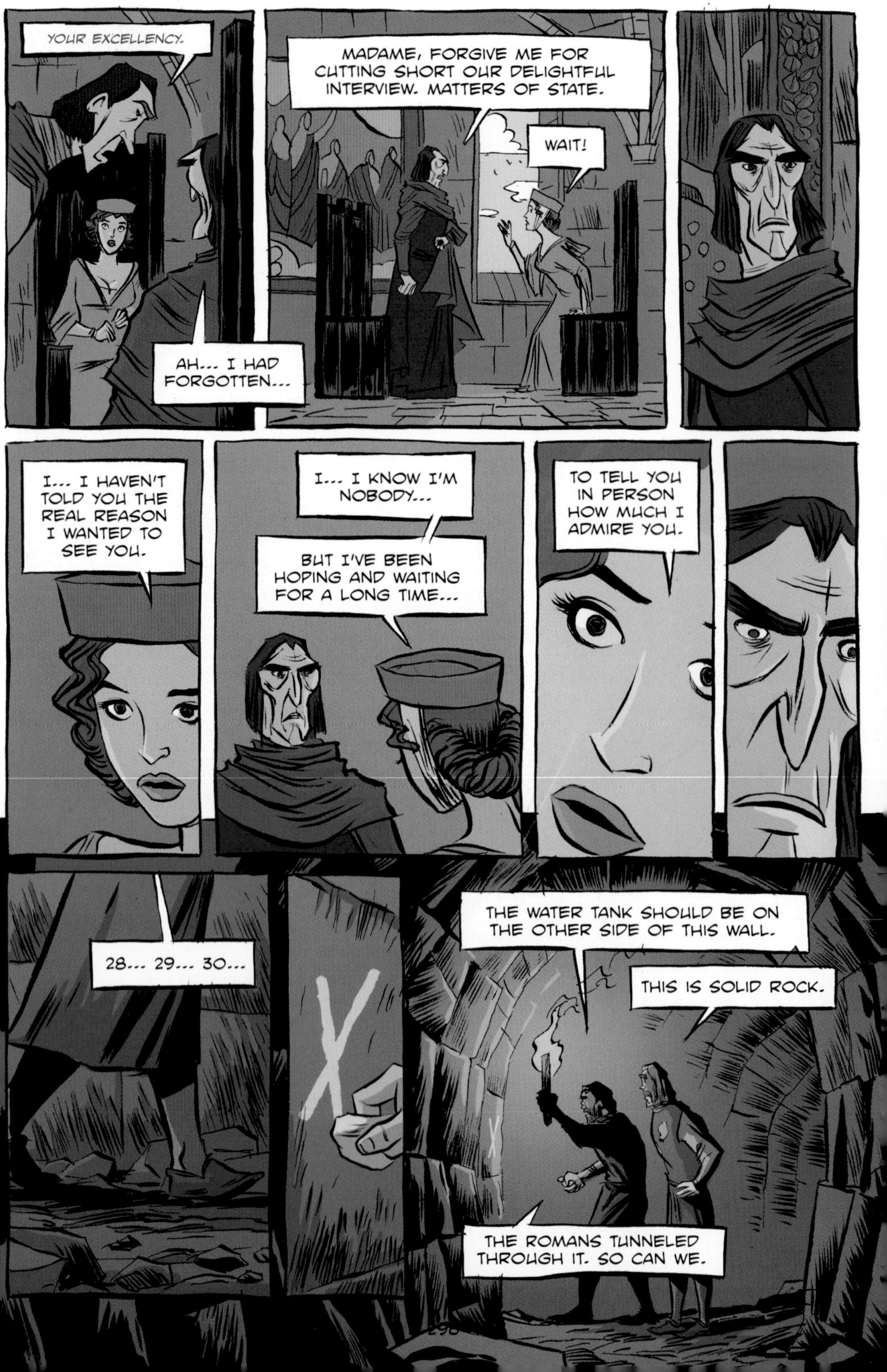
YOUR EXCELLENCY.
AH... I HAD FORGOTTEN...
MADAME, FORGIVE ME FOR CUTTING SHORT OUR DELIGHTFUL INTERVIEW. MATTERS OF STATE.
WAIT!
I... I HAVEN'T TOLD YOU THE REAL REASON I WANTED TO SEE YOU.
I... I KNOW I'M NOBODY...
BUT I'VE BEEN HOPING AND WAITING FOR A LONG TIME...
TO TELL YOU IN PERSON HOW MUCH I ADMIRE YOU.
28... 29... 30...
THE WATER TANK SHOULD BE ON THE OTHER SIDE OF THIS WALL.
THIS IS SOLID ROCK.
THE ROMANS TUNNELED THROUGH IT. SO CAN WE.

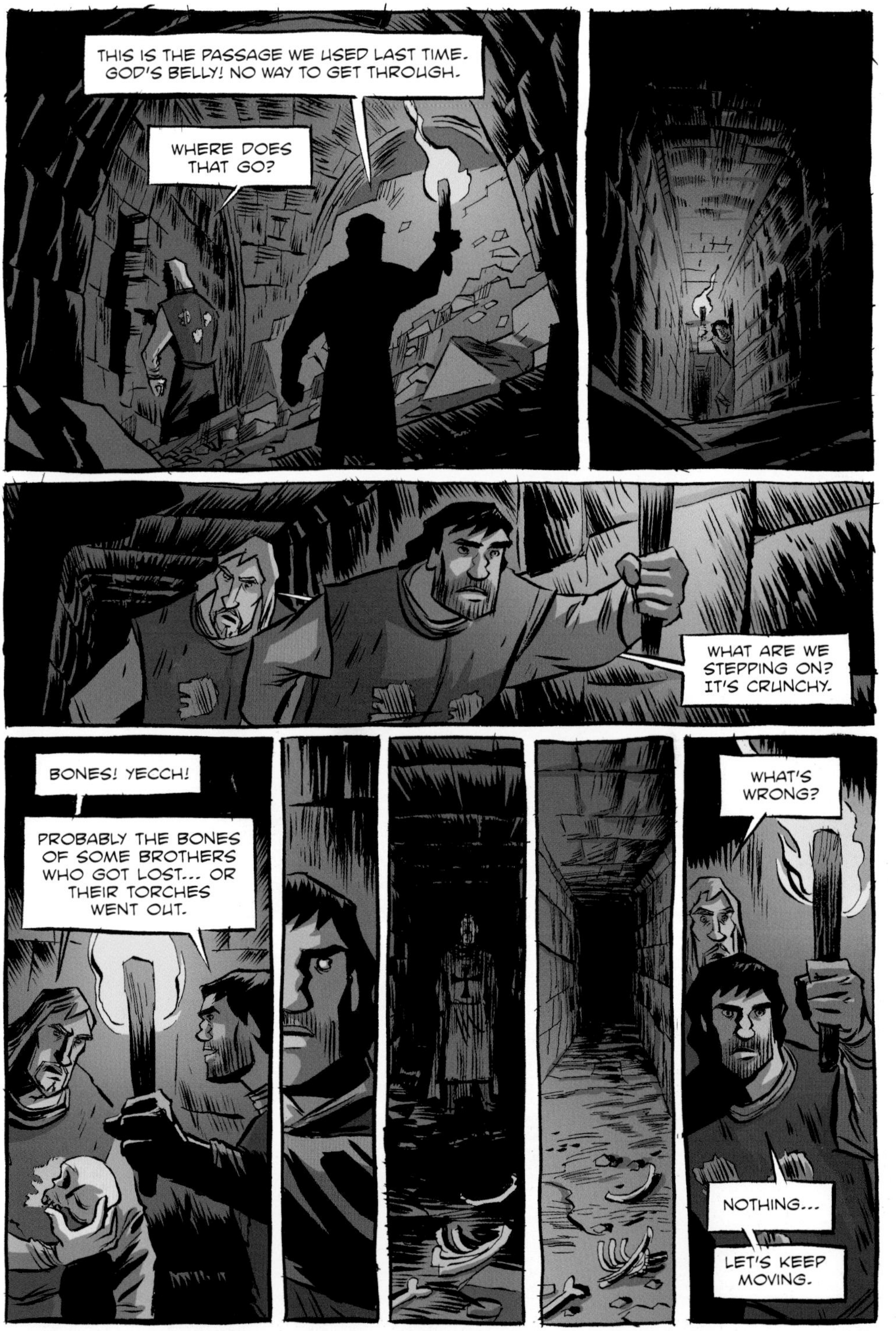

THIS IS THE PASSAGE WE USED LAST TIME. GOD'S BELLY! NO WAY TO GET THROUGH.
WHERE DOES THAT GO?
WHAT ARE WE STEPPING ON? IT'S CRUNCHY.
BONES! YECCH!
PROBABLY THE BONES OF SOME BROTHERS WHO GOT LOST... OR THEIR TORCHES WENT OUT.
WHAT'S WRONG?
NOTHING...
LET'S KEEP MOVING.

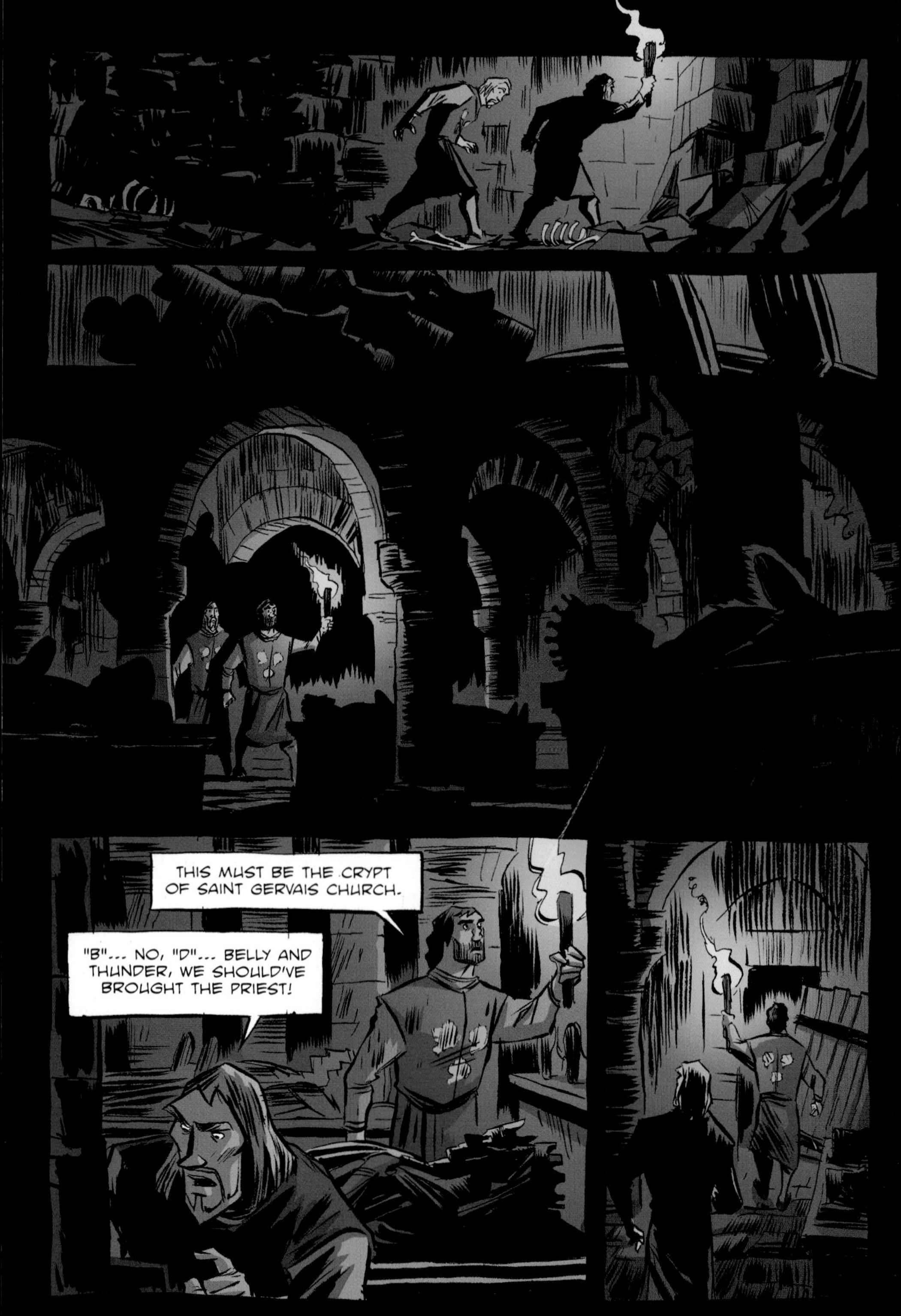
THIS MUST BE THE CRYPT OF SAINT GERVAIS CHURCH.
"B"... NO, "D"... BELLY AND THUNDER, WE SHOULD'VE BROUGHT THE PRIEST!

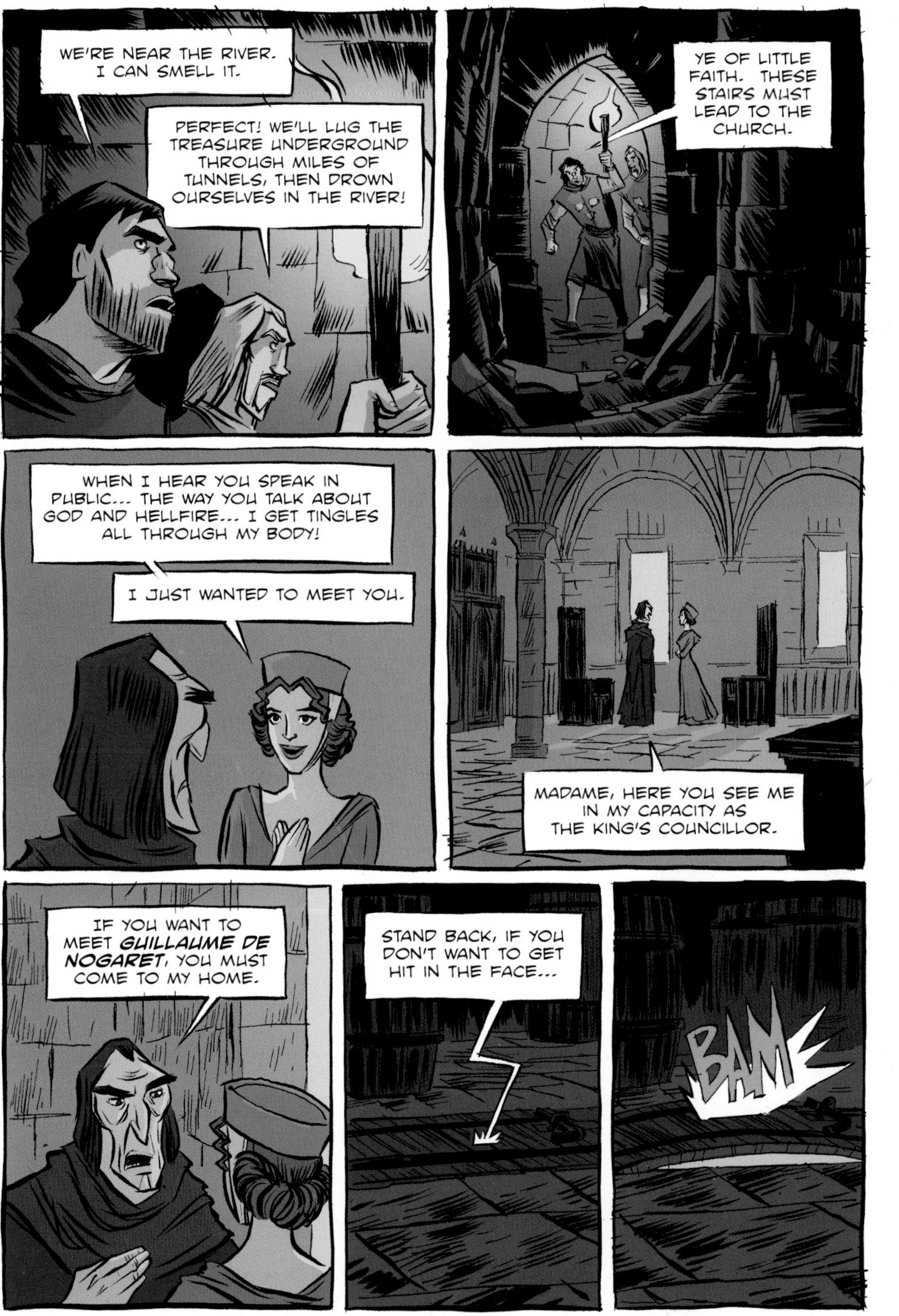
WE'RE NEAR THE RIVER. I CAN SMELL IT.
PERFECT! WE'LL LUG THE TREASURE UNDERGROUND THROUGH MILES OF TUNNELS, THEN DROWN OURSELVES IN THE RIVER!
YE OF LITTLE FAITH. THESE STAIRS MUST LEAD TO THE CHURCH.
WHEN I HEAR YOU SPEAK IN PUBLIC... THE WAY YOU TALK ABOUT GOD AND HELLFIRE... I GET TINGLES ALL THROUGH MY BODY!
I JUST WANTED TO MEET YOU.
MADAME, HERE YOU SEE ME IN MY CAPACITY AS THE KING'S COUNCILLOR.
IF YOU WANT TO MEET ***GUILLAUME DE NOGARET***, YOU MUST COME TO MY HOME.
STAND BACK, IF YOU DON'T WANT TO GET HIT IN THE FACE...
BAM

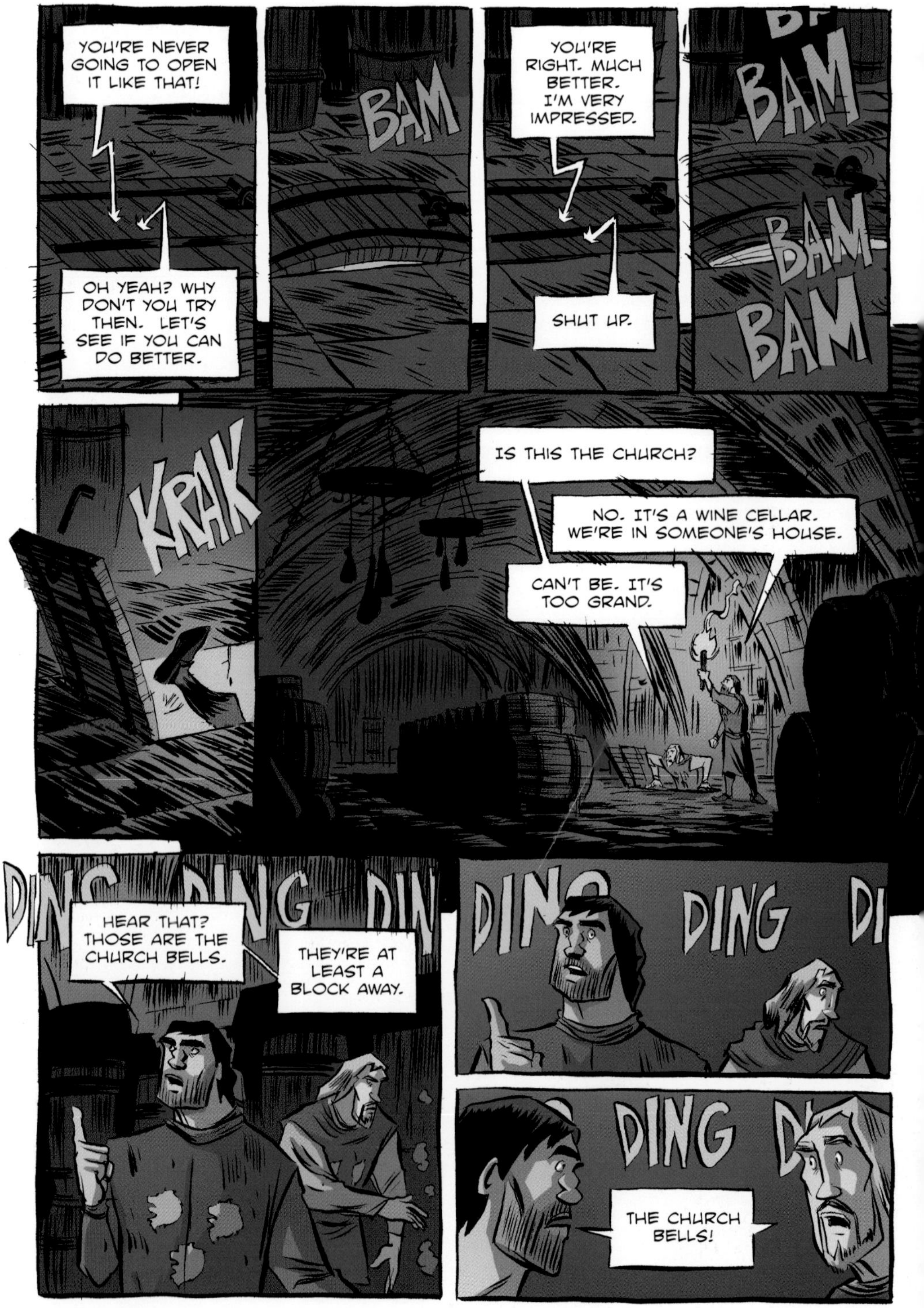
YOU'RE NEVER GOING TO OPEN IT LIKE THAT!
OH YEAH? WHY DON'T YOU TRY THEN. LET'S SEE IF YOU CAN DO BETTER.
BAM
YOU'RE RIGHT. MUCH BETTER. I'M VERY IMPRESSED.
SHUT UP.
BAM
BAM
BAM
KRAK
IS THIS THE CHURCH?
NO. IT'S A WINE CELLAR. WE'RE IN SOMEONE'S HOUSE.
CAN'T BE. IT'S TOO GRAND.
DING
HEAR THAT? THOSE ARE THE CHURCH BELLS.
THEY'RE AT LEAST A BLOCK AWAY.
DING
DING
THE CHURCH BELLS!

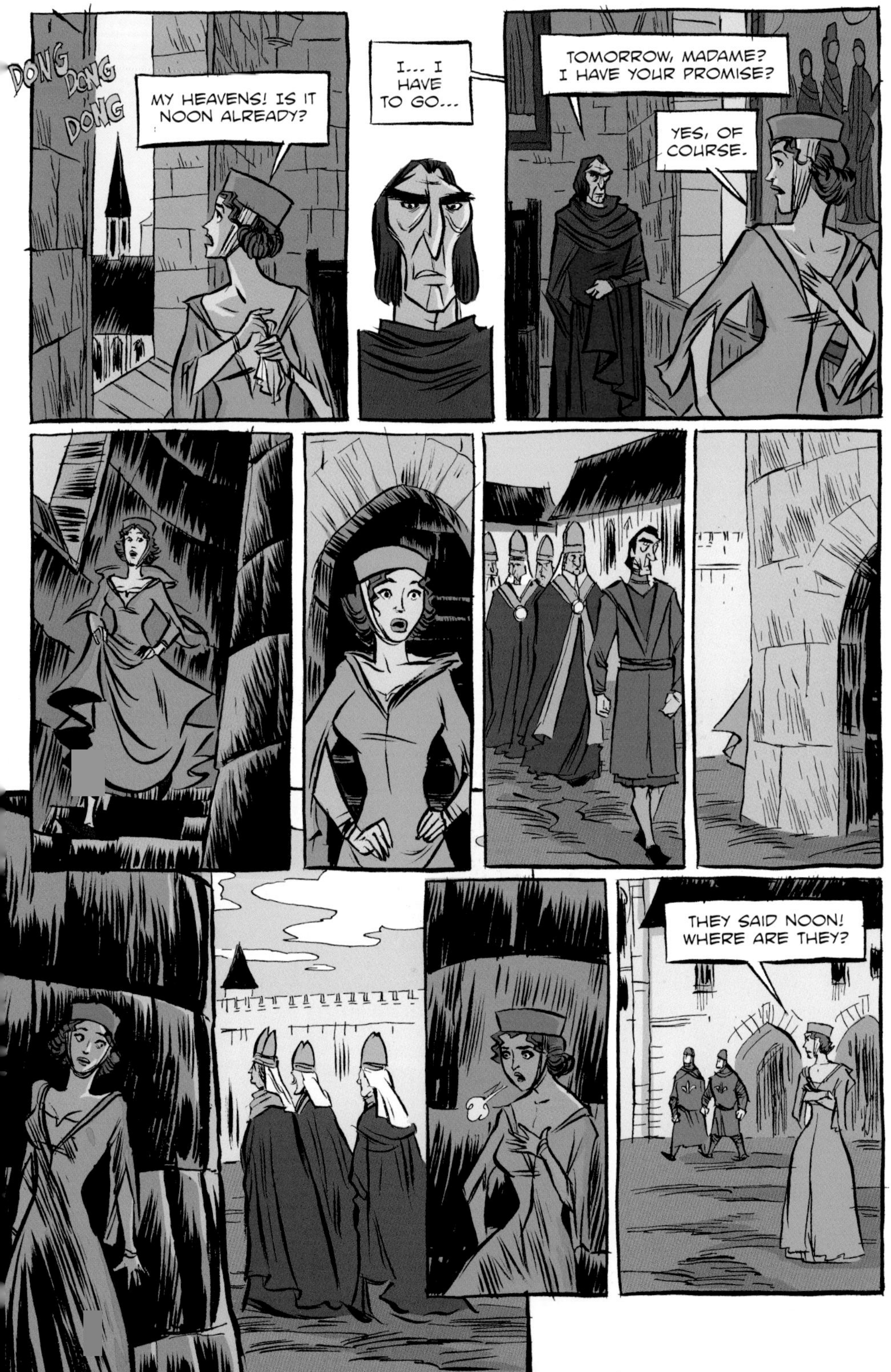
DONG DONG DONG
MY HEAVENS! IS IT NOON ALREADY?
I... I HAVE TO GO...
TOMORROW, MADAME? I HAVE YOUR PROMISE?
YES, OF COURSE.
THEY SAID NOON! WHERE ARE THEY?

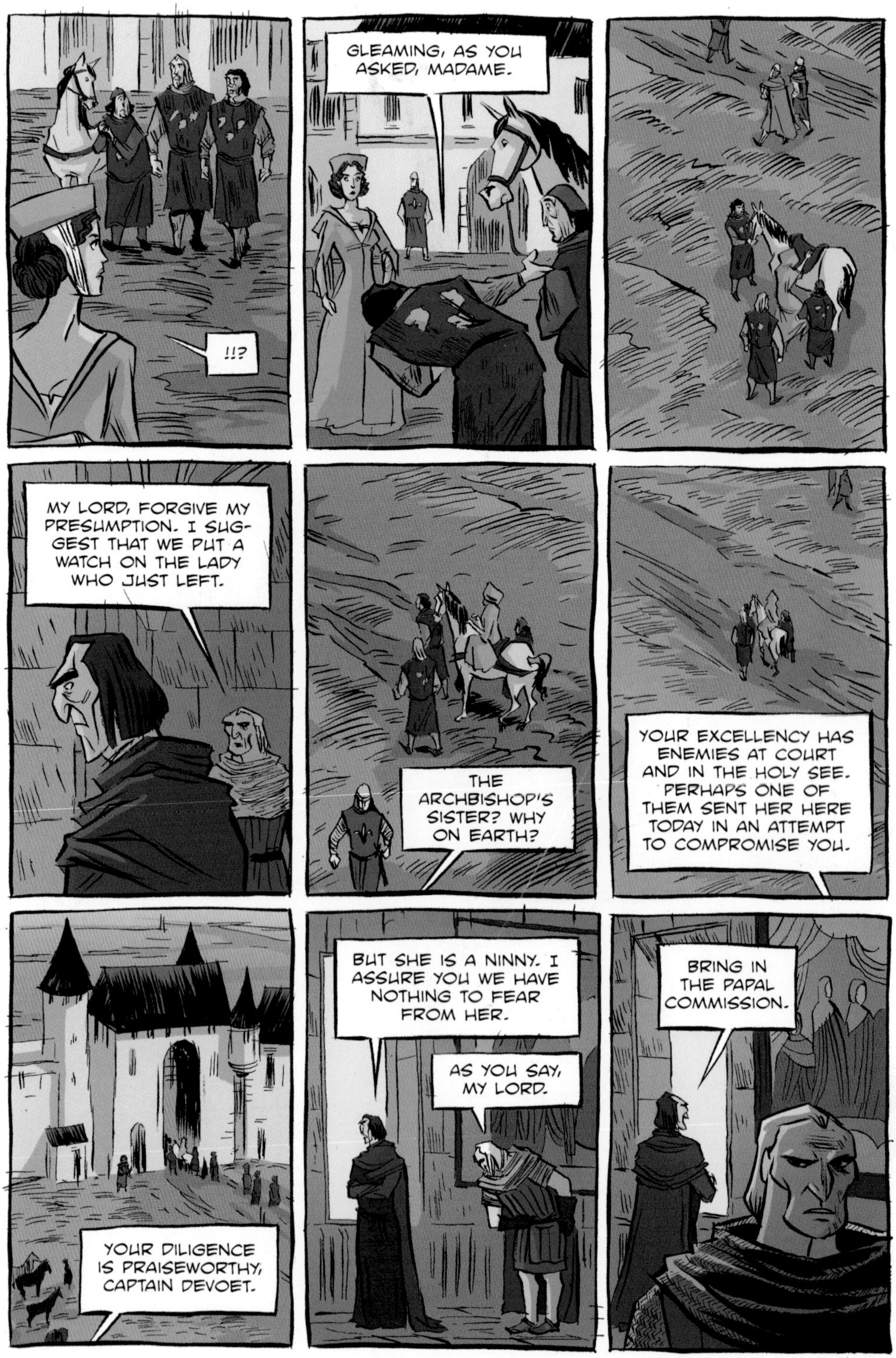
!!?
GLEAMING, AS YOU ASKED, MADAME.
MY LORD, FORGIVE MY PRESUMPTION. I SUGGEST THAT WE PUT A WATCH ON THE LADY WHO JUST LEFT.
THE ARCHBISHOP'S SISTER? WHY ON EARTH?
YOUR EXCELLENCY HAS ENEMIES AT COURT AND IN THE HOLY SEE. PERHAPS ONE OF THEM SENT HER HERE TODAY IN AN ATTEMPT TO COMPROMISE YOU.
YOUR DILIGENCE IS PRAISEWORTHY, CAPTAIN DEVOET.
BUT SHE IS A NINNY. I ASSURE YOU WE HAVE NOTHING TO FEAR FROM HER.
AS YOU SAY, MY LORD.
BRING IN THE PAPAL COMMISSION.

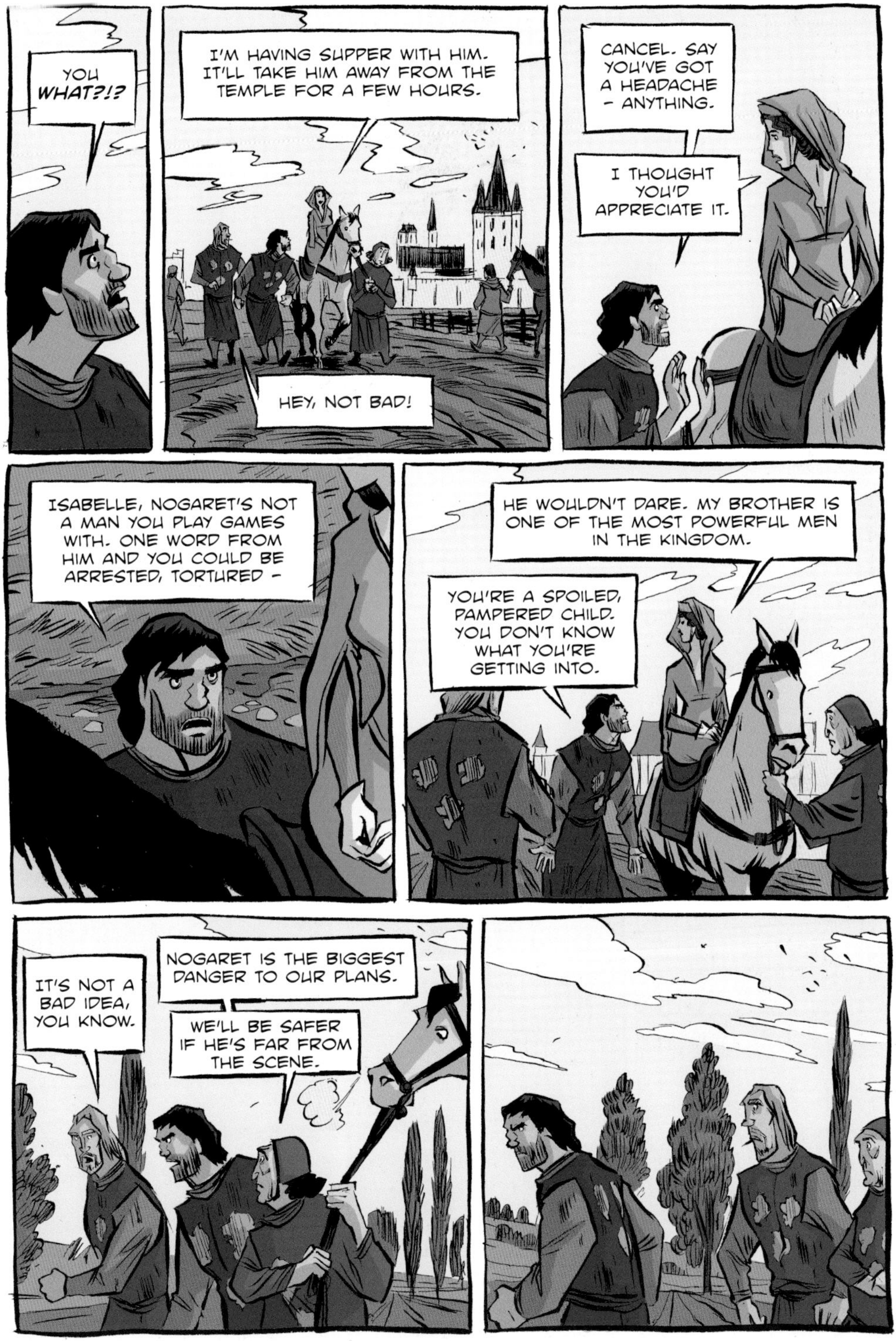
YOU *WHAT?!?*
I'M HAVING SUPPER WITH HIM. IT'LL TAKE HIM AWAY FROM THE TEMPLE FOR A FEW HOURS.
HEY, NOT BAD!
CANCEL. SAY YOU'VE GOT A HEADACHE – ANYTHING.
I THOUGHT YOU'D APPRECIATE IT.
ISABELLE, NOGARET'S NOT A MAN YOU PLAY GAMES WITH. ONE WORD FROM HIM AND YOU COULD BE ARRESTED, TORTURED –
HE WOULDN'T DARE. MY BROTHER IS ONE OF THE MOST POWERFUL MEN IN THE KINGDOM.
YOU'RE A SPOILED, PAMPERED CHILD. YOU DON'T KNOW WHAT YOU'RE GETTING INTO.
IT'S NOT A BAD IDEA, YOU KNOW.
NOGARET IS THE BIGGEST DANGER TO OUR PLANS.
WE'LL BE SAFER IF HE'S FAR FROM THE SCENE.

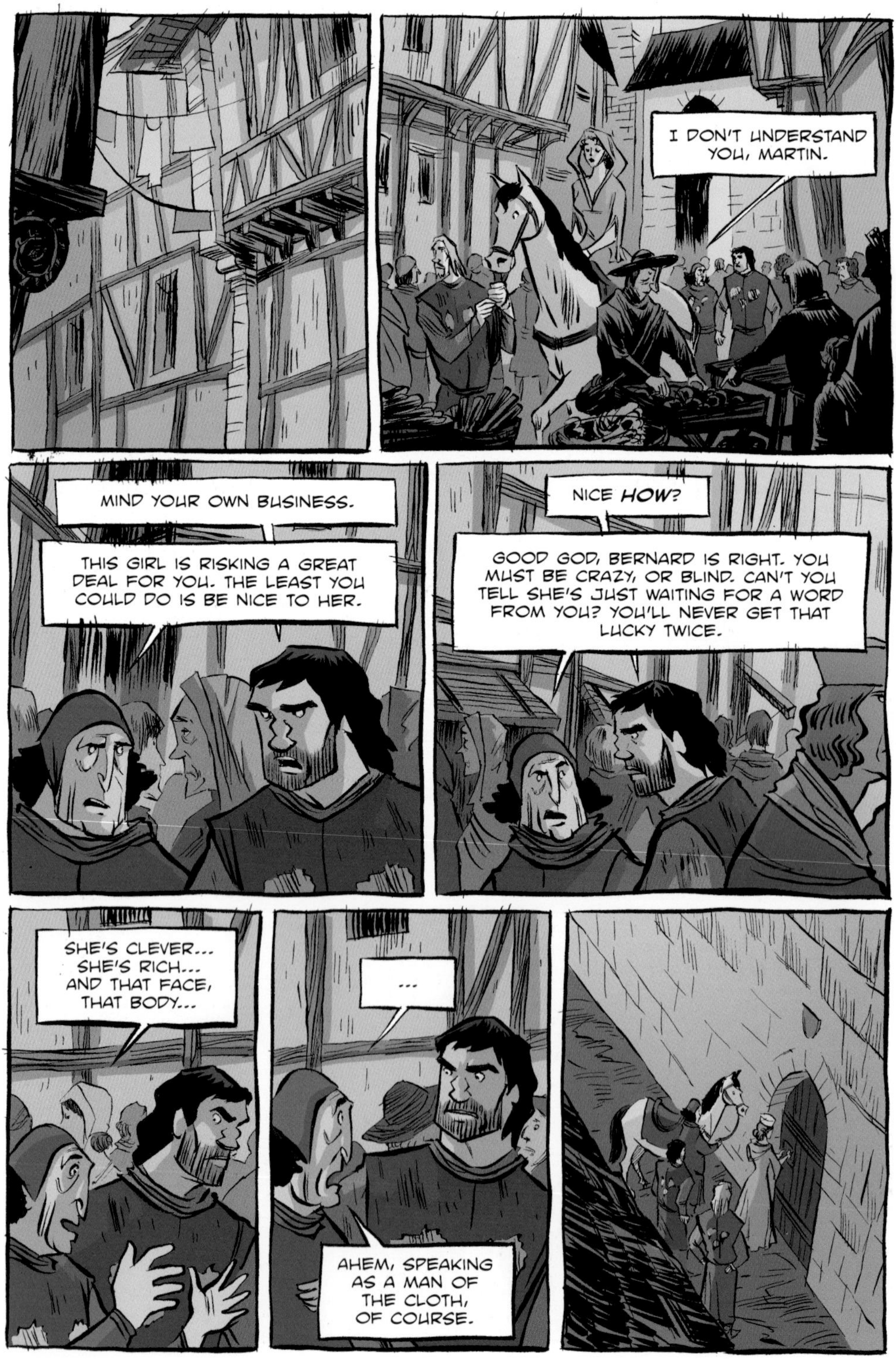
I DON'T UNDERSTAND YOU, MARTIN.
MIND YOUR OWN BUSINESS.
THIS GIRL IS RISKING A GREAT DEAL FOR YOU. THE LEAST YOU COULD DO IS BE NICE TO HER.
NICE *HOW*?
GOOD GOD, BERNARD IS RIGHT. YOU MUST BE CRAZY, OR BLIND. CAN'T YOU TELL SHE'S JUST WAITING FOR A WORD FROM YOU? YOU'LL NEVER GET THAT LUCKY TWICE.
SHE'S CLEVER... SHE'S RICH... AND THAT FACE, THAT BODY...
...
AHEM, SPEAKING AS A MAN OF THE CLOTH, OF COURSE.

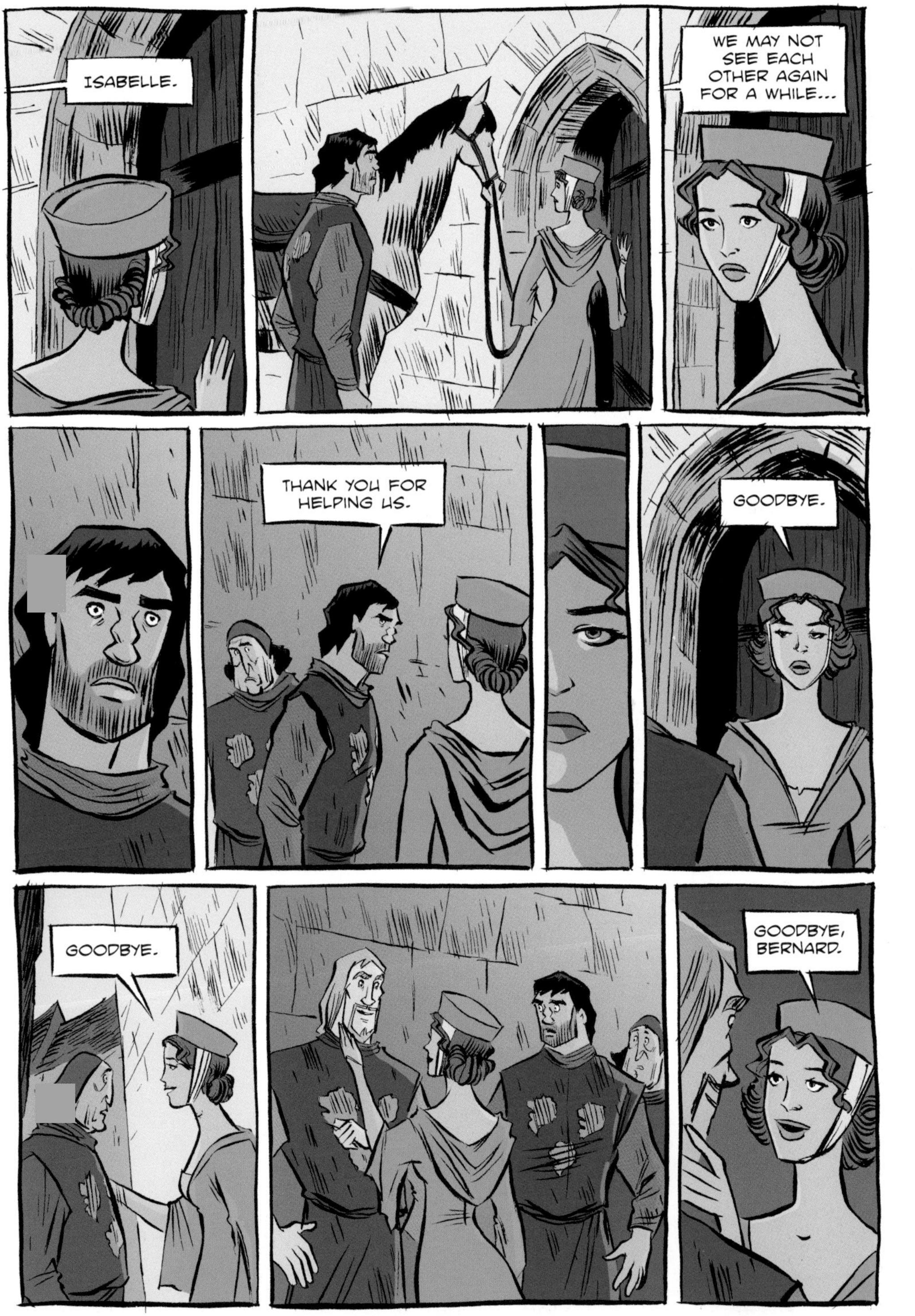
ISABELLE.
WE MAY NOT SEE EACH OTHER AGAIN FOR A WHILE...
THANK YOU FOR HELPING US.
GOODBYE.
GOODBYE.
GOODBYE, BERNARD.

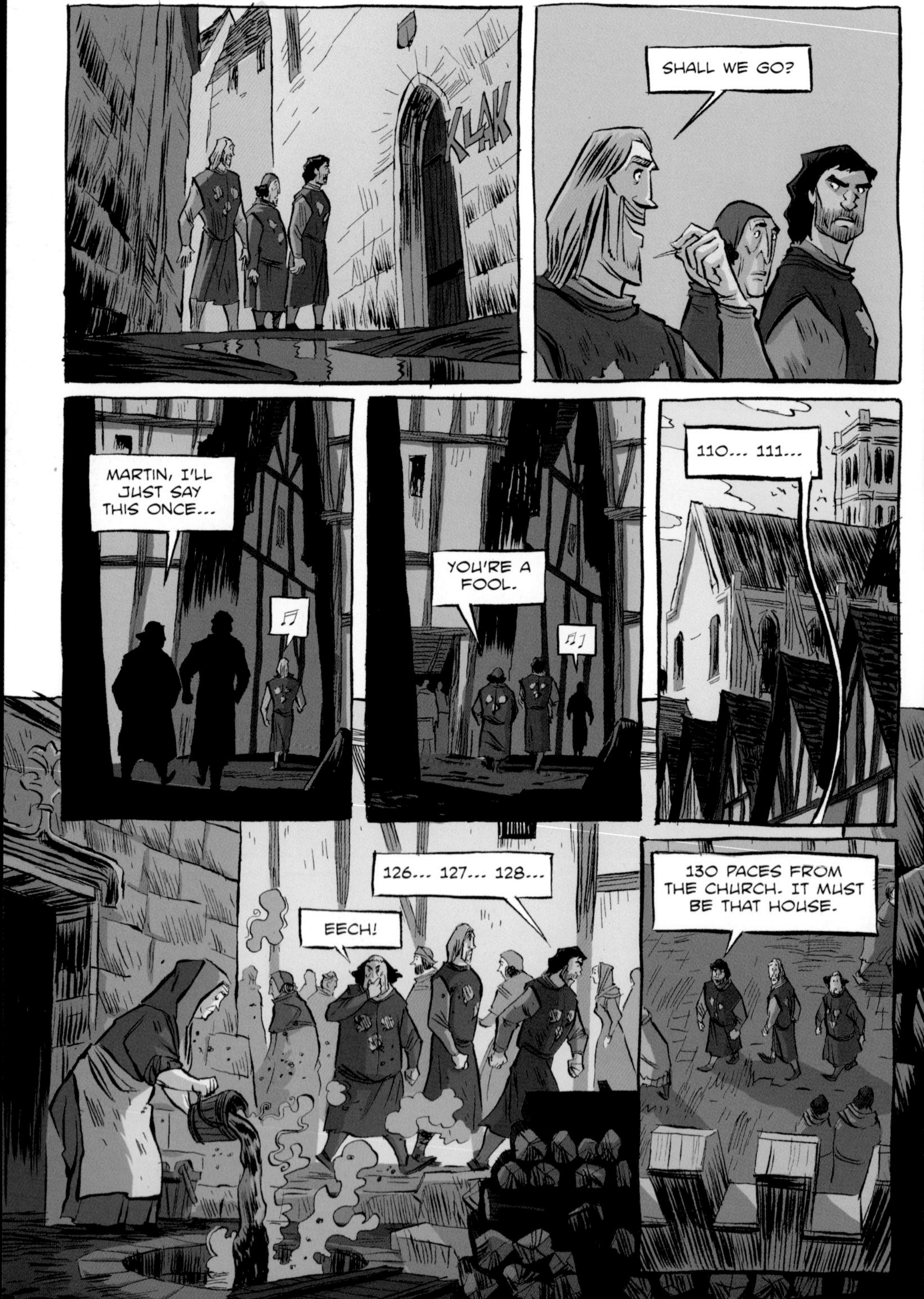
KLAK
SHALL WE GO?
MARTIN, I'LL JUST SAY THIS ONCE...
YOU'RE A FOOL.
110... 111...
126... 127... 128...
EECH!
130 PACES FROM THE CHURCH. IT MUST BE THAT HOUSE.

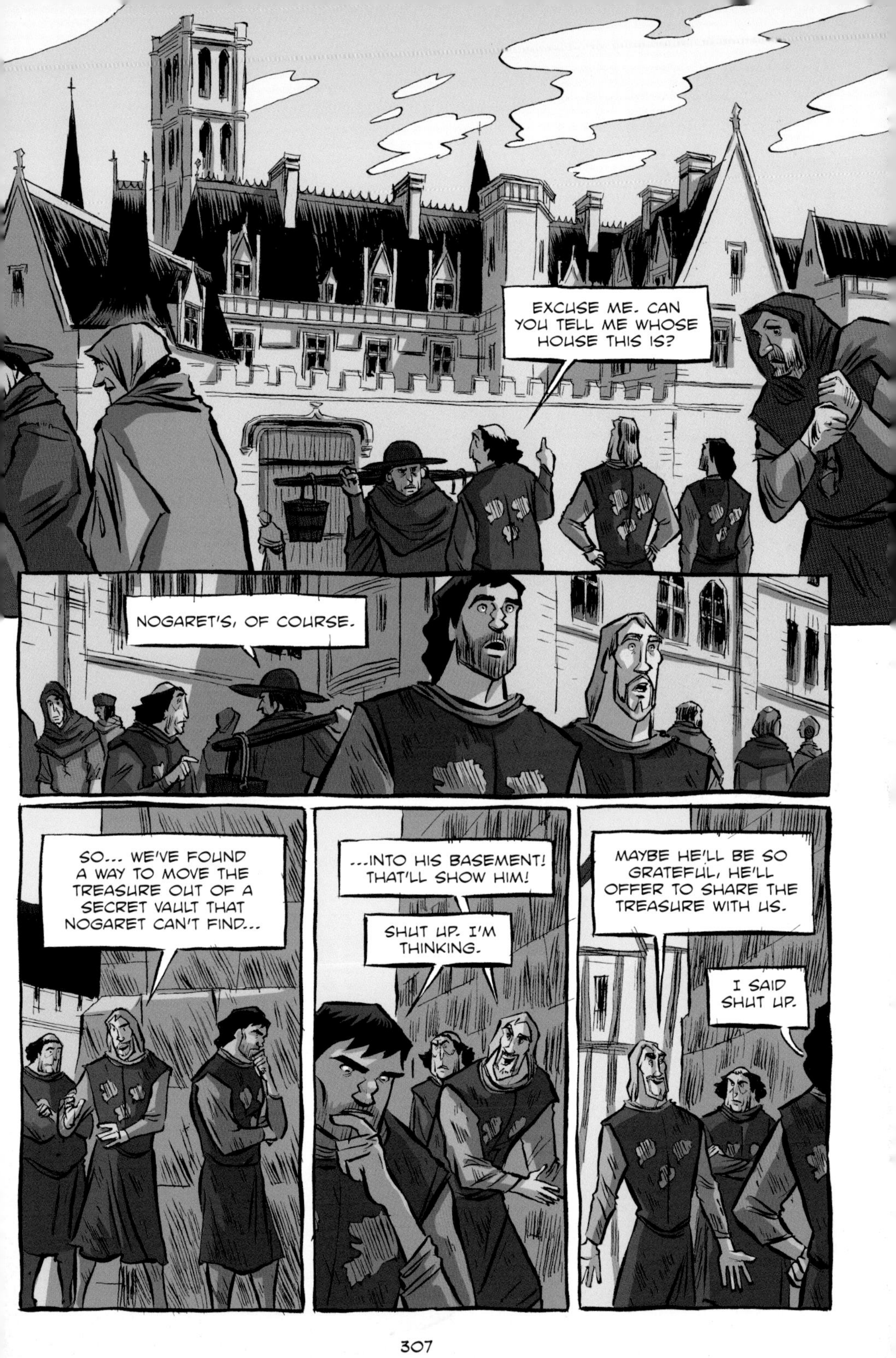
EXCUSE ME. CAN YOU TELL ME WHOSE HOUSE THIS IS?
NOGARET'S, OF COURSE.
SO... WE'VE FOUND A WAY TO MOVE THE TREASURE OUT OF A SECRET VAULT THAT NOGARET CAN'T FIND...
...INTO HIS BASEMENT! THAT'LL SHOW HIM!
SHUT UP. I'M THINKING.
MAYBE HE'LL BE SO GRATEFUL, HE'LL OFFER TO SHARE THE TREASURE WITH US.
I SAID SHUT UP.

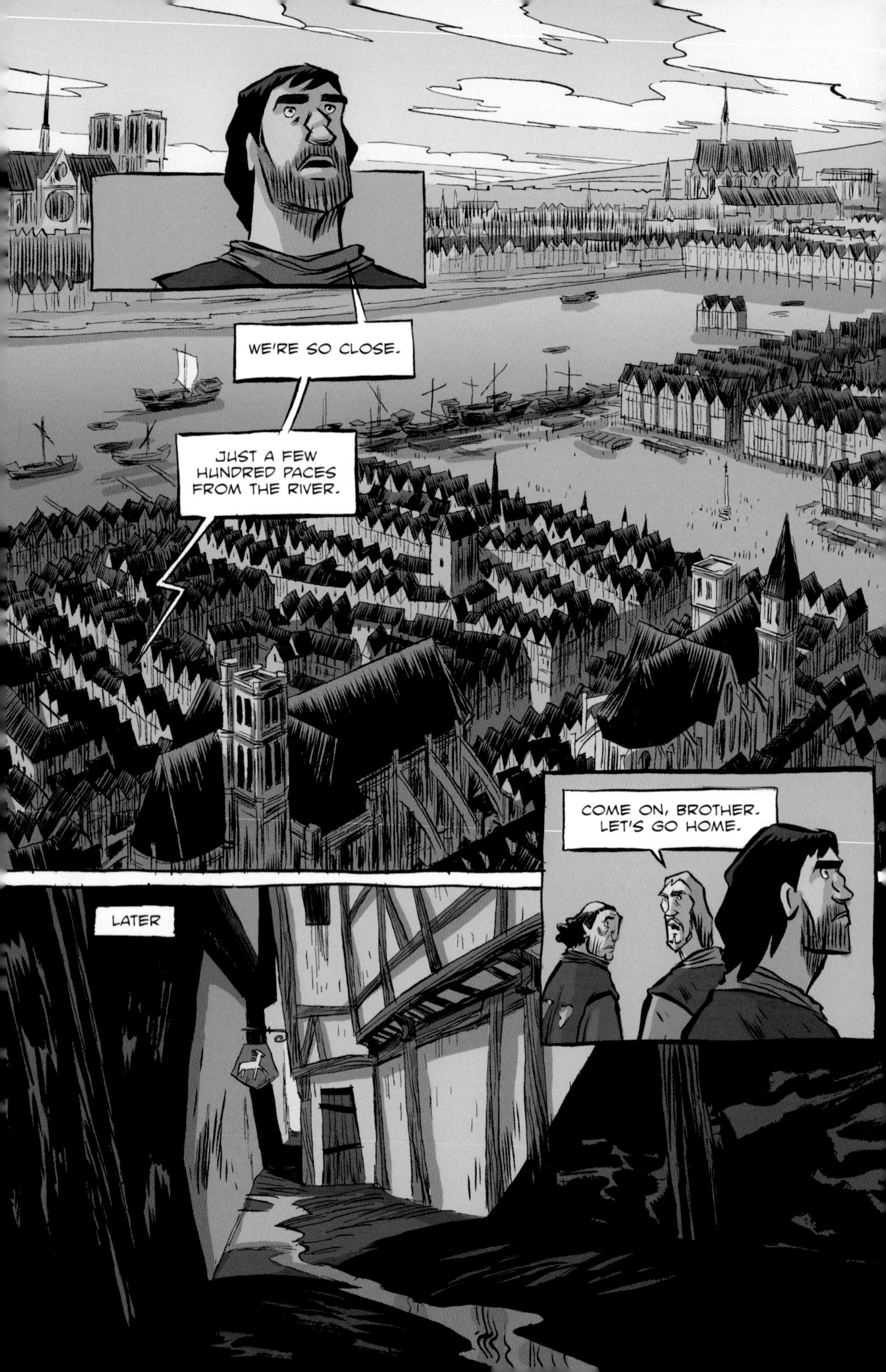
WE'RE SO CLOSE.
JUST A FEW HUNDRED PACES FROM THE RIVER.
COME ON, BROTHER. LET'S GO HOME.
LATER

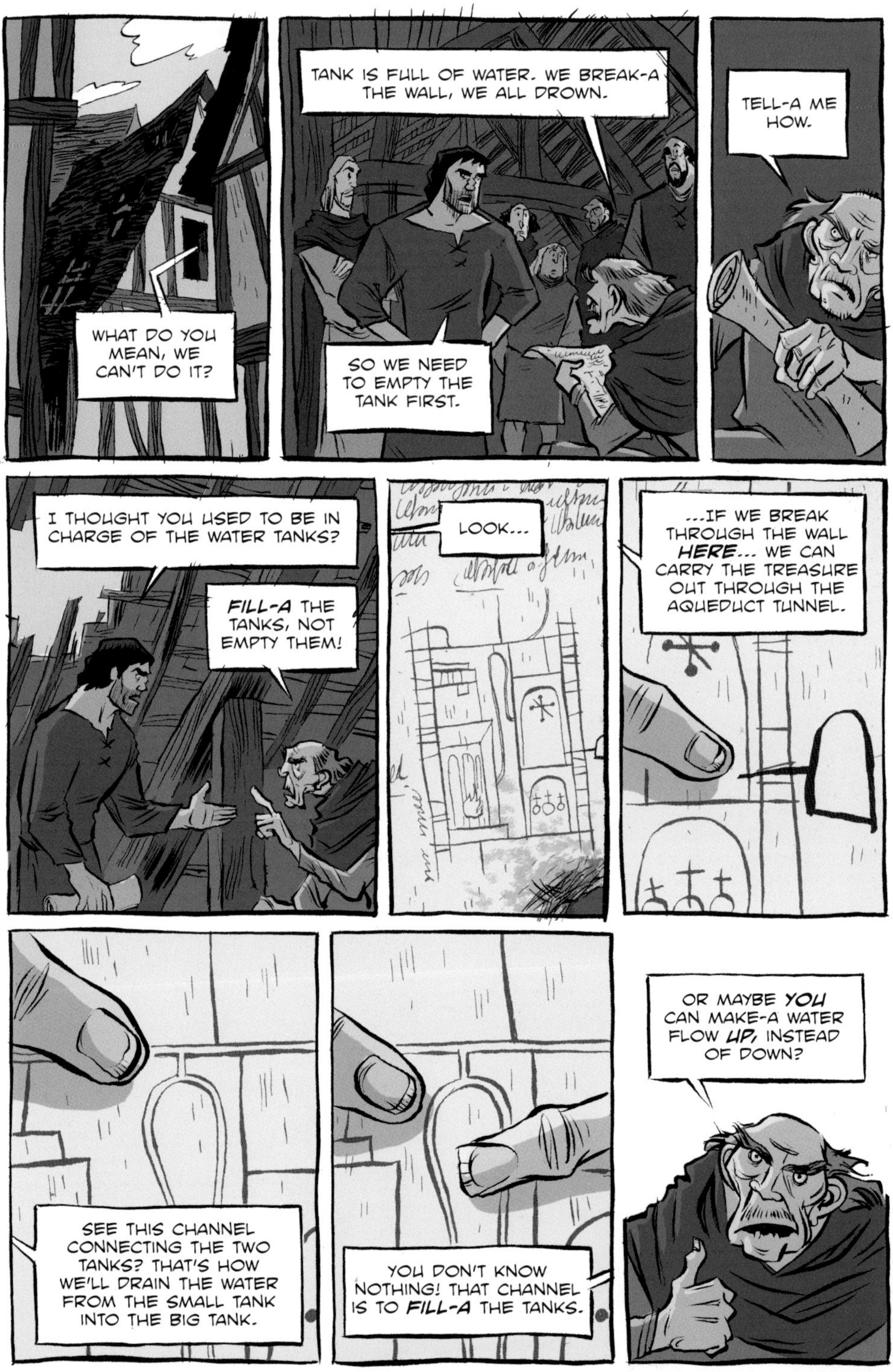
WHAT DO YOU MEAN, WE CAN'T DO IT?
TANK IS FULL OF WATER. WE BREAK-A THE WALL, WE ALL DROWN.
SO WE NEED TO EMPTY THE TANK FIRST.
TELL-A ME HOW.
I THOUGHT YOU USED TO BE IN CHARGE OF THE WATER TANKS?
FILL-A THE TANKS, NOT EMPTY THEM!
LOOK...
...IF WE BREAK THROUGH THE WALL HERE... WE CAN CARRY THE TREASURE OUT THROUGH THE AQUEDUCT TUNNEL.
SEE THIS CHANNEL CONNECTING THE TWO TANKS? THAT'S HOW WE'LL DRAIN THE WATER FROM THE SMALL TANK INTO THE BIG TANK.
YOU DON'T KNOW NOTHING! THAT CHANNEL IS TO FILL-A THE TANKS.
OR MAYBE YOU CAN MAKE-A WATER FLOW UP, INSTEAD OF DOWN?

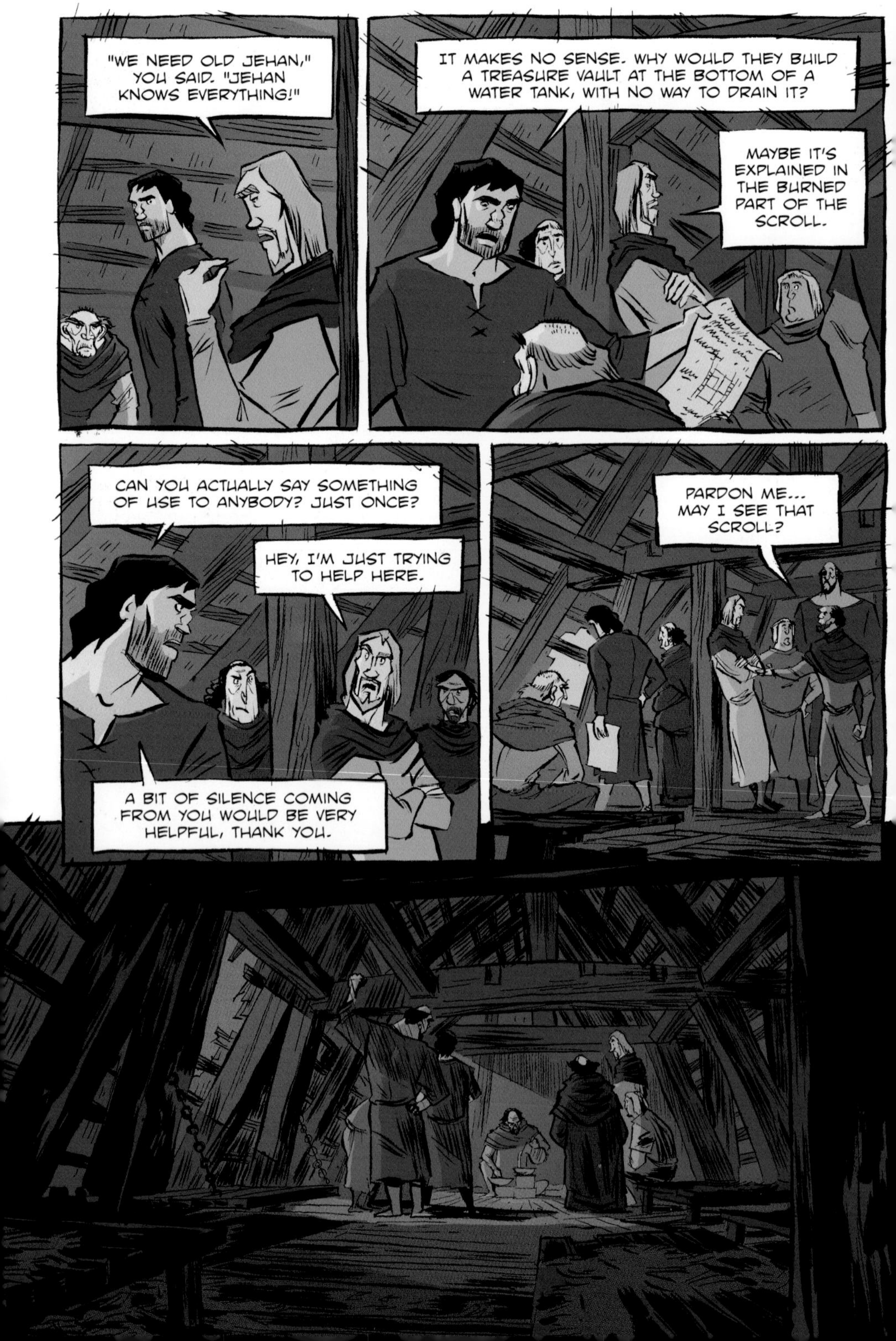
"WE NEED OLD JEHAN," YOU SAID. "JEHAN KNOWS EVERYTHING!"
IT MAKES NO SENSE. WHY WOULD THEY BUILD A TREASURE VAULT AT THE BOTTOM OF A WATER TANK, WITH NO WAY TO DRAIN IT?
MAYBE IT'S EXPLAINED IN THE BURNED PART OF THE SCROLL.
CAN YOU ACTUALLY SAY SOMETHING OF USE TO ANYBODY? JUST ONCE?
HEY, I'M JUST TRYING TO HELP HERE.
A BIT OF SILENCE COMING FROM YOU WOULD BE VERY HELPFUL, THANK YOU.
PARDON ME... MAY I SEE THAT SCROLL?

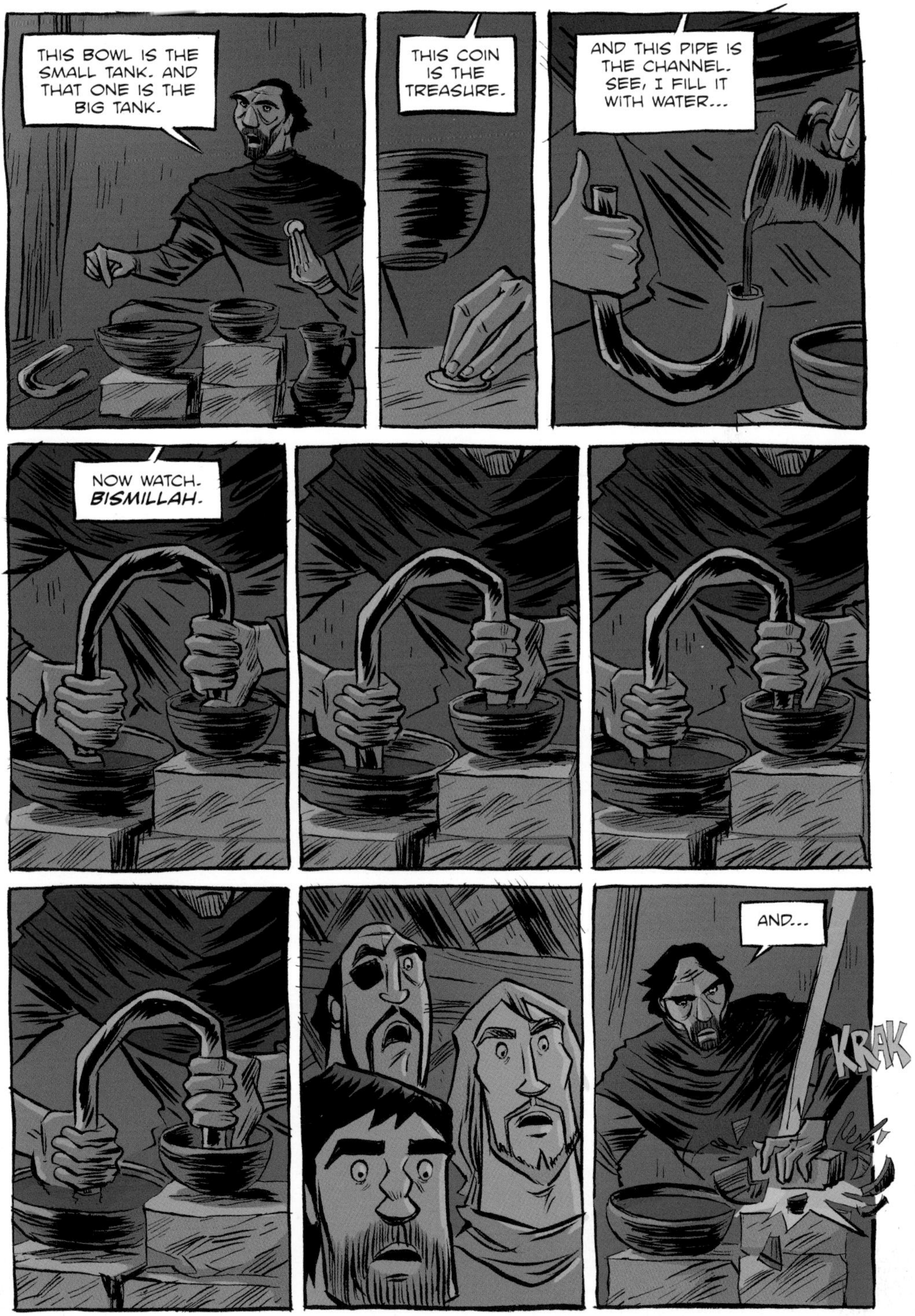
THIS BOWL IS THE SMALL TANK. AND THAT ONE IS THE BIG TANK.
THIS COIN IS THE TREASURE.
AND THIS PIPE IS THE CHANNEL. SEE, I FILL IT WITH WATER...
NOW WATCH. BISMILLAH.
AND...
KRAK

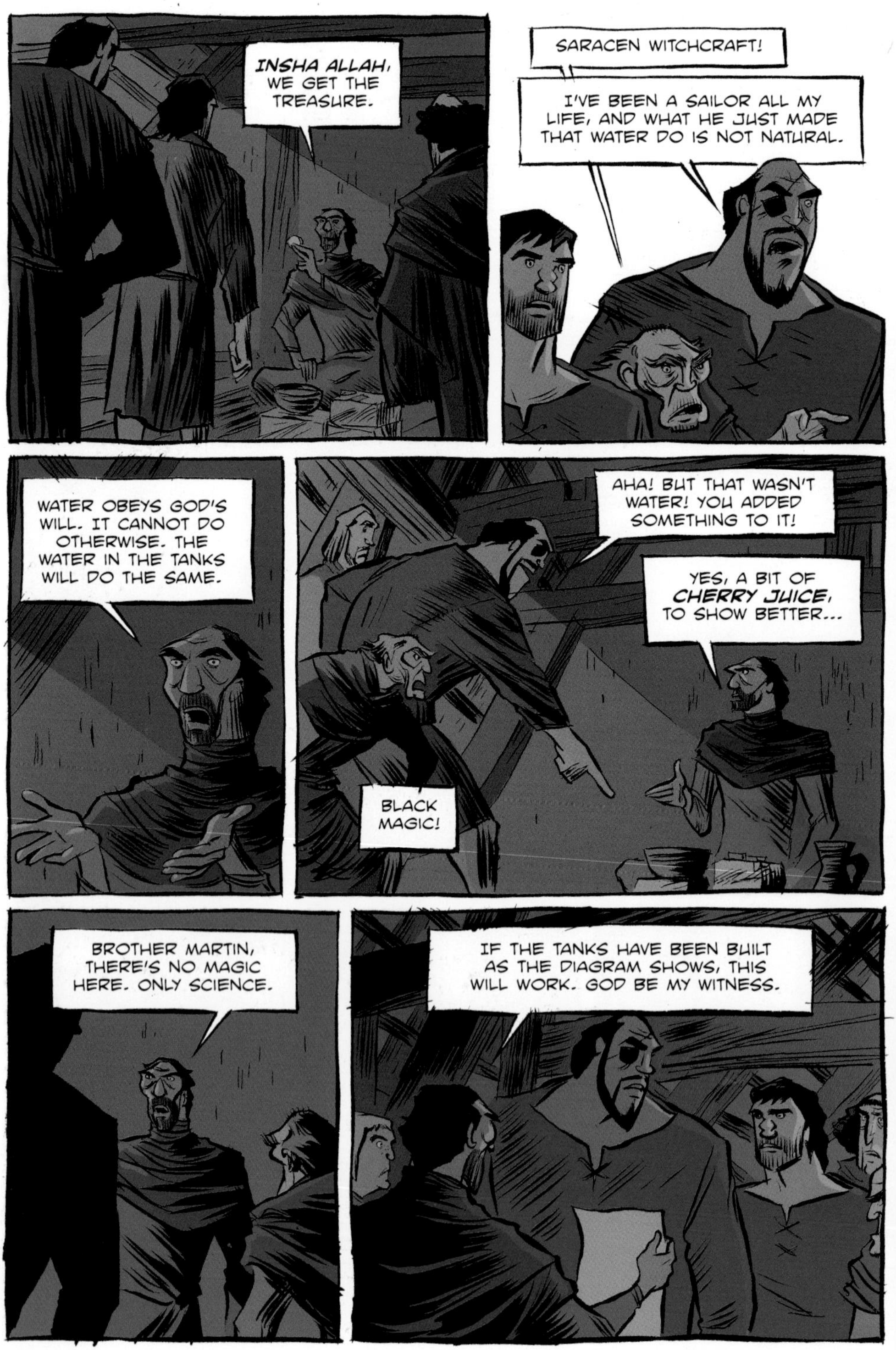

INSHA ALLAH, WE GET THE TREASURE.
SARACEN WITCHCRAFT!
I'VE BEEN A SAILOR ALL MY LIFE, AND WHAT HE JUST MADE THAT WATER DO IS NOT NATURAL.
WATER OBEYS GOD'S WILL. IT CANNOT DO OTHERWISE. THE WATER IN THE TANKS WILL DO THE SAME.
AHA! BUT THAT WASN'T WATER! YOU ADDED SOMETHING TO IT!
YES, A BIT OF CHERRY JUICE, TO SHOW BETTER...
BLACK MAGIC!
BROTHER MARTIN, THERE'S NO MAGIC HERE. ONLY SCIENCE.
IF THE TANKS HAVE BEEN BUILT AS THE DIAGRAM SHOWS, THIS WILL WORK. GOD BE MY WITNESS.

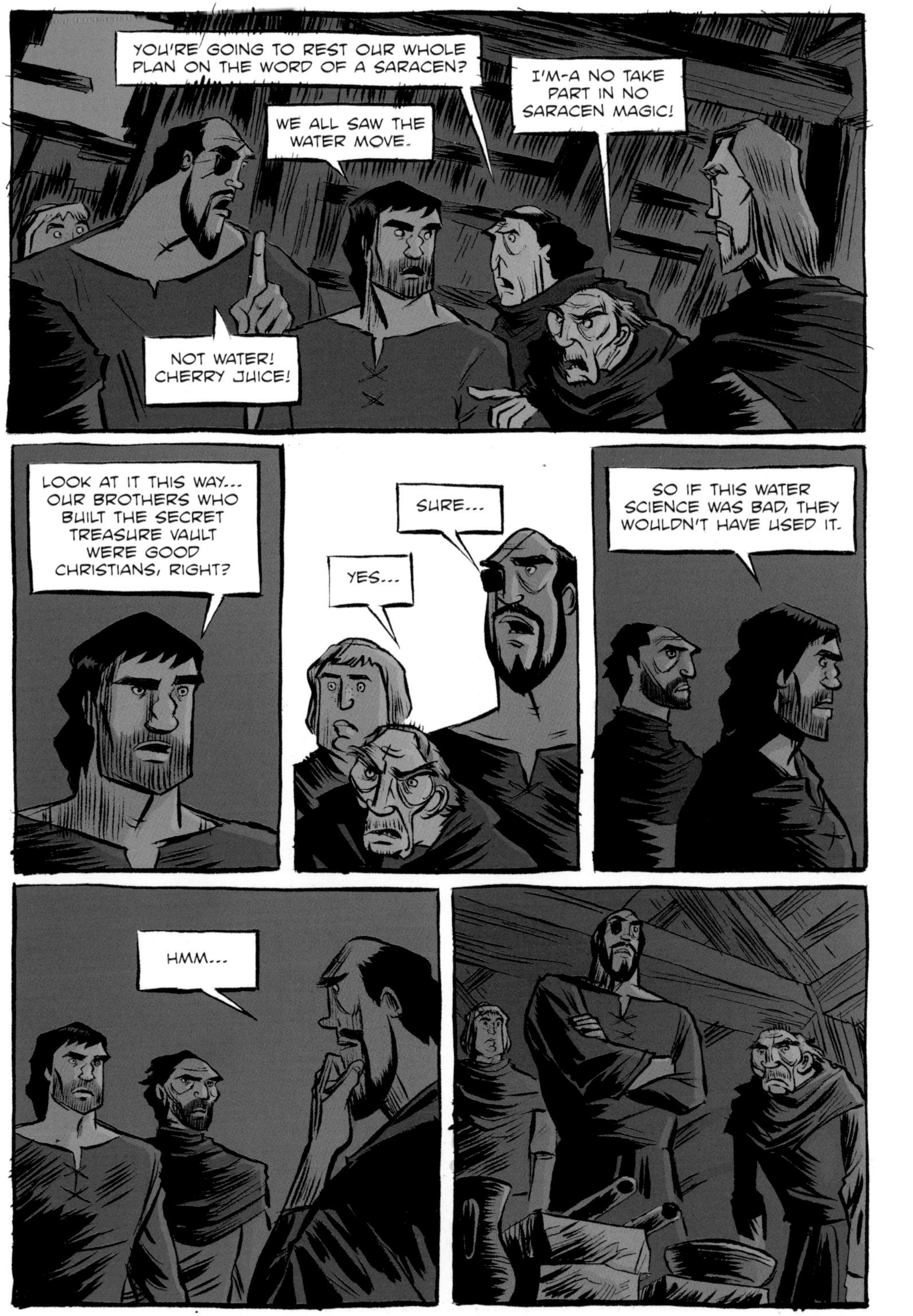
YOU'RE GOING TO REST OUR WHOLE PLAN ON THE WORD OF A SARACEN?
WE ALL SAW THE WATER MOVE.
I'M-A NO TAKE PART IN NO SARACEN MAGIC!
NOT WATER! CHERRY JUICE!
LOOK AT IT THIS WAY... OUR BROTHERS WHO BUILT THE SECRET TREASURE VAULT WERE GOOD CHRISTIANS, RIGHT?
SURE...
YES...
SO IF THIS WATER SCIENCE WAS BAD, THEY WOULDN'T HAVE USED IT.
HMM...

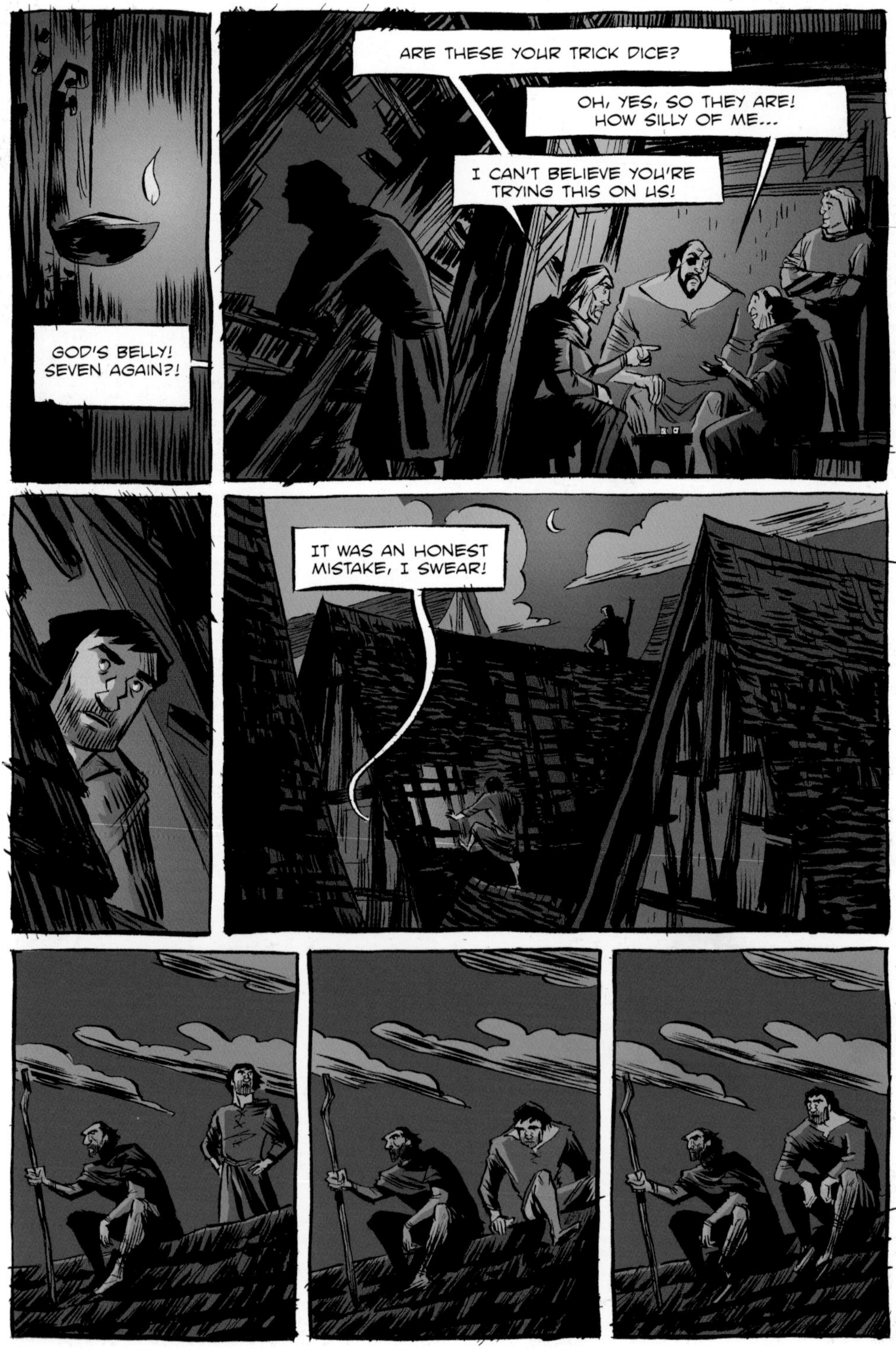
GOD'S BELLY! SEVEN AGAIN?!
ARE THESE YOUR TRICK DICE?
OH, YES, SO THEY ARE! HOW SILLY OF ME...
I CAN'T BELIEVE YOU'RE TRYING THIS ON US!
IT WAS AN HONEST MISTAKE, I SWEAR!

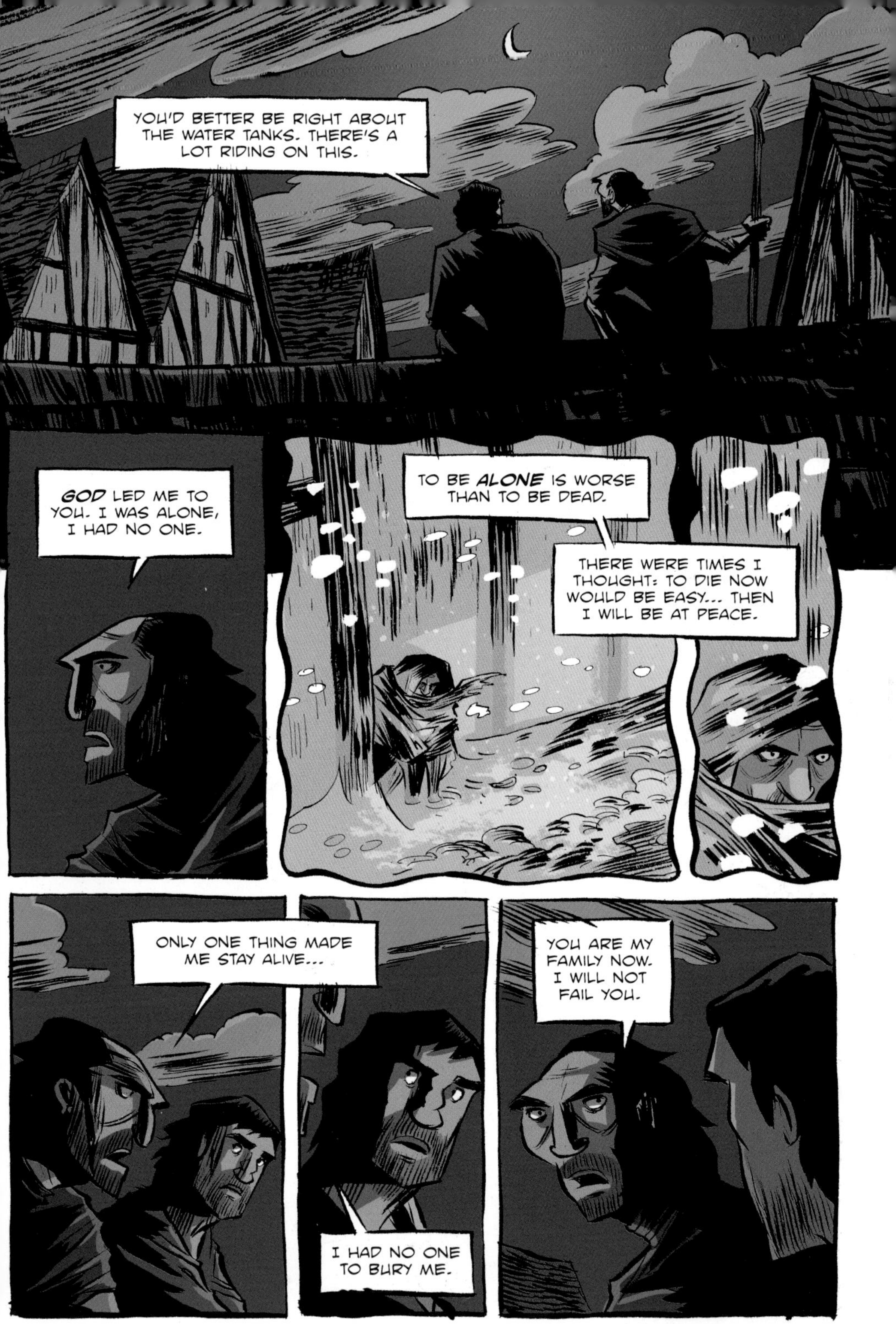
YOU'D BETTER BE RIGHT ABOUT THE WATER TANKS. THERE'S A LOT RIDING ON THIS.
GOD LED ME TO YOU. I WAS ALONE, I HAD NO ONE.
TO BE ALONE IS WORSE THAN TO BE DEAD.
THERE WERE TIMES I THOUGHT: TO DIE NOW WOULD BE EASY... THEN I WILL BE AT PEACE.
ONLY ONE THING MADE ME STAY ALIVE...
I HAD NO ONE TO BURY ME.
YOU ARE MY FAMILY NOW. I WILL NOT FAIL YOU.

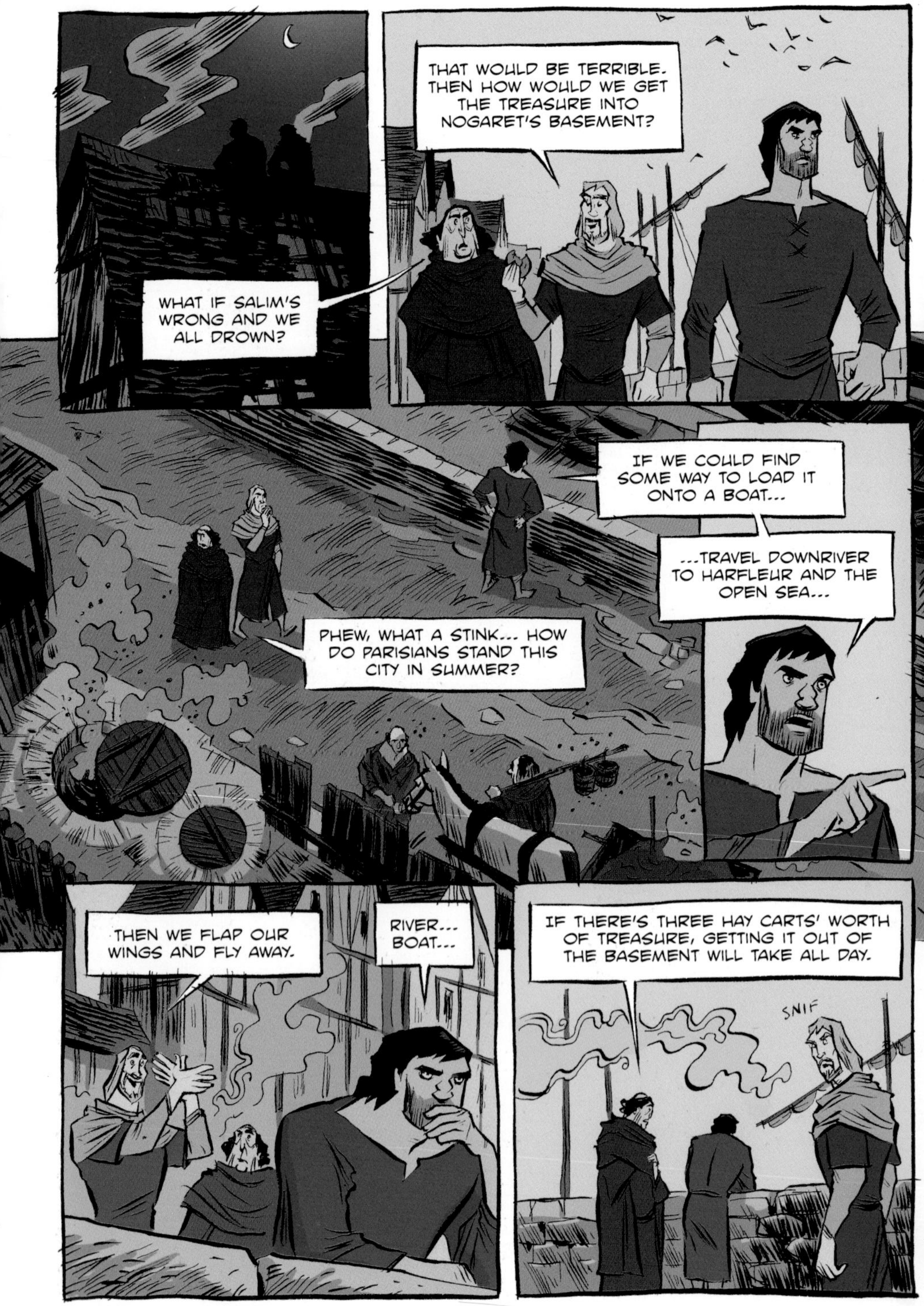
WHAT IF SALIM'S WRONG AND WE ALL DROWN?
THAT WOULD BE TERRIBLE. THEN HOW WOULD WE GET THE TREASURE INTO NOGARET'S BASEMENT?
IF WE COULD FIND SOME WAY TO LOAD IT ONTO A BOAT...
...TRAVEL DOWNRIVER TO HARFLEUR AND THE OPEN SEA...
PHEW, WHAT A STINK... HOW DO PARISIANS STAND THIS CITY IN SUMMER?
THEN WE FLAP OUR WINGS AND FLY AWAY.
RIVER... BOAT...
IF THERE'S THREE HAY CARTS' WORTH OF TREASURE, GETTING IT OUT OF THE BASEMENT WILL TAKE ALL DAY.
SNIF

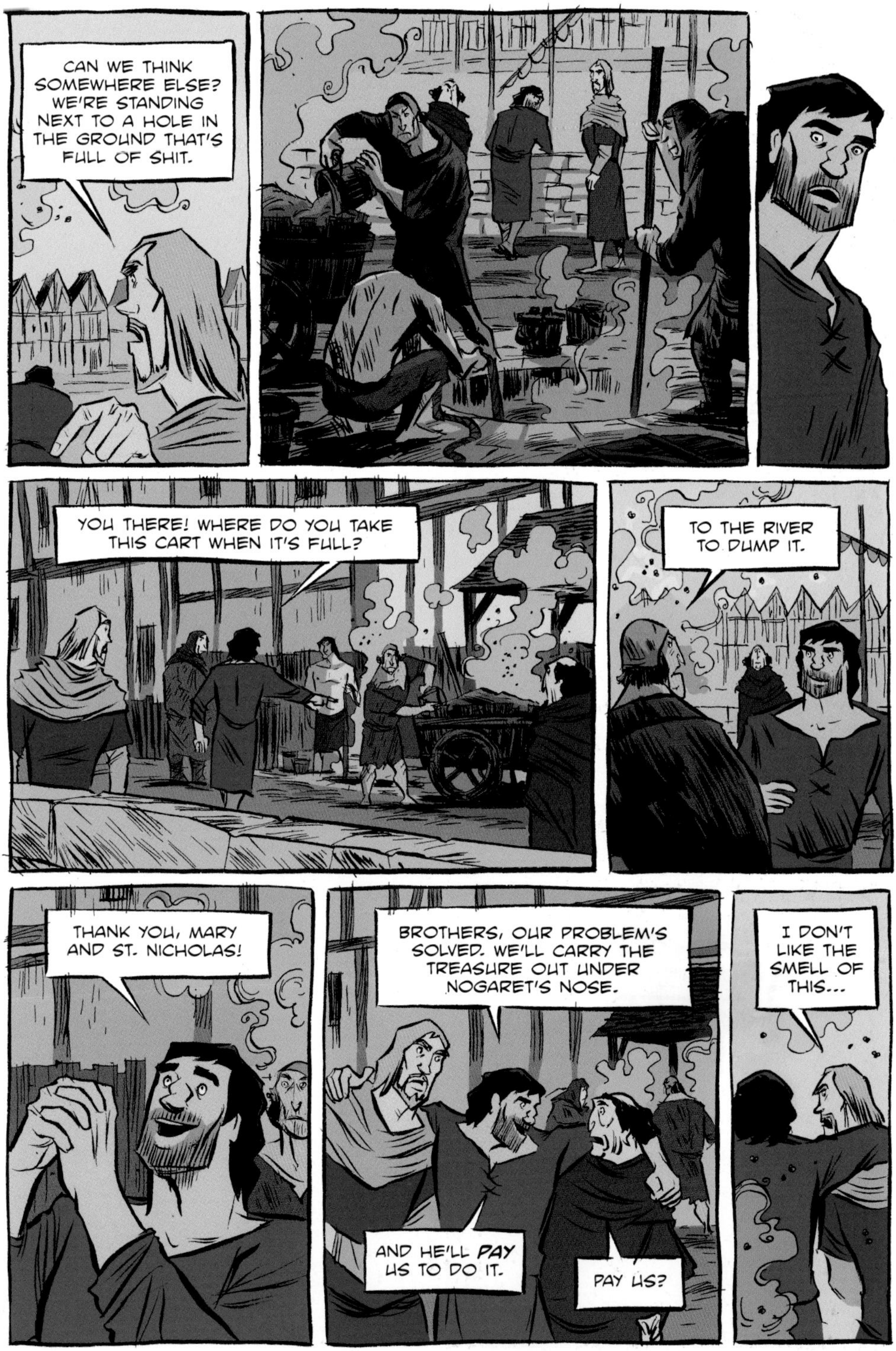
CAN WE THINK SOMEWHERE ELSE? WE'RE STANDING NEXT TO A HOLE IN THE GROUND THAT'S FULL OF SHIT.
YOU THERE! WHERE DO YOU TAKE THIS CART WHEN IT'S FULL?
TO THE RIVER TO DUMP IT.
THANK YOU, MARY AND ST. NICHOLAS!
BROTHERS, OUR PROBLEM'S SOLVED. WE'LL CARRY THE TREASURE OUT UNDER NOGARET'S NOSE.
AND HE'LL *PAY* US TO DO IT.
PAY US?
I DON'T LIKE THE SMELL OF THIS...

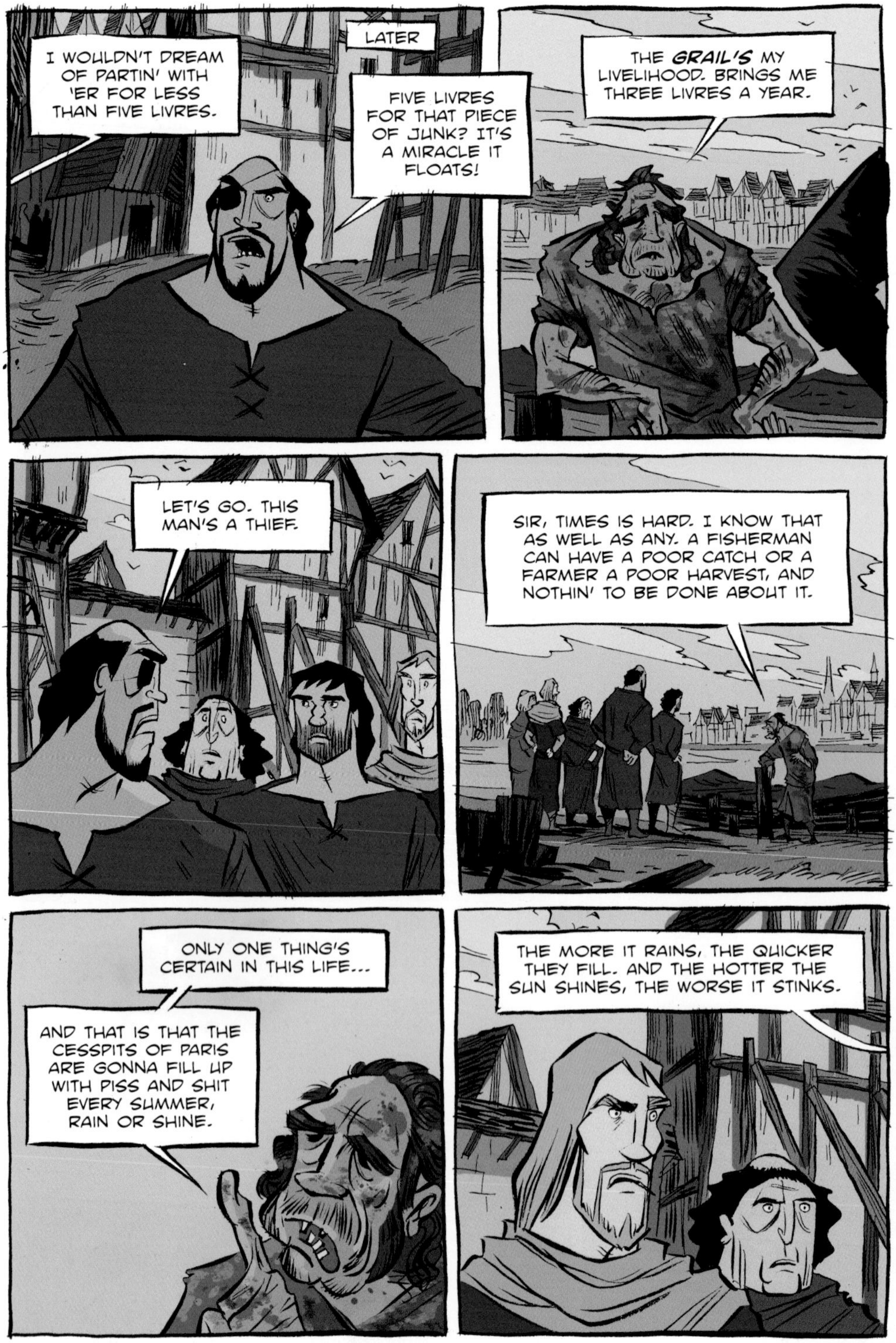
I WOULDN'T DREAM OF PARTIN' WITH 'ER FOR LESS THAN FIVE LIVRES.
LATER
FIVE LIVRES FOR THAT PIECE OF JUNK? IT'S A MIRACLE IT FLOATS!
THE GRAIL'S MY LIVELIHOOD. BRINGS ME THREE LIVRES A YEAR.
LET'S GO. THIS MAN'S A THIEF.
SIR, TIMES IS HARD. I KNOW THAT AS WELL AS ANY. A FISHERMAN CAN HAVE A POOR CATCH OR A FARMER A POOR HARVEST, AND NOTHIN' TO BE DONE ABOUT IT.
ONLY ONE THING'S CERTAIN IN THIS LIFE...
AND THAT IS THAT THE CESSPITS OF PARIS ARE GONNA FILL UP WITH PISS AND SHIT EVERY SUMMER, RAIN OR SHINE.
THE MORE IT RAINS, THE QUICKER THEY FILL. AND THE HOTTER THE SUN SHINES, THE WORSE IT STINKS.

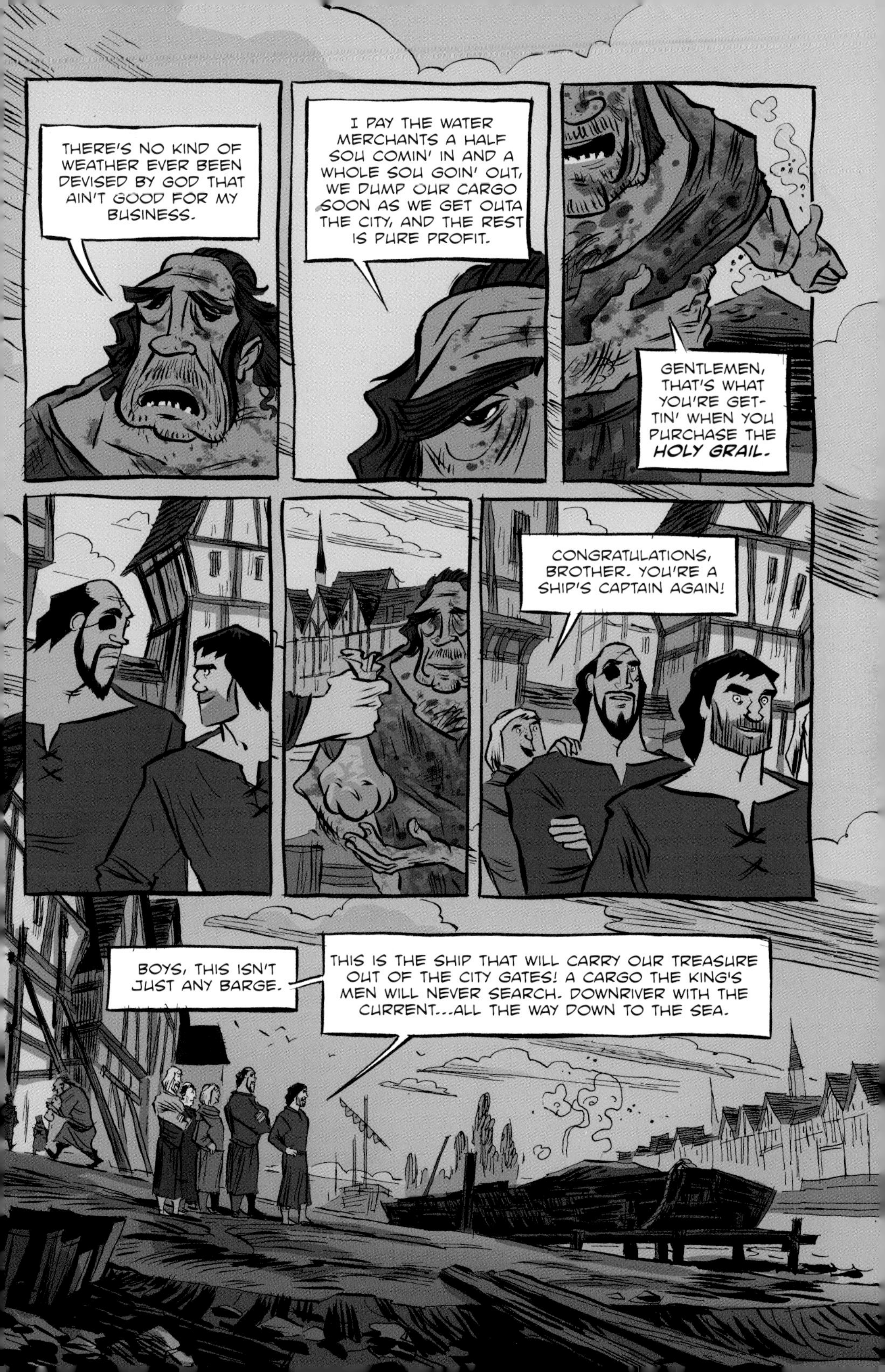
THERE'S NO KIND OF WEATHER EVER BEEN DEVISED BY GOD THAT AIN'T GOOD FOR MY BUSINESS.
I PAY THE WATER MERCHANTS A HALF SOU COMIN' IN AND A WHOLE SOU GOIN' OUT, WE DUMP OUR CARGO SOON AS WE GET OUTA THE CITY, AND THE REST IS PURE PROFIT.
GENTLEMEN, THAT'S WHAT YOU'RE GETTIN' WHEN YOU PURCHASE THE HOLY GRAIL.
CONGRATULATIONS, BROTHER. YOU'RE A SHIP'S CAPTAIN AGAIN!
BOYS, THIS ISN'T JUST ANY BARGE.
THIS IS THE SHIP THAT WILL CARRY OUR TREASURE OUT OF THE CITY GATES! A CARGO THE KING'S MEN WILL NEVER SEARCH. DOWNRIVER WITH THE CURRENT...ALL THE WAY DOWN TO THE SEA.

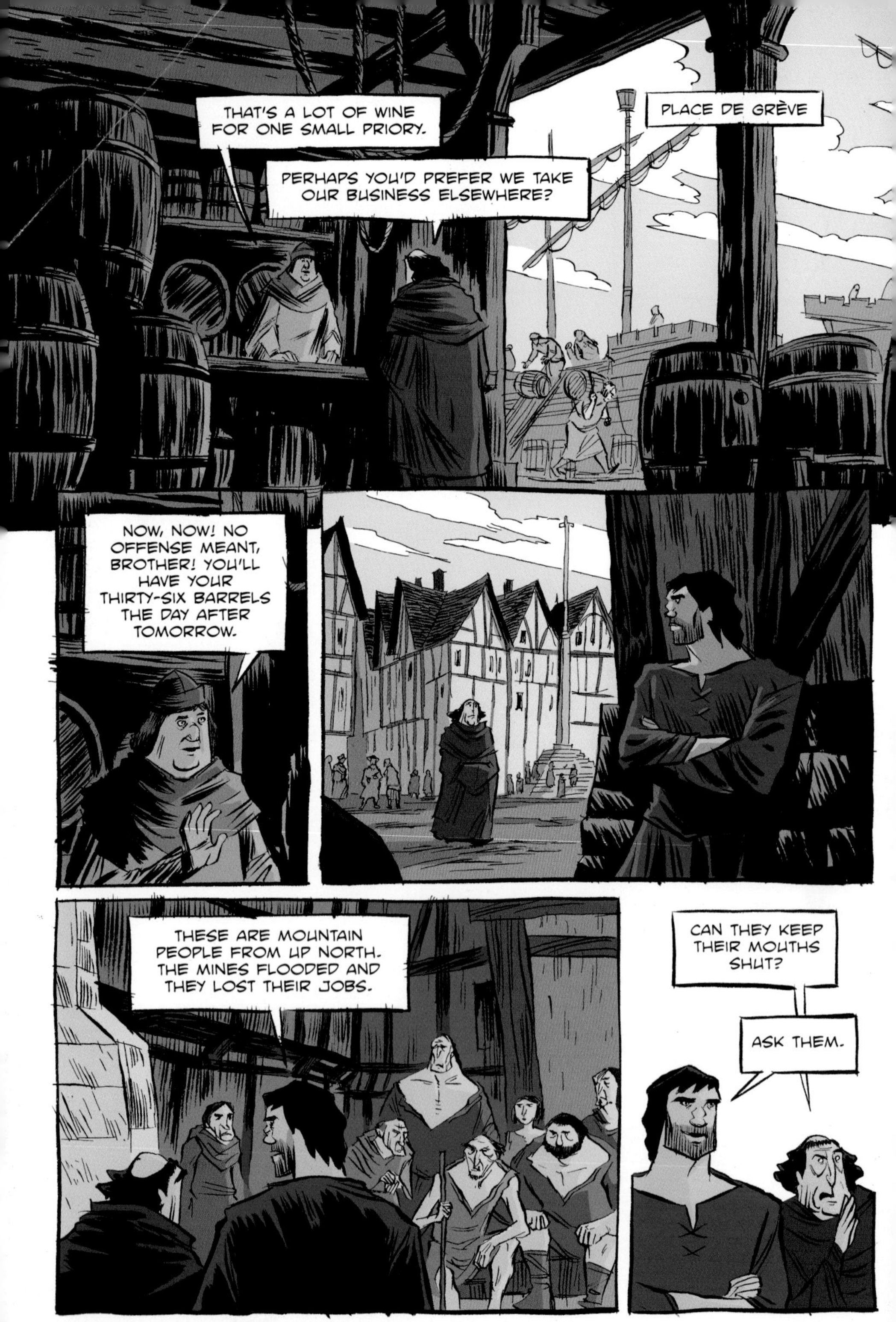
THAT'S A LOT OF WINE FOR ONE SMALL PRIORY.
PLACE DE GRÈVE
PERHAPS YOU'D PREFER WE TAKE OUR BUSINESS ELSEWHERE?
NOW, NOW! NO OFFENSE MEANT, BROTHER! YOU'LL HAVE YOUR THIRTY-SIX BARRELS THE DAY AFTER TOMORROW.
THESE ARE MOUNTAIN PEOPLE FROM UP NORTH. THE MINES FLOODED AND THEY LOST THEIR JOBS.
CAN THEY KEEP THEIR MOUTHS SHUT?
ASK THEM.

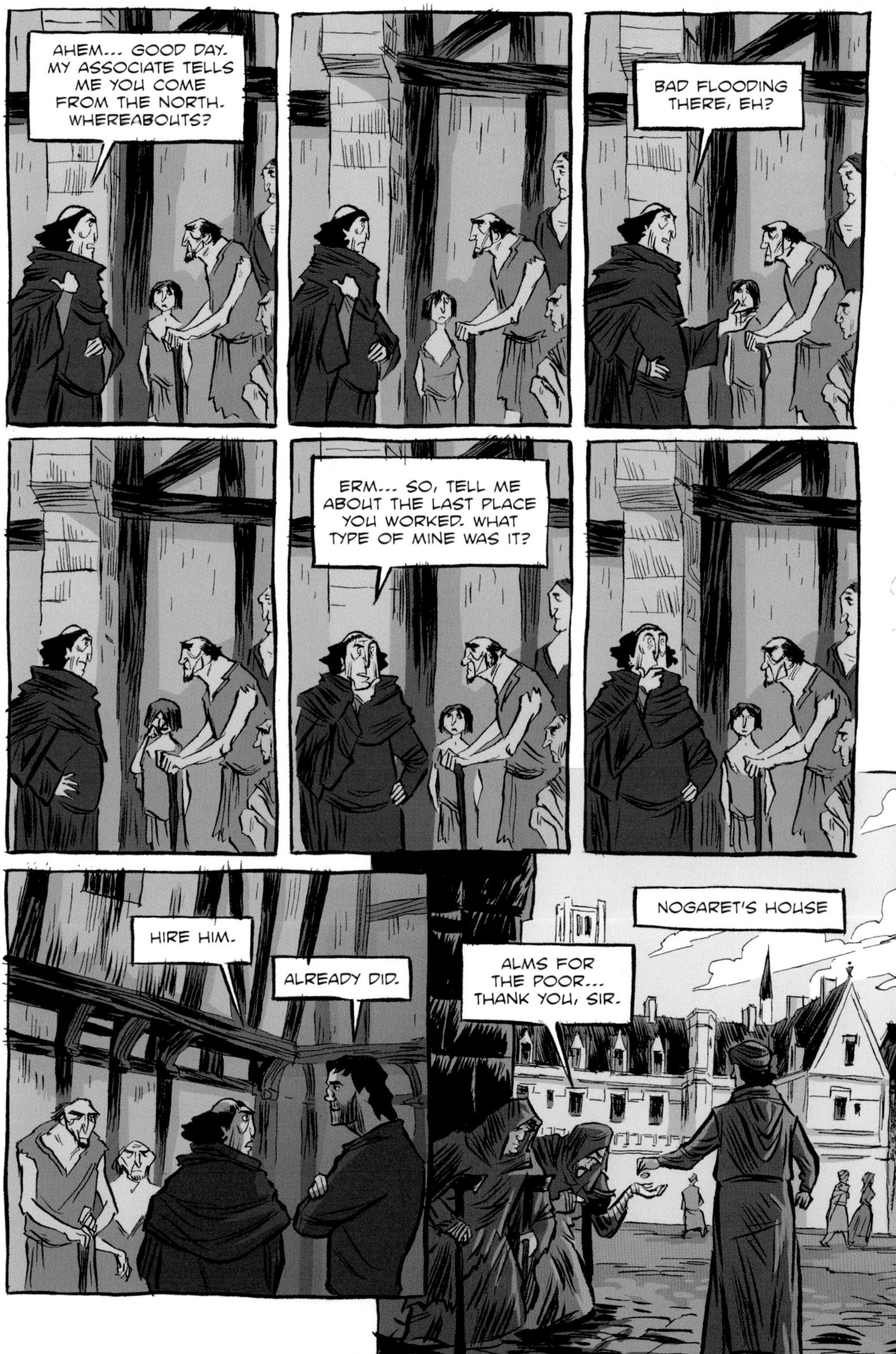
AHEM... GOOD DAY. MY ASSOCIATE TELLS ME YOU COME FROM THE NORTH. WHEREABOUTS?
BAD FLOODING THERE, EH?
ERM... SO, TELL ME ABOUT THE LAST PLACE YOU WORKED. WHAT TYPE OF MINE WAS IT?
HIRE HIM.
ALREADY DID.
NOGARET'S HOUSE
ALMS FOR THE POOR... THANK YOU, SIR.

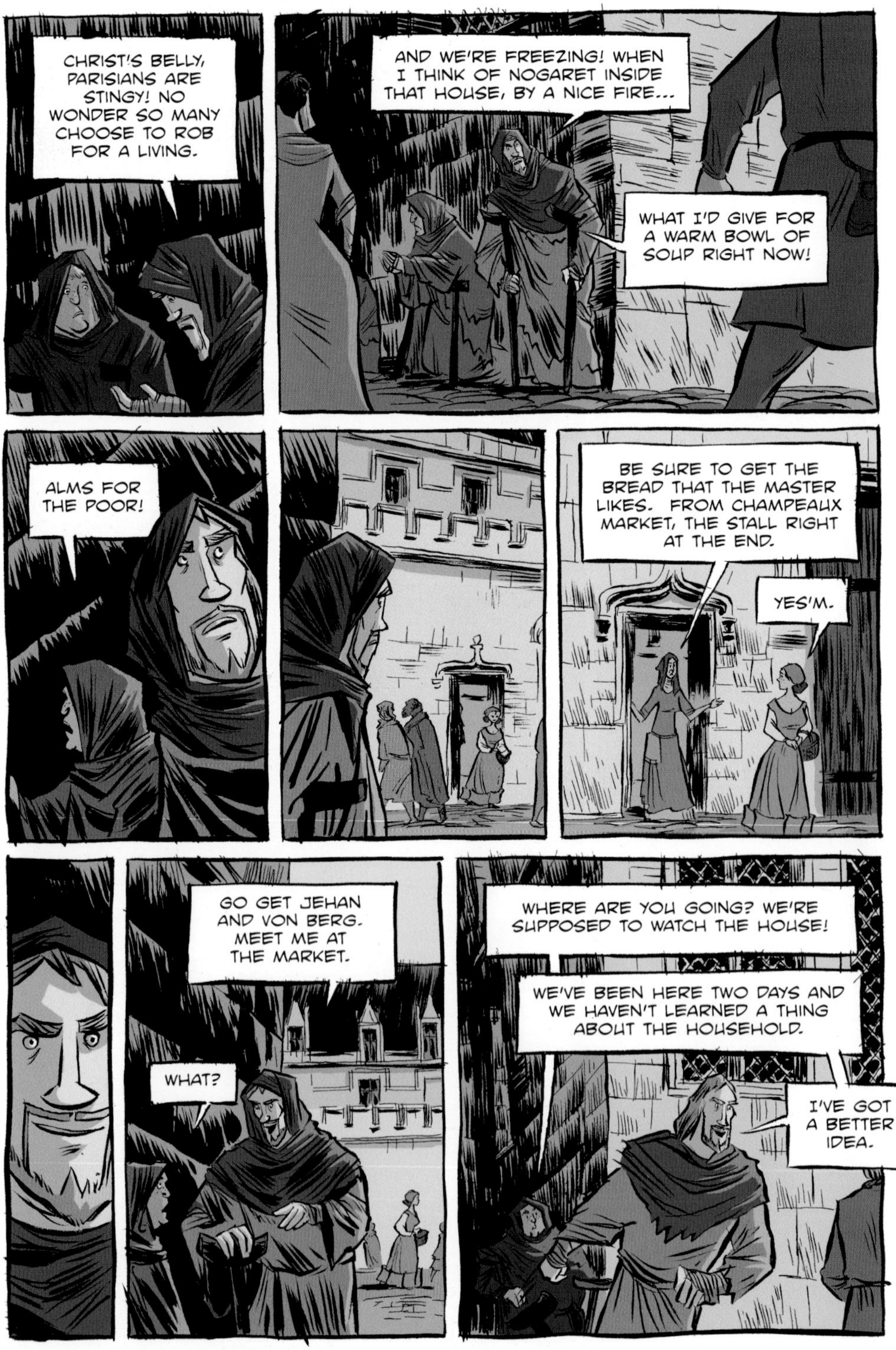
CHRIST'S BELLY, PARISIANS ARE STINGY! NO WONDER SO MANY CHOOSE TO ROB FOR A LIVING.
AND WE'RE FREEZING! WHEN I THINK OF NOGARET INSIDE THAT HOUSE, BY A NICE FIRE...
WHAT I'D GIVE FOR A WARM BOWL OF SOUP RIGHT NOW!
ALMS FOR THE POOR!
BE SURE TO GET THE BREAD THAT THE MASTER LIKES. FROM CHAMPEAUX MARKET, THE STALL RIGHT AT THE END.
YES'M.
GO GET JEHAN AND VON BERG. MEET ME AT THE MARKET.
WHAT?
WHERE ARE YOU GOING? WE'RE SUPPOSED TO WATCH THE HOUSE!
WE'VE BEEN HERE TWO DAYS AND WE HAVEN'T LEARNED A THING ABOUT THE HOUSEHOLD.
I'VE GOT A BETTER IDEA.

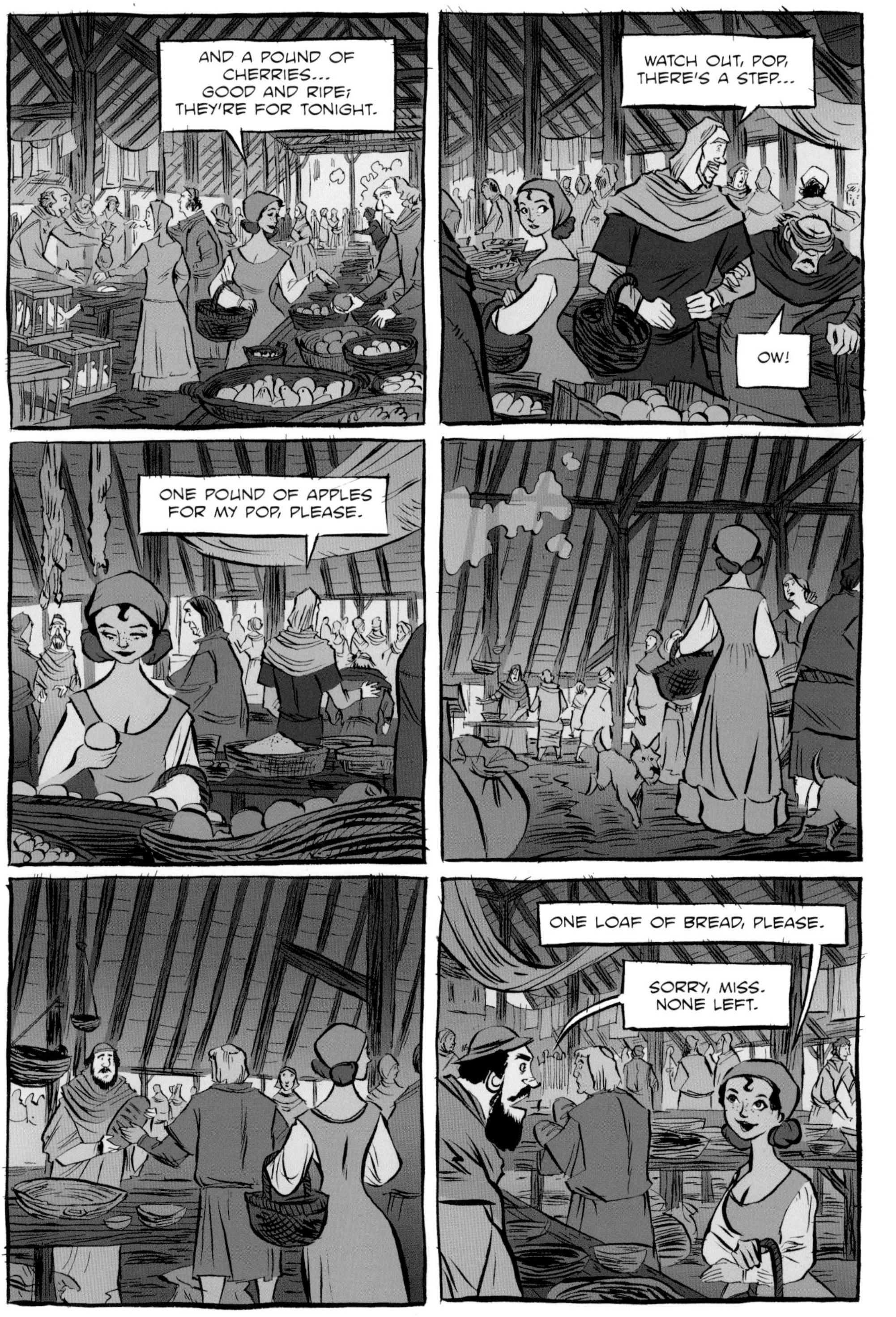
AND A POUND OF CHERRIES... GOOD AND RIPE; THEY'RE FOR TONIGHT.
WATCH OUT, POP, THERE'S A STEP...
OW!
ONE POUND OF APPLES FOR MY POP, PLEASE.
ONE LOAF OF BREAD, PLEASE.
SORRY, MISS. NONE LEFT.

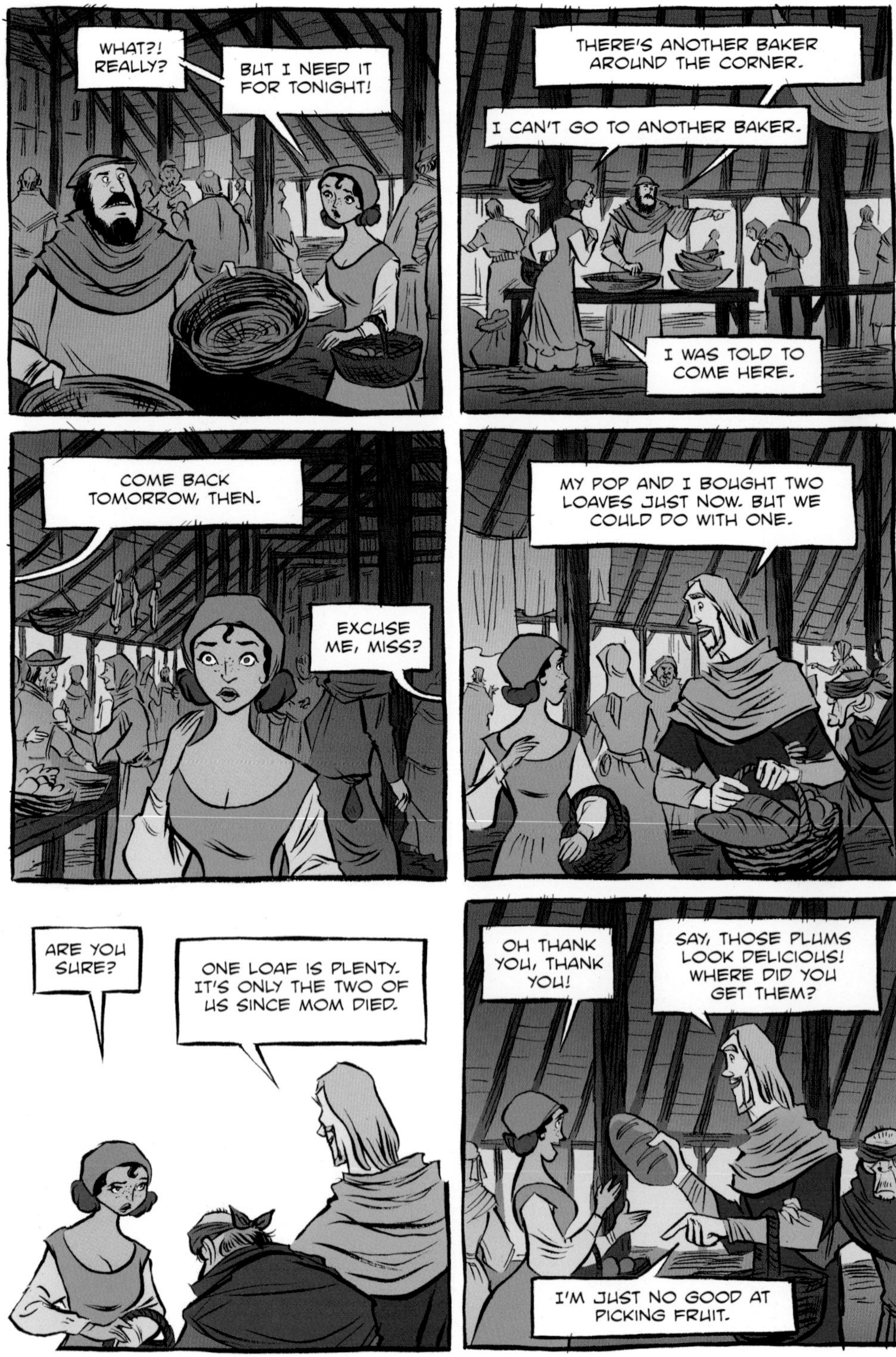
WHAT?! REALLY?
BUT I NEED IT FOR TONIGHT!
THERE'S ANOTHER BAKER AROUND THE CORNER.
I CAN'T GO TO ANOTHER BAKER.
I WAS TOLD TO COME HERE.
COME BACK TOMORROW, THEN.
EXCUSE ME, MISS?
MY POP AND I BOUGHT TWO LOAVES JUST NOW. BUT WE COULD DO WITH ONE.
ARE YOU SURE?
ONE LOAF IS PLENTY. IT'S ONLY THE TWO OF US SINCE MOM DIED.
OH THANK YOU, THANK YOU!
SAY, THOSE PLUMS LOOK DELICIOUS! WHERE DID YOU GET THEM?
I'M JUST NO GOOD AT PICKING FRUIT.

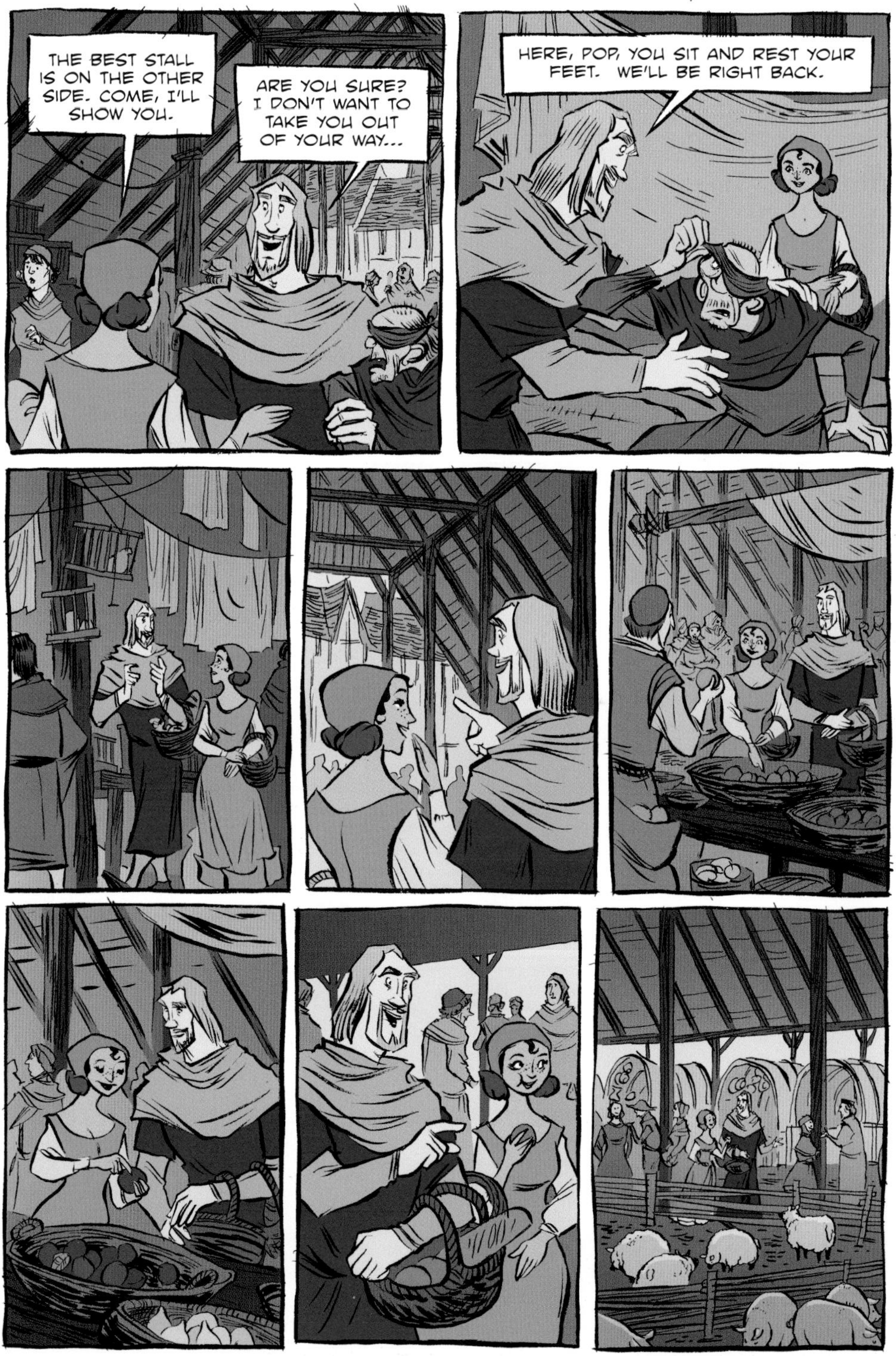
THE BEST STALL IS ON THE OTHER SIDE. COME, I'LL SHOW YOU.
ARE YOU SURE? I DON'T WANT TO TAKE YOU OUT OF YOUR WAY...
HERE, POP, YOU SIT AND REST YOUR FEET. WE'LL BE RIGHT BACK.

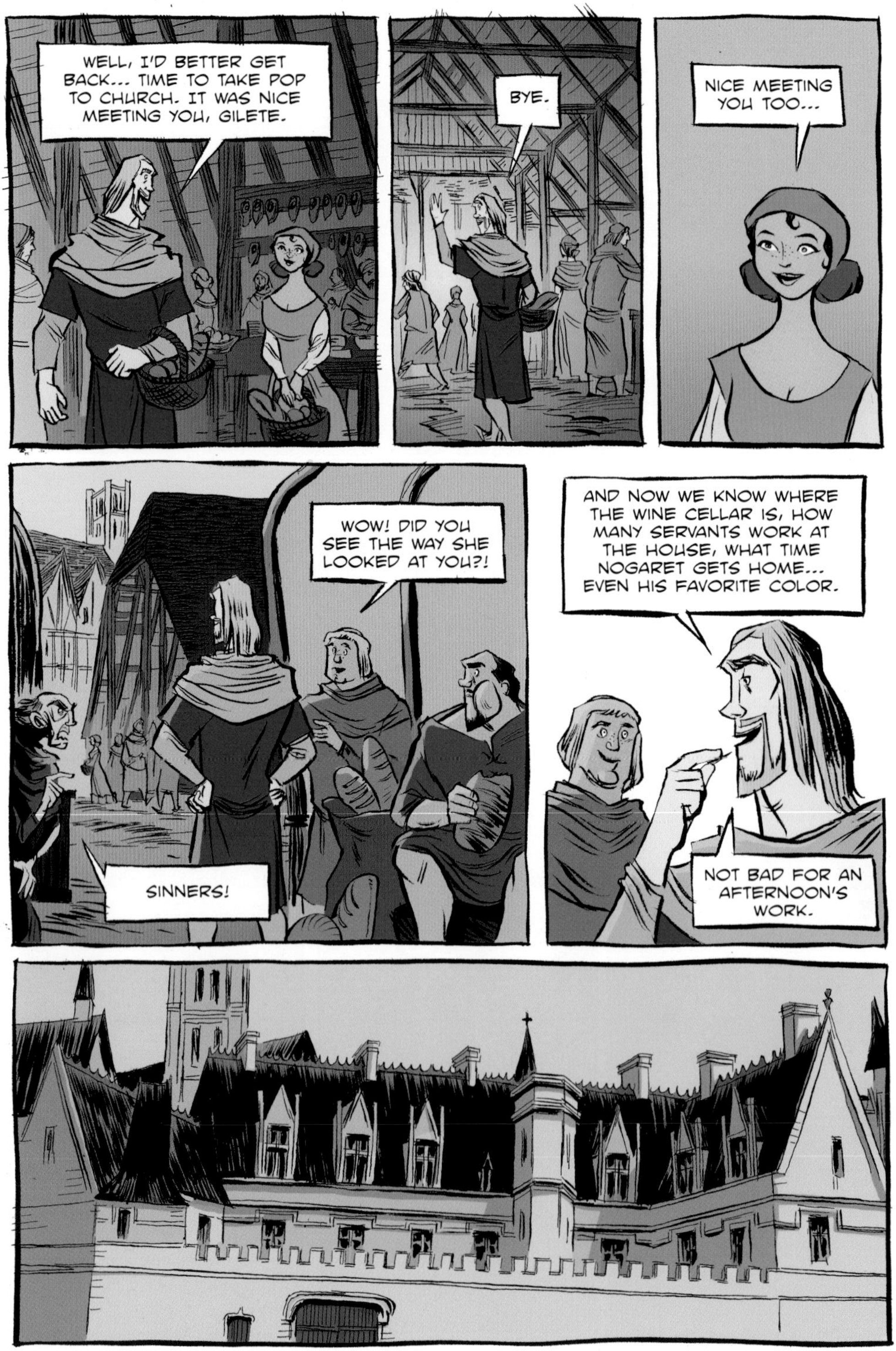
WELL, I'D BETTER GET BACK... TIME TO TAKE POP TO CHURCH. IT WAS NICE MEETING YOU, GILETE.
BYE.
NICE MEETING YOU TOO...
WOW! DID YOU SEE THE WAY SHE LOOKED AT YOU?!
SINNERS!
AND NOW WE KNOW WHERE THE WINE CELLAR IS, HOW MANY SERVANTS WORK AT THE HOUSE, WHAT TIME NOGARET GETS HOME... EVEN HIS FAVORITE COLOR.
NOT BAD FOR AN AFTERNOON'S WORK.

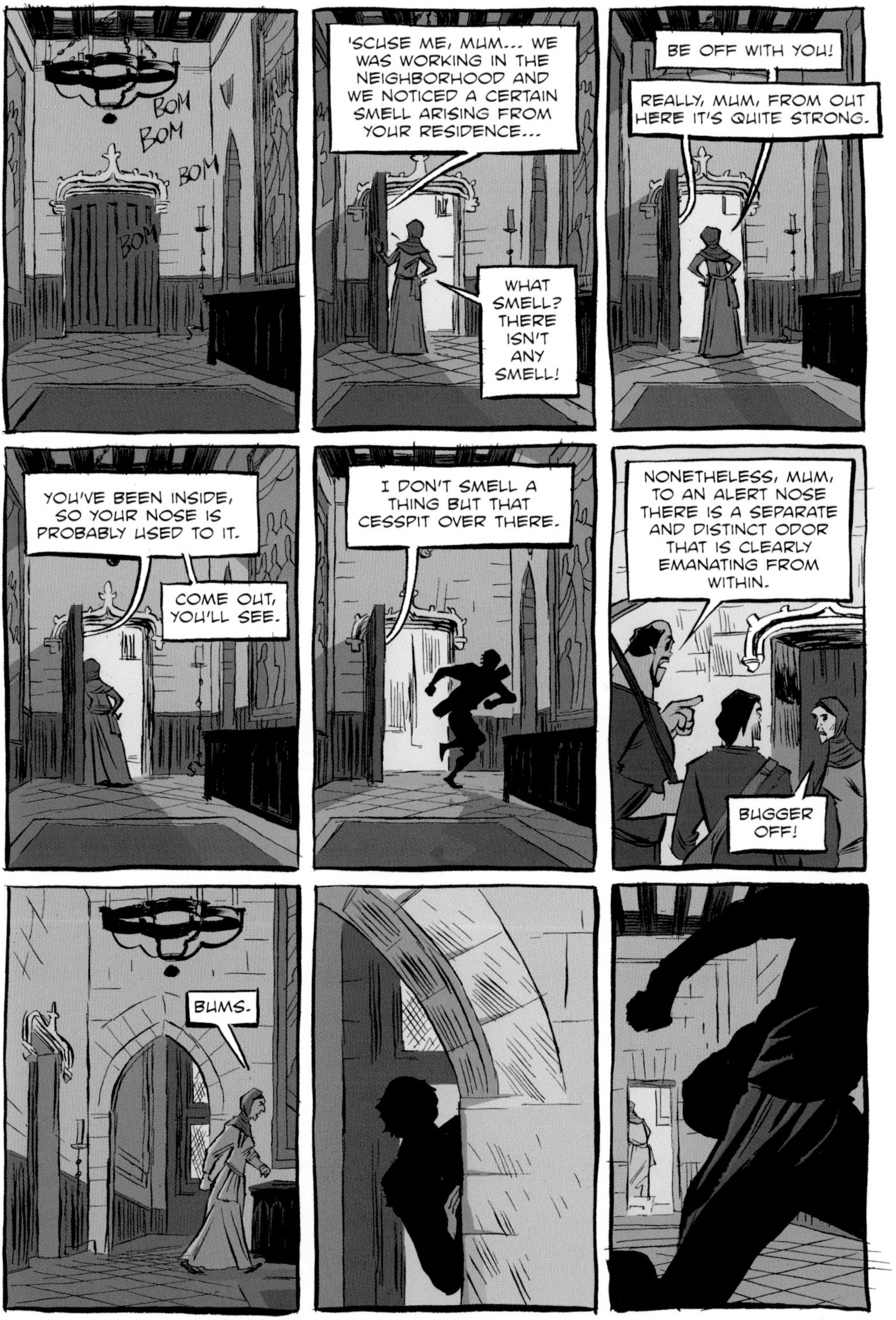
BOM
BOM
BOM
BOM
'SCUSE ME, MUM... WE WAS WORKING IN THE NEIGHBORHOOD AND WE NOTICED A CERTAIN SMELL ARISING FROM YOUR RESIDENCE...
WHAT SMELL? THERE ISN'T ANY SMELL!
BE OFF WITH YOU!
REALLY, MUM, FROM OUT HERE IT'S QUITE STRONG.
YOU'VE BEEN INSIDE, SO YOUR NOSE IS PROBABLY USED TO IT.
COME OUT, YOU'LL SEE.
I DON'T SMELL A THING BUT THAT CESSPIT OVER THERE.
NONETHELESS, MUM, TO AN ALERT NOSE THERE IS A SEPARATE AND DISTINCT ODOR THAT IS CLEARLY EMANATING FROM WITHIN.
BUGGER OFF!
BUMS.

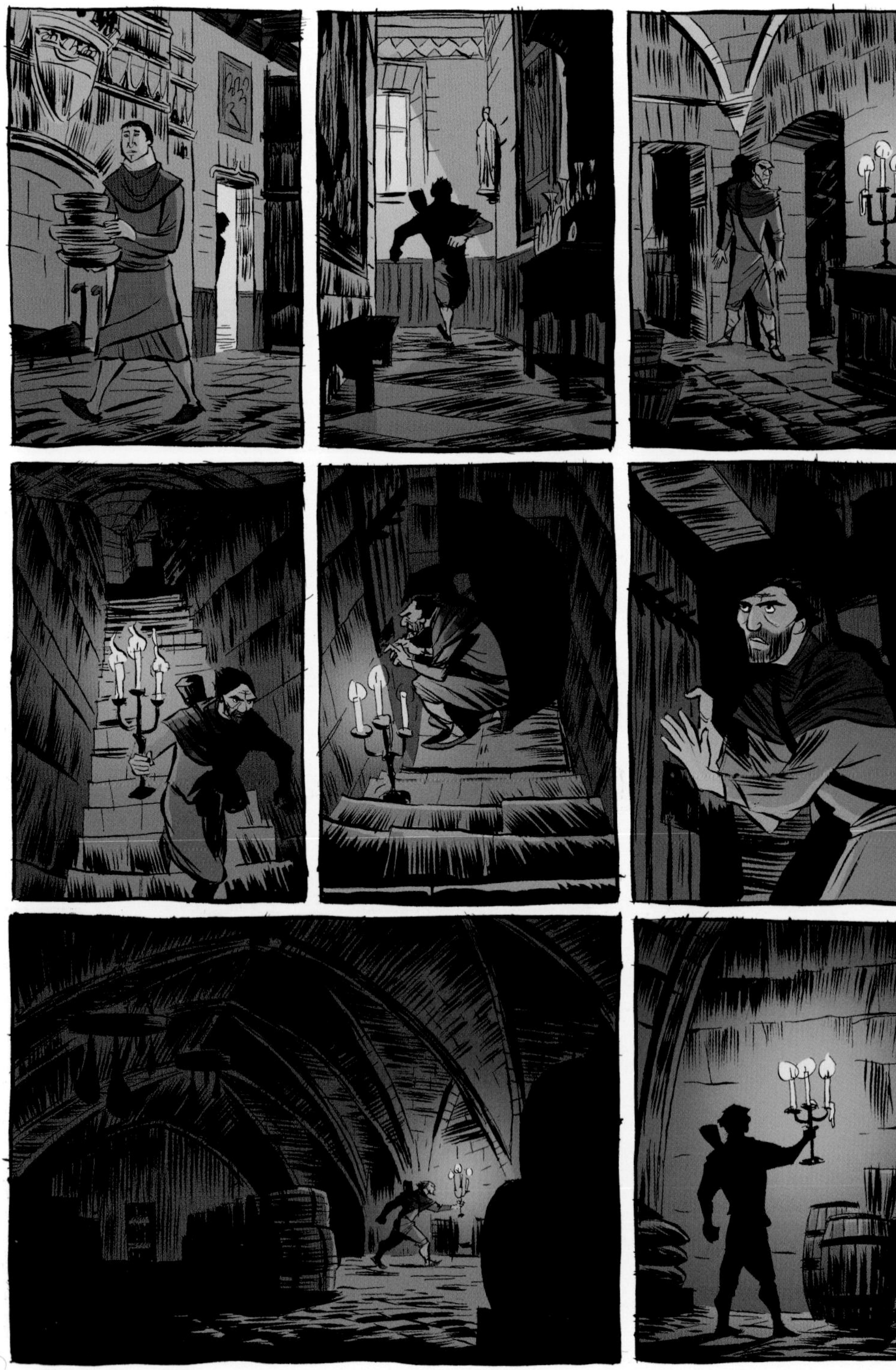

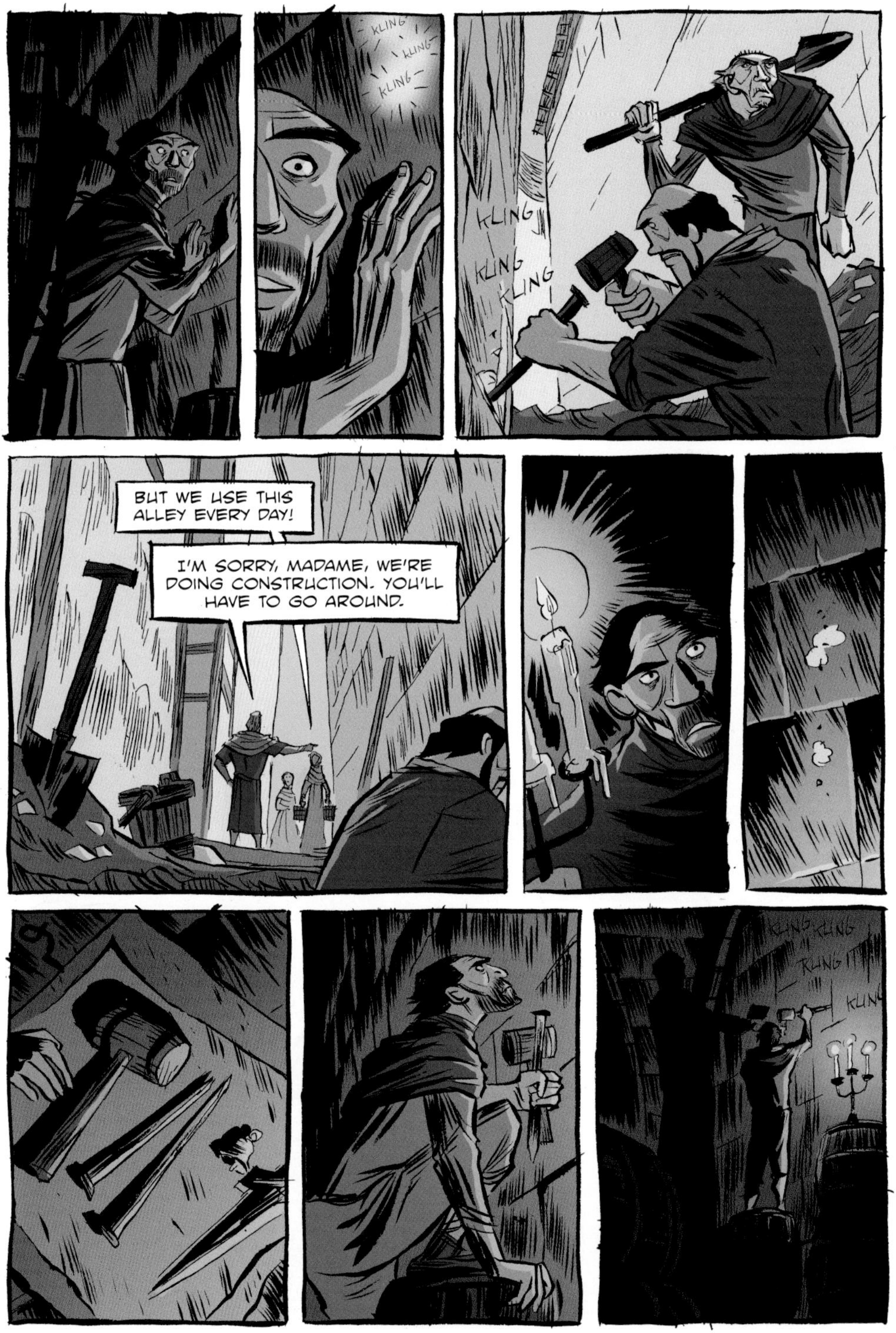
KLING
KLING
KLING
KLING
KLING
KLING
BUT WE USE THIS ALLEY EVERY DAY!
I'M SORRY, MADAME, WE'RE DOING CONSTRUCTION. YOU'LL HAVE TO GO AROUND.
KLING KLING
KLING

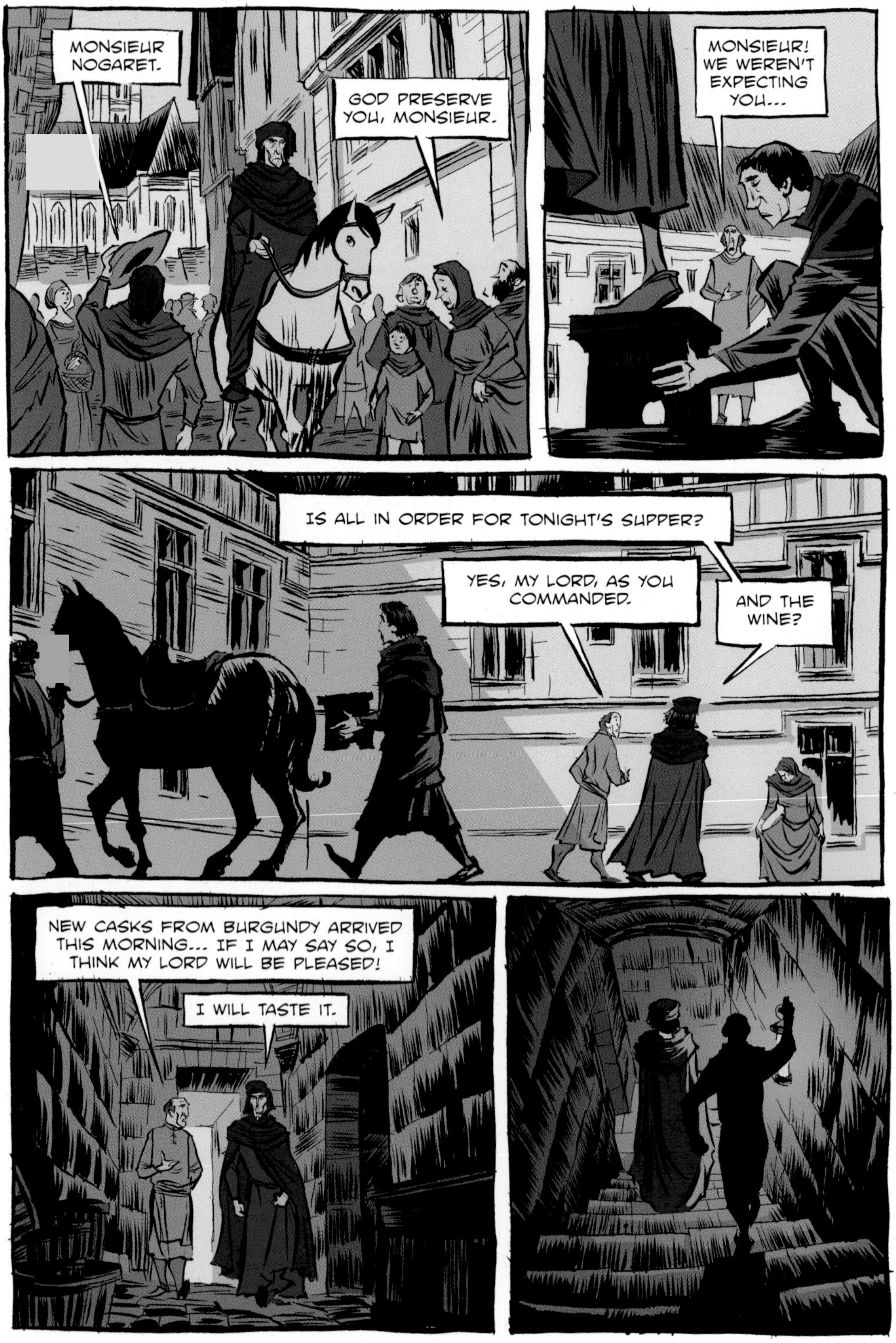

MONSIEUR NOGARET.
GOD PRESERVE YOU, MONSIEUR.
MONSIEUR! WE WEREN'T EXPECTING YOU...
IS ALL IN ORDER FOR TONIGHT'S SUPPER?
YES, MY LORD, AS YOU COMMANDED.
AND THE WINE?
NEW CASKS FROM BURGUNDY ARRIVED THIS MORNING... IF I MAY SAY SO, I THINK MY LORD WILL BE PLEASED!
I WILL TASTE IT.

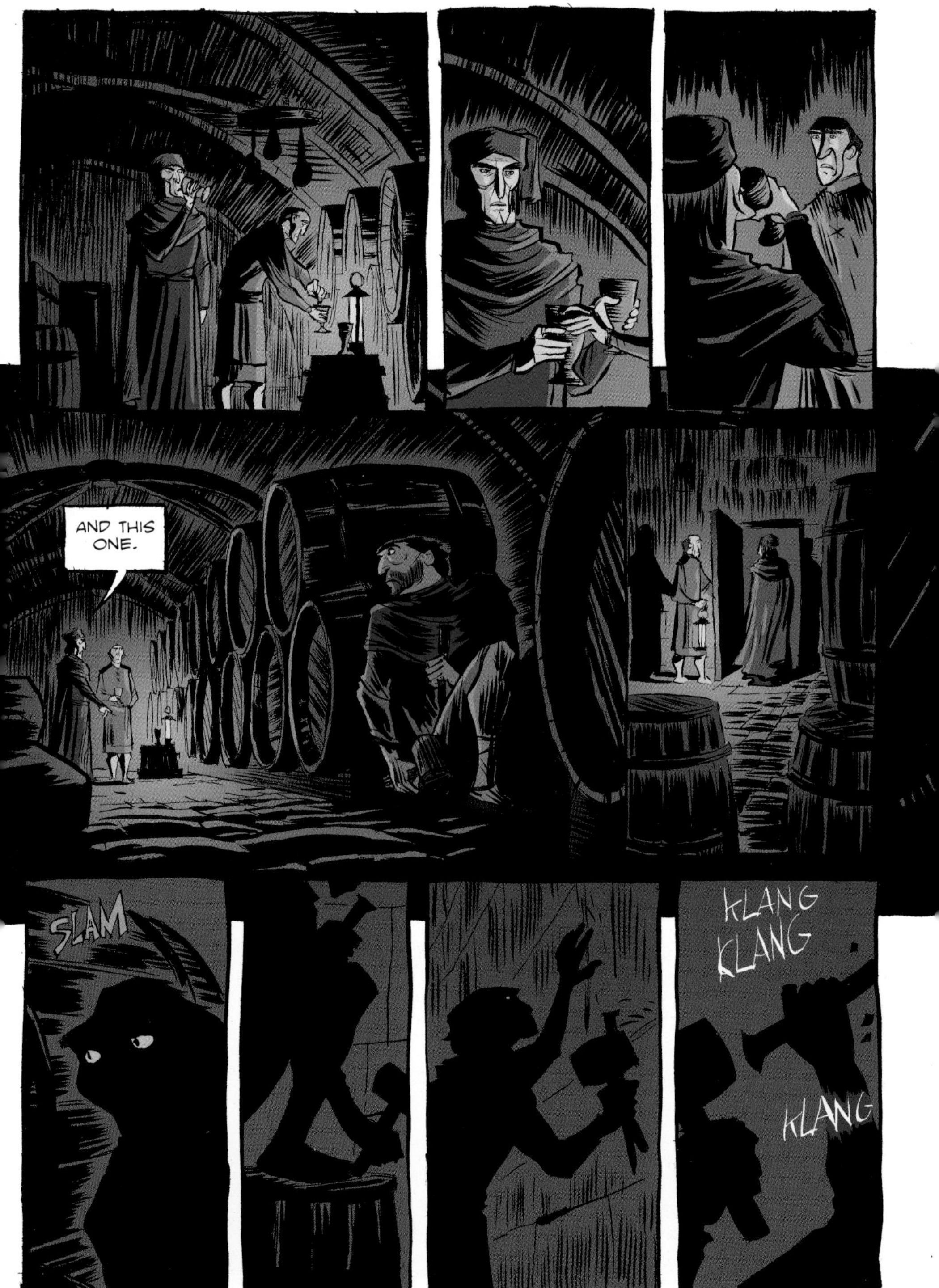
AND THIS ONE.
SLAM
KLANG
KLANG
KLANG

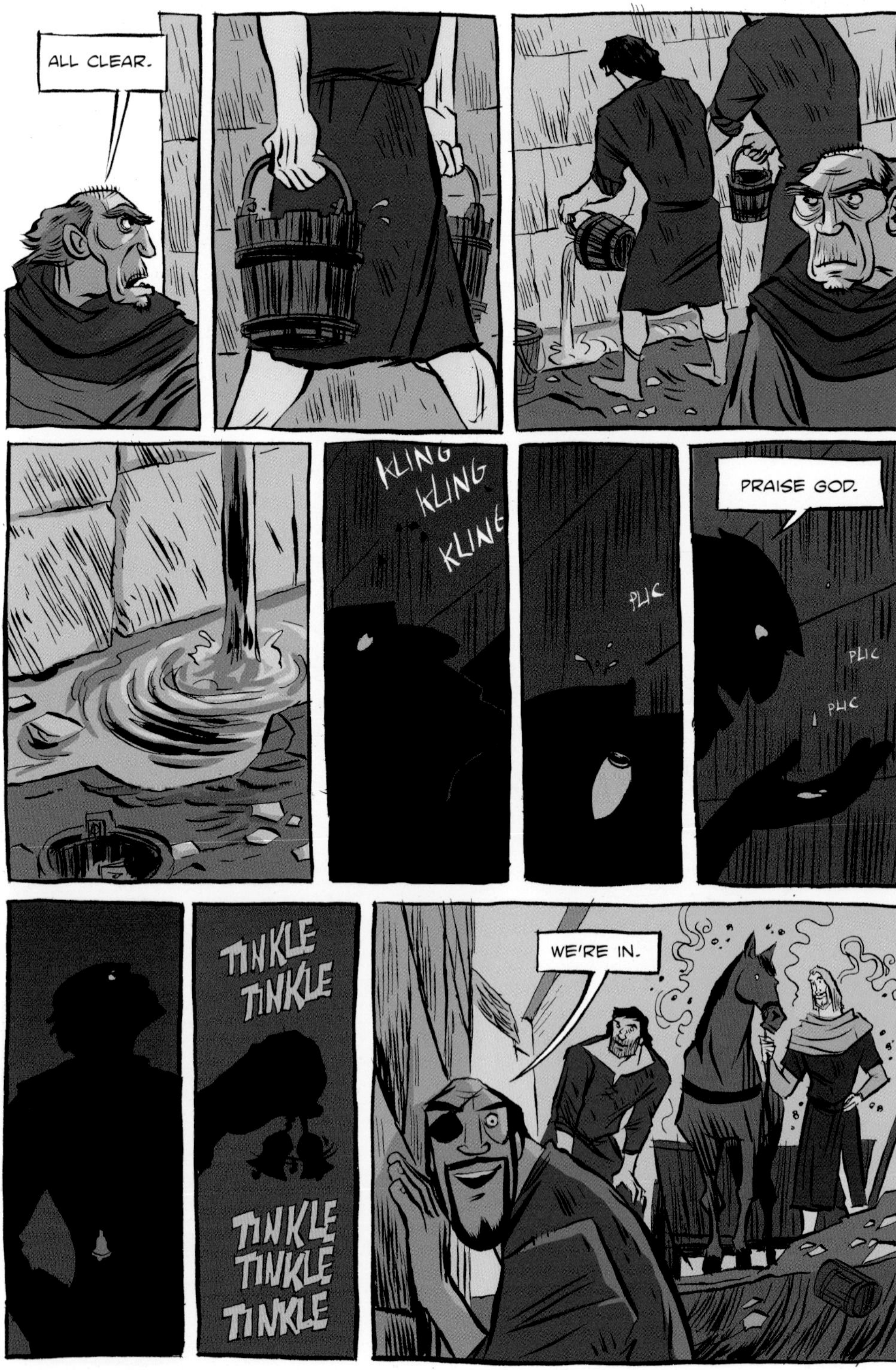

ALL CLEAR.
KLING
KLING
KLING
PLIC
PRAISE GOD.
PLIC
PLIC
TINKLE
TINKLE
TINKLE
TINKLE
TINKLE
WE'RE IN.

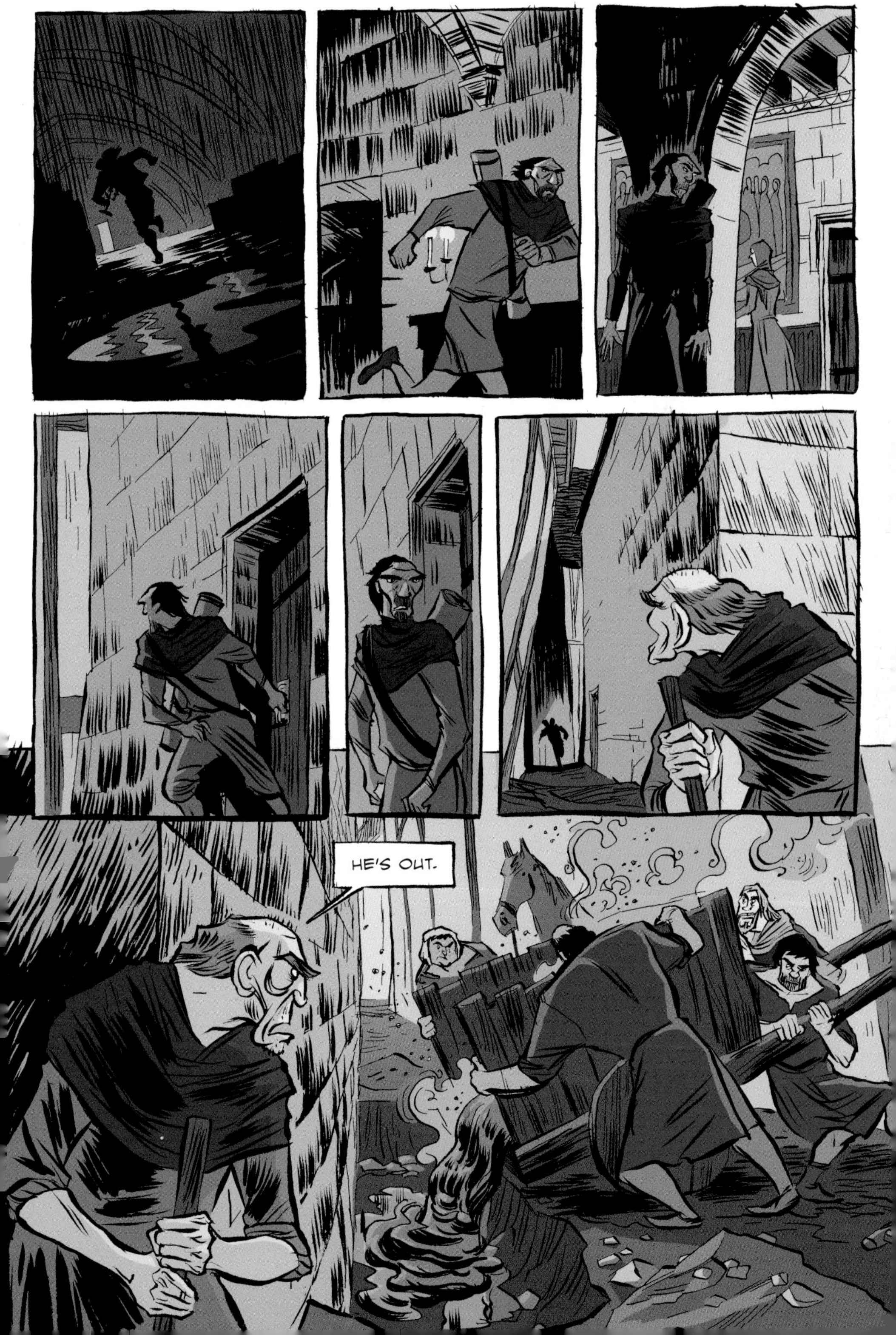
HE'S OUT.

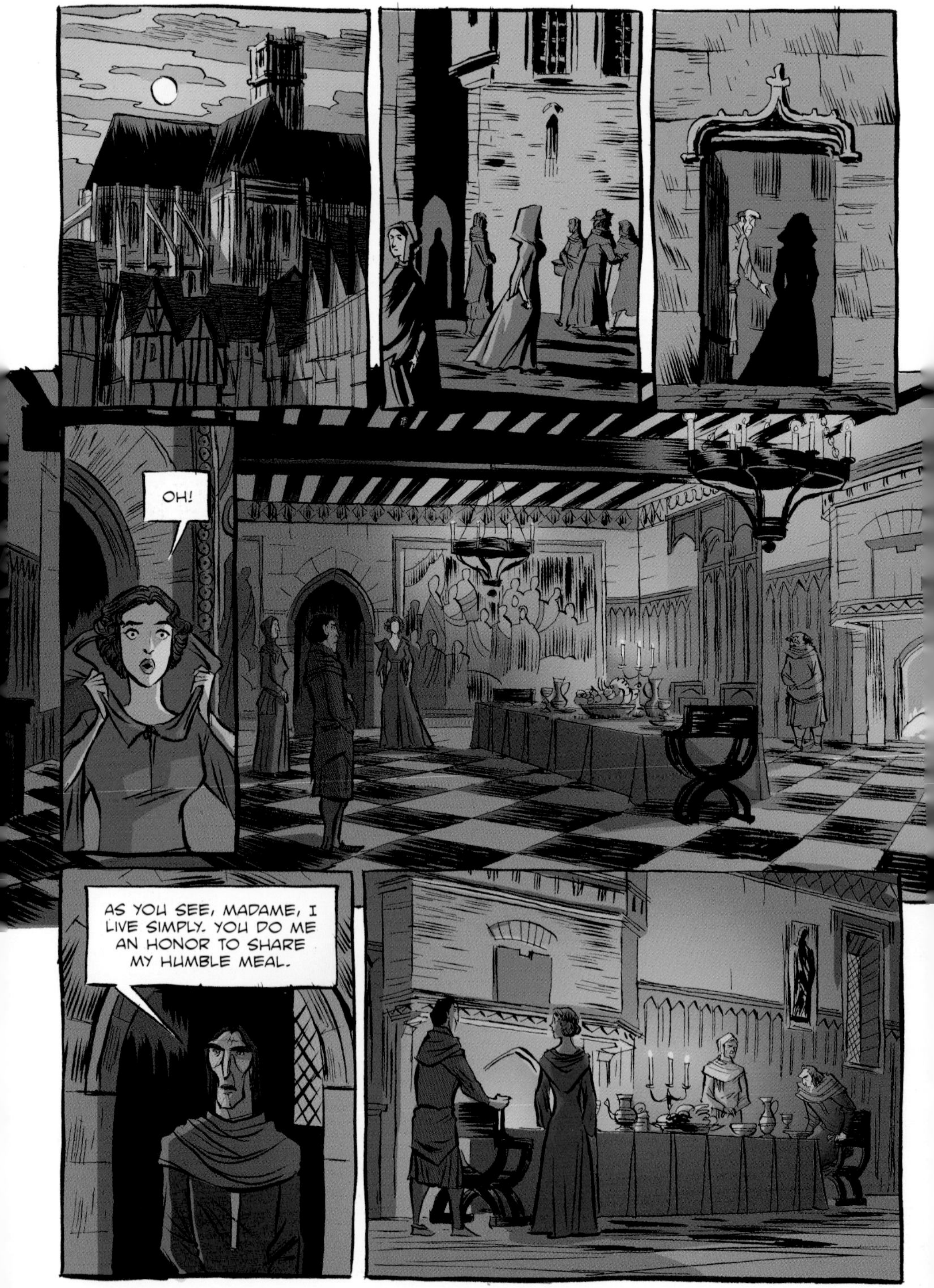
OH!
AS YOU SEE, MADAME, I LIVE SIMPLY. YOU DO ME AN HONOR TO SHARE MY HUMBLE MEAL.

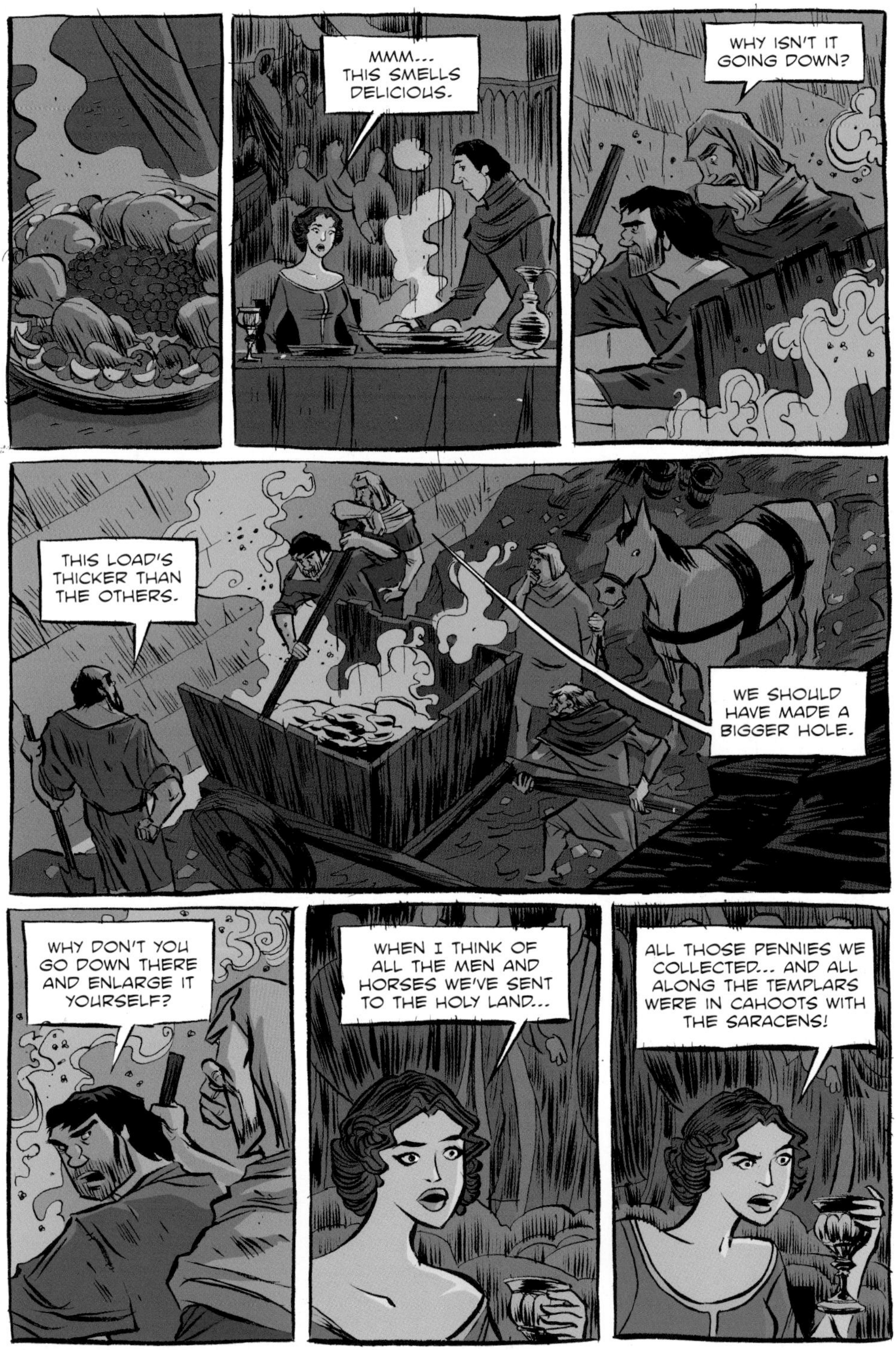
MMM... THIS SMELLS DELICIOUS.
WHY ISN'T IT GOING DOWN?
THIS LOAD'S THICKER THAN THE OTHERS.
WE SHOULD HAVE MADE A BIGGER HOLE.
WHY DON'T YOU GO DOWN THERE AND ENLARGE IT YOURSELF?
WHEN I THINK OF ALL THE MEN AND HORSES WE'VE SENT TO THE HOLY LAND...
ALL THOSE PENNIES WE COLLECTED... AND ALL ALONG THE TEMPLARS WERE IN CAHOOTS WITH THE SARACENS!

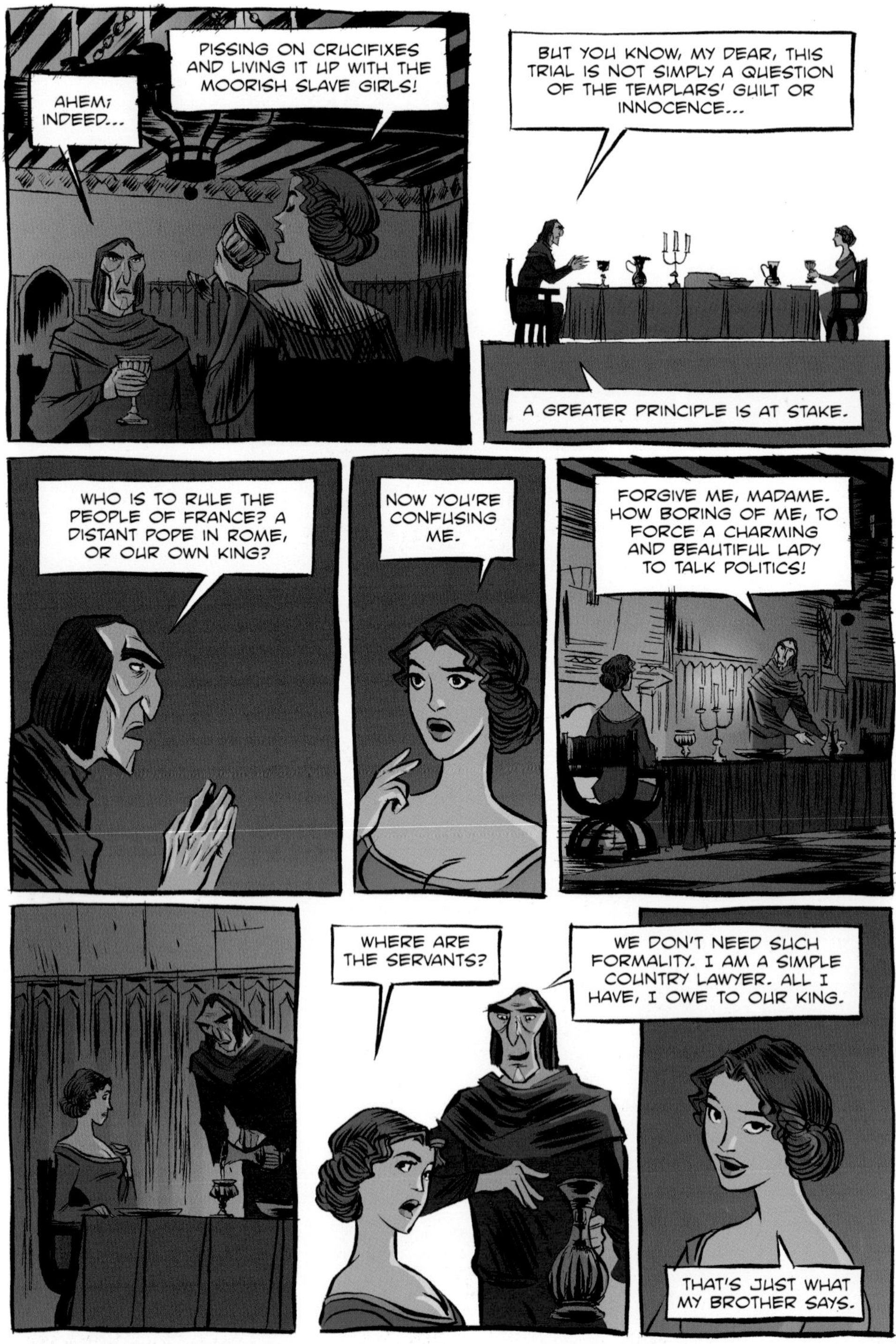
AHEM; INDEED...
PISSING ON CRUCIFIXES AND LIVING IT UP WITH THE MOORISH SLAVE GIRLS!
BUT YOU KNOW, MY DEAR, THIS TRIAL IS NOT SIMPLY A QUESTION OF THE TEMPLARS' GUILT OR INNOCENCE...
A GREATER PRINCIPLE IS AT STAKE.
WHO IS TO RULE THE PEOPLE OF FRANCE? A DISTANT POPE IN ROME, OR OUR OWN KING?
NOW YOU'RE CONFUSING ME.
FORGIVE ME, MADAME. HOW BORING OF ME, TO FORCE A CHARMING AND BEAUTIFUL LADY TO TALK POLITICS!
WHERE ARE THE SERVANTS?
WE DON'T NEED SUCH FORMALITY. I AM A SIMPLE COUNTRY LAWYER. ALL I HAVE, I OWE TO OUR KING.
THAT'S JUST WHAT MY BROTHER SAYS.

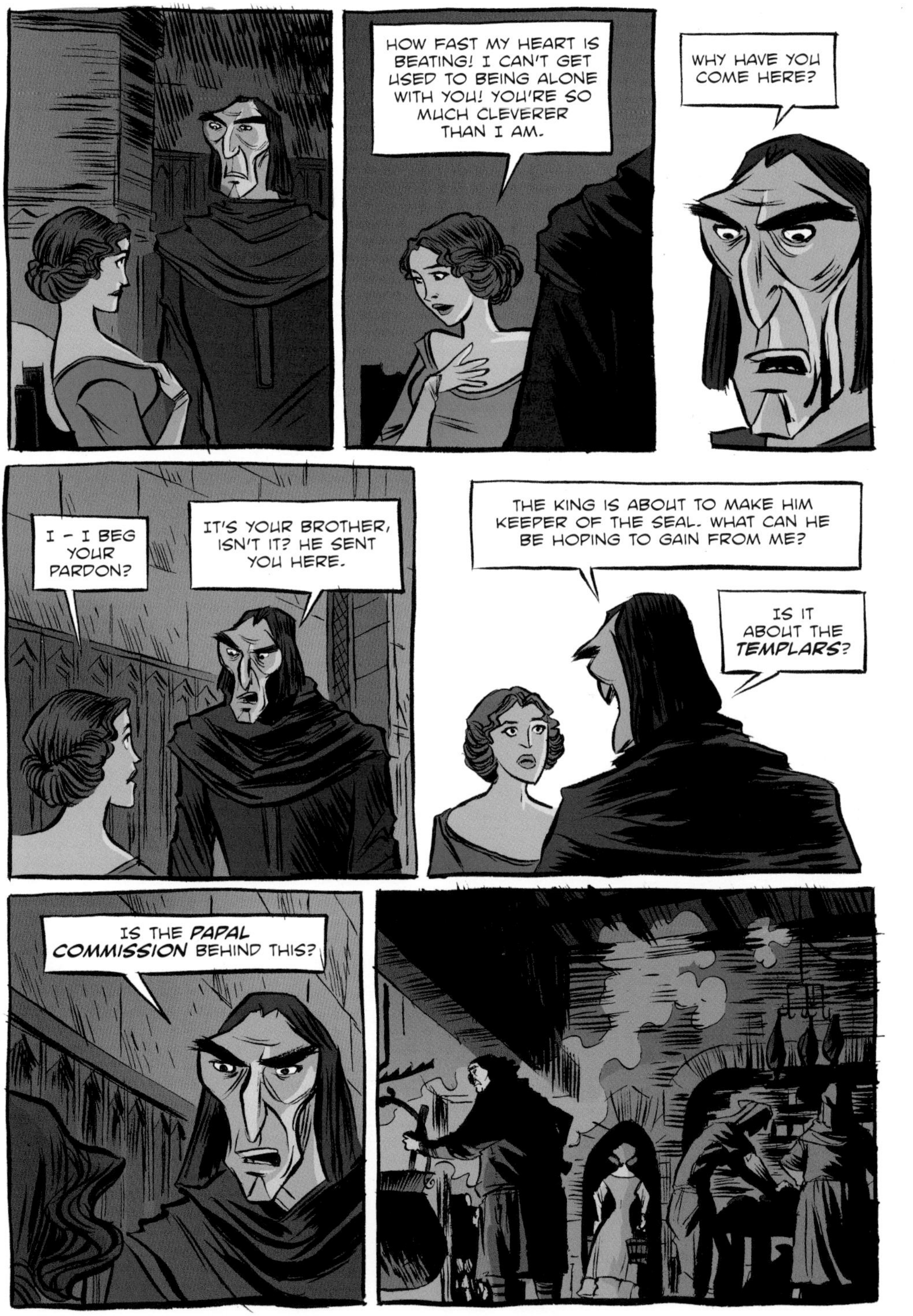
HOW FAST MY HEART IS BEATING! I CAN'T GET USED TO BEING ALONE WITH YOU! YOU'RE SO MUCH CLEVERER THAN I AM.
WHY HAVE YOU COME HERE?
I - I BEG YOUR PARDON?
IT'S YOUR BROTHER, ISN'T IT? HE SENT YOU HERE.
THE KING IS ABOUT TO MAKE HIM KEEPER OF THE SEAL. WHAT CAN HE BE HOPING TO GAIN FROM ME?
IS IT ABOUT THE TEMPLARS?
IS THE PAPAL COMMISSION BEHIND THIS?

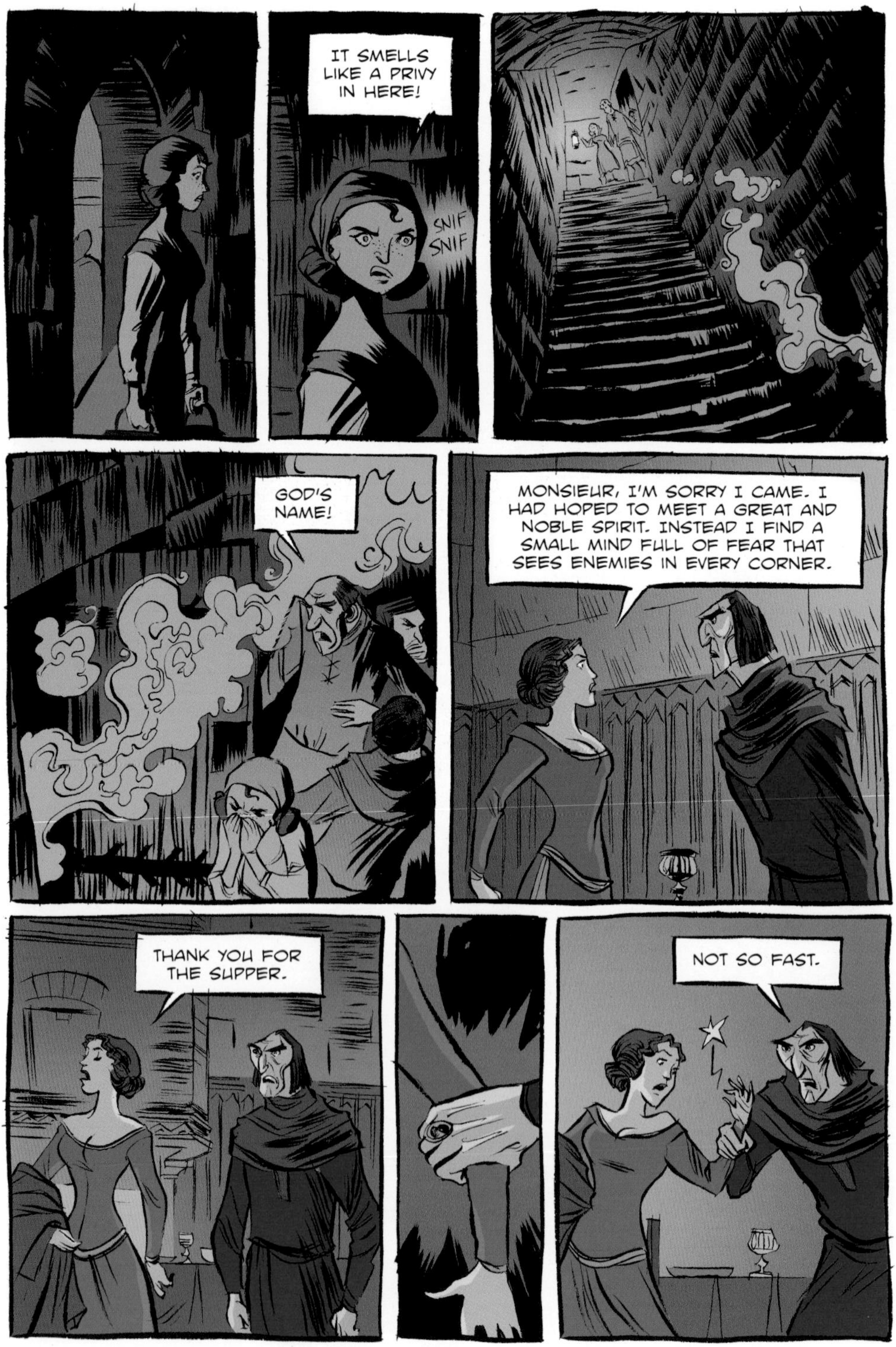
IT SMELLS LIKE A PRIVY IN HERE!
SNIF SNIF
GOD'S NAME!
MONSIEUR, I'M SORRY I CAME. I HAD HOPED TO MEET A GREAT AND NOBLE SPIRIT. INSTEAD I FIND A SMALL MIND FULL OF FEAR THAT SEES ENEMIES IN EVERY CORNER.
THANK YOU FOR THE SUPPER.
NOT SO FAST.

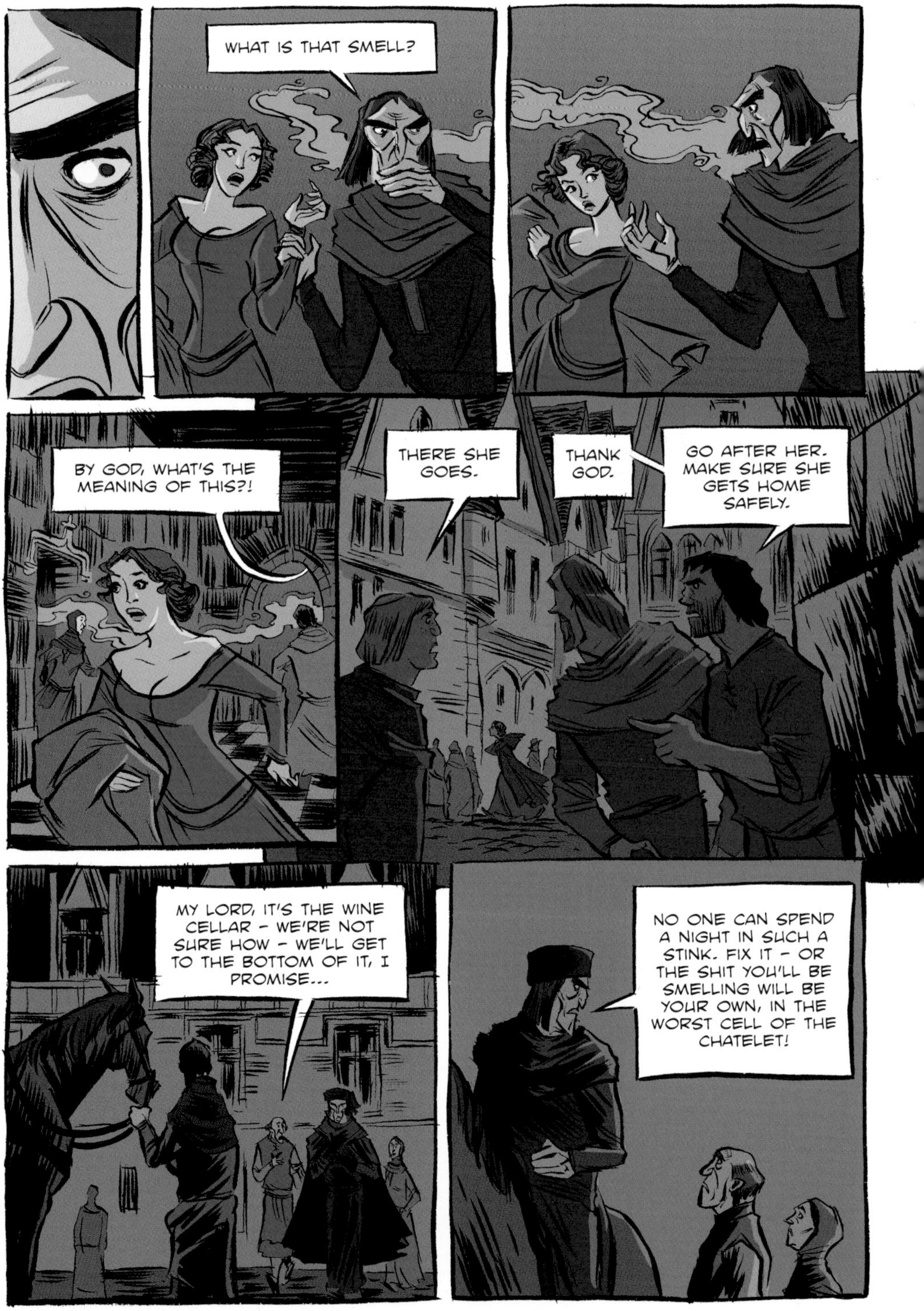
WHAT IS THAT SMELL?
BY GOD, WHAT'S THE MEANING OF THIS?!
THERE SHE GOES.
THANK GOD.
GO AFTER HER. MAKE SURE SHE GETS HOME SAFELY.
MY LORD, IT'S THE WINE CELLAR - WE'RE NOT SURE HOW - WE'LL GET TO THE BOTTOM OF IT, I PROMISE...
NO ONE CAN SPEND A NIGHT IN SUCH A STINK. FIX IT - OR THE SHIT YOU'LL BE SMELLING WILL BE YOUR OWN, IN THE WORST CELL OF THE CHATELET!

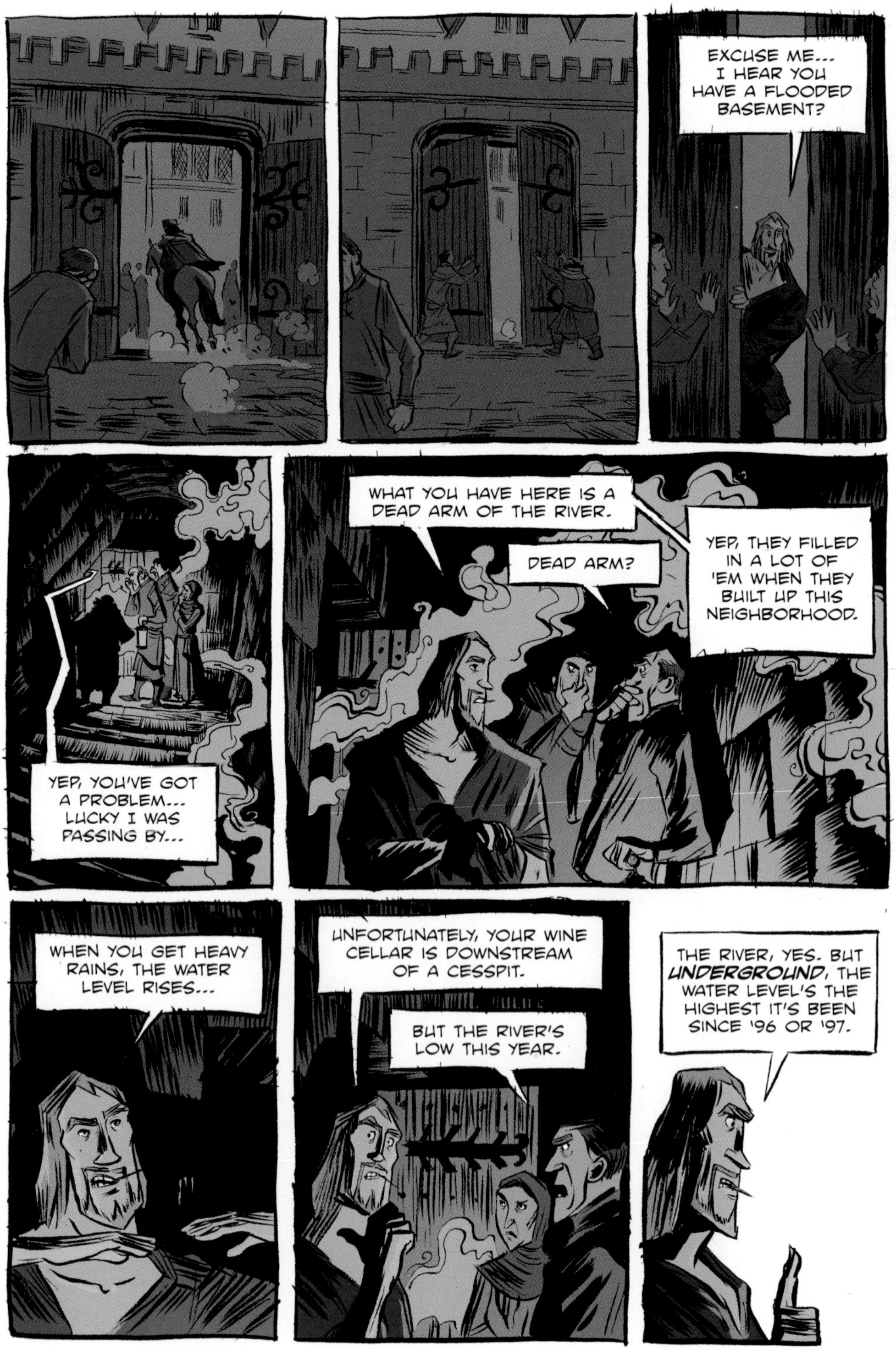
EXCUSE ME... I HEAR YOU HAVE A FLOODED BASEMENT?
YEP, YOU'VE GOT A PROBLEM... LUCKY I WAS PASSING BY...
WHAT YOU HAVE HERE IS A DEAD ARM OF THE RIVER.
DEAD ARM?
YEP, THEY FILLED IN A LOT OF 'EM WHEN THEY BUILT UP THIS NEIGHBORHOOD.
WHEN YOU GET HEAVY RAINS, THE WATER LEVEL RISES...
UNFORTUNATELY, YOUR WINE CELLAR IS DOWNSTREAM OF A CESSPIT.
BUT THE RIVER'S LOW THIS YEAR.
THE RIVER, YES. BUT *UNDERGROUND*, THE WATER LEVEL'S THE HIGHEST IT'S BEEN SINCE '96 OR '97.

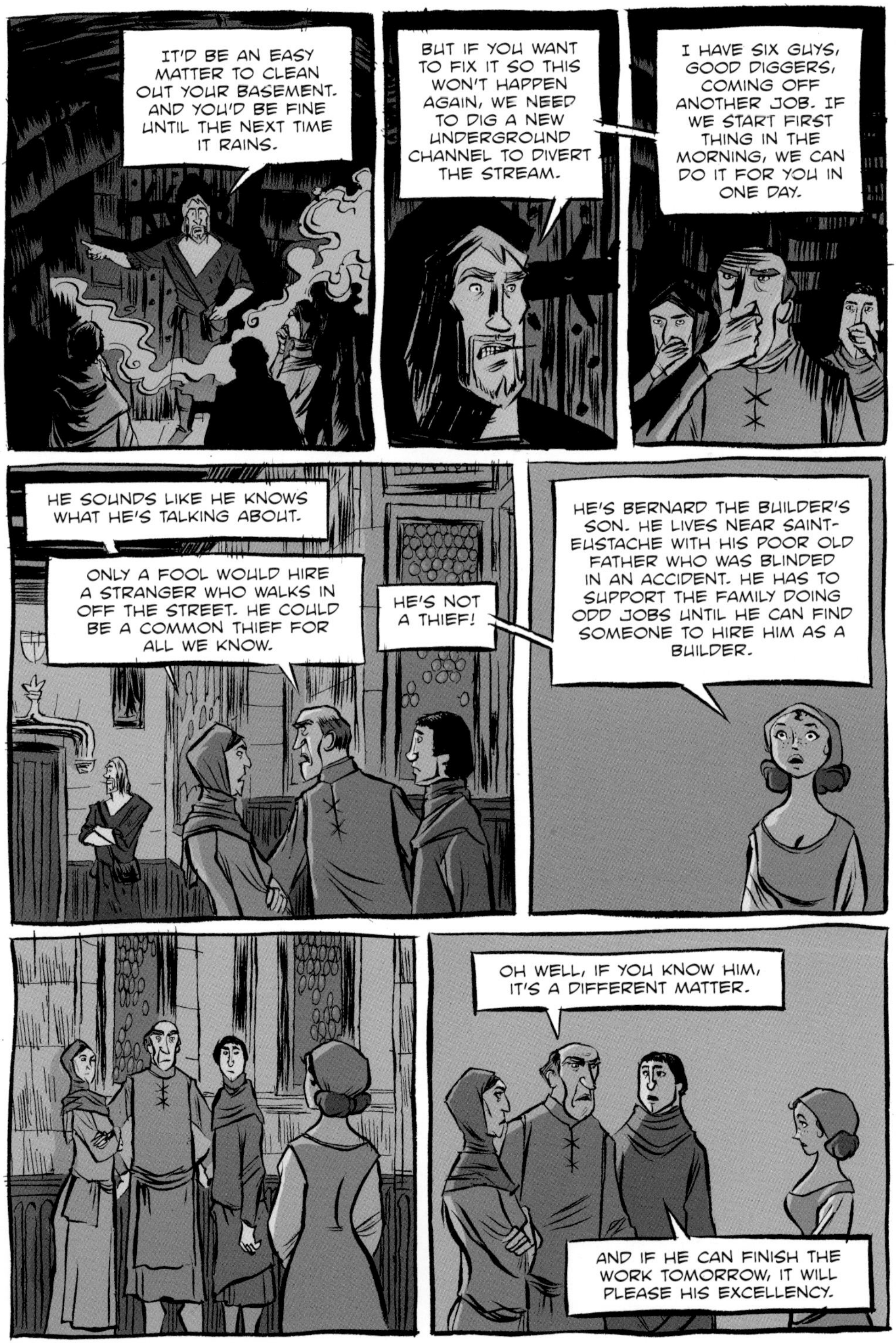
IT'D BE AN EASY MATTER TO CLEAN OUT YOUR BASEMENT. AND YOU'D BE FINE UNTIL THE NEXT TIME IT RAINS.
BUT IF YOU WANT TO FIX IT SO THIS WON'T HAPPEN AGAIN, WE NEED TO DIG A NEW UNDERGROUND CHANNEL TO DIVERT THE STREAM.
I HAVE SIX GUYS, GOOD DIGGERS, COMING OFF ANOTHER JOB. IF WE START FIRST THING IN THE MORNING, WE CAN DO IT FOR YOU IN ONE DAY.
HE SOUNDS LIKE HE KNOWS WHAT HE'S TALKING ABOUT.
ONLY A FOOL WOULD HIRE A STRANGER WHO WALKS IN OFF THE STREET. HE COULD BE A COMMON THIEF FOR ALL WE KNOW.
HE'S NOT A THIEF!
HE'S BERNARD THE BUILDER'S SON. HE LIVES NEAR SAINT-EUSTACHE WITH HIS POOR OLD FATHER WHO WAS BLINDED IN AN ACCIDENT. HE HAS TO SUPPORT THE FAMILY DOING ODD JOBS UNTIL HE CAN FIND SOMEONE TO HIRE HIM AS A BUILDER.
OH WELL, IF YOU KNOW HIM, IT'S A DIFFERENT MATTER.
AND IF HE CAN FINISH THE WORK TOMORROW, IT WILL PLEASE HIS EXCELLENCY.

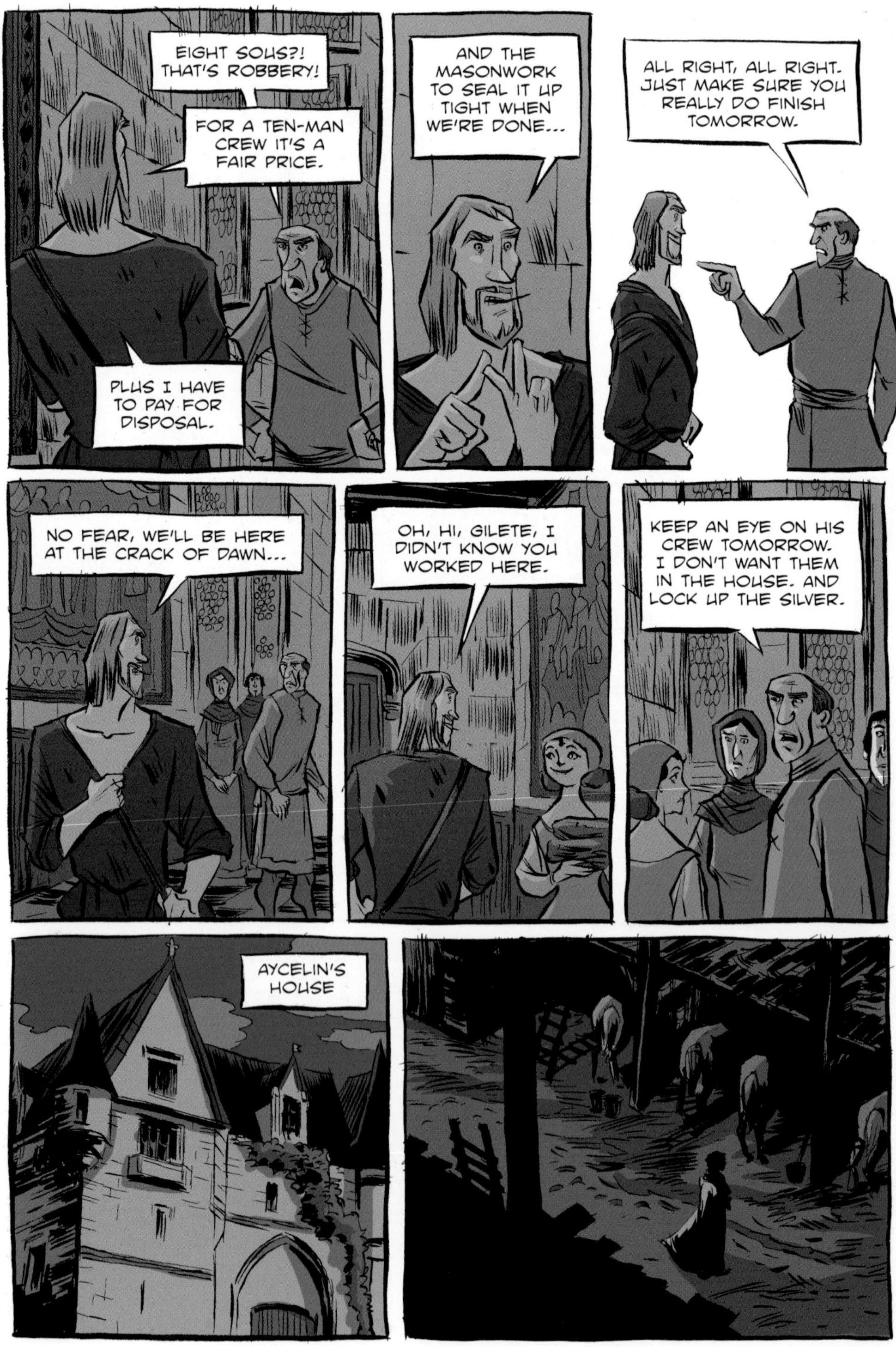
EIGHT SOUS?! THAT'S ROBBERY!
FOR A TEN-MAN CREW IT'S A FAIR PRICE.
PLUS I HAVE TO PAY FOR DISPOSAL.
AND THE MASONWORK TO SEAL IT UP TIGHT WHEN WE'RE DONE...
ALL RIGHT, ALL RIGHT. JUST MAKE SURE YOU REALLY DO FINISH TOMORROW.
NO FEAR, WE'LL BE HERE AT THE CRACK OF DAWN...
OH, HI, GILETE, I DIDN'T KNOW YOU WORKED HERE.
KEEP AN EYE ON HIS CREW TOMORROW. I DON'T WANT THEM IN THE HOUSE. AND LOCK UP THE SILVER.
AYCELIN'S HOUSE

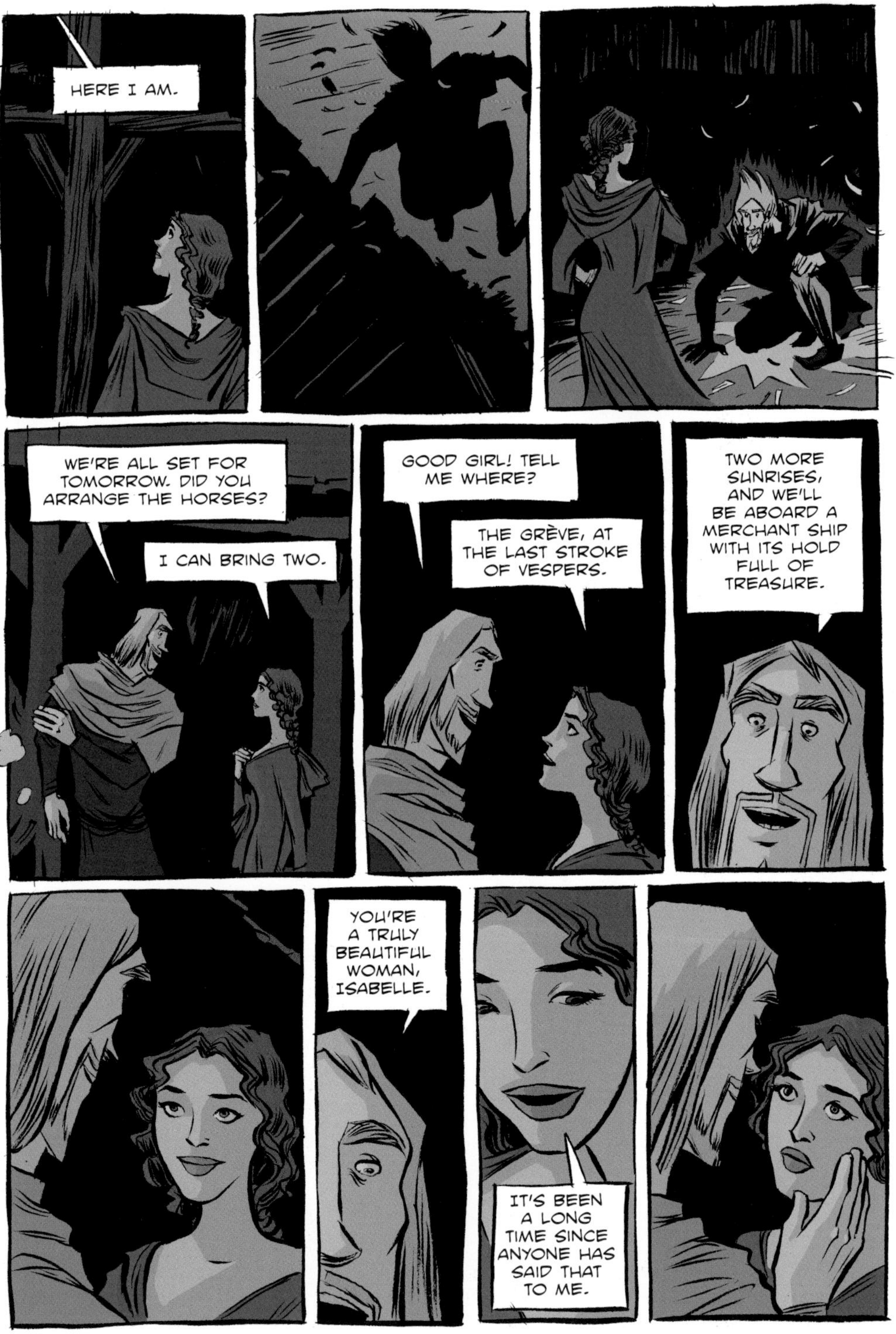
HERE I AM.
WE'RE ALL SET FOR TOMORROW. DID YOU ARRANGE THE HORSES?
I CAN BRING TWO.
GOOD GIRL! TELL ME WHERE?
THE GRÈVE, AT THE LAST STROKE OF VESPERS.
TWO MORE SUNRISES, AND WE'LL BE ABOARD A MERCHANT SHIP WITH ITS HOLD FULL OF TREASURE.
YOU'RE A TRULY BEAUTIFUL WOMAN, ISABELLE.
IT'S BEEN A LONG TIME SINCE ANYONE HAS SAID THAT TO ME.

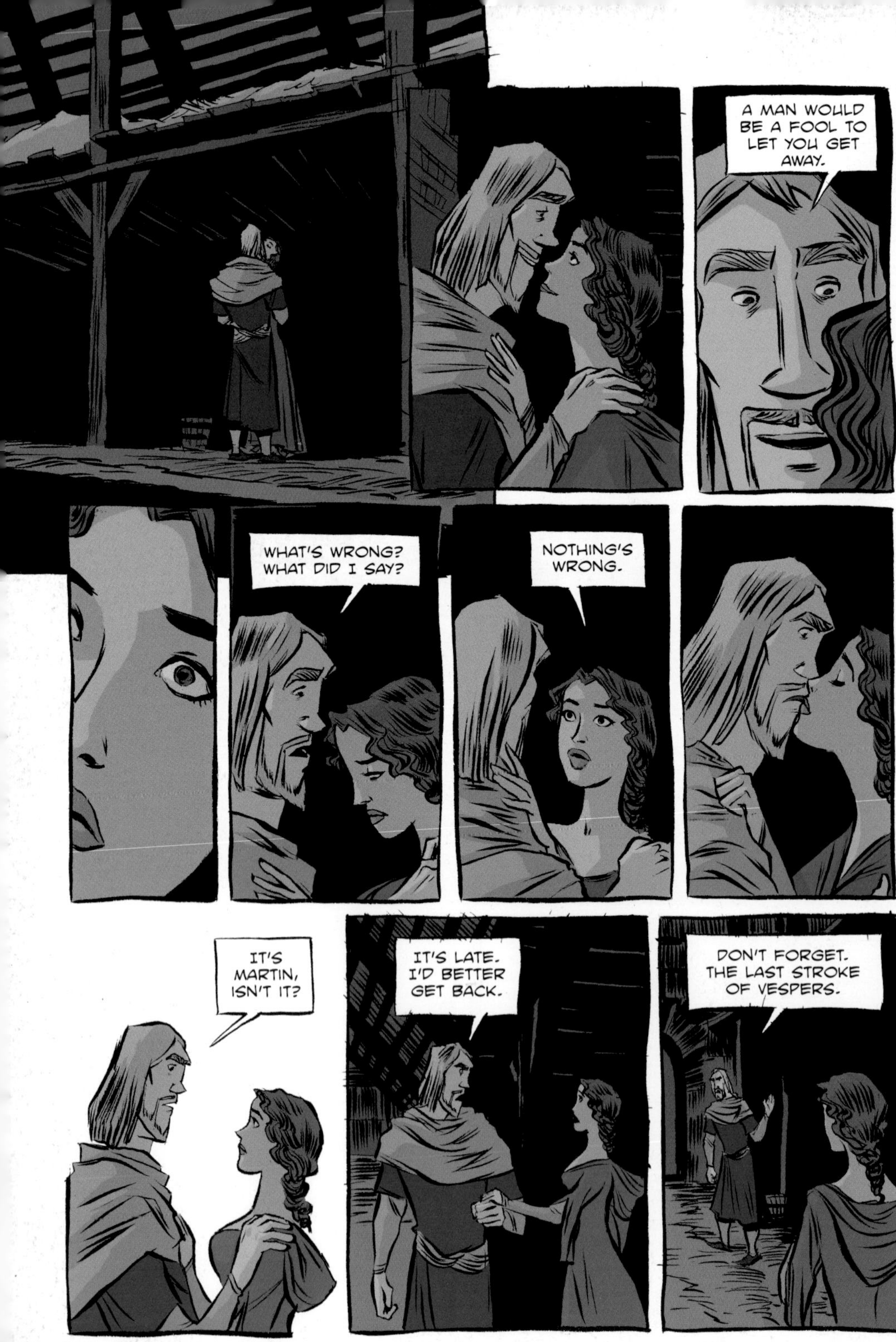
A MAN WOULD BE A FOOL TO LET YOU GET AWAY.
WHAT'S WRONG? WHAT DID I SAY?
NOTHING'S WRONG.
IT'S MARTIN, ISN'T IT?
IT'S LATE. I'D BETTER GET BACK.
DON'T FORGET. THE LAST STROKE OF VESPERS.

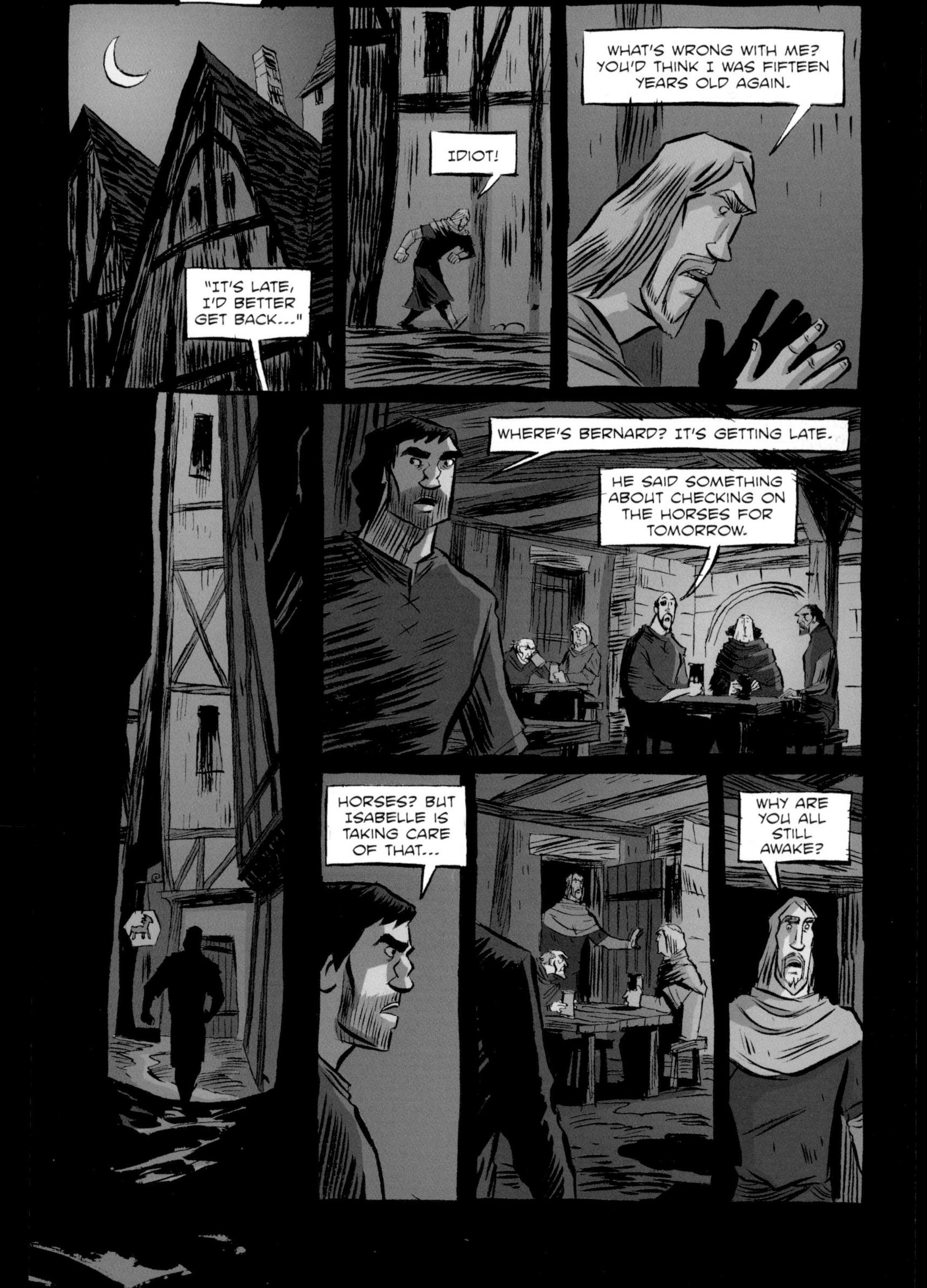
"IT'S LATE, I'D BETTER GET BACK..."
IDIOT!
WHAT'S WRONG WITH ME? YOU'D THINK I WAS FIFTEEN YEARS OLD AGAIN.
WHERE'S BERNARD? IT'S GETTING LATE.
HE SAID SOMETHING ABOUT CHECKING ON THE HORSES FOR TOMORROW.
HORSES? BUT ISABELLE IS TAKING CARE OF THAT...
WHY ARE YOU ALL STILL AWAKE?

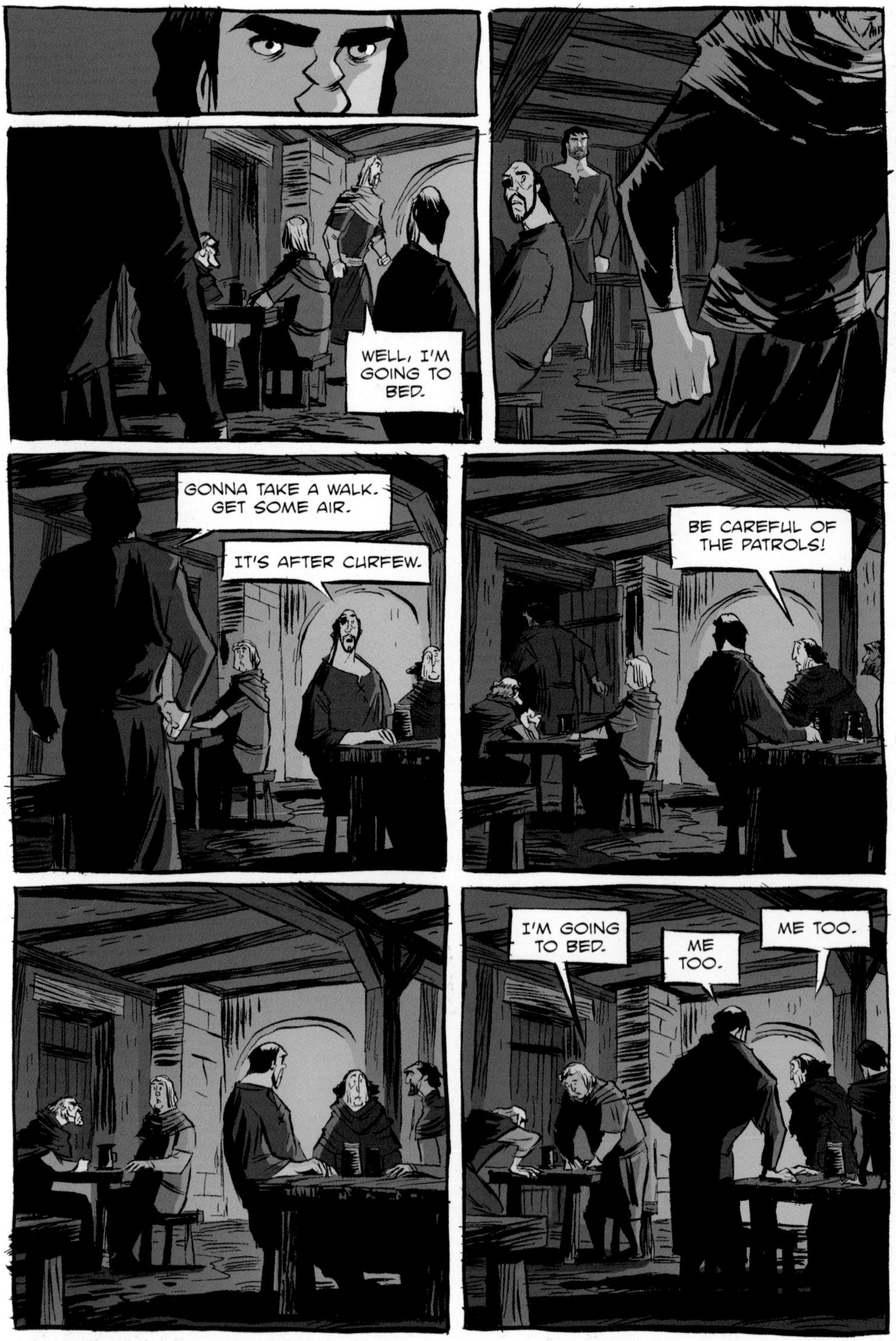
WELL, I'M GOING TO BED.
GONNA TAKE A WALK. GET SOME AIR.
IT'S AFTER CURFEW.
BE CAREFUL OF THE PATROLS!
I'M GOING TO BED.
ME TOO.
ME TOO.

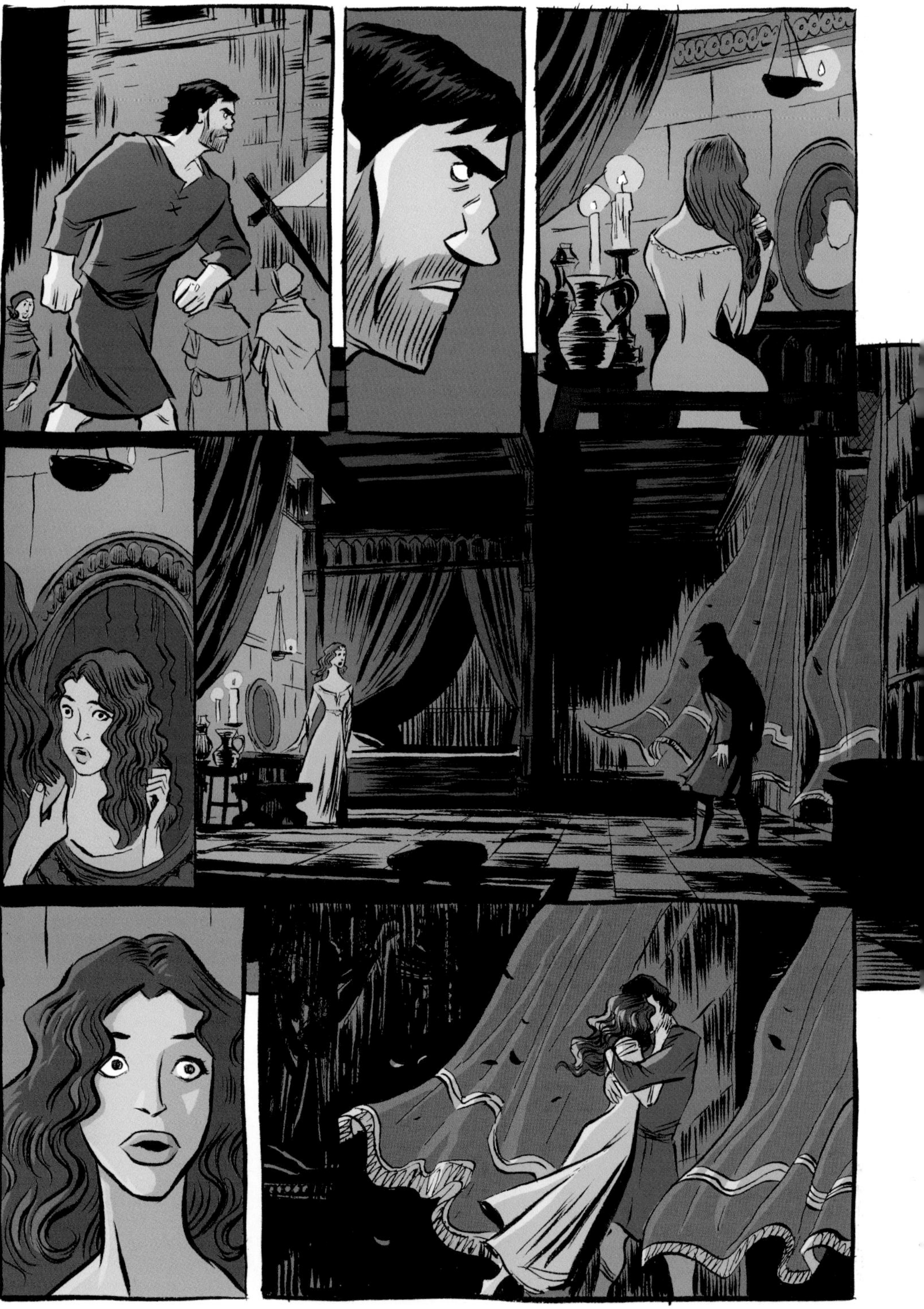

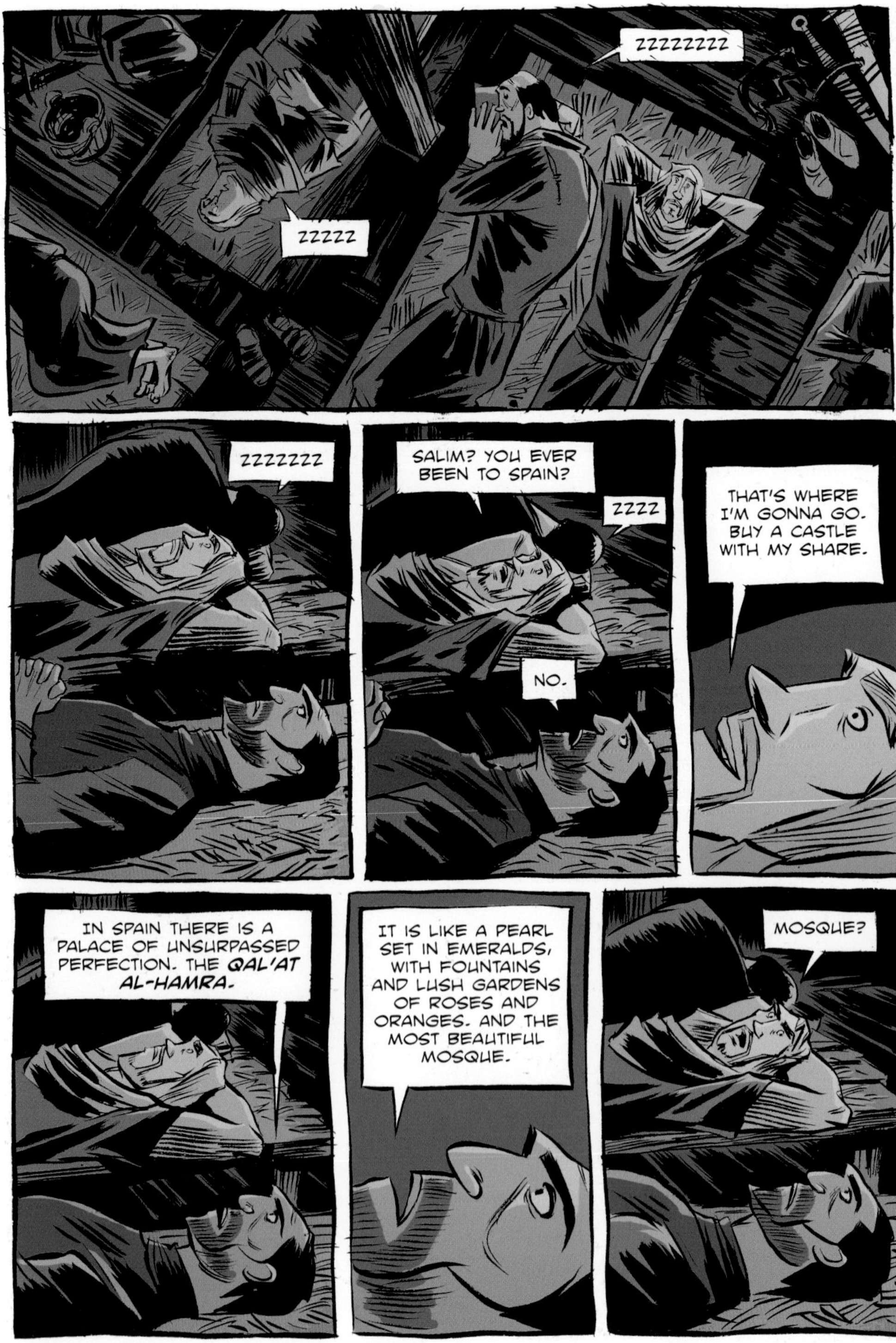
ZZZZZZZZ
ZZZZZ
ZZZZZZZ
SALIM? YOU EVER BEEN TO SPAIN?
ZZZZ
NO.
THAT'S WHERE I'M GONNA GO. BUY A CASTLE WITH MY SHARE.
IN SPAIN THERE IS A PALACE OF UNSURPASSED PERFECTION. THE *QAL'AT AL-HAMRA*.
IT IS LIKE A PEARL SET IN EMERALDS, WITH FOUNTAINS AND LUSH GARDENS OF ROSES AND ORANGES. AND THE MOST BEAUTIFUL MOSQUE.
MOSQUE?

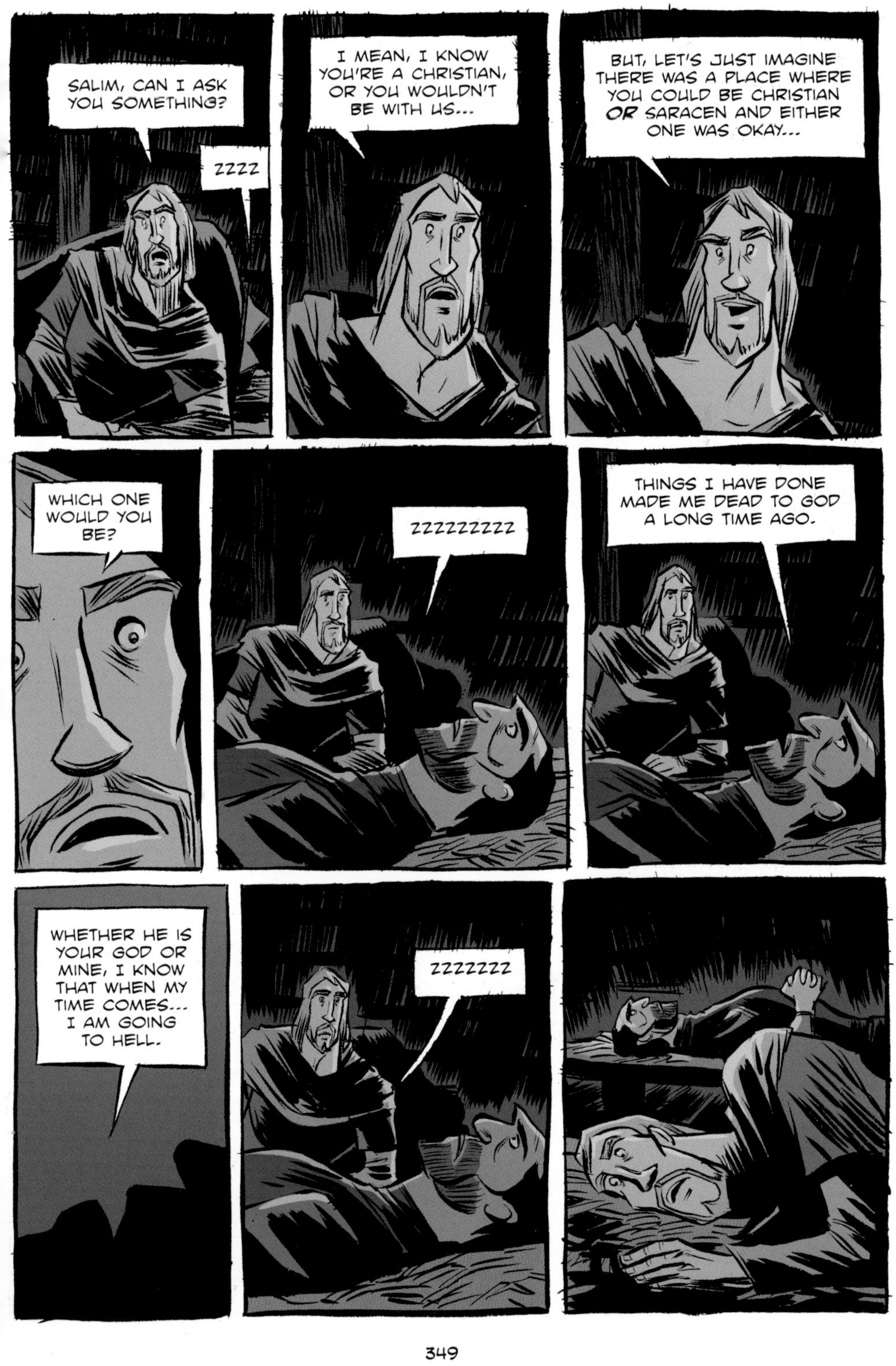
SALIM, CAN I ASK YOU SOMETHING?
ZZZZ
I MEAN, I KNOW YOU'RE A CHRISTIAN, OR YOU WOULDN'T BE WITH US...
BUT, LET'S JUST IMAGINE THERE WAS A PLACE WHERE YOU COULD BE CHRISTIAN *OR* SARACEN AND EITHER ONE WAS OKAY...
WHICH ONE WOULD YOU BE?
ZZZZZZZZZ
THINGS I HAVE DONE MADE ME DEAD TO GOD A LONG TIME AGO.
WHETHER HE IS YOUR GOD OR MINE, I KNOW THAT WHEN MY TIME COMES... I AM GOING TO HELL.
ZZZZZZZ

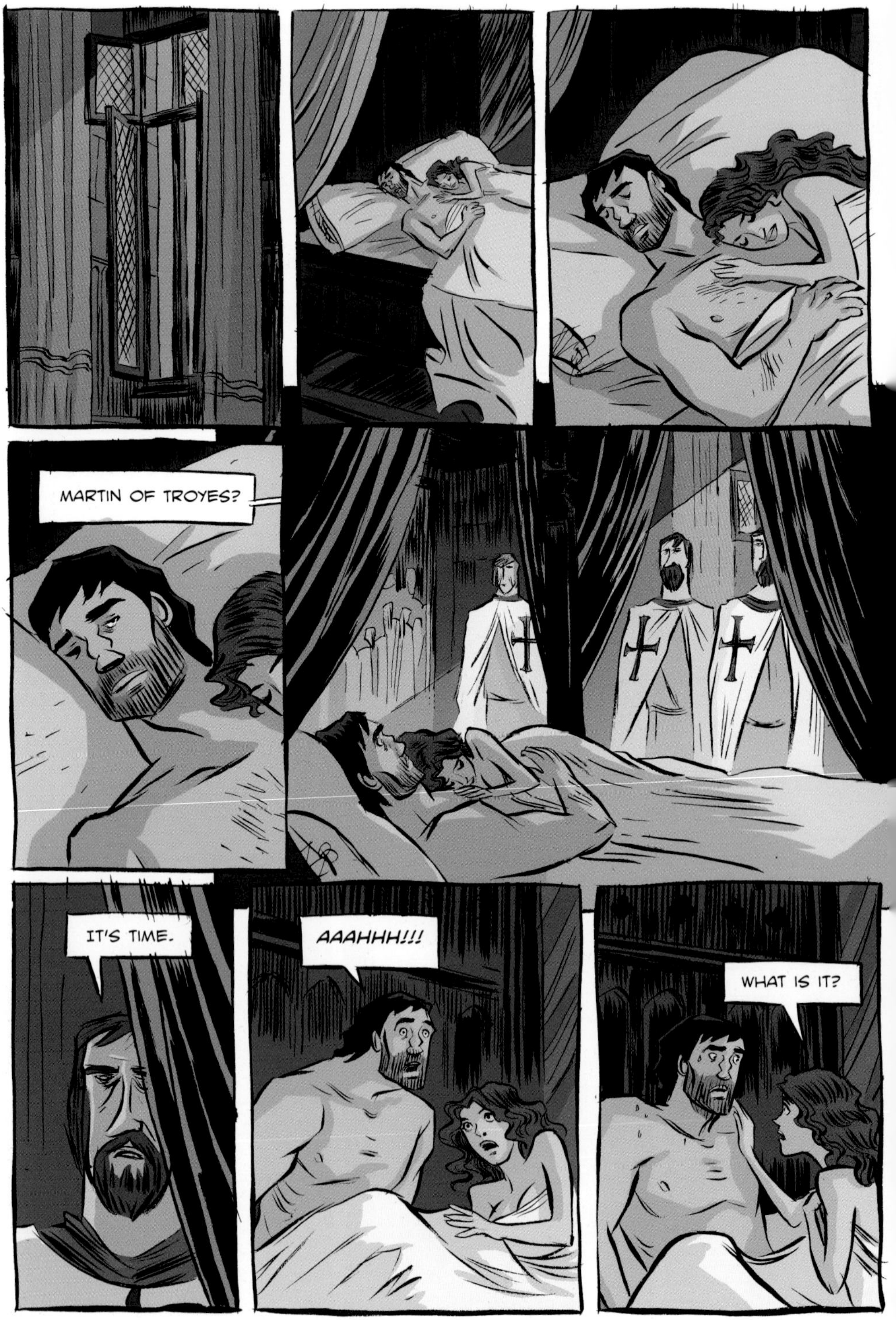
MARTIN OF TROYES?
IT'S TIME.
AAAHHH!!!
WHAT IS IT?

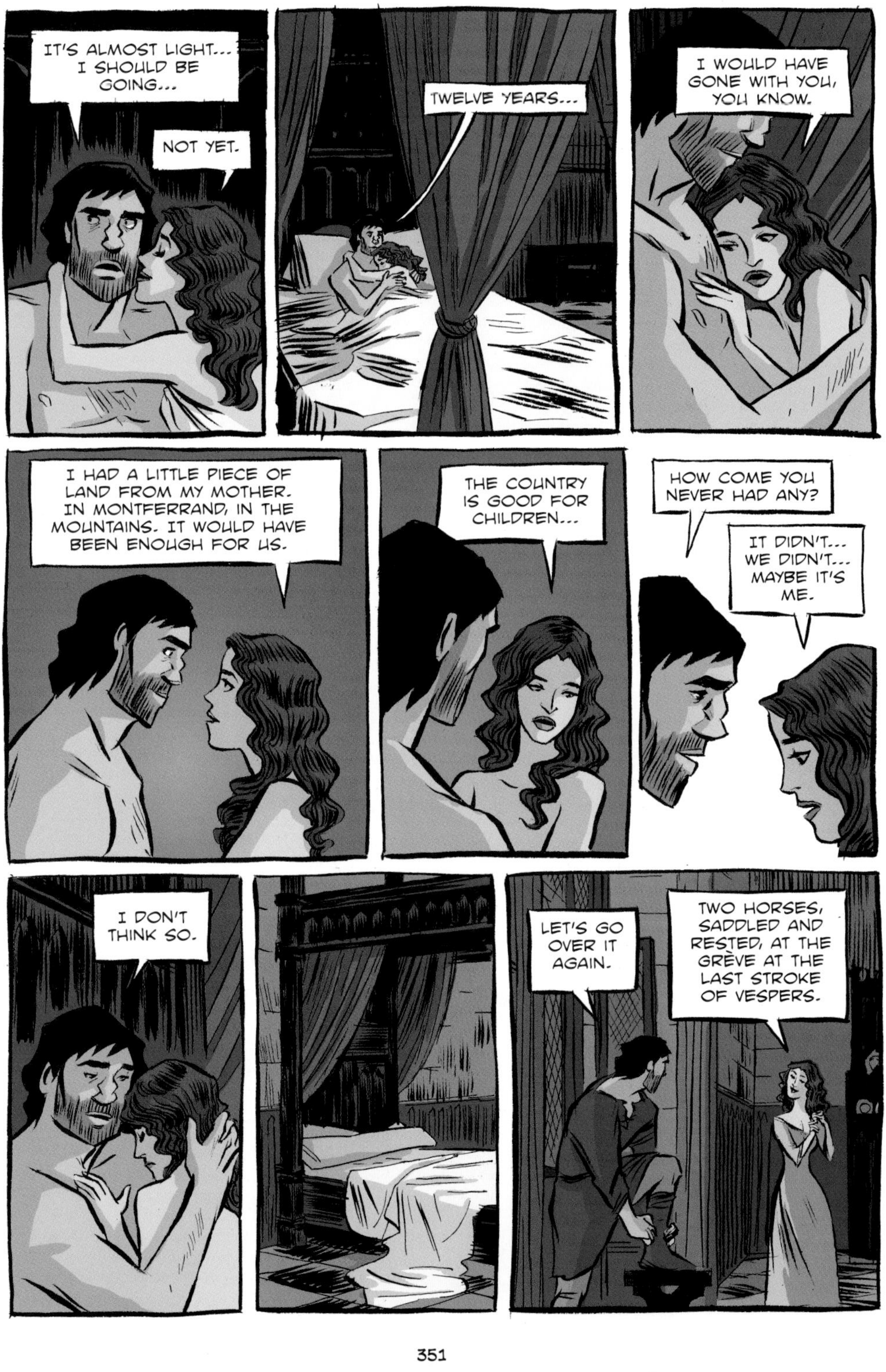

IT'S ALMOST LIGHT... I SHOULD BE GOING...
NOT YET.
TWELVE YEARS...
I WOULD HAVE GONE WITH YOU, YOU KNOW.
I HAD A LITTLE PIECE OF LAND FROM MY MOTHER. IN MONTFERRAND, IN THE MOUNTAINS. IT WOULD HAVE BEEN ENOUGH FOR US.
THE COUNTRY IS GOOD FOR CHILDREN...
HOW COME YOU NEVER HAD ANY?
IT DIDN'T... WE DIDN'T... MAYBE IT'S ME.
I DON'T THINK SO.
LET'S GO OVER IT AGAIN.
TWO HORSES, SADDLED AND RESTED, AT THE GRÈVE AT THE LAST STROKE OF VESPERS.

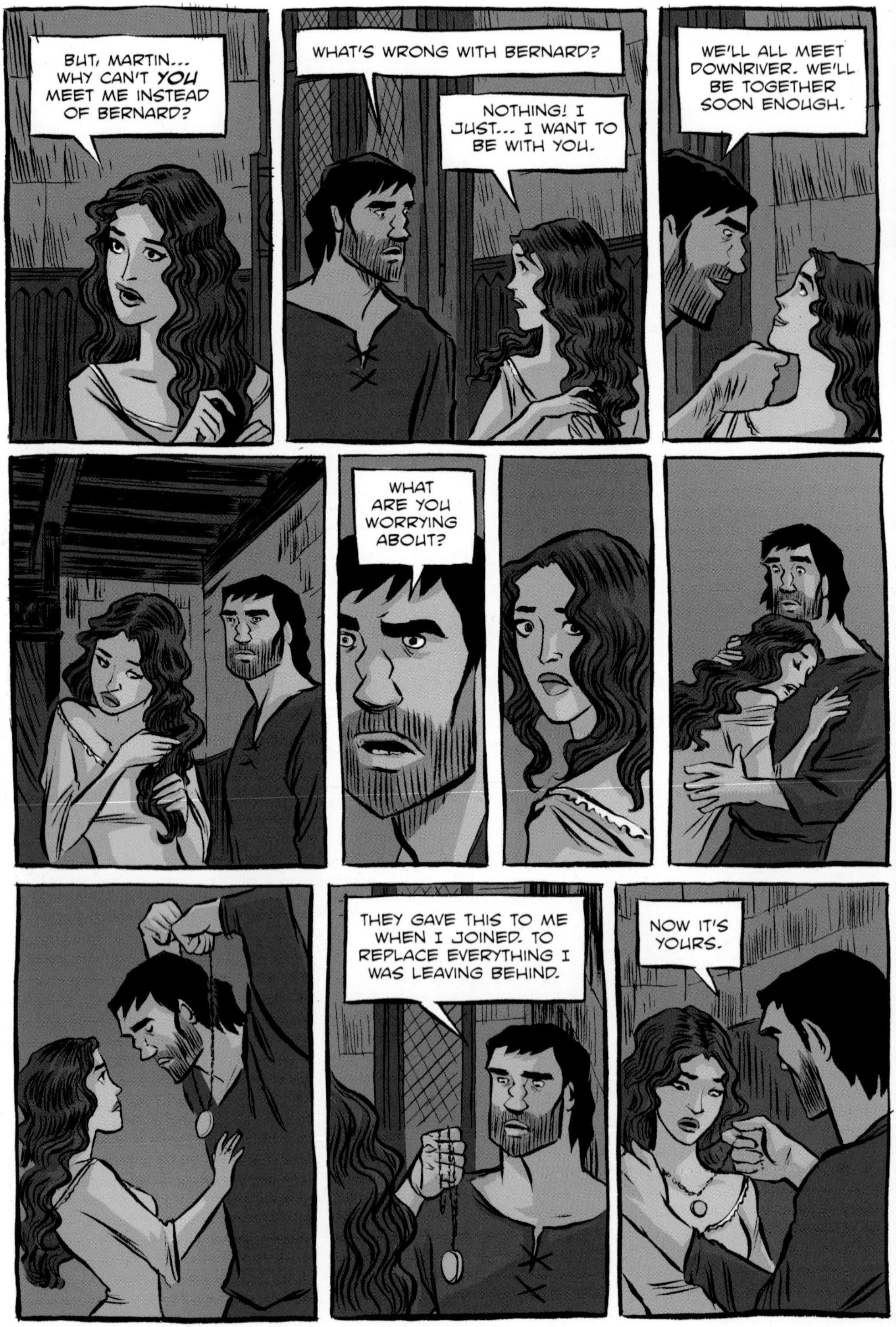
BUT, MARTIN... WHY CAN'T YOU MEET ME INSTEAD OF BERNARD?
WHAT'S WRONG WITH BERNARD?
NOTHING! I JUST... I WANT TO BE WITH YOU.
WE'LL ALL MEET DOWNRIVER. WE'LL BE TOGETHER SOON ENOUGH.
WHAT ARE YOU WORRYING ABOUT?
THEY GAVE THIS TO ME WHEN I JOINED. TO REPLACE EVERYTHING I WAS LEAVING BEHIND.
NOW IT'S YOURS.

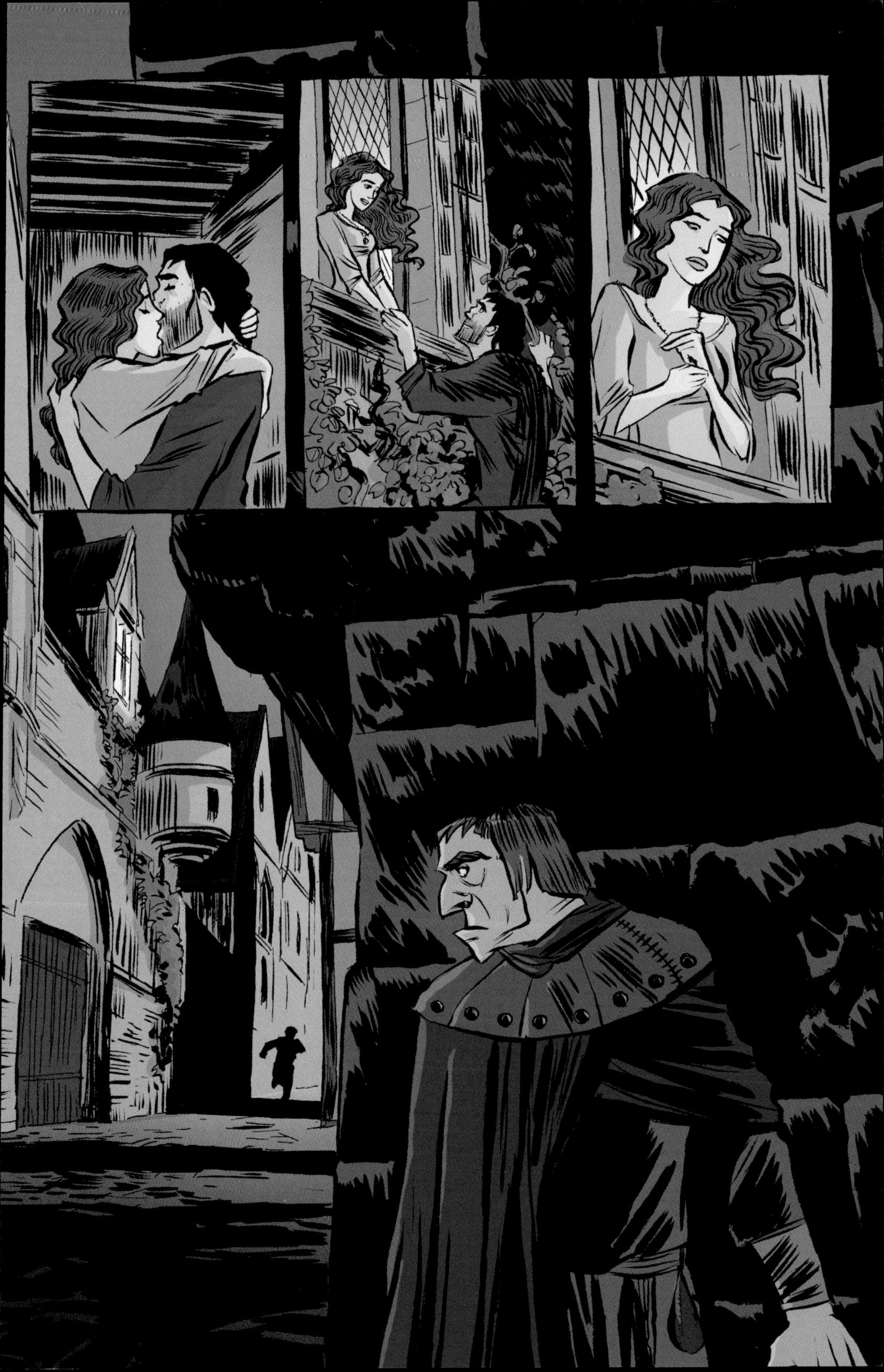

8. Solomon's Treasure

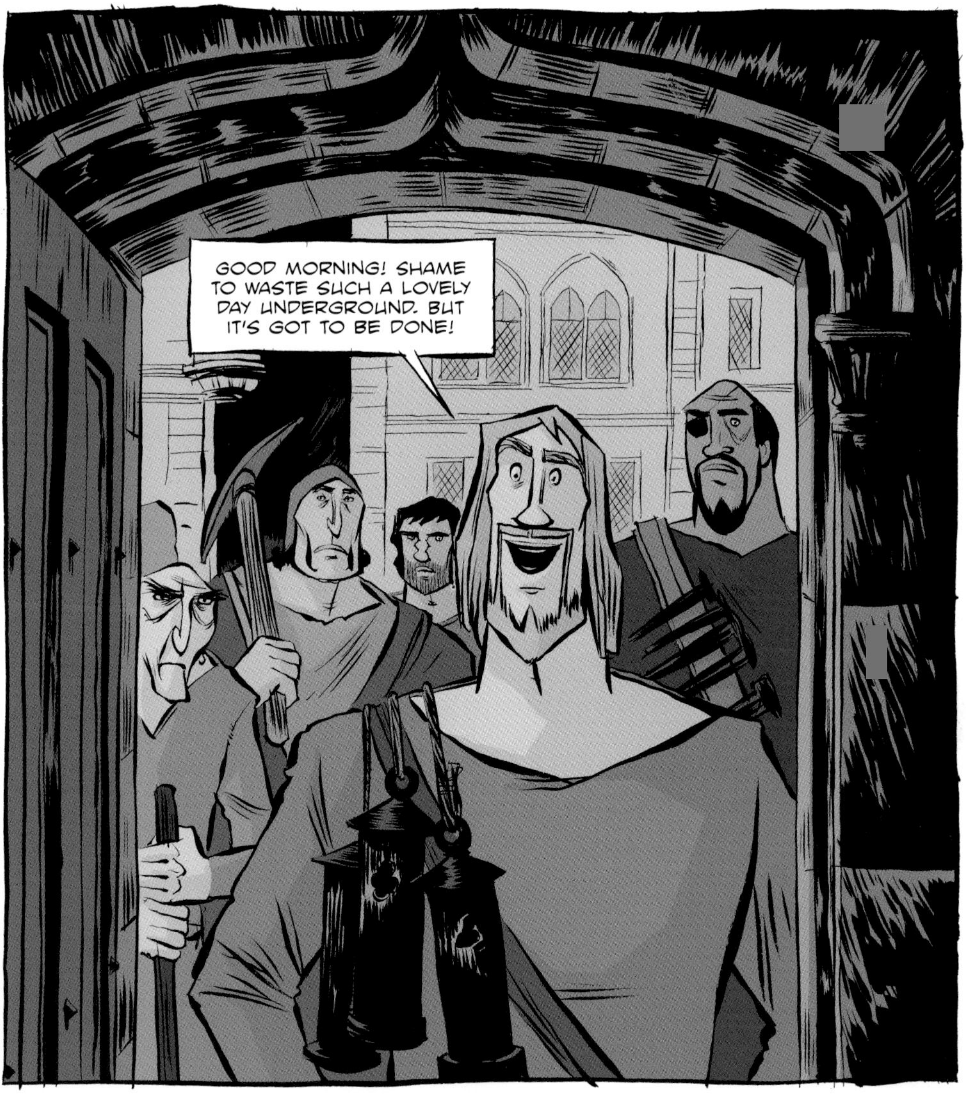
GOOD MORNING! SHAME TO WASTE SUCH A LOVELY DAY UNDERGROUND. BUT IT'S GOT TO BE DONE!

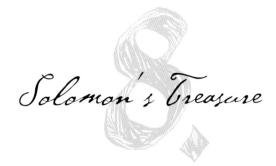

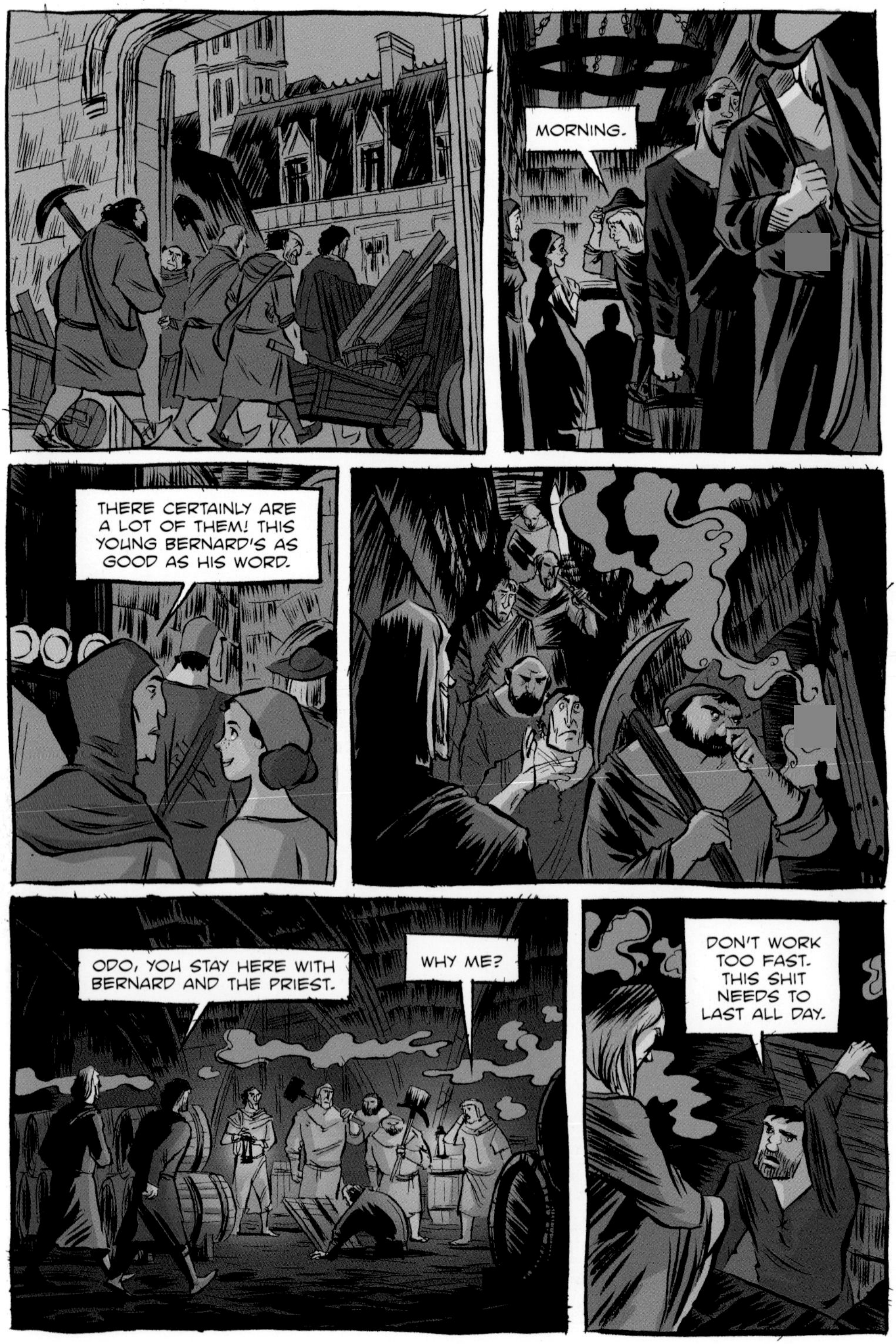
MORNING.
THERE CERTAINLY ARE A LOT OF THEM! THIS YOUNG BERNARD'S AS GOOD AS HIS WORD.
ODO, YOU STAY HERE WITH BERNARD AND THE PRIEST.
WHY ME?
DON'T WORK TOO FAST. THIS SHIT NEEDS TO LAST ALL DAY.

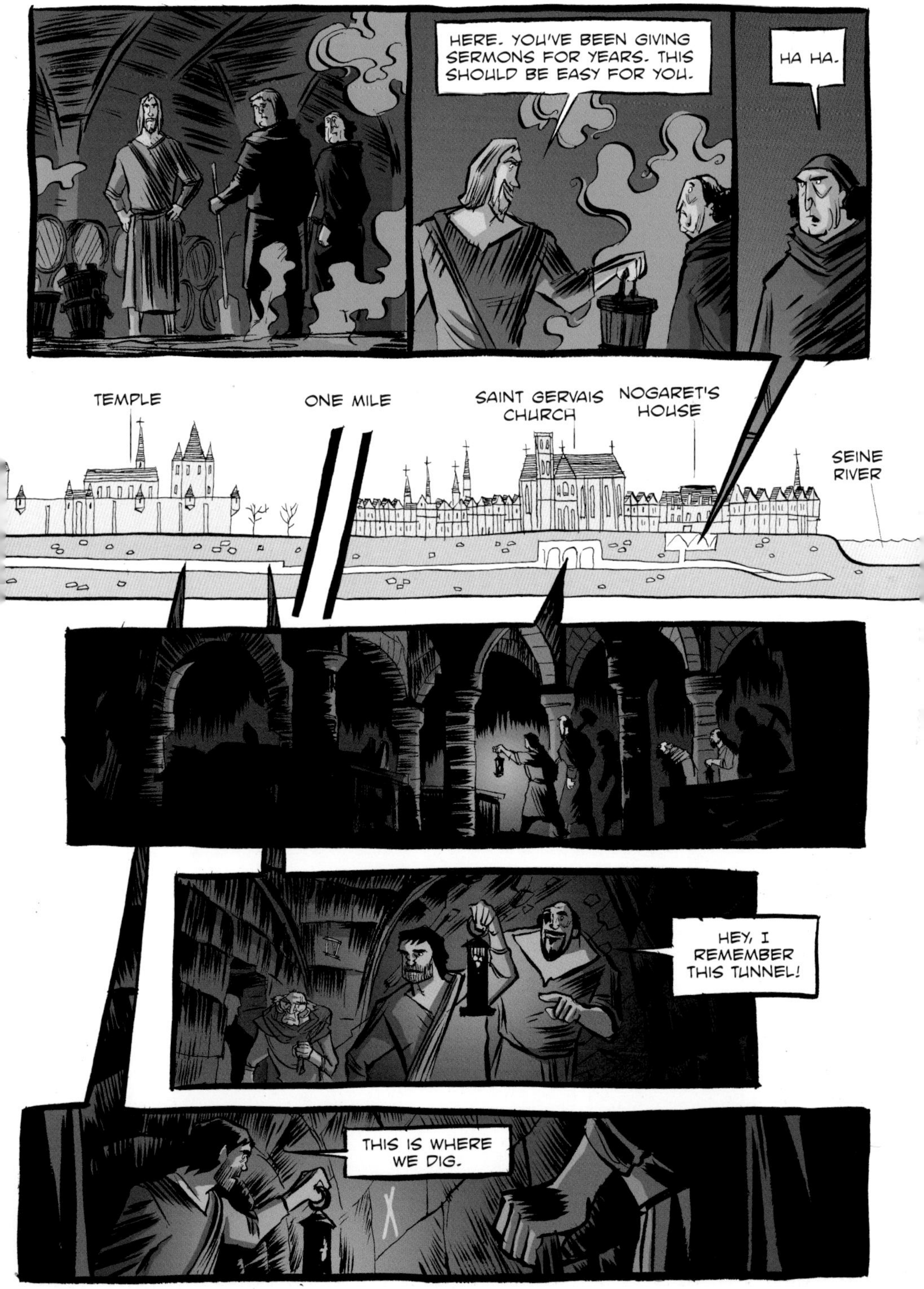
HERE. YOU'VE BEEN GIVING SERMONS FOR YEARS. THIS SHOULD BE EASY FOR YOU.
HA HA.
TEMPLE
ONE MILE
SAINT GERVAIS CHURCH
NOGARET'S HOUSE
SEINE RIVER
HEY, I REMEMBER THIS TUNNEL!
THIS IS WHERE WE DIG.

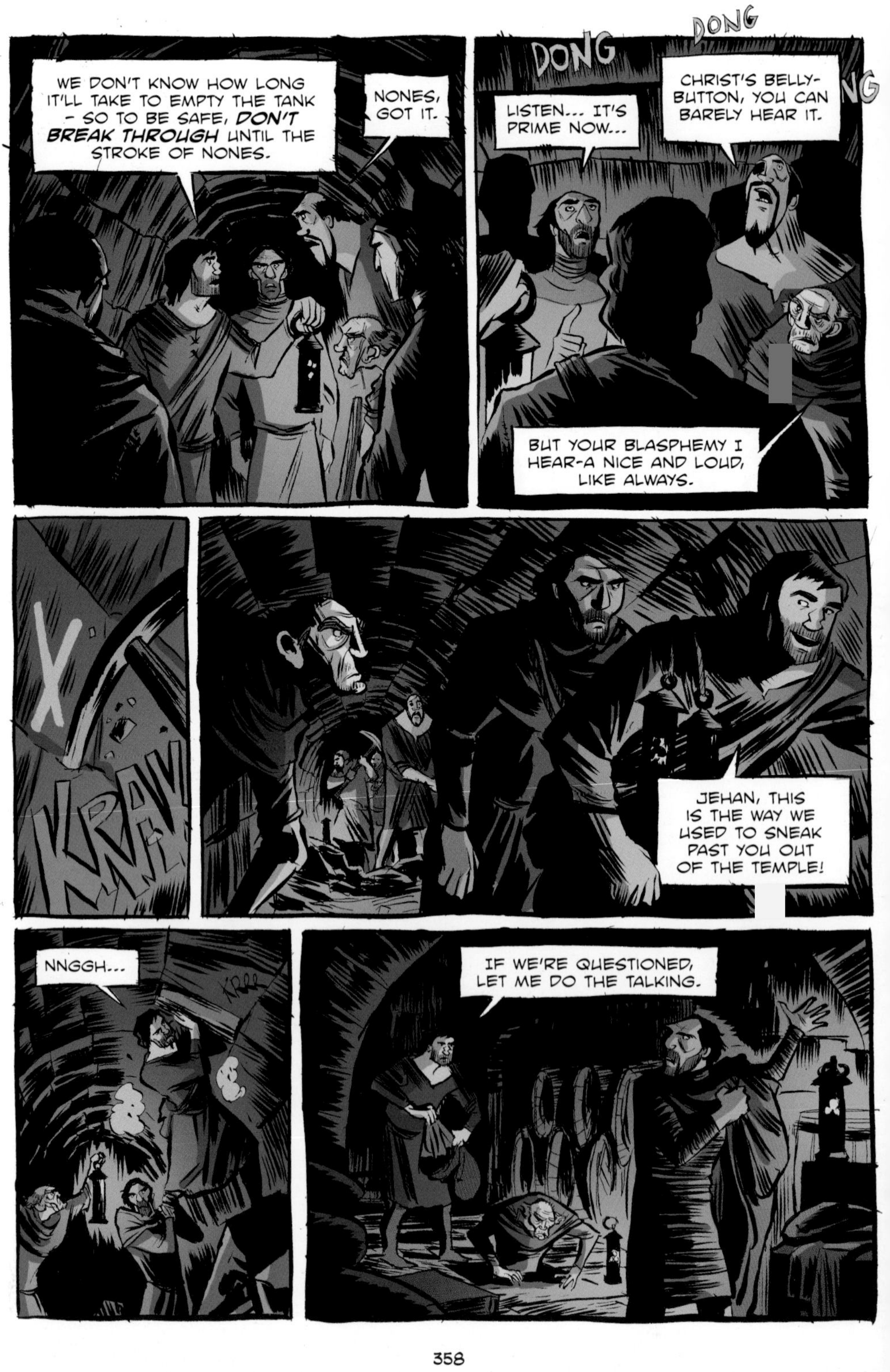

WE DON'T KNOW HOW LONG IT'LL TAKE TO EMPTY THE TANK - SO TO BE SAFE, ***DON'T BREAK THROUGH*** UNTIL THE STROKE OF NONES.
NONES, GOT IT.
DONG
DONG
LISTEN... IT'S PRIME NOW...
CHRIST'S BELLY-BUTTON, YOU CAN BARELY HEAR IT.
BUT YOUR BLASPHEMY I HEAR-A NICE AND LOUD, LIKE ALWAYS.
JEHAN, THIS IS THE WAY WE USED TO SNEAK PAST YOU OUT OF THE TEMPLE!
NNGGH...
IF WE'RE QUESTIONED, LET ME DO THE TALKING.

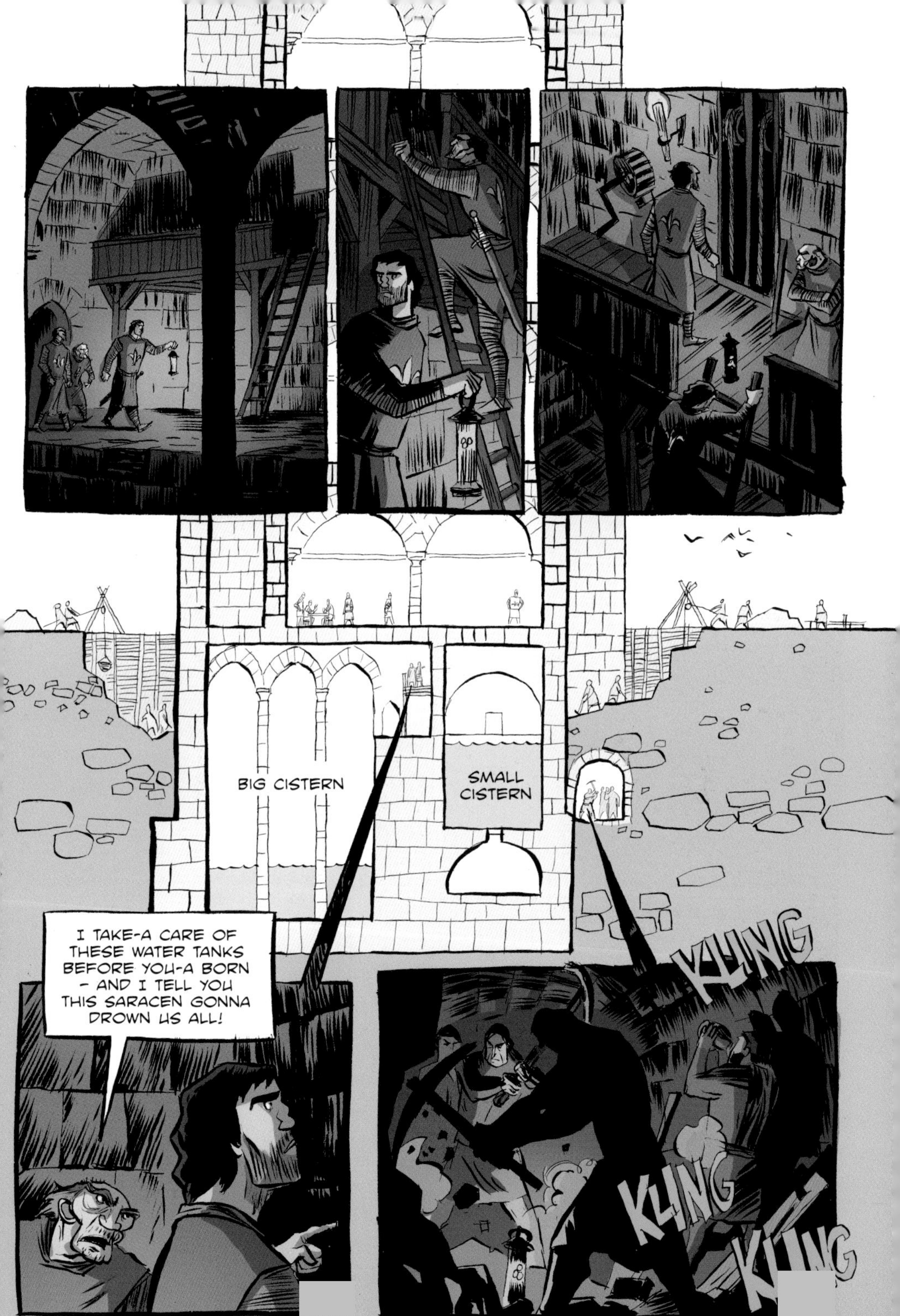
BIG CISTERN
SMALL CISTERN
I TAKE-A CARE OF THESE WATER TANKS BEFORE YOU-A BORN - AND I TELL YOU THIS SARACEN GONNA DROWN US ALL!
KLUNG
KLUNG
KLING

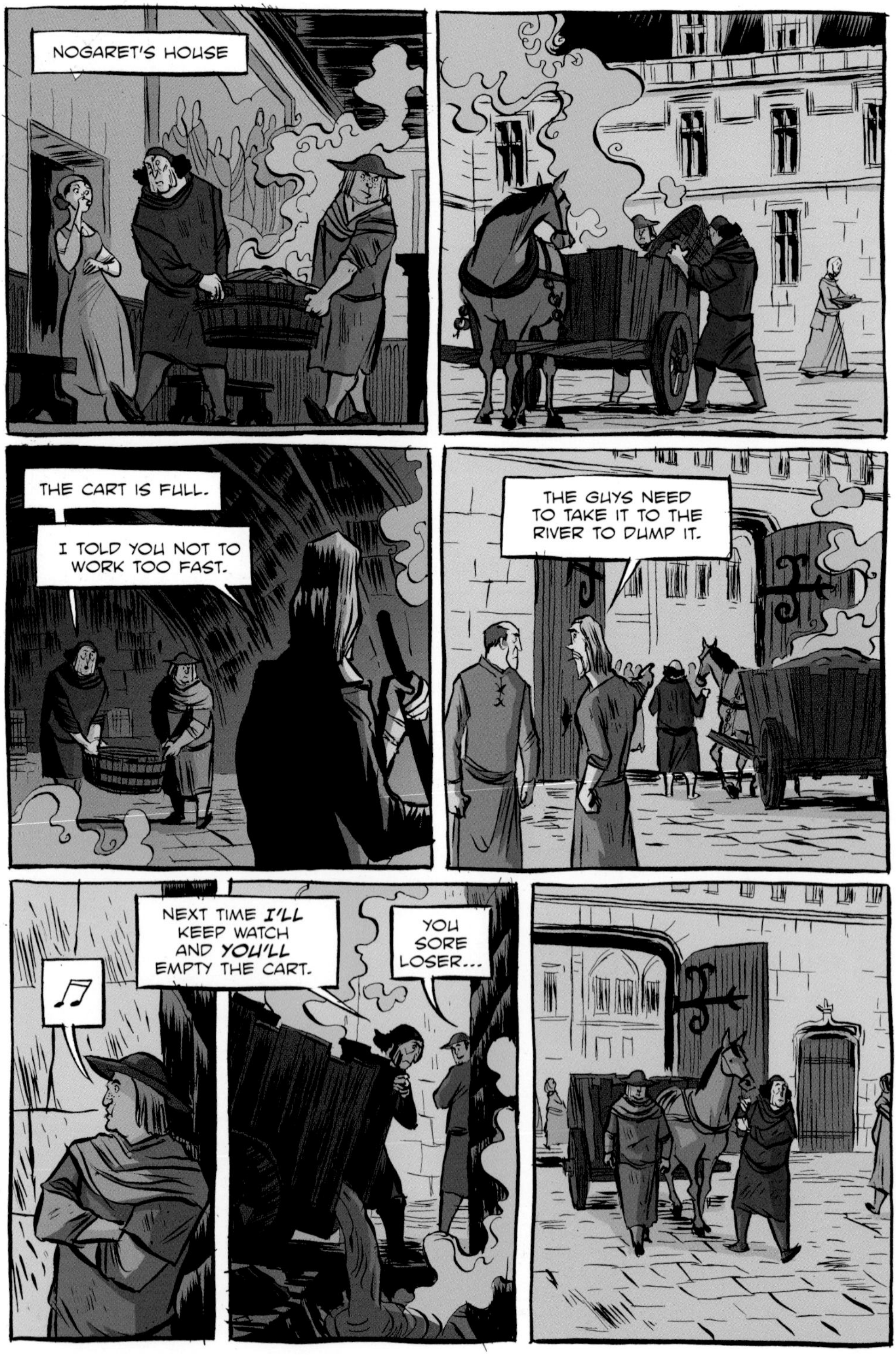
NOGARET'S HOUSE
THE CART IS FULL.
I TOLD YOU NOT TO WORK TOO FAST.
THE GUYS NEED TO TAKE IT TO THE RIVER TO DUMP IT.
♫
NEXT TIME *I'LL* KEEP WATCH AND *YOU'LL* EMPTY THE CART.
YOU SORE LOSER...

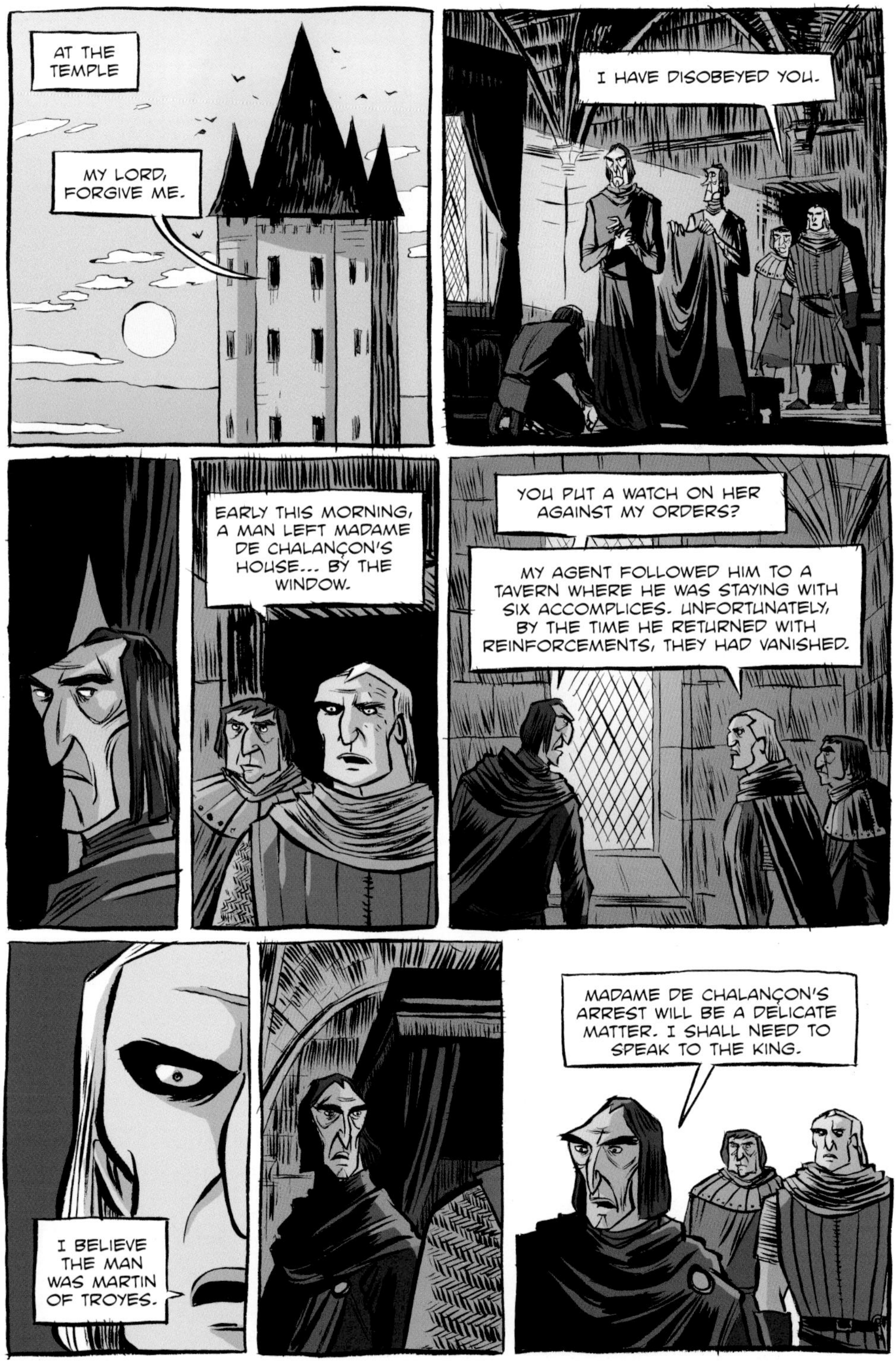
AT THE TEMPLE
MY LORD, FORGIVE ME.
I HAVE DISOBEYED YOU.
EARLY THIS MORNING, A MAN LEFT MADAME DE CHALANÇON'S HOUSE... BY THE WINDOW.
YOU PUT A WATCH ON HER AGAINST MY ORDERS?
MY AGENT FOLLOWED HIM TO A TAVERN WHERE HE WAS STAYING WITH SIX ACCOMPLICES. UNFORTUNATELY, BY THE TIME HE RETURNED WITH REINFORCEMENTS, THEY HAD VANISHED.
I BELIEVE THE MAN WAS MARTIN OF TROYES.
MADAME DE CHALANÇON'S ARREST WILL BE A DELICATE MATTER. I SHALL NEED TO SPEAK TO THE KING.

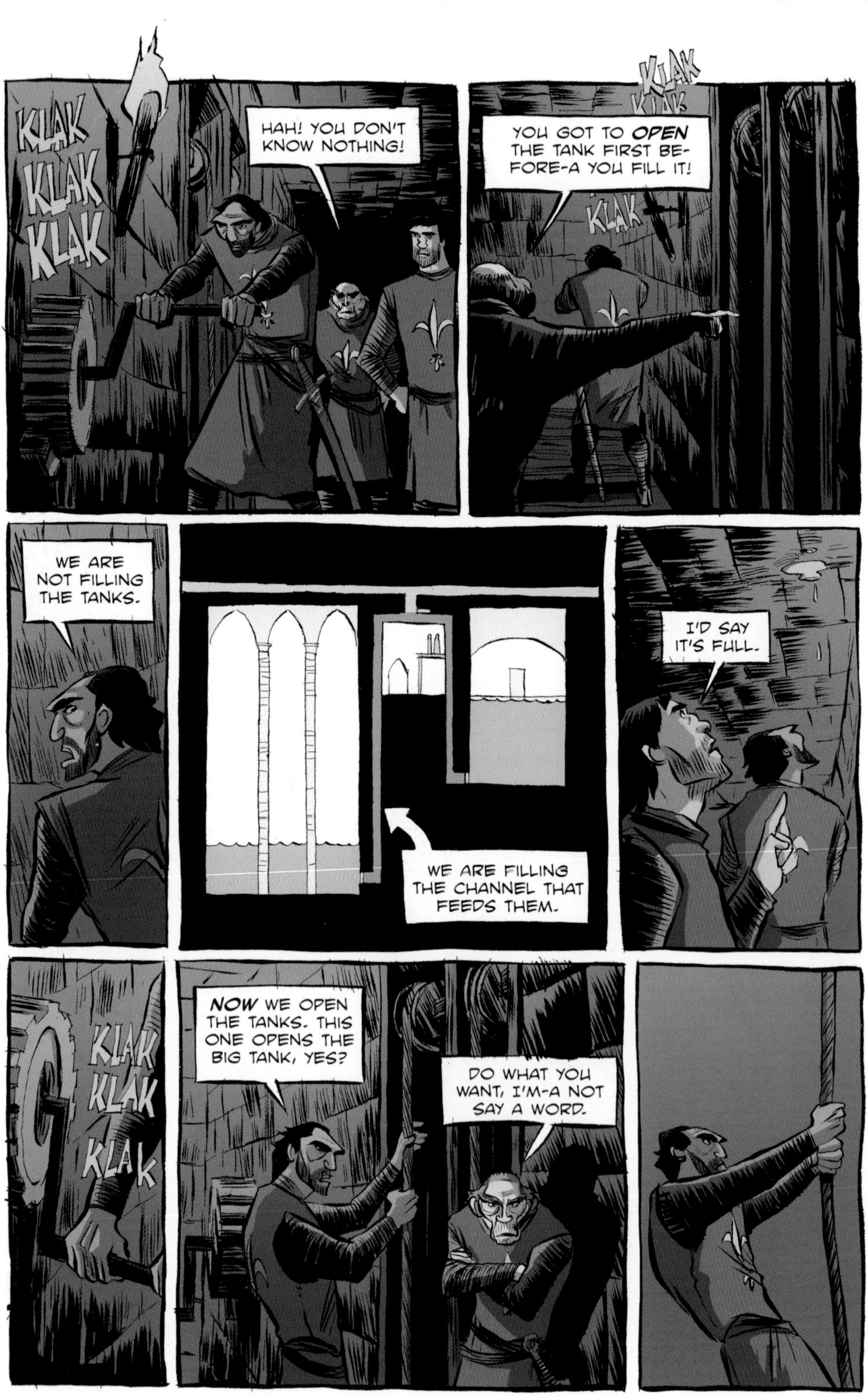

KLAK KLAK KLAK
HAH! YOU DON'T KNOW NOTHING!
KLAK
YOU GOT TO OPEN THE TANK FIRST BE-FORE-A YOU FILL IT!
KLAK
WE ARE NOT FILLING THE TANKS.
WE ARE FILLING THE CHANNEL THAT FEEDS THEM.
I'D SAY IT'S FULL.
KLAK KLAK KLAK
NOW WE OPEN THE TANKS. THIS ONE OPENS THE BIG TANK, YES?
DO WHAT YOU WANT, I'M-A NOT SAY A WORD.

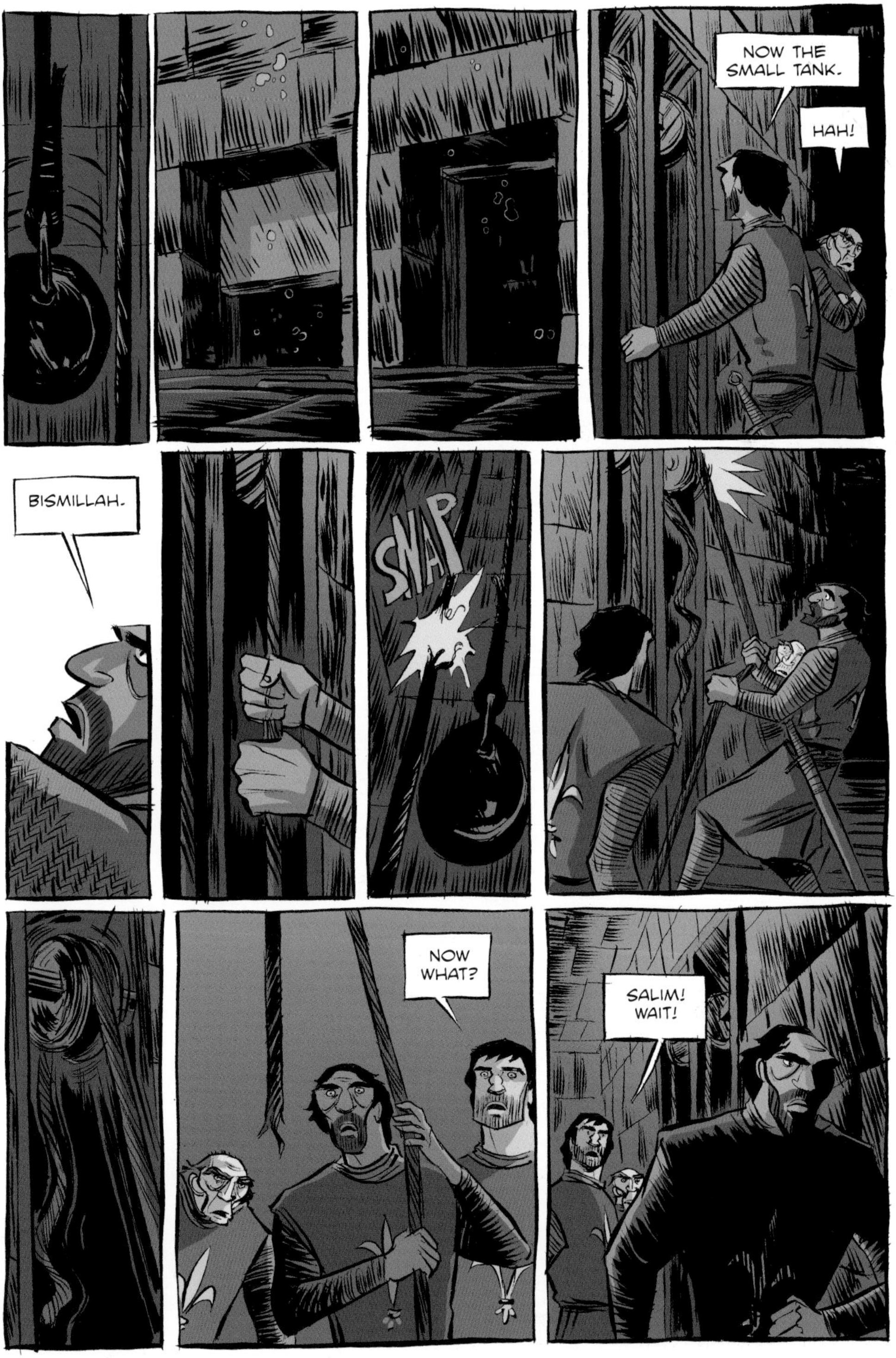
NOW THE SMALL TANK.
HAH!
BISMILLAH.
SNAP
NOW WHAT?
SALIM! WAIT!

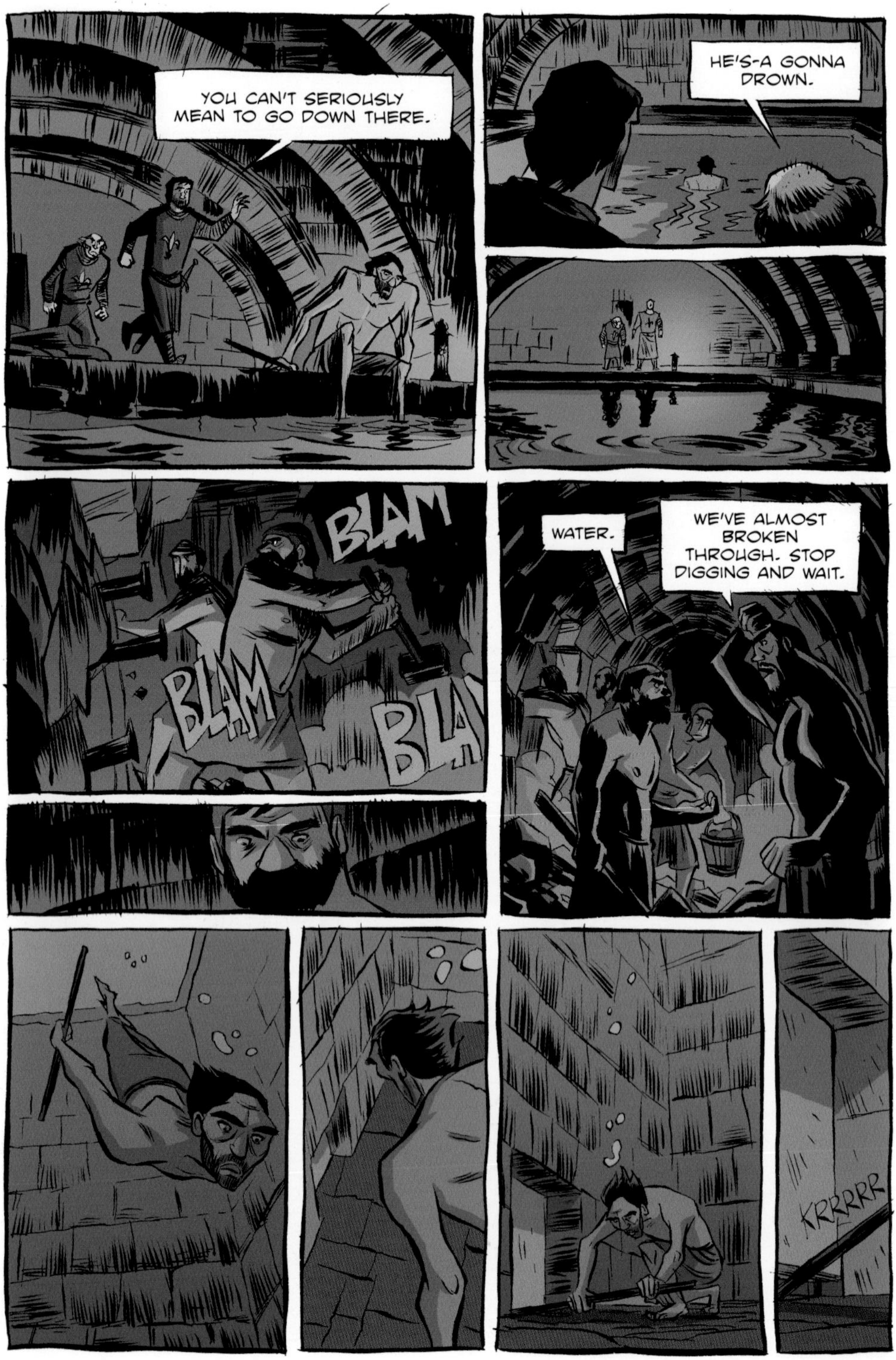
YOU CAN'T SERIOUSLY MEAN TO GO DOWN THERE.
HE'S-A GONNA DROWN.
BLAM
BLAM
BLA
WATER.
WE'VE ALMOST BROKEN THROUGH. STOP DIGGING AND WAIT.
KRRRRR

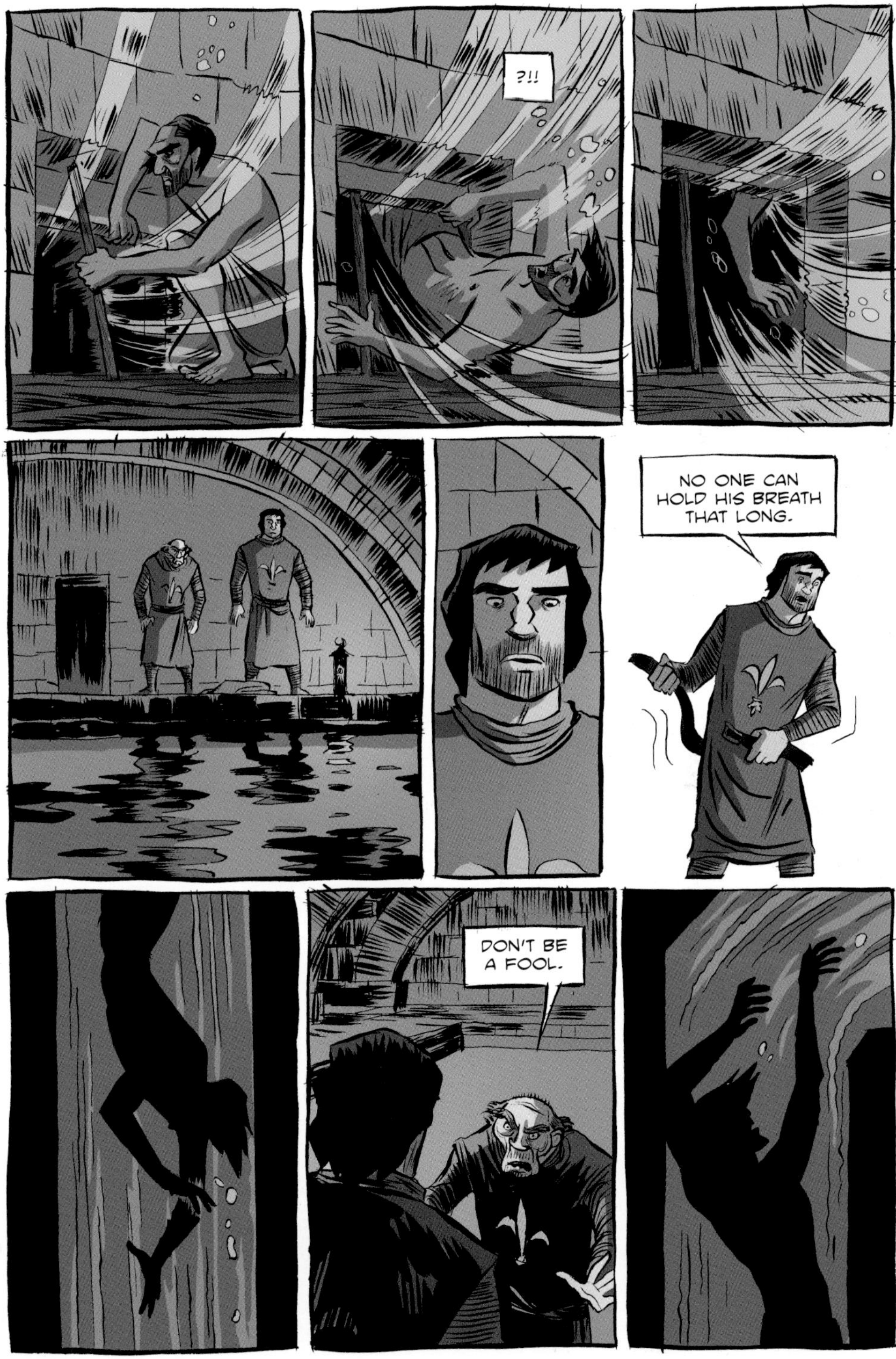
?!!
NO ONE CAN HOLD HIS BREATH THAT LONG.
DON'T BE A FOOL.

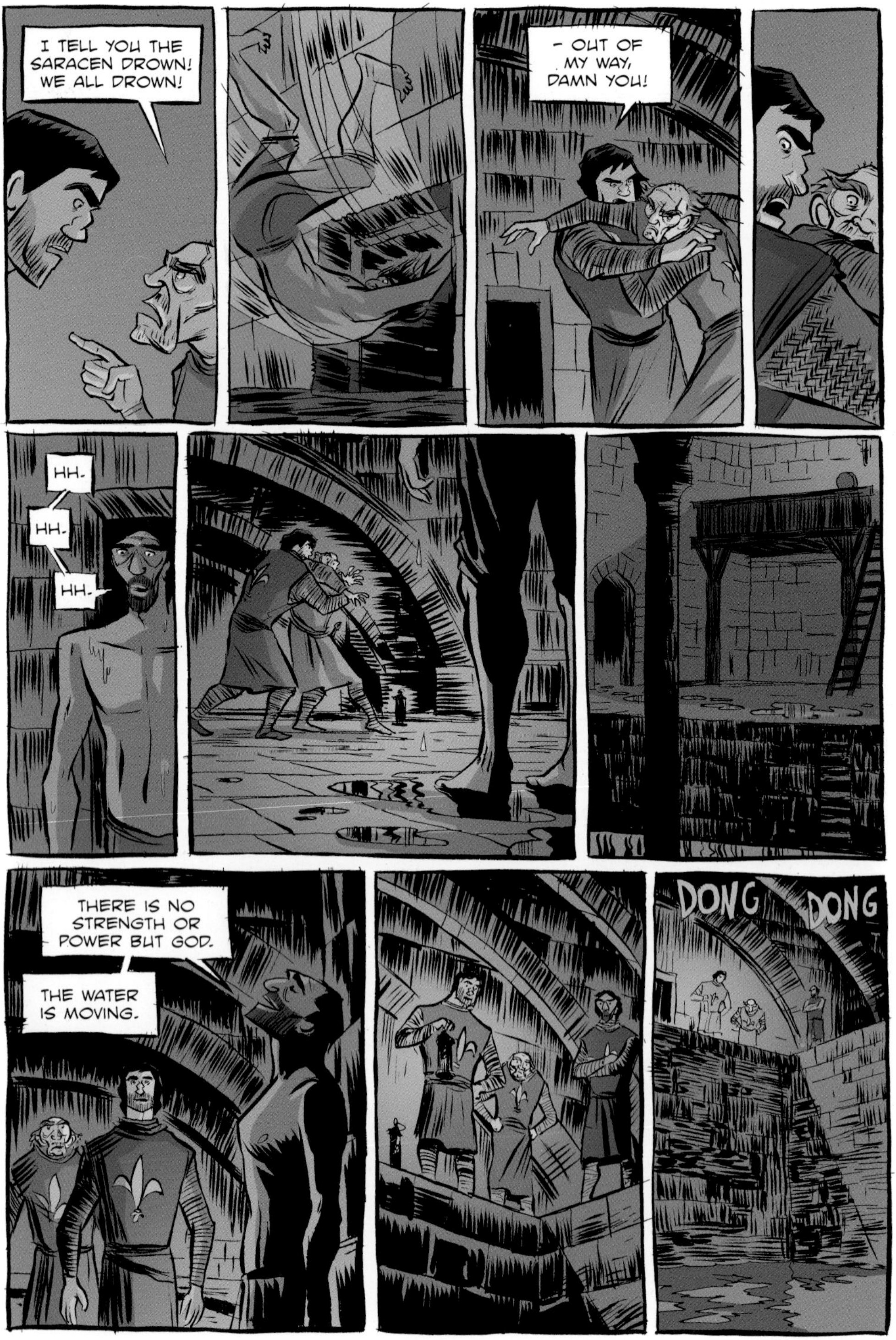
I TELL YOU THE SARACEN DROWN! WE ALL DROWN!
- OUT OF MY WAY, DAMN YOU!
HH-
HH-
HH-
THERE IS NO STRENGTH OR POWER BUT GOD.
THE WATER IS MOVING.
DONG
DONG

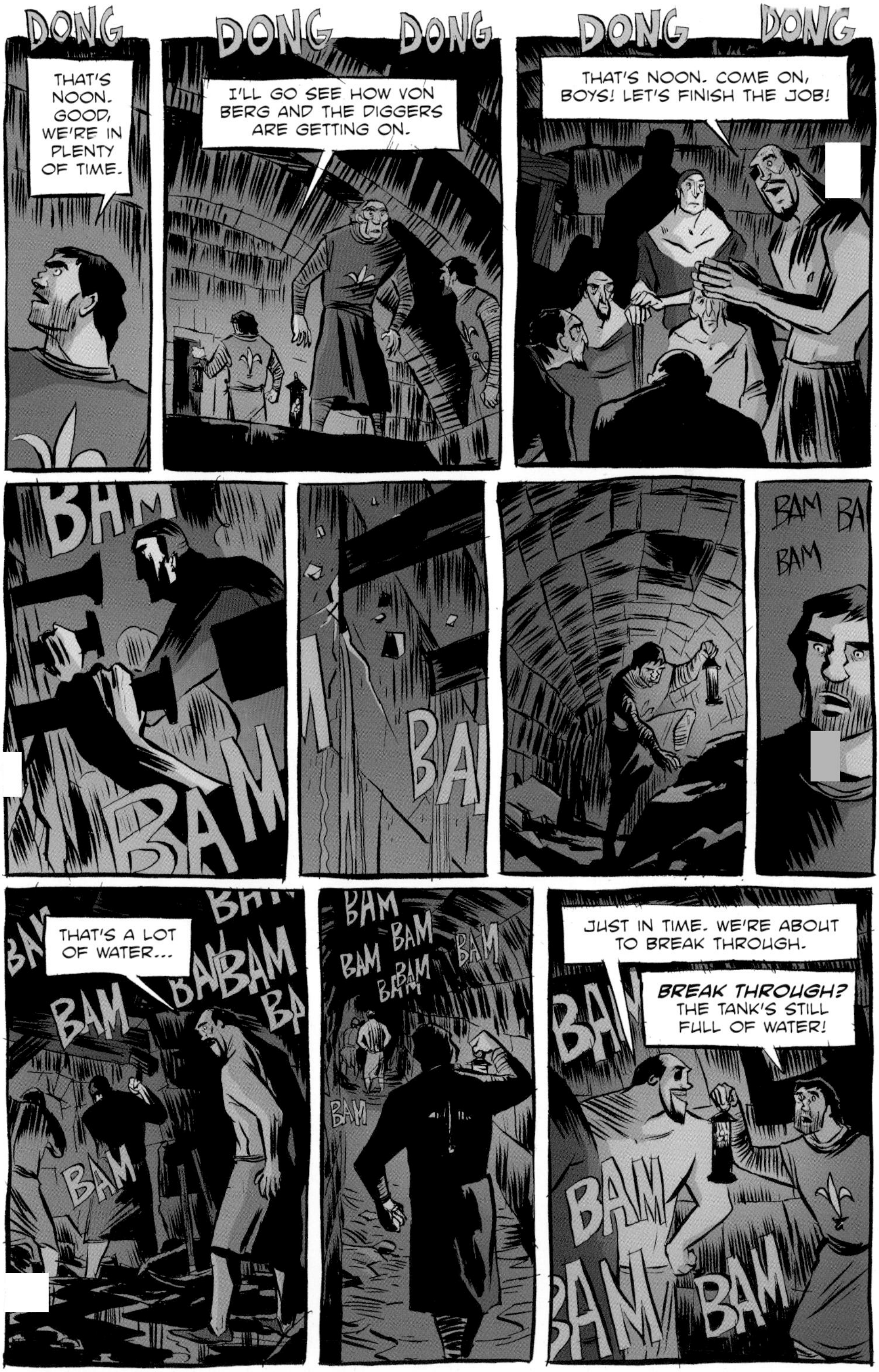
DONG
THAT'S NOON. GOOD, WE'RE IN PLENTY OF TIME.
DONG
DONG
I'LL GO SEE HOW VON BERG AND THE DIGGERS ARE GETTING ON.
DONG
DONG
THAT'S NOON. COME ON, BOYS! LET'S FINISH THE JOB!
BAM
BAM
BAM
BAM BA
BAM
THAT'S A LOT OF WATER...
BAM
BAM
BAM
BAM
BAM
BAM
BAM
BAM
BAM
BAM
JUST IN TIME. WE'RE ABOUT TO BREAK THROUGH.
BREAK THROUGH? THE TANK'S STILL FULL OF WATER!
BAM
BAM
BAM
BAM

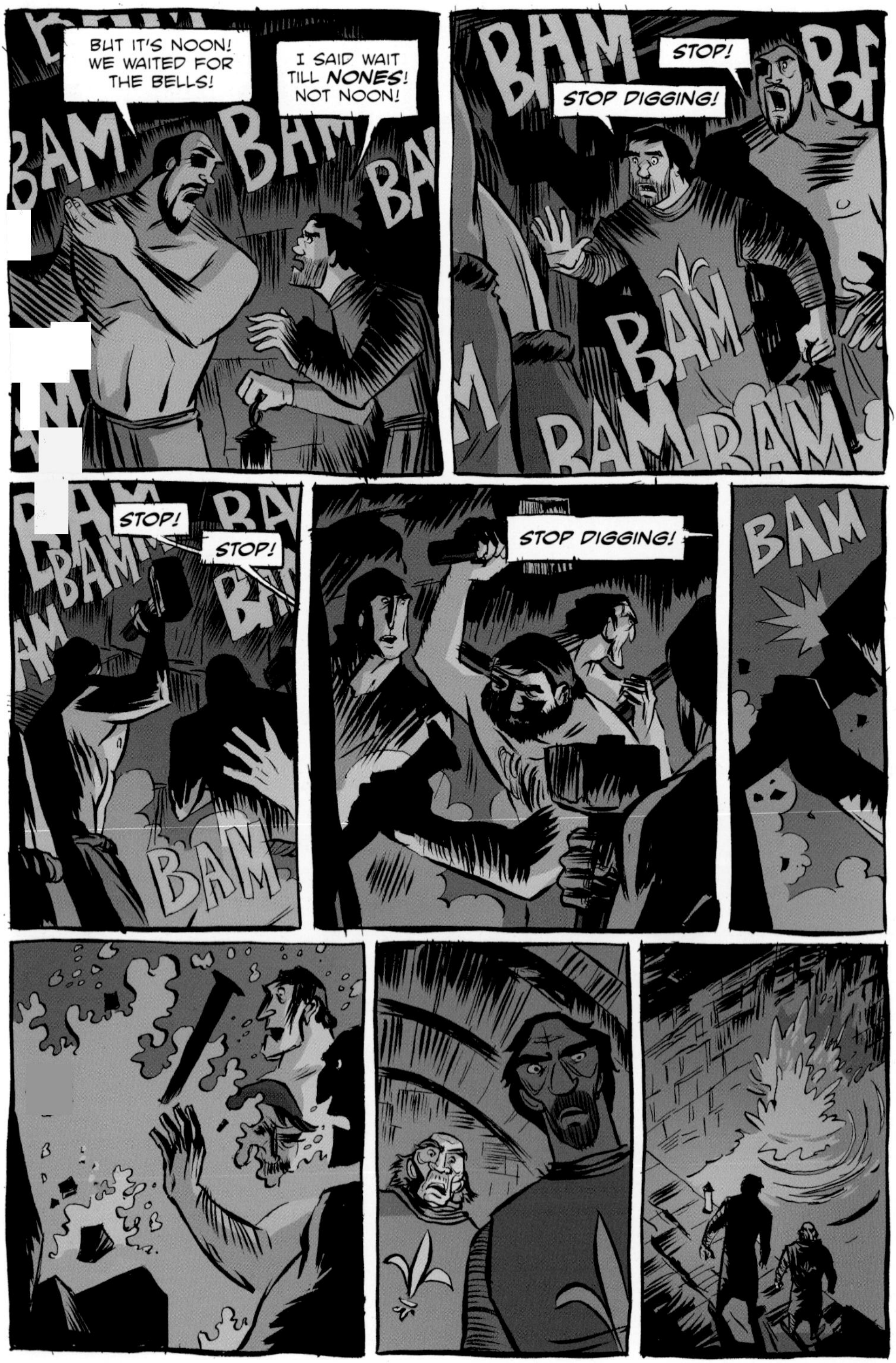
BAM
BUT IT'S NOON! WE WAITED FOR THE BELLS!
I SAID WAIT TILL **NONES**! NOT NOON!
BAM
BAM
BA
BAM
STOP!
STOP DIGGING!
BA
BAM
BAM BAM
BAM
STOP!
BAM
STOP!
BA
BAM
STOP DIGGING!
BAM

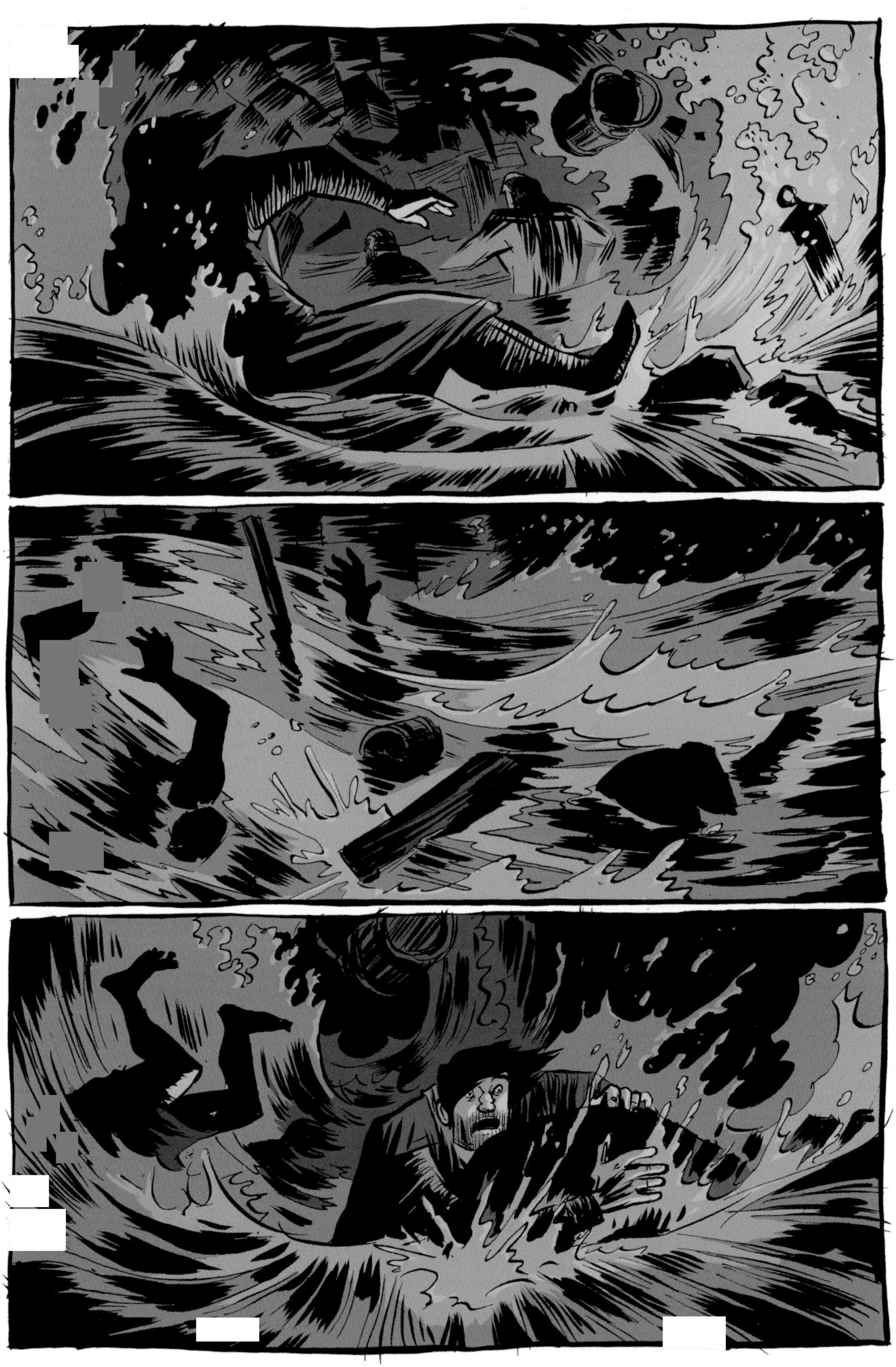

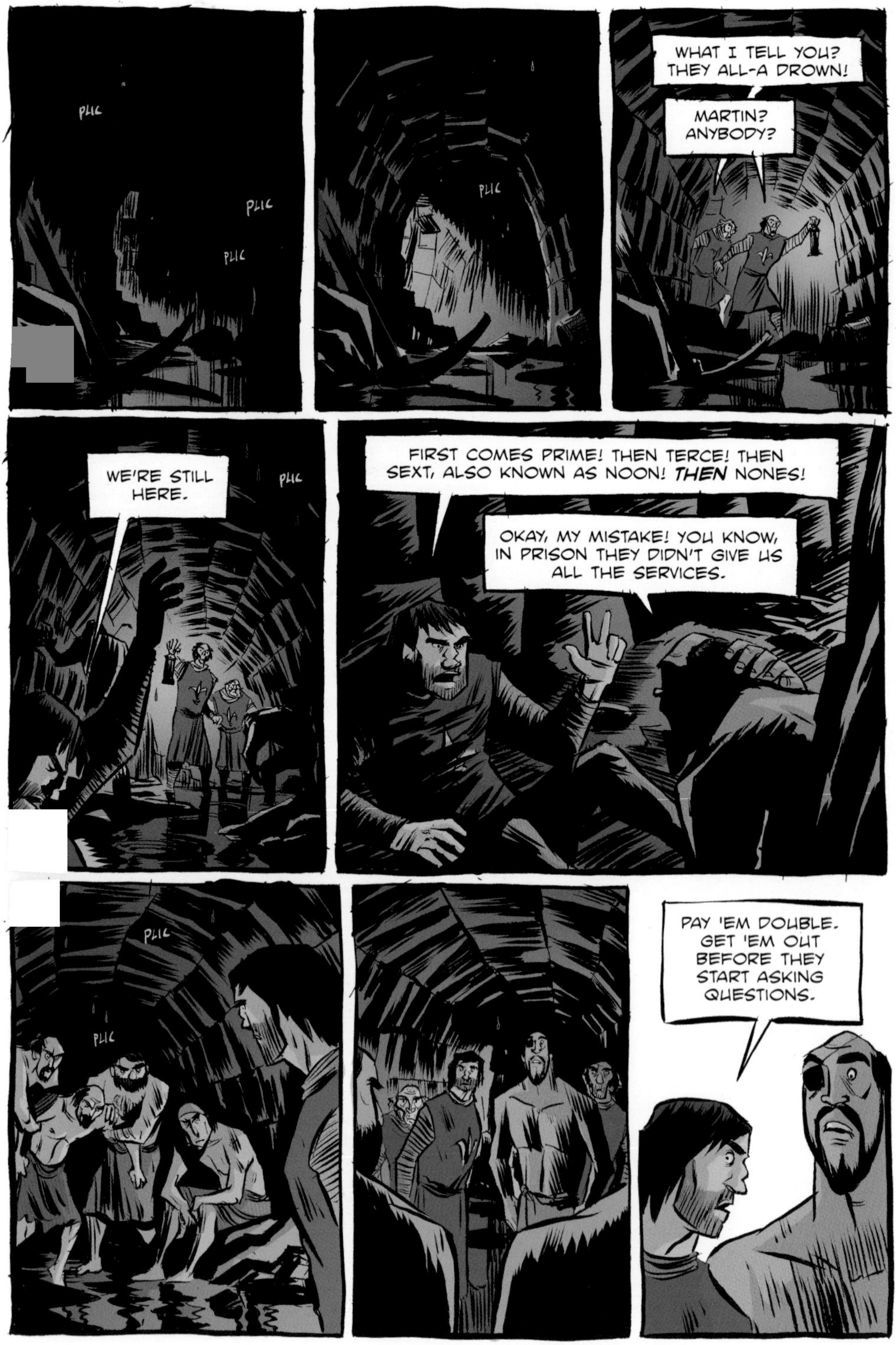
PLIC
PLIC
PLIC
PLIC
WHAT I TELL YOU? THEY ALL-A DROWN!
MARTIN? ANYBODY?
WE'RE STILL HERE.
PLIC
FIRST COMES PRIME! THEN TERCE! THEN SEXT, ALSO KNOWN AS NOON! THEN NONES!
OKAY, MY MISTAKE! YOU KNOW, IN PRISON THEY DIDN'T GIVE US ALL THE SERVICES.
PLIC
PLIC
PAY 'EM DOUBLE. GET 'EM OUT BEFORE THEY START ASKING QUESTIONS.

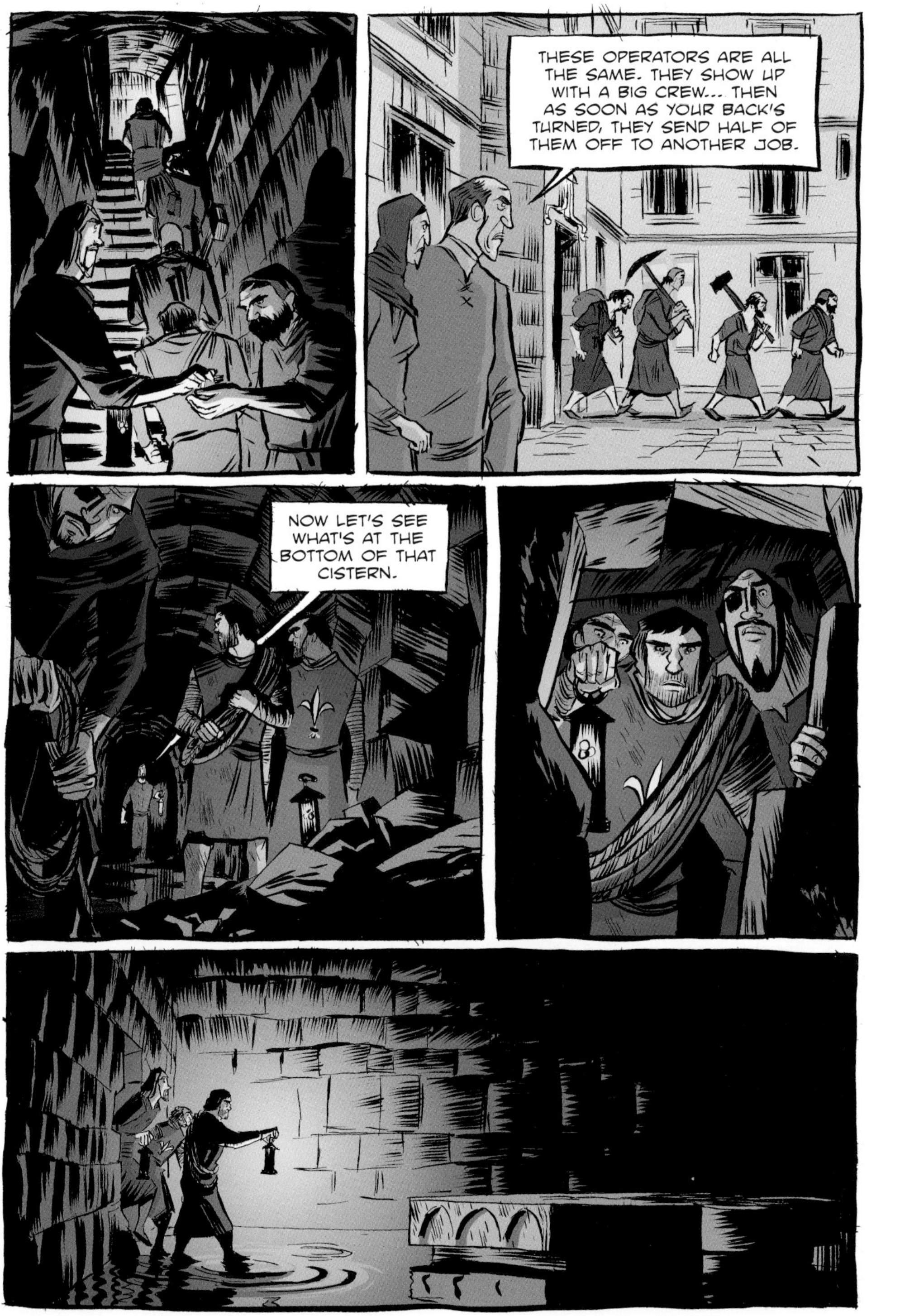
THESE OPERATORS ARE ALL THE SAME. THEY SHOW UP WITH A BIG CREW... THEN AS SOON AS YOUR BACK'S TURNED, THEY SEND HALF OF THEM OFF TO ANOTHER JOB.
NOW LET'S SEE WHAT'S AT THE BOTTOM OF THAT CISTERN.

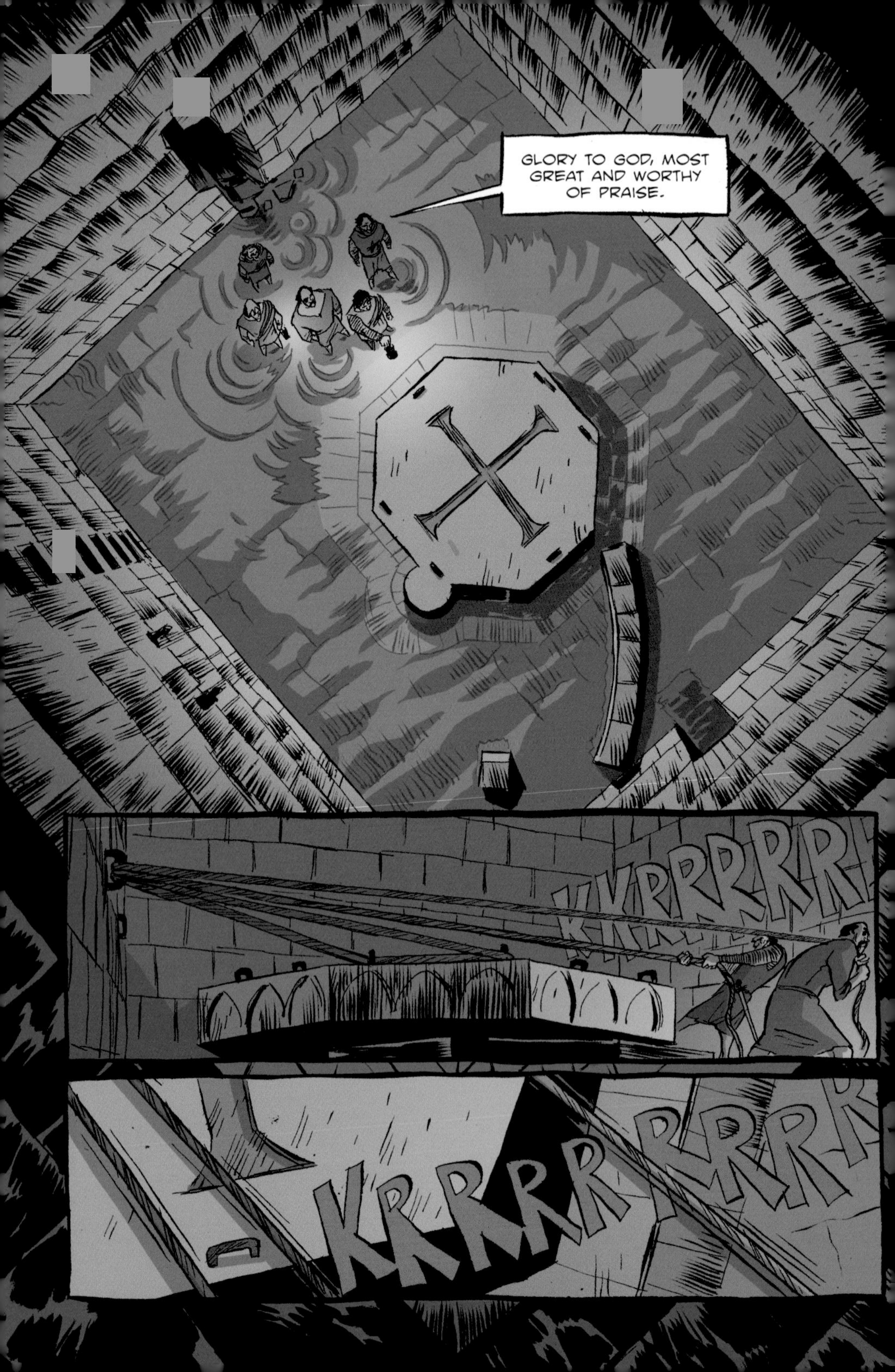
GLORY TO GOD, MOST GREAT AND WORTHY OF PRAISE.

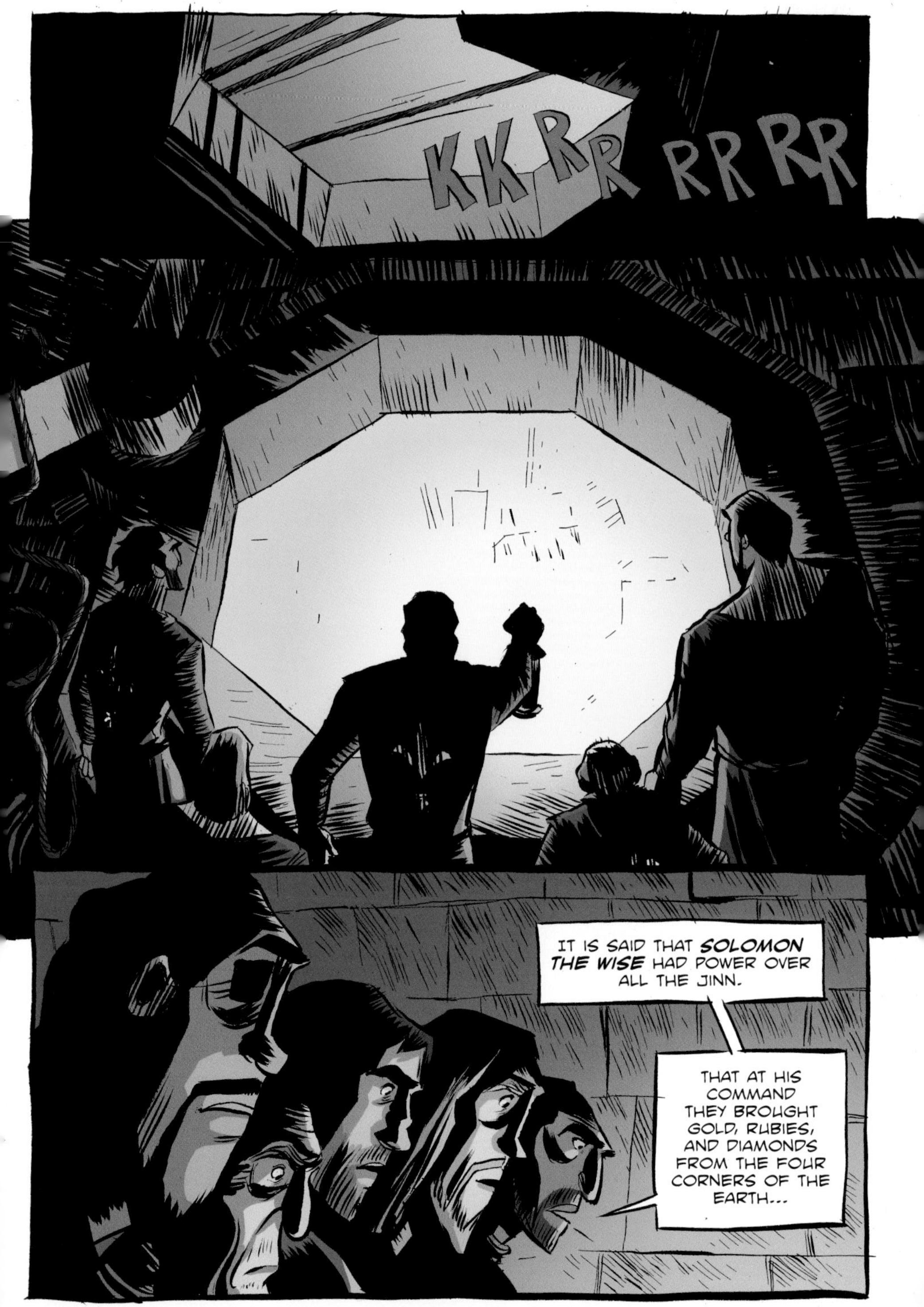
KKRRRRRRR
IT IS SAID THAT **SOLOMON THE WISE** HAD POWER OVER ALL THE JINN.
THAT AT HIS COMMAND THEY BROUGHT GOLD, RUBIES, AND DIAMONDS FROM THE FOUR CORNERS OF THE EARTH...

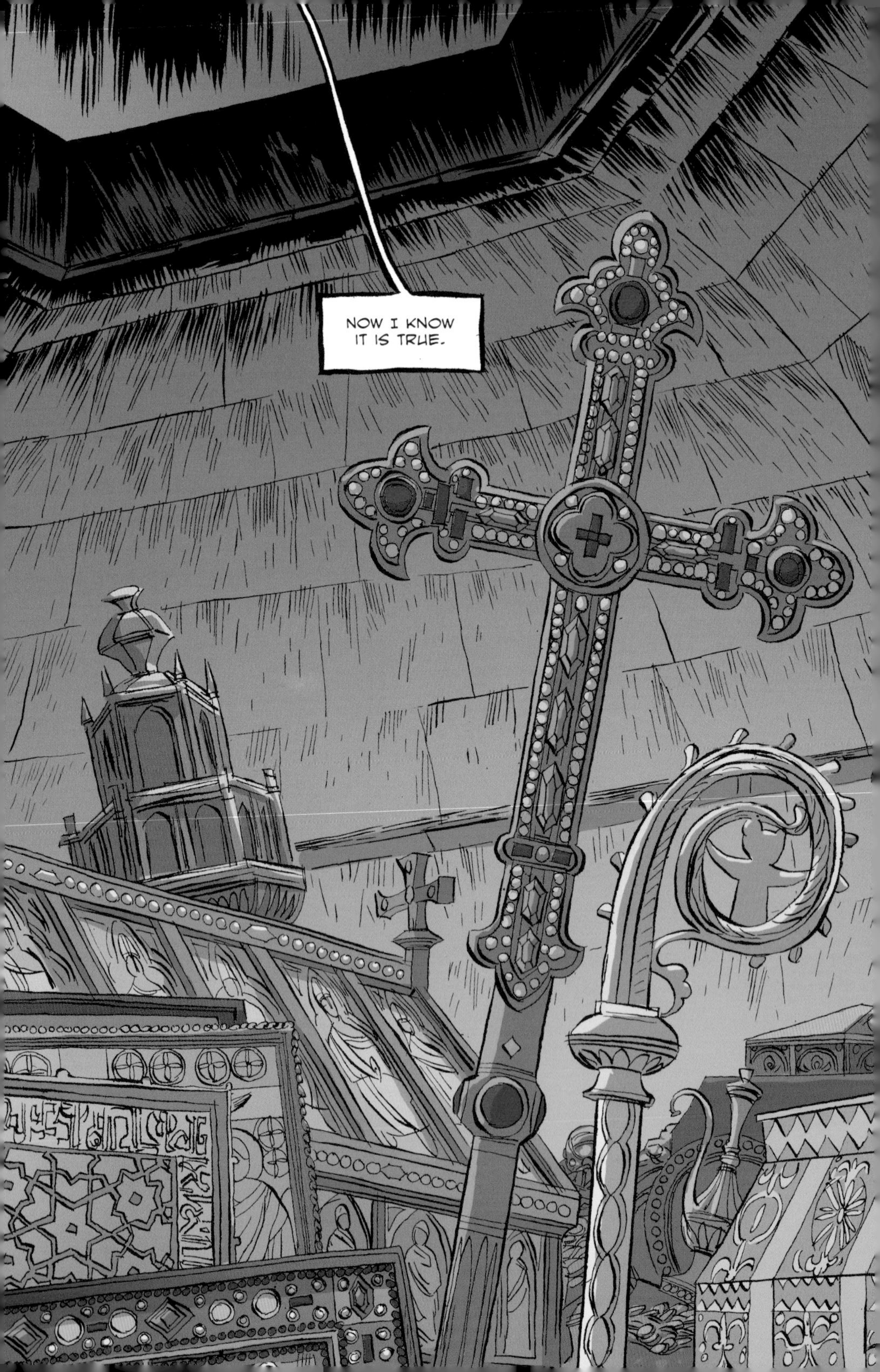
NOW I KNOW IT IS TRUE.

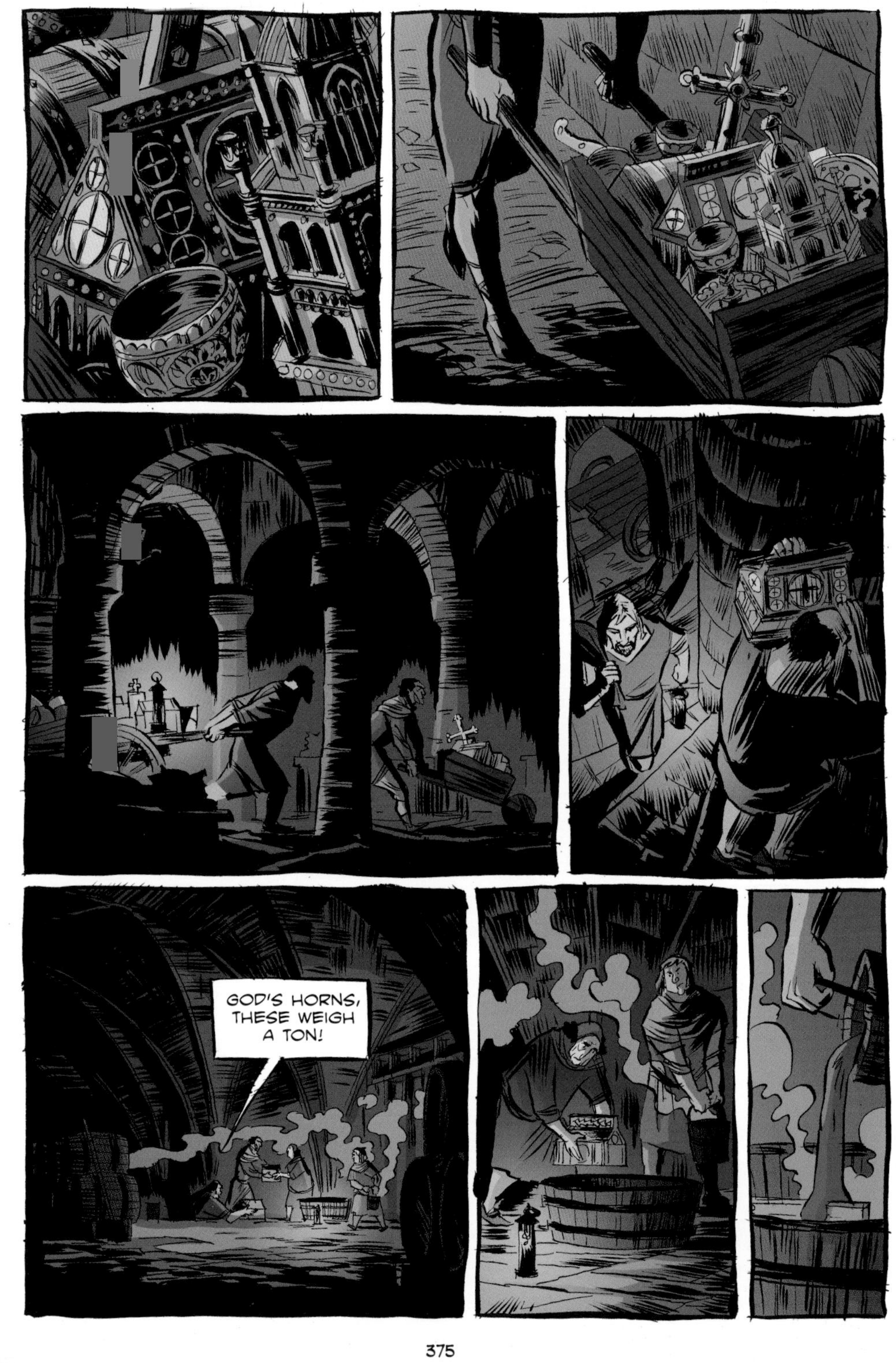
GOD'S HORNS, THESE WEIGH A TON!

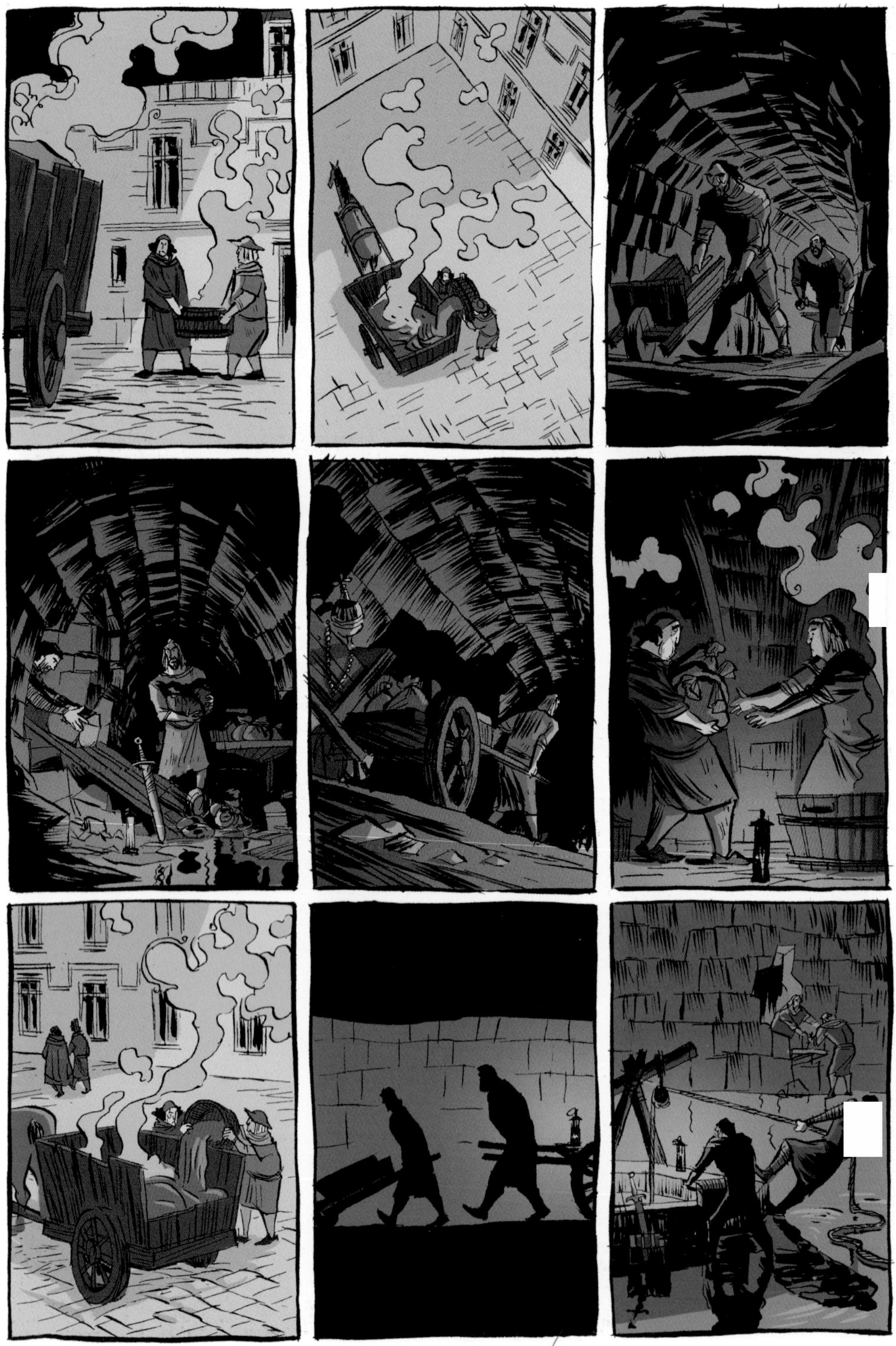

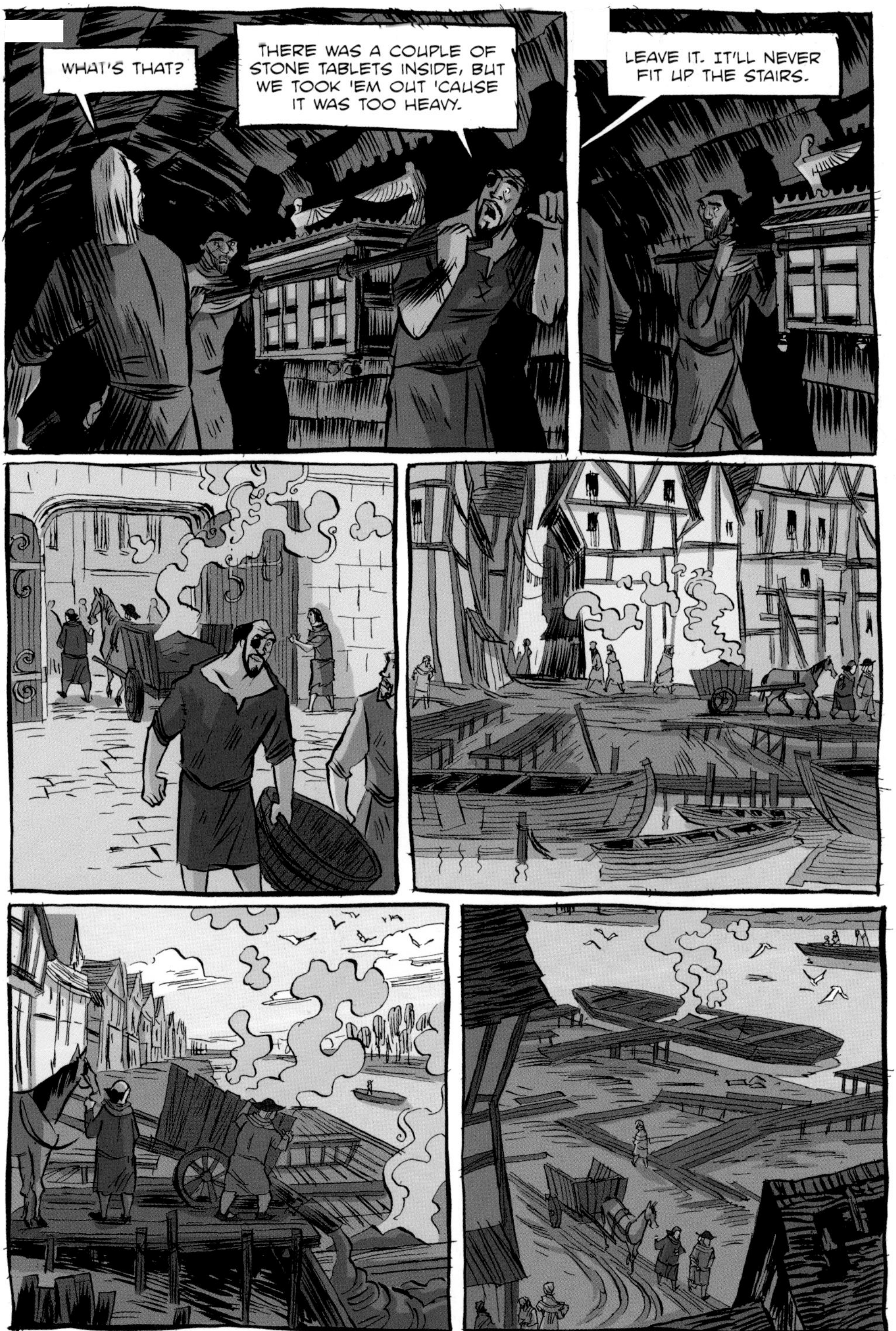
WHAT'S THAT?
THERE WAS A COUPLE OF STONE TABLETS INSIDE, BUT WE TOOK 'EM OUT 'CAUSE IT WAS TOO HEAVY.
LEAVE IT. IT'LL NEVER FIT UP THE STAIRS.

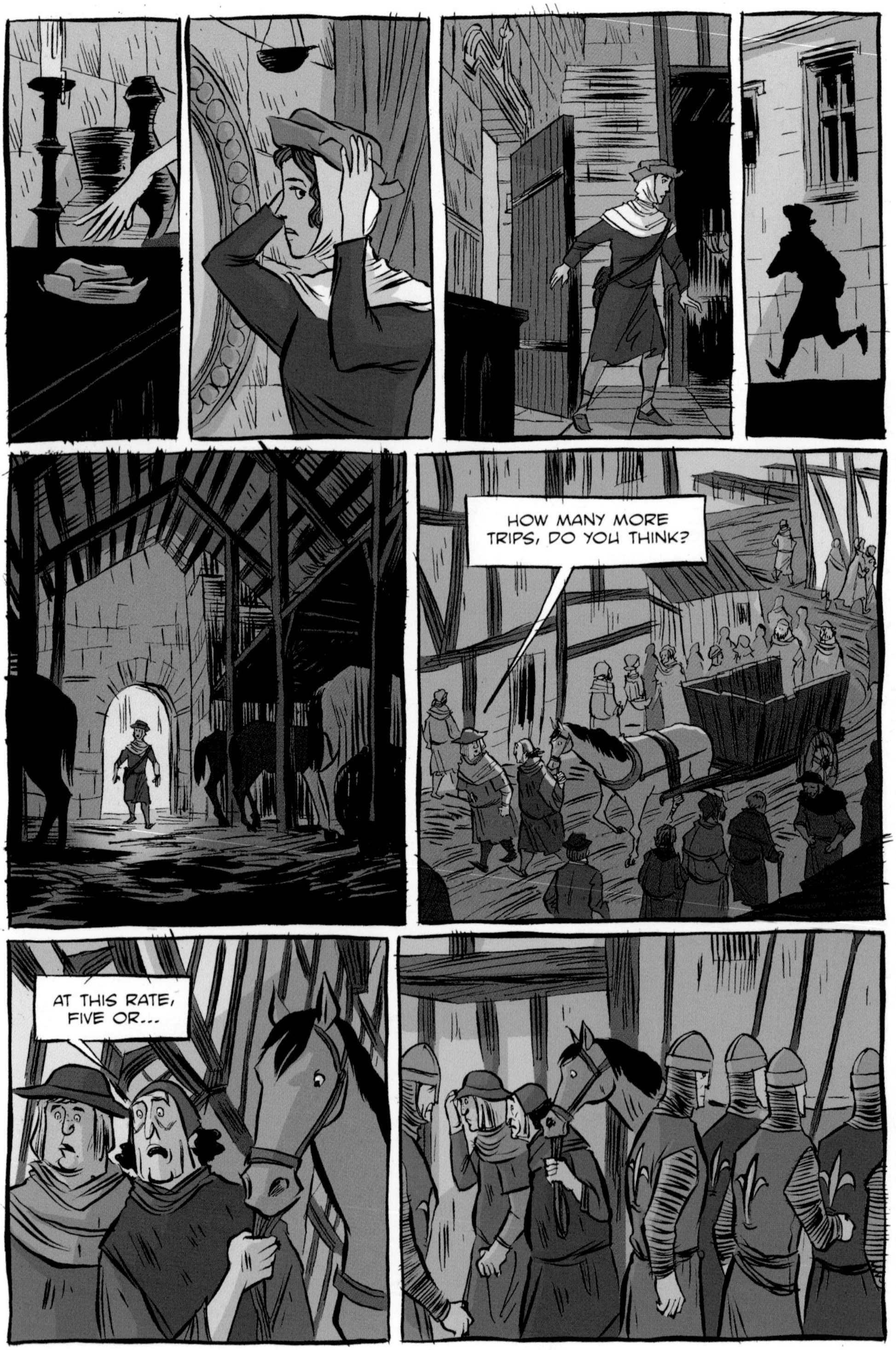
HOW MANY MORE TRIPS, DO YOU THINK?
AT THIS RATE, FIVE OR...

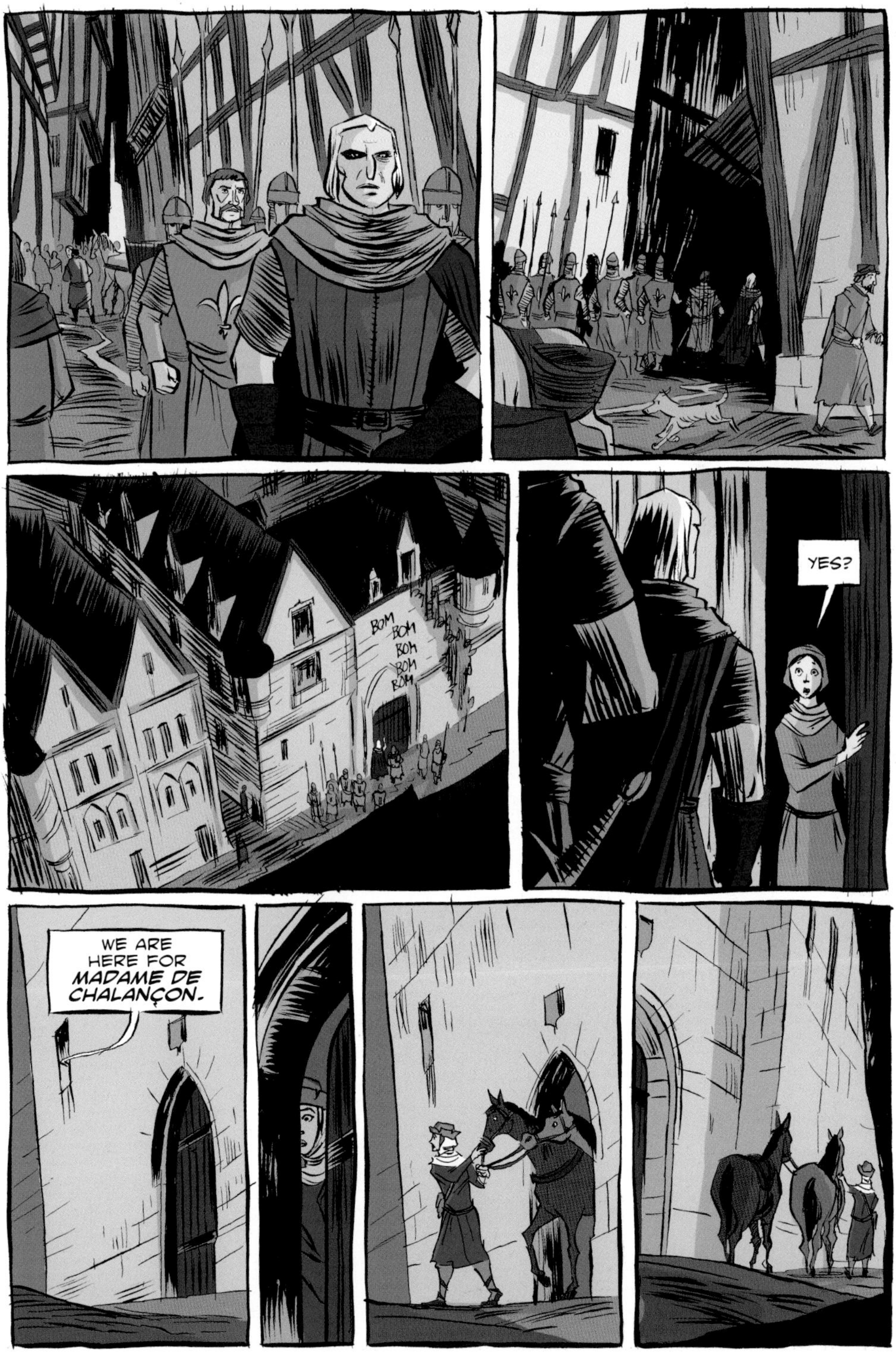
BOM BOM BOM BOM BOM
YES?
WE ARE HERE FOR *MADAME DE CHALANÇON.*

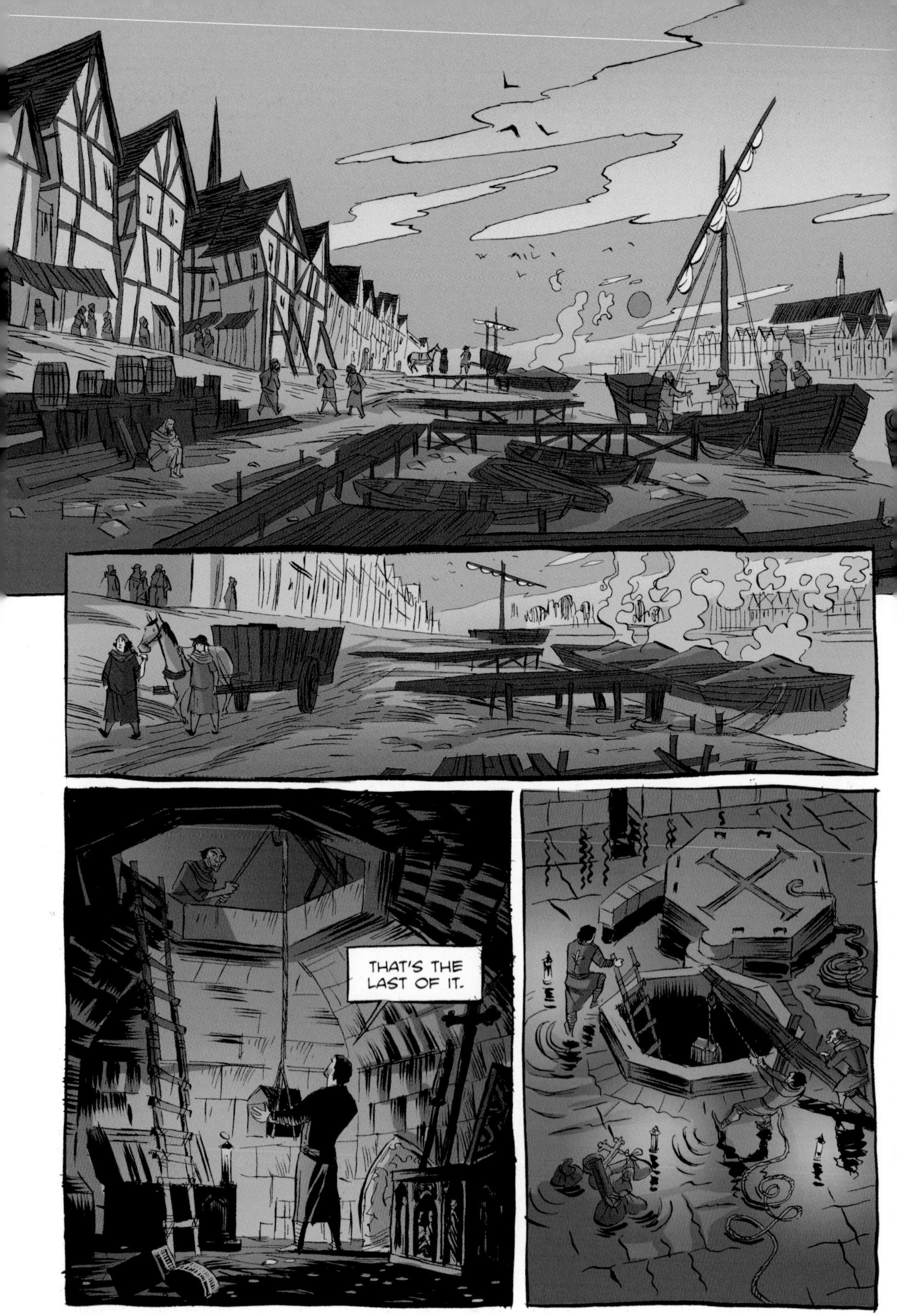
THAT'S THE LAST OF IT.

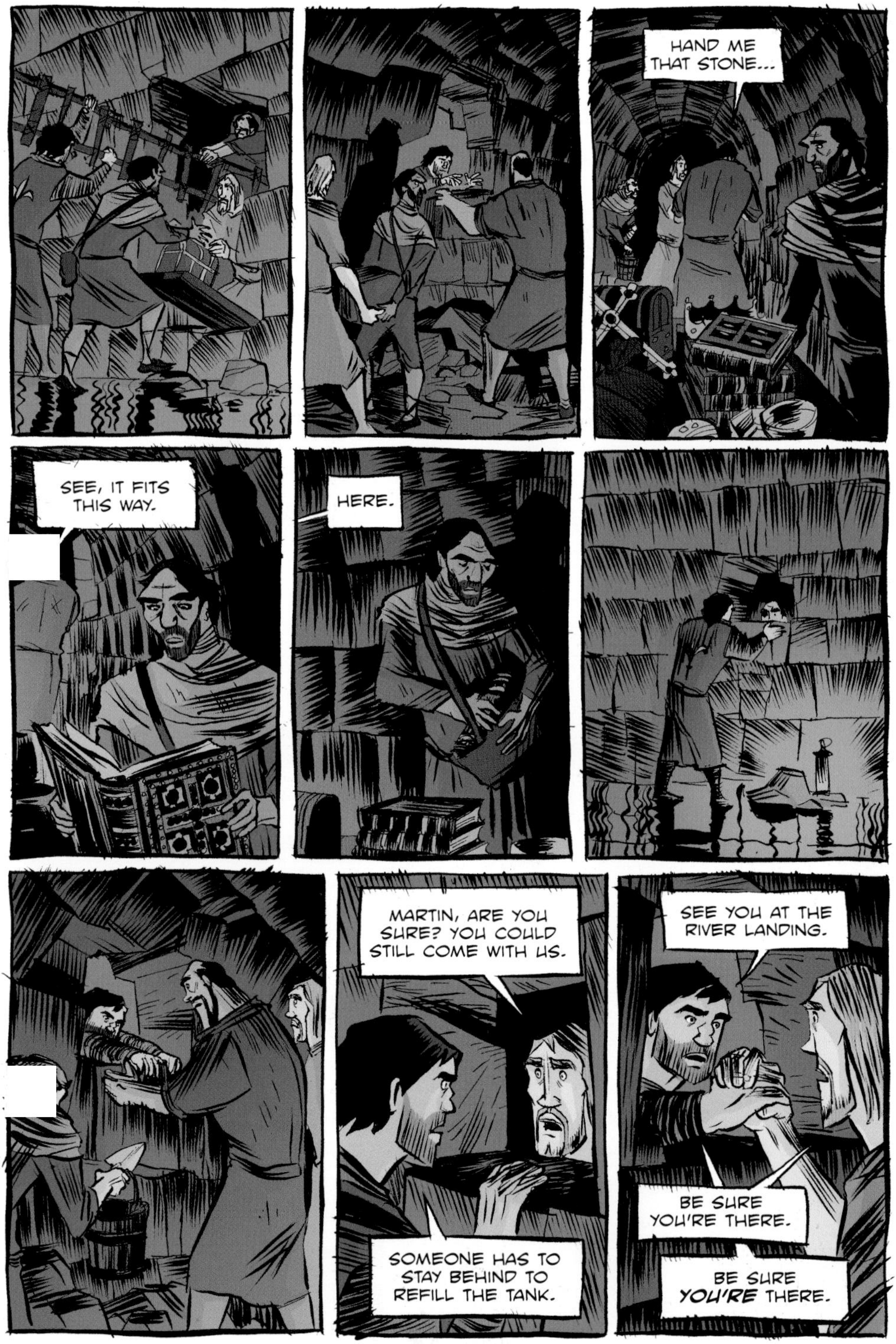
HAND ME THAT STONE...
SEE, IT FITS THIS WAY.
HERE.
MARTIN, ARE YOU SURE? YOU COULD STILL COME WITH US.
SOMEONE HAS TO STAY BEHIND TO REFILL THE TANK.
SEE YOU AT THE RIVER LANDING.
BE SURE YOU'RE THERE.
BE SURE *YOU'RE* THERE.

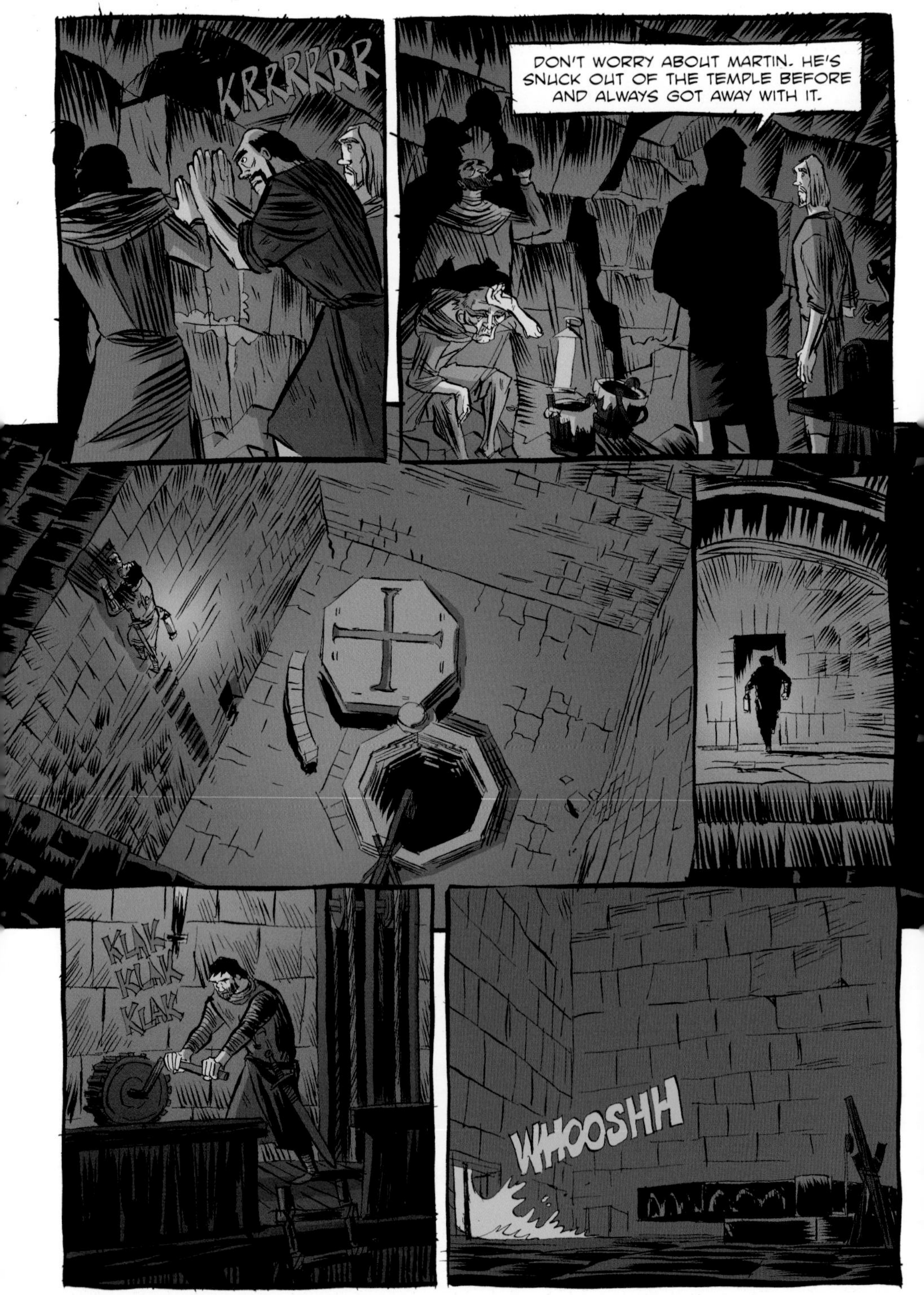
KRRRRRR
DON'T WORRY ABOUT MARTIN. HE'S SNUCK OUT OF THE TEMPLE BEFORE AND ALWAYS GOT AWAY WITH IT.
KLAK KLAK KLAK
WHOOSHH

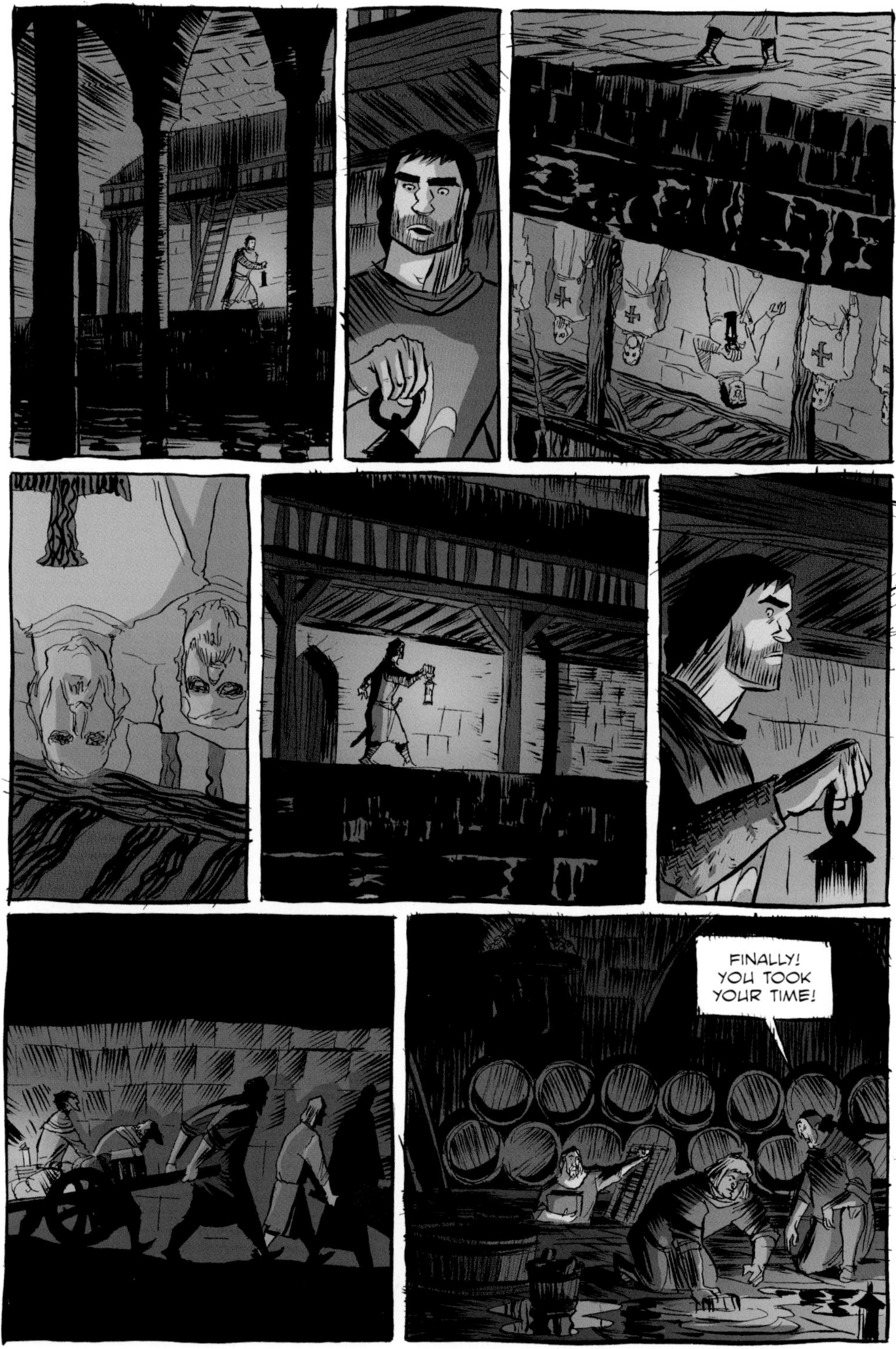
FINALLY! YOU TOOK YOUR TIME!

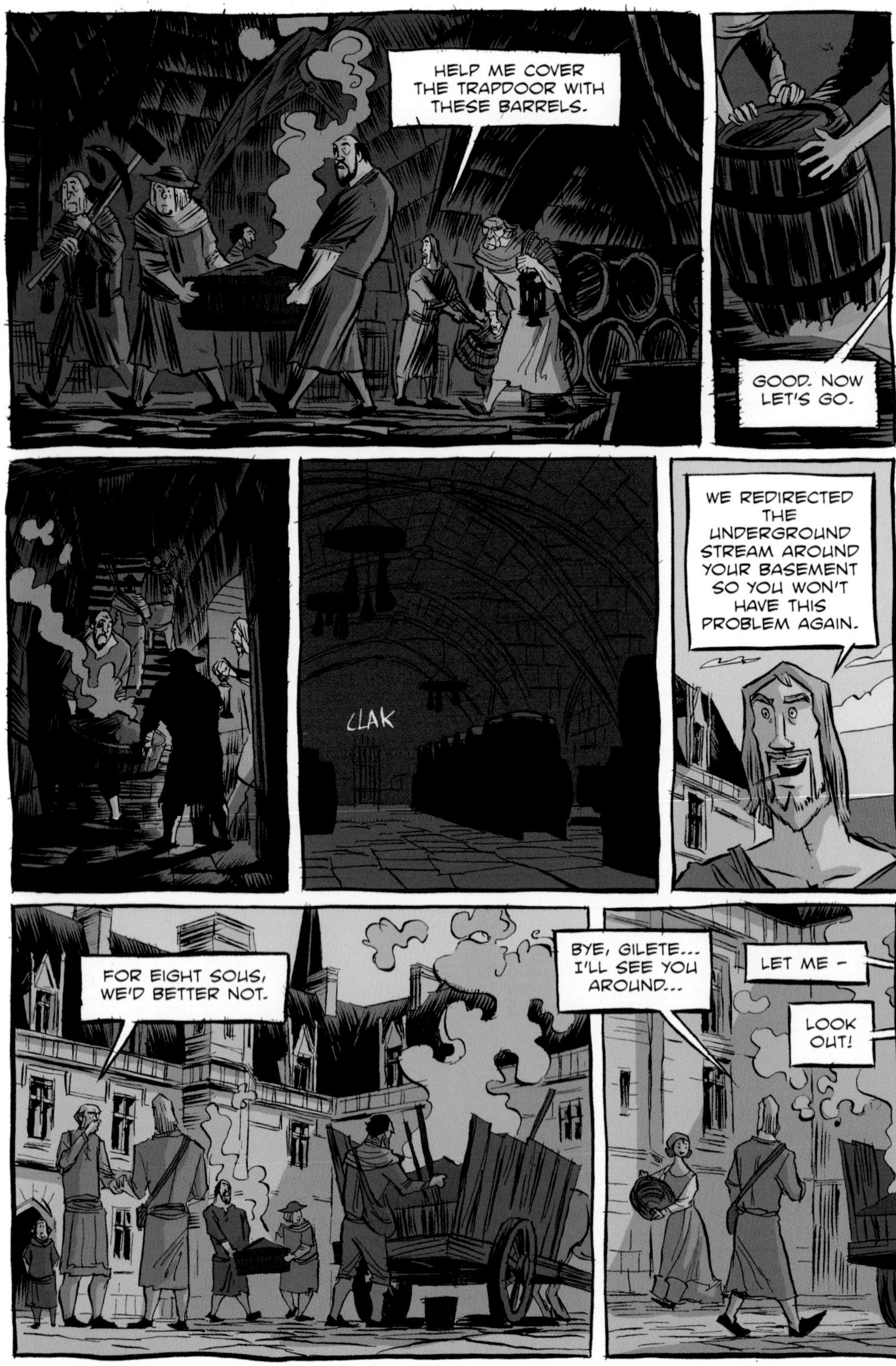
HELP ME COVER THE TRAPDOOR WITH THESE BARRELS.
GOOD. NOW LET'S GO.
CLAK
WE REDIRECTED THE UNDERGROUND STREAM AROUND YOUR BASEMENT SO YOU WON'T HAVE THIS PROBLEM AGAIN.
FOR EIGHT SOUS, WE'D BETTER NOT.
BYE, GILETE... I'LL SEE YOU AROUND...
LET ME –
LOOK OUT!

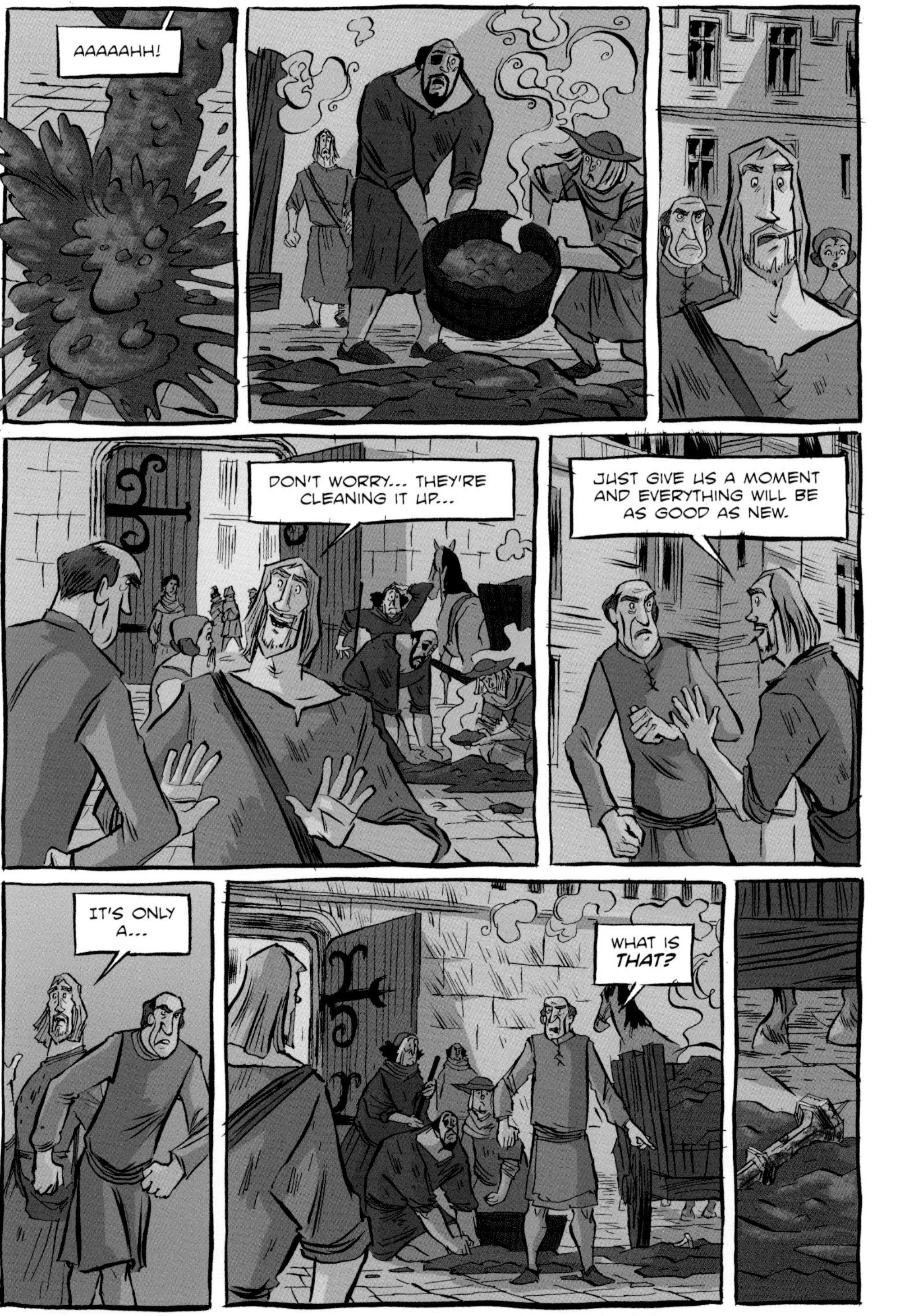
AAAAAHH!
DON'T WORRY... THEY'RE CLEANING IT UP...
JUST GIVE US A MOMENT AND EVERYTHING WILL BE AS GOOD AS NEW.
IT'S ONLY A...
WHAT IS *THAT?*

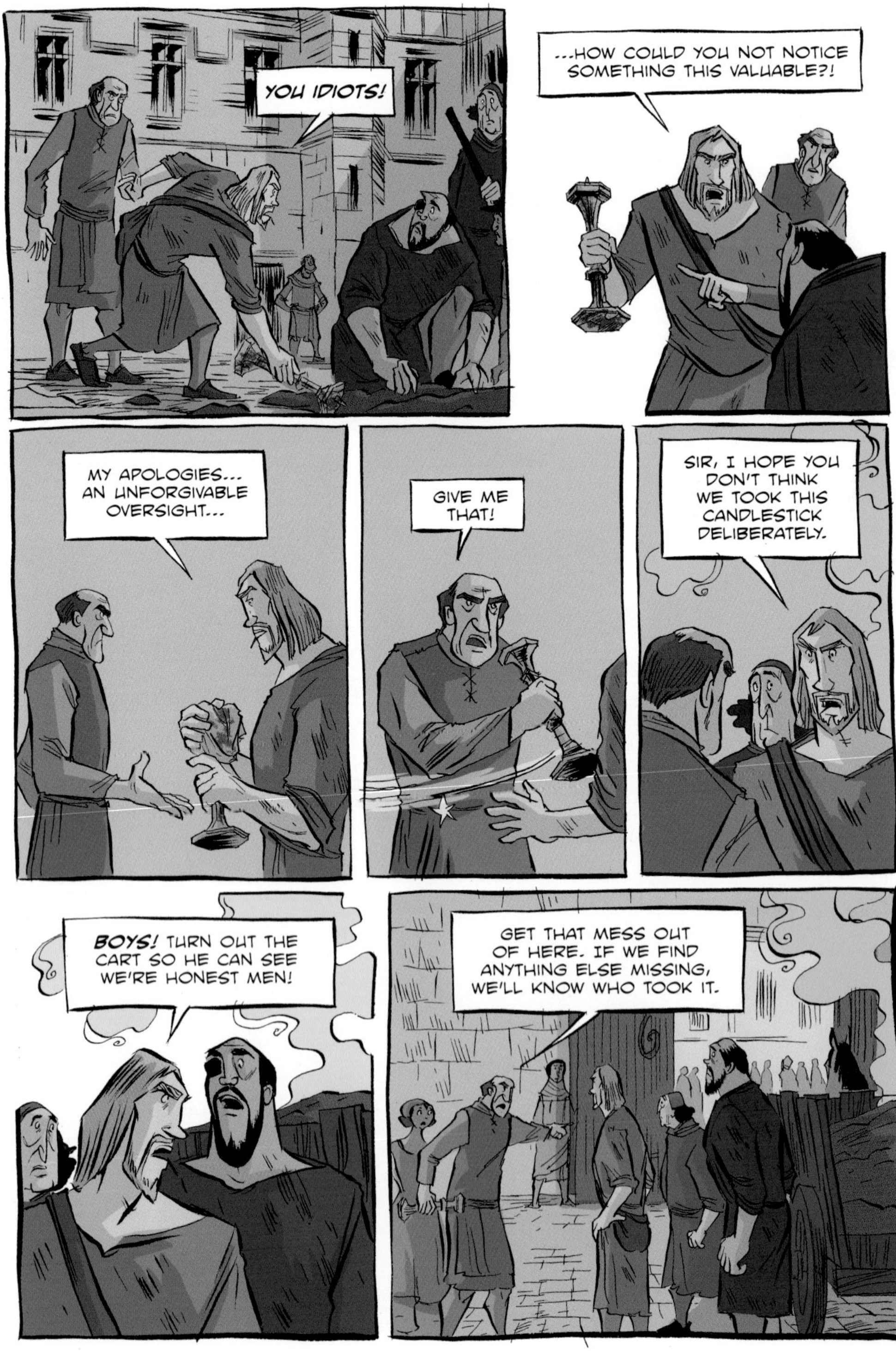
YOU IDIOTS!
...HOW COULD YOU NOT NOTICE SOMETHING THIS VALUABLE?!
MY APOLOGIES... AN UNFORGIVABLE OVERSIGHT...
GIVE ME THAT!
SIR, I HOPE YOU DON'T THINK WE TOOK THIS CANDLESTICK DELIBERATELY.
BOYS! TURN OUT THE CART SO HE CAN SEE WE'RE HONEST MEN!
GET THAT MESS OUT OF HERE. IF WE FIND ANYTHING ELSE MISSING, WE'LL KNOW WHO TOOK IT.

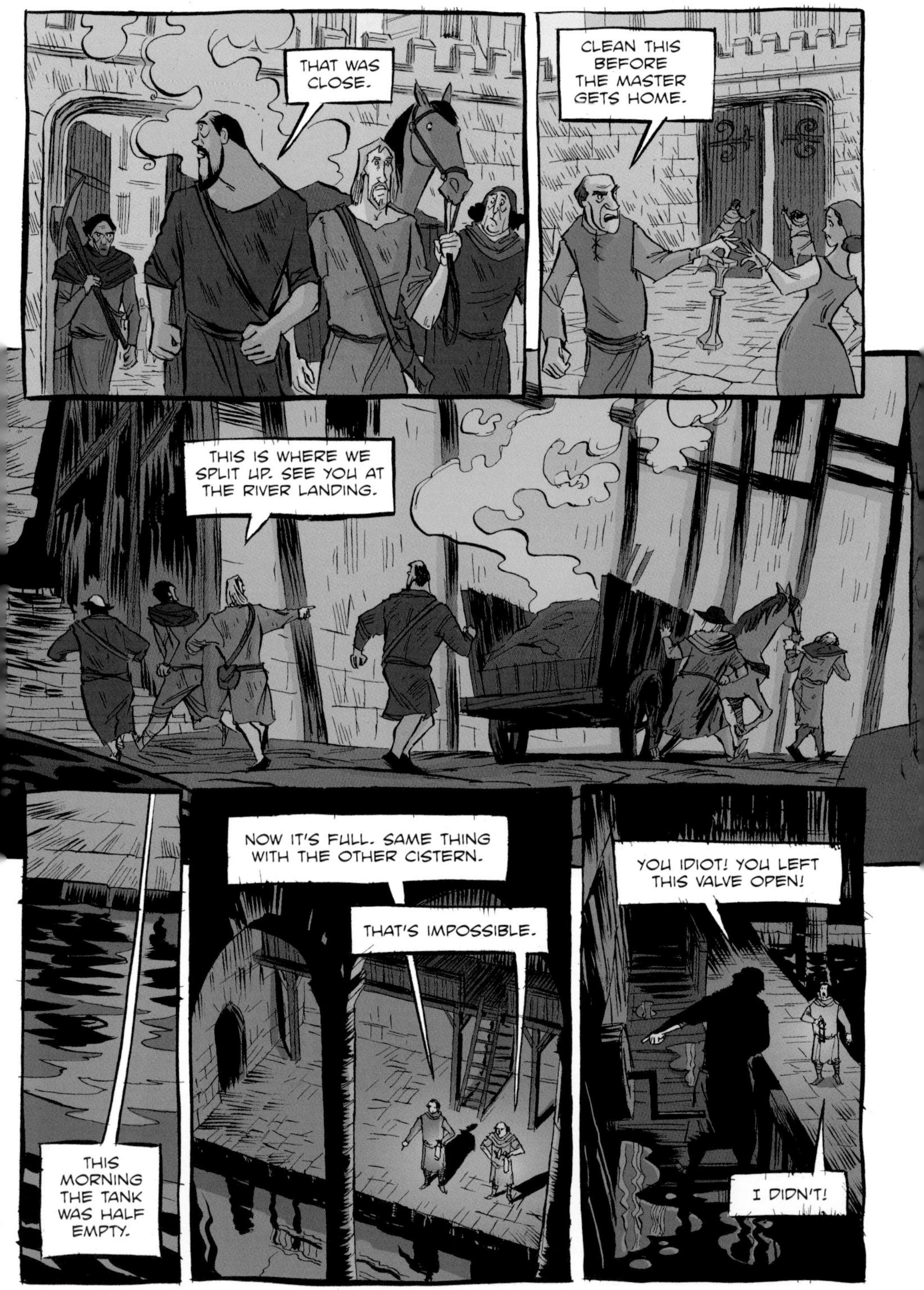
THAT WAS CLOSE.
CLEAN THIS BEFORE THE MASTER GETS HOME.
THIS IS WHERE WE SPLIT UP. SEE YOU AT THE RIVER LANDING.
THIS MORNING THE TANK WAS HALF EMPTY.
NOW IT'S FULL. SAME THING WITH THE OTHER CISTERN.
THAT'S IMPOSSIBLE.
YOU IDIOT! YOU LEFT THIS VALVE OPEN!
I DIDN'T!

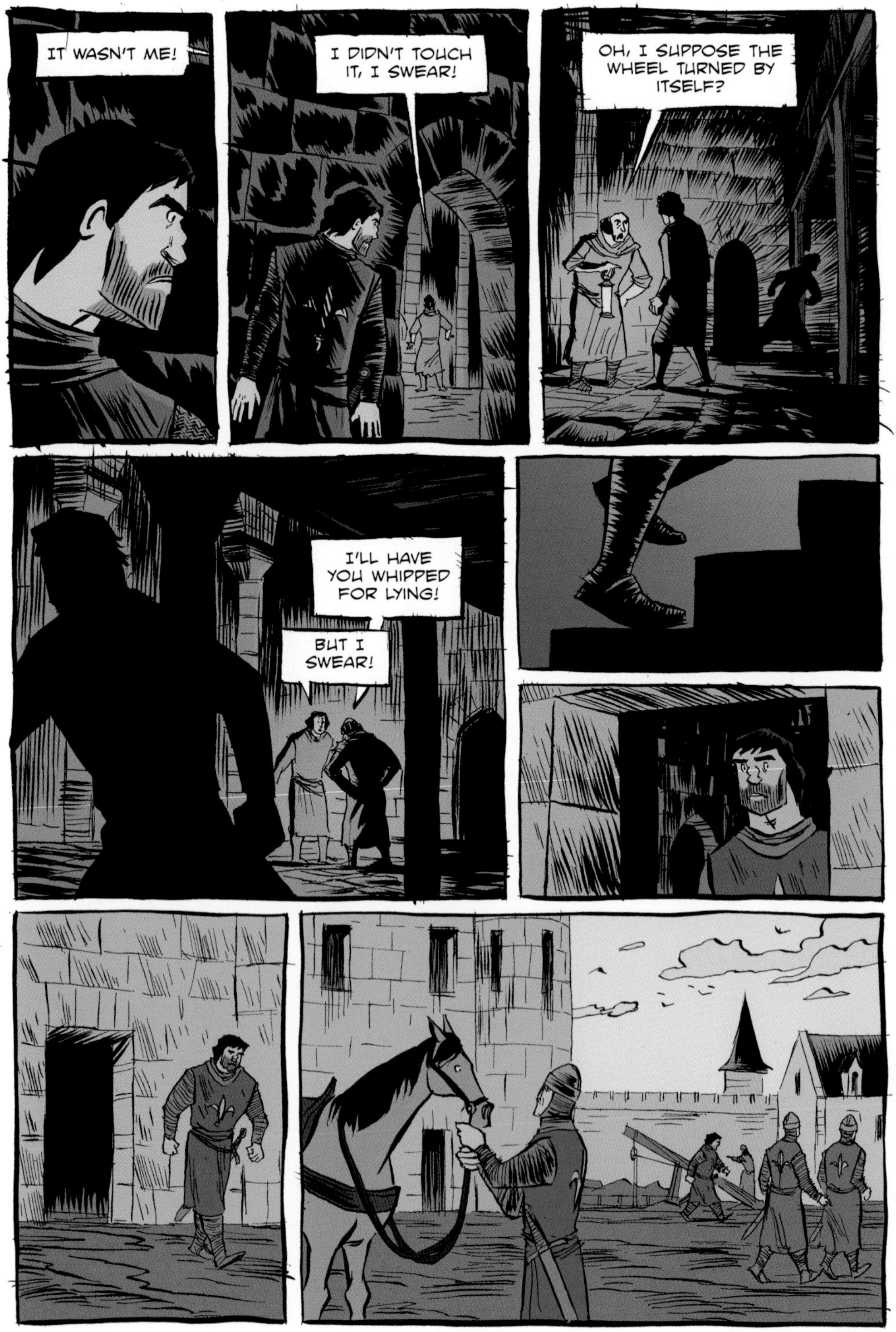
IT WASN'T ME!
I DIDN'T TOUCH IT, I SWEAR!
OH, I SUPPOSE THE WHEEL TURNED BY ITSELF?
I'LL HAVE YOU WHIPPED FOR LYING!
BUT I SWEAR!

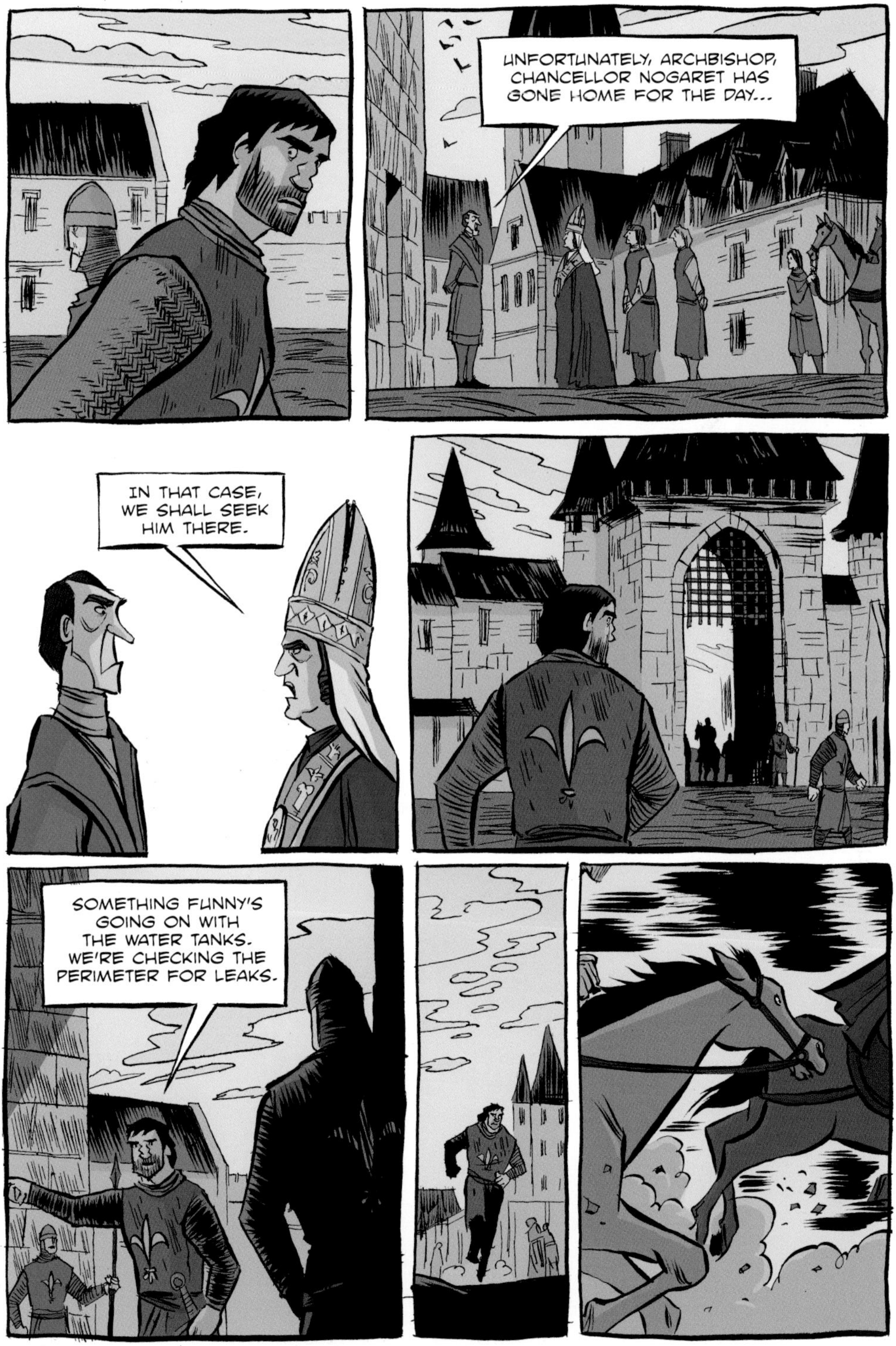
UNFORTUNATELY, ARCHBISHOP, CHANCELLOR NOGARET HAS GONE HOME FOR THE DAY...
IN THAT CASE, WE SHALL SEEK HIM THERE.
SOMETHING FUNNY'S GOING ON WITH THE WATER TANKS. WE'RE CHECKING THE PERIMETER FOR LEAKS.

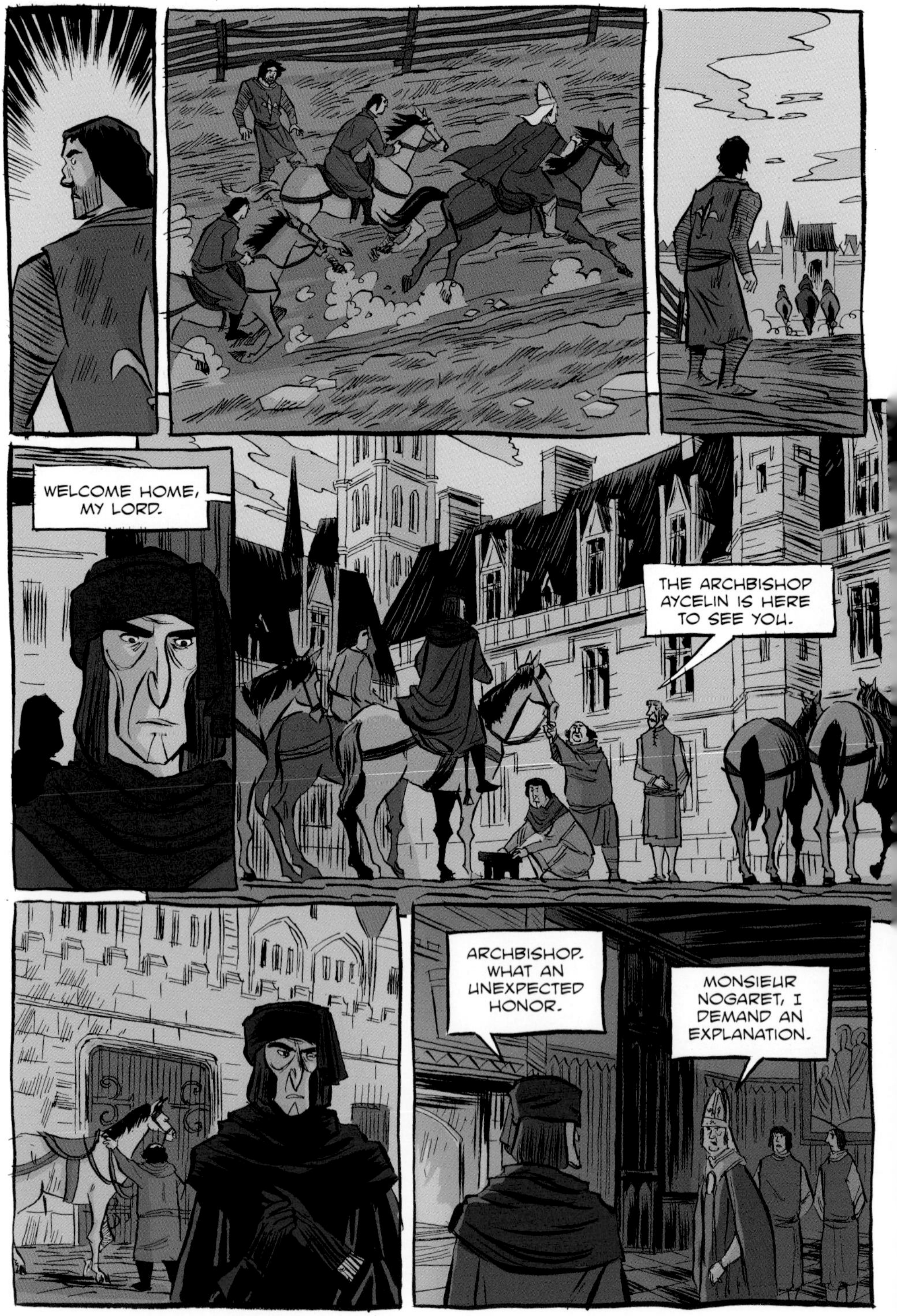

WELCOME HOME, MY LORD.
THE ARCHBISHOP AYCELIN IS HERE TO SEE YOU.
ARCHBISHOP. WHAT AN UNEXPECTED HONOR.
MONSIEUR NOGARET, I DEMAND AN EXPLANATION.

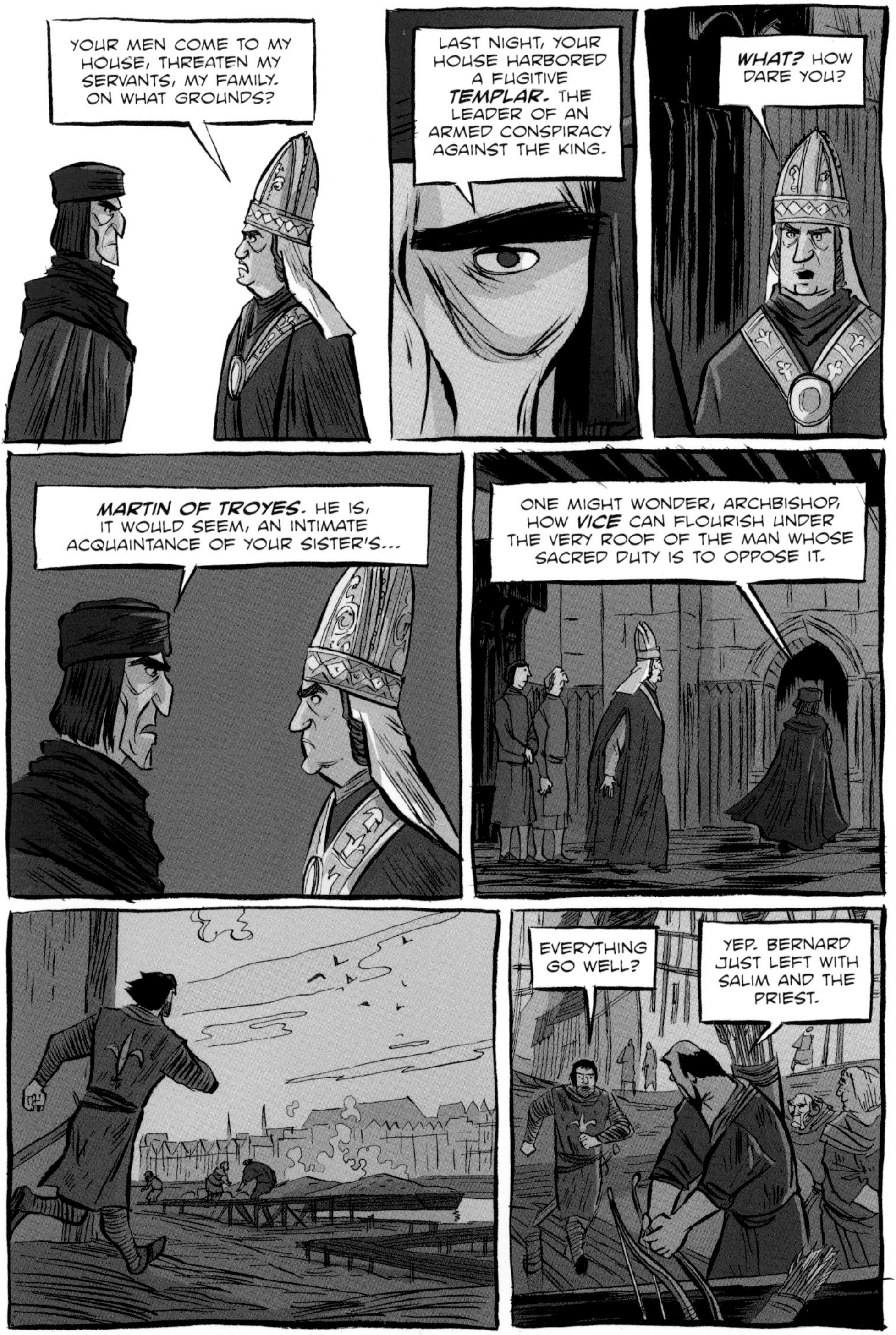
YOUR MEN COME TO MY HOUSE, THREATEN MY SERVANTS, MY FAMILY. ON WHAT GROUNDS?
LAST NIGHT, YOUR HOUSE HARBORED A FUGITIVE TEMPLAR. THE LEADER OF AN ARMED CONSPIRACY AGAINST THE KING.
WHAT? HOW DARE YOU?
MARTIN OF TROYES. HE IS, IT WOULD SEEM, AN INTIMATE ACQUAINTANCE OF YOUR SISTER'S...
ONE MIGHT WONDER, ARCHBISHOP, HOW VICE CAN FLOURISH UNDER THE VERY ROOF OF THE MAN WHOSE SACRED DUTY IS TO OPPOSE IT.
EVERYTHING GO WELL?
YEP. BERNARD JUST LEFT WITH SALIM AND THE PRIEST.

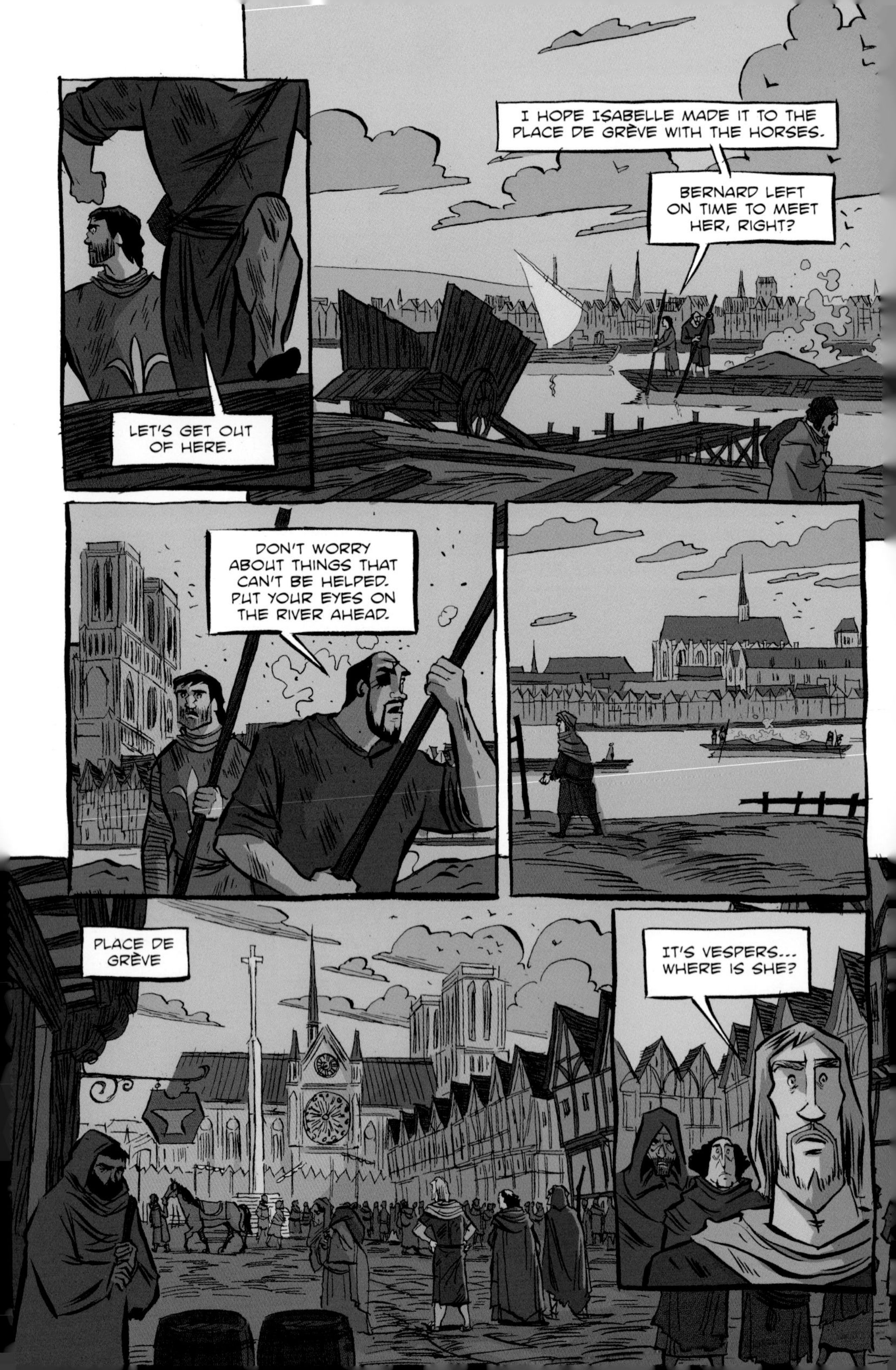
LET'S GET OUT OF HERE.
I HOPE ISABELLE MADE IT TO THE PLACE DE GRÈVE WITH THE HORSES.
BERNARD LEFT ON TIME TO MEET HER, RIGHT?
DON'T WORRY ABOUT THINGS THAT CAN'T BE HELPED. PUT YOUR EYES ON THE RIVER AHEAD.
PLACE DE GRÈVE
IT'S VESPERS... WHERE IS SHE?

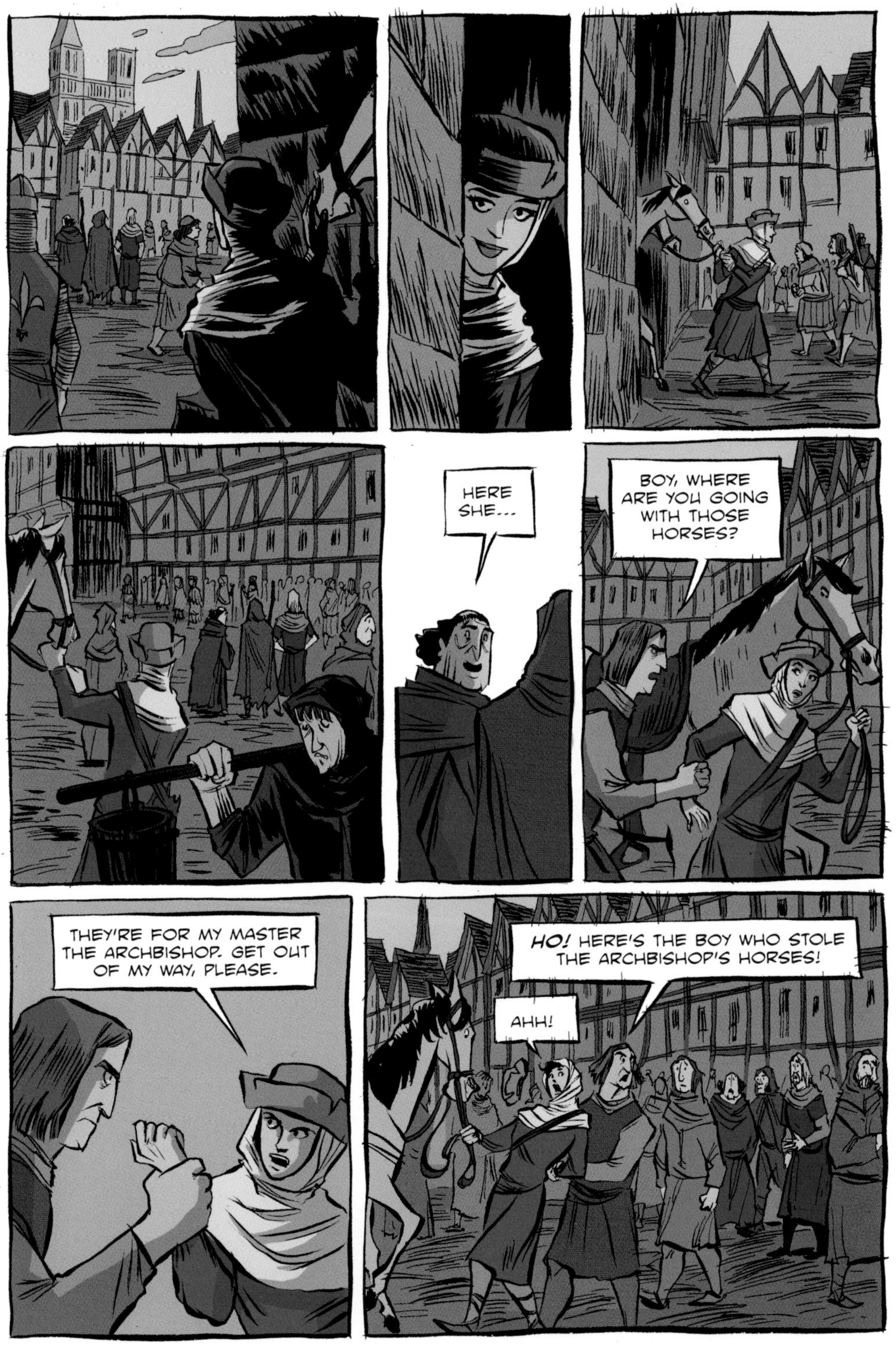
HERE SHE...
BOY, WHERE ARE YOU GOING WITH THOSE HORSES?
THEY'RE FOR MY MASTER THE ARCHBISHOP. GET OUT OF MY WAY, PLEASE.
HO! HERE'S THE BOY WHO STOLE THE ARCHBISHOP'S HORSES!
AHH!

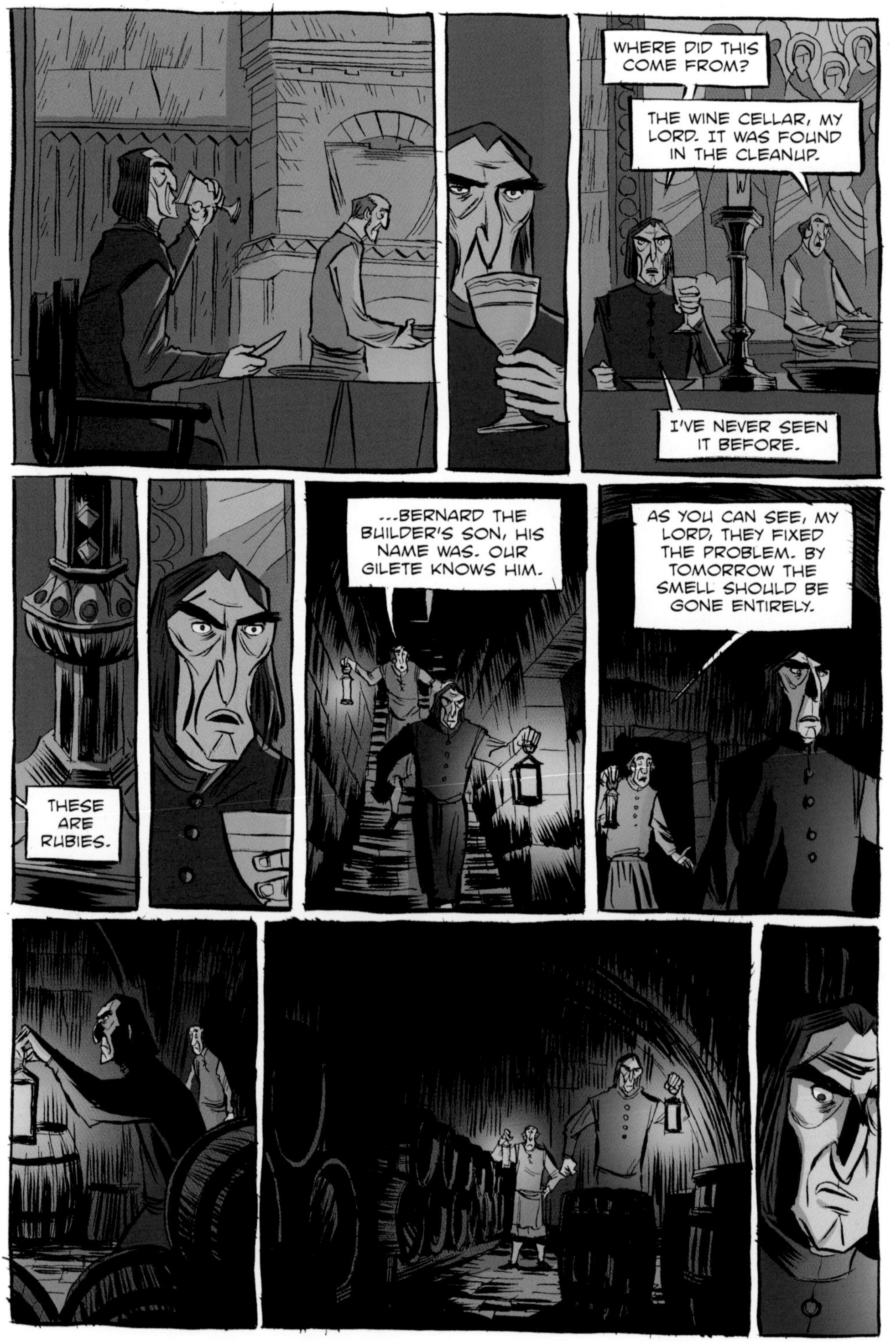
WHERE DID THIS COME FROM?
THE WINE CELLAR, MY LORD. IT WAS FOUND IN THE CLEANUP.
I'VE NEVER SEEN IT BEFORE.
THESE ARE RUBIES.
...BERNARD THE BUILDER'S SON, HIS NAME WAS. OUR GILETE KNOWS HIM.
AS YOU CAN SEE, MY LORD, THEY FIXED THE PROBLEM. BY TOMORROW THE SMELL SHOULD BE GONE ENTIRELY.

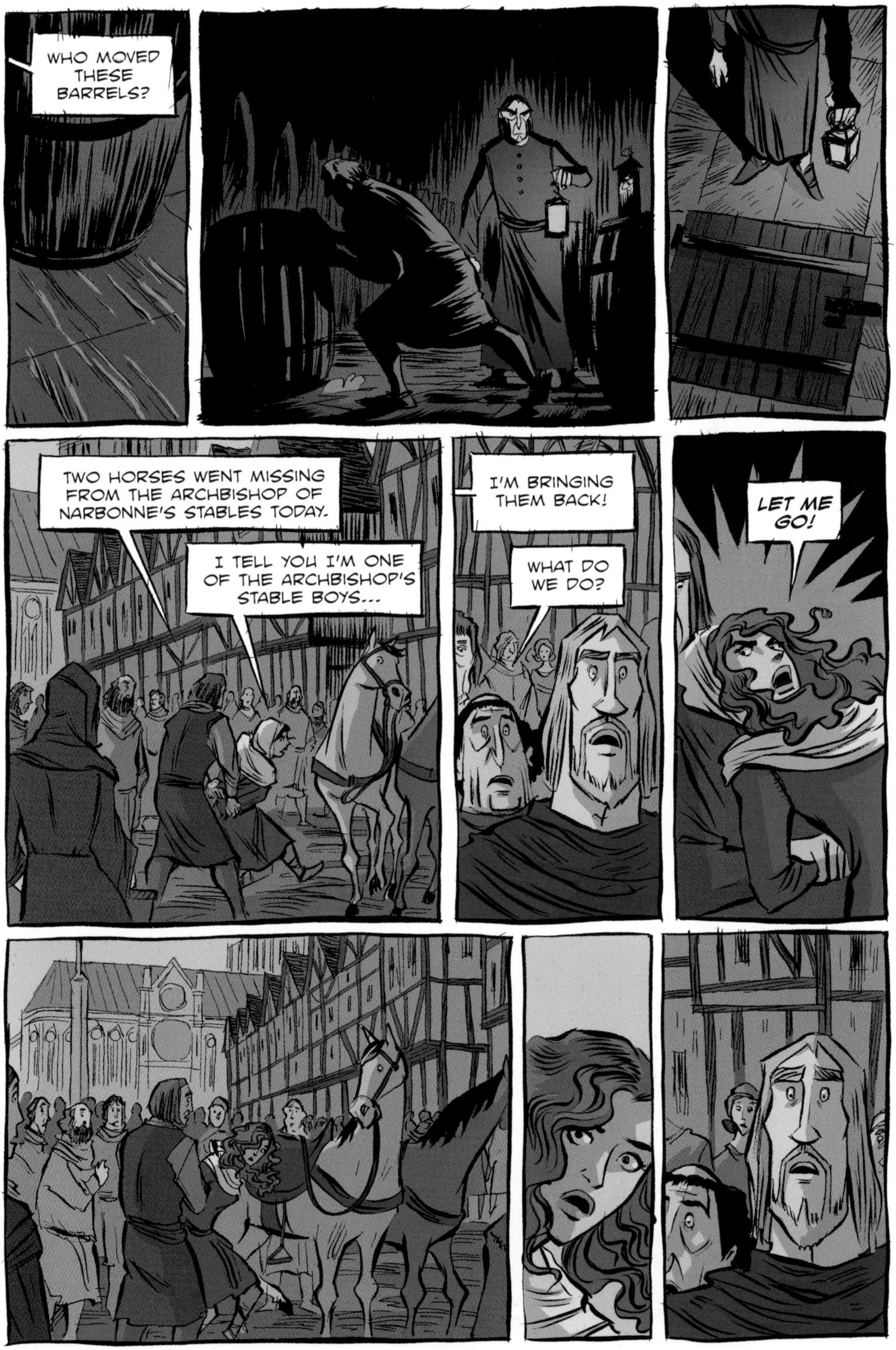
WHO MOVED THESE BARRELS?
TWO HORSES WENT MISSING FROM THE ARCHBISHOP OF NARBONNE'S STABLES TODAY.
I TELL YOU I'M ONE OF THE ARCHBISHOP'S STABLE BOYS...
I'M BRINGING THEM BACK!
WHAT DO WE DO?
LET ME GO!

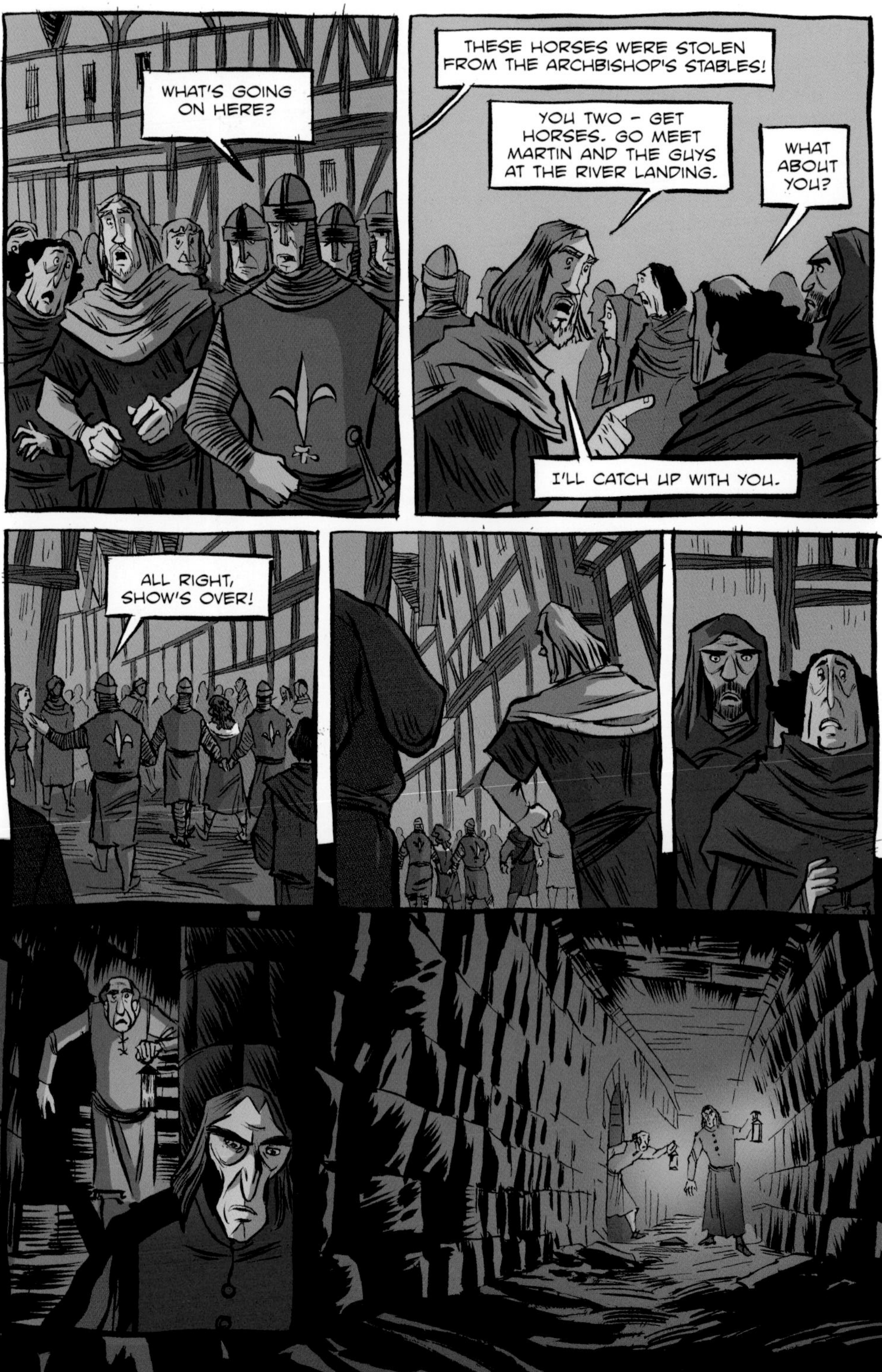
WHAT'S GOING ON HERE?
THESE HORSES WERE STOLEN FROM THE ARCHBISHOP'S STABLES!
YOU TWO - GET HORSES. GO MEET MARTIN AND THE GUYS AT THE RIVER LANDING.
WHAT ABOUT YOU?
I'LL CATCH UP WITH YOU.
ALL RIGHT, SHOW'S OVER!

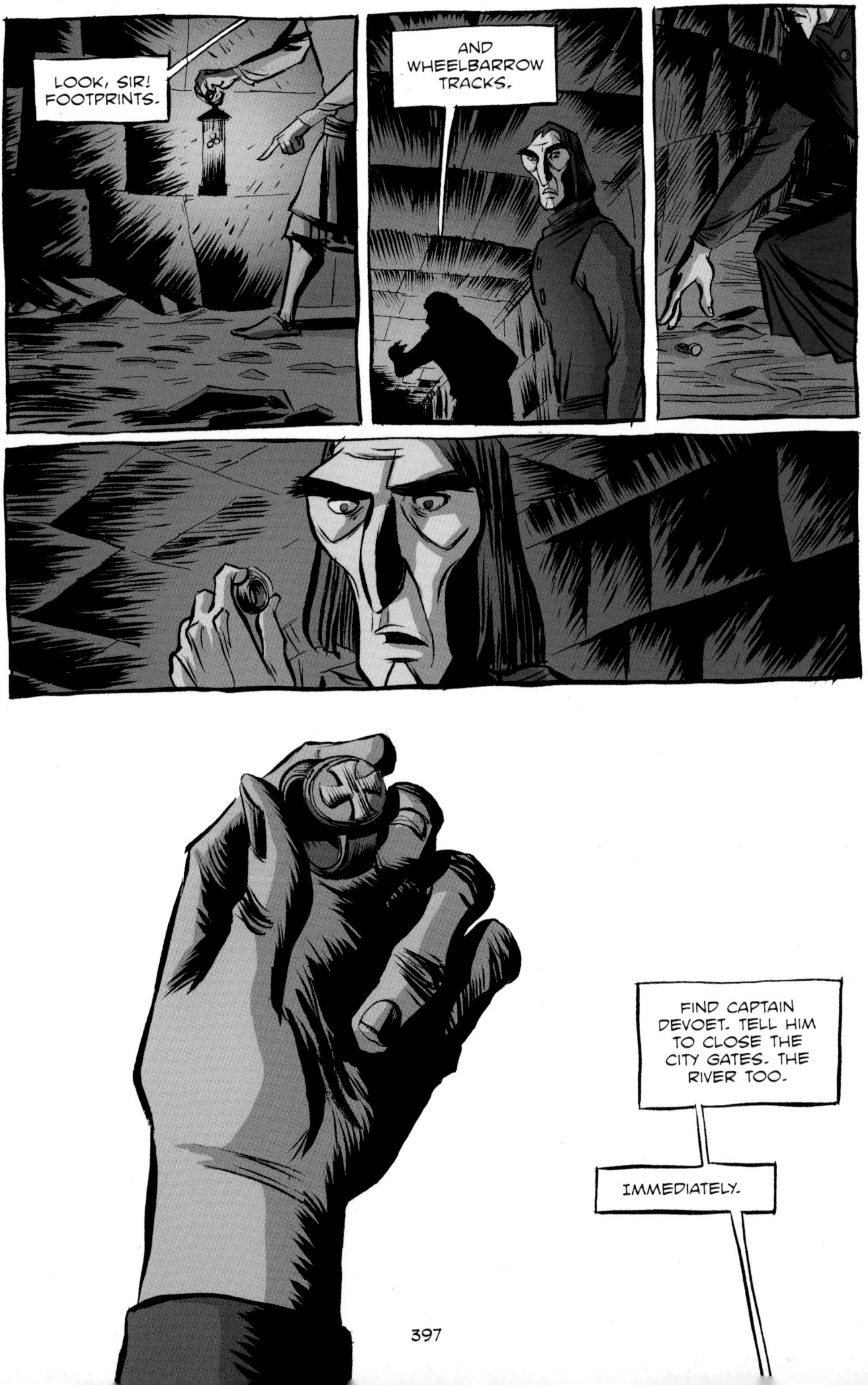
LOOK, SIR! FOOTPRINTS.
AND WHEELBARROW TRACKS.
FIND CAPTAIN DEVOET. TELL HIM TO CLOSE THE CITY GATES. THE RIVER TOO.
IMMEDIATELY.

9. The River

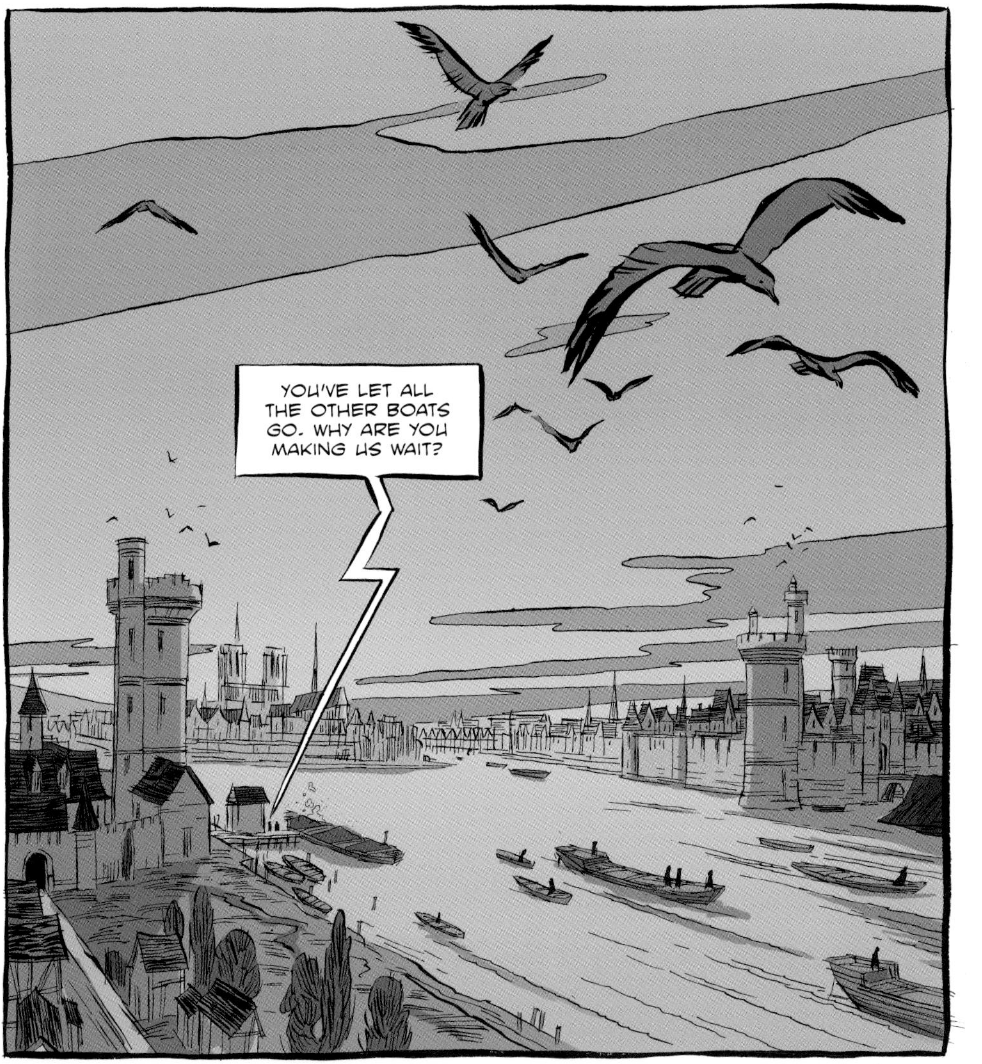
YOU'VE LET ALL THE OTHER BOATS GO. WHY ARE YOU MAKING US WAIT?

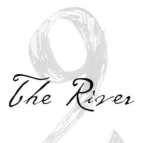

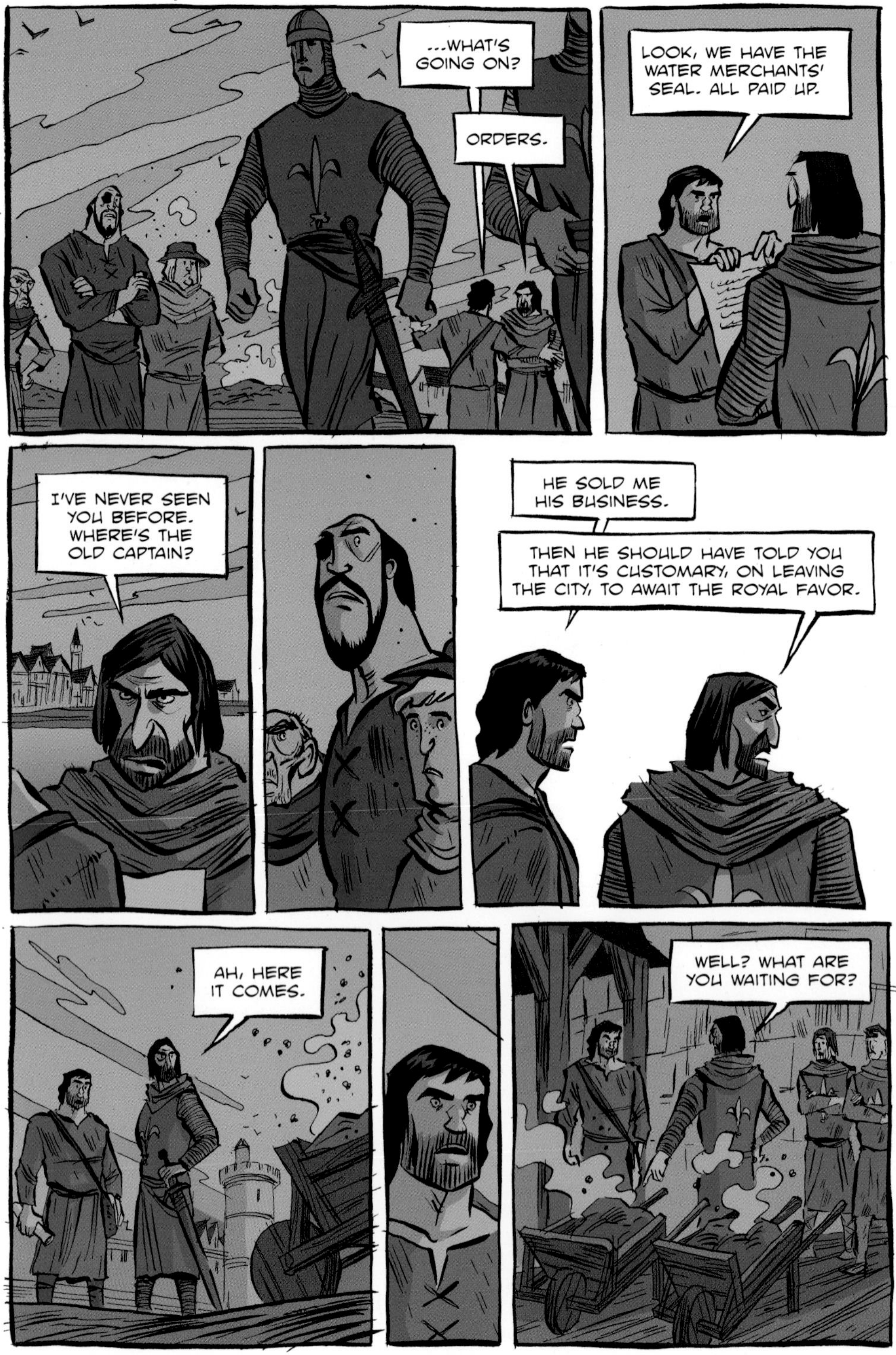
...WHAT'S GOING ON?
ORDERS.
LOOK, WE HAVE THE WATER MERCHANTS' SEAL. ALL PAID UP.
I'VE NEVER SEEN YOU BEFORE. WHERE'S THE OLD CAPTAIN?
HE SOLD ME HIS BUSINESS.
THEN HE SHOULD HAVE TOLD YOU THAT IT'S CUSTOMARY, ON LEAVING THE CITY, TO AWAIT THE ROYAL FAVOR.
AH, HERE IT COMES.
WELL? WHAT ARE YOU WAITING FOR?

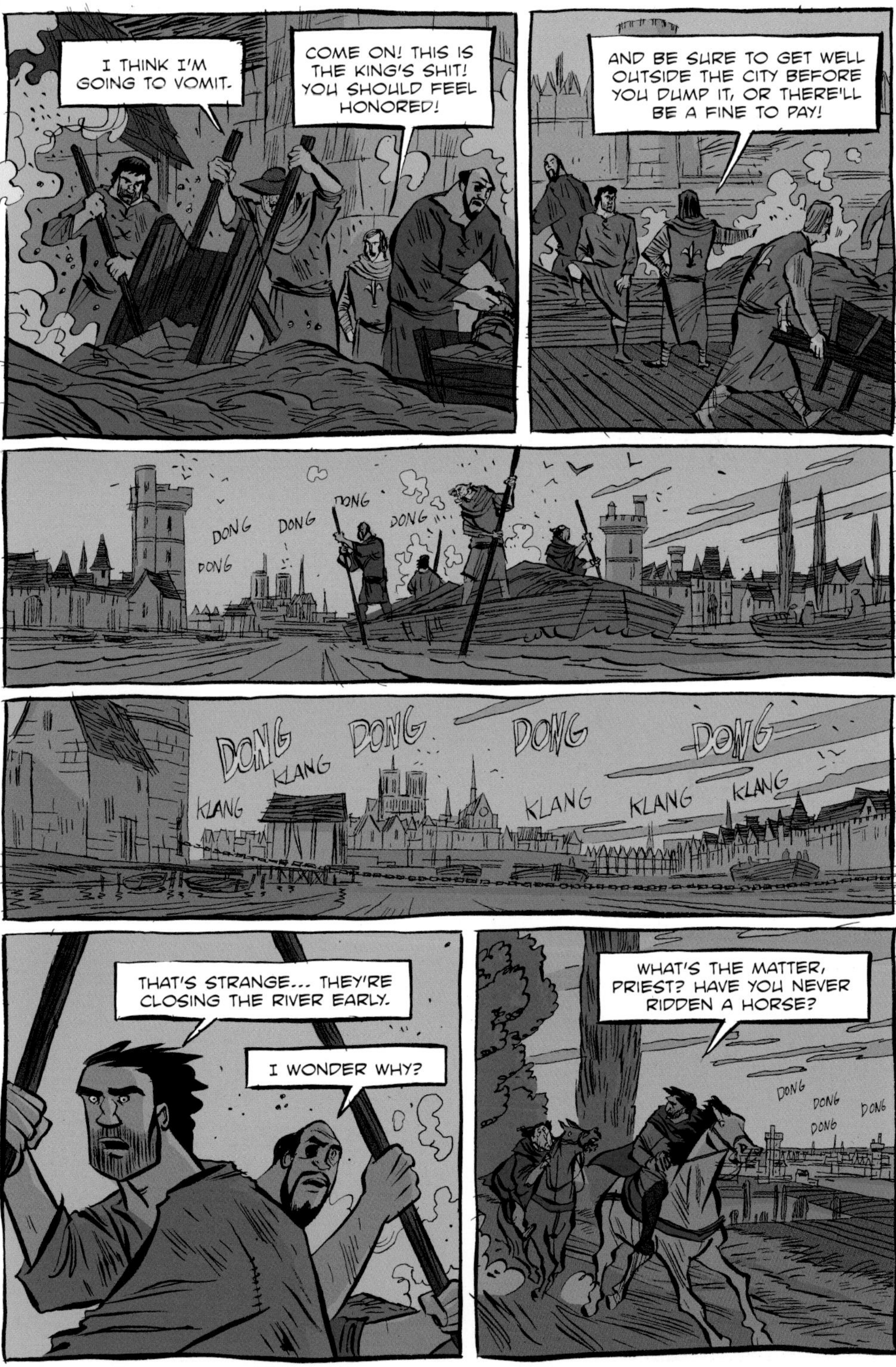
I THINK I'M GOING TO VOMIT.
COME ON! THIS IS THE KING'S SHIT! YOU SHOULD FEEL HONORED!
AND BE SURE TO GET WELL OUTSIDE THE CITY BEFORE YOU DUMP IT, OR THERE'LL BE A FINE TO PAY!
DONG DONG DONG DONG DONG
DONG KLANG DONG DONG DONG KLANG KLANG KLANG KLANG
THAT'S STRANGE... THEY'RE CLOSING THE RIVER EARLY.
I WONDER WHY?
WHAT'S THE MATTER, PRIEST? HAVE YOU NEVER RIDDEN A HORSE?
DONG DONG DONG DONG

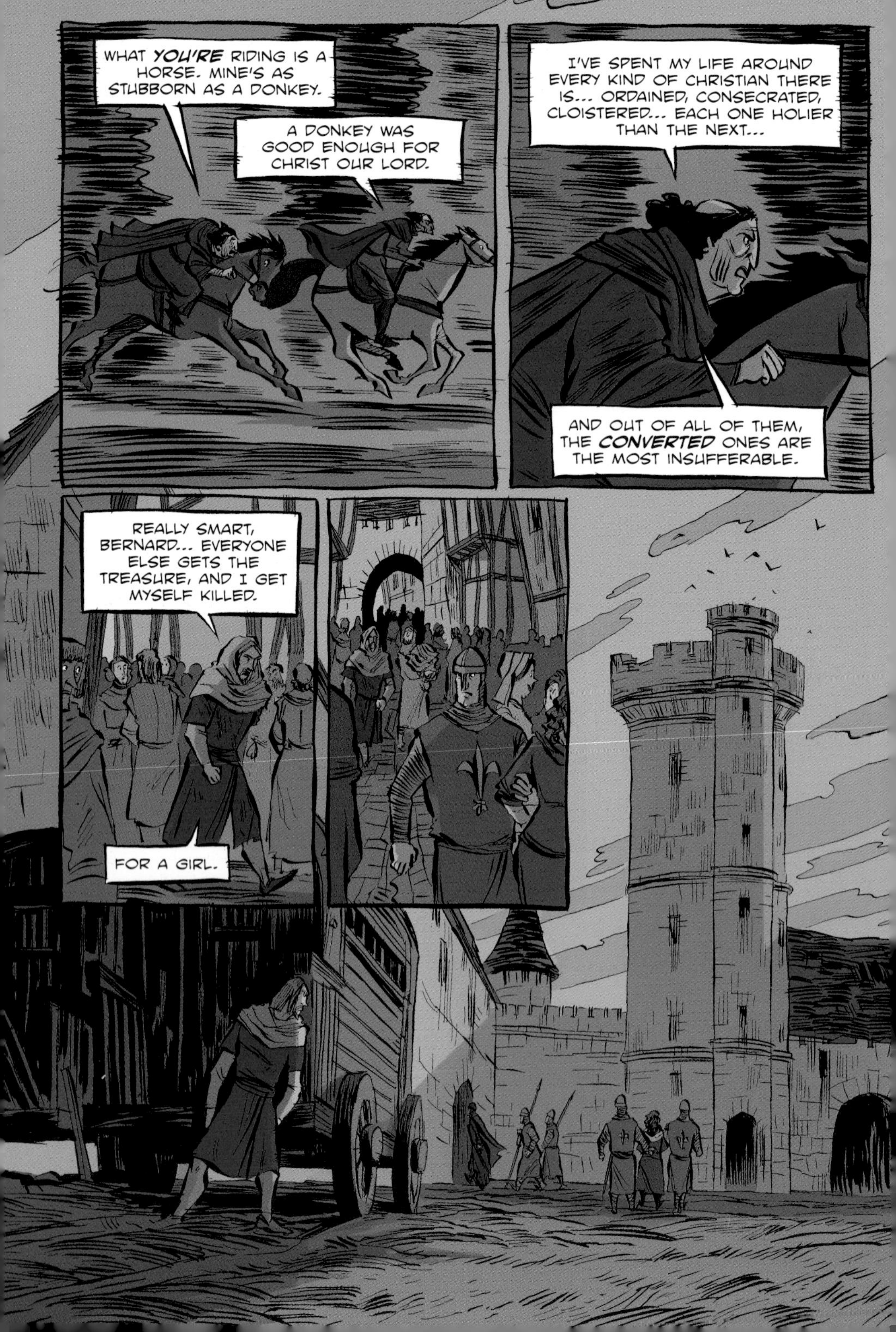
WHAT YOU'RE RIDING IS A HORSE. MINE'S AS STUBBORN AS A DONKEY.
A DONKEY WAS GOOD ENOUGH FOR CHRIST OUR LORD.
I'VE SPENT MY LIFE AROUND EVERY KIND OF CHRISTIAN THERE IS... ORDAINED, CONSECRATED, CLOISTERED... EACH ONE HOLIER THAN THE NEXT...
AND OUT OF ALL OF THEM, THE CONVERTED ONES ARE THE MOST INSUFFERABLE.
REALLY SMART, BERNARD... EVERYONE ELSE GETS THE TREASURE, AND I GET MYSELF KILLED.
FOR A GIRL.

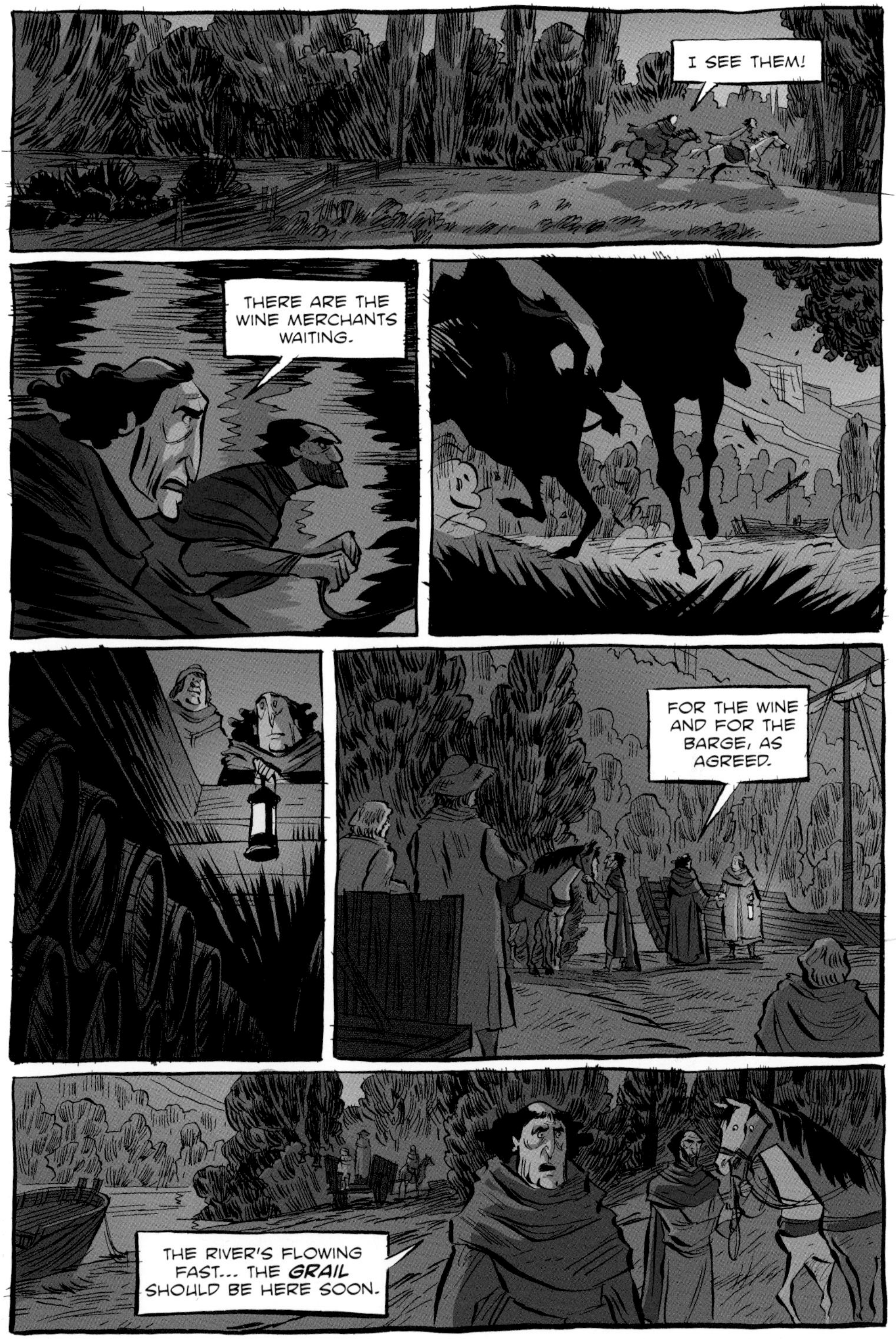
I SEE THEM!
THERE ARE THE WINE MERCHANTS WAITING.
FOR THE WINE AND FOR THE BARGE, AS AGREED.
THE RIVER'S FLOWING FAST... THE ***GRAIL*** SHOULD BE HERE SOON.

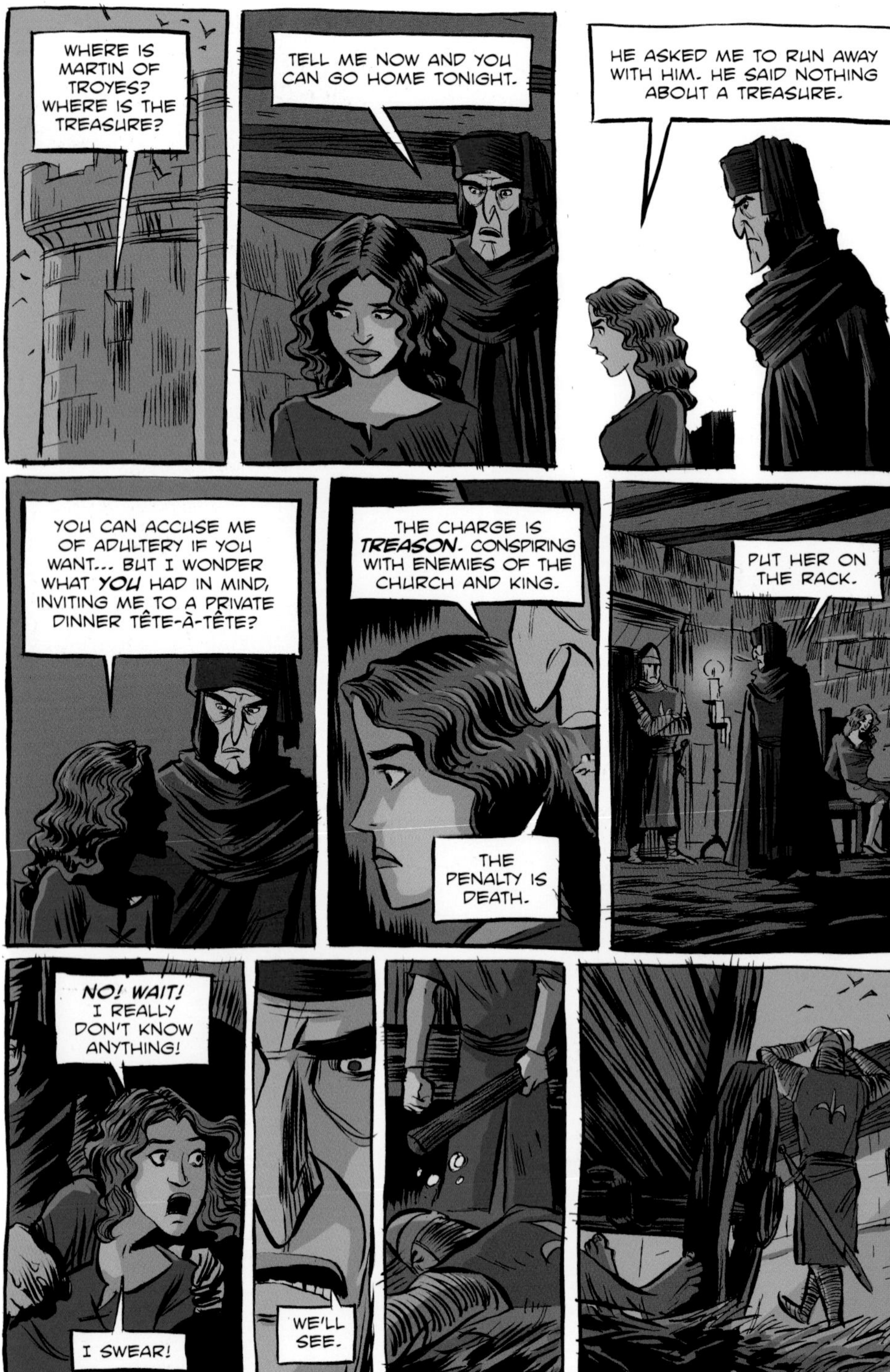
WHERE IS MARTIN OF TROYES? WHERE IS THE TREASURE?
TELL ME NOW AND YOU CAN GO HOME TONIGHT.
HE ASKED ME TO RUN AWAY WITH HIM. HE SAID NOTHING ABOUT A TREASURE.
YOU CAN ACCUSE ME OF ADULTERY IF YOU WANT... BUT I WONDER WHAT *YOU* HAD IN MIND, INVITING ME TO A PRIVATE DINNER TÊTE-À-TÊTE?
THE CHARGE IS *TREASON*. CONSPIRING WITH ENEMIES OF THE CHURCH AND KING.
THE PENALTY IS DEATH.
PUT HER ON THE RACK.
NO! WAIT! I REALLY DON'T KNOW ANYTHING!
I SWEAR!
WE'LL SEE.

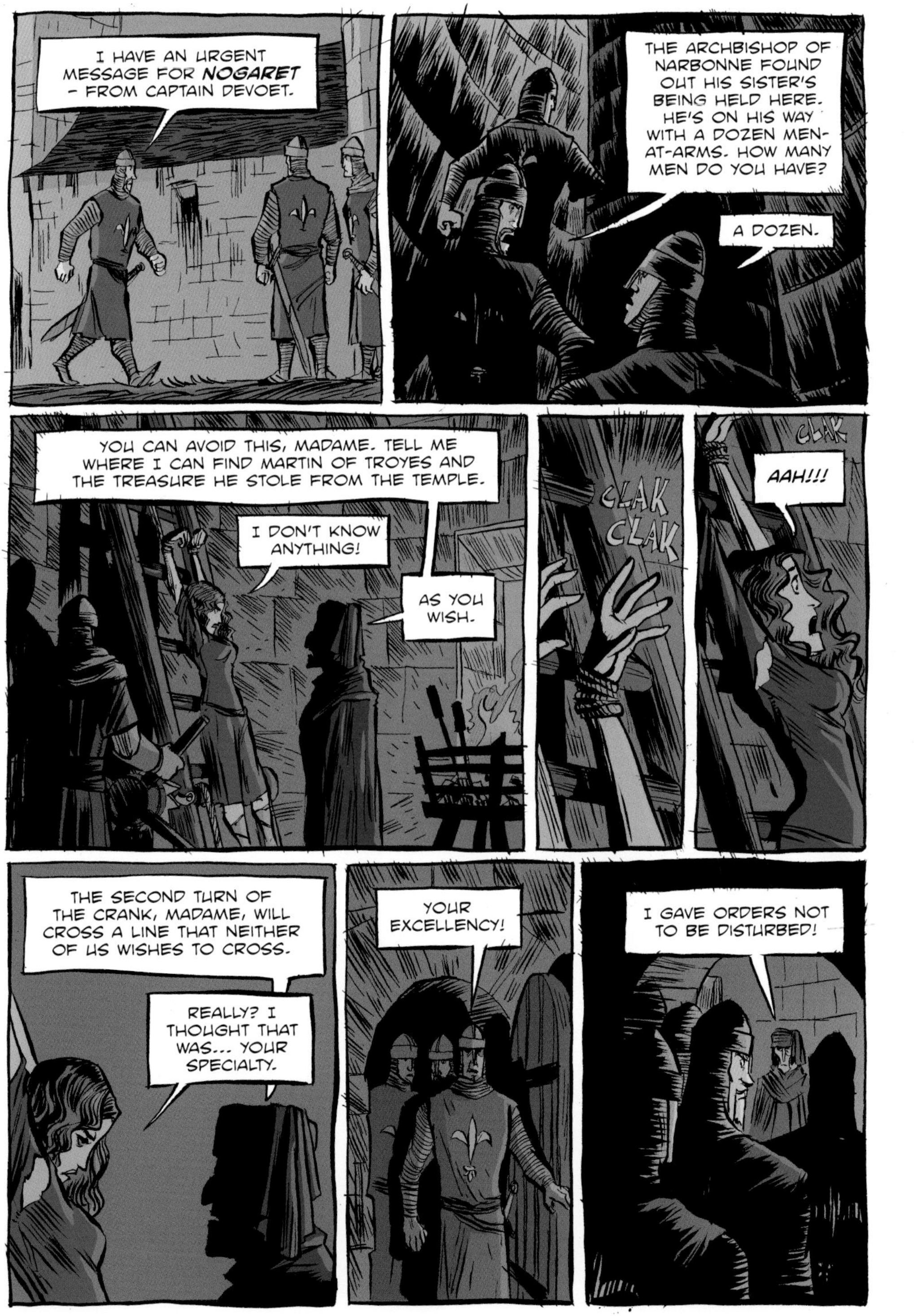
I HAVE AN URGENT MESSAGE FOR NOGARET - FROM CAPTAIN DEVOET.
THE ARCHBISHOP OF NARBONNE FOUND OUT HIS SISTER'S BEING HELD HERE. HE'S ON HIS WAY WITH A DOZEN MEN-AT-ARMS. HOW MANY MEN DO YOU HAVE?
A DOZEN.
YOU CAN AVOID THIS, MADAME. TELL ME WHERE I CAN FIND MARTIN OF TROYES AND THE TREASURE HE STOLE FROM THE TEMPLE.
I DON'T KNOW ANYTHING!
AS YOU WISH.
CLAK CLAK
CLAK
AAH!!!
THE SECOND TURN OF THE CRANK, MADAME, WILL CROSS A LINE THAT NEITHER OF US WISHES TO CROSS.
REALLY? I THOUGHT THAT WAS... YOUR SPECIALTY.
YOUR EXCELLENCY!
I GAVE ORDERS NOT TO BE DISTURBED!

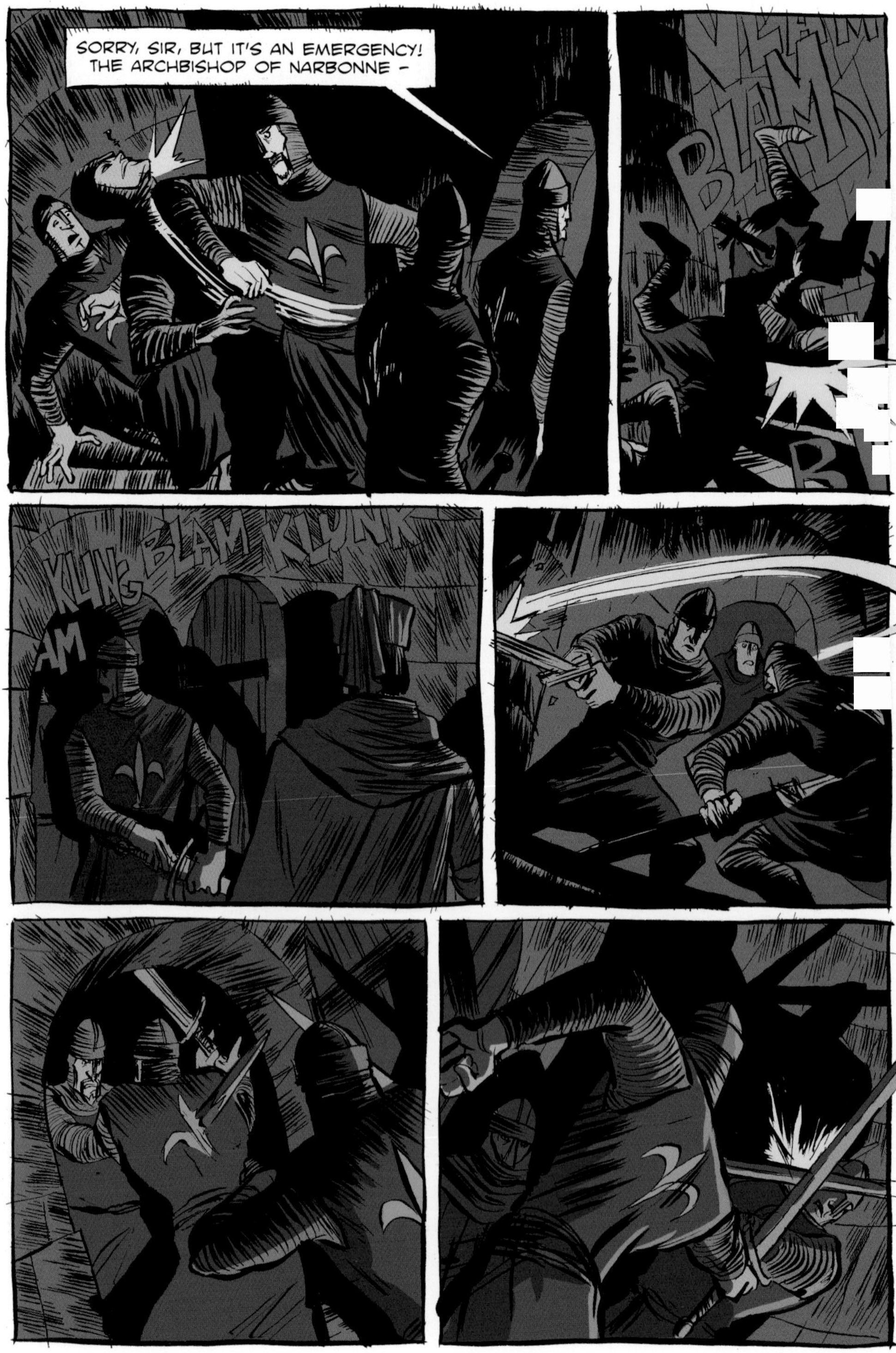
SORRY, SIR, BUT IT'S AN EMERGENCY! THE ARCHBISHOP OF NARBONNE –
BLAM
KLUNG BLAM KLUNK
AM

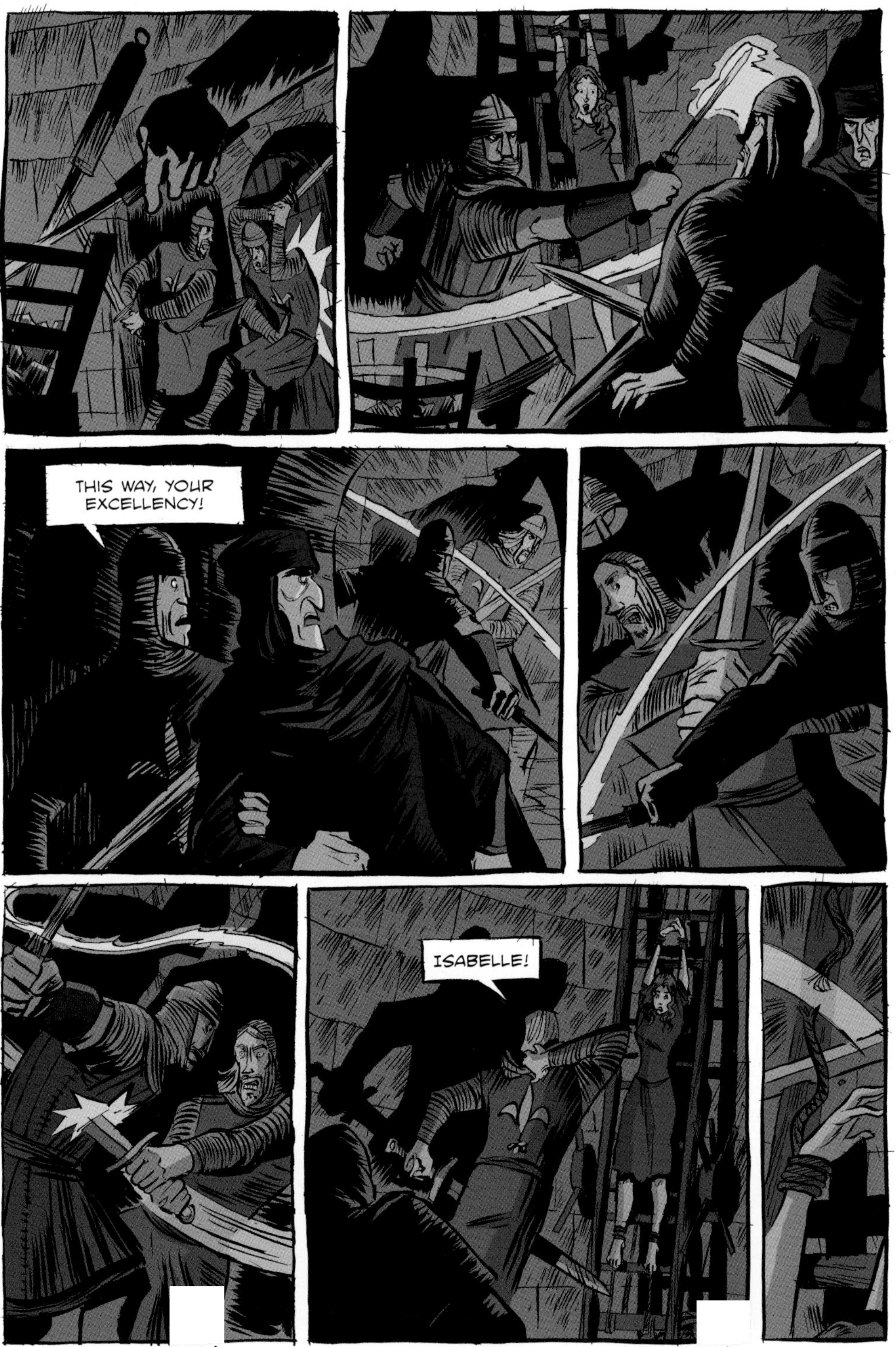
THIS WAY, YOUR EXCELLENCY!
ISABELLE!

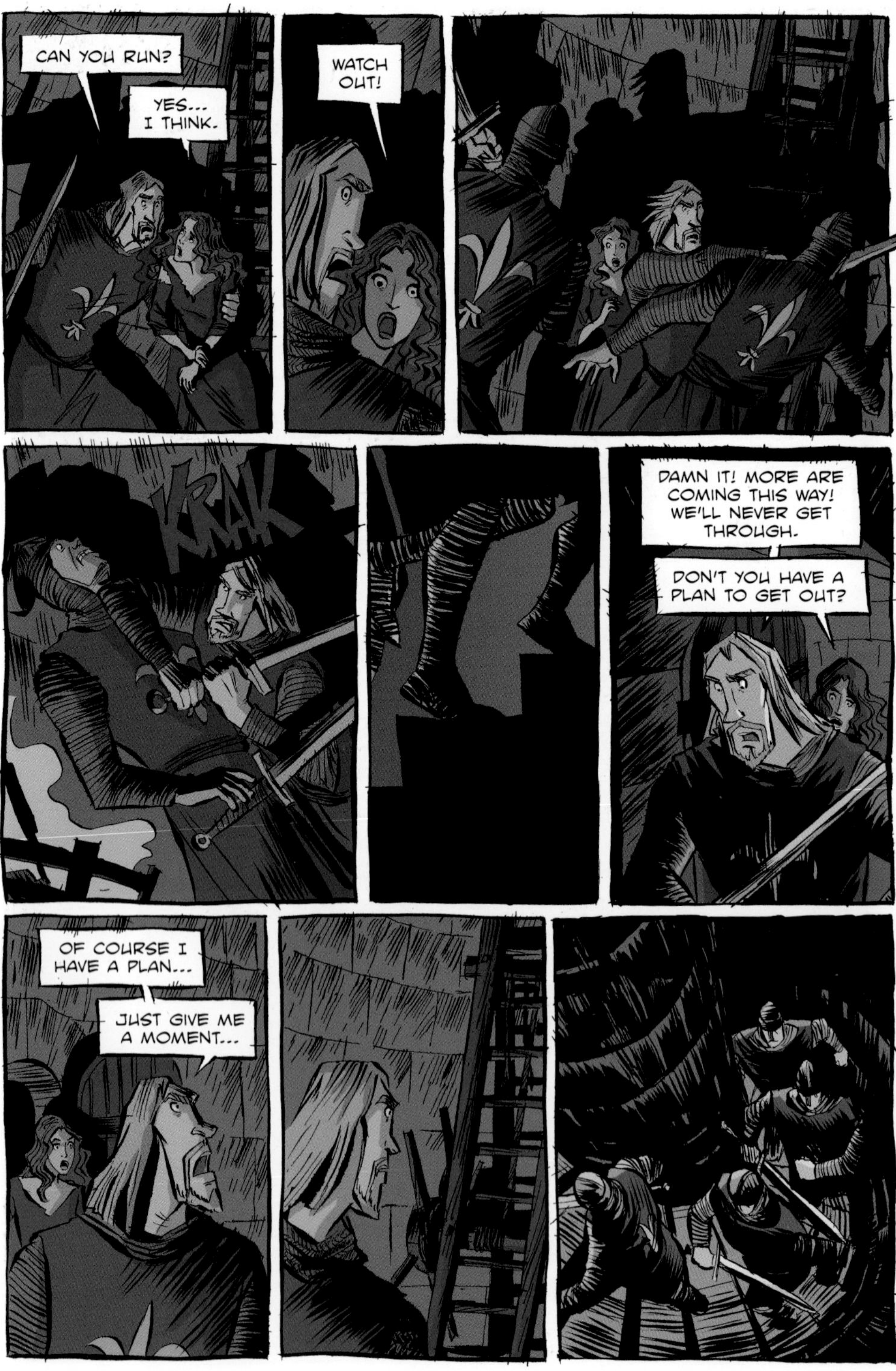
CAN YOU RUN?
YES... I THINK.
WATCH OUT!
KRAK
DAMN IT! MORE ARE COMING THIS WAY! WE'LL NEVER GET THROUGH.
DON'T YOU HAVE A PLAN TO GET OUT?
OF COURSE I HAVE A PLAN...
JUST GIVE ME A MOMENT...

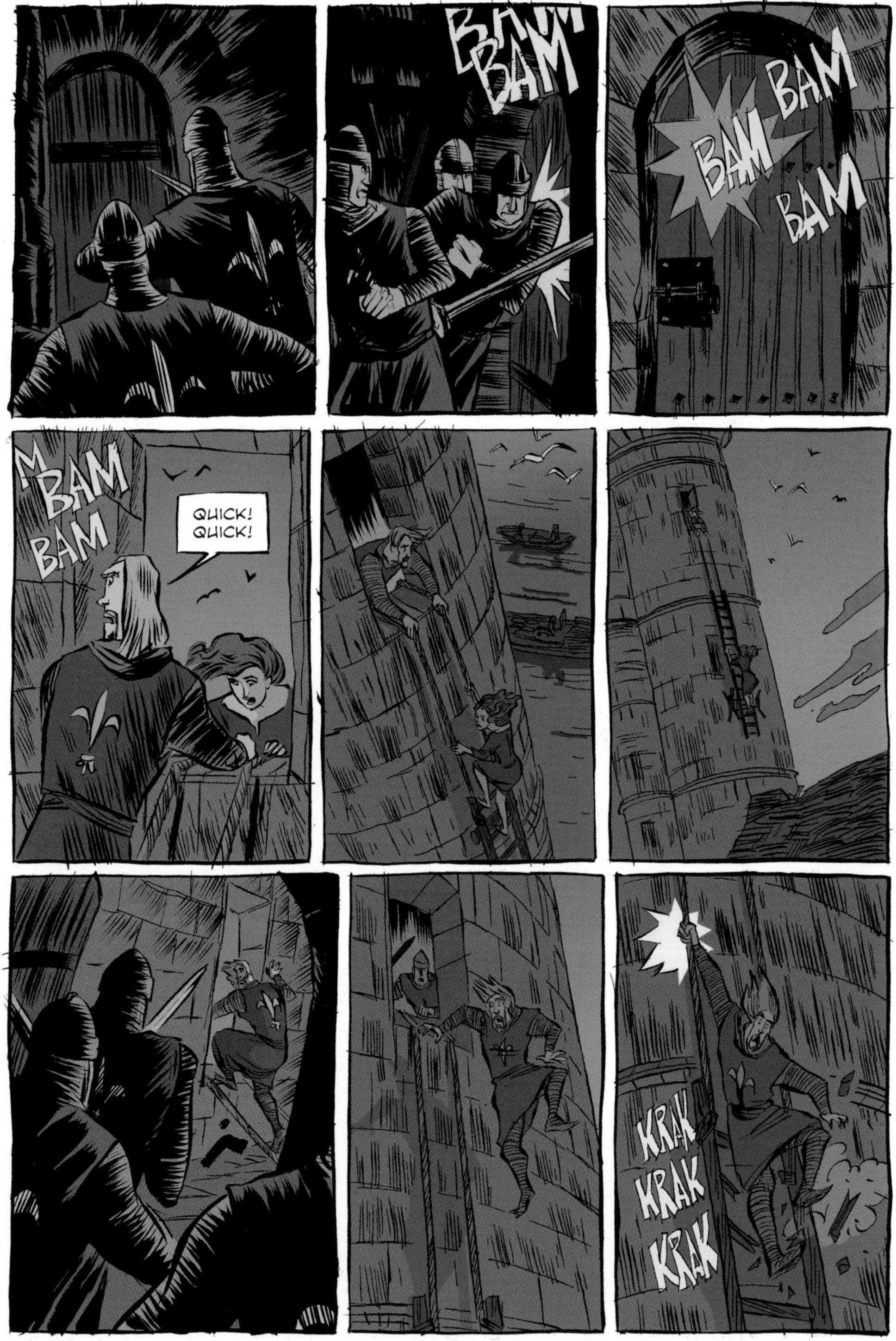
BAM
BAM
BAM
BAM
BAM
BAM
M
BAM
BAM
QUICK! QUICK!
KRAK
KRAK
KRAK

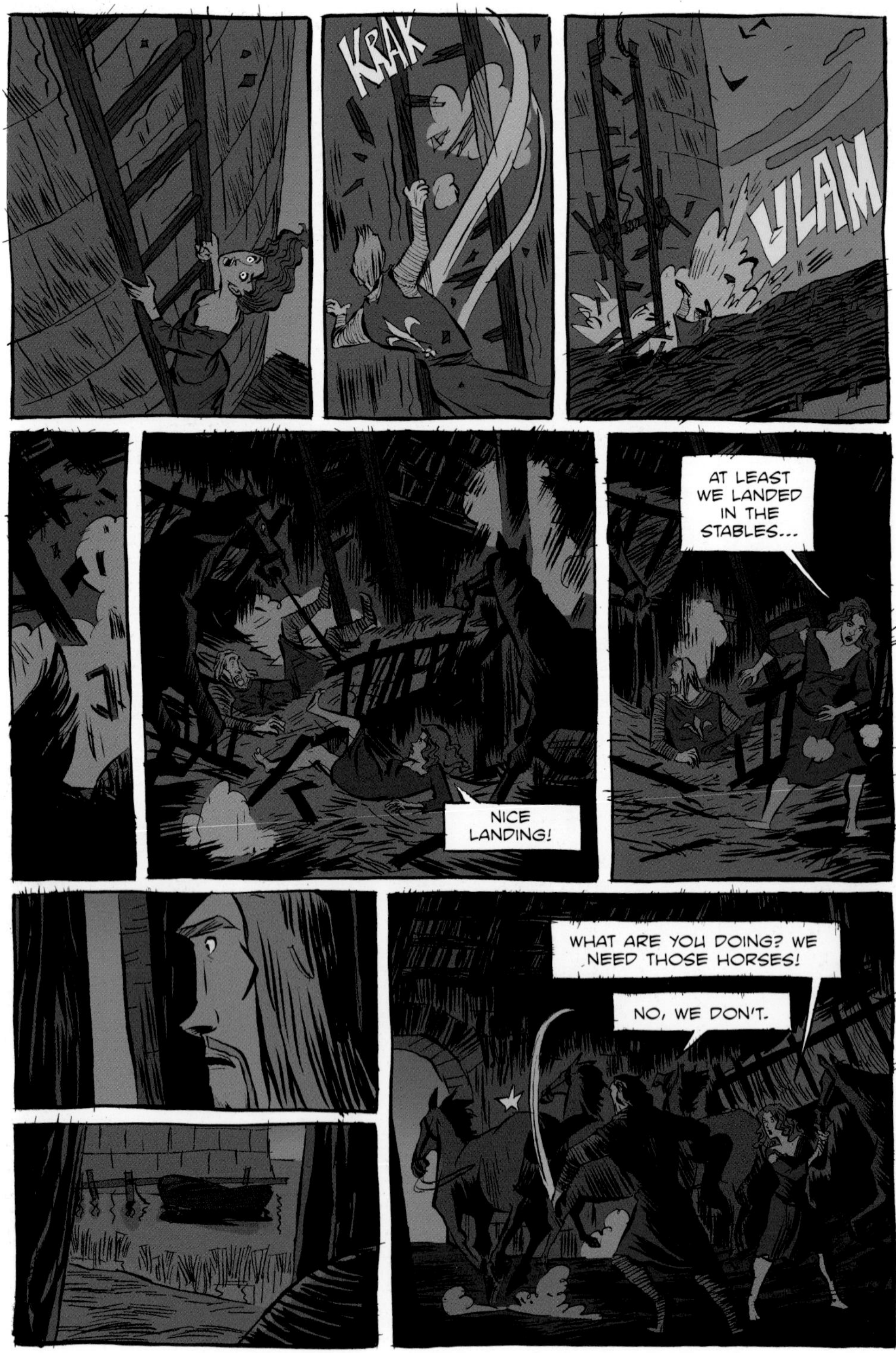
KRAK
VLAM
NICE LANDING!
AT LEAST WE LANDED IN THE STABLES...
WHAT ARE YOU DOING? WE NEED THOSE HORSES!
NO, WE DON'T.

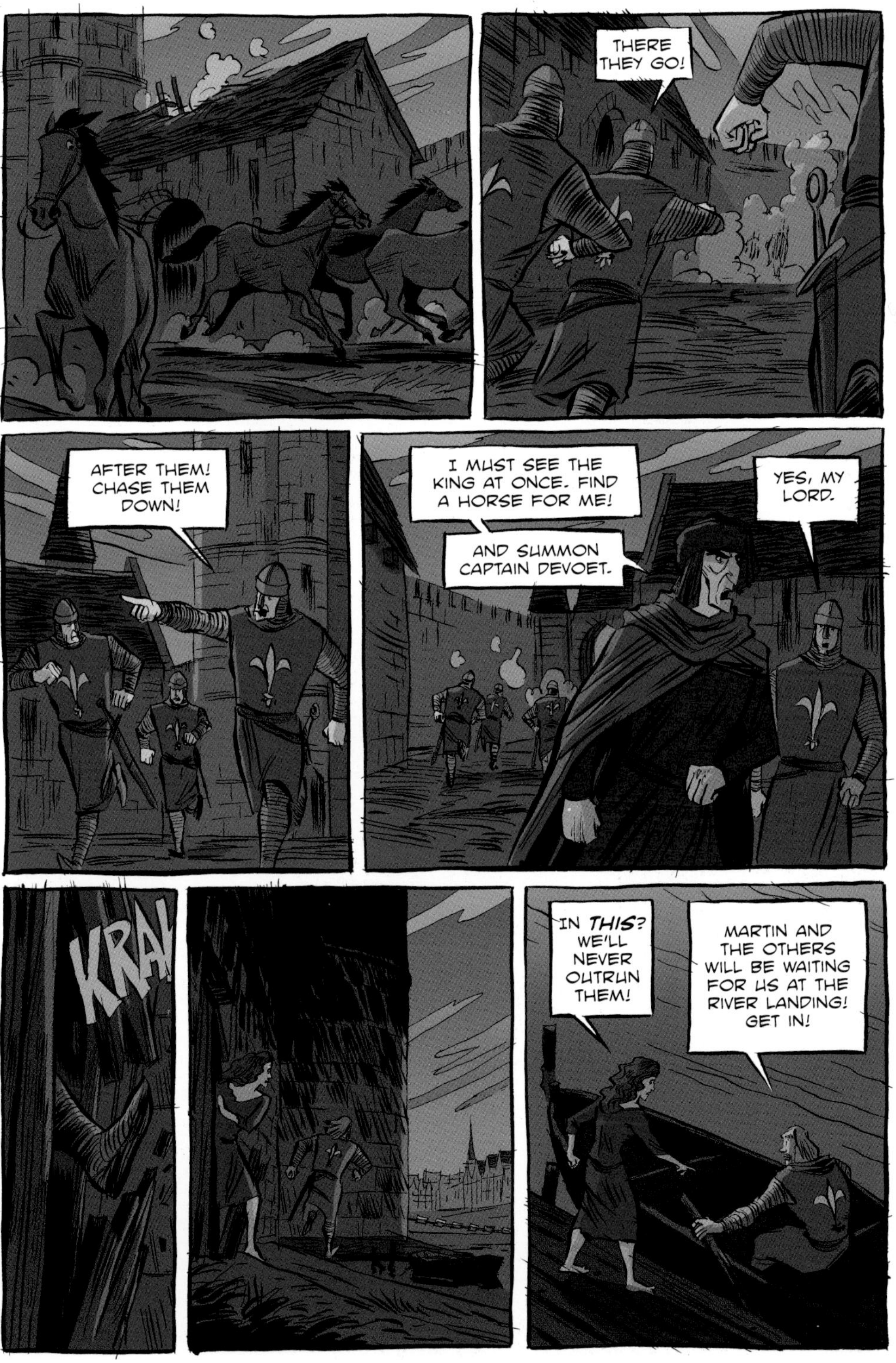
THERE THEY GO!
AFTER THEM! CHASE THEM DOWN!
I MUST SEE THE KING AT ONCE. FIND A HORSE FOR ME!
AND SUMMON CAPTAIN DEVOET.
YES, MY LORD.
KRA
IN *THIS*? WE'LL NEVER OUTRUN THEM!
MARTIN AND THE OTHERS WILL BE WAITING FOR US AT THE RIVER LANDING! GET IN!

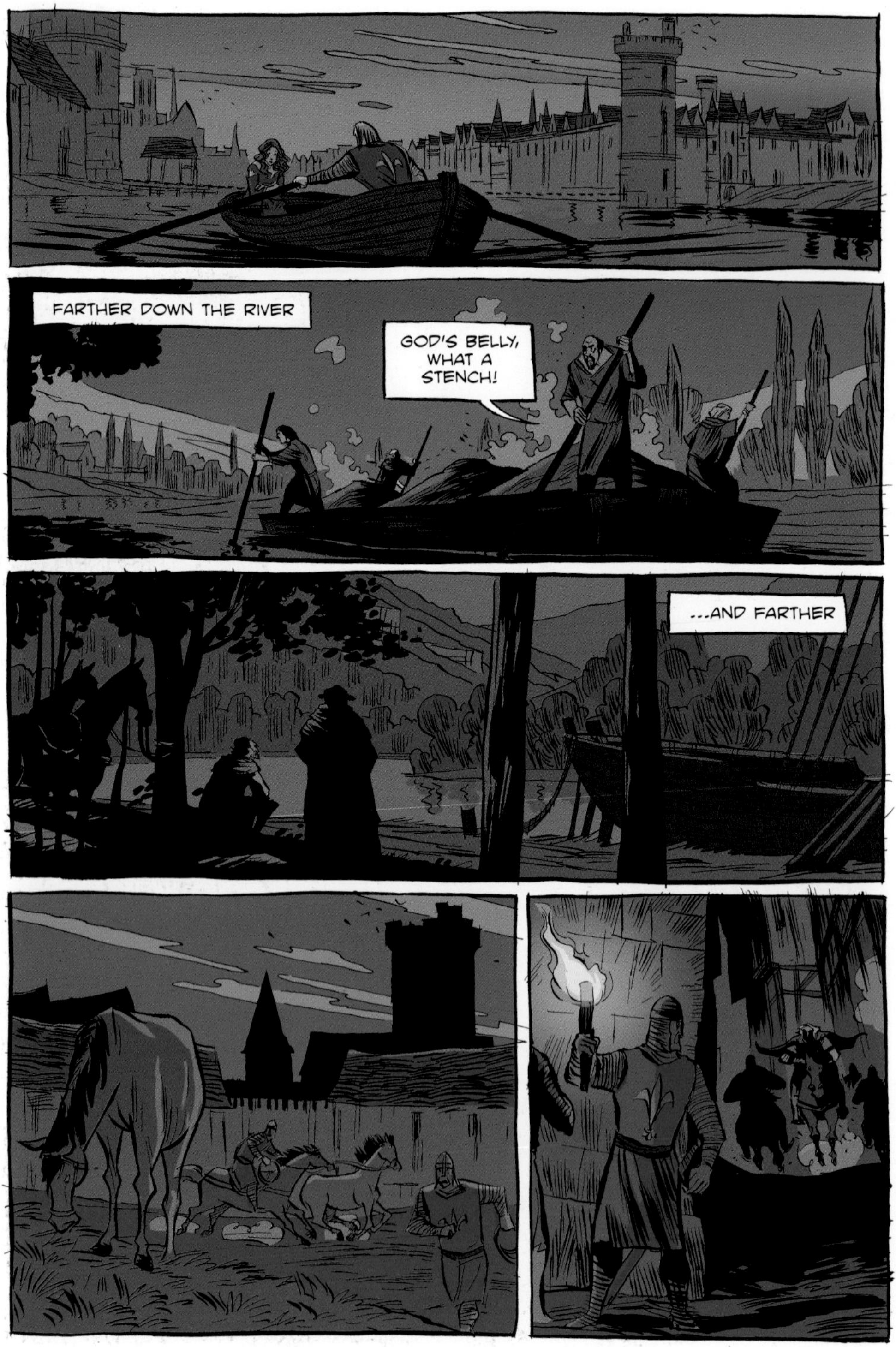
FARTHER DOWN THE RIVER
GOD'S BELLY, WHAT A STENCH!
...AND FARTHER

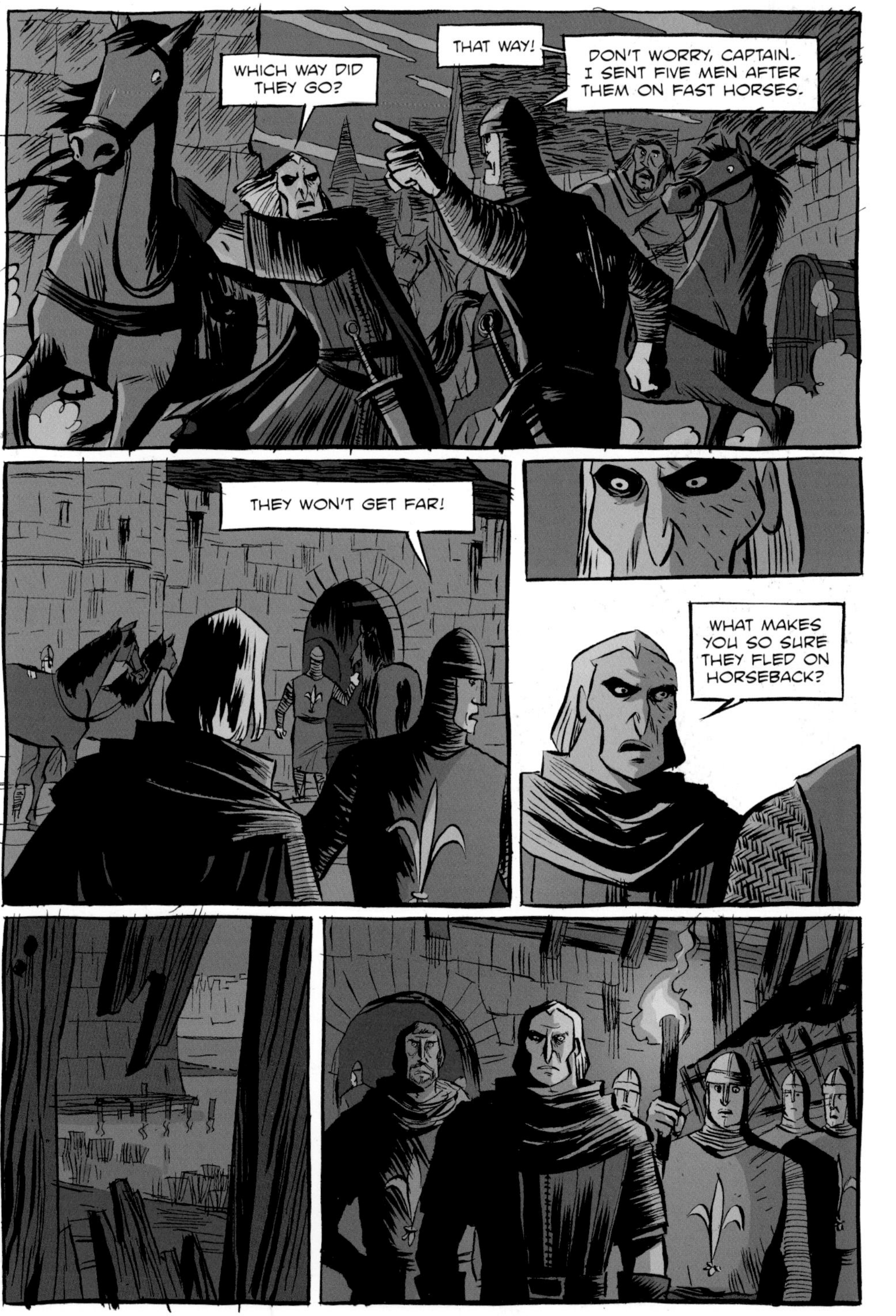
WHICH WAY DID THEY GO?
THAT WAY!
DON'T WORRY, CAPTAIN. I SENT FIVE MEN AFTER THEM ON FAST HORSES.
THEY WON'T GET FAR!
WHAT MAKES YOU SO SURE THEY FLED ON HORSEBACK?

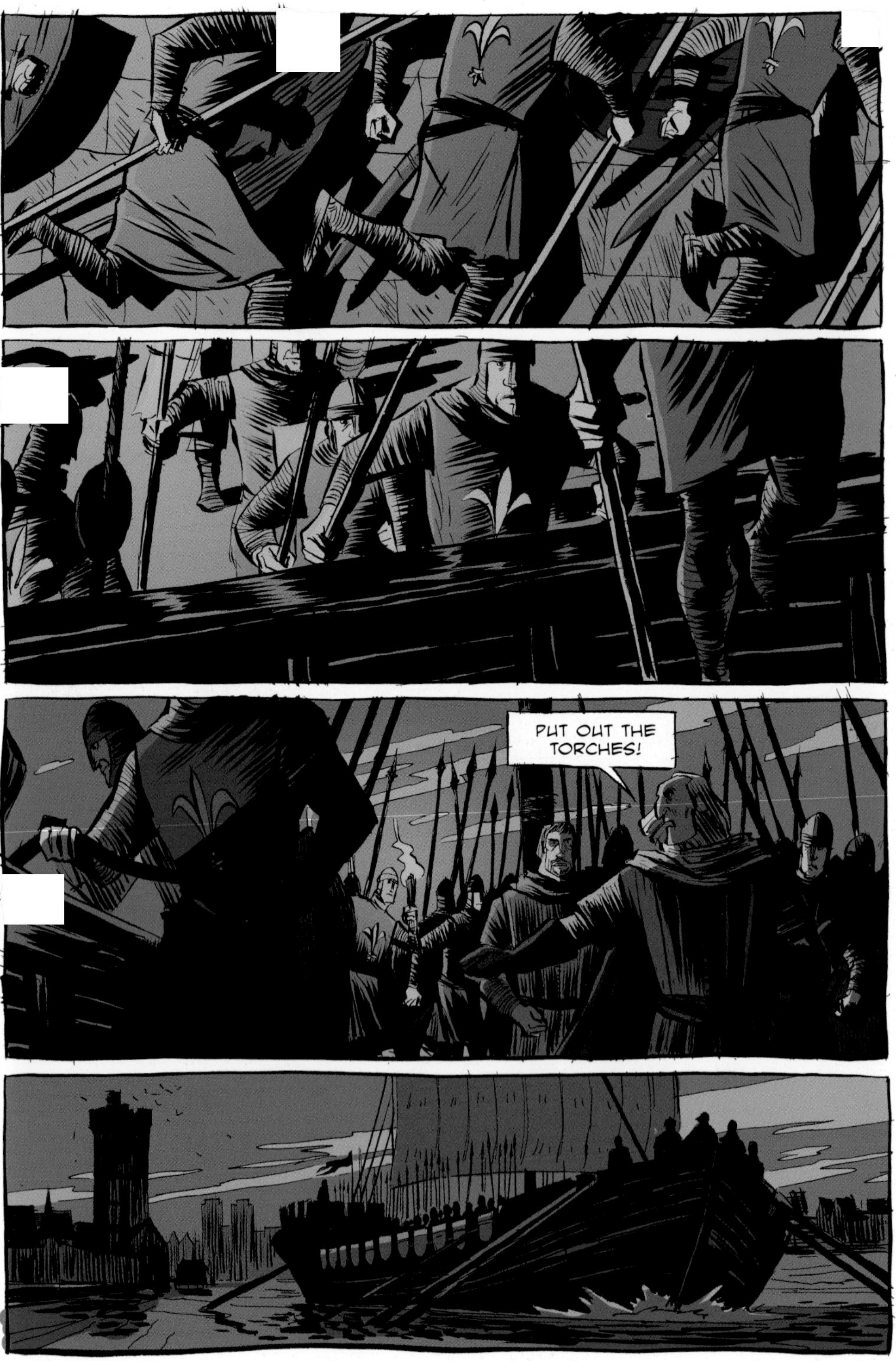
PUT OUT THE TORCHES!

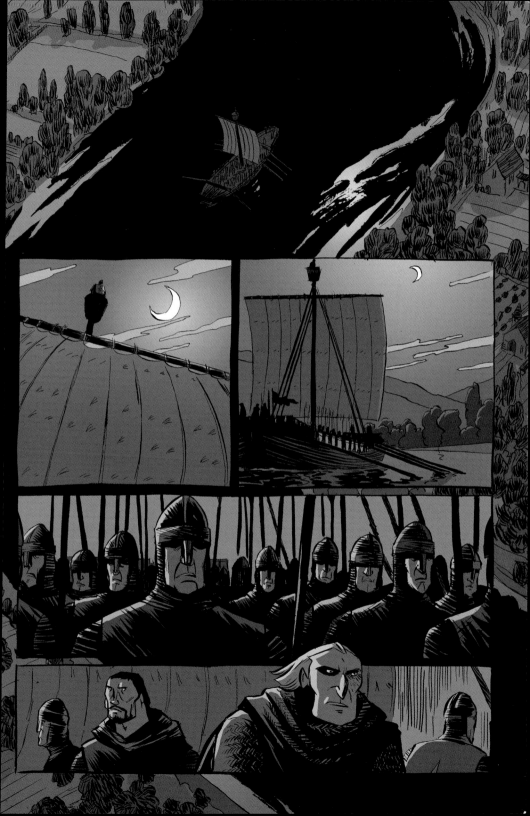

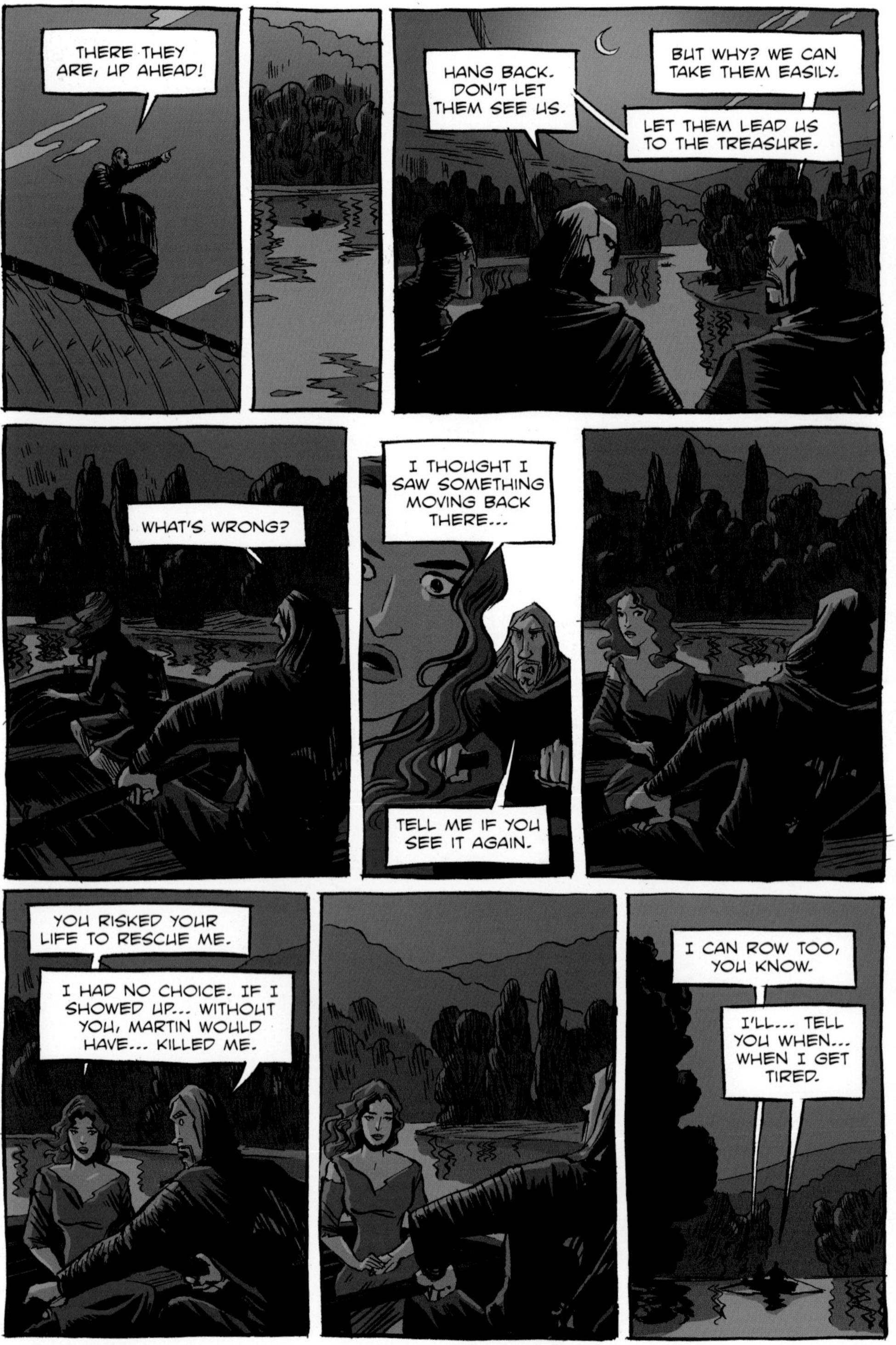
THERE THEY ARE, UP AHEAD!
HANG BACK. DON'T LET THEM SEE US.
BUT WHY? WE CAN TAKE THEM EASILY.
LET THEM LEAD US TO THE TREASURE.
WHAT'S WRONG?
I THOUGHT I SAW SOMETHING MOVING BACK THERE...
TELL ME IF YOU SEE IT AGAIN.
YOU RISKED YOUR LIFE TO RESCUE ME.
I HAD NO CHOICE. IF I SHOWED UP... WITHOUT YOU, MARTIN WOULD HAVE... KILLED ME.
I CAN ROW TOO, YOU KNOW.
I'LL... TELL YOU WHEN... WHEN I GET TIRED.

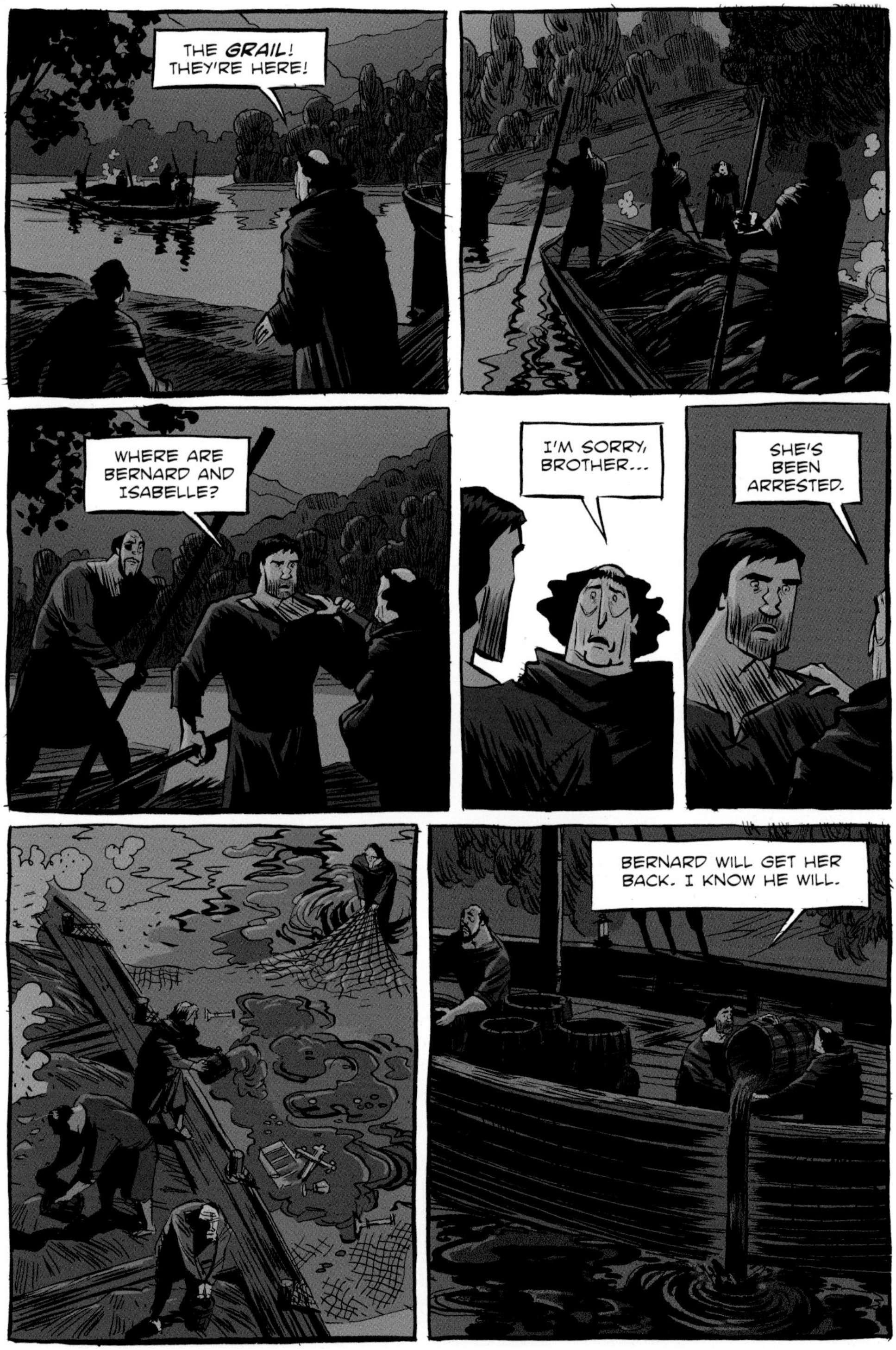
THE GRAIL! THEY'RE HERE!
WHERE ARE BERNARD AND ISABELLE?
I'M SORRY, BROTHER...
SHE'S BEEN ARRESTED.
BERNARD WILL GET HER BACK. I KNOW HE WILL.

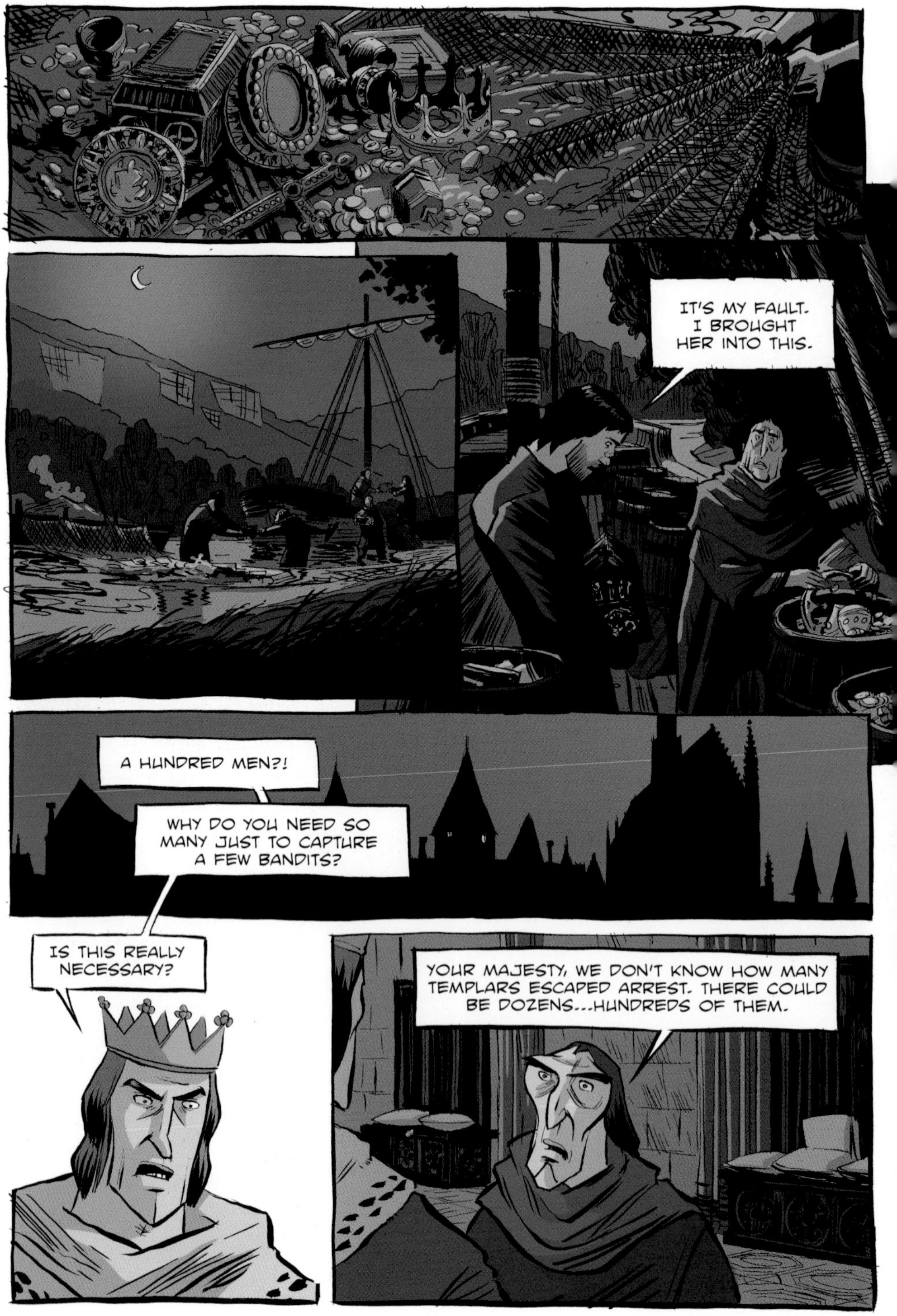
IT'S MY FAULT. I BROUGHT HER INTO THIS.
A HUNDRED MEN?!
WHY DO YOU NEED SO MANY JUST TO CAPTURE A FEW BANDITS?
IS THIS REALLY NECESSARY?
YOUR MAJESTY, WE DON'T KNOW HOW MANY TEMPLARS ESCAPED ARREST. THERE COULD BE DOZENS...HUNDREDS OF THEM.

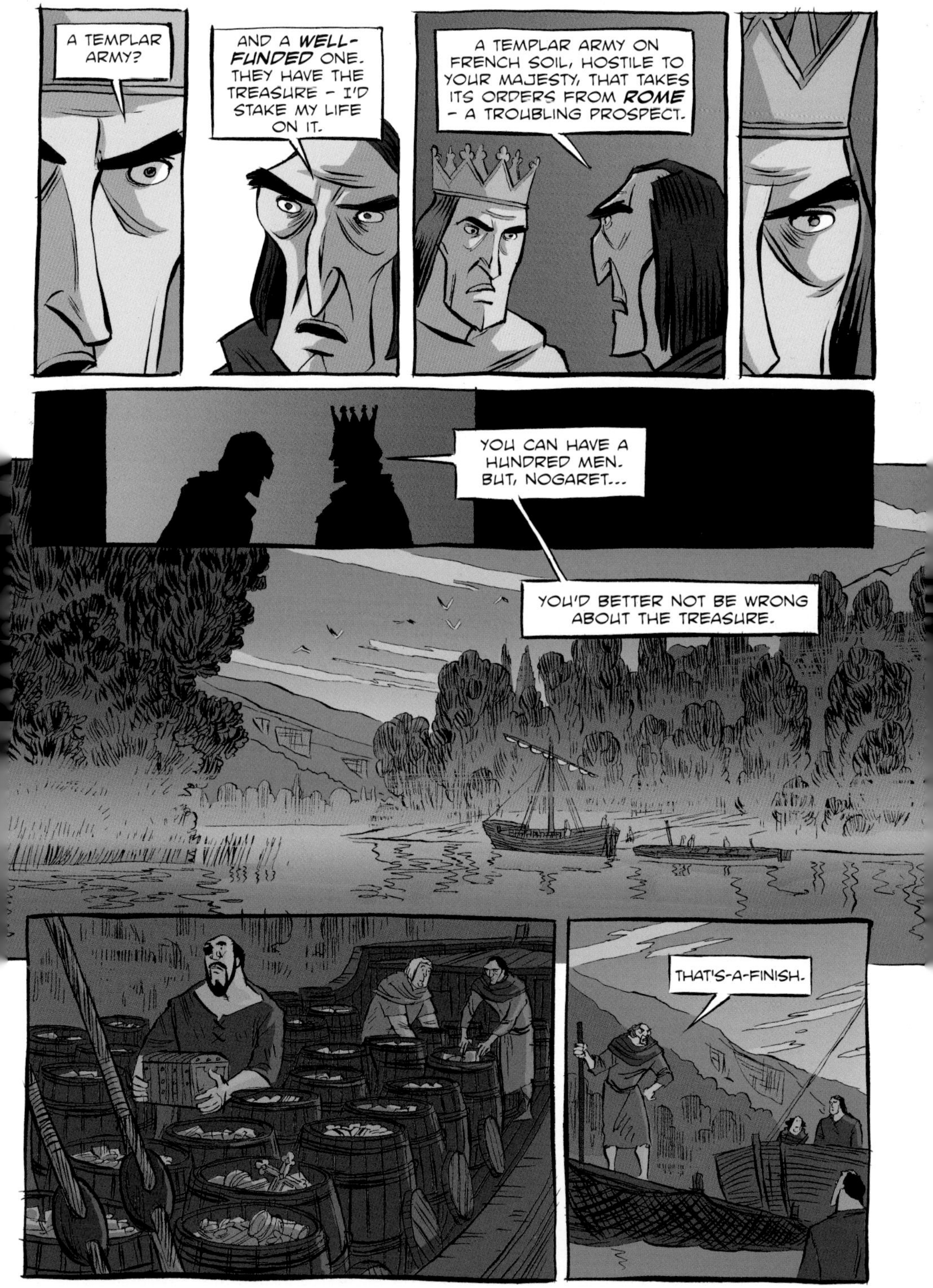
A TEMPLAR ARMY?
AND A WELL-FUNDED ONE. THEY HAVE THE TREASURE - I'D STAKE MY LIFE ON IT.
A TEMPLAR ARMY ON FRENCH SOIL, HOSTILE TO YOUR MAJESTY, THAT TAKES ITS ORDERS FROM ROME - A TROUBLING PROSPECT.
YOU CAN HAVE A HUNDRED MEN. BUT, NOGARET...
YOU'D BETTER NOT BE WRONG ABOUT THE TREASURE.
THAT'S-A-FINISH.

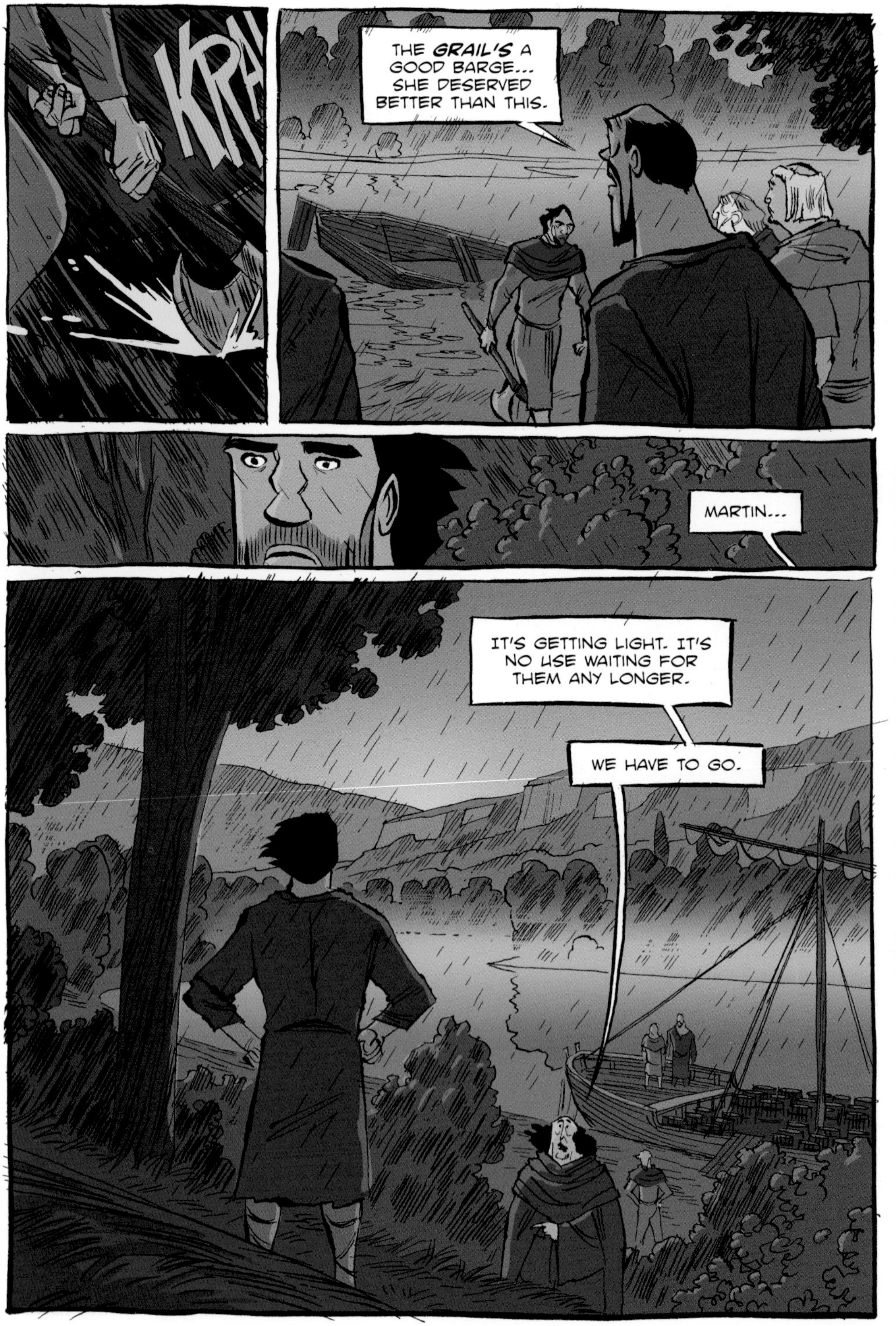
KRA
THE GRAIL'S A GOOD BARGE... SHE DESERVED BETTER THAN THIS.
MARTIN...
IT'S GETTING LIGHT. IT'S NO USE WAITING FOR THEM ANY LONGER.
WE HAVE TO GO.

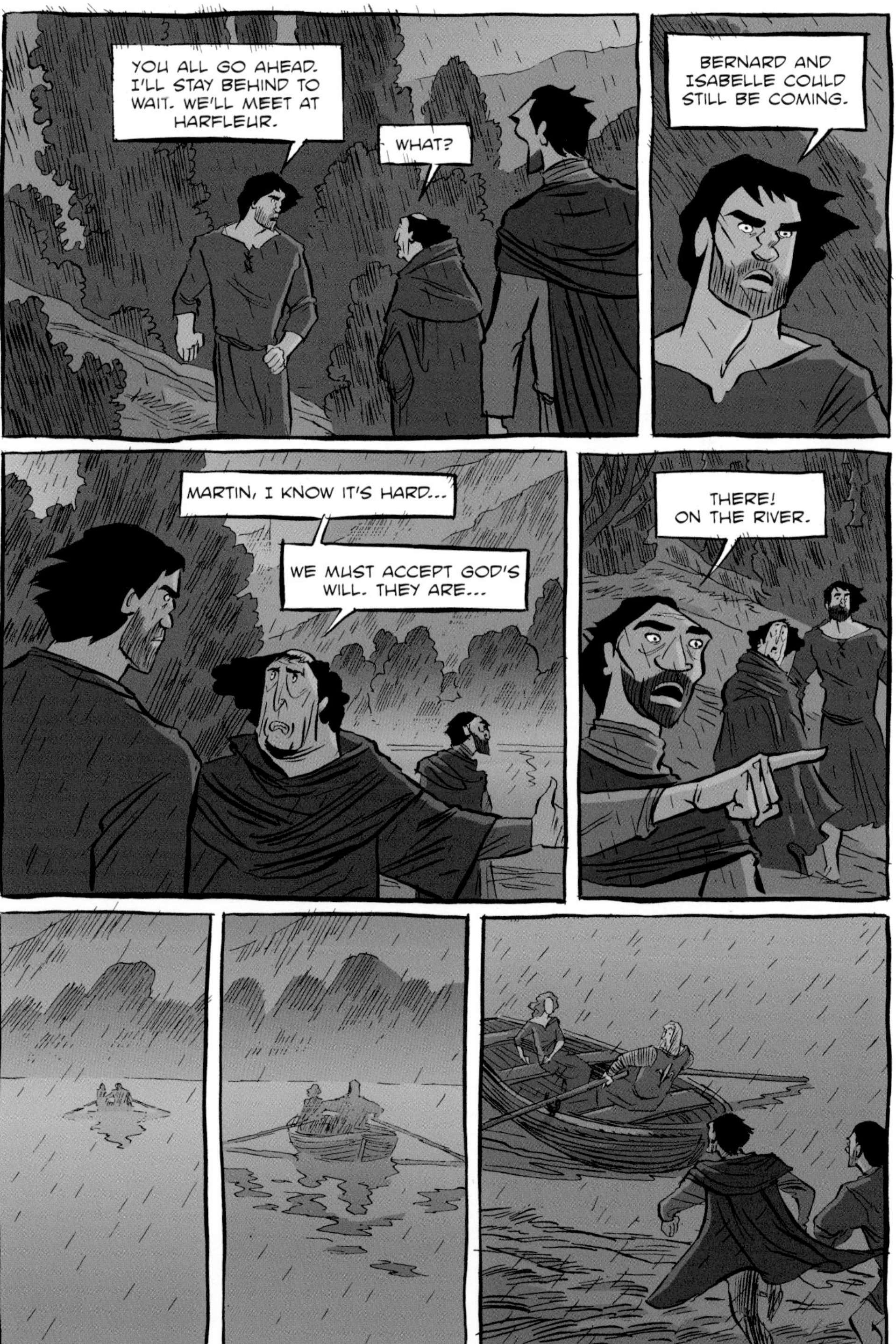

YOU ALL GO AHEAD. I'LL STAY BEHIND TO WAIT. WE'LL MEET AT HARFLEUR.
WHAT?
BERNARD AND ISABELLE COULD STILL BE COMING.
MARTIN, I KNOW IT'S HARD...
WE MUST ACCEPT GOD'S WILL. THEY ARE...
THERE! ON THE RIVER.

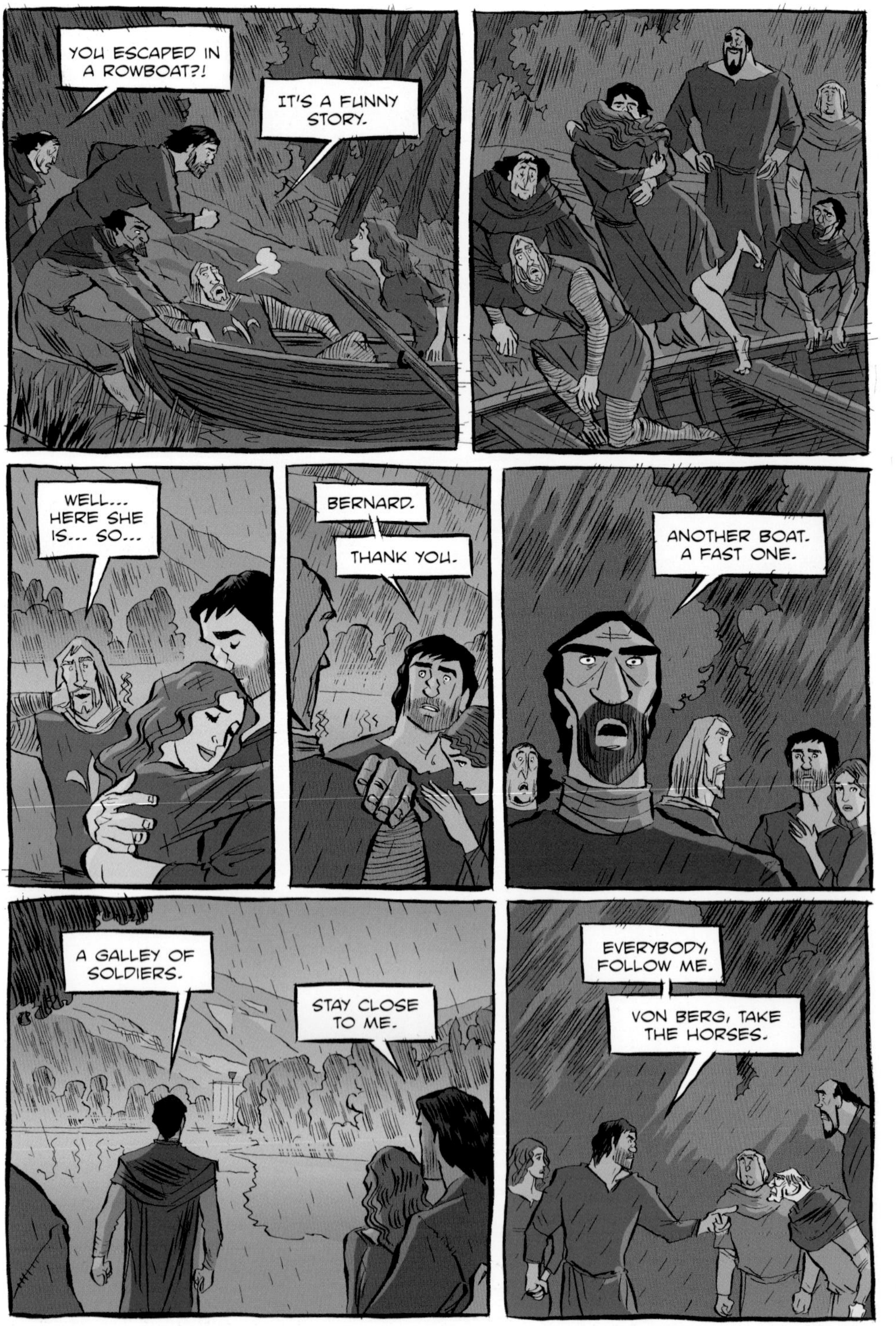

YOU ESCAPED IN A ROWBOAT?!
IT'S A FUNNY STORY.
WELL... HERE SHE IS... SO...
BERNARD.
THANK YOU.
ANOTHER BOAT. A FAST ONE.
A GALLEY OF SOLDIERS.
STAY CLOSE TO ME.
EVERYBODY, FOLLOW ME.
VON BERG, TAKE THE HORSES.

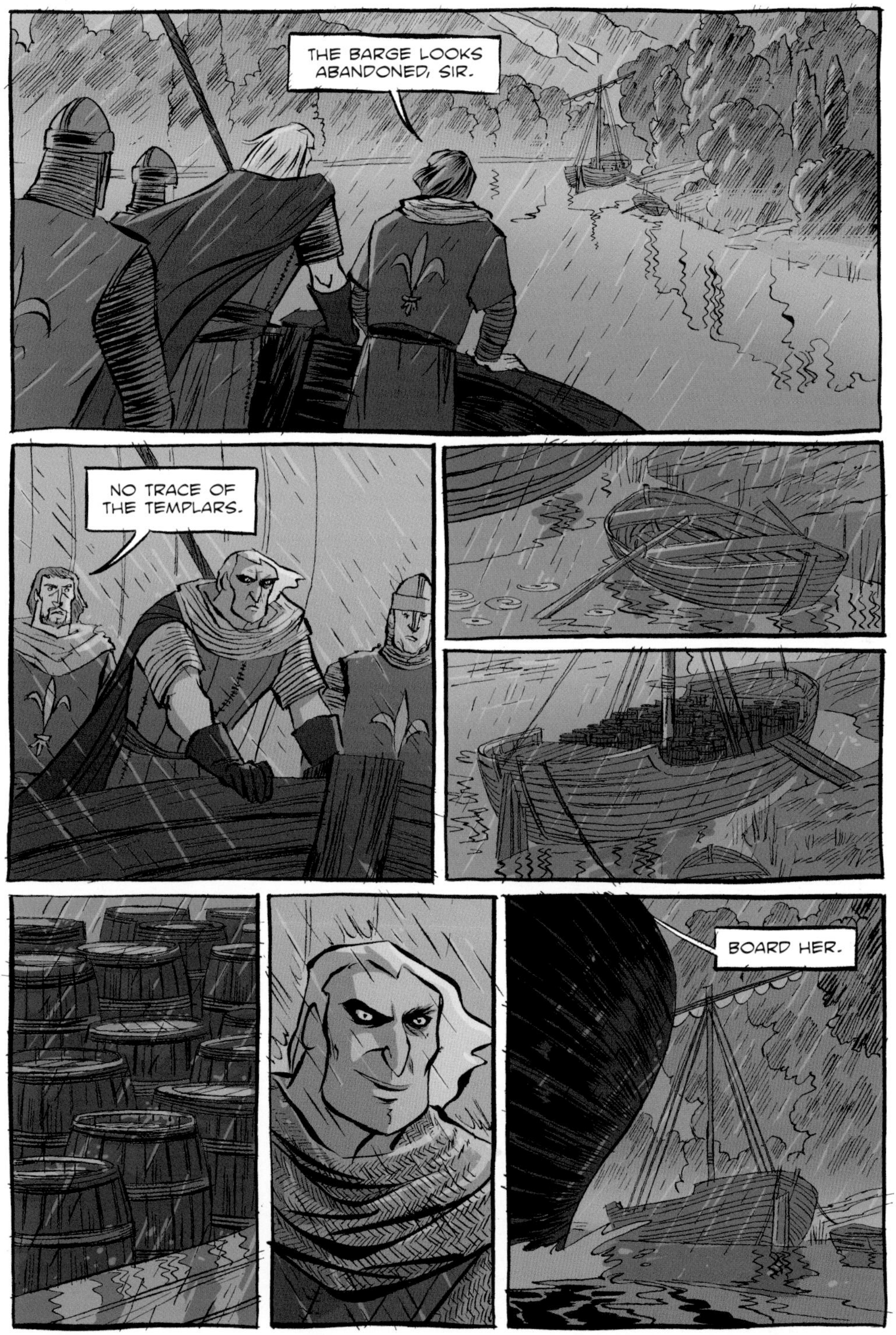
THE BARGE LOOKS ABANDONED, SIR.
NO TRACE OF THE TEMPLARS.
BOARD HER.

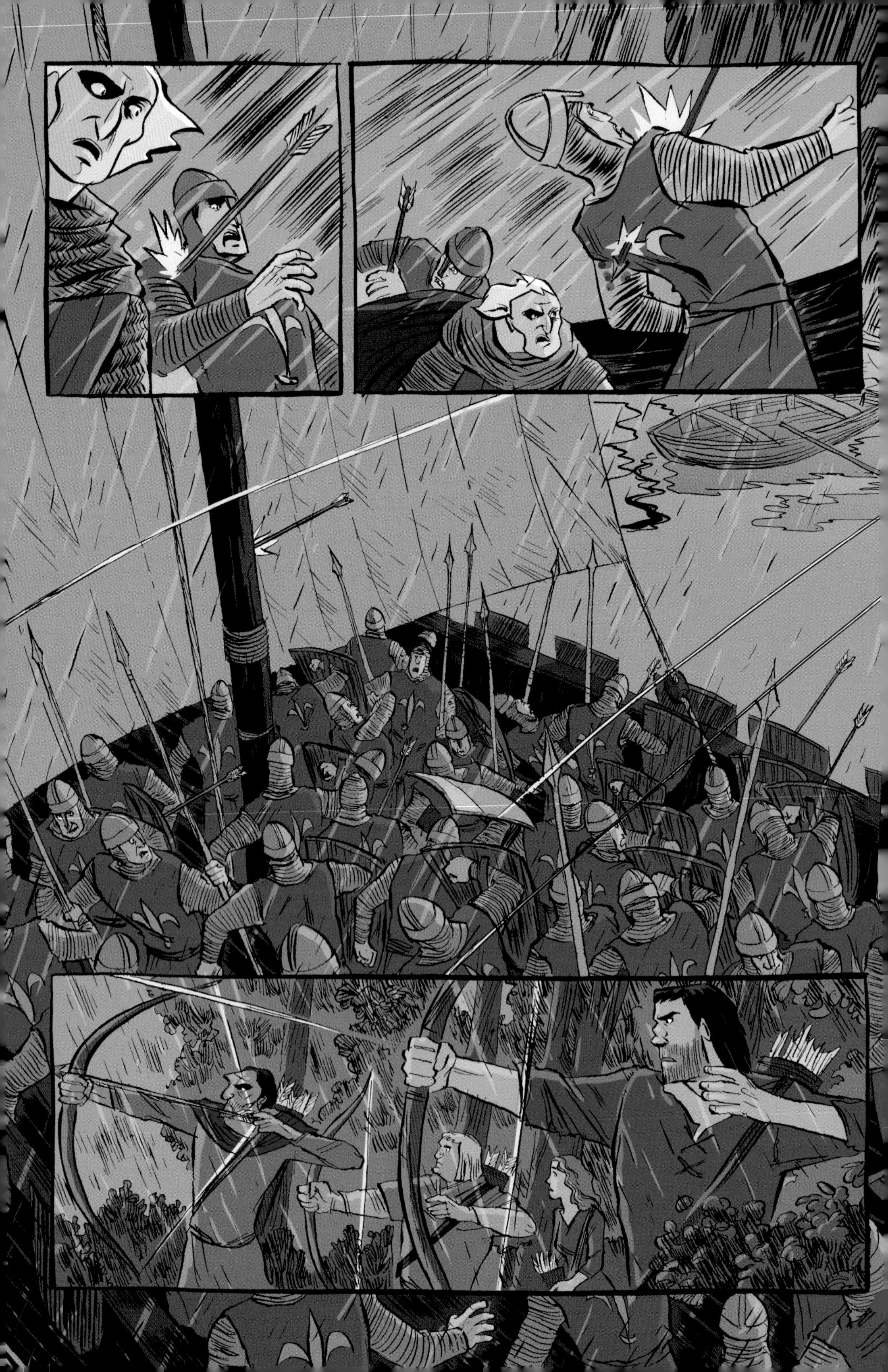

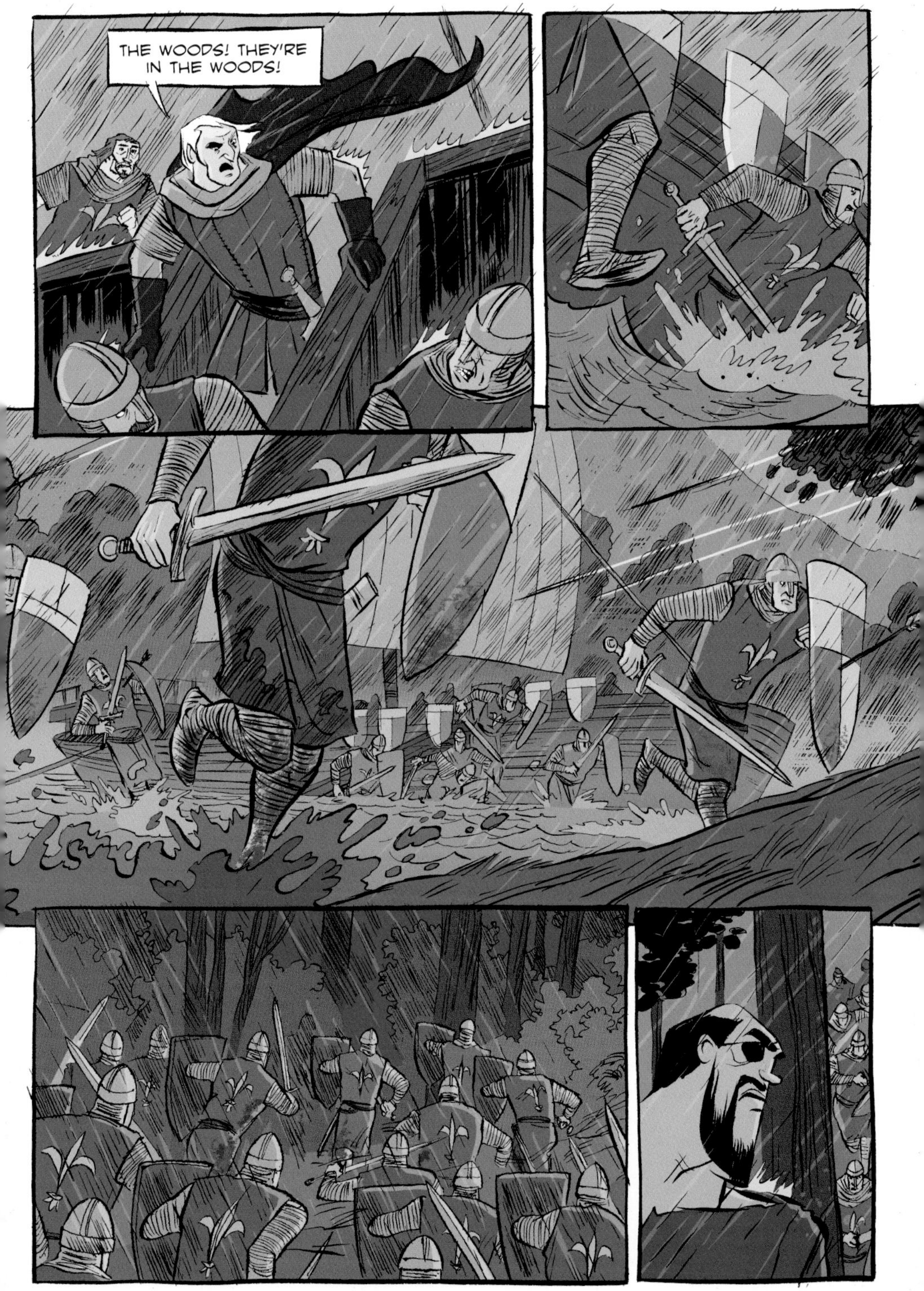
THE WOODS! THEY'RE IN THE WOODS!

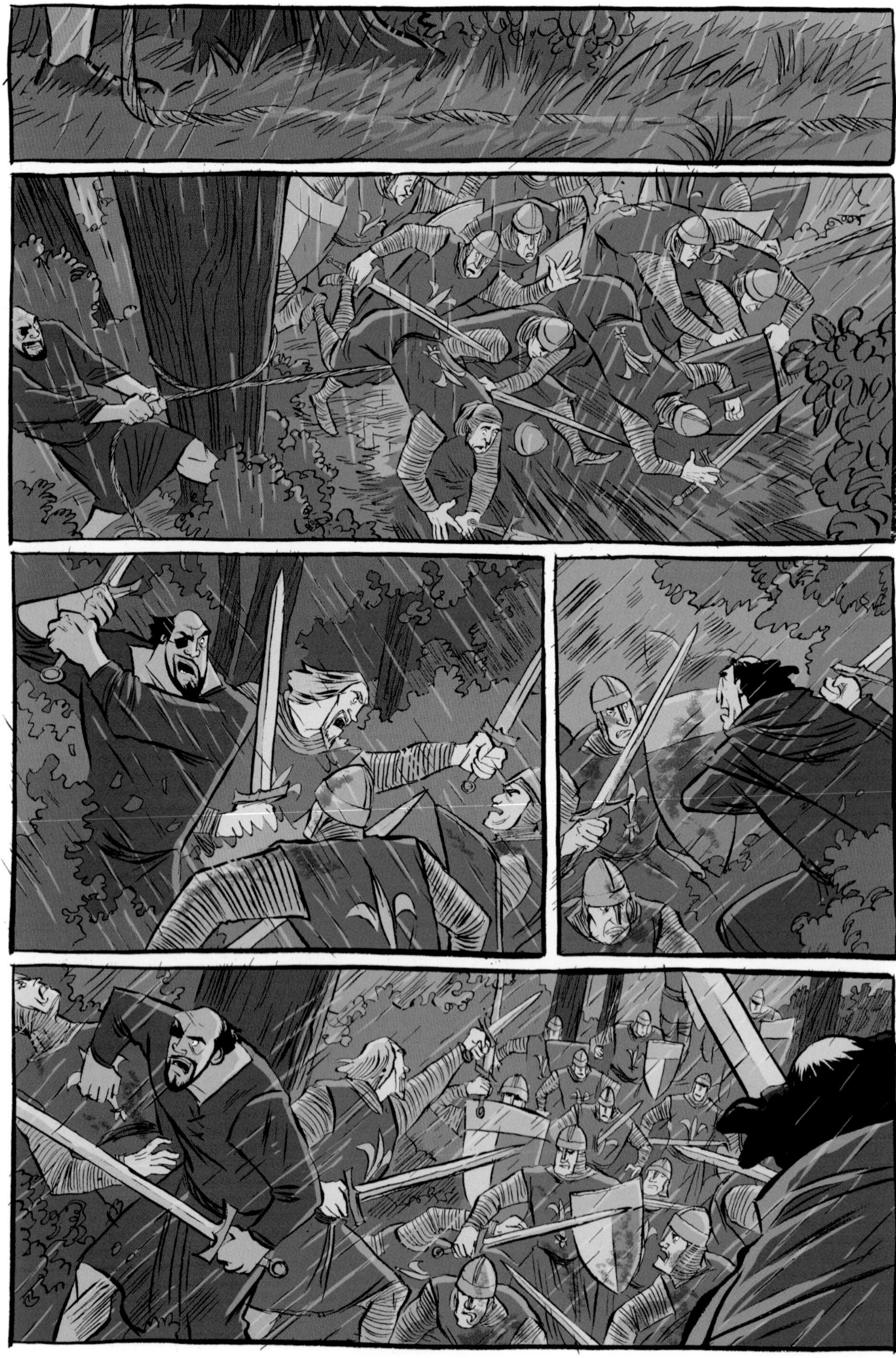

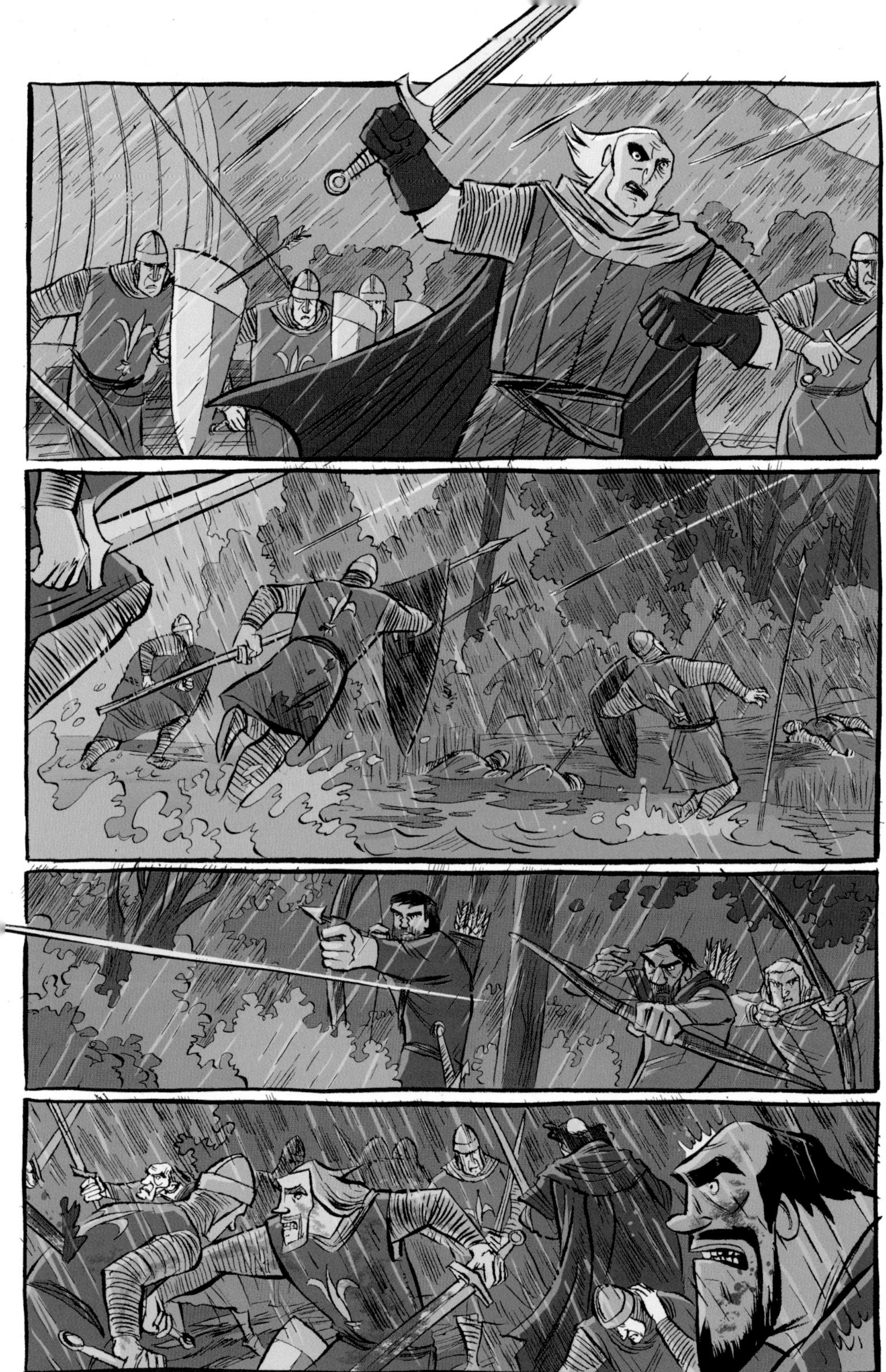

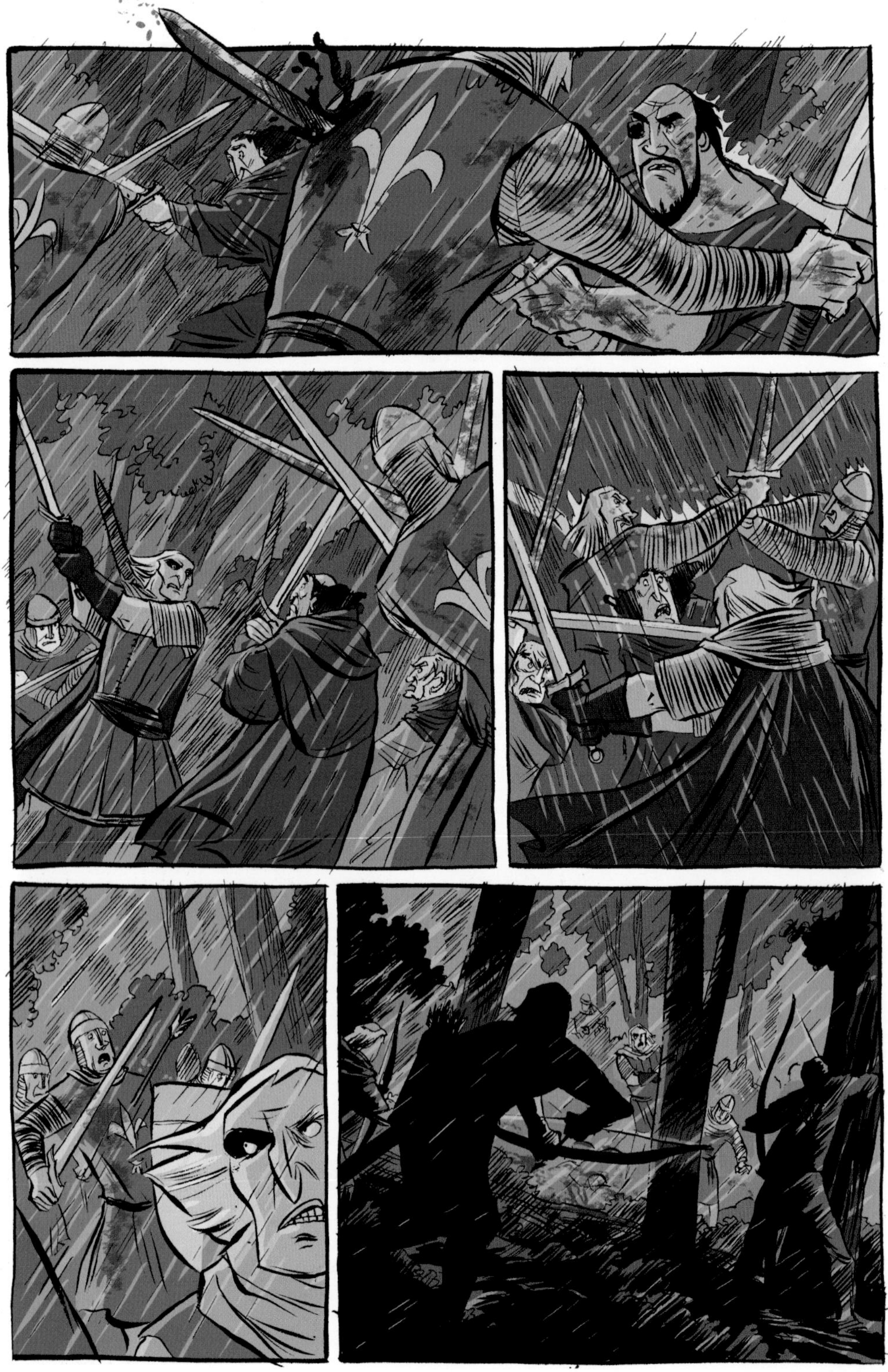

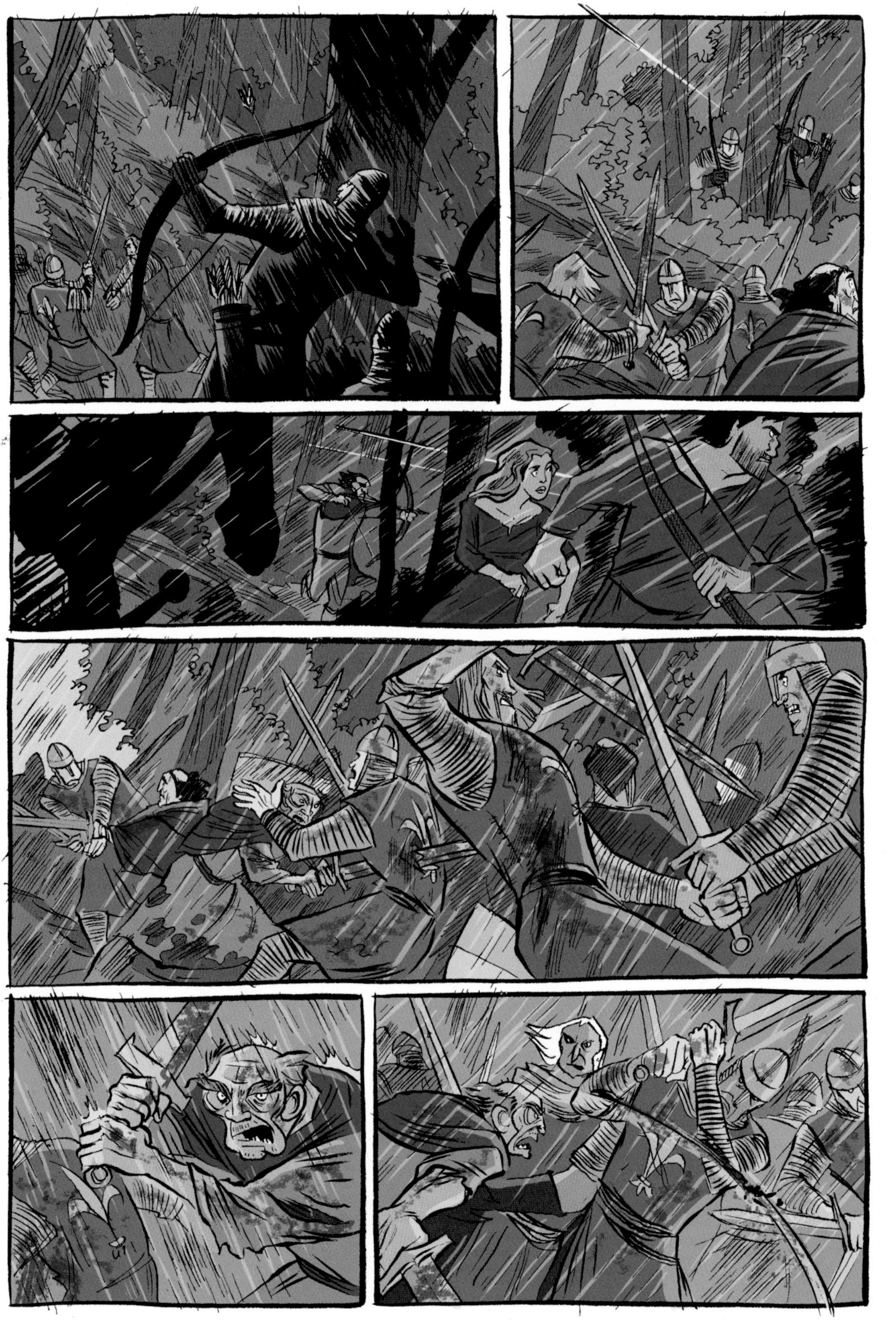

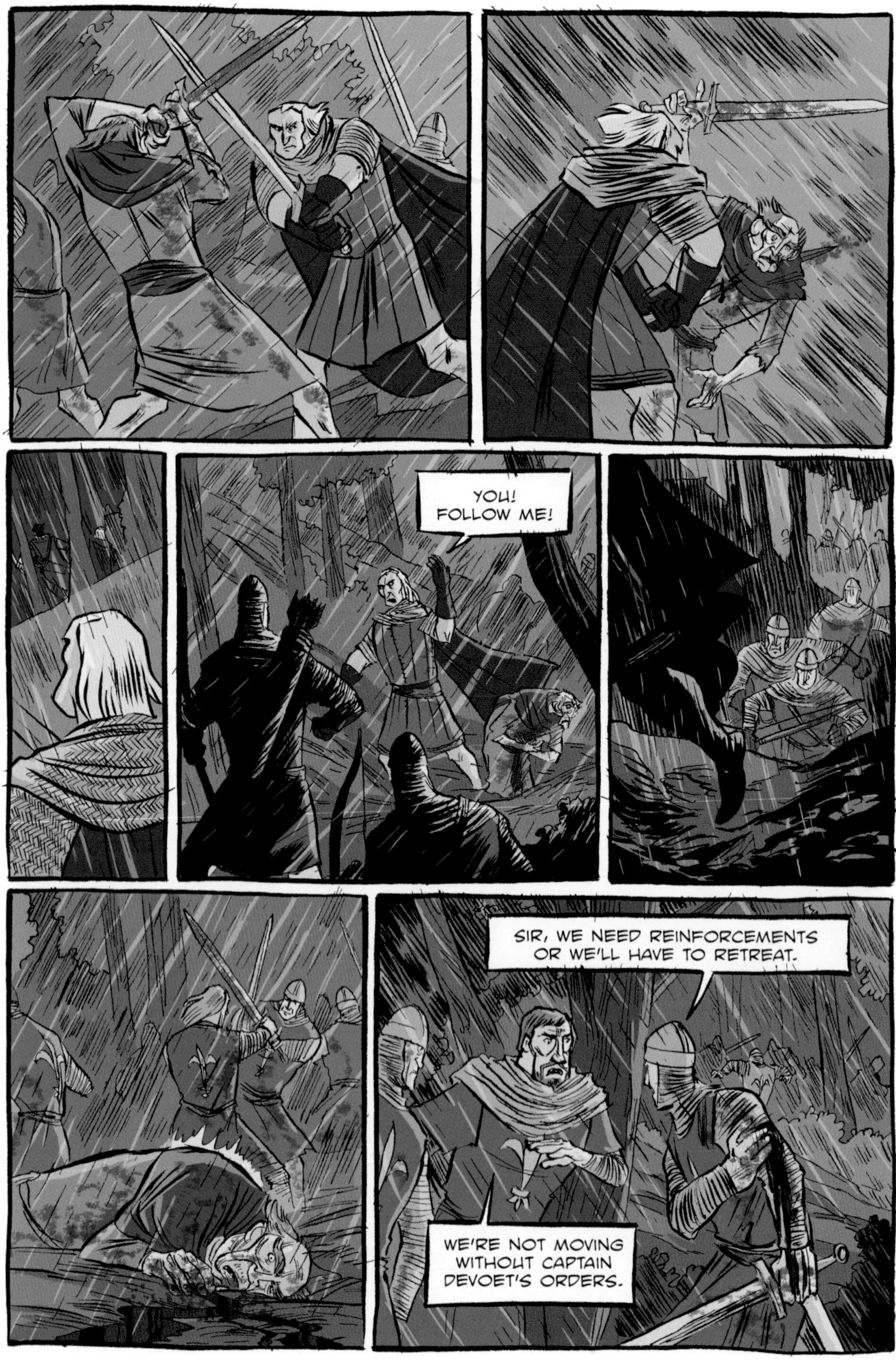
YOU!
FOLLOW ME!
SIR, WE NEED REINFORCEMENTS OR WE'LL HAVE TO RETREAT.
WE'RE NOT MOVING WITHOUT CAPTAIN DEVOET'S ORDERS.

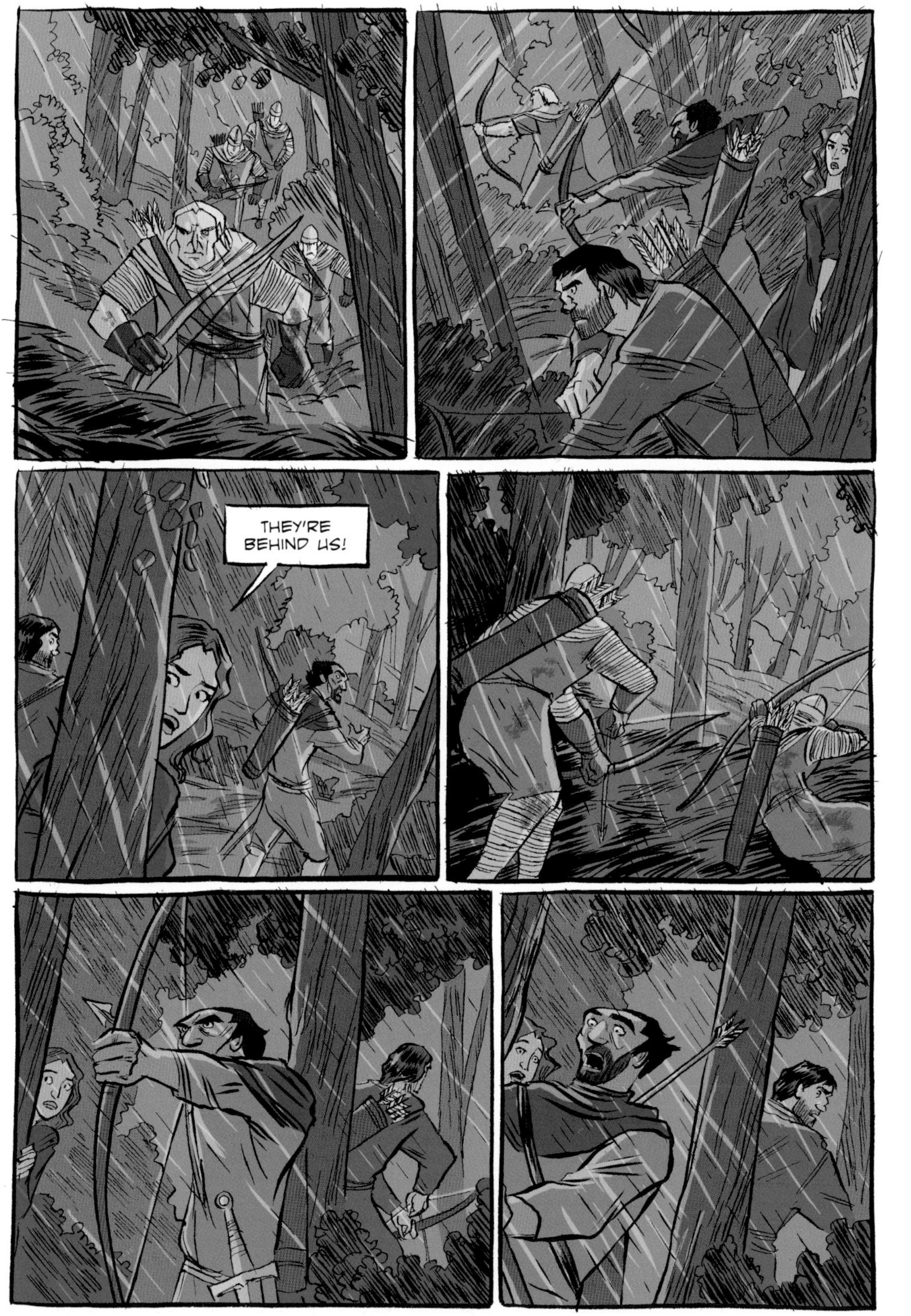
THEY'RE BEHIND US!

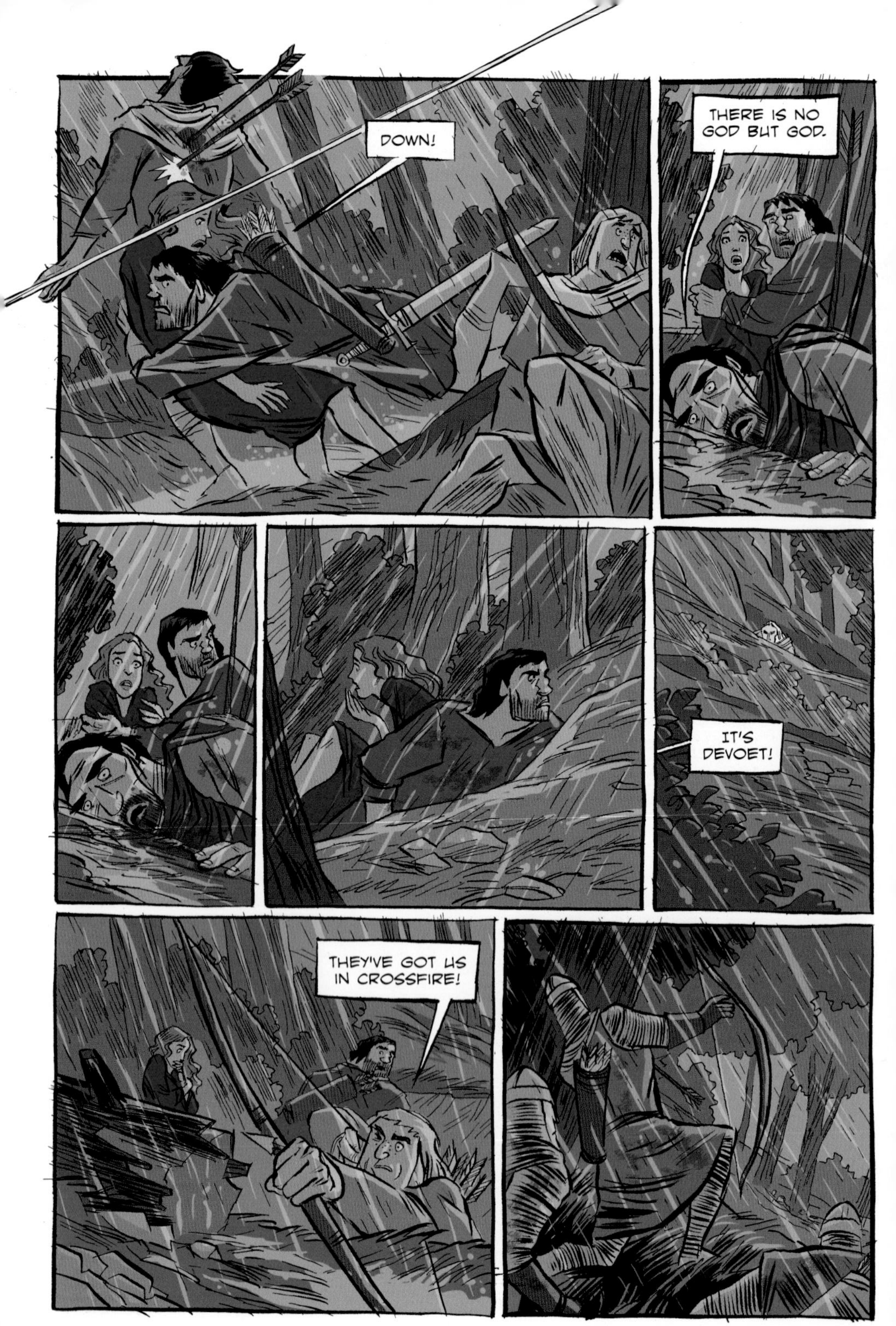
DOWN!
THERE IS NO GOD BUT GOD.
IT'S DEVOET!
THEY'VE GOT US IN CROSSFIRE!

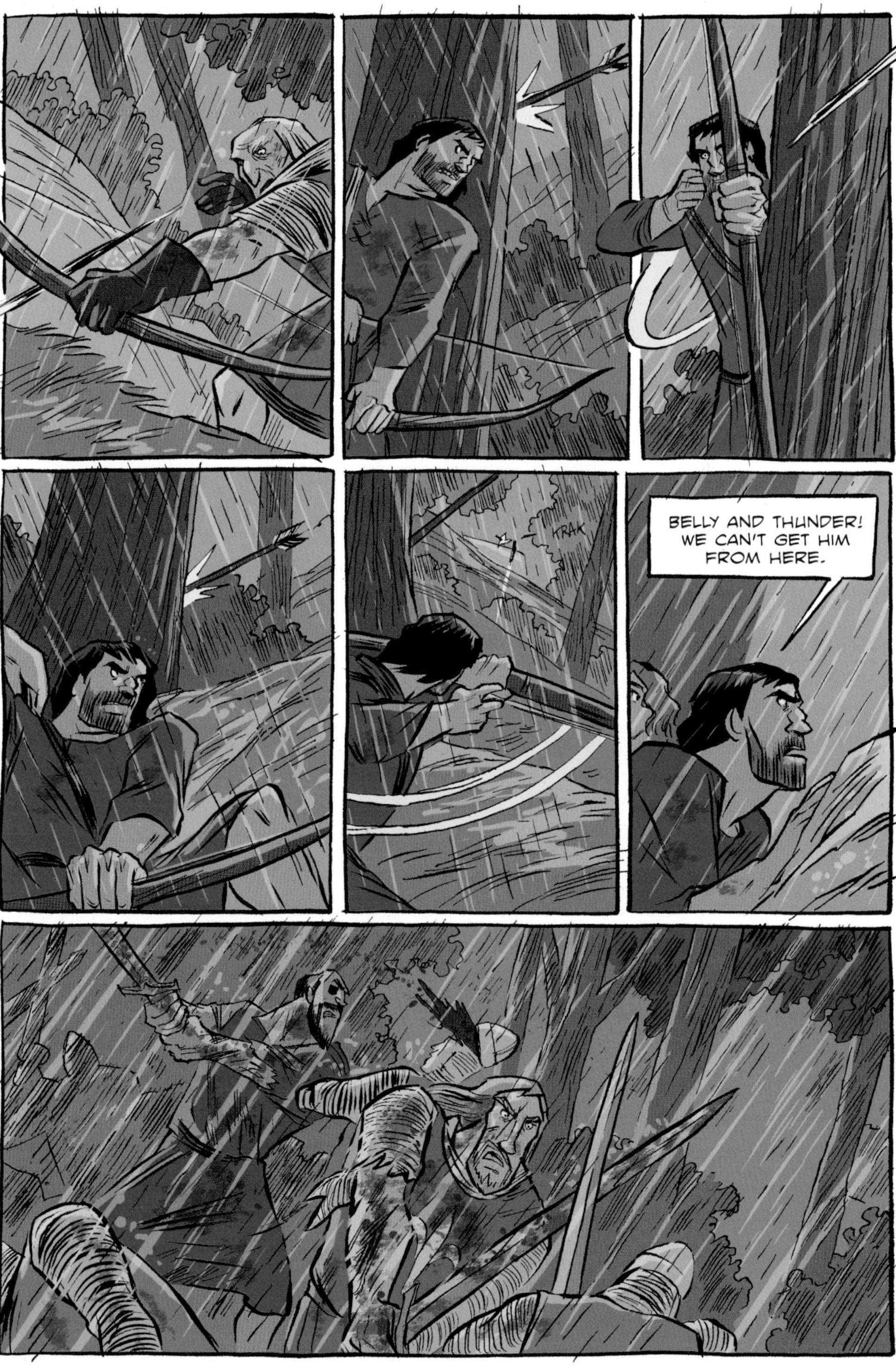
KRAK
BELLY AND THUNDER! WE CAN'T GET HIM FROM HERE.

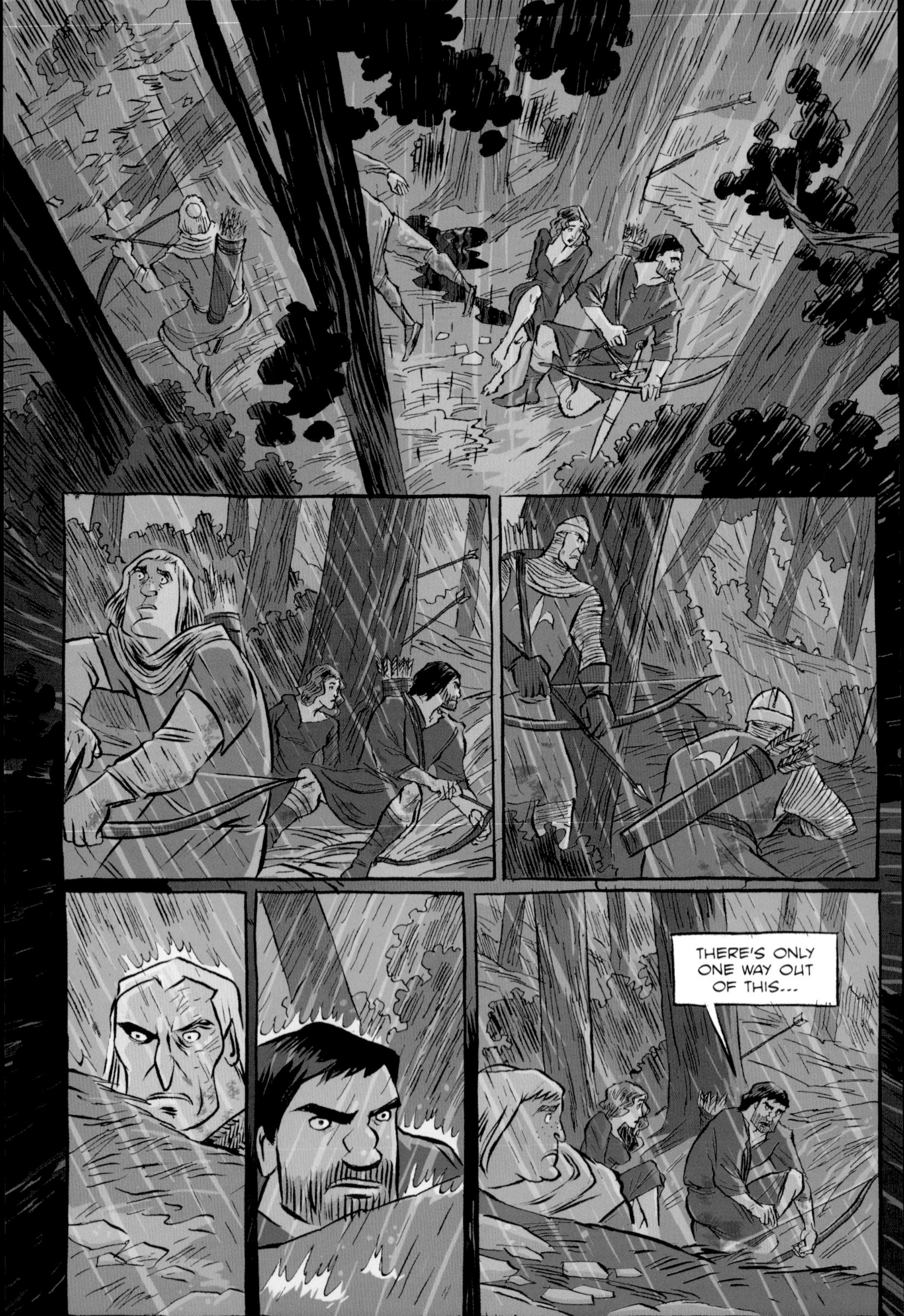
THERE'S ONLY ONE WAY OUT OF THIS...

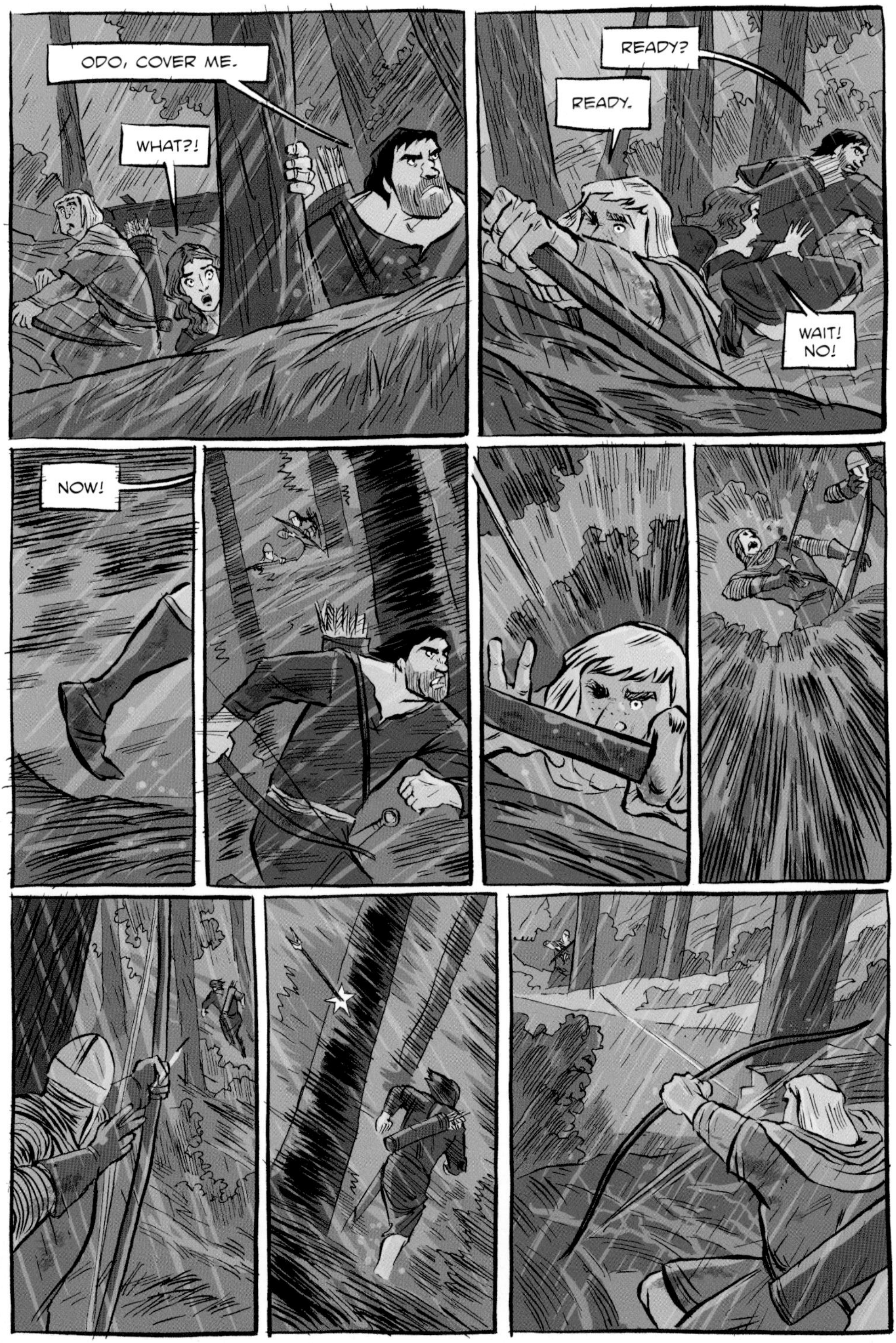
ODO, COVER ME.
WHAT?!
READY?
READY.
WAIT! NO!
NOW!

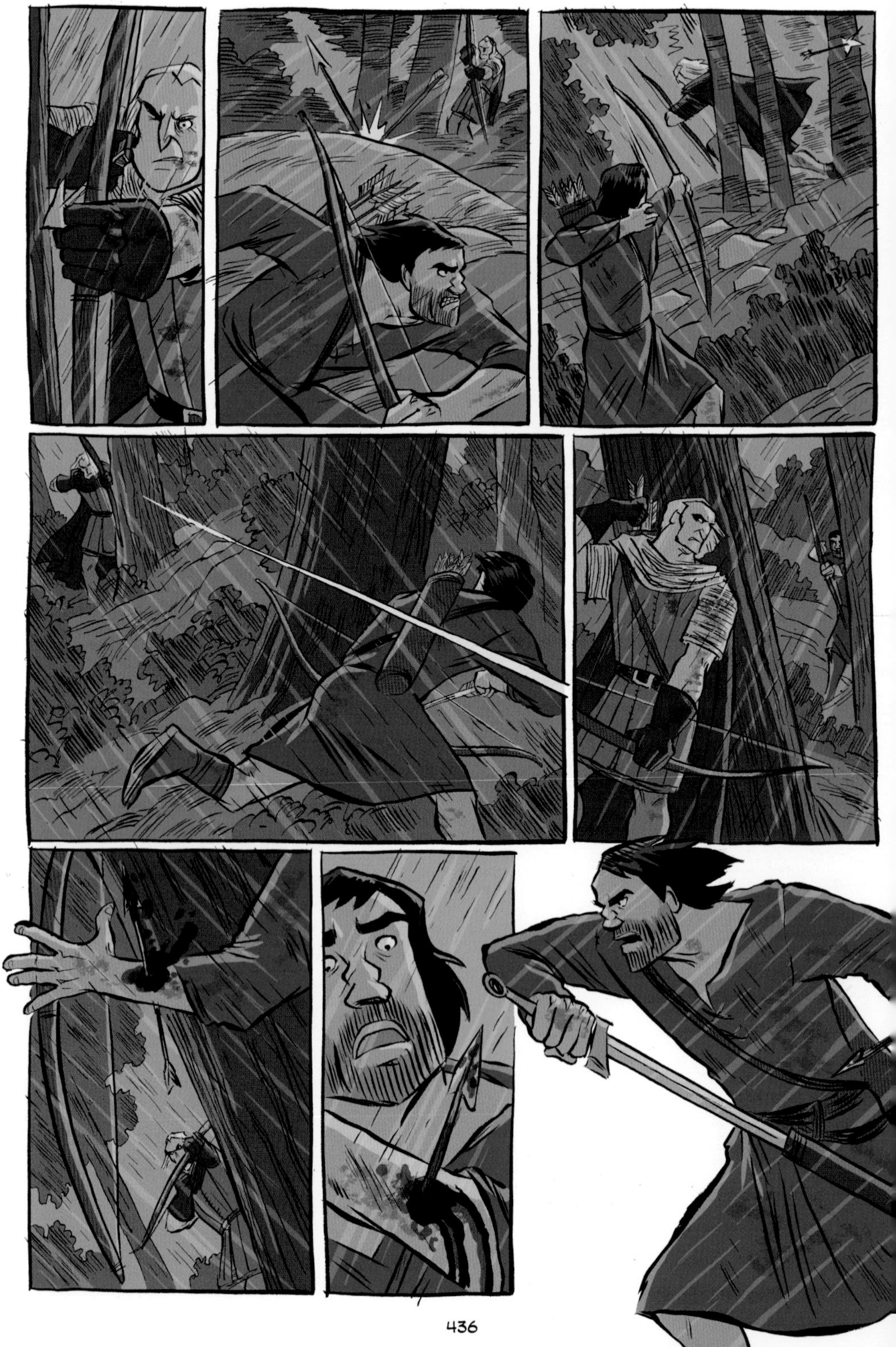

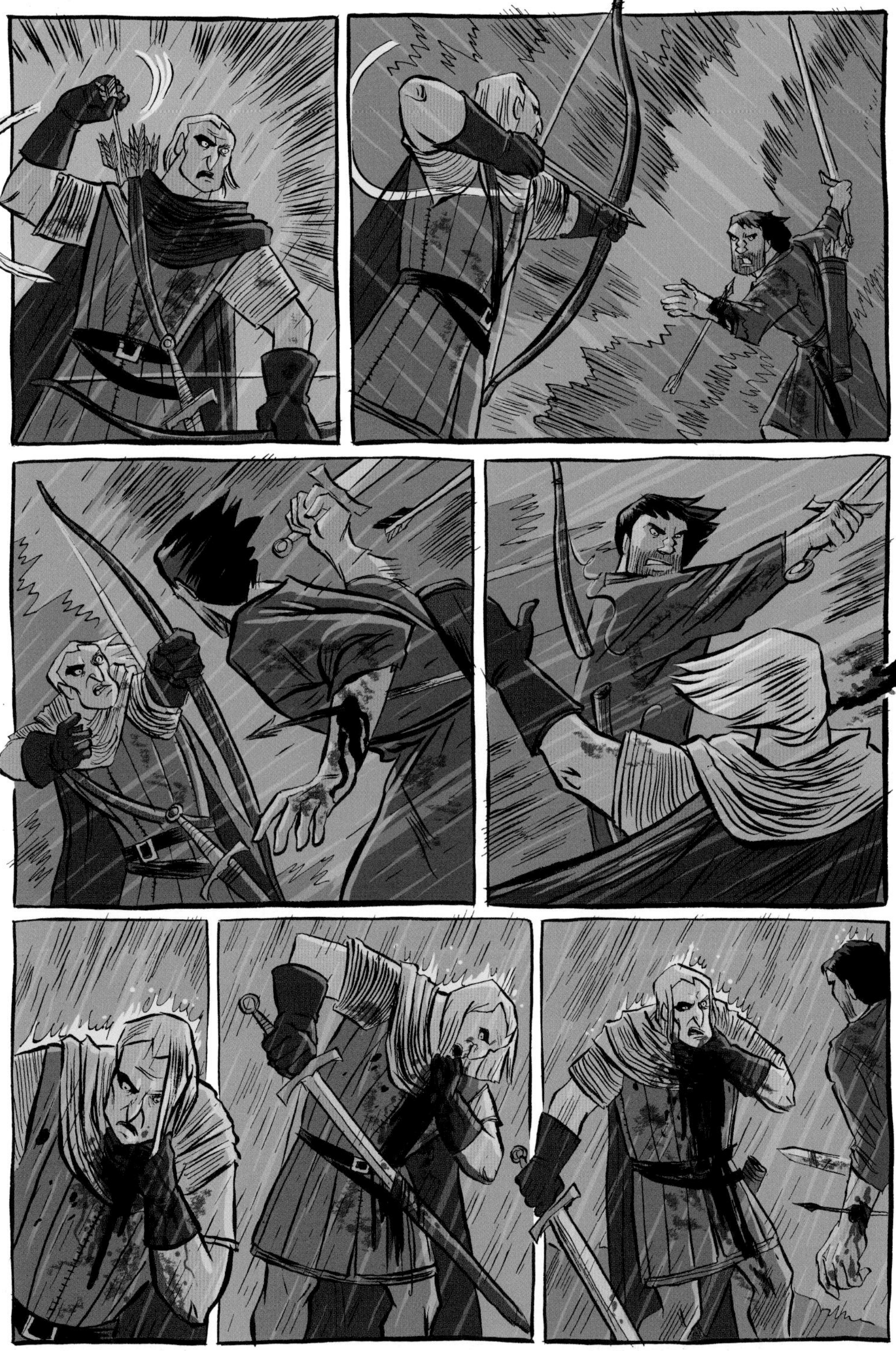

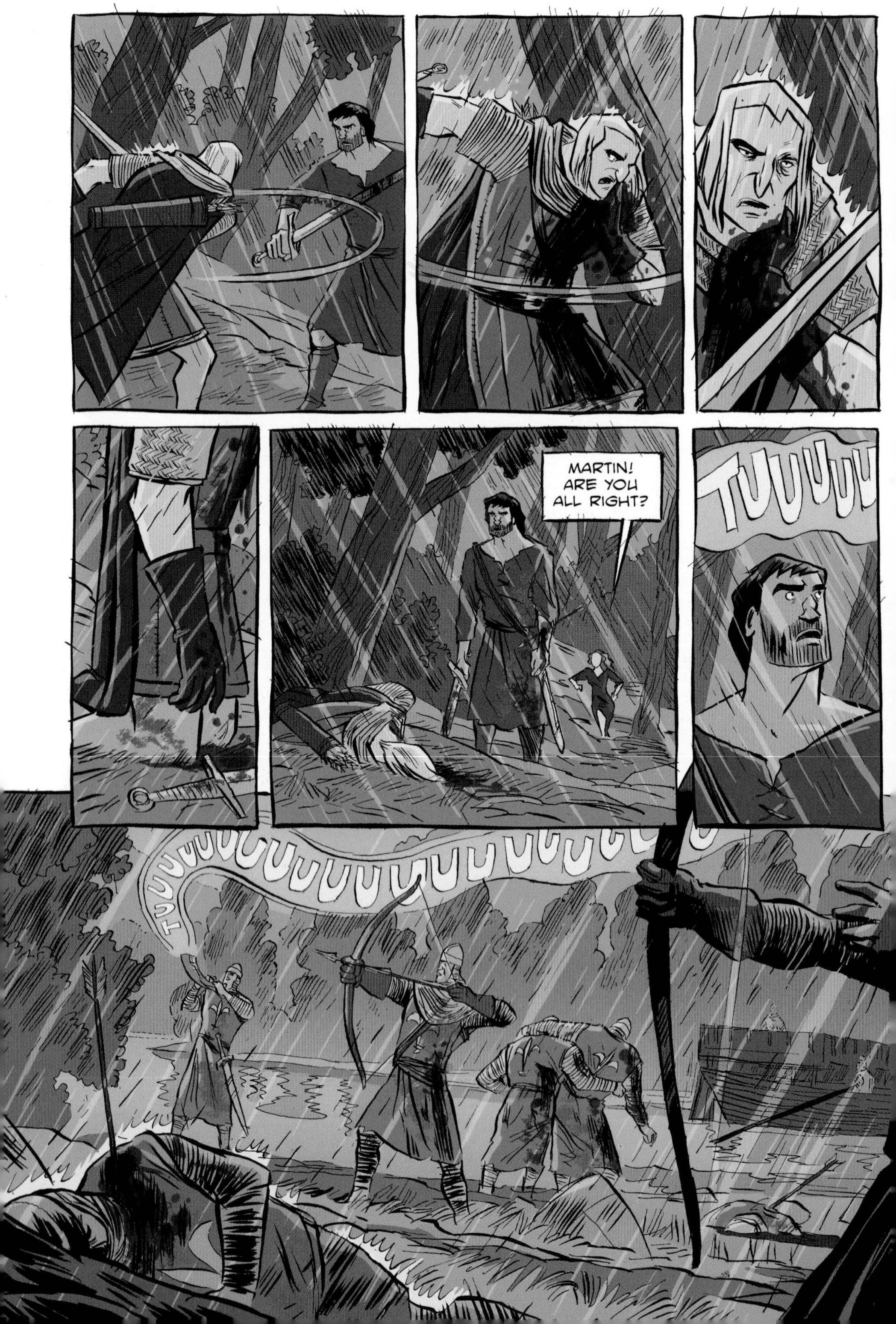

MARTIN! ARE YOU ALL RIGHT?
TUUUUU
TUUUUUUUUUUUUUUUUUUUUUUUU

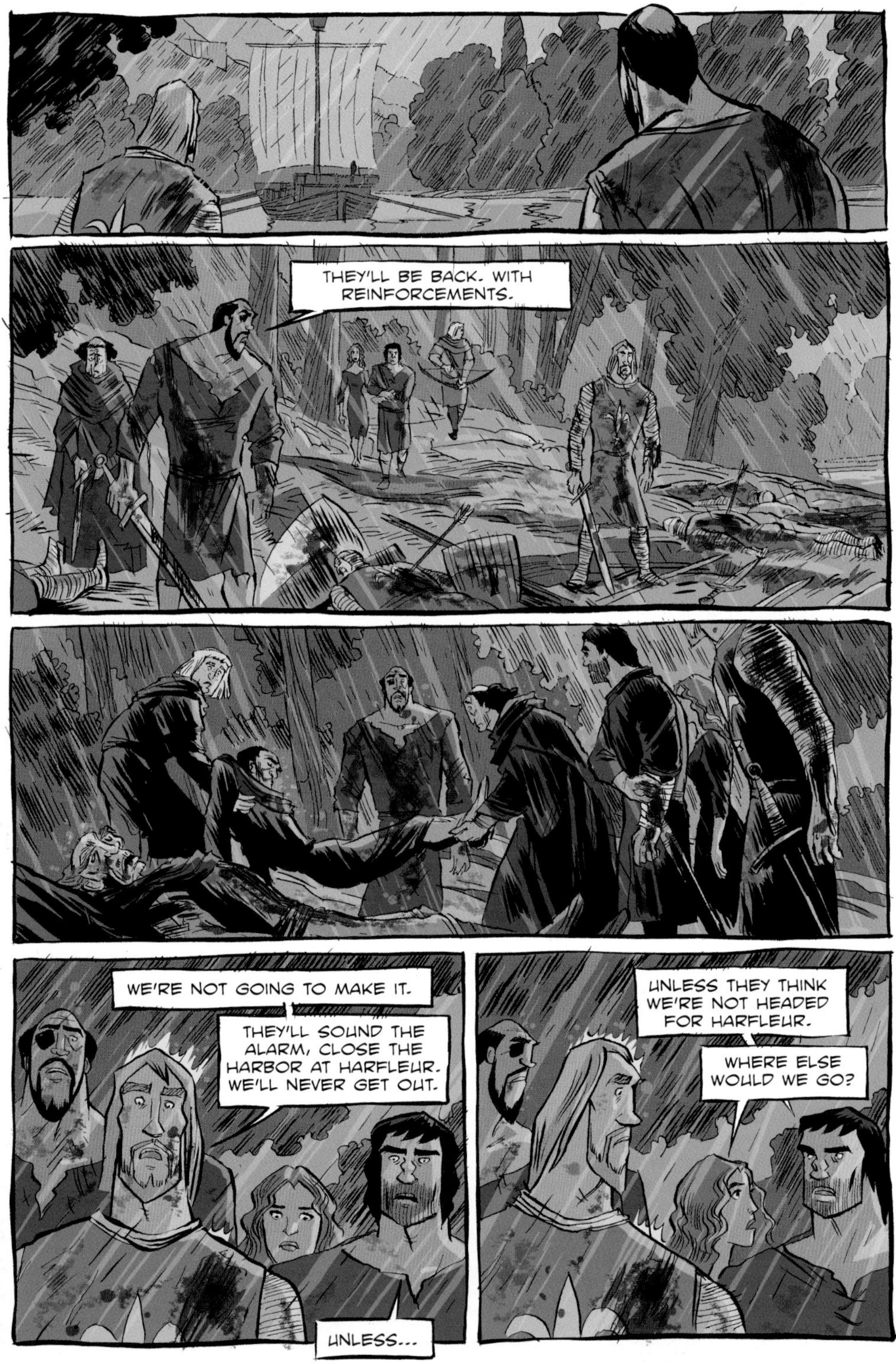
THEY'LL BE BACK. WITH REINFORCEMENTS.
WE'RE NOT GOING TO MAKE IT.
THEY'LL SOUND THE ALARM, CLOSE THE HARBOR AT HARFLEUR. WE'LL NEVER GET OUT.
UNLESS...
UNLESS THEY THINK WE'RE NOT HEADED FOR HARFLEUR.
WHERE ELSE WOULD WE GO?

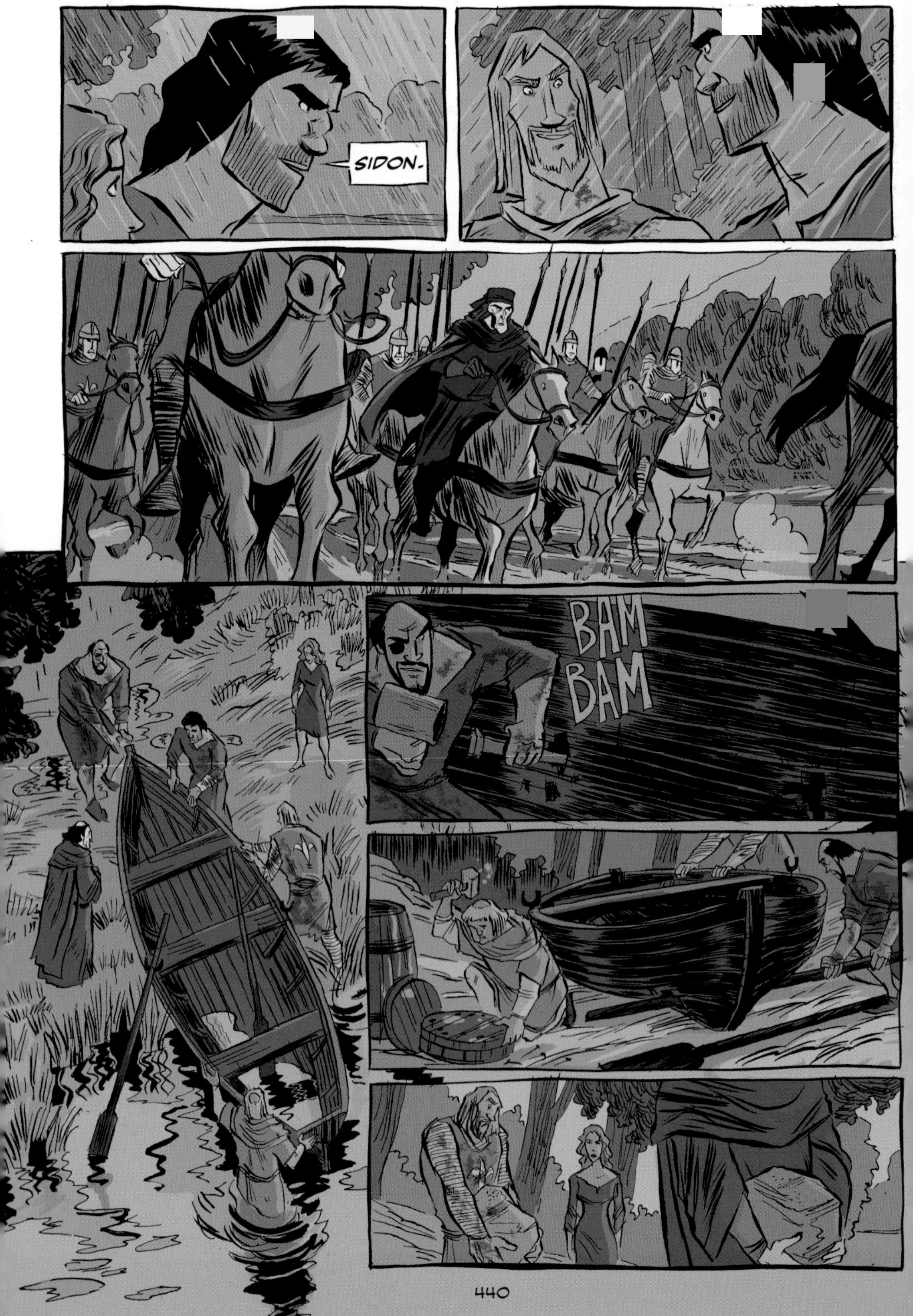
SIDON-
BAM
BAM

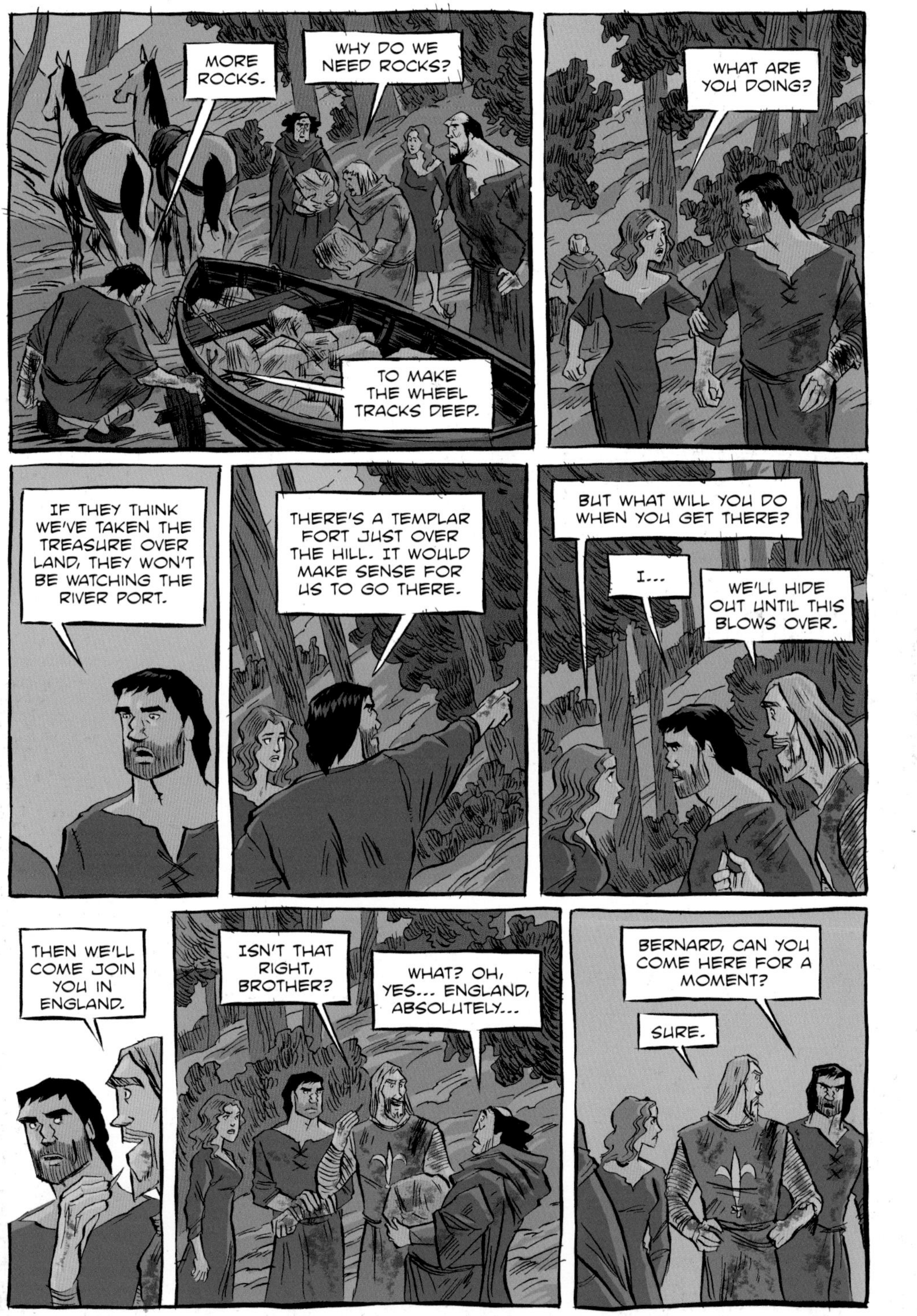
MORE ROCKS.
WHY DO WE NEED ROCKS?
TO MAKE THE WHEEL TRACKS DEEP.
WHAT ARE YOU DOING?
IF THEY THINK WE'VE TAKEN THE TREASURE OVER LAND, THEY WON'T BE WATCHING THE RIVER PORT.
THERE'S A TEMPLAR FORT JUST OVER THE HILL. IT WOULD MAKE SENSE FOR US TO GO THERE.
BUT WHAT WILL YOU DO WHEN YOU GET THERE?
I...
WE'LL HIDE OUT UNTIL THIS BLOWS OVER.
THEN WE'LL COME JOIN YOU IN ENGLAND.
ISN'T THAT RIGHT, BROTHER?
WHAT? OH, YES... ENGLAND, ABSOLUTELY...
BERNARD, CAN YOU COME HERE FOR A MOMENT?
SURE.

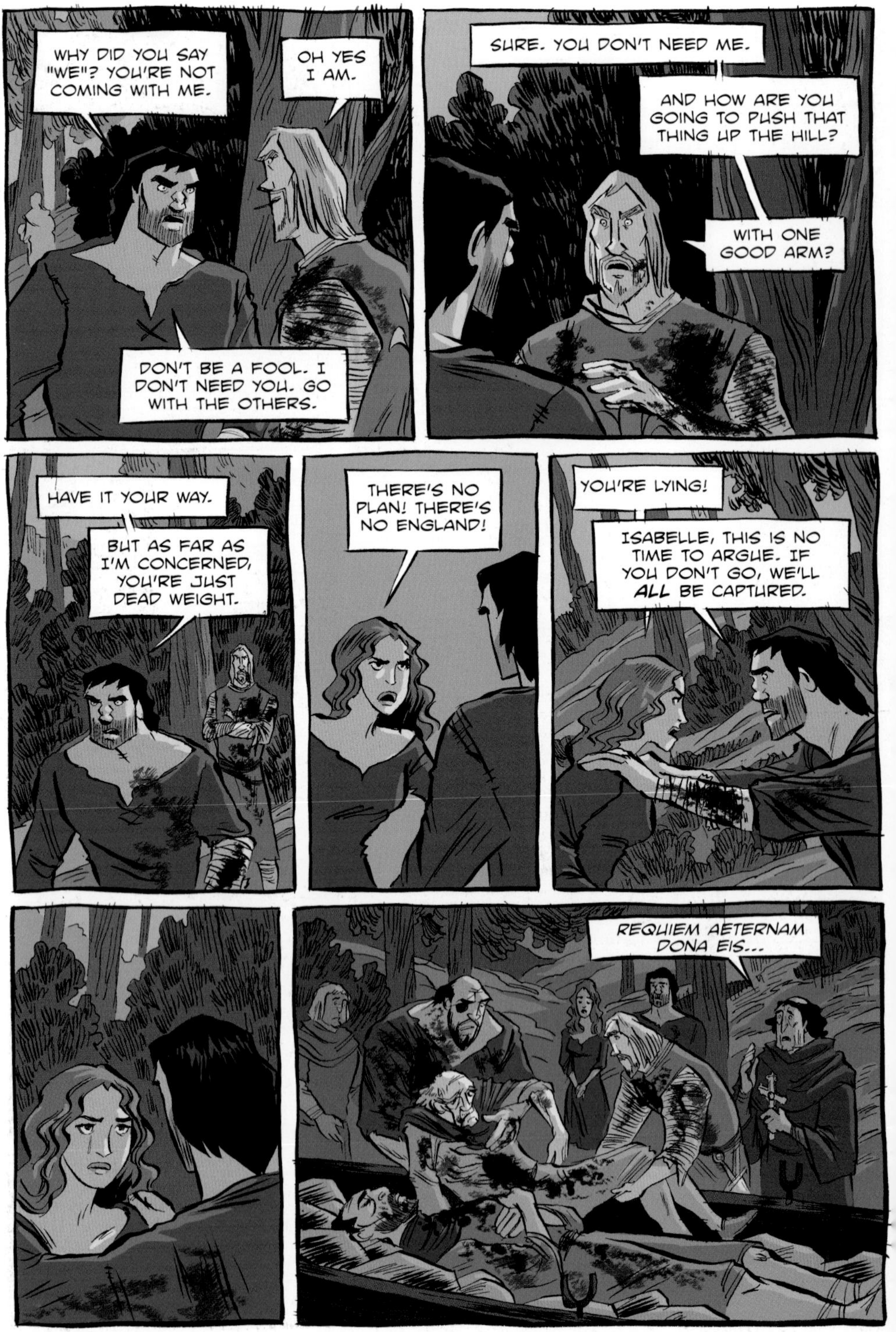
WHY DID YOU SAY "WE"? YOU'RE NOT COMING WITH ME.
OH YES I AM.
DON'T BE A FOOL. I DON'T NEED YOU. GO WITH THE OTHERS.
SURE. YOU DON'T NEED ME.
AND HOW ARE YOU GOING TO PUSH THAT THING UP THE HILL?
WITH ONE GOOD ARM?
HAVE IT YOUR WAY.
BUT AS FAR AS I'M CONCERNED, YOU'RE JUST DEAD WEIGHT.
THERE'S NO PLAN! THERE'S NO ENGLAND!
YOU'RE LYING!
ISABELLE, THIS IS NO TIME TO ARGUE. IF YOU DON'T GO, WE'LL ALL BE CAPTURED.
REQUIEM AETERNAM DONA EIS...

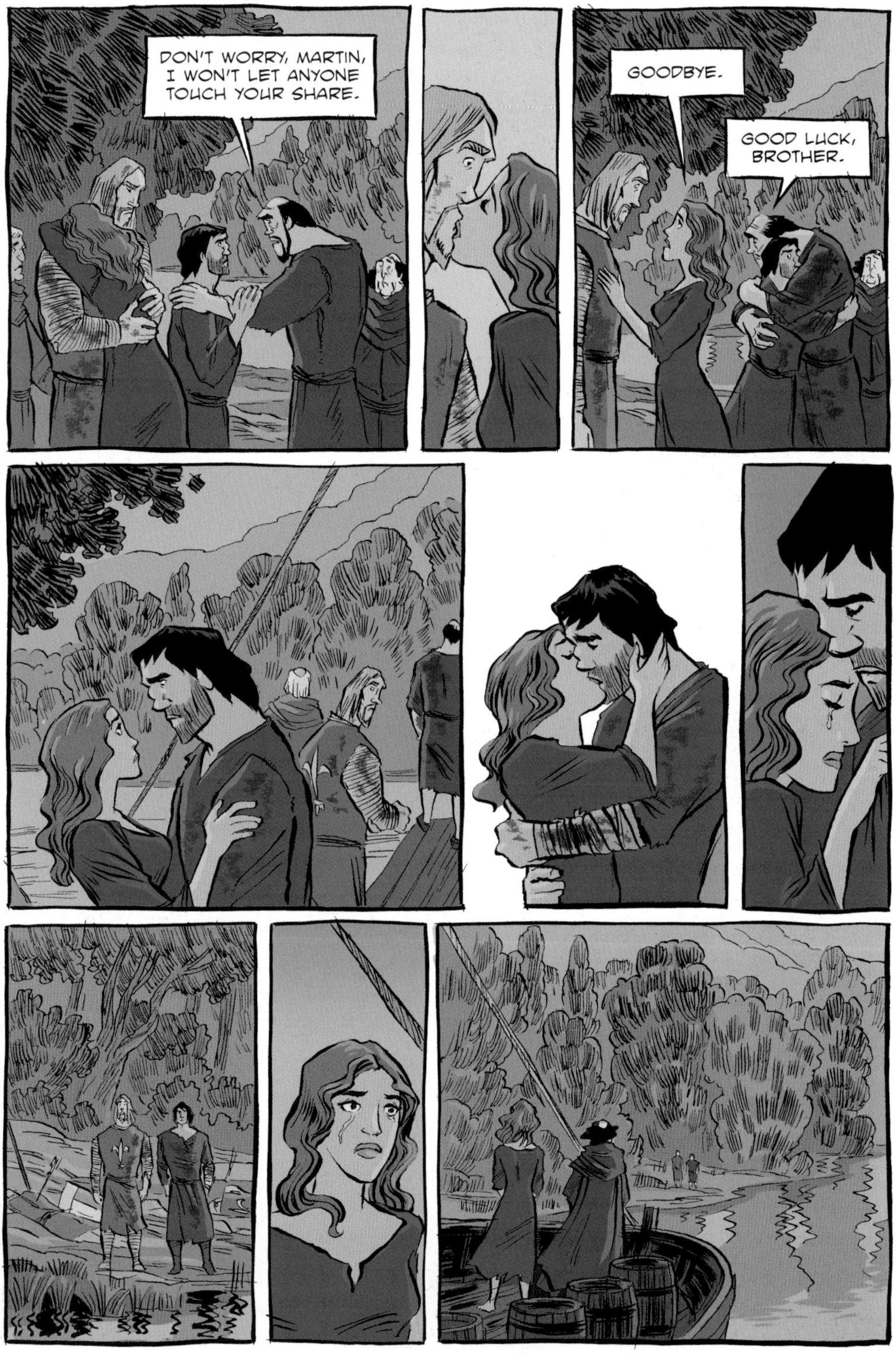
DON'T WORRY, MARTIN, I WON'T LET ANYONE TOUCH YOUR SHARE.
GOODBYE.
GOOD LUCK, BROTHER.

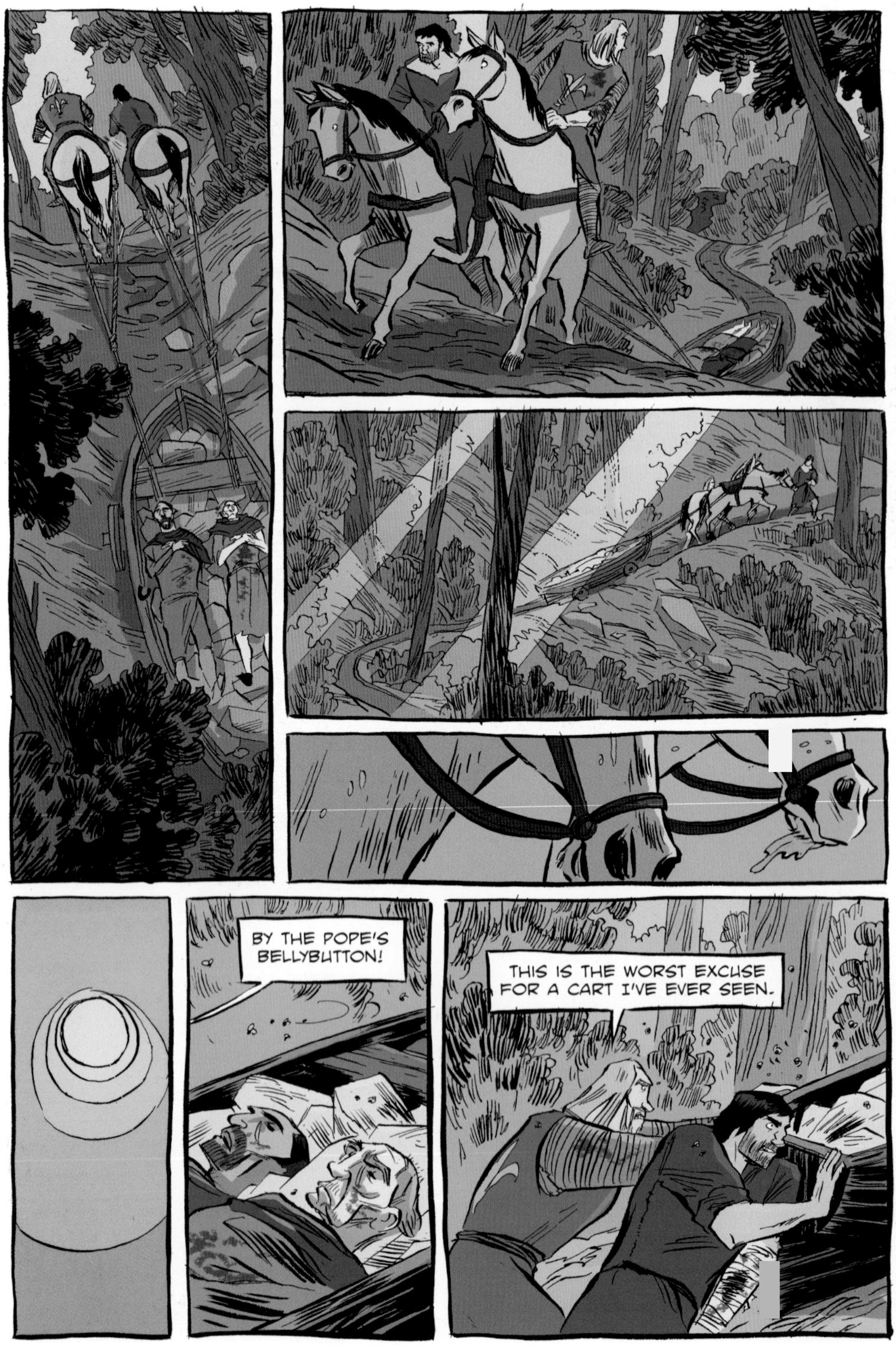
BY THE POPE'S BELLYBUTTON!
THIS IS THE WORST EXCUSE FOR A CART I'VE EVER SEEN.

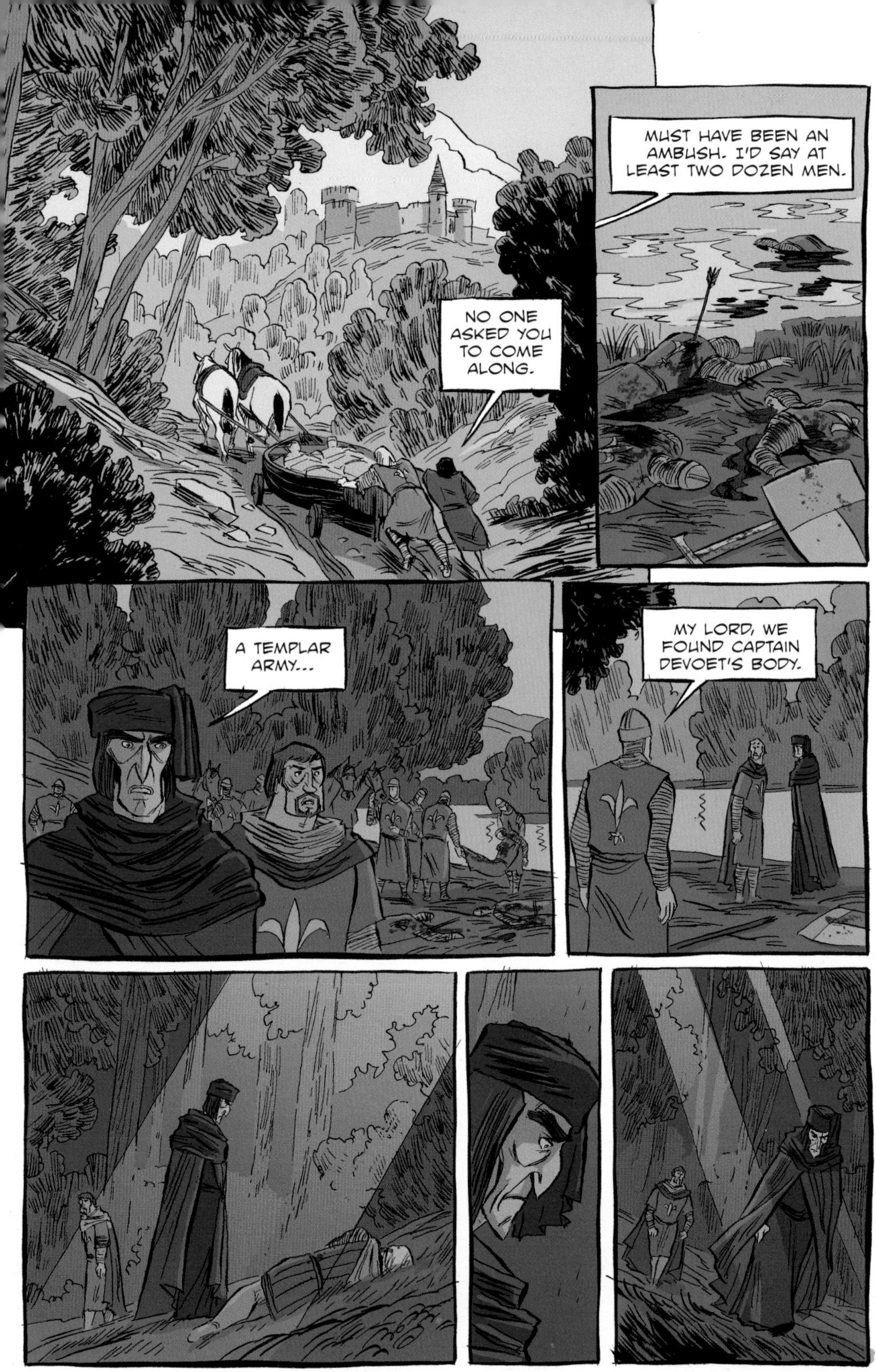
MUST HAVE BEEN AN AMBUSH. I'D SAY AT LEAST TWO DOZEN MEN.
NO ONE ASKED YOU TO COME ALONG.
A TEMPLAR ARMY...
MY LORD, WE FOUND CAPTAIN DEVOET'S BODY.

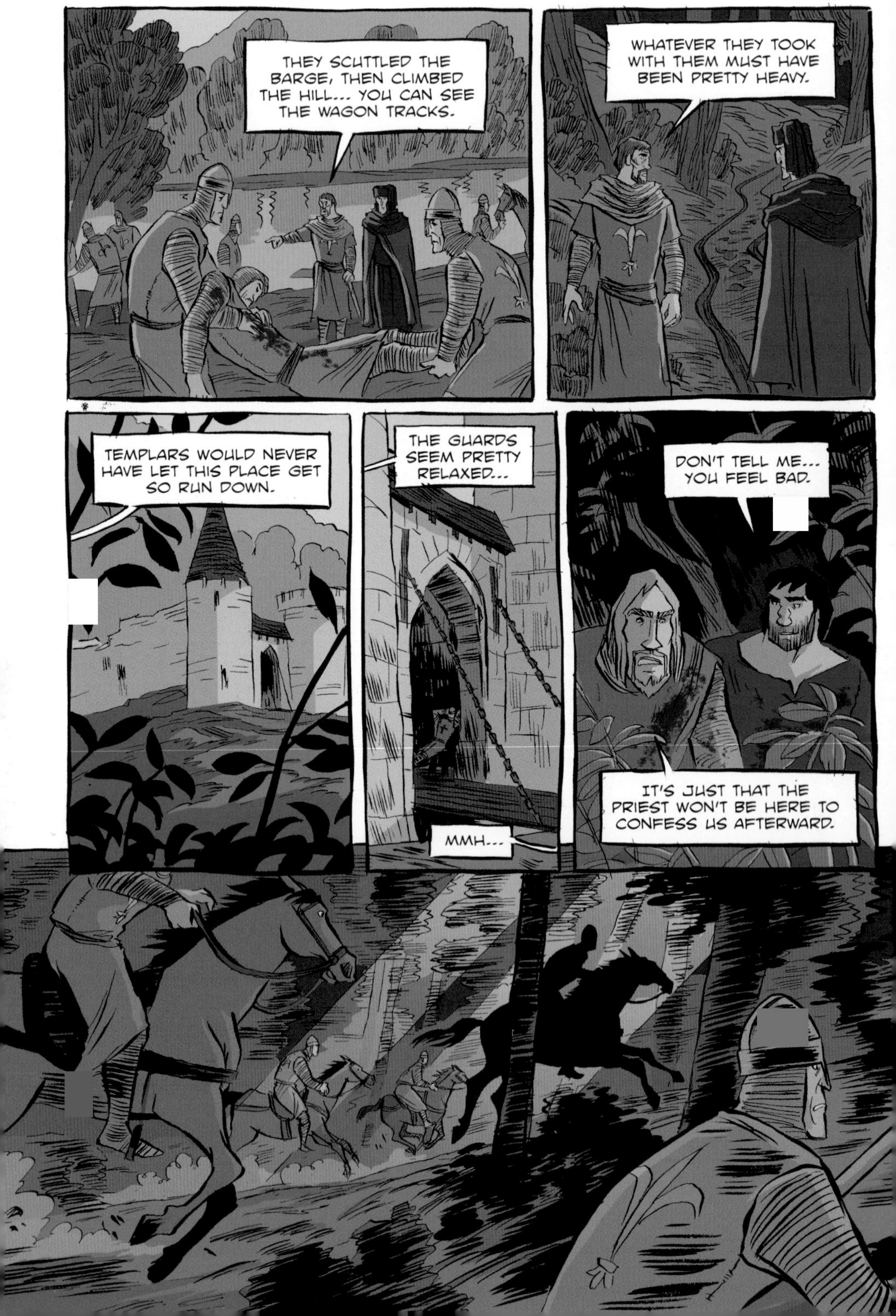
THEY SCUTTLED THE BARGE, THEN CLIMBED THE HILL... YOU CAN SEE THE WAGON TRACKS.
WHATEVER THEY TOOK WITH THEM MUST HAVE BEEN PRETTY HEAVY.
TEMPLARS WOULD NEVER HAVE LET THIS PLACE GET SO RUN DOWN.
THE GUARDS SEEM PRETTY RELAXED...
MMH...
DON'T TELL ME... YOU FEEL BAD.
IT'S JUST THAT THE PRIEST WON'T BE HERE TO CONFESS US AFTERWARD.

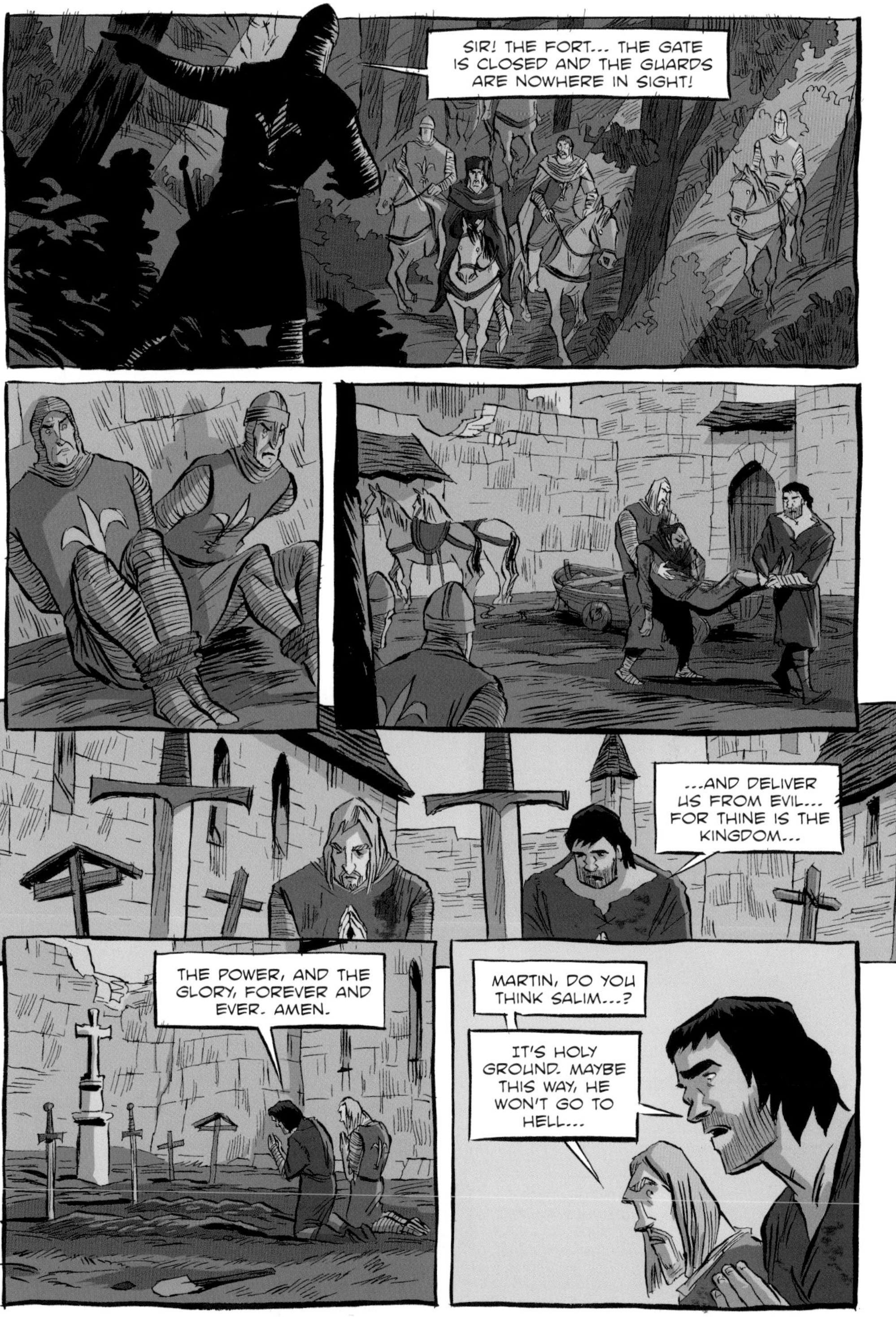
SIR! THE FORT... THE GATE IS CLOSED AND THE GUARDS ARE NOWHERE IN SIGHT!
...AND DELIVER US FROM EVIL... FOR THINE IS THE KINGDOM...
THE POWER, AND THE GLORY, FOREVER AND EVER. AMEN.
MARTIN, DO YOU THINK SALIM...?
IT'S HOLY GROUND. MAYBE THIS WAY, HE WON'T GO TO HELL...

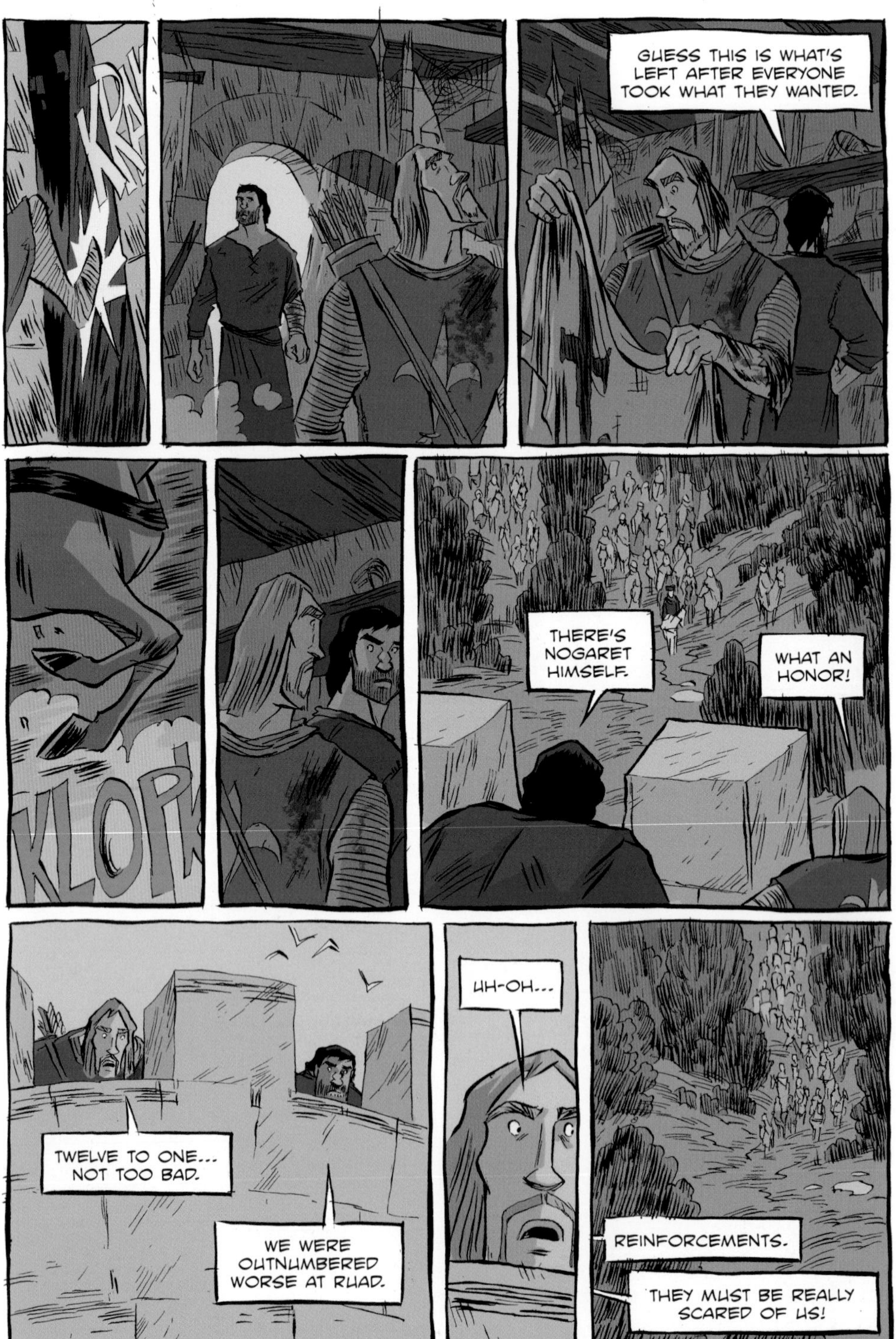

KRAK
GUESS THIS IS WHAT'S LEFT AFTER EVERYONE TOOK WHAT THEY WANTED.
KLOP
THERE'S NOGARET HIMSELF.
WHAT AN HONOR!
TWELVE TO ONE... NOT TOO BAD.
WE WERE OUTNUMBERED WORSE AT RUAD.
UH-OH...
REINFORCEMENTS.
THEY MUST BE REALLY SCARED OF US!

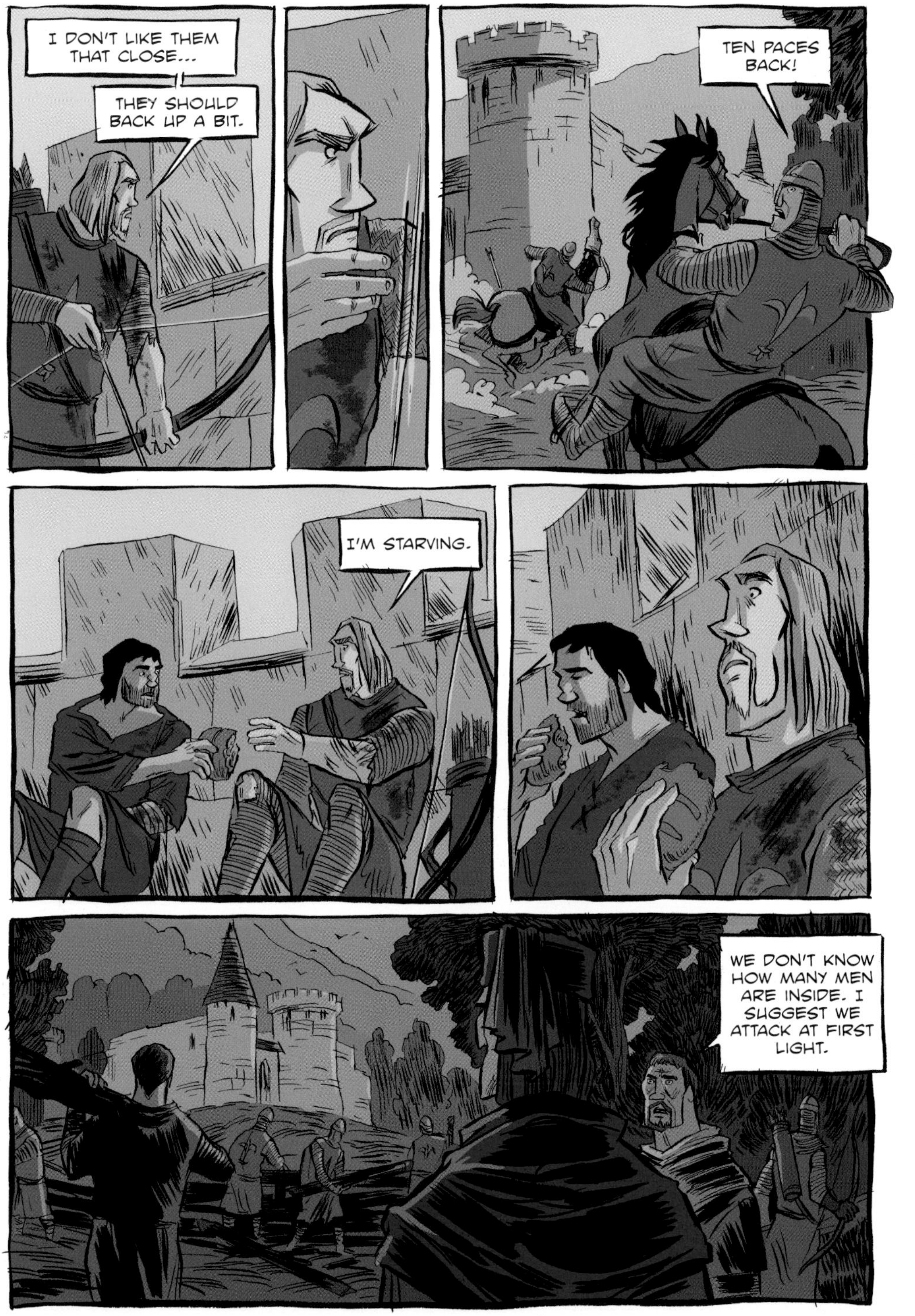
I DON'T LIKE THEM THAT CLOSE...
THEY SHOULD BACK UP A BIT.
TEN PACES BACK!
I'M STARVING.
WE DON'T KNOW HOW MANY MEN ARE INSIDE. I SUGGEST WE ATTACK AT FIRST LIGHT.

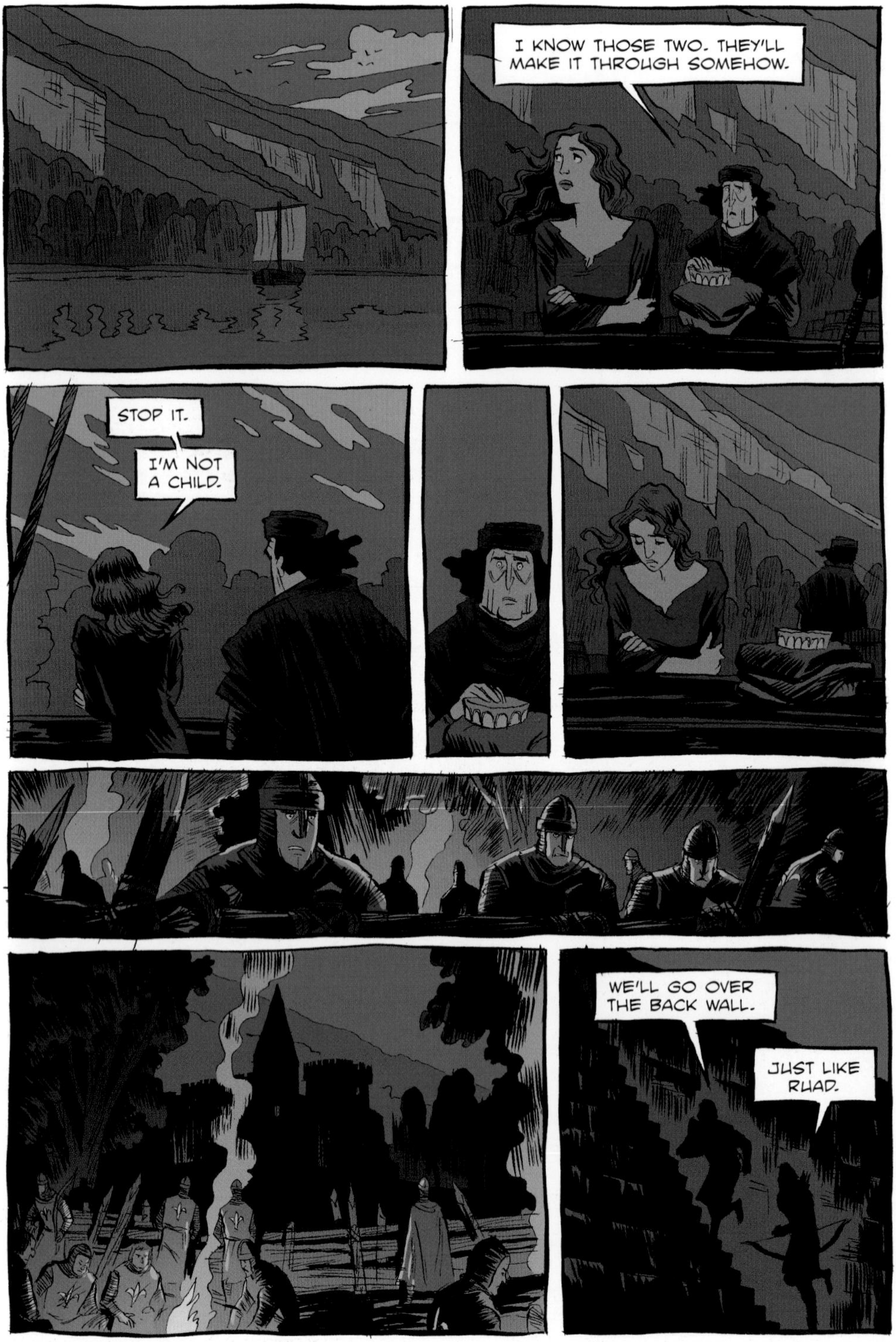
I KNOW THOSE TWO. THEY'LL MAKE IT THROUGH SOMEHOW.
STOP IT.
I'M NOT A CHILD.
WE'LL GO OVER THE BACK WALL.
JUST LIKE RUAD.

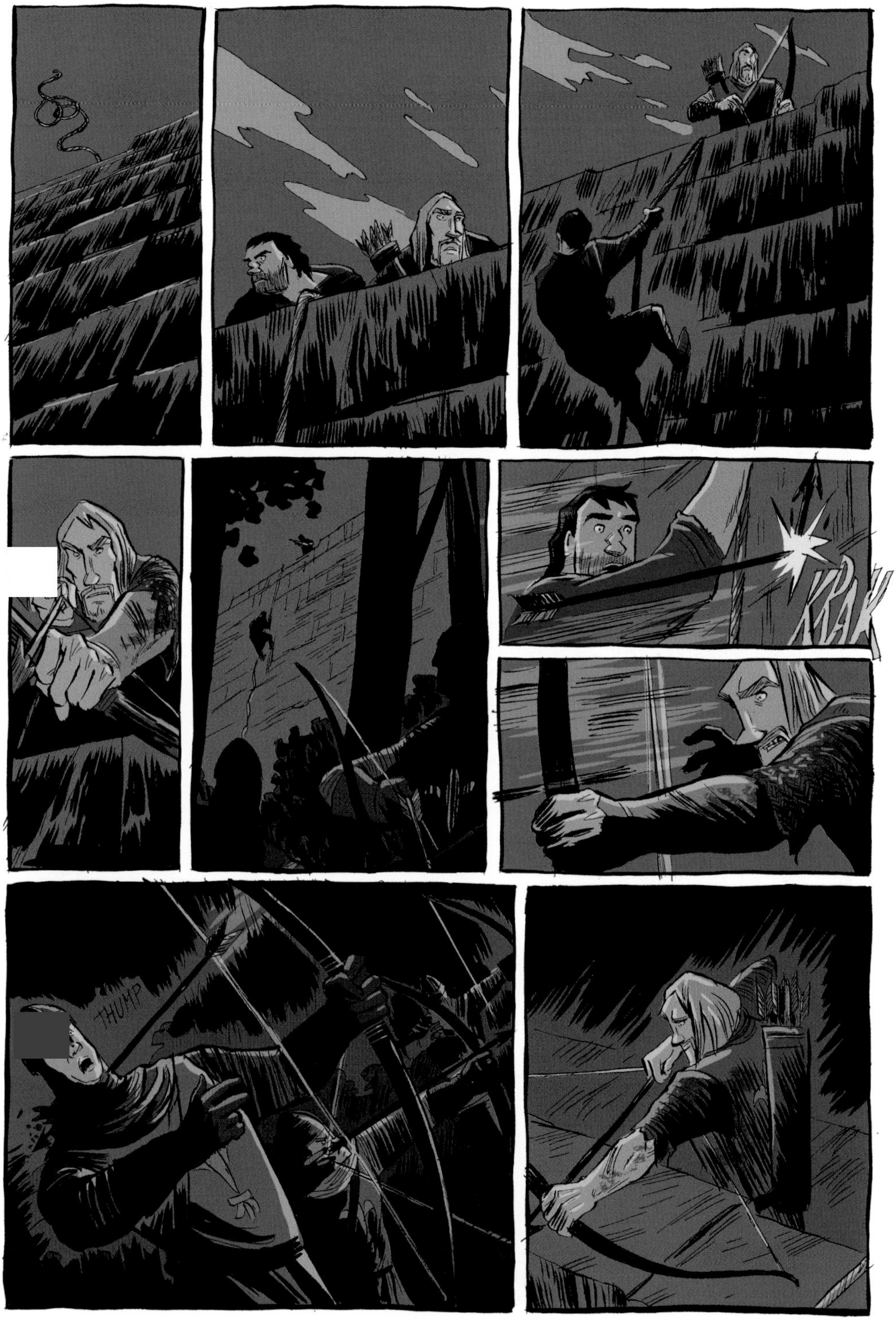
KRAK
THUMP

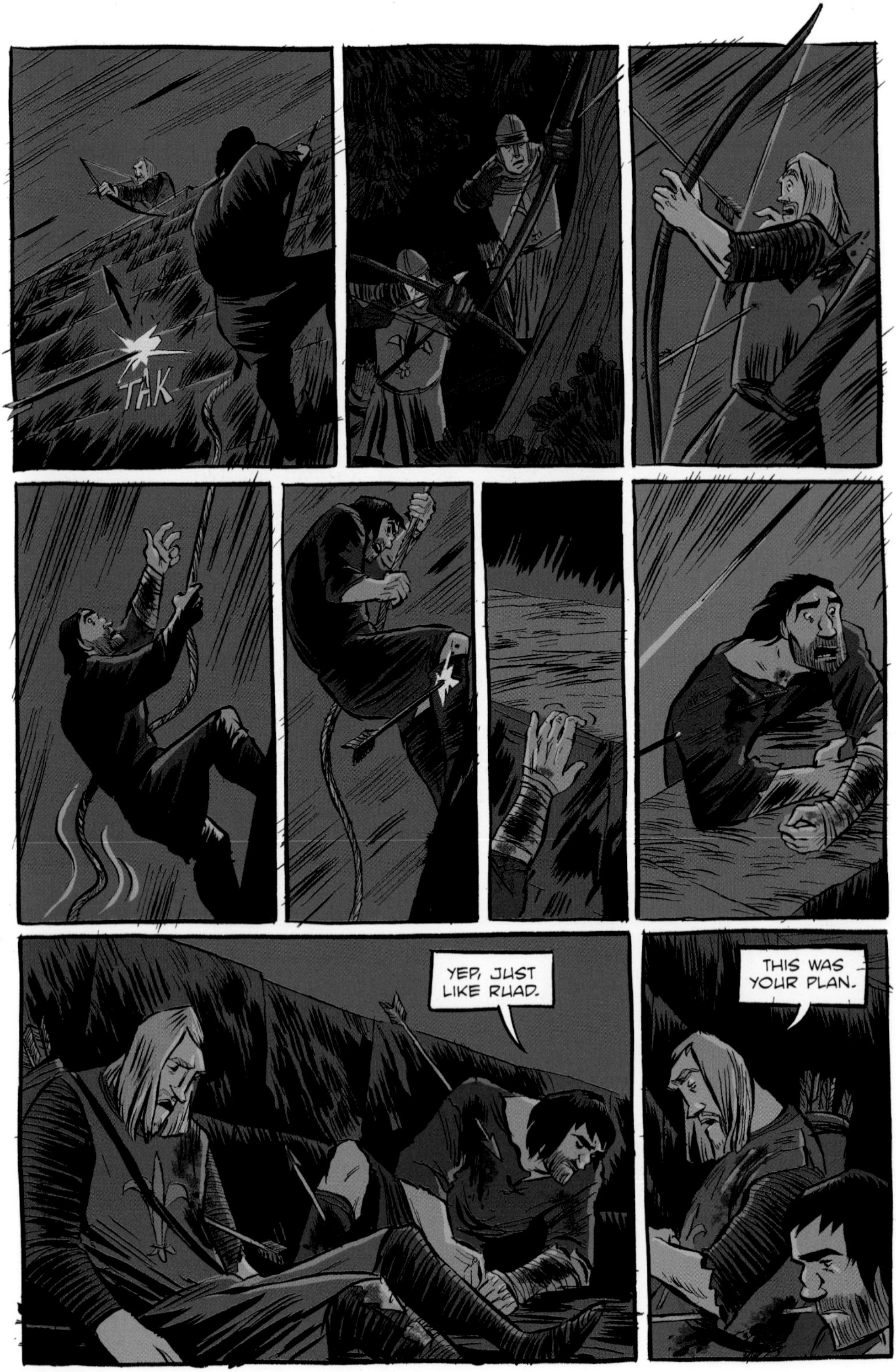
TAK
YEP, JUST LIKE RUAD.
THIS WAS YOUR PLAN.

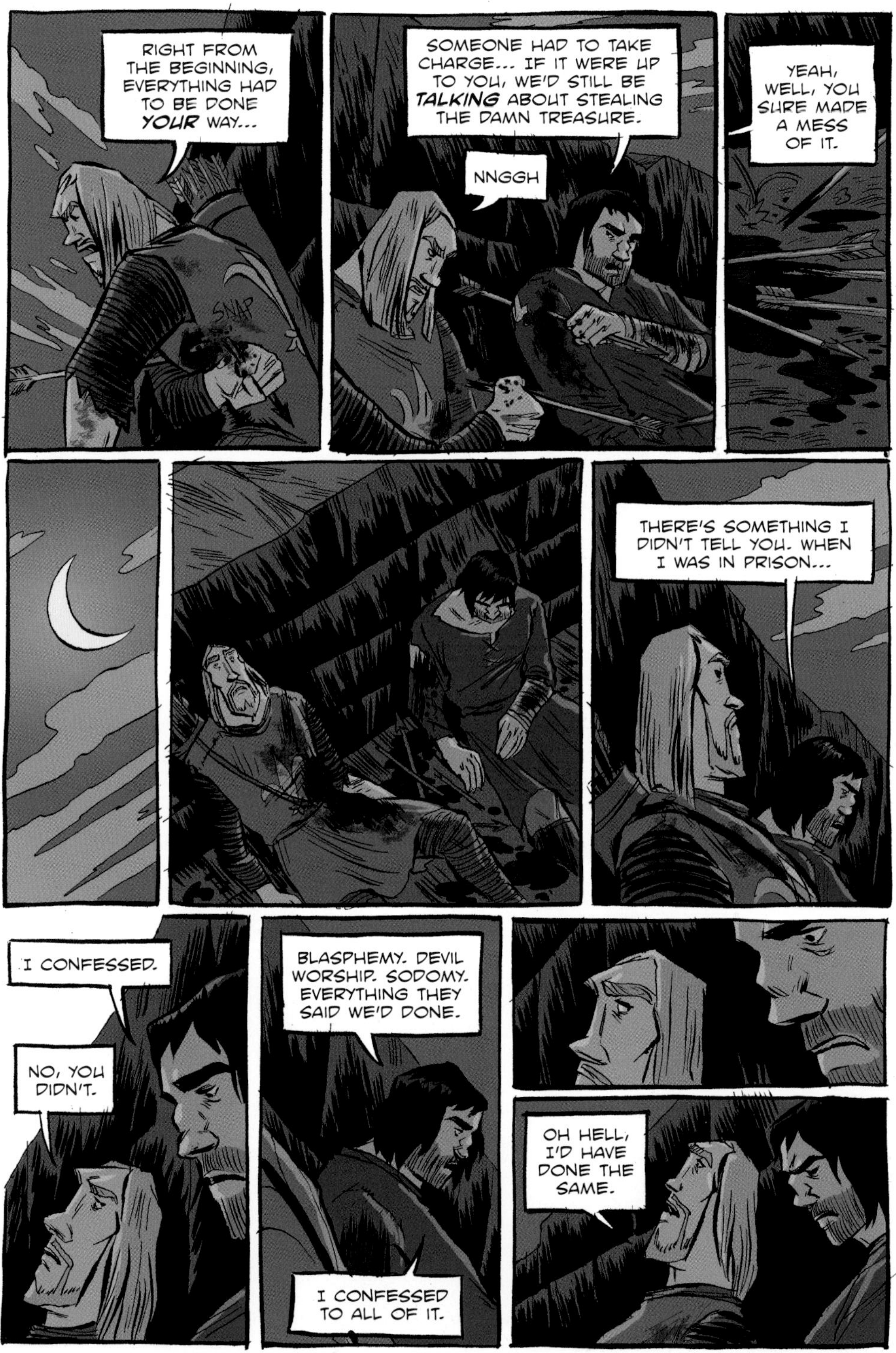
RIGHT FROM THE BEGINNING, EVERYTHING HAD TO BE DONE *YOUR* WAY...
SNAP
SOMEONE HAD TO TAKE CHARGE... IF IT WERE UP TO YOU, WE'D STILL BE *TALKING* ABOUT STEALING THE DAMN TREASURE.
NNGGH
YEAH, WELL, YOU SURE MADE A MESS OF IT.
THERE'S SOMETHING I DIDN'T TELL YOU. WHEN I WAS IN PRISON...
I CONFESSED.
NO, YOU DIDN'T.
BLASPHEMY. DEVIL WORSHIP. SODOMY. EVERYTHING THEY SAID WE'D DONE.
I CONFESSED TO ALL OF IT.
OH HELL, I'D HAVE DONE THE SAME.

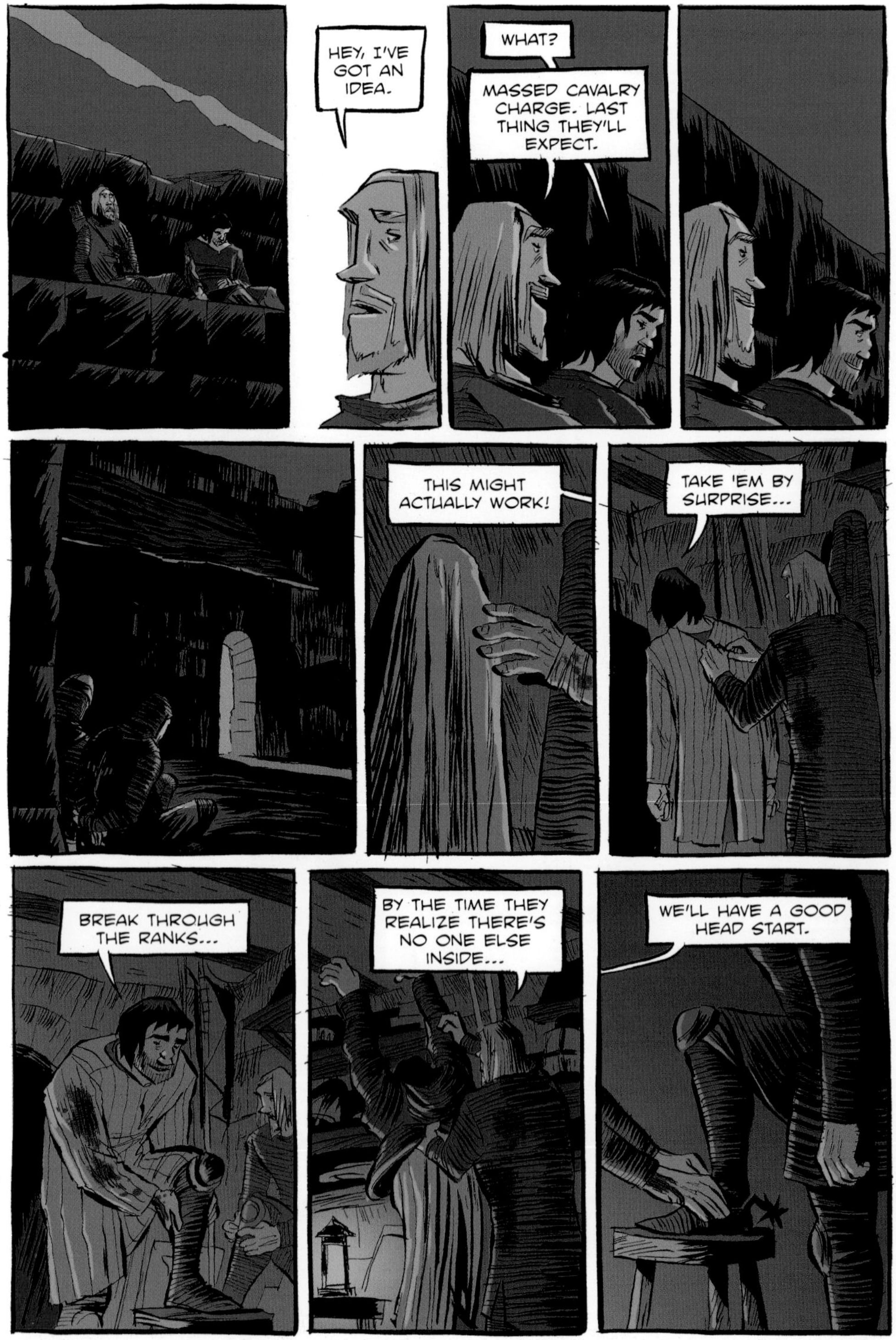
HEY, I'VE GOT AN IDEA.
WHAT?
MASSED CAVALRY CHARGE. LAST THING THEY'LL EXPECT.
THIS MIGHT ACTUALLY WORK!
TAKE 'EM BY SURPRISE...
BREAK THROUGH THE RANKS...
BY THE TIME THEY REALIZE THERE'S NO ONE ELSE INSIDE...
WE'LL HAVE A GOOD HEAD START.

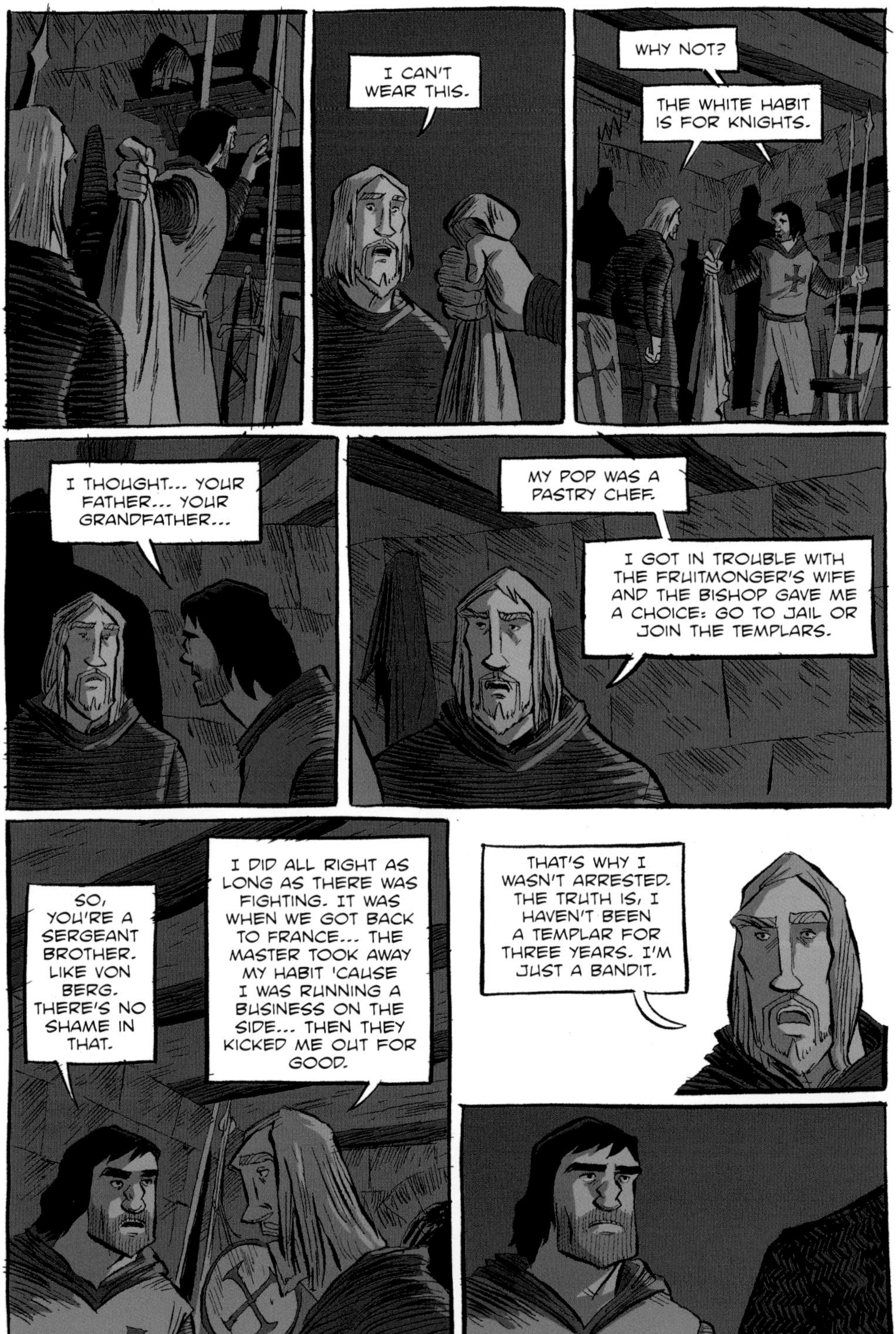
I CAN'T WEAR THIS.
WHY NOT?
THE WHITE HABIT IS FOR KNIGHTS.
I THOUGHT... YOUR FATHER... YOUR GRANDFATHER...
MY POP WAS A PASTRY CHEF.
I GOT IN TROUBLE WITH THE FRUITMONGER'S WIFE AND THE BISHOP GAVE ME A CHOICE: GO TO JAIL OR JOIN THE TEMPLARS.
SO, YOU'RE A SERGEANT BROTHER. LIKE VON BERG. THERE'S NO SHAME IN THAT.
I DID ALL RIGHT AS LONG AS THERE WAS FIGHTING. IT WAS WHEN WE GOT BACK TO FRANCE... THE MASTER TOOK AWAY MY HABIT 'CAUSE I WAS RUNNING A BUSINESS ON THE SIDE... THEN THEY KICKED ME OUT FOR GOOD.
THAT'S WHY I WASN'T ARRESTED. THE TRUTH IS, I HAVEN'T BEEN A TEMPLAR FOR THREE YEARS. I'M JUST A BANDIT.

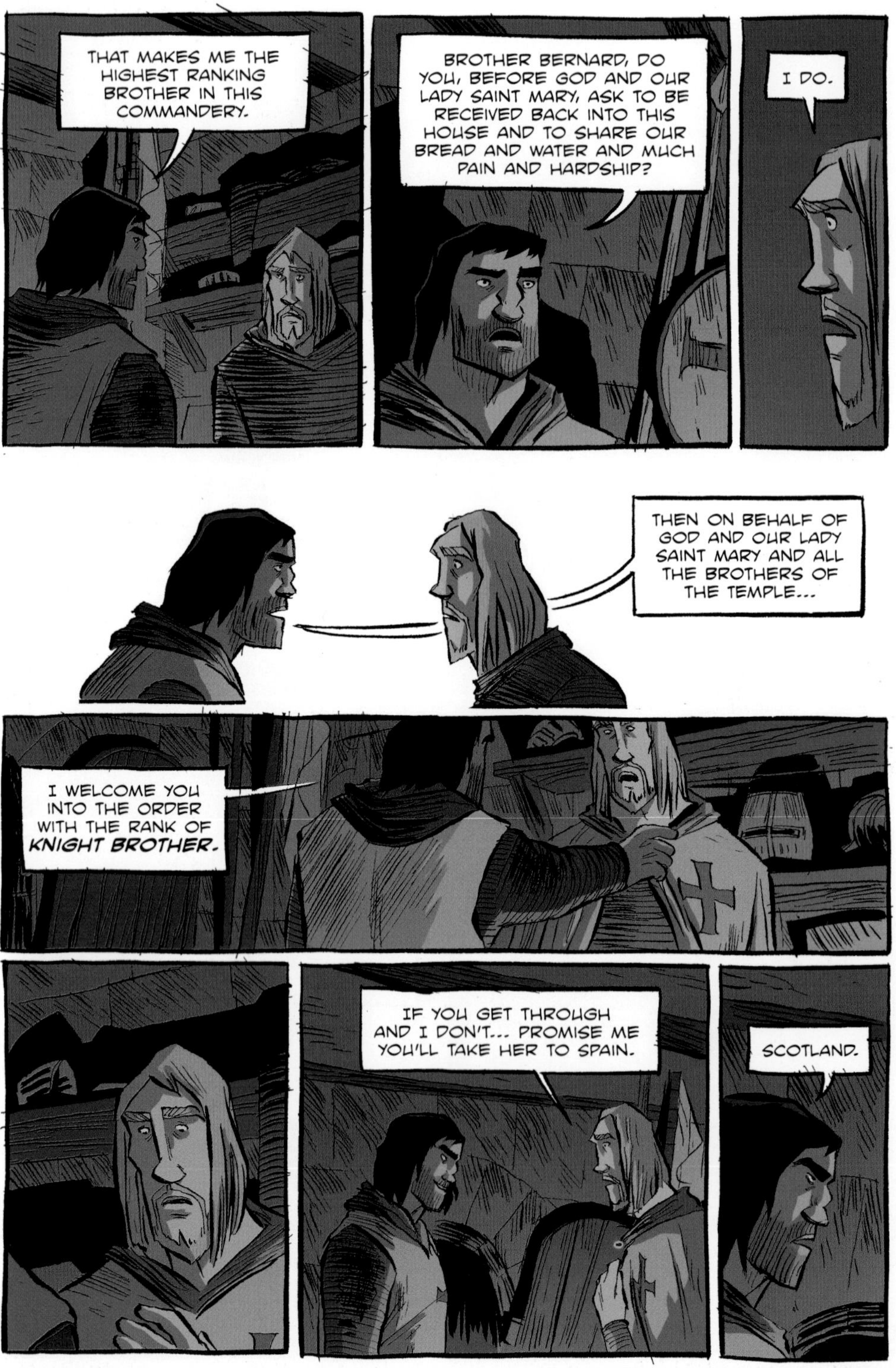
THAT MAKES ME THE HIGHEST RANKING BROTHER IN THIS COMMANDERY.
BROTHER BERNARD, DO YOU, BEFORE GOD AND OUR LADY SAINT MARY, ASK TO BE RECEIVED BACK INTO THIS HOUSE AND TO SHARE OUR BREAD AND WATER AND MUCH PAIN AND HARDSHIP?
I DO.
THEN ON BEHALF OF GOD AND OUR LADY SAINT MARY AND ALL THE BROTHERS OF THE TEMPLE...
I WELCOME YOU INTO THE ORDER WITH THE RANK OF *KNIGHT BROTHER*.
IF YOU GET THROUGH AND I DON'T... PROMISE ME YOU'LL TAKE HER TO SPAIN.
SCOTLAND.

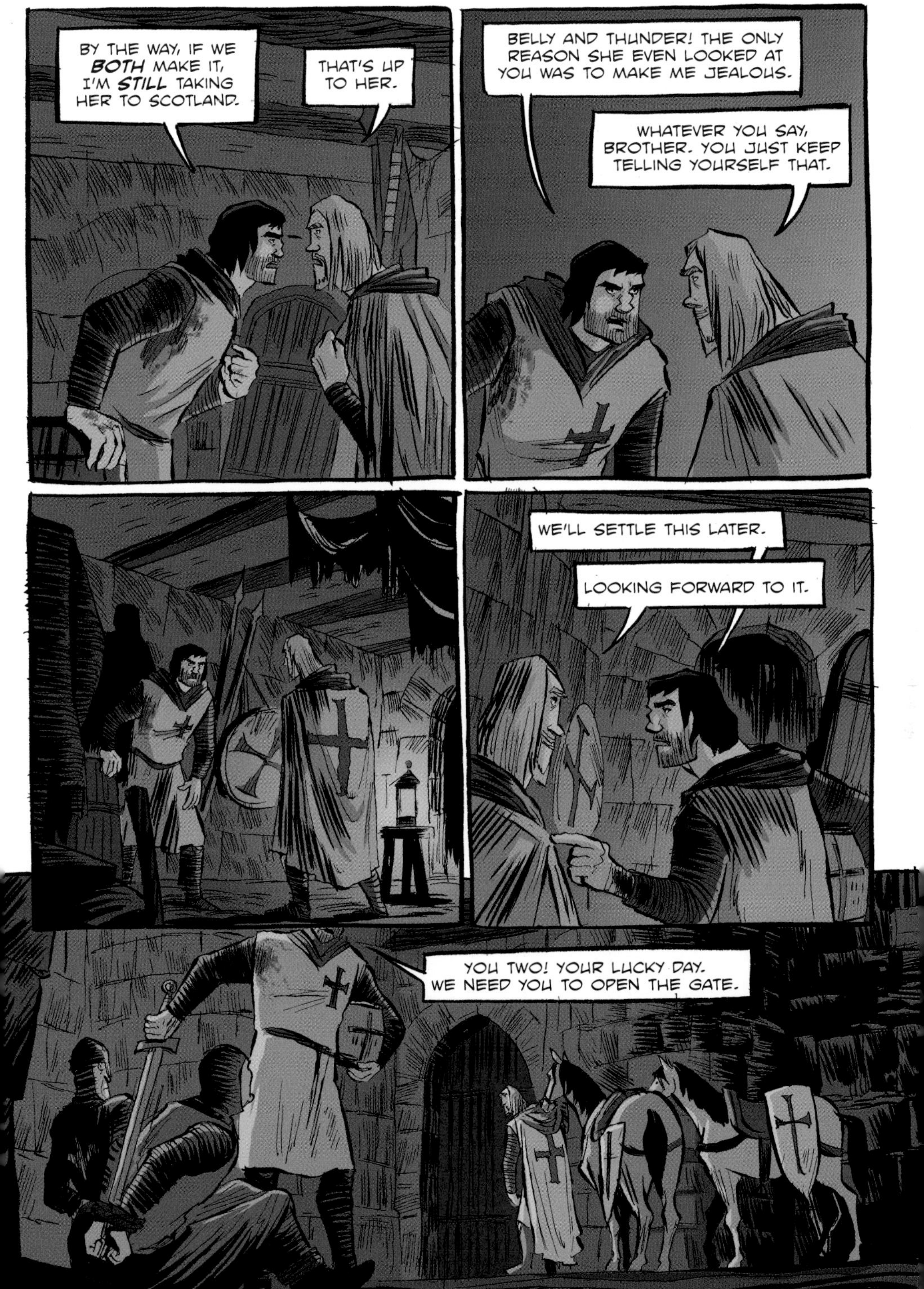
BY THE WAY, IF WE BOTH MAKE IT, I'M STILL TAKING HER TO SCOTLAND.
THAT'S UP TO HER.
BELLY AND THUNDER! THE ONLY REASON SHE EVEN LOOKED AT YOU WAS TO MAKE ME JEALOUS.
WHATEVER YOU SAY, BROTHER. YOU JUST KEEP TELLING YOURSELF THAT.
WE'LL SETTLE THIS LATER.
LOOKING FORWARD TO IT.
YOU TWO! YOUR LUCKY DAY. WE NEED YOU TO OPEN THE GATE.

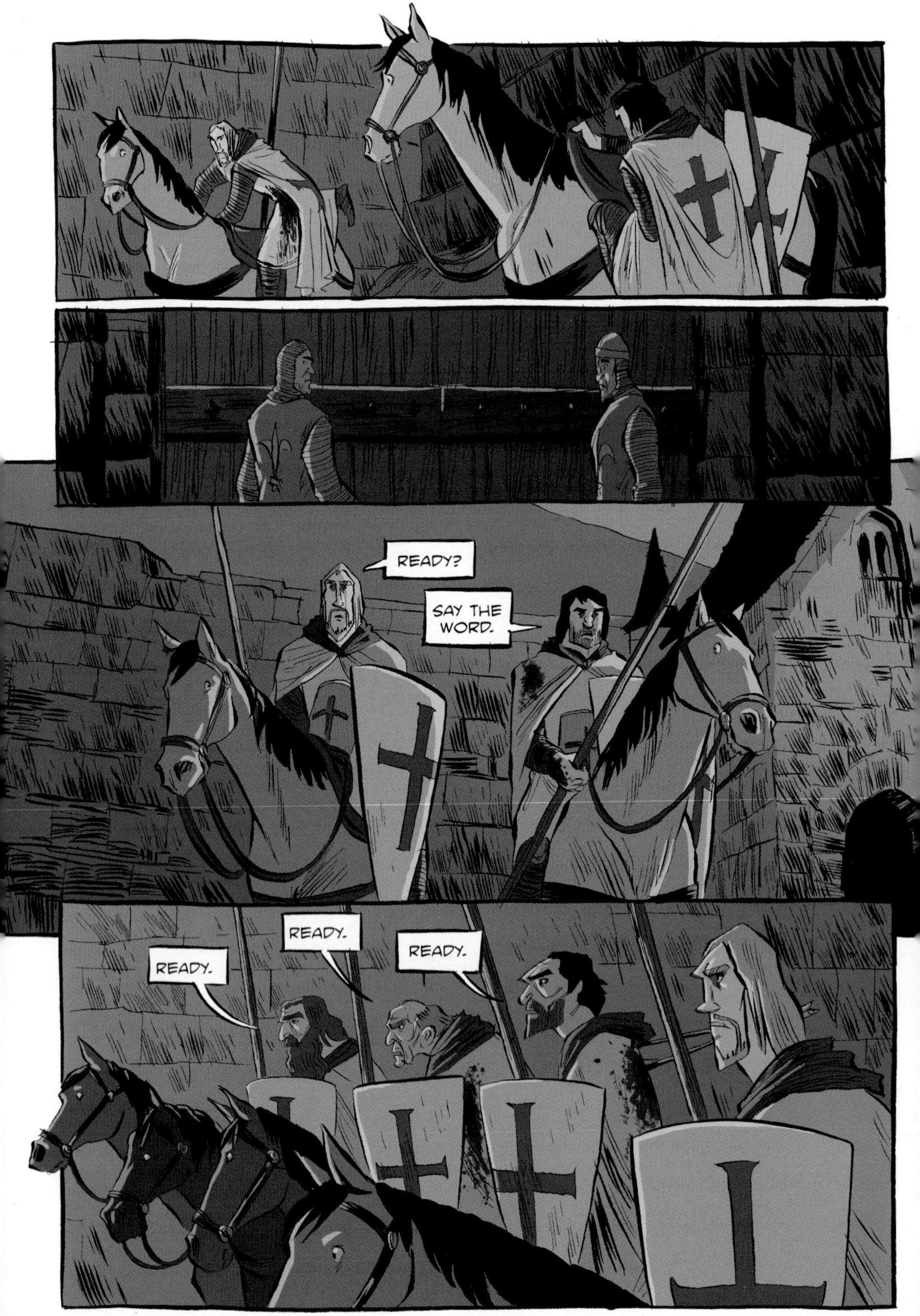
READY?
SAY THE WORD.
READY.
READY.
READY.

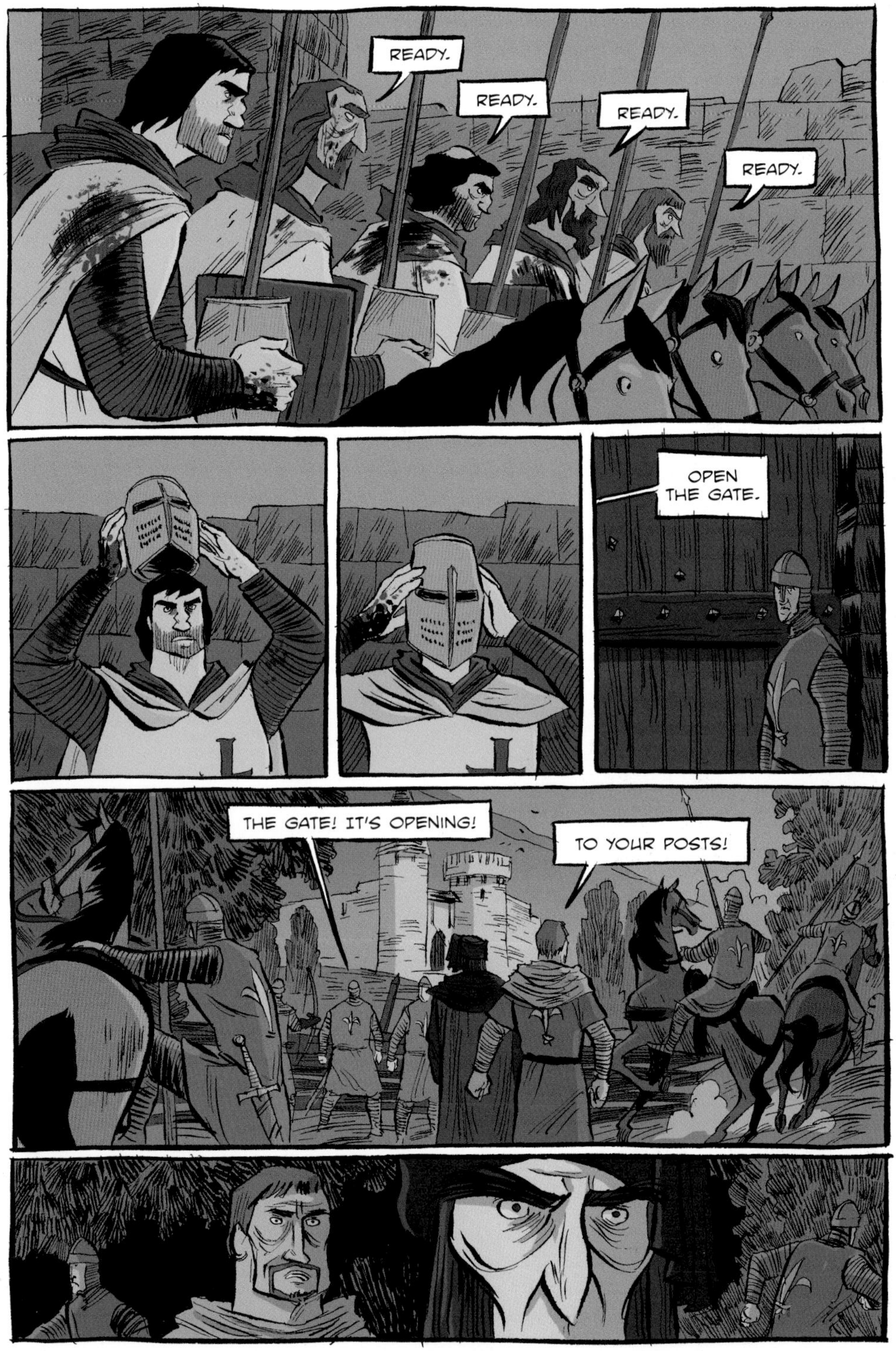
READY.
READY.
READY.
READY.
OPEN THE GATE.
THE GATE! IT'S OPENING!
TO YOUR POSTS!

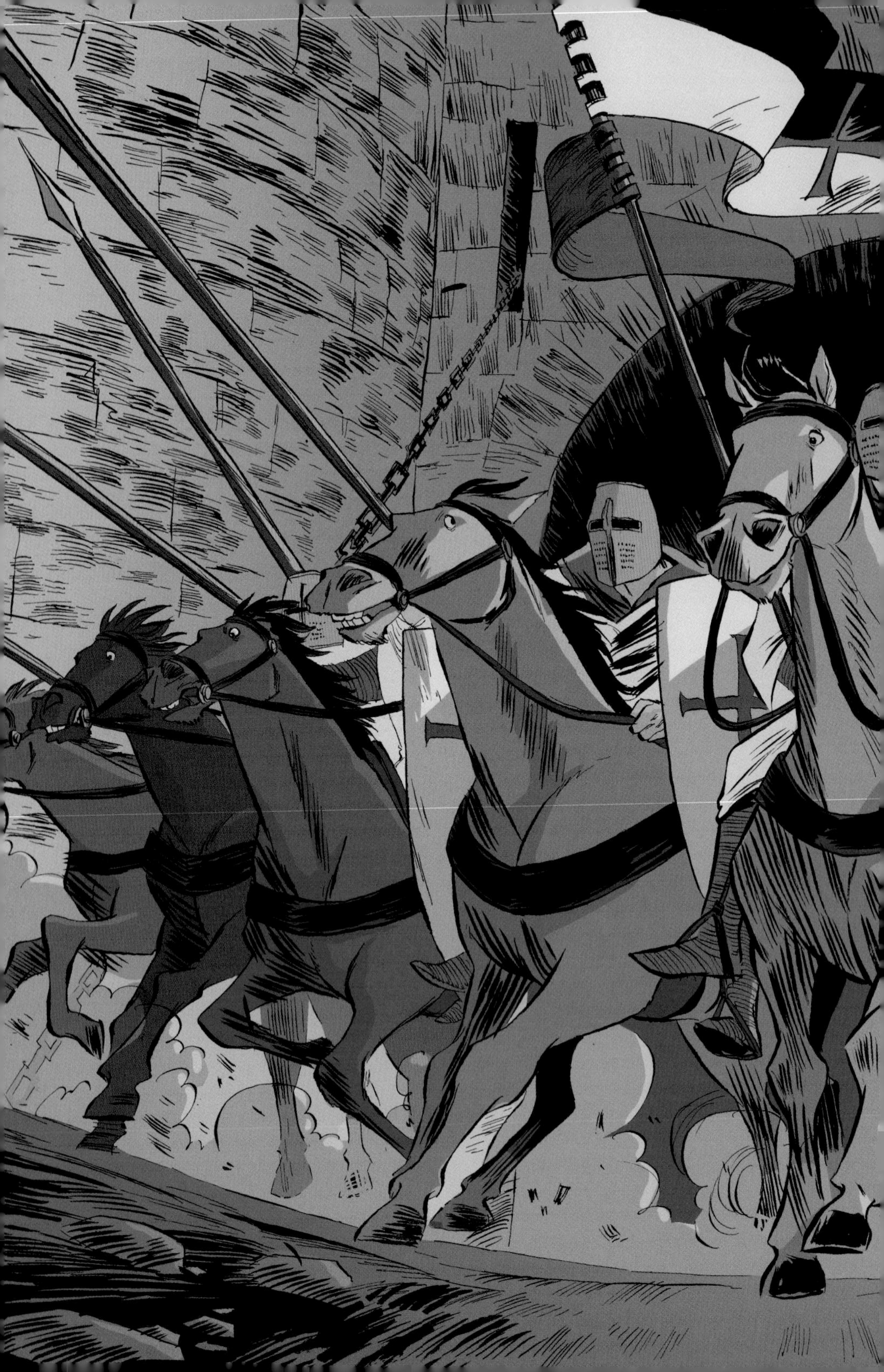

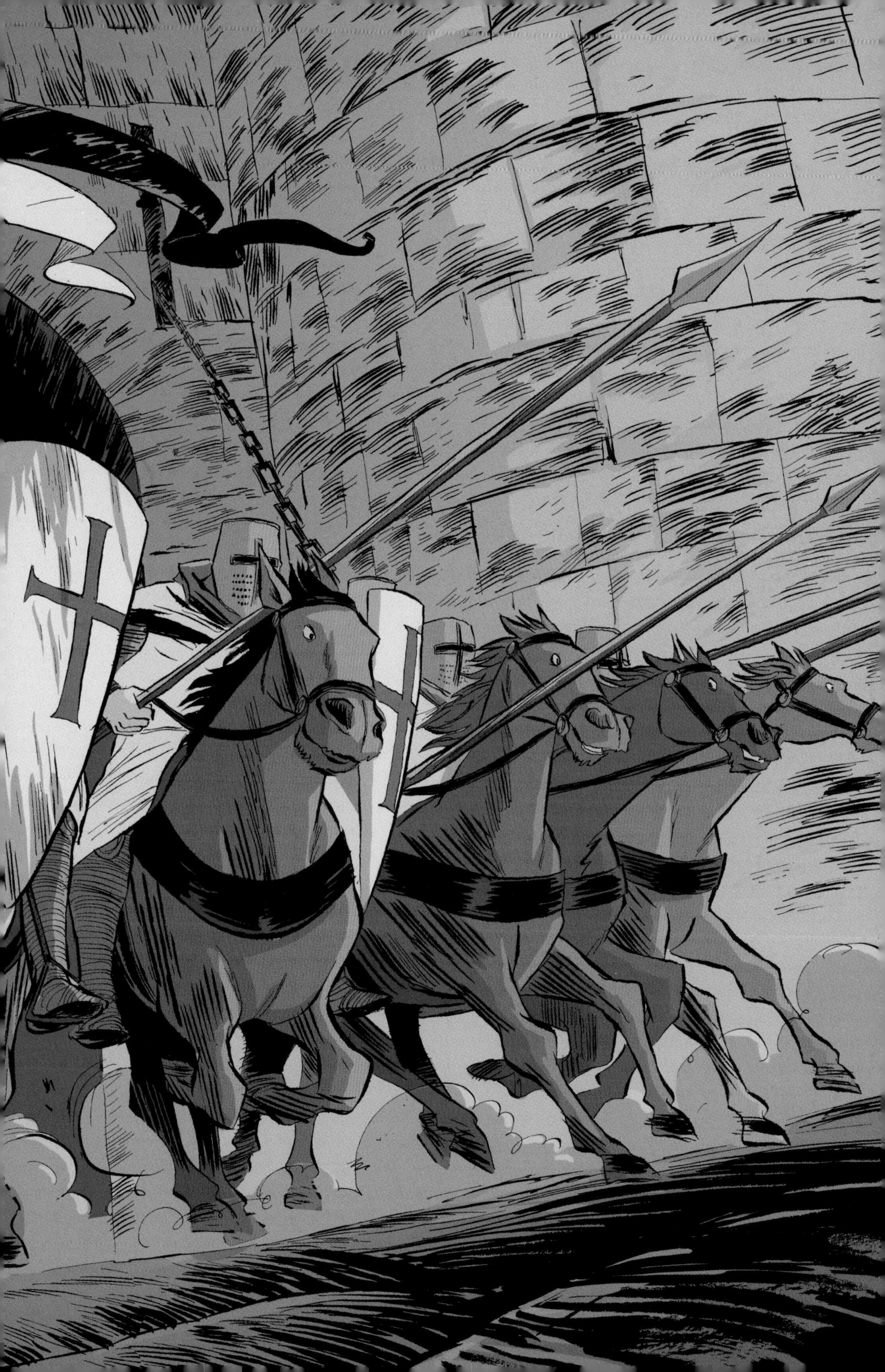

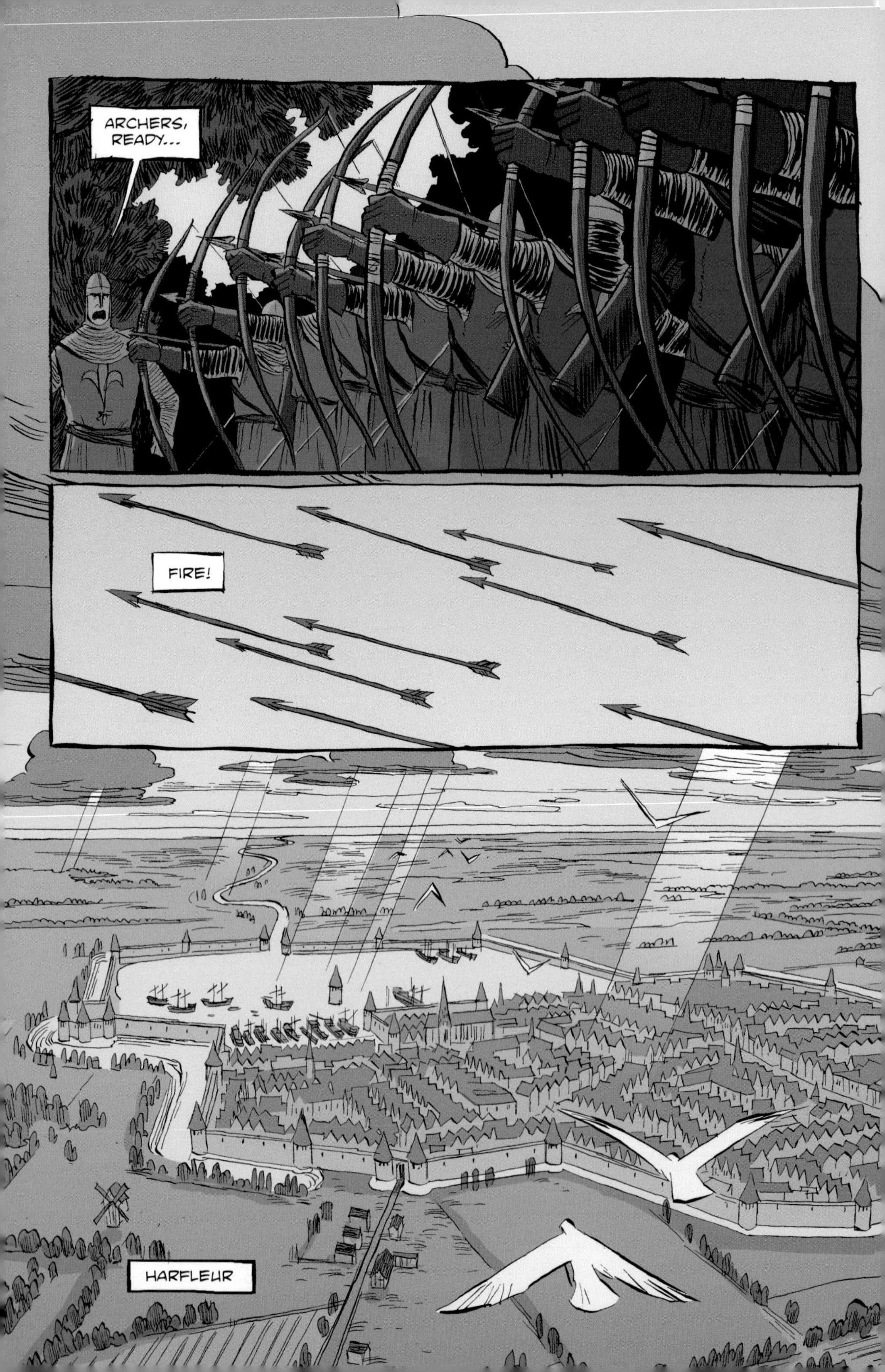
ARCHERS, READY...
FIRE!
HARFLEUR

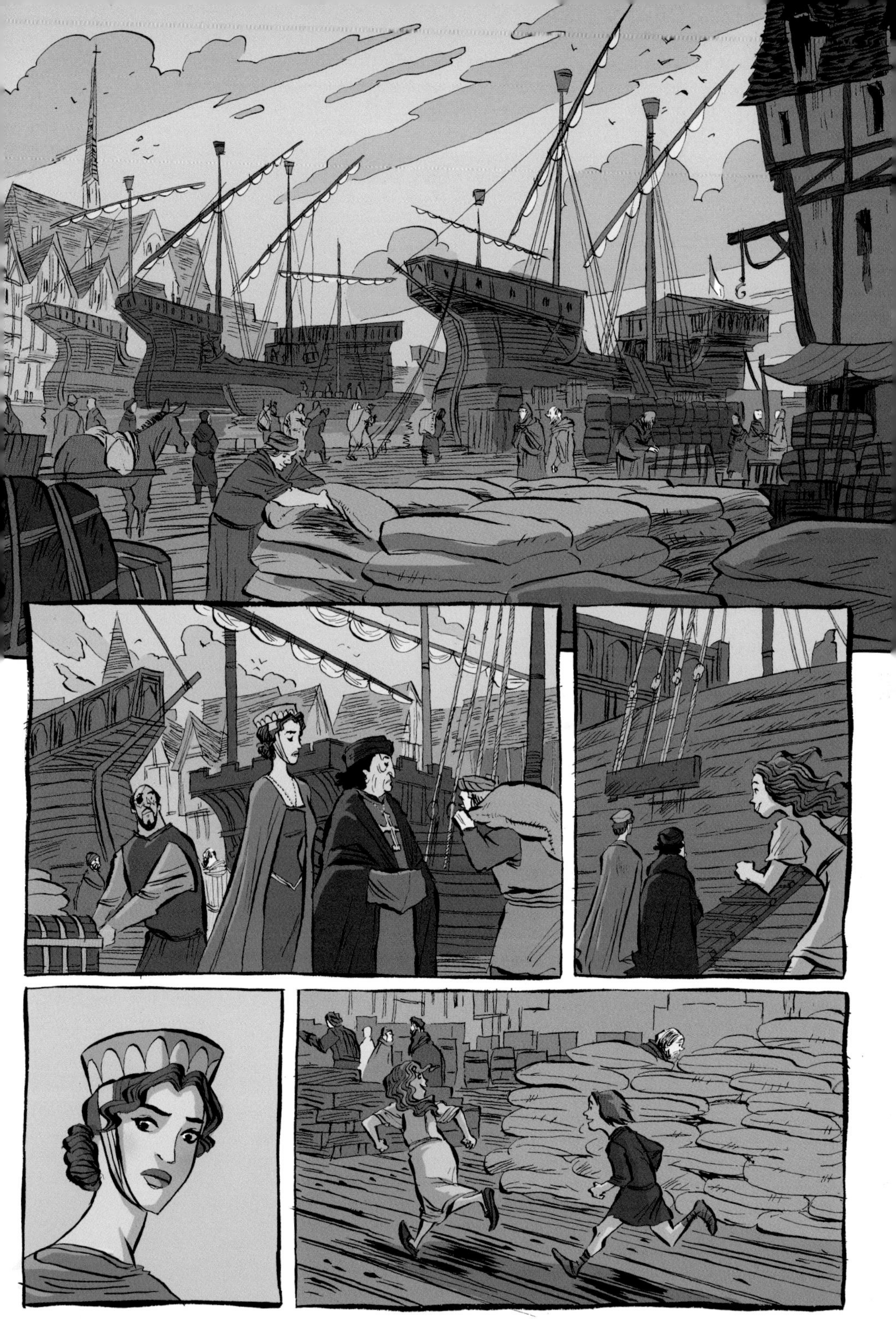

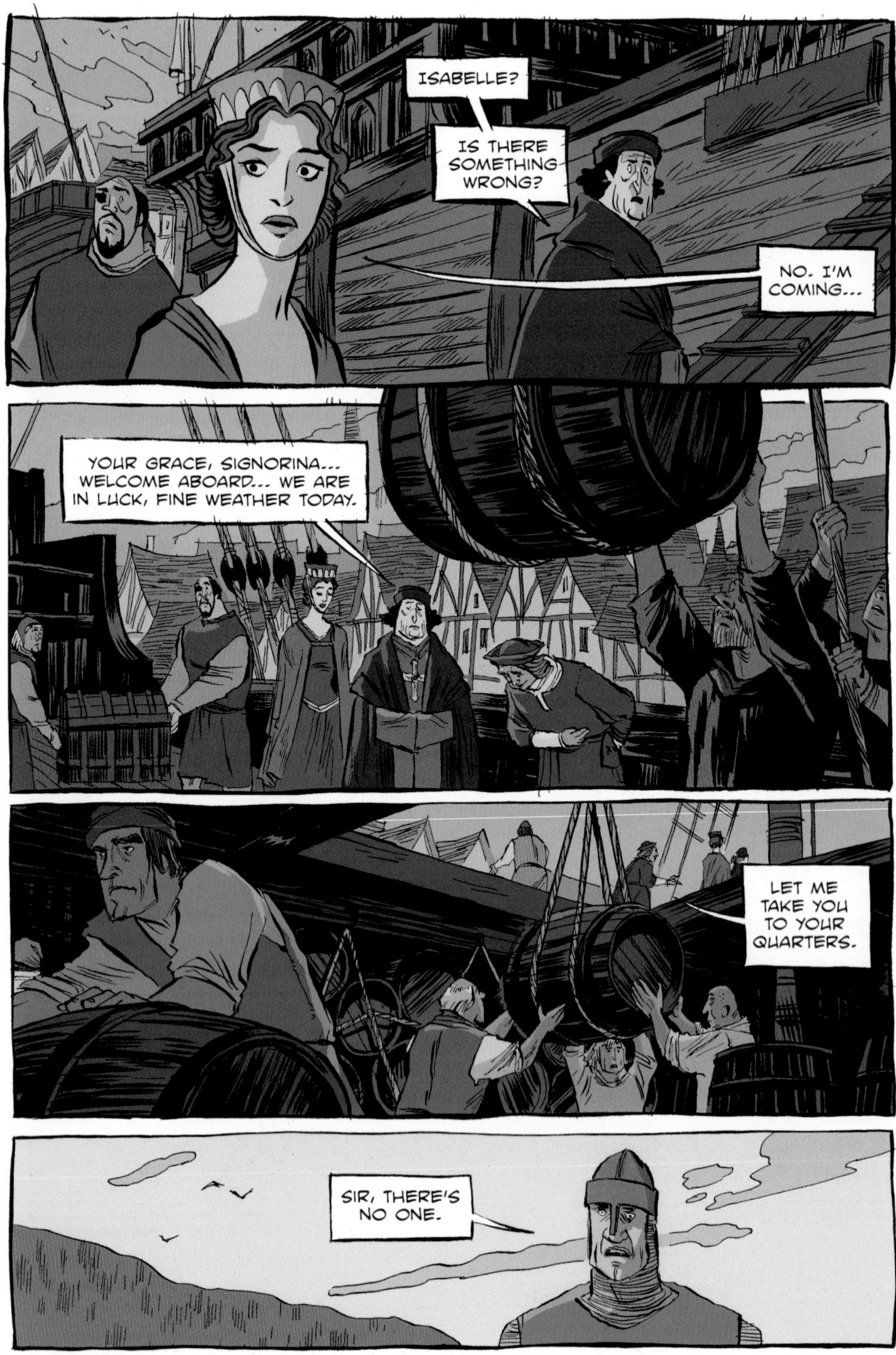
ISABELLE?
IS THERE SOMETHING WRONG?
NO. I'M COMING...
YOUR GRACE, SIGNORINA... WELCOME ABOARD... WE ARE IN LUCK, FINE WEATHER TODAY.
LET ME TAKE YOU TO YOUR QUARTERS.
SIR, THERE'S NO ONE.

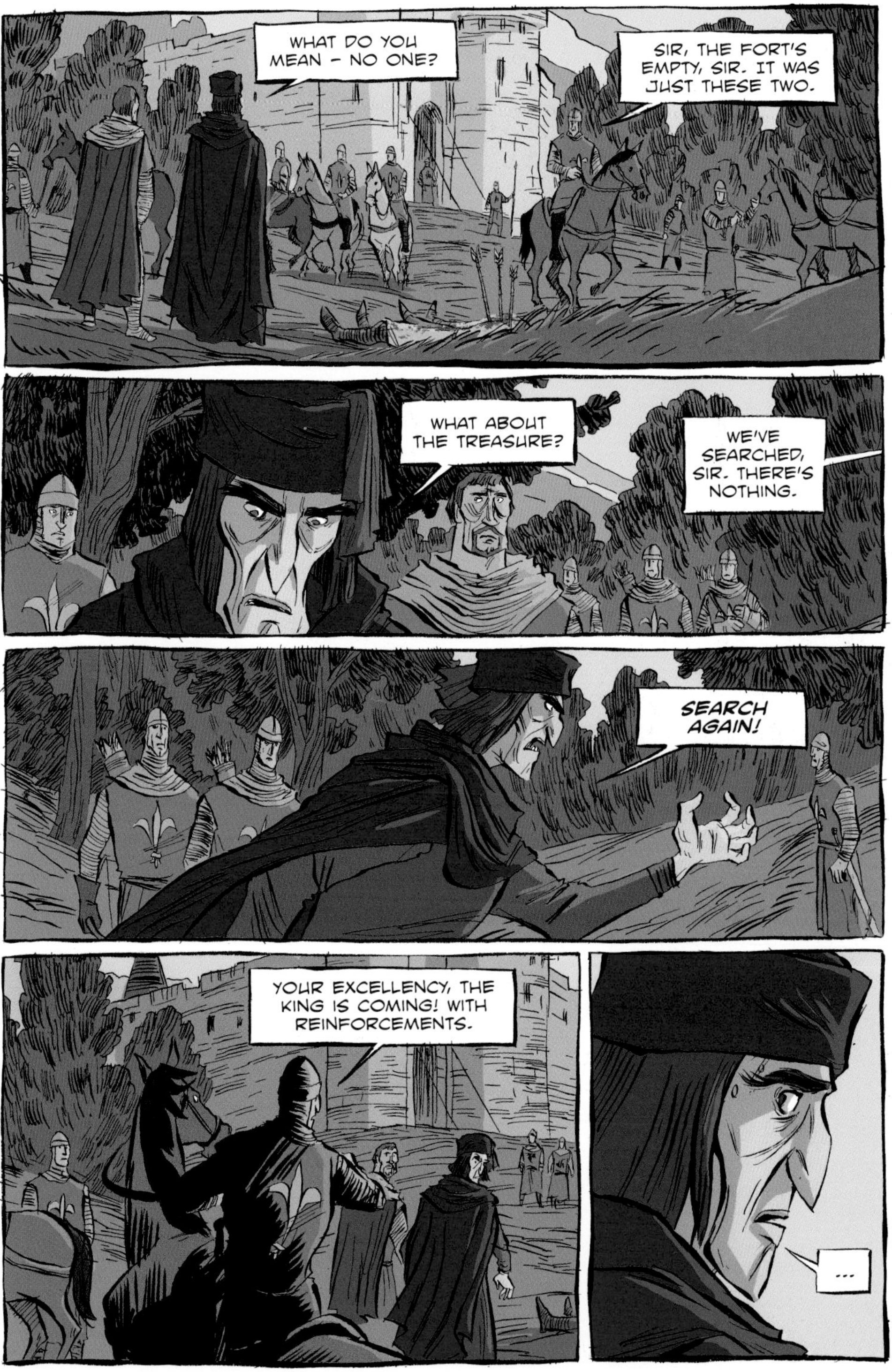
WHAT DO YOU MEAN - NO ONE?
SIR, THE FORT'S EMPTY, SIR. IT WAS JUST THESE TWO.
WHAT ABOUT THE TREASURE?
WE'VE SEARCHED, SIR. THERE'S NOTHING.
SEARCH AGAIN!
YOUR EXCELLENCY, THE KING IS COMING! WITH REINFORCEMENTS.
...

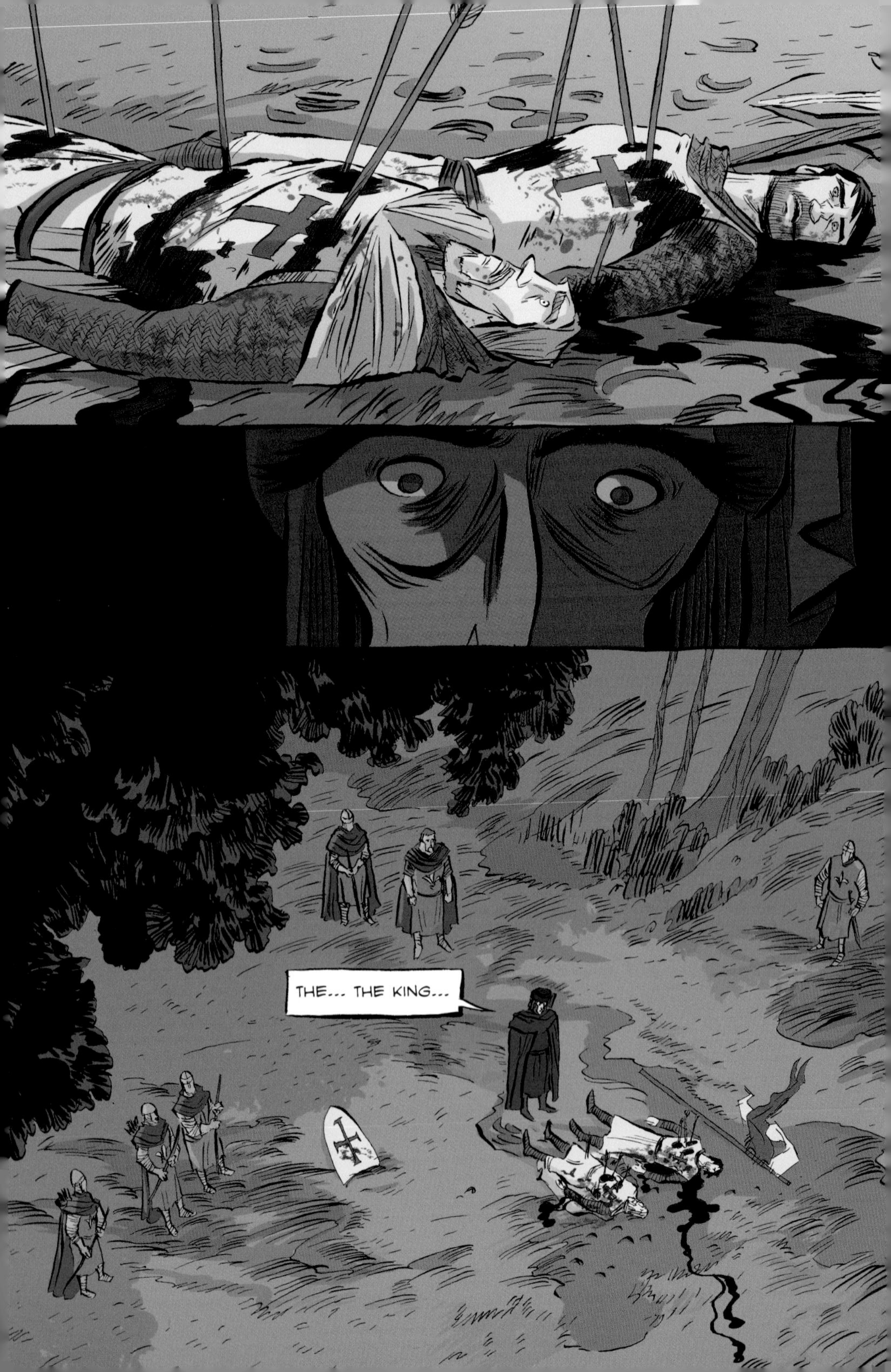
THE... THE KING...

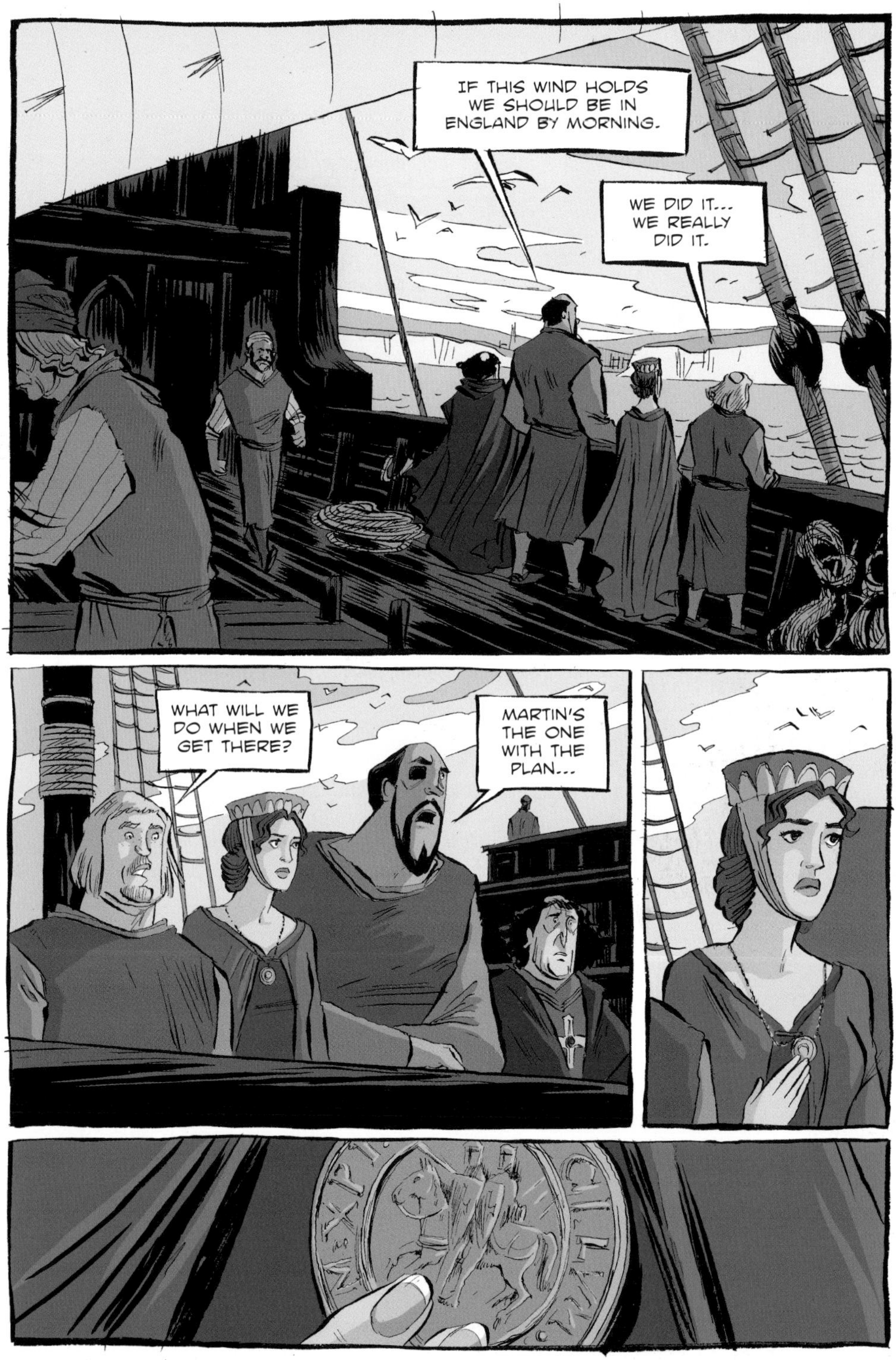
IF THIS WIND HOLDS WE SHOULD BE IN ENGLAND BY MORNING.
WE DID IT... WE REALLY DID IT.
WHAT WILL WE DO WHEN WE GET THERE?
MARTIN'S THE ONE WITH THE PLAN...

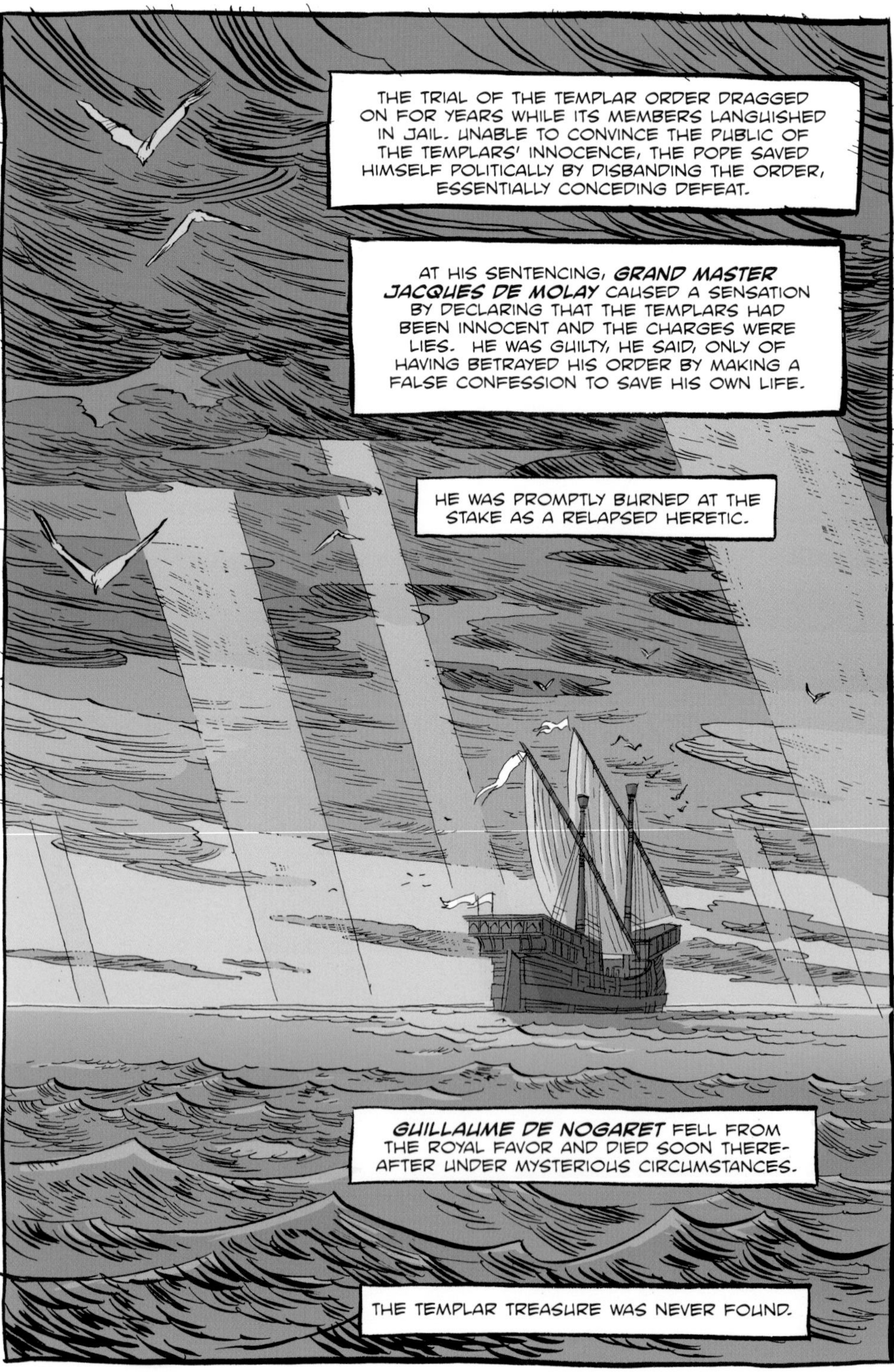
THE TRIAL OF THE TEMPLAR ORDER DRAGGED ON FOR YEARS WHILE ITS MEMBERS LANGUISHED IN JAIL. UNABLE TO CONVINCE THE PUBLIC OF THE TEMPLARS' INNOCENCE, THE POPE SAVED HIMSELF POLITICALLY BY DISBANDING THE ORDER, ESSENTIALLY CONCEDING DEFEAT.
AT HIS SENTENCING, GRAND MASTER JACQUES DE MOLAY CAUSED A SENSATION BY DECLARING THAT THE TEMPLARS HAD BEEN INNOCENT AND THE CHARGES WERE LIES. HE WAS GUILTY, HE SAID, ONLY OF HAVING BETRAYED HIS ORDER BY MAKING A FALSE CONFESSION TO SAVE HIS OWN LIFE.
HE WAS PROMPTLY BURNED AT THE STAKE AS A RELAPSED HERETIC.
GUILLAUME DE NOGARET FELL FROM THE ROYAL FAVOR AND DIED SOON THERE-AFTER UNDER MYSTERIOUS CIRCUMSTANCES.
THE TEMPLAR TREASURE WAS NEVER FOUND.

FIN

Afterword

MUCH NONSENSE HAS BEEN WRITTEN ABOUT THE KNIGHTS TEMPLAR over the years. I'm proud to say that this book has added to that sum.

But some of what's been written *isn't* nonsense, and I owe those writers and historians a special debt of gratitude. For readers interested in learning more about the Templars and their world, I've attached a selected bibliography of works I found especially valuable while writing *Templar*.

As portrayed in this graphic novel, the events of the Templar trial itself—including the arrests, subsequent interrogations, testimony, and legal machinations that culminated in the burning of fifty-four prisoners in a field outside Paris—match the historical record (allowing for a bit of time compression and ordinary dramatic license). Key speeches from the mouths of Guillaume de Nogaret, Gilles Aycelin, and other bishops, archbishops, and cardinals who figured in the trial, as well as Grand Master Jacques de Molay and legally versed prisoner Pierre de Bologna, are paraphrased from actual trial transcripts. LeUyen and Alex's depiction of the city of Paris as it might have looked then is likewise as accurate as our research could make it.

While the trial records do indicate that a group of knights led by Gerard de Villiers fled the Paris Temple with hay carts the night before the arrests, their actual fate (and cargo) is unknown. I'm pretty sure that the heist portrayed in this book didn't happen. I'll leave it to the reader to decide whether my version is more or less fanciful than other alternatives that have been proposed.

As to our main characters, Aycelin did have a younger sister, and a handful of Templars did escape arrest. Within those broad outlines, Martin, Bernard, Isabelle, and their gang are pure invention. They were born when I read the following passage in Malcolm Barber's *The Trial of the Templars:*

A small number of Templars did escape, twelve according to official sources, although there seem to have been at least twelve others; but only one of the escapees, Gerard de Villiers, Preceptor of France, was a figure of any importance... For some, like the knight Pierre de Boucle, the respite was only temporary; although he discarded the Order's mantle and shaved off his beard, he was still recognized and taken into custody. Two others, Jean de Chali and Pierre de Modies, who had made off together, were later apprehended in the striped clothes which they had adopted as a disguise.

I felt immediately drawn to those "figures of no importance," and knew that they would be the heroes of my story.

Pseudo-History and Fiction

I highly recommend Umberto Eco's novel *Foucault's Pendulum*, which not only precedes and supersedes *The Da Vinci Code, Holy Blood, Holy Grail*, and other Templar conspiracy-theory books, but brilliantly encompasses them. Aside from its sheer entertainment value as the conspiracy thriller to end all conspiracy thrillers, *Foucault's Pendulum* contains one of the best-written digests of the real Templar history to be found anywhere.

Templars

If you're looking for a pocket history, *The Knights Templar: The History and Myths of the Legendary Military Order*, by Sean Martin, is a quick read and packs a lot of good information.

For more in-depth, scholarly reading, these three general histories are excellent: *The New Knighthood: A History of the Order of the Temple*, by Malcolm Barber; *The Templars*, by Piers Paul Read; and *The Murdered Magicians: The Templars and Their Myth*, by Peter Partner.

The dramatic saga of the Templar arrests and trial is well documented in *The Trial of the Templars*, by Malcolm Barber. Grounded in medieval legal documents and trial records, it's fascinating reading.

Knight Templar 1120-1312, by Helen Nicholson. Part of the Osprey Warrior series, this slim paperback is full of concrete details about the Templars' actual daily experience and mindset, both in the West and during military operations.

This may be deeper than you want to go, but *The Templars: Selected Sources Translated and Annotated*, by Malcolm Barber and Keith Bate—a collection of documents from the time, including trial transcripts, legal documents, and even a poem written by a Templar—gives an amazing feeling of being in the presence of the actual people and events, rather than as interpreted by historians.

Knights and Crusades

The Templars were only one of many groups of Christian knights that went to the Middle East to fight in the Crusades—a series of wars and civil wars that lasted two centuries, and changed the medieval world (and ours) forever.

Of the many excellent books on the Crusades, one I especially like is *Chronicles of the Crusades*, edited by Elizabeth Hallam. It's vivid, epic, and beautifully illustrated, with excerpts from first-hand accounts on all sides.

Another is *The Crusades through Arab Eyes*, by Amin Maalouf, a well-written, informative, and gripping account of the Crusades from start to finish, drawing from eyewitness accounts by Muslim chroniclers of the time.

Two very different books reconstruct the life stories of individual knights: *William Marshal: The Flower of Chivalry*, by Georges Duby, and *The Last Duel*, by Eric Jager. Both provide fascinating insight into the chivalric mindset of the period, and are so well written that they read like novels.

Life in the Middle Ages

I found *Daily Life in Medieval Europe*, by Jeffrey Singman, to be an invaluable resource for writing a story set in medieval times.

A Distant Mirror, by Barbara Tuchman, is all about the calamitous fourteenth century that was to come, right after the period of *Templar*. Wide-ranging, brilliant, and highly readable, like all her books.

My very favorite medieval historian is Jacques Le Goff; he just "gets" the period, and manages to convey its essence, in a way all his own. His books explode a lot of clichés about the Middle Ages. If you read French, I especially recommend *A la recherche du Moyen Âge* and *Le Moyen Âge expliqué aux enfants*.

And if you ever need to find your way around medieval Paris, the indispensable book is *Atlas de Paris au Moyen Âge*, by Philippe Lorentz and Dany Sandron. Beautifully designed and printed, chock full of maps and architectural drawings, this is an extremely thorough and reliable resource that the artists and I went back to time and again.

Happy reading!

J.M.

SELECTED BIBLIOGRAPHY

Barber, Malcolm. *The New Knighthood: A History of the Order of the Temple.* Cambridge and New York: Cambridge University Press, 1995.

___. *The Templars: Selected Sources Translated and Annotated.* Malcolm Barber and Keith Bate, translators. Manchester (UK): University of Manchester Press, 2002.

___. *Trial of the Templars.* 2nd ed. Cambridge and New York: Cambridge University Press, 2006.

Duby, Georges. *William Marshal: The Flower of Chivalry.* New York: Pantheon, 1987.

Eco, Umberto, and William Weaver. *Foucault's Pendulum.* William Weaver, translator. Boston: Houghton Mifflin, 2007.

Hallam, Elizabeth M. *Chronicles of the Crusades.* New York: Weidenfeld and Nicolson, 1989.

Jager, Eric. *The Last Duel.* New York: Broadway Books, 2004.

Le Goff, Jacques. *À la recherche du Moyen Âge.* Paris: Louis Audibert, 2003.

___. *Le Moyen Âge expliqué aux enfants.* Paris: Seuil, 2006.

Lorentz, Philippe, et al. *Atlas de Paris au Moyen Âge.* Paris: Parigramme, 2006.

Maalouf, Amin. *The Crusades through Arab Eyes.* New York: Schocken Books, 1989.

Martin, Sean. *The Knights Templar: The History and Myths of the Legendary Military Order.* New York: Thunder's Mouth Press, 2004.

Nicholson, Helen. *Knight Templar, 1120-1312.* Gloucestershire (UK): Sutton, 2004.

Partner, Peter. *The Murdered Magicians: The Templars and Their Myth.* Oxford and New York: Oxford University Press, 1982.

Read, Piers Paul. *The Templars.* New York: Macmillan, 2000.

Singman, Jeffrey. *Daily Life in Medieval Europe.* Westport, CT: Greenwood Publishers, 1999.

Tuchman, Barbara. *A Distant Mirror.* New York: Random House, 1979.